GERMANY
2000 YEARS

By

KURT F. REINHARDT, Ph. D.
STANFORD UNIVERSITY
CALIFORNIA

THE BRUCE PUBLISHING COMPANY
MILWAUKEE

TO MY WIFE

PREFACE

This book, the fruit of many years of teaching and study, aims at filling a real gap in the field of German historiography. There are available in the German language several comprehensive works dealing with either the political or cultural history of Germany. And there are some recent publications in the English language which in their discussion of German political history pay at least passing attention to the cultural context and background. This is true in particular of such presentations as E. F. Henderson's *A Short History of Germany* (New York: The Macmillan Co., 1916), 2 vols.; George N. Shuster's and Arnold Bergstraesser's *Germany: A Short History* (New York: W. W. Norton & Co., 1944); Prince Hubertus zu Loewenstein's *The Germans in History* (New York: Columbia University Press, 1945); and Veit Valentin's *The German People* (New York: Alfred A. Knopf, 1946). Ernst Richard's *History of German Civilization* (New York: The Macmillan Co., 1911) was at the time of its publication an interesting and praiseworthy attempt to present a condensed survey of German cultural history with occasional sidelights on political history. But to the present-day reader its perspective and scope appear as too limited. There is thus completely lacking a comprehensive and up-to-date survey presenting the history of Germany in its entirety, *in both its political and cultural aspects*.

The attempt to write such a history is, however, such a formidable undertaking that it might almost seem presumptuous. If the author of this book has nevertheless embarked upon this venture, he has done so fully conscious of the necessarily fragmentary nature of a work of this scope and of certain almost inevitable weaknesses in the intended synthesis. He has approached his task prompted and guided by the conviction that political and cultural history are historically and actually inseparable, mutually illuminating and supplementing each other, so that the one cannot really be comprehended and appreciated apart from the other. In trying to integrate both, the author has scrupulously endeavored to avoid shallow popularization on the one hand and the technical intricacies of detailed specialized knowledge on the other. To what extent he has been successful in this endeavor is for the reader to judge.

Each section dealing with a particular period in German history opens with a chronological table and a cursory account of political events. This is followed by a discussion of the major cultural trends and movements in the several fields of human endeavor and accomplishment: in the spheres of state and society; in political, economic, and social theory and practice; in literature, the plastic arts, and in music; in science and technics; in education, philosophy, and religion.

That the historical survey comes to a halt in 1933, the year of the National Socialist revolution, may at first glance seem rather arbitrary. The reason for not going beyond that date is twofold: in the first place there is no lack of able (if at times one-sided) presentations of the rise and fall of Germany under National Socialism; and, secondly, the author is convinced that this most recent phase of German history is too close to the historian's field of vision to allow for a perspective that is duly proportioned and therefore objectively valid. The author has thus confined himself to making visible and intelligible certain trends in recent German history which eventually converged in the rise of National Socialism. "There exists," writes Karl Jaspers in *Die Schuldfrage* (Heidelberg, 1946), "something in our national tradition, something mighty and threatening, which has become our moral ruin." But, he continues, "what erupted in Germany has been on its way in the entire western world as a spiritual crisis, a crisis of faith. This fact does not diminish our guilt. . . . But the consciousness of the common human crisis liberates us from the feeling of absolute isolation. And, as it concerns every human being, it may teach others a lesson. . . . If the chain of evil is not radically broken, the victors may eventually find themselves in the same situation in which we found ourselves, and with them all mankind."

The history of Germany is viewed in this book as embedded within the larger frame and context of Europe and European history and thus as an integral part of the "Western Tradition" of thought and culture. If there is any lesson to be gleaned from two thousand years of German history, it may be said to be the realization that Germany is always most substantially herself when and as long as she remains conscious of her European anchorage, inheritance, and responsibility, and that the temporary loss of this consciousness entails a betrayal that invites disaster and exacts retribution. As a bridge — politically and culturally — between eastern and western Europe, Germany has fulfilled an important function in the European past, and she may well be destined to fulfill a similar function in the future. However, the author has in this book no thesis to advance and no ax to grind. He merely hopes that to some extent, at least, he may have succeeded in telling (to use Leopold von Ranke's words) *"wie es eigentlich gewesen ist."*

Both the author and the publisher wish to express their gratitude to the *Herder Verlag* in Freiburg im Breisgau, and especially to Dr. Theophil Herder-Dorneich, the present head of the German publishing firm, for permission to utilize several of the excellent historical maps produced by the members of Herder's editorial staff (with whom the author had the privilege of being associated from 1922 to 1925) and contained in the volumes of the encyclopedia *Der Grosse Herder*. The perusal of two standard works on German cultural history, published by the *Herder Verlag* (F. Zoepfl's *Deutsche Kulturgeschichte*, 2 vols., 1929–1930, and Franz Schnabel's *Deutsche Geschichte im Neunzehnten Jahrhundert*, 4 vols., 1929 sqq.), has been an invaluable aid in preparing the manuscript for this book. The author is also greatly indebted to Dr. Bayard Quincy Morgan, professor emeritus and former executive head of the Department of Germanic Languages at Stanford University, for much pertinent advice and constructive criticism and for his assistance in reading the page proofs.

Kurt F. Reinhardt

Stanford University, California
October 15, 1949

INTRODUCTION

The Heirs of Rome. Germany, placed by nature and historic fate in the center of Europe, is intrinsically linked up and interwoven with what is generally known as the European Tradition. For centuries she not only constituted a factor but represented a major exponent of that tradition. Europe, in turn, taken as a cultural, social, and intellectual whole, has been determined in its physiognomy to a large extent by the destinies, the character, the creative efforts, and the cultural achievements of those Germanic tribes which were the heirs of the civilization of the ancient world.

The form of the tradition of antiquity with which the Northern barbarians became acquainted was the political and social structure of the Roman Empire in the period of its decline. Roman civilization was still imbued with the splendor of a rich and mature intellectual, artistic, and civic life, and it could point to a high level of material prosperity, though it was lacking in spiritual depth and cultural initiative. The philosophic teachings of a Marcus Aurelius and similar representatives of high ethical standards had been supplanted by widespread naturalism and materialism, a cult of pleasure and success. Public opinion endorsed a philosophy of life which is thus scathingly described by St. Augustine (A.D. 354-430): "They do not trouble about the moral degradation of the Empire; all they ask is that it should be prosperous and secure. They say: What concerns us is that everyone should be able to increase his wealth so that he can afford a lavish expenditure and keep the weaker members of society in subjection. Let the laws protect the rights of property and leave man's morals alone. Let there be gorgeous palaces and sumptuous banquets, where anybody can play and drink and gorge himself and be dissipated by day or night. Let the noise of dancing be everywhere, and let the theatres resound with lewd merriment and with every kind of cruel pleasure. As for the rulers who devote themselves to giving the people a good time, let them be treated as gods and worshipped accordingly. Only let them take care that neither war nor plague nor any other calamity may interfere with this reign of prosperity."*

Naturally enough, such a civilization was in no way prepared to cope with those mighty forces which challenged the imperialism of the totalitarian Roman State: the biological vitality of the primitive Germanic warriors and

---

* Cf. *De Civitate Dei*, II, XX; *Ep.*, CXXXVIII, 3, 14.

forest dwellers of the North, and the spiritual vitality of Christianity, which had risen as a foreign element in the very heart of the Empire.

Out of these conflicting forces and tendencies, as they prevailed in an age of transition and violent change, Germany has grown as an integral part of European civilization, burdened and blessed with the heritage of the ancient world, destructively and constructively engaged in a constant interchange and interplay with the remnants of the old and the experiences and realities of the new.

If it is true that the character of an individual shapes his destiny, the same may be said of a people, a nation, a civilization. The character, however, of a civilization is an even more complex entity than the character of an individual. It can be analyzed, evaluated, and understood only as it displays itself in the process of historic evolution, thus mutually illuminating the significance of historical events on the one hand, and innate bents as well as acquired habits on the other. The present is linked to the past as much as to the future, and the story of the past will aid in the interpretation of the present and the shaping of the future.

The Scope of Cultural History. The history of civilization, whether it concerns itself with several, a few, or only one cultural unit, is always more ambitious and broader in scope than political or national history. Although it deals in part with an identical set of factual occurrences, it approaches, views, and interprets historical facts and events from altogether different angles. However, the fact that the history of civilization covers a much larger territory than does political historiography is not the decisive distinction. What gives cultural history or the history of civilization its peculiar character and flavor is its attempt to break through the surface of political events of a circumscribed extension and dimension in order to discover and comprehend the fundamental cultural and social unity that underlies a given civilization as a whole. This unity is evident wherever we deal with formations that owe their origin and evolution to a community of race, environment, occupation, and thought.*

Cultural Evolution: Necessity and Freedom. While race, environment, and occupation constitute important factors in historic and cultural evolution, it is the community of thought that is truly essential. Without it there could be no civilization properly so called. Through the elimination of thoughtfully planned and freely determined action the evolutionary process would be reduced to the growth of a biological species. Man, who is the chief actor on the historical stage, the actual center of all cultural life, would no longer be the determining but the completely determined element. Quite logically, then, all theories of historic determinism are compelled to link cultural development to a chain of biological and mechanical causation. These theories have been advanced in various forms and guises, the better

---

* Cf. Christopher Dawson, *The Age of the Gods* (London and New York: Sheed & Ward, 1933), Introduction.

known of which are those of Hegel (1770–1831), Marx (1818–1883), Spengler (1880–1936), and Rosenberg (1893–1947).

According to Hegel it is the "World Spirit" that manifests itself in historic and cultural evolution, achieving an ever higher degree of consciousness, and reaching an absolute climax in the divinized totalitarian state. In the system of historic materialism as designed by Karl Marx the development culminates in the classless and stateless society of communism. Oswald Spengler, who, like Marx and Rosenberg, is largely indebted to Hegel, conceives of cultural history as proceeding in monumental "cultural cycles," plantlike cultural organisms following their predestined course through the successive stages of generation, growth, maturity, and decay. The "maternal landscape" is their vital principle and life-imparting force. Alfred Rosenberg,* who had tried to formulate the philosophical convictions of National Socialism, has espoused the "Myth of the Twentieth Century," the myth of blood, as the vital force that "is the most profound law of every genuine culture," and "is to give conscious expression to the vegetative quality of a race." For both Marx and Rosenberg an absolute cosmic energy is focused in human society and rules its destinies. In all these theories there is, of course, no room for a freely operating social and cultural activity, without which the establishment of social and cultural traditions seems inconceivable. Even Hegel, in contradiction to his own premises, criticizes Plato's ideal Republic for having neglected "the principle of the independent personality of the individual," and considers the recognition and adoption of this principle the distinctive mark of Germanic-Christian civilization.

Human Reason and Cultural Integration. There is no doubt, then, that in all cultural growth and social transformation human reason and intelligence, planning, and initiative play a most conspicuous part, providing for a continual enlargement of experiences and their integration and incorporation in the material, social, and intellectual universe. Thought, philosophical and religious, is a great molder of the destinies of individuals and of nations. The great individuals themselves, for better or worse, are not only the exponents of definite and historically rooted concepts and modes of life and thought, but the molders as well, transformers and reformers, pioneers, prophets, and leaders. Civilization and its history is a continuous manifestation of the intelligent integration of new experiences, a documentation of man's co-operation with the forces, the laws, and the ends of nature. This co-operation begins in each cultural unit with the development of higher agriculture, the shaping of materials into adequate tools and instruments, the development of the mechanical arts and crafts, and the creation of the means of self-expression and communication in writing, measuring, and reading. Social forces grow into social institutions, into various forms of secular and religious rule within an organized society and a civil state. This is a kind of general framework within which civilizations in different

---

* Cf. Alfred Rosenberg, *Der Mythos des 20. Jahrhunderts* (1930; placed on the Index, 1934).

climes and zones seem to erect their particular and individual structures. Within this framework there seems to be an amplitude admitting of well-nigh infinite varieties of realizations, so that no civilization is committed to a predestined course.

The human element, so strong in each civilization, is the correcting and controlling factor. Any *laissez-faire* attitude in regard to cultural evolution is oblivious of some of its most real forces. It overlooks forces which address this modern age even across the boundary lines of generations and centuries past; the cultural energies that are alive in the great personalities of the emperors and popes of the Middle Ages, in the synthetic minds of the Schoolmen, in the voices of the ages that were inspired and informed by the messages of Luther and Calvin, the genius of Leibniz and Kant, of Goethe and Schiller, the idealism of Fichte, the cultural pessimism of Schopenhauer, and the feverish and ecstatic optimism of Nietzsche.

German Idealism. The history of German civilization is not identical indeed with the history of her great creative minds. But it may be safely maintained that this history owes its particular shape and character to the cumulative intellectual incentives supplied by many generations of men and women who, in different stations of life and engaged in varying labors and occupations, constitute a community of thought as well as of life. These have jointly contributed to the major currents of cultural achievement and social tradition.

There is a certain dramatic tenseness, occasionally involving an aspect of tragic frustration, in the rugged outline of German cultural history. There are certain major incisions which mark an end as well as a beginning, which provide a scenic setting full of contrasts and seeming contradictions that set German civilization apart from the more epically composed development of many other nations and races. Perhaps more than in any other European nation the course of cultural movements and political events in Germany is inspired and directed by ideas and ideologies. The ideal and material strength of centuries was spent in the passionate and futile attempt to perpetuate the concept and force the realization of the Holy Roman Empire of the German Nation; or to maintain the claims of the "Imperium" as against the demands of the "Sacerdotium," Empire versus Papacy.

German Interiority. There is a specific brand of German inwardness or interiority (*Innerlichkeit*) that asserts itself no less in the great mystics of the thirteenth and fourteenth centuries than in Martin Luther's doctrine of salvation "by faith alone" (*sola fide*): the "fiducial faith" of "pure interiority" which he proclaimed as the sole requisite for justification (cf. p. 219). There is the same immediacy and directness of emotional appeal and inner experience in the pietistic movement (cf. p. 364 sqq.) of the pre-Classical age and the mystical or "magical" idealism of the post-Classical Romantic school (cf. p. 470 sqq.). This mystical idealism permeates German thought and German life, and a profoundly personal interiority imparts to the German language and diction its heavily laden and richly ornamented texture. The fervent thoroughness of German idealism inspired in part the social and religious revolts and wars of the sixteenth and seventeenth centuries. But without this generative power the material and cultural devastations of the Thirty Years' War could never have issued in the cultural renascence that characterized the age of German Classicism, little over a hundred years after the Treaty of Westphalia (1648).

German Romanticism. It has been said that mystical and romantic yearning, a longing which is infinite by its very nature, is of the essence of the German mind. It manifests itself in the concepts of German mythology and nature philosophy in ancient and modern times; in the major themes of German folk song and lyric poetry; in the "longing infinite" of the Romantic painters, writers, and philosophers; and in the ecstatic frenzy of the towering German-Gothic cathedral, which in its heavenward flight is a mystical dream come true. Spengler has spoken of the eternal restlessness of the "Faustian" soul, taking Goethe's greatest dramatic character as a profound symbol of the aspirations of the Germanic race: a restless striving which fulfills itself eternally *in statu viae,* considering the way not as a means to an end but as the end and the goal itself.

Gotthold Ephraim Lessing (1729–1781) attributes a higher value to the quest for truth than to the possession of truth. He, too, felt the fascination of the *Faust*-theme, and composed a *Faust*-fragment. Thomas Mann (1875–), the creator of many romantic characters, has his Savonarola in the play *Fiorenza* confess: "Longing is a gigantic force but possession emasculates." And yet, with all the apparent lack of a conventional formal quality approved by the canon of classical aesthetics, it seems that the German mind possesses and commands a form-character specifically its own, unique and incomparable in its kind. It is when we make the acquaintance of some of the greatest of German artists and writers, such as Dürer and Holbein, Goethe and Schiller, that we realize that this spiritual unrest is far from being aimless and endless. In between long stretches of seeking there appear blessed isles of finding, islands of fulfillment and sublime achievement, where the German mind has come to rest in happy balance and harmony.

Methods of Approach and Critical Evaluation. Evaluations in the field of cultural history are difficult and never infallible. Is classical form better than romantic form? Is Gothic architecture the creation of a barbaric race, as Goethe thought when his aesthetic judgment received its rules from the art forms of antiquity? Or was he right when, in the prime of youth, he stood in front of the Strasbourg Minster and was delighted and transported beyond measure by that monumental spiritualization of matter that met his eye in the sublime craftsmanship of Erwin von Steinbach? Was eighteenth-century rationalism right when it looked at cultural progress as a uniform law of nature, so that the bigger and better things would inevitably fall into the lap of an evolving civilization? Is contemporary German art more mature or more perfect than the art of Dürer and Holbein and Grünewald? Has modern literature improved and advanced beyond the scope and workmanship of the "Lay of the Nibelungs," Wolfram's "Parzival," Goethe's "Faust," Schiller's "Wilhelm Tell"? Is contemporary philosophy sounder or truer than the systems of Albert the Great, Leibniz, and Kant? Are the new forms of government and social organization, the administration of social and distributive justice more progressive or more humane than similar functions and institutions of the preceding centuries? The answers to all these questions depend upon the standard of measurement.

Cultural gain and loss, however, cannot be measured in the abstract. It can be measured only by taking into consideration concrete, historical situations and conditions. From Johann Gottfried Herder (1744–1803) we have learned how to understand and appreciate cultural history as a discipline dealing with individual organisms that must be interpreted and judged from their own premises. These vary according to climate, race, and place, and to their ethnological, geographical, and sociological environment. The interpretation of genetic relations within cultural organisms of a definite time and place becomes thus the foundation of methodology which does away with the one-sided views of a purely descriptive, or purely pragmatic, or purely normative approach.*

Past, Present, and Future. To understand those facts, events, currents, and movements that display themselves significantly within a given historical frame of reference, in the light of particular premises and circumstances, and to refrain from simplified and single-tracked judgments, becomes singularly imperative in viewing the cultural landscape of a Germany which even now appears in a process of complete liquefaction. Past and present, tradition and progress seem to meet in the form of an open challenge which has to be accepted and comprehended in the interest of the welding process of a future Germany and a future German civilization. Friedrich Nietzsche (1844–1900) has well expressed the plight and the hope of a Germany-in-the-making: "We do not yet know the goal toward which we are being driven after having thus broken away from our ancient foundations. But it is these foundations that have implanted in us the strength which now urges us on into the distant future, into adventure. . . . "

---

* Cf. H. A. Hodges, *Wilhelm Dilthey* (New York: Oxford University Press, 1944).

CONTENTS

A. *Merovingians*

The Merovingian Kingdom of the Franks. The Baptism of
Clovis. Christianity and Paganism Among the Franks. Social
Conditions. Law and Legal Procedure. Currency and Trade.
Learning. Language: The High German Sound Shift. The
Influence of Latin Culture and the Roman Church. Christianity
As a State Religion. Christianity As the Heir of the Classical
Tradition. Monasticism. The Monks of the West. Anglo-Saxon

Ritterorden"). Social Divisions in the Middle Ages. The Peasants. The Medieval German City. City Leagues. The Hanseatic League. Trade Fairs. The External Appearance of the City. Public Buildings. Private Residences. City Administration. Care of the Poor and the Sick. Merchant and Craft Guilds ("Gilden" and "Zünfte"). Medieval Economic Theory. Religion and the Church. The Religion of the People. The Mendicant Orders: Franciscans and Dominicans. Albigenses and Waldenses. Heresy and the Inquisition. The Universities: Organization and Curriculum. The Revival of Learning: Theology and Philosophy. Gothic Architecture. Gothic Arts and Crafts. Court Epic; Folk Epic; Didactic and Lyric Poetry. The Medieval Theory of Art.

LIST OF MAPS AND ILLUSTRATIONS

PART I. THE GERMANIC PAST AND THE CREATION OF THE EMPIRE OF CHARLEMAGNE

A. MEROVINGIANS

B. CAROLINGIANS

I

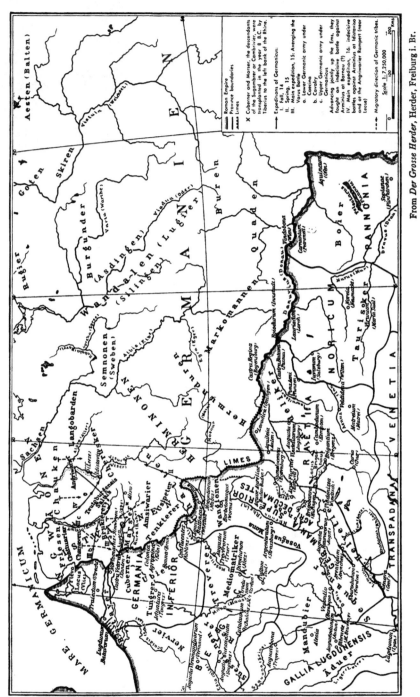

Germany at the Time of Tacitus (End of the First Century).

From *Der Grosse Herder*, Herder, Freiburg i. Br.

Chapter 1

ORIGINS

Germans and Indo-Europeans. The Germanic peoples of prehistoric and historic times represent one branch of the Indo-Germanic or Indo-European family of nations. The majority of contemporary anthropologists, ethnologists, and linguists consider the unity that existed among the Indo-Europeans as one of speech rather than of race. There is no doubt, however, that most of these peoples belonged racially to the nordic dolicocephalic (long-skulled) type. Comparative philology names as linguistic members of the Indo-European family the ancient inhabitants of India, Persia, Greece, the old Italic and modern Romanic nations, Celts, Slavs, and the various Germanic peoples. Exact knowledge as to their origins, their homes, their culture, and their migrations is lacking. No literary documents are extant to tell us of their lives and their activities; our only sources of information are a common stock of words, and a certain amount of archaeological and ethnological evidence.

It is quite possible that the unity of the Indo-Europeans came to an end with the passing of the Neolithic Age (*c.* 2000 B.C.). It seems to be ascertained that the Indo-Europeans were peasants with a rather advanced agriculture, that their social life rested on patriarchal customs and institutions, their family life on monogamy. Their religion included, among a pantheon of minor deities, belief in the supreme power and majesty of the sky-god (Dyaus-Pitar, Jupiter, Zeus, Tyr, Thor, Wodan, etc.).

As to their original homes, the opinions are divided. The two major theories point to inner Asia and northern Europe, in particular to the Baltic region. This latter theory assumes that the Indo-Germanic peoples spread from northern Europe and ultimately penetrated into Turkestan and India. C. M. Schroeder* is most emphatic in his assertion that the testimony of comparative linguistics, prehistory, and ethnology definitely establishes the regions north of the Caspian Sea as the cradle of the Indo-Germanic peoples.

The Prehistoric Germanic Peoples and Their Culture. In prehistoric times most of the territory that is today occupied by the German people was inhabited by the Celts. But even the Celts were not the original inhabitants

---

* Cf. C. M. Schroeder, *Rasse und Religion* (München, 1937), pp. 76–98.

3

of this region. They were preceded by three much more primitive types of Illyrian, Celtic, and Germanic culture. Ancient Thuringia, occupying a central position, must have acted as a unifying and co-ordinating focus, the result being the creation of a Celtic cultural center in the southwestern part of what is today the territory of Germany.

In the second millennium B.C. these aboriginal populations were seized by a typically Indo-Germanic *wanderlust* which carried them into Russia and Greece. Bastarnians and Cimbers began to grow restless and started upon their migrations, some time during the first millennium B.C. The Slavs took possession of those districts that were vacated by the Goths, the Burgundians, the Alemans, and the Marcomans. The Thuringians were the main carriers of a steadily gaining Germanization in the North of present-day Germany. At the same time, they were an important factor in the creation of the highly developed "Lusation Culture" (*Lausitz-Kultur*) of the middle Bronze Age (*c.* 1200 B.C.), which had its center in the east and southeast.

By 500 B.C. the greater part of northern Europe was inhabited by Germanic tribes, and the aboriginal Celts found themselves hard pressed. In the southwest the Germanic advance was temporarily checked by Celtic strongholds, but during the last centuries of the pre-Christian era the Celts gradually receded toward the Alps.

Archaeological finds illustrate the successive stages of this advancing Germanic culture. Some of the tools and implements of the Stone and Bronze ages show exquisite workmanship and an original arrangement of ornamental and decorative design. The oldest musical instruments of Germanic culture that have been unearthed date back to *c.* 800 B.C. They are called "lurers" (from Old Norse *"ludhr"*), alphornlike, S-shaped wind instruments, from four to six feet long, made of bronze and sometimes beautifully decorated. They have been found in pairs perfectly tuned one to the other. Comprising the diatonic scale and major triad, they allow for twenty-two notes and produce musical sounds of a solemn and majestic, noble and war-

From *Der Grosse Herder*, Herder, Freiburg i. Br.

Runic Alphabets. Top Row: Old German; Second Row: Norse;
Bottom Rows: Anglo-Saxon.

like character. Twenty-three "lurers" are in the possession of the National Museum in Copenhagen. Their tonal quality has been tested in several public concerts in Denmark.

An ancient Germanic script, based on an alphabet of symbolic signs which are known as "runes" (from Gothic *run,* "secret, mystery") has come down to us in the form of inscriptions on weapons and monuments. The inscriptions and symbols are of a ritualistic, magic, or oracular significance, but as they all date from the post-Roman period it is very doubtful whether they were known to the prehistoric tribes. It is much more likely that the runic symbols were derived from Italic alphabets. They occur in all Germanic regions and are characterized by their rugged, angular shape. The symbols were scratched or carved on wood, metal, or stone. Altogether nearly 3000 such inscriptions have been discovered, most of them in Scandinavia. The knowledge of runic symbols is still alive in some parts of present-day Sweden.

The existence of a primitive Germanic poetry, of religious dances and cultic ceremonies is, in the absence of documents, more or less a matter of conjecture. Certain conclusions may be drawn with a reasonable amount of probability by referring to analogical customs and habits of other primitive peoples. So it may be assumed that the various arts and crafts of the ancient Germanic peoples were organically interrelated; that there prevailed a unity of poetry, music, and the dance; that music, poetry, and dances were strongly rhythmical and constituted part of the religious cult and of all those rites and ceremonies in which the meaning of group life manifests itself.

The Germanic Peoples Enter the Historic Stage. The Germanic tribes had ceased to be full-fledged barbarians when they finally made their appearance in the history of Europe. They represented a peasant culture of at least a thousand years' duration and of a definite physiognomy in its agriculture, its craftsmanship, and its standard of living.

Pytheas of Massilia (Marseilles), a contemporary of Alexander the Great (356–323 B.C.), who traveled from Marseilles to Britain and the coast of the North Sea, was the first one to mention the early Germanic peoples of historic times. He also tells of amber fisheries that he found on the west coast of Jutland. Julius Caesar (100–44 B.C.) knew the Germanic lands and tribes from personal contact and experience, and so did Cornelius Tacitus (A.D. 54–120) whose *Germania* contains the most comprehensive and detailed information on Germanic culture as it existed at the beginning of the Christian era. As a writer of history, Tacitus was a pragmatist: in his desire to castigate the physical and moral decadence of Imperial Rome he painted the picture of the vigorous young barbarians in bright and glowing colors, putting strong emphasis on their virtues and passing mildly or silently over their vices.

The documentary evidence that is available suggests that light and shade were more evenly distributed. The same qualification applies to some of the highly idealized statues that were produced by Roman artists, although there can be no doubt that the makers of these sculptures were deeply impressed with the vigor and the noble bearing of these young Germanic giants. Vivid scenes of Germanic life are depicted on Roman triumphal arches and columns, commemorating imperial victories over the barbarians. Most illuminating of all, for prehistoric and early historic times alike, are, of course, the finds that have been unearthed in all parts of Germany, from moors and lakes, fields and forests, caves and tombs.

The Country. As early as in Caesar's time the Germanic tribes had advanced far into central and southern Germany. Germanic settlements had been established on both banks of the Rhine, in Bohemia, and along the Danube, not to speak of the Germanic population of the Scandinavian North, of England, Greenland, and Iceland. The surrounding Celtic states in the south and west had been conquered and dispersed.

According to the Romans Germany at that time consisted mainly of impenetrable forests and impassable swamps. "Who would ever think of leaving Asia, Africa, or Italy and migrate to Germany?" asks Tacitus. "It is a wild country under an inclement sky, hard to cultivate, a gloomy sight for anyone who does not call it his home." This description applied especially to the northwestern frontier districts. There were indeed moors and swamps and huge, densely grown forests extending through a large part of the Germanic regions and, often enough, seriously impeding the advancing Roman armies. The climate was rough and damp. On the other hand, approximately one fifth of the area known to have been inhabited by Germanic tribes, and especially the plains and valleys alongside the big rivers and the coast regions, was richly populated and well cultivated.

The People. In the latter part of the first century A.D. from three to four million people were living on approximately the same territory that in modern times marked the geographical boundaries of Germany up to 1945. It is the prevailing opinion today that the Germanic variety of the Nordic and Phalic races originated in the coastal region of the Baltic as the result of a process of miscegenation. In Julius Caesar's time three major divisions, the same that characterize the Germanic nations to this day, may be distinguished: (1) the *eastern Germans,* who lived on the Oder and Vistula, comprising, among others, the Visigoths, the Ostrogoths, the Burgundians, and the Vandals; (2) the *northern Germans,* who occupied the southern part of Scandinavia, the adjacent islands, and Jutland; (3) the *western Germans,* who dwelled in the most southerly part of Jutland and in the oblong space between the Elbe, the North Sea, the Rhine, and the Main. The name *German* is probably of Gallic-Celtic origin. It has come into general usage since Caesar's time, and may imply the meaning of "neighbor" or "brother." The name *deutsch* (Old High German *diutisk,* from *Theoda,* "people, tribe") is of later origin and occurs first in its latinized form *theodiscus* (*lingua theodisca*) in documents of the eighth and ninth centuries.

Among the three major groups of Germanic peoples the northern Germans, due to their remoteness from the influence of the Mediterranean civilizations, have best preserved their ancient Germanic traits. The eastern Germans played a most significant part in the final destruction of the Roman Empire and the formation of the new Romanic civilizations. The descendants of the Western tribes are the present-day Germans, the French, the Dutch, the Flemings, and the Anglo-Saxons.

Appearance. Despite specific tribal characteristics the Germans appear as a unity when compared with the Italic and other Mediterranean populations. They were people of fair complexion, with reddish-blond hair, and of powerful build. Ausonius, a Roman rhetorician and poet of the fourth century A.D., has left a poetical description of one of his slaves, a girl named Bissula of the tribe of the Suevians: "Bissula, born and brought up on the Rhine, the wintry river, German her features, golden her hair, her eyes of blue color; Bissula, inimitable in wax or by the brush of the painter; adorned by nature with charms which defy all artificial tricks. Well may other maidens use powder or rouge, her face does not owe its rosiness to the deftness of her fingers. Painter, mix the whiteness of the lilies with the purple of the roses: thus you will get the proper colors for Bissula's portrait."

While the women may have refrained from using powder and rouge, Tacitus tells us that the men used artificial dyes to give their hair a color of flaming red, probably to make themselves appear more fearful to their enemies on the battlefield. Their clothing was simple, and male and female fashions were almost identical. They wore tight-fitting sleeveless undergarments of linen or wool, breeches or trousers of the same material, and a coarse woolen outer garment in form of a cloak, often adorned with fine furs and held together on the right shoulder by an artfully shaped metal pin or brooch. Shoes were made of one piece of leather and fastened with a string around the ankles. Both men and women were fond of metal adornment which they fastened to their necks, arms, ears, fingers, and feet. The women wore necklaces of metal, amber, or glass.

The characteristic weapons were: the *framea*, a short javelin that could be thrown as well as used in hand-to-hand fighting; a hatchet called the *francisca* (Frankish: *weapon*); slings; and bows and arrows. Later on, a daggerlike sword appears as distinguished from the long, double-edged sword which is infrequently found in the earlier period. The only defensive weapon was a huge wooden shield, either oval, square, or round in shape and fortified on the outside with leather or iron bands. It was painted in the different tribal colors: white with the Cimbers, red with the Saxons, brown with the Frisians. The shield was the symbol of manhood and of freedom, and its loss in battle was proof of disgraceful cowardice. The Germans frequently crossed rivers on their shields or, using them as sleighs, slid down the icy slopes of the Alps into the Italian plains.

Domestic Living and Community Life. In Tacitus' time the Germanic house had lost some of its original primitive appearance. The Germans had, however, not yet learned from the Romans how to build in stone. Most of their dwellings were simple log houses. They were either constructed of firm wooden beams or consisted of a wooden framework (*Fachwerk*), filled in with clay, rock, and brushwood. The simplest form was the round hut, made of wood and wickerwork. Most of the houses had steep roofs covered with straw or brushwood, extending almost to the ground on one side as a protection against adverse climatic influences. Ordinarily the huts had only one room, in the center of which stood the open hearth. Chimneys were unknown, so the smoke escaped either through the door or a dormer window. Tables and stools were used, and benches ran along the walls.

The Germanic and Roman villages differed in their layouts. The Roman village had a planned regularity of design, while the typical Germanic village consisted of irregularly scattered houses, fenced off from each other and from the outside world, with a wicker fence surrounding the whole group of houses. Caves were dug in the ground outside the house and covered with leaves and dung. They served as storerooms, as a protection against the severe climate or in case of danger, and, according to Pliny, as workshops for the women and maids engaged in weaving.

The fields and plowlands were owned and cultivated by the community. All the arable land of a village was divided up and apportioned to the members of the community, with lots being redistributed every year so as to give each one the same advantages and disadvantages of soil and sun. The methods of cultivation and the seeding and harvesting periods were decreed by the village community. Outside the arable area lay the pastures and woods, the *allmende* or commons, which were likewise owned by the community, and in the use of which each one shared equally. Cities were unknown to the ancient Germans, and in the beginning they even refrained from settling down in those Roman cities which they had gained by conquest.

Standard of Living, Manners and Customs. As is to be expected, the early Germans lived simply and unpretentiously. Their main subsistence consisted of bread, vegetables, and meats. Cattle were bred for dairy purposes, sheep for their wool. Next to pork, horse meat was the principal animal food. Westphalian ham was known and appreciated even by the Romans. The Christian Church finally succeeded in eradicating the habit of eating horse meat, which it opposed on account of its intimate connection with pagan sacrificial rites. Salt was used for seasoning in the earliest times, some of the salt mines having been inherited from the Celts and worked by Celtic slaves. It was obtained in the simplest way: the brine was poured over burning logs or glowing charcoal; the water evaporated, and the salt remained. Mead (*Met*) and various kinds of beers were extensively brewed. "As a drink the Germans consume a liquid made of barley or wheat which is adulterated into a sort of wine," says Tacitus. Some of the tribes held a strong prejudice against the importation of Roman wines as contributing to enervation and effeminacy.

The slaves worked in the fields, the women in the house, and the men attended to the hunt and the business of war. The craft that was regarded as especially honorable and almost the only one worthy of a freeman was the art of smithing, manufacturing arms and ornaments. It is also the only handicraft that stands out in the world of Germanic mythology, in the heroic sagas and epics. The work of the women included the household arts of cooking, sewing, spinning, and weaving. The garments, found in excavations in all regions of Germanic influence, are adorned with embroideries which show that interlacing band ornament which is so typical of all Germanic ornamentation. It is characterized by a phantastic interplay of lines: lines with apparently no beginning and no end, entirely abstract in design, but feverishly agitated and indicative of the forceful expressionism of Germanic mentality.

The freeman had much time for leisure and loafing. He was fond of outdoor life, but he felt no pangs of conscience when he lay on a bearskin for days, sleeping, dreaming, and meditating in front of his hearth fire. Periods of inertia and introspection alternated with periods of alertness and wide-awake, energetic action. The long, dark nights of the winter season encouraged the German's natural bent for meditative brooding. But the long winters also contributed to that healthy intimacy of family life which aroused the admiration of Tacitus.

Family Life. "Strictly upheld there," says the Roman historian, "is the marriage bond, and there is no aspect of their cultural life that deserves higher praise." Although marriage had passed through the usual primitive stages of rape and purchase, it was early considered as the most important civil contract. The father was the head of the family and of the household. In the earliest times he even possessed the judicial power of life and death over wife, children, and slaves.

At the time of Caesar and Tacitus monogamy was the generally prevailing practice. Juridically the women occupied an inferior position, although actually they were highly respected and even credited with an intimate relation to supernatural powers, and with the gifts of prophecy, divination, and healing. Their advice was sought and greatly esteemed, particularly in matters of vital concern for the well-being of the community. Motherhood was woman's supreme title of honor, chastity her prime virtue. Adultery on the part of a woman was cruelly punished by the outraged husband: stripped of her garments, she was whipped through the village and frequently killed during or after the ordeal. Infidelity on the part of the husband was more frequent and went unpunished. As is the case with several Indo-Germanic peoples, earlier customs had made it obligatory for the wife to follow her husband in death.

Marriage consisted of two major phases: the ceremony of betrothal, and the nuptials. Betrothal signified the transferring of the guardianship of the future wife from her family to her husband who was usually chosen by the girl's father or guardian (*Muntwalt, Vormund*). The day after the nuptials the husband presented his newly wedded wife with her dowry (*Morgen-*

gabe) which was to offer her protection and security in the case of widowhood, desertion, or divorce.

Tacitus shows himself impressed with the large size of the Germanic family: "It is considered shameful to limit the number of children or to kill one of the offspring." Nevertheless, infanticide was not infrequent in the case of sickly or otherwise undesirable children.

Virtues and Vices. The ancient Germanic peoples possessed, as we have shown, a culture decidedly their own, but it was a culture of peasants and warriors, lacking the finish and refinements of more advanced types of civilization. They were children of nature, and there was something childlike in the mixture of violence and sentimentality, of harshness and tenderness that characterizes their lives. Their lust of adventure and love of warfare made them frequently oblivious of humane considerations and inhibitions. They tortured criminals, occasionally killed their prisoners of war, and broke solemnly sworn treaties without scruples. They indulged in immoderate drinking and gambling, a man frequently losing his property and his liberty in a game of dice. On the other hand, unswerving loyalty and unbending heroism are the two outstanding virtues of the Germanic warrior, virtues that are glorified again and again in the heroic epics and sagas. Honor and glory rank higher in the scale of values than life itself, so that even women preferred death to slavery and disgrace.

These character traits were supported and complemented by a rich and deep emotional and imaginative life (*Gemüt*) which animated tree and forest; brook, river, and lake; wind, cloud, and sky; weaving the raiment of Germanic folklore out of the threads of creative fancy.

We have here, then, a society of armed and warlike peasants whose ethics of loyalty and honor and heroic deeds is opposed to an ethics of humility, compassion, and charity as taught by some of the higher world religions, above all by Christianity. Germanic loyalty and sense of honor inspires the exaltation of vengeance. But self-respect and honor demand that the enemy be honorable and respectable.

This whole ethical code is highly personalistic: superindividual motivations, such as patriotism or religious idealism, are strangely lacking.

Tacitus devotes a special chapter to the Germanic virtue of hospitality, which was indeed practiced to the highest degree. The visitor remained with his host as long as there was food and drink left in the house, and afterward both guest and host went to a neighbor's house where they were received with the same generous hospitality. No distinction was made between strangers and friends, and friendships that had such a casual beginning frequently endured through generations.

The salesman was almost as graciously received as the traveler. Roman merchants sold their German customers weapons of bronze and iron and ornaments of silver which were preferred to those of gold. All commercial intercourse was based on barter. The monetary value of Roman coins went unappreciated. They were, however, worn as ornaments or stored away in treasure chests. The word used for the measure of barter indicates that cattle provided its standard and fixed value: *pecunia* in Latin; *Faihs* in Gothic; *fihu* in Old Saxon and Old High German; *fee* in English; *Vieh* in modern German. The great highway by which Roman civilization entered Germany was the valley of the Moselle river.

The Tribes. The tribal organization of the Germanic peoples was based on the natural organism of the family. The Germanic tribes are natural units distinguished by specific hereditary character traits which are the result of a community of race, the influence of a common ethnological and geographical environment, and similar or identical social and cultural experiences. A knowledge of Germanic tribal life will aid in the understanding of the complex character of the German nation and the appreciation of its cultural achievements.

The process of the formation of the Germanic tribes continued well into the thirteenth century A.D. Three important phases may be distinguished: (1) the *High Germanic* tribes, crossing the Rhine and Danube rivers, penetrated into Gaul and the Alpine districts; (2) the *Saxons* expanded and spread into parts of present-day Franconia and Thuringia; (3) the third movement, in which all the original tribes participated, took place east of the Elbe, the Saale, and the middle Danube.

The individual tribes are marked off from one another by dialect, custom, popular traditions, racial characteristics, literary and artistic expression. Some of them have fulfilled definite functions in the formative stages of German civilization. The Franks were the most important factor in welding the political, social, and intellectual frame of the western European tradition to the foundation of the cultural heritage of pagan and Christian Rome. The Alemans were next in taking over the reins of the Empire, proving exceptionally gifted in statesmanship, and presenting Germany with a series of great dynastic leaders. The Bavarians in their Austrian branch inherited and administered the task of ruling over the destinies of the *Reich* until, with the rise of Prussia, the younger tribes (*Neustämme*) of the north and northeast began to dominate the historic scene. The Frank Charlemagne forced the Saxons into the unity of the Roman Empire of the German nation, and the Saxon emperors were soon to take a decisive hand in the political and cultural development of the realm. The Franks and Thuringians were entrusted with the great and difficult work of colonization east of the Elbe and Saale. And it was the territory of the new colonial settlements that gave birth to the idea of German national unity and to the unified New High German language.

State and Society. The tribal organization was made up of groups of related families which were united by the strong ties of blood relationship. The gradual growth of the Germanic State may serve to illustrate the fallacy of Rousseau's and Hobbes' theories of the origins of organized civil society. The ancient Germans had not yet developed the conception of the state, and when it finally came into being, it was the outgrowth of a natural expansion of the family, not the result of an artificial and arbitrary contract based on considerations of utility and expediency. The Germanic tribesman had a strong sense of the primacy of the family as an organism endowed with specific natural and inalienable rights of its own.

Sons and daughters stayed with their families until they were married, and even then the sons continued to cultivate their family bonds and traditions. The male blood relations formed the Germanic *Sippe* (*syb*, "clan"). A certain number of clans constituted what might be called the ancient Germanic State. The head of the clan enjoyed some special privileges in regard to property and authority. Verbal offenses, bodily injuries, and murder were dealt with by the clan by means of the blood feud. Usually it was not the culprit who became the object of vengeance or was bound to offer restitution or compensation, but the most prominent member of the *Sippe*. The amount of compensation (*weregild, Wergeld*) was fixed in later times by a regular tariff which is preserved in the oldest written laws. The compensation was received by the *Sippe,* and so strong was the concept of personality and personal responsibility that he who could induce the most influential freemen to vouch for him was judged right.

The larger units of the Germanic tribes and peoples grew out of the smaller units of the *Sippe*. A *Sippe* comprised from fifty to one hundred families. The annual redistribution of land was made by drawing "lots." The different lots of the fields and the homestead together formed the "hide" or *hufa* (*Hufe*). Private ownership of land makes its appearance during and after the period of migrations.

A more artificial unit than the clan was that of the "hundreds," the "Mark Community" or *Hundertschaft,* comprising from 100 to 120 households. Geographically the territory owned by a "Mark Community" was designated as a *Gau* (Latin, *pagus;* English, *shire*).

The population was divided into two classes: the freemen and the slaves. Only the freemen, that is, only those who descended from free parents, were full-fledged members of a tribe or a village community. And only the freemen shared in the common ownership of land, were permitted to take up arms in case of war, and were admitted to the popular assemblies. The most prominent members of the class of freemen were the noblemen (athelings) who stood out by virtue of distinguished ancestry, superior capabilities, or special merits, but enjoyed no legal prerogatives. The caste of the slaves was made up chiefly of prisoners of war and their children. Members of the tribe who had gambled away their liberty were usually sold to foreign traders. The slaves were regarded as pieces of personal property or merchandise, and marriages between freemen and slaves were prohibited. Whenever such a marriage occurred, the children belonged to the class of the unfree. Otherwise, according to Tacitus, the treatment of slaves was relatively humane. Slaves who had acquired their freedom were rare exceptions, and their social position was ambiguous and indefinite, although

Tacitus claims that with tribes that were ruled by kings the freedmen sometimes rose to positions above freemen and noblemen.

The assembly of freemen expressed the sovereign power of the people in its legislative, judicial, and executive branches. These assemblies were called the *Ding* (*mahal, moot,* "thing"). Custom and tradition were important factors in their decisions, making for elasticity and flexibility of procedure. The popular assembly elected the king or *Herzog* (duke), who was given unlimited power in time of war, but who had to give up his office when peace was restored. The *Ding* also acted as a court of justice in all cases referring to public peace and order, and in grievous offenses which involved or endangered the commonweal, such as disturbances of the public peace, high treason, desertion, cowardice, moral turpitude, sacrilege. Capital punishment was decreed as a propitiatory sacrifice to the gods, and priests* were the executioners.

The *Ding,* whether convening as the representation of the Mark Community or of the whole tribal community, was called together and presided over by the "leader" or chieftain. A village community was headed by the "alderman" or "senior"; the hundreds by a distinguished member of the nobility (*Markgraf, Gaugraf*). The chiefs of the combined mark community constituted in many cases the leadership of the tribe. With some of the eastern tribes a limited monarchical rule under the leadership of a hereditary king seems to have been customary.

The followers of the chief were called the *thegans* (*Degen*) or thanes, representing in their entirety the *gasindi* (*Gesinde*) or *trustio*. "It is disgraceful for the chief," says Tacitus, "to be outdone in bravery by the thanes, disgraceful for the thanes not to equal the bravery of the chief. But it brings reproach and lifelong infamy to survive the chief after he has fallen in battle." The relationship between leader and thanes provided ample opportunity for the practice of the Germanic virtue of loyalty, the *Nibelungentreue* of the sagas and epics. The basis of this relationship is an unwritten contract of mutual service, trust, and obligation, and the thane was willing to subordinate his own judgment completely to the superior authority of the leader. However, violation of the trust on the part of the chief immediately invalidated the contract.

Civil law and criminal law in the modern sense were unknown to the Germanic tribes. Custom, however, frequently acquired the force of law, establishing definite legal traditions which were handed on by word of mouth and in symbolic language. Laws fixed in writing do not occur until after the migration period. Even in much later times Roman law has never been able to obliterate the survival of important legal elements of indigenous tribal concepts, and the reform of the German law codes under National

---

* The Germanic tribes had no special caste of priests but designated some worthy members of the community as *Ewarte* (protectors of Sacred Law).

Socialism was primarily concerned with the elimination of the so-called "alien" spirit of Roman Law.

Mythology and Religion. It is perhaps in their mythological and religious concepts that peoples are truest to themselves and most expressive of their innermost being. Early Germanic religion must not be judged according to the mature religious ideology of the North Germanic Edda, which received its shape as late as the eighth century A.D. and is partly influenced by Christianity. On the other hand, pre-Christian documents and reports on Germanic religion are completely lacking, because the written tradition begins only with the conversion of the Germanic tribes. The Roman historians, on the other hand, are no unbiased observers, and their reports moreover refer primarily to the southern tribes. The judgment of the early Christian missionaries is similarly colored by their uncompromising opposition to Germanic paganism. It is therefore very difficult to give an objective account of ancient Germanic religious beliefs and cultic observances. Our most reliable guides and informants are the old Icelandic sagas and the many archaeological finds of the Stone and Bronze Ages.

The gods of the genuinely Germanic religion were conceived as personal powers to which the Germanic tribesman maintained a personal relationship. They were feared and revered as superhuman guardians and protectors, of whom the worshiper expected certain favors and advantages. His relationship to his gods was very much like his relationship to his chiefs: it was based on an attitude of *"do ut des,"* of mutual service, trust, and loyalty. The god is man's *fulltrui* (the term is familiar to the Icelanders), one who can be trusted implicitly, the god-friend, and the Germanic warrior-peasant's heroic philosophy of life is projected into the skies where he visualizes the cosmic strife that rages between gods and giants, ending with the *Götterdämmerung* (twilight of the gods) and the destruction of the gods by the giants.

Both gods and giants are "beyond good and evil." Neither are exemplary moral types to be imitated or even approximated, with the possible exception of Balder, who appears as the just and peace-loving judge. Both gods and giants are shrewd and powerful, but neither omnipotent nor eternal. Their battle is one between cosmic powers, not one between moral forces or ethical principles. Man approaches them in awe and fear, trying to propitiate their wrath and gain their favor by offering them human and other sacrifices.

There are antagonistic elements, then, in the Germanic concept of the divine, the trust inspiring and the awe inspiring in close proximity. Although they seem hard to reconcile, they supplement each other, and together they express the spirit of the Germanic pagan religion. Donar-Thor is the friendly, good-natured god of a peasant religion, the real *fulltrui,* while Wodan-Odin represents the mysterious and demonic elements in Germanic religion. Thor is the guardian of the pastures, the god who watches over the changing seasons and climates, the donor of rich harvests, prosperity, and honorable peace. He is the protector of married life and the guarantor of justice. But even Thor is at the same time the god of war, thus in himself combining the contrasting elements of friendly guardianship and dark and dangerous irrationality. With his hammer he smashes the enemies of men. He seems to be related to the ancient Aegaean thunder-god whose emblems were the double ax and the bull. To the Roman historians he is known as Hercules and Jupiter, and the Romans named after him the fifth day of the week (Thor's Day, Thursday, *Donnerstag*).

Ziu-Sachsnot is the war-god of the Saxons. The Romans called him Mars, naming after him the second day of the week (Ziu's Day, Tuesday, *Dienstag*). Wodan, whom the Scandinavians know as Odin, is the youngest of the Germanic sky-gods, the majestic god of death, of storm, of the battlefield, of wisdom, and of witchcraft. He is the leader of the army of disembodied souls, familiar to the Roman writers as Mercurius, and living on in the name of the third weekday (Wodan's Day, Wednesday). Even after having been raised to the position of the supreme sky-god he retained his original character of incalculable and unfathomable irrationality. He destroys heroes and protects cowards; he sows discord among friends and relations. He changes his attachments and affiliations, deserting his friends when they need him most. In his unreliability the arbitrariness of Fate appears personified and rationalized. In his capacity as the "father of all" (*Allvater*) he represents a symbolization of superindividual care and concern: he links the destinies of men with the cosmic fate of the gods and giants, gathering the proven heroes of the battlefield into *Valhalla* to save them for the final and monumental contest.

All Germanic peoples worshiped the great Mother Goddess Nerthus (*Hertha*, later *Njödr, Hödur*) whose cult has an almost exact parallel in that of Cybele, the mother of the gods, in Asia Minor. Some Germanic tribes call her *Frija* or *Frigg,* making her the patroness of love and matrimony. The Romans connected her with Venus and named after her the sixth day of the week (*Dies Veneris*, French "*Vendredi,*" Frija's Day, Friday, *Freitag*). Nerthus and her cult apparently belonged to the religion of the earth, of vegetation and sexual reproduction of the more ancient peasant culture, while the high gods or sky-gods are the creation of the more advanced warrior society which had, however, retained its peasant traditions. This dualism is even more manifest in the Old Norse mythology of early medieval times: the Scandinavians know two divine races or families, *Vanir* and *Aesir,* the former gods of the earth, the latter gods of the sky.

Heaven and earth, mountain and forest were populated by friendly and hostile spirits, elves, nymphs, dryads, dwarfs, goblins, witches, and werewolves. The spirits of the dead were believed to live on for a certain period of time in the trees and springs near the scenes of their former lives and activities.

Summarizing, it may be said that Germanic mythology and religion offer no final answer to the quest of the purpose and meaning of life. Even the best and most heroic life is ultimately lived and spent in vain. The gods, too, are subject to the decrees of Fate. And the final combat terminates the existence of the earth, of the gods, and of men. When *Ragnarök*, the fatal time, has arrived, "the sun will turn black, the earth sinks into the sea, the stars disappear from the skies, smoke and fire rage, burning flames lick the skies" (*Wöluspa*). The heroes cannot save the gods, but must perish with them, vanquished by the hostile powers. But what will happen to those hostile powers which survive the twilight of the gods, no tale will ever tell.

Thus Germanic mythology and religion dismiss us with an open question. This question was answered in the stormy centuries of the migrations with the reception of a new world religion in which the Germanic warrior-peasant rose above and beyond the stature of the gods of his cultural childhood.

Chapter 2

MIGRATIONS

Causes. The mass-movement of Germanic peoples (*Völkerwanderung*) which coincided with and in part contributed to the downfall of the Roman Empire and brought about decisive changes in the political map of Europe, appears as one of the last phases of the Indo-European migrations. The final outburst of these cataclysmic forces swept the European continent, leaving behind it ruin and destruction, to be sure, but also the seeds of a regeneration of Mediterranean culture and the formation of a Germanic and European civilization.

What was it that caused these peoples to abandon their native lands and, in many cases accompanied by their wives and children, their livestock and all their movable possessions, to look for new homes? One of the main reasons was the increase in population and the growing scarcity of habitable and arable land. The culture of the southern countries with their mild climate and their highly developed art of living exercised a strong power of attraction and fascination. Lust of adventure and the warlike spirit of ambitious leaders added a further motive. The increasing pressure of neighboring tribes, adverse social and political conditions, defeat in war, intertribal quarrels and rivalries were also back of the desire for a radical change in the form of a new start in more favorable surroundings. Finally, it may be said that the migrations were a manifestation of Germanic restlessness, a response to the romantic urge to seek out and conquer the distant unknown, the outgrowth of *"Fernweh"* and *"Wanderlust."*

Expansive Forces. The basis of the collective migratory movements was originally given in the organizations of the *Sippe* (clan) and *Stamm* (tribe). Later on, this basis grew broader, other communities and entire tribes following the lead of one group, thus giving the movement momentum and intensifying the force of its impact.

We see eastern and western Germans adopting different methods in the ways in which they migrate and settle in the newly acquired territories; while Visigoths and Ostrogoths, Vandals, Burgundians, and Langobards migrate in compact groups, carrying their movements in sweeping strides into Italy, Spain, and North Africa — Franks, Alemans, Bavarians, and Thuringians proceed more slowly and hesitatingly, maintaining close contact with their former homes. Of the northern Germans only the surplus popula-

17

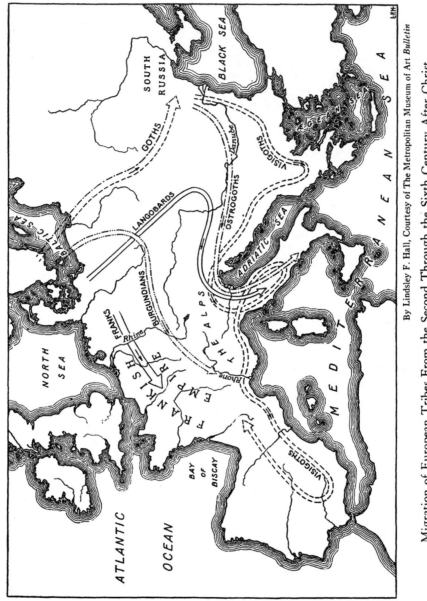

By Lindsley F. Hall, Courtesy of The Metropolitan Museum of Art *Bulletin*

Migration of European Tribes From the Second Through the Sixth Century After Christ.

tion leave their native shores on the North Sea, setting out for the conquest and settlement of Britain.

The Germanic migrations are often rather arbitrarily dated from the arrival of the Huns in Europe in A.D. 375. However, the migratory movement of the Germanic tribes had actually started long before that time. The Germanic expansion at the expense of the Celts lasted until Caesar's time. The Romans had early realized the danger which threatened from the northern barbarians. In vain they used force and cunning to break the power and spirit of their potential Germanic enemies. Roman armies marched into the Germanic lands, subjecting the conquered populations to Roman rule. They fortified the new boundaries, encouraged discord and rivalry among the different tribes, and even admitted increasing numbers of individuals and finally entire tribes into the Empire as imperial soldiers, army officers, and commanders, as semiservile agricultural workers, and as *foederati* or allies. This gradual infiltration of barbarians into the Empire acted in itself as a subversive element, and weakened further the already undermined structure of a waning civilization.

Beginnings: Bastarnians, Cimbers, and Teutons. The migrations of the Cimbers and Teutons mark the prelude of the more decisive events that were to follow. The first Germanic tribe to reach the frontiers of the Mediterranean world were the East Germanic Bastarnians who, at the beginning of the second century B.C., settled in the region between the lower Danube and the Black Sea. Toward the end of the pre-Christian era they were decisively defeated by the Romans and later mingled with the Goths and other tribes.

About 120 B.C. the Cimbers and Teutons started from their homes in Jutland and Schleswig-Holstein respectively, migrating in a southerly and southwesterly direction, finally entering Gaul and defeating several Roman armies, spreading fear and terror wherever they went (*"Terror Cimbricus," "Furor Teutonicus"*). They failed, however, to take advantage of their victory, so that the Romans were given ample time to prepare for an efficient counterattack. In two battles Teutons and Cimbers were annihilated by the Roman general Marius (156–86 B.C.), the Teutons at Aquae Sextiae (102 B.C.), the Cimbers on the Raudian Fields in the plain of Vercellae (101 B.C.), in the region of the upper Po river.

The first Germanic invasion of Italy thus ended in tragedy and defeat. As was customary in Germanic warfare, women and children, the aged and infirm, awaited the outcome of the battle barricaded behind the bulwark of wagons (*Wagenburg*), the women encouraging the warriors with singing and shouting, even repulsing with clubs and axes those who attempted to flee. After the victors had denied the women's request to permit them to enter the service of the Vestal Virgins,* so that their honor would be

---

* *Vesta* is the ancient Helic goddess of the hearth fire (Greek, *Hestia*). The "Vestal Virgins" in ancient Rome guarded the hearth fire in Vesta's Temple. They were chosen by lot and enjoyed special privileges in the city of Rome.

protected, the wives of these Germanic warriors first killed their children and then committed suicide.

The destruction of the Teutons and their subsequent disappearance from historical records proves conclusively that, aside from their being one of the Germanic tribes, there is no etymological or other connection between "German" (*deutsch*) and "Teutonic."

Suevians and Cheruscans: Caesar, Ariovistus, Arminius. About three decades after the extinction of the Cimbers and Teutons we find Ariovistus in Gaul. Ariovistus was the leader of the powerful tribe of the Suevians with whom Julius Caesar struggled for the possession of the Gallic province. He was defeated by Caesar's superior man power and strategy and had to withdraw across the Rhine, which therewith became the temporary boundary line between German and Roman territory.

The threatening neighborhood of the warlike tribes caused the emperor, Augustus (63 B.C. — A.D. 14), to occupy and fortify the Germanic lands up to the Danube, while his stepsons Drusus and Tiberius penetrated into the interior of Germany and conquered the territory between the Rhine and the Weser. Roman imperialism had already visualized an expansion of the colonial empire east to the river Elbe and south through Bohemia to Budapest, when these ambitious plans were thwarted and the Roman advance into Germanic territory halted by a major German victory.

The Roman colonial policy in Germany suffered its first severe setback at the hands of Arminius (Hermann), a Cheruscan prince who, in the famous battle in the Teutoburg Forest (A.D. 9), attacked and defeated the powerful Roman legions which were under the command of the provincial governor, Varus. At the end of the third day Varus fell upon his own sword, not daring to face his emperor after the annihilation of three legions. The battle marked a turning point in the destinies of Rome as well as of Germany, and Roman pride and prestige never quite recovered from this severe blow. Arminius, who had received his military training in the Roman armies, proved himself the docile disciple of sophisticated Roman strategies. The victory had been effected by a conspiracy of several Germanic tribes and, with the aid of cunning and deceit, resulted in the liberation of the greater part of Germany from Roman domination. Augustus' grandson, Germanicus, failed in several attempts to regain the former supremacy.

Once more the Rhine became the boundary line, until a few decades later the Romans proceeded to reoccupy some of the territory on the eastern bank of the river, concluding their colonial expansion into Germany with the construction of the *limes* or frontier wall which was begun under Emperor Claudius and completed under the emperors of the Flavian dynasty (first century B.C.). It was to facilitate the protection and supervision of the frontier districts, and extended into present-day Austria and Hungary. The *Saalburg* in the Taunus Mountains is part of the "limes," owing its restoration to Emperor William II. The fertile lands of the Rhine and Danube became the seat of a rich Roman provincial culture whose memory is still preserved in the ruins of irrigation works, aqueducts, baths, temples, and palaces, among which the *Porta Nigra* (Black Portal) in Treves (Trier) is the most monumental (first century B.C.). German cities of Roman origin, such as Strasbourg (*Argentoratum*), Mainz (*Mogontiacum*), Köln (*Colonia Agrippinensis*), Augsburg (*Augusta Vindelicum*), Regensburg (*Castra Regina*), Wien (*Vindobona*), and the net of highways linking these centers of urban life and culture, give evidence of the Romans' amazing building activity. Agricultural methods were greatly improved, and the commercial transactions of Roman merchants extended far to the north, including the rich amber trade of the Baltic.

New National Formations. For about 150 years relative peace was maintained between the Romans and the Germanic tribes. In the meantime, the beginning of the major phase of the great Germanic migrations was foreshadowed by a steady increase of the Germanic populations and a growing restlessness among the tribes. Their agricultural methods were relatively undeveloped and too inefficient to extract from the soil the necessary amount of food supplies. Their large herds of cattle made them look out for new pastures.

By the beginning of the fourth century A.D. we find that the political events of the recent past had led to the formation of several new nations. Wars, conquests, new alignments and alliances had strengthened the national consciousness, so that a number of smaller tribes joined in larger national confederations. On the eve of the second and major phase of the migrations two great East Germanic groups occupied the territory along the Rhine: the Franks were settled on the lower Rhine and the Alemans on the upper Rhine; in the northwest, along the coast of the North Sea and in the Danish peninsula, were the Saxons, Angles, and Jutes, the future conquerors of England; the Frisians, too, were located on the North Sea, the Vandals on the upper reaches of the Oder, the Langobards (Lombards) between the Oder and the Vistula, while the Burgundians drifted westward from the Vistula to the Main, and the Thuringians retained their ancient central position. Far in the southeast we find the kingdoms of the Ostrogoths (*Ostgoten*) and Visigoths (*Westgoten*), the greatest of the new Germanic nations. In the second century A.D. they had migrated from their old homes on the Baltic to southern Russia and advanced to the Black Sea.

Bishop Ulfilas and the Visigoths. The Visigoths, settled on the lower Danube in the immediate neighborhood of the Romans, were the first successful invaders of the Empire. They were the first of the Germanic peoples to accept Christianity, through their Bishop Ulfilas, who began his missionary activity among his countrymen in 341. Having been taken to Constantinople in his younger years as a hostage, he had acquired a mastery of Latin and Greek and later utilized this knowledge in his famous translation of the Bible into the Gothic tongue. He had invented for this purpose a special alphabet that followed the Greek pattern, thereby providing the most essential instrument for the creation of a written German literature.

Arianism. Ulfilas' translation of the Bible aided greatly in the spread of Christianity among the Visigoths, and through them among the Ostrogoths, Vandals, Burgundians, and other Germanic peoples. But while the Romans were adherents of the Catholic form of Christianity as embodied in the Roman Mother Church, the Visigoths, their bishop, and all those peoples that followed their example professed the creed of Arius (256–336), the founder of Arianism, who was born in Lybia and died in Constantinople. His Christology, which denied the divinity of Christ and the consubstantiality of the Father and the Son, and thereby attacked the Catholic dogma of the Trinity, was condemned as heretical by the First General Church Council of Nicaea (325).

The Arian sect gained immeasurably in power and prestige after the Vandals in North Africa, the Visigoths in southern Gaul and Spain, the Ostrogoths in Italy, and the Burgundians in southern France had succeeded in establishing powerful kingdoms, making Arianism their state religion, so that the terms "Arian" and "Germanic" were henceforth used synonymously, in polemical opposition to "Roman."

As a state religion Arianism had identified itself with these Germanic nationalities to such a degree that it did not survive their downfall and destruction. The adoption of Roman Catholicism by those nations which lived through the stormy centuries of the migrations and emerged victoriously from the disaster dealt the deathblow to the remnants of the Arian Sect. It lingered on to the seventh century and then disappeared from ecclesiastical and secular history.

The First Gothic Invasion and the Appearance of the Huns. When the Visigoths finally invaded the Roman Empire, they did so not so much of their own volition as under the pressure thrust upon them by the advancing Huns who, after having conquered the Ostrogoths in 375, threatened to overrun the territory of the Visigoths. The Huns were fierce and barbaric Mongolian or Tartaric nomads. For centuries they had been the scourge of civilized China until they were expelled by the emperors of the Han dynasty. As early as 49 B.C. they started on their westward movement, in search of new pastures.

The Gothic historian Jordanes describes them as short, broad-shouldered, and bowlegged, with hideous and beardless faces of yellow complexion, inseparable from their horses, living, fighting, eating, and sleeping on horseback.

With the appearance of the Huns in eastern Europe the prolonged border warfare between Romans and Germans enters upon a new stage. Shortly after the Mongolians had conquered the Ostrogoths and subjected them to their rule, the Visigoths, in fear and horror of the irresistibly advancing savages, asked permission of the Romans to cross the Danube and enter Roman territory. After having been admitted under humiliating terms and with much abuse and ill treatment by Roman officials, they took up arms and destroyed the imperial army, which joined battle with them at Adrianople

(378) under the personal command of the eastern Emperor Valens, who was killed in battle.

The End of the Western Empire. The battle of Adrianople marked the beginning of the end of the Roman Empire of the West. After Constantinople had been established as the second capital of the Empire by Emperor Constantine (A.D. 330), the center of gravity had shifted to the East. The growing estrangement between the eastern and western parts of the Empire was deepened by the adoption of Arianism in the East.

After the death of Emperor Theodosius (395) the Roman commonwealth was divided into the Eastern Empire under Arcadius, and the Western Empire under Honorius. While Constantinople and the Eastern Empire were spared the harassing experiences of the barbarian onslaught, and were capable of continuing the revival of the cultural traditions of classical Rome, the Western Empire was exposed to the full and brutal force of the invasions. About the middle of the fifth century West Rome found herself thrown back upon her original Italian boundaries. The East Germanic mercenary soldiers who were put in charge of Rome's defense, the Romans having grown unfit for military service, deposed Romulus Augustulus, the last emperor of the West, mockingly called "the little emperor," and proclaimed their leader Odovacar of the tribe of the Scirians as their king (476).

Thus the western Roman Empire of glorious memory came to an end, a disaster of extraordinary dimensions which shocked the pagan and Christian world alike. It seemed that the end of all things had come. In 396, when the storm was only beginning and the worst was yet to come, St. Jerome wrote: "The mind shudders when dwelling on the ruin of our day. For twenty years and more, Roman blood has been flowing ceaselessly over the broad countries between Constantinople and the Julian Alps, where the Goths, the Huns, and the Vandals spread ruin and death. Bishops live in prison, priests and clerics fall by the sword, churches are plundered, altars are turned into feeding-troughs. How many Roman nobles have been the prey of the barbarians! On every side sorrow, on every side lamentation, everywhere the image of death." And at the end of the sixth century Pope Gregory the Great, looking back from the chaotic disorder of the end phase of the migration period to the material prosperity of the early Christian centuries, repeated the words of Jerome: "Everywhere death, everywhere mourning, everywhere desolation! In the age of Trajan, on the contrary, there was long life and health, material prosperity, growth of population. Yet while the world was still flourishing, in men's hearts it had already withered."

The Visigoths Continue Their March of Conquest. The battle of Adrianople in 378 was an epochal event in that it sounded the death knell for the almost legendary superiority and invincibility of Rome. Theodosius (379–395), who had succeeded the defeated Emperor Valens, permitted the Visigoths to settle in Thrace, exempting them from taxation and enrolling 40,000 of them in the Roman armies. The events that followed center in the political and military leadership of Alaric, king of the Visigoths (398–410). For a while his aggressive ambition was checked by the Roman general, Stilicho, who was himself of Germanic race. Their forces and talents were evenly matched. But after Stilicho had fallen a victim to the jealousy of Emperor Honorius, Alaric led his people down into Italy, marched three times upon Rome, and, in the year 410, entered and sacked the city. He died in the same year. His brother-in-law Ataulf married Gallia Placidia, half sister of Honorius, and obtained from the emperor the permission to settle his people in southwestern Gaul, from where they expanded into Spain, establishing there a new Visigothic kingdom which lasted in Gaul until the coming of the Franks in the sixth century, and in Spain till the Mohammedan invasion of 711.

The Vandals. The Visigoths had been preceded in the possession of Spain by the Vandals who, coming from the German East, had reached the Spanish peninsula in 406. Invited by the imperial ruler of North Africa, Count Boniface, to come to his assistance in his rebellion against Rome, they crossed the straits of Gibraltar in 429, under the inspired leadership of Gaiseric (428–477), entered Africa, and devastated the region of the North African seaboard. While they besieged the city of Hippo (430), St. Augustine, its bishop, died inside the city walls.

In 439 Gaiseric captured Carthage, the largest city and the most important harbor on the African coast, which he used as a naval base to strike at the dwindling commerce of the Empire. In 455 the Vandals sacked and pillaged Rome, sparing, however, the Christian churches, and carrying the golden roof of the temple of Jupiter back to their own capital. Their African kingdom lasted until 534, when it was destroyed by the armies of the Eastern emperor, Justinian (527–565).

That the Vandals were not the beasts of prey and wanton savages which they are frequently depicted to be — the term "vandalism" was coined by a French bishop in the eighteenth century — is suggested by the words of Salvianus, a Roman-Gallic priest who weighs the merits of Romans and barbarians against each other: "Whose wickedness," he asks, "is as great as that of the Romans? There is none of that kind found among the Vandals, none among the Goths. One thing is certain: the Vandals have been very moderate. Who can help but admire their tribes who, although entering the richest cities, concerned themselves with the pleasures of the corrupt only in so far as they scorned their moral corruption, and adopted only their good qualities? Among the Goths there are no unchaste people but Romans, and among the Vandals not even Romans; not that they alone are chaste, but, to relate something new, incredible, and almost unheard of: they have made even the Romans chaste."

And again he says: "They are growing from day to day, and we decline; they prosper, and we are humiliated; they flourish, and we wither." This may be as one-sided a statement as some of the reports of Tacitus, and it may have been prompted by the same reasons. We hold no brief for the Vandals: they were barbarians and, to a certain degree, they acted as savages, destroying, looting, marauding wherever they went. But they were not unsusceptible to higher cultural influences and impulses: they let themselves be persuaded by Pope Leo I to spare the lives of the civilian population of Rome, the churches, and some of the art treasures of the city. Only too quickly they succumbed to the sophistication, the luxuries, and the moral corruption of Mediterranean culture, paying for the surrender of their national traditions with the loss of their national existence.

Attila, Leader of the Huns. After having forced the Visigoths across the Danube into Roman territory (cf. p. 22), the Huns had organized an empire of their own north of the Black Sea and the lower Danube, thus being a constant threat to the peace and stability of the Eastern Empire. Under their great leader Attila who, as King Etzel, lives on with his people in the idealized account of the greatest of German folk epics, the Lay of the Nibelungs (*Nibelungenlied*), they crossed the southern frontier (445), and ravaged the provinces south of the Danube to the walls of Constantinople. Then they turned on the Western Empire, crossed the Rhine, and invaded Gaul.

Repulsed in 451, in the fierce but undecisive battle on the Catalaunian Fields (near Châlons-sur-Marne), by the combined efforts of Romans and barbarians, Attila returned in the following year, entered Italy, and, after sacking several cities in the north, returned to the region of the Danube and died shortly afterward. We are told that this unexpected retreat and the fact that Attila refrained from attacking and destroying Rome was due to the interference and persuasive power of Pope Leo I. Attila's empire crumbled almost immediately after his death. The Huns as a tribe disappeared from Europe and from the historic scene even more suddenly than they had originally emerged from the Asiatic steppes, although their race was partially absorbed by the Turks and Hungarians.

The Ostrogoths. After Odovacar of the tribe of the Scirians had deposed Romulus Augustulus (cf. p. 23) and subsequently taken over the government (476), he was granted the title of "Patrician" by the Eastern emperor, Zeno. This was nothing but an official acknowledgment of an actual situation, Italy having been ruled by barbarian generals for the past two decades. But in 489 Odovacar himself met the fate of the emperors whose place he had usurped. After Attila's death the Ostrogoths had freed themselves from the rule of the Huns and, under their capable leader and King, Theoderic (the Great), who is commemorated as Dietrich von Bern (Verona) in the German sagas and epics, waged war upon Odovacar. Not being able to prevail over him in battle, Theoderic resorted to trickery, invited Odovacar to negotiate a peace treaty, and assassinated him. Thereupon he conquered Italy and established his court at Ravenna.

As a ruler (489–526), Theoderic was relatively just and progressive, and is thus portrayed by Procopius, the historian of the Eastern Empire: "His manner of ruling over his subjects was worthy of a great emperor; for he maintained justice, made good laws, protected his country from invasion, and gave proof of extraordinary prudence and valor." He called philosophers and poets to his court and fostered a literary revival. Formally he recognized the superiority of the Eastern emperor Anastasius, he too holding the title of "Patrician"; actually, however, he was not only the king of the Ostrogoths but the independent ruler of Italy.

The problems of Theoderic's rule were complicated by the fact that Italy was now composed of two distinct races whose members lived side by side, preserving their own traditions, practicing their own laws, cultivating their own religion: Romans and Goths; Catholics and Arians. The military rule and caste was purely Gothic, the civil government purely Roman. And Theoderic insisted that these divisions be strictly observed and maintained. In this he succeeded to a remarkable extent, even in handling the difficult religious situation. "We cannot," he wrote, "impose religion, because no one can be compelled to believe against his will." Theoderic's death coincided with the splendid revival of the Eastern Empire under Justinian (527–565). Factional strife soon weakened the resistance of the Gothic kingdom, and made it the prey of Justinian's armies. And thus the powerful Ostrogoths, too, disappeared from the history of civilization.

Revival of Classical Learning Under Theoderic. The revival of learning and literature, which Theoderic encouraged, was to serve as an important link between the classical culture of antiquity and the Christian humanism of the early Middle Ages. Under Theoderic's rule the civil administration was in the hands of highly cultured Roman officials who carefully preserved the classical inheritance. Boethius (480–525) and Cassiodorus (490–583), scholars and educators of great distinction, were both in the service of Theoderic. Boethius has been called "the last of the classics and the first of the schoolmen." He transmitted to the medieval West the knowledge of Aristotelian logic and Greek (Euclidean) mathematics. While in prison and awaiting his execution for an alleged conspiracy against Theoderic, he composed his *Consolations of Philosophy,* a perfect blend of classical tradition and a thoroughly Christian philosophy of life.

Cassiodorus, in his position as Minister of State, tried to reconcile the Germanic and Roman types of culture. After his plan of a Christian university had failed and the outbreak of the Gothic wars began to impede his cultural activities, he founded a monastery at Vivarium, in the region of his Calabrian estates, collected a library, and drew up two programs of monastic studies ("Institute of Divine and Secular Letters"), including a compendium of the seven Liberal Arts. It was his idea to harmonize the essential features of the classical Roman curriculum with the needs and requirements of the new Christian society. Thus he made Vivarium the cradle of the Western tradition of monastic learning.

The Lombards. The last of the invaders of Italy were the West Germanic Lombards (Langobards, *longo bardi,* the long-bearded ones), who settled in the northern and central parts of Italy and whose influence extends to medieval history and civilization. They invaded northern Italy in 568, and were able to maintain their rule over the conquered territories for about two hundred years. In 774 their power was destroyed by Charlemagne, who himself assumed the title of "King of the Lombards." Racially they were absorbed by the new Romance populations, the name of the province of Lombardy being one of the few reminders of their national identity.

The Anglo-Saxons. After the Roman legions had been withdrawn from Britain at the beginning of the fifth century, to come to the rescue of the Romans in Italy and Gaul, the Jutes, Angles, and Saxons sailed from their homes on the North Sea and conquered the British Isles in the course of the two succeeding centuries. The Romanized Celtic population was destroyed or pushed back into the hill country of Wales and Cornwall. They remained apart from the race of the Germanic and pagan invaders, who developed Germanic institutions along the same lines as the Germanic peoples on the Continent.

After the Migrations. The Germanic kingdoms which originated during the centuries of the migrations were of relatively short duration, with the exception of those of the Franks and the Anglo-Saxons. The conquest of Gaul by the Frankish tribes, completed early in the sixth century, marks one of the milestones of German and European history, and transcends in scope, substance, and consequences the confines of the migration period. All the other tribes and nationalities were soon absorbed by the numerical and cultural superiority of the native Roman populations.

This process of assimilation and fusion, which ultimately issued in the formation of medieval and modern Europe, worked to the mutual advantage of the two cultures and races: the barbarians adopting the habits, attitudes, and outlook of the higher civilization, and the Romans experiencing the regenerative and purgative effects of a young and undespoiled cultural vitality. The new Romance (Latin) nations whose languages grew out of the vulgar Latin of the provincial populations of the Empire, owe their cultural and national existence to this Germanic-Roman synthesis. But while with them the Roman tradition remained the dominating element in life and thought, in art and literature, in religion and philosophy, the Franks and Anglo-Saxons instilled the vigorous individuality and originality of their own national heritage into the receptive molds of pagan and Christian Rome. The culture of the Franks, in particular, stands out as the fountainhead and pattern of a future German civilization.

It appears, then, that despite so many instances of a stupendous waste and loss of spiritual and material goods, the listless squandering of an inherited treasury of ideas and accomplishments by ruthless barbarians, the age of the migrations represents the incubation period of German culture. It ended with a considerable expansion of the habitable area of the German peoples, and it provided the natural and ideal setting for those national entities that had proven culturally most healthy, promising, and creative in the sifting process of these dark centuries.

Chapter 3

THE FRANKS AND THE CHRISTIANIZATION OF GERMANY

A. MEROVINGIANS

The Merovingian Kingdom of the Franks. We have seen that of all those Germanic tribes who played a prominent part in the migrations, only the Franks and the Anglo-Saxons succeeded in creating civil organizations that survived the dark centuries of destruction and ruin. And among those peoples who stayed within the confines of their homelands the Franks were destined to become the founders of a civilized German state and the pioneers of the German civilization of the future.

The name "Franks" probably means "the free ones," i.e., the people on the right (east) bank of the Rhine who were nontributary to the Romans. They are first mentioned in A.D. 241, located in the region of the middle and lower Rhine, and comprising the two major groups of the Salians and Ripuarians. After A.D. 400 we find them in northern Gaul and in present-day Holland and Belgium. By virtue of a long tradition of contact and association with the Roman Empire, they formed the real bridge between the civilizations of ancient Rome and medieval Europe. In Gaul the Roman and barbarian societies met and complemented each other, providing through their fusion the basis of new social and cultural organisms.

In the year 486 Clovis (Clodovech), a Salian Frank of the family of Meroveus, became the absolute ruler of a strong Germanic kingdom of mixed Germanic-Roman population. He had cleared his way to the throne by the murder of all possible rivals and, after his accession, consolidated his rule by successive victories over the Gallo-Romans under Syagrius at Soissons (486), the Alemans (496), the Visigoths (507), and subsequently all the Frankish tribes, including the Ripuarians. Under Clovis' successors the Burgundians, Thuringians, Bavarians, Langobards, and Saxons were made tributaries of the Merovingian kingdom.

However, the remaining two and a half centuries of the Merovingian dynasty were characterized by internecine struggles among the rulers and pretenders, by crime, corruption, and degeneracy which undermined the prestige of the crown and let the actual rulership pass into the hands of the chief ministers, the "mayors of the palace," who governed the country.

In the seventh century the Frankish kingdom was split into three parts,

	Frankish Kingdom in 481		Original possession of Clovis
	Conquests of Clovis		Boundaries of Kingdom of Clovis
	Conquests of his sons		Conquests of Pepin

From *Der Grosse Herder*, Herder, Freiburg i. Br.

Kingdom of the Franks From Clovis to Charlemagne (481–768).

known as Austrasia, Neustria, and Burgundy, each under its own king and mayor of the palace. The customary Frankish law for the inheritance of private property applied also to the order of royal succession, the Frankish king regarding his kingdom as his private domain which he divided among his sons. Thus each of the three kings of Austrasia, Neustria, and Burgundy had retained the title "Rex Francorum," King of the Franks. Neustria (New Land) included the territory north of the Loire with the principal cities of Paris, Soissons, and Orléans; Austrasia (East Land) comprised the eastern part of the Frankish kingdom, the territory of the later province of Lorraine with its capital Metz; Burgundy was located in the southern region of the Rhone, and included the cities of Lyon, Vienne, and Geneva.

Unity was restored in 687, when the ruling power was concentrated once more in the hands of Pepin of Heristal, the former mayor of Austrasia. Among his successors, Charles Martel (the "Hammer"), regent and mayor of the palace (*maior domus*), has earned the reputation of having saved Western civilization from the attack of the Mohammedan Arabs who, on their steady advance from the Arabian desert, along the northern coast of Africa, through Spain and into Gaul, were defeated by the Franks near Poitiers in 732. Upon Charles Martel's death the kingdom was again divided between his two sons, Pepin the Younger and Carloman. After Carloman had retired to a monastery, Pepin felt that his sovereign power was firmly enough established to warrant the deposition of the Merovingian puppet king and to claim the crown for himself and his family. With the moral support of Pope Zacharias he had himself crowned king of the Franks and solemnly consecrated by Boniface, the papal nuncio and primate of Germany, thereby establishing an important precedent regarding the future relations of Church and State. In thus obtaining the title of King of the Franks Pepin the Younger became the first royal member of that family of mayors of the palace who for three generations ruled the destinies of the Frankish realm, and who have come to be known as Carolingians from the greatest of their number, Charlemagne.

The Baptism of Clovis. When Clovis first took possession of the throne, there was one great remaining obstacle to prevent the union of Romans and Franks in the territory in which they lived side by side: the Franks were heathens, the Romans were Catholic Christians. Persuaded by his Burgundian wife Clotilde and prompted by political considerations, King Clovis had himself solemnly baptized, and was received into the Church at Reims on Christmas Day, 496, together with three thousand of his followers. This event marked a turning point in the history and civilization of Europe and of Germany. It inaugurated the close alliance between the Frankish kingdom and the Church, an alliance which, in turn, provides the background of Western medieval culture. As the champion of Roman Catholicism against Arianism, Clovis undertook his campaign against the Visigoths in 507, naïvely veiling his desire of conquest in the words reported by Bishop Gregory of Tours: "Verily it grieves my soul that these Arians should hold a part of Gaul; with God's help let us go and conquer them and take their territories."

Christianity and Paganism Among the Franks. That Christianity was frequently embraced reluctantly and practiced only nominally by the Franks, may well be imagined. The Germanic peoples in their heroic age were pagans at heart, and they remained so for some time to come, even when giving lip service to the Christian God. Pagan rites continued in the guise of Christian ceremonies and Christian forms of worship; the pagan deities lived on in the images and character traits of Christian saints; magical beliefs and practices eagerly fastened themselves on the devotion to sacred objects and places, relics and shrines. At the time of the summer solstice, burning wheels, symbolizing the sun, could still be seen rolling down the mountain slopes; pagan dances and love feasts were performed in Christian churches to honor the saints on their feast days; Christian priests moved into the places that had been vacated by the Germanic witches, sorcerers, and weathermakers.

The external routine of Roman administration was almost slavishly imitated by the barbarian king. He had his "sacred palace" with its hierarchy of officials, headed by the "mayor of the palace." The administrative unit was no longer the Germanic "hundreds" but the Roman *civitas* with its surrounding territory. The *civitas* or municipality was divided into hundreds and under the authority and jurisdiction of a count (Old English: *gerefa;* "sheriff," *Graf*) who was the king's appointee. This adaptation of Roman institutions was however outweighed by the prevalence of barbarian elements in the Merovingian State. What consolidated society was not so much the civil authority of the State, but the personal loyalty of the tribesman to his chief and his kinsfolk, of the warrior to his leader.

Social Conditions. Class distinctions, which in the earliest times seem to have been based upon the amount of freedom enjoyed, were more and more determined in Merovingian times by the possession of property, although the concept of absolute ownership was still unknown. We may roughly distinguish between freedom, semifreedom, and slavery. The large freeholders were mostly members of the aristocracy, constituting the king's mounted bodyguard, and taking the place of the old Germanic thanes. As military leaders they became more and more indispensable to the rulers. An increasing number of vassals thus received their lands as loans or fiefs (Latin: *feodum, beneficium*) from the king, the land theoretically remaining the king's property and the vassal or steward taking an oath of lifelong fidelity (fealty). The small freeholders frequently renounced their freedom and gave up their lands to some powerful secular or clerical overlord to receive it back as a "fief," in order to escape indebtedness or military service and, at the same time, to enjoy the protection of the liege lord.

As the king's vassals grew more influential they acquired important privileges, especially the so-called "immunity" which freed them from the jurisdiction of the royal courts, thus weakening the central power and authority of the State. This development marked the beginnings of "feudalism" or the "feudal" system which was to provide the political, economic, and social pattern of medieval society, and which signified the transition from the public ownership of the primitive Germanic tribes to the age of private property and the eventual rise of capitalism.

Slave trading had gained considerably, and the number of slaves increased during the migrations, because many members of the subdued populations had been reduced to the status of slaves. In Merovingian times it was still considered legal for a creditor to enslave an insolvent debtor, and enslavement was the lot of those convicted of treason, rape, and other major crimes.

Although the Church did not immediately abolish slavery — slaves were held on ecclesiastical estates to the end of the sixth century — the ecclesiastical authorities did much to ease their lot, granting them a certain amount of protection within Church territory, and gradually working toward their liberation. The institution of slavery disappeared only in proportion to the growing estimation of human life and personality.*

Law and Legal Procedure. Judicial power had passed from the tribe and the hundreds to the king. He (later on the mayor of the palace) was the supreme judge. Following the Roman model he established "the King's Court," in which the count administered justice and pronounced judgment in the local centers of the hundreds in the king's name. To determine the guilt or innocence of the accused, the old Germanic "ordeal" or appeal to "God's Judgment" (*Gottesurteil*) was still in favor. So was the duel or trial by combat, which was fought with swords, clubs, or axes. Duels between members of the opposite sexes were not uncommon, the woman as the weaker combatant being granted certain advantages. The ordeal is known in various forms, the most common being the "cauldron test" (*Kesselprobe*), in which the suspect had to take with his bare hand a stone or a ring out of a cauldron of boiling water; the "fire test" (*Feuerprobe*) which consisted in walking a certain distance, carrying red-hot irons in one's hands, or in walking barefoot over glowing plowshares; and the "water test" (*Wasserprobe*), requiring the victim to be bound and thrown into a tank. His floating upon the surface of the water was considered proof of his guilt.

The crude and barbaric administration of justice was gradually modified by the codification of Germanic law in the Latin language which followed closely upon the codification of Roman Law under Justinian I of the Eastern Empire (527-565). All the German tribes believed that every man should be judged according to the traditional legal concepts of his own people (*Volksrecht*). Thus each of the tribes had its own ancestral code. The tribal laws of the Franks, the Alemans, the Bavarians, and the Saxons were written down in Merovingian times. Even earlier the Romanized East Germanic Visigoths, Ostrogoths, and Burgundians had committed their legal concepts to writing. From the later years of Clovis' rule (508-511) dates the oldest code of German tribal law which is completely preserved: the *Lex Salica* (Salic Law), containing a detailed scale of punishments that range from simple offenses to major and capital crimes.

Currency and Trade. In Merovingian times fines and compensations were paid largely in coin, which presupposes the adoption of some system of currency, although a money economy in the medieval and modern sense was still lacking. The barter system was still commonly practiced, money being valued as a treasure rather than a means of exchange. However, the Franks were acquainted with Roman money, and Clovis introduced the

---

* During the Middle Ages the institution of slavery was gradually transformed into various forms of serfdom (*Leibeigenschaft*), which in some European countries persisted well into the eighteenth and nineteenth centuries.

gold standard of coinage as the unit of measurement (gold *solidus* or *shilling*), a shilling representing the value of approximately three dollars.

In the course of the seventh century the silver shilling replaced the gold shilling as the standard of coinage.* In order to counteract avaricious and usurious practices in commercial dealings, the first general prohibition of the taking of interest was decreed by the Church in 787, thereby opening a new field of remunerative activity to the Jews, who were outside the jurisdiction of canon law and therefore able to monopolize the money trade to the end of the Middle Ages.

Learning. In almost every department of civilization, then, we find a crossing and blend of Roman and barbarian, Christian and Germanic impulses and influences, frequently with a marked preponderance of the barbarian elements. As regards the field of education, the Romans had continued and further developed the Druidic (Celtic) schools which they had found well established in Gaul, with a curriculum that included the teaching of theology, philosophy, rhetorics, astronomy, mathematics, and law. Marseille, Toulouse, Bordeaux, Reims, Lyon, among other cities, were such Druidic and afterward Roman centers of learning.

The founding of cathedral schools and monastic schools as well as of those parish schools that were recommended by the Council of Vaison (529) contributed to the continuation and revival of learning when, toward the end of the Merovingian period, it was in danger of disintegration. Books, which had replaced the rolled manuscripts of antiquity in the fifth century A.D., were now being collected by the newly founded monasteries on German soil, and the crude script of the Merovingian age experienced a considerable refinement at the beginning of the Carolingian epoch, probably owing to the influence of the Irish missionaries (cf. p. 37 sq.).

Language: The High German Sound Shift. Roman, Germanic, and Celtic elements mingled in the linguistic expression of Merovingian times, symbolically revealing the struggle of two ages, two races, two cultures. Between 500 and 800 the speech of the Franks, the Alemans, and the Bavarians was considerably altered by the so-called Second or High German Sound Shift,** which resulted in a sharper distinction between the High (i.e., south) and the Low German (including Anglo-Saxon, Dutch, and Flemish or Walloon) languages, literatures, and cultures. This sound shift affected principally old Germanic *p, t,* and *k,* which changed their character in High German dialects, as in the following examples.

Germanic *p* became *pf* or *f* in High German (but not in Low German), for example, Gothic: *slêpan;* High German: *schlafen;* English: sleep.

---

* The following examples may give some idea on the purchasing power of the shilling: a cow cost 3 sh. or $9; an ox 2 sh. or $6; a steer 3 sh. or $9; a horse 12 sh. or $36; a serf 12 sh. or $36; a long sword (*spatha*) 3 sh. or $9; a long sword with belt 7 sh. or $21.

** The First or "Germanic Sound Shift," which created the dividing line between the Germanic and other Indo-European languages, had occurred about 500 B.C. At that time the tenues (voiceless stopped consonants), *t, p, k* were transformed into voiceless spirants (fricative consonants); the Indo-European aspirated mediae (voiced stopped consonants) *dh, bh, gh* into voiced spirants; the Indo-European mediae *d, b, g* into tenues.

Germanic *t* acquired a *ts* sound (spelled z or tz) or an *s* sound, for example, Gothic: *twai;* High German: *zwei;* English: two. Gothic: *itan;* High German: *essen;* English: eat.

Germanic *k* became *ch,* for example, Gothic: *juk;* High German: *Joch;* English: yoke. There is still no agreement among philologists as to the cause of these phonetic changes.

The Influence of Latin Culture and the Roman Church. On the whole, then, the Frankish State in Merovingian times showed relatively small evidence of the influence of Christian culture. Greed, avarice, treachery, and moral depravity was evidenced in many actions of the rulers. The dominant force was still the spirit of the primitive warrior tribe. And yet Christian impulses were strong enough to leave an enduring impress on the culture of the Frankish kingdom, and to work almost imperceptibly as a leaven to prepare the medieval synthesis of Germanic, Roman, and Christian elements.

The power that acted as the principle of integration in the new political and cultural organism of the Frankish kingdom was the Roman-Christian tradition. In the early period of the Empire Rome had been an international city, and Greek was then the language of the Roman Church. With the growing estrangement of the eastern and western parts of the Empire the Roman Church gradually became Latinized. Latin culture was henceforth embodied in Roman Catholicism, and with the conversion of the barbarians Christianity rose from its subordinate role as the religion of conquered populations to a dominating and culturally formative force in the new civilization.

Christianity As a State Religion. Christianity thus confronted the Germanic peoples, the Franks especially, as a compelling force which challenged and tested their adaptive and creative cultural capacities, causing a cultural "break," signifying the transition from primitivity to maturity. The idea of divine providence and omnipotence imparted a new meaning and value to the life and work of the Germanic warrior, whose faith in the protective power of his national deities had been shaken even before Christian missionaries cut down Donar's sacred oak trees and destroyed the heathen sanctuaries.

Since Christianity had become a State religion under Emperor Constantine (306–337) it felt, even more strongly than before, the necessity of combining its historic continuity with its universal mission. The Church is a supernatural society, recognizing the State in its own right as a natural society. Before it had become a State religion, Christianity had shown itself radically opposed to the social and moral conditions that prevailed in the Roman Empire, and it had refused to co-operate with a society that bore the marks of corruption and decadence. The Church, with its own organization and hierarchy, its system of government and administration, its rules of membership and initiation, was an autonomous society whose social philosophy would never come to terms with the culture of the Empire.

Yet with all these glaring antagonisms, certain typically Roman characteristics were also embodied in the primitive Christian Church. Pope Clement I, in his Epistle to the people of Corinth (A.D. 96), insisted that that order which he calls the law of the universe should likewise be the principle of the new Christian society. He stressed moral discipline and subordination as essential virtues. Constantine himself considered a church which proclaimed such ideals the logical ally of the universal claims and traditions of the Empire.

Christianity As the Heir of the Classical Tradition. The fourth century finds the Church organized according to the model of the Empire. While the eastern churches began to look to Constantinople as their spiritual and political center, Rome, the capital of the Empire in the West, became also a center of the Church. While the East shows itself creative in the fields of philosophy and the arts, among the Christian thinkers of the West only Augustine stands out as highly original, whereas the majority are eclectics, utilizing the riches of eastern Christian wisdom, and being satisfied with the cultivation of the traditional Roman civic virtues of order and discipline. This western Roman tradition is alive in Bishop Ambrose of Milan (340–397) and, coupled with a strong moral sense and the fervor of his Christian faith, it makes him the first exponent of the ideal of a Christian state in the West. Early in the fifth century Ambrose's ingenious disciple, St. Augustine (354–430), constructed a system of thought that was to stimulate and occupy the Western mind for more than a thousand years. Later in the fifth century, Pope Leo I combined Ambrose's conviction of the providential mission of the Roman Empire with the doctrine of the primacy of the see of the bishop of Rome as the successor of Peter, the "Prince of the Apostles."

Thus the Roman Church had developed an autonomy and a social and religious authority which embodied some of the most constructive elements of Roman culture, and which enabled it to stand on its own feet when the Empire collapsed, fully equipped to become the heir of ancient Rome and to transmit its cultural assets together with Christian doctrine to the new barbarian peoples. The survival of classical literature and the rhetorical tradition, and its cultivation by the Christian theologians and poets of the "patristic age" (the age of the "Church Fathers"), prepared the way for the rise of the medieval literatures of Europe. Church and Scriptures on the one hand, Hellenistic and classical cultural tradition on the other — these heterogeneous aspects of waning and rising social orders were certainly powerful stimuli in a period of transition.

The Graeco-Roman schools of rhetorics represented, it is true, only the literary side of ancient culture, while its scientific aspects were assimilated by the Christian and Moslem East. The West was affected only by the late revival of Greek philosophy in the form of Neo-Platonism (second and third centuries A.D.) which so strongly influenced medieval thought and culture. Just as there would be no medieval philosophy without Augustine, so without Dionysius the Areopagite (fifth century A.D.) one important branch in the tradition of mystical theology and in particular the linguistic splendor and speculative depth of the German mystics of the thirteenth and fourteenth centuries would be unthinkable (cf. p. 146 sq.).

Both writers were greatly indebted to Neo-Platonism, Augustine being a professional rhetorician, and deriving from his acquaintance with the system of Plotinus (204–269) his idea of God as the source of being and intelligence, and of the soul as a spiritual substance that finds beatitude in mystical union with the Uncreated Light. Even after his conversion to Christianity, so elaborately described in his *Confessions,* he retained the Graeco-Roman and Platonic emphasis upon the elements of order and rationality in the universe, and the conviction of the metaphysical goodness and beauty of all created being as emanating from the eternal source and exemplary paradigm of all goodness and beauty. To be sure, the strict religious orthodoxy of the following centuries temporarily obscured this heritage of Christian Platonism, only to restore it to full and sovereign splendor in the thought and life of the later Middle Ages and the early Renaissance.

Monasticism. The conversion of the Franks and a number of other Germanic tribes during the Merovingian Age was chiefly due to the missionary zeal and fearless enthusiasm of Irish and Anglo-Saxon monks. It was toward the end of the migration period (*c.* A.D. 500) that the monastic movement became the leading force in the political and cultural formation of Europe. Monasticism originated in the East, where hundreds of hermits and ascetics had secluded themselves in the Egyptian and Libyan deserts, forsaking all human association and cultural attachments in order to live the pure and simple life that Christ recommended in the Evangelical Counsels (Matt. 19:12; 21:29). The ideals of poverty, chastity, and obedience thus became the foundation of monastic life. But while Eastern monasticism negated and even abhorred cultural values and felt inclined to practice an extreme asceticism as an end in itself, the West gradually developed its own conception of the monastic community, in which cultural activities received due consideration but were ordered to the supreme end of Christian life, the vision and possession of God, and the imitation of Christ as a means to that end.

The Monks of the West. When Rome had been conquered by the Germanic peoples, the time seemed to have arrived to realize the genuine Western type of monasticism. In 520 Benedict of Nursia founded the monastery of Montecassino in the hill country between Rome and Naples, completing the work that had been begun by Cassiodorus at Vivarium in Calabria (cf. p. 26). "The Patriarch of the Monks of the West," as he has been called, was a descendant of the provincial Roman nobility, endowed with the Latin genius for law and order, and possessing the gifts of a great educator and organizer. In contrast to the irregularity and eccentricity that marked the lives and habits of the ascetics and hermits of the Eastern deserts, the Benedictine order from its beginning was conceived as a co-operative and economically self-sufficient society, emphasizing the necessity of a well-organized, familylike community life. The same sense of moderation that knew how to practice true devotion without submitting to the unsound precepts of extreme asceticism, dividing monastic life between prayer, work, and recreation, is embodied in Benedict's famous "Rule," which henceforth was to shape and influence the mode and standard of life in Western monasteries.

In learning and research, in agriculture, horticulture, and the mechanical arts and crafts, Benedictine monks became the teachers of the Germanic peoples, and numerous Latin loan words in German point to the educational influence of the Benedictines in these occupations. They taught the Germans the dignity of manual labor, which even the most brilliant minds of antiquity, a Plato, an Aristotle, a Cicero, had considered a fitting occupation for slaves only. Now labor for the first time was conceived of as cooperation with the laws of nature, and as the value-creating collaboration with the designs of the Author of nature.

Anglo-Saxon Missionaries. Pope Gregory the Great (590–604), himself a Benedictine monk, scholar, and mystic, was directly responsible for the Benedictine missions in England and Germany. Roman Benedictines went forth to Britain to convert the Anglo-Saxons, and inspired their Anglo-Saxon disciples to continue their crusade and carry it back to the Continent. Providing Latin texts with vernacular glosses, the Anglo-Saxon monks in Germany aided in creating the beginnings of a vernacular German culture and literature.

Wynfrith (Boniface), "The Apostle of the Germans." Wynfrith (672–754), who received the name of Boniface when he was made a bishop in 722, is known as the great organizer of the Frankish-German Church. A native of Wessex, he united in his character and work Germanic initiative and a Roman-Benedictine sense of proportion. He carried the message of Christianity into the heart of the German land, converted the inhabitants of Hesse and Thuringia, reorganized and revived ecclesiastical discipline in Bavaria, established abbeys and bishoprics on the sites of the Germanic folkburgs and heathen sanctuaries, and was finally slain with fifty-two of his companions by pagan Frisians to whom he was preaching the Gospel. In 732 he had been made archbishop and in 738 primate and papal nuncio of Germany. He lies buried in the crypt of the Cathedral of Fulda, where he had founded the famous abbey of the same name, and where the German bishops still meet annually in solemn convention to carry on their deliberations near the tomb of the Apostle of Germany.

Irish Missionaries. Even before the Anglo-Saxon Benedictines had organized their missionary work in Germany, monks from Ireland had come to the kingdom of the Franks to preach Christ and His kingdom. Their methods, however, were altogether different, as different as was their race, their temper, and their mentality. They were representatives of that Celtic population that even in prehistoric times had played a prominent part in the development of Western culture (cf. p. 3 sq.). We know that they had originally inhabited the greater part of Germany as well as the British Isles, that the Germanic tribes owed them their acquaintance with the cultures of the Bronze and Iron Ages. Most of the Celts were conquered by the Romans, and the Christian religion reached them simultaneously with the influence of Roman culture. Only gradually did they give way to the pressure of the expanding Germanic tribes. Ireland as such had never been conquered by the Romans, and therefore remained the actual center and focus of Celtic civilization. Christianity had penetrated into the island of Erin (British: *Iwerddon;* Latin: *Hibernia*), as Ireland was originally called, during the first half of the fifth century. It was enthusiastically received, and as early as the sixth century we witness the missionary activities of Irish monks on Frankish territory.

The monasteries of Ireland were characterized by a rigid and even cruel discipline as much as by their preoccupation with scientific and artistic problems and endeavors. The monks wrote prose and poetry, prayed and conversed in their Celtic mother tongue. They excelled in the ornamentation of biblical manuscripts, which they adorned with the symbols and major characters of the Scriptures, revealing their rich and involved imaginative life in beautifully painted initial letters and lines, interspersing the spiral movement of intertwining lineament with a phantastic imagery of stylized animal motifs.

In organization and administration the Irish monasteries differed from the Anglo-Saxon and German Benedictine abbeys in that they had no uniform monastic rule. Here, too, to be sure, the vows of poverty, chastity, and obedience were considered the basis of community life. But the life in common revealed distinctly the clannish organization of national life in Ireland. One or several monks occupied the simple and primitive wooden huts which together made up the monastic settlement. The members of the congregation were members of the same tribe or clan, and the tribal chieftain usually appointed as abbot a member of his own family. Despite such peculiarities and certain deviations from the ideal type of Western monasticism, the authority of the Roman Church was recognized in Ireland, and there was no doctrinal cleavage.

The inborn unrest of the Irish temper soon found an outlet for its suppressed energies in the missionary work among the Franks which began at the end of the sixth century.

Columbanus and Gallus. With twelve companions, Columbanus the Younger had left his monastery at Bangor in Ulster about the year 590, and soon afterward we find him in Frankish Gaul where, according to his report, "the love of mortification was scarcely to be found even in a few places." He himself founded the monasteries of Luxeuil in the French Jura Mountains, at Fontaines, and at Anegray. The name of his disciple, Gallus, is linked with his world-renowned foundation, St. Gall in Switzerland, which for a considerable length of time was the most distinguished seat of German scholarship.

Statue of St. Boniface, Apostle of Germany, at Fulda.

The Cathedral in Aachen.

In contrast to the disciplinary regulations in the Benedictine abbeys, Irish monasticism shows no consideration for the inherent weakness of human nature, and breathes the spirit of harsh and unbending autocracy. This uncomprising attitude, coupled with certain defects in matters of organization, accounts for the partial failure of the Irish monks' enthusiastic and untiring efforts. Nevertheless, their energy was not misspent. At a time when the decadent Merovingian dynasty had handed over its power to the "mayors of the palace," the Irish and Anglo-Saxon missionaries aided the advancement of culture and brought about the reform and restoration of the Frankish Church. Their work was sympathetically viewed and actively supported and supplemented by Charles Martel and his successors Pepin and Carloman, and henceforth the Carolingians became the promoters and patrons of ecclesiastical reform. They utilized the forces of the Christian religion and the institution of monasticism for their work of political, social, and cultural reorganization.

B. CAROLINGIANS

The "Donation of Pepin." When Boniface in the year 752 anointed Pepin, the erstwhile Merovingian mayor of the palace, he not only gave ecclesiastical sanction to the new Carolingian dynasty, but confirmed in a symbolical act the sacerdotal mission of the Frankish monarchy. The Merovingian State had been predominantly secular and national, its church had been primarily a national church, only loosely linked with Rome and the papacy. The Carolingian State was to be universal and theocratic, resting upon the alliance between the Frankish monarchy and the papacy, the monarch acting as the recognized champion and protector of the pope.

In the very same year (751) in which Pepin had been made king of the Franks, the Lombards had destroyed the Byzantine (East Roman) province of the Exarchs of Ravenna in central Italy, thus depriving the popes of their traditional protectors. In the winter of 753-754 Pope Stephen II crossed the Alps to meet Pepin at Ponthion, near Bar-le-Duc, to implore his aid against the Lombards. In 754 and 756 Pepin defeated the Lombards, and forced them to surrender to the papacy the exarchate of Ravenna, together with the duchies of Spoleto and Benevento. The Pope conferred on Pepin the dignity of "Patrician" of the Romans, a title traditionally held by the Exarchs of Ravenna, the highest Byzantine officials in Italy.

These events marked the foundation of the Papal States (States of the Church) and the beginning of the temporal power of the papacy, which was to endure until 1870, when Rome was captured by Italian troops, and which was restored to some small extent by Benito Mussolini in the *Lateran-Treaties* of 1929. But the "Donation of Pepin" also marks the beginning of the protectorate of the Carolingians and their successors in Italy and of their intense interest in Italian affairs. It was about the time of Pepin's rule that the bold forgery of the so-called "Donation of

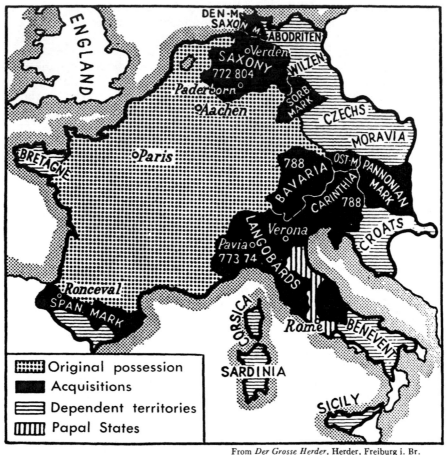

From *Der Grosse Herder*, Herder, Freiburg i. Br.
Kingdom of Charlemagne (768–814).

Constantine" made its appearance, contending that Emperor Constantine through a similar deed had willed all Italy to Pope Sylvester I (314–335).

Pepin, "Patrician" of the Romans. What had actually happened in that memorable meeting of King Pepin and Pope Stephen II was that the papacy and the Frankish kingdom had come to each other's support. For if Pepin wanted to establish his family firmly on the throne and carry through his ideas of political and social reform, he needed the moral support of the papacy. In return for his gift "to the Roman Church, to St. Peter, and his successors the popes" he was hailed as the "New Moses" and the "New David" who had been anointed by the High Priest of the New Dispensation.

Charlemagne and the Creation of the Carolingian Empire. What had been begun by Pepin was completed by his eldest son Charles. The "Patrician" became the "Imperator." The king of the Franks accepted the universal mission of uniting all the Western nations under the dome of a Christian-Germanic civilization. For although Charles received the imperial crown from the pope, the Church in Germany retained many of its Frankish-national features, and Charles was ambitious enough to include the papacy in his far-reaching schemes. He acquired an exalted view of his authority as the divinely appointed leader of the Christian peoples, holding the two swords of spiritual and temporal power, and imposing his will on Church and State alike.

Charles earned his surname "the Great" by coping successfully with ever new and increasingly complex situations. Defeating the Lombards in 774, he redeemed Pepin's pledge to the papacy. Placing the Langobard crown on his own head, he celebrated Easter in Rome and renewed the promises of Pepin. His bitter and relentless wars with the heathen Saxons, extending over a period of more than thirty years (772–804), ended with a complete victory of Charles and the Saxons' submission to Frankish rule and to the Christian religion, which was forced upon them together with political domination. Thousands of Saxons were slaughtered at Verden on the river Aller in 782, after they had been delivered into Charles's hands by members of their native nobility. Thousands of others were deported to be employed as colonists in different parts of the Frankish kingdom. Deposing the dukes of Bavaria, Charles brought this province of southern Germany into closer union with the Frankish kingdom. He fought successfully against the Avars in the region of present-day Austria and against Slavic tribes in the eastern Alps. The famous *Chanson de Roland,* the greatest of medieval French epics, as well as the German *Rolandslied* (c. 1170), commemorate Charles's campaign in Saracen Spain (778). While he was on his return march through the Pyrenees, the rear guard of the Frankish army under the command of Count Hruotland (Roland) was cut off and destroyed by the Basques in the mountain pass of Roncesvalles. But Charles succeeded in getting control of a strip of land south of the Pyrenees, where he established the strongly fortified Spanish "march."

As the eighth century drew to a close, Charles's kingdom included the territories of modern France, a part of Spain, Holland, Belgium, Austria, Bohemia, Moravia, and the greater part of Italy. Since the fall of the Roman Empire the West had not seen such a vast territory under one ruler. The Frankish king was the unchallenged sovereign of Western Christendom. The pope called him the "new Constantine" and the defender of St. Peter. The princes of Scotland and Ireland paid homage to him, and the patriarch of Jerusalem offered him the keys of the Holy Sepulcher.

Thus the stage was perfectly set for the epoch-making scene that took place in Rome on Christmas Day of the year 800. After the pontifical High Mass in St. Peter's Cathedral Pope Leo III placed an imperial crown upon Charles's head, hailing and venerating him in Byzantine fashion as the august emperor of the Romans.

If we may believe Charles's biographer Einhard, Charles was in no way prepared for this honor and not only surprised but positively embarrassed. Yet he soon learned to look upon this historic hour as an event of providential significance, and he fully lived up to its vast implications and promises.

An Empire had thus been created which was Roman, Christian, and Germanic in one, and its ruler was courageous enough to visualize the creation of a league of chosen nations which would establish the kingdom of God upon earth, translating into reality the ideal state and society of Charles's favorite book, St. Augustine's *City of God*. Even if these far-reaching dreams remained largely unfulfilled, so much is true: the Western family of nations rose under Charles's leadership to an unprecedented cultural pre-eminence.

The Personal Regime. Beginning Disintegration. The Empire of Charles did not live much longer than did the genius of its founder. It lasted less than a century. Built upon the personal rule of one man who acted as the autonomous leader of his people, it was too large and unwieldy an organism to withstand for any length of time the attacks of foes from without and of disruptive forces from within. The idea of personal leadership in the Germanic past and present is based upon an unwritten sacred contract between the one who governs and those who are governed. This personal relationship, which distinguishes Germanic rule from the legalistic and abstract Roman concept of government, underlies the structure of the feudal system, and accounts for the moral greatness and the political weakness of medieval and modern Germanic State organisms. On the whole, the Empire of Charles is more noteworthy because of its historical and cultural significance than because of its material achievements. Economically and socially it never attained to that cohesion and unity that characterizes a thoroughly civilized State.

Relapse Into Barbarism. The decades that followed Charles's death witnessed the rapid disintegration of the Empire he had created. Empire and papacy alike became immersed in an abyss of anarchy and barbaric lawlessness. The governing principles of society were the law of force on the one hand and the need for protection on the other. In the course of the ninth century the State lost all contact with the urban tradition and became completely agrarian. The life of the feudal nobility was spent in warfare and private feuds. From their strongholds the feudal lords terrorized peaceful villagers and passing travelers. Bishops like other feudatories received investitures from the princes, holding their estates in return for military services, while the papacy reached the climax of depravity in the tenth century, becoming a passive tool in the hands of the Roman Consul Theophylact and the women of his house. The records of this period read like the accounts of the Germanic migrations: "The cities are depopulated, the monasteries ruined and burned, the country reduced to solitude. The strong oppress the weak, the world is full of violence against the poor. Men devour one another like the fishes in the sea" (Acts of the Synod of Troslé of the year 909).

Louis the Pious and His Sons. What had happened? Charles the Great died in 814, and was survived by only one of his sons, Louis (the "Pious"), king of Aquitaine. The year before he died Charles himself had bestowed the imperial crown upon Louis because apparently he was disinclined to surrender to the papacy the privilege of sanctioning the choice of his successor. But Louis had Pope Stephen V repeat the ceremony of coronation at Reims, three years later. Complying with the customary Frankish law of inheritance, Louis announced his plan of dividing the Empire after his death among his three sons, Lothar, Pepin, and Louis. Meanwhile Judith, Louis' second wife, was scheming to gain the greater part of the Frankish heritage for her own son Charles. The three sons of Louis' first marriage rose up in arms against their father, and when Louis the Pious died in 840, the question of the division of the Empire was still unsettled. The death of Pepin left the three brothers Lothar, Louis, and Charles as pretenders, while the functions of government were neglected and the imperial authority suffered irreparable damage. The insurgent nobility and the ambitious princes vied in their attempts to wrest as much power and prestige as possible from the central government.

The Treaties of Verdun (843) and Mersen (870). At last Louis and Charles came to an understanding, when they met at Strasbourg in 842, taking an oath of perpetual loyalty to each other. This meeting revealed the cultural cleavage that now separated the eastern and western parts of the Frankish kingdom. While the East Frankish tribes, including the Alemans, Thuringians, and Bavarians, who were united under Louis (the "German"), had preserved their old Germanic dialects, the language of the West Frankish tribes, owing to its mixture with Gallo-Latin, had developed into the Romance tongue, the ancestor of modern French. The two assembled armies no longer understood each other's language, so that the oath had to be read in German (*theodisca lingua*) and in Romanic.

The new alliance compelled Lothar to come to terms with his brothers, and in 843 the Treaty of Verdun put an end to the protracted family feud, granting Lothar the imperial title and a strip of land that ran through the center of the Empire, from the North Sea to Rome, including most of the valleys of the Rhine and Rhone. The two younger brothers retained the title of kings, Charles receiving the territories of the Romanic West, Louis those of the Germanic East. The future countries of Germany, France, and the "Lotharingian" middle kingdom were thus geographically and politically marked off. The Treaty of Mersen (870), concluded between Charles (the "Bald") and Louis (the "German") after the death of Lothar II (Lothar's son), gave Louis some additional territory in the West. After the extinction of Lothar's line Charles the Bald obtained the imperial title over the protest of Louis the German.

Charles the Fat and the End of the Carolingian Dynasty. The whole

Carolingian Empire was united once more in 884 under the rule of Charles the Fat (876–887), the son of Louis the German and the only surviving adult member of the Carolingian dynasty. Unable to cope with the ravages wrought by the invasions of Viking raiders who threatened and devastated the northern provinces of the Empire, Charles was deposed by the Frankish nobility and died shortly afterward. With his death the Carolingian Empire broke up into a disorganized mass of regional units which were badly harassed by the continued attacks of the Scandinavian Vikings of the north and the Saracens of the Mediterranean. But, strange as it seems, while this process of disintegration was going on, the idea of a united Christian-Germanic Empire of the West remained alive under the ashes of the gigantic conflagrations of the ninth century. Out of the darkness of this age the new nations of Europe were born, and the German emperors of the Saxon dynasty (919–1024) carried on the work of Charles the Great. Otto the Great (936–973), the most imposing figure among the Saxon rulers, was the great-grandchild of that Saxon atheling Widukind, at whose baptism in 785 Charles the Great, once his fiercest opponent, served as his godfather. Continuing the Carolingian tradition, Otto the Great imbued it with the tribal characteristics of the Saxons.

Charles the Great, King and Emperor. The whole epoch to which the great Charles has bequeathed his name feasted on the memory of his rule but wasted his inheritance. It was Charles who had inspired his people with new hope and confidence, showing them a definite goal to live and work for: the creation of a new and better society and civilization. In his *Life of Charles (Vita Caroli Magni)* Einhard, the royal secretary, has vividly portrayed the personality of his friend and king. There we learn that Charles was not only the greatest warrior and conqueror of his age but a farseeing statesman with definite ideals and aims which he pursued uncompromisingly.

Despite his imperial title Charles remained a Frank in word and deed, a man of simple and somewhat barbaric habits. At his request the heroic songs of his people were collected and written down, he gave German names to the four winds and the twelve months, and he even attempted to compose a grammar of the Frankish tongue, though he never succeeded in mastering the art of writing, spending many a sleepless night with honest but fruitless calligraphic exercises. Charles habitually wore Frankish dress, and only twice he acceded to the request of the Pope to appear in a large Roman tunic and shod with Roman sandals. Germanic and Frankish was his passion for hunting and swimming, not quite so thoroughly Germanic his moderation and temperance in the use of food and drink. Although a kindhearted father, he was not a model husband: his mistresses bore him a number of illegitimate children. Viewing with an open mind the cultural accomplishments of foreign nations, he preferred Frankish manners and customs to all others. On Frankish soil he wanted to be laid to his eternal rest, and workmen from all parts of the Empire co-operated in the construction of the mighty Minster at Aachen (Aix-la-Chapelle).

Administration Under Charles. The Empire of Charles was a theocratic Church-State, and the emperor exercised the functions of government as a priest-king, somewhat in the fashion of an Egyptian pharaoh, a Moslem kadi, or a Byzantine emperor. Consequently, in all his administrative institutions and political enterprises secular and religious aspects were inextricably intermingled. Thus his campaigns against the Saxons and the other Germanic tribes were political as well as religious wars, and the cross and the sword were inseparable companions. True enough, the aim of these wars was the unity and security of the Empire, but this unity was to be guaranteed and cemented by the universal acceptance of the established State religion.

The mayor of the palace and the lay referendary of Merovingian times had been supplanted by the archchaplain and the chancellor, the latter being in charge of the ministries of the interior and of finance. The organization of the chancery followed closely the Byzantine model, and included a graduated series of clerical officials. It was the emperor who laid down the rules of conduct and ritual for the clergy, who issued minute regulations for the observance of the Sunday, rules for liturgical art and music, and for monastic discipline. The emperor's emissaries (*missi dominici*) went on circuit through the counties of the Empire, two by two, a clergyman and a layman, to supervise local administration. The way in which they addressed their charges illustrates the dual secular-religious aspect of their function: "We have been sent here," we read in one of the typical exhortations, "by our Lord, the Emperor Charles, for your eternal salvation, and we charge you to live virtuously according to the law of God and justly according to the law of the world. We would have you know first of all that you must believe in one God, the Father, the Son, and the Holy Ghost." Then the king's messenger proceeds to enumerate the duties of all social classes and estates, from husbands and wives to bishops and counts, concluding as follows: "Nothing is hidden from God. Life is short, and the moment of death is unknown. Be ye therefore always prepared."

Charles regarded the Pope as his chaplain and told him that it was the emperor's duty to govern as well as defend the Church. In the famous Iconoclast Controversy that followed the Second Church Council of Nicaea (787), he went so far as to call together an anti-Council of all the Western bishops, which met at Frankfurt in 794, Charles presiding and directing the deliberations according to his superior will. The *Libri Carolini* (Carolingian Books) were prepared at his request, containing a refutation of the Greek doctrine that advocated the veneration of religious images and that had been adopted in part by the Nicaean Council. Charles's pronounced sympathy with the Oriental iconoclast movement and his refusal to recognize the authority of the Second Council of Nicaea threatened to lead to serious complications. The strain in Frankish-Roman relations was eased, however, by Pope Leo III's countermove, the coronation of Charles as Roman emperor. Thus new dignity and additional prestige was given to the Frankish king, but at the same time Charles was forced into a definite juridical relationship and close association with Rome and the papacy.

The absolutism of Charles's rule implied a paternalistic concept of government. As the father of his people the emperor felt responsible for their temporal and eternal welfare, attempting to enforce morality and religion by legislation and, if necessary, by the power of the sword. Frankish custom made him consider the Empire and its revenues as his family property. Although the general assembly of freemen, the so-called "May Field" (*Maifeld*) still met once or twice a year, it had retained only a nominal significance as far as the legislative and judicial power of the people was concerned. The agenda were carefully prepared by a special imperial synod and were then submitted to the popular assembly for formal approval. The consent of the king-emperor, however, was required to give any resolution the force of law.

These resolutions were laid down in the *Capitularies,* so called because of their being arranged according to chapters or headings. They deal with the most varied and minute matters and aspects of administration. Those that applied to public affairs concerning the whole Empire had to be published by the counts and bishops who were in charge of the local districts. Charles himself had no permanent local domicile, but traveled about among his several imperial palaces (*Pfalzen*), accompanied by the Count Palatine (*Pfalzgraf*), who represented the imperial judiciary power and was in charge of the supervision of markets and highways.

Growing Feudalization of Society. Many of the *Capitularies* deal with the economic conditions of the Empire and the management of the royal estates. We gather from these accounts that the imperial officials were not paid with money but with land that belonged either to the State or to the Church, Charles making no distinction between crown lands and Church lands, claiming title of ownership to both.

Identical obligations, including that of military service, were imposed on secular and ecclesiastical landowners alike. The imperial revenues were derived from "The King's Land," i.e., from the agricultural produce of the undistributed crown lands; from the rights of coinage; from tolls and customs duties; from the tributes paid by conquered peoples as well as by Jews and foreigners, in return for royal protection. The giving away of increasingly large territories of the royal and ecclesiastical domains to ambitious nobles in order to secure their military assistance and good will not only strengthened the power of the territorial lords at the expense of the crown, but wrought havoc in the ecclesiastical sphere by making the ruler the arbitrary dispenser of benefices and Church offices, the result being the secularization of Church institutions in addition to the secularization of Church property. The clergy had become indispensable to the emperor not only because they held the monopoly of education but because of the nonhereditary nature of their fiefs, which made them largely dependent on the royal favor and therefore much more reliable than the secular vassals.

As had been customary in Merovingian times, bishops and abbots had again become the armed leaders of their troops, thus fulfilling the obligations attached to their fiefs.

The military aristocracy, no longer controlled by the king, had the people at their mercy. Under Charles's successors the feudal lords were the only ones to whom one could turn for protection. This whole development marks the growing feudalization of the society of the ninth century. As the land grants to secular lords became increasingly hereditary, the vassals began to feel like small sovereigns, freely disposing of their land, giving away parts of their territories to their subordinate followers, so that through continuous "subinfeudation" there arose eventually a graduated system of vassalage, a symmetrical pyramid of ascending ranks, with the king at the apex. This description anticipates the structure of the fully grown feudal system of the following centuries. However, even in Charles's time the general trend and the essential features of this future development can be clearly recognized.

Serfdom and Tenancy. The economic life of the Carolingian period centers in the *Maierhof* (estate of the "mayor") or *Fronhof* (estate of the lord), and is closely linked with the institution of serfdom (*Leibeigenschaft*), which in itself admitted of different grades of social status and different degrees of income and freedom. The land was divided into estates which were self-sufficient units, administered by the king's or the lord's steward (*"maior domus," Hausmaier, Maier*). The king's seneschal or high steward was in charge of the royal estates in their entirety. In the center of each estate was located the *Maierhof,* surrounded by the huts of the peasants, each of whom had a small strip of land attached to his dwelling. Such a "village" usually also comprised a mill, a blacksmith's shop, and a church or chapel with the parish house. Part of the arable land that surrounded the village was set aside for the exclusive use of the king or lord. What remained was parceled out among the peasant tenants. The fields were divided into three parts (three-fallow system, *Dreifelderwirtschaft*), one of which was used for the planting of the summer crop, the second for the winter crop, while the third part would lie fallow. In the absence of scientific methods of fertilization this system permitted a rotating treatment of the fields, thus preventing the exhaustion of the soil. The cultivation of the fields was a communal and co-operative enterprise, although each peasant harvested the crop from his own strips of land.

The same relationship of mutual service and obligation that formed the cornerstone of the whole feudal system and that bound vassal to lord or lord to king, determined likewise the unwritten contract that tied the peasant to the lord or his steward. The lord gave the peasant protection, furnished the land, built a mill and a village church, and administered justice in the territory that he had learned to consider as his own, either by inheritance or by special grant. The peasant, in turn, enjoyed the security that went with the hereditary right to the possession of his strip of land, he took his share of the agricultural produce, and returned the privileges extended to him by making certain payments and rendering certain services to the lord, exactments whose extent and nature were determined by custom. Theoretically still a serf, the peasant of the Carolingian period had actually become a tenant, and although still unfree, this peasant tenant, being exempt from the burden of military and court service, was envied by many a small freeholder. A traditional body of legal concepts gradually developed out of the peasant-lord relationship (*Hofrechte, Weistümer,* manorial statutes), which were, however, not committed to writing until the end of the thirteenth century.

Law and Order. The administration of justice in Carolingian times was seriously handicapped by the fact that public opinion still upheld the law of the stronger or the principle that might creates right. In the almost total absence of official organs of public safety, the freeman was in duty bound to protect and defend himself, his belongings, and his family against attack and injury. Thus the peasants formed protective associations which were called "gilds" and bore close resemblance to the old Germanic "oath helpers" (*Eideshelfer, Schwurgenossen*). The members of these brotherhoods were bound by solemn oaths to assist each other in time of danger or distress, and continued to cultivate pagan rites and customs at their communal feasts and social gatherings. One of the *Capitularies* deals with these abuses, prohibiting the taking of oaths, but not interfering with the gild's aim of mutual protection. Under the influence of Christianity these "gilds" were gradually transformed into Christian brotherhoods and eventually into the vocational groups of the medieval city.

The "King's Court" concerned itself with cases of high treason and plots against the safety of the ruler and the nation. The majority of law suits fell under the jurisdiction of the "Count's Court," and the "Court of the Hundreds." Minor offenses were dealt with by the "Jurors' Court" (*Schöffengericht*), consisting of the presiding judge (*Zentner*) and usually seven jurymen (*Schöffen*).

Currency and Commerce. Some of the *Capitularies* deal with the prices of food and clothing. A decree fixes the price for the finest fur at thirty shillings, while for an ordinary one the maximal price should be ten shillings. In order to stabilize the silver denarius (*Pfennig,* penny), which had been recently devaluated by the growing scarcity and increased value of gold, its weight had been raised from 1.36 g. to 1.7 g. The value of the shilling was established as the twentieth part of a pound (*Pfund*), and new coins had been issued (twelve pence to the shilling), so that we arrive at the following currency tabulation which was to remain the same to the end of the Middle Ages: 1 pound = 20 gold shillings = 20 × 12 silver denarii (*pfennigs,* pence). With the dwindling supply of precious metals the purchasing power of money rose as compared with the Merovingian period. According to a tariff of the year 794 a bushel (*Scheffel* = fifty to sixty liters) of oats cost four to six pence; a bushel of wheat, four to six pence;

a bushel of rye, three to four pence; twelve loaves of wheat bread (of two pounds each), one penny; a chicken, half a penny; a sheep, six pence; a cow, two shillings.

Domestic and foreign trade experienced a short-lived revival under the influence of the political unification of the Frankish kingdom under Charles the Great. Commercial relations not only extended to the Germanic North, the Scandinavian countries, and England, but included even Russia and the Orient. Itinerant merchants went from Saxony to Denmark and Finland; Danes, Swedes, and Norwegians visited the markets of the Frankish kingdom. Articles of luxury, such as fancy cloths, silks, furs, rugs, jewels, and spices were imported from the Orient. Commercial activities were especially lively in the newly founded and slowly developing cities.

Following the advice of the popes, Boniface had founded most of the German bishoprics in the most thickly populated regions, in order to emphasize the significance of the episcopal sees. Thus he had considered the ancient Roman settlements on German soil as the most suitable centers of ecclesiastical life. In the period of Charles the Great we find approximately thirty bishoprics which were gradually developing into marketing and trading communities, and were endowed with special royal privileges. These Carolingian markets soon became the permanent abodes of merchants and craftsmen and present in a rudimentary form the essential features of the later medieval city. Hamburg, Bremen, Magdeburg, Erfurt, Regensburg, among others, were such marketing centers of the Carolingian period.

A regular postal service was still unknown in Charles's time. Special messengers or traveling friends served as mail carriers. The use of public highways and bridges was subject to toll. Not only the king but also the territorial lords derived part of their revenues from tolls and customs' duties, and the feudal lords made a gainful occupation of the exploitation of the itinerant merchant. Charles issued a number of decrees for the protection of trade and commerce, exempting pilgrims, courtiers, and warriors from the payment of tolls, and giving the merchants letters of safe-conduct. But despite these and other protective and preventive measures the great Charles was too much a child of his age to recognize and attack the fundamental evil of the times, which consisted in the growing accumulation of territorial possessions in the hands of secular and ecclesiastical princes and lords. The "father of the poor, of widows and orphans," as he was called after his death, was unable to defeat the forces that were to cause poverty and destitution, breeding the anarchy, lawlessness, and despair of the succeeding century.

Carolingian "Renaissance." Charles's biographer, Einhard, hails the emperor as the new Augustus, and Bishop Modoin of Auxerre speaks of the renaissance of classical antiquity. These are undoubtedly euphemistic epithets, exaggerating the scope and significance of the Carolingian revival of ancient culture. Charles was not interested in resurrecting the empires of Augustus, Constantine, or Justinian. He felt himself to be the leader of a young and vigorous nation which had conquered the Western Roman Empire and had rightfully inherited its power and tradition. As the "New David" he was the *"rex iustus"* and *"rex pacificus"* (king of justice and peace) of a new dispensation and legislation, the educator of his people, the Christian ruler of a new empire.

The "School of the Palace." The "Carolingian Renaissance," therefore, is not so much a genuine revival of antiquity as a strengthening of the continuity of the elements of ancient thought, learning, and education. Charles himself threw all his personal energy and influence into the work of restoring the time-honored principles and methods of classical learning. The educational activities had their center in the "School of the Palace," headed from 782 on by Alcuin (Alchvin, 730–804), formerly director of the famous school of York, whom Charles put in charge of three of the most prominent abbeys of the Empire. His teaching was based on the old classical curriculum of the seven liberal arts, consisting of the so-called *Trivium* (grammar, rhetorics, dialectics), and the *Quadrivium* (arithmetic, geometry, music, astronomy). Alcuin was commissioned with the revision of the Bible and the service books and thus inaugurated the Carolingian liturgical reform which provided the foundation of medieval Christian liturgy.

The "School of the Palace" set the educational standard for all the other monastic schools which were diffused throughout the Empire, such as St. Gall, Reichenau, Lorsch, Tours, Orléans, Auxerre, Pavia, and many others.

From Italy Charles had called to his court the grammarians and poets Petrus of Pisa and Paulinus of Friaul, and the Lombard Paulus Diaconus (Paul the Deacon), author of the *Historia Langobardorum* (*History of the Langobards*) and biographer of Pope Gregory the Great. From Spain came the Goth Theodulfus, a neo-classical poet and a severe critic of Germanic criminal law. And there were the Franks Angilbert, abbot of St. Riquier; Hildebold, Charles's archchaplain and later on archbishop of Cologne; and the illustrious Einhard, annalist, poet, and architect, a native of the Main district, who although a layman, was to succeed Alcuin as head of the Palace School. In his biography of Charles he shows himself influenced by the style of the classical Roman historians, especially by Suetonius. Charles made him his chief architect and put him in charge of several abbeys.

Charles's Academy.   Following Oriental models Charles organized his circle of scholarly friends and advisers in the form of a court academy, in which even women, such as Charles's sister Gisela and his daughters Hruodtrut and Bertha, were received as members. Each member of the Academy was given a symbolical name, taken from the Bible or from classical literature. Charles himself was David, the poet-king of the Old Testament; Alcuin was Horatius Flaccus; Angilbert was Homer; Einhard, because of his architectural gifts, was given the name of Beseleel, the builder of the Jewish tabernacle. The entire Academy used to accompany Charles on his travels throughout the Empire. The customary readings during meals comprised poetic and prose passages from classical and patristic literature, preferably from Augustine's *De Civitate Dei.* The conversation was carried on in Latin, in which language Charles was as well versed as in his native Frankish.

The "Caroline Minuscule" and Miniature Painting. Preoccupation with classical writers in the Carolingian period led to the copying of many of the famous documents of ancient literature. We owe most of our knowledge of these masterpieces to the zeal of Carolingian copyists. Their manuscripts reveal a remarkable improvement over the crude and frequently illegible scripts of the Merovingian Age. This new style of writing, known as the "Caroline Minuscule," became the standard type for western Europe, excepting Spain, Ireland, and southern Italy. It is the precursor of the "Humanist Script" of the Italian Renaissance of the fifteenth century and of the modern printed Latin type.

The Carolingian manuscripts were richly adorned with miniature paintings and picturesque illuminations. The name "miniature" is derived from their prevailingly vermilion color (*minium, Mennig,* "cinnabar"), and the scribes were called "miniators." Special artistry was displayed in the beautifully designed initial letters and marginal adornments. They show Carolingian art at its best, revealing in their elaborate spiral and fretted designs Oriental-Byzantine, Oriental-Moslem, and Anglo-Celtic influence. There is a peculiar restraint in the rendering of natural objects and human characters, an absence of thematic variations, and a lack of verisimilitude that endows these miniatures with a solemn and sublime monumentality. From here a straight line may be drawn to the Rhenish schools of painting of the tenth and eleventh centuries. Most of the monasteries succeeded in developing their own style of miniature painting, so that when speaking of the art schools of Reichenau, Regensburg, Tours, etc., we are able to distinguish specific local characteristics.

Architecture. Byzantine influence is noticeable in Charles's famous palace church (*Palastkapelle,* Münster) at Aachen which shows a central octagonal ground plan of Oriental origin. The palace church was to represent a partial replica of the East Roman Emperor Justinian's *Hagia Sophia* in Constantinople, the symbol of the emperor's theocratic power and majesty. The Church of San Vitale in Ravenna had to serve the Carolingian architect as the nearest model. From Ravenna, too, Charles had transferred the bronze monument of Theoderic the Great, placing it in the court of his palace in Aachen.

The excavations at Ingelheim in the Rhineland give us an idea of the appearance and organization of a Carolingian palace (*Pfalz*). A vast building served as living quarters for the retinue of the imperial court. It comprised porticoes, chapels, and halls of varying size and shape. As an economically self-sufficient unit the palace included the surrounding dwellings of the laborers, artisans, brewers, bakers, weavers, spinners, carpenters, metalworkers, and so forth.

The ecclesiastical architecture of the Carolingian Age followed the model of the simple and longitudinal early Christian basilica rather than the more complex central or circular plan of the Byzantine and Iranian styles and of Charles's palace church. The form of the basilica itself had evolved from the late Roman court and market hall and the Roman *villa*. The early Christian basilica (*c.* 350–600) is a modest and ascetic-looking building, consisting of one high central nave and two (or four) lower aisles, a flat roof, and a semicircular apse which contained the altar and the throne of the bishop. In Carolingian times the primitive style of the basilica developed into the Romanesque style, so called because of the several motifs of Roman architecture embodied in it. The main innovation was the introduction of a transept that rendered the ground plan cruciform and provided additional space for the common recitation of the Office that had become the rule under Benedictine influence. In Germany churches of great age or large size were called *Münster* ("minster," from the Latin *monasterium*).

Despite his patronage of the arts and crafts, Charles was convinced that "the adornment which is derived from the moral goodness of a congregation is of greater value than a beautiful church." And in the *Libri Carolini*, which were written to reject the cult of images, we read: "In the realm that God has entrusted to Our care, the basilicas abound with gold and silver, with jewels and lovely ornaments, and even if we decline to burn candles and incense in front of images, we nevertheless adorn with the most precious of objects and materials the places which are dedicated to the divine service."

Music. In connection with the general liturgical reform Charles emphasized the importance of Church music. The primitive water organ, which had been invented in Alexandria in the second century B.C., was introduced in the Frankish kingdom through a gift of the Eastern Emperor Constantine V (757) to King Pepin. Charles had several instruments sent from the East to be copied by Frankish craftsmen and installed in the major churches of the Empire. To insure correct liturgical singing, he had Roman teachers instruct clergy and laity in different parts of the Frankish kingdom. Especially favored was the *Cantus Gregorianus* (*cantus plenus,* "plain song," "plain chant") which, originally derived from Greek and Jewish temple chants, had become an integral part of early Christian liturgy and had been revised and reorganized by Pope Gregory the Great (590–604).

Gregorian singing, which is unaccompanied and for one voice only, and characterized by its free rhythmical movement, flourished through the greater part of the Middle Ages but declined after the fourteenth century with the advent of polyphony. It experienced a modern revival at the end of the nineteenth century, when it recovered its ancient status as the official liturgical chant of the Roman Catholic Church. Its so-called "neumatic notation" (from Greek: *neuma* = "wink," "gesture," "sign"), of unknown origin, differs in tact, measurement, and appearance from modern notation, but we now know how to transpose the notes into their modern

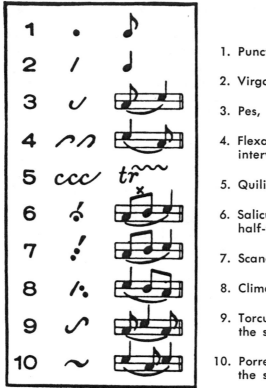

Neumes

1. Punctus, Punctum (short note)

2. Virga (higher tone)

3. Pes, Podatus (ascending interval)

4. Flexa or Clivis (descending interval)

5. Quilisma (tremolo)

6. Salicus (2 ascending tones with half-tone beat)

7. Scandicus (2 ascending tones)

8. Climacus (2 descending tones)

9. Torculus or Pes flexus (3 tones in the sequence: low, high, low)

10. Porrectus or Resupina (3 tones in the sequence: high, low, high)

equivalents. The most famous modern schools of Gregorian Chant are the Benedictine abbeys of Beuron and Maria-Laach in Germany and Solesmes in France.

Carolingian Culture After Charles the Great. The cultural revival that owed its splendid achievements to Charles the Great was more long lived than were his political and social creations and innovations. Carolingian culture grew into its full stature in the generation that followed Charles's death, finding home and shelter in the institutions of monastic learning. Under Charles the Bald the director of the Palace School was Johannes Scotus Erigena (810–877), a native of Ireland and the greatest scholar and philosopher of the ninth century, representing an important link between Neo-Platonism and the scholasticism of the twelfth and thirteenth centuries (cf. p. 141 sqq.).

Among the many pupils of Alcuin one of the outstanding men is Hrabanus Maurus (780–856), abbot and later on archbishop of Fulda, the author of an encyclopedia of knowledge and of poetical as well as catechetical works. At the head of the abbey of Reichenau at Lake Constance (*Bodensee*) we find his pupil Walafrid Strabo (809–849), a native Aleman, a scholar and poet

of vivid imagination and strong emotional appeal, who has left us a sample
of nature poetry in the descriptive poem "My Little Garden." In the
monastery of St. Gall taught Notker Balbulus (the "Stammerer," 840–912),
the greatest of the religious poets of the Carolingian epoch and the author
and compiler of the stories and legends concerning the life of Charles the
Great which are contained in the collection *Gesta Caroli Magni.* Likewise
at St. Gall we find Tutilo († 915), a man of universal tastes and interests,
equally versed in commercial and literary matters, architect, painter, goldsmith, poet, and composer.

The Carolingian Abbey. While war, famine, and death, the apocalyptic
triad, were driving the Carolingian empire to the brink of complete destruction, the Benedictine monasteries kept the flame of culture alive. The
Carolingian abbey, which provided the background for these many-sided
cultural activities, was at the same time a great social and economic center,
a great landowning corporation. In the eighth century the abbey of Fulda
owned 15,000 plowlands, while Lorsch possessed 911 large estates in the
Rhineland. But St. Gall in Switzerland perhaps more than any other
monastic community represented the ideal type of a Carolingian abbey.
A plan that dates from the beginning of the ninth century shows the abbey
as a miniature city, with churches, schools, workshops, granaries, hospitals,
baths, mills, breweries, farm buildings, gardens, and cemeteries. Material and
intellectual culture, agrarian economy, and the cultivation of the arts and
sciences went hand in hand.

It must have been relatively easy for an organization of such dimensions
and such resources to accomplish the difficult task of transforming waste
lands and swamps into flourishing settlements, clearing the forests, draining
the fens, and creating centers of agricultural and commercial life and
enterprise. The monasteries were among the first to establish markets and
to develop the institutions of banking and social insurance on a small scale.
Landowners could purchase pensions or become resident members of the
monastic community as "oblates." Freemen would surrender their liberty
in order to join the number of those serfs and tenants who were living within
the confines of the "patrimony of the Saint" in whose name an abbey or
church was dedicated. They were called *Homines Sanctorum* (the "Saint's
Men"; French: *Sainteurs*), and usually enjoyed the benefits of that mild and
humane rule that has given rise to the proverb: "There is good living under
the crozier" (*Unter'm Krummstab ist gut leben*).

Vernacular Literature in German Monasteries. It is to the credit of the
German monasteries that they bridged over the abyss that still separated
the Latin language of the educated from the *lingua theodisca,* the language
of the people. The "interlinear glosses," which provided the Latin texts with
an interspersed German vocabulary, and the "glossaries," a primitive type
of Latin-German dictionaries, represent the first attempts at making use
of the German language for the purposes of education. The oldest glossary
was compiled in Bavaria about the year 750. The still older "Wessobrunn

Prayer," discovered in the monastery of Wessobrunn in Bavaria, is written in Bavarian dialect and dates back to the missionary activity of Boniface. It consists of a description of the creation of the universe in alliterative verse, and concludes with a prayerful invocation in prose. As a cultural document it illustrates an early stage of the Germanic reception of Christian ideas.

The period of Charles the Great witnessed the translations of the Benedictine rule and the hymns of Ambrose (Reichenau), of the Psalms and several theological tracts (St. Gall), of the Gospel of Matthew, several sermons of Augustine, and a large number of liturgical and homiletic texts. A translation of Tatian's (second century) Gospel Harmony is dated in the ninth century, being a continuous narrative of the life of Christ based on the four Gospels. *The Lay of Hildebrand (Hildebrandslied)*, copied about the year 800 by two monks, who wrote the fragmentary alliterative poem on the outer leaves of a theological manuscript, was found in the abbey of Fulda. Representing the only surviving document of Old High German heroic poetry, the *Hildebrandslied* tells of the probably fatal encounter between Dietrich of Bern's (Theoderic of Verona, cf. p. 25 sq.) armor-bearer Hildebrand and his son Hadubrand.

A heroic poem, although of a different kind, is also the Old Saxon *Heliand (Heiland,* "Saviour"), written in alliterative verse by an unknown Saxon author during the earlier part of the ninth century. Here the life of Christ is assimilated to the everyday life and thought of the recently converted Saxon people. Christ is depicted as a great king and heroic leader, the Church is the king's palace, the disciples are the faithful thanes and vassals who have sworn lifelong fidelity in truly Germanic fashion. The landscape of Saxony with its fields, forests, and castles provides the scenic background. But we must not exaggerate the significance of certain deviations from the biblical account, recalling that early Christian art, literature, and liturgy quite generally cherish the conception of Christ as a victorious king rather than the humiliated sufferer on the cross. The Saxon *Heliand* combines Germanic form with Christian content in a true synthesis. While the advice to offer the attacker the other cheek would still have appeared incomprehensible to the Saxon temper, the poem nevertheless elaborates on the Sermon on the Mount, praising the hero whose heroism is tempered by gentleness, whose loyalty is adorned with the virtues of justice and charity.

In some respects the simple contours of the Old Saxon *Heliand* offer an even more eloquent testimony to the Christianization of the German mind than the velvety outline of its Frankish counterpart, Otfrid von Weissenburg's *Gospel-Harmony* of Christ (*Krist*), which was written by its scholarly author between 850 and 868. The rhyme at the end of the metrical line, familiar from Latin hymnology and vernacular charms and incantations, was adopted by the Alsatian monk, Otfrid, in place of alliteration. But both *Heliand* and *Krist* are German as well as Christian, each reflecting the tribal characteristics of their authors and the different ways in which Franks and Saxons responded to Christian ideas. The more immediate and naïve response is contained in the *Heliand*. Otfrid's narrative is more flexible and slightly sentimental, and at the same time more didactic, inspired by the monastic reform movement under Louis the Pious and its attempts to extirpate secular and pagan heroic poetry.

National Diversity and Cultural Unity. Such literary documents as *Heliand* and *Krist* are powerful manifestations of the new national life that for the first time began to assert itself at the end of the Carolingian period, coinciding with the dissolution of the Empire of Charles the Great. In view of this at first gradual and afterward phenomenal rise of the national states of Europe, it is a fact well worth remembering that Charles the Great, the creative master builder of the epoch that bears his name, is claimed as a national hero by Frenchmen and Germans alike, thus forcefully symbolizing the common cultural roots that underlie the two major branches of continental European civilization.

PART II. MEDIEVAL CIVILIZATION UNDER THE SAXON, SALIAN, AND HOHENSTAUFEN DY-NASTIES (919 - 1254)

919–1024	Saxon Emperors
919– 936	Henry I, founder of the German Empire
928– 934	Successful wars against Wends and Danes
933	Henry defeats the Hungarians on the river Unstrut
936– 973	Otto I, the Great, son of Henry I
955	Otto I defeats the Hungarians on the Lechfeld
962	Otto I receives the Imperial Crown in Rome and founds the "Holy Roman Empire of the German Nation"
973– 983	Otto II, son of Otto I
983–1002	Otto III, son of Otto II
1002–1024	Henry II, the Saint, great-grandchild of Henry I, great-nephew of Otto I
1024–1125	Salic-Frankish Emperors
1024–1039	Conrad II, duke of Franconia, founder of the Salic-Frankish dynasty
1032	The Kingdom of Burgundy is united with the German Empire
1039–1056	Henry III, son of Conrad II
1056–1106	Henry IV, son of Henry III
1073–1085	Pope Gregory VII (Hildebrand)
1075–1122	Struggle of Investiture
1076	Henry IV has a synod of German bishops depose Pope Gregory VII, and is excommunicated by Gregory
1077	Henry IV goes to Canossa and is absolved from the ban
1084	Henry IV is crowned emperor by the antipope Clement III (1084–1100)
1104	Henry IV is forced by his son Henry (V) to abdicate
1106–1125	Henry V, son of Henry IV
1122	Concordat of Worms
1125–1137	Lothar of Supplinburg, a Saxon noble, chosen by the electoral college, without hereditary claims German eastern colonization is resumed (Albrecht the Bear, Otto of Bamberg)
1138–1254	The Hohenstaufen dynasty
1138–1152	Conrad III, a Hohenstaufen, elected despite the hereditary claims of the Welf, Henry the Proud, son-in-law and heir of Lothar
1147–1149	Conrad III takes part in the unsuccessful Second Crusade
1152–1190	Frederick I (*Barbarossa*), half Welf, half Hohenstaufen, a nephew of Henry the Proud through his mother and of Conrad III through his father
1154–1155	Frederick's first expedition into Italy: he receives the crown of the Lombard kingdom in Pavia, the imperial crown in Rome
1158–1162	Frederick's second expedition into Italy: he defeats the cities of Lombardy, calls an Imperial Diet on the Roncaglian Fields, and destroys Milan

1166   Frederick's third expedition into Italy: he captures Rome but is forced by an epidemic to withdraw to Germany

1176   Frederick's fourth expedition into Italy: he is decisively defeated by the Lombard army at Legnano

1177–1178   Peace between Frederick I and Pope Alexander III at Venice and truce between the emperor and the Lombard League

1183   Peace of Constance, confirming the preliminary peace treaties and granting a large degree of self-government to the Lombard cities

1184   The great *"Reichsfest"* of German Chivalry at Mayence, attended by over 70,000 knights

1189–1192   The Third Crusade under the leadership of Frederick Barbarossa

1190   Frederick Barbarossa is drowned in Asia Minor

1190–1197   Henry VI, son of Frederick Barbarossa

1190   Founding of the Order of Teutonic Knights

1191   Henry VI is crowned emperor in Rome

1194   Henry VI conquers his hereditary kingdom of Sicily, Hohenstaufen supremacy extends over all Italy, with the exception of the Papal States

1198–1208   Philip, duke of Swabia, younger son of Frederick Barbarossa, elected by the German nobles

1198–1215   The Welf, Otto IV of Brunswick, younger son of Henry the Lion, elected antiking by the Welf faction of German nobles, struggle for the throne between Welfs and Hohenstaufens

1208   Philip of Swabia is assassinated

1212–1250   Frederick II, son of Henry VI of Hohenstaufen

1220   Frederick II receives the imperial crown in Rome

1226   The Order of Teutonic Knights is called into Prussia for the purpose of Eastern colonization

1227   Frederick II is excommunicated by Pope Gregory IX (1227–1241) for his failure to fulfill his vow to undertake a Crusade

1228–1229   The Fifth Crusade under the leadership of Frederick II

1230   Peace between Frederick II and Gregory IX

1230–1283   Conquest of heathen Prussia by the Order of Teutonic Knights

1235   Legal enactment of the *Land Peace* at the Diet of Mayence, the first publication of an imperial law in Latin and in German

1236–1237   Victorious struggle of Frederick II against the cities of Lombardy

1237   Expansion of the territory of the Teutonic Knights to include Kurland, Livland, and Estland

1241   The Mongolians are repulsed at Liegnitz

1245   Following a resolution of the Council of Lyon, Frederick II is deposed and excommunicated by Pope Innocent IV (1243–1254)

1246–1247   Henry Raspe, landgrave of Thuringia, first antiking

1247–1256   William of Holland, second antiking

1250–1254   Conrad IV, son of Frederick II

1256–1273   *"Interregnum"* (*"die kaiserlose, die schreckliche Zeit"*): Germany without an emperor

1268   Conradin, the last member of the Hohenstaufen dynasty, executed at Naples; collapse of imperial government in Germany

Chapter 4

THE SAXON DYNASTY AND THE REBIRTH OF THE EMPIRE

The Medieval Synthesis. The Carolingian ideal of a universal Christian empire under the leadership of emperor and pope survived the century of decline, and contact with the Carolingian tradition was restored by the ascendancy of the Saxon dynasty. The tenth and eleventh centuries completed the synthesis and cultural consolidation of Europe and at the same time allowed the individual nationalities to assert their character and express themselves freely within the general frame of a supranational civilization. Nationalism in the modern sense of the term, denoting the autonomous expansion and development of European nations and their cultures, did not become a historical reality until medieval society was being disrupted by the social, religious, and political upheavals of the fifteenth and sixteenth centuries. Until this happened Germany remained the leading member of the European commonwealth of Christian nations, owing her leadership primarily to the glamour and glory of the idea of the Empire which symbolically expressed the continuity of past, present, and anticipated future.

While presenting on the surface the spectacle of an organic unity, embedded within the structure of a universal State and a universal Church, Germany actually constituted a *coincidentia oppositorum*. She presented a unity of opposites, achieved and held together by virtue of the fundamental conviction that was shared by Greek and Christian civilization alike: that life could and should be molded according to ideal patterns, that religious and social ideas were to inform material reality and impress upon it the mark of the ideal and the spiritual. Within the Christian commonwealth of nations this ideal pattern had assumed the form of a natural-supernatural organism which, in a rationally arranged order, tied the particular to the universal, the individual to the group, the State to the Church, nature to supernature. It is this concept of the organic structure of society, derived from the biblical idea of the Church as the "Mystical Body of Christ" (1 Cor. 10:17; Eph. 4:22; Gal. 4:9), that made it possible to combine seeming opposites in a unified system of graduated orders and relations.

Every type of being receives its individual character and intrinsic value from its relation to its infinite source and cause, which permeates and sustains the entire cosmos of nature and mind. "Be what thou art" — realize all your potentialities in your God-given station in society — becomes the imperative of a Christian humanism which rests upon the foundation of Greek and Christian wisdom and is absorbed by the European mentality, so that it is as vigorously alive in Dante and the German mystics of the Middle Ages as in the thought of Leibniz, Goethe, and Hegel. Knowing himself as an instrumental cause in the hands of his Creator, man freely collaborates with the plans and designs of a metaphysically significant world and civilization. Cultural formation out of a philosophical and religious ideology becomes the ideal goal of the Christian and German Middle Ages.

It is only when looking at it in this way that the medieval "unity of opposites" becomes comprehensible. Life is full of contrasts, but they are ultimately reconciled in the synthesis of a God-centered civilization. Love of the world and flight from the world, the ideals of knighthood and the ideals of the cloister, cruelty and tenderness, sensuality and spiritual ecstasy, penetrating rational analysis and implicit and childlike faith, the claims of an authoritarian State and Church and respect for the dignity of the individual and the social group, exploitation of the peasant and tender consideration for the poor and downtrodden, for widows and orphans and the sick and suffering, for lepers and outcasts: the cleavage between the ideal demand and the imperfect reality is overcome by a generally accepted and approved standard of moral values whose violation is condemned as a sinful infringement upon a divinely sanctioned order. This medieval synthesis had constantly to be reconquered, with the supernational unity of medieval Europe as the scene of the struggle, harboring under its roof the three major forces of Greek, Christian, and Germanic cultures.

This European unity under Germanic leadership was one of faith and morals, of thought and action, manifesting itself in State and Church, in their antagonisms as much as in their common idealism and enterprise. Struggles were waged for the supremacy of State or Church, among and between classes and vocational groups, between emperors and popes: campaigns and crusades, peaceful colonization and violent conquests, irenic missionary activity and cruel inquisition, persecution, and extermination of heretics. And the Saxon emperors were destined to symbolize the vital cultural and social energies and ambitions of an ecclesiastically colored civilization, to resurrect the Roman Empire of the Frankish Nation in the more imposing structure of the "Roman Empire of the German Nation."

Saxon Leadership. The disintegration of the Carolingian dynasty had greatly encouraged the spirit of rebellion against a centralized authority among the hereditary sovereigns of the great tribal duchies of Germany. Saxony, Bavaria, Franconia, Swabia, and Lorraine formed the so-called "stem" duchies (*Stammesherzogtümer*), each of them representing a feudal state within the German realm. Any ruler who wanted to restore the dignity and authority of the imperial crown had first of all to restrain the ambitions and aspirations of the overbearing territorial lords. The situation was rendered even more complex by the fact that the dukes and other magnates constituted the electoral college and, in electing a new king, were naturally inclined to give their vote to a man whom they could hope to control to some extent and who would not endanger their relative independence. Considering this state of affairs, the historian marvels at the number of brilliant and powerful leaders who, with firm determination and farseeing vision, were to rule the destinies of the German nation through the centuries that followed the downfall of the Carolingian empire.

It was the tribal vigor and patriotism of the Saxons that was resplendent in the extraordinary qualities of some of the Saxon rulers. They succeeded in welding together into a new cultural unity the discordant and disjointed forces of the German lands. Under Henry I (919–936) and Otto I (the Great, 936–973) German cultural and political leadership in the Western World reached an unprecedented summit. The new Empire, it is true, rested on a narrower basis than the Carolingian Germanic-Romanic civilization. The western part of the Frankish kingdom had now become an independent national organism (France), and Italy as well as Burgundy were autonomous administrative units. However, this new Empire was more interested in serving the cultural advancement of the Western World than in establishing an imperialistic rule. The Germans of this period may therefore truly be called the great organizers among the European nations, taking upon their shoulders the world-historic responsibility of shaping the Christian Middle Ages. It was Otto the Great who saved the papacy from an abyss of depravity, who profoundly comprehended and realized the immense task of renewing German civilization in harmony with the spirit of the Christian and classical tradition.

As Saxons the rulers belonged to a racial group that had been scarcely touched by the culture of classical antiquity. As German kings and emperors, however, they soon transcended the narrow limits of tribal politics and restored a definite relationship with the social background and heritage of Western Christendom.

Of special significance for the future development of German civilization were the ties that soon began to link inextricably the German and Italian interests and policies. In 962 Otto the Great responded to several appeals of Pope John XII by entering Italy and restoring law and order, which for several decades had been at the mercy of rival secular and ecclesiastical factions. He married Adelaide (Adelheid), the heiress of the crown of Lombardy, and pronounced himself king of Italy. The Pope bestowed upon him the imperial crown, and this event marked the actual beginning of the "Holy Roman Empire of the German Nation" (*Sacrum Romanum Imperium Nationis Germanicae*), although the name itself was not applied until the fifteenth century.

The continuity of tradition with the ancient Roman as well as with the

Carolingian empire was virtually re-established. Northern Europe once more came in contact with Mediterranean and more especially with Byzantine civilization. Otto's and Adelaide's son, Otto II (973–983), married the Greek princess Theophano, the daughter of the Byzantine emperor, Romanos II. With her and even more with the son of Otto II and Theophano, Otto III (983–1002), Byzantine manners and customs were introduced into the life of the imperial court of the West, and were reflected in the arts and crafts as well as in social and religious practices and institutions. In Otto III the Christian empire had come to life again in its dual aspect of an Eastern and Western, a Byzantine Greek and Carolingian Roman ancestry. The emperor's scholarly friend and adviser, Gerbert of Aurillac (940–1003), later Pope Sylvester II (999–1003), impressed upon Otto the superior claims and titles of the Western Roman tradition. It was he who made Otto see and appreciate the great heritage of Western civilization: "Ours, yea ours, is the Roman Empire. Its strength rests on fruitful Italy and populous Gaul and Germany. Our Augustus art Thou, O Caesar, the Emperor of the Romans. . . . " Gerbert and Otto visualized Dante's ideal Empire, the commonwealth of Christian nations, ruled by the dual authority of emperor and pope.

Under Otto III Rome became the capital of the Empire, the emperor exercising a practically unlimited control over the papacy, while at the same time his influence on German affairs was steadily waning. For more than one German emperor it proved an impossible task to rule both Germany and Italy, to do justice to German and Italian interests alike, and to wield both the secular and the spiritual sword. Otto III died at the early age of twenty-two, leaving to his successors the difficult task of once again restoring royal authority in Germany. With Henry II (the Saint, 1002–1024), a great-nephew of Otto I, the Saxon dynasty came to an end. Henry used the bishops, whom he had invested with their offices and endowed with land and administrative authority, to control and curb the unruly lay nobility.

The general physiognomy of the age is more and more characterized by the growing influence of Church civilization upon secular life, a development which began with the rule of Otto the Great and lasted unto the days of Henry IV (1056–1106) of the Salian-Frankish dynasty. The Saxon as well as the early Salian emperors were relying chiefly on the loyalty and support of the ecclesiastical princes. To insure this loyalty the king invested the bishops with the symbols of their ecclesiastical office. On the occasion of Henry II's coronation in Rome in 1014, Pope Benedict VIII handed the emperor a golden apple, richly adorned with jewels and a cross, the apple signifying the universal aspect of imperial power. But Henry had the apple sent to the monastery of Cluny, in order to indicate his devotion to the ideals of the ecclesiastical reform movement, which inspired the political and cultural activities of the Ottonian and the Salian periods and co-operated with the forces of secular and ecclesiastical administration.

The Beginnings of German Colonization. It has been pointed out that the German territory of the Saxon emperors compared unfavorably with that of the Carolingian empire. The Slavs in the east and the Hungarians in the southeast constituted an increasing danger to the stability of the Empire, so that the Saxon emperors considered it as one of their primary tasks to establish their supremacy in these outlying frontier districts. This was accomplished both by conquest and by peaceful penetration and colonization. Peasants and missionaries under the leadership of dukes and princes, abbots and bishops, acted as the emissaries and became the guarantors of German culture in these religions. But better protection of the frontiers was only one of the reasons for the Germanization of the eastern and southeastern districts. Another and even more compelling motive was the scarcity of land in view of a rapidly increasing population, subsequent to the restoration of order and security under Henry I and Otto the Great. Continuing the work of his father, Otto vanquished the Wends and established marches and bishoprics between the Elbe and Oder rivers. On the Lechfeld near Augsburg he dealt a decisive blow to the Hungarian invaders (955) and reconquered the eastern Bavarian march, thereby laying the foundations for a future Austria.

In his personal appearance Otto the Great exemplified the vigor and youthful optimism of the people over whom his rule extended and whose labors, struggles, and achievements he faithfully and joyfully shared. Physical and intellectual alertness made him equally fitted for warlike and peaceful pursuits. His erudition comprised a wide range of interests, and he spoke several languages, having acquired a mastery of Latin rather late in his life. The two Ottos that succeeded him were his equals in cultural and intellectual awareness but lacked his sense of proportion. This lack was the main cause of their inefficiency in handling the affairs of Germany.

The Electoral College. The German monarchy under the Saxon and Salian emperors was still hereditary, though not in name. Nominally, the ecclesiastical and secular electors (*Kurfürsten*) formed the electoral college, but in reality the more powerful ones among the German emperors exercised their authority to secure the succession of their eldest sons.

Up to the year 1257 the ecclesiastical electors were the archbishops of Mayence (Mainz), Cologne (Köln), and Treves (Trier); the secular electors were the Count Palatine, the duke of Saxony, and the margrave of Brandenburg. In that year, however, the number of secular electors was increased by one through the addition of the king of Bohemia. The number of seven electors in all was legally established by the "Golden Bull" (1356, cf. p. 165). In 1623 the electoral dignity was transferred from the Count Palatine to the ruler of Bavaria, while in 1648 the Palatinate was once more added as the eighth and in 1692 Hanover (Brunswick-Lüneburg) as the ninth electoral district. After 1803 additional electoral provinces were created in Baden, Hesse-Kassel (Kurhessen), Württemberg, and Salzburg. The title *Kurfürst* (elector), however, became meaningless after the dissolution of the "Holy Roman Empire of the German Nation" in 1806.

The Army. The old Germanic army, recruited from the people (*Volks-heer*), had been transformed into an army of vassals, of professional soldiers and warriors. The dukes, counts, bishops, and abbots who had been endowed with fiefs were to furnish the king a certain number of armed men, proportionate to the size of their holdings. These subordinate vassals usually dwelt in their castles (*Burgen*), and were summoned by their liege lord to render military service in time of war.

Castles and Cities. Up to the twelfth century the terms *burg* ("borough"; Greek: *polis*; Gothic: *baurg*) and *stat* (town, city) are used synonymously to designate a fortified place, surrounded by walls. This original meaning is still evident in the names of numerous German cities: Augsburg, Freiburg, Hamburg, and so forth. The inhabitants were called *Bürger* (burghers), their legal statutes, *Burgrechte* (burghership, civic rights).

The arts of fortification developed in the later Middle Ages from primitive beginnings to a high degree of perfection. From the early Middle Ages on methods and materials were frequently adopted from ancient Roman models. A fortified settlement enjoyed the special privilege of the "Peace of the King" (*Burgfriede; Königsfriede*), granting the inhabitants the king's protection in their peaceful pursuits and prohibiting feuds inside the city walls. It was this element of security that contributed greatly to the growth of the cities and to making their walled-in territories centers of trade and commerce. It was in the cities, too, that with a rising class of "burghers" a new conception of civic liberties and of personal freedom came into being that found its expression in the proverbial saying: *"Stadtluft macht frei"* (the air of the city makes a man free).

Even a small village might be fortified by a surrounding wall and moat, but it could not be called a city unless it had obtained the privilege of holding a weekly market. The inhabitants of the larger and more thickly populated settlements depended on the agricultural produce of the surrounding farming districts. The peasants, on the other hand, were in need of the commercial and industrial products of the cities. Thus the development of a fortified settlement into a marketing center was the outcome of a natural process of economic intercourse and expansion. The privilege of holding a market was granted by the king, who issued special charters, at first to the lord, later to the city magistrates. Frequently we find the medieval city simply designated as "market" or *koufstat* (trading place), its inhabitants are called *koufliute* (trading people); *marktrecht* (marketing right) is used synonymously with *statrecht* (city rights, civic rights).

The lord is the guarantor of the "King's Peace" and represents the judicial power within the territory of the city. He appoints a judge and puts him in charge of legal administration. While the lower judiciary powers were soon to be transferred to the city magistrates, the lord reserved for himself the higher judiciary and the power over life and death (*Blutbann*). As soon as the lords began to realize that the cities represented a new and substantial source of income, they proceeded to create a large number of new urban settlements upon their territories and secured for them the usual royal privileges. At least 350 new towns originated in this way in the course of the twelfth and thirteenth centuries in the northeast of Germany alone. Some of them never developed beyond the size of village communities. Among the most famous founders of German cities are the counts of Zähringen (Freiburg im Breisgau, Bern in Switzerland) and Henry the Lion (1129–1195; München, Braunschweig, etc.).

Social Organization. The social structure of the period of the Saxon emperors as well as that of the succeeding Salian-Frankish dynasty was characterized by the political and economic supremacy of the dukes and counts, the bishops and abbots as the representatives of the secular and ecclesiastical nobility. Their power rested upon the ownership of land. Several victories over the Hungarians and Slavs had added considerably to their territorial possessions. The royal domains, which had been temporarily increased by the conquests in the East, diminished rapidly in size under the later Saxon emperors, owing to the continued necessity of rewarding the services of the nobles by territorial grants.

To the steadily increasing power of the secular and ecclesiastical landowners corresponded the decreasing number and significance of the freemen. The free or partially free peasantry of former times was no more. The majority of the people were living in some form of bondage or serfdom. The status of actual slavery was restored to some extent following the wars of conquest in the eastern Slavic regions. Most of the Slavic prisoners of war were reduced to an extreme form of serfdom, and slave trading became once more a remunerative occupation. Legally the serf was still considered as a piece of merchandise: he could be sold, exchanged, or given away.

Agriculture, Trade, Commerce. Despite the seemingly low social esteem in which the tillers of the soil were held, this whole society of the early Middle Ages still rested upon a solid agricultural foundation. Agriculture and horticulture were closely allied, and men and women took an equal share in the cultivation of fields and gardens. The monasteries excelled in the cultivation of vineyards as well as of fruit, vegetable, and flower gardens.

Industrial activities were still in a rudimentary stage. Many of the articles of consumption were produced by the consumer, and the home industries flourished. The small homesteader built his own home and stables, manufactured his own plows, carts, and tools. Bread, butter, and beer were homemade. Spinning, weaving, sewing, embroidering were some of the favorite occupations of women and were practiced by women of every social rank.

The restoration of a reasonable amount of security under Otto the Great safeguarded and encouraged the development of trade and commerce. The new territories in the East furnished the raw materials and absorbed the finished products of the mother country. The trade routes to Italy and the Orient were opened anew, and the Saxon emperors held their protecting arm over the "emperor's merchants," as the German tradesmen were then called. Jews, Lombards, and Venetians held a kind of trade monopoly, particularly as far as the trade with foreign countries and money transactions was concerned. If the needy wanted to obtain small loans they usually turned to the monasteries, thus avoiding the payment of interest.

Those merchants who had their permanent abode in the city were artisans and craftsmen. Their commercial activities were confined to the city territory, while the traveling merchants exported domestic goods and imported the merchandise of foreign countries. Outstanding commercial centers in the eleventh and twelfth centuries were Zurich, Basel, Strasbourg, Konstanz, Augsburg, Regensburg in the south; Mainz and Köln in the west; Magdeburg in the east. The southern German cities were the intermediaries of the German-Italian-Byzantine trade; the western Rhenish cities were important outposts for the commercial intercourse with Flanders, France, and England, while Magdeburg occupied a key position in regard to the newly developed Slavic East.

Mining. City life with its increasing and much more complex demands, its luxuries, and the ensuing spirit of competition stimulated the development of free commercial enterprise. Not only were new industries created, such as the manufacture of glass, but old industries, such as mining, smithing, and the furrier's and currier's trade, experienced a vigorous revival. The ore deposits in the southeast of Germany, in the Tyrol, in Styria, Bohemia, the Hartz, the Ore Mountains (*Erzgebirge*), and the Giant Mountains (*Riesengebirge*) provided the raw materials for the manufacture of arms.

The eleventh and twelfth centuries witnessed the formation of the first trade unions: they were unions of miners, and it was the German miner who became the teacher of Europe in the art of mining.

Money. The significance of money and its circulation was greatly increased by the development of trade and commerce. The working of gold and silver mines resulted in new forms of wealth, and new methods in the acquisition and the administration of property were soon to be adopted. Money began to circulate more and more freely and accumulated in the urban centers of trade. Into a world that still lived and thought in accordance with the ideal patterns of the self-sufficing village community and the feudal hierarchy, the growth of city life and commercial economy introduced a new concept of the function and purpose of money. As soon as opportunities for investments offered themselves, money began to lose its stigma of sterility: money began to breed money. The seed of a capitalistic money economy was planted in medieval soil.

The Slavic and Italian regions abounded with precious metals, and the German rulers received tributes and various duties and taxes in silver or gold coin from these countries. The right of coinage, originally a royal privilege, was gradually extended to the dukes and counts, the bishops and abbots, and finally to the cities, where the "master of the mint" occupied an important and respected position. As the local coins frequently differed in value according to their place of origin, the traveling merchant found himself compelled to go through the troublesome and costly process of a repeated currency exchange. To forge coin was considered a capital crime and avenged by capital punishment. In this as in other respects economic theory and practice is characterized by its strong ethical implications, an ethical bias which is prompted by theological and philosophical considerations and which remains practically unchanged until the advent of modern times.

Chapter 5

THE SALIC-FRANKISH DYNASTY AND THE REFORM MOVEMENT OF CLUNY

Imperial Power Under the Early Salic Franks. After the death of the last Saxon emperor, Henry II, in 1024, the crown passed to Conrad II (1024–1039), duke of Franconia, who became the founder of the Salic-Frankish dynasty. He followed the example of Henry II in further strengthening the royal power and creating respect for lawful authority. Under his rule the kingdom of Burgundy (not to be confused with the duchy of Burgundy which belonged to France) became through inheritance part of the German Empire (1032). It occupied the region of the Rhone Valley, territories which today belong partly to France, partly to Switzerland.

Both Henry II and Conrad II had prepared the way for the further extension of imperial power that took place under Conrad's son, Henry III (1039–1056), with whom the Salic-Frankish rule reached its greatest dignity and strength. Once more the German emperor was able to assert his authority in ecclesiastical as well as in secular matters. Once more it was the Empire which came to the rescue of a degraded papacy, the emperor deposing three rival popes and appointing to the papal see Clement II, formerly bishop of Bamberg. A number of German popes, following each other steadily by imperial appointment, were to become the exponents and leaders in the ecclesiastical reform movement that had its origin in the tenth century in the French-Burgundian monastery of Cluny. Its strongest and most efficient supporter and protector was Emperor Henry III. It was due to his relentless activism and enlightened idealism that for a brief interval Empire and Papacy harmoniously co-operated in a combined effort to purify and renovate Church and society.

Growing Antagonism Between Empire and Papacy. But Henry III's successful attempt to strengthen the spiritual power and influence of the Church, and to free the clergy from secular bonds and attachments, was to result in new and unprecedented complications and conflicts, which came to a dramatic climax shortly after the emperor's death, stirring the Christian commonwealth of nations to its very depths.

When Henry III died in 1056, his son Henry IV (1056–1106), who was to succeed him on the throne, was only six years old. The king's widow, Agnes, who acted as regent until 1062, was unable to uphold the imperial authority in view of the unreliability and unbridled selfishness of the secular nobles. As chaos and anarchy threatened anew, it became all the more essential for the imperial government to preserve its prerogatives in appointing bishops and abbots. The ecclesiastical vassals, endowed with nonhereditary fiefs, were the emperor's most valuable advisers in time of peace and his most loyal supporters in time of war. It was therefore understandable from a political point of view that the emperors made every effort to oppose the attempts of the Church to free herself and her episcopate from secular control and influence.

As an outgrowth of the austere spirit of Cluny, the monastic rule of celibacy was made binding on all priests. It was imposed on the clergy in their entirety, in the face of stubborn resistance and widespread opposition among the German priests. Shortly after the death of Henry III a decree enforcing earlier enactments was passed by the Lateran Council, which vested the right of electing a pope in the College of Cardinals and the clergy of the City of Rome, thereby eliminating the influence of the Roman aristocracy and the German emperors.

Pope Gregory VII. The most outspoken advocate of the ecclesiastical demands was the Cluniac monk Hildebrand, who, in 1073, succeeded to the papal throne as Gregory VII (1073–1085). At the time when Henry IV had reached maturity, then, he found himself confronted with a powerful papacy, led by a representative of the ascetic rule of Cluny, where Benedictine monasticism had been restored to its original purity. The pope counted among his friends and allies not only the counts of Tuscany, but the Lombards in northern Italy and the Norman conquerors of southern Italy as well. After their first landing at Salerno in 1016 the Normans had returned at regular intervals, building up their own small but powerful states in the southern part of the Italian peninsula and especially in Sicily. In return for aid and protection that he had received from the Normans, Pope Nicholas II (1058–1061) had invested the Norman leader, Robert Guiscard, with power over Apulia, Calabria, and Sicily. In this way the papacy had prepared itself for the coming contest with the Empire.

Simony and Lay Investiture. Under the leadership of Pope Gregory VII the Church launched its major attack upon the practice of *simony* and upon *lay investiture. Simony* denotes the sale of ecclesiastical offices, which had become a widespread abuse as a consequence of the holding of temporal powers and possessions by the clergy. Lay investiture refers to the right of the king, or the feudal lord of a bishop or abbot, to invest these clerical dignitaries with ring and crozier, the symbols of ecclesiastical power. It was the contention of the popes of the Cluniac reform and especially of Gregory VII that the insignia of a Church office carried a spiritual significance, and that no layman should have the right to bestow them. The spirit of Cluny demanded the complete liberation of the Church from imperial and secular influences. But Gregory VII demanded more than that: with his iron will and all the tenacity that he had inherited from his peasant ancestors, he fought for the absolute supremacy of the ecclesiastical authority over both spiritual and temporal affairs, thus actually trying to reduce the imperial dignity to a position of vassalage. As the soul is superior to the body, he argued, so spiritual authority is superior to temporal authority. It is the duty of the successors of Peter, the Prince of Apostles, to admonish and, if need be, depose wicked rulers, because the vicar of Christ is responsible for the souls of all men.

Thus the prohibition of lay investiture was only one item in Gregory's far-reaching and revolutionary program. For the emperor, however, it was an issue of capital importance, not only his prestige but the very structure of imperial power and authority being involved. And so the attack upon the practice of lay investiture was bound to develop into a life-and-death struggle between Empire and Papacy, a struggle which could only end with the virtual obliteration of one of the two powers.

The German bishops, as we know, were at the same time members of the nobility, holders of royal fiefs and therefore vassals of the king-emperor. To give up the right of investiture meant in the emperor's opinion that he had to divest himself of the support of his ecclesiastical vassals and to put himself at the mercy of the lay nobility. On the other hand, to grant the emperor continued control of ecclesiastical appointments and elections meant that the pope had to abandon his plans of gaining complete independence from secular interference in Church affairs.

Henry IV at Canossa. The struggle for supremacy that raged between these two powers unleashed not only torrential floods of human passion, but also strong currents of idealism and enthusiasm. It cut into the very marrow of State and Church, entailing division and disruption of empire and papacy, the banishment of kings, and the deposition of kings and popes, undermined religious convictions and social institutions, and broke the heart and spirit of both Gregory and Henry, the two principal characters of the tragedy.

Gregory VII, in the year 1076, demanded universal renunciation of the practice of lay investiture. Henry IV's answer was the convocation of a synod of German bishops, who declared Gregory deposed and proceeded to elect an antipope. Gregory, in turn, excommunicated the emperor, absolving his subjects from their oath of allegiance. The German lay nobles promptly seized the opportunity to start a rebellion against the emperor. As Henry's situation grew more and more desperate, he made up his mind to offer his unconditional submission to the papal demands and to ask for absolution. In 1077 Henry and Gregory met at Canossa, in the castle of Countess Mathilda of Tuscany, where the pope, interrupting his intended journey across the Alps and into Germany, had sought shelter and protection in view of the approaching imperial forces. After having spent three days barefoot in the snow in front of the gates, Henry, wearing the garb of a penitent sinner, was admitted and freed from the ban of excommunication. Considering the spirit of the age, this scene in itself — an emperor humbly confessing his sins and begging for the priestly absolution — is by no means unusual, but Henry, in recognizing the authority of a pope whom he himself had deposed and declared unworthy of wearing the triple crown, had silently acknowledged political defeat.

Nevertheless, the immediate result of Canossa was a temporary restoration of imperial prestige that enabled the emperor to regain the support of a majority of the German nobles and bishops. Was Henry's submission prompted by a temporary change of heart or was it merely a shrewd political move on his part? The emperor was a spoiled, ego-centered young ruler, passionate, impulsive, and lacking in self-control. Yet his character shows traces of a genuine nobility of heart and mind, coupled with a sincerity of endeavor that seems to preclude mere deceptive scheming and cheap hypocritical dissimulation.

The reconciliation, at any rate, was of short duration. When Henry resumed the practice of lay investiture, he was once more deposed by Gregory, and Rudolf, duke of Swabia, the choice of the rebellious nobles, was given papal recognition. But the situation had changed: with the moral and active support of the greater contingent of the German nobility and clergy, Henry deposed Gregory a second time and had Clement III elected as antipope. With his victorious army the emperor entered Rome in 1084 and was crowned by Clement, while Gregory, seemingly defeated, died in exile in southern Italy where he had sought refuge in Norman territory.

The Concordat of Worms. Henry's triumph, to be sure, was short lived. While in the Church the schism continued, the emperor's own son Henry V (1106–1125) concluded an alliance with the papacy and rose in arms against his father, imprisoning the emperor and forcing him to renounce the throne. Henry IV, however, escaped and was about to begin a punitive campaign against his treacherous son when death put an end to his colorful and tragic career. The struggle continued between Church and State. Henry V carried on his father's fight for the imperial control of ecclesiastical elections. A pope was imprisoned and another rebellion occurred in Germany before the struggle was brought to a temporary conclusion by a compromise that was actually a victory for the papal claims.

In the Concordat of Worms (1122) it was decided that bishops and abbots were to be invested with their fiefs (as a symbol of their secular office) by the emperor, but that they were to receive ring and staff (the insignia of their spiritual authority) from the pope. In Germany the act of consecration was to follow the act of investiture, whereas in Burgundy and Italy consecration was to take precedence. Being represented at the elections, the emperor retained a limited control over ecclesiastical appointments and over the German clergy. But just the same, the struggle over investiture left the imperial authority considerably impaired and greatly contributed to that turbulent and unsettled state in which the German nation found itself upon the death of Henry V in 1125. Since the emperor died without a direct heir, the Salic-Frankish dynasty came to an end, and once again the princes were offered the opportunity of exercising their legal rights in electing a new monarch.

Kingship and Priesthood. It is an ingredient of the Germanic tradition that the political organization of the State expresses a community of interests that rests on the two pillars of royal authority and individual freedom. The Germanic chieftains, princes, and kings were never absolute rulers in the Oriental and Byzantine fashion. They were the leaders of their people and as such they were held personally responsible for the common welfare of all and could be deposed if they failed to fulfill the terms of the unwritten contract from which they derived their title of leadership. Furthermore, royal power, according to the Germanic concept of government, is never above the law but always subject to its rules. "The royal power, like the whole people," we read in the *Forum Iudicum,* an early Visigothic law code, "is bound to observe the laws."

The attitudes taken by both Henry IV and Gregory VII signified a departure from these ancient principles of Western political theory. Henry IV, and after him Frederick Barbarossa (cf. p. 89 sq.), appealed to certain principles in Roman Law to substantiate their absolutistic claims, principles that were opposed to those upon which medieval civilization had risen under Germanic leadership. Likewise, the divinely ordained sovereignty of Dante's (1265–1321) concept of a universal monarchy introduces an idea which is foreign to the Germanic tradition. In his *Monarchia* the principle of liberty is sacrificed to a legalistic concept of order that is arbitrarily divorced from the demands of reason and the natural law. Gregory VII's attempted establishment of a theocracy (a Church-State) at well as Henry IV's and Barbarossa's inclination toward "caesaro-papism" (imperial absolutism, totalitarianism) tended to undermine the constitutional structure of the Germanic Middle Ages. However, it should be noted that even during their most heated controversies the representatives of Empire and Papacy never surrendered the idea that State and Church mutually depended on each other and that their destinies were therefore closely intertwined. It was not in order to destroy the papacy that Henry IV launched his attack against Gregory VII, but in order to depose a pope who in his opinion endangered the unity and harmony of the ecclesiastical and secular powers: "For our Lord Jesus Christ has called Us to the Kingship but not Thee to the Priesthood" (*Mon. Germ.* LL. II, p. 47).

It was the same ideology that motivated the actions of Henry's papal opponent. The fight against simony and lay investiture and the enforcement of celibacy among the secular clergy were means to the same wished-for end, the harmony of *regnum* and *sacerdotium,* this time, to be sure, emphasizing the supremacy of the papacy.

Canossa, therefore, is a symbol as well as a turning point. It marks the end of Charlemagne's and Otto the Great's protectorship and actual domination of the ecclesiastical realm. Henceforth the German emperor and the Empire as such relinquish their claims to the spiritual sword. The monasteries, in accordance with the demands of the Cluniac reform movement, are placed under the direct supervision and authority of Rome, so that the struggle over lay investiture constitutes the first major phase in the creation of a strictly ecclesiastical medieval civilization.

The Church in Germany. An external symptom of a religious revival and a direct outgrowth of the reform movement was the foundation of several new religious orders, all animated by the desire to restore the rigorous discipline of the earlier stages of western monasticism. Bruno, a canon from Cologne, retired with several companions into a solitary wilderness, the Chartreuse mountains near Grenoble, and became the founder of the Carthusian Order (1084); Robert, abbot of Molesme and founder of the Cistercian Order (1098), introduced into his monastic communities the revised and invigorated Benedictine rule; St. Norbert of Xanten on the Rhine founded the Premonstratensian Order at Prémontré (1121).

The Carthusians were to become famous as writers and copyists of manuscripts, while Cistercians and Premonstratensians indulged in hard, bodily labor, contributing to the economic development of their age and taking a prominent part in the work of colonization in the eastern frontier districts of Germany. As missionaries they penetrated into the region between the Elbe and Oder rivers, clearing the forests, draining the swamps, and teaching the German settlers who had followed them from different parts of Germany how to cultivate the soil and protect alluvial lands against floods and other elemental forces of nature. Thus numerous German villages grew up in the immediate neighborhood of these eastern monasteries.

But the spirit of Cluny also made itself felt in the ranks of the secular clergy, where the vices of venality and bribery had exerted a corrupting influence, ecclesiastical offices being sold or given away by the secular lords who were the owners of churches and church lands. The decrees of Gregory VII which imposed celibacy upon all the members of the clergy caused, as we have heard, a storm of indignation in Germany; priests, bishops, and even synods expressed their violent opposition. But Gregory did not yield and even went so far as to forbid the people to receive the sacraments from married priests or to attend their services. It is an interesting fact that in Italy as well as in Germany the pope found his strongest support among the laity. In Italy popular feeling ran high against the worldly possessions and the luxury of the higher clergy, while in Germany the people at large approved of the ascetic ideals of Cluny and showed themselves deeply concerned with the reformation and purification of the Church.

The ecclesiastical penal codes are contained in the Penitential Rituals (*Bussbücher*). Under the influence of the reform movement disciplinary measures became more and more severe. To understand the significance of this ecclesiastical administration of justice it is necessary to point out that the medieval church in many respects performed judiciary functions that were later entrusted to the State. Lacking an organized police force and a centralized judicial power, the State was frequently not in a position to exercise or even command a judicial authority.

Faith and Superstition.   The Penitential Rituals and the Communion Books give evidence of the amount of ancient pagan beliefs which still survived in a Christian garb. Throughout the medieval centuries pagan superstitions and Christian faith were closely allied, particularly among the peasant population with their stubborn adherence to ancient customs and traditions. The Cluniac reform destroyed many of these pagan remnants of the Germanic past, while the preceding and again the following period frequently made use of pagan beliefs and practices in order to give the Christian message a wider popular appeal. The unlettered people, living in close contact with nature, its phenomena and forces, were unfamiliar with the finer distinctions of theological and philosophical speculation, and attributed magical powers to their favorite saints and even to the sacraments of the Church. The relics of saints, sacred numbers, altars, altar cloths, the vestments of priests were supposed to be endowed with miraculous powers.

The blessings with which the Church consecrated and elevated nature and its implements, salt, oil, bread, wine, wax, herbs, fields, and pastures, were frequently mistaken for magical rites and in this way encouraged superstitious beliefs. The most sinister and consequential residue of ancient paganism was the belief in witchcraft and sorcery, an offshoot of the demonology of the Chaldeans, the Jews, the Greeks, the Romans, and other ancient peoples. Germanic mythology and religion knows of evil spirits who dwell in the forests and are the enemies of man, threatening to destroy or corrupt him. In the Christian era these superstitions sometimes blended with the Christian doctrine of the fallen angels (devils), repeatedly gripping the imagination of an entire epoch of Western civilization with the force of a mental disease and associating themselves with the most inhuman perversions and aberrations. The historically and culturally significant "Penitential Ritual" of Bishop Burchard of Worms (*c.* 1020) opposes many of the superstitious beliefs of his age and prescribes severe punishments for uncritical credulity in such matters.

Symbolism and Emotionalism.   According to the medieval view of the world, all natural and human life is symbolical and analogical: it points beyond itself to its eternal source and cause. Life thus assumes the appearance of a monumental morality play in which everything receives significance in view of the momentous decisions that precede and determine the end. This symbolical character of reality adds weight and meaning to the seemingly most indifferent things, words, thoughts, and deeds. Life itself thus becomes a kind of continuous liturgical ritual. This explains the important part that gestures and attitudes, formal social etiquette, religious ceremonial, meaningful verbal patterns, play in the plastic and literary arts of these centuries.

Men and women of every station in life were given to violent outbursts of emotionalism. In an age of contrasts the free and easy flow of tears alternated with childlike expressions of gaiety, laughter, and merrymaking. Self-abasement in public was quite commonly practiced, and at times assumed the curious forms of a standardized ritual: it was customary that a bishop-elect at first refused to accept the dignity conferred upon him, fleeing into the wilderness to hide his unworthiness. The emperor was expected to weep profusely at his coronation. A penitent sinner had to lie prostrate on the ground, manifesting his repentance by moaning and weeping. Embraces and kisses were freely exchanged on every conceivable occasion. Expressions of love and hatred, joy and sorrow, gentleness and cruelty were found side by side, symbols and symptoms of a life that was manifold in its outlets and manifestations, but unified and single-tracked in purpose and end.

"Treuga Dei" (The Truce of God). Under Feudal Law (*Fehderecht*) private feuds and wars were practically unrestricted in number and extent. It is one of the greatest merits of the ecclesiastical reform movement, and one of the symptoms of the growing influence of Church legislation, that the French bishops succeeded at the end of the tenth century in imposing the so-called Peace of God (Latin: *Pax Dei*) upon the lawless nobility, compelling the nobles under penalty of excommunication to respect the person and property of peasants, merchants, churchmen, and other noncombatants. As a direct outgrowth of the spirit of Cluny must be considered the institution of the "Truce of God" (Latin: *Treuga Dei*), promulgated by a French synod and prohibiting any kind of private warfare from every Wednesday evening until the next Monday morning, the days that were hallowed by the suffering, death, and resurrection of Christ, and during the season of Lent.

Later on the "Truce of God" was extended to include certain other seasons and feasts of the ecclesiastical year. The Salic emperors worked unceasingly for the general promotion and the universal acceptance of the Truce of God. Henry IV regulated its observance by legal decree (1085). And when Pope Urban II in 1095 called upon the knights of Europe to come to the rescue of the Holy Sepulcher in Jerusalem, he referred to the "Peace of God" in these words: "Those who formerly have misused their feudal right in fighting against the faithful, shall now start out upon a battle that is worthy of their efforts and that will end in victory. Those who formerly have taken the field against their brethren and blood-relations shall now wage a just war against the barbarians."

Family Life and the Position of Woman. It was due to the generally strengthened position of the Church that it gained an increasing influence upon family life. The priest, taking the place of the guardian (*Muntwalt*), now joined man and woman in holy wedlock, and the marriage ceremony was held in the church and followed by a nuptial Mass. But married life was anything but pure happiness and bliss. Sexual appetites were only partly checked by moral and religious restrictions and inhibitions, and adultery was widespread among both sexes. Abortions were frequent, and malformed or crippled children were often exposed or killed.

Aside from general religious instruction only a small percentage of the young men and women received a liberal education or some kind of intellectual training. Those who were given the opportunity of attending the cathedral or convent schools were usually either members of the nobility or candidates for the priesthood and ecclesiastical offices.

The civilization of the Middle Ages shows a strongly masculine character. Men are the dominating agents in Church, State, and society. Despite the chivalresque glorification of love and womanhood, women occupied an inferior social position throughout the Middle Ages. The social prejudices of ancient biology and sociology were too firmly entrenched to be overcome by a Christian dogmatics which theoretically recognized in woman man's equal, destined to reach the same degree of perfection in this life and in the life to come. But in practice even the leading philosophers of thirteenth-century scholasticism considered woman as a biologically underprivileged male and withheld from her the equality of social status. "She exists for the sake of man, and yet she is not a slave; she is free, and yet she is not a full-fledged citizen; there is no strict legal relationship between man and woman as there is between free man and free man, and yet she is man's partner and his companion of equal rank" (Thomas Aquinas, *Summa Theologica*, 2-2, q. 10, a. 8).

It is nevertheless true that we meet with a large number of highly educated women, some of them of noble birth, some outstanding in literary accomplishments or adepts of mystical theory and practice, yet all of them confined to a circle that is marked by the cultural domination of the Church. Secular education and therefore also the education of women in secular pursuits is the exception rather than the rule.

The legislative power of the Church (Canon Law) made itself most strongly felt in the enactment and enforcement of marriage laws. While in other respects Roman Law served as a suitable basis for ecclesiastical legislation, the marriage laws were an immediate expression of Church doctrine. According to Roman and Germanic Law the marriage bond could be solved either by mutual agreement of the two parties to the marriage contract or by the wish of one of the partners. The Church, on the other hand, maintained that only death solved and terminated the marriage bond. As one of the seven sacraments, marriage was endowed with religious sanctions and consecrated by the Church. The Church, therefore, claimed exclusive legislative and judicial power in all matters pertaining to the state of matrimony. The tenth and eleventh centuries witness the gradual disappearance of state legislation in matrimonial affairs.

Nature, Animals, and Plants. Medieval man, still largely depending on the soil for his livelihood, was firmly rooted in maternal Nature. He was deeply attached to reality in all its aspects, the visible and the invisible, the sensuous and the spiritual. His confidence in the world of phenomena was sustained and guaranteed by that supreme reality of which everything else was a symbol and feeble image. Field and forest, wind and cloud,

St. Michael's Church, Hildesheim.

Interior of St. Godehard's Church, Hildesheim.

plants and animals evoked brotherly thoughts and affections. The plant and animal ornaments with which the copyists adorned their manuscripts and the masons their handiwork in sculpture and architecture give evidence of their faithful and accurate observation. The philosophers never doubted that mind and reality were proportioned to each other, so that the theory of cognition plays a rather negligible part in medieval speculation.

The artists and poets loved to personify the forces of nature, endowing sun and moon, wind and cloud with human features as they share emotionally the moods of sadness and joy, of crucifixion and resurrection. Animals were honored and commemorated in legend and satire, they were man's inseparable companions at home and in public. Knights and noble ladies surrounded themselves with falcons, magpies, daws, starlings, ravens, cranes, and parrots. Hunting with hounds or hawks was a favorite pastime of both sexes. The presents that kings and princes received from foreign potentates regularly included some lions, leopards, or monkeys. Legal procedure dealt with animals as with intelligent and responsible beings that were indicted, judged, sentenced, punished, and sometimes executed.

Arts and Crafts. At the beginning of the eleventh century the arts of the Western World found themselves in a new situation. The persecutions of Christianity and the struggles for recognition were a matter of the past, and the Romanesque style (*c.* 950–1150), having come into its own, proudly displayed its riches in the different countries of Europe. Christian doctrine, reinforced by the reform movement of Cluny, provided the inspiration for the artistic accomplishments in architecture, sculpture, painting, and the minor arts and crafts. The supernational unity of this inspirational source did not result, however, in uniformity of artistic creation, but left room for the individual national temperaments to speak in their own voices.

German architecture of the Romanesque period is characterized by an intense struggle between the horizontal and vertical forces and directions, verticality being emphasized by the tallness of an increasing number of church towers and spires. The Romanesque church rests upon the earth in its walls, its round arches, its vaults, its pillars, and its porches, but it rises toward heaven in its towers, its choirs, and its gables. It combines the massive and plastic self-sufficiency of classical antiquity with the soaring flight of Christian spirituality. Romanesque church architecture in Germany grows out of the German landscape: it embodies the hopes, fears, beliefs, and superstitions of the period of which it is a monumental symbol. The Romanesque style expresses that graduated and hierarchical order of values that characterizes the civilization of the Middle Ages, a hierarchy that, reaching down from God to the atom, allots to each type of being its proper place in the universal organism of Church, State, and society. Life, nature, and art acquire a symbolical value by sharing in that cosmos of Nature and Grace which, by means of the sacramental system of the Church, consecrated the objects of nature and daily life: vegetative life, animal life, and life on the human level.

It is in two major points that the Romanesque style in church architecture departs from the earlier type of the Christian basilica: (1) pillars replace the columns, supporting the arches of the nave arcade; (2) the nave is divided into a series of sections or "bays," retarding the continuous horizontal movement of the basilican interior and introducing in its place a diversity of clearly proportioned and self-sufficient architectural parts.

In view of future developments special emphasis must be placed on the resumption of the ribbed groined vault (already known to the Romans), which in the eleventh century replaced the early wooden ceiling as well as the intermediate form of the barrel vault. The ribbed groined vault was supported by a series of six arches, resulting normally in a vault of domical shape.

Bishops, abbots, and princes tried to outdo each other in their building activities and in their encouragement and sponsorship of the arts. St. Gall, Regensburg, and Hildesheim continued to stand out as illustrious centers of artistic activities and accomplishments. Bishop Bernward (993–1022) of Hildesheim, the tutor of Emperor Otto III, was one of the most influential protectors of the arts and is especially remembered as the builder of St. Michael's Church in Hildesheim (1001–1022), the most outstanding contribution of Saxony to the early Romanesque style. The cathedral of Magdeburg owes its existence to Emperor Otto I, that of Bamberg to Henry II. The great Rhenish cathedrals of Spires (Speyer), Mayence (Mainz), Worms, the abbey church of Maria-Laach, and the several Romanesque churches of Cologne (Maria im Kapitol, Apostelkirche, St. Gereon) were erected during the rule of the Saxon and Hohenstaufen emperors. Many of these monuments were completely destroyed during World War II.

Secular architecture played a rather insignificant part in a prevailingly ecclesiastical age. Of the representative secular architecture of the Saxon and Salic epochs only a few samples have survived. The most beautiful and the one best preserved is the Imperial Palace (*Kaiserpfalz*) at Goslar in the northern part of the Hartz Mountains that was begun by Henry II and completed by Henry III (*c.* 1050). Within its walls Henry IV was born. The building was restored during the years 1867–1878. Secular building activity was greatly aided and stimulated by the rise of a knightly aristocracy, the spread of the ideals of chivalry, and the growth of the cities.

Romanesque architecture ruled over the other arts of the period. Sculpture as well as painting were subordinated to architecture, which provided their *raison d'être*. Romanesque sculpture is filled with a sense of lasting existence, abiding in childlike confidence in the manifold forms of reality that are presented as sensible symbols and images of the purely intelligible.

The arts and the crafts are still undivided, united by the general characteristics and criteria of skill, usefulness, beautiful shape, and social significance. The anonymous masters, those artist-monks, who created altar tables, choir screens, baptismal fonts, crucifixes, ornate columns and capitals, and the solemn cathedral sculptures: they were both artists and craftsmen. The art of goldsmithing reached a high degree of perfection in the creation of altar vessels and cultic furniture, of tabernacles, monstrances, reliquaries, book covers, and chandeliers. The cathedral of Aachen contains a pulpit wholly wrought of gold, dating back to the days of Emperor Henry II.

The pelican, who nourishes his young with his own blood; the phoenix, who rises to a new life out of his own ashes: they are symbols of Christ. The poisonous glance of the basilisk signifies the spirit of evil; the virginal bee tells of Mary, the immaculate maiden. Minerals, plants, animals, men, and angels, the book of nature and the book of life repeat a thousandfold the story of creation, fall, and redemption. The arts are integral parts of the lives of the people, and life itself in its plenitude is enshrined in artistic creation.

Romanesque painting, like sculpture, served the adornment and enhancement of the architectural frame and background. The huge wall spaces of the cathedrals were frequently decorated with representations of biblical themes of the Old and New Testaments. The figural composition in its rigid and angular design seems to be influenced by the style of miniatures and mosaics. The illumination and illustration of manuscripts, missals, gospel books (*Evangeliare*), psalters, legends, calendars, and Latin classics reached new heights of perfection with the gradual emancipation from Irish and Byzantine patterns. In the art school of Reichenau originated the "Evangeliary" of Otto III, containing a famous miniature painting of the nations doing homage to the emperor. The art of painting on glass, being still in the earliest stage of its development, was practiced in Romanesque times at St. Emeram (Regensburg) and at Tegernsee near Munich. Some of the stained-glass windows in the cathedral of Augsburg date from the middle of the eleventh century and are among the oldest specimens of this sublime art which achieved its full splendor in the later Gothic period.

Music. Together with architecture and its allied arts, music also served religious, social, and educational ends. To be sure, there were the popular tunes of the wandering students and minstrels, who accompanied their songs on the harp or the fiddle, the former being one of the most ancient musical instruments, while the latter was introduced from Asia by way of Byzantium in the tenth century. But music as a fine art occurs in the early Middle Ages chiefly in the form of the ecclesiastical and monastic choral chant, which in the Romanesque period at times introduces even polyphonic motifs. The music of the Antiphonaries (choral songbooks) of St. Gall in Switzerland of the ninth and tenth centuries represents the authentic version of the liturgical Gregorian Chant (cf. p. 54 sq.).

The Latin system of *neumatic* notation was developed in Rome before the eighth century, and remained in use to the end of the fourteenth century. The neumatic signs were derived from the signs and accents of the grammarians. The necessity of fixing the intonation of the notes led to the invention of several tentative systems of notation after the ninth century and to the introduction of the "staff," consisting at first of one, then of two, and finally of four lines (five lines in modern notation). The transformation of the neumatic signs into square notes was practically completed at the end of the thirteenth century. Of greater importance were the several modal systems, because they expressed the psychological and sociological implications of different musical styles. The three major phases of modality are represented by the Greek, the medieval (Church modes), and the modern polyphonic modes which date from the beginning of Renaissance polyphony in the fifteenth century.

The first theoretical treatises on the medieval Church modes were written at the beginning of the ninth century. Hermann Contractus of Reichenau († 1054) gives a complete description of eight modes which he calls *tropi*, while the Italian Benedictine monk Guido d'Arezzo († 1050) first introduced the term *modus* instead of *tonus* or *tropus*. Adam of Fulda, an outstanding German musicologist of the fifteenth century, quotes a little poem by Guido d'Arezzo that illustrates the changing emotional contents that are expressed by the different Church Modes:

> "For every mood the first will be good; the second so tender to grief;
> If anger the third one provoke, then the fourth will bring the relief;
> The fifth be the mood for the joyous; the sixth one the pious will prize;
> The seventh is pleasing to youth, but the last is the mood of the wise."

On the whole it may be said that medieval German and European music followed the peculiarities of the Latin language with its characteristic measuring or counting of syllables, the same principle that has left its indelible impress upon the metric forms of all the Romance languages and literatures. It took Germany several more centuries to emancipate herself in her musical and literary arts from this foreign rhythmical and metrical technique and to rediscover the qualitative principle of accentuation. Of all the Indo-European nations the Germanic peoples alone emphasize the quality rather than the quantity of word syllables, putting the stress on the root syllable, the one that imparts substantial meaning to the verbal pattern. Medieval liturgical chant, on the other hand, depended entirely on the quantity of syllables, the neumes being sung as a succession of long and short tones, following the example of oratory and the declamation of poetry. The German manuscripts of St. Gall, Einsiedeln, and Metz of the ninth and tenth centuries mark the long and short tones by means of signs and letters. The growing influence of the spoken vernacular languages after the close of the tenth century tended to corrupt the classical tradition of Latin elocution and likewise the ancient style of musical performance.

Literature. Latin was the language of the Church, it was the language of the clergy, who represented learning and culture in most of its aspects. The vernacular Old High German language with its full sounding vowels and sonorous endings appeared as inferior to the velvety smoothness and the elegant flow of the Latin rhymes and rhythms. Whoever wanted to be recognized as a poet had to write Latin verse, carefully heeding the metrical rules of the ancient classical authors.

The poetry of monks and nuns dealt with the most diversified subject matter: biblical themes and the lives of Christian saints, historical events and legends, proverbs and satires. While all the German monasteries encouraged the practice of poetry and song, the didactic and epical elements prevailed, and only a few of the writers excelled in the field of the drama and the creation of church hymns. The Benedictine abbeys of Gandersheim, Tegernsee, and St. Gall stood out as centers of literary activities.

Hrotsvitha (Roswitha, *c.* 932–1001), a learned canoness of a secular convent for ladies of the Saxon nobility, affiliated with the monastery of Gandersheim, commemorated about the year 980 the accomplishments of Otto the Great in her epic *Gesta Odonis*. In her poems she celebrated the foundation of Gandersheim, the resurrection of Christ, the life of Mary, and, basing her story on a Greek model, she approached the *Faust* theme in *The Conversion of Theophilus*. The latter is a poetic description of Theophilus' pact with the devil and his final salvation through the intercession of the Virgin Mary. In her dramas, which were written in rhythmical prose and were to serve as substitutes for the widely read but objectionable pagan comedies of the late Roman playwright Terence (*c.* 190–159 B.C.), she described the conversion of harlots, glorified Christian virgins and martyrs, and gave evidence of great skill and a naïve and sprightly sense of humor. The period of the Saxon emperors could offer no equivalent to the stage of the age of Terence, so that Hrotsvitha's dramatic works were not written with a view to stage production. While Hrotsvitha composed these clever and amusing dialogues, medieval drama, properly so called, originated at about the same time from the liturgy of the Church.

Religious poetry flourished above all in the monastery of St. Gall in Switzerland. It was the home of Germany's leading poets, writers, and teachers in the tenth century. Out of the spirit of music was born the literary form of the "sequence," in which words and music blended and whose influence is noticeable in the works of the *"Minnesänger"* of the age of chivalry (cf. p. 155 sq.).

Latin in their form, but German in their content are the epic poems of *Walter with the Strong Hand* (*Waltharius Manu Fortis*) and *Ruodlieb*. The *Song of Walter* (*Waltharilied*) was written about 930 in Latin hexameters by Ekkehard I and metrically revised by Ekkehard IV († 1060). The poem tells of Walter and his betrothed Hildegund, who flee from the court of Attila, king of the Huns, their encounter with the greedy King Gunther of Burgundy, and the final triumph of their love and loyalty. It is typically Germanic in its mixture of heroism and tenderness, and Walter appears as the first German representative of Christian knighthood, the undaunted yet humble protector of noble womenhood.

In *Ruodlieb* (*c.* 1030) the colorful world of the eleventh century has come to life. The anonymous author, belonging to the Bavarian monastic community of Tegernsee, has been called the first master of realism in German literature. The description of the knightly hero's travel experiences and adventures manifests not only an accurate factual observation, but reveals wisdom, human understanding, love of nature, and a keen sense of humor.

During the eleventh and twelfth centuries a growing missionary zeal finds its literary equivalent in an increasing output of didactic poetry and prose. The attempts at popularization issued in the gradual adoption of the German vernacular, in sermons as well as in religious poetry. Closely related to the ascetic spirit of Cluny is the *Ezzoleich* (*Lay of Ezzo, c.* 1060), a lyric poem, written in German, but following the formal model of the Latin sequences. Linguistically it marks the transition from Old High German to early Middle High German. As to its content, it represents the first lyrical attempt to tell the story of creation and redemption in the German tongue. Ezzo, its author, deserves high credit for the harmonious combination of didactic and poetic values.

The institution of the Feast of the Immaculate Conception in Lyon (*c.* 1140) led to the creation of hymns, sequences, and epic poems in praise of the Virgin Mary, the mediatrix between Christ and suffering mankind. At the beginning of the twelfth century many members of the clergy began to turn to worldly themes. *The Lay of Anno* (*Annolied*), composed between 1080 and 1110 by a monk of the monastery of Siegburg near Bonn on the Rhine, is a kind of world chronicle, centering in the figure of St. Anno, archbishop of Cologne (1056–1075) and tutor of the young Emperor Henry IV. The *Lay of Alexander* (*Alexanderlied*) was written between 1120 and 1130 by the cleric Lamprecht (*Pfaffe Lamprecht*), who used as his model a French epic of the same name. The life of the great conqueror Alexander is described as futile and misspent because of his entanglement in worldly concerns.

At about the same time (*c.* 1130) Conrad, a priest from Ratisbon (Regensburg) in Bavaria, adapted his *Lay of Roland* (*Rolandslied*) from the French *Chanson de Roland,* telling of the heroic deeds of the most famous of Charlemagne's paladins (cf. p. 43). Roland is depicted as the typical knight of the age of the Crusades, the servant of God whose life has been consecrated by his exalted calling. Despite this religious tinge the description of camp life in the army of Charlemagne emphasizes the worldly aspects and elements of the period. *The Emperors' Chronicle* (*Kaiserchronik*), the work of a Bavarian priest (*c.* 1150), goes so far as to praise the power of worldly love (*minne*) over all creatures, as an indispensable requisite for knightly and courtly education. The work belongs in the category of popular rhymed chronicles, presenting a medley of historical and legendary elements.

Secular literature of an inferior order is represented in the poetry of the gleemen (*Spielmannsdichtung*), of wandering students and scholars who included among their number all kinds of entertainers, jugglers, and jesters. These in their own way perpetuated the ancient heroic legends and sagas, but primarily fulfilled the role of a living news chronicle, singing of contemporary events in Church and State, telling fairy stories and fables, performing on the village green or in the castle, catering in every way to the taste of the popular fancy of the unlettered and worldly minded. It was only later in the twelfth century that the wandering minstrel recovered a finer sense of literary values and prepared himself for the great task that the age of chivalry had in store for him.

Scholarship and Education. The primary goal of learning and education in the Ottonian and Salic periods was the formation of a religious and moral personality. The pre-Christian classical curriculum of the seven liberal arts was to provide the foundation upon which the structure of Christian dogma should rest. As in Charlemagne's time, the higher learning was patronized and greatly encouraged by the German emperors. But the members of the clergy were the representatives and carriers of intellectual life. Many of the bishoprics became now important seats of learning.

Each monastery had two separate schools, one of which served the education of the future clergy, while the second one was attended by the sons of nobles who aspired to leading positions in secular life. The strictest discipline ruled in both schools, corporal punishment being frequent and severe. Next in importance and influence ranked the cathedral schools which were attached to each bishopric. The director of the cathedral school was called "Master" (*Magister Scholarum, Scholasticus*), and to him was entrusted the supervision of the several parish schools of his bishop's diocese.

The curriculum in both monastery and cathedral schools consisted of a preparatory course, followed by instruction in rhetoric, dialectic, music, astronomy, arithmetic, and geometry. The preparatory training included the reading, recitation, and memorization of Latin psalms, writing upon wax tablets and parchment, and the acquisition of a vocabulary comprehensive enough to enable the student to begin with the reading of the more popular Latin authors of antiquity. The study of grammar made the student familiar with the classical Roman grammarians, writers, and poets, reading and translation being equally stressed. The class in rhetoric had to learn the art of letter writing, the drawing up of legal documents and diplomas, the making of wills, and all the agenda of the medieval chancery. Style and composition were further improved by the study of Cicero, Quintilian, St. Augustine, or some compendium of the art of rhetorics. The study of dialectic served the sharpening of the intellect to make it a suitable instrument for logical thought and disputation. Some of Aristotle's works were read in Latin translations alongside with Boëthius (cf. p. 26), Cassiodorus (cf. p. 52), and other pagan and Christian philosophers. Greek was not taught in these early medieval schools, and consequently very few had any knowledge of it.

The *Trivium* of sciences was, as we know (cf. p. 26), followed by the *Quadrivium*. The class in music studied the Church modes and the interrelation of tonal values, following in the main the theories laid down in Boëthius' tract *On Music* (*De Musica*). Astronomy was chiefly concerned with calendaric calculations in connection with the fixing of ecclesiastical feast days and seasons, and the hours of monastic devotions. Arithmetic, following in the footsteps of Pythagoras († 497 B.C.) and the Church Fathers, was closely tied up with speculations on the symbolism of numbers. More realistic but less popular was the study of geometry, including geography and the rudimentary beginnings of natural science. Maps and globes were known and frequently used. The maps of the world showed Asia with an indication of the location of the biblical Paradise in the upper half, Europe in the lower left, Africa in the lower right part of the map. The continents, surrounded on all sides by water, were arranged in the form of a "T" (T-maps).

The convent schools for women, attached to their respective monasteries, were attended by girls who were preparing themselves for a religious vocation as well as by daughters of noble families who would leave the convent after their educational curriculum was completed. Versatility in the reading, writing, reciting, and singing of Latin was emphasized, while the curriculum of the seven liberal arts was otherwise reduced to a minimum of fundamental principles of general education.

Outside of the monastic and metropolitan schools education was at a low ebb. Even in the ranks of the nobility the eleventh century witnesses a growing contempt of the higher learning. We find, for example, honorable mention of the fact that Emperor Henry IV was able to read the letters that he received. And even the splendor of the following period of courtly culture is not without the blemish of widespread illiteracy among the laity.

Chapter 6

THE HOHENSTAUFEN DYNASTY AND THE AGE OF CHIVALRY

Lothar and Conrad III: Welf and Waiblingen. With the death of Henry V in 1125 the Salic-Frankish dynasty had come to an end, and the German nobles, in choosing Lothar of Supplinburg (1125-1137) as their new king, reasserted once more the validity of the time-honored elective principle of Germanic kingship. Henry V had died without direct heirs, and the electors had disregarded the hereditary claims of the two nephews of the late emperor, Frederick of Hohenstaufen and his younger brother Conrad. Thus originated the feud between the two powerful feudal families of the *Welfs* (Guelfs) and the *Waiblingens* (Ghibellines; their name possibly derived from one of the family possessions of the *Hohenstaufens*), which later on spread to Italy and continued for several centuries.

Lothar's election caused the Hohenstaufens to rise in armed rebellion and to wage private warfare against Henry the Proud (1126-1139). Henry was head of the Welfs; son-in-law and heir of Lothar; duke of Bavaria, Saxony, and Swabia; count of Tuscany; and, by the end of Lothar's reign, the most powerful territorial lord of Germany. True to their traditional policy of checking any considerable growth of the imperial power, the electors chose the Hohenstaufen, Conrad III (1138-1152) to succeed Lothar. Now it was the Welfs' turn to feel themselves slighted and offended, and this Welf-Waiblingen family feud added to the general turmoil and confusion that characterized this period of feudal license. Conrad's participation in the unsuccessful Second Crusade (cf. p. 107), undertaken in alliance with the king of France, tended to undermine further the prestige of the German emperor.

Frederick I (1152-1190) and the Consolidation of the Empire. Conrad III wisely passed over his own young son in favor of his nephew, Frederick, who was destined to rescue the Empire from anarchy and disintegration. Being the nephew of Henry the Proud through his mother, he was half Welf and half Waiblingen, thus acceptable to both parties and able to reconcile temporarily their conflicting ambitions.

Frederick I, named *Barbarossa* (red beard, *Rotbart*), is the most brilliant and attractive figure among the Hohenstaufen emperors, the symbol of all chivalrous virtues, and the favorite of the Romantic writers of the early nineteenth century. It was the ambition of his life to resurrect the ancient glory and power of the Roman Empire under German leadership, and he succeeded to a remarkable extent in realizing his aims. True representative of the social standards and prejudices of knighthood that he was, he underestimated the significance of the rising commercial and industrial forces embodied in city life and their new ideals of citizenship. An idealist in his vision of a greater empire and in his exalted view of the mission' of chivalry, he was a realist in the execution of his far-reaching plans and in the practical application of his sound and noble principles.

His first major objective, the restoration of order and stability in the German lands, was at least partly achieved by the promulgation of a general land peace (*Landfriede*), forbidding private wars and feuds, and guaranteeing a stricter enforcement and a more universal application of the existing local enactments. Next he re-established imperial supremacy over Poland, Bohemia, Hungary, and Burgundy.

The emperor's nephew and the current head of the Welfs was Henry the Lion (1156–1180), the son of Henry the Proud. To gain the friendship and military support of this ambitious prince, Frederick made him duke of Saxony and Bavaria and thereby the most powerful lord in the Empire. Henry accompanied Frederick on the first two of his six expeditions into Italy, and aided German expansion and colonization in the East (cf. p. 110 sq.). He is also remembered as the founder of the bishoprics of Lübeck, Ratzeburg, Schwerin, and of the city of Munich (München). Banned by the emperor in 1179 for his refusal to come to Frederick's aid in the Italian campaign of 1174, he went into exile in England, retaining only Brunswick (Braunschweig) and Lüneburg as his family possessions. The duchies of Saxony and Bavaria were divided up into smaller units, and the greater part of Bavaria was given to Otto Wittelsbach, whose descendants occupied the Bavarian throne until the German revolution of 1918.

Frederick experienced a most severe setback in his attempt to recover imperial control of Italy. His relations with the Roman Curia appeared to be of a friendly nature when he started upon his first Italian expedition in 1154. Pope Adrian IV (1154–1159), the first and only Englishman to sit on the papal throne, had sought Frederick's aid against the citizens and the Senate of Rome, who under the leadership of Arnold of Brescia attempted to regain the ancient freedom of the city from papal supremacy. Frederick had Arnold of Brescia executed and, in 1155, received the imperial crown from Adrian. However, when Frederick refused to act as the pope's squire by holding his bridle and stirrup, and thus seemed to deny implicitly the papal claim that the imperial crown was a feudal benefice conferred by the pope — affirming rather the origin of imperial power from God through the election of the princes — the relations between the two potentates became very strained. These incidents, as a matter of fact, marked the beginning of the last great struggle between Empire and Papacy that finally led to the decline and almost complete disintegration of both powers in the fourteenth century. Both emperor and pope tried to substantiate their claims by legal argumentation, having recourse to Roman and Canon Law respectively. Both legal branches had received a new impetus from the revival of learning in the twelfth century, and Canon Law, mainly based on the Scriptures and the decrees of popes and Church councils, received its classical form in the *Decretum* of Gratian (*c.* 1140), famous jurist of the University of Bologna.

The natural allies of the papacy were the cities of Lombardy, which felt themselves hampered in their commercial and industrial growth and thwarted in their desire for civic rights and self-government by imperial administration and supervision. Most of these North Italian communities were involved in factional and internecine strife, and Milan in particular exercised an oppressive rule over her smaller neighbors. Frederick took it upon himself to have the royal privileges formulated by a council of jurists from Bologna, and to appoint royal officers to safeguard these imperial prerogatives. On his second expedition to Italy in 1158 Frederick captured Milan and publicly promulgated his imperial rights before the Imperial Diet at Roncaglia. These rights included the appointment of imperial administrative officers and the collection of taxes from tolls, markets, mints, and law courts. But the Lombard cities offered at first passive and later active resistance, and turned to the pope for protection.

In the meantime, Adrian's death had caused a papal schism, a majority of the cardinals voting for Alexander III (1159–1181), a minority for Victor IV. The emperor's support of Victor and several other antipopes was of no avail, as practically all the rulers of Europe stood solidly behind Alexander. Thus Frederick found himself facing the combined opposition of a united Italy, and in Alexander III he was confronted by a masterful politician who was fully his equal in circumspection, determination, and practical realism. Despite all the odds against him, the emperor at first seemed successful in the execution of his plans. He destroyed Milan in 1162, crushed the Lombard cities on his third expedition to Italy in 1166, and even besieged and captured Rome, while Alexander had to seek refuge in Sicily. But this victory was almost immediately followed by disaster: a pestilence destroyed the imperial army, and Frederick had to withdraw to Germany.

His withdrawal was the signal for the Lombard cities to unite in renewed efforts to offer an organized and impregnable resistance. Under the leadership of a newly risen Milan they formed the Lombard League, building at the same time a strongly fortified city which they named Alexandria in honor of their papal ally. When the emperor returned to Italy in 1174, this city withstood all his attempts to conquer it, and in 1176 Frederick was decisively defeated at Legnano. The Lombard cities emerged triumphant from the struggle for their civic liberties, and Frederick had to come to terms with the Lombard League as well as with his papal adversary. He ended the papal schism by making his peace with Alexander, and in 1183 he confirmed the self-government of the Lombard cities in the Peace of Constance. The royal prerogatives had to be surrendered, but the cities in return recognized the imperial sovereignty.

Although Frederick seemed to have failed in his struggle against the papacy, neither emperor nor pope had abandoned their respective claims to supremacy, so that at best a new compromise was effected which bore in itself the symptoms of latent discontent and a future crisis. Stubbornly persisting in the traditional aims of imperial policy, Frederick brought about the marriage of his eldest son Henry with Constance, heiress of the kingdom of Sicily, thus paving the way for a future alliance between southern Italy and the Empire that would be a formidable asset in a renewed conflict with the papacy, while at the same time it established a new basis for the commercial relations with the Orient.

Frederick paid his final tribute to the spirit of the age when he took the cross in 1189 and led twenty thousand of his knights on the noble adventure of the Third Crusade. He was seventy years of age when he started upon this crowning event of his colorful career, only equaled in splendor and enthusiasm by the great festival of Chivalry of the year 1184 at Mayence (Mainz), where more than seventy thousand nobles had gathered to witness the knighting of the emperor's sons, Frederick and Henry. Frederick Barbarossa never reached the Holy Land, meeting his death in 1190 in the icy waters of the river Saleph in Asia Minor. The chaotic times of the *Interregnum* (cf. p. 96) gave birth to the Kyffhäuser legend, which attached itself first to Barbarossa's grandson, Frederick II, then to be transferred in the sixteenth century to his great ancestor. Popular imagination, coupled with certain prophecies of the Italian Benedictine historian Joachim of Fiore (*c.* 1140–1205) relating to the coming of the Third Empire, pictured the emperor asleep in the depths of the Kyffhäuser Mountain in Thuringia, waiting for the day of his return to lead his people to unity and renewed glory.

Frederick II and the Disintegration of the Empire. The Hohenstaufen period is marked from its beginning by an intense nationalization of both the imperial and the papal claims and ambitions. While the German historian Otto von Freising (*c.* 1111–1158) still visualized the ultimate realization of Augustine's universal kingdom of peace and justice under imperial leadership, the Church as well as the Empire nourished the idea of national independence. The Hohenstaufen emperors saw in the Empire the source of all law, investing the imperial dignity with totalitarian titles and predicates.

a) The Imperial Policy of Henry VI. Potentially Frederick Barbarossa's son Henry VI (1190–1197) represented the gravest threat to the power of the papacy, and his final victory was only prevented by his premature death. He succeeded in isolating the pope in central Italy by enforcing his authority in the kingdom of Sicily, to which he had a claim through his wife

Constance, and at the same time he secured the loyalty of northern Italy by granting the largest measure of independence to the Lombard cities. He appointed his own vassals in the Papal States, thus limiting the suzerainty of the pope to the duchy of Rome. His cruel and relentless will to power envisaged a hereditary Empire of the Hohenstaufens, with Italy as its center, extending over the territories of both the Western and the Byzantine Empires. Feeling himself the true heir of the Roman Caesars, he revived and invigorated the political ideology of Otto III (cf. p. 64). During the seven years of his reign he built up a system of personal power and imperial influence that is almost unparalleled in medieval history.

b) Frederick II and Innocent III. Once more the tense drama that had reached its climax at Canossa (cf. p. 72 sq.) was re-enacted on the European stage, but this time the two major characters were more evenly matched than Henry IV and Gregory VII.

When Henry VI died he left as his heir his four-year-old son Frederick, and immediately rival candidates began to struggle for the imperial crown. Philip of Swabia, Henry's brother, was the choice of the Waiblingen faction, while the candidate of the Welfs was Otto of Brunswick, son of Henry the Lion. After ten years of factional strife Philip was murdered in 1208, Otto was proclaimed German king and received the imperial crown in 1209. When he tried to assert his imperial claims in Italy and threatened the Papal States, he met with the opposition of Pope Innocent III (1160–1216), the most powerful of the medieval popes, who carried the theocratic ideas of Gregory VII to their logical conclusion. As a result of the excommunication of Otto of Brunswick a Hohenstaufen rebellion in Germany returned Frederick, king of Sicily, the son and heir of Henry VI, to the throne of his ancestors. Civil war continued in Germany to the year 1214, when Otto of Brunswick was defeated by Philip Augustus, king of France (1180–1233), who was one of the supporters of Frederick's claims to the imperial crown. After having received the desired assurances and guarantees, including Frederick's promise to give up the kingdom of Sicily to his infant son Henry, Pope Innocent confirmed the election of the new emperor, who now ascended the throne as Frederick II (1212–1250).

In Barbarossa's grandson one of the most fascinating personalities of Western civilization enters upon the historical stage. Frederick II has been called the first modern man, a precursor of the great figures of the Renaissance, a humanist, and a skeptic. To his friends he appeared as the Messiah, the herald of universal peace, the god-emperor of a new age, while his enemies saw in him a ruthless tyrant and the incarnation of the antichrist whose coming spelled ruin and the end of the world. The modern historian recognizes in Frederick the antagonistic elements of a historic constellation in which two epochs meet and clash: the ecclesiastical civilization of the Middle Ages and the secularized modern world.

When Frederick at the age of eighteen proceeded triumphantly from Sicily to his northern German kingdom to receive the royal crown at

Aachen (1215), he completed the encirclement of the Papal States and precipitated the beginning of the final phase of the life-and-death struggle between Empire and Papacy.

From his father, Henry VI, Frederick had inherited the cunning that was needed to master the adverse forces of political intrigue, and an implicit consciousness of his exalted mission. The cosmopolitan environment of Sicily with its mixture of racial, religious, and social forces had equipped his mind with keenness of observation and a mild, sometimes cynical, skepticism. And Pope Innocent, to whose guardianship the years of his early intellectual formation had been entrusted, had not only influenced the future emperor's ideas of rulership and statecraft but had also put at his disposal the broad educational facilities of the new age of learning, thus laying the foundations for those extraordinary mental qualities which made Frederick one of the most advanced and independent thinkers of his epoch.

Pope Innocent III had been trained in the law schools of Bologna and Paris, and he based his universal claims on the tradition embodied in Canon Law. "God," he proclaimed, "has instituted two high dignities: the Papacy, which reigns over the souls of men; and Monarchy, which reigns over their bodies. But the first is above the second." Innocent III lived entirely in the world of medieval ideas, and he attempted to formulate and realize his political plans according to the principles and methods of scholastic philosophy and theology (cf. p. 141 sqq.). In contrast to the inspirational asceticism of Gregory VII, the papal adversary of Frederick II represents a legalistic and casuistic mentality which is guided by considerations of formal logic. Accordingly, the gigantic struggle between the two potentates had now become a competitive contest of legal principles rather than a conflict between historical powers.

c) Frederick's Struggle With the Papacy. The final act of the Hohenstaufen tragedy began with Frederick's return to Italy in 1220. Pope Innocent III had died in 1216. After having wrested from Innocent's successor, Honorius III (1216–1227), the concession to remain in possession of his Sicilian kingdom, Frederick reorganized the whole governmental system of Sicily, issued a new legal code based on the principles of Roman Law, and lent his encouragement to industry, commerce, and agriculture. He founded the University of Naples and made southern Italy a center of intellectual and cultural activities. Although the emperor was primarily interested in Italy and cared but little about Germany, he did not lose sight of the idea of a universal and united empire. Less than eight of the thirty-eight years of his rule were spent in Germany, where imperial government was almost exclusively carried on through the princes. In order to gain the support of the German secular and ecclesiastical lords he gave them almost absolute sovereignty within their domains. The "Constitution in Favor of the Princes" (*Constitutio in Favorem Principum*), promulgated by the emperor in 1231, created a fateful community of interests and privileges among the nobility as against the rising citizenry of the towns, and established a legal basis for the future particularistic dismemberment of the Empire.

While in this way the Church in Germany gained a much desired independence of imperial control, in Italy Frederick's territorial ambitions came into sharp conflict with the sovereign rule of the popes in the Papal States and their feudal supremacy over Sicily. Honorius' successor, Gregory IX (1227–1241), took advantage of Frederick's unfulfilled promise to undertake a Crusade and excommunicated the emperor. When Frederick finally started upon his Crusade in 1228, he did so in defiance of the pope, and succeeded in winning Jerusalem by diplomatic negotiations with the sultan. A peace treaty, concluded in 1230, established a temporary truce between Empire and Papacy.

When Frederick returned to Italy from Germany where, in 1235, he had subdued a rebellion instigated by his son Henry, he found himself confronted with an alliance between the Lombard League and the papacy, the same combination of forces that had brought disaster to his grandfather, Frederick Barbarossa. Pope Gregory's fight for the theocratic claims of the Church was carried on by his successor, Innocent IV (1243–1254), and the struggle was still undecided when Frederick's death in 1250 released the forces of anarchy in the German lands.

d) Frederick, the "Antichrist"?   In judging Frederick's character and in trying to evaluate the struggle between waning and rising cultural forces that are symbolically expressed in his conflict with the papacy, one does well to take into consideration the emperor's own estimate of his world-historic mission. After his peaceful conquest of Jerusalem he issued a manifesto in which he interpreted his victory as a token of the Lord Almighty, who is powerful and terrible in His glory, who changes the times to make them suit His will and welds the hearts of the nations to unity. The emperor speaks here as the Chosen One of the Lord, who has been raised miraculously above the princes of the earth. Making use of the terminology of the Old Testament, Frederick assumes the full autocratic power of the reborn Roman Imperator, and he rationalizes his political philosophy by means of the newly discovered Aristotelian metaphysics (cf. p. 143). The ancient Roman idea of the universal rule of peace and justice within the framework of a totalitarian State, thoroughly organized by the power of the sword, takes the place of the Augustinian ideal of the Peace of the City of God.

Gregory IX, on the other hand, the last of the papal representatives of the medieval philosophy of life and civilization, recognized the fundamental change that was involved in the imperial proclamations and policies and publicly declared the emperor to be the self-avowed emissary of the Prince of this World and the personification of the antichrist: "Out of the depths of the sea rises the beast, filled with the names of blasphemy, raging with the paw of the lion and opening the lion's mouth to blaspheme the Divine name. . . . Openly it displays its machinations . . . to destroy the Tables of the Covenant of the Saviour! Behold the head, the middle, and the end of this beast, Frederick, the so-called Emperor."

The emperor, in turn, calls the pope the Pharisee occupying the chair of perverted dogma, planning the reversal of the divinely established order of the Realm, an apocalyptic monster, the red horse risen from the sea, the great dragon, the antichrist, the false vice-regent of Christ. The Roman Curia is characterized as the Council of the High Priest, scheming against the "Anointed One of the Lord." The Romans must be awakened from their sleep of inertia to rise once more to their ancient greatness. The Messianic age has arrived when everyone must be converted to worship the new and true Messiah. From the emperor's birthplace, as from a new Bethlehem, will come forth the new leader, the *Dux,* the Prince of the Roman Empire. The emperor is the supreme lawgiver whose will must be done, whose name must be adored, to whom earth and sea pay homage.

When the emperor was on his triumphal march upon the city of Rome, it was Gregory, then one hundred years of age, who rallied the wavering Romans to his support, pointing to the relics of Peter and Paul, and who, crowning them with the papal tiara (triple crown), explained: "This, Romans, is your antiquity." Frederick passed by the city of Rome, and afterward all his remaining plans were doomed to failure.

In viewing the profound significance of these events the modern historian is forced to the conclusion that both Empire and Papacy failed to recognize the mutual interdependence of *Imperium* and *Sacerdotium,* that both powers overstressed their claims to absolute supremacy, and that both thereby not only undermined the foundations of their own political power but contributed to the dissolution of the supernational unity of Western civilization.

The End of the Hohenstaufen Dynasty. As if to seal outwardly the ultimate failure of the imperial policy of the Hohenstaufens, the last member of their family, Frederick II's grandson Conradin, was captured by Charles, duke of Anjou, and executed together with his friend, Frederick of Baden (1268).

The German nobles had used Frederick II's Italian entanglements to establish fully their own independence. During the last ten years of Frederick's reign the antikings, Henry Raspe and William of Holland, were elected by the papal party. After Frederick's death his son Conrad IV (1250–1254) carried on the campaign in Italy, and his short reign was followed by the *"kaiserlose, schreckliche Zeit"* (the terrible period of Germany's being without an emperor, 1256–1273) of the so-called *Interregnum,* leaving the Empire deprived of a central power and at the mercy of rival factions.

Disregarding for the moment the frustration of the Hohenstaufen policies, with the resultant political disintegration of the Empire, we recognize the age of Hohenstaufen rule as the most brilliant period of medieval civilization, its climax as well as its beginning decay. It is the age of the great accomplishments in philosophy and the arts, in the realm of mind and letters, and it marks the consummation of the formative forces of a religiously guided and inspired civilization and the incubation period of the modern world.

The Age of Chivalry. The Hohenstaufen emperors embody in their personalities and their interests the type of culture that is generally associated with the Age of Chivalry and the ideals of knighthood. For the first time in the history of Western civilization we meet here with a genuine class culture that is characterized by secular or semisecular features. Ecclesiasticism and monasticism have moved from the center to the periphery, and their place has been occupied by the knightly castle and the princely court.

The fully developed knightly culture of the twelfth and thirteenth centuries was the result of a gradual transformation of the social organism. One of the factors that contributed to the formation of the international society of knights (French, *chevalier;* German, *Ritter* — "horseman") was the development of a mounted army, replacing the foot soldiery of the early Middle Ages. This change dates back to the time of Charles Martel and his fight against the Saracens in the eighth century (cf. p. 30) and the Mongolian invasions of the ninth century. The feudal environment with its social and cultural implications provided the setting for the evolution of knightly etiquette and class consciousness. The fourteenth century saw the decline of knighthood, heralding at the same time the phenomenal rise of the new burgher class with their corresponding social ideology. During the twelfth and thirteenth centuries, when the spirit of chivalry was at its height, knighthood had become a legally established institution, to the extent that only descendants of three generations of freeborn nobles were admitted to the Order of Knighthood, while in the period of decline the class restrictions were virtually obliterated, and an intermixture with the newly developed city aristocracy took place.

Knightly culture (*höfische Kultur*) was characterized by definite rules of social behavior, stressing the knightly virtues of moderation (*diu mâze*), discipline, self-control, courage, perseverance, and loyalty. The law of the strong hand or the principle that might creates right (*Faustrecht,* "club-law") gave way gradually to the rules of the "Peace of God" (cf. p. 77), which protected the poor, women, and traveling merchants from the former lawlessness of feudal aristocracy. Promulgated as an ecclesiastical commandment by Pope Urban II (1088–1099), the *Treuga Dei* was embodied in Canon Law in the twelfth century. It expressed the endeavor of the Church to infuse religious motivations into the institutional etiquette and the practices of knighthood. The ideals of Cluny (cf. p. 70 sq.) are reflected to some extent in the concepts of knightly honor and knightly virtue. It is this aspect of chivalry that is strikingly presented in the romances of the twelfth century, of which the French *Chansons de Geste* are beautiful examples and notably, among them, the *"Chanson de Roland."*

The knightly cult of noble womanhood likewise shows a peculiar mixture of purely secular and religious or even mystical elements. It was chiefly due to the influence of the French *Troubadours* that the German *Minne-*

sänger (cf. p. 155 sq.) developed a highly conventionalized etiquette in the service of the noble Lady who was, at least in theory but frequently also in reality, placed upon a pedestal of exalted dignity. However, the artificiality of this rationalized sexuality of chivalry, the external gloss of courtliness (*hoevescheit*) or courtesy (*courtoisie*) only thinly veils the inherent frivolity of a knightly ethics which does not hesitate to make God the confidant of lovers and the helper and guardian of adulterers. Furthermore, it is the married woman and frequently the one of higher social rank who is made the object of knightly yearning and wooing; an ideal object that is all the more worthy of devotion and veneration because its attainment would of necessity meet with innumerable obstacles and difficulties. On the other hand, the more religious and ascetic components of the spirit of chivalry were further developed by the knightly orders and especially by the Order of Teutonic Knights (cf. p. 113 sq.), whose members solemnly forswore the knightly love code and submitted to a semimonastic discipline.

The cradle of knighthood as a social order is to be looked for in southern France, in the homeland of the *Provençal Troubadours,* and it is there that the secular elements are most conspicuous. Fashion and poetry, etiquette and external behavior of the French knights of the *Provence* developed in close contact with and under the influence of the highly civilized Arabs, the conquerors of Spain, who had established cultural centers at the courts of the caliphs, especially the court of Cordova. The Crusades (cf. p. 106 sqq.) further strengthened the influence of Islam and its culture upon those knights and their retinue who visited the Moslem countries and observed at firsthand the social and cultural customs and conditions of the Arabs. At the same time the Crusades contributed to the greater refinement and cultural education of the German knight by subjecting him to the polishing influence of French elegance of manners and a highly cultivated sense of literary and artistic form. Thus the creation of a supernational knightly aristocracy is largely to be attributed to the supernational enterprise of the Crusades. But whatever significance may be attached to these foreign importations and adaptations, they acted merely as external stimuli to which the German mind responded in a thoroughly original way. They left their marks on the cultural surface without changing the essential indigenous forces of German civilization. Thus German *Minnesang,* the German court epic, German mysticism, German Gothic reflect to a large extent the Romanic pattern, but they nevertheless represent typically German adaptations and variations of a general European theme.

German Knighthood. As far as Germany is concerned, the new culture of chivalry is associated with the Swabian, Bavarian-Austrian, and Frankish regions. Southern Germany was in closer touch with the international movements of the age and therefore more susceptible to influences from East and West. The Saxons of the German Northwest were more conservative by nature and at the same time geographically farther removed from the new focus of cultural exchange. The splendor of the rule of the Swabian dynasty of the Hohenstaufens made their native stem duchy the actual center of the courtly display of German knighthood.

In an age of feudal aristocracy with vertical rather than horizontal divisions of social strata, it is not surprising to find the structure of the knightly pyramid hierarchically ordered and graduated. The king was the knight supreme. Then followed in a descending scale the dukes, margraves, counts, and nobles. Lowest in the social scale of knighthood ranked the "ministerials," the descendants of those unfree tenants who in the Frankish empire of the Carolingians had become the personal attendants of the lord and thus the nucleus of a new caste of the lower nobility. During the twelfth century they had obtained the right to acquire independent fiefs, and the thirteenth century witnessed their ascendancy to the class of free knights.

Strict dividing lines separated the various ranks of knights from other social groups and estates, from which they were distinguished by social etiquette, dress, standards and manners of living and habitation, and the code of feudal law.

Knightly Education. The training for the profession of knighthood started at an early age. The small boy who was destined to become a future knight was usually sent to the castle of his father's liege lord or some other nobleman to serve as a page (*Knappe*) and to be educated in the social etiquette of chivalry. Not infrequently he was sent to the court of some French noble or was given a French tutor. Military education began at the age of fourteen. As one of his lord's squires he received a thorough training in the knightly sports and games, such as racing, jumping, swimming, wrestling, riding, fencing, hunting, the art of archery, and the intricate ceremonials and finesses of the knightly tournament. He had to learn the full etiquette of social behavior, the rules of dressing, walking, conversation, salutation, and the strict requirements of social intercourse. At the age of twenty-one the young squire was considered sufficiently prepared to be solemnly received into the order of knighthood.

The ceremony of knighting (*Schwertleite*) provided an occasion for an elaborate display of knightly splendor and was an exorbitantly expensive affair for the youth's family. The Church took an important part in the proceedings. The night preceding the great event was spent by the knight-to-be in vigil before the altar of the family chapel. After having attended Mass in the morning and having received the sacraments of Penance and Communion, the youth had his sword blessed by the priest and he was once more entreated to be loyal to the virtues of his new calling: to be magnanimous, helpful, courteous, truthful, loyal, and brave; to aid the Church; to protect and defend widows, orphans, pilgrims, and the poor and oppressed; to obey the Roman emperor in all temporal matters; and to keep himself untainted in thoughts, words, and deeds. The ceremony reached its climax with the handing over of shield, sword, and golden spurs, followed by the "accolade" (*Ritterschlag*), three blows on neck or shoulder, administered by the king, the prince, the liege lord, the bishop, or some distinguished knight or noble lady. The festivities were usually concluded by a tournament, the favorite and most picturesque of knightly sports and entertainments. The actual tournament (German: *Turnier;* from Latin, *torneamentum;* French verb, *tourner:* "to turn") was distinguished from the lighter and less hazardous sportly encounters of two knights in single combat: the *Buhurt* (from late Latin, *hurtus:* "thrust"; French, *heurter*) and the *Tjost* (Latin, *justa;* French, *jouste:* "joust"), by its almost warlike character: two groups of knights meeting in armed contest, with prisoners being taken and ransomed, frequent fatalities being the rule rather than an exception.

An important and indispensable element of these knightly spectacles was the presence of noble ladies, whose favor and admiration was coveted by the display of knightly courage, skill, and cunning. Many a knight took part in the tournament in honor of the lady of his choice, wearing upon his shoulder or helmet her veil or colors as a symbol of his devotion. A flower wreath, a belt, a falcon, a sword bestowed upon him by his beloved seemed ample reward for his bravery.

Knightly Armor and Knightly Warfare. The armored knight is still a favorite subject of popular imagination, and it is indeed hard to conceive of knightly life without evoking at the same time the colorful picture of knightly armor, which was considered a habit of honor and a symbol of social distinction. The armor consisted of a cone-shaped steel helmet, a shield, and a loose cloak of linked mail which covered the body from the helmet to the knees. Closed visors to protect the face, and full-plate armor as well as the more fanciful types of headgear and silk coats, made their appearance toward the end of the thirteenth century. The knight's offensive weapons were sword, dagger, and spear. The dagger, sometimes called the *misericorde,* was used as a "dagger of mercy" to administer the coup de grace to a mortally wounded enemy. The knight's horse was protected by a heavy blanket, consisting of metal rings, which was covered by a more elaborate *covertiure,* a second cover of costly material and adorned with the coat of arms. The foot soldiers among the knight's attendants wore a partial-plate armor and were equipped with swords, spears, and halberts (from *helmbarte,* "battleax"), clubs, bows and arrows (*Armbrust,* popular adaptation from Middle Latin, *arcubalista,* "crossbow"). This foot soldiery was made up of mercenaries and servants, frequently recruited from urban communities. Although snubbed by the knights as their social inferiors, they represent the nucleus of all modern armies and were soon to outgrow the knights in military efficiency and strategic significance.

The knightly armies were of relatively small size, rarely exceeding two thousand in number, not including the attendants and the baggage train. The crusading army of Frederick Barbarossa is estimated to have numbered one hundred thousand, an exceptionally formidable contingent of soldiers. Army discipline was strictly regulated by the decrees of martial law. Barbaric cruelty frequently characterized the treatment of wounded or captured

Evangeliary of Otto III.

Rheinstein Castle.

enemies; and the conquered territories, cities, and castles were ruthlessly pillaged and destroyed; the men killed, the women violated, the children murdered.

The Castles and Their Inhabitants. The castle is as inseparably linked with knightly life and culture as is military training, feudal warfare, and knightly armor. It was home and fortress in one, the knight's abode in time of peace as in time of war. To get a true insight, therefore, into the spirit of chivalry it will be necessary to observe the nobleman's life inside the castle walls.

The German equivalent for castle is the word *Burg,* derived from the verb *bergen,* denoting a protecting and protected dwelling. The beginnings of the medieval type of *Burgen* date back to the ninth and tenth centuries. The plans of fortification followed in the main the rules laid down by the Roman writers and architects Vitruvius (88–26 B.C.) and Vegetius (*c.* A.D. 400). Important innovations and improvements were due to the influence of Oriental military science during the period of the Crusades.

The invention and perfection of firearms toward the end of the Middle Ages greatly diminished the military significance of the castles, many of which were destroyed during the peasant wars of 1524-1525 and again during the Thirty Years' War (1618-1648), and a large number decayed and fell to ruins when their owners abandoned them and moved into the cities. It was the Romantic movement of the early nineteenth century that rediscovered the rugged beauty of these witnesses and symbols of knightly civilization, glorifying them in poetry, songs, and pictures, and reviving a general public interest in their preservation and restoration. The total number of *Burgen* on German soil at the end of the Middle Ages was in the neighborhood of 10,000, about 400 of which are still extant and habitable.

The site of the *Burg* was chosen for its defensibility rather than for the beauty of the surrounding scenery or easy accessibility. Preferred locations, therefore, were hilltops, islands, or marshy regions. The castle could be approached from one side only, and a series of obstacles had to be overcome by an attacking enemy. The moat (*Graben*) which wholly or partly surrounded the castle was usually filled with water and spanned by a draw-bridge. Above the moat rose the mighty wall (*Mauer*), built of solid blocks of stone and crowned with battlements (*Zinnen*). To render the defense more efficient towers of various shape were intermittently inserted in the wall, the center of which was occupied by the great gate, wrought of heavy oakwood and reinforced with iron bands.

In case the attackers succeeded in breaking through this outer wall, they found themselves in the outer courtyard and had to face a second line of defense. In this outer courtyard were located the stables and barns, the bakery and the washhouse, a small fruit and vegetable garden, the lady's rosary, and frequently a small square where, in the shade of linden trees, knightly sports and games would be practiced by the lord's sons and their companions. In the inner court rose in lonely majesty the main tower with its thick and heavy walls (*Bergfried;* Old French, *beffroi;* English, *"belfry"*), overlooking the countryside, thus permitting to spy an approaching enemy from afar, and serving as the last refuge of the castle's inhabitants in time of war. In its lower stories the great tower contained the storerooms and the subterranean dungeon. Next to this fortresslike and awe-inspiring structure was located the lord's palace (Latin, *palatium;* German, *Pfalz*), with kitchen, bath, storerooms, and the servants' living quarters on its main floor, and the big festival hall, the sleeping rooms, and the lady's apartments (*Kemenate,* from Middle Latin, *caminata;* Old High German, *cheminata:* a room equipped with a "chimney") in the upper stories. In the larger castles the women's living quarters frequently occupied a separate building. The palace-chapel was architecturally connected with the palace.

The knightly castle as a whole was a very imposing structure from a military point of view, but crude and primitive as far as comfort, convenience, and hygienic conditions were concerned. As glass windows were unknown well into the thirteenth century, the openings that were set in the masonry were narrow open slits through which wind and rain could pass practically unobstructed, or they might be covered with horn sheets, parchment, oiled paper, or linen. Despite the fire that burned in the open chimneys of the larger rooms, cold, dampness, and drafts must have caused great inconvenience.

Social life in the castle centered in the big vaulted hall, benches running alongside the walls, chandeliers and candles shedding their light, Oriental rugs being spread out on the floors or being affixed to the walls, and cushions of precious materials being used for added comfort as well as for decorative purposes. Indoor games of various kinds, such as chess, checkers, backgammon, and dice games, were enjoyed by the inhabitants of the castle in the wintertime. Otherwise, the winter must have been a most dreary and depressing season, so that spring was universally hailed as the great harbinger of joy, the bringer of all the good things in nature as well as in human life. But despite the narrowness and primitivity of his home life the knight felt such a strong sentimental attachment to his castle that he even made it an integral part of his family name (*Herr Georg von Frundsberg; Herr Heinrich von Mindelberg,* etc.).

Knightly Dress, Manners, and Customs. The Crusades were in part responsible for the more extravagant tastes and habits of living, for the increased craving for luxuries as manifested especially in the manner of dressing, eating, and drinking. Precious silks and furs added to the splendor and dignity of the personal appearance of lord and lady. Lively and even glaring colors were quite fashionable, red and yellow being highly favored, before the later Middle Ages made yellow the distinguishing color of harlots and Jews. Make-up, which had been popular with the peoples of antiquity, was now lavishly used by noble ladies, and the women of Austria were so entranced by the new custom that even the peasant women began to imitate it. The trains of men's and women's costumes became so long that they had to be carried by pages. Some of the preachers refer to them as the "devil's coaches." The shoes became narrow and pointed. The upper garment had detachable sleeves which were widened and lengthened to such an extent that they would drag on the ground. Men and women adopted the fashion of having the dress cut low about the neck and tightly fitting about the body, with slits in various places allowing for freer movement and at the same time adding a new decorative element.

The manners and pleasures of the table were largely influenced by the French. A growing variety of food and drink from different parts of the world was gradually made available. The extensive use of spices called for heavy drinking, wine being the most popular beverage. Knives were used but forks were still unknown in the fourteenth century. One plate, one knife, and one drinking cup usually served two persons, a lord and his lady. The knight was fond of a generous and lavish display of food, drink, and social entertainment in the presence of guests, but left alone with the members of his family he practiced the virtue of economy and was satisfied with a most frugal bill of fare.

The knights were skillful and enthusiastic hunters, both for sportly and utilitarian reasons. The kitchen had to be provided with meat, and the forests had to be cleared of wild animals, such as lynx, bear, wolf, boar, bison, and so forth. The knight reserved the right to the chase of big game, while small-game shooting (rabbits, squirrels, partridges, blackcocks, etc.) was left to the peasant. The taming of falcons for hunting purposes was originally an Oriental custom but became one of the most distinguished forms of the knightly chase. Frederick II and Albert the Great (cf. p. 144 sq.) are among the famous authors of special treatises on the art of falconry and falcon breeding. The tamed falcon was taught how to hunt and kill herons and other game in an air fight. For centuries the falcon hunt remained one of the favorite entertainments of the knightly aristocracy.

The ceremonious and rhythmical dances were accompanied by singing and the playing of the lute or the fiddle, the latter being the forerunner of the violin that was introduced from the Orient via Byzantium in the tenth century. Customarily the noble lords and ladies were skillful makers of verse and tunes which they sang and accompanied on their own instruments. The nobleman's and noblewoman's musical teacher was the wandering minstrel (*Spielmann,* pl., *Spielleute*). He was messenger, news reporter, singer, and poet in one, and he was hailed and feted in the knight's castle, at the bishop's court, and on the village green.

The small, heatable bathroom of the castle contained a wooden bathtub in which the knight would spend many hours, enjoying the aromatic fragrance of his perfumed bath, being waited on by maidservants, taking his meals or carrying on lengthy conversations.

The feudal marriage was one of convenience and was entered into on the basis of economic considerations, usually involving a transfer of land or the union of two families of nobility. The formal consent of the bride had become a prerequisite for the validity of the marriage contract, although the husband was as a rule chosen by the parents or other relatives of the bride-to-be or even by the feudal overlord of the knightly family. The nuptial festivities would last for days or even weeks, the attending knightly guests adding to the splendor of the occasion by arranging tournaments, dances, and other social entertainments.

The general political disintegration of the waning Middle Ages, together with the gradual dissolution of the agrarian basis of medieval society and its replacement by the rising money economy, resulted in the material and cultural decay of the knightly class. It was only in the newly colonized territories of the Germanic East that the spirit of chivalry experienced a brief and glorious belated flowering in the stern and ascetic heroism of the Teutonic Knights (cf. p. 113 sq.).

The Crusades. The phenomenal rise and spread of the religion and culture of Islam after the death of Mohammed (570–632) had led to the foundation of great Mohammedan states in the Near East, in North Africa, Spain, and Sicily. Islamic culture in the early medieval centuries was far superior to the still semibarbarous civilization of western Europe. It was not until the beginning of the eleventh century that the stupendous dynamic force of Mohammedanism began to slacken, while Christian Europe, on the other hand, was well on its way to political and intellectual superiority. The two cultural forces which, due to their mutually exclusive ideological convictions and their strong missionary zeal, had developed a growing antagonism, were nearing the crucial moment of a decisive clash and contest.

During the eleventh century the Saracens were driven out of Sicily, and the firmly entrenched Moslem outposts in Spain became the object of the awakening crusading spirit of the West. The earlier phases of the disputes and struggles between Empire and Papacy had sufficiently enhanced the authority of papal power to allow its representative in Rome to speak as the leader and exponent of a united Christendom. The ascetic spirit of Cluny (cf. p. 70 sq.) and the monastic reform movement had in turn aided in creating a religious enthusiasm that was eager to spend its pent-up energies.

Thus the way was well prepared when Pope Urban II (1088–1099) summoned the peoples of Europe to take up arms to recover the Holy Land and the City of Jerusalem from the hands of the infidels. The Byzantine emperor, Alexius I, had appealed to the pope to aid him in his defensive struggle against the Seljuk Turks who, after having taken over the remnants of the once flourishing empire of the caliphs of Bagdad, were advancing westward and threatening Constantinople.

Pope Urban's appeal found ready and universal response, and his message was carried to the corners of the Christian commonwealth of nations by

Peter the Hermit and other preachers whose oratory aroused the enthusiasm of feudal Europe.

There were seven Crusades in all, not including the grotesque adventure of the "Children's Crusade" of the year 1212, which brought death or slavery to many of the thousands of boys and girls from France and Germany who did not get farther than to the ports of Genoa and Marseilles. Although Germany was profoundly stirred and vitally affected by each one of these expeditions to the Holy Land, only three of them were conducted with the official support and participation of German knighthood and under the full or partial leadership of the German emperor.

The first Crusade (1096–1099) was also the most successful one, leading to the conquest of Edessa, Antioch, and Jerusalem, and to the establishment of several Christian feudal states in the East, among them the kingdom of Jerusalem. The crusaders' army consisted chiefly of Flemish, French, and Norman knights. The high command was given to the papal legate, Adhemar of Puy. Among the knightly leaders were Count Raymond of Toulouse and Duke Godfrey of Bouillon.

The second Crusade (1147–1149), which was given its start and its élan by the powerful preaching of St. Bernard of Clairvaux (1090–1153), and in which King Louis VII of France and the Hohenstaufen Emperor Conrad III were the leading figures, turned out to be a complete failure. As a consequence the situation of the Christian population in the Holy Land became increasingly precarious, especially as rivalries and jealousies had caused multiple divisions among the Christian settlers, while on the enemy's side the great Sultan Saladin succeeded in uniting most of the Moslem world under his rule.

Saladin's conquest of Palestine and the City of Jerusalem in 1187 was the danger signal that was needed to prepare the European mind for the effort of the third Crusade (1189–1197). This time the German emperor, Frederick Barbarossa, was the first one to start upon the new expedition, followed by the kings of France and England, Philip Augustus and Richard the Lion-hearted. But Frederick Barbarossa was drowned while crossing the river Saleph in Asia Minor. The command was taken over by his son, Frederick of Swabia, who died during the siege of the city of Acre on the coast of Palestine. After futile battles with the Moslem armies and quarrels between the kings of France and England and their followers, Philip Augustus returned home, while Richard the Lionhearted concluded a truce with Sultan Saladin in 1192. The Christians were given a strip of the Palestine Coast from Acre to Ascalon and obtained the permission of free entry to the City of Jerusalem.

The fourth Crusade (1202–1204), inaugurated by Pope Innocent III, got under way while civil war raged between the rival emperors in Germany (cf. p. 93). The campaign became a series of shameful dealings between the French crusaders and the Venetians, whose greedy doge, Enrico Dandalo, was largely responsible for diverting the Crusade from its original purpose and turning it into a looting expedition that ended with the capture of Constantinople and the establishment of the Latin Empire of Constantinople (1204-1261).

The fifth Crusade (1228-1229) was undertaken by the excommunicated Hohenstaufen Emperor Frederick II (cf. p. 95), who succeeded in gaining Jerusalem by peaceful negotiations with the sultan, thus resurrecting once more the kingdom of Jerusalem in his own name.

France's saintly king, Louis IX (1226-1270), was the leader of the remaining two expeditions. The sixth Crusade (1248-1254) was aimed against Egypt, whose sultan had conquered the kingdom of Jerusalem (1244). The French king was captured with his army and had to be ransomed. He died in Tunis in the course of the seventh Crusade (1270), while the crusaders under the leadership of Prince Edward of England went on to Syria without accomplishing anything. After the loss of Tripolis (1289) and Acre (1291) the Christians had to give up their claims to the Holy Land.

Significance and Motivations of the Crusades. It can easily be seen that the Crusades were a strange combination of various motives and impulses, ranging from the loftiest to the basest. Medieval man is fully human in that he exhibits all potentialities from the greatest exaltation and sublimity to the most pitiful depravity. It is not surprising, therefore, to find among the crusaders those inspired by religious idealism and true devotion side by side with those who had left their native soil because adventure, lust, and rich booty beckoned in the mysterious East. And religious enthusiasm, the spirit of adventure, and the love of fighting not infrequently resided in the same breast. It is true: the fight against the infidels was all too often taken as a pretext for plunder or as a subterfuge to satisfy the land hunger of a feudal society that was beginning to feel the effects of the growing shortage of land. But there was also to be found that splendid conception of the loyalty of the Christian knight to his divine Liege Lord who had called him to arms through His representative, the pope. And there were the large numbers of knights who were desirous of expiating their human failings by a life of heroic sacrifice, by joining the army of pilgrims on their way to the sepulcher of Christ.

Results of the Crusades. The political failure of the Crusades is obvious enough. Lack of adequate leadership, and those frequent dissensions in the ranks of the crusading armies that reflected the factional discord of medieval Europe, contributed to the ultimate paralyzation of even the most heroic and unselfish efforts. The consequence was a growing disillusionment and a steadily diminishing enthusiasm, while at the same time the interests of the European peoples were diverted into new channels. With military feudalism involved in a slow but inevitable process of decline, the national monarchies and the new commercial middle class were manifestly establishing themselves as the dominating forces of the future. Although the Church had taken a leading part in inaugurating and encouraging the Crusades, the fact that neither the political nor the religious aspirations of the papacy in the East were realized, engendered, in the end, a loss of ecclesiastical prestige. The new cultural and religious contacts that were established with the Mohammedan and Byzantine civilizations resulted not only in a broadening of interests and the acquisition of new departments of knowledge but likewise in the growth of criticism and even skepticism.

As far as Germany was concerned, there had been some cultural and economic intercourse with the Arabic-Islamitic world long before the beginning of the Crusades. But these commercial and cultural bonds were now strengthened and broadened. Eastern science, philosophy, artistry, nautical knowledge, military science, manners and customs of living began to exert a direct influence upon the German lands. Among the newly imported products of the soil were maize, rice, sugar, pepper, cinnamon, lemons, and oranges (Arab., *nârandsch*); among the new fabrics were damask, baldachin silk (*Baldach* = "Bagdad"), colorful Oriental rugs and embroideries, and leather articles. The Germans began to grow fond of the use of Oriental dyes, cosmetics, salves, and perfumes; they decorated their homes and castles with Oriental mattresses, cushions, and divans; they learned from the Arabs a more courtly and genteel social behavior, so that much of the courtly etiquette of knighthood may be traced to Arabic or Byzantine sources; they adopted from the Arabs new methods of fortifying their German cities and castles and learned to prepare a kind of gunpowder from sulphur, charcoal, and saltpeter; they enlarged their knowledge of stellar constellations and enriched the sailors' language by Arabic terms, such as zenith (*Zenit*), *Bussole* (compass), admiral, and so forth; the merchants' language by such words as bazaar (*Basar*), magazine (*Magazin*), tare (*Tara*), tariff (*Tarif*), and so forth. In architecture the horseshoe arch and the highly ornamental "arabesques" are of Arabic origin. The art of goldsmithing received new inspiration from the Oriental smiths and carvers in whose Eastern workshops some of the German goldsmiths had been apprentices in the age of the Crusades. Arabic legends and sagas provided new motifs for the German epic and lyric poetry of the Age of Chivalry.

But it was chiefly Arabic science and philosophic speculation that left its profound impress on all Western civilization. The Arabs became the teachers of Europe in astronomy, geography, arithmetic, physics, and alchemy, and the influx of the new scientific ideas was due to the newly established contacts with the Arabic outposts in Spain as well as in the Near East. Their medical science was highly developed, not only theoretically but in practical application, as is documented by the model organization of their hospitals and the variety of their medicaments. In theology and philosophy Arabic thinkers such as Alfarabi (philosopher, † 950), Avicenna (physician and philosopher, 980–1037), Ghasali (Algazel; philosopher and theologian, 1059–1111), and Averroes (philosopher, 1126–1198) proved themselves masters of original and ingenious speculation and presented the West with their translations of and commentaries on the works of Aristotle, thus facilitating the Christian-scholastic synthesis of the Platonic and Aristotelian traditions (cf. p. 143).

The results and consequences of the Crusades in the intellectual and cultural spheres were manifold, and while some of these results would have been achieved by way of Spain and Sicily, that is, without the direct contacts established by the Crusaders, the whole process of the intellectual and cultural expansion of Europe was intensified and speeded up by the crusading spirit with its emotional stimuli and by the actual acquaintance with life and thought in the Near East.

It is, however, symptomatic of the growing astuteness of German culture that neither the Romanic nor the Oriental influences that acted upon the German mind in the Age of Chivalry, and especially during the two centuries of the Crusades, were able to silence the voice of a genuine Germany that speaks so unmistakably in German art and poetry, in the games of war and the diversions of peace, in bold political action and in the silence of mystical contemplation.

Colonization and Expansion in the East. The territories to the north and east of Germany were the scene of a number of crusading enterprises in the broader sense of the term, campaigns that had for their goal as much the conquest of new arable land and the security of the outlying frontier districts of the German empire as the conversion of heathen populations. These expeditions were rewarded by lasting success not only because of a more competent leadership but because they found an invaluable ally in the healthy energy and inexhaustible working capacity of the German peasantry.

Byzantine missionaries had begun the conversion of the Bohemian Slavs in the ninth century. These Bohemians soon turned their allegiance from the Greek Orthodox to the Roman Catholic Church. Otto the Great incorporated Bohemia in the Empire but granted its rulers a fair degree of autonomy. In the second half of the tenth century Roman missionaries succeeded in converting the Slavic population of Poland. St. Stephen, king of Hungary (997–1038), converted the partly Slavic but predominantly Magyar population of Hungary, Poland's southern neighbor, at the beginning of the eleventh century. He organized the nomadic peoples of his country in a unified state that followed closely the Frankish pattern. During the thirteenth century Poland and Hungary together acted as buffer states of the Empire to ward off the repeated attacks of Mongolian hordes.

But most important and consequential for Germany was the expansion of the Germans in the northern and eastern frontier districts and the subsequent colonization of the newly acquired territories. The beginning of the colonization of the regions east of the Elbe dates back to the days of Henry I (cf. p. 65) and Otto I (cf. p. 65), but the preoccupation of imperial policy with the problems of southern Europe and especially with Italy had nullified many of the initial results. It was not until the twelfth century that colonization in the North and East was consistently and energetically resumed by some of the powerful princes of northern Germany, among them Henry the Lion, duke of Saxony and head of the Welf party, Albrecht the Bear, Adolf II of Schauenburg, and the archbishops of Bremen and Magdeburg.

In a proclamation of the year 1108 the secular and ecclesiastical princes of northeastern Germany issued the following appeal to the various tribes of Germany: "Oppressed by many and unending calamities and acts of violence that we have endured at the hands of the heathen, we implore your mercy, that you may come to our aid in halting the ruin of your mother, the Church. The most cruel of heathen peoples have risen against us and have become all-powerful: men without mercy, glorying in their inhuman malignity. Arise, then, spouse of Christ, and come! Thy voice shall sound into the ears of the faithful, so that all will speedily join the army of Christ. Those peoples are the most wicked of all, but their land is the best of all, abounding in meat, fowl, honey, and corn. It need only be cultivated in the right manner to overflow with all the fruits of the soil. . . . Well, then, you Saxons, you people of Lorraine, you Flemings, you renowned conquerors of the earth: here is an opportunity not only to save your souls but, if you wish, also to acquire the finest land as your dwelling place. . . . "

This is a manifesto that is as strange as it is illuminating. Even if it should be verified that it was penned not by the nobles of eastern Saxony but by a Flemish author who dwelt in the Slavic border regions, this proclamation would still reveal in a very striking way the several motives that prompted the Germans of the later Middle Ages to start upon their eastward drive into the wide open spaces beyond the river Elbe.

The motivations are threefold, and they are stated with naïve and almost disarming frankness. In the first place, the princes and nobles of northeastern Germany felt it necessary to protect the open and almost defenseless boundary line, beyond which dwelt semibarbarous and politically unstable populations. Widukind of Corvey, famous Saxon historian of the tenth century, tells of the stubborn resistance of the Slavs who "preferred war to peace, ignoring the greatest of misery when it was a question of defending their precious freedom." But, as time went on, Slavic resistance weakened, and the Germans began their advance beyond the boundary lines of the old marches.

The second impulse to eastern colonization was a direct outgrowth of the crusading spirit of the twelfth century, as exemplified by the campaign against the heathen Wends in the year 1147, the harsh alternative as formulated by Bernard of Clairvaux allowing only for conversion or destruction. In this second impulse, missionary zeal and a very worldly will to power were mingled in constant interaction. The military subjugation of the heathens was immediately followed by missionary efforts, the religious activities being frequently contaminated by all those inconsistencies and ambiguities that forever attach to the use of physical force and coercion in the realm of the spirit. Charlemagne's conversion of the Saxons and the deeds and misdeeds of the Spanish Conquistadores in South and Central America belong in the same category with the methods employed in the colonization of the Slavic lands in the Germanic East. The chronicles of the twelfth century tell of the greed and cruelty of some of the Saxon dukes and margraves and make them responsible for the refusal of the Slavs to submit voluntarily to Christian-Germanic rule.

The third impulse was the desire to find an outlet for a growing population and to relieve the economic pressure caused by an increasing scarcity of arable soil.

National ambitions and national consciousness were still in a very rudimentary stage, and they are not even mentioned in our manifesto. It is only the retrospective view of the modern historian that ascribes a momentous national significance to the colonization of the Germanic East. The feeling of racial superiority was likewise conspicuously absent, and marriages between Germans and Christian Slavs were frequent and were considered unobjectionable.

Despite the fact that the German emperors and imperial policy had no direct share in the Eastern colonization, it is nevertheless obvious that the authority of the *Imperium Christianum* provided the indispensable foundation for German policy in the East. Ever since the days of Charlemagne the emperors considered themselves as the protectors, defenders, and pioneers of Christendom and were always prepared to extend their claims to heathen territories and populations. It was Charlemagne himself who had started the drive to the East in his powerful thrust against the Avars that opened up the regions of the lower Danube and the vital road into Austria. It was Otto the Great who had succeeded in incorporating in the Christian-Germanic realm the vast territories of the Northeast. But it was only in the period of Hohenstaufen rule and afterward under the leadership of the Teutonic Knights that the policy of colonization received its solemn sanction as a partial realization of the universal mission of the Christian Empire of the German nation.

Knights, clerics, peasants, and burghers shared in the colonization and settlement of the Germanic East. These settlements went economically through the same stages as the motherland, the establishment of marketing centers being followed by the founding of cities. The thirteenth and fourteenth centuries witnessed the growth of important urban communities in Brandenburg, Pomerania, Saxony, Silesia, Prussia, and Livonia (Livland). Most of the settlers came from the Low German lands, i.e., from Holland, Flanders, Friesland, and from the Rhenish districts. The farmers in particular were attracted by promises of a higher standard of life, better working conditions, and increased personal liberties.

The villages that originated east of the Elbe were distinguished from those of the motherland by their regularity, the houses with their apportioned lots of land being located alongside the main road (*Reihendorf, Marschen-*

dorf). In tenacity and working capacity the German peasant was superior to the Slav and therefore considered as a desirable settler even by Slavic princes who would call German peasants to their territories and permit them to live and work there "under German law."

The Order of Teutonic Knights ("Deutscher Ritterorden"). Beyond the Vistula, in the territory between Poland and the Baltic, lived the heathen Prussians, a savage and warlike tribe of Letto-Lithuanian stock. Early in the thirteenth century the Poles appealed to the Order of Teutonic Knights for aid in their struggle with their Prussian neighbors. After they had been promised the exclusive possession of all the territory they would be able to conquer, and after this promise had been confirmed by the special privilege of Emperor Frederick II of the year 1226, the Knights started upon their crusade in 1230 and, by the year 1283, had made themselves the uncontested masters of Prussia. They established a strong German state on the eastern Baltic and thereby created a political organism which combined in a perfectly unique way certain fundamental character traits of medieval and modern times.

In its origins the Order dates back to the year 1190, when it was founded during the siege of Acre by the armies that took part in the Third Crusade. The Knights pledged themselves to the care of the poor, the sick, and the wounded, and to the fight against the infidels. The members comprised German knights, priests, and lay Brothers. A white mantle with a black cross was the distinguishing feature of their habit. White and black subsequently became the national colors of Prussia. The fifteenth century marked the beginning of the Order's decline. Its remaining possessions in the German Reich were secularized in 1805, while its Austrian branch still existed early in the twentieth century.

The state that was founded by the Teutonic Knights at the end of the thirteenth century was the embodiment of contrasting ideas: a belated fruit of the waning Middle Ages, based upon a spiritualistic conception of chivalry, including the ascetic features of monasticism and the religious fervor of the Crusades, but at the same time vigorously documenting the absolutistic and centralistic tendencies of modern statecraft. This ideal of a monastically colored knighthood was merely one more manifestation of that spiritualistic absolutism that animated the political aspirations of the papacy in the final phase of its struggle with the secular totalitarian ambitions of the Empire. And when, at the beginning of the sixteenth century, the realm of the Teutonic Knights was nearing its doom, it was Martin Luther who, in 1523, commented on the situation in a letter addressed to the Order of Teutonic Knights: "Your Order," he wrote, "is truly a strange order, and especially because it was founded to fight against the infidels. For this reason it must make use of the worldly sword and must act in a worldly manner, and yet it should be spiritual at the same time, should vow chastity, poverty, and obedience, and should keep those vows like the members of other monastic orders. How well these two things harmonize we know from daily experience and from the use of our reason."

Sociologically the Teutonic Order was organized according to the Germanic principle of leadership and loyalty, the members blindly obeying their freely chosen "leader" who could be deposed by the community only in case of serious infractions of fundamental rules and laws of the Order. Out of this centralized administration grew an absolutely reliable officialdom that facilitated the exact and efficient handling of state finances and guaranteed a maximum of political and economic self-sufficiency. But this very same sociological structure produced a certain inflexibility in the theory and practice of government, and prevented the Order from adapting itself to the changing conditions of time and environment. As a social organism the Order was and remained a foreign element in the conquered Prussian lands, and it failed to educate the indigenous population in the rights and duties of citizenship and thus to employ them usefully and constructively in social and political life. It was therefore not unnatural that the native burghers and nobles in their growing opposition resorted successively to treasonable conspiracies with the Polish enemy, to revolution, and finally to outright desertion in the decisive battle of Tannenberg (1410).

The Order of Teutonic Knights owes its fame to its accomplishments in the field of rural and urban colonization and economico-political administration. Its cultural achievements are limited to the creation of a certain type of architecture that is a true mirror of the ideas that inspired its life and work. The East Prussian castles of the Order, above all the magnificent Marienburg, the seat of the Grand Master (*Hochmeister*), are a remarkable combination of monastery, castle, and palatial residence. This architecture is stern, solemn, and matter of fact. Although the characteristic features of the Gothic style (cf. p. 148 sqq.) are unmistakable, it lacks all the more intimate charm of an artistically refined taste.

The Order of Teutonic Knights enacts the final chapter in the story of Eastern colonization. The result of this ruthless and heroic conquest of land as well as of the earlier stages of the eastward drive was the approximate doubling of the area of habitable and arable German territory. The frontiers that were reached and secured at the end of the Middle Ages are the racial frontiers of Germany to the end of Word War II. It is the settlement of the Eastern marches (*Ostmarken*) that has laid the foundations for the growth of the modern state organisms of Brandenburg-Prussia and Austria-Bavaria.

Social Divisions in the Middle Ages. Individualism in the modern sense was unknown in medieval society. The individual received his sanctions from the group with which he shared his concepts of right, honor, and responsibility. The social order was conceived as an essentially static one, in which each class or estate had to fulfill definite God-given functions. All the members of the social organism were expected to collaborate for the good of the whole. This was the ideal. It permeated to some extent the

Marienburg Castle.

The Town Hall in Braunschweig.

whole edifice of feudal society: the property concepts of the nobles, the labor concepts of peasants and craftsmen, the concepts of honor and bravery of the warriors. "The health of the whole commonwealth will be assured and vigorous, if the higher members consider the lower and the lower answer in like manner the higher, so that each is in its turn a member of every other" (John of Salisbury, bishop of Chartres, 1115–1180). It was a faultless theory whose attempted realization met with all the imponderabilities of human nature, human frailty, greed, and passion.

But medieval man was more than a mere member of his social class (*Stand*): as a social being (*animal sociale*) he was at the same time a moral personality, endowed with reason and the faculty of moral self-determination. This personal quality remained theoretically unaffected by his social position, so that master and servant were both considered as equals before God but as legally distinguished according to their social function. These social distinctions were largely dependent on the definitions of Roman Law which as such was rooted in the traditions of antiquity.

This system of social order is ideally fashioned in analogy to the graduated order and continuity of the universe and its divine rulership, so that Thomas Aquinas (cf. p. 145 sq.) could designate the principle of order as "the most excellent thing in the universe" (*Ordo est Optimum Universi*). Man, by virtue of his intellect, shares in the government of the universe and is called upon to realize the principle of order in the cosmos of human relations. Every title of human authority, from the head of a nation to the head of a family, is derived from this divinely instituted universal order. The "law of nature," reflecting divine law, is recognized as the all-pervading universal law that serves as a guiding principle and an absolute norm for the ordering of human relations and the fulfillment of the demands of social justice. Human reason establishes the identity of the natural and the moral law and by doing so becomes capable of collaborating with the aims and ends of the universe.

The Peasants. The agricultural basis of medieval society made for an economic system that reduced the peasant quite generally to the position of a serf. In the graduated scale of estates the peasant, therefore, ranged at the bottom. He had to perform compulsory labor, he was expected to pay all kinds of special fees and taxes, and he was legally tied to the lord's manor. If he wanted to leave the manor, he had first to obtain the lord's permission and pay a special fee. He was subject to the private court of justice of his lord, he had to grind his grain at the lord's mill and bake his bread in the lord's oven. In case of death the serf's personal belongings, his cattle and household goods, could be seized wholly or in part at the lord's pleasure, and the heir would have to buy a special license to acquire the movable property that was bequeathed to him.

It is an undeniable fact that the medieval mind was firmly convinced that the institution of some sort of servitude was contained in the natural law and could never be entirely done away with. And yet the position of the peasant was better than that of a slave. The corporative spirit of the Middle Ages created the march and village associations, where the peasants united for the protection of their interests, and by means of which they secured for themselves a certain minimum of human dignity and economic independence. The peasant could generally be assured of food, clothing, and shelter for himself and his family. He was required to work on the lord's demesne land from two to four days a week and was frequently called upon to perform various extra services (*Frondienste*), but he was usually able to devote several days of the week to the cultivation of his own land.

The Church insisted that the serfs were not tools but men, although Canon Law seems to have recognized and enforced serfdom, and Pope Innocent III (1198–1216) merely described an actual situation when he wrote: "The serf serves; he is terrified with threats, wearied with forced labor, afflicted with blows, despoiled of his possessions; for, if he possess nought, he is compelled to earn; and if he possess anything, he is compelled to have it not; the lord's fault is the serf's punishment; the serf's fault is the lord's excuse for preying on him. . . ." (*De Contemptu Mundi:* "On the Contempt of the World.") And yet the disappearance of serfdom was chiefly due to the general shift of economic forces and not to interference on the part of the Church. The peasant revolts in England (1381), Flanders (1382), and Germany (1524–1525) reveal a deep-seated resentment on the part of the peasant class that finally resulted in desperate acts of violence.

There were groups of peasants in Saxony, Flanders, Friesland, and in the valleys of the Alps who were practically freemen, dwelling on their own land and only subject to the emperor. They had to pay military taxes and were entitled to take part in the judicial administration of their county. The majority of the German peasants, however, were half-free or unfree tenants.

At the end of the thirteenth century the peasant's lot had considerably improved, owing primarily to the general change in economic conditions and the opening up of new markets and new colonial territory. The value of arable land had increased many times over, and the cultivation of fruits and of the vine would yield a rich surplus that could be traded at the lord's market or in the nearest city. Many peasants, of course, joined the huge army of emigrants to the Eastern marches to establish themselves as free tenants.

The Medieval German City. Despite the fact that the city dwellers did not rank as a real class or estate in the social pyramid of the Middle Ages, it was nevertheless the burgher who proved the most dynamic and disruptive element of medieval society, who in the end successfully opposed his own independent concept of culture to the medieval idea of a universal cultural organism. In his own personal self he discovered the power of his own thought and will, the bases of his new concept of freedom. Thus the medieval city became the cradle of a new middle class, a new corporative legal code, a new economic system, and a new philosophy of life.

The new money economy was developed first in the Italian cities, whose leading merchants and bankers created a number of free and legally independent republican communes. Their fight against the feudal privileges of the ecclesiastical and secular princes is paralleled by a similar struggle of the German and French cities for a complete autonomy of city trade and city administration. Some of the German cities developed likewise into free city republics, while others joined the newly formed city leagues.

In Germany alone about two thousand cities and towns of varying size were founded during the medieval centuries, the most important of which were Cologne (Köln) in the Rhineland, the largest of medieval German cities, with a population of about fifty thousand; Nuremberg (Nürnberg) in Franconia; Munich (München), later the capital of Bavaria and the cultural center of southern Germany; Augsburg, likewise in Bavaria, one of the foremost commercial centers, an important link in the trade route from Italy to northern Europe and home of some of the wealthiest burgher families of the later Middle Ages; Strasbourg in Alsace; Mayence (Mainz), the "golden city," one of the foremost centers of the secular and ecclesiastic culture of the Empire; the great seaports of Hamburg (at the mouth of the Elbe), Bremen (at the mouth of the Weser), and Lübeck (on the Baltic); Danzig, the port for German-Polish trade; and Vienna, southeastern outpost of the Empire, the leading city of the Eastern march and later on the capital of the Austro-Hungarian monarchy. Most of the principal cities of Germany had an average population of from ten to twenty thousand. The important commercial centers were connected by trade routes, one such commercial artery leading from Venice across the Alps via the Brenner Pass, through Germany, and up the Rhine valley to the prosperous cities of Flanders.

City Leagues. The Hanseatic League. The Lombard League, which had fought for the freedom of the cities of northern Italy against the ambitions of the Hohenstaufen emperors (cf. pp. 91, 95), furnished the pattern for the formation of several German city leagues, among which the Rhenish League (founded 1254-1255), the Swabian League (founded 1331), and the *Hanseatic League* were the most powerful. The word *Hansa* (Gothic and Old High German: "union," "group," "association") was applied in the thirteenth century to the guild of Rhenish-Westphalian merchants in their London settlement, the Steel-Yard (*Stahlhof*), and was later used to designate the character of the German city leagues as co-operative associations for the protection of mutual commercial interests. By the end of the thirteenth century the Hanseatic League controlled the mouths of the Elbe, Weser, Oder, and Vistula (Weichsel), and had secured trading privileges and foreign markets in London, Bruges (Netherlands), Bergen (Norway), and Novgorod (Russia). The League comprised the most important cities of northern Germany, among them the new cities of the Germanic East, in the territory that had been recently acquired from the Slavs. With the emperor busying himself in Italian affairs, these cities, for the sake of self-protection, had to rely on close co-operation. Only in this way were they able to maintain a fleet that was large and strong enough to guarantee safe trading. Hamburg and Lübeck had started the movement about the middle of the thirteenth century, and the largest known membership in the League at any one time was close to one hundred. Leading cities were Danzig, Lübeck, Brunswick, and Cologne. The League held a monopoly in the Baltic trade and controlled especially the important herring and cod industries. But the Hanseatic merchants also shipped furs, amber, lumber, grain, and flax from Russia, Sweden, Poland, and Prussia, and traded these articles in Bruges and London for raw wool, cloth, and minerals. The settlements in these foreign lands were equipped with extensive warehouses and living quarters and protected by surrounding walls.

The Hanseatic League reached its greatest prosperity in the second half of the fourteenth century. In the course of the fifteenth century the power and prestige of the League were steadily weakened by the rise of a capitalistic economy, the growth of the commercial power of the Netherlands, that caused the shifting of trade routes to the West, and by the disintegration of the Baltic and Russian trade as a consequence of the Polish conquest of the Teutonic Knights and the political unification of Scandinavia (Union of Kalmar, 1397). Nominally the Hansa existed for two more centuries, and the cities of Lübeck, Bremen, and Hamburg were still known as the three "Hansa-Cities" at the end of the nineteenth century.

Trade Fairs. Any merchant, whether an inhabitant of the city or not, who paid his toll and the rent for his booth could trade freely at the international city fairs which were held once or twice a year under the protectorate of either the municipal government or, more frequently, the king, bishop, abbot, or lord. The German city fair is known as *Messe* (Mass), because it usually began on solemn religious feast days, immediately following the celebration of the Mass. It lasted for several days or several weeks, and after it was all over the foreign merchants would pack up their remaining goods and would continue their troublesome and dangerous voyage to the next city where a fair was to be held. The most celebrated city fairs in the middle of the twelfth century were those in the prosperous district of Champagne in France. But they were soon equaled in fame by the fairs of Bruges.

The External Appearance of the City. The medieval city was small in extent, the streets were narrow, and the houses crowded together. But the general appearance was highly picturesque and never monotonous. Regular city planning can only be observed in the colonial cities in the conquered Slavic regions, while ordinarily the city presented a highly irregular maze of streets, squares, nooks, and corners.

The city was surrounded by a high, massive wall and a deep moat. Numerous inserted towers surmounted the wall, and admission was gained through several city gates which in turn were strongly protected by bridges, towers, and palisades. Many medieval city gates are beautiful examples of the exquisite craftsmanship of the medieval stonemason.

The contour of the city was dominated by the cathedral with its towers and spires, symbolically expressing the subordination of all secular life to religious incentives. One or more main streets, from fifteen to twenty feet wide, led from the gates to the centrally located market square, and from there on to the opposite gate. The remaining streets were crooked, narrow, usually unpaved, and without a drainage system. As the city grew it frequently became necessary to enlarge the encircling wall or to construct a second and even a third one with a larger diameter.

Surrounding the market square were the main municipal buildings: the church, the town hall (*Rathaus*), and the merchants' hall (*Kaufhaus*). The large size of the market place corresponded to its significance as the focus of municipal life, its civic center for trading, public assemblage, and city administration and jurisdiction.

The houses were usually four or five stories high, the upper stories jutting out beyond the lower ones so as to utilize every bit of available space. As a result of these building methods the already congested living conditions in the cities often became quite intolerable. Frequent epidemics were a natural outgrowth of these unsanitary surroundings.

Public Buildings. Special care was taken to make the public buildings true symbols of the dignity and self-assurance of the burghers. Many surviving city halls are marvels of architectural art, testifying to the excellent taste and the great wealth of the cities. Among the most renowned of German city halls are those of Braunschweig, Goslar, Hildesheim, Hanover, and Lübeck in the north, and Regensburg, Ochsenfurt, and Überlingen in the south. Most of the famous southern town halls are of later date and therefore largely influenced by models of the Italian Renaissance (Konstanz, Augsburg, Nürnberg, etc.).

The interior of the city hall contained the subterranean city prison or dungeon, called the "dogs' hole" (*Hundeloch*) or "black bag" (*Schwarzer Sack*). Likewise in the basement was located the *Ratskeller* (council cellar), where the municipal supply of wine and beer was stored, on which the city usually held a monopoly. The City Council, one of whose duties was the arrangement of public festivals, employed a "city cook" and provided rooms for banqueting and dancing in the city hall. The main floor contained a certain number of booths that were used as shops and rented to trades people. The larger part of the second floor was occupied by the imposing and richly decorated *Ratssaal* (council hall), which served as the assembly hall of the City Council, as municipal courtroom, and as official reception room.

The *Kaufhaus* vied with the *Rathaus* in the artistic taste and solemn dignity of its external appearance. The oldest *Kaufhäuser* date from the thirteenth century, but most of them were built during the following two hundred years. From the merchants' halls we must distinguish the "guild halls" constructed and owned by the members of the different merchant and craft guilds (cf. p. 125 sq.), to serve as places of consultation and social recreation. Of simpler taste and appearance were the remaining municipal buildings, such as the granary (*Kornhaus*), the weighhouse (*Waage*), the mint (*Münze*), the armory (*Zeughaus*), the apothecary's shop (*Apotheke*), and the bathhouse (*Badestube*).

Private Residences. Even less ostentatious was the dwelling place of the ordinary citizen. The protruding upper stories of the houses were adorned with bays (*Erker*) and bay windows (*Erkerfenster*). Most of the houses were built of wood and covered with thatched roofs. Quite popular but in the main confined to Germany was the technique of supporting stone walls with timber framing (*Fachwerk*). Up to the thirteenth century only the bishop's residence and the houses of wealthy patricians were built of stone. This explains the large number of devastating conflagrations. Leather buckets and a big water tub were the only known implements for extinguishing a fire. The first fire engine was invented in Nuremberg in the fifteenth century.

Almost every house bore the owner's special mark on its front; it was either related to his calling or derived from the name of his patron saint. The owner's mark imparted a kind of personal life and dignity to his dwelling place. Windows were few in number; they were small, and could be closed with wooden shutters, oiled paper, parchment, or wickerwork. The beginning of the thirteenth century brought Germany the benefits of imported Venetian glass windows. They consisted of several small sections of glass panels with leaden frames (bull's-eye glass, *Butzenscheiben*).

If a benignant moon was not shedding some rays of light, the city was enveloped in darkness during the night, the interiors of the houses being scantily lit by means of tallow candles, small oil lamps, lanterns, and chandeliers. For heating purposes the stove was given preference over the open hearth that was quite universally used in the Romanic countries. Originally made of bricks, after the beginning of the thirteenth century the German type of stove was built of green or yellow glazed tiles which were covered with relieflike ornaments and figurative compositions of biblical themes, mostly of high artistic quality.

The household furniture included several heavy oak benches, running alongside the walls and provided with solid backs and arms; some chairs and stools; a heavy rectangular table; a large, iron-plated chest; a tall, massive, and artistically decorated cupboard. The beds were large and wide, and so high that a footboard was needed to climb in. They were crowned by a rooflike canopy (baldachin) that was covered with paintings or carvings, with curtains hanging down on either side.

City Administration. Personal freedom was the one precious possession that all the inhabitants of the city had in common. If a serf escaped from some manor and lived in a city for a year and a day, he was free and could no longer be claimed by his former lord. On the basis of this consciousness of personal liberty there developed the specific laws and regulations of the social and economic life in the city as manifested in democratic forms of self-government. Some cities in Germany acquired an almost complete independence (*Freie Reichsstädte,* "free imperial cities"), while others voluntarily accepted the overlordship of the king or some powerful noble. They paid their taxes to the legitimate political authority and were otherwise left free to manage their own affairs. Many of the cities had to fight for their freedom and their civic rights, while others obtained charters from the king or the lord by peaceful negotiations. A city could consider itself fully emancipated when it was granted representation in the Imperial Diet.

The city administration was in the hands of the City Council (*Stadtrat*), whose members were chosen either jointly by the burghers and the overlord of the city or, in free cities, by the burghers alone. The City Councils could usually rely on the co-operation and sympathy of the emperors, who were their natural allies in their struggle against the ambitions of the territorial princes. The weakening of imperial power toward the end of the Middle Ages was therefore the cause for the subjection of many a German city to princely rule.

Membership in the City Council was at first limited to the indigenous city aristocracy, the nobles and ministerials (cf. p. 99) who had achieved the liberation of the city from the domination of the overlord. Gradually the big landowners and the merchants were admitted to the governing class, whose members constituted a distinct patrician aristocracy. The cities grew strong and prosperous under their rule. But it was not long before the demands of the lower classes for a proportionate share in city administration led to severe struggles for political power and supremacy, which in turn were followed by a progressive weakening of the political influence of the cities. In many cases these social conflicts ended in compromise. In the Hansa cities the patricians maintained their supremacy, in other places (Augsburg, Nürnberg, Ulm) the patricians as well as the merchant and craft guilds were represented in the City Council, while in the city of Mainz the guilds became the uncontested masters of their city in 1444.

One or several Bürgermeister (mayors) presided over the City Council. The councilors (*Ratsherren*) employed a number of paid officials, the most important of whom was the city clerk (*Stadtschreiber*) who was in charge of records, protocols, and city archives, and who was originally a member of the clergy. He had to be an experienced jurist and was aided by several legal advisers.

Imperial cities obtained the status of independent republics and combined the functions of city and state government. They had to concern themselves with foreign politics, they waged wars, and they made treaties and concluded alliances with other cities or with territorial princes.

The City Council also administered the judicial branch of government. The city had its own code of civil and criminal law that was binding upon all citizens with the exception of the clergy, whose members were subject to Canon Law. Another important function of city government was the organization of military defense. In the beginning every citizen was bound by duty to take up arms, the poorer classes providing the foot soldiery, the patricians the cavalry. Most of the city armies were excellent, outstanding in attack and defense. When the growing economic development of the cities made it desirable to release the burghers from military service, the City Councils began to employ mercenary soldiers, sometimes even hiring impoverished knights and princes.

The privilege of coining money was a right of the city government that had only been won after a long struggle. Their administration of the mint contributed to the stabilization and unification of the currency. A unified system of currency had not yet been attained by medieval economy, and the granting of the right of coinage to great and small lords had created an increasing monetary confusion.

At the end of the Middle Ages the *Pfennig* could be considered as a kind of monetary unit. Half a *Pfennig* was a *Heller,* so named after the city of Halle in Swabia, the place of its coinage. Twelve pfennigs made up one *Schilling;* 240 pfennigs were one *Pfund* (pound). Various silver coins, such as the *Groschen* (from Latin, *grossus,* "thick pfennig") or the *Weisspfennig* (*Albus*), were used locally. In the latter part of the thirteenth century the standard basis of currency became the Rhenish *Goldgulden* ("gold guilder," "florin," first coined in Florence in 1252). The currency agreement of the Rhenish Prince-Electors of 1386 fixed the value of one *Goldgulden* at 20 *Weisspfennigs* which was the equivalent of 240 *Heller.* The Saxon *Gulden-groschen* (a silver coin) and *Joachimstaler Silbergulden* were used side by side with the Rhenish *Goldgulden* from the beginning of the sixteenth century. The standard currency in the German north and northeast was the *Mark,* the equivalent of half a *Taler.* Several currency unions (*Münzvereine*) worked for a unification of the different currencies. The fraudulent devaluation of coins was a frequent occurrence and led to the enactment of stringent city laws against counterfeiting. According to a register from Niederaltaich in Bavaria of the year 1243 a large horse cost three pounds, a pig 25–50 pfennigs, a sheep 10 pfennigs, a package of special Christmas cheese 1 pfennig, a bushel of oats 14 pfennigs. Skilled masons received a weekly pay of 38 pfennigs, unskilled laborers 19 pfennigs. Money was worth approximately six times as much as it is today.

The life of the citizens was regulated and controlled by a number of city ordinances that laid down rules for the construction and maintenance of houses and streets, for the preservation of public health and the prevention of the spread of epidemics, for the prevention of fires, against immodesty and indecency in dress and entertainment, for the protection of the consumers of food and drink, together with a host of similar regulations that might pertain to almost any department of human and social activity.

Care of the Poor and the Sick. The care of the poor and the sick was in the hands of several monastic and semimonastic orders which were founded toward the end of the Middle Ages. Very numerous were the members of the sisterhood of Beguines who spread from the Netherlands over the greater part of Germany. Their congregations could be found in almost every German city of medium size. They answered a real social need in a period when Crusades, wars, and epidemics had led to a definite surplus of women, a considerable proportion of whom could never expect to get married. The Beguines took the vows of chastity and obedience for the period of their stay in the beguinage (*Klause, Samnung*), earning their livelihood with spinning, sewing, nursing, and teaching. Frequently there developed in their circles enthusiastic and exaggerated forms of piety which brought upon them accusations of heresy and persecutions by the ecclesiastical and secular authorities.

Outside the city walls were located the hospitals for the sufferers from leprosy (*Siechenhäuser*). They were built during the twelfth and thirteenth centuries when this disease began to claim more and more victims, partly because of the crowded and unsanitary conditions in the cities. A specially assigned priest ministered to the lepers in their own hospital chapel, and they were buried in their own church yard. They were excluded from human society by solemn ecclesiastical rites. They were then given a gray or black habit, gloves, a cane, a drinking cup, and a bread bag, and were escorted to the lepers' home where they would have to spend the rest of their earthly days. They were forbidden to drink from public wells, and they had to warn the approaching stranger by the sound of a rattle or a horn. The order of St. Lazarus that was founded in Palestine in the twelfth century was especially devoted to the care of lepers. St. Elizabeth of Thuringia (1207–1231), the wife of landgrave Ludwig, and St. Hedwig, duchess of Silesia (1174–1243), founded *Siechenhäuser* and personally nursed the unfortunate ones who were afflicted with leprosy.

Merchant and Craft Guilds ("Gilden" and "Zünfte"). While the city as a corporate economic unit of marked independence presented a united front to those who were not members of its community of interests, the social divisions within the city were in turn corporatively organized and strictly delimited. The organizations of the merchants and artisans who represented the most numerous classes of the population were known as guilds. The German word *Zunft* is derived from the Old High German verb *zeman* (to become, befit, beseem) and refers to the regulative and restrictive character of the guilds. The guilds were the channels through which the city government exercised its control of business. The "masters" worked out the rules, the magistrates confirmed them, and henceforth they were considered as binding on all the members of the guild.

The origin of the guilds is rather obscure. They may derive from the old Germanic religious brotherhoods, or they may simply be an outgrowth of the desire of the merchant and artisan classes for mutual protection and social security. The first records of organized guilds date from the twelfth century.

The guild was closely linked with the religious life of its members, and religious and social incentives were intertwined in all their activities. Each guild had its patron saint, whose image was represented on its banners and shields and whose feast day was solemnly commemorated. In fraternal intercourse they cultivated the social virtues. They revolutionized the conventions of the feudal age and revived the social heritage of the German past for the benefit of a new epoch of German civilization.

Sociologically the guild is a corporation of individuals that become a unity by means of the voluntary association of its members. This association imparts to the individual a new consciousness of his personal value, freeing him from his attachment to the soil and placing him in an organic relationship to city, state, and corporation. While the individual thus frees himself in one respect, he imposes upon himself new ties and obligations.

To safeguard the efficient control of social economy, to uphold the "honor of the trade," and to serve the interest of the common good, membership in the guild was made compulsory, so that ordinarily nonmembers could neither buy nor sell at retail within the city. The guilds regulated prices, set definite standards for wages and hours of labor, and controlled the quality of goods. But more important than these restrictions on unlimited profits and unfair competition was the positive promotion of trade and commerce, and the encouragement that the individual merchant and craftsman received from a reasonable equality of opportunity.

The merchant guilds achieved their greatest power and influence in the twelfth century. While their main purpose remained an economic one, they began to take an active part in the administration of the city. With the growing specialization of industry the influence of the merchant guilds declined, and their place was taken by the craft guilds, whose members were artisans. They sold the products of their hands directly to the consumer without needing the services of a middleman.

The craft guilds were highly specialized, and each branch of industry was represented by its own guild. Membership was limited to the skilled trades, and the guild statutes and regulations were even more strict and exclusive than those of the merchant guilds. The methods of manufacture, the quality of materials, prices, and wages were closely supervised, and the total number of local masters, journeymen, and apprentices was limited by special rules.

A long period of training was required to advance from apprenticeship to mastership. The master had to obtain the permission of the guild if he wanted to take on an apprentice. The permission was granted if the apprentice was of free and legitimate birth and of German nationality, and if the particular trade was not crowded. The apprentice (*Lehrling*) was usually ten or twelve years of age when he entered the service of his master. He lived in the master's house, but his training was supervised by the guild. The master gave him food and clothing and a small fee. The master exercised the authority of a father and was responsible for the boy's physical and moral well-being. The apprenticeship would last from two to ten years, depending in part on the skill that was required in a particular trade. At the end of this period the apprentice was promoted with solemn rites to the rank of a journeyman (*Geselle*). He was given a certificate (*Lehrbrief*) and was now free to set out upon several years of travel (*Wanderjahre*) in order to acquire more experience and greater skill. He was paid by the day or by the week and tried to save enough money to be able to stand on his own feet at the earliest possible time. His working day lasted from five or six o'clock in the morning until darkness and often late at night. But holidays were frequent, and Monday was the journeyman's special day off, so that he would be able to attend to his personal affairs, visit the bathhouse, and cultivate his social and political interests ("good Monday," "blue Monday").

When the end of his years of travel had come, the journeyman would apply for full membership in the guild. He was required to submit a sample of his work (*Meisterstück*) and had to pass an examination before being received into the guild as a master (*Meister*). He would then establish a workshop in his own house, where he would manufacture his goods with his own hands and hire his own journeymen and apprentices. As an employer he considered himself as socially on the same level as his employees, who would some day be masters themselves. The self-imposed rules of the guild prevented him from making excessive profits at the expense of his competitors, while at the same time they guaranteed him a decent standard of living.

The rise of capitalistic tendencies at the end of the Middle Ages tended to undermine the bases of the guild system. The guild principle of "production for use" gave way to the methods of "production for profit," and the masters began to misuse their monopolies to the detriment of their competitors.

Medieval Economic Theory. The new economic system that was no longer based on the personal tenure of land, but on the impersonal power of money, found its strongest supporters in the cities. It was there that the new kind of wealth was created and the methods for its acquisition developed. Payments in the feudal age were mostly made in the form of services or produce, and trade was carried on primarily by barter. Money, if it existed, was usually hoarded. With the revival of trade that followed the Crusades, and with the rise of the new urban centers of commerce, the opportunities for investment increased, and the new money economy began to revolutionize the structure of medieval society. Economic forces no longer have their meaning circumscribed by the needs of the consumer, but they become the instruments of the producer, who artificially creates ever new needs that in turn require ever new satisfactions.

The economic theories of the Middle Ages, as embodied in the works of the scholastic philosophers and theologians of the thirteenth and fourteenth centuries (cf. p. 141 sqq.), were prompted by and immediately concerned with those economic and social transformations that were gradually brought about by the growth of trade and the rise of the cities. Their economic speculations dealt in the main with private property, money, prices, and the taking of interest (usury).

a) Private Property. They maintained that the right to own property was a natural and moral one, springing from the nature of man and finding its expression in the institution of private property. On the other hand, it was considered as equally obvious that the actual distribution of private property was in no way sacred or absolute but a matter of social convenience and human relations. "Man has a twofold relation to external things, of which one is the power of producing and consuming. For this it is lawful that man should possess property. . . . The other relation to external things is their use, and as far as this goes no man ought to have anything proper to himself but all in common, so that thus each may communicate easily to another in his necessities" (Thomas Aquinas, *Summa Theologica,* I, 2, 66, 2). The reasons listed in defense of the institution of private property were derived from Aristotle and were repeated over and over again in medieval treatises on social science.

The principle of contract that permeated all human relationships in the feudal age and that was binding on king and serf alike, knew only of the conditional exercise of the right of ownership. The owner was a steward, and while the means of production were thus actually in private holding, they remained theoretically in the hands of the community.

b) Money. The medieval attitude in regard to money, its nature, acquisition, and use, was based on the fundamental conviction that economic goods were mere means and as such subordinated to the moral ends of life, and that any economic activity was subject to the moral law. In his *Commentary on the Politics of Aristotle* (Parma edition, Vol. IV, p. 390), Thomas Aquinas wrote: "Political economy, which is concerned with the using of money for a definite purpose, does not seek unlimited wealth, but wealth such as shall help towards its purpose, and this purpose is the good estate of the home." If the prime object of the trader was to make money, he was engaged in a condemnable economic activity. If he was motivated by the desire to provide a decent living for himself and his family, his profession was lawful and laudable, provided that his business practices were beyond reproach. "He who has enough to satisfy his wants," wrote Heinrich von Langenstein (1325–1397), "and nevertheless ceaselessly labors to acquire riches, either in order to obtain a higher social position, or that subsequently he may have enough to live without labor, or that his sons may become men of wealth and importance — all such are incited by a damnable avarice, sensuality, or pride" (*Tractatus Bipartitus de Contractibus Emptionis et Venditionis,* 1, 12). About two hundred and fifty years later Martin Luther used even stronger language to condemn the same economic practices.

c) The Just Price (Justum Pretium). It was the conviction of the medieval thinkers that a "just price" for articles that were bought and sold could be determined and fixed by law. It was admitted, however, that the price level would have to be adjusted to local conditions and circumstances. "Sometimes the just price cannot be determined absolutely, but consists rather in a common estimation, in such a way that a slight addition or diminution of price cannot be thought to destroy justice" (Thomas Aquinas, *Summa Theologica,* II, 2, 77, 1, ad m). The ideal standard by which the justice of economic practices could be measured was provided by the natural law: "Every law framed by man bears the character of a law exactly to that extent to which it is derived from the law of nature. But if at any point it is in conflict with the law of nature, it at once ceases to be a law; it is a mere perversion of law" (Thomas Aquinas, *Summa Theologica,* I, 2, 95, a. 2). The just price would guarantee a man a sufficient profit to live his life according to the standards that public opinion associated with his social status.

d) The Taking of Interest. The prohibition of the taking of interest was defended in the Middle Ages by reference to the Scriptures, to the Church Fathers, to Aristotle, and to the law of nature. It had thus become an integral part and a major issue of medieval economics. It was a prohibition well suited to a system of agricultural economy but out of tune with the new money economy that depended more and more on the credit system. Paradoxically enough, the very Church which had promulgated and for centuries enforced the laws and decrees prohibiting the taking of interest, joined the State in becoming in many instances a protagonist of money economy and of the spirit of early capitalism.

The ethical theory of the Middle Ages in regard to the taking of interest held that money was barren and sterile and therefore could not breed money. It was considered contrary to the natural law that a man should live and earn without labor. It was considered immoral to charge money for a loan on which no such payment should have been asked. The profits raised by a monopolist, the beating down of prices, the rack-renting of land, the subletting of land by a tenant at a higher rent than he paid himself, the cutting of wages, the refusal of discount to a tardy debtor, the excessive profits of a middleman—all these practices were condemned by medieval ethics, which grouped them all under the title of "usury."

There were, however, certain loans on which interest might be lawfully demanded. Thus it was considered lawful to charge interest if the lender, in loaning the money, suffered a loss which he would not have incurred otherwise; or if the lender by loaning the money deprived himself of a profit which he would otherwise have made; or if the borrower of the money used it in a manner that involved the risk of losing it, and if he had mentioned the nature of that risk to the lender. There were other exceptions to the general rule, but they were few, and most of them could be grouped among the above cases.

The Church councils which were strongest in their condemnation of usury in any form were the Lateran Councils of 1139 and 1179, and the Councils of Lyon (1274) and Vienne (1311). Any kind of financial speculation was branded as illegal and immoral. The moneylender was considered virtually an outlaw. Under pain of excommunication or interdict individuals and communities were required to expel usurers from their midst, and they were to be refused the sacraments and Christian burial until they had made restitution. The Council of Vienne decreed that moneylenders be compelled to submit their accounts to examination, and those who defend usurious practices are to be punished as heretics.

e) The Jews and Lombards as Moneylenders. One of the results of this ecclesiastical legislation on interest was the concentration of credit transactions in the hands of the Jews who were not bound by the prohibition laws of the Church. An imperial edict of the fourteenth century decreed a rate of 43 per cent as the upper limit of charges on loans! However, the Jews not only demanded excessive rates of interest but dead pledges (*Faustpfänder*) and promissory notes as well, so that they became the possessors of increasing wealth in the form of money, land, and real estate. By the payment of large sums they secured the protection of emperors, princes, and cities. The people at large, however, began to hate and despise them as usurers and oppressors. They were excluded from citizenship, restricted in their movements, relegated to certain streets and quarters of the city (*Judengassen, Judenviertel*). They were not admitted to the public baths and places of social entertainment and had to wear special dress and other distinguishing marks. Despite the enactment of protective laws, violent outbreaks against the Jews were frequent. They were reproached with ritual murders, sacrilege, and blasphemy, with the poisoning of public wells and a host of other crimes. In 1285 the Synagogue in Munich was burned by an angry populace, with one hundred Jews who had sought refuge in the building, and the long series of cruel persecutions reached their climax about the middle of the fourteenth century, when there raged wholesale murder of Jews in Switzerland, along the Rhine, in Swabia, Bavaria, and Austria. They were banished from Augsburg in 1438, from Munich in 1440, from Würzburg in 1488.

The repression of the Jews was good news for the financially no less efficient and equally ruthless Lombards, who took the place of the Jews as moneylenders and, by cunning and casuistry, successfully endeavored to circumvent the ecclesiastical laws. The Italians in general felt no scruples in asking interest, not even from the pope when he needed money to finance his undertakings. To protect the poor from the exploitation of Jews and Lombards the cities established special organizations in the form of fraternities, guilds, and hospitals, where money could be borrowed cheaply. Such loan banks were called *Montes Pietatis* (Mounts of Piety); they were founded in most European countries in the course of the fifteenth century.

But the most dangerous competitors of Jews and Lombards were the big merchants who began to monopolize the money trade toward the end of the Middle Ages. The bulk of their income was derived from the working of rich mines of silver, gold, iron, copper, zinc, quicksilver, and lead. The mining industries of Bohemia, Bavaria, Saxony, Silesia, Styria, Carinthia, and the Tyrol provided all Europe with the much coveted metals, ores, and minerals. The fifteenth century witnessed a regular "gold rush" in Germany. According to tradition the mines were still owned by the territorial lords. But the big merchants took them over as security for loans and began to exploit them for themselves, so that the masters of the mines soon became the owners of the precious metals as well. When they found out that money trade was the most lucrative of all, most of them went into the banking business.

The papal Curia became involved in the practices of the new money economy after the beginning of the thirteenth century, when the papacy had reached its peak as a political power and when scholastic philosophy had just completed its anticapitalistic system of economic ethics. The Curia needed money to keep up its world-wide political organization, but money could only be obtained by taxing the clergy and the laity and by paying interest to lenders. Many representatives of the Church, becoming more and more entangled in worldly affairs, were in the end more interested in the raising of funds than in the salvation of souls. Some popes became the most important customers of the new Italian and German bankers. These latter had their agents and advisers at the papal court, and they were in charge of the administration of the receipts from indulgences, and other sources of papal income. Like the emperors, some of the popes began to take part in the competitive economic struggles and established capitalistic monopolies for certain industries. Thus Church and State both paid their tribute to the changing spirit of the age, and the Church in particular became in many instances the ally of forces that undermined the foundations of medieval civilization.

Religion and the Church. In Germany as elsewhere the Middle Ages were formed, dominated, and permeated by religious forces. Even the seemingly most insignificant event or activity was endowed with a strong religious accent, so that practically nothing was relegated to a sphere of neutrality or indifference. A definite scale of values was accepted as inherent in the universal order of things, establishing a "hierarchy of being" (minerals, plants, animals, human beings, angelic beings, God) that might be resented, criticized, or challenged, but which was entrenched strongly enough in the medieval mind to constitute a general rule of life and a standard of public opinion.

The sacramental system of the Roman Catholic Church was accepted as the normal framework within which Christian life and culture displayed themselves, and for centuries the Church and religion were almost synonymous. This implicit confidence in the legitimacy of ecclesiastical authority was challenged for the first time by the contact of the Christian West with non-Christian forms of civilization that followed the Crusades (cf. p. 108 sq.). It was further undermined by the growing secularization of Church institutions and practices and a general lowering of moral standards among the members of the ecclesiastical hierarchy. It was finally destroyed by revolutionary movements in theology, philosophy, economics, politics, art, and literature. At the end of the Middle Ages regional nationalism in Church and State began to replace the universal ecclesiastical rule.

The administrative center of the medieval Church was the papal Curia with its head, the pope, the College of Cardinals, and its large number of clerical officials. The right of the cardinals to elect the pope had been established by the decree of Pope Nicholas II in 1059. The chief administrative officers in the many national provinces of the Church were the archbishops and bishops who presided over their dioceses. Most of the members of the higher clergy were of noble birth, and many of them lived the lives of feudal lords and were oblivious of the spiritual significance of their position. They surrounded themselves with vassals and servants, court singers and entertainers. They loved the excitement of the hunt and the adventures of war, and they were so thoroughly entangled in worldly affairs that a popular saying in Germany maintained: the hardest thing to take on faith was the salvation of a German bishop.

The cathedral, which was located in the principal city of each diocese, was the church of the bishop. The "cathedral chapter" consisted of a certain number of canons (priests) who were in charge of the services, took part in the administration of the diocese, and elected the new bishop. The acquisition of land made the cathedral chapters more and more independent of the bishop. As many of the canons likewise belonged to the nobility, they frequently neglected their priestly duties, appointed a poorly paid curate (vicar), and lived like the worldly lords and knights. The "prebend" (office) of a canon was coveted by many a young nobleman because it guaranteed a considerable revenue from some piece of land. Many such officeholders were attracted by nothing but these material advantages and were therefore utterly lacking in the spirit of religion and morality.

In contrast to the richly endowed prebends of the canons, the income that the average parish priest drew from his share in the land of the village, town, or manor was very small. The payment of the tithe (*der Zehnte*), representing a compulsory tax on one tenth of the agricultural and industrial produce and originally promulgated by the Carolingians as a compensation for the confiscation of Church property, was exacted only in a few places. Besides, part of the parish priest's income went to the bishop in the form of taxes and another part to the "patron" of the church who had bestowed the parish upon the priest as a feudal "benefice."

Most of the parish priests were recruited from the peasant class. They were poorly equipped for their office, and frequently they lacked even the most elementary forms of secular and religious education. Many of them tried to increase their incomes by engaging in secular businesses, such as agriculture, trading, medical or legal practice, or more despicable activities. In the later Middle Ages the law of celibacy was frequently not observed, and the wives and concubines of priests became the objects of popular resentment and of the eloquent denunciations of the preaching friars.

The rise of the cities and the newly founded universities (cf. p. 137 sqq.) contributed greatly to the gradual improvement of clerical training. But at the same time the improved and increased educational facilities created a kind of academic proletariat, as many of the students, after having completed their university course, were unable to find positions. These "goliards" (from Goliath, their patron) roamed about as wandering minstrels and vagabonds, as composers and singers of *Vaganten-Lieder,* praising wine, women, and song. One of their number, "Walther, the arch-poet," is known as the author of the Latin student song *"Mihi est propositum in taberna mori"* (it is my destiny to die in a tavern). Its author belonged to the retinue of Reinald of Dassel, archbishop of Cologne (1120–1167).

Ecclesiastical jurisdiction was exercised in the episcopal courts according to the rules of Canon Law. Episcopal jurisdiction extended to all the members of the clergy, including students and deacons, likewise to widows and orphans and to those who took part in a Crusade; also to all who were engaged in dealings of a moral and religious nature, such as marriages, certain business transactions that were sanctioned by an oath, and offenses against religion (heresy, sacrilege, blasphemy, etc.). The sentences imposed by the ecclesiastical courts were usually lighter than those of the civil courts, and never involved the death penalty. According to Canon Law the Church should never shed blood, and formally the ecclesiastical authorities complied with this principle by reserving the imposition of capital punishment to "the secular arm" of the civil government, to which an unrepentant sinner was ordinarily handed over. In doing so, however, the Church knew exactly what the judgment would be, with what methods it would be executed, and how the admissions of guilt were obtained.

The Religion of the People. Religious life in the Middle Ages was essentially informed by the theological concepts of the Church, but it was enriched and colored by the imagination of the common people.

The people were anxious to have visible and tangible objects for their devotion and adoration. During the period of the Crusades the veneration of the relics of the saints increased greatly in fervor and frequency. Jacobus de Voragine's "Golden Legend" (Latin, *Legenda Aurea*) describes the mourning and the great devotion of the people when they learned of the death of their benefactress, St. Elizabeth of Thuringia (1207–1231). They cut off some curls of her hair and pieces of her garment to keep them as relics of the dead saint. The people rejoiced when Frederick Barbarossa in 1164 had the bones of the Three Wise Men of the East (*die heiligen drei Könige*) transferred from Milan to Cologne. In their honor the artisans of Cologne created in the thirteenth century one of the most imposing cathedrals and one of the most magnificent reliquaries of Germany. The "shrine of relics" soon became quite generally the most precious implement of the churches and the object of innumerable pilgrimages.

Pilgrimages became more numerous and gained greatly in popularity during the age of the Crusades. The new shrines in Canterbury (England), Mont-Saint-Michel (France), St. Patrick's Cave (Ireland), and Maria-Einsiedeln (Switzerland) began to attract as many pilgrims as the ancient ones in Rome, Jerusalem, and Santiago de Compostela (Spain). But very much like the Crusaders, some of the pilgrims were prompted by worldly incentives, by love of adventure, curiosity, or greed. Brother Berthold of Regensburg († 1272), one of the most popular and influential German preaching friars of the Franciscan Order, expressed the opinion that it was better to journey to find devout people who are alive than to see dead saints: "I pity you, because every now and then you journey to St. James. And what do you find at Compostela when you arrive? St. James's head! That is all right; but, after all, it is only a dead skull whose better part is in the heavens beyond. But you run to St. James and neglect your business at home, so that your children and good wives grow poorer and poorer, and you yourself become more and more indebted and oppressed."

The Mendicant Orders: Franciscans and Dominicans. Some of the ancient Benedictine monasteries had been responsible for the reform movement of Cluny (cf. p. 70 sq.). The Cistercian and Carthusian Orders represented reform movements which led to a revival of strict monastic discipline with the Benedictine order itself (cf. p. 36 sq.). In the meantime, however, the Benedictine monasteries had again fallen into decline, chiefly owing to their excessive wealth. The Church in general had greatly relaxed its moral discipline and turned from the purity and simplicity of the early Christian centuries, when Francis of Assisi (1182–1226) and Dominic, a native of Calaroga in Castile (1175–1221), appeared and became the founders of the Franciscan and Dominican Orders respectively. Both the Italian and the Spaniard were sons of wealthy parents, but both renounced the possessions and honors that awaited them and chose poverty as their lot. No member of the two new orders was allowed to possess more than the bare necessities of life, and their communities lived entirely on the charity of their fellow men. They were therefore called the mendicant or begging orders and were also known as *friars* (from Latin, *frater:* "brother").

While St. Francis stressed the preaching of the Gospel and the imitation of Christ in aiding the poor, the sick, and the sinners (*Ordo Fratrum Minorum;* abbr.: O.F.M.; "minor brothers," "little brothers"), St. Dominic and his followers were more exclusively concerned with the task of preserving and restoring the purity of religious doctrine by scholarly sermon and disputation (*Ordo Praedicatorum;* abbr.: O.P.; "preaching friars"). St. Francis was a man of great simplicity, animated by a childlike devotion to Christ and the Church; Dominic was a penetrating thinker, a born leader and organizer, whose mind was endowed with a rare sense of proportion and moderation. Both men wanted the members of their congregations to come in close contact with the people, and the Dominicans more than the Franciscans were destined to play an active part in social and political affairs.

Whereas the Benedictine settlements were mostly located in the countryside, the Franciscans and Dominicans established themselves in towns and cities. Even while Francis of Assisi was still alive Franciscan settlements were founded in such German cities as Augsburg, Regensburg, Mainz, and Worms. And the Dominican Order likewise gained a foothold in Austria before the death of its founder. The German Dominican, Jordanus of Saxony († 1237), was chosen to succeed Dominic as general of the order in 1222.

The greatest of medieval theologians, philosophers, and scientists in all European countries were either Franciscans or Dominicans. They met at the new centers of learning, the universities, and added greatly to their growth and reputation. But soon rivalries and heated controversies disturbed the good relationship between the two orders, and they began to oppose each other on doctrinal grounds.

The Franciscan friars were closer to the hearts of the people than the learned Dominican preachers. David of Augsburg (1200–1272) and his pupil, Berthold of Regensburg, were both Franciscans, and the common people enjoyed listening to them because in their sermons they recognized their own language, their own thoughts and emotions, their own joys and woes.

Albigenses and Waldenses. The same dissatisfaction with the actual conditions in Church, State, and society that led to the foundation of the mendicant orders was at the root of a number of heretical movements which threatened the Church from within, and whose adherents were persecuted and finally suppressed by force. The several heretical sects that originated in the twelfth century were all opposed to the sacramental system of the Church and to the clergy as a privileged and socially distinguished class or caste. Like the Franciscans, they demanded the return to the apostolic ideals of primitive Christianity, proclaiming the general priesthood of all Christians.

The Albigenses (from the city of Albi) and Waldenses (the followers of the merchant Peter Waldo from Lyon; also called *Cathari:* "the pure ones") lived and preached in the south of France, but their teachings soon spread to Germany. They denounced avarice and selfishness but went so far in their extreme asceticism as to identify everything material and physical with the forces of evil. They thus revived the ancient Manichaean doctrine of the radical corruption of nature and matter, to which St. Augustine had given allegiance before his conversion to Christianity. They rejected all external symbols, such as sacraments, liturgical ceremonies, sacred vessels, vestments, and images. They denounced marriage, private property, the eating of meat, the use of force, and the shedding of blood. They threatened the unity of Church and State with anarchy and nihilism by preaching a double morality for two essentially different classes of men: the chosen ones who belonged to the inner circle of the religious elite and were no longer in need of religious and civil authority; and the uninitiated masses who still walked in utter darkness. Peter Waldo and his followers were more moderate in their views, and several groups of Waldenses escaped persecution and were allowed to survive in various European countries.

Heresy and the Inquisition. Ever since the days of Emperor Constantine heresy had been considered as a major crime that implied an attack against God and a divinely instituted authority, and that was to be punished in accordance with both ecclesiastical and secular legislation. Thomas Aquinas makes a distinction between those who, like pagans and Jews, have never known and professed the Christian faith, and actual apostates. The former should be left free to follow their consciences, while the latter are to be considered as traitors and are to be dealt with by force. Generally speaking, he thinks, no one should be compelled to accept the teaching of Christianity, and even children should not be baptized against the wish of their parents to whom God had given authority and responsibility in their regard. But anyone who had once voluntarily accepted Christianity should be compelled to live up to his promises. To the medieval mind such a promise constituted a simple contract whose legal obligations were enforceable by law. And the law of heresy followed the pattern of the law of treason: no one could be compelled to belong to one State rather than another, but once he had sworn allegiance to a certain State, he could then be compelled to fulfill his obligations toward that State.

Many a ruler encouraged the destruction of heretics as a welcome means to enlarge his possessions at their expense or to rid himself of dangerous enemies and rivals. In 1232 Emperor Frederick II decreed for the whole Empire that heretics should either be burned or have their tongues cut out. At about the same time Eike von Repkow's *Sachsenspiegel,* the oldest law-book written in German, whose legal concepts are based on national tradition and custom as well as on imperial legislation, demands that heretics be burned at the stake.

Finally, the extermination of heresy was methodically organized by Pope Gregory IX (1227–1241), who authorized certain religious orders, and especially the Dominicans, to try cases of heresy, thereby establishing the Papal Inquisition or Holy Office. The trials were held in secret, a counsel of defense was often denied, the names of the accusers remained unknown to the accused, and the confessions were extorted by the application of torture. The cruelty of these trials, in which accuser and judge were united in the person of the inquisitor, contributed to the growth of anticlerical feeling. Conrad of Marburg, inquisitor of Germany and confessor of St. Elizabeth of Thuringia, was assassinated in 1233, and his fate could hardly claim any sympathy on the part of the German hierarchy. Bishop Conrad I of Würzburg was killed on his way to the cathedral in 1202. It is not surprising, therefore, that Pope Boniface VIII (1294–1303), the last of the great medieval pontiffs, speaks of the hatred of the laity for the clergy as if it were a matter of course. Both the sectarian heretical movements and

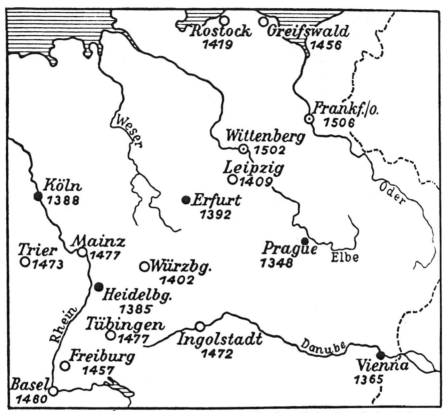

From *Der Grosse Herder*, Herder, Freiburg i. Br.

The Oldest German Universities (to 1500).

the growing opposition of the orthodox laity indicate the dangers with which the ecclesiastical structure was being threatened from without and from within. The clerical element is gradually outnumbered and outweighed by a laity whose members adopt the self-contained culture of the new urban civilization.

The Universities: Organization and Curriculum. The expansion of trade and commerce and the concentration of prosperity and culture in the cities made not only for a richer life but for a more complex concept of living. New problems had to be faced whose solution demanded a depth and acuteness of mental training that could no longer be provided by the old monastery and cathedral schools (cf. p. 87 sq.). And so there arose between the twelfth and the sixteenth centuries — mostly under the sponsorship of the Church — those institutions of higher learning which became known as universities and which were henceforth the main carriers of theoretical and practical knowledge.

By the beginning of the thirteenth century six such Centers for General Studies had been established, among them Salerno and Bologna in Italy, Paris in France, and Oxford in England. Eight more developed during the following hundred years in Italy, Spain, Portugal, France, and England. Twenty-two more universities were founded during the fourteenth century, five in Germany, and by the year 1500 their number had increased to eighty.

While the intellectual life of Germany suffered from the aftereffects of the struggles between Empire and Papacy, France more than any other nation experienced a cultural and intellectual rebirth. As early as the eleventh century Paris had become the center of learning and the "city of philosophers." Its university served as a model for all the *Studia Generalia* in the northern countries, including Germany and England. The neighboring outposts of Arabic and Jewish learning that had been established in Spain proved a mighty stimulus in the educational renascence of France. The University of Paris, where the liberal arts as well as theology and philosophy were especially cultivated, had developed out of the cathedral school of Notre Dame. Among its famous professors in the eleventh and twelfth centuries we find Peter Abelard (1069–1142), the "master of opposites," who first developed the scholastic method of argumentation (cf. p. 145 sq.); Hugh of St. Victor (1069–1141), of German origin, who was called the "second Augustine"; and Peter Lombard († 1164), the author of the famous *Four Books of Sentences* that became the standard text for all the theological schools up to the sixteenth century.

The first university on the soil of the German empire was established in Prague, the capital of Bohemia, in 1348, by Emperor Charles IV, to be followed by the foundation of the Universities of Vienna (1365), Heidelberg (1385), Köln (1388), Erfurt (1392), Würzburg (1402), Leipzig (1409), Rostock (1419), Greifswald (1456), Freiburg (1457), Basel (1460), Ingolstadt (1472), Trier (1473), Mainz (1477), Tübingen (1477), Wittenberg (1502), and Frankfurt on the Oder (1506).

The organization of the medieval university followed the general sociological pattern of the craft guilds (cf. p. 125 sqq.). Students and professors were related to each other like the members of a guild who had united for the purpose of study. The students were the apprentices, the bachelors the journeymen, the professors the masters (*Magister Artium:* Master of Arts, M.A.). The master's degree was granted after the student had passed a thorough examination in which he had proven his ability in defining, discussing, and defending certain propositions. The doctor's degree was granted to those who wished to specialize in one of the professions, and an examination in public was one of the requirements. The term *Artium Baccalaureus* (A.B.) merely indicated that a student had started to do advanced work.

As an essentially ecclesiastical institution the university was exempt from civil jurisdiction and subject to the disciplinary powers vested in the faculty, whose members were only responsible to the pope. The charter for the founding of a university might be granted by the emperor, the king, or the pope.

The students flocked to the universities from different countries, attracted by the reputation of certain schools in their respective fields. They were not hampered by language barriers, Latin being the universal language of higher learning. The university usually consisted of four "faculties": liberal arts, theology, law, and medicine. Each faculty was headed by a dean who was subordinate to the rector and possibly a chancellor, who was the representative of the bishop. Masters and students were divided into several "nations" (*Landsmannschaften*) according to the countries of their origin, and the rector was chosen by these national societies. In the thirteenth century four "nations" were represented at the University of Paris: the French, the Picards, the Normans, and the English. The latter group included the Germans, Scandinavians, Poles, Hungarians, and Bohemians. All the "nations" together were called *universitas nationum* (university).

The material equipment of the medieval university was of the most primitive kind: there were no campus grounds, no lecture halls, no laboratories, no libraries. Teachers and students were practically the only assets that the university possessed. The professor would lecture in his own home or in a hired hall, surrounded by a group of students who might be seated on the floor. The lectures were based on standard texts, and the professor would dictate the text itself, together with his commentaries (glosses). To the beginning of the fifteenth century the students used wax tablets on which they inscribed their notes.

The course in the liberal arts included the work of the beginners, part of which was taught in the monastery and cathedral schools. The *trivium* and *quadrivium* (cf. p. 87 sq.) still provided the general framework of the curriculum, but more emphasis was now placed upon the strictly philosophical disciplines, while grammar and rhetoric were merely considered as valuable tools for the better mastery of the more important subjects of logic and metaphysics.

The study of nature was still in its infancy. The "book of nature" presented a panoramic display of divine works, "written by God Himself, so that in it man might be able to read eternal truths" (Hildegard of Bingen). In flower and tree, mountain and river, rock and animal, medieval man saw symbolic hieroglyphics of a supernatural design. The originally Oriental collection of allegorical descriptions of the world of animals and minerals, known as the *Physiologus,* presents a true picture of the medieval outlook on nature, traces of which are also found in art, literature, and culture. According to Freidank, a German poet of the thirteenth century, nothing on earth is without symbolical or allegorical meaning (*bezeichenheit*).

On the other hand, the thirteenth century shows considerable progress in the accuracy of scientific observation and in the empirical collection and classification of scientific facts and data. It was the conviction of Albert the Great (1193–1280, cf. p. 144 sq.) that "a logical conclusion that contradicts sense perception is not acceptable. A fundamental principle which does not agree with the experimental data of sense knowledge is in reality no fundamental principle at all but a fundamental error." Albert recognized that the milky way consisted of a multitude of stars, he knew about the existence of our antipodes, discussed the influence of the axial direction of mountain ranges on climatic conditions, and he gave accurate descriptions of plant and animal organisms. His English colleague, the Franciscan friar, Roger Bacon (1214–1294), the "admirable doctor" (*Doctor Mirabilis*), was the most progressive scientist of his age. He was actively engaged in mathematical, astronomical, optical, chemical, and medical research. He recognized the laws of the refraction of light and described the phenomenon of the rainbow and the burning glass. He constructed optical instruments and designed plans for automobiles, microscopes, telescopes, steamboats, and airplanes. In order to determine the nature of the original human language he developed the idea of a science of comparative linguistics. Being thus far advanced beyond the scientific knowledge of his time and very outspoken in his criticism of contemporary conditions and institutions, he was suspected of heresy, until he found a protector and defender in the person of Pope Clement IV (1265–1268).

Medieval chemistry was almost invariably linked with the pseudo science of alchemy, just as astronomy seemed inseparable from astrology. The alchemists were still in search of the philosopher's stone (*Stein der Weisen*), the fundamental substratum of all metals, and they tried with indefatigable zeal to change iron into gold or copper into silver.

In the absence of anatomical studies the students often had to be satisfied with the book knowledge gathered from the works of the ancient Greek and Roman physicians Hippocrates (the "father of medicine," 490 to *c.* 370 B.C.) and Galenus (second century A.D.) and their Arabic translators and commentators. It was Emperor Frederick II who prescribed practical studies in anatomy and on the dissecting table for all the medical schools of the Empire. The people at large had little confidence in new medicinal methods and medicaments and clung steadfastly to their old beliefs in the healing power of magical charms and miracle-working salves, roots, and plants.

Contacts with the Orient stimulated and enriched geographical and ethnological studies. The earth was still considered the center of the universe and the stage for divinely directed drama. It was believed to be of globular shape, immovably fixed in space, while around it revolved the celestial spheres, consisting of fire, water, air, and the different constellations and circles of stars. Beyond these starry circles were the dwellings of the blessed in heaven, while the place of the condemned was thought to be located in the interior of the globe. The surface of the earth came to be better known in consequence of Crusades and commercial and missionary expeditions, the latter leading some members of the mendicant orders into the interior of Asia even before the fourteenth century. Nevertheless, the people were only too willing to believe the most wondrous tales of distant countries and continents.

The study of law was chiefly concerned with Roman civil law as embodied in the Code of Justinian (482–565) and Canon Law, based largely on Gratian's *Decretum*. The Universities of Bologna, Padua, and Orléans were among the most renowned centers of legal studies, while Salerno, Toulouse, and Paris were famous for their medical schools.

The Revival of Learning: Theology and Philosophy. The curriculum of the medieval university received its formal justification from the place that was allotted to theology and philosophy, the supreme sciences, from which all knowledge and learning had to take its directions. It is because of the major changes and innovations that occurred in the course of the twelfth and thirteenth centuries in these sciences and their mutual relations, and because of the cultural significance of these transformations, that theology and philosophy occupy a unique position in the general revival of learning and therefore require special treatment.

a) Scholasticism. Up to the twelfth century the leading clerical scholars of the West had been primarily interested in theological speculation from a theological point of view, leaving little or no room for rational argumentation, but referring their discussions and arguments to divine authority as supreme arbiter. There is, therefore, hardly any systematic and independent philosophical thought from the decline of the Neo-Platonic Greek schools of the second and third centuries to the medieval schools of the thirteenth century, if philosophy be understood as a natural interpretation of the universe and a general evaluation of being from the point of view of pure reason. The centuries that lie in between were taken up by the development of theological doctrine and dogma as embodied in the works of the Church Fathers of early Christian times (patristic epoch) and the writers of the early medieval centuries (Origines, Clement of Alexandria, Gregory of Nyssa, Augustine, etc. — Scotus Erigena, Gerbert of Aurillac, Anselm of Canterbury, etc.).

In the period from the sixth to the ninth century a new civilization was gradually built up on the ruins of the Roman empire and with the aid of the northern barbarians. Roman Law was adopted and codified, and the Carolingian Renaissance (cf. p. 51 sqq.) emerged from the "dark ages" of the migrations like a symbolical synthesis of the pagan and the Christian, the southern Mediterranean and the northern Germanic-Frankish forces of civilization. And this first great cultural awakening, retarded as it seemed by political anarchy, was nevertheless soon followed by decisive developments in the sphere of human thought. The period from 900 to 1200 prepared the way for the formation of a so-called "scholastic" theology and philosophy, whereby the limitations and respective claims of both disciplines were redefined, the problem of universals (universal ideas) received its classical formulation, and a definite method of rational disputation was worked out.

The redefinition of theology and philosophy amounted in reality to a declaration of independence on the part of human reason within its own proper sphere. Was human reason then henceforth considered as capable of grasping all the truth that there is? The philosopher-theologian would reply with Thomas Aquinas that there were certain truths which by their very nature transcended the capacity of human reason and would therefore have to be accepted on divine authority. Reason and revelation both proceeding from the same divine source, it seemed inconceivable to the scholastic philosopher that they could ever contradict each other, as long as man made the proper use of his God-given faculties.

In the fourteenth century the followers of the Franciscan friar William of Occam (c. 1300–1349) introduced the doctrine of the so-called "twofold truth," maintaining that what was philosophically true might be false theologically, and vice versa. This Occamist teaching, which exercised such a strong influence on Martin Luther's theological concepts ("I am of Occam's school"), grew out of a disregard for human reason for the sake of an overemphasis upon a supernaturally infused faith. Scholasticism, on the other hand, as developed by the Thomistic schools (the schools influenced by Thomas Aquinas) insisted that the theologian must refer in his arguments to God as the first cause of all things, whereas the philosopher's argumentation must be strictly rational, in that he considers things as they are constituted individually in themselves and, by making use of his sensory and intellectual experience, step by step works his way upward to the First Cause. The theologian argues deductively from cause to effect; the philosopher argues inductively from effect to cause. Under the influence of this revolutionary departure in the field of philosophical speculation Thomas Aquinas created a new theory of knowledge and completely reshaped the proofs of the existence of God as well as the traditional philosophical groundwork of moral philosophy.

The solution of the problem of universal ideas at which Thomistic scholasticism arrived is known as moderate or Aristotelian realism. It has been erroneously stated that scholasticism was nothing but an endless theorizing about the nature of universal ideas. The problem, however, is one that every philosophy in every part of the world has had to face. It concerns the reality of human concepts or ideas. To the so-called extreme realist (e.g., Plato) universal ideas, such as humanity, goodness, whiteness, have a real existence independent of the objects in which they are embodied. For the "nominalist" (e.g., Epicurus, William of Occam, our contemporary pragmatists and behaviorists, etc.), on the other hand, ideas have no reality whatsoever but are merely conventional symbols and names (*nomen, nomina*) that serve to signify and classify human perceptions.

Moderate realism or the realism of the Thomistic schools strikes a middle path between these extreme positions, admitting both the ideal and real validity of the universal concept. Perceptions inscribe the experiences of particular, individual objects of thought upon the mind as upon an "empty slate" (*tabula rasa*), but the spontaneity of the "active intellect" (*intellectus agens*) is capable of abstracting the universal qualities that are inherent in the individual objects of thought, thus forming an idea or universal concept. According to this theory, then, the individual is the real substance, and the universal idea owes its clear formulation to the abstractive and conceptual faculty of the human mind.

Thus the Thomistic philosopher affirmed with strong arguments the significance of individual objects and their lawful activities, and thereby established a solid basis for the investigations of natural science. Once created, each individuality rests in itself, standing on its own ground, but is sustained in its substantiality by that divine power to which it owes its existence. All created things together in their manifoldness and their individualization resemble their Creator and reveal His perfection in varying degrees. Individually and united they partake of the highest good, thus constituting an ordered universe. Man, finding himself placed in the center of such a universe, at the crossing point of matter and spirit, the highest animal and the lowest spirit, evidently a "mixed being," endowed with the irrational nature of the brute as well as with the faculties of intellect and free will, became more convinced of his personal value as philosophy encouraged him to be conscious of his own self, telling him that only a free contractual agreement could bind him to any individual or any authority.

b) Aristotle Rediscovered. The great intellectual revival of the thirteenth century would have been impossible without the abundance of philosophical stimulation that was received from the acquaintance with the great Arabic, Saracen, and Jewish thinkers whose works were introduced in Latin translations in the schools of France, England, Germany, and Italy. The Spanish city of Toledo provided an ideal meeting ground for Moslem and Christian civilization. The Arabic thinkers had not only preserved the Neo-Platonic tradition which was partly embodied in the Augustinian and Franciscan schools of Europe, but in Syria and Persia they had also become familiar with Aristotle (384–321 B.C.), the greatest speculative and scientific mind of antiquity and the tutor of Alexander the Great. It was through Arabic translations and interpretations that European speculation became re-acquainted with the writings of the great sage from Stageira, whose major works for centuries were believed to have been lost, following the suppression of philosophical studies in Athens by Emperor Justinian in 529. To the end of the twelfth century the knowledge of Aristotle had been confined to his *Logic* as expounded by the Neo-Platonist Porphyry and in the translation of Boëthius (470–525).

But the Aristotle who was now transmitted to the West was so strongly colored by the philosophical and theological convictions of the Mohammedan world that he had to be retranslated and reinterpreted to make his philosophy a suitable instrument for the expression of Western thought. Two Dominican scholars, Albert the Great ("the German") and his pupil, Thomas Aquinas, accomplished the great synthesis of Platonic, Aristotelian, and Christian philosophy.

Such an undertaking required courage as well as genius, at a time when Aristotelian philosophy was opposed in many quarters as being at odds with Christian doctrine, and when some Aristotelian writings had been condemned by the Church Synods of 1210 and 1215. Notwithstanding these obstacles, Albert and Thomas went about to demonstrate that Christian doctrine could find a natural support and solid foundation in the Aristotelian physics, metaphysics, and ethics.

c) *St. Albert the Great* (Albertus Magnus, *1193–1280*) *and St. Thomas Aquinas* (*1226–1274*). Being the greatest German scholar of the Middle Ages, Albert the Great was surnamed "the universal Doctor" (*Doctor Universalis*). He was a descendant of the counts of Bollstädt and a native of the town of Lauingen in Swabia. He was won for the Dominican Order by its general, Jordanus of Saxony. He taught in Hildesheim, Freiburg, Regensburg, Strasbourg, Cologne, and Paris; acted as provincial for the German Dominicans from 1254-1257; became bishop of Regensburg in 1260; and resumed teaching in Cologne in 1269. He built up his encyclopedic structure of knowledge on the foundations of Aristotelian thought, following the example of Aristotle in using both the inductive and deductive methods and in showing great interest in the natural sciences. In his long life he learned how to combine action with contemplation, never losing sight of the human, social, and practical implications and obligations of knowledge and wisdom. From the study of books he turned to his laboratory to work on the construction of mechanical instruments, to carry on chemical research, or to experiment with animals. And from the laboratory he might turn to the monastery gardens to give the gardener some advice as to the care of vineyards and vegetables or to tell some peasant about the best methods of cattle breeding. He trained falcons, wrote a book on falconry, and displayed great skill as an artisan.

In medieval legends Albert the Great lives on as a miracle worker and a magician. Nature and life were to him open books of whose perusal he never tired. He studied the literatures and philosophies of the Jews, the Arabs, and the Greeks; he devoted twenty years of his life to the commentation and interpretation of the works of Aristotle. His zeal led him far beyond the confines of his monastery, his pulpit, and his confessional. It became one of his major concerns to work for peace and co-operation among men, classes, and nations, so that he was many times called upon to settle religious, social, and political disputes by arbitration.

Albert's thoroughly human nature comes out frequently in his dealings with philosophical opponents. When accused of teaching indiscriminately the system of Aristotle, he answered that his commentaries represented an explanation of Aristotle rather than his own doctrine, and went on to say: "I mention this point because some of my opponents have grown so petrified in their indolence that they read and search the books of more talented writers for the sole purpose of exhibiting their own destructive criticism. It was this type of men who murdered Socrates; they drove Plato from Athens; they intrigued and plotted against Aristotle. They are in the councils of scholars what the liver is in the human body. For when the bile which issues from the liver flows into the body, it makes it bitter. Similarly, there are some scholars who are very bitter and bilious. And they pour their biliousness over all the others because they cannot tolerate the thought that others want to strive harmoniously for the attainment of the truth."

The sane and practical nature of Albert's thought and of his art of living is well summed up in these excerpts from his sermons: "That you weep one tear of love: that is more pleasing to God than that you weep tears of sorrow, even if they would flow as abundantly as the waters of the Danube. . . . Go out and find God yourself. That is more profitable to you than that you send all the saints and all the angels. . . . Judge and condemn nobody. That is more pleasing to God than that you shed your blood. . . . Accept with patience the dispensations of God's providence. That is more pleasing to Him than that you be carried away in rapture and ecstasy."

It was in Paris, the "city of philosophers," that the first meeting took place between Albert the German and his great pupil, Thomas Aquinas, the "angelic doctor" (*Doctor Angelicus*), who was destined to complete the imposing synthesis of ancient and medieval wisdom. Thomas was born at Rocca Sicca in Italy, in the hereditary castle of the counts of Aquino. After having received his earliest education at the ancient Benedictine abbey of Monte Cassino, he took up the study of the liberal arts at Naples. In 1244 he joined the Dominican Order despite the protests of his family, and suffered a year's imprisonment at the hands of his brothers. After having regained his freedom he went to Paris (1245), and followed Albert to Cologne when the latter took charge of the new house of studies in that city. He returned to Paris in 1252 and passed the regular examinations to obtain the higher degrees. He taught at the University of Paris from 1256–1259, at the Pontifical Curia in Rome from 1259–1268, and returned to Paris once more to take a hand in the struggles between the Aristotelians and the followers of the Arabic philosopher Averroes as well as the conservative Augustinian-Franciscan theologians. In 1272, Thomas began to teach at the University of Naples, the foundation of Emperor Frederick II. He died in 1274, forty-eight years of age, on his journey to the General Church Council that was to be held in the French city of Lyon.

Seventy major works are listed in the official index of Thomas' writings, the most important ones being his commentaries on the Aristotelian physics, ethics, and metaphysics, the *Summa Contra Gentiles* (against the errors of the non-Christians), and the *Summa Theologica* (in three major parts, unfinished). The latter work contains a comprehensive exposition of the system of nature and grace in their hierarchical interrelation, intended as an irrefutable basis of Christian civilization. The method used in the *Summa Theologica* is the dialectical one, first developed in a rudimentary form by Peter Abelard (1069–1142) in his *Sic et Non* (Yes and No) principle, presenting successively argument and counterargument. The method was perfected by the English Franciscan philosopher, Alexander of Hales (1170–1245), and Thomas Aquinas. In its classical form it involves a triadic process, consisting of a prefatory statement of the arguments and counter-arguments of a given proposition, then follows the solution of the problem (the "body" of the article: *corpus articuli*); and, finally, the initial objections are answered point by point on the basis of the solution contained in the main part of the article.

When Thomas Aquinas first entered the University of Paris, his heavy build and his taciturnity caused his fellow students to nickname him the "dumb ox." After his death the faculty of arts referred to him as "the shining morning star, that sublime light that is destined to enlighten the whole world."

d) Mysticism. Scholasticism as such includes both theological and philosophical speculation. As a philosophical discipline it considers in its Thomistic form the intellect as the highest of human faculties, convinced that human reason is capable of penetrating deeply into the mysteries and causal relations of the universe, and of acquiring an analogical knowledge even of the supernatural. Mysticism, on the other hand, is a branch of theology and as such is concerned with a knowledge that transcends the realm of physical nature, in its mode as well as in its object. Christian mysticism aspires to the ultimate reunion of the spiritual soul with its divine origin, brought about by a contemplating love that is informed and infused by divine grace. The "mystical union" (*unio mystica*), of which all the mystics speak as the culminating point of their experience, signifies the blending of cognition and love, of intellect and will, and their unification with the divine will. Visions, ecstasies, and other extraordinary phenomena are entirely lacking on the highest levels of mystical experience. On the other hand, the mystic is transformed into what the Flemish mystical writer Ruysbroek (1294–1381) calls "the true social being," and what Thomas Aquinas has in mind when he discusses the interrelation of the active and contemplative forms of life. To the mystic all earthly things are interwoven with eternity. Elevated to the life of contemplation, he returns to his daily life and occupation to do the works of charity with a higher degree of intensity and efficiency. The pinnacle of Christian mysticism, therefore, is nothing but the highest possible earthly development of Christian life.

e) Mysticism and the German Language. It becomes quite intelligible, then, why Christian mysticism is not opposed to scholastic philosophy, even if some of the mystics use their own terminology to express experiences which have a tendency to escape hard-and-fast verbal patterns. Many of the great leaders of medieval philosophy were both philosophers and mystics, simply because they were both philosophers and theologians. This is especially true of the German mystics of the thirteenth and fourteenth centuries, men and women alike, even if they clothed their religious experiences at times in Neo-Platonic phraseology. Whenever they avail themselves of the German tongue they become linguistically creative, coining new words and imparting new meaning to old and conventional ones. If, like Meister Eckart, they are given charge of convents or beguinages (cf. p. 125), they find themselves compelled to adapt their sermons to the mental capacity of their listeners, thereby simultaneously softening and vitalizing the formalistic rigidity of the scholastic syllogisms. Thus they must be credited with having created a German philosophical language and terminology.

Meister Eckart (1260–1327) is the first German philosopher to use the German language in discussing problems of psychology, metaphysics, ethics, and speculative and practical theology. Not until the eighteenth century did the German language become the accepted medium of philosophical speculation, when Christian Thomasius (1655–1728, cf. p. 360 sq.) departed once more from the traditional use of Latin. Many of the German abstract nouns ending in the suffixes *"-heit,"* *"-keit,"* and *"-ung"* owe their origin to the German mystics (e.g., *Wesenheit, Heiligkeit, Tröstung*).

f) Mysticism and German Literature. One of the centers of mystical devotion in the second half of the thirteenth century was the Cistercian convent of Helfta in the present province of Saxony, the home of Gertrud the Great, Mechthild of Hackeborn, and Mechthild of Magdeburg. While Gertrud and Mechthild of Hackeborn wrote in Latin, Mechthild of Magdeburg's *Fliessendes Licht der Gottheit* (the effluence of the divine light) is the first great mystical work in the German language; it is saturated with the sentiments of mystical lyricism and makes use of the motifs and verbal patterns of knightly and courtly culture. It was in the latter part of the thirteenth century that the Dominicans were given charge of a large number of convents in Germany. Out of sermons, lectures, and letters developed a special category of mystical literature, consisting of tracts, legends, verse, epistles, prayers, sentences, and biographies. A favorite literary form was the dialogue. Centers of German mysticism and mystical literature were Cologne, Basel, Strasbourg, and numerous Dominican monasteries and convents in Switzerland, Swabia, and Franconia.

Francis of Assisi's *Hymn to the Sun* sounded the *leitmotif* of mystical nature feeling and the love of nature. The world is resplendent with a beauty that the mystic does not esteem for its own sake but as the raiment of its Maker. Henry Suso (1295–1366) sees everywhere in nature the radiation of the uncreated Light: "If you take a close look, there is no creature so small that it could not serve as a stepping stone to carry you nearer to God."

g) Eckart, Suso, Tauler. Meister Eckart of Hochheim (1260–1327), a native of Thuringia, is the most ingenious of the German mystics, a metaphysician, preacher, and speculative theologian whose Latin works grow out of the Thomistic tradition of the Dominican Order. He has influenced later Catholic and Protestant mysticism as well as the nature philosophy and speculation of the German Romanticists and idealists of the nineteenth century. The "little spark of the soul" (*das Fünklein*) is the innermost part of the human being, the apex of the human mind, where the birth of the divine Logos and the mystical union with the Godhead takes place. Meister Eckart's style is dialectical, antithetical, and full of paradoxes, his terminology colored by Neo-Platonism; his statements are hyperbolical, unconventional, and daring to such a degree that he was not spared the accusation of heresy and the censorship of the Inquisition. Despite the sublimity of his speculative intuition he never lost sight of the near and the concrete, as is evidenced by this often quoted and characteristic utterance: "If a man were carried away in ecstasy like St. Paul, and he knew of a sick person who was in need of a plate of soup: I should consider it far better that you leave your rapture for charity's sake, so that you might serve with greater love that needy person."

Henry Suso (1295–1366), likewise a Dominican friar of noble descent and a native of Swabia, is the *Minnesänger* among the German mystics, a pupil of Meister Eckart's but less intellectualistic and more given over to lyrical sentiment. His *Booklet of Eternal Wisdom* is one of the most precious gems of mystical literature and the most widely read manual of devotion of the German Middle Ages.

John Tauler (*c.* 1300–1361) of Strasbourg, a Dominican preacher like Eckart and Suso, is more ethically and practically inclined than either of them. His style is popular and direct, but not lacking in depth and formal beauty. His personality and his writings are in conformity with the religious outlook of the new middle class, the inhabitants of the cities and the builders of the Gothic cathedrals. He was greatly admired by Martin Luther and exercised a profound influence on Luther's theology in its earlier phase.

Gothic Architecture. It has been said that the Gothic cathedral is a theological *Summa* in stone, the architectural manifestation of those spiritual forces that are alive in scholasticism and mysticism. But Gothic architecture is more than that: it embodies the culture and splendor of knighthood, the enthusiasm of the Crusader, the Individualism of the burgher. It is, in short, the most striking expression of the changing and changed spirit of the age, the symbol of a new rhythm and meaning of life. It expresses the longing of a heart whose attachment is divided between heaven and earth, and whose restlessness heralds a radical break in the continuity of European civilization.

Gothic architecture is a European phenomenon, and Germany received it from northern France, where it had developed in the course of the twelfth and thirteenth centuries, only to adapt it to her own needs and shape it according to her own national spirit. A transitional style with mixed Romanesque and Gothic characteristics is occasionally found in the first half of the thirteenth century, while strict Gothic becomes the general method of building in Germany after the middle of the thirteenth century.

The term "Gothic art" was first used by Giorgio Vasari and other Italian artists and art critics of the sixteenth century who, enthralled by the art works of antiquity, considered Gothic architecture as a creation of the northern barbarians, the "Goths." The German Romanticists of the beginning nineteenth century in their enthusiasm for medieval art and culture made the epithet "Gothic" a title of honor.

The transformation from Romanesque to Gothic was then a gradual one. As an artistic style Gothic held sway over most of Europe to the middle of the fifteenth century. According to certain stylistic changes it is divided chronologically into early, high, and late Gothic.

The later examples of the Romanesque style (cf. p. 81 sqq.) suggest an increasing vertical tendency, owing especially to the tallness and the growing number of towers and spires. But the Romanesque architect was unable to achieve that strict verticality and extreme height of the building that seemed to be desired by the northern temperament, as long as he continued to use round arches for the construction of the nave vaults. The Gothic master builder broke with this tradition by dividing the nave into a series of oblong bays in place of square ones, and he vaulted these spaces with pointed arches instead of semicircular ones. As a result, the whole building began to take on a different shape, suggesting a dynamic vertical movement and rising to much greater height. However, the full utilization of the new structural tendencies depended on the even more important invention of the buttressing system. The flying buttresses and the nave piers, while introducing fascinating new aesthetic motifs in the external appearance of the building, fulfilled at the same time the practical function of carrying the lateral thrust of the roof and the vaults to the outside of the cathedral, so that the walls become actually disembodied. Being no longer required to carry the heavy load of masonry, they serve as a framework for the increasingly large stained-glass windows which in their turn add a new element to the artistic effects of the interior.

Ground plan and general appearance of the Gothic cathedral are characterized by a complication of detail and a simultaneous simplification of the structural whole. The choir frequently becomes double aisled, providing for an ambulatory with many small private chapels that radiate from it, indicating a growing desire for private devotions and a more personal relationship to the Deity. The façade becomes the dominating part of the building and symbolizes the Gothic striving for extraordinary effects.

The Gothic cathedral stands in the world no longer as a stranger as did the early Christian basilica, but as a princely ruler, conscious of the tasks and functions of the *Sacrum Imperium* of medieval civilization at its height. The interpenetration of spiritual and secular rulership and the increasing secularization of life appear in the many plant and animal motifs that characterize Gothic tracery and ornamentation. The artisan carves naturalistically and in motley array the foliage of maple, ivy, thistle, hops, strawberry, geranium, clover, violets, and others. The slender spires are crowned with the cruciform finial flower, the symbol of faith, hope, and charity, the theological virtues.

While Romanesque architecture was a monastic type of art, executed under monastic leadership, Gothic architecture is largely the result of the communal religious spirit of the laity in the cities. The guilds of stone-masons have their own local workshops (*Bauhütten*), their patron saints, their special trade-marks, carefully guarding the secrets and symbolisms of their profession. For the first time in the history of Western architecture the will of the masses becomes a decisive element in the stylistic development. They are the creators of those immense spaces of naves and aisles, the centers of the worshiping thousands (the Dome of Milan has a capacity of forty thousand) who listen to the oratory of preaching friars, watch the display of the colorful liturgical drama, and take part in religious spectacles and processions. "Here body and soul are immersed in a deep sea. . . . Human intellect loses itself in divine intellect. It is drowned as in a bottom-less sea" (John Tauler). Here the "pure inwardness" (*reine Innerlichkeit*) of Martin Luther and early Protestantism, the idea of a general priesthood, and the pantheistic nature-philosophy of the Renaissance are foreshadowed. The interior of the cathedral of the "late Gothic" style (*Spätgotik*) acquires, especially in Germany, more and more the character of a huge hall (*Hallenkirche*), the nave and side aisles reaching equal height and the pillars growing slender and tall like ever so many trees that spread their branches across the vaulting, where they form a netlike pattern of inter-twining lines (*Netzgewölbe*).

Gothic Arts and Crafts. Gothic sculpture has no independent existence but is subordinated to the laws and requirements of architecture. The body seems to move under a transcendental law. Its well-known *S* line appears as a fragment of an infinite movement that aims beyond itself and beyond the natural sphere. The female figure is depicted in frail and soft outlines, of slender build, with narrow shoulders and long, sensitive hands.

Worldly motifs and grotesque forms again indicate an increasing secular tendency. The glass windows of the northern aisle of the cathedral of Strasbourg depict the idealized portraits of the twenty-eight German kings who had ruled up to the year 1275. A wild and grotesque sense of humor is rampant in the gargoyles (*Wasserspeier*) and masks, in the stone-cut demons, goblins, dragons, and other phantastic imagery that were attached to buttresses, choir stools, moldings, vaulting shafts, and so forth.

The statuary of the cathedral in its inexhaustible wealth of invention confronted the individual with the totality of life, its possibilities and realities, embracing nature and supernature, birth, growth, and decay, health and sickness, alertness, weariness, and soft melancholy. The cathedral sculpture relates the epic of the Christian economy of salvation, beginning with the Old Testament (creation, patriarchs, prophets, kings, and queens), then proceeding to the dramatic events of the New Testament (birth and life of Christ, Apostles, confessors, virgins, martyrs), and finally culminating in the scenes of the Last Judgment and the themes of the Apocalypse (resurrection of the dead; the angels with the trumpets of doom; St. Michael with the scales; Christ in His glory, surrounded by the nine choirs of angels, etc.). Side by side are portrayed the Synagogue (Old Testament) with veil and broken lance and the *Ecclesia Triumphans* (New Testament). The starry sky with the signs of the zodiac, the motherly earth with the seasonal symbols of growth and decline, the months with their respective activities and benefits, the seven liberal arts as friendly helpers in the intellectual and moral formation of the Christian personality: they all share in illustrating and paraphrasing the meaning and the end of human life; they all want to impress upon man the necessity of that momentous decision that involves his sanctification and eternal happiness.

The special contribution of the Gothic style to the art of painting was the creation of the stained-glass window with its peculiar and intricate technique that has never again been equaled. Considering that some of these windows consist of several thousand pieces of glass, it is obvious that great skill and patience were required for their creation. The glass had to be cracked with the aid of glowing iron or coal, and in each and every piece the color had to be fixed by firing. Then the pieces had to be fitted together and held in place by strips of lead. The black lines of the leading served at the same time to separate color from color and keep the different colors from fusing in the eye of the spectator.

In the later phases of the development of Gothic architecture the stained-glass windows began to occupy more and more space, so that in the end the artists created veritable walls of glass, color, and light. But the life of the colored windows depends on the co-operation of the sunlight. They change their appearance according to the changing hours of the day and the changing seasons of the year. Living an unreal and transfigured life, they are the last thin walls to separate the church interior from the world outside, the last frail barrier erected between nature and spirit.

A special significance attaches to the "rose window," one of the favorite decorative motifs of the Gothic style. It is a large circular wheellike window that was inserted in the façade or other prominent parts of the building and consists of a multitude of glass panels separated by spokes of masonry. The "rose window" is a kind of mystical mathematics, symbolizing the convergence of supreme lawfulness and impenetrable mystery in the concept of the divine. From the inside of the cathedral it looks like a wheel of fire or a whirling sun of the skies.

The excellence of Gothic craftsmanship is manifested in the many works of the minor arts and crafts. Great care was taken in preparing dignified monuments for the dead. On top of the sarcophagus the defunct person was usually represented in either lying or kneeling position, clothed with the insignia of his office and dignity. Goldsmiths used the ornamental patterns of Gothic architecture in their shrines, reliquaries, monstrances, chandeliers, and crucifixes. The art of manuscript and book illumination flourished to the end of the medieval period. The Gothic miniatures frequently turn to secular subject matter, such as the description of tournaments, festivals, and hunting scenes. The *Hortus Deliciarum* (Garden of Delight) of the Abbess Herrad of Landsperg is a kind of encyclopedia, illustrated with 636 drawings.

The most outstanding German monument of miniature painting and book illumination is the Heidelberg Manesse Codex (*Heidelberger Liederhandschrift*) which originated in Zürich in Switzerland about 1330 and on its 854 pages contains about 7000 stanzas of 140 German *Minnesänger* and 131 illustrations. This manuscript belonged originally to the Swiss Councilor Manesse von Maneck, was temporarily in the possession of the Vatican Library, and, in 1888, was given to the University of Heidelberg by the crown prince of Germany. The artist-monks and secular painters began to take an equal share in the creation of these and similar works.

While the Gothic period was not favorable to the development of an independent art of painting, the stained-glass windows occupying most of the available clear wall space, the easel picture made its appearance at the end of the medieval period, calling for new techniques, new subject matter, and new objectives.

Court Epic; Folk Epic; Didactic and Lyric Poetry.

a) *Court Epic.* The age of the Hohenstaufen emperors; the struggles between emperors and popes; the adventures of knights and crusaders; the period of scholasticism, mysticism, and Gothic art gave Germany her first great literary awakening. The French versions of Greek, Byzantine, Carolingian, and Celtic themes, the French *chansons de geste,* the romances dealing with Charlemagne, Roland, Alexander, King Arthur, Parzival, Tristan provided the German authors with their subject matter. They sang and told about the heroic and idyllic past and present in a language that is known as Middle High German (*c.* 1100–1450) and Middle Low German (*c.* 1200–1600) and that was distinguished from Old High German by a flattening of the full sounding middle and end syllables (from *o* and *u* to *e:* OHG *salbôtum* to MHG *salbeten,* etc.) and by the partial diphthongization of *î, û, iu* to *ei, au, eu* (*hûs* to *haus,* etc.) and the monophthongization of *ie, uo, üe* to *î, û, ü̂* (*stuol* to *stûl,* etc.).

The German court epic is truly national in tone and feeling, in its passionate longing, its joyous exaltation, its sweet melancholy, its somber brooding and doubting. It is international and cosmopolitan in its themes, its social and conventional setting, and in the characters of its heroes. The higher and lower nobility are the standard-bearers and protectors of poetry. Princely courts, such as the Babenbergers in Vienna or the counts of Thuringia on the Wartburg, become centers of literary movements. The place of the old Germanic hero is taken by the courtly cavalier. This new society was partly educated by its poets and singers, who were its servants as well as its rulers. It was the function of poetry as a social art to serve the entertainment and cultural education of the knightly class.

Henry of Veldeke (twelfth century), the first of the great German *Minnesänger,* is also the founder of the courtly epic, the singer of the love of Dido and Aeneas (*Aeneid*). The Swabian ministerial, Hartmann von Aue (*c.* 1160–1210), the perfecter of a classical Middle High German style, adopts some of the themes of the Old French poet, Chrestien de Troyes (*c.* 1140–

1191) in the Arthurian romances of *Erec* and *Ivein* and creates his own version of *Oedipus Rex* in the legend of Gregorius, the "virtuous sinner" who atones for having unwittingly married his own mother by lifelong penance on a barren rock in the open sea. In his *Poor Henry (Der arme Heinrich)* he strikes a theme that was later on treated by both Longfellow (*The Golden Legend*) and Gerhart Hauptmann: the Swabian knight who is cured of leprosy by the unselfish devotion and sacrifice of a peasant girl from the Black Forest.

Wolfram von Eschenbach (1165–1220) was an unlettered ministerial of the lower nobility. He never achieved in his works Hartmann's formal perfection and harmony of style, but his personality was richer and deeper, his language dark and heavy, expressing a dynamic vitality of thought, emotion, and imagination that would never submit to the clarity and symmetry of the literary conventions of the age.

A comparison of Wolfram's greatest work, *Parzival,* with its French source, *Li Conte de Graal* by Chrestien de Troyes, shows the originality and thoroughly Germanic quality of Wolfram's epic. The theme of the inborn nobility of man who through doubt, error, and complexity unwaveringly proceeds on his way to the castle of the Holy Grail and to that simplicity and wholeness of thinking and doing that constitutes the ideal of spiritual knighthood, is really an early version of the *Faust* problem and a true mirror of German mentality in the Hohenstaufen age.

The saga cycle centering in the Holy Grail is closely connected with the legends of King Arthur (*Artus*) and the knights of his Round Table. Arthur is the leader of the British Celts in their campaigns against Scots, Angles, and Saxons. Gavein, Ivein, Erec, Tristan, Parzival are among the most distinguished knights of the Round Table. The Holy Grail (German, *Gral;* from Romanic, *gréal;* Middle Latin, *gradalis:* "vessel") is that precious vessel that was used by Christ at the Last Supper and by Joseph of Arimathea to receive the blood of the Crucified. To be a guardian of the Grail is the privilege and reward of that highest order of spiritual knighthood whose members are called Knights Templar. According to the legend, Titurel, the son of a French king, erected the castle of the Holy Grail, Montsalvage (MHG: *munsalvâtsche,* "wild mountain") on Spanish soil, in the midst of a wild, impenetrable forest.

Parzival's life receives its meaning and sanction from the German knightly culture of which he is a part, and his vocation to the kingship of the Holy Grail reads like a commentary on the political and spiritual implications of the Hohenstaufen claims to the *Sacrum Imperium.* Parzival's doubts are alleviated and resolved not by the administration of the sacrament of penance and the priestly absolution, as was the case in Chrestien's version, but by his trust in the consoling word of Trevrizent, his uncle, and by divine grace, whose all-pervading presence he has divined in the awakening of nature on Good Friday morning: "First of all he thought of his Creator who had made this whole world."

The author of the first German literary work that glorifies the passion of earthly love was probably a cleric. Master Gotfrid von Strasbourg's († c. 1215) epic fragment, *Tristan and Isolt,* surpasses even Hartmann von Aue's epic art in its clarity and purity of form. Gotfrid's poem follows the model of the story told by the Anglo-Norman poet, Thomas, but the subject matter is treated with originality and ingenuity. All the forms and forces of the age of chivalry, with light and shade evenly distributed, refined and with a considerable amount of sophistication, are psychologically interwoven with the overmastering passion that draws the hearts of Tristan and Isolt inevitably into an abyss of sinful bliss and moral anarchy.

b) Folk Epic (Heroic Epic). Unknown poets are the authors of those great literary monuments of the twelfth and thirteenth centuries that are known as folk epics or heroic epics (*Heldenepos*). They differ in form and content from the knightly and courtly literature of the same period and seem to follow different ethical standards and social ideals. The author of the *Lay of the Nibelungs (Nibelungenlied, c.* 1170) draws his themes from the Germanic past, especially from the centuries of the migrations, and he uses a style that is less refined and more rugged than that of the court epics. In place of the knightly virtues of steadiness (*staete*), discipline (*zucht*), moderation (*mâze*), we find the irrepressible and imponderable forces of unrestrained passion, in love and hatred, in doing and suffering, in victory and defeat, in life and death, loyalty (*triuwe*) being the only Germanic character trait that is glorified in folk and court epics alike. The knightly and Christian concepts are merely an external gloss, barely covering the brutal and unbridled rule of the instincts of a seemingly different race of men and women. A sense of tragic frustration permeates the *Lay of the Nibelungs,* which in its unmitigated pessimism deprives this monumental work of a final metaphysical significance. The Middle Ages added a sequel to the poem, entitled *The Lament (Die Klage),* in which the attempt was made to explain the inexorable immensity of the Nibelungen tragedy and to introduce into it an element of conciliation.

Siegfried's death through the treachery of Hagen, and Kriemhild's revenge that leads to the destruction of the Nibelungs, are the major themes of the poem. Interest is focused upon the personal destiny of its heroes and heroines, and no attention is paid to the world-historic setting or the social background of its events. From the point of view of the Middle Ages the geographical setting of the *Lay of the Nibelungs* must have appeared as an unreal one, reaching back into the remoteness of the fifth and sixth centuries of the Christian era. Even more unreal in its setting and almost wholly lacking in distinct historical contour appears the second of the great heroic epics of the German Middle Ages, the *Lay of Kudrun (Gudrun-lied)* that was composed about 1230. The scene is laid in the North Germanic regions of the North Sea. If the *Nibelungenlied* conjures up the period of the migrations, the *Lay of Kudrun* re-creates the atmosphere of the Viking Age, thereby again transcending and evading the conventional requisites of the age of chivalry and the courtly epic. The poem tells of the abduction of Kudrun by an unsuccessful suitor, her years of trials and sufferings, and her final rescue by her lover, Herwig. This main theme is preceded by a parallel set of motifs in the Viking story of the abduction of Hilde, the daughter of Hagen. While artistically the Kudrun epic equals the poem of the Nibelungs, it does not reach the latter's scope as a symbol of Germanic mythology and psychology. It combines the features of family chronicle and idyl, relating its episodes of Viking raid, rape, revenge, reunion, and happy end in orderly sequence, but lacking the dramatic intensity and suspense of the Nibelungen tragedy.

c) Didactic Poetry. In a category by itself but not without a didactic implication is the poem *Meier Helmbrecht,* which was composed about the middle of the thirteenth century by Wernher "the gardener." Written in the vein of the later village novel, it presents a vivid and realistic picture of the age of decaying chivalry, relating the story of a young farmer who, dissatisfied with his lowly social position, becomes a highwayman and is finally hanged by angry peasants.

Didactic rules of life as well as acrimonious attacks upon immoral practices in Church and State are contained in Freidank's poem *Bescheidenheit* (a book of useful advice, *c.* 1230). Manuals of knightly discipline and behavior were composed by the author who is known by the name of "Winsbeke" (*Herr von Windsbach*) and by Thomasin von Zirclaria (*c.* 1216). With a didactic purpose the Franconian poet named "Stricker" wrote the story of a clerical impostor (*Der Pfaffe Amis, c.* 1230), and moralizing tendencies are embodied in Hugo von Trimberg's realistic poem *Der Renner* (1300) and in the Dominican friar Ulrich Boner's *Edelstein* (*Jewel*, 1330), a collection of fables and parables.

d) Lyric Poetry ("Minnesang"). The period of court epic and heroic epic was also the great age of a unique type of lyric poetry known as *Minnesang* (love song). It is a form of social love poetry and as such is distinguished from the later *Liebeslied* as well as from the simple *Volkslied.* It is the expression of the knight's homage to some noble lady and is therefore determined in form and content by the code of knightly etiquette.

The literary pattern of *Minnesang* was originally developed in the Arabic court circles of Andalusia and later on adapted to the social environment of the knightly aristocracy of the Provence, where the Hellenistic and Latin sense of poetic form had never been lost. The art of the Provençal *troubadour* (inventor) was intimately associated with music. His song was accompanied on the lute or the fiddle.

From the Provence, where it had developed at the beginning of the twelfth century, the art of the *troubadour* migrated to the north of France and from there to the German Rhineland. The forms of the *Minnesang,* however, soon became stereotyped and artificial, and only poets of more than average talent were capable of breaking through the wall of conventions to give vent to natural and personal feeling.

Among those who were thus able to rise above the limitations of a poetic honor code, Walther von der Vogelweide (*c.* 1170–1230) stands out as the greatest lyrical genius prior to Goethe. What imparts to his poetry its distinctive character is the perfect blend of form and content, the universality of his outlook, the integral realism and absolute sincerity of his poetic experience.

Walther was in all probability a native of the southern Tyrol. As a member of the lower nobility and a man without means he wandered as a gleeman from court to court, from country to country, from the Adriatic to the Baltic, from Styria into France, thereby gaining that broad knowledge of human nature and worldly affairs that is reflected in his works. He was drawn into the feud of the Welfs and Waiblingens (cf. p. 89), and in the end the young Hohenstaufen, Frederick II (cf. p. 92 sq.), rewarded Walther's allegiance with a small fief that brought with it long-desired economic security.

Walther's poems are based on personal experience, and they deal with every phase of life that entered into the circumference of his personal vision. He affirmed wholeheartedly the universalistic tendencies of his age, which confronted him practically in the rival claims of Empire and Papacy. He sided with the Hohenstaufens in their rejection of papal theocracy. The education, outlook, and social form of knightly culture are Walther's own, but he animates them with the breath of his genius.

In accordance with the broad scope of his interests and his knowledge Walther's poetry extends from the praise of "uncourtly" love (*niedere Minne*) to the mystical veneration of the Madonna; from trifling yet intimate observations to the passionate call to arms in the interest of some great political, social, or religious cause. The treasury of Walther's lyrical themes is thus well-nigh inexhaustible. He sees the universal significance in individual things and events, and he derives personal applications from general rules and universal principles. His nature poetry combines realism with idealism; it is as naïve and direct as it is artful and thoughtful. His ardent love for his German land, for German breeding, German women, German scenery, for everything German made him wish for the rebirth of an enlightened German-Christian Imperium under Hohenstaufen leadership.

Thus in Walther von der Vogelweide the disparate forces of medieval German culture were once more united, integrated, and poetically trans-figured, while in State and Church the cleavage of minds had already begun to disrupt the ideological bases of medieval society. In one of his last poems Walther looks back upon his life and upon the waning splendor of knightly culture, and he realizes that the world that is his world begins to grow old, and that winter and death are approaching. Thus his singing, that had begun with the joyous jubilation of the awakening spring, ends with a note of resignation, intimidation, and sadness.

The Medieval Theory of Art. It is rather amazing that in an age that abounded with works of sublime beauty there should not be developed a definite philosophy of art. As a matter of fact, medieval views on art and beauty have to be gleaned from the works of philosophers who, aside from occasional remarks, gave no special attention to the aesthetic problem as such. Art in the Middle Ages, it seems, was a social phenomenon to such an extent that its manifestation in human works was taken for granted, constituting an integral element in the everyday experience of every man, woman, and child.

If we try to disengage the few references to artistic creation in the works of the schoolmen from their metaphysical frame, it appears that a work of art was considered as proceeding from the exercise of right reason in the sphere of creative activity. It was the business of the artist to make things that needed making and to make them as well as possible, so that they would fit their purpose. In this way art signified a triumph of mind over matter, impressing some ideal form upon some proportionate material.

Prudence was required for *doing* things in the right way. Artistic skill was required for *making* things in the right way. Prudence was primarily concerned with the effect of an action upon the doer; art was primarily concerned with the effect of the creative act upon the work that was to be created. Both activities proceeded from the exercise of right reason.

Any human work that was governed by the rule of right reason was therefore a work of art, whether it was a question of making shoes or illuminating manuscripts or building cathedrals. God, as the world's Creator, was the supreme Artist; man was "His workmanship," "His husbandry," but also the continuator of God's creation and so His collaborator and a creator in the second degree. Thus there was no distinction between artist and artisan: every artisan was an artist and every artist an artisan.

All the arts were considered both useful and beautiful; all were socially and religiously significant. Some arts are more closely related to matter, while some are of greater appeal to the mind, and so the medieval philosopher made a distinction between "servile" and "liberal" arts. In the contemplation and appreciation of beauty, mind, will, and sense rejoice because they are immersed in the superabundance of being. In other words, the beautiful is a free gift that is superadded to works that are properly planned, fashioned, and executed.

It was the opinion of Thomas Aquinas that art followed the ways of nature, and that nature followed the ways of God (*Summa Theologica,* I, 145, 8). That does not mean that it is the task of the artist to imitate or duplicate the works of nature, but rather to follow nature in its ways of operation. Thus the medieval artists did not copy nature, but interpreted, deciphered, transfigured it. Nature was a sealed book, full of miracles and mysteries. It was the privilege of the artist to open its seals and to disclose the meaning of its pages, pictures, and signs. The artist was an interpreter of life, having experienced life in the fullness of its meaning and having touched the splendor of that form that determines the essence of all things.

PART III. DECLINE, REVOLT, REFORM, RESTORATION

1261	Rudolf wages war against King Ottokar II of Bohemia
1273–1291	Rudolf of Hapsburg, king and emperor of Germany
1278	Rudolf's victory over Ottokar on the Marchfield establishes the dynastic power of the house of Hapsburg
1291	Foundation of the Swiss Confederation of Schwyz, Uri, and Unterwalden
1292–1298	Emperor Adolf of Nassau, a Rhenish count, Rudolf's successor, is defeated and slain in 1298 by Rudolf's son, Duke Albrecht of Austria
1298–1308	Emperor Albrecht I of Austria; assassinated by a member of his own family (John Parricida, duke of Swabia)
1308–1313	Emperor Henry VII, count of Luxemburg
1309–1376	The "Babylonian Captivity" of the popes at Avignon
1310–1313	Henry VII's expedition to Italy and his coronation in Rome. He wins Bohemia for his son, John
1313–1330	Frederick "the Fair" of Hapsburg and Louis, duke of Bavaria, struggle for the imperial crown
1314–1347	Emperor Louis IV, the Bavarian, opposed by Pope John XXII (1316–1334)
1327–1330	Louis's expedition to Italy and his coronation by the people of Rome
1338	The "Electors' Union" (*Kurverein*) of Rense establishes the validity of imperial elections without papal approval
1347–1378	Charles IV, of the House of Luxemburg, German emperor and king of Bohemia, son of King John of Bohemia
1349–1350	The "Black Death," the flagellants, and the persecution of the Jews
1356	The "Golden Bull," defining the methods of imperial elections, making the electoral princes virtually independent sovereigns
1378–1400	Emperor Wenceslaus (Wenzel), the elder of Charles's two sons, deposed by the Rhenish Electors in 1400
1378	Beginning of the "Great Schism" in the Western Church
1386	Victory of the Swiss Confederation over Duke Leopold of Austria near Sempach
1400–1410	Emperor Rupert (Ruprecht), count palatine of the Rhine
1410–1437	Emperor Sigismund, king of Hungary (since 1387), younger brother of Wenceslaus
1410	Battle of Tannenberg: the Poles vanquish the Teutonic Knights
1414–1418	Church Council of Constance; end of the "Great Schism"
1415	John Huss is burned at the stake
1419–1436	The Hussite Wars
1438–1439	Emperor Albrecht II, son-in-law of Sigismund; the imperial crown returns to the house of Hapsburg
1440–1493	Emperor Frederick III, cousin of Albrecht II
1440–1450	Civil war in Switzerland. The last Hapsburg possessions in Switzerland are lost.
1448	Concordat of Vienna between Frederick III and the Holy See

c. 1450	Invention of the art of printing by John Gutenberg (*c.* 1400–1468) of Mainz
1452	Frederick III receives the imperial crown in Rome, the last coronation of a German emperor in Rome
1457	The "Marienburg," stronghold of the Teutonic Knights, taken by the Poles
1460	Personal Union of Schleswig-Holstein with Denmark
1466	The territory of the Order of Teutonic Knights (West Prussia plus Ermland) is ceded to Poland; East Prussia becomes a feudatory of Poland
1477	Frederick's son Maximilian, by his marriage to Mary, the daughter and heiress of Charles the Bold of Burgundy, secures the Netherlands and the Free County of Burgundy for the Hapsburg family possessions
1483–1546	Martin Luther, reformer
1491–1556	Ignatius of Loyola, founder of the Society of Jesus
1491	Frederick III negotiates a treaty with Ladislas IV, the Polish ruler of a united Bohemia and Hungary, to secure for the Hapsburgs the hereditary succession in Hungary
1493–1519	Emperor Maximilian I, son of Frederick III
1495	The Diet of Worms; constitutional reform and promulgation of a perpetual Land Peace (*ewiger Landfriede*)
1504	Francis of Taxis establishes the first postal route between Brussels and Vienna
1508	Maximilian I accepts the title "Chosen Roman Emperor"
1512	The Diet of Cologne; the Empire is divided into ten major judicial districts (*Landfriedenskreise*)
1517	Martin Luther nails ninety-five theses on the portal of the castle church in Wittenberg
1519	Ulrich Zwingli's reformation in Zurich (Switzerland)
1519–1556	Emperor Charles V, son of Philip the Fair and Joanna the Insane
1520	Publication of Luther's three revolutionary pamphlets: (1) *To the Christian Nobility of the German Nation;* (2) *On the Babylonian Captivity of the Church;* (3) *On the Freedom of a Christian Man* — Condemnation of forty-one sentences in Luther's writings by the Papal Bull *"Exsurge Domine"* (June 15) — Luther is threatened with the ban of the Church; he burns the papal Bull and a copy of the book of Canon Law (Wittenberg, December 10)
1521	Luther is banned by the Church (Bull, *"Decet Romanum"* of January 3) — Diet of Worms — Luther refuses to recant and is declared under the ban of the Empire by the "Edict of Worms" — Charles V's brother Ferdinand receives the Austrian possessions of the Hapsburgs
1521–1526	Charles V's first war against Francis I, king of France
1522	First edition of Luther's translation of the *New Testament;* 1534: first edition of his translation of the entire *Bible*
1522–1523	Diet of Nuremberg — revolt of the knights of the Empire
1524–1525	The Peasants' War
1525	Luther's marriage to Katherine of Bora (June 13); he publishes

his pamphlet *Against the Murderous and Rapacious Hordes of Peasants*

1526   Peace of Madrid between Charles V and Francis I — the First Diet of Speyer — Ferdinand (I) inherits Bohemia and Hungary

1526–1529   Charles V's second war against Francis I

1529   Peace of Cambrai between Charles V and Francis I — The Second Diet of Speyer: the "evangelical" estates of the Empire protest against the decrees prohibiting the spread of the Lutheran doctrines ("Protestants") — Vienna is threatened by the Turks — Disputation of Marburg between Luther and Zwingli, concerning the doctrine of the Eucharist (the Lord's Supper)

1530   Coronation of Charles V in the cathedral of Bologna by Pope Clement VII, the last coronation of an emperor by a pope — Diet of Augsburg: Presentation of the Protestant "Augsburg Confession" (*Confessio Augustana*), composed by Melanchthon — Formation of the Protestant League of Schmalkalden — Promulgation of the "*Carolina*" (imperial code of criminal law)

1531   Ferdinand (I) becomes Roman-German king — Death of Zwingli in the battle of Kappel against the Catholic cantons of Switzerland.

1532   The religious peace of Nuremberg

1533   Peace between King Ferdinand and Sultan Soliman

1534–1535   Rule of the Anabaptists in Münster

1536–1538   Charles V's third war against Francis I

1540   Foundation of the Society of Jesus (Jesuit Order) by Ignatius of Loyola

1541   John Calvin's reformation in Geneva

1542–1544   Charles V's fourth war against Francis I

1544   Charles V invades France; Peace of Crespy — Diet of Speyer: Charles V and the Protestants unite for the purpose of defending the Empire against France and the Turks

1545–1563   Council of Trent: the Catholic Restoration

1546–1547   War of Schmalkalden between Protestants and Catholics

1548   The Diet of Augsburg accepts the "Interim," a provisional settlement of the religious dispute

1552   Duke Maurice of Saxony betrays the cause of the emperor; Occupation of the bishoprics of Metz, Toul, and Verdun by King Henry II of France — Treaty of Passau, favoring the Protestant cause — Unsuccessful campaign of Charles V against Henry II

1555   The religious peace of Augsburg

1556   Emperor Charles V abdicates and retires to a Spanish monastery; he dies in 1558

1556–1564   Emperor Ferdinand I, brother of Charles V

1564–1576   Emperor Maximilian II, son of Ferdinand I

1576–1612   Emperor Rudolf II, son of Maximilian II

1583–1634   Albrecht von Wallenstein, duke of Friedland and Sagan

1585–1642   Cardinal Richelieu

1602–1661   Cardinal Mazarin

1608   Foundation of the Protestant Union, headed by Frederick IV, elector palatine

1609	Foundation of the Catholic League, headed by Duke Maximilian of Bavaria
1612–1619	Emperor Matthias, brother of Rudolf II
1618–1623	*The Bohemian Revolt.*
1619–1637	Emperor Ferdinand II, grandson of Emperor Ferdinand I, cousin of Emperor Matthias
1619	Election of Frederick V, Elector Palatine, son-in-law of King James I of England, as king of Bohemia
1620	The combined armies of the emperor and the Catholic League under General Tilly defeat the Bohemians on the White Hill near Prague
1623	Duke Maximilian I of Bavaria (1598–1651) receives the Upper Palatinate and Frederick V's Electorate
1624–1629	*The Saxon-Danish War*
1626	Wallenstein defeats Count Mansfeld at Dessau — Tilly defeats King Christian IV of Denmark at Lutter am Barenberg (Brunswick)
1628	Wallenstein besieges unsuccessfully the city of Stralsund
1629	The Edict of Restitution, restoring to the emperor all ecclesiastical estates, secularized after the Treaty of Passau (1552)
1630	Dismissal of Wallenstein
1630–1635	*The Swedish War*
1630	Gustavus Adolphus, king of Sweden (1611–1632), lands on German soil (Pomerania)
1631	Tilly storms the city of Magdeburg and is defeated by Gustavus Adolphus at Breitenfeld
1632	Wallenstein is called back and given the supreme command of the imperial armies — Death of Tilly — Death of Gustavus Adolphus in the Battle of Lützen
1634	Wallenstein is assassinated in Eger (Bohemia)
1635	Peace of Prague
1635–1648	*The Swedish-French War*
1637–1657	Emperor Ferdinand III, son of Emperor Ferdinand II
1640–1688	Frederick William, the Great Elector (of Brandenburg)
(1643–1715)	Louis XIV, king of France
1644–1648	Peace assemblies at Münster and Osnabrück (Westphalia)
1648	*Peace of Westphalia*
1683–1699	The Great Turkish War
1683	Siege of Vienna
1684	Formation of the "Holy League" between Austria, the republic of Venice, and the papacy
1687	Victory of the "Holy League" at Mohács (Hungary)
1697	Victory of Prince Eugene of Savoy at Zenta (Hungary)
1699	Peace of Karlowitz
1715–1718	The Second Turkish War
1716–1717	Victories of Prince Eugene at Peterwardein and Belgrade
1718	Peace of Passarowitz

Chapter 7

THE END OF THE MIDDLE AGES: DISINTEGRATION OF THE EMPIRE AND THE RISE OF THE TERRITORIAL STATES

The End of the Interregnum. Rudolf of Hapsburg. The period of the *Interregnum* with its unchecked lawlessness was brought to an end in 1273, when the leading German princes elected Rudolf of Hapsburg as German king, thus at least nominally restoring the "Holy Roman Empire of the German Nation." The fourteenth and fifteenth centuries saw the continuance of the imperial dignity under different houses, finally reverting to the Hapsburgs, who were to retain the imperial title until the dissolution of the Empire in 1806. But while France and England developed during the following two centuries into powerful centralized nations with a unified civilization, the German Empire developed a progressive weakness in its political organization that found only partial and temporary compensation in the flourishing culture of its individual territorial states, under the rule of secular and ecclesiastical princes. The emperors no less than the territorial lords were primarily interested in the aggrandizement of their family possessions or their social prestige, and thus they mostly lost sight of the greater national and international issues at stake. Protective leagues of cities and districts within the Empire were organized for the defense of national and communal interests, a defense which the emperor could not and would not provide.

Rudolf of Hapsburg (1273–1291) owed his election to the fact that the German princes had been on the lookout for a ruler who would be strong enough to put an end to the anarchical conditions in the Empire, yet whose prestige and personality would constitute no danger to their own particularistic and dynastic ambitions. The new emperor was a prince of moderate wealth and influence, whose family possessions were located in the German south, extending from the Alpine passes into the Alsatian regions. His upright and noble character won him the confidence of the people, and he succeeded in checking lawlessness and securing peace in the Empire.

He wisely abstained from reviving the Italian policies of the Hohenstaufens, but concentrated his energies on the acquisition of land and power for his family, thus laying the foundation for the future greatness of the Hapsburg dynasty.

Ottokar II of Bohemia, who had refused to recognize the validity of Rudolf's election, was defeated and fatally wounded on the Marchfield near Dornkrut (Lower Austria) in 1278, and Rudolf took from him Austria and its dependent territories. The emperor gave some of these conquered lands to his son Albrecht and thereby aroused the fear and suspicion of the electoral princes to such an extent that upon Rudolf's death in 1291 they passed over Duke Albrecht of Austria and gave their vote to Adolf of Nassau (1292–1298), an obscure Rhenish count, adventurer, and ruthless politician, who was defeated and slain by a dissenting group of German princes under the leadership of Duke Albrecht.

The Hapsburg, Wittelsbach, and Luxemburg Emperors (1298–1438). Emperor Albrecht I (1298–1308) is described in contemporary chronicles as a stern and energetic ruler, "hard as diamond." In his attempt to stand up for his imperial rights he had to cross swords with the electoral princes and was assassinated by his own nephew, John "the Parricide," duke of Swabia. The Electors had gotten a rather bitter taste of the menacing power of the house of Hapsburg and decided to offer the crown to Count Henry of Luxemburg, who succeeded Albrecht as Emperor Henry VII (1308–1313). His exalted conception of the imperial dignity prompted him to embark on an expedition to Italy to pacify the warring members of the Welf and Waiblingen factions and to receive the imperial crown in Rome in the traditional fashion. He was hailed by the exiled Florentine poet Dante (1265–1321) as the bringer of peace and justice and was crowned Roman emperor in 1312. But he proved himself a partisan of the Waiblingen cause and died only one year later, without having succeeded in settling the family feud. Before leaving for Italy Henry had secured an Eastern outpost for the territorial power of the house of Luxemburg by obtaining the election of his son, John, as king of Bohemia.

In Germany Henry's death was followed by another disputed election, and this time the Hapsburgs in the person of Frederick "the Fair," son of the late Emperor Albrecht I, met with the opposition of Louis of Bavaria, pretender of the house of Wittelsbach. A civil war that broke out after Frederick and Louis had both been crowned by their respective adherents ended with Louis' victory and Frederick's imprisonment. Louis subsequently used Frederick as a pawn in his dealings with Pope John XXII (1316–1334), the last great character on the papal throne in the drawn-out struggle between Empire and Papacy in the Middle Ages. Frederick was released after a captivity of two years and a half and was later on accepted by Louis as coregent.

When Pope John XXII interfered in the struggle between Louis and Frederick, claiming that Louis should have appealed to Rome for arbitration, and demanding Louis' resignation under penalty of excommunication, it seemed as if the times of Henry IV, Frederick Barbarossa, and Frederick II had once more returned, with accusations and counteraccusations being hurled back and forth. But the political constellations had changed, and the events that had preceded the papal threat aided in rendering it ineffective. Louis had started upon an expedition to Rome and had been crowned on the Capitoline Hill by the Roman people and anointed by two excommunicated Italian bishops. The pope's residence was no longer in Rome but in Avignon, where the papacy in its "Babylonian Captivity" (1309–1376, cf. p. 172 sq.) was more and more becoming a servile instrument of the French monarchy. Louis heaped a flood of invectives upon John XXII, declared him deposed, and secured the election of an antipope. But only ten weeks later both emperor and antipope had to flee from Rome for fear of being stoned by the populace. Louis tried to make his peace with Benedict XII, the successor of John XXII, but was appalled by Benedict's demands, including unconditional surrender of all his imperial rights and dignities until his claims and titles should have been vindicated by the Church. The result was a joint proclamation of the "Electors' Union" (*Kurverein*), issued at Rense (1338), in which the Electors came to the defense of Louis and the imperial prerogatives. The proclamation stated that "since the Empire depends on God alone, he who is elected by a majority of votes can take the title of king and exercise all sovereign rights without need of consent or confirmation of the Pope."

Louis failed to take advantage of the strength of his position and antagonized the German princes by the inconsistency and selfishness of his political moves. The opposition party rallied around the house of Luxemburg, demanded the deposition of Louis, and secured the election of Charles of Luxemburg, one year before Louis' death (1347). The new emperor, Charles IV (1346–1378), had inherited the kingdom of Bohemia from his father, King John, the son of Emperor Henry VII. He had been educated in France, Bohemia, and Italy, and had received an intellectual training and diplomatic schooling that proved a great aid in the troublesome times into which he was born and in which he tried to steer a middle course between social, political, and religious extremes. It was his supreme ambition to restore the glory of the German empire, with his native and hereditary state of Bohemia as the center of gravity, and with the acceptance of a hereditary succession of the house of Luxemburg. In his autobiography he appears as a man of strong religious convictions with definite leanings toward mysticism.

Charles's interest was so much centered in his Bohemian lands that Emperor Maximilian I (cf. p. 167 sq.) was to refer to him later on as "the arch-father of Bohemia and the arch-stepfather of the Empire." Bohemia developed under his rule into one of the best organized states of the Empire, and its flourishing culture found an external expression in the foundation of the University of Prague (1348), the first university in German-speaking lands and the personal creation of Charles IV. By means of diplomatic schemes, financial transactions, and marriage unions he incorporated in the Bohemian kingdom the territories of Brandenburg, Lower Lusatia, and part of the Upper Palatinate. Brandenburg, which he took from the house of Wittelsbach, fell to his son, Sigismund, upon the emperor's death in 1378, who bestowed it on Frederick of Hohenzollern in 1415. Alliances with Poland and Hungary assured the security of the eastern boundaries of the Empire.

As far as the Empire at large was concerned, Charles nourished no illusions as to the solidity of its political and social structure. He was conscious of the inherent weakness of the Imperial Diet and of the partyism among princes and nobles which was to blame for the internal disintegration and for a weak and vacillating foreign policy. He felt that the best he could do was to take a number of measures to prevent further decline and to enforce at least a semblance of order. At the Diet of Nuremberg in the year 1356 Charles IV promulgated the famous "Golden Bull," whose significance has been compared by some authors with that of the British *Magna Charta Libertatum* of 1215. It defined the powers of the electoral princes, dealt with the proceedings at elections and the order of succession to an Electorate, and most of its provisions remained valid to the very end of the Holy Roman Empire in 1806. One of its major effects was a remarkable increase in the prestige and independence of the members of the electoral college. They were to have full sovereign power within their territories, and from the judgments of their courts no one could henceforth appeal to the emperor. The electorates were to be hereditary, and the territories of the secular electors were to be inherited according to the rule of primogeniture (succession of the first-born son). There were to be seven electors, four of them secular princes (the king of Bohemia, the duke of Saxony, the margrave of Brandenburg, the count palatine of the Rhine), and three ecclesiastical princes (the archbishops of Mainz, Köln, and Trier).

In laying down the provisions of the rudimentary form of a written national constitution Charles had tried to make the best of an extremely precarious situation. Without curtailing the privileges of the territorial princes he had managed to secure the possession of two of the most important electoral votes, those of Bohemia and Brandenburg, for the German emperor and the house of Luxemburg. The elections in the future were to be held at Frankfurt, and the ceremonious display of the imperial insignia, the crowns of Aachen and Milan, the orb, the staff, the scepter, and the sword were to enhance the splendor of such an occasion.

While Charles had thus undeniably consolidated the power of his house and outwardly added to the territorial possessions and the prestige of the Empire, it is none the less apparent that the prestige of the imperial office itself had suffered greatly from the surrender of so much power to the territorial princes. The rule of Charles's sons marked a further step in the gradual decline of imperial power. Wenceslaus (Wenzel, 1378-1400), the

elder of the two, was an habitual drunkard, and in 1400 he was deposed
by the electors and replaced by Rupert, count palatine of the Rhine (1400–
1410). After his death the crown was offered to Wenzel's younger brother,
Sigismund (1410–1437), who had been king of Hungary since 1387 through
his marriage with the heiress of that country. While his diplomatic skill
in directing the proceedings of the Council of Constance (1414–1418)
achieved a major triumph by putting an end to the "Great Schism" of the
Church (cf. p. 173 sq.), he became involved in the ferocious Hussite Wars
that followed the burning of John Huss (cf. p. 176 sqq.) in 1415. It was in the
same year that Sigismund gave the March of Brandenburg to Frederick
of Hohenzollern (the name derived from the ancestral castle atop Mt.
Zollern in Swabia), Count (*Burggraf*) of Nuremberg, whose descendants
became the creators of the kingdom of Prussia and the later German empire
of the Hohenzollern dynasty.

Under Wenzel's and Sigismund's rule disorder in the German lands
increased, the Burgundian state in the West and the Polish nation in the
East reaping the profits of the virtual breakdown of imperial power. The
Teutonic Knights were decisively defeated by the Poles at Tannenberg
(1410, cf. p. 114), and the Swiss peasant communes in the South emancipated
themselves from the domination of the house of Hapsburg (1386).

The Rise of the Hapsburg Dynasty. When Sigismund died without a
male heir in 1437, the crown reverted once more to the Hapsburgs. The
short reign of Albrecht II (1438–1439) was followed by the election of his
cousin, Frederick III (1440–1493), who devoted most of his energy to the
consolidation of his family possessions, so that the power of the Hapsburgs
soon overshadowed completely the other principalities of the Empire, and
the imperial dignity was never again wrested from the Hapsburg dynasty
to the very end of the Austro-Hungarian monarchy in 1918.

During the fifty-three years of Frederick's rule German affairs of state
were drifting from bad to worse, while the emperor looked on, unable to
make up his mind one way or the other. Verifying the traditional saying
"Bella gerant alii; tu felix Austria nube" ("Let the others wage wars; you,
happy Austria, may rely on marriage alliances"), he secured the Burgundian
succession for his house by joining his son, Maximilian, in matrimony to
Mary, the heiress of Charles the Bold of Burgundy. In addition, he negotiated
a treaty in the East, whereby the Hapsburgs were to become the heirs of
Ladislaus, king of a united Poland and Bohemia, upon the expiration of
the male line of succession. The son of Mary of Burgundy and Maximilian,
Philip "the Handsome" (*Philipp der Schöne*), was to inherit not only the
Burgundian estates, including the Free County (*Freigrafschaft*) of Burg-
undy, but also Luxemburg and the wealthy provinces of the Netherlands.
Philip was married to Joanna (1496), the daughter of Ferdinand and
Isabella of Spain and the heiress of Castile and Aragon. When Philip died
and Joanna was pronounced insane (1509), their young son Charles inherited
not only the immense territorial possessions of his parents but, upon the

death of his maternal grandfather Ferdinand in 1516, became the sovereign of the kingdoms of Spain, Sardinia, Sicily, Naples, and the Spanish-Castilian possessions in the New World. When Emperor Maximilian I died in 1519, the domains of his grandson, Charles, were further increased by the vast hereditary Hapsburg territories in Germany, so that Emperor Charles V stated the truth when he said: "In my realm the sun never sets."

When Charles was nineteen years of age, his Empire extended over Germany, Burgundy, Italy, and Spain with her possessions overseas, an aggregation of power that was unparalleled since the days of Charlemagne. However, it was too artificial a structure, composed of too many heterogeneous elements, to last for any considerable length of time.

Maximilian I (1493–1519), "the last of the knights" (*der letzte Ritter*), was a ruler of charming personality; a poet and a scholar; a patron of art, culture, and education. His interests were broad and cosmopolitan, his ideas lofty and often spectacular, but he lacked the realistic sense of proportion that makes the great statesman. He attempted to remedy the clumsy and inefficient administrative and political organization of the Empire by decreeing several constitutional reforms at the Diet of Worms (1495), including the establishment of a standing national court of justice (*Reichskammergericht*) and the promulgation of a perpetual Land Peace (*ewiger Landfriede*).

The realization of some of his major projects was seriously hampered by rising war clouds and political complications in the East and West of the Empire. In the East the Turks were sweeping across the plains of Hungary, threatening Austria with invasion, while, in the West and Southwest, France and Spain were embarking on a definitely imperialistic policy of expansion, with the conquest of Italy as one of their major objectives. Owing partly to his constant lack of funds, partly to the unreliability and indifference of the German princes, Maximilian was unable to prevent the French from becoming the masters of northern Italy and the Spaniards from conquering Naples and Sicily. If Maximilian had not reverted to the traditional Austrian policy of letting peaceful matrimonial alliances make up for military losses, the Empire would undoubtedly have had to bow before the rising stars of Spain and France.

"The last of the knights" was at the same time one of the foremost among the moderns, and actually dealt the knightly form of warfare a deadly blow by adopting the new methods and inventions of military science, replacing the old-fashioned cavalry with their heavy armor and their elaborate showing by artillerymen and foot soldiers whose organization followed the model of the Swiss mercenaries (*Landsknechte*). The emperor himself invented new types of cannon and transport wagons, taking a lively interest in all matters pertaining to military science.

All the external splendor of which Maximilian himself was an exponent cannot obscure the fact that the German empire at the end of the Middle Ages lacked the essential elements of order, solidarity, and unity. The processes of decentralization went on practically unchecked, and the larger territorial principalities of the Electors were surrounded by a growing number of the smaller domains of sovereign barons and free knights, and of the ecclesiastical estates of archbishops, bishops, and abbots. To these must be added some fifty to sixty free imperial cities, subject only to the nominal authority of the emperor. The fourteenth and fifteenth centuries witnessed innumerable private feuds, border skirmishes, wars of succession, and endless struggles and clashes between princes, cities, and nobles, between clergy and laity, patricians and guilds. But despite the absence of a central, controlling, directing, and law-enforcing power the general cultural level was high, trade and commerce flourished, and the prosperity of the burgher class favored the development of higher education and creative endeavor in the arts and crafts.

The Rise of Austria. It seems necessary, at this juncture, to trace the growth of that German state which, with the rise of the Hapsburg dynasty, assumed the cultural leadership of Germany for centuries to come. That state is Austria.

After Otto the Great (cf. p. 65) had successfully checked the westward migration of the Magyars (Hungarians) by his victory on the Lechfeld (955) and driven the Slavs eastward from the river Elbe, he re-established the eastern march (Ostmark), which had been created originally by Charlemagne after his victory over the Avars (790–803). The name Austria (*Ostarrîchi*) was first used in the tenth century to designate the German settlements of the eastern marches, which owned nominal allegiance to the duke of Bavaria but which, since 976, actually had been governed quite independently by the margraves of Babenberg. Frederick Barbarossa made Austria an independent duchy in 1156. In the course of the twelfth and thirteenth centuries Styria (*Steiermark*), parts of Carniola (*Krain*), and Upper Austria were added to the Austrian domains.

The last member of the house of Babenberg died in the battle against Bela IV of Hungary (1246), and the duchy of Austria as well as the province of Carinthia (Kärnten) were occupied by King Ottokar II of Bohemia (1251). Rudolf of Hapsburg seized the German fiefs of Ottokar II and gave Austria, Styria, and Carniola to his sons, Albrecht and Rudolf, thereby firmly establishing the stronghold of Hapsburg supremacy in southeastern Germany.

The Austrian regions had become predominantly Germanic in the centuries of the migrations, their ethnological and national structure being decisively influenced by the immigration of the Bavarians in the beginning of the sixth century. The Bavarians were the descendants of the ancient Marcomans, who had originally occupied the territory of Bohemia and for that reason had been named "Boivarii." They were an agricultural Germanic tribe of great vitality and tenacity and endowed with other qualities that predestined them for cultural leadership. They rapidly acquired the habits of a frontier people, dwelling in partial autonomy in the outlying eastern border regions of the Frankish empire. They were severely hampered in the peaceful cultivation of their lands and even found their territorial possessions endangered by the onslaughts of the fierce Avars and several auxiliary Slavic peoples with independent cultures of their own. Partly subjected by the Avars, who drove the rest of them westward, they advanced into the Alpine valleys and had reached Styria and Lower Austria by the end of the sixth century. Charlemagne's victory over the Avars led to the definitive incorporation of the eastern marches in the Frankish empire and to the creation of an ecclesiastical province with its center in Salzburg. Politically and ecclesiastically these eastern Alpine regions, extending far into the plains of Hungary, formed part of Bavaria. The subsequent subjection and absorption of the several Slavic enclaves, according to the opinion of some scholars, led to the verbal and semantic equation of *servi, sclavi, Slavi* (slaves, Slavs).

The day of the battle on the Lechfeld (955), with its decisive victory over the Magyars, was the actual birthday of Hapsburg Austria. It reestablished the eastern march and created for Bohemia and Hungary the foundation for their later unification with Austria. At the same time it provided a suitable background for the cultural achievements of these regions in the Middle Ages. It was in the Eastern March that the *Lay of the Nibelungs* (cf. p. 154) and the Gothic and Bavarian saga cycles were given their final touch. These were the regions where *Minnesang* achieved its most vital expression in Walther von der Vogelweide (cf. p. 156), where Austrian historiography developed in intimate connection with a specific monastic culture, where during the seventeenth and eighteenth centuries flourished the courtly as well as the popular arts, crafts, and literatures of the Austrian Baroque and Rococo (cf. p. 337 sqq.).

It was in the tenth century, then, that the genius of Austria came to life, that very definite and homogeneous type of national culture that perpetuated itself through the centuries, displaying its humane and artistic riches in song and dance, fashions and manners, arts and crafts, political and social formations, religious and philosophical ideas.

Rudolf of Hapsburg was responsible for the shift of the center of gravity of German dynastic rule to the eastern part of the Empire. It was this shift that made the combination Hapsburg-Austria a constellation of world-historic significance. Even the Mark Brandenburg, the nucleus of the later kingdom of Prussia, and the German empire under Prussian leadership, were an outgrowth of this development. When Napoleon I destroyed the last remnants of the Holy Roman Empire of the German Nation, political leadership passed to the combined East German powers of Austria and Prussia, an alliance which successfully defended the German heritage and freed Germany from French domination and oppression. It is for this reason that the history of Austria can only be understood with a view to the larger context of the history of central Europe.

The House of Hapsburg and the Swiss Confederation. The independence of Switzerland was achieved in a prolonged struggle of the free Swiss peasant and city communes against the absolutistic claims of the rising territorial state of Austria. The Swiss Confederation originated in the league of the three Alpine cantons of Schwyz, Uri, and Unterwalden. The inhabitants of these rural districts had formed a defensive alliance against their Hapsburg overlords and more specifically against Rudolf of Hapsburg. After the latter's death the league developed into a formal confederation, whose peasant armies won their first decisive victory over the Hapsburg knights at Morgarten (1315). They were afterward joined by neighboring cities and cantons and defeated the Hapsburgs again at Sempach (1386) and Näfels (1388), thereby consolidating their political autonomy. The last Hapsburg attempt at restoration of the *status quo ante* was successfully frustrated in the so-called "Zurich-War" (*Zürich-Krieg*) of 1436–1450. By 1516 the number of cantons had increased to 13, including Zug, Glarus, Lucerne, Zurich, Berne, Basel, the southern French-speaking Valais with the valley of the upper Rhone, and the Italian-speaking Ticino (*Tessin*), south of the Saint Gotthard Pass.

The new Swiss peasant democracy of Europe rested ethnologically upon a combination of Alemanic and Romanic tribal and racial characteristics; it rested politically and culturally on the semiautonomy of individual cities and cantons. During the following centuries various subdivisions brought the number of cantons to 22, and this cantonal system of administration was acknowledged and preserved by the powers at the Congress of Vienna (1814–1815, cf. p. 454 sqq.). Nominally the Swiss Confederation remained a part of the Holy Roman Empire to the end of the Thirty Years' War (1648).

Decline of Feudal Law, and the Holy Veme. The victories of the Swiss peasant armies over the heavily armored Austrian knights was one of the many symptoms of the approaching doom of the age of knighthood. The knights would indeed have become the forgotten men of the new age, if a goodly number of them had not disgraced their name and calling by exhibiting a complete disregard for law, order, and decency. As highwaymen and robber-knights they became the parasites and playboys of the age. The rising money economy had reduced their means of livelihood, while the new methods of warfare steadily reduced their military superiority. When they were not passing their days in enforced idleness in their castles, they would ravage and ransack the countryside, taking their revenge on the prospering though despised "pepper-bags" (merchants) from the cities, who had undermined the bases of their subsistence. Feudal law, whose provisions for self-defense were deeply rooted in ancient Germanic legal concepts, now degenerated into "club law" (*Faustrecht*) and was used as a pretense for attacks upon monasteries, villages, and traveling merchants. Imperial power had grown too weak to act as a law-enforcing agency. The people, therefore, unwilling to tolerate the outrages of the knightly robber bands, began to organize for the suppression of crime and lawlessness.

The "Holy Veme" was originally a Westphalian peasant court, deriving its methods of legal procedure from the old free courts of Carolingian times, judgment being passed by bailiffs (*Schöffen*), who were presided over by a *Freigraf* (count). The Veme developed into a secret society of vigilantes, who counted among their members many noblemen and even Sigismund, the German emperor, who welcomed the organization as an efficient means to check the legal anarchy that had risen in the Empire. The trials were surrounded with great secrecy, and a solemn oath bound all members "to hold and conceal the Holy Veme from wife and child, from father and mother, from sister and brother, from fire and wind, from everything upon which the sun shines or the rain falls, from everything between earth and heaven." The proceedings were conducted with elaborate rites and cere- monial symbolisms. The death penalty was inflicted by hanging. In case the accused person refused to appear before the court, he was solemnly pronounced as outlawed (*vogelfrei*), and every member was in duty bound to carry out the dread sentence of the law. The later development of the Veme in the fifteenth century led to an increasing abuse of its power and to its final suppression by law. The authority of these secret tribunals had never been established by due legal process but was based chiefly on the moral force of public opinion.

Emancipation of the State and Beginning Decline of the Church. The three major events that left their indelible mark on European civilization in the fourteenth and fifteenth centuries were the struggle between Emperor Louis the Bavarian and Pope John XXII; the "Babylonian Captivity" of the papacy at Avignon; and the Conciliar Movement.

a) Boniface VIII and the Bull "Unam Sanctam."   When Pope Boniface VIII (1294–1303) tried to restate and reassert the political claims of the papacy, he met with the strong resistance of the rising territorial monarchies of France and England. Although Boniface was as firmly convinced as Gregory VII (cf. p. 71 sqq.) that there was only one real head of the Christian commonwealth and that the papacy had been endowed by Christ with temporal as well as spiritual power, the feudal might of the Church was thoroughly broken, and the days of the feudal state were likewise numbered. Boniface, whom Dante's *Divine Comedy* relegates to the "Inferno," was a character of the early Renaissance: haughty, vainglorious, avaricious, and also extremely practical minded, a canonist who was fond of any outward display of power but oblivious of all strictly spiritual motivations. In his Bull *"Unam Sanctam"** of 1302 he solemnly declared that "for salvation it is absolutely necessary for every creature to be subject to the Roman pontiff." A few years earlier (1296) the Bull *"Clericis Laicos"* had forbidden the clergy of any country to pay subsidies to secular rulers without the pope's consent. Both documents had been drafted in connection with Boniface's quarrels with King Philip IV (the Fair) of France. The im- mediate result of these controversies was an open rebellion of the French

---

* Papal bulls and encyclical letters are usually named after the first two words of their text.

king and the French National Assembly and their appeal to a general Church council. Boniface was taken prisoner by the French chancellor but released shortly afterward. He died in 1303, leaving the authority of the Papal See at the mercy of the French crown.

b) Louis the Bavarian and Pope John XXII. The king of France succeeded in persuading the College of Cardinals to elect Clement V (1305–1314), a Frenchman, to the papal throne. Clement then established the papal capital in the city of Avignon (1308), which was a fief of the Holy Roman Empire and, though located on the border of France and thus within the sphere of French influence, was not actually a French city. Clement V appointed twenty-eight cardinals, twenty-five of whom were Frenchmen, in this way ensuring an unbroken line of French popes, seven in all. The period of predominating French influence in papal elections and papal policies is known in the history of the Church as the "Babylonian Captivity" (1309–1376).

Clement V was followed by John XXII (1316–1334), who revived the claims of Boniface VIII and went so far as to demand the right to appoint the German king. The result was his clash with Louis the Bavarian, one of the two claimants to the imperial crown.

c) The "Defensor Pacis." In his counterattack Louis made use of the services of his court physician, Marsilius of Padua (*c.* 1290–1342), who with his famous political tract *Defensor Pacis* (Defender of the Peace) popularized the traditional medieval theory of the State which in its essential features was based on the political philosophy of Aristotle and Thomas Aquinas and only deviated from tradition when it subordinated papal authority to the State and denied the primacy of the bishop of Rome (the pope). It had been one of the main tenets of medieval political theory in the West from the ninth to the thirteenth century to extol the supremacy of the law of the State over all its members, even over kings and princes. This theory maintained that positive State law, in order to be valid, must be based on the natural law and that as such it expressed the traditions, customs, and wishes of the whole community.

It is this point of view that distinguishes the political philosophy of Thomas Aquinas or John of Salisbury (*c.* 1115–1180, scholastic philosopher of the School of Chartres) from the concepts of an Oriental State absolutism, based on the presumption of a "divine right of kings." The community being the ultimate source of all State authority, its members may legitimately take action against unjust rulers and unjust laws. The idea of the sovereignty of the people is thus deeply embedded in medieval political theory, but inseparably linked with the sanctions that are embodied in the divine law, the natural law, and the law of reason. According to John Quidort of Paris, a Dominican friar of the end of the thirteenth century (✝ 1306), royal power is derived from God but with the consent and elective power of the people (*a populo consentiente et eligente*). The innovation in Quidort's position is his rejection of the temporal power of the papacy and the strict separation of ecclesiastical and secular jurisdiction. The Church is confined to the sacramental order, while the State is conceived of as an autonomous and completely secularized organism. As Christ rules only over a spiritual kingdom and not over earthly goods, so the pope can claim no domination but only ministration.

These arguments are repeated with even greater emphasis in regard to the autonomy of the secular State by Marsilius of Padua and John of Jandun (✝ 1328), his collaborator. Quidort's political liberalism issues in undisguised naturalism, anticipating Machiavelli's complete emancipation of politics from moral sanctions (cf. p. 247 sqq.).

The *Defensor Pacis* calls the claims of the Bull *"Unam Sanctam"* — papal jurisdiction over the affairs of the Empire and the right of controlling elections — a "laughable arrogation." No bishop is head of the Church by any other title than by a spiritual life and by human delegation. But the Roman bishop has usurped secular power and thereby perverted ecclesiastical legislation. He intends to destroy the authority of the princely electors by denying that the king or emperor-elect is invested with full legal power. By opposing such papal claims to temporal authority, the emperor acts as "defender of the peace." As the adviser of Louis the Bavarian, Marsilius of Padua staged a practical demonstration of his political theories when, in 1328, he had Louis proclaimed emperor by the people of Rome and, shortly afterward, had an antipope (Nicholas V) chosen in the same way.

d) The Great Schism and the Conciliar Movement. Marsilius had demanded that in all matters of dogma and doctrine the final decision should not rest with the pope but with a general council of the whole Church. Not being derived from the Scriptures, papal authority, according to Marsilius, could only be delegated by a general council or by State legislation.

The popular movement that favored the authority of a standing committee of the Church or a general Church council to replace the centralized power of the Roman pontiff received a new impetus from the events which led to the "Great Schism." The "Babylonian Captivity" ended with the return of Pope Gregory IX (1371–1378) to Rome. He died shortly afterward, and the following conclave (the electoral assembly of cardinals) conferred the papal dignity on the Neapolitan Urban VI (1378–1389). Because of the latter's refusal to return to Avignon, the French cardinals, maintaining that the election had been influenced by the pressure of the Roman mob, elected Clement VII (1378–1394) as antipope and thereby started that disastrous division of the Church known as the "Great Schism" (1378–1418). The rival pope set up his residence at Avignon.

The Council of Pisa (1409) summoned both popes, and upon their refusal to appear and to recognize the authority of the council, it declared them deposed and proceeded to elect Alexander V, formerly archbishop of Milan; after Alexander's early death (1410) they gave their votes to the wily and energetic John XXIII, whose shady past (he had been a freebooter) could but further discredit the dignity of his office. Since neither the aged Gregory XII (1406-1415), the third of the successors of Urban VI in Rome, nor Benedict XIII (1394-1424), Clement VII's successor in Avignon, would recognize the decisions of the Council of Pisa, the year 1410 witnessed three rival claimants to the papal throne, while in the same year three rival candidates — Wenceslaus, Sigismund, and Jodocus of Moravia — contended for the secular rulership of the Christian commonwealth.

At the Council of Constance (1414-1418) all three popes were forced to abdicate, the schism was ended with the election of Martin V, a Roman cardinal of the Colonna family (1417-1431), and the papacy returned to Rome. While the Council of Constance could do little to do away with the abuses which had led to the schism, it issued a decree which asserted the superiority of a general council over the pope, and aided the Conciliar Movement by providing for future convocations and deliberations of general councils of the Church.

A new attempt to accomplish what the Council of Constance had failed to bring about was made at the Council of Basel (1431-1449). Its main objectives were: reform of the Church "in head and members," and re-union with the schismatic Greek Orthodox Church, which had been separated from Rome since the eleventh century. Both moves failed to materialize in the end, and factional disputes as well as a general lack of clear thought and concerted action were soon to paralyze the efforts made in behalf of the conciliar theory.

Pope Martin V had been succeeded by Eugenius IV (1431-1447), who was uncompromisingly opposed to the theory that the pope should be merely the first official of a constitutional assembly. He tried to gain control of the general council by transferring it from Basel to Ferrara and later to Florence. Thereupon the members of the rump council who stayed in Basel, ignoring a papal decree of dissolution, declared the pope deposed and elected Felix V as antipope. Eugenius, however, succeeded in rallying most of the European powers to his support, thus forcing his papal rival into submission and resignation. By declaring itself dissolved in 1449, the Council of Basel silently acknowledged the defeat of the Conciliar Movement.

The principle that the decisions of general Church councils should take precedence over papal decrees, which had been agreed upon at Constance and Basel, was voided by Aeneas Sylvius Piccolomini, who had been Frederick III's secretary and poet laureate at his court, and who ascended the papal throne as Pius II (1458-1464). He was one of the leading Humanists (cf. p. 244 sqq.) and without any doubt the greatest representative of the papacy in the fifteenth century. After having at first supported the antipope, Felix, he afterward sided with Eugenius IV and was instrumental in bringing about the Concordat of Vienna (1448). In concluding this solemn treaty with the Holy See, Germany followed the example of France which had secured her national and political autonomy by the "Pragmatic Sanction" of Bourges (1438), which clearly defined the limits of papal interference in ecclesiastical elections as well as in matters of papal taxation and jurisdiction. The Concordat of Vienna contributed to the temporary appeasement of the relations of State and Church, redefining the mutual spheres of influence, and conferring certain benefits and material advantages on both partners. In his Bull *"Execrabilis"* (1460) Pius II denounced any future appeal to a general council as an "execrable abuse," thereby giving the lie to his own former convictions and wiping out the last vestiges of the conciliar theory.

Black Death, Flagellants, Persecution of the Jews. In the years 1349–1350 Europe was visited by the most devastating epidemic in all its history, the Black Death or bubonic plague. It was an event of such enormous dimensions that it left a lasting impress on the physiognomy of the age, and some historians have even attributed epochal significance to the plague and its consequences. It added to the many sinister forebodings of the waning Middle Ages an aspect of gloom and despair, so that henceforth the dreaded figure of Death and the "Dance of Death" becomes a familiar theme in preaching and teaching, thinking and living, in theology as well as in literature and the arts.

It is estimated that twenty-five million of the population of Europe died as victims of the plague, which in all probability had been introduced from the Far East, spreading from Asia Minor and North Africa to the ports of southern Europe and from there across the whole continent, including England. In Germany there was hardly a village that was spared the horrible visitation.

The populace and their ecclesiastical and secular leaders felt inclined to look upon the plague as a judgment of God, passed upon a faithless generation whose members in Church and State had rent the seamless garment of Christ by revolt, discord, and anarchy. The bloody struggles between the Welfs and Waiblingens (cf. p. 89 sqq.), the Mongolian invasions, earthquakes, floods, and upheavals of every kind were the common experience of everyone and, together with the prophecies of the Benedictine theologian Joachim of Fiore († 1202) and others, had given rise to the general expectation of the approaching end of the world.

As early as the thirteenth century groups of penitents had organized mass processions and pilgrimages in the Romanic countries, but the movement reached its climax in the years of the Black Death. Intimidated and frightened people from every walk of life joined the processions of the "Flagellants," religious fanatics who went from town to town, carrying crosses, singing hymns, burning candles and incense, and lashing themselves with iron-spiked scourges. Wherever they went, they were met by large numbers of enthusiastic and credulous people, often by the entire population of a town or village, so that they themselves became the most dangerous carriers of the plague. They preached repentance and mortification, attacking not only the widespread and flagrant abuses in State and Church but all civil and ecclesiastical authority. It is hardly surprising, then, that in the end they were branded as heretics and proscribed as enemies of society.

The cruel and fanatical persecution of the Jews that took place about the middle of the fourteenth century was partly instigated and generally encouraged by the Flagellants. The Jews were suspected of having poisoned the wells and thereby caused the Black Death. Social, religious, and racial hatreds combined brought about the massacres of the years 1348–1351. A contemporary Strasbourg chronicle describes the burning of Jews on a funeral pyre that was erected in the cemetery. Similar scenes were enacted in scores of towns. In many cases the Jews put fire to their own houses and perished in the flames. The imperial government made no attempt to punish the excesses. The property of the victims was confiscated and fell to the crown or the municipalities.

John Huss and the Hussite Wars. The trial and burning of John Huss (1369–1415) and the bloody civil war that followed it offers an interesting illustration of the growing nationalistic feeling in Europe. John Huss was the hero, leader, and exponent of a movement that represented a compound of religious, national, and social motivations. Theologically Huss was influenced by the doctrines of the Oxford scholar, John Wyclif (c. 1324–1384), who demanded that the Church be expropriated and reduced to the simplicity and poverty of the early Christian centuries. Wyclif defended the superiority of the State over the Church in temporal matters, defined the Church as the community of those who are predestined for salvation, appealed to the authority of the Bible as against that of dogma and canon law, and denied the dogma of "transubstantiation" (the real transformation of the substance of bread and wine into the substance of Christ's body and blood in the consecration of the Mass).* He insisted that only a worthy priest could validly administer the sacraments and thereby renewed the Donatist heresy against which St. Augustine in the fifth century had asserted the objective character of sacramental grace. He urged a thorough reform of ecclesiastical organization and discipline, and attacked the veneration of saints, the granting of absolution from sins in the sacrament of penance, and the practice of indulgences (the remission of temporal punishment, as distinct from eternal punishment, through the application of the accumulated merits of Christ and the saints). Wyclif was expelled from Oxford but enjoyed the backing of the British crown and parliament. After the peasant revolt in England of the year 1381 his followers, the "Lollards" ("lullers," poor, singing priests), were persecuted as heretics.

Wyclif's ideas had spread to Bohemia, where they provided John Huss, who held a professorship at the University of Prague, with his arguments against the corrupt Bohemian clergy. But Huss went beyond an attack on religious doctrines and practices. He was a Czech nationalist and a fierce and eloquent preacher of social reform, and as such he advocated the use

---

* The dogma of "transubstantiation" maintains that while the "substance" is thus transformed, the "accidents" or properties (color, shape, extension, etc.) remain unchanged.

of the vernacular in the liturgy and launched a campaign against the wealth of the clergy as well as against the dominating influence of German ecclesiastics in the Bohemian Church. His demand for the use of the vernacular in the liturgy became the battle cry and symbol for a national revival movement of the Czechs. After the "Golden Bull" (1356, cf. p. 165) had confirmed the independence of the kingdom of Bohemia and had urged the teaching of the native Czech language, Slavic nationalism rose in full force, extending to secular and religious matters alike. A national Czech literature was in the making, and the Bible was translated into the national language. Thus the political implications of the Hussite movement were soon to overshadow its religious significance.

John Huss, who enjoyed the backing of King Wenceslaus and a large part of the population of Prague, was urged by Emperor Sigismund to appear before the Council of Constance to answer to the charge of heresy. As early as 1412 Huss had been indicted and excommunicated by the archbishop of Prague, but now he received from the emperor a guarantee of safe-conduct and hoped that once he were given a chance to answer his enemies in public, he would easily sway them with the power and fire of his oratory.

However, Huss reached Constance before Sigismund, and the emperor upon his arrival learned with dismay that the safe-conduct had been violated and that after a brief hearing Huss had been thrown into a dungeon. Huss's enemies argued that, first, a heretic was beyond the pale of even the protection of the emperor and that, second, it was not necessary to keep faith with one who himself had broken faith with God. On the other hand, it seems that only now did the emperor learn the seriousness of the charges that were advanced against Huss, and that he was shocked and horrified by the radical views of the would-be reformer. Huss was given no opportunity to explain and defend his doctrines, but at four council hearings was urged to recant. After the second hearing the emperor left John Huss to his fate with these words: "If you persist in your errors, it is for the council to take its measures. I have said that I will not defend a heretic; nay, if anyone remained obstinate in heresy, I would burn him with my own hands." Huss was found guilty of heresy, handed over to the secular arm, and burned at the stake.

The Hussite party of Bohemia almost immediately rallied to avenge the martyrdom of their national hero. The clergy, nobles, and cities sent a strongly worded protest to Constance, while a group of Huss's followers seized half a score of the city councilors of Prague and hurled them through the windows of the city hall to the street below, where the frenzied mob tore them to pieces. This event marked the beginning of the Bohemian revolt and the Hussite wars (1415–1436).

The uprising, aside from being anti-German, soon became distinctly socialistic in character, giving exaggerated emphasis to certain democratic and liberalistic aspects in Wyclif's and Huss's teachings. The war was waged on the part of the Hussites with all the ferocity and fanaticism of a national crusade. Imperial armies were repeatedly sent against the Bohemians, but they crumbled before the invincible courage of the rebels. Not until the year 1436 could actual peace be restored, and then only by a compromise on the part of the Empire and the Church. The so-called "Compactates of Prague" secured for the Bohemians some of their religious objectives: communion in both kinds (the host and the chalice as well, which in the Roman Catholic rite is allowed to the celebrating priest only), the free preaching of the Gospel, and the right to try members of the clergy before secular courts. The more radical wing of the Hussite party formed the nucleus of the sect of the "Moravian Brethren" whose members were to play an important part in the pietistic revival movement of the seventeenth and eighteenth centuries (cf. p. 364 sqq.). King Wenceslaus had died as one of the first victims of the war. Emperor Sigismund, his brother, could enter Prague in 1436 as king of Bohemia, but he died in the following year.

William of Occam, Nicholas of Cusa, and the Political Reform. It was significant that at the meetings of the Council of Constance the participating nations and their ecclesiastical representatives were holding separate sessions, formulating their policies by majority vote, before they met the other nations in plenary session. In doing so they acted as national parliaments, and it was undoubtedly the parliamentary type of government in England, as established in a rudimentary form by the Magna Charta of 1215, which provided the pattern for the proceedings at general councils of the Church, the cardinals constituting a standing committee of the Church, and the pope presiding as the chosen executive.

a) William of Occam and Nominalism. Two essential innovations are implied in the theories that underlie the political structure of the Council of Constance. The one points to the nationalization of the Church, the other to the transfer of the idea of the sovereignty of the people from the State to the Church. The credit for having provided the intellectual bases of these fundamental changes belongs to William of Occam († 1349 in Munich), a Franciscan theologian and philosopher, who was born in England, taught at the University of Paris, was excommunicated in 1328, and found refuge and protection at the court of Emperor Louis the Bavarian. A great scholar and a prolific writer, he must be considered as the most important forerunner of Martin Luther, some of whose central theological convictions he anticipated.

As a representative of the nominalistic branch of scholastic philosophy (cf. p. 142), Occam deprives religion of its rational foundations, substituting the irrationality of a dark, miraculous, and paradoxical unintelligibility. Tertullian's (c. 160–220) famous saying: *"Credo quia absurdum"* (I believe, because the object of my faith is an incomprehensible paradox) expresses the quintessence of Occam's theology. His God is an arbitrary and absolutistic ruler, who is bound neither by the laws of nature nor by the laws of reason. In his denial of the law of causality Occam anticipates

Hume's and Kant's criticism, while in his denial of substances and universals he is in essential agreement with the pragmatism and behaviorism of today. His denial of an objective universal order of nature leaves no room for a rational ethics which could be based on such an order. If realities, such as good, evil, order, law, truth, falsehood, and every kind of universal concept and predication is a mere nominal label and an expedient convention, there remains nothing but the testimony of the individual conscience, whose authority and judgment must be final, because it constitutes the only certainty which exists. In this emphasis upon the subjective certitude of individual consciousness Occam points forward to Descartes's (1596–1650) *"Cogito, ergo sum"* (I think, therefore I am), who made this kind of certitude the starting point of his philosophy. Furthermore, the denial of causality implies the denial of finality, and with the rejection of a teleological universe (one of graduated causes, means, and ends) the road is cleared for the rise of the *"nuova scienza"* (new science) of mechanical physics.

In his social ideals as well as in his struggle against the papacy William of Occam is to some extent determined by his Franciscan heritage. He belonged to that radical group of "Spiritual" Franciscans who had been condemned by Pope John XXII for their uncompromising adherence to the ideal of absolute poverty and a voluntary communism on a religious basis. In opposing the theories on property and private ownership advanced by John XXII, Occam wrote a monumental work on social philosophy (*Opus Nonaginta Dierum,* "The Work of Ninety Days"), outlining in 126 chapters a comprehensive system of Christian communism, designed for the reorganization of the Church. The secular order, on the other hand, is pessimistically conceived as being perverted and corrupted by sin and therefore subject to the rule of force and violence. William of Occam no longer believes in the possibility of a just and reasonable social order in the secular sphere, and therefore relinquishes the norm of the natural law, on which Thomas Aquinas had built the system of his social and political philosophy. Occam quite logically, then, proclaims an almost complete autonomy of the political and economic spheres. In his teaching, Church and laity, God and world, supernature and nature are separated by an unbridgeable chasm.

Occam's masterpiece is the *Dialogus* (Dialogue), in which he attacks the papal claims to temporal authority and sets definite limits to the spiritual power of the papacy by appealing to the authority of the Bible. It is in this work that he applies the principle of the sovereignty of the people to the ecclesiastical realm. All rulers, including the pope, have received their power indirectly from God but directly and immediately from the people and the commonwealth. The sovereignty of the people may be exercised in the form of a referendum, each parish or community delegating their representatives to a bishop's council or royal parliament, whose members in turn elect delegates for a general council, in which laymen as well as women may be represented. The pope like any other ruler is limited in his authority by the will and the general welfare of his constituents.

In examining the leading ideas of the political and religious reformation in the following centuries it is impossible to avoid the realization of the fact that William of Occam's thought has proven a most vital influence in the making of the secularized modern world.

b) Nicholas of Cusa's Attempted Reform. The period from the middle of the fourteenth to the middle of the fifteenth century marks the beginning of the modern world. The major events and movements — the "Great Schism," the Councils of Constance and Basel, the rise of the great city republics of Italy and Flanders, the German city leagues, the European peasant revolts — they all signalize the dissolution of medieval civilization and the approaching political, social, and religious revolution and reformation.

While in England and France the nationalistic tendencies in the Church were firmly anchored in the national State, in Germany the mystical movement prevented such a consolidation. German mysticism (cf. p. 146 sqq.), the *"philosophia Teutonica,"* prepared the way for a nonecclesiastical form of piety, a religion without a priestly hierarchy, a devotion with an anticlerical bias. Especially in the Netherlands this new form of piety (*devotio moderna*) gained considerable influence on the thought and culture of the new age. It was here, in the circles of the "Brethren of the Common Life," that the *Imitation of Christ* originated, a manual of Christian devotion, which, notwithstanding its strict orthodoxy, owes its modernity and universal appeal to the same practical and communal bent of mind that made the schools of the Brethren in Deventer and Windesheim model institutions of humanistic education. In Deventer (Holland) the great Erasmus of Rotterdam (cf. p. 249 sq.) received his early training.

A similar religious atmosphere and environment furnished the background for the life and thought of Nicholas (Krebs) of Cusa (1401–1464), a native of the Moselle district, who grew up in the still orthodox but broad and many-colored world of ideas as advanced by men like Gerard Groote (1340–1384), Florentius Radewyn (1350–1400), and Thomas à Kempis (1379–1471). These influences left their marks on the mind of the future bishop and cardinal, while at the same time the numerous heretical, anticlerical, and antiauthoritarian societies in the Rhineland and in Holland, the "Brethren of the Free Spirit," the "Friends of God," and the "Lollards," impressed upon him the need for ecclesiastical reform. In 1432 we find Nicholas of Cusa at the council tables of Basel and afterward of Florence and Ferrara. We see him turn against the conciliar theory which he had at first defended and become an eloquent advocate of papal rights at the Diets of Mainz, Nuremberg, and Frankfurt. As a papal legate he traverses Germany, Austria, and the Netherlands, carries on negotiations with the Hussites and the Greeks, trying to arbitrate and to reconcile opposing points of view in political and religious matters.

Nicholas of Cusa is one of the great philosophers of Germany and the first one of her speculative geniuses in modern times. In a unique way he combines tradition and progress, being as much at home in antiquity as in the medieval and modern worlds. He combines a Greek sense of form, proportion, and moderation with Gothic spirituality and modern individualism. His keen critical sense recognized the shortcomings of the feudal system and the danger of a narrow and selfish particularism and partyism for Church and State. If he could have had his way, Germany might have been spared many of the upheavals that followed the Lutheran reformation. "Nicholas of Cusa appeared in Germany as an angel of light and peace in the midst of darkness and confusion. . . . He was a man of faith and love, an apostle of piety and learning," wrote John Trithemius, abbot of Sponheim (1462–1516).

The scholastic pattern of his philosophy was enriched and invigorated by a strong overtone of Neo-Platonic mysticism. His God is the "unity of opposites" (*coincidentia oppositorum*); He is beyond all that is knowable and finite and yet the innermost essence of everything that there is; the greatest and the smallest ("*Deus est omnia, quae esse possunt, maximum et minimum*"), comprising in Himself every type of being and becoming, while the universe, conversely, in its entirety and in every part is a mirror and representation of the Godhead. All human knowledge is a "learned ignorance" (*Docta Ignorantia*), and only the Socratic philosopher who realizes his own ignorance may hope to approach the mysteries of reality and to explore the depths of the unknown. All creatures are related to God, glorifying Him as the supreme Artist, the Creator, and Father of all.

Some of the ideas of the great Cardinal of Cusa live on in the philosophical system of Leibniz (1646–1716); his mathematical speculations in Leibniz' discussions of the infinitesimal calculus; his theory of individual monads — vital centers of energy, forming the ultimate constituent parts of the universe — in Giordano Bruno's (1548–1600) and Leibniz' *Monadology*. And, like Leibniz, Nicholas of Cusa drew up a program for the reunion of the separated churches and the unification of religious creeds, inspired by a visualization of a unified Christendom under the rule of Christ the King.

The New City Culture. The inhabitants of the newly developed city communes were the creators of new forms of life and civilization, which they cultivated in conscious opposition to the medieval culture of chivalry. The feudal idea of a social pyramid and the system of mutual services and obligations which it entailed was replaced by the self-sufficiency and the pride of the burgher class. Human value was no longer inherent in social functions and in privileges of birth but was found in human nature as such, in personal vision, individual initiative, and in critical search and research.

Rudolf of Hapsburg (cf. p. 162 sq.) was the first German ruler whose personality bore the imprint of the new age and who was therefore an emperor with a great popular appeal. When he was still governor (*Landvogt*) in his ancestral province of Alsace, he sided with the citizens of Strasbourg in their struggle with their bishop, and he held his protecting hand over the merchants who traveled across the peaks of the Alps. He preferred the company of simple city folk, of artisans and craftsmen, to that of minnesingers and courtiers.

a) Fashion in the Fifteenth Century. The increasing wealth of the burgher class as well as their contact with foreign manners and customs led to a growing extravagance in the world of fashion. Many city ordinances and imperial as well as local statutes attempted to put a check on the immoderate indulgence in luxuries. In 1445, the city of Regensburg enacted a law that set eighteen dresses and eighteen coats as an upper limit for a woman's wardrobe.

The modes of apparel for men grew more and more effeminate. The lords and knights began to wear their hair long and curly and tried to imitate women in dress and gait. They bared their necks and shoulders and wore necklaces and bracelets. Men and women alike were fond of many-colored costumes, fashioned of costly imported materials, such as damasks interwoven with gold and silver threads, velvet, brocade, fur, and Flemish lace. The shoe points became so long that they rendered walking difficult and had to be tied to the knees by means of a chainlet. (A Regensburg city ordinance of 1485 restricts the maximal length of shoe points to two inches.) The detachable sleeves of the upper garments were either so tight that they hindered the freedom of movement or so wide that they would drag on the ground. The tight-fitting costumes, as they prevailed especially in the Burgundian fashion, were slit open at different places, showing the silk lining and the finely plaited silken French shirt underneath. Bells of different size and shape were often attached to hems, belts, and shoes.

b) Family Life. Craftsmen, artisans, merchants, and professional men who kept careful records of their families in the form of chronicles give evidence of a strong clannish feeling. The overplus of women still forced a large number of the female members of the family to join religious communities, either regular convents or semimonastic beguinages (cf. p. 125).

Sex life in the fourteenth and fifteenth centuries had become very irregular. Adultery and concubinage were no longer as strongly resented by law and public opinion as in the earlier medieval centuries or in Germanic antiquity. Illegitimate children were often brought up together with the legitimate ones, and they even inherited part of the family possessions.

The dowry of a burgher's daughter usually represented a considerable amount of money, and each house father took pride in providing in the best possible way for the security and comfort of his offspring. Marriages were contracted at an early age, and frequently, especially in the wealthier classes, the married couple continued to live in the parental household. Early marriages among the poorer burghers and peasants, on the other hand, caused a good deal of social misery and destitution.

Prolific families were the rule rather than an exception, and infant mortality was correspondingly high. Ecclesiastical and secular legislation protected mother and child and provided severe penalties for abortion.

The number of servants was much larger than in later centuries. They were considered as part of the family, sharing in the weal and woe of their employers. Wages were very low, legal protection was entirely insufficient, and there were no provisions for old age and sickness. The relationship between employer and employee was accordingly a patriarchal one, based on considerations of charity rather than of social justice.

All classes indulged in eating and drinking without any sense of moderation, especially on festive occasions. The culinary arts developed under foreign influence. Spices were used in increasing quantities, and every kind of food and drink was strongly seasoned. Meat was preferred to any other food, and strongly salted gravies were served with meat, fish, and vegetables. Many varieties of pastries, puddings, cakes, and tarts are indications of the growing refinement of the German cuisine. The first cookbooks were written by hand and date back to the fourteenth century. The most comprehensive of the earliest printed cookbooks is the one by Marx Rumpolt (Frankfurt, 1576). When Bishop John II of Speyer solemnly took office in 1461, the bill of fare on this festive occasion consisted of the following courses: (1) Mutton and chicken in almond milk; fried baby pigs, geese, carp, and pike, with baked dumplings; (2) venison in black pepper sauce; rice with sugar and baked trout, gingered all over; sugar cakes; (3) fried geese, filled with eggs; carp and pike in gravy and berry jam; baked pastry with white and red wine.

Wine and beer were the most popular drinks. Mead was consumed chiefly by peasants. Brandy was at first (fourteenth century) used exclusively as a medicine. "Whoever drinks half a spoonful of brandy every morning, he will never be sick," says a pamphlet of the year 1483. Beer was consumed in large quantities, and its quality had considerably improved. Home-brew was less frequently manufactured, while the community breweries became more and more numerous. Beer trade increased greatly in volume, especially in the North, where the Hansa-cities acquired almost a monopoly. The North also produced the best-quality beers, the brews of Erfurt, Naumburg, Einbeck (*Bock*), Goslar, and Magdeburg taking the lead. The famous Brunswick brew (*Braunschweiger Mumme*) was the favorite beer of Martin Luther.

In the South, Nuremberg and Schwabach were outstanding brewing centers. But the South quite generally gave preference to the excellent products of the growing wine industry, the wines of the Rhine, Moselle, and Neckar regions, and those of Franconia ranking highest in quality. From Austria came the Tyrolese and Danubian wines, from Hungary the "Eastern wine" (*Osterwein*), from foreign countries the various Greek and Italian wines. The Swabian city of Ulm was the center of the German wine trade. The Scandinavian countries were Germany's chief customers.

Drunkenness, which the Roman Tacitus had mentioned as one of the weaknesses of the Germanic tribes, again became the national German vice in the fifteenth and sixteenth centuries. We read in Aventinus' (1477-1534)

Chronicle of Bavaria: "All the other nations speak evil of us, scolding us as a people who are no good except in carousing and revelling, drinking and slumming, and they call us the coarse, senselessly drinking Germans, always intoxicated, never sober."

Drinking bouts were held in the private drinking rooms of the guilds and in the homes of patricians as well as in hostels, taverns, and public houses. The day laborer, the servant, the wandering student, the peasant, the journeyman would frequent the public houses and taverns, where manners were coarse and service poor. The tavern (*Weinhaus*) could be recognized by its house mark, from which its name was usually derived. This symbolic emblem might have the shape of a green wreath, a barrel hoop, or a jug; or it might represent the coat of arms of some distinguished traveler who had stopped over and hung up his escutcheon.

Tablecloths and table utensils were now quite generally used, the plates being made of tin or wood. Knives and spoons were fashionable but forks were still missing, and the fingers were still considered the most suitable instruments in eating.

c) Feasts and Holidays. Most of the feasts of the ecclesiastical year were family festivals as well. At the end of the Middle Ages they were celebrated with greater splendor than ever before. Early in Advent, on December 6, St. Nicholas (Santa Claus), accompanied by his servant Rupert (*Knecht Ruprecht*), the mythical wanderer, in whom Odin (Wodan), the supreme god of the Germanic pantheon, lived on, went from house to house offering apples, walnuts, sweets, and pictures to well-behaved children. The children placed little paper boats in front of doors and windows so that St. Nicholas, the patron of skippers, might fill them with his gifts.

The sacred twelve nights between Christmas (*Weihnacht*) and Epiphany were the period of the turning of the year, and were filled with mysterious forebodings. Green branches adorned with colored ribbons and tinsel served as decoration, later replaced by the Christmas tree (first mentioned in Alsace about the middle of the sixteenth century). The crib with the Christ Child originally derives from the Christmas celebration of St. Francis of Assisi (1223), but in its present form it is a German creation of the later Middle Ages. The realistic rendition of the events of the holy night was developed to artistic perfection in the sixteenth century, in connection with the popular Christmas plays. From that time on the art of crib making can be traced through the centuries, experiencing unprecedented heights in Sicily and Naples at the beginning of the eighteenth century and later on in Bavaria, Austria, Silesia, the Rhineland, and Westphalia. In the later Middle Ages the children, masquerading as angels, shepherds, and kings, would wander from house to house, singing Christmas carols. Street singing likewise introduced the New Year (*Neujahr*); and Epiphany, the feast of the Three Wise Men from the East (*Dreikönigsfest*), again offered an opportunity to do homage to the child in the manger. At nightfall three boys in royal attire would carry a star on top of a tall pole, singing their "star-songs" (*Sternlieder*).

Preceding the season of Lent the old pagan instincts would come to life again in the celebration of "shrovetide" (*Fastnacht*). Reverting to the tradition of the Roman *"Saturnalia,"* men, women, and children, clergy and laity alike, disguised their identity and plunged into unchecked merriment and sensual pleasure. Among the floats of the shrovetide pageant (*Fastnachts-zug*) was the *carrus navalis,* a ship filled with masqueraders, from which the word "carnival" is derived. The ship symbolized originally the resumption of the shipping trade and traffic after the gloomy winter season.* The climax of the pageant was usually the performance of a shrovetide play in the market square.

The hilarity of the shrovetide was followed by the sorrow and lament of Ash Wednesday. Equipped with torches and lanterns people would go out and search for the defunct *Fastnacht;* they would conduct a mock funeral for her, while in the church choir the huge Lenten veil (*Fastentuch*) would be affixed to the wall, on which various scenes of Christ's Passion were depicted.

On Palm Sunday the children brought to the church bundles of palm leaves, which were blessed by the priest. They were then carried in solemn procession, children and members of the clergy impersonating young Hebrews and disciples, drawing or carrying a wooden statue of Christ, seated on a donkey. During Holy Week, Passion plays were performed in many German cities.

Easter, commemorating the resurrection of Christ, was the central feast of the Christian world. Its events, as they are embodied and dramatized in the liturgy of the Church, formed the nucleus for the development of a European drama. Many of the popular Easter customs point back to pre-Christian times. The jubilant sound of the Christian Easter bells mingled with the old Germanic joyful welcome extended to the awakening spring. In the countryside the Maypole was surrounded by dancing lads and maidens, a May Queen (*Maienkönigin*) or a May Count (*Maigraf*) was chosen and paraded about village and town. The "Easter fires" (*Osterfeuer*) were believed to protect the crops and to aid the fertility of the soil. The blessing of the elements at the entrance of the church on the morning of Holy Saturday includes the solemn kindling and blessing of fire. The most popular custom, however, was the giving away of the motley-colored Easter eggs (*Ostereier*), known and practiced all over Europe and apparently dating back to very ancient times. The Easter rabbit (*Osterhase*), who is supposed to lay the Easter eggs, probably owes this title of honor to his being widely known as a symbol of fertility, while the Easter lamb (*Oster-*

---

*Sebastian Brant appropriated this symbol when he wrote his *Ship of Fools* (*Das Narrenschiff*).

lamm) symbolizes the Paschal Lamb of the Old Testament, which fore-shadows Christ's sacrificial death.

The most magnificent ecclesiastical pageant was the Corpus Christi procession, which was held on the Thursday after Trinity Sunday and was instituted in 1246. It was a feast of thanksgiving to the eucharistic Christ and was celebrated with the participation of all classes of the population, clergy and laity alike. The day of *Corpus Christi* (*Fronleichnam*: the body of the Lord) stimulated the creation and production of "sacramental plays" (*Sakramentsspiele*), of which the great Spanish playwright Calderón de la Barca (1600–1681) became the unsurpassed master (*Autós Sacramentales*).

The festival enjoyment of the summer season was climaxed by the celebration of St. John's day (*Johannistag*), the birthday of John the Baptist, fraught with memories and superstitions of Germanic-pagan antiquity. As in olden times it was celebrated as the feast of the summer solstice, with fires kindled on the mountain peaks and the young folk jumping across the flames. Fiery wheels were rolled down the slopes and hillsides, while the ashes of the fires of St. John were poured over the fields.

Many German cities celebrated their own local feasts of a semisecular or secular and popular character, some of which have survived to the present day. Festivities were also customarily connected with the visits of high dignitaries of State and Church and with secular and ecclesiastic gatherings (diets and councils).

The knightly tournament (cf. p. 100) had become in the fourteenth and fifteenth centuries a favorite sport and entertainment not only of patricians but of members of the merchant class and even of peasants. Each city had its special playgrounds and rose gardens, which served for recreation and diverse kinds of sports and amusements, such as bowling, handball, dancing, and fencing. The love of dancing became a craze, so that not only guild halls, dance halls, and taverns would be invaded by dancing crowds, but churchyards, monasteries, and church porches were at times used indiscriminately as public ballrooms. Quite different from the light, loose, and lively popular dances of the younger generation were the solemn and heavy dance rhythms that had survived from the age of courtly culture. Obscenity and licentiousness characterized not only the peasant dances but sometimes those of the educated classes as well. The popular dance tunes of former times were partially replaced in the fourteenth and fifteenth centuries by instrumental accompaniment, the favorite instruments of the wandering minstrels and gleemen being the fife, the pipe and the bagpipe, the trumpet, the trombone, the harp, the lute, and the drum. Music was introduced in the urban home as a new form of social entertainment.

The riflemen of the cities were organized in guilds, the so-called brotherhoods of St. Sebastian, whom they had chosen as their patron saint. In the course of the fourteenth century the crossbow began to replace the heavy wooden bow, which with the invention of gunpowder gave way to the firearm. The great festivals of the rifle guilds (*Schützenfeste*), originating in the fourteenth century, were usually held in the season of Pentecost. The outstanding marksmen were given awards that varied in value and kind, such as geese, oxen, horses, cloths, banners, beakers, rings, belts, coins, and so forth. The winner of the first prize was pronounced "king of the marksmen" (*Schützenkönig*).

Card and dice games became a favorite pastime in the fourteenth and fifteenth centuries and were practiced openly or clandestinely in gambling houses. Playing cards, which had originated in the Orient, came to be manufactured in large quantities, especially as the invention of the printing press (cf. p. 189 sq.) facilitated mass production. Some of the foremost engravers tried their artistic skill in the making of playing cards. The oldest extant German deck, consisting of forty-eight cards, dates from the year 1475 and was printed in Ulm.

d) Public Baths, Immorality, and Prostitution. Of cultural interest are the customs and abuses connected with public and private bathing. It was generally believed that frequent bathing was an effective weapon against diseases and epidemic plagues. Private bathing facilities were provided in monasteries, castles, and the homes of the well-to-do burghers. The public bathhouses of the cities were leased to bath keepers (barber; German, *Bader*). These bathing establishments became more and more houses of public amusement and finally of moral depravity and prostitution. The bathers would spend many hours in the bathhouse, being waited on by maidservants, eating, drinking, gambling, singing, gossiping, and talking politics. Instead of being an aid to public health and hygiene, the bathing houses thus became centers of contagion, favoring the spread of epidemic diseases, such as cholera, syphilis, and the plague.

Besides these private and public baths there were the spas or natural mineral-water baths (*Wildbäder, Heilbäder, Naturbäder*), for the benefit chiefly of the upper strata of society. We have a description of Baden in the canton Aargau in Switzerland by Francesco Poggio Bracciolini, a citizen of Florence, who visited this spa when he attended the Council of Constance in 1417. He found gathered together there a motley crowd of statesmen, army officers, members of the secular clergy, monks, and nuns. The bathing establishments were frequented by men and women alike, and the baths were equipped with floating tables, upon which food and drink was served. The evenings were spent in dancing and other social diversions.

Public morals were quite generally at a low ebb in the fourteenth and fifteenth centuries, and no social class was exempt from the decline and confusion of ethical standards. Brothels (*Frauenhäuser*) were condoned by public opinion and legalized by the administration. On the occasion of princely receptions these houses were festively adorned with flowers and garlands, and the distinguished visitors of the town were greeted and presented with bouquets by the inmates (*Hübscherinnen*). The life of a prostitute was regulated by city ordinances. She was required to wear distinctive dress or a special mark, such as a yellow or red veil, a green or yellow cloak and red headdress. In old age they were abandoned to misery, destitution, crime, and disease, unless they had mended their ways and found refuge in one of the many "homes of St. Magdalen" (*Magdalenenheime*).

e) Commerce, Banking, Mining. Despite political factionalism and growing social unrest the country was still prosperous and filled with the spirit of venture and enterprise. At the turn of the fifteenth century the expansion of German commerce was evidenced by the thriving Hansa cities in the North, the fishing industries of the North Sea, the wealthy communities of the Rhine valley; the rich iron, copper, and silver mines of Austria, Bohemia, and central Germany. Frankfurt, Nuremberg, and Augsburg had their equals only in the leading Italian trade centers, such as Venice, Florence, or Genoa. The Medicis of Florence and the Fuggers of Augsburg were the most influential banking-houses of the fifteenth century.

These bankers were the pioneers of international finance in the modern sense. When Hans Fugger, a weaver from the district of Augsburg, died in 1409, he left his sons a considerable fortune. The younger son, Jacob († 1469), became the actual founder of the trading company of Fugger, while in turn his three sons, Ulrich, Georg, and Jacob, Jr., carried on their father's business, intermarried with noble families and, in 1473, received a patent of nobility from Emperor Frederick III. In 1519 the three brothers established in their native city of Augsburg a model settlement for the poor, consisting of fifty-three duplex houses (*Fuggerei*), constituting a section of the city that was well preserved at the beginning of World War II and was one of the major attractions shown to tourists. Emperor Maximilian I borrowed from the Fuggers the equivalent of two and one half million dollars, and Charles V as well as several of the popes obtained similar loans. Like the Medicis of Florence the Fuggers were generous patrons of the arts and of learning.

Much of the Fugger fortune was acquired by the exploitation of the German silver mines and by securing a monopoly of mining rights for certain districts. Banking and mining mutually depended on each other, banking capital facilitating the introduction of improved technical methods and wielding sufficient political and economic power to make the operation of the mines a worth-while and productive undertaking. With the general growth of the volume of trade and commerce the opportunities for profitable investment became more numerous and money circulation increased, especially with the importation of gold and silver from the mines of Mexico and Peru in the sixteenth century.

f) Means of Transportation and Communication. The use of the compass had been known to the Arabs, and important discoveries in the fields of cosmography and meteorology during the fourteenth and fifteenth centuries led to a notable advancement of overseas traffic. The ships of the Hansa advanced to the entrance of the Mediterranean. Nautical geography was greatly aided by the calculations of the German cosmographer, Martin Behaim (1459-1507), who undertook an expedition to the west coast of

Africa (1484–1486) and constructed the first globe. Transportation on land, on the other hand, was carried on in traditional primitive forms. The ordinary traveler usually rode across the country on horseback, while elderly and sickly people were either carried in a sedan chair or traveled in a closed carriage or coach.

Regular postal service was established at the end of the fifteenth century. Up to that time the exchange of written communications was complicated and difficult. In the Middle Ages princes, cities, monasteries, and universities had transmitted their messages by a special messenger and courier service. The Teutonic Knights had developed a very efficient system of relay posts. The cities in the interior of Germany followed their example in developing their own system of postal messengers. The imperial chancellery of the Hapsburg rulers employed special couriers and developed a fairly regular postal communication system during the reign of Frederick III.

From 1489 on we find members of the family of Taxis (later Thurn and Taxis) as imperial postmasters. In 1520 they were given charge of postal administration in all imperial territories. They controlled two main postal highways, the one running from the Netherlands through France and Spain, the other through southern Germany and Austria down to Venice, Milan, Rome, and Naples. In 1595 Emperor Rudolf II appointed Leonard of Taxis as "postmaster general." Later on, the territorial princes and the great urban trade centers established their own postal services, thereby becoming competitors of the imperial post and cutting in on its big revenues. The dissolution of the Holy Roman Empire (1806) invalidated most of the postal privileges of the Taxis family. The German-Austrian Postal Union of 1850 created a unified postal territory for the German and Austrian states. After the unification of the German states and the foundation of the new German Empire of 1871 the Imperial Postal Administration (*Reichspostverwaltung*) absorbed all the remaining local administrative units, with the exception of Bavaria and Wurtemberg (*Swabia*), which retained some degree of autonomy until 1919.

The Invention of Printing. The expansion of trade, commerce, and industry in the fifteenth century was accompanied by a growing desire for more efficient means and methods of education, which would give the average citizen access to the intellectual and scientific achievements of the past and present. The new craving for reading and for a broad general education was satisfied and received an even greater impetus through the invention of book printing with movable type.

Up to the middle of the fifteenth century books had to be written by hand. The manuscripts (*manu scribere;* "to write by hand") were the work of monks, and they were almost exclusively used in monastic libraries. The "Brethren of the Common Life" (cf. p. 180) were among the first professional copyists of religious books who tried to make their products available to the people at large. The fifteenth century witnessed the growth of a class of professional scribes in the cities.

It is only partly correct to speak of the "invention of printing" in the fifteenth century and to credit John Gensfleisch Gutenberg (*c.* 1400–1468) of Mainz with this discovery. The art of printing had been known to the Chinese, the Babylonians, the Romans, and other peoples of the ancient world. The Chinese had produced printed books before the beginning of the eleventh century A.D. Pictures, playing cards, pamphlets, and even books had been printed in Europe since the twelfth century by means of carved metal or wooden blocks (woodcuts, block prints). The invention of the manufacture of paper from rags considerably reduced the cost of the manuscripts and led to the gradual development of a regular book trade, which was in the hands of the so-called *stationarii* (stationers).

Gutenberg's important contribution to the art of printing was the invention of the movable metal types, which were cast separately with the aid of a "matrix" or model and could be assembled in any desired combination for any number of books. It was the great advantage of this innovation that books could now be printed in large quantities and at very moderate cost. Before the close of the fifteenth century more than one thousand printing presses had been established in Europe and more than thirty thousand editions had been published. In the sixteenth century Germany alone contributed nearly one million volumes to the general output. The most famous of the early printing firms were the Aldine Press at Venice, the Froben Press at Basel, and the Plantin Press at Antwerp. Five presses had been established at Mainz, six at Ulm, sixteen at Basel, twenty at Augsburg, and twenty-one at Cologne. More than one hundred German presses were operated in Italy. The first geographical maps were printed by Konrad Schweinsheim in 1471, and Erhard Oeglin invented the art of printing musical notes in movable type.

The earliest books printed with movable type are called *incunabulae* (*Inkunabeln, Wiegendrucke*). In type, format, and material they follow closely the old paper and parchment manuscripts. The Latin (*Antiqua*) type of letters, which resembled the old minuscules (cf. p. 53), was introduced into Germany from Italy, partly replacing the Gothic characters.

The invention of movable type aided greatly in providing the broadest possible forum for the teachings of the Humanists and the Reformers, and in arousing a widespread popular interest in political, social, and religious affairs. In the age of the Reformation the art of printing served as one of the most efficient weapons in the religious struggle. Germany as a nation prided herself on having given to the world a new method of education and public enlightenment. Everyone probably agreed with Jacob Wimpheling, one of the leaders of early German Humanism, when he wrote in 1507: "As in former times the apostles of Christianity, so now the disciples of the new sacred art of printing go out from Germany into all the lands, and their printed books become the heralds of the Gospel, the preachers of truth and knowledge."

Arts and Crafts. The German craftsman and artisan of the fourteenth

Section of the Virgin's Altar in Creglingen, by Tilman Riemenschneider.

and fifteenth centuries was justly proud of his exquisite workmanship. The products of his hands were highly praised and esteemed at home and abroad. The "Tomb of St. Sebald" in St. Sebald's Church in Nuremberg, containing the relics of the city's patron saint, and the famous tabernacle in St. Lawrence Church (*St. Lorenz*), in the same city, are adorned with the self-portrayals of their makers, Peter Vischer (*c.* 1460–1529) and Adam Krafft (*c.* 1455–1508), the former depicted with his leather apron and hammer, the latter shown in the company of two of his journeymen. The fame of the goldsmiths and metalworkers of Augsburg, Nuremberg, Cologne, Vienna, Ratisbon, Prague, and Ulm extended all over Europe, their crafts being greatly aided and encouraged by the brief revival of the spirit of knighthood under Emperor Maximilian I. The Tyrolese masters excelled in cabinetwork, such as the making of chests, cupboards, decorative portals, chancels, choir stools, and so forth.

In the age of prospering cities and expanding trade the wealthy merchants became the patrons of the arts. The artists themselves were little concerned about the originality of their work or their personal fame, so that it is often difficult to distinguish between the creations of the masters and those of their apprentices and journeymen. The public buildings, secular and ecclesiastic, were the result of the communal effort of the city, each social group contributing its proper share. Thus an intimate contact was established between the people, the artists, and the art works. The interrelation of art and life in the fourteenth century is reflected in the more realistic observation of the near and the concrete, the occurrences of everyday life, the small, the genrelike, and the idyllic.

German architecture of the fifteenth century lacks the depth and vitality of many monuments of the preceding age, but it excels in magnificent and imposing creations of ecclesiastical and secular art, cathedrals, town halls, and castles. The great works of late Gothic sculpture forego the solemnity and sublimity of the high Gothic and, in accordance with the taste of the burgher class, turn to the descriptive, the intimate, and the psychological. The statues partake of the fast and vigorous rhythm of city life. They are close to nature and indulge in phantastic decorative design, the abstract lineament of folds, exaggerated gesticulation, and a complex scale of emotions. In Nuremberg we find the artists Veit Stoss, Adam Krafft, and Peter Vischer; in Würzburg Tilman Riemenschneider (*c.* 1460–1531), the master of late Gothic wood sculpture in Franconia, whose works combine the religious inwardness of medieval sculpture with the psychological realism of the early Renaissance. In the peasant wars of 1524–1525 (cf. p. 240 sq.) this master joined the peasant armies who fought against the bishop of Würzburg, and was captured and subjected to severe torture.

The growing realism and individualism in the arts was most strikingly manifested in the Netherlands, whose culture was strongly and proudly Germanic and where the full national emancipation of occidental painting was brought about in the fifteenth century by such ingenious innovators as the brothers Hubert (*c.* 1370–1426) and Jan van Eyck (*c.* 1385–1440), the creators of the famous Altar of Ghent, who had been educated in the tradition of book illumination. Together they painted the Ghent altarpiece, the central panel depicting the "Adoration of the Lamb," symbolizing Christ and his sacrificial death, an illustration of the words of the Apocalypse: "I looked, and Lo, a Lamb stood on Mount Sion." In the background is the likewise symbolic Fountain of Life, in the foreground a realistically rendered landscape, while the groups of worshipers represent the different strata of Christian society. The altarpiece consists of twenty separate panels, reaching a new height of individualistic portrayal and a richness of color which bears witness to the greatly improved technique of oil painting. This newly perfected technique of the artists of the Netherlands and those of Burgundy became the model for the great painters of Italy, Spain, England, and especially Germany. Under the leadership of the Van Eycks oil painting on canvas or wood replaced the older method of painting on a specially prepared panel with colored pigment that had been mixed with egg (*tempera*-technique).

The classical land of book painting (illumination, miniature painting) was Burgundy, but the Netherlands and Germany benefited from the achievements of the Burgundian schools, appropriating and imitating their advanced technique of perspective and verisimilitude. The school of miniature painting in Prague enjoyed the friendly interest and support of Emperor Charles IV and King Wenceslaus.

The school of Cologne took the lead in the development of oil painting in Germany. The works of the Rhenish masters combine the spiritual depth of the mystics of the Rhineland with the gracefulness and fragrant beauty of the painters of Burgundy. Stephan Lochner († 1451), the most prominent member of the Rhenish school, is the author of many religious paintings, among which his Madonnas and especially the solemn and sublime "Adoration of the Child" in the Cathedral of Cologne (*Dreikönigsbild*) rank highest.

After the middle of the fifteenth century the leadership in oil painting passed to the south of the Empire, with the Swabians, Lukas Moser and Konrad Witz, and the Tyrolese, Michael Pacher (painter and carver), forcefully striking a new and more virile note. In the Alsatian regions Martin Schongauer's (*c.* 1450–1491) workshop attracted the outstanding talents among the younger generation, and from him they adopted a new sense of form and proportion. His influence is especially noticeable in the works of the masters of Ulm, Augsburg, and Nuremberg.

Dürer, Holbein, and Grünewald. It is against this general artistic background that the three greatest geniuses of German painting — Albrecht Dürer, Hans Holbein the Younger, and Matthias Grünewald — must be seen to be fully appreciated. In Dürer and Holbein the inner life of the late Gothic style in the North blends with the formal beauty of the Italian Renaissance, while in Grünewald the spirituality of the Germanic North reaches out even beyond the stylistic boundaries of the sixteenth century

Knight, Death, and the Devil, by Albrecht Dürer.

Madonna With Child, by Matthias Grünewald.

and anticipates the religious fervor of the period of Baroque (cf. pp. 330–354) and Catholic Restoration (cf. pp. 253–259).

a) Albrecht Dürer (1471–1528). The sober realism and solid craftsmanship that characterize the Frankish school of painting, and that were practiced in the workshop of Michael Wohlgemut (1434–1519) in Nuremberg, were to reach unprecedented heights in the timeless art of Wohlgemut's greatest pupil, Albrecht Dürer. A native of Nuremberg, a city which in the fifteenth century embodied everything that was great and admirable in German culture, Albrecht Dürer learned the art of drawing in the workshop of his father, who was a well-known goldsmith. From 1486–1490 he worked as one of Wohlgemut's apprentices. As a journeyman he traveled along the valley of the upper Rhine, to Colmar, Basel, and Strasbourg. Twice he visited Italy, and in his later years he journeyed to the Netherlands.

During his travels he eagerly absorbed new experiences and technical innovations but never lost his identity and strongly marked personality. Foreign lands and their people, personal contacts and social intercourse rather proved an invaluable aid in developing his individual style, and the acquaintance with foreign mentalities helped him to understand more profoundly himself, his own art, his country, and his people. Some of the leading Humanists he called his friends, and during his stay in the Low Countries he met Emperor Charles V and Erasmus of Rotterdam (cf. p. 249 sq.). Clever and ingenious artist and craftsman that he was, Albrecht Dürer never lost sight of the material and mechanical bases of his work and happily combined sound theory with faultless execution. In the graphic arts he stands out as a bold innovator who perfected the techniques of woodcut and engraving, both arts having originated in Germany during the first half of the fifteenth century, while the technique of etching was invented by Daniel Hopfer of Augsburg about the year 1500.

The sentiments of the age as well as Dürer's own outlook on life are symbolically illustrated in two of his most celebrated engravings: "Knight, Death, and Devil" (1513) and "Melancholia" (1514). The former shows a knight on horseback, in heavy armor, proceeding on his way through vale and forest, in grim determination and with courage undaunted, while the weird specters of Death and Devil try in vain to waylay him and shake his trust in life. The engraving that bears the title "Melancholia" depicts an enigmatic woman, seated on the ground and surrounded by all the paraphernalia of sciences old and new, but with the despairing glance of utter skepticism and frustration in her eyes. Clearly, Albrecht Dürer is suggesting the growing complexity of life as it weighed heavily on the individuals of a new epoch that was about to emerge from the shelter of a common heritage of faith and order, embarking upon adventures of body and soul, which were as alluring as they were intimidating.

b) Hans Holbein the Younger (1497–1543). The second of the great German masters in the sixteenth century deserves the predicate "classical" in a fuller sense than even Dürer did. He emancipated himself completely from the Gothic tradition which was as yet unbroken in the warm color harmonies of his own father, Hans Holbein the Elder (*c.* 1470–1524), a prominent member of the Swabian school of painting. The son owes his fame to the purity of his artistic form and the clarity of pattern which helped him to achieve a detachment and tranquillity that make him a faithful recorder of reality and one of the greatest portrait painters of all time. In him the northern Renaissance reaches its culminating point.

At the age of seventeen Holbein moved from his native city of Augsburg to Basel in Switzerland, where he had intercourse with Erasmus of Rotterdam and other scholars and publishers of the humanistic circles. The iconoclast movement of some groups of the reformed churches in Switzerland forced him to abandon religious painting and finally prompted him to leave his native land to become the official painter to the court of King Henry VIII of England.

Even the religious paintings of Holbein's early period are religious in name and theme only, but classical, cool, and worldly in their matter-of-factness and in the calculated stateliness of their poses. His "Madonna of the Burgomaster Meyer" is a German family picture, the document of a ripe city culture and of bourgeois taste. An element of irony and mild skepticism permeates many of Holbein's works, introducing a satirical note even into his treatment of the "Dance of Death," a series of woodcuts that present a running commentary on one of the favorite themes of the later Middle Ages: the gruesome figure of Death approaching the representatives of different social groups and impressing upon them the universal democracy of the great Reaper's merciless rule: "Here God judges justly, the masters lying with the servants: now mark well and, if you can, tell the master from the servant!" (from the so-called *Little Dance of Death* of Basel). In these woodcuts Holbein becomes the spokesman of his age as well as of his class, the defender of the democratic claims of the cities against the aristocracy of imperial and princely rule.

c) Matthias Grünewald (c. 1470–1528). The most unconventional and extraordinary of the three German master painters, entirely untouched by the Italian Renaissance and deeply rooted in the intellectual clime and maternal soil of the Germanic North, is Mathis Gothard Neithard, better known as Matthias Grünewald. Beyond the fact that he was born in Würzburg, died in Halle on the Saale, and worked in Mainz, Frankfurt on the Main, and Aschaffenburg, little is known about his life. In his masterpiece, the "Isenheim Altar" in Colmar (Alsace), he appears as the great mystic visionary among the German painters, the interpreter of the inner life, in whose works a sense of inexorable tragedy is mitigated only by the spiritual powers of mercy and love. His colors are symphonically arranged, with loud dominants striking the key notes.

The "Isenheim Altar" was originally painted for a hospital church in southern Alsace and depicts, on some of its panels, scenes of the Annunciation, the Birth of Christ, the Crucifixion, and the Resurrection. Grünewald's treatment of the theme of the Crucifixion illustrates best the artist's indifference to conventional concepts of beauty, harmony, and symmetry, whenever it was a question of expressing inner experiences that transcend the normal scope of human joy or human suffering. The body of Christ is rendered in proportions much larger than life, yet with a naturalistic over-description of somber detail, in livid, greenish colors as if in the process of decomposition. It is suspended from the cross against the backdrop of a dark night sky, the emaciated arms outstretched, with hands nailed to the cross-beams and fingers convulsively upturned. Beneath the cross the pointing finger of John the Baptist gives pictorial emphasis to his spoken words: "He must grow, and I must diminish," offering an effective counterbalance to the group of mourners on the opposite side: Christ's mother in the protecting embrace of John the Evangelist, and the kneeling figure of Mary Magdalen, with hands raised in fervent supplication.

Gloom and suffering of the Crucifixion are contrasted with the jubilant tones and colors of the Incarnation and the "Angels' Concert": one panel, but divided into two parts, with a dual background of late Gothic decoration and a bright, sunlit landscape. The minute and naïve observation of human life adds to the poetic and idyllic beauty of the composition.

As the ripest bloom of the Gothic-medieval world the "Isenheim Altar" with its masterly orchestration restates and summarizes the spirituality of the past, anticipating at the same time the synthesis of nature and super-nature which was to become the central problem and the supreme ambition of Baroque art (cf. p. 337 sq.). The antithesis of life and death, the dualism and tension that penetrates reality to its innermost depth, but is reconciled in the ecstatic exuberance of feeling, point forward to the mystical and pietistic forms of devotion that characterize the religious temper of the age of the Catholic Restoration (cf. p. 253 sqq.).

Language and Literature. During the thirteenth, fourteenth, and fifteenth centuries the German language was used in an increasing number of legal documents, deeds, and contracts of sale, donation, and arbitration. The law code of the Saxons (*Sachsenspiegel*), originally written in Latin, had been translated into German by Eike von Repkow about the middle of the thirteenth century. The Swabian law code (*Schwabenspiegel*) was written in German about 1275. Various imperial edicts, such as Rudolf of Hapsburg's Land Peace of 1287, were likewise promulgated in German. The German language became more and more a true mirror of the social changes that were taking place and, owing to the influence of the German mystics (cf. p. 146 sqq.) and the rising city culture, acquired a closer affinity to the everyday life of the people. Poetry descended from its aristocratic heights and put on the simpler and popular features of a workaday world of burghers and peasants.

a) Folk Songs. The singers, too, descended from the castles to the valleys and plains, mingled with the people, singing with them the songs of their loves and yearnings, their woes and worries, their deeds and aspirations: working songs, hunting songs, nature songs, religious songs, pastoral songs, drinking songs, student songs, soldiers' songs, and so forth. Some of the oldest German folk songs have the form of the ballad, and they frequently manifest, in their moods, themes, and rhythms, dramatic and tragic elements.

The folk songs of the Germans, like every type of folk song, are an expression of the communal experiences of an entire people. They mirror the folk spirit that is shared by the many individuals that constitute the natural units of the several social groups, classes, and estates. Melody and text become inseparably linked, after having undergone a process of gradual mutual adaptation and solidification. As to the question of authorship, it seems impossible to establish a general rule: many of the German folk songs are anonymous, while others were composed by well-known poets but were appropriated by the people and underwent considerable transformations.

Stylistically the German folk songs are simple and direct in text and tune without ever becoming monotonous. The dialogue and the refrain are favorite devices, adding rhythmical stress and color accents.

The oldest German folk songs date from the middle of the thirteenth century. The first collection is contained in the *Locheimer Liederbuch* of 1460. Herder (cf. p. 396 sq.) in the eighteenth and the Romanticists of the beginning nineteenth century (cf. p. 470 sqq.) extolled the folk poetry of all nations as genuine manifestations of the folk spirit (*Volksgeist*). The very term *Volkslied* was coined by Herder. He published an anthology of the folk songs of forty-eight different nations (*Stimmen der Völker,* "Voices of the Nations," 1778). The most popular collection of German folk poetry was edited by the two Romantic writers, Achim von Arnim and Clemens Brentano (*Des Knaben Wunderhorn,* "The Boy's Magic Horn," 3 vols., 1806–1808). The interest in German folk song was revived in recent decades by the several groups of the German Youth Movement (cf. p. 709 sq.).

Next to the folk songs the folk books (*Volksbücher*) stand out as monuments of German life and German culture. Like the folk songs they were handed down from generation to generation, wandering from village to village and from one German tribe to the other. They, too, were probably written down originally by some individual author but soon became the property of the people as a whole. Historical personages (Faust, Eulenspiegel, Kaiser Octavianus, etc.) were frequently surrounded with a wreath of poetic fancy, embodying the thoughts and feelings of the people. Again the Romantic writers of the early nineteenth century must be credited with the rediscovery and just appraisal of these literary documents of the German past.

b) The Beginnings of German Drama. Medieval drama originated in the liturgy of the Church and therefore was essentially an accessory of the religious service. It was closely associated with the sacrifice of the Mass, its stage being the church choir and its purpose the dramatization of the mysteries of the Redemption. Its spiritual center was the Gospel narrative of the Incarnation and Resurrection of Christ. The absence of all the elements of metaphysical or individual tragedy sets this liturgical drama apart from Greek and modern drama alike. The gloom of Golgotha was always followed by the gladness of Easter, so that in the end tragedy issued in "Divine Comedy."

In Italy, France, and England the origins of these morality and miracle plays can be traced back to the eleventh and twelfth centuries, while in Germany they were not universally known and produced until the beginning of the fourteenth century. The oldest plays were all performed in Latin, the texts strictly following the biblical and liturgical books; later on, German and Latin passages were used alternatingly. A purely German drama finally emerged in the fourteenth century.

The actors were originally priests, who dramatized the antiphonies of the Easter chants, especially the scene that depicts the two Marys and the angel at the tomb of the risen Christ. This so-called "Easter-Tropus" (verses which introduce and surround the liturgical texts) was composed around the biblical question: "Whom do ye seek?"; the answer of the two Marys: "Jesus of Nazareth, the Crucified," and the angel's response: "He is risen, He is not here; go ye and make it known." To this nucleus new and more realistic motifs were gradually added, until the preponderance of satirical and comical elements made it necessary to transfer the performance from the interior of the church to less cultic surroundings, monastic chapter halls or public buildings and squares. Additional religious themes were provided by the inclusion of other parts of the liturgy, so that in the end medieval drama embraced almost every major event of the ecclesiastical year, including the prefigurative symbols and prophecies of the Old Testament.

The development of the Passion play marks a certain humanization and secularization of the purely religious and cultic character of the early miracle plays. The dramatization of Christ's Passion required not only a more elaborate display of technical and artistic devices, made possible by the share that the inhabitants of the prosperous cities of the fifteenth century took in these spectacles, but it also put the emphasis on the human and emotional elements in the performance of the actors: torture and agony, human suffering, and motherly care. The Passion and morality play of the fifteenth century becomes a cyclical and panoramic spectacle, the production of which might occupy a period of several days, enacted no longer by priests and clerics but by students and choirboys, burghers and lay brotherhoods. Of the several Passion plays which have survived the disintegration of religious drama, the one of Oberammergau in Bavaria is the best known. It owes its origin to a revised edition and compilation of two Augsburg moralities of the fifteenth and sixteenth centuries. The oldest authentic text dates from the year 1662. Its periodical performance (normally every tenth year) was instituted by a solemn vow of the population of Oberammergau in 1633, when the town was visited by the plague.

A purely secular type of play developed apart from religious drama, but was of less decisive influence on German dramatic art. It dates back to the farces and burlesques of the Carolingian period and, in the form of the "shrovetide play," reached its maturest form in the *Fastnachtsspiele* of Hans Sachs (1494–1576), Hans Rosenplüt (*c.* 1450), and Hans Folz (*c.* 1450–1515), all connected with the circles of the *Meistersinger* Schools of Nuremberg, but none of them ascending to the level of a pure dramatic style.

c) The Schools of the "Meistersinger." With the decay of the culture of chivalry the "Minnesänger" (cf. p. 155 sq.) had become silent, and the castle could no longer serve as the abode of the Muses. The art of poetry had to adapt itself to the simple and sober tastes of the burgher class, and it found a new home in the workshops and festival halls of the guilds and glee clubs. These so-called schools of the "mastersingers" emerge at the beginning of the fifteenth century, and their members apply the strict rules and statutes of the guild system to the free spirit of poetry, thus cutting the wings of poetic imagination and stifling creative genius.

The apprentice of the art of poetry had to undergo a rigid training until he would be allowed to graduate from "scribe" (*Schreiber*) and "friend of the schools" (*Schulfreund*) to the rank of "poet" (*Dichter*) and "master" (*Meister*). The rules were set forth in the "tablature" (*Tabulatur*) and had to be pedantically observed, if the candidate wished to avoid failure. Meter and subject matter were likewise meticulously prescribed, and specially appointed judges (*Merker*) presided over the public competitions to add up the errors and the infractions of the rules and to award the winner a silver chain with a medallion. The whole procedure was, of course, profoundly oblivious of the true spirit of poetry. Even Hans Sachs, the Nuremberg shoemaker-poet and the greatest talent among the members of the schools, hardly ever succeeded in transcending the unnatural limitations imposed on his art by the social prejudices and artistic misconceptions of his age. Among his 6200 poetic creations there are 4275 master songs. However, some of his *Fastnachtsspiele* and farces (*Schwänke*) stand out as models of wit, healthy realism, and common sense. Hans Sachs joined the forces of the Reformation, praising Luther as the "nightingale of Wittenberg."

Education and the Schools. The changing standard of living, the difference in vocational training and interest, and the increasing number of people who actively participated in the social, economic, and cultural life of the cities required new means and methods of education. Many of the secondary schools of the fourteenth and fifteenth centuries were founded, administered, and supervised by the city councils. The cathedral and monastery schools continued in existence, but had grown too small to take care of the rapidly growing number of pupils. The schoolmaster (*Schulmeister*), appointed by the city council, was in most cases a layman who had acquired his education at some university. He was assisted by one or several teachers (*Unterlehrer, Provisoren, Locati*). The larger part of the headmaster's and the assistants' salaries was paid from tuition fees. In addition, the pupils were required to present their teachers with various contributions paid in kind, such as Christmas hens, shrovetide cakes,

Easter eggs, flour, wood, and so forth. The teacher might earn some extra money by making woodcuts or drawing up legal documents.

The well-to-do children had their private tutors or preceptors, who supervised their homework and accompanied them on their way to and from school. The poorer children obtained the money needed to pay their board and tuition by begging or singing, if they were not fortunate enough to secure one of the few available stipends (endowments for choirboys, etc.).

The curriculum usually included writing, reading, reckoning, religion, liturgical singing, and Latin. The three standard textbooks were the *tabula* (primer), Donatus' time-honored grammar, and the *Doctrinale puerorum,* composed by the Franciscan grammarian, Alexander de Villa Dei, in 1199. According to the texts used on different class levels the students were known as Tabulists, Donatists, and Alexandrists. Discipline was severe and corporal punishment frequent.

Private German schools, as distinguished from the public and municipal Latin institutions, make their appearance after the middle of the fourteenth century. Coeducation was not infrequently practiced in private German schools as early as the fifteenth century. Separate public schools for girls (*Maidlin-Schulen*), with women as teachers, are traceable in the fourteenth century. They were mostly attended by the children of the poor, while the daughters of wealthy burghers and nobles received their training in convent schools. The standard of general education was relatively high in the fifteenth century. It seems evident that the majority of the population had acquired the essentials of reading, writing, and arithmetic.

Students attending the university lived together in a students' hall or dormitory (*Burse*), under the supervision of a *Magister* (master). Here, too, an almost monastic discipline was rigidly enforced. Dress, the hours of study and recreation, and rules of conduct were prescribed in every detail. The student's day began at four o'clock in the morning and ended at nine o'clock at night. Meals were taken in the common refectory. The strictness of the rules was perhaps responsible for the many infractions of academic discipline, as evidenced by unending complaints and reprimands. Various excesses were traditionally committed during the initiation ceremonies for freshmen. In the presence of the *Magister* the newcomer would be subjected to almost any imaginable kind of mischief and vexation; with his face disfigured by mud or salves, teeth broken or pulled out, his beard shorn, and powerful purgatives administered by force, the neophyte must have cut a sorry figure, especially when he considered that he had to pay for the ensuing drinking bout. Nevertheless, he had the satisfaction that henceforth he was entitled to call himself "scholar" or *Bursche*.

The Changing Spirit of the Age. The fourteenth and fifteenth centuries witnessed the growth of modern humanity as it stands revealed in the movements of Renaissance, Humanism, Reformation, and Catholic Restoration, which stir and occupy the following two hundred years. The symptoms of the impending transformation are manifold, and they affect life and civilization in all their aspects. The change is primarily one of religious ideology and social philosophy, and it is therefore most clearly manifested in the religious attitudes of individuals and groups and in their relationship to life and death.

The religion of the later Middle Ages bears the marks of paradoxical contrasts: superficiality and carefree hedonism on the one hand, and a terrifying metaphysical anxiety, loneliness, and a frenzied and almost hysterical preoccupation with the mysteries of the supernatural and preternatural on the other. Church festivals are celebrated with an ever increasing splendor and the outward display of lavish popular entertainment. The interior of the church building becomes a favorite social meeting place: the people attending the services in the company of their dogs or other pets; the traveling merchants offering their wares for sale; and announcements of public auctions being read from the pulpit. But this desecration of the spiritual and this intemperate joy of living was accompanied by morbid fear, resignation, and wayless despair—a mood that is well expressed in a touching little poem, composed by a certain Master Martinus of Biberach in the year 1498:

> *Ich leb', weiss nit wie lang*
> *Ich sterb und weiss nit wann;*
> *Ich geh', weiss nit wohin:*
> *Mich wundert dass ich fröhlich bin.**

The hour of death is filled with all the horror of the awful unknown. The soul is overwhelmed by dryness, lack of faith, distrust and doubt, and by its attachment to things transitory. The dying person, however, clings desperately to the sacraments and the other aids and consolations that the Church has to offer, such as extreme unction, holy water, blessed candles. The funerals become most elaborate and even extravagant affairs. The mourners wear black garments and carry crosses, candles, torches, and banners. The burial is followed by a funeral repast or burial feast.

This dualism, which sounds so shrill and discordant in the death throes of the Middle Ages and the birth throes of the modern world, finds a remarkable illustration in a literary document of the early fifteenth century. Johan von Saaz, author of *Der Ackermann aus Böhmen* (*The Ploughman of Bohemia,* 1400), after having lost his beloved wife, has a plowman and Death discuss in dialogue form the position of man in the universe, in view of death, retribution, and eternal salvation. The plowman defends the intrinsic value of earthly beauty, vigor, and joyfulness, of human life in its plenitude, as against the medieval subordination of creature to Creator, of nature to supernature. This glorification of life and nature as ends in themselves—however problematic and restrained its expression—sounds the major theme of Renaissance and Humanism.

---

* I live, don't know the end;
  I die, and don't know when;
  I go, and don't know where;
  I wonder I am free from care.

Chapter 8

REFORMATION, PEASANT WARS, AND CATHOLIC RESTORATION

Charles V and the Empire. After the death of Emperor Maximilian I, in 1519, the choice of the Electors was his grandson Charles, the son of Philip the Fair, duke of Burgundy, and Joanna the Insane, the eldest daughter of Ferdinand and Isabella of Spain. At the age of sixteen Charles had become king of Spain, and he was nineteen years old when he assumed the burden of governing one of the vastest empires of all time. The dominion of the new ruler of the Hapsburg dynasty extended over the hereditary Hapsburg possessions in Germany: the Burgundian states of Franche-Comté, Luxemburg, and the Netherlands; the newly conquered Spanish possessions in South America; the Spanish kingdoms of Castile and Aragon; as well as Naples, Sicily, and Sardinia, Spain's possessions on Italian soil.

In contrast to France, which had achieved unity and strength as a centralized monarchy, Charles's possessions were scattered through many lands, and communications were difficult. The royal power was further weakened by the lack of a hereditary imperial succession, the absence of a definite political center of gravity, and the constant rivalry of the several princely houses.

The election of 1519 had been preceded by an electoral campaign, in which King Francis I of France (1515–1547), King Henry VIII of England (1509–1547), Charles's own younger brother Ferdinand, and Frederick, the prince-elector of Saxony, were at various times candidates for the imperial office. Leo X (1513–1521), the Renaissance pope of the Medici family, only reluctantly withdrew his initial objection to Charles's election and his support of the candidacies of Francis I and Frederick "the Wise" of Saxony. When the German Electors finally voted unanimously for Charles, their decision was chiefly influenced by the fact that, with the withdrawal of Frederick of Saxony as a candidate and with Charles's refusal to withdraw his own claims in favor of his brother Ferdinand, the choice left to them was between a member of the Hapsburg family and a potentate of wholly foreign blood and nationality. They also hoped that personal interest in the fate of his hereditary Austrian lands would impel Charles to take up the fight against the Turkish menace in the eastern provinces of the Empire, and that the strongly Catholic tradition of the Austrian and Spanish Hapsburgs would make the new emperor a stanch defender of the Roman Catholic position against the rising tide of the Reformation. Nevertheless, before giving Charles their votes, the Electors had made him sign a "capitulation" (electoral compromise) that was to guarantee their own prerogatives as well as safeguard Germany from the infiltration of Spanish soldiers and officials and from a cultural prevalence of Spanish influence.

The solution of the problems with which the young emperor found himself confronted would have required a large measure of statesmanlike vision, determination, and actual power, a combination of qualities which Charles could in nowise call his own. He grew but slowly into the stature required by his exalted calling, and was at all times both too sensitive and too inflexible to direct or control the rapidly shifting events on the European scene. Being no match for the shrewd and frivolous king of France, and the scheming territorial princes of Germany, and handicapped besides by the fact of his never ceasing to be a foreigner on German soil — a Spaniard in his manner, his tastes, and his mentality — Charles experienced a long series of partial achievements and total disappointments. Finally, reaching a point where, in his utter loneliness, dynastic power had no more allurements for him, he laid down the burden of ruling the mightiest empire on earth and retired to a Spanish monastery (1556).

Charles V and Francis I: The Conflict Between Hapsburg and Valois. The main factors that decided the future destiny of the Empire were the conflict between the houses of Hapsburg and Valois and the Lutheran revolt in Germany. Most of the wars that Charles waged against Francis I were fought on foreign soil, which necessitated the absence of the emperor from Germany and provided the German princes with the opportunity of strengthening their territorial independence and of preventing the centralization of the imperial government. Charles's foreign entanglements required his exclusive attention and used up most of the material resources of the Empire, so that little consideration could be given to the settlement of the religious disputes and to the readjustment of the social order.

Between the two opposing monarchies of Hapsburg and Valois stood the less powerful but equally determined and ever watchful representative of the house of Tudor, Henry VIII of England. He and his minister of state, Cardinal Wolsey, encouraged, chiefly with vague promises, either side at different times, thus upholding what is euphemistically known as the "European balance of power."

The ruler of France, finding his country surrounded by the Hapsburg lands in the south (Spain) and in the east (the Empire), had set his mind on the destruction of what he considered the Hapsburg menace. In Italy, the possessions of the two houses were spread out over the peninsula, Francis holding the duchy of Milan and Charles ruling over the kingdom of Naples, with both monarchies challenging the legality of each other's claims.

The cause of Charles was hampered not only by the traditional shortage of money and supplies of the German emperors, but likewise by the political, social, and religious unrest in different parts of the unwieldy Empire. Hostilities started in 1521, after Charles had presided over the Diet of Worms, and had entrusted his brother Ferdinand with the administration of the German and Austrian crown lands of the house of Hapsburg. While Charles was engaged in his struggles with the house of Valois, the task of protecting the eastern frontiers of the Empire from the attacks of the Turks was left to Ferdinand. He became king of Bohemia and Hungary by marriage, after his wife's brother, Louis II, the last king of Hungary, was killed by the Turks at Mohács in 1526.

Charles's first war against Francis was fought in Italy and ended with what looked like a decisive victory for the emperor — the capture of the French king. In the Treaty of Madrid (1526) Francis solemnly renounced the duchy of Burgundy as well as the French claims to the disputed territories in the Netherlands, Navarre, and Italy. In this first campaign Henry VIII and Pope Leo X had been the allies of the German emperor.

Francis, however, never intended to keep the solemn pledges of the Peace of Madrid. Once safely back on French soil he succeeded in organizing the "League of Cognac," which included the Italian states as well as the successor of Leo X, Pope Clement VII (1523-1534), another Medici on the papal throne, during whose reign the separation of the Anglican Church from Rome was consummated. In Germany, meanwhile, the affairs of State were carried on by a "governing council" which had been created by the Diet of Worms and which was composed of delegates chosen by the Electors and the emperor. It was during this second campaign against Francis I that the ill-famed and brutal "sack of Rome" (1527) occurred. The constable of Bourbon, after having deserted the cause of the French king and after having obtained the command of the imperial army in northern Italy, led his mutinous troops to the Eternal City so that they might collect their overdue pay from the spoils of pillage and plunder. Spanish troops and German mercenaries vied in acts of wanton savagery and sacrilege.

Clement VII, after an imprisonment of seven months in the castle of San Angelo, conferred the imperial crown on Charles V in the cathedral of Bologna in 1530, this being the last coronation of a German emperor by a pope. In the Peace of Cambrai (1529) Francis I again renounced his claims to the contested territories in Italy, but was allowed to retain the duchy of Burgundy. Several times Charles's impending defeat had been turned into victory, and by 1529 Hapsburg domination of Italy was definitely established.

The *"Sacco di Roma"* had taken place without Charles's knowledge, but though he disapproved of the acts of violence, the conquest of Rome and the siege of Clement VII in San Angelo served his ends and strengthened his strategic position. The terms of the Treaty of Cambrai gave him sufficient prestige and a free hand to deal with the dual dangers of Turkish aggression and religious revolt.

The Turks had captured Constantinople in 1453 and had constantly advanced westward during the following decades. At the time of Charles's election they were in possession of the territory of the ancient Byzantine empire and of the Balkan States, carrying their advance under Sultan Suliman "the Magnificent" (1520–1566) up the river Danube and threatening Vienna in 1529. After a temporary setback they resumed their march on Austria in 1532, when Charles V joined forces with his brother Ferdinand, repulsing the aggressors and liberating part of Hungary. In 1533 a peace was concluded between Ferdinand, who in 1531 had been elected Roman-German king, and Sultan Suliman. The final result of twelve years of warfare with the Turks was the partition of Hungary in 1541, which left the greater part of the country in the possession of the enemy. The Turkish domination of Hungary lasted for some 150 years and brought the country to the brink of ruin. Not until the end of the seventeenth century did the house of Hapsburg succeed in restoring the integrity of Hungary.

The Peace of Cambrai was hardly more than a truce, and hostilities between Charles and Francis started again in 1536, with a French attack on Milan and Piedmont, ending in another truce (Nice) and another treaty (Toledo, 1538). The French king repeatedly sided with the Protestant princes of Germany and with the Turks against Charles V. The year 1542 witnessed the grand alliance of the French, the Turks, the Swedes, and the forces of the duke of Cleves, and in 1544 Charles invaded France and advanced on Paris. In the Peace of Crespy (1544) Francis surrendered all his former gains, renouncing all his claims to Hapsburg territory but retaining Burgundy and the towns of the Somme districts. The feud was once more resumed under the successor of Francis, King Henry II (1547–1559), when through the treachery of Duke Maurice of Saxony and other rebel princes of Germany the German bishoprics of Metz, Toul, and Verdun were lost to France (Treaty of Chambord, 1552). The self-styled "vindicator of the liberties of Germany" (Henry II) was to hold the three bishoprics as "Vicar of the Holy Empire."

Charles V and the Reformation: The Wars With the German Princes. It becomes necessary at this point to recount the major events of the reform movement that had been initiated by Martin Luther, as far as they affected the course of German political history in the sixteenth century. The religious, cultural, and literary aspects of the Reformation will be treated separately.

When German mercenaries, most of them Lutherans, stormed Rome on Easter, 1527, they actually made Charles V the undisputed master of Italy, a fact that was later on confirmed by the Treaty of Cambrai, 1529. The march on Rome was almost symbolical, inasmuch as it gave vent to a general and popular German resentment against the papacy. Oddly enough, the emperor's victory over Clement VII and the following reconciliation of the two rulers made it possible for Charles to turn now with full vigor against the Lutheran reform movement. When Charles returned to Germany in 1530, it was with the firm resolve to settle the religious issue once and for all.

Charles was a native of the Spanish Netherlands, a Spaniard at heart, and a foreigner in Germany and Italy alike. His religious and political convictions were predetermined by his strictly Catholic education and by the ideas of the Catholic Reform in Spain that had been inaugurated by Francisco Ximenez de Cisneros (1436–1517), cardinal and primate of the Church in Spain and later on regent of that kingdom. Charles furthermore was intellectually and emotionally attached to the tradition of the Holy Roman Empire and its universal mission, as the embodiment of the Christian commonwealth of nations. He was therefore by nature as well as by inherited characteristics opposed to political and religious particularism and regionalism. These were the factors that influenced his attitude in dealing with the Lutheran Reformation.

On October 31, 1517, Martin Luther had posted his ninety-five theses on the portal of the castle church in Wittenberg, attacking the practice of the sale of indulgences and other abuses as well as dogmatic teachings of the Catholic Church. Luther's refusal to recant at the Diet of Augsburg (1518), the ensuing controversy with the famous theologian Dr. John Eck of the University of Ingolstadt (1519), and the burning of the papal bull of excommunication (1520) had made the German Augustinian monk a figure of international significance and the logical protagonist of ecclesiastical reform.

The disputation with Eck at Leipzig almost coincided with the election of Charles V as German emperor. In the following year (1521) Charles solemnly opened his first imperial diet in the city of Worms. According to ancient imperial law the ban of the Church called for an immediate proclamation of the ban of the Empire. The diet, because Luther's position had already grown so strong, decided to grant him another hearing with an added guarantee of safe-conduct. The "Edict of Worms," declaring Luther under the ban of the Empire, was pronounced and signed by Charles and a number of the German princes, after Luther had again refused to retract any of his statements, unless he should be convinced "by witness of Scripture or by plain reason." Charles decreed that the safe-conduct should be respected but that henceforth Luther should be prosecuted as a convicted heretic. To avoid any possible resistance on the part of pro-Lutheran forces, the edict, which had been drawn up on May 8, was not published until May 26, when most of the representatives of the Estates of the Empire had left the city.

Instead of quelling the incipient reform, the Edict of Worms had the opposite effect of strengthening the adherents of Luther and of further weakening the authority of the emperor. Charles's renewed absence from Germany made it possible for the Lutherans to complete their organization and to overthrow the established ecclesiastical regime in all the territories they controlled. At the First Diet of Speyer (1526) the States of the Empire passed a "recess," in which they agreed that each of them should be permitted to manage its own religious affairs according to the dictates of conscience, until the time when a general council would decree a permanent settlement of the religious issues. This declaration, which practically made ecclesiastical policy a matter of the independent sovereignty of individual states, was supported by the Lutheran and Catholic princes alike. It was repealed, however, by the Second Diet of Speyer in 1529, where it was decreed that the existing dividing lines between the religious factions should be recognized and respected, but that further interference with the religious practices of the Catholic tradition should not be tolerated. The six princes and fourteen cities whose signatures were obtained to a formal protest against these decrees were henceforth known as the "Protestant" party.

In the following year (1530) Charles returned to Germany and presided over the Diet of Augsburg. The "Confession of Augsburg," drawn up on the emperor's request by Luther's friend and collaborator, Melanchthon, and designed to prepare the way for a mutual understanding and a possible reunion between Catholics and Lutherans, was read in public. Its conciliatory tone was met by a firm Catholic "confutation," adopted and confirmed by Charles in its entirety. The emperor then gave the Protestant party six months to reconsider their position, after which their heresy should be suppressed by force. Luther, still under the ban of the Empire and the Church and therefore prevented from being personally present at the Diet of Augsburg, was kept well informed of every phase of the proceedings and threw the weight of his influence and advice on the side of those who were convinced that reconciliation was impossible and that civil war had become virtually unavoidable.

In 1531 a number of Protestant princes and delegates of free cities joined together in a defensive alliance, known as the League of Schmalkalden (the name of a town in Hesse). The leadership was alternately in the hands of the Elector John of Saxony and Duke Philip of Hesse. The League became the spearhead of all opposition against the imperial regime, and was at various times supported by the kings of France and England and even by the Catholic Dukes of Bavaria. When the Turkish menace became more acute, the members of the League refused to defend Germany against foreign invasion unless they were granted freedom of religious propaganda in all the territories of the Empire. The so-called First Religious Peace of Nuremberg (1532) established another truce between the opposing forces and provided the basis for joint action against the Turkish aggressors. The following fourteen years, during which Charles V was preoccupied with embroilments and military campaigns in the Mediterranean, in France, and in the Netherlands, gave the members of the League ample time to consolidate their position. Their cause was further strengthened by the death of Duke George of Saxony, a stanch Catholic, who was succeeded by his Protestant brother, Henry (1539), and by the inclusion of Brandenburg among its member states. The German North had now become a solid bulwark of the Lutheran faction, which by the year 1546 could boast of a following that included more than half of Germany and four of the seven Electors of the Empire.

If Charles V nevertheless could open his campaign of 1546 with a fair chance of success, it was due not only to the inadequate leadership of the armies of the League but also to the discords, rivalries, and selfish policies of the Protestant princes. The Spanish foot soldiers of Charles's army, though inferior in numbers, represented the crack troops of the military forces of Europe and were commanded by the duke of Alva, one of the greatest and at the same time most ruthless military leaders of his century.

Another contributing factor to the eventual defeat of the Protestant League was the unexpected alliance of Landgrave Philip of Hesse with the emperor, the outgrowth of an unsavory family affair of this prince. With Luther's and Melanchthon's consent the landgrave had contracted a second marriage, while his first wife was still alive, and though Luther had urged that the whole affair be kept secret, the truth had come out, alienating many of the members of Philip's own party. The additional fear of having to face indictment and punishment for bigamy caused the landgrave to become a traitor to the cause of his allies and to join secretly the imperial forces. Although according to Canon Law the validity of Philip's second marriage was not recognized, he was satisfied as long as he was allowed to stay with Margarete von Sale, his second wife.

Charles very shrewdly used the discord among the Protestant princes to his own advantage, and succeeded in winning over two Hohenzollern princes as well as Maurice, duke of Saxony, the successor of Duke Henry. Pope Paul III (1534–1549), successor to Clement VII, concluded an alliance with Charles and supported the emperor with troops and money. The defeat of John Frederick, Elector of Saxony,* in the battle of Mühlberg (1547) broke the resistance of the League of Schmalkalden, leaving the Protestant princes at the mercy of the victorious emperor. Martin Luther had died in the previous year, and the Catholic Reform Council of Trent (cf. p. 257 sqq.) had held its first session in 1545. King Francis I of France and King Henry VIII of England died in 1547. Charles V could feel himself for once the undisputed master of the Empire, and as such he is represented on Titian's famous painting: in full armor, seated on horseback, with "dark red, golden-fringed saddle-cloth; a broad red, gold-edged sash over his burnished breast-plate; on his head a German helmet, in his hand a short spear."

The Diet of Augsburg (1548) brought a provisional settlement of the religious dispute, known as the "Interim," which, it was hoped, would soon be superseded by the definitive and lasting decrees of the general Church

---

* The electorate of Saxony had been divided in 1485 between the Dukes Ernst and Albrecht (Ernestine and Albertine line) of the Wettin dynasty, Ernst receiving the electoral title, the duchy of Saxony, northern Thuringia, and part of Franconia, while Albrecht was given the Mark Meissen and southern Thuringia. John Frederick belonged to the Ernestine, Maurice to the Albertine line of succession.

council. But the terms of the "Interim" were never really accepted in good
faith, nor were they observed by the Protestant princes and their subjects,
who felt that the concessions of the Catholic party were by no means far
reaching enough. Any hopes that Charles might have nourished as to the
durability of the religious truce were bitterly disappointed by the rebellion
of the Protestant princes of 1552. This time Duke Maurice of Saxony
made common cause with King Henry II of France (1547–1559), and
Charles narrowly escaped being captured by Maurice's troops at Ingolstadt.

The emperor not only had failed to take advantage of a situation which
in every respect favored his cause, but had wasted the fruits of his victory
by a series of tactical and psychological mistakes. He had alienated many
of his sympathizers by the continued presence of Spanish troops on German
soil and, above all, by his attempt to secure the imperial succession for his
son, Philip of Spain. At a meeting of the German princes at Passau,
Charles's brother Ferdinand presided as the representative of the emperor,
securing the latter's consent to a treaty which was to grant equal protection
to Catholics and Protestants. Ferdinand, in his capacity as Roman-German
king, was again commissioned by Charles to preside over the Diet of Augsburg in 1555, negotiating the Religious Peace of Augsburg, which finally
settled by decree some of the most controversial issues, and whose enactments served to maintain an armed peace for the rest of the sixteenth
century. The compromise arrived at in the deliberations of the Diet was by
no means to the liking of Charles, who remained unwaveringly opposed to
the concessions as contained in the major provisions of the Treaty of Augsburg. He had staked his life and his honor on the destruction of Protestantism, and he withdrew from the political arena when he realized his
failure and partial defeat.

The Diet of Augsburg laid down the following four principles as a
modus vivendi for the Catholic and Lutheran factions: (1) The Lutheran
principalities and free cities should be free to choose between the Catholic
and Lutheran creeds, but the rulers were entitled to impose the religion
of their choice upon their subjects. Those people who professed a religion
different from that of their rulers were permitted to move with their belongings to other territories. This principle is expressed in the phrase:
cuius regio eius religio (the religion of the ruler determines the religion
of those ruled). (2) An "ecclesiastical reservation" (*reservatum ecclesiasti-
cum*) decreed that ecclesiastical princes who wished to join the Lutheran
faith were to surrender their territories, which would then remain under
the control of the Catholic Church. Lutherans living in such ecclesiastical
holdings should be permitted to practice their religion. (3) Protestant states
should retain all Church property that they had confiscated prior to 1552.
(4) The principle expressed in the phrase *cuius regio eius religio* should
apply only to Catholics and Lutherans, but not to Calvinists.

The terms of the Religious Peace of Ausburg as contained in these declarations marked one further step in the dissolution of the traditional order

of Europe. By endowing the secular princes with the prerogatives of ecclesiastical (episcopal) dignity and jurisdiction it prepared the way for the absolutistic and totalitarian forms of secular government in the following centuries. Additional power and prestige was added to princely rule and accelerated the disintegration of the Empire.

Armed Peace and Formation of Rival Leagues. Charles V, realizing that the Electors could not be persuaded to accept the Spanish Philip as his successor, had finally decided to divide his inheritance between his son Philip and his brother Ferdinand, the former receiving Spain and Burgundy, the latter the German Hapsburg possessions as well as the imperial crown. The new German emperor, however, was a weak monarch. Repeatedly he had to call upon the aid of his Hapsburg cousins in Spain to defend his lands against foes within and without.

The German princes, Protestant and Catholic alike, had acquired too much secular and ecclesiastical power to accept the dictates of imperial rule. They embarked upon separatistic policies and adventures and frequently crossed and counteracted the political designs of the emperor. All the same, the Religious Peace of Augsburg might have provided a workable basis for a stabilized national policy if the selfishness of the princes had not been greatly encouraged by the constant interference of foreign powers. The situation was further complicated by the gradual shift in the religious balance of power that had been brought about by the Catholic reform movement following upon the successful conclusion of the Council of Trent (cf. p. 257 sqq.).

The Religious Peace of Augsburg coincided with the first vigorous attempts on the part of the Catholic Church to recover its former power and prestige, and to regain Germany for the Catholic faith. The Roman Curia, aided by the militant Order of Jesuits (cf. p. 254 sqq.), had become exceedingly active in all parts of the world, but especially in the territories of the Empire. The larger part of southern Germany and the ecclesiastical principalities of the Rhineland were thus recovered for the Catholic faith, and the principles of the Peace of Augsburg were rigorously enforced. Lutheranism, on the other hand, had fallen into a state of political apathy, thereby manifesting some of that passive quietism in regard to political authority that had characterized Luther's own theological attitude in his earlier years. On the Protestant side the law of political action, backed by strong moral conviction, was now dictated entirely by the forces of Calvinism (cf. p. 236), which had established its German strongholds in some parts of the upper Rhineland in the West and in Bohemia in the East. It had gained the adherence of the elector palatine and the elector of Brandenburg and was prepared to challenge the Catholic Restoration. Any co-operation between Calvinists and Lutherans was precluded by the sharp cleavage of minds that separated the two denominations from each other as much as from the Catholic Church. Thus the Lutheran princes remained passive onlookers in the initial stages of the Calvinist-Catholic struggle, trying to follow a policy of detached neutrality.

To appreciate the rapid and dynamic growth of Calvinism, we do well to remember that in the Religious Peace of Augsburg its adherents had not even been given a legal status. Now, only seven years later (1572), the Calvinists felt strong enough to incite the Rebellion of the Netherlands under the leadership of Prince William of Orange, which led to the secession of the seven northern provinces from Spain and from the Empire (1581), followed by the destruction of the Spanish Armada by the English in 1588.

The struggle for the possession of Cologne was fought in the years 1582–1584. Westphalia and the lower Rhenish districts were saved for Catholicism with the aid of Spanish troops and owing to the indifference of the Lutheran princes as well as the Catholic fervor of the population. The incident which at last aroused the Lutherans from their lethargy and from a false feeling of security was the forced conversion of the Bavarian city of Donauwörth by Duke Maximilian of Bavaria (1598–1651), the militant leader of the Catholic princes. At Donauwörth Protestant interference with a Catholic procession had led to the military occupation of the town and the ensuing religious decrees.

These events occurred in 1608, and in the same year a number of Protestant princes under the leadership of the Calvinist elector palatine, Frederick IV, united to form a defensive alliance, known as the "Protestant Union." The Catholic answer was given in the following year (1609), when Maximilian of Bavaria assumed leadership in the newly organized "Catholic League." Civil war was not far off, and an immediate outbreak of hostilities was perhaps only halted by the realization that the impending conflict would soon assume the dimensions of a general European war and that it would have to be fought on German soil.

The mere fact that the German emperor was not a member of the Catholic League speaks eloquently of the rather pitiable role that the imperial government played in national affairs. The Hapsburg emperors, Ferdinand I (1556–1564), the brother of Charles V; his son, Maximilian II (1564–1576); and the latter's son, Rudolph II (1576–1612), all Catholics, were chiefly concerned with preserving and expanding their hereditary lands, including the kingdoms of Bohemia and Hungary. The Catholic princes of the Empire, on the other hand, were ever watchful lest the central authority might be strengthened by a decisive imperial victory over Protestantism. And, as it was perfectly obvious that any war would involve both the Austrian and Spanish branches of the Hapsburg family, none of the Catholic princes was anxious to precipitate such a concentration of imperial power as would inevitably result from an armed conflict.

But the events that issued in the final catastrophe happened in such rapid succession that considerations of diplomacy and expediency had to be disregarded. Emperor Rudolph II, a lover of astrology and black magic and the admiring protector of John Kepler and Tycho de Brahe, was politically unstable and incompetent and in his later years suffered from persecution mania. Under pressure, and while his brother Matthias in union with the Hungarian and Austrian nobles was working for his deposition, he attempted to appease the Protestant Estates of Bohemia and to win their support by issuing the Bohemian "Royal Charter" of 1609, granting free exercise of religion to all his Bohemian subjects. The head of the Catholic opposition against these concessions was Duke Ferdinand of Styria, the emperor's cousin, a docile pupil of the Jesuits and, together with Maximilian of Bavaria, champion of the Catholic Restoration in the Empire. Matthias finally achieved the overthrow of his brother's regime in Bohemia and, upon Rudolph's death in 1612, succeeded him as German emperor (1612–1619). After some attempts at conciliation Matthias aroused the violent opposition of the Bohemian Protestants when he designated as his heir and the future king of Bohemia his cousin Ferdinand, who was known and feared for his intolerance and for the ruthless suppression of Protestantism in his own lands. An open rebellion of the Czech nobles in 1618 gave the signal for the beginning of the Thirty Years' War (cf. pp. 284–293). Emperor Matthias died in the following year, after having been deprived by Ferdinand of his Bohemian, Austrian, and Hungarian possessions. Exactly one hundred years after the election of Charles V as emperor of the Holy Roman Empire the electors met again in Frankfurt on the Main to cast their votes for a successor to Emperor Matthias, this time under the shadow of the great religious war which had become a grim reality.

Martin Luther: His Personality and His Work. There are few characters in the history of civilization who have caused such profoundly revolutionary changes in the general outlook of their age and who have determined the destiny of their own nation to such an extent as Martin Luther. Although his thought and work were in many respects a continuation and fruition of certain tendencies of the preceding centuries, supplemented by influences of education and environment, the amount of spontaneous and creative innovation that remains Luther's personal contribution to his age testifies to a unique and ingenious personality. Although the picture of Luther has been colored by partisan likes and dislikes, by prejudice and wishful thinking, his dynamic vitality as well as his passionate sincerity have seldom been denied, and it thus becomes the privilege of the historian to view and evaluate the significance of the reformer and his work with the dispassionate detachment of a retrospective analysis.

a) Childhood and Early Manhood. Martin Luther was born on November 10, 1483, at Eisleben, in the province of Saxony. His father, Hans Luther, a small peasant and mine digger, had moved with his family to the Saxon town from Möhra in Thuringia shortly before Martin's birth. One year later (1484) the father was again on the move, this time settling at Mansfeld, the center of the growing mining industry of Saxony. "My great-grandfather, my grandfather, and my father were real peasants," says Martin Luther in his *Table Talk*. His proud assertion: "I am the son of a peasant," receives added emphasis in the further statement: "Kings and emperors have been of peasant stock."

Martin's childhood was by no means a very happy one. The sternest discipline ruled in the house of his parents as well as in the Mansfeld school where he received his elementary education. The son complained later on that father and mother were incapable of understanding the inner life of their children and that their strictness had driven him into a state of pusillanimity (*usque ad pusillanimitatem*). At the age of fourteen Martin was sent to the school of the "Brethren of the Common Life" (cf. p. 180) in Magdeburg to continue his studies. The schools of the Brethren counted among their more famous pupils such men as Thomas à Kempis, the mystic; Gabriel Biel, one of the German followers of William of Occam (cf. p. 142); Nicholas Copernicus, the great astronomer; and Cardinal Nicholas of Cusa (cf. p. 180 sq.), the ingenious philosopher. Their doctrines were on strictly orthodox ground, but in their devotional life they stressed the social aspects and impulses of the *devotio moderna*.

Luther spent only one year with the Brethren in Magdeburg. In 1498 he entered the Latin school in Eisenach in Thuringia, following his father's wish, who wanted him to get acquainted with some family relations in that city. In Magdeburg as well as in Eisenach Martin had to earn his livelihood by begging and singing in the streets. We are told by Luther's pupil, Mathesius, that even the sons of well-to-do parents were sent on these begging and singing tours to acquire the virtue of humility and to develop a feeling of compassion with the poor and unfortunates. Martin soon found a home and with it the warmth and benignity of family life in the house of Kuntz Cotta and his wife, Ursula, who began to take a motherly interest in the development of the boy.

Hans Luther wanted his son to become a jurist, and Martin again followed his father's advice when he left Eisenach after a stay of three years and entered the Saxon University of Erfurt (1501). The city had become known as the "new Prague," after the mass emigration from the capital of Bohemia that followed the Hussite struggles (cf. p. 176 sq.). Before taking up his professional studies Luther had to complete his course in the faculty of arts, including the study of the classics (Ovid, Vergil, Horace, Terence, etc.), and an extensive training in the essentials of philosophy. The leading philosophical authority was still Aristotle, but Erfurt more than most of the other European institutions of higher learning was committed to the nominalistic (cf. p. 142) interpretation of the Greek master, following the example of William of Occam and other members of the Franciscan schools. It was the period of decadent scholasticism, and the classical philosophical synthesis of Thomas Aquinas (cf. p. 145 sq.) was no longer sufficiently known and appreciated. The Bible was familiar to Luther at that time only in the form of homilies (*Postillen*), pericopes (passages of the Gospels and Epistles, used in the liturgy), and of the "Biblical Histories" (*Historienbibeln*), all of which were known in German translations to clergy and laity. Luther tells us that he was twenty years old when he first saw the complete Bible in the university library at Erfurt.

Luther received the degree of Bachelor of Arts in 1502, that of Master of Arts in 1505. Soon afterward he began his studies for the legal profession. His later criticism of the contents and methods of jurisprudence indicates that his rich emotional life found itself thwarted by the unimaginative dryness of his subject matter. He may have found an emotional outlet in his association with some of the members of the Humanist movement (cf. p. 251 sq.), known as the "Erfurt poets." Luther was especially attracted by the brilliance of their literary style and admired their proficiency in the Latin tongue. His enthusiasm for the Latin classics bore fruit in the fluency and formal perfection of his own literary style, both in Latin and German. The pagan aspects of the Humanist movement left no impression on Luther's mind. His growing interest in the Bible made him virtually immune to any such influence.

b) Luther, the Augustinian Monk. It seems that the cheerless atmosphere of his parental home predisposed Luther to take a gloomy and pessimistic view of life and human nature. A letter of the year 1528 speaks of an innate inclination to religious melancholy and even despair. It must have been such a state of mind that prompted his sudden decision to quit his legal career and enter the local monastery of the Augustinian Eremites. On his way back to Erfurt, from Mansfeld, where he had paid a visit to his parents, he was thrown to the ground by a stroke of lightning and, convinced of having received a sign and call from heaven, he immediately vowed to become a monk. Luther was twenty-two years old when the portals of the monastery closed behind him. In 1506 he was made a subdeacon and deacon, and in 1507 he was ordained to the priesthood. While celebrating his first Mass he was so overcome with the tremendous majesty of the Almighty that the assisting priest had to restrain him from running away.

In 1508 Luther was sent by his superiors to the new University of Wittenberg, recently founded by Frederick the Wise, elector of Saxony. He stayed at the Augustinian monastery in that city and was immediately commissioned to teach a course on Aristotle's Nicomachean Ethics. Upon the recommendation of the vicar of his order, John Staupitz, Luther was made a Bachelor of Sacred Scripture in 1509.

His inner life during these years was darkened by the unbearable thought of an eternal predestination of man for either heaven or hell: "My heart trembled when I thought of God's grace. The name of Jesus frightened me, and when I looked at Him crucified, He appeared to me as a flash of lightning." Luther had such a strong sensation of the terrors of God's judgment that he felt his hair stand on end. Some of his lecture notes reveal his beginning rejection of Aristotle, whom he calls a "rancid philosopher" and a comedian whom he intends to unmask. At the same time we read of his growing admiration of the writings of St. Augustine, whose teachings were traditionally given preference in the Augustinian and Franciscan Orders.

In the late autumn of 1510 we find Luther on a journey to Rome, where he went as a delegate of his order to settle some disputed matters of ecclesiastical administration. He had expected to find a holy city and was shocked and grieved when he discovered that the Rome of the Renaissance was a center of art, taste, sophistication, and luxury, but that the religious spirit was drowned in worldliness and moral corruption. Luther stayed in Rome for about four weeks and then returned to the Augustinian monastery in Wittenberg, where he resumed his teaching at the university and, in 1512, received the degree of Doctor of Theology.

The lectures of the new professor dealt with scriptural exegesis and showed a strongly mystical inclination. He was particularly fond of the sermons of John Tauler (cf. p. 148) and an anonymous mystical treatise, known as *Theologia Germanica*. He was fascinated by his discovery that these mystical doctrines emphasized the weakness of the human will and the all-pervading efficiency of divine grace. For Luther these teachings seemed to imply a complete passivity of human nature in the process of salvation, a quietude born of the conviction — which resulted from his own tormenting experiences — that all human endeavor was incapable of overcoming the fatal consequences of original sin. Shortly after having prepared a new edition of the *Theologia Germanica* he declares in a sermon of the year 1516: "The man of God goes wherever God may lead him. He never knows whither he goes. He does not act himself, but God acts through him. He is on his way, whatever this way may be. . . . Such are the men who are guided by the divine spirit."

In 1515, Luther had been chosen as his order's vicar of the districts of Meissen and Thuringia and entrusted with the supervision of eleven monasteries. His many administrative duties left him little time for the observation of monastic rules: "I could use two clerks or chancellors. My chief occupation is writing letters. Besides, I have to preach in the monasteries, in the refectories, in the parish church. I am director of studies and vicar, i.e., I do the work of eleven priors. . . . I lecture on St. Paul and collect the explanations of the Psalter. . . . Rarely do I have time to recite the canonical office and to celebrate Mass, to say nothing of the temptations of the flesh, the world, and the devil."

Luther's interpretation of certain mystical doctrines led him to more and more violent attacks against the Catholic teaching on the merits of "good works" (*Werkheiligkeit*), such as the veneration of saints, sacraments, pilgrimages, indulgences, fasting, and almsgiving. While he was still a devout member of his monastic congregation, the seeds of his new gospel had already been firmly embedded in his soul. Why should there be confession of sin and penance, if good works were unsuitable instruments to procure a lasting peace with God? When Luther was told by his friend and superior, Staupitz, that peace and consolation were hidden in the love of Christ, these words were balsam for Luther's aching and longing heart. He was ready to challenge a religious and social system that had grown too complacent to see that its own faults were writing its doom.

c) Luther's New Gospel. The dramatic events that made Luther's name and personality a blazing signal of opposing creeds were a direct outgrowth of his religious scruples concerning the problem of predestination and the share of divine grace and human works in the economy of salvation. While lecturing on Paul's Epistle to the Romans, Luther was struck by the Apostle's insistence that neither the natural law nor the Mosaic law could justify a man before God, but that justification was exclusively due to God's grace as revealed in the New Testament. This statement was interpreted by Luther as implying the negation of the natural human faculties, so that man would be "justified by faith *alone,* through the merits of Christ being attributed to the sinner." If that was true, then "good works" were not only unnecessary, but they were actually impossible, due to that weakness and corruption of human nature that was the consequence of the "Fall of Man" (original sin). Human self-abnegation was thus effectively contrasted with God's all-pervading power and majesty. There was no doubt in Luther's mind that those who were predestined for salvation would be given the gift of faith and, with faith, the confidence and conviction of being children of God, saved by His redeeming love. The stain of corruption remains, but the sinner uses the merits of Christ as a shield to cover up his weakness and sinfulness.

The position of the Roman Catholic Church in this matter makes clear the extent of the innovation: according to the pre-Reformation as well as post-Reformation Catholic teaching, man's essential natural faculties and the freedom of his will were not radically corrupted but only deeply wounded by original sin. As it is God's will that all be saved, everyone is called upon to co-operate freely with divine grace. The amount of grace given is sufficient to enable the sinner to remain a child of God by his own free choice, after having been adopted by Christ through the sacrament of baptism. The disposition for sin is constantly diminished, and the potency for moral action strengthened by the aid of the other sacraments.

Luther calls William of Occam (cf. p. 142) his spiritual ancestor, and it is interesting to note how much of the substance of Luther's teaching can be attributed to that dynamic court theologian of Louis the Bavarian. Occam had denied that the existence of God, the freedom of will, and the spirituality of the soul could be rationally demonstrated. He had espoused the doctrine of the "double truth" (what is true philosophically may be false theologically, and vice versa), and he had exalted the Deity beyond the distinctions of good and evil, thus making the divine will entirely arbitrary and irrational.

Luther follows Occam in his contempt of reason and in his ideas on the nature and all-pervading power of God, whose testimony in the "inner word" enlightens the faithful as to the true meaning of the Scriptures, independent of ecclesiastical authority. The contention that God's exalted majesty had been minimized by Catholic theologians and philosophers in favor of the human faculties of reason and free will is Luther's main argument against the scholastic *Sautheologen*. On the other hand, he characterized William of Occam, Gabriel Biel (1430–1495), and other nominalists as empty dialecticians, who had neglected the study and testimony of the divine "word" as revealed in the Bible. Positively as well as negatively, therefore, the influence of Occamistic teaching, together with the main body of traditional Franciscan theology that it contains, represents an important force in the formation of Luther's religious convictions.

d) Luther's Ninety-Five Theses; Fight Against Indulgences; Disputation of Leipzig. The event that brought the latent crisis into the open was the public sale of indulgences by the Dominican friar, John Tetzel, in the year 1517. Pope Leo X (1513–1521), the friend and protector of Raphael and Michelangelo, the splendor-loving Renaissance pope of the Medici family, had proclaimed a papal indulgence in order to obtain the funds needed for the reconstruction of St. Peter's Cathedral in Rome in accordance with the designs of Michelangelo. Leo had commissioned Albrecht of Brandenburg, archbishop of Mainz, with the task of collecting the money in Germany. Tetzel, in his turn, acted on the orders of his superior when he went from town to town, offering varying spiritual benefits upon the payment of certain amounts of money.

"Indulgences" were customarily granted by the Church on different occasions, not to effect the remission of sins but as a form of penance consisting in the performance of good works. Not until the fourteenth century do we find the partial substitution of money gifts for works of mercy and charity. In Luther's time the theory and practice of indulgences was rather indefinite, lending itself to all kinds of misinterpretation and abuse. Yet as late as 1516 Luther himself had been of the opinion that whatever abuses might be connected with the practice of granting indulgences, "it is a great benefit that indulgences are offered and obtained." It was therefore not the institution or practice as such that aroused his anger and prompted his attack when, on the eve of the Feast of All Saints, 1517, he expressed his disapproval in the form of ninety-five theses, which he nailed on the door of the castle church in Wittenberg.

Although Luther's theses were written in Latin, they immediately caused a sensation. They voiced a resentment that was quite universally felt, aggravated by the overbearing manner in which such contributions had been solicited in Germany and by their matter-of-fact acceptance by the Roman Curia.

Luther had declared his willingness to discuss and defend his theses in public, but the immediate result was the publication of a number of counter-theses by Tetzel and a summons to Luther to appear before a chapter meeting of his order at Heidelberg. Luther knew that at Heidelberg he would be asked to recant and that his refusal to do so might bring upon him the severest penalties. He therefore appealed to the Elector Frederick of Saxony, whose interference in his behalf was to make it possible for him to return safely to Wittenberg.

Contrary to his own expectations, the disputation at Heidelberg in 1518 resulted in a victory for his cause, and on his way back to Wittenberg he enjoyed the further satisfaction of being allowed to preach in Dresden before Duke George of Saxony and his court. Greatly encouraged by his success, he now edited a revised edition of his theses in the form of "resolutions," in which he further elucidated his new dogmatic views and which he dedicated to Pope Leo X. Although firm in his insistence that he could not recant, he asked Leo for advice and guidance and concluded with the following fervent supplication: "Most holy father! I prostrate myself at the feet of thy Holiness with all that I am and all that I have. Do what thou wilt, give life or death, call or revoke, approve or disapprove! In thy voice I will recognize the voice of Christ, who dwelleth and speaketh in thee. If I have deserved death, I do not refuse to die."

When Luther was asked to appear in Rome within sixty days to answer the charges preferred against him, Frederick the Wise of Saxony again interceded, with the result that the inquiry was entrusted to the famous Dominican theologian, Cardinal Cajetanus de Vio, and Luther was allowed to stay in Germany. He met Cajetanus at Augsburg in 1518, where the Imperial Diet was in session, and again he refused to recant, claiming that he had not contradicted any papal definition. He appealed to the pope against his accusers and asked that his case be submitted to a general Church council. In this appellation he promised to speak or do nothing against the Roman Church and the pope, as long as the latter was "well advised" (*bene consultus*). Frederick the Wise also took the stand that Luther's teachings had not been proven heretical.

To secure the co-operation of the Saxon elector in the Lutheran controversy, the pope ordered the papal notary and chamberlain, Charles von Miltitz, a Saxon nobleman, to present Frederick with the "golden rose," which had been blessed by the pope and which was customarily awarded each year to some prince as a symbol of special favor. Miltitz approached Luther and succeeded in effecting a further truce by persuading the reformer to dispatch a conciliatory letter to Rome.

In the meantime, the quarrel over the granting of indulgences had begun to develop into a more fundamental controversy concerning the primacy of the Roman See. It was this ancient claim of papal supremacy and authority over the universal Church, redefined by a papal decree of the year 1518, that was next attacked by Luther and that became the major issue in the Disputation of Leipzig in 1519.

The disputation was held between Martin Luther and his friend, Andrew Bodenstein, called Carlstadt, on the one side, and John Eck (Mayr), professor of theology at the University of Ingolstadt, on the other. The verbal duel took place in the largest hall of the Pleissenburg, in the presence of the duke and his court and a large number of local and visiting scholars. Eck succeeded in evoking from Luther the reluctant admission that he even questioned the authority of general Church councils, and that he considered some of the condemned teachings of John Huss (cf. p. 176 sq.) as Christian and evangelical.

   e) Revolutionary Writings and Excommunication. In 1520, John Eck was called to Rome to report on the Lutheran struggle, and he took with him copies of Luther's publications. Immediate action on the part of the Curia had been delayed by the imperial election of 1519 (cf. p. 205). In order to gain the support of Frederick the Wise, Charles V had promised that Luther should not be condemned without having been given an opportunity to present his case before the Imperial Diet. This delay was used by Luther to formulate his convictions in several writings, some of which are equally important as theological and literary documents.

   In June, 1520, he published his book *On the Papacy in Rome.* It was written in German and demonstrated for the first time his ability to adapt his style to the taste and understanding of the broad audiences to which many of his writings were henceforth addressed. He proclaimed that, being a spiritual, invisible realm, the Church needed no visible head and that its mark of identification was the community of the faithful, united and distinguished by baptism, communion (the Lord's Supper), and the preaching of the divine word. The "power of the keys" (power to forgive sins) was not confined to the priesthood or an ecclesiastical elite, but was possessed by all Christians who were capable of awakening in the consciences of their brethren the certitude of divine mercy.

   News had reached Luther that Rome was about to bring his trial to conclusion by pronouncing the Great Ban against him. Far from being intimidated by this prospect, he was roused to passionate and almost feverish literary activity. His *Address to the Christian Nobility of the German Nation on the Improvement of the Christian Estate* and the following pamphlet *On the Babylonian Captivity of the Church* have become famous as the two major polemical manifestoes of the Lutheran Reformation. The former was written in German and contained an ardent appeal to the Estates of the Empire to revolt against the tyranny and corruption of the papacy. The Roman Curia is accused of having exploited the good-natured Germans for the sake of material gain and political power. The distinction between priesthood and laity is termed a hellish invention, and the doctrine of a general priesthood of all the faithful is proclaimed for the first time. The national states are called upon to establish their secular jurisdiction over the ecclesiastical hierarchy. The papacy is designated as the embodiment of the antichrist, and among the ecclesiastical institutions that are attacked, monasticism and the law of celibacy rank foremost. The violent language of this pamphlet won Luther the enthusiastic support of the revolutionary knights Ulrich von Hutten (cf. p. 251 sq.) and Franz von Sickingen (cf. p. 251 sq.), and of some of the younger set of Humanist writers.

   In the same year in which Luther published his *Address to the Nobility* and was working on the Latin pamphlet *On the Babylonian Captivity of the Church,* he addressed a letter and a "protestation" to Charles V, in which he calls himself an obedient son of the Holy Catholic Church, who only reluctantly, against his will and for the sake of truth, had left the solitude of his cell to take part in the theological controversies: "In vain do I ask forgiveness, in vain do I offer silence . . . in vain do I ask for better information." He concludes by asking the emperor for a just trial, addressing Charles as the "king of all kings," before whom he (Luther) appears "humbly as a little flea." When the letter was handed over to Charles V at the Diet of Worms, he tore it to pieces with his own hands.

The pamphlet *On the Babylonian Captivity of the Church* identifies the papacy with the kingdom of Babylon, which has subjugated and corrupted the Church of Christ. Only three sacraments as against the seven* of the Catholic tradition are recognized as valid: baptism, penance, and the Lord's Supper. The doctrine of "transubstantiation" (cf. p. 231) is denied, and the reception of the sacraments is described as a voluntary act of the individual, not demanded by Christ. The celebration of the Mass has no sacrificial significance and is not even a meritorious act. "Neither Pope nor bishop nor anybody else has the right to impose even one syllable on a Christian without his consent."

Shortly after Luther had learned that the bull of excommunication had arrived in Germany, he published the famous tract *On the Liberty of a Christian Man,* in a German and Latin edition. Following the advice of Miltitz, he sent the Latin version to Leo X, together with a letter in which he once more emphasized his peaceful intentions, but at the same time asserted that the institution of the papacy was dead: Leo was like a sheep among the wolves and like Daniel in the lions' den. The Roman Church was a den of thieves and rogues.

In his treatment of the concept of Christian liberty Luther reiterates his definition of faith, which is an act of simple confidence in God's mercy. The result of such an act is the true liberty of a Christian: "That is Christian liberty: we no longer need any works to attain true devotion. . . . By virtue of his faith a Christian man is raised so highly above all things that he becomes their master in a spiritual way: nothing can impair his road to beatitude" (*Seligkeit*). However, the Christian as a social being must exercise self-control and be charitable to others. Such charity grows out of his faith and his pure love of God. The works of mercy are without merit in themselves and cannot lead to beatitude. Therefore, it is quite useless to look upon the good works and count their number: "Good works never make a good, devout man, but a good, devout man does good and devout works." He does them, knowing that Christ has already fulfilled for him all the commandments, and that therefore a just man needs neither the law nor good works. Luther's argumentation was intended to refute the

---

* (1) Baptism; (2) confirmation; (3) Sacrament of the Altar [Eucharist, the Lord's Supper]; (4) penance [confession and absolution of sins]; (5) extreme unction [of the dying]; (6) holy orders [ordination of priests]; (7) marriage.

Catholic teaching that hope of eternal reward and fear of eternal punishment were legitimate motives of Christian faith and works.

Meanwhile, Luther's case had been judged by the Roman Curia, and the Bull *Exurge Domine et iudica causam tuam* ("Rise, O Lord, and judge Thy cause") of 1520 had condemned forty-one of Luther's propositions and had threatened him with excommunication unless he retracted within sixty days. Among the condemned teachings were those that referred to man's inability to perform good acts, those that dealt with justification by faith alone; with the efficacy of the sacraments; his teachings concerning purgatory, penance, and indulgences; and those that denied the authority of the pope and of general councils.

Luther took this condemnation of his major tenets as a declaration of war and answered immediately with another pamphlet, entitled *Against the Execrable Bull of the Anti-Christ (Adversus execrabilem Antichristi bullam)*. In his own German edition of this pamphlet he asked the question: "Who would be surprised if princes, nobles, and laymen should beat the Pope, the bishops, priests, and monks over the head and drive them out of the country?" On December 10, 1520, a gathering of students and professors of the University of Wittenberg, who had assembled in front of the Elster-Gate, witnessed the solemn burning of a collection of the papal decretals and the canon law. Luther himself stepped forward and, committing a printed copy of the papal bull (*Exurge Domine*) to the flames, exclaimed: "As thou hast destroyed the truth of God, so the Lord today destroyeth thee, by means of this fire. Amen." This symbolic act was the signal for the actual beginning of religious revolution in Germany.

After the time limit set for Luther's submission had expired, a new bull (*Decet Romanum Pontificem*), dated January 3, 1521, declared the excommunication in force. Copies of Luther's writings and a wooden statue of the reformer were ceremoniously burned in Rome. Leo X addressed a letter to Charles V, asking for the full co-operation of the Empire in making the ban of the Church effective.

A meeting of the Imperial Diet had been called in the city of Worms, for January, 1521, and Luther, upon the suggestion of Frederick the Wise, declared his willingness to appear before the assembled Estates to have his cause tried and judged. Over the objections of the papal legate the Estates petitioned the emperor to summon Luther to Worms, in order to prevail once more upon him to retract, before pronouncing over him the ban of the Empire.

The summons reached Luther in Wittenberg on March 26, together with an imperial safe-conduct. The reformer's journey from Wittenberg to Worms was one triumphal procession, confirming his conviction that he could rely upon the sympathy of the majority of the German people, an experience which strengthened in him the resolution not to recant, come what might. Defiance and self-assurance are the characteristic traits in Luther as portrayed by Lucas Cranach in the year of the Diet of Worms.

The first hearing before the assembled electors, princes, prelates, nobles, and other delegates took place in the palace of the local bishop. Luther seemed intimidated by the august assemblage and, when asked by the speaker whether he was ready to recant, answered with a subdued voice, demanding that he be given more time for deliberation. He was granted a delay of twenty-four hours. The emperor, unimpressed by Luther's appearance, remarked: "That man will never make a heretic of me."

At the decisive second hearing that was held on the following day, Luther had regained his courage and composure and delivered the famous speech, in which he defended his convictions, with a firm and steady voice. After he had finished, the speaker asked him for an unequivocal answer: was he willing to recant or not? Whereupon Luther declared: "Unless I shall be convinced by witness of Scripture or by valid argument, I shall stay convinced by those sacred Scriptures which I have adduced, and my conscience is imprisoned in the word of God. I neither can nor will recant anything, for it is neither safe nor right to act against one's conscience. So help me God. Amen."

Luther left Worms a few days after the hearing. Meanwhile, Frederick the Wise had worked out a plan that would protect Luther against the dangerous consequences of the impending ban of the Empire. Five of the elector's horsemen, feigning an attack on Luther's traveling coach, kidnaped him on the road that leads from Möhra to Gotha, and brought him safely to the Wartburg near Eisenach in Thuringia, the property of the elector of Saxony. The hiding place had been selected by the councilors of Frederick who, claiming complete ignorance as to Luther's whereabouts, saved himself unnecessary embarrassment.

The "Edict of Worms," dated May 8, declared Luther under the ban of the Empire. He was condemned as a heretic, ten times worse than John Huss; as the author of writings which served to incite revolt, schism, and bloody civil war; as a subverter of all law, and a devil in human form. No one might shelter him or offer him food and drink. When apprehended, he must at once be handed over to the emperor. Whoever should protect him would share in his crime and incur identical penalties.

f) Luther in the Wartburg. Clothed in knightly attire and partly disguised by a beard, Luther stayed in the Wartburg as "Squire George" (*Ritter Görg*) for almost a full year. He occupied a small room and used his enforced solitude to continue his writing. He tells of temptations of the flesh and of frequent vexations by the devil, who appeared to him in various shapes and disguises. He calls the Wartburg his "Patmos,"* because of the large number of visions and hallucinations that he experienced there. There is no evidence, however, that Luther threw his inkstand at the devil, thereby causing the famous stain on the wall of his cell that is even to this day shown to visiting tourists.

---

* The name refers to the city of Patmos on the Dodecanese Islands where St. John the Evangelist is said to have written the inspired text of the Apocalypse.

Luther's *Interpretation of the Magnificat,** written in the Wartburg and dedicated to the son of the Saxon elector, rejects the Catholic belief in the intercession of Mary in behalf of the faithful, but retains the doctrines of the virgin birth and of the Immaculate Conception (Mary's being born without the stain of original sin, in view of her being destined to become the mother of the Redeemer).

The greatest and most far-reaching accomplishment of the year in the Wartburg, however, was Luther's translation of the *New Testament* from Greek into German, a work whose literary significance was almost immediately recognized by friend and foe alike. It is hard to understand how Luther could have completed this monumental work, in addition to all his other plans and labors, within the short span of one year. The translation of the *Old Testament* followed later, and Luther's complete German Bible was published in 1534. The fifth printing of the year 1545 is regarded as the standard edition.

Luther's desire to fortify his theological system and especially to anchor his doctrine of "justification by faith alone" (fiducial faith) in scriptural authority induced him to consider the different sacred books as of unequal value and to eliminate several of them, among others the Epistle of James, which he called an "epistle of straw." By using for his translation the written language of the Saxon chancelleries and by blending this Middle German with elements of High German dialects, while at the same time he imparted to his work the flavor, vigor, and vitality of his own personality, he became the creator of a unified High German language, whose structure, syntax, and vocabulary have remained essentially unchanged to the present day. His acquaintance with mysticism on the one hand, and with the life, thought, and speech of the people on the other, made him capable of enriching his native tongue by means of individual and communal experience, which called for and issued in new and striking word formations.

As it was Luther's intention to substitute the authority of the Bible for almost the entire body of discarded Church tradition, he employed every device to make his work as readable and easily accessible as possible. Woodcuts served to emphasize the anti-Catholic tendency of his translation. Thus, the scarlet woman of the Apocalypse is crowned with the papal tiara, and Catholic dignitaries as well as the German emperor pay homage to this symbol of blasphemy and iniquity.

g) Luther's Return to Wittenberg and His Marriage. While Luther was working in his cell on the Wartburg, some of his followers in Wittenberg and elsewhere had carried his teachings to such extreme conclusions that he felt his presence was needed to call a halt to such excesses as the burning of sacred images, and the demolition of the statues of saints. Even more dangerous was the movement of the "Prophets of Zwickau,"

---

* *"Magnificat anima mea Dominum"* (my soul doth magnify the Lord): Mary's hymn of praise, in which, during her visit with her cousin Elizabeth, she gives thanks for being chosen to become the mother of Christ. The "Magnificat" forms part of the canonical office.

who adopted the teachings of the Anabaptists and their leader, Thomas Münzer (cf. p. 242), and who turned against Luther's doctrine on infant baptism, arguing that if Luther's contention was true and faith was the only requisite for the efficacy of the sacrament of baptism, then children must not be baptized until they had reached the maturity that was required for an act of faith.

Luther was fully conscious of his religious mission when he defied all the dangers that threatened him and returned to Wittenberg in 1522. He soon disappointed many of his friends and followers by turning out to be much more conservative in his views than they had anticipated. It had become clear to him that religious and social anarchy could only be avoided if he succeeded in organizing a church in which freedom was curbed by unity through authority. Although many vital changes in cult, liturgy, and dogmatic theology were introduced, much of the traditional Catholic doctrine and practice was retained. The authority of the Scriptures was declared supreme, but the practical exercise of the new creed was placed under the absolute control of the civil government. Superintendents, replacing the Roman Catholic bishops, were the appointees and officers of the state.

If the religious and social radicals felt repelled by Luther's conservatism, many of his Humanist sympathizers were estranged by the schismatic character that the Lutheran reform movement had assumed. Thus their hopes were frustrated that the reform could be carried out within the old Church by a gradual process of enlightened education. They were also unable to accept Luther's metaphysical and ethical rigorism and pessimism, his denial of free will, and his denunciation of human nature.

Luther's ideas were realized step by step in the organized structure of the new church: of the sacraments there now remained only baptism and the Lord's Supper; pilgrimages, fasts and abstinence, the veneration of the saints and their relics were done away with; the monastic orders were dissolved, and all the members of the clergy were allowed to marry. Thus the barriers that had separated ecclesiastics and laymen were broken down. Luther resumed his lectures in the University of Wittenberg and at the same time reorganized the religious cult and ecclesiastic discipline of his church. The liturgy of the Mass was largely retained, the Latin texts being gradually replaced by German translations (*German Mass and Order of the Service,* 1526). The sacrificial character of the Mass, however, was definitely denied.

As time went on, more and more significance was attached to congregational singing. Recognizing in the religious hymn a powerful force in spreading the new faith, Luther delved into the treasury of the past and drew on his own religious experience, utilizing his poetic gifts to provide the Lutheran Reformation with its great, warlike, lyric manifestoes. Ancient Latin hymns were translated into German, secular songs were revised and turned into church hymns. Luther himself created thirty-six hymns, for which his friend, John Walter, the musician, composed the melodies. Twenty-four of these songs were first published in 1524 (*Geistliches Gesang-büchlein*). The powerful and defiant *Trutzlied: "Ein' feste Burg ist unser Gott"*) ("A Mighty Fortress Is Our God"), whose melody is based on motifs of medieval "plain song" (Gregorian chant, cf. p. 83 sq.), originated in 1527, reflecting a period of critical strife and strain in the progress of the Lutheran Reformation. Frequently the melodies of ancient Latin church hymns or of pre-Reformation German religious and folk poetry served as textual and musical patterns.

In 1524 Luther threw off the habit of the Augustinian Order, and in the following year married the former Cistercian nun, Katherine of Bora. His friends were jubilant, his opponents scandalized. The newly married couple made their home in the former Augustinian monastery in Wittenberg, and Luther's "Käthe" rented the former monastic cells to university students, who henceforth shared the family life of Luther's household.

h) Luther and the Peasants. The same year 1525 marked the climax of the great German Peasants' War (cf. p. 240 sq.), with whose origin, conduct, and infamous end Luther was at first indirectly and later on directly concerned. The views that he had expressed in his book *On the Freedom of a Christian Man* had been interpreted by the peasants as a vindication of their revolt against social injustice and oppression. Luther's *Exhortation to Peace* (April, 1525) referred to the "Twelve Articles" of the peasants, their demand of the "Gospel without human addition," and was an attempt on his part to reconcile the opposing parties by mediation. He addressed both lords and peasants, telling them that they were both wrong and at odds with Christian teaching: "Both tyrants and mobs are enemies of God." His admonition having failed to persuade either party, Luther then turned passionately against the peasants in his pamphlet "Against the Murderous and Rapacious Hordes of the Peasants," in which he not only claimed that the peasants have no just cause of complaint, but ended by calling them "mad dogs and specters of hell," urging the princes and lords to "strike them down, throttle and stab them in secret and in public": "A prince can now deserve mercy better by shedding blood, than others can by prayer." Even years after the revolt had been savagely put down, Luther, himself a peasant's son, was to write: "I am very angry at the peasants, who cannot see how well off they are, sitting in peace through the help and protection of the princes. You impudent, coarse asses, can you not understand this? May thunder strike you dead!"

Such violent outbursts of anger can only be understood if we remember that Luther had originally attacked ecclesiastical and secular authorities, not because he found them too rigorous and too exacting but because of their laxity and corruption. With most of the medieval writers he shared the conviction that society rested on serfdom. In addition, the sharp dividing line that he had drawn between the external realm of secular power and the inner kingdom of the spirit had issued in a political theory that favored an extreme absolutism of the secular powers, whose function it was to act as law-enforcing agents in a world that was hopelessly entangled in sin and corruption. Thus, when the peasants wrote: "Christ has delivered and redeemed us all, the lowly as well as the great, without exception, by the shedding of His precious blood," Luther felt all the horrors of approaching anarchy and answered promptly: "This article would make all men equal and so change the spiritual kingdom of Christ into an external, worldly one. Impossible! An earthly kingdom cannot exist without inequality of persons. Some must be free, others serfs, some rulers, others subjects." The problems of social ethics and social reconstruction were to be left to the discretion of the state. They were foreign to Luther's conception of the functions of the Church: "Christians are rare people on earth. Therefore, stern, hard, civil rule is necessary in the world, lest the world become wild, peace vanish, and commerce and common interests be destroyed. . . . No one need think that the world can be ruled without blood. The civil sword shall and must be red and bloody."

i) Predestination and Free Will. In 1523 Erasmus of Rotterdam (cf. p. 249 sq.) had published his work on the freedom of the human will (*De Libero Arbitrio Diatribe*), in which he attacked Luther's determinism. Luther's answer was given in 1525, in a work that he himself considered his masterpiece and the capstone of his theology, and to which he gave the title *De Servo Arbitrio* (On the Enslaved Will). Employing a large number of biblical quotations, Luther tries to establish once and for all that God works everything in everyone and that man, by his own nature, is entirely unable to recognize and choose the good: "Everything that is created by God, is moved by His omnipotence. . . . " Human will, like a saddle horse, stands between God and the devil: "If God mounts into the saddle, man goes as God wills it. . . . If the devil mounts into the saddle, man goes as the devil wills it. It is not in man's power to run to one of the two horsemen and offer himself to him, but the horsemen fight against one another to gain hold of the horse. . . . If we believe that Satan is the Prince of this World, who constantly besets the Kingdom of Christ and does not release his grip on the enslaved human beings unless he is forced to do so by the power of God, then it is evident that there can be no free will." In this way Luther tries to explain the predestination of the condemned souls, who will suffer the torments of eternal hell-fire. But if man lacks the freedom of choice, who then is responsible for the sins he commits? Luther answers: "God is God, and for His will there is neither reason nor cause. . . . He is the rule of all things." We are reminded once more that Martin Luther was "of Occam's school."

j) The Two Catechisms and the Book on Marriage. The more Luther's reformation lost the character of a sectarian movement and acquired the sociological characteristics of a church organism, which received and embraced saints and sinners, the more was he compelled to stress the authoritarian elements as against the individualism and liberalism of religious enthusiasts and pseudomystics. In the end he was to deny explicitly the mystical inclinations of an earlier period of his own life and to construe instead an antagonism between a "faith," which was based on the objective authority of the Scriptures, and a "mystical" subjectivism, which claimed personal illumination by an "inner light."

The development in the direction of authoritarianism included the justification of force, compulsion, and persecution of heretics as means to crush divergent views and movements within and without the Lutheran Church. The demand of freedom of conscience and religious conviction was completely abandoned. In serious cases of heresy, such as adherence to the teachings of the Anabaptists (cf. p. 241 sq.), capital punishment was recommended, while in milder forms of disbelief or in the case of moral offenses the disciplinary action consisted in the exclusion of the sinner from the sacrament of communion. The Lord's Supper in the Lutheran congregations was now (after 1526) generally administered in both kinds, the bread and the wine.

In 1529 Luther published two manuals of religious instruction, known as the *Little* and the *Great Catechisms.* The *Little Catechism,* designed "for children and people of a simple mind," was a model of clear and straightforward exposition of doctrine, omitting all polemic agitation against the Catholic Church. The *Great Catechism* was primarily intended for the use of Lutheran pastors. No reference was made to the right of individual interpretation of the Bible, nor to Luther's previous emphasis on the fatal consequences of original sin and the dogma of predestination for eternal damnation. After Luther's death the two catechisms were incorporated in the "Form of Concord" (*Konkordienbuch*) as *"symbola"* (articles of faith) of the Lutheran Church.

In his book *On Matrimony* (*Von Ehesachen*) of 1530 Luther emphasizes that marriage is not a sacrament but "an external, worldly thing, like clothes and food, home and hearth, subject to secular authority." Nevertheless he praises the state of married life as a worthy and even sublime and divine institution. Divorce he considers permissible in the case of adultery and desertion.

k) *Luther and Zwingli.* At about the time when Luther had taken his monastic vows at Erfurt, Huldreich (Ulrich) Zwingli (1484-1531) was ordained a priest. His relations to the radical wing of the Humanist movement awakened his interest in the ideas of the Lutheran reform. Shortly after having accepted the ministry of the Great Minster (*Grossmünster*) in Zurich, he succeeded in winning the city council over to his views, and in introducing the "reformed" creed in that city. Celebration of the Mass was prohibited, all images were either destroyed or removed from the churches, and all citizens were in duty bound to listen to Zwingli's sermons. Even singing and organ music were originally excluded from church services.

In a Socratic manner Zwingli declared that virtue was the result of knowledge. Yet, quite inconsistently, he denied the freedom of the will and taught absolute predestination. His radicalism and rationalism, however, resulted in several clashes with Luther, especially concerning the words of institution in the commemoration of the Lord's Supper. It was Zwingli's conviction that Christ's sacramental words "This is My body, this is My blood" must be understood symbolically, not literally, meaning "this signifies My body, this signifies My blood," while Luther insisted on a strictly literal interpretation, maintaining that Christ was really present on the altar, but only for those who believed in His presence and only as long as the ceremony lasted (doctrine of *impanation*).

In 1529 Luther and Zwingli met in the city of Marburg for a disputation (*Religionsgespräch*) on the controversial issue. Despite Zwingli's conciliatory attitude Luther refused to yield to the rational arguments of the Swiss reformer, with the repeated assertion: "Your spirit is different from ours." In the same year the rural cantons of Switzerland, which had preserved their Catholic heritage, concluded an alliance with Catholic Austria, and the following armed conflict ended with the defeat of the reformed forces in the battle of Cappel (1531). Zwingli died on the field of battle.

l) Luther and Melanchthon. With the "Protestation" of the Lutheran princes and cities of the year 1529 (cf. p. 210) a "Protestant party" had come into actual existence. At the Diet of Augsburg in 1530 the Lutherans presented the so-called "Augsburg Confession" (*Confessio Augustana*) that had been drawn up by Philip Melanchthon (1497–1560), Luther's close friend and collaborator. It was a carefully and shrewdly worded document that left the door ajar for a compromise with the Catholic party. Some of Luther's main tenets, such as the doctrine of the general priesthood of all the faithful, the denial of the primacy of the Roman See, the denial of free will, and the doctrine of absolute predestination, were not even mentioned.

The author of this document was a classical philologist and a teacher of great erudition, whose impressionable mind had been fascinated by Luther's genial and dynamic personality. He was a man of letters rather than a man of action, and it was in his capacity as a scholar that he effectively supplemented the Lutheran teachings, by providing the reformed theology with a philosophic basis, thus systematically preparing the way for the development of a Protestant scholasticism that was indebted to Cicero and Aristotle. A native of Bretten in Baden, he showed his predilection for the Humanist trend of the age by adopting the name "Melanchthon," a Greek translation of his family name, Schwarzerd. Retiring, introspective, and peace loving by nature, of frail physical constitution, he was drawn into theological controversies and political quarrels against his will, so much so that he remarked in the hour of his death that he felt happy to be freed at last from the wrath of the theologians (*a rabie theologorum*). The great services that Melanchthon rendered to his country by reorganizing the system of higher learning, especially his reforms in the field of Protestant secondary education, earned for him the title of honor, *"Praeceptor Germaniae"* (the Teacher of Germany).

Although Luther had somewhat reluctantly approved of Melanchthon's formulation of the *Confessio Augustana,* he subsequently declared himself opposed to all further attempts at mediation and compromise. He admitted that he was not able "to tread as gently and softly" as Melanchthon. On April 15, 1530, he had arrived at the castle of Coburg on the southern slope of the Thuringian mountains, to watch the proceedings at Augsburg. From here he sent an *Admonition to the Ecclesiastics Assembled at the Diet of Augsburg,* designed to impress upon the members of the Diet the momentous importance of their decision. "If I live," he explains in this pamphlet, "I shall be as a pestilence to you; if I die, I shall be your death; for God has called me to run you down. . . . I shall not leave you in peace until you either mend your ways or perish."

m) Completion of the German Bible. Twelve years after the edition of his translation of the New Testament, the entire Bible in German, richly illustrated with woodcuts, was published by Hans Luft in Wittenberg. Luther had taken as a basis for his translation the original Greek text of the Scriptures in place of the Latin Vulgate. In this he followed the humanistic tendencies of his age. Erasmus of Rotterdam (cf. p. 249 sq.) had pointed the way with his Greek edition of the New Testament. But it was Luther's great merit that the Bible soon became the most widely read book in German lands.

Many of the illustrations are violently polemical. The scarlet women of Babylon and the apocalyptic dragon appear again, crowned with the papal tiara, and the title page of the Wittenberg edition of 1541 portrays the devil with a cardinal's hat, driving a man into the jaws of hell.

Luther's translation of the Bible was a work of eminent literary merit, but it was by no means the first German translation. The author of the first complete German Bible, printed by Mentel in Strasbourg in 1466, is unknown. One hundred and fifty-six different Latin editions of the complete Bible were printed between the years 1450 and 1520. Thereto must be added a large number of earlier manuscripts as well as the numerous editions of specific parts of the Scriptures in Latin and German, especially the Psalter and the Gospels and Epistles of the ecclesiastical year, taken from the Old and New Testaments. They were collected in the so-called "plenaries" or "homilies" (*Postillen*), which had gained great popularity among people of every walk of life.

n) Luther's "Table Talk." The students who lived as boarders in Luther's household, friends of the family, and invited guests gathered almost daily around the family table to listen to Luther's informal talks or to carry on spirited discussions. Luther's utterances were usually written down in shorthand by some zealous student or friend, and it is to these gatherings in the family circle that we owe the famous collection of "Table Talks" (*Tischreden*), dealing with various theological and philosophical problems,

Luther at the Age of 37, by Lucas Cranach.

Erasmus, by Hans Holbein.

personal experiences and reminiscences, and multiple related subjects. The *Tischreden* are an invaluable aid in any attempt to establish a historically reliable picture of Martin Luther, his personality and his work. The directness and spontaneity of the speech, the blend of natural simplicity, genial humor, and biting satire make this collection a source of genuine delight, notwithstanding an obvious lack of consistency, moderation, and premeditation. The almost unbelievable coarseness of many passages and expressions must be largely attributed to the growing degeneration of taste and style in the sixteenth century. The records begin with the year 1531 and extend to the end of Luther's life. "Frau Käthe" was not only an attentive listener but frequently took part in the discussions.

Luther's family life was a happy one. The children were brought up in a deeply religious atmosphere, and Katherine Luther proved herself a strong and brave comrade in the many struggles that weighed dark and heavy on the last decades of Luther's life.

o) Luther's Last Years and Death. Dissensions in the ranks of his own church, controversies with the leaders of separatistic sects, the realization of the gradual regeneration of the Catholic Church, and, in addition, Luther's failing health were factors that produced in his mind frequent moods of doubt, weariness, skepticism, and even despair: "Let everything fall to pieces, let it stand, let it perish, let it go as it will . . . ," he exclaims in 1542. And again: "Germany is no more; never again will she be the same that she was in the past."

The "invisible" church that Luther had hoped to establish in the hearts of all the faithful had grown into a very visible human institution, which had to rely on the support of the secular state for its existence and perpetuation. In order to preserve the unity of his creation, Luther found himself compelled to maintain it by force and to turn against his own principles of individual freedom and toleration.

From the beginning of the fourth decade of the sixteenth century the thought of his approaching death recurred again and again. When he celebrated his sixty-first birthday in the company of friends (1545), he thought that he would not live through the Easter season of that year. He spoke gloomily of a threatening defection of the brethren in the faith, by which they would do more harm to the Gospel than the mostly ignorant and epicurean papists.

Once more, however, his hatred of the papacy prompted Luther to take up his pen to denounce the Church of Rome as the creation of Satan (*Against the Papacy in Rome, an Invention of the Devil,* 1545). Lucas Cranach's drawings and woodcuts, inspired and commentated by Luther and designated by himself as his "testament to the German nation," served the same purpose. In other writings of this last period he dealt with the practices of usury and the part played by the Jews in the money trade. While in an earlier period of his life he had hoped to convert the Jews to his new gospel, he now attacked their race and religion in most violent terms. In his views on usury Luther adhered strictly to the medieval tradition, in an age in which the gradual adoption of the credit system in trade and commerce had rendered meaningless the prohibition of the taking of interest. He felt that the devil himself is in the complicated mechanism of financial organization: "The greatest misfortune of the German nation is the traffic in interest. . . . The devil invented it, and the Pope, by giving his sanction to it, has done untold evil throughout the world." Usurers should be refused the Lord's Supper and Christian burial. The luxury trade with the East, the machinations of international finance, speculation, and monopolies are denounced: "Foreign merchandise which brings from Calicut and India and the like places wares such as precious silver and jewels and spices . . . and drain the land and people of their money, should not be permitted."

In 1541 John Calvin (1509–1564) had established his theocratic rule in Geneva. Born in Picardy (France) and educated in Paris and in the law schools of Orléans and Bourges, he had been influenced by the reading of Luther's works, when he began to work out his own version of the reformed creed and gave it a doctrinal foundation in the *Institutes of the Christian Religion* (1534). His legally trained mind made him averse to all halfhearted measures, and though he recognized his indebtedness to Luther, he became the most relentless advocate of the doctrine of absolute predestination and an integral determinism that went far beyond Luther's position. Luther's separation of the worldly and ecclesiastical spheres he likewise rejected and, by conceiving of God as an all-powerful, all-penetrating, stern, and unbending Judge, he established the moral code of Calvinism on the basis of an Old Testament concept of divine law.

Calvin's theocratic state embraces the most minute details of public and private life and tries to realize a commonwealth of saints by the application of the most rigid discipline and a system of constant control and supervision. By denying the real presence of Christ in the Eucharist Calvin approached the position of Zwingli. His teachings, accordingly, were sufficiently at variance with Luther's fundamental convictions to make an open conflict between the two men highly probable. Luther's death, however, forestalled this. In the following decades Calvinism spread from Switzerland to other countries, notably France, the Netherlands, Bohemia, and Scotland, making also considerable inroads into southern Germany, where in some districts it replaced Lutheranism.

Martin Luther died on February 18, 1546, of a prolonged heart ailment, at Eisleben, the city of his birth. He had gone there to mediate a quarrel between the counts of Mansfeld. Two of the friends who surrounded his deathbed asked him whether he wished to remain faithful to his teachings. His affirmative answer was his last utterance. His wife and children had remained in Wittenberg and could not be with him in the hour of his death. He lies buried in the castle church in Wittenberg.

p) Germany and the Reformation. It depends upon the historian's point of view whether he looks upon the Lutheran Reformation as a blessing or a curse. To designate it as a typically German phenomenon, and to oppose it as such to a Romanic or un-Germanic type of religious devotion, may be correct in so far as Luther's movement shows a definite preference for a religion of "pure inwardness" (*reine Innerlichkeit*) and personal experience as against a form of worship which stresses the importance of external form and dogma, liturgical ritual, and cultic imagery. However, we shall do well not to put too much emphasis on such distinctions, in view of the fact that Luther's ideals of spiritual freedom, individual judgment, and pure inwardness were never actually embodied in the completed structure of his church; most of the ideas that had brought about his break with Rome had to seek refuge in the shelter of those separatistic sects that were persecuted with fire and sword by the three reformed churches.

On the other hand, while Luther's own mentality was undoubtedly more medieval than modern, he nevertheless inaugurated that secularization of life and culture which came to its fruition partly without his doing and partly even against his will. As far as Germany is concerned, the fatal consequence of his movement was the division of the German nation, its best minds and its cultural energies, into antagonistic camps, intellectually, socially, politically. But even here it is hard to determine whether the searching thoroughness of the German mind, its deep and vital concern with the ultimate problems of human existence, with truth, goodness, and beauty, was not intensified rather than crippled by the spiritual challenge that was Luther's gift to the German people.

Revolution and Civil War. The Lutheran Reformation represents only one aspect of the deep-seated unrest and dissatisfaction that produced the violent social reactions of the early sixteenth century. Socially and politically, the age was characterized less by attempts at reform than by the spirit of revolt, issuing in class warfare and social disintegration. The end of the Middle Ages and the beginning of modern times is marked by the revolt of the have-nots, the socially disinherited, those who for some reason or other were not able to keep pace with the changing economic and political constellations of the time. But, as is always the case, these economic and political transformations were only surface phenomena which pointed to a more fundamental change in the intellectual and moral attitudes and convictions. The have-nots in the beginning of the sixteenth century were the peasants, the proletarians in the cities, and the impoverished knights.

a) *Peasantry and Early Capitalism.* The peasant, who had been relatively well off in the agrarian society of the early Middle Ages, had become virtually a slave in the course of the fourteenth and fifteenth centuries, concomitant with the advent of the new money economy, city trade, and capitalistic enterprise. The rights to the piece of land that he held either on a long or short lease (*Erbpacht* and *Zeitpacht*), had been constantly diminished, while at the same time his duties had become correspondingly heavier and, finally, almost unbearable. With the waning of imperial power questions of right and social justice had become more and more questions of might, to the exclusion of any moral motives and obligations.

Roman law, after the eleventh century, had been gradually adopted by most European countries and had supplanted the traditional tribal laws in Germany during the fourteenth and fifteenth centuries. It was used with legalistic ingenuity and seemingly inexorable logic to the advantage of princely and capitalistic interests. It superseded and invalidated the principles that had been embodied in the ancient law codes of the peasants (*Weistümer*). "According to the damnable teaching of the new jurists, the prince is to be everything in the country, but the people nothing, the people having nothing to do but obey, serve, and pay taxes," wrote Jacob Wimpheling (1450–1528), a priest and one of the leaders of early Humanism. Furthermore, the steady increase in population led to a growing scarcity of available land and to the parceling out of farmland in smaller and smaller units.

The peasantry at the end of the Middle Ages was becoming more and more dependent on city capital. This increasing indebtedness led to hatred and resentment against the professional money lenders, the Jews, usurers, merchants, and quite generally against all the representatives of the new money economy, who dominated and cornered the markets, controlled the prices, and destroyed the bases of agrarian activity and economy. The great merchants and merchant-princes of the fifteenth century, such as the Medicis in Italy and the Fuggers, Welsers, and Hochstetters in Germany, represented the growing power of international finance and were the powers behind the European thrones and the directors of the destinies of European states. They fixed the prices of commodities and necessities at their will and controlled the domestic and foreign markets. Mining and banking were the two main sources of the income of these early capitalists. The Fuggers in Augsburg, for instance, acquired the greater part of their wealth through the operation of German silver mines. With an organized credit system still in its infancy, the possession of coined money in gold and silver was an absolute prerequisite for business transactions on a large scale. The restrictions imposed on unrestrained competition by the guilds (cf. p. 126) were felt as so many shackles and were thrown off to give way to the freedom of capitalistic venture and initiative. Merchant companies and, later on, joint-stock companies were to provide added opportunities for profit for their individual members and facilitated the formation of monopolies. The joint-stock company, which appears fully developed in Germany at the end of the sixteenth century, implies joint liability for the indebtedness of the whole company, while in the ordinary merchant company each member carried on his transactions on his own capital and risk.

The anticapitalist spirit called forth plans for social reconstruction as well as many get-rich-quick schemes, supposed short cuts to Utopia. Some writers suggested that all merchant companies should be done away with. Ulrich von Hutten (cf. p. 251 sq.) fought against merchants, knights, lawyers, and clergymen, while Geiler von Kaisersberg (1445–1510), the famous preacher and moralist, found the monopolists more detestable even than the Jews and asked that they be exterminated like wolves.

A resolution passed by the Austrian Diet of 1518 reads as follows: "The great companies have brought under their control . . . all goods which are indispensable to man, and they are so powerful by the strength of their money that they cut off trade from the common merchant who is worth from one to ten thousand florins; they set the prices at their pleasure and increase them at their will, by which they visibly grow fewer in number; but a few of them grow into a princely fortune to the great detriment of the country." Some of the inflated big business houses broke down after a short-lived boom, involving in their downfall the savings of small investors. The failure of the Hochstetters in 1529 amounted to 800,000 florins, about $6,500,000 in our present value of money. With the disintegration of the craft and merchant guilds the hitherto friendly relations between masters and journeymen gave way to growing antagonism. Labor was on the way to become a commodity that could be bought and sold, and the working-man, selling his labor to the highest bidder, was gradually forced into a proletarian existence.

The revolts of the peasants were essentially a last attempt of an agrarian society to hold its own against the superior forces of the new capitalistic system of economy. The peasants appeared as the reactionary and retrogressive forces in an age that had introduced the profit motive as the chief factor in economic endeavor and that adhered to the formerly condemned and despised theory that money can breed money. With increasing opportunities in commercial enterprise the investment of capital in ever so many ways became the order of the day and was universally practiced by states, cities, and individuals. The newly discovered trade routes to Africa, India, and the Americas added even greater stimulus and allurement to an expanding international trade, based on large-scale investment and commercial credit. But this whole process of transforming an agrarian into a financial society was accompanied by almost constant conflicts, convulsions, and explosions.

It is not surprising that despite his conservatism the peasant, too, wanted his share of the goods of this world; that he, too, had been seized by the desire to advance his social position and to raise his standard of living. In addition, Luther's message concerning the "Freedom of a Christian Man" had provided him with a moral incentive and justification in his demand for social justice and for due consideration of his human rights. The spirit of revolt was fanned by the news of the successful struggle of the Swiss peasants against the oppressive rule of the Hapsburgs (cf. p. 170) and by the sympathizers among the city proletariat, groaning under the burden of excessive taxation. From the beginning, therefore, we find the lower classes in the cities involved in the uprisings of the peasants.

b) Beginnings of the Peasants' Revolt. The first revolutionary wave started in the southwestern corner of the Empire, those districts that were closest to the free peasant republic of Switzerland. Within a short time the movement spread to Swabia, Franconia, and Thuringia. The symbol of the rebellious peasants was the *"Bundschuh,"* the common laced boot worn by the peasants, which was depicted on their banners — a sign of protest against the costly buckskin footwear of the nobles.

The first major uprising occurred in the Alsatian regions in 1493. It was prematurely discovered and bloodily crushed. The same fate befell the second major revolt of the year 1502. But Joss Fritz, the leader of the peasants, escaped and, after another unsuccessful attempt and another escape, he reappeared in 1525, when the Great Peasant War had already gotten well under way. Minor uprisings in Wurtemburg and in the eastern part of the Empire had likewise ended in failure.

c) The Great Peasant War (1524-1525). "Nothing but God's Justice" had been the battle cry of the peasants at the beginning of the revolt, but now they demanded the liquidation of all the intermediate powers that stood between the emperor and the people: (princes, lords, bishops, abbots, etc.). They formulated their demands in the famous "Twelve Articles" of 1525, to which the peasants in all parts of Germany subscribed. The authors of the articles accepted Luther's new gospel as their spiritual creed and designated all opponents as enemies of Christ. In the name of the gospel they demanded freedom of choice in the election of their pastors; the abolition of serfdom and the tithe; the free use of water, woods, and pastures; and the abolition of the death tax (*Todfall*) which deprived widows and their children of a large part of their inheritance. Reference to scriptural authority was again made in the concluding words: "If one or several of these articles be contrary to the word of God, we will not defend such propositions."

The more considerate among the ruling powers recognized that there was just cause for complaint on the side of the peasants, and if their counsel had been heeded, the following excesses could have been averted. A number of city magistrates and several territorial and imperial Diets passed resolutions against usurious practices and trade monopolies. Berthold of Henneberg, the imperial chancellor, elector, and archbishop of Mainz, had spoken for the cause of the peasants when he advocated a thorough reform of imperial administration at the Diet of Worms in 1495. However, the shortsightedness and selfishness of the imperial and local governments prevented the adoption of any socially progressive legislation.

After the rather moderate demands of the Twelve Articles had been rejected, the peasant movement developed into a social revolution. Direct communications between the peasants and the dissatisfied elements in the cities were soon established. The armies of the peasants received further moral and material support from the ranks of the rebellious imperial knights who, in 1522-1523 under the leadership of Ulrich von Hutten (cf. p. 251 sq.) and Franz von Sickingen, had risen in revolt against ecclesiastical and secular princes to establish an empire that was to be free from Rome and from princely domination. Some of the knights and nobles came to the aid of the peasants for idealistic reasons, among them Götz von Berlichingen and Florian Geyer, who even assumed temporary leadership of the peasant troops. Fanatics, adventurers, mercenary soldiers, and others were prompted by ambition, lust of adventure, or greed to join the ranks of the peasants. In Würzburg we find on their side Tilman Riemenschneider, the sculptor.

The Great Peasants' War which had started in May, 1524, in the region of Lake Constance (*Bodensee*) near the Swiss border, had soon spread to most parts of southern and central Germany. An assembly held at Memmingen in Bavaria voted death to all nobles and asked for the destruction of all monasteries. During the following period of violence cities were· captured, castles destroyed, monasteries and churches desecrated and burned, and the instincts of the peasant mobs satisfied their desire of .revenge in many acts of savage cruelty. In the course of seven major encounters the peasants were finally subjugated by the well-trained armies and the superior strategy of their opponents. The peasant armies were well equipped but lacked adequate, unified, and unselfish leadership. The lords followed Luther's advice and drowned the revolt literally in blood. Over one hundred thousand peasants were slain, many other thousands were wounded, tortured, and crippled for life. Terrible vengeance was meted out to the survivors: their arms were confiscated, their liberties revoked, their burdens increased. An official estimate puts the number of those executed at ten thousand. The lords devised the most inhuman tortures for their victims.

The lot of the peasants after the end of the war was much worse than it had ever been before. The winners were the princes and territorial lords. They made the Lutheran Reformation, that had been so enthusiastically welcomed by the peasants, serve their own selfish and dynastic ends, feeding their lust for power on both social revolt and religious reform. In 1555 serfdom was legally recognized throughout the Empire. The lower classes fell into a state of apathy and degradation, while the educated classes cherished a pedantic Latin culture, built on legalistic concepts and rationalized theological formulas.

d) *The Anabaptists.* In the cities the revolutionary movement had its center in the sect of the Anabaptists. In their literal interpretation of the Scriptures they went to such extremes as to run about without clothes or to play with toys in order to appear "as little children." They gathered together, waiting for the food that their heavenly father would send them, if only they "took no heed as to what they should eat." They refused military service, would not bind themselves by oaths, denied the doctrine of eternal damnation, the existence of the Trinity, the divinity of Christ, and derived the sanctions for their actions from visions and inspirations. They were opposed to private property and the authority of State and Church and, above all else, they denied the validity of the baptism of infants.

From Switzerland, where the movement originated, the Anabaptist teachings spread to the North and gained an enthusiastic following in the Saxon towns of Zwickau and Wittenberg, at the time when Luther was a voluntary prisoner in the Wartburg (cf. p. 225). Their leader, Thomas Münzer (1498–1525), a native of Thuringia, adopting a hammer as the symbol and emblem of his party, led his followers in their fight for a new communistic society, built on the inspired guidance of those in whom the divine word burned as a living flame that devoured all "godless," that is, all who were opposed to the new order. The Anabaptists succeeded in converting Luther's friend, Carlstadt, but Luther's unexpected return from the Wartburg shattered their hopes of making Wittenberg the center of their movement.

After the outbreak of the Great Peasants' War Thomas Münzer dreamed of making Mühlhausen in Thuringia the nucleus of his kingdom of God on earth. He secured for himself a position in the city government, established a "Christian regime," raised (contrary to the antimilitarist creed of his sect) an army, and called for the extermination of all his opponents, especially of all monks, priests, and nobles. Scores of churches, monasteries, and castles were sacked and burned by his fanatical followers. Countless works of art and literature were destroyed.

Thomas Münzer reappeared on the day of the decisive battle of Frankenhausen (May 15, 1525), leading his peasant hordes to their destruction. He was captured, subjected to torture, and executed, after having confessed and received Communion according to the Catholic rites.

After Münzer's death the Anabaptist movement was revived in 1531 in the city of Münster in Westphalia. The cruel persecutions of the preceding years had strengthened rather than weakened the vitality of the sect. Under the leadership of Bernard Rothmann, Bernard Cnipperdolling, and John of Leyden the Anabaptists overthrew the magistrates of the city, took the government into their own hands and banished all the "godless" from the city. A communistic regime was established and polygamy was officially decreed, the women being distributed among the men. What was to happen again in the days of the French revolution of 1789 was proclaimed in the "Kingdom of Zion" of 1534: all church towers were to be cut down, so that "everything that is exalted might be humbled." John of Leyden assumed the title of king, calling himself "John the Just, on the throne of David," proclaiming his dominion over all the world and sending out twenty-eight apostles to preach the new dispensation.

After a year's duration the "Kingdom of Zion" succumbed to the imperial armies that had been sent against the city of Münster. The Anabaptists and their leaders offered heroic resistance, and those who had to pay with their lives died with the fortitude of religious conviction. The doctrines of the Anabaptists were once more revived in a milder and saner form by Menno Simmons (1492–1559), the founder of the Mennonite sect.

The Age of Discoveries. The Spaniards and the Portuguese were the great seafaring peoples and the discoverers of new continents at the beginning of modern times (fourteenth and fifteenth centuries). The Germans, who had practically no share in the expeditions themselves, were nevertheless deeply affected by the cultural changes that followed the discovery of new countries, peoples, and entire civilizations. Their outlook was broadened, their geographical and astronomical concepts revolutionized, their thinking and living was directed into new channels.

The first great family of explorers were the Polos of Venice, Nicolo, Matteo, and Nicolo's son, Marco, who undertook two expeditions to Asia, in the closing decades of the thirteenth century. They reached the Chinese city of Pekin, and young Marco Polo spent seventeen years in the service of the Tartar emperor, Kublai Khan. Up to this time trade between Italy and the Far East had been controlled by Moslem middlemen, who had reaped immense profits. It was for this reason that the Western merchants were eager to discover a direct sea route which would make it possible for them to avoid the difficult and costly journey through central Asia and to establish direct communication with India and China. Their spirit of enterprise and adventure was soon encouraged and backed by the centralized states and the money interests of Europe.

After Henry the Navigator (1394–1460), a Portuguese prince, had devoted his untiring efforts to the exploration of the west coast of Africa, his country-man, Bartolomeu Diaz, reached the Cape of Good Hope, the southern-most point of Africa, in 1486. About one decade later (1497–1498) another Portuguese, Vasco da Gama, discovered the sea route to the East Indies and landed in the harbor of Calicut. In the meantime, Cristoforo (Juan) Colombo (latinized form: Columbus; germanized form: Cristoffel Dauber, 1451–1506), a native of Genoa (Italy) in the service of the Spanish crown, had set out to explore the eastern coasts of Asia and had discovered the islands of Guanahani (San Salvador), Cuba, and Haiti. He undertook four expeditions in all and died in the conviction that all he had accomplished was to find a new sea route to East India, when in reality he had re-discovered the American continent, once known to the seafaring Norman Vikings and long since forgotten.

The final conquest of the American continent was due to the initiative of Spanish military leaders and adventurers, such as Fernando Cortez and Francisco Pizarro, who in the opening decades of the sixteenth century conquered Mexico and Peru. Streams of gold and silver began to flow from the New to the Old World, greatly strengthening the capitalistic trends in European society and at the same time making Spain its foremost and most powerful exponent.

The newly discovered continent received its name (America) from the Florentine cartographer, Amerigo Vespucci († 1512), who had made several journeys to the New World. The name "America" was first proposed by Martin Waltzenmüller, a native of Freiburg, in his *Cosmographiae Introductio* ("Introduction to Cosmography," 1507). Fernando Magellan, a Portuguese nobleman in Spanish services, was the first explorer who succeeded in sailing completely around the world (1519–1522).

The Germans, like all other Europeans, were fascinated and entranced by the fabulous treasures and luxuries that the age of discoveries had made available for Western civilization. They stood amidst a changing world with mixed feelings of jubilation, awe, admiration, and a pride which throve on visions of unlimited power and manifested itself in greed, unrest, and dissatisfaction. When Albrecht Dürer was shown in Brussels a display of all the wondrous and precious things imported from Mexico, he wrote: "Never in all my life have I seen anything that has elated me as much as these goods; for among them I noticed wonderfully artistic things, so that I marvel at the subtle ingenuity of these peoples in foreign lands."

The Renaissance. The beginning of modern times is generally associated with the *Rinascita* or "Renaissance," as the movement was called by Voltaire and the French Encyclopaedists. The term signifies an attempted revival of the arts, literatures, and ideas of classical Graeco-Roman antiquity, a culture that was characterized as much as the medieval philosophy of life by a definite concept of man, who now enthusiastically experienced his newly acquired power in the conquest and technical mastery of the realms of nature and mind. The objects of nature are submitted to closest scrutiny and to the test of the scientific experiment, while at the same time they are divested of the partly symbolical and partly mystical veil which had enveloped and harbored them in the cosmic universe of a spiritually and ecclesiastically determined world view. Nature and supernature are broken asunder, and the natural provinces of life, the realms of philosophy, morality, art, politics, economics, and so forth, are proclaimed autonomous, subject only to their own intrinsic laws.

Properly speaking, the Renaissance is a phenomenon of the European South and more specifically of Italy, where the spirit of antiquity had never died. It was still alive to some extent in the structures of ancient temples and palaces, in Roman Law, and in the documents of classical Greek and Roman literature. But the philosophic, artistic, and literary Renaissance forced these ancient contents into new molds, and its great representatives proudly felt themselves to be the legitimate sons and heirs of the classical past of their nation.

Dante Alighieri (1265–1321), the great Florentine poet, had summarized for a last time the medieval system and mode of life in the tripartite setting of his *Divine Comedy,* man's journey through hell, purgatory, and paradise. But the personal style, national consciousness, and strongly individualistic outlook of this master foreshadowed the spirit of a new age. The vernacular Tuscan dialect had served him as the medium of his literary language and, together with Petrarch (1304–1374) and Boccaccio (1313–1375), he created the modern Italian idiom. Petrarch, like Dante, embodied contradictory motives in his life and work: the lover of solitude and introspection praises friendship and social intercourse; the ascetic despiser of things transitory hungers for the acclaim and applause of the masses; the lover of freedom humbly submits to ecclesiastical rule and discipline; the defender of an enlightened and supernational humanism passionately proclaims the political and cultural supremacy of Rome. While Petrarch in the sonnets that he addressed to Laura created a distinct pattern for the poets of the Italian Renaissance, the witty, sensuous, and superbly balanced prose style of Giovanni Boccaccio's *Decamerone* became the model for the later Italian novelists. Translations of Boccaccio's works were among the first books printed in Germany.

The Renaissance movement and the largely secularized Church of the fifteenth and early sixteenth centuries were on excellent terms, the representatives of the Roman Church giving their sanction and blessing to the cult of Christian as well as pagan antiquity. Clerical writers adopted the style of the Attic comedy, and the Vatican became one of the great centers of Renaissance culture. Girolamo Savonarola (1452–1498), the ascetic Dominican prior of San Marco in Florence, who had raised his lonely voice in passionate protest against the extravagance and moral depravity of the papal court of Alexander VI (1492–1503), was burned at the stake as a heretic, while Pope Leo X of the house of Medici (1513–1521) surrounded himself with the most famous artists, writers, and orators of his age. The popes of the Renaissance were no hideous monsters but splendor-loving secular princes, who shared in the virtues and vices of their contemporaries. Some were even very able administrators, but most of them had little realization of the spiritual responsibilities of their office.

The most distinguished protagonists of the political and artistic Renaissance were the Florentine Medicis. Cosimo de Medici (1389–1464), the son of a merchant, founded the Platonic Academy in Florence and made himself the undisputed political leader of his native city. His grandson, Lorenzo "the Magnificent," himself a poet and art collector, told his son Giovanni, the future Pope Leo X, that the fine art objects and beautiful books of antiquity were of much greater value than gold and other material possessions. He held his protecting hand over the arts and sciences and employed the famous painters Ghirlandajo (1449–1494) and Botticelli (1444–1510) at his court. He founded the academy for sculptors in which Michelangelo received his training.

One of Giovanni's closest friends was the philosopher Pico della Mirandola (1463–1494), in whose works the Jewish, Greek, and Christian traditions blend. In his *Discourse on the Dignity of Man,* Pico gave expression to the religious creed of a Christian Platonist, when he had God address Adam in these words: "Thou hast the seeds of eternal life within thyself. I have set thee in the center of the universe, so that thou mayest see everything that existeth therein. I have created thee neither a heavenly nor an earthly being, neither mortal nor immortal, so that thou mayest be thine own sculptor and conqueror, so that thou mayest model thine own countenance. Thou canst degenerate into an animal, but by virtue of thy free will thou

canst also regenerate thyself and become a godlike being." Pico della
Mirandola and his contemporary, Marsilio Ficino (1433–1499) signify the
turn from Aristotle to Plato that characterizes the philosophical outlook
of the foremost thinkers of the Italian Renaissance.

The first of the Renaissance popes was Nicholas V (1447–1455), who
told the College of Cardinals shortly before his death: "I have adorned the
Holy Roman Church with magnificent buildings, with the most beautiful
forms of an art that abounds with pearls and jewels, with books and
tapestries, with vessels of gold and silver, with precious vestments. I have
practiced every kind of magnanimous liberality, in building activities, in
the purchase of rare books and manuscripts, in the copying of Latin and
Greek masterpieces, in the employment of great scholars." One of his
collectors of manuscripts, whom he had sent to Germany, discovered the
long-lost *Germania* of Tacitus (cf. p. 5) in the monastery of Hersfeld.
Lorenzo Valla (1405–1457), one of the pope's advisers, a master in the new
science of literary and historical criticism, offered conclusive proof that the
so-called "Donation of Constantine" (cf. p. 41 sq.), on which the medieval
papacy had based their claims to Italian territory, was a bold forgery of the
ninth or tenth century.* The fraudulent nature of the document of the
"Donation" was independently substantiated by Cardinal Nicholas of Cusa
and by the English Bishop Reginald Pecock. Pope Nicholas' lasting creation was the foundation of the Vatican Library, which grew to approximately five thousand volumes during the period of his pontificate.

Pope Pius II (1458–1464), the former Aeneas Sylvius Piccolomini, who
succeeded Nicholas after the short reign of Calixtus III, acquired fame as a
scholar, poet, and orator. For years he had been the secretary of the Imperial Chancellery and was therefore excellently acquainted with conditions
in Germany, on which he comments at length in his "History of Europe."
Under the pontificates of Sixtus IV (1471–1484), Innocent VIII (1484–1492),
and Alexander VI (1492–1503) the institution of the papacy became almost
completely secularized and corrupted, chiefly by the practice of "nepotism."**

Under Julius II (1503–1513) the reconstruction of St. Peter's Cathedral
was begun, which was completed under his successor, Leo X (1513–1521),
the last of the Renaissance popes. It was Julius who called Michelangelo
(1475–1564), the great architect, sculptor, painter, and poet, to his court and
entrusted to him the task of adorning the Sistine Chapel with monumental
paintings and of designing the pope's own tomb.

Raphael (Santi), 1483–1520, a native of Urbino, worked as court painter
and architect under Julius II and Leo X. In his "Disputa" Raphael depicted the most brilliant figures of world history, gathered around the exposed Eucharist, and in his monumental "School of Athens" he conjured

---

* This, of course, does not invalidate the legitimacy of the donations of Pepin and
Charlemagne (cf. p. 41 sq.).

** Nepotism (from Latin, *nepos* = "nephew"): favoritism, practiced among the members
of the papal families in order to increase their dynastic power, including appointments to
important offices and the creation of entire new principalities.

up the entire culture of antiquity in the figures of its leading representatives. A large number of mural paintings record the high points of ecclesiastical history and the victories of the papacy.

Under Leo X Rome became the capital city of the Renaissance, the magnificent center and meeting place of a motley array of artists, writers, and scholars, but also of vainglorious courtiers and venial parasites. Under Leo's two successors, the Dutch Hadrian (1522–1523), the last of the popes of non-Italian nationality, and Clement VII (1523–1534) of the house of Medici, the structure of the Church was badly shaken by the storms of the Lutheran Reformation. In 1527 Rome was pillaged by Spanish and German mercenary soldiers, and the death knell had been sounded for the splendor of the Roman Renaissance. Among the defenders of Rome we find Benvenuto Cellini (1500–1571), the illustrious goldsmith, sculptor, musician, and engineer, whose autobiography was to be translated by Johann Wolfgang von Goethe.

All the smaller Italian courts of the Renaissance vied with Rome in the attempt to become centers of art, learning, and brilliant social culture. The great Florentine painter Leonardo da Vinci (1452–1519), a master of all the arts and an engineer and scientist besides, worked at the court of the Sforza in Milan. In the literary atmosphere of the court of Urbino, Baldassare Castiglione (1478–1529) wrote his *Cortegiano* ("The Courtier"), glorifying the social ideals of the Italian Renaissance. Venice, the great commercial metropolis, abounded with art collections and libraries, palaces and churches. Here Giovanni Bellini (*c.* 1430–1516) and Titian (1477–1576) created their immortal works, and here also Aldus Pius Manutius (*c.* 1449–1515) had established his famous printing press, the cradle of many highly artistic and rare specimens of printing, known as the Aldine books.

The ecclesiastical as well as the secular Renaissance paid homage to the ideal of an individualism that realizes all the potentialities of human nature, striving for a harmonious development of the physical and intellectual faculties of the *uomo universale* (the "total man"). In the political perspective the "total man" is Nicolo Machiavelli's ideal "Prince," who became the model of all the political absolutisms of the following centuries. This "Prince," as depicted in Machiavelli's famous book of the same title, bore the features of Cesare Borgia (1475–1507), the most ruthless and unscrupulous of the Renaissance rulers, who paid his own peculiar tribute to his age by developing even murder into a fine art. Divorcing political action from all principles of morality, Machiavelli makes the political leader a law unto himself, whose might creates his right, and who feels justified in using any conceivable means that serves the end of political power. "Whoever makes the attempt," we read in the fifteenth chapter of *The Prince,* "to act morally in all things, must of necessity perish among a crowd who pay no heed to morality. Therefore, a prince who wishes to assert himself must know how to act immorally whenever the opportunity arises, always conforming his actions to political necessity."

To be sure, the prince must use frequently such terms as "justice" and "religion," but only to cater to the fools. Moral values are determined by power, not by religion. Christianity in particular is to blame for having emasculated the political will and, by educating man for a world to come, made him an easy prey for scheming scoundrels.

German Humanism. When the Renaissance crossed the Alps about a century after the death of Petrarch and Boccaccio, it underwent a thorough transformation. Despite the many points of contact and interrelation between Germany and Italy, the spirit of the *Rinascita* never became an adopted philosophy of life in the north. The Italian Renaissance was too much and too essentially a culture of external form and a philosophy of sensuous beauty to suit the serious and introspective mood of the northern mind. The Germans in particular were traditionally much more concerned with the substances than with the appearances of things. The Lutheran Reformation had strengthened rather than weakened this innate tendency. But there was one aspect of the southern movement that struck sensitive organs in the north: the intellectual leaders of the German nation were deeply in sympathy with those scholarly efforts that dealt with the timeless values and interests of humanity.

When the Turks conquered Constantinople in 1453 many of the Byzantine scholars had sought refuge in Italy, making their living by copying and translating Greek manuscripts. The Italian scholars who subsequently devoted themselves to the study of the classical writings in Greek and Latin, the *litterae humaniores,* and who brought about a splendid revival of ancient literature, called themselves "Humanists." German students attending Italian universities, and those Italians who represented their nation at the Church councils in the north, carried the movement across the Alps. But whereas Italian Humanism had been essentially an intellectual and philological movement, in Germany it became a strong moral and educational force. The Italians were interested primarily in the pagan documents of Greece and Rome, while the Germans rediscovered many of the treasures of Christian antiquity, the writings of the Church Fathers, and the original texts of the Scriptures.

Just as in Italy, German princes took pride in becoming the patrons and protectors of the new movement and its representatives. Emperor Charles IV (cf. p. 164 sq.), the founder of the University of Prague, has been called the "father of German Humanism." His son Sigismund surrounded himself with poets and scholars, and Emperor Maximilian, the "last of the knights" and the contemporary of Pope Leo X, cultivated more than any of the other rulers the humanistic spirit in his many-sided interests and activities. The courts of Wurtemberg, Saxony, Brandenburg, and the Palatinate became centers of humanistic culture and education. By the end of the fifteenth century the movement was firmly entrenched in the Universities of Heidelberg, Vienna, Prague, and Erfurt. Among the ecclesiastical princes, Cardinal Albrecht, elector and archbishop of Mainz, stood out as a patron of humanistic culture, and Bishop Johann von Dalberg of Worms was on friendly terms with some of the foremost Humanist writers. Humanists were employed in the imperial, princely, and municipal chancelleries, and the cities of Augsburg and Nuremberg were renowned Humanist havens. Ulrich von Hutten (cf. p. 251 sq.) voiced the general conviction of his contemporaries when he exclaimed: "The arts and sciences are gaining more strength and vitality, the spirits wake up; banished is barbarism; Germany has opened her eyes."

a) *John Reuchlin and the "Letters of Obscure Men."* "The two eyes of Germany" was the epithet applied to John Reuchlin (1455-1522) and Desiderius Erasmus (*c.* 1466-1526), the two leading Humanists in the north. Reuchlin had revived the study of Hebrew and published the first Hebrew grammar in Germany. A jurist by profession, he mastered Greek and Latin with equal ease, and his scholarly endeavors encouraged the critical and comparative study of the scriptural texts. Although he was on orthodox ground in his theological convictions, he became involved in a partly theological, partly linguistic controversy which brought him into close alliance with some of the antiecclesiastical Humanists.

His intense interest in the mystical doctrines of the postbiblical Jewish *Cabbala* made him oppose a scheme for the destruction of all nonbiblical Hebrew books, as advocated by John Pfefferkorn, a baptized Jew. Asked for his opinion by Emperor Maximilian, Reuchlin condemned Pfefferkorn's proposal as an unjust and barbarous undertaking. The following personal quarrel with Pfefferkorn soon became a public issue, the Humanists siding with Reuchlin, and a number of obscurantist theologians supporting Pfefferkorn. In the course of this struggle the Humanists dealt a blow to their opponents which made these the laughingstock of Europe. Some of Reuchlin's friends and sympathizers, among them Ulrich von Hutten, published anonymously the famous 118 *Letters of Obscure Men* (*Epistolae Obscurorum Virorum,* 1515 and 1519), addressed to Ortuin Gratius, a theologian of Cologne and one of Reuchlin's chief opponents. The letters were supposedly written by a number of anti-Humanist theologians, and in their barbarous mixture of Latin and German were a most convincing exhibition of vanity, ignorance, stupidity, and obscenity. So skillfully were they composed that the deception went at first unnoticed. When the truth finally leaked out, the discovery proved decisive for the victory of Humanism in Germany.

b) *Desiderius Erasmus of Rotterdam.* The "Prince of the Humanists" was "the shadow of a man" — of frail physique, sensitive and mildly skeptical, but endowed with a penetrating mind that embraced with its keen observation the widest possible range of interests. Witty, a good entertainer, yet not free from vanity, Erasmus knew how to gain the favor of the mighty by flattery and adulation. Opposed to extremes and excesses, he loved moderation, harmony, peace, and in all things the golden mean, avoiding a clear "Yes" and "No" whenever possible. Cosmopolitan of mind, he felt himself to be the intellectual ruler of the most illustrious minds of a European family of nations, and he considered it his major duty to live the life of a true Humanist, to develop in himself a perfect harmony of human faculties and performances. His life was spent in the great cultural centers of France, England, Italy, Germany, and Switzerland.

Erasmus was born in Rotterdam, the son of a cleric; he was educated in the school of the Brethren of the Common Life (cf. p. 180) in Deventer and entered one of the monasteries of the Windesheim Congregation of the Brethren. He was ordained a priest in 1492 but soon afterward left the cloister with the permission of his superiors to start on his wanderings and to pursue the studies which made him the most brilliant scholar of his age. Not unlike Dürer and Holbein the painters, Erasmus combined Germanic inwardness with a Romanic sense of form and proportion. As a man and a thinker he lived in the ancient past rather than in the present, feeling perfectly at home in the Greek and Latin tongues and developing a classical diction entirely his own. As a philosopher and theologian he advanced the studies of textual and biblical criticism by his new editions of the classical writers, the Church Fathers, and the Greek New Testament (1516), preparing the way for the rationalistic sociology and theology of the age of Enlightenment.

On his first visit to England in 1499 he met the leading Christian Humanist in that country, Sir Thomas More. More was the internationally known author of the *Utopia,* a work that visualized an ideal pagan Humanist state established on the bases of natural reason, and as such a trenchant reproach against the so-called "Christian" states of Europe. Thomas More eventually suffered martyrdom for his opposition to King Henry VIII. Erasmus was bound to him by a lifelong friendship. Adhering to Christianity as the guiding philosophy of his life, Erasmus was nevertheless very outspoken and full of scorn and sarcasm in his criticism of ecclesiastical personalities and institutions, of scholastic philosophy and monastic theory and practice. His most widely read book, the *Praise of Folly (Encomion Moriae,* 1509), presents Dame Folly, bragging about her large following among all nations and estates, while her most faithful sons and servants are the theologians, especially the monks. Despite such attacks on the Catholic tradition Erasmus disappointed the expectations of those who had hoped that he would join the forces of the Lutheran Reformation. His initial admiration of Martin Luther turned gradually into aversion and definite opposition. Commotion, excitement, and revolt had never been to his liking. To the same men who had hailed him as the shining star of Germany, he appeared after his defection from Luther's cause as a snake in the grass, a cowardly renegade, a sophistic juggler.

In his *Querela Pacis* (Lament of Peace) of the year 1517 Erasmus appears as an ardent advocate of enduring peace among the members of the Christian family of nations. He shows himself influenced by the political ideas of Cicero, Seneca, St. Augustine, and even the scholastics, Thomas Aquinas and Cardinal Cajetanus de Vio, agreeing with the latter in their rejection of an unqualified pacifism. In his capacity as privy councilor of the young King Charles of Spain (the future Emperor Charles V) he composed, in 1515, an instruction for the guidance of a Christian ruler (*Institutio Principis Christiani*), an interesting and noteworthy refutation of Machiavellian principles in political theory. When Paul III (1534–1549) succeeded Clement VII on the papal throne, and the idea of a Catholic Reform Council was nearing its realization, Erasmus declared his willingness to co-operate in the restoration of peace and order in the Church. There was even some talk of making him a member of the College of Cardinals. But Erasmus for once recognized his limitations: he knew he was a king in the realm of letters and learning, but a stranger in the arena of political action.

c) Ulrich von Hutten, Franz von Sickingen, and the "Younger Humanists." The most colorful, spectacular, and erratic figure among the German Humanists was Ulrich von Hutten (1488–1523). He and his companions, who called themselves "the poets," belonged to a group of so-called "Younger Humanists," most of them highly talented but ruthless and undisciplined, and in their boundless vanity thinking of themselves as the reborn Homers, Ovids, and Ciceros. Beyond the fact that they adopted Greek and Latin names in place of their inherited German ones, there was little that they had in common with the world of antiquity.

Ulrich von Hutten was a descendant of Franconian nobility, whose family shared in the general decay of the knightly estate to such an extent that in Hutten's generation they had sunk to the level of robber-knights. However, Ulrich had been destined by his father for the monastic life, and his first act of rebellion was to flee from the monastery of Fulda and join the ranks of the Humanists. He was above all a fiery German nationalist who was untiring in his efforts to arouse Germany to wage a life-and-death struggle against the power of the Roman Catholic Church and all "ultramontane" influence in the north. He used the brilliance of his mind and the dynamic force of his pen to castigate and excoriate the objects of his wrath. Through his great talents as a writer, poet, and orator he gained the favor of Emperor Maximilian who, in 1517, personally crowned him with a laurel wreath. But, living recklessly, Hutten wasted his gifts, ruined his health, and died prematurely of the dread "French disease" (syphilis).*

For a short time Hutten's name was associated with that of Martin Luther, but Hutten's radicalism led to an early estrangement. With words of unrestrained hatred and wild passion the warring knight called upon his countrymen to rise in bloody revolt against Rome: "They have sucked our blood, they have gnawed our flesh, they are coming to our marrow; they will break and crush our every bone! Will the Germans never take to arms, will they never rush in with fire and sword?" To render his appeal

---

* This disease, first recorded toward the end of the fifteenth century, is said to have been brought to Western Europe by the Spanish conquerors of South America.

more effective Hutten relinquished the Latin tongue and began to write
in German. He made common cause with Franz von Sickingen (1481–1523),
one of the robber-knights, whose deeds and misdeeds were often inspired
by noble motives and by his compassion with the oppressed and downtrodden. Sickingen played a leading part in the revolt of the Imperial
Knights of 1522–1523 and, in the end, having failed in his attempt to better
the economic and legal position of the knightly estate by means of constitutional amendments, was mortally wounded during the siege of his castle
of Landshut in the Palatinate. From the Ebernburg near the city of Worms,
where Sickingen had been born and where in the days of the Diet of Worms
he offered shelter to a number of friends and sympathizers of the Lutheran
Reformation, Hutten sent out a veritable flood of pamphlets, attacking and
vilifying the assembled delegates: "The measure is full," he wrote. "Away
from the pure springs, ye filthy swine. Out from the sanctuary, ye cursed
money-lenders. . . . Can ye not see that the breezes of freedom are blowing;
that men are wearied of the present state of things and want to bring
about a change?"

Hutten's end was tragic: after the Diet of Worms and Sickingen's defeat
he lost all his bearings, so that his actions began to resemble those of
a common highway robber. Without means of subsistence and tormented
by his disease, broken in body and spirit, haunted by his enemies, he fled
to Basel, where he hoped Erasmus of Rotterdam, with whom he had once
been on friendly terms, would give him shelter, so that he might die in
peace. But Erasmus sent word that he was very much afraid Hutten might
not be able to live in his unheated rooms, for he, Erasmus, could never
endure the heat of a stove! Hutten gave vent to his disappointment in one
last pasquil, in which he referred to Erasmus' vanity, thereby inviting an
answer which for once was stripped of all subtle irony and showed the
dignified Humanist in a genuine, red-blooded rage. Banished from Basel,
Hutten spent his last days on the tiny islet of Ufenau on Lake Zurich, which
had been offered him by Huldreich Zwingli, from whose report we learn
that Hutten "left behind him positively nothing of value: no books, no
household effects — nothing but a pen."

The German Humanists expressed their ideals in poetry and prose, in
speeches and epistles, in word and in deed. Here and there they followed
the example of the Italian academies and formed literary societies. Heidelberg and Vienna became outstanding centers of the movement. It was not
easy for the new spirit to gain a foothold in the universities of the Empire,
but gradually the faculties of art and letters had to adapt their curriculums
to the demands of the Humanists, who had their largest following among
the younger generation. Basel, Erfurt, and Heidelberg became the foremost
seats of Humanist education. The Latin secondary schools in the cities
benefited greatly from the Humanist influences. The increased enrollment
and improved methods of instruction prompted Luther to write in 1521:
"A boy of twenty knows more today than twenty doctors did formerly."

Nevertheless, despite the wider range of studies and a definite enlargement of the historical and scientific horizon in the upper strata of society, the people at large were hardly affected by the Humanist movement. It remained essentially confined to scholarly circles, who drew a sharp line of demarcation between themselves and the uneducated rabble. Many a German Humanist, on the other hand, pursuing historical studies and witnessing the pride the Italian people took in the glories of their national heritage, came across some of the important documents of the Germanic past. This slowly awakening nationalism was greatly stimulated by the strong antipathy to everything that was associated with the Roman Curia. This explains the temporary alliance between the younger German Humanists and the leaders of the Lutheran Reformation. They had in common the objects of their hatred but were divided by what they loved and esteemed. It did not take the younger Humanists long to discover that Luther was not greatly interested in dialectics, aesthetics, and linguistics, but rather in theology, faith, and the Bible. And when the Lutheran Reformation had really gotten under way, its reverberations proved vital enough to overshadow completely the scholarly endeavors of the Humanists.

The Catholic Restoration (Counter Reformation). Of those European countries which remained practically untouched by the waves of the Protestant Reformation (Italy, Spain, Portugal, Poland, Ireland), Spain ranked foremost as a political power. Emerging successfully from her armed contests with France, she had been able to assert her will in the north and south of Italy as well as in the Netherlands and in the Free County of Burgundy. The family relations between the courts of Madrid and Vienna made the house of Hapsburg the European center of gravity. Owing to this political constellation it had been possible for Spain to approach and solve the question of ecclesiastical reform at a time when the Roman Curia had not even been awakened to a full realization of the threatening dangers, and several decades before the beginning of the Lutheran Reformation in Germany.

The leader of the reform movement in Spain was the archbishop of Toledo (1495–1517), Cardinal (1507) Ximenes de Cisneros (1436–1517), the confessor of Queen Isabella of Castile and a member of the Franciscan Order. Supported in his efforts by the rulers of Castile and Aragon, Ximenes restored the integrity of the Catholic Church throughout Spain, revived and vitalized the theological and philosophical studies, and founded the University of Alcalá (1500). Like the Protestant and Humanist leaders he was convinced of the necessity of a thorough reform, but he also felt certain that this could and should be accomplished within the framework of the established Church. It was the spirit of this Spanish Restoration that dominated and permeated the Catholic reform movement in other European countries.

While official Italy in Church and State was still imbued with the semi-paganism of the Renaissance, increasing numbers of devout individuals began to organize in religious brotherhoods, aiming at a revival of the religious spirit among the masses. Under the pontificate of Leo X the "Oratory of Divine Love" was founded, and in 1524 Bishop Gian Pietro Carafa of Naples established the new Theatine Order (Theate or Chieti was the name of his episcopal see), while the Capuchin Order, founded in 1526, restored the original rigor of the Franciscan monastic discipline.

Within a relatively short period (c. 1535–1648) the Catholic reform movement had not only restored faith and order in the Roman Church but had impressed its ideas on the culture of those countries in which it was victorious. The Catholic Restoration, in the countries of its origin as well as in the territories that were reconquered and reconverted from Protestantism, succeeded in rallying once more the intellectual, social, religious, artistic, and literary forces around an ideological center, manifesting itself in the élan of the Baroque style (cf. p. 337 sq.) which superseded the Renaissance. It was a form of expression that was less naïve and more fraught with inner contradictions than the preceding Christian styles, but it was forceful and aggressive, a blend, as it were, of pagan and Christian elements, of Gothic spirituality and the sensuous beauty of the Renaissance. Its chord of emotions with a corresponding scale of formal values reached from the ecstatic heights of the mystical revival in Spain (St. Teresa of Ávila, St. John of the Cross) to the gay and colorful exuberance of ecclesiastical and secular architecture, sculpture, and painting in Spain, Italy, southern Germany, and Austria; from the austere serenity of Calderón de la Barca's (1600–1681) dramas and sacramental plays to the dazzling phantasmagoria of the new Jesuit stagecraft (cf. p. 346 sq.); from stern religious asceticism to festive courtly splendor, uniting Church and State in powerful and soul-stirring displays of undisguised propaganda.

a) *Ignatius of Loyola and the Jesuit Order.* In spite of the fact that with the accession of Paul III (1534–1549) the Catholic reform movement began to make itself felt in the leadership and guidance of the Church, its sweeping successes and victories would have been impossible without the two events which marked a turning point in the history of the Catholic Church: the foundation of the Jesuit Order and the Council of Trent.

Ignatius (Íñigo) of Loyola (1491–1556), the founder of the Jesuit Order, a native of the province of Guipúzcoa, was of Basque origin and the heir of the knightly traditions of his family. Born in the ancient castle of his ancestors, near the town of Azpeitia, and having received a knightly and military education, he was thirty years of age when his normal career as an officer in the Spanish army was abruptly cut short by a serious wound which he received while defending the fortress of Pamplona against the French. During a long period of convalescence, partly spent in the ancestral castle, being aware of the fact that his physical injury would never permit him to re-enter the military service, and influenced by some spiritual readings, he conceived of the idea of devoting his future life to the service of

Christ, his divine Liege Lord. His health restored sufficiently, he made a pilgrimage to the Benedictine abbey on the Montserrat. After a knightly vigil before the image of the Madonna, he deposited his armor and his sword on the altar, continuing on his way in the garb of a penitent, equipped only with a pilgrim's staff. The harbor of Barcelona being closed on account of an epidemic, Ignatius had to relinquish temporarily his plan of boarding a ship for Jerusalem. He stayed in Manresa for almost a year, during which time he familiarized himself with some of the important documents of medieval mysticism and with the spirit of the *"devotio moderna"* (cf. p. 180). He was especially impressed with the "Spiritual Exercises" (*Ejercitatorio de la Vida Espiritual*) as devised by Garcia de Cisneros, the abbot of Montserrat, which manual in turn was based on the teachings of some of the leading French, German, and Dutch mystics of the Middle Ages.

Garcia's spiritual meditations suggested to Ignatius the principal structure of his own *Spiritual Exercises (Exercitia Spiritualia)*, which were to become the theological, ascetic, and psychological basis of Jesuit training, education, character formation, and institutional organization. Ignatius' original contribution and addition to the older methods of meditation lie in his profound psychological insight, his knowledge of the human soul and its faculties. He used these means to the end of training the human mind and bending the human will so as to become obedient instruments of any purposeful direction and command: instruments hard as steel, ready to submit to any kind of sacrifice or privation, willing to serve at any place, any time, and in any circumstances. All the senses and all the powers of the imagination are called upon to contribute their full share to the formation of mental and moral habits and decisions. The *Imitation of Christ* is made a tangible reality by contemplating vividly and in drastic nearness the Lord's suffering and humiliation in order to arouse the Christian's generous love and devotion, in view of an ultimate union with the source of all beauty, goodness, and truth.

The most conspicuous element of the *Spiritual Exercises* is the spirit of military regulation and discipline, transferred to a set of spiritual ends. Man is to be so transformed that he no longer "prefers health to sickness, wealth to poverty, honor to disgrace, a long life to a short one — and so on in everything else, so that we learn to desire and choose only those things which are helpful in reaching the end for which we have been created." Christ is depicted as the supreme War Lord, whose honor and glory are the final goal of the individual's every thought and deed. All disorderly inclinations are to be ordered, adjusted, and subordinated to the divine will. Education for Christian action is considered as all important, and it is this principle of activity, *"Ad Maiorem Dei Gloriam"* (for the greater glory of God), which further distinguishes Ignatius' *Exercises* from purely contemplative forms of devotion, and which greatly appealed to an age of political conquest, geographical expansion, and scientific invention.

After having finally satisfied his yearning for a pilgrimage to the Holy Land (1523), Ignatius returned to Barcelona by way of Venice and Genoa and subsequently completed his liberal and theological education at the Universities of Alcalá, Salamanca, and Paris. He received the degree of Magister of Arts from the College of Ste. Barbe in 1534. In the same year he and six of his companions and disciples on the Montmartre solemnly vowed to devote their lives to missionary activity in the Holy Land, or, if this plan should prove impracticable, to offer their services to the pope for whatever kind of work he would assign to them.

Several times Ignatius and his companions suffered persecution and incarceration at the hands of the Inquisition and had to clear themselves of the suspicion of being sympathizers of Martin Luther. Their apostolic zeal among the poor and unlearned and the plain gray habit which they had chosen as their dress seemed to make them conspicuous as innovators and agitators. In 1535 we find Ignatius back in his home town, to recover from a chronic infection of the gall bladder, taking up his residence in the asylum for the homeless, preaching and teaching in the immediate neighborhood of the castle of the Loyolas. A reunion with his Paris companions in Venice was followed by a recurrence of his illness. After his recovery he decided to make Italy his abode and the center of his future activities.

On their way to Venice the companions of Ignatius visited the tomb of Erasmus of Rotterdam in Basel. After their arrival in Venice Ignatius ordered them to proceed to Rome to obtain the papal permission for their pilgrimage to Jerusalem. The permission was granted by Paul III, but the threatening war between Venice and the Turks prevented them from making the journey. Shortly afterward Ignatius and his companions were ordained to the priesthood.

Meanwhile, in Rome, the friends of the ecclesiastical reform had greatly strengthened their influence. The scholarly statesman and diplomat, Gasparo Contarini, had been made a member of the College of Cardinals and of the committee in charge of the preparations for the forthcoming Church council. He and a group of like-minded friends became the nucleus of a new generation of cardinals who carried the reform to its final victory.

After Ignatius and his companions had offered unconditionally their services to the pope, the "Society of Jesus" (*Compañía de Jesús*) was formally instituted in June, 1539. A special vow of absolute obedience to the pope was added to the customary three monastic vows of poverty, chastity, and obedience. The members were to be freed from the observance of the choral recitation of the liturgical office, so that more time might be available for the service to their fellow men. They were not required to wear monastic habit, so that they might not be mistaken for just another variety of the then ill-famed and partly degenerate older religious orders. The original decree of the foundation was confirmed by a special bull of Julius III on July 21, 1550, and Ignatius was elected general or *praepositus* of the Society. Despite his feeble health he guided the destinies of his order with circumspection and indefatigable energy for fifteen years. The absolute authority with which the constitution of the Society invested the office of its general reflected the spirit of the age of rising absolute monarchies and national armies. The democratic-parliamentary constitutions of the mendicant orders (cf. p. 134 sq.) had given way to the spirit of autocracy, with the principles of leadership and subordination as its bases.

When Ignatius died, his foundation comprised fifty-eight colleges, in addition to numerous seminaries and novitiates. The first companions of Ignatius had received a humanistic education during their years of study in Paris, and they retained their high respect for the principles of liberal education and handed it down to their associates and successors. During the lifetime of the founder, houses of study were established in most of the larger cities of Europe and in all the centers of academic learning. The spirit of Ignatius was the lifeblood of all these institutions of higher learning, the spirit of a personality whose genius for organization was akin to that of John Calvin, and whose depth and breadth of religious experience was comparable to the spiritual fire that burned in the soul of Martin Luther.

b) *The Council of Trent* (*1545-1563*). It was not long after the foundation of the Jesuit Order that the papacy itself took the lead in the Catholic reform movement. In vain had Cardinal Contarini made the attempt to bring about a reconciliation of Protestants and Catholics at the Diet of Regensburg in 1541. He had only drawn upon himself the suspicion of heresy and had died in the following year without having been able to clear his reputation. The same year, 1542, witnessed the resurrection of the Inquisition (cf. p. 136) for the suppression of heresy, wherever it might raise its head. At the same time a strict censorship of the printing press was set up to stamp out all heterodox opinions, preparing the way for the publication of the *Index of Forbidden Books* and the creation of a permanent *Congregation of the Index* (*1571*), the former promulgated during the Council of Trent, the latter under the pontificate of Pius V (1566-1572).

The preliminary efforts to restore the doctrine and discipline of the Church were finally crowned by the convocation of the Council of Trent (Trient), so named after the southernmost city of the Empire, where the assembly was solemnly opened in 1545. Four popes (Paul III, Julius III, Marcellus II, Paul IV) died during the eighteen years that the council was in session. The deliberations were several times interrupted and the meeting place temporarily removed to Bologna and back again to Trent. The militant leader of the reform was for some time Pope Paul IV (1555-1559), the former Gian Pietro Carafa, the compiler of the first *"Index,"* who attempted to recover for the papacy the power and prestige that it had possessed in the Middle Ages. His failure to understand the vastly different spirit of his own age, his ineptitude in dealing with political realities, and his anti-Spanish bias involved him in a number of futile controversies and in a useless and unsuccessful war with King Philip II of Spain (1555-1598), the son of Emperor Charles V. He reproached Ferdinand I (cf. p. 214) for being too lax in dealing with German Protestantism, and refused to recognize him as German emperor. He made the Inquisition the supreme tribunal in all matters of faith and morals, and by his uncompromising attitude he provoked a rebellion of the Roman people, who gave vent to their anger by setting fire to the building of the Inquisition.

It was Paul IV's successor, Pius IV (1559–1565), who brought the Council of Trent to a successful conclusion. A sober and sane student of jurisprudence, he preferred mediation and persuasion to force. The twenty-fifth and last session of the council was held in December, 1563. Among the 255 assembled ecclesiastics there were 4 cardinal legates, 2 cardinals, 3 patriarchs, 25 archbishops, 168 bishops, 7 abbots, 39 procurators (representing absent members), and 7 generals of religious orders.

While the council failed in healing the breach between Catholics and Protestants, still its chief objective was fully secured, namely that of firmly laying the foundations for a thorough restoration of the Roman Catholic Church. The hierarchical constitution had been preserved, abuses had been recognized and rectified with utter rigorism, and the ancient ideological structure of the Church had been reaffirmed and redefined.

Some of the more important decrees dealt with the contested nature of the process of justification. Luther's doctrine of "justification by faith alone" was rejected; the human will was declared to be not entirely unfree; human nature, human emotions and passions were considered as not radically corrupted but as capable of being educated, ordered, and used for moral ends. Special decrees dealt with the intellectual and moral training of the clergy, the importance of the integrity of the Christian family, and the indissolubility and sacramental character of the marriage bond. As against the Protestants' appeal to the exclusive authority of the Bible, the council decided that Scriptures and Tradition (all the dogmas and definitions preserved and handed down by the teaching office of the Church) were equally valid sources of divine authority and revelation; that Church Tradition existed prior to the Scriptures, and that therefore the Bible was merely an inspired written documentation and reflection of oral tradition.

c) Peter Canisius and the Catholic Restoration in Germany. The pontificate of Pius V (1566–1572) marks the climax of the Catholic reform movement. "Fra Scarpone" (Brother Sabot or "Wooden Shoe"), as the new pope was called on account of his monkish habits, was neither a warrior nor a politician but exclusively interested in the salvation of souls. Frugality, strictest economy, and moral austerity began to rule at the papal court. It was under Pius V's successor, Gregory XIII (1572–1585), whose name remains associated with his reform of the calendar (cf. p. 274 sq.), that the Catholic Restoration made itself felt as a formative cultural force beyond the confines of the Italian nation.

The Jesuits had exerted considerable influence on the proceedings of the Council of Trent, and they had been active in near-by and distant countries (China, India, etc.) in ever so many fields of religious and educational endeavor. But their order derived the greatest amount of encouragement from the favor of Pope Gregory XIII. The fifth general, Claudius Aquaviva (1581–1615), the author of the famous *Ratio Studiorum* ("Order of Studies"), obtained from the pope a new confirmation of the original constitution and invaluable support in the organization of theological seminaries and institutions of higher learning.

Some of the most significant educational work of the Jesuits was done in Germany, where Catholic education was revived under the leadership of Peter Canisius (1521–1597), to whom the German Catholics refer as a "Second Apostle of Germany" (the first being St. Boniface, cf. p. 39). A native of Nymwegen in Holland, he had been influenced by the *devotio moderna* as cultivated by the Brethren of the Common Life (cf. p. 180) and by the reading of manuals of mystical contemplation of the later Middle Ages. He had attended the first sessions of the Council of Trent as the "procurator" of Cardinal Otto Truchsess von Waldburg and soon afterward had been called to Rome by Ignatius of Loyola himself. The special field of his activity was to be a number of southern German districts, where he succeeded in winning over the Catholic princes for his plans and where he worked as a teacher and preacher.

Canisius considered it one of his major tasks to raise educational standards among the Catholic youth, so as to match the unquestionably superior training and discipline of the Protestant schools, which had attained such great efficiency under the influence of Philip Melanchthon's (cf. p. 231 sq.) school reforms. Canisius was engaged in educational work in Vienna, Ingolstadt, Augsburg, and Fribourg (Switzerland), and was commissioned by Emperor Ferdinand I to compose the new Catholic catechism, first in Latin (1555) and later on in German (1560). The Antwerp edition of 1589 was illustrated with 102 engravings. The *Imperial Catechism* was translated into twenty-five languages and was still used in many Catholic schools as late as the nineteenth century.

Peter Canisius was the first German member of the Society of Jesus. Shortly after his death the *Ratio Studiorum* was officially introduced in the German schools of the Jesuit Order. The curriculum included the humanities as well as mathematics and the natural sciences. The scholastic standards were high enough to make the Jesuit secondary schools model institutions of their kind. Gradually the Jesuits extended their influence to the leading Catholic universities of the Empire, and the great successes of the Society as the vanguard of the Counter Reformation were mainly achieved by means of their firm grip on the educated classes, especially on the future political and dynastic leaders. Under the direct or indirect guidance of the Jesuits the Catholic Restoration was carried forward by force in several German lands. Protestantism was utterly destroyed in Bavaria. When the archbishop of Cologne joined the Protestant reformers, he was driven from his see by Bavarian and Spanish troops, and a Bavarian prince was placed at the head of his diocese. At the end of the sixteenth century all the bishoprics in the German West were held firmly by the Catholic Church. The eastern dioceses had been secularized by the Protestant princes. In the Austrian Alpine regions Duke Ferdinand of Styria carried the Counter Reformation to a complete victory. Catholic and Protestant princes alike adopted and enforced the principle *"cuius regio eius religio"* (cf. p. 212).

Social and Cultural Conditions: (a) *Peasants, Burghers, Nobles, and Princes.* Of the four estates (*Stände*) of the Empire, as they existed after the Great Peasants' War of 1524–1525 (clergy, nobility, burghers, and peasants), the *peasants* ranked so low in the social scale that Wimpheling, one of the spokesmen of German Humanism, does not even consider them a *Stand* in the juridical sense of the term. Their condition was worst in the German East, where they were completely at the mercy of the powerful feudal landowners, and where in some districts (Mecklenburg, Pommern) they were reduced to the status of actual slavery. But everywhere the peasant was an object of social oppression and exploitation, especially after serfdom had been legally established by the Imperial Diet of 1555.

The *burghers* enjoyed prosperity and social prestige in the earlier part of the sixteenth century, but their estate began to show symptoms of decline and diminishing influence after 1550. The trading privileges of the Hansa (cf. p. 119 sq.) were revoked by Queen Elizabeth of England in 1579, and the Steel Court (*Stahlhof*) in London was closed in 1598. Hamburg was the only one of the member cities of the Hanseatic League which succeeded in maintaining and improving its trade relations with England and in establishing commercial contacts with Amsterdam, the new Dutch trading center, thereby developing into the "most flourishing emporium of all Germany."

The commercial districts of upper (southern) Germany were able to maintain their prosperity to the end of the sixteenth century, when they gradually had to give way to the competitive pressure of the British and Italian money interests. The Dutch revolt against Spain and the sack of Antwerp by Spanish mercenaries (1576) eliminated one of the chief markets of the merchants of upper Germany, but at the same time it established the commercial supremacy of Amsterdam and the Dutch trading interests. Frankfurt on the Main, on the other hand, benefited by the fall of Antwerp, as is indicated by the growing significance of the *Frankfurter Messe* (Trade Fair).

The numerous bank failures and crashes of the second half of the sixteenth century were partly caused by the growing indebtedness and final bankruptcy of Spain and France, partly by reckless financial speculation and the excessive luxury that characterized the wealthy burgher class. The static nature of the guild system (cf. p. 125 sq.) made it too rigid to provide the frame for the rapidly shifting forces of the money trade. Capital rose as a monstrous and wholly impersonal power that could only with difficulty be controlled by the undeveloped financial techniques of the age of early capitalism. The wholesale middleman, a figure that had been unknown to the Middle Ages, began to dominate the markets and to secure trade monopolies. The separation of the producer from the consumer transformed and finally destroyed the fundamental character of the guild system. The guilds were becoming more and more exclusive, the masters establishing themselves as an oligarchic group, subjecting to their financial power not only the journeymen but also those fellow masters who lacked the means to invest the capital required for wholesale production, or who were determined to preserve their independence. A sharp social division began to line up merchant employers against a class of wage earners whose members had little chance of ever rising from the rank of journeyman to that of employer. In the sixteenth century the journeymen began to form their own guilds to defend their rights against the vested interests of capitalist masters who, in their turn, established employers' guilds to impose their will on the wage earners and to facilitate mass production.

The burgher who, in the fifteenth and the early sixteenth century, had been proud of his social status and had developed cultural, artistic, and literary tastes, forms, and standards, began to cast envious glances at the members of the nobility, trying to imitate their style and manner of living. The outward appearance of the burgher's residence assumed more and more the palatial pomp and elegance of the Italian Renaissance, and many a wealthy citizen moved into the abandoned castle of some impoverished nobleman. Increasing numbers of burghers' sons attended the universities of the Empire and of neighboring lands to prepare themselves for a career in the imperial or princely chancelleries or, as privy councilors, professors, and members of the higher clergy, to exert an influence on political and cultural affairs.

The social and cultural crisis of the *nobility* had preceded the decline of the burgher class by more than a century. It has been pointed out how the nobles were deprived of their livelihood and the *raison d'être* of their social existence by the transformations that had taken place in the technique of warfare and in military science. The manufacture of gunpowder and the introduction of firearms had largely done away with the mounted armies of knights, replacing them with mercenary foot soldiers.* As a disinherited class, the nobles hated and despised the burghers. Nevertheless, marriages between the two estates were frequent, the burgher coveting a distinguished name and an exalted rank in the social ladder, the nobleman frequently trying to salvage his shattered finances by choosing a bride from among the city plutocracy. In the German East more than in any other part of Germany the nobility shared in agricultural and commercial activities, trading and speculating in wool, wine, wood, and grain. Only in a very few instances were the nobles interested in the intellectual and cultural

---

* The Chinese were familiar with gunpowder and the use of hand grenades in the twelfth century, and in the thirteenth century the Arabs had brought this knowledge to the Western World, where both Albert the Great and Roger Bacon, the most advanced scientific observers of their time, had described it in detail (*c.* 1250). About 1380 the German, Berthold Schwarz, is said to have considerably improved the efficiency of gunpowder as an instrument of warfare.

pursuits of their nation, and the majority of them are reprimanded and denounced in contemporary chronicles for their extravagance and their riotous living. The honor code and etiquette of the old-time knight and noble became an object of ridicule and satire in Bojardo's (1434–1494) *Orlando Innamorato* ("The Enamored Roland"), in Ariosto's (1474–1533) *Orlando Furioso* ("The Raging Roland"), and especially in Cervantes' (1547–1616) immortal *Don Quixote*.

A new avenue for members of the nobility was opened up by the development of a centralized system of administration at the princely courts. The creation of a large number of professional court officials (*Berufsbeamtentum*) made it possible for a new generation of nobles to obtain positions as councilors, ambassadors, chamberlains, pages, and so forth.

The *princes* themselves, with their prestige greatly enhanced after their decisive victories over the peasants and other social rebels, their coffers swelled with the expropriated Church possessions, moved swiftly in the direction of absolutism. In the case of Protestant princes, their newly acquired position as titular heads of national and regional churches had brought the administration and supervision of ecclesiastical affairs, public morals, education, public health under their jurisdiction. Economically, they became the protectors and promoters of capitalistic interests, realizing that the welfare of their states depended on a prosperous business life and on a maximal amount of taxable income. By creating a unified territorial economy they were able to finance the maintenance of the official bureaucracy of their chancelleries and to meet the growing expenditures of their mercenary armies. In many cases they monopolized the mining privileges, leased the rights of coinage, pawned the princely domains, and sold the secularized Church properties. Thus their policy of aggrandizement and enrichment was strictly guided by Machiavellian principles. Considerations of honor, square dealing, or patriotism were in most instances subordinated to economic and financial calculations. Although the fully developed system of "mercantilism" (cf. p. 328 sq.) and State paternalism is a creation of the seventeenth and eighteenth centuries, its beginnings are clearly distinguishable in the sixteenth century.

The wasteful extravagance of the princely household, with its constant need of money and the ensuing search for new sources of income, explains the profound interest of the rulers in the art of "gold making" and the pseudo science of alchemy. "Gold makers" are found in the service of practically all the princely courts, and many of the princes spent days and weeks of hard labor in their court "laboratories," in the vain hope of producing gold synthetically. Emperor Rudolph II (1576–1612) kept two hundred alchemists busy at his court, and the princes of Saxony, Brandenburg, and so forth, followed his example.

The social and intellectual culture of the courts of the Italian Renaissance is conspicuously lacking at the German courts. In its place there is found an external and superficial display of gorgeous pageantry and perpetual festive entertainment. The great passion of the average prince was the hunt, with all the sportly thrills that it involved and all the infringements on the property rights of the peasantry that it entailed. Tremendous sums of money were spent on artificial fireworks, mythological *tableaux vivants,* romantic and exotic pageants and masquerades.

Some of the German princes were collectors of all kinds of rarities, curiosities, and antiquities, and in this way the arts and crafts derived some benefit from the princely tastes and interests. It was the chief task of the court painters to flatter the vanity of their employers by idealized portraiture of the different members of the princely families. "Art chambers" (*Kunstkammern*) were established at most courts to house the many oddities that the traveling collectors of the prince had brought together from many lands and regions. Genuine artistic taste was shown by the Hapsburg Emperor Rudolph II, the "German Medici," who had assembled 413 valuable paintings in his art gallery in Prague, by Archduke Ferdinand of Austria, the founder of the splendid collection of the castle of Ambras, and by some of the Bavarian princes. Augustus I of Saxony (1533–1586), who was chiefly interested in astronomical and mechanical instruments, started the court collection in Dresden which was to become famous under his successors. Of the higher arts, music was greatly appreciated at the Bavarian court, where Albrecht V (1528–1579) appointed Orlando di Lasso (1532–1594), the great composer, as conductor of the princely orchestra (1563).

The gradual weakening of the indigenous national elements in German culture in the course of the sixteenth century was responsible for an increasing admiration of foreign modes of living and the imitation of un-German artistic and literary styles. The German princes and nobles visited the famous Italian universities and learned to live and breathe in the atmosphere of Italian Humanism. The graphic and decorative arts copied Italian models and motifs, and princes as well as wealthy patricians had their residences either built by Italian architects or by German workmen who had learned their trade in Italy.

The family relations between the German Imperial and the Spanish courts account for the influence of Spanish style and etiquette in fashion, behavior, and literary expression. The Spanish writers Antonio Guevara (c. 1480–1545) and Luis de Gongora y Argote (1561–1627) had developed an *"estilo culto,"* a pompous, flowery, and ornate but empty and shallow style, which became known as "Gongorism." It had its equivalents in Italy and in England, in the works of Giambattista Marini (1569–1625) and John Lilly (1554–1606), known as "Marinism" and "Euphuism" (from Lilly's novel *Euphues, Anatomy of Wit*), respectively. Likewise from Spain came the phantastic and bombastic novel of *Amadis,* the son of King Perion of Wales and the British Princess Elisena, who, after numerous adventures, marries the daughter of King Lisuarte of England. The novel conquered all Europe and had reached the monstrous size of twenty-four volumes when the German translation of 1569 was published by Sigmund Feyerabend in Frankfurt. For a long time the *Amadis* was considered as the manual of correct and exemplary social behavior. It represents a last flickering of the courtly chivalresque tradition and was duly satirized in Cervantes' *Don Quixote* (1605, 1615). The Spanish "picaresque" novel (*Schelmenroman*) inspired Grimmelshausen's masterpiece, *Simplicissimus* (cf. p. 300). Popular taste in Germany reacted negatively to these foreign fads and fashions, but the people at large had no say in the matter, and by the end of the sixteenth century the Spanish style in dress and social behavior had become widely accepted.

Much of the Spanish influence reached Germany by way of France. Under Louis XI (1461–1483) and Louis XII (1498–1515) the French court had become the center of the national and cultural life of the country and, as in the days of chivalry, the German princely aristocracy considered France as the model country of the refined arts of living and learning. While the ruling dynasty of France was involved in its struggles with the Hapsburg emperor (cf. p. 206 sq.), the French court made capital out of the selfishness and greed of the German princes, many of whom received "pensions" from the French king, their reward for political services or even for treasonable activities. Many of the German nobles joined the French armies and fought the battles of the French monarchy. French tutors were called to Germany to educate the sons of nobles and princes, and German students traveled to France to attend the Universities of Paris, Orléans, and Montpellier, to learn the French language, acquire the polish of French manners, and get acquainted with the much heralded French culture.

The general fondness of everything foreign reached its culminating point during and following the Thirty Years' War (cf. p. 284 sqq.). But even at the end of the sixteenth century the national substance of Germany had become so diluted that Pastor Johannes Sommer, in the preface to his *Ethnographia Mundi* (a description of the modern world), published in 1609, was quite serious in asserting that people who had died twenty years ago would not recognize their own children: if they were to step back into life, they might think that there were no Germans left but "only Frenchmen, Spaniards, Englishmen, and other peoples." Those foreign countries and cultures, to whose influence and dictates the Germans too willingly submitted, seemed to share this opinion: they looked down upon Germany with scorn and contempt, calling her inhabitants semibarbarians, brutal, uncultured, and intellectually inferior. "No nation is more despised than the Germans," exclaims Martin Luther. "The Italians call us beasts, and France, Italy, and all the other countries heap ridicule upon us."

Social and Cultural Conditions: (*b*) *Clergy and Scholars. Religion and Superstition.* Reformation and Counter Reformation alike had stimulated the interest in theological problems and religious discussions among all classes of the population, but after the middle of the sixteenth century this preoccupation assumed the nature of a real obsession, with all the earmarks of religious fanaticism. Not only the Bible but theological pamphlets and dogmatic compendia were read and discussed by men and women, by princes, scholars, burghers, artisans, and peasants. Political and social life, the arts and the sciences bore the imprint of theological tutelage, and the court theologians became more and more the intellectual leaders of the age. Religion was the topic of conversation in universities and on street corners, in chancelleries and taverns, in cities and villages. The rapidly multiplying sects, all convinced of their exclusive possession of religious truth and all basing their claims on the concept of "evangelical freedom," engendered a spirit of hatred, suspicion, abuse, and persecution. The pulpits and lecture halls, hymns and morality plays, paintings, engravings, and woodcuts served to indict and calumniate the religious opponents. Protestant artists pictured the pope and the cardinals suffering the tortures of hell-fire, while the Catholic artists meted out the same punishment to Luther and his followers. Parties and individuals accused each other of being possessed by the devil, of being the devil's allies, of being devils in disguise.

In Geneva, John Calvin (cf. p. 236) had established his tyrannical regimentation of faith, and there, in 1553, the physician Michael Servet was burned because of his anti-Trinitarian views. In Basel, the Dutch Anabaptist David Joris, the founder of the Jorist sect, was exhumed three years after his death (1556), to be solemnly burned, together with his portrait and his writings. Similar tyranny and bigotry were prevalent in Catholic Austria: in 1527 Leonard Käser, a priest who had embraced Lutheranism, was seized at the deathbed of his father and burned. Many who had accepted the reformed doctrines had done so because of the promised liberties, completely forgetting about the sacrifices and obligations that were implied. Thus Melanchthon complains as early as 1528 that "no one hates the Gospel more bitterly than those who claim it as their own." When he looks at the conditions of the age he feels fear that transcends all imagination, and twenty years later (1548) he speaks of the hatred of the majority of the German people for the Gospel and its preachers. As a matter of fact, in the later decades of the same century the dogmatism and fanaticism of the theologians meets with a growing indifference, laxity, and ignorance on the part of the masses.

In 1549 Johann Oldecop, a German chronicler of Hildesheim, had the following inscription affixed to his house: "The Church is shaken; the clergy is corrupt; the devil rules." While popular religious devotion and the people's participation in ecclesiastical life were on the decline, it was the element of fear that now as formerly in the fourteenth and fifteenth centuries held sway over men and women.

The decline of religious life was due in part to the corruption of the clergy. Both the Catholic and Protestant clergy had become the objects of popular hatred. Many of the priests and pastors lived in dire poverty, like beggars, and many others lacked the most elementary training for their office. Those few who held the flame of the Gospel alive were usually disliked and defamed by their colleagues or even denounced as heretics. Thus,

Johann Arndt (1555–1621), the author of the *Four Books of True Christianity,* was attacked as an enthusiast, a Calvinist, a papist. "The devil will give him his reward for his heretical doctrines," wrote John Corvinus, a Lutheran pastor.

The devil quite generally was uppermost in the imagination, the speeches, and the writings of all and sundry. Superstitious beliefs, partly inherited from the previous centuries, partly rediscovered in the documents of antiquity and in the panpsychism of Platonic and Neo-Platonic nature philosophy, generated a pathological craving for the miraculous, the mysterious, and the occult. Some of these superstitions showed a host of morbid, sinister, and pernicious aspects and components. The unexpected, extraordinary, unheard-of might occur at any time and in any place. In 1522 a cow was said to have given birth to a monster, and Luther promptly published an *Explanation of the Monkish Calf of Freiberg in Saxony,* wherein he described the monster as a symbol and counterfeit of the horrible institution of monasticism, a miracle wrought by God Himself. Melanchthon followed with a publication on *The Popish Ass in Rome,* referring to the offspring of a donkey that had been found in the Tiber, pointing to an early end of the papacy. Tales were rampant of animals that had given birth to human children, of women who had begotten young devils, of dragons who had caused conflagrations, of dead persons who had risen from their graves, of angels who had descended from heaven, of all kinds of evil forebodings: events that are recorded in letters, chronicles, house books, dream books, nativity books, books of magic and sorcery. Prophetic visionaries claimed to be able to read the future in the stars (astrology), in the storm, in the fire, in metal mirrors, in human features, or in the lines of the palm.

An atmosphere of black magic and sorcery surrounds the mysterious figure of Doctor Georg Faust (*c.* 1507-1540), a native of Knittlingen in Swabia, the archsorcerer, physician, and alchemist, the "philosopher of all philosophers," who claimed with his black magic to have effected the victory of the imperial army at Pavia and the conquest of Rome (1527). He captivated the imagination of his contemporaries and inspired the poetic fancy of centuries to come (Marlowe, Lessing, Goethe, Lenau, Grabbe, etc.). The first *Faust-Book,* the *Story of Doctor Johann* Faust, the Widely Renowned Sorcerer and Magician,* was first published by Johann Spiess in Frankfurt.

The hero of the Faust-Legend, the *Faust-Book,* and the popular puppet play of the archsorcerer is in a way a true mirror of the sixteenth century. Faust's pact and companionship with the Evil One illustrates the importance that was attributed to the influence of the demonic powers and the vile, cruel, and sinister tyranny of the devil. In Luther's life and works references to the devil are frequent. While in the Wartburg, he claims to have seen him twice in the disguise of a dog. In Wittenberg he saw him

---

* In legend, fiction, and drama Georg Faust lived on as "Johann" Faust.

in the form of a black cat, and in Eisleben he beheld him from his window, seated on a near-by fountain, his mouth opened in a wide grin. "The devil is about us everywhere; he puts on a mask, as I have seen with my own eyes, appearing in the guise of a sow, a bundle of straw, and the like," we read in Luther's *Hauspostille*. Everything that stands in the way of the spread of the Gospel is the work of the devil. Even the best man must fall if the devil rides him. Theologians of all denominations agreed with Luther, suspecting His Satanic Majesty as the cause of every human passion, weakness, and vice. The "trouser-devil" was responsible for the bizarre fashions of mercenaries and burghers; the "drink-devil" caused drunkenness and debauchery; the "dance-devil" lurked behind the immorality of dance-crazed couples; and the "hunting-devil" inspired the passion of the chase. This preoccupation with the devil produced a special type of literature (*Teufelsliteratur*), works that were often profusely illustrated, the devil frequently being clothed in the habit of a monk.

Persons afflicted with mental diseases, also sleepwalkers and epileptics, were suspected of being possessed by the devil. "Far and near, on all sides the number of possessed persons is getting so large that it is a pity and a wonder," wrote Andreas Celichius, superintendent of Mecklenburg (1595). Exorcisms designed to drive out devils were practiced by Catholics and Protestants. Celichius published a treatise on "Possessions," in which he pointed out that most of the afflicted persons were women. This he finds not surprising, in view of the fact that sin and death were brought into the world by a woman and that women were full of pride, curiosity, and sensuality, and therefore more attracted by devilish sorcery than men.

The darkest chapter in this story of aberrations of the human mind was written by the instigators and perpetrators of the trials for witchcraft. It was the crowning superstition of all and it swept over Europe with the irresistible force of an epidemic, affecting the young and the old, the wise and the unlettered, men and women of every station in society. The *Witches' Hammer* (*Malleus Maleficarum*), edited by the two Dominican inquisitors, Heinrich Krämer (Institoris) and Jacob Sprenger (1487), makes it possible for us to gain some insight into the follies and manias that poisoned the imagination of the waning Middle Ages and that came to life again after the middle of the sixteenth century.

In 1484 the two authors of the *Witches' Hammer* succeeded in inducing Pope Innocent III to issue the Bull *"Summis Desiderantes,"* which defined witchcraft as a form of heresy and thereby placed the prosecution of alleged witches under the jurisdiction of the Inquisition. In the first decades of the sixteenth century the numerous accusations still met with a healthy skepticism, and Hans Sachs very soberly speaks of "vain imaginings." But the majority of scholars and educators, both Catholic and Protestant, were of a different opinion. After initial doubts even Luther became firmly convinced of the actual existence of witches, whom he denounced from his pulpit as milk thieves and weathermakers who traveled on magic carpets and induced people to fornication and prostitution. "I would burn them myself, according to the custom of the Law, as the priests of old stoned the evildoers," he wrote. John Calvin, too, demanded the merciless destruction of witches, and the prisons in Geneva were overcrowded with the unfortunate victims of superstition. Although himself a mortal enemy of the Dominicans, the German poet and satirist Johann Fischart (*c.* 1546–1590) prepared a new edition of the *Witches' Hammer* in 1588 and translated the *Daemonomania* of the French jurist, Jean Bodin (1530–1596), a work which served as a great encouragement to one of the worst persecutions.

As a matter of fact, many people actually engaged in fortunetelling, stargazing, gold making, and manifold other magical practices, and it was by no means exceptional that overscrupulous or hysterical persons voluntarily accused themselves of having had sexual intercourse with the devil and other evil spirits and of having committed other horrible crimes. The number of trials increased greatly after the middle of the sixteenth century, when the cruelty and semibarbarism of the age; the sadism of judges, spectators, and executioners; and the application of the most inhuman devices of torture added new notes of terror to the proceedings. The "witches" were forced to confess that they had traveled through the air on broomsticks, on goats, calves, and pigs, that they had attended the "Witches' Sabbath" on a desolate mountain peak in the Hartz, known as the "Brocken" or "Blocksberg," there to celebrate "Walpurgis-Night" (the eve of May 1) in wild orgies with Satan. They were forced into the admission that they had paid homage to demons, sacrificed children, and practiced cannibalism.

In the later sixteenth century and throughout the seventeenth century the witchcraft trials extended all over Germany. It is estimated that during that period approximately one hundred thousand victims were executed. Among them were men, women, and children; princesses and other ladies of noble birth; councilors and princes; priests, monks, and pastors; and even some of the judges and accusers were themselves accused and convicted.

Rules for the legal procedure in trials on witchcraft had been laid down by the *Carolina,* the law code of Emperor Charles V (1532), which served as the standard for German criminal law for a period of about 250 years. Its statutes were relatively moderate and sane, but they were frequently invalidated and disregarded by the territorial law courts. In Germany, the tribunals of the Inquisition played an insignificant part in the trials, the "secular arm" becoming more and more the sole administrator of justice. Absolute lawlessness characterized the final phase in the evolution of this collective insanity. No one was safe and beyond suspicion and, once accused, he was considered an outlaw, caught in a legal net from which there was no escape.

The belief in witchcraft and the persecution of witches was not a German but a European disease and affliction, and in some countries the mania persisted even after it had died down in Germany. In Scotland, where the trials were especially cruel, the legal statute dealing with witchcraft was not repealed until 1735. In North America we read of sporadic persecutions during the seventeenth century in Massachusetts, Connecticut, Virginia, culminating in the outbreak of a regular epidemic in Salem, Massachusetts, in the year 1692. The last burning of a "witch" in Germany took place in Würzburg in 1749. In Glarus (Switzerland) a servant girl was accused of witchcraft and executed by the sword in 1782.

The first German author who courageously expressed his condemnation of the trials for witchcraft was the Calvinist physician Johann Weyer, whose Latin work on sorcery and demonology was translated into German in 1565 and was almost immediately placed on the *Index* of forbidden books. Gradually the voices of reason grew stronger, and Protestant as well as Catholic theologians and scholars attempted to put an end to the trials and executions. In the seventeenth century the Jesuits, Adam Tanner (1572–1632) and Friedrich Spee (1591–1635), stood in the forefront of those who were opposed to the witchcraft trials. In 1631 Spee published anonymously his *Cautio Criminalis,* a book of 400 pages whose contents were the fruit of the personal experiences of the author who, in his capacity as a priest and confessor, had accompanied many of the victims on their way to the stake and had convinced himself of their innocence. The brunt of his attack was aimed at the injustice of the procedure, especially as regards the application of torture: "Is torture to be abolished?" he asks. "I answer: either torture must be wholly done away with or it must be so changed that it no longer endangers innocent persons. This is a matter that concerns the consciences of the princes, a matter for which they as well as their councillors and confessors will have to render account before their eternal judge. . . . My blood boils when I hear mentioned the names of those unjust inquisitors who even declared our devout Father Tanner as deserving of torture, for the sole reason that he has written very reasonably concerning these witchcraft trials. This is one of their arguments for indicting persons and committing them to torture. Why don't you make me an inquisitor! I should immediately proceed against all German magistrates, prelates, canons, and religious. If they want to defend themselves, I will not listen to them, but I will torture them, good and solidly, and they will yield, and: behold! I shall exclaim, where the witches hide themselves . . . I declare: we are all witches as soon as we are subjected to torture."

The venom of theological strife and the cancerous growth of superstition had by no means deadened the voices of true and simple faith and devotion. Mystical piety had withdrawn from the official churches but was alive in private conventicles and in the hearts of religiously inspired individuals. Caspar Schwenckfeld (1489–1561) of Ossig (Luther called him "Stänkfeld" or Stenchfield) was a Silesian nobleman whom the intolerance of the Protestant orthodoxy had forced to roam about without rest or haven. Sebastian Franck of Donauwörth (1499–1542) was first a Catholic priest, then a Protestant preacher, then a soap boiler and a printer, but always a

"Schwarmgeist" (enthusiast), a mystic visionary, and the author of the first comprehensive history of Germany (*Chronicle,* 1531). Valentin Weigel (1533–1588), a native of Saxony, lived the quiet life of a saintly Protestant parson, stressing the value of mystical inwardness and placing the kingdom of God in the individual soul: "Paradise, Christ, or the Kingdom of God is then not outside but within. Therefore we must not seek heaven here or there. If we do not find it within ourselves, if we do not feel and taste it there, we shall seek it in vain and shall never find it."

Quaint and fanciful was the life, personality, and work of Jacob Böhme (1575–1624), the unlettered shoemaker-philosopher of Görlitz in Lower Silesia, whose mystico-theosophical speculations on God, man, and the world were drawn from his rich inner life, and whose originality of style and thought have exercised a decisive influence on the German thinkers of the early nineteenth century, especially on Fichte, Schelling, Hegel, Novalis, and Franz von Baader. For Böhme a strong dualism is inherent in the "abyss" of the Deity. Purity, goodness, and beauty are from eternity opposed by darkness and evil, and out of this aboriginal antinomy God constantly generates His own essence into the world, which consequently includes good and evil as the necessary requisites of the process of cosmic evolution. In contemporary philosophy Max Scheler's anthropology with its dualism of "urge" and "spirit" is indebted to Böhme's theosophy. But his influence extends even to British and North American speculation. The English theosophists, Bromlay and John Pordage, and the visionary, Jane Leade, adopted Böhme's fundamental ideas, and the "Behmenists" play a significant part in English Church history in the seventeenth century. In modern times the vitality of Böhme's thought is reflected in some of the concepts of Ralph Waldo Emerson and the New England Transcendentalists.

With the exception of Jacob Böhme, these mystical representatives of unorthodox Protestantism continued the medieval tradition of Eckart, Suso, Tauler, and the *Theologia Germanica* (cf. p. 218), with an added pantheistic note which made them maintain with Sebastian Franck that "God is all in all: nature, happiness, the essence of all beings and natures, the virtue of all virtues, He in whom all things are contained." Not sharing in the vilification of opponents and the intolerance of the orthodoxy, they also agreed with Franck when he wrote: "To me a Papist, a Lutheran, a Zwinglian, a Baptist, yes, even a Turk is a dear brother."

Both the old and the new churches in some of their best representatives gave testimony of their conviction that any true faith must be tested and proven in acts of mercy and charity. Faith and charity in their interplay are described by Luther in his book *On the Freedom of a Christian Man* as follows: "A Christian man does not live in himself but in Christ and in his fellow men; in Christ through his faith, in his fellow men through his love. By virtue of his faith he rises above himself to God; from God he descends again by virtue of his charity, and yet he always remains in God and in the divine love."

Social and Cultural Conditions: (c) *Education and the Schools.* Scholastic-dogmatic interests on the one side and humanistic tendencies on the other determined the educational ideas of the sixteenth century. The humanistically trained scholar was the standard-bearer and model type of intellectual culture. Those who had hoped that the German written language would preserve and further develop the fluency and brilliance with which Luther's tongue had endowed it were bitterly disappointed. The New High German language had to face the dangerous competition of the New Latin idiom of the scholars with its pedantic and unimaginative conventionality, whose influence was felt in the official German style of the chancelleries. Many of the scholars and educators went so far as to discourage the instruction and use of the German language altogether and, by means of the strictest supervision of the students, to enforce the exclusive use of Latin. The cultivation of a neo-classical style became the primary aim of the philologically minded Humanist teachers.

Martin Luther, on the other hand, was chiefly interested in religious education, and he seized upon every means that seemed to further that end. To combat certain destructive forces in education, such as a popular hostility toward the higher learning, a widespread distrust of scholars and clergymen, and a growing neglect of learning in favor of money-making, Luther wrote his address *To the Councillors of All German Cities: that they may uphold and reconstruct the Christian Schools* (1524). Melanchthon, the author of the constitution of the schools of the province of Saxony (1528), praised the sciences as the most splendid ornament of religion and emphasized their importance for the well-being of the national state. His grammars were adopted in a large number of secondary Latin schools, and in his capacity as a professor in the University of Wittenberg he influenced and educated a generation of prospective teachers. The spirit cultivated in these circles was that of Christian Humanism. Special emphasis was placed on religious instruction, prayer, church attendance, and the development of moral habits. Greek and Latin were the major subjects in the liberal curriculum, and dramatic productions in Latin were to facilitate self-expression in the languages of the classical masters.

To be sure, Melanchthon's beneficent influence did not extend much beyond his lifetime. Toward the end of the sixteenth century complaints about the Protestant secondary schools became very outspoken. We learn that the teachers were poorly paid, that they had to petition annually for their reappointment, that they had to earn extra money as musicians, innkeepers, and fortunetellers. Even more numerous are the complaints about the studying youth: their lack of discipline and due respect for authority; their indecent dress; their drinking, fighting, and swearing.

The Catholic schools which went through the same critical stage were greatly improved by the endeavors of the Jesuit teachers. The curriculum followed the directions laid down in Ignatius of Loyola's *Ratio atque Institutio Studiorum Societatis Jesu* (cf. p. 254 sqq.), but in their Christian-

Humanist aim they were very similar to those institutions which had adopted Melanchthon's educational ideals.

The universities began to flourish again after an initial decline that had followed the religious upheavals of the beginning Reformation. New foundations of the sixteenth and early seventeenth centuries were the Catholic universities of Dillingen (1549), Olmütz (1574), Würzburg (1582), Graz (1586), Paderborn (1615), and Salzburg (1623); and the Protestant universities of Marburg (1527), Königsberg (1544), Jena (1558), Helmstedt (1574), Giessen (1607), Rintelen (1621), and Altdorf (1623). Most of the newly founded Catholic institutions served primarily the education of the future clergy and had only a philosophical and theological faculty.

All of the new universities were founded by territorial princes; they were no longer self-governing but State institutions; the professors had become the servants and employees of the princes and had lost many of their former privileges. The denominational character of the university was strongly marked, and the freedom of teaching was much more restricted than in the Middle Ages. Whenever the prince found it expedient to change his religious affiliations the teaching staff of the university had to follow suit. Objectors were summarily dismissed or imprisoned. The professors were poorly paid and had frequently to rely on extra earnings as tradesmen, innkeepers, court jesters, and so forth. Their venality, servility, and indolence became the subject of many complaints. The Catholic universities came more and more under the exclusive influence of the Jesuit Order.

With the dissolution of monastic and clerical institutions the medieval students' unions (*Bursen*) had gradually disappeared. They lived on only in the seminaries of the Catholic universities. Numerous sources tell of the breakdown of academic discipline, of dueling, carousing, strikes, and revolts among the students, and of their clashes and quarrels with the townspeople.

Although there were no essential changes in the program of studies, and most of the universities had retained the four medieval faculties, scholarship as such became less and less creative and constructive but was either controversial or purely factual, historical, and philological in a narrowly restricted sense of the term.

The Sciences. Renaissance, Humanism, and the era of discoveries had greatly stimulated the general interest in man and the physical world that was his abode. But nature was still a great mystery, and science and occultism were close allies. Chemistry and alchemy, astronomy and astrology were still inseparably linked together. Sebastian Münster's *Cosmographia* (1543), pretending to be a compendium of geography, history, physics, and linguistics, gives evidence of a queer mixture of careful observation, childlike credulity, and uncontrolled imagination. The sixteenth century finds Germany taking the lead in cartography and in the manufacture of globes. Gerhard Krämer's map of the world of 1569 served as a model for the cartographers of other European countries. Mineralogy and geology were considerably advanced by the investigations and studies of Georg Bauer

(Agricola, † 1555), a physician who spent many years of his life in the mining district of Joachimsthal and published the results of his research in numerous writings (*Bermannus, Sive de Re Metallica; De Re Metallica Libri XII,* etc.). Though a scientific mind in the modern sense, he nevertheless believed firmly in the existence of gnomes and mountain goblins.

The science of botany had made but little progress since the days of Albert the Great (cf. p. 144 sq.). It was due to the influence of the Humanists that the botanical works of antiquity and of the Middle Ages were studied anew, leading to a growing preoccupation with living plant organisms. Conrad Gesner († 1565), professor of natural science and a physician in the city of Zurich, composed two comprehensive works on botany and zoology and grew rare alpine and exotic plants in his private botanical garden. The "herb-books" (*Kräuterbücher*) by Hieronymus Bock and Leonard Fuchs (the fuchsia is named after him) acquired great popularity.

The sciences of anthropology and anatomy benefited from the physicians' new interest in the mysterious functioning of the human body. Andreas Vesalius († 1564), physician at the imperial court, saw in the authority of the ancient Roman physician Galenus (second century A.D.) the most formidable handicap for a fruitful development of medical science. Vesalius' *De Humani Corporis Fabrica Libri VII* (Basel, 1542), richly illustrated with excellent woodcuts, was the result of his anatomical studies and marks the beginning of modern medical science.

A pioneer in the fields of medical science and nature philosophy and likewise opposed to the chiefly theoretical knowledge of ancient medicine was Theophrastus Bombastus Paracelsus von Hohenheim (1493-1541), a Swiss physician, scientist, and theosophist, and one of the most fascinating personalities of the sixteenth century. A revolutionist in his thoughts and methods, he favored practical observation and experimentation and burned in public the works of Galenus and Avicenna (Arabic physician and philosopher, 980-1037). Nature he considered the greatest of all teachers and healers, and man was the mediator and interpreter of its laws. He placed chemistry in the service of medicine, praising the human mind, imagination, and will as the most important sanative powers. He criticized the use of Latin and Greek in writing and teaching and was the first professor to deliver his lectures in German (Basel, 1526-1528). His philosophical teachings may be characterized as a kind of panpsychism, claiming a magical affinity between plant organisms and certain organs of the human body and stressing the influence of the planets on human life. His eccentricity and doctrinal rigorism won him many enemies and few friends. Wandering restlessly from place to place, he died in poverty and misery at the age of forty-seven and lies buried in the Church of St. Sebastian at Salzburg. His writings have been re-edited and reinterpreted in recent years.

With surgery still in its infancy and medical science in general on a low level, ignorance and superstition were widespread among the members of the medical profession, and most people had to entrust their well-being to the crude methods and medicaments of the barbers. The majority of physicians were firm believers in the "science" of astrology, but their preoccupation with the planets and their movements prepared the way for the rise of astronomy.

Nicholas Copernicus (1473–1543), the son of a merchant of German ancestry, a native of the then Polish city of Thorn (East Prussia), and a canon of the Cathedral of Frauenburg, the father of modern astronomy, roused a storm of opposition with his epochal work *De Revolutionibus Orbium Coelestium* ("On the Revolutions of Heavenly Bodies"; completed in 1535 and published shortly before his death), wherein he described the sun as a fixed body in the center of the universe, around which revolve the earth and the other planets. He furthermore contended that the earth rotated on its own axis once every twenty-four hours (heliocentric view). The Middle Ages, on the other hand, had considered the earth the immovable center of the universe, around which the other heavenly bodies revolved once in every twenty-four hours (geocentric or Ptolemaeic theory, advanced by Ptolemaeus of Alexandria, second century A.D.). The theologians found fault with the discovery of Copernicus because it seemed to be at variance with the Scriptures. Nevertheless he dedicated his work to Pope Paul III. It was temporarily placed on the *Index of Prohibited Books* (1616–1757), in connection with the controversies concerning the teachings of Galileo.

Following in the footsteps of Copernicus, the great Swabian astronomer, John Kepler (1571–1630), expressed the planful motion of the universe in three fundamental laws: (1) the orbit of the planets has the form of an ellipse, the sun being fixed in one of the foci; (2) the radius vector of a planet traverses equal areas in equal times, its speed increasing and diminishing in proportion to its nearness to or remoteness from the sun; (3) the time interval required by a planet to complete its way around the sun depends on its average distance from the sun: the square of a planet's periodic time is proportional to the cube of its mean distance from the sun.

But even Kepler, great scientist that he was, devoted himself to the making of calendars, prognostics, and horoscopes. "I serve," he says, "the foolish little daughter Astrologia, so that her highly rational mother, Astronomia, may not have to starve." Theological bigotry was up in arms against Kepler's scientific discoveries, and his Protestant coreligionists attacked him severely for having recommended the acceptance of the "new calendar," promulgated by Pope Gregory XIII in 1582. In Protestant Germany and the Netherlands this "Gregorian Calendar" was not adopted until 1700. In Denmark it was introduced in 1710 and in England and the American colonies in 1752.

The hitherto accepted "Julian Calendar," introduced by Julius Caesar in 46 B.C. and improved by Emperor Augustus in A.D. 4, had been based on an assumed solar year of 365¼ days, whereas actually the solar year is eleven minutes and a few seconds shorter. This accumulated annual error prompted Gregory XIII to publish his Bull *Inter Gravissimas* of 1582, annulling ten days and restoring the original date of the equinox to the twenty-first of March. A leap year was proposed for every fourth year, but three of the leap years occurring within a period of 400 years were to be considered as common years (leap years at the close of the centuries, ending in oo and not divisible by 400). The improvement that was achieved by the new calendar is indicated by the fact that on its basis an error of only one day would accumulate after a period of approximately 4000 years. Before the final steps for the adoption of the calendar were taken, the Fifth Lateran Council (1512–1517) and the Council of Trent (1545–1563) had devoted some of their deliberations to this much disputed question, and in 1514 the papal commission had asked for and received the advice of Corpernicus. The Gregorian Calendar in its final form was largely the work of the Bamberg Jesuit, Christopher Clavius (1538–1612), who furnished an explanation of the reformed calendar in his *Apologia* (1588) and *Explicatio* (1603).

Foremost among the great minds of the age of the rising natural sciences ranks the genius of Galileo Galilei (1564–1642) of Pisa, the inventor of the telescope; the discoverer of the mountains of the moon, the rings of Saturn, the moons of Jupiter, the phases of Venus and Mercury, and the sun spots. His defense of the Copernican system led to his being compelled by the Inquisition to forswear his belief in the movement of the earth. Summoned to Rome in 1615, he promised neither to teach nor defend henceforth the heliocentric theory. Nevertheless, he wrote a defense of the Copernican system in form of a dialogue (1632).

A worse fate befell Giordano Bruno (1548–1600), the brilliant Italian nature philosopher who, influenced by Stoic and Neo-Platonic trends of thought, taught a system of aesthetic pantheism, in which he proclaimed the infinity of the world and the identity of man, God, and the universe. Returning to Italy after a stay of five years in Germany, he was arrested by the Inquisition, accused of heresy, and after a lengthy trial handed over to the secular authorities to be burned at the stake.

Philosophy and Historiography. The revival of Aristotelianism and Thomistic Scholasticism (cf. p. 141 sqq.), in the seventeenth century was preceded by a period of philosophical stagnation, eclecticism, and decadence. The reformers, with the exception of Melanchthon, had no use for philosophy as a rational discipline, and it was therefore neglected in the curriculums of the Protestant schools. In the Catholic system of education, on the other hand, Aristotle retained his time-honored position, but Germany and Europe in general lacked philosophical ingenuity and preferred the dusky labyrinths of occultism and mystagogy to the light of reason.

Historiography flourished in the sixteenth century in both the ecclesiastical and secular fields. Among the new and improved editions of historical documents of the past were the works of the Church Fathers and the acts of the Church councils. Matthias Flacius (1520–1575), one of the leaders of the Lutheran orthodoxy, wrote with several collaborators the first Protestant church history (1559 sq., 13 vols.), the so-called *Magdeburg Centuries (Magdeburger Zenturien)*, which found its Catholic counterpart in the *Annales Ecclesiastici* (1588–1593, 12 vols.) of the Italian historian, Cardinal Caesar Baronius (1538–1607).

The classical historiographical works of Switzerland and Bavaria respectively are Gilg Tschudi's (1505–1572) *Swiss Chronicle*, 1000–1470 (first printing, 1735), and John (Aventinus) Turmair's (1477–1534) *Annales Boiorum* (Bavarian Annals), first written in Latin (1554) and later on in German (1566). Of equal merit from the point of view of political and cultural history are the historical works of the Swabian Lutheran preacher and mystic, Sebastian Franck (1499–1542), whose sincerity and objectivity have netted him the title of a "modern thinker of the sixteenth century" (*German Chronicle, Cosmography,* etc.). Both his historical and mystical writings are inspired by his belief in the manifestation of a divine principle in the changing forms and aspects of historic evolution, as reflected in the destiny of peoples. The "Eternal Word" is "spirit and life, not just a letter, not written with ink or pencil on paper, parchment, or stone, but impressed as a seal into the hearts of all men by the finger of God."

Language and Literature. Martin Luther's significance in connection with the history of the German language has been mentioned (cf. p. 226). Luther's language and style as well as the depth of his religious experience exercised a decisive influence on the form and content of German prose and poetry in the sixteenth century, an influence which is even noticeable in the writings of his most bitter foes. The people as a whole, every group and each individual, had been taught to read, sing, and pray in Luther's tongue, thus gradually imparting color and life to the adopted idiom of the Saxon chancellery. The philologico-grammatical exercises and the Ciceronian mannerisms of the younger German Humanists could not prevent the final and permanent victory of popular feeling and expression in language and literature. The printed and written German script (Gothic letter type) owes its modern form to John Neudörffer (1497–1563), who taught students from all parts of Germany in his Nuremberg writing school.

As far as German literature is concerned the century of the Reformation is a period of decline. Most of the literary products of theological zeal, whether written in German or Latin, were didactic, academic, and eclectic. The greatest literary talent in the ranks of Luther's Catholic opponents was the eloquent Franciscan friar, Thomas Murner (1469–1537). A native of Alsace, he became the leader of the Upper Rhenish branch of German Humanism and earned international fame by his passionate German satire *On the Great Lutheran Fool (Von dem grossen lutherischen Narren)*. A masterful German satirist like Murner, influenced by François Rabelais' (c. 1494–1553) great French satire of *Gargantua and Pantagruel* (1532), was John Fischart (c. 1546–1590), who used polemical wit and a baroque ornamental and gaudy style in his violent attacks on Catholic institutions and traditions. Ulrich von Hutten (cf. p. 251 sq.), likewise writing with a strong anti-Catholic bias, is next to Luther the first German author whose German style achieves true greatness of lyrical expression and whose revolutionary pathos is born of the depth of social and personal experience.

Following in the footsteps of Martin Luther, the singers of Protestant hymns impart in their songs religious significance to the entire breadth of life and culture. Defiance, fear, trust, and jubilant rejoicing are the principal motifs of their lyrics, varying according to temperament, mood, and religious climate. Many of the Protestant church songs were taken over into Catholic hymnals before the close of the sixteenth century. The realization of the fact that the production of hymns had proven an invaluable aid in spreading the Protestant convictions led to the publication of several Catholic songbooks (Michael Vehe, 1537; John Leisentritt, 1567).

Next to religious poetry the historical folk song came into its own during and immediately following the Reformation. It was inspired by the great events of the early sixteenth century: Luther's and Hutten's fight against Rome and the national resistance to the advancing Turks. Many of these folk songs originated around the campfires of mercenary soldiers, and their texts and tunes expressed the soldier's longing for home, love, happiness, and peace. The creative forces of poetry were still alive among the common people, nourished by the reminiscences of inherited motifs of the *Volkslieder* and *Minnelieder* of the fourteenth and fifteenth centuries.

The endeavors of the Humanists and of Hans Sachs in the dramatic field were chiefly documents of pedagogical tendencies, issuing in the post-Reformation period in a new type of "school drama" that combined ancient classical with contemporary elements, didacticism with psychological introspection. The German drama of the sixteenth century consciously cultivates a "bourgeois" atmosphere and a set of emotions and ideals that were characteristic of the new middle class of the cities: inwardness (*Innerlichkeit*), righteousness, honesty, simplicity of heart and mind, humility, morality, and all the virtues of a healthy and homely family life. The treatment of the biblical parable of the Prodigal Son by Burkard Waldis (*c.* 1490–1556) and others gives evidence of the same emphasis upon the redeeming and forgiving love of the father for his lost child that appears so strongly accentuated in Luther's translation of the Bible and in his doctrine of "salvation by faith alone."

German narrative prose in the sixteenth century exists in the two major forms of the folk tale or folk novel (*Volksroman*) and the art novel (*Kunstroman*). The folk novel has its roots in traditional popular anecdotes and is always close to the events that move the hearts and minds of the common people. The art novel, on the other hand, is more intimately linked to the social pattern of the new middle class (*Bürgertum*). The mostly anonymous folk novel reaches its peak in the *Faust-Book* of 1587 (cf. p. 266), the most characteristic example of the didactic middle class literature of the period following the Reformation. The typical art novel of the age was created by George Wickram (1520–1561), the founder of the "Meistersinger School" of Colmar in Alsace. The art novel does not grow out of the anecdotal tradition but follows the pattern of courtly and knightly fiction, with a new emphasis on social distinctions and a growing self-assertion of middle class consciousness. Wickram's *Goldfaden* ("Golden Thread") presents the civic virtuousness of the German middle class in effective contrast with knightly decadence. The entire set of knightly virtues and courtly emotions and passions is viewed with growing suspicion and disgust. But already the following generation adopts an attitude of scorn, disdain, and critical satire toward the self-centered complacency of middle class morality, and the era of princely despotism leads to a devaluation of conservative civic ideals.

Arts and Crafts. The Reformation had shown its hostility toward the plastic arts in the iconoclast movements which were inspired by the theological spiritualism of the reformers and which were especially violent in those countries and regions where the teachings of Calvin and Zwingli had been adopted. Religious paintings and sculptures, altars, organs, monstrances, crucifixes, chalices, and chandeliers were in many places removed from the churches and destroyed. We have observed how Luther successfully tried to halt the misguided enthusiasm and fanaticism of the despoilers of religious art. Though opposed to the veneration of saints and their relics and to those cultic practices (the sacramental system, the Mass, etc.) around which the arts had crystallized in the past, he was not hostile to religious art as such and found words of highest praise for ecclesiastical music, "that magnificent gift of God, which is so close to sacred theology."

The secularization of ecclesiastical institutions and possessions was another factor that worked to the detriment of religious art, depriving especially the Protestant churches of the necessary means to carry on their protectorate over the arts and crafts. The new employers of the artists were the princes, nobles, and patricians.

As in former times they had worked for the greater glory of God and the Church, so now the artists and artisans served the glorification of the secular State and its princely rulers. The architects, mostly of Italian and Dutch nationality, were entrusted with the task of constructing a host of magnificent princely palaces and castles, with flights of halls and chambers, with huge courts and extended parks and gardens. The castles of Heidelberg and Stuttgart and the Belvedere in Prague are some of the outstanding monuments of princely pride and splendor in sixteenth-century Germany. Compared with these palatial residences even such stately and ornate structures as the city hall in Bremen or the Peller-House in Nuremberg appear rather small and insignificant.

The courts of the castles and palaces and the public squares in front of them, the parks, portals, and stairways were adorned with a rich display of statuary and plastic ornamental design. The castle church or chapel was lavishly decorated and equipped with imposing altars and pulpits. An

Heidelberg Castle.

artistically designed tombstone, sarcophagus, or mausoleum was to perpetuate the name of the ruler. German cities, gardens, residences, public fountains, even churchyards and churches, abounded with mythological sculptures of a pagan pantheon of gods and goddesses, of nymphs and dolphins, of Greek heroes and courtesans.

German *painting* of the sixteenth century likewise reflects the tastes and whims of the princely or patrician employers. Mythological scenes and figures animate the atmosphere of landscape painting, and "nothing was dearer to the heart of the most august princes and lords and their most serene spouses and relations than the glorious portraits of their own countenances." It goes without saying, therefore, that the art of portrait painting achieved new and unprecedented heights under the influence of an exaggerated cult of personality. Most of the princes gave steady employment to specially appointed court painters.

The *graphic arts,* including engraving, etching, and woodcut, had greatly aided the propagandistic activities of the adherents as well as the opponents of the Reformation. These relatively new techniques had facilitated the inexpensive mass production of polemic subject matter without excluding or diminishing artistic values. Many of the leading painters of the age (Dürer, Holbein, Altdorfer, Aldegrever, the brothers Barthel and Hans Sebald Beham, etc.) created outstanding graphic works in the form of book illustrations or designs for goldsmiths and other craftsmen, some of them owing the greater part of their fame to their masterful command of the new techniques (the Neat Masters or *Kleinmeister*).

The applied and mechanical arts and crafts flourished in the workshops of the goldsmiths, carvers, and cabinetmakers. The products of southern Germany, profiting by close contact with the accomplishments of the Italian Renaissance, were superior in number and quality to the output of the German North. In the year 1588 we find in Augsburg alone 170 masters in the art of goldsmithing. The preferred materials in which the German artisans exercised their craftsmanship were ivory, alabaster, mother-of-pearl, amber, gold and other precious metals, ebony and cedarwood. Many of the finished products served to enrich the "art chambers" of princes and patricians.

The art of *music* had been introduced into secular society by the Italian Renaissance, whose favorite form of musical expression was the madrigal, based on lyrical texts and sung by from four to six different voices, with or without instrumental accompaniment. The form of the madrigal marks the disappearance of the Ecclesiastical Modes (cf. p. 83 sq.), the upper voice taking the lead and dissonances becoming the common device of musical composition. Among the German practitioners of this new musical form Hans Leo von Hasler (1564–1612) of Nuremberg stands out. He had held a Fugger scholarship in Venice and had been taught by the great Venetian master, Andrea Gabrieli (*c.* 1510–1586). For the Lutheran Church Hasler created a famous book of chorals.

The first of the great German composers is Heinrich Finck (*c.* 1445–1527), whose works reveal the influence of the great Dutch masters, William Dufay (*c.* 1400–1474) and Josquin des Près (*c.* 1450–1521). German music like German painting received decisive inspiration in the sixteenth century from Italy as well as from the Netherlands. The Dutch composer Josquin des Près spent the last years of his life in the service of the German imperial court. The courts of Vienna, Munich, Heidelberg, and Dresden opened their portals to music and song and took pride in employing some of the outstanding composers of the age.

Dutch and German polyphony reached its classical height in the works of Orlando di Lasso (1520–1594). He had received his musical training in Italy and had traveled in England, France, and the Netherlands. From 1557 until his death he lived in Munich at the court of Duke Albrecht V. Emperor Maximilian II raised him to the status of nobility and the pope conferred upon him the title of a "Knight of the Golden Spur." He is to the North what the great Palestrina (1526–1594) is to Italy, and his *Seven Penitential Psalms* rank with Palestrina's *Missa Papae Marcelli* (a Mass dedicated to the memory of the Reform pope, Marcellus II) as crowning achievements of modern polyphony.

Luther's description of the polyphonic technique of vocal composition gives evidence of his appreciation and understanding of this musical form: "Is it not remarkable and admirable," he says, "how one sings a plain melody or tenor voice against which these four or five voices take part, gamboling and playing round this single tune, decking it with wondrous art and sound; seeming to take the lead in a heavenly dance, meeting, greeting, and embracing one another, so that all who have an understanding for such art agree that there is nothing in the world more remarkable than such a song decked round with many voices." Luther himself had some of the Protestant chorals polyphonically arranged, in the manner of the Dutch Motets. The collection of *New German Sacred Hymns* (*Neue deutsche Geistliche Gesänge*) of 1544 contains polyphonic arrangements of the works of the early composers of the Lutheran Reformation, among them the Swiss master, Ludwig Senfl, and Arnoldus de Bruck, conductor at the court of Vienna. The singing of polyphonic chorals required specially trained church choirs, under the direction of a precentor (*Kantor*). The schools took an important part in the rendition of these works, and Luther strongly insisted that instruction in musical theory and practice be made compulsory.

Gradually, in the course of the sixteenth century, the strict boundary lines between ecclesiastical and secular music disappeared, and instrumental music acquired an increasing significance. Among the favorite musical instruments were the horn, bassoon, flute, cornet, trumpet, trombone, violin, and the newly improved organ which, with the varieties of its tonal expression, represented an orchestra by itself.

At the beginning of the sixteenth century the medieval fiddle (rebec) with only three strings gave way to the modern violin, in the dual form of the *viola da braccio* and the *viola da gamba* (violincello). Violinmaking has been practiced as a craft and an important home industry in Füssen and later on in Mittenwald in Bavaria ever since the beginning of modern times.

Chapter 9

THIRTY YEARS' WAR AND
TURKISH WARS

The Bohemian Revolt and the "Winter-King" (1618–1623). The war which started with the violent uprising of the Bohemian nobles, in answer to the enforced acceptance by the Bohemian Diet of the Catholic Duke Ferdinand of Styria as future king of Bohemia, was to last for thirty years and, as time went on, it involved almost every state in Europe. Its first phase is marked by the fierce opposition of Bohemian Calvinism to the religious and dynastic ambitions of the Hapsburgs. By designating his cousin Ferdinand as his heir and successor on the Bohemian throne, Emperor Matthias had violated the ancient elective principle embodied in the Bohemian monarchy. The opportunity beckoned for the Czech nationalists to free their country once and for all from the hated Hapsburg domination.

On May 23, 1618, a group of nobles entered the council chamber of the royal palace at Prague and hurled the emissaries of the emperor into a ditch below the window, where they landed unharmed. With this somewhat symbolical act the Bohemians had given the signal for the outbreak of open rebellion. Their representatives met at a specially convened Diet and pronounced Ferdinand dethroned. When Emperor Matthias died early in 1619, the duke of Styria succeeded him as Emperor Ferdinand II, and this newly added prestige gained for him the support of Spain, the Catholic League (cf. p. 214), and the papacy. The Bohemians, on the other hand, turned for aid to Frederick, the young Calvinist prince-elector of the Palatinate, the head of the Protestant Union (cf. p. 214) and the son-in-law of King James I of England, offering him the Bohemian crown. They hoped that in so doing they would be able to enlist the active support of England as well as of the Protestant princes of Germany. Both parties involved in this struggle thus must bear the responsibility for having turned a local rebellion into a European religious war.

The hopes of the Bohemian Calvinists were not fulfilled: King James of England, who was engaged at that time in negotiations for a marriage alliance with Spain, was unwilling to aid Frederick's campaign, and the Lutheran princes of Germany felt utterly reluctant to risk possible defeat at the hands of the powerful Catholic League by throwing in their lot with the Calvinists. The combined armies of the emperor and the Catholic League under the command of General Tilly defeated the Bohemians in the battle of the White Hill near Prague (1620), and Frederick had to flee the country, leaving Ferdinand in undisputed possession of Bohemia and Austria. Thus the bold adventure of Frederick's campaign had come to an inglorious end, and the Jesuits had been proven right in their prediction that the reign of the "winter-king" would not last a full year.

The Catholic reaction was ruthless, the persecution of Calvinism violent in the extreme. All the religious privileges that had been granted to the Bohemians were revoked, the estates of the rebel nobles were confiscated, and large parts of the population were faced with the alternative of either conversion or emigration. Duke Maximilian of Bavaria, whose armies had had a major share in securing the victory for the emperor, was awarded the electoral title and the domains of Frederick (1623). The scene of action had been shifted to the Palatinate, where Spanish troops had been quartered and where the outlawed Frederick, aided by the soldiers of General Mansfeld and the margrave of Baden-Durlach, had made a last stand. The Palatinate was subjugated by Tilly, and the Protestant troops retired in a northerly direction, leaving the combined forces of Austria, Bavaria, and Spain as the victors in this first major phase of the war.

Albrecht von Wallenstein and the Saxon-Danish War (1624–1629). The collapse of German Protestantism on the field of battle had given a vastly superior strength to the forces of the Catholic League and to the house of Hapsburg, thus seriously upsetting the religious balance of power. Fear of a complete re-Catholization of Germany aided in enlisting foreign support for the cause of the German Protestants and at the same time led to a fateful extension of the bases of warlike operations. The neighboring Protestant nations, Holland, England, and Denmark, were aroused by the impending danger of a Catholic supremacy in Europe, while the French monarchy, though Catholic, disliked the increasing power and prestige of the rival Hapsburg dynasty and was ready to offer subsidies and diplomatic aid to the German Protestants. James I's marriage negotiations with Spain had come to naught, and the British ruler had decided to improve the relations between England and France by marrying Henrietta Maria, the sister of King Louis XIII of France. He was busy with cementing a coalition of states to force the restoration of Frederick of the Palatinate to his hereditary possessions. Holland was anxious to join any alliance directed against Spain, and King Christian IV of Denmark was willing to lend material aid to his German-Lutheran coreligionists in their fight against the German emperor and the Catholic League.

It was at this juncture that the brilliant and enigmatic figure of Albrecht von Wallenstein stepped into the limelight of European affairs to dominate the theater of war during the following decade. A native of Bohemia of Protestant parentage, but nominally a Catholic, he twice rose to power to become the generalissimo of the imperial armies and to save the emperor from imminent disaster, and twice he fell from the heights of success, to be dismissed in disgrace and deposed. Wallenstein belongs among those mysterious and fascinating political or military genuises who, like Alexander, Caesar, Napoleon, or Hitler, consider themselves as the chosen instruments of fate or providence and who, exclusively possessed by the dynamic force of an idea and impelled by demonic ambition, follow a meteorlike course to their inescapable downfall. Compared with the far-flung planning and scheming of Wallenstein, Tilly's military bravery appears as the efficiency of a devout and honest but utterly unimaginative subaltern officer.

Having acquired a considerable fortune and social prestige by the purchase of lands that had been confiscated after the Bohemian revolt, Wallenstein raised an army for the emperor at his own expense, demanding in return the right to support his soldiers by levying contributions in conquered territories, and to be invested with almost unprecedented political power. His army included the most heterogeneous elements, Catholics as well as Protestants, men picked from various nationalities, all blindly devoted to their leader, unified and co-ordinated in aim and action by Wallenstein's personal magnetism.

With over fifty thousand men the generalissimo marched northward to join the army of the Catholic League. His troops broke the resistance of Count Mansfeld of Savoy, leader of an army of mercenaries and an ally of the Bohemians. Mansfeld was defeated at Dessau on the Elbe and withdrew into Bohemia, hotly pursued by Wallenstein, while Tilly at the same time (1626) defeated the Danes at Lutter am Barenberg and forced them to withdraw from German soil. With the Catholic-Imperial forces gaining a firm foothold in northern Germany, Wallenstein envisioned the establishment of a sovereign state of his own in the conquered territories along the Baltic coast. Emperor Ferdinand appointed him as general of the imperial navy and of the Baltic and North Sea and made him "Duke of Friedland."

It was Wallenstein's favorite idea to make the German emperor as absolute and independent a sovereign as the kings of France and England and, to achieve this end, to make the imperial office hereditary. A powerful imperial fleet in the Baltic was to forge an important link between the Hanseatic cities and the Spanish sea power. The great general's interest in the religious issues of the war was completely overshadowed by his political plans and ambitions, which in turn could only be realized if the German emperor were willing to sacrifice the issues of the Catholic Restoration to the ideal of a superdenominational German monarchy. This, however, Ferdinand was not prepared to do. Even if he could have been persuaded to follow Wallenstein in his visionary political ideology, he would have met with the stubborn opposition of the princes of the Catholic League and the ecclesiastical electors. The members of the League were apprehensive lest a strong and centralized imperial authority might endanger their sovereign prerogatives, while the ecclesiastical princes were most anxious to gain back for the Church the confiscated, secularized, and protestantized ecclesiastical domains.

Wallenstein suffered his first setback in 1628, when the city of Stralsund withstood successfully the siege of his army. In the following year Emperor Ferdinand issued the "Edict of Restitution," calling for the restoration to the Catholic Church of all ecclesiastical lands which had been handed over to the Protestants since the Treaty of Passau (1552, cf. p. 212). Wallenstein, well aware that the enforcement of the "Edict" would lead to a severe aggravation of the religious conflict and necessitate the continuation of the war, declared himself opposed to it. Faced with the choice of losing the support either of the Catholic League or of his commander in chief, Ferdinand decided on the latter course. In carrying out the resolution of the Diet of Regensburg (1630), Ferdinand notified Wallenstein of his unqualified dismissal and appointed Tilly as supreme commander.

Gustavus Adolphus, Wallenstein, and the Swedish War (1630–1635). In the very year of Wallenstein's dismissal Gustavus Adolphus, king of Sweden (1611–1632), the "Lion of the North," had landed on the coast of Pomerania. A descendant of the house of Vasa, he was enthroned at the age of seventeen and in scarcely two decades had made Sweden one of the most formidable and best organized military powers of Europe. He had driven the Russians back from the Baltic and had concluded a treaty with Poland, which gave him access to a number of Prussian ports and strengthened his resolution to make the Baltic a "Swedish Lake."

The two pillars of Swedish supremacy in the North were the spiritual force of Lutheran Protestantism and the political domination of the Baltic. Both appeared to be threatened by the sudden expansion of the Catholic-Hapsburg empire along the Baltic coast. It is doubtful, nevertheless, whether Gustavus Adolphus would have acted without the encouragement and the assurances he received from France's Cardinal Richelieu, the powerful prime minister of King Louis XIII (1610–1643). It was the political combination of the power politics of Sweden and France which proved decisive for the final stages of the Thirty Years' War and which forced the religious ideologies to yield to the objectives of Spanish-Austrian, Swedish, and French imperialism.

In 1629 Richelieu persuaded his king that it was necessary to intervene in the European conflict in order to guarantee France's greatness and security for centuries to come. In bringing about an alliance between Catholic France and Protestant Sweden Richelieu placed political expediency above religious loyalty and sacrificed the Catholic to the nationalistic idea.

It was Swedish aid which had encouraged the inhabitants of Stralsund to resist successfully Wallenstein's attack in 1628. Now, with the promise of financial support from France, Gustavus Adolphus decided to start armed intervention on a large scale. Strange to say, he was not favorably received by those forces whom he came to rescue. Not only were the Lutheran princes intimidated by the strength of the imperial forces, but they also seemed to be apprehensive of the political implications of further foreign intervention. Thus, the elector of Brandenburg could only be won over to the Swedish cause by force, after his territory had been invaded. The tactical mistake on the part of Tilly, of attempting to scare John George of Saxony to his side by threats of force, caused the Saxon elector to join hands with the Swedes. Thus reinforced by an alliance with the two leading Protestant powers of northern Germany, Gustavus Adolphus attacked and defeated the imperial army at Breitenfeld near the city of Leipzig (1631). From then on the Swedish king proceeded on a triumphal march, westward through the bishoprics on the Main and Rhine rivers and finally southward into Alsace and southeastward into Bavaria. He entered Munich in the company of the outlawed "winter-king," Frederick of the Palatinate. Tilly had been defeated again at the crossing of the Lech river and had died shortly afterward of the wounds received on the field of battle (1632).

Emperor Ferdinand was quick to realize that there was only one man who could save the imperial armies from annihilation — Wallenstein! Living in involuntary retirement on his estates, smarting from the blow to his dignity and his pride, and still resenting what he considered ignoble ingratitude on the part of the emperor, Wallenstein had to be begged to raise an army and to accept the supreme command. When he finally agreed it was with the understanding that he be given dictatorial powers and princely prerogatives.

Gustavus Adolphus and Wallenstein, the two greatest military geniuses of the age, met in the bloody battle of Lützen near Leipzig (1632). The Swedes were victorious, but the victory cost them their king and leader, who died in action. The Swedish military command was taken over by Duke Bernard of Weimar, while the political destinies of Sweden were entrusted to chancellor Oxenstierna, acting as regent for Queen Christina who was not yet of age. Despite partial successes the Swedish cause waned with the death of Gustavus Adolphus, while the stars of the Duke of Friedland and his emperor ascended.

Wallenstein, too, was nearing the end of his dramatic career. Encamped in Bohemia and Silesia with his army of sixty thousand, he relapsed into political dreaming and scheming, being determined that his own political ambitions should receive their full share in the remaking of the political map of Europe. He visualized himself as the future elector of Brandenburg and as the sovereign ruler of a state that was to extend from Friedland in Bohemia to the Baltic and North Sea. Convinced that his destiny was written in the constellations of the stars, he let his judgment be influenced by astrological speculation and began to lose more and more of his freedom of choice and determination. His inactivity as well as his personal ambitions aroused the suspicion of the imperial court in Vienna. Suspected of carrying on secret and treasonable negotiations with the Swedish enemy with a view to dictating a political peace to the Empire based on the equality of religious creeds, Wallenstein was deserted by most of his officers and men and assassinated in the Bohemian town of Eger by the Irish Colonel Butler and some fellow conspirators (1634).* His fortune and extended possessions were confiscated by the emperor and distributed among the officers and troops of the dead general.

In the year of Wallenstein's assassination the Swedes under Bernard of Weimar were defeated by an imperial army at Nördlingen in Bavaria and had to give up most of the territories that they had previously conquered. In the following year (1635) the emperor negotiated the Peace of Prague with the electors of Brandenburg and Saxony. Under the terms of this treaty the two electors were to relinquish their alliance with Sweden, and all disputed German Church lands were to be restored to those who had held them in 1627. The "Edict of Restitution" of 1629 was thereby virtually annulled.

Richelieu, Mazarin, and the Swedish-French War (1635–1648). With the signing of the Treaty of Prague peace could have been restored if the aims of French imperialism had not prevented it. Richelieu had not yet achieved the ardently desired destruction of Hapsburg power in Europe. He found a willing tool to carry out his political plans in the Capuchin monk, Père Joseph of Paris, the former François du Tremblay, Baron de Maffiers. In lending his aid to Richelieu's Machiavellian policies Père Joseph was attempting to revive the mystical dream and prophecy that dated back to the times when King Louis VII of France started on the Second Crusade. In this prophecy the French king was described as the future supreme sovereign of a universal Christian empire that was to embrace Orient and Occident. The house of Hapsburg appeared as the major obstacle in the realization of this ambitious scheme.

In 1635 France declared war on Spain and concluded an alliance with Holland and Savoy. Bernard of Weimar, the Swedish commander, was placed on the French payroll. Thus France was not only responsible for the continuation of the war for another thirteen years, but she also became the leading power as far as military strategy and efficiency were concerned. Most of the battles were fought on German soil, and the final peace negotiations were conducted under French pressure and concluded at the expense of Germany.

In 1642 Richelieu was succeeded by Cardinal Mazarin, an ambitious politician of Italian descent, who assumed truly dictatorial powers and continued with even greater energy and ruthlessness the struggle for the aims of French imperialism. It was chiefly due to his influence that France now became a thoroughly militarized nation. The French armies under the command of General Turenne and the prince of Condé fought with varying success on the Neckar and Rhine and in the Spanish Netherlands, where the Spaniards suffered a crushing defeat at Rocroi in 1643. In 1646

* Cf. Friedrich Schiller's Wallenstein trilogy (*Wallenstein's Camp; The Piccolomini; Wallenstein's Death*) and the same author's *History of the Thirty Years' War*.

the Swedish army under General Wrangel and a French army under Turenne joined their forces on Bavarian soil, and in 1648 the Swedes stormed Prague, while the prince of Condé annihilated a Spanish-Austrian army near Lens (France). Peace negotiations had been under way for the past four years, carried on by two parallel assemblies, the Catholic and Protestant powers meeting separately in the Westphalian cities of Münster and Osnabrück. On October 24, 1648, the peace treaty of Westphalia was signed.

The Peace of Westphalia (1648). The peace treaty of Münster and Osnabrück marked the end of the Holy Roman Empire of the German Nation as a political power. From 1648 on, it existed only nominally and on the map. The profits of the war were reaped by those foreign powers whose intervention had prolonged the conflict and whose armies had devastated the German lands. In the Westphalian Peace Conference Sweden and France sat in judgment on the destiny and the future boundaries of Germany, with the German princes and the German emperor too power-less to withstand their dictation. Each of the almost three hundred petty principalities of Germany was represented at the conference table, and each of them was given sovereign rights, including the privileges of coining money, raising their own armies, and concluding alliances with foreign powers ("*ius foederis*"). And in addition to their votes, those of France and Sweden were required in any important decision that was to be taken by the Imperial Diet.

France and Sweden were doing a thorough job in paralyzing the arm of the central government and in destroying German unity of purpose and political action. The war which had begun as a religious struggle ended with a peace that bore all the earmarks of modern imperialism, leading to the economic and national strangulation of the weaker by the stronger. The injustices embodied in the terms of the settlement bore in themselves the seeds of future armed conflicts, of a series of wars that were to be fought for dynastic supremacy, territorial gains and readjustments, and for economic domination.

In the Treaty of Westphalia the Thirty Years' War was described as a "struggle of liberation," waged by the German Estates and Principalities against the autocracy of the emperor, and France and Sweden came forward as the guarantors of "German Liberty." Freed from its diplomatic verbiage and elaborate trimmings, this meant simply that Germany had become a French protectorate.

France accordingly received the largest share of the booty: the Hapsburg possessions in Alsace, in addition to the bishoprics of Metz, Toul, and Verdun, which she had held since 1552 (cf. p. 208). Richelieu in his memorandum of 1629 had already designated the acquisition of Lorraine and the city of Strasbourg as objectives of France's foreign policy, "*pour acquérir une entrée en Allemagne*" (in order to gain a gateway into Germany). With the possession of these territories France would obtain a strategic position in the German Southwest; from here she would be able to control the activities of the princes of southern Germany and check the movements and designs of Austrian politics. Although the free city of Strasbourg was not included in the French grab at the end of the war, the new boundary was marked by the Rhine river, from the Rhenish Palatinate (*Rheinpfalz*) up to the Swiss border.

Sweden, the second great European power to entrench itself on German soil, received the bishoprics of Bremen and Verden and the western part of Pomerania. She thereby gained a strong foothold on the southern coast of the Baltic and control of the Oder river and the mouth of the Elbe.

Brandenburg, in return for the surrender of western Pomerania to Sweden, received several secularized bishoprics and a guarantee of her territorial rights in eastern Pomerania. The Palatinate was divided between Duke Maximilian of Bavaria and Charles Louis, the son of the "winter-king" (Frederick V), each of them receiving the electoral title. Holland and Switzerland, which nominally had still belonged to the Empire, were formally recognized as independent European powers. The great German seaports on the North Sea and the Baltic, Hamburg, Bremen, and Lübeck, lost their freedom and were made subject to the political and economic influence of Denmark and Sweden.

As to the religious settlement, the status of the year 1624 was to be recognized as a binding norm, and secularized Church lands were to remain in the hands of those who held them at that time. In this way a large number of north German bishoprics as well as the lands of Wurtemberg and the Palatinate were retained by the Protestants. On the initiative of the elector of Brandenburg the Calvinists were now included in the privileges of the Religious Peace of Augsburg (cf. p. 212). Calvinist princes thus were given the right to determine the religion of their subjects. Although theoretically the three major rival denominations, Catholic, Lutheran, and Calvinist, were granted equal rights, religious toleration was no more in evidence at the end of the great war than it was at its beginning.

Cultural Collapse. The Thirty Years' War engraved itself on the consciousness of contemporaries as the greatest scourge of mankind since the days of Attila and his Huns. Its horrors are vividly described in memoirs and letters, in sermons and pamphlets, in chronicles and narratives. These documents speak of an *"excidium Germaniae"* (the destruction of Germany), of a *"Germania expirans"* (a dying Germany). They tell a sordid tale of the lust of bloodshed; of slain and tortured men, women, and children; of destroyed cattle and farm land; of devastated and pillaged cities, towns, and villages. We read of the rapidly shifting alliances and allegiances and of how, as time went on, everybody became everyone's foe: Swedes, Croats, Spaniards, Frenchmen, and mercenaries from all countries ravaging and ransacking the German lands. We learn of a whole generation growing up and knowing the blessings of peace only from hearsay. We are told about the deserted schools and universities, the decline of morality and religion, about empty workshops, burned churches and desecrated church-yards. It is hardly surprising then that Gustav Freytag (1816–1895), in his *Pictures from the German Past* (*Bilder aus der deutschen Vergangenheit;* first printing in 5 vols., 1859–1867), wonders how "after such losses and such corruption of the survivors, a German people has remained in existence, a people which was able after the conclusion of the peace to till the soil, to pay taxes and, after miserably dragging along for a hundred years, to bring forth new energy and enthusiasm, and a new life in the arts and sciences."

And yet, truthful as some of the contemporary reports on the social and cultural collapse of Germany may be, many others will have to be accepted with reservation. For one thing, the seventeenth century in general leans toward exaggeration, no less in its historiographical accounts than in its art, its literature, its fashion, its social behavior. Again, we have learned today from experiences that are close to our own memories that times of extraordinary stress and duress generate various modes of wishful reportage and outright propaganda, born of the urge to indict the political, social, or religious opponent and to blacken his record by atrocity tales which usually are a composite of truth and imagination. To judge the frightful events of the war adequately it becomes necessary to submit the above-mentioned horror tales to the tranquil searchlight of historical criticism and thus reduce them to their true proportions.

It is obvious that the Thirty Years' War, judged by its original motivating causes and aims, was one of the most futile and unnecessary wars ever fought. During its last phases the war dragged on by its own momentum. In viewing its dire course from the beginnings of the conflagration down to its last flickerings, it becomes almost impossible and evidently quite meaning-less to even raise the question of war guilt: the war had been born of the convulsions of a disintegrating civilization, and its changing constellations were merely symptoms and symbols of one of the major crises in the history of the European peoples.

Some figures may illustrate the extent to which the vitality of the German people was taxed and depleted by the successive waves of destruction. The city of Augsburg lost 62,000 of its 80,000 inhabitants. The population of the duchy of Wurtemberg was reduced from 400,000 to 48,000. It is reliably estimated that the density of the population of Germany as a whole decreased by nearly two thirds. The national health was weakened for generations to come by hunger and epidemic disease. The purity and strength of the racial stock suffered from miscegenation as well as from inbreeding. The economic decline which in its beginnings reached back to the preceding century was fatally accelerated and consummated by the war. The work of reconstruction was hampered by the lack of raw materials, building mate-rials, and skilled labor. Peasants, craftsmen, artists, and merchants were equally hit by the instability of the times and by the reduction of national income. The chaotic conditions of trade and commerce led to an increasing confusion of the money market and a devaluation of the currency, while on the other hand money became a mere commodity and the object of reckless speculation. The disproportion between the increasing prices and the decreasing purchasing power grew appalling.

Bleeding from innumerable wounds, Germany in a supreme effort had to draw upon the moral and spiritual reserves of her people if she wanted not only to survive but also to revive. That strength of conviction, a strong will to action, and a realistic appraisal of the difficult tasks ahead were not wholly lacking, is evidenced by the text of a pamphlet of the year 1647, in which the anonymous author appeals to the national spirit of the German people in words like the following: "The Frenchmen and Swedes boast loudly of having subdued Germany. Our banners are displayed in Paris and Stockholm. . . . Kings, formerly obeying the call of the German Emperor . . . have become our masters by our own discord. . . . These so-called liberators approach us as with the kisses of Judas. . . . From the Rhine, from the North Sea, and the Baltic they look out from their watch towers, spying for every opportunity and conflict that might arise . . . and not unlike the ancient Romans in Greece, they begin as friendly advisers, then become arbiters, and finally masters. Awake, O Germany! Consider what thou really art! Arise from this deadly fight! The Empire can only be revived by the Empire; Germany can only be reborn by Germany. . . . As members of one body, of one state, as brethren we all must embrace each other in love, and with all our faculties and virtues strive heroically toward the great goal. . . . "

Austria Amidst Warring Ideologies. The Thirty Years' War in its later phases had developed into a life-and-death struggle between the French Bourbons and the Austrian-Spanish Hapsburgs. With the steadily diminishing prestige of the Spanish crown the burden of defending the dynastic aims and possessions of the Hapsburgs against French aggression fell more and more on the Austrian branch of the Hapsburg family. In the seventeenth century we find Austria engaged in a world-historic struggle on two fronts, *France* launching her attack from the West and the *Ottoman Turks* advancing from the East.

The battle that had to be fought against the encroachment of the dynastic interests of France, the ally of the Turks, was rendered all the more difficult because it required both repulsion of foreign attack and defense of the central authority of the Empire against the autonomous German princes, some of whom had concluded alliances with the French crown.

Three rival interests and ideologies clashed in the Thirty Years' War, Emperor Ferdinand II representing the unity of imperial power and Catholic tradition, Gustavus Adolphus advancing the idea of a Nordic Protestant empire, and Wallenstein fighting for a centralized monarchy, based on religious toleration and headed by the house of Hapsburg. It was Wallenstein's dream to create a monumental German superstate extending from the Baltic in the North to the Adriatic Sea in the South. Such a German imperium if realized would have established German hegemony in the Western World and would have provided an impregnable basis for unified operations against the Turks.

But it was the idea of religious toleration and a political unification without unity of faith which was unacceptable to Emperor Ferdinand and which caused Wallenstein's defection and downfall. The emperor felt in duty bound to follow the example of his much admired Spanish cousin, King Philip II, in restoring the Christian-Catholic unification of the Western World. The idea of political unity without unity of faith was inconceivable to him. Thus Wallenstein was dismissed, and France and the autonomous German princes became the beneficiaries of his defeat. The emperor, in turn, had to compromise his religious ideology by concluding a separate peace with the Protestant Saxons, and the religious war became a regional struggle for a European balance of power. The house of Hapsburg was forced to concentrate its efforts on the creation of a strong Danubian state within the confines of its hereditary domains. Mazarin's war aims culminated in the separation of the Spanish and Austrian branches of the Hapsburg dynasty; the separation of Austria from the rest of the Empire; and the establishment of the French-German boundary on the Rhine. In 1658 the first Rhenish League, headed by the archchancellor of the Empire, lined up the German princes against the central imperial power; while the Peace of the Pyrenees of 1659, terminating the struggle between France and Spain, marked the decline of Spanish power and the rise of France to European supremacy. The Peace of the Pyrenees was sealed by the marriage of the young French king, Louis XIV (1643–1715), to Maria Theresa, the daughter of King Philip IV of Spain. The political ambitions of Richelieu had finally reached their goal.

In the East, on Austria's second frontier, the Ottoman Turks, who had invaded the Balkan Peninsula about the middle of the fourteenth century, had held the European continent in suspense over a period of three hundred years. As the Franks under Charles Martel had saved the Christian civilization of the West from the advancing Arabs in the eighth century, so the house of Hapsburg preserved the essential integrity of Europe by the repulsion of Turkish-Islamitic expansion.

In 1453 the Turks had conquered Constantinople and subsequently driven the Venetian Republic from its outposts in the Aegean Sea and in Greece. They threatened the entrance to the Adriatic and conquered Egypt in 1516, thus erecting a wall between the economic spheres of the Mediterranean and Indian Oceans. Under Soliman II (1520–1566), their greatest sultan, they crossed the Danube and advanced into Hungary, took the city of Belgrade and annihilated the Hungarian army in the swamps of Mohács in 1526. Once again the claims of emperor and pope to supremacy over the Christian West was met by the Ottoman Sultan's idea of a theocracy of the East, including in its orbit the Western World.

By 1529 the Turks had advanced to the gates of Vienna, to put an end to the rule of "those miserable lords of Vienna." A small contingent of scarcely 20,000 defenders, drawn from the hereditary Hapsburg domains and from other parts of the Empire, was faced with the almost impossible task of holding the city against a besieging army of 150,000 men. The Turks were masters in the art of mine-warfare but unequal to the superior strategic resourcefulness of western military science. Their indecision and several blunders saved Vienna, but the westward advance of the Turks resulted nevertheless in the tripartition of Hungary, leaving the invaders in possession of the largest slice of that country. Austria had to agree to pay an annual tribute to the Turkish "Sublime Porte" and went through a period of constant anxiety, insecurity, and incessant border warfare which ended only in 1606, when the sultan was compelled to recognize the political equality of the Hapsburg emperor.

The remainder of the Turkish drama was enacted in the latter part of the seventeenth century. The second siege of Vienna of 1683 opened the period of the Great Turkish War, in the course of which the house of Austria, united with the pope, the king of Poland, and the republic of Venice in the "Holy League," and entrusting its armies to the brilliant leadership of Duke Charles of Lorraine and Prince Eugene of Savoy, gained victory after victory over the Turks. With the decisive battle near Zenta on the Theiss river, the resistance and military prestige of the enemy were shattered, and the kingdom of Hungary with its dependencies was regained for the Austrian crown. The great victories of Prince Eugene of 1716 and 1717, at Peterwardein and Belgrade, were won in alliance with Venice in the course of the third major Turkish war. The heroic deeds of the great Savoyan leader live on in the stanzas of the dramatic folk ballad *"Prinz Eugenius, der edle Ritter . . ."* (Prince Eugene, the Noble Knight . . .). The house of Hapsburg extended its influence far into the Balkans and began even to nourish dreams of a revived Byzantine Empire under Hapsburg leadership. Prince Eugene is commemorated as the statesman and general who, though of Italian birth and French breeding, fought his battles for the liberation of Europe from French and Ottoman imperialism, co-ordinating the dynastic interests of the Hapsburgs with the vital necessities of German and European civilization as a whole.

Soldiers and Military Science. The period of the Thirty Years' War had further developed and perfected the system of mercenary armies and the methods of recruiting these hired troops from many lands. The princes entrusted the business of recruiting to their generals, who were frequently held responsible for the maintenance of the armies and who reimbursed themselves by marauding, pillage, and by the imposition of heavy contributions on conquered territories and populations. The soldier was attracted to the colors not by love of country or other ethical motives but primarily by greed and love of adventure. Some of the great military leaders, such as Wallenstein, Tilly, and Gustavus Adolphus, made repeated attempts to enforce discipline and the observance of some degree of lawfulness among their troops. Thus Wallenstein's *Military Law* of 1617 enjoins the soldiers to refrain from "ungodly, frivolous, and evil living; from blasphemy, oppression of the poor, and debauchery. Therefore, all lords, squires, and their servants shall listen to the word of God every Sunday and whenever the sound of the bugle calls them to service or sermon. Likewise, though money or payment may not always be ready in due time for distribution, everyone shall observe the rules of equity and fair play and shall make out receipts and keep accounts." However, there was a wide gap between theory and practice, and after the death of the great generals the last remnant of discipline and humane consideration was thrown to the winds, and cruelty and inhumanity became the order of the day.

Military science was directed into new channels by that eminent military strategist, Gustavus Adolphus. He reorganized the Swedish army and made it the most powerful military machine of Europe. He was the first to introduce compulsory military service (conscription) among some of his Swedish contingents. He armed his foot soldiers with muskets instead of pikes, emphasized the tactical and strategical significance of the cavalry, and heightened the flexibility of his armies by introducing new and lighter uniforms and more adequate equipment. The square formation of the troops was replaced by formations of threefold echelons, resulting in a considerable lengthening of the fighting line. Light artillery units were created by a general diminution of the cylinder bore (caliber) of the cannon, by the shortening of the gun barrel, and by the introduction of "leather cannon" whose barrels were made of thin copper sheathing, covered with leather.

It was the soldier as a social type who became the symbol and the ruler of the age. Booted and spurred, a martial-looking and colorful figure and an insufferable braggart, this new *"miles gloriosus"* is portrayed in the Silesian dramatist Andreas Gryphius' (1616–1664) satire *Horribilicribrifax*. Informed of the conclusion of a peace treaty between the emperor and the king of Sweden, he thunders indignantly: "Can he make peace without even asking me? . . . Does he not owe all his victories to me? Have I not shot down the Swedish king? . . . Have I not conquered Saxony? Have I not earned my reputation in Denmark? How would the battle on the White Hill have ended without me? What glory have I not earned in the battle with the Grand Turk? Fie upon you! Get out of my sight; for I get mortally vexed when I fly into a real rage: overpowered by hot and boiling wrath and savage ire I am capable of seizing the spire of St. Stephen's Cathedral in Vienna and bending it down so hard that the whole world will turn upside down like a skittle-ball."

The horrors of the great war had made the soldier an object of popular fear, hatred, and contempt. It was the general conviction that the calling of a soldier was outside the pale of decent and humane occupations. The soldier had made himself an outlaw and an outcast.

Fashion "à la Mode." The superiority which France had achieved as a result of the Thirty Years' War strengthened greatly the French prestige and influence in matters of artistic taste and social behavior. Even during the initial stages of the war the French *monsieur à la mode,* the fashionable beau, made his appearance in German cities and at the German courts. The stiff and tight Spanish fashion for which the standard had been set by Emperor Charles V and his court, with its "millstone collars" and the enormous wire constructions which had become a requisite of women's dresses (the "farthingale" or *"cache-bâtard"*), familiar from Velasquez' paintings, gave way to looser, wider, and softer garments of precious materials and imposing splendor.

About the middle of the seventeenth century the change from the Spanish to the French fashion was completed: the men wore wide, soft, sacklike pleated breeches, adorned with laced ribbons. The upper part of the body was covered with a sleeveless vest and a comfortable long-tailed coat. The stiff frill was replaced by a soft, broad linen or lace collar. The hair was worn either braided on one side or in long, flowing curls, covered usually with ribbons and jewels. A soft felt hat with broad rim, adorned with colorful feathers, took the place of the tall and stiff Spanish headdress. A pointed "Vandyke" beard or goatee, long gauntlets, a rapier dangling from a sword belt, and spurred boots completed the martial appearance of the gentleman: a queer mixture of Frenchman and Swede, of ruffian and dandy.

The ladies relinquished the wire contraptions of their crinolines or hoop petticoats, and the contours of the female figure reappeared under the easy and natural flow of the folds. The skirts were very long and ended in a train. The upper garments were cut low around the neck and were framed by a lace collar. The sleeves were wide, pleated, and likewise adorned with costly lace and multicolored ribbons. The loud colors gradually gave way to subdued halftones and nuances of blue, green, pink, brown, and yellow. The "tower coiffure" or *"Turmfrisur,"* with the hair combed over tall frames of wire, was abandoned in favor of freely flowing curls, parted in the middle, braided, and dressed in the form of a chignon on the back of the head. Powder was used to give the hair the desired color to match the dress. Men and women covered their faces with tiny black plasters, the "beauty patches" or "mouches." "I noticed many women," remarks Hans Michael Moscherosch (1601–1669), one of the leading satirists of the age, "whose faces looked as if they had had themselves cupped, pricked, or hacked. For in all those places to which they wanted to draw attention, they were pasted with small black plasters and with round and pointed little flies, fleas, and other quaint man-traps."

Literary Trends. German literature in the period of the Thirty Years' War presents a medley of eclectic imitations of foreign models, living mainly on borrowed form and subject matter. The reaction against such an artificial and colorless internationalism found its expression in the linguistic societies whose endeavors to purify and invigorate the national German idiom reach back to 1617, the year of the foundation of the "Fruitbringing Society." Other groups with similar aims were organized during the following decades, but on the whole the literary products of their members were no less pedantic, artificial, and lacking in social significance than the works which they criticized and upon which they wanted to improve. It was their conviction that poetry could be taught and learned like any trade or craft, and one of their number, the Nuremberg councilman George Philip Harsdörffer, composed the famous *Poetischer Trichter* ("Poetic Funnel"), to "pour in the German art of verse and poetry within six hours."

Like the members of the "Meistersinger Schools" these writers preferred biblical subjects, but introduced pastoral and idyllic motifs to emphasize their desire for the primitive and indigenous. Others cultivated a ceremonious courtly formalism with which they paid their tribute to the fashions and tastes of princely despotism. Conspicuously lacking were the truly poetic elements of creative imagination, melodious rhythm, and the warmth and sensuous richness of life and nature. They did not write and sing out of the fullness of their hearts, but as the representatives of a certain class, group, or convention. Nevertheless, their works were indicative of a significant social transformation which was characterized by the disintegration of the middle class and the birth of the aristocratic culture of the gentleman *à la mode,* with its petrified code of a conventional and unreal philosophy of life.

At the same time these writers mark the transition from a poetry that was limited by religious precepts and patterns to a secular style and worldly themes. The world is seen as a play of the forces of good and evil, but sensuous and natural beauty are positively valued and affirmed. In the religious speculation of Jacob Böhme (cf. p. 270) the forces of evil figure as vital and formative necessities. It is this thought that Böhme names as the fundamental cause of his spiritual unrest which was born when he "contemplated the great depth of this world, the sun and the stars and the clouds, rain and snow and the whole of creation, and man, that little spark, and what he may be worth in the judgment of God as compared with this great work of heaven and earth. But because I discovered that good and evil dwelled in all things, in the elements of nature as well as in creatures, and that in this world the ungodly fare as well as the devout . . . I was seized by a deep melancholy."

The strong note of doubt and insecurity which is felt in Jacob Böhme's utterances is almost wholly absent in the poetic works of those writers who continue the tradition of the Protestant and Catholic church hymn. Here trust in the rational administration of world affairs, confidence in the dispensations of divine providence, are the prevailing motifs, while the praise of nature as a revelation of the wisdom and supreme beauty of the Godhead is added as an element of mystical piety. While Luther's hymns (cf. p. 227 sq.) had been expressions of the religious experiences, longings, and victories of his social-ecclesiastical group, the lyrics of Paul Gerhardt (1606–1676) and

Paul Fleming (1609–1640) sing of the yearning of the individual soul, rising at the same time above the artificial conventions of their contemporaries. Friedrich Spee (1591–1635), the Jesuit writer and poet, and the convert Johann Scheffler, surnamed "Angelus Silesius" (the Silesian Angel, 1624–1677), the two outstanding Catholic hymn writers of the seventeenth century, show themselves influenced by the mystical speculation of past centuries as well as by the pastoral poetry of their own time. The works of both authors reveal originality of form and depth of ideas despite the shackles imposed upon them by mechanical rules and patterns. On Andreas Gryphius (1616–1664), on the other hand, the horrors of the times weighed too heavily, inhibiting and stunting a creative genius who under more favorable conditions might have become one of the leading dramatists and lyricists of Germany. His sensitivity was struck by the disheartening breakdown of all those values that he cherished, and his sonnets paint a gloomy picture of the transitoriness of all earthly things.

What the seventeenth century relished and desired was not a great poet but a clever theorist who could offer a clear-cut and comprehensible program. Martin Opitz (1597–1639), a member of the "Fruitbringing Society," was so widely acclaimed because he offered just such a program in his *Prosodia Germanica* (*Book on German Poetry*, 1624). It proved a most influential work whose rules and prescriptions were gratefully obeyed by several generations of German writers, and whose author was enthusiastically proclaimed as the "father of modern German poetry." It was Opitz' ambition to teach his German contemporaries how to achieve a literary greatness that equaled that of ancient Greece and Rome. He succeeded to some extent in freeing the secular forces of German culture from the dogmatic bonds of Protestant Reformation and Catholic Restoration alike and in utilizing literary talent for social purposes. Both he and Friedrich Spee independently established a new principle for German poetics and metrics by their demand that the mechanical counting of syllables in German verse should be replaced by the alternating use of stressed and unstressed syllables, in accordance with the normal and natural rhythm and meaning of the word. By following the model of Dutch literary patterns he transformed the Romanic metrical devices so as to adapt them to the Germanic laws of prosody.

The German imitation of foreign fashions and the corruption of courtly culture find a severe critic in the Silesian epigrammatist, Friedrich von Logau (1604–1655), and in the prose satires of Hans Michael Moscherosch (1601–1669). Logau speaks of Germany as the slave of France, a "lumberroom where other nations store their crimes and vices," and Moscherosch asks questions like the following: "Are you a German? And you wear your hair like a Frenchman? . . . Why do you wear that silly French kind of a beard? Your ancestors considered an honest full-grown beard their greatest pride, and you . . . treat and trim and curl it every month, every week, every day! . . . Is nothing good enough for you that is made in your own country, you despisers and traitors of your fatherland?"

The greatest cultural and literary document of the period of the Thirty Years' War is, however, the masterly novel that bears the title *The Adventurous Simplicissimus* (1669) and whose author was Jacob Christoffel von Grimmelshausen (1625-1676). After his conversion to Catholicism he became an advocate of the reunion of all Christian denominations and emphasized the practical values of religious conviction. His *Simplicissimus* has often been compared with Wolfram von Eschenbach's epic *Parzival* (cf. p. 153), and the parallelism of theme and character development is very close indeed. Though largely autobiographical and highly personal and direct in style and atmosphere, Grimmelshausen's work achieves the objective plasticity of the great epic. The novel tells us of the physical and spiritual growth of its hero from early childhood to a manhood tempered and balanced by that practical wisdom which is the result of experience, great suffering, and frequent trial and error. The ways of both Parzival and Simplicissimus lead from original harmony and childish innocence through complexity and sinful entanglements to a second and richer unity and simplicity in the vision and possession of God. But Parzival's social "milieu" was that of courtly culture at its best, while the cultural barrenness in the environment of Simplicissimus offers a sharp contrast and an almost insurmountable obstacle to the spiritual aspirations of the hero. While the cultural and social frame of Wolfram's epic is essentially static, that of *Simplicissimus* is dynamic, depicted in a continuous process of change and evolution and beset with conflicts and tensions which symbolically reflect a world composed of good and evil, beauty and sordidness, orderliness and chaos. Simplicissimus is a fool like Gerhart Hauptmann's *Emanuel Quint*, Dostoievski's *Idiot*, and Wolfram's *Parzival*, a fool before God in the end, after having been nature's and the world's fool in the earlier parts of the novel. The author seems to visualize the end of an historic epoch, the end of his time, and with the apocalyptic laments over the impending dissolution are mingled the voices of faith in humankind, hope for regeneration, and love of this strange world of incomprehensible mystery.

PART IV. RATIONALISM — ENLIGHTEN-MENT — GERMAN IDEALISM — ROMANTICISM

1658–1705	Emperor Leopold I, son of Emperor Ferdinand III
1658	Formation of the first "Rhenish League" (*Rheinbund*) for the preservation of the terms of the Peace of Westphalia
1663–1806	The "Permanent Diet" at Regensburg
1670	Louis XIV drives Duke Charles IV out of Lorraine
1674	The Empire declares war on France
1675	Frederick William, the "Great Elector" (of Brandenburg) defeats the Swedes at Fehrbellin
1678	Peace of Nymwegen; Freiburg im Breisgau is ceded to France; continued French occupation of Lorraine
1679	The Peace of St. Germain compels the Great Elector to return all his Pomeranian conquests to Sweden
1680	Louis XIV institutes his "Chambers of Reunion" to determine the historical territorial rights of France and to justify Louis' annexations in Alsace, Lorraine, and Franche-Comté (Free County of Burgundy)
1681	The French occupy the city of Strasbourg
1684	Truce of Regensburg with Louis XIV
1687	The Diet of Pressburg confers the male line of succession in Hungary on Austria
1688–1697	Louis XIV's invasion of the Palatinate
1688	Alliance of the emperor, Spain, Sweden, the foremost imperial princes, England, Holland, and Savoy against France
1689	Devastation of the Palatinate by the French armies under General Mélac
1697	Peace of Ryswyk: France retains the occupied regions of Alsace but returns Freiburg and the territories on the right bank of the Rhine — The duke of Lorraine is reinstated in his rights
1699	Peace of Carlowitz: Hungary, Transylvania (*Siebenbürgen*), part of Slavonia, and Croatia are united with Austria; the Austro-Hungarian monarchy becomes one of the Great Powers of Europe
1701	Frederick III, elector of Brandenburg, son of the "Great Elector," assumes the title of "King *in* Prussia" (Frederick I)
1701–1714	The Spanish War of Succession
1705–1711	Emperor Joseph I, son of Emperor Leopold I
1711–1740	Emperor Charles VI, younger brother of Emperor Joseph I, the last in the male line of Hapsburg succession
1713	Promulgation of the "Pragmatic Sanction" by Charles VI, proclaiming the indivisibility of the Hapsburg possessions and providing for the succession of the emperor's daughter, Maria Theresa
1713–1740	Frederick William I, king of Prussia, son of the elector of Brandenburg, Frederick III (Frederick I, after his adoption of the royal title)
1740–1786	Frederick II (the Great), king of Prussia, son of King Frederick William I

1740–1780   Maria Theresa, empress of Austria (queen of Hungary), married to Francis Stephen, duke of Lorraine
1740–1742   The First Silesian War
1741–1748   The Austrian War of Succession
1742–1745   Emperor Charles VII (of Bavaria), the only non-Hapsburg emperor between 1438 and 1806
1744–1745   The Second Silesian War
1745–1765   Emperor Francis I of the Lorraine-Hapsburg line, husband of Maria Theresa (*cf. above*), elected as German emperor after the death of Charles VII
1756–1763   The Seven Years' War (Third Silesian War)
1765–1790   Emperor Joseph II of the Lorraine-Hapsburg line, son of Maria Theresa
1772   The first partition of Poland between Prussia, Austria, and Russia
1778–1789   The Bavarian War of Succession
1781   Emperor Joseph II issues the Edict of Toleration
1785   Foundation of the League of Princes (*Fürstenbund*) by Frederick the Great
1786–1797   Frederick William II, king of Prussia, nephew and successor of Frederick the Great
1789   Outbreak of the French Revolution
1790–1792   Emperor Leopold II, brother of Emperor Joseph II
1790   Convention of Reichenbach between Prussia and Austria
1792–1797   First Coalition War between Prussia-Austria and France
1792–1806   Emperor Francis II (Francis I as emperor of Austria, 1804–1835) of the Lorraine-Hapsburg line, son of Emperor Leopold II
1793   The second partition of Poland between Prussia and Russia
1795   Separate peace between Prussia and France at Basel — The third partition of Poland between Prussia, Austria, and Russia
1797–1840   Frederick William III, king of Prussia, son of Frederick William II
1797–1799   Congress of Rastatt
1799–1802   Second Coalition War between Austria and France
1803   Principal Decree of the Imperial Deputation (*Reichsdeputationshauptschluss*) of Regensburg concerning the secularization and expropriation of all ecclesiastical principalities and imperial cities — The French occupy the electorate of Hanover
1804–1814   Napoleon I, emperor of the French
1805   Third Coalition War between Austria and France
1806   Creation of the Rhine Confederation (*Rheinbund*) — Abdication of Francis II as German emperor — The End of the Holy Roman Empire
1807   Peace of Tilsit between France and Prussia
1809   Peace of Schönbrunn between France and Austria

Chapter 10

RISE AND DECLINE OF ABSOLUTISM AND ENLIGHTENED DESPOTISM AND THE END OF THE HOLY ROMAN EMPIRE

Princely Despotism and the Theory of the Absolute Monarchy. The Thirty Years' War had carried France to a leading position in European affairs, but it had greatly weakened Austria, Spain, and the German principalities. The Holy Roman Empire dragged on merely by its historical momentum, and the feudal system was discredited and damaged beyond repair. The Treaty of Westphalia had given full sovereignty to the German princes and, lending every encouragement to their selfish ambitions, had taught them how to reap personal benefits from the conclusion of foreign alliances and from their disloyalty to the emperor. Imitating the pattern of the French court, they established an autocratic type of regime, disregarding the traditional prerogatives of the Estates and provincial Diets. Their principalities became autonomous (self-governing) territorial units, ruled by absolute monarchs who exercised the functions of government by "Divine Right" and who were thus the originators and infallible interpreters of divine, natural, and human law. The code of princely absolutism had been written by Machiavelli (cf. p. 247 sq.), and Louis XIV followed its precepts to the letter. Though he may never actually have spoken the words *"L'Etat c'est moi"* ("I am the State"), they summarize admirably his political philosophy.

In his *Instructions for the Dauphin* Louis XIV wrote: "My first step was to make my will supreme; everything that is comprised in our states, all the money in public treasuries as well as all the money in circulation, belongs to us. You, the Dauphin, must be convinced that the kings, as good patriarchs, have the absolute disposal of all property, whether it belongs to clergymen or laymen. The life of the subjects belongs to their princes, and the princes must preserve it as their property. . . . We are the representatives of God. Nobody has a right to criticize our actions. Whoever is born as a subject must obey without asking."

Similar ideas were expressed in England by the philosopher Thomas

Hobbes (1588–1679), to whom the State appeared as a "mortal God" and who saw in despotism the only efficient protection against anarchy. The change that political theory had undergone between the fifteenth and seventeenth centuries becomes evident when we compare the above statements with certain pronouncements of Cardinal Nicholas of Cusa (cf. p. 180 sq.), who expressed the sentiments of his age when he wrote: "It is much better that the commonwealth should be ruled by laws than even by the best man or king" (*De Concordantia Catholica,* Book III). This principle of the supremacy of the law had been upheld by political theorists throughout the Middle Ages. The German *Sachsenspiegel* of the thirteenth century (cf. p. 199), speaking of the right of free election, states that this principle is not derived from the authority of one man but from the natural and divine law. All "majesty" comes from God, but also from man, so that any monarchical rule is limited and conditioned by law and the common good of the citizens.

In the earlier part of the sixteenth century this principle of the relative and limited authority of the ruler was still upheld by some of the most important writers on political theory, and even Machiavelli insisted upon the subordination of rulers to the law, citing France as a kingdom that lived in security because its rulers were bound by many laws. Martin Luther's position is somewhat ambiguous, and while in his earlier writings he defended the absolute authority of the ruler as the representative of God, whose will must not be resisted even if he be a tyrant, we find that after 1530 Luther took account of the constitutional law of the Empire, admitting that the electors might agree to depose an unjust ruler.

The Jesuit writers of the sixteenth and seventeenth centuries (Vitoria, Mariana, Suarez, Bellarmine, etc.) are unanimous and very definite in their rejection of the theory of an absolute "Divine Right" and in their insistence that the community is the ultimate natural source of political authority and therefore of all law. They declare that it is the characteristic vice of the tyrant to invalidate existing laws and to show no consideration for legal traditions. These authors are joined in their condemnation of the claims of the absolute prince by most of the political thinkers and the theologians of the Established Church in England (Richard Hooker, George Buchanan, William of Orange, etc.), by the leaders of the Whig party (John Selden, Edmund Burke, etc.), and by the Huguenot writers in France. Some of them go even so far as to defend tyrannicide.

The theory of the Absolute Monarchy, or the doctrine that the king was above the law, was systematically defended for the first time by Jean Bodin (1530–1596), the French jurist, in his work *On the Republic.* Absolute monarchy appeared to him as the best form of government, and even the rule of a tyrant he deemed better than the rule of the people. William Barclay, a Scotch jurist, in a work on royal power published in 1600, maintains that it is the king who decides what is to be law, that the ruler's authority is truly divine, and that to revolt against the king is to revolt against God. Theory and practice blended in the personality of King James I of England (1603–1625) who, as James VI of Scotland, before he succeeded to the English throne, had written a work on *The True Law of Free Monarchies* (1598, 1603), in which he combined the secular theory of the absolute monarch with the theological doctrine of absolute authority by divine right.

Like Luther and the early Church Fathers, James referred to the scriptural testimony of the appointment of the Old Testament kings, Saul and David, directly by God, thus making God the remote cause of all constituted authority. The major components of this theory are the ideas of government as embodied in Roman Law; the Oriental conception of royal power; and the Judaistic idea of the king as the appointee of God. In holding such views James I reverted to the political convictions of the early Christian centuries, when the injustices of the political and social order were regarded as a consequence of the fall of man from his original innocence and therefore had to be passively accepted and endured. The Jesuits, St. Robert Bellarmine (1542–1621) and Francisco Suarez (1568–1617), on the other hand, resumed and continued the medieval tradition, and the latter urged the people to retain supreme power in themselves and to delegate the task of legislation to a senate or some appointed leader who was to act in conjunction with some legislative body. The same doctrine had been stated in the thirteenth century by the famous jurist and cleric Bracton in these words: "The king is subject to God and to the Law."

When Charles I of England (1625–1649) tried to carry further his father's absolutistic claims he provoked the rebellion that sent him to the block of the executioner. Nevertheless, the same claims were revived by Charles II (1660–1685), and by the year 1660 royal absolutism was firmly established in every part of Europe, with the exception of Holland and Switzerland. In England the absolute supremacy of the crown was finally done away with by the "Glorious Revolution" of 1688 which made the ruler responsible to a parliament.

The Calvinists, in the course of their struggles with Catholic governments, took exception to the doctrine of the Divine Right of Kings, asserting the right of resistance to "ungodly rulers." The representative system as embodied in the Reformed Presbyterial Church-Order offers one of the first examples of representative government in the modern sense, based on a "social contract" that was fashioned in accordance with the model of the covenants of Israel, from which the Jews derived their kings and laws. The Calvinist idea of the State, however, was strictly governed by religious principles, and truly democratic institutions were anticipated only in the administration of the New England states, where the European class system was nonexistent and where political institutions were derived directly from church institutions. And yet there was a vast difference between these patriarchally ruled state organisms with their stern ethico-religious discipline, anchored in the divine and natural law, and Rousseau's (cf. p. 376) naturalistic Contract State, the product of the arbitrary will of fluctuating majorities.

Despite the changes from limited to unrestricted absolutism that took place in most European countries in the course of the seventeenth century, the real and radical break with the medieval idea of civilization occurred first in Oliver Cromwell's (1599–1658) "Commonwealth," in which the separation of State and Church was proclaimed and different denominations were (in theory) to be tolerated side by side.

Louis XIV and the German Empire. The Peace of Westphalia had given France the much coveted opportunity to influence and control to a large extent the future destinies of Germany. Louis XIV was firmly resolved to continue his anti-Hapsburg policies and to bring about the permanent enfeeblement of Austria. To achieve this end and at the same time to keep the Empire in a state of confusion and disruption, he made use of the princes' opposition to the emperor, assuming the role of a protector of their prerogatives. When Emperor Ferdinand died in 1657 Louis tried in vain to secure the succession of the elector of Bavaria. Much against his wishes, the Hapsburg Leopold I (1658–1705), archduke of Austria and king of Bohemia and Hungary, received the votes of the electoral princes. But the new emperor found himself immediately confronted by the "Rhenish League" (*Rheinbund*), a powerful combination of German princes, headed by the elector of Mainz and in alliance with France. The avowed purpose of the League was the protection of the liberties of the princes against possible imperial encroachments, and the preservation of the terms of the Westphalian Peace.

A few years later the Imperial Diet, as constituted by the same peace treaty, composed of the three colleges of the princes, the nobility, and the cities, established itself on a permanent basis in the city of Regensburg, the several states and principalities being represented by delegates and ambassadors. This "Permanent Diet" continued its shadowy existence for the next 143 years (1663–1806) and died a belated death in the year of the dissolution of the Holy Roman Empire. It was merely a debating society, in which France's voice carried more weight than all the others combined, and it accomplished little in the realm of practical politics. The imperial court (*Reichskammergericht*), established in Frankfurt on the Main in 1495, was moved to Speyer in 1527 and to Wetzlar in 1693, where it likewise lingered on to the end of the Empire in 1806, when it was found that 6000 law suits were still pending and that some of the unfinished business dated back one hundred years. The German empire as such included over 1700 independent or semi-independent princes and nobles, vassals of the emperor in name only, three hundred of whom were secular or ecclesiastical sovereigns of German principalities.

Louis XIV, conscious of the strength of his position and well aware of the inherent weakness of the Empire, carried out a comprehensive program of national aggrandizement at German expense. His designs aimed at the realization of what he called France's "natural frontiers," meaning the acquisition of all of Alsace and most of the other territories on the left bank of the Rhine, including Franche-Comté, the Rhenish Palatinate, the Spanish Netherlands, and part of the Dutch Republic. If these plans were crowned with success, Louis would not only be strong enough to prevent a reunion of the Spanish and Austrian Hapsburgs, but he would be able to establish an undisputed hegemony of France in Europe. Feeling himself to be the heir of Charlemagne, he dreamed of disinheriting the Hapsburgs and of resurrecting the Frankish Empire under French leadership. In this grandiose political scheme the river Rhine was to become the natural and national boundary of France. In advancing his claims Louis could count not only on the sympathy and support of most of the German princes, but also on the aid of Sweden, which owed her position as a great power to her collaboration with the policies of Richelieu and Mazarin (cf. p. 287 sq.). The anti-imperial sentiment in Poland and the Franco-Turkish alliance (cf. p. 293 sq.) forged the remaining links in the combination of powers which encircled the German Empire on all sides.

All the odds seemed to be against the Empire. If Louis had confined himself to his anti-imperial policies he might have succeeded in his far-reaching plans. However, the aspirations of French imperialism transcended Louis' continental European ambitions. In his attempt to extend French political and economic supremacy to the colonial possessions overseas, he challenged the rival claims of Spain, England, and the Netherlands alike. Louis overreached himself and, though partly successful in his aggressive policies against the Empire, suffered ultimate defeat at the hands of the Great Powers of Europe.

In 1667 Louis attacked the Spanish Netherlands and in the following year invaded Franche-Comté. Sweden decided to join a Dutch-English alliance against the French king, and in the Peace Treaty of Aix-la-Chapelle (Aachen, 1668) Louis returned Franche-Comté but retained eleven cities in Flanders. In 1670 he drove Duke Charles of Lorraine out of his hereditary domains and annexed this province of the Empire. In 1672 he launched an unprovoked attack against the Dutch who, commanded by Prince William of Orange (1650-1702), the subsequent King William III of England, broke the force of the invasion by opening the dikes and flooding the countryside. In its defensive war Holland was aided not only by Emperor Leopold and the elector of Brandenburg but eventually also by Denmark, Spain, and England. An ironclad alliance between the Empire and Spain was answered by Louis with the annexation of the ten imperial towns of Alsace and the first devastation of the Palatinate by the troops of General Turenne. In the Peace of Nymwegen (1678) France obtained Franche-Comté from Spain and retained a number of border towns in the Spanish Netherlands and the imperial city of Freiburg im Breisgau.

In the years after the conclusion of the Peace of Nymwegen Louis tried to achieve one of his major aims, the annexation of Alsace. He instituted the

"Chambers of Reunion" (*Chambres de Réunion*), specially appointed French law courts, whose task it was to establish by means of casuistry and sophistry the historical French titles of sovereignty to the contested territories. Military occupation followed promptly every legal decision of these courts, and the seizure of the imperial city of Strasbourg in 1681 completed the annexation of Alsace.

While a number of German princes gradually awoke to a realization of the ignominious position of the Empire, concerted opposition to France was hampered by the pro-French sympathies of some of the most influential principalities, among them Brandenburg, whose elector was completely drawn into the orbit of French imperialism. Nevertheless, many of the princes joined with the emperor and the kings of Spain and Sweden in the defensive League of Augsburg (1686). When Louis violated the terms of the Truce of Regensburg of 1684 (which had left him in possession of all the recently annexed territories) by a renewed attack on the Rhenish Palatinate (1687), he found himself confronted not only by a suddenly aroused and united Germany but simultaneously by a European coalition of powers, headed by England.

In the meantime the Turks, France's allies, had been halted in their westward advance, and this Franco-Turkish friendship as well as Louis' persecution of the French Protestants (Huguenots) had alienated many of France's sympathizers among the Protestant princes of Germany. About 200,000 Huguenots, deprived of the freedom of worship and education, left France and found refuge in Holland, England, and Prussia, the same powers that were now solidly lined up against further French aggression.

The winter of 1688–1689 witnessed a second and even more cruel and senseless devastation of the Palatinate by order of General Mélac, and the destruction of the cities of Worms, Speyer, Mannheim, and Heidelberg with their historic monuments and art treasures. The Heidelberg castle, beautiful even in ruins, stands to this present day as an eloquent witness of wanton destruction.

The Peace of Ryswik (1697) marked the end of the war against the Palatinate and brought humiliating terms for Louis: he was forced to return all the territories which had been adjudged to France by the Chambers of Reunion, with the exception of the city of Strasbourg and the occupied regions of Alsace, and the duke of Lorraine was to be reinstated in his sovereign rights and lands. That Louis was able to retain part of his booty on the left bank of the Rhine was due to the fact that the attention of the Empire was absorbed a second time by the Turkish threat of invasion in the East. The emperor decided to sacrifice Alsace in the West in order to be able to put up an impregnable wall of defense in the East. The Peace of Carlowitz (1699) made Hungary part of Austria and raised the Austro-Hungarian monarchy to the rank of a Great Power.

With the following War of the Spanish Succession the Empire was only indirectly concerned. That it was eventually drawn into the conflict was due to the fact that Charles, the Hapsburg pretender to the Spanish crown, was the son of the German emperor (Charles VI, 1711–1740). The other claimant to the Spanish throne was Philip of Anjou, the grandson of Louis XIV, whom the testament of King Charles II of Spain had named as his successor. When Louis XIV tried to press the claims of his grandson by threat of arms, he met with the determined opposition of the *"Grande Alliance,"* consisting of a coalition of Austria, England, Holland, Savoy, and Brandenburg. The French suffered defeat at the hands of the brilliant English strategists John Churchill and the duke of Marlborough in the North, and Prince Eugene of Savoy in the South. The fact that after ten years of struggle Charles, the candidate of the *"Grande Alliance,"* was called to succeed his brother Joseph on the imperial throne, reviving the threat of a reunited Spanish-Austrian Hapsburg empire, created uneasiness and dismay in the war councils of the allies and more particularly among the English and the Dutch, who were as much opposed to a European hegemony of the Anjous and Bourbons as they were to that of the Hapsburgs, considering either one to be contrary to the cherished principle of the European "balance of power." The peace treaties of Utrecht (1713) and Rastatt (1714) reflected the conflicting ideas among the member states of the *"Grande Alliance"* and their endeavor to keep France powerful enough to check Hapsburg ambitions.

The Bourbon Philip V was allowed to succeed to the Spanish throne, with the stipulation that the crowns of Spain and France were never to be reunited. The emperor received the Spanish Netherlands, Milan, and Naples, while the elector of Brandenburg, Frederick III (cf. p. 312), obtained the privilege of assuming the title of "King *in* Prussia." France retained Alsace but had failed in her designs to dominate Germany by making the Rhine her national boundary. The states of Louis XIV were financially exhausted by a series of long and costly wars, whose net gain was out of proportion to the material waste and physical exertion involved. Germany's position as a nation was not much stronger than it had been after the catastrophe of the Thirty Years' War: she was still a pawn in the hands of scheming European politicians; foreign potentates were still represented among the German Estates; and German princes were still entangled in foreign political interests and alignments. The Swedish king ruled part of Pomerania and was represented in the Diet at Regensburg, while the elector of Saxony became king of Poland in 1697, and a member of the Welf dynasty of Hanover ascended the English throne as George I (1714–1727), thus linking Hanover to England by a bond of personal union. The imperial house itself had large possessions in Hungary, the Netherlands, and Italy, finding it more and more difficult to harmonize its European with its specifically German interests and obligations.

The Rise of Brandenburg-Prussia. The constellation of the European powers experienced a decisive change toward the end of the seventeenth and at the beginning of the eighteenth century. Two newcomers, Prussia and Russia, had been added to the three Great Powers of Europe: France, Austria, and England. While the gigantic struggle for economic and colonial supremacy between France and England eventually overshadowed every other event, the attempted realization of a balance of power met with ever increasing difficulties, and the two youngest arrivals among the European nations advanced their national and territorial claims with great vigor and determination.

The great Nordic War (1700–1721), fought by King Frederick IV of Denmark, Augustus the Strong of Saxony-Poland, and Tsar Peter the Great of Russia against the young ruler of Sweden, Charles XII, had ended with Sweden's defeat in the battle of Poltawa (1709). The allies were joined in 1714 by Prussia and Hanover, and the Peace of Stockholm (1720) restored to Prussia the larger part of Pomerania (annexed by Sweden during the Thirty Years' War), including the mouths of the Oder and Vistula rivers. Sweden yielded her position as a Great Power to Russia, which had been able to conquer Estonia and Livonia and thus dominated the Baltic. In their pursuit of the Swedes the Russian armies had advanced into the territories of Pomerania, Mecklenburg, and Holstein, and during one phase of the war Peter the Great had visualized the acquisition of these lands for Russia. French-Russian rivalry finally prevented the full realization of the Russian ambitions, but Russian influence nevertheless extended henceforth into the German empire, adding another element of foreign pressure and thereby increasing the internal instability.

a) *The Great Elector (1640–1688) and the Construction of the Prussian State.* The meteoric rise of Brandenburg-Prussia from a petty North German state to a leading European power was due to the political and military leadership of three members of the Hohenzollern family: Frederick William (the "Great Elector"), King Frederick William I (grandson of the Great Elector, 1713–1740), and King Frederick II ("the Great," great-grandson of the "Great Elector," 1740–1786). Frederick III of Brandenburg (1688–1713), the son of the Great Elector, was inefficient and wasteful in his administration but a patron of the arts and sciences and, as a reward for his support of the emperor in the Spanish War of Succession, was given the privilege of calling himself "King Frederick I *in* Prussia" (West Prussia still being part of Poland).

The Hohenzollerns of both the Swabian and the Frankish-Brandenburg-Prussian Line derived their name from their ancestral castle on top of Mount Zollern in Swabia. As counts of Nuremberg the members of the family increased their possessions by inheritance as well as by their repeated support of imperial policies and military campaigns. Frederick VI was given the Stadtholdership and later on the hereditary possession of the Mark Brandenburg (1415). The Great Elector, margrave of Brandenburg, after having freed East Prussia from Polish overlordship in the course of the Thirty Years' War, acquired eastern Pomerania and some other territories in the Treaty of Westphalia. By inheritance the three small duchies of Cleves, Mark, and Ravensberg on the lower Rhine had become part of Brandenburg-Prussia in 1614. All these territories were widely scattered, disorganized, and without natural cohesion. It was the Great Elector's historic accomplishment to have turned this conglomeration of lands into a unified state that was animated by the definite political and cultural will to assume leadership among the principalities of northern Germany and to make Brandenburg-Prussia the foremost Protestant power of the Empire.*

The Great Elector achieved his goal by circumspection, thrift, and political shrewdness. Despite the tenacity with which he clung to his constructive ideas for Prussia, he did not lose sight of the larger issues of imperial policy, and when Louis XIV in 1658 attempted to bribe him into supporting the French king's aspirations to the imperial throne, Frederick William gave his decisive vote to the Austrian candidate (Leopold I). In 1672 he came to the defense of the Dutch Republic against Louis' unprovoked attack, and when the Swedish allies of France invaded the Mark Brandenburg in 1675 and the armies of the Great Elector found themselves outnumbered two to one, he achieved a major victory over the enemy in the battle of Fehrbellin. In 1686 his army joined the imperial troops in the war that was waged against Turkey for the reconquest of Hungary, and in 1688 he concluded a secret treaty with Prince William of Orange, according to which 6000 Brandenburg soldiers were to assist the prince in his struggle for the British throne.

If the Great Elector's foreign policy was naturally confined to efforts that aimed at territorial unification and national consolidation, his internal reforms offered remarkable evidence of prudent and constructive government. A small standing army represented a powerful weapon of defense and provided that amount of security that was necessary to carry out the intended social reforms. The Great Elector, realizing that the well-being of his state rested on a well-balanced system of production and consumption, on a healthy integration of agrarian and industrial interests, improved the system of land tenure and the methods of soil conservation and at the same time encouraged trade and industry.

Colonists from Holland and Huguenot exiles from France were settled on Prussian soil, and their efficiency and skill contributed greatly to the rising prosperity of the country. The desertlike regions around Berlin developed into flourishing provinces, and the capital itself doubled its population during Frederick William's reign. A regular postal service connected outlying districts of the state, breaking down the monopoly of the Empire-supported Thurn and Taxis posts (cf. p. 189). The Frederick William Canal was constructed, connecting the Spree with the Oder and, by joining up with the Havel and Elbe rivers, provided an uninterrupted waterway to the North Sea. The colonial foundations overseas, however, the East India Company, and the settlements on the West Coast of Africa, while

* Lutheranism was first overtly adopted by the Elector Joachim II of Brandenburg in 1539.

proving the Great Elector's spirit of enterprise, did not warrant the expenditure involved and were short lived. When Frederick William died the Prussian State was strong enough to command the attention and respect of the leading European statesmen.

b) King Frederick William I (1713-1740) and the Growth of Prussian Militarism. The Great Elector's son, Frederick III (Frederick I as "King *in* Prussia," 1688-1713), proved unworthy of the heritage bequeathed to him, and his love of splendor and ostentation as well as the corruption and extravagance of the royal household brought the state to the verge of bankruptcy. An iron will was needed to restore the continuity of the policies pursued by the Great Elector. Frederick's son and successor, Frederick William I, the soldier-king, was a ruler who possessed those qualities that were to make Prussia not only respected but feared as well. He possessed a brutal and tyrannical will, free from the inhibitions of sentiment and untouched by the refinements of taste and culture, an indefatigable working capacity coupled with frugality and economy, and a sense of duty that was rooted in religious convictions. These were the qualities that made Frederick William I at once admired and feared, a tyrant in the family circle and an autocrat in his country. What adds a human touch to the harsh features of this character is his unswerving devotion to the service of his country, an almost humble modesty in his personal needs and wants, his high sense of responsibility, and a self-effacement that was ever willing to sacrifice personal happiness for the sake of the commonweal. If he demanded much of others, he demanded even more of himself, and his own life was a perfect paradigm of the sternest of discipline.

During the rule of Frederick William I, Sweden ceased to exist as a great military power, and the Treaty of Stockholm (1720), concluded at the end of a series of wars with Poland, Russia, Denmark, and Prussia, adjudged the greater part of western Pomerania to the Prussian king. When Frederick William I died he left to his heir a state that was recognized as the most thoroughly militarized power of Europe and one of the most self-sufficient and prosperous of contemporary absolutistic monarchies. The king of Prussia had created an army that in numerical strength was surpassed by few in Europe and in military efficiency was second to none. The "long fellows" (*die langen Kerle*) of the regiment of the royal guards, recruited from many lands by notoriously dubious methods, were the king's greatest pride, and he took a childish delight in everything that pertained to military drill and soldierly display. He went even so far as to force marriages between especially tall men and women, in the hope of breeding a generation of giants.

Following the mercantilistic trend of his age, Frederick William I furthered the development of domestic agriculture, encouraged the home industries by protective tariffs, and strove in every way to make his country economically self-supporting. In his *Instructions for the General Directory of Finance, War, and Domains* he pledged his adherence to the creed of all absolute monarchs: "We are lord and king, and can do what we will." He strove to do away with inefficiency in government, with "red tape" and legal quibbling. If the members of the General Directory keep their minds on the service of the king, they "will all have their hands full and will not need to campaign with law suits against each other. But the lawyers, these poor devils, will be as futile as the fifth wheel on a cart."

The king had achieved his aim and established Prussian sovereignty on a "rock of bronze." He had built an impregnable political organism which the superior statesmanship of his son was to endow with the social and cultural substance of a civilized state.

c) King Frederick II ("the Great," 1740–1786) and Prusso-Austrian Dualism. Emperor Charles VI had died in 1740 without a male heir. Before his death he had secured the Hapsburg territories for his daughter Maria Theresa by invoking the "Pragmatic Sanction" of 1713. Frederick II had succeeded his father as king of Prussia in the same year (1740) in which Maria Theresa, the archduchess of Austria, became queen of Hungary and Bohemia and advanced her claims to the imperial succession. Frederick, who at the age of thirty had become the ruler of the powerful Prussian State, made his recognition of Maria Theresa's succession dependent on the cession of the province of Silesia to Prussia. Under the pretext that Austria was no longer strong enough to protect the liberties of the Silesians, Frederick occupied that province in a surprise coup, at the same time offering Maria Theresa an alliance in return for a full recognition of his claims to the Silesian crownlands. Maria Theresa's refusal led to the first Silesian war (1740–1742), running concurrently in part with the Austrian War of Succession (1741–1748), which was fought for the possession of the imperial crown. Both the Elector Charles of Bavaria and Frederick Augustus of Saxony had married daughters of the late Emperor Joseph I and laid claims to the imperial succession.* Following the example of Prussia, and with the approval and support of France, the German electors gave their votes not to Francis Stephen of Lorraine, Maria Theresa's husband, but to the Elector Charles of Bavaria (1742–1745) who, as Charles VII, thus became the only non-Hapsburg emperor between 1438 and 1806. Austria's claims

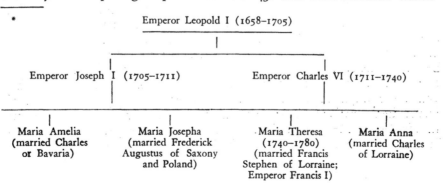

*

	Emperor Leopold I (1658–1705)		
Emperor Joseph I (1705–1711)		Emperor Charles VI (1711–1740)	
Maria Amelia (married Charles of Bavaria)	Maria Josepha (married Frederick Augustus of Saxony and Poland)	Maria Theresa (1740–1780) (married Francis Stephen of Lorraine; Emperor Francis I)	Maria Anna (married Charles of Lorraine)

were supported by Russia, Holland, and England, while France, Spain, Bavaria, and Saxony fought on Frederick's side. In the Treaty of Breslau (1742) Prussia gained Upper and Lower Silesia.

In the second Silesian war (1744–1745), Prussia, France, and Bavaria were opposed by Austria, England, and Sardinia, and the Treaty of Dresden (1745) confirmed Frederick in the possession of Silesia. The death of Emperor Charles VII and the election of Francis Stephen (Francis I, 1745–1765) as emperor strengthened Maria Theresa's cause by adding considerably to the prestige of the house of Hapsburg. The general European war ended with the Treaty of Aix-la-Chapelle (Aachen) in 1748, whereby Frederick's annexation of Silesia was once more confirmed.

As far as the adversaries, Austria and Prussia, were concerned, the results of the two Silesian wars were undecisive, inasmuch as the fundamental issue, the rivalry between the houses of Hapsburg and Brandenburg-Prussia, remained unsettled. The struggle of France and England for supremacy in their colonial empires in the New World (the "French and Indian War") coincided with the Seven Years' War (1756–1763) on the European continent, which was fought by Frederick almost singlehanded against a triple alliance of Austria, Russia, and France. Political allegiances and coalitions shifted so rapidly that it is sometimes difficult to give a rational account of the changes on the European chessboard which made partners in arms one day, implacable foes the next. While in the War of the Austrian Succession (1741–1748) England and Austria stood together against France and Prussia, in the Seven Years' War France and Austria were aligned against England and Prussia. Hapsburg and Bourbon, archenemies for the past two hundred years, made common cause against the king of Prussia, whose aggressive policies seemed to constitute the latest threat against the European balance of power.

Frederick invaded Saxony and Bohemia and for five years fought with varying success, aided only by insignificant military forces from some of the minor German princes and by subsidies from England. Nevertheless, he held at bay a coalition of three empires whose population outnumbered that of Prussia twelve to one. The labors of Frederick's ancestors now bore fruit, and the long-established discipline of the Prussian armies, the solid structure and admirable organization of the Prussian State, combined with Frederick's strategic genius, were rewarded by the successive victories over the French at Rossbach (Province of Saxony, 1757), over the Austrians at Leuthen (Silesia, 1757), and over the Russians at Zorndorf (Brandenburg, 1758). Serious reverses failed to shake the Prussian king's confidence in his ultimate triumph. In the sixth year of the war the Empress Elizabeth of Russia died (1762) and Tsar Peter III followed her on the throne; he was an admirer of Frederick and proposed an immediate peace and a Russo-Prussian alliance. France, exhausted by her colonial war with England, likewise deserted the Austrian cause by concluding the separate Peace of Fontainebleau (1763). Maria Theresa, in the Peace of Hubertusburg of the same year, had to reconcile herself to the definitive surrender of Silesia to Prussia.

Despite the fact that as far as the geographical map of Europe was concerned the Seven Years' War had resulted in but few territorial changes, it had created an entirely new situation with respect to the prestige and relative significance of Prussia and Austria. Prussia had proven and established herself as the second great power within the German Empire. The Prusso-Austrian dualism of interests and ambitions had come into the open and provided a keynote in the following struggle for national unity and the cultural integration of modern Germany. The cession of Silesia to Prussia made Austria more than ever before a southeastern border state of the Empire. Austria's foreign policy in the second half of the eighteenth century was determined by her desire to revenge the rape of her former province. This explains the otherwise incomprehensible alliance with the French monarchy, an alliance which involved the severance of those ties that had bound Austria to England ever since the days of Prince William of Orange. It was this new alignment of powers that provided the bases for England's victorious colonial wars against France, so that William Pitt was correct in saying that England conquered America in Germany. The distribution of the colonial empires of the future was in part at least decided on German soil, with Germany having neither a say nor a share in the matter.

The Prusso-Austrian dualism was not only due, however, to rival political claims, but just as much to the dynamism of spiritual forces that were embodied in the two powers. Austria was the traditional bulwark of German Catholicism, while Prussia had made herself the spearhead of an active and aggressive Protestantism. The two countries developed their respective cultures in accordance with different intellectual and moral patterns. The almost constant political tension provided not only for frequent conflicts and clashes, but likewise in the end for a growing enrichment and variety of German civilization as a whole. The integration and utilization of these polar forces within the political structure of a "Greater Germany" loomed as a faint possibility even in the eighteenth century, but the factors that worked against its realization — the particularism of the German principalities, the shortsightedness or selfishness of political leaders, and the complexity that characterized the general European struggle for spheres of interest and economic power — were obstacles that proved too formidable. Thus the following two centuries offer the sad spectacle of a relentless Prusso-Austrian contest for supremacy rather than that of a constructive effort for co-ordination and unity.

A most unfortunate result of the Prusso-Austrian rivalry in the eighteenth century was the ever growing influence of foreign powers in German politics. Austria, to gain the support of France and Russia, sacrificed the formerly Spanish Netherlands (the territory of Belgium) to France, and East Prussia to Russia (Russian occupation, 1758–1762). Almost in the same measure in which the French danger in the West subsided, the Russian pressure in the East increased. The rival interests of Prussia and Austria offered an opportunity for Russia to assume the role of an arbiter in German affairs. Both Austria and Prussia tried to further their political interests by courting the favor of Russia. When Catherine II of Russia (1762–1796), who succeeded her husband, Tsar Peter III, after the latter's assassination, showed her determination to make Poland part of the Russian empire, it was Frederick the Great who suggested the first partition of Poland (1772) between Prussia, Russia, and Austria. Although Prussia's share in that shady deal was smaller than that of either Austria or Russia, Frederick acquired West Prussia, which for the past three hundred years had been under Polish sovereignty, and thus united East Prussia with the province of Brandenburg. The city of Danzig* remained Polish for the time being owing to the pressure of England, which had a big stake in the Polish trade and did not want to see that important Baltic seaport change hands.

The empress of Russia felt that it was to her country's advantage to perpetuate the Prusso-Austrian dualism. She showed her hand again in negotiating the Peace of Teschen (Silesia), ending the Bavarian War of Succession (1778–1789), the last in the series of wars that Frederick the Great waged against Austria, in which he frustrated the attempt of Maria Theresa's son, Emperor Joseph II (1765–1790, cf. p. 302) to annex part of Bavaria. The peace treaty gave Austria only a tiny fraction of the desired territory, while Prussia emerged from this conflict without any territorial gain. The foundation of the "League of Princes" (*Fürstenbund*) in 1785 represented Frederick's final and crowning attempt to check Hapsburg expansion in the empire.

d) *Frederick the Great: An "Enlightened Despot."* The forty-six years of Frederick's rule were almost evenly divided between the exploits of war and the works of peace. The twenty-three years that followed the bloody Seven Years' War were only interrupted by the brief campaign of the Bavarian War of Succession. It was in his peaceful and constructive endeavors that Frederick proved himself the model representative of "enlightened despotism."

The king considered himself "the first servant of the state" and ruled his country in a benevolent and patriarchal, but nevertheless thoroughly autocratic and absolutistic, fashion. The evaluation of his accomplishments as a German prince and statesman differs in accordance with the political theories and attachments of his biographers. Those who favor the idea of a "Greater Germany," either with the inclusion of both Austria and Prussia

---

* Danzig, first mentioned in 997, was added in 1308 to the territories of the Teutonic Knights and, after the decline of the Order, was linked with Poland by Personal Union (after 1454). It reached the peak of its prosperity about 1600 and lost much of its former significance in the following period of Polish decline. In 1793 Danzig was given to Prussia, was made a "Free City" by Napoleon (1807), returned to Prussia in 1814, and became the capital of West Prussia in 1878. It was separated from Germany by the Treaty of Versailles (1919) and declared a "free city" under the protectorate of the League of Nations. The Treaty of Potsdam (1945) gave Danzig to Poland.

and the co-ordination of their forces and spheres of interest or under Hapsburg leadership, see in him the destroyer of the integrity and prestige of the Holy Roman Empire. Those who read and interpret German history from the Prussian point of view praise him as the great pioneer of the unification of Germany under Prussian leadership, the ruler who laid the foundations for the powerful national state of Bismarck and William II (cf. p. 546 sqq.). Whatever judgment the individual historian may feel inclined to make his own, it is certain that Frederick, like most of the other German princes, was guided in his political plans not by the interests of Germany as a whole but by the interests and needs of his own Prussian State and its aggrandizement.

It makes one of the most startling chapters in the study of human psychology to follow the development of this enigmatic character from a rather effeminate and indolent poetical dreamer to one of the most imposing and uncompromising political figures of modern history. The hard school of experience through which Frederick went under the one-sided military education of his early youth, in humiliating subjection and violent opposition to the tyrannical regime of his father, explains in part the bitter cynicism and utter disillusionment of his later years. His thwarted emotional life and the forced marriage to Princess Elizabeth Christine of Brunswick undoubtedly contributed to making Frederick the avowed misogynist he was, whose anti-Austrian policies were stimulated and intensified by the fact that the Hapsburg lands were ruled by a woman, and who in the course of the Seven Years' War complained that he was persecuted by the "Three Furies" (Maria Theresa of Austria; Elizabeth of Russia; and Madame de Pompadour, the all-powerful mistress of King Louis XV of France). His attempted and frustrated desertion and flight and the following execution of his youthful friend and accomplice, Lieutenant Hans Hermann Katte, marked the decisive break in the life of the crown prince of Prussia, after which he resigned himself to the destiny that his position imposed upon him.

After his accession to the throne Frederick's primary concern was the development of the army to an even greater efficiency. He considered the heritage of military organization that his father had bequeathed to him as the most precious asset in the consolidation of the Prussian State. By the end of the seventeenth century standing armies had become a common institution in all German principalities. At the end of the Seven Years' War Frederick had raised the strength of his armed forces from eighty thousand to two hundred thousand men. Prussia had become one of the foremost military powers of Europe, and as most of the contingents of the Prussian army were recruited among the native population, the Prussian soldier developed a sense of duty and a patriotic sentiment which were invaluable in both war and peace. Prussia became the first and foremost of modern nations to cultivate a Spartan ideal of military discipline, combined with a consciousness of national solidarity.

The internal policies of Frederick the Great were inspired by certain principles that he had adopted from some of his favorite writers and philosophers: among the ancients, the Stoics; and among the moderns, Leibniz (1646–1716), Christian Wolff (1679–1754), and Voltaire (1694–1778). "Philosophers should be the teachers of the world and the guides of princes," he wrote. In his youth he had written a book entitled *Anti-Machiavell* (1739), in which he set forth his own ideas on the obligations of the ruler toward his subjects, and in general opposed the amoralistic political doctrines of Machiavelli (cf. p. 247 sq.). But in practice and especially after the bitter experiences of the Seven Years' War Frederick developed more and more into one of Machiavelli's most docile disciples. By that time "the first servant of the state" had become an exceedingly lonely individual, cut off from all family ties and associated with hardly any man or woman whom he could call his friend. He had correctly foreseen that his marriage would turn out to be a failure and that there would be "one more unhappy princess in the world." Even in the colloquial atmosphere of the "tobacco college" at Potsdam and Sans-Souci, where the king used to spend merry evenings in the circle of scholars and artists whom he had drawn to his court, where he would play the flute or read from his own manuscripts — even here real human warmth was strangely lacking and Frederick's lonely majesty seemed to erect invisible but unscalable barriers. The king's real friends were his dogs and horses, with whom he would converse in German, while on most other occasions he gave preference to French.

Frederick's admiration for French *esprit,* the French language, French literature and culture was almost boundless, while he was unaware of the great classical revival of German literary and intellectual life that was gradually taking shape under his very eyes. He had nothing but praise for the tragedies of Corneille and Racine and despised the works of the young Goethe (cf. p. 407 sqq.) as a "detestable imitation of the abominable plays of Shakespeare." Among the famous Frenchmen who contributed to making his court a great center of enlightened thought was Maupertuis (1698–1759), the French physician and mathematician, who conducted an arctic expedition to Lapland to prove the flattening of the poles of the earth. In 1741 Frederick made him president of the Academy.

With Voltaire, whom Frederick had likewise invited to his court and whom he considered the greatest genius of the age, his relations were more complex. It was a kind of love-hate that bound him to the great French "philosophe," historian, playwright, and satirist. Frederick was fascinated by Voltaire's keen and critical mind, by his wit and *esprit,* and by his sectarianism. The initial familiarity between Frederick and Voltaire ended abruptly when the king ordered the confiscation of one of Voltaire's satires, aimed at Maupertuis. Voltaire's intercepted flight from Prussia and his following arrest were the remote cause for the satirist's publication of *The Private Life of the King of Prussia,* the bitter fruit of a pent-up resentment.

In accordance with his moral and political convictions Frederick proceeded in his work of social reform in the highhanded manner of paternalistic government. He imposed his ideas and his will on all and sundry — on men and institutions alike. The royal decrees extended to the procedures of criminal and civil law; to military, financial, and social administration; to agriculture, industry, and commerce; to the modes and manners of thinking and living.

One of his first measures provided for the abolition of torture in Prussia. In matters of religion he favored a spirit of toleration that was to make it possible for "everyone to get to heaven in his own fashion" (*Jeder kann nach seiner Façon selig werden*). Accepting the ideas of eighteenth-century "Deism" (cf. p. 356 sq.), he had no use for theological dogma and established churches, although he would not interfere with their cults. He considered it politically expedient to grant complete freedom of worship and even invited the Jesuits to teach in the Prussian schools after their order had been expelled from most European countries and temporarily suspended (1773–1814) by papal decree.

The hardest work of social reconstruction had to be done after the sufferings and devastations of the Seven Years' War. Within a few years Frederick had accomplished the task of healing most of the wounds inflicted on Prussia by the invading armies and the prolonged state of siege. By means of a state-controlled inflation of the currency he managed to emerge from the war with a balanced budget. By a systematic policy of colonization and settlement he added several thousand people to the population of Prussia, increased the area of the arable land, and, by encouraging agriculture and the home industries, made his states practically independent of foreign markets. The manufacture of silk was introduced by a royal decree which commanded the planting of mulberry trees and the cultivation of the imported silkworm. Settlers from foreign countries were granted exemptions from taxes and customs duties, and with their aid 225,000 acres of waste land and marsh were reclaimed along the shores of the Oder, the Warthe, the Vistula, and the Netze. High protective tariffs practically eliminated foreign competition, and an administrative board, composed entirely of French officials, was entrusted with the enforcement of these highly unpopular measures. As coffee could not be grown in Prussia, Frederick had his "coffee smellers" enter and search private homes at will, to prevent wholesale smuggling.

The same Spartan discipline that ruled in the Prussian army was made the basis of the life and occupations of the entire aristocracy. They were under the constant supervision of the crown and had to pay dearly for belonging to a caste whose special privileges were outweighed by the heavy burdens they had to carry in the service of their government. Frederick's attempted abolition of serfdom among the peasantry met with the determined opposition of the landed nobility of Pomerania and proved unsuccessful for that reason.

In all his endeavors Frederick II was guided by a fundamental conviction that is best expressed in the preamble of the *"Codex Fridericianus,"* the code of Prussian common law that was published after the king's death: "The welfare of the state and its inhabitants is the object of society and the limit of legislation; laws must limit the liberty and the rights of the citizens only in the interest of general welfare."

The king's mind was as fertile in the speculative as in the practical realm: his collected works, including historical writings, poetry, and musical compositions, fill thirty-one volumes in the edition of the Berlin Academy (1846–1887), to which the over forty-odd volumes of his political correspondence (1879–1931) must be added.

Austria and Prussia After Frederick the Great. Maria Theresa's eldest son, Emperor Joseph II (1765–1790), was another representative of the ideas of "enlightened despotism." His noble intentions, however, lacked so much in practical sense and moderation that Frederick the Great could justly say of him that "he always wishes to take the second step before he has taken the first." In the brief span which followed his mother's death and during which he ruled independently (1780–1790), his far-flung undertakings met with such wholesale failure that in his self-composed epitaph he spoke of himself as a man "who, with the best of intentions, was unsuccessful in everything that he undertook."

In his foreign policy he made the mistake of attacking the Turks (1788) in alliance with Catherine of Russia, thereby strengthening Russia's hand in the region of the Black Sea at the expense of Austria's Eastern sphere of interests. His attempts to follow the example of Prussia in creating a strong military state by winning the Bavarian lands for Austria, in exchange for the Austrian Netherlands, were frustrated by Frederick's watchfulness and superior diplomacy. With the aid of his recently created "League of Princes" the Prussian king succeeded in checking Joseph's every move. His endeavors to make German the official and "universal" language in all the territories of Austrian administration, and to Germanize racially and ethnically non-Germanic populations, resulted in dangerous uprisings in Flanders, Hungary, and the Tyrol. When he tried to enforce by decree the principles of enlightened despotism, abolishing torture, advocating religious toleration ("Edict of Toleration," 1781), curtailing the autonomy of ecclesiastical administration and the privileges of the nobles, and in general aiming at a more equitable social order, he met with a negative response, with passive resistance, censure, or open rebellion in each individual case.

Whatever may be said in just criticism of many of Joseph's hasty and sometimes ill-considered reforms, there is little doubt that both he and his brother Leopold II (1790–1792), who succeeded him on the throne, were undeviating in their loyalty to the idea of the German empire as the embodiment of a unified Central Europe. They kept this idea alive amidst all the vicissitudes of the Prusso-Austrian struggle for power and supremacy. It was their profound conviction that the Empire was doomed if a way could not be found to unite and rally Austria and Prussia in a common effort for a common cause.

To the detriment of the Empire neither King Frederick William II of Prussia (1786–1797), the nephew and successor of Frederick the Great (his marriage remained childless), nor Emperor Francis II (1792–1806), the son of Emperor Leopold II, who succeeded his father and, in 1804, assumed the title of Emperor of Austria (1804–1835) — neither of these two rulers was big and farseeing enough to place the interests of the Empire above small regional politics. Frederick William II was a frivolous despot who possessed none of the moral qualifications of his predecessor, whose anti-Austrian policy he abandoned without offering any constructive political idea as a substitute. He showed himself opposed to the plan that had been advocated by Duke Charles Augustus of Weimar, calling for the transformation of the "League of Princes" into a North German League under the leadership of Prussia. But the attempted co-operation with Austria, symbolically sealed by the Convention of Reichenbach (1790), was rendered

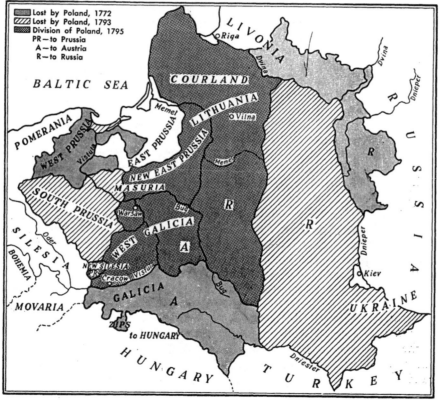

From *Der Grosse Herder*, Herder, Freiburg i. Br.

Partitions of Poland.

ineffective by continued rivalry and mutual distrust. Francis II likewise was motivated in his policies by Austrian rather than common German interests. He dealt a deathblow to the idea of the Empire when, contrary to imperial law, he made himself emperor of Austria.

It was during the reign of Francis II and Frederick William II that the *second and third partitions of Poland* took place. The first dismemberment of the Polish State (cf. p. 316) had been followed by a political and social reform movement in the territory that was left of the once proud Polish kingdom. But to prevent Poland's recovery and to create a new pretext for foreign intervention, Catherine of Russia fostered a rebellion against the new Polish constitution, and in 1793 Russia and Prussia agreed to renew the criminal procedure of 1772. Russia took by far the largest slice, while Prussia received Danzig, Thorn, and the districts of Posen and Gnesen.

In the third partition, which followed in 1795, Austria was once more allowed to share in the robbery: Prussia was given Masuria and the districts around Warsaw; Austria received West Galicia; Russia took the rest. Poland had ceased to exist as a State and was resurrected only when Russia, Germany, and Austria-Hungary were defeated in World War I (1914–1918).

The three partitions of Poland and especially the last one had given Prussia a considerable increase in territory, but at the same time a foreign population which became more and more unmanageable and whose assimilation proved impossible. Russia, on the other hand, had not only gained territorially but also ethnically and politically by bolstering her power with the annexation of a Slavic country.

French Revolution. Coalition Wars. Napoleon. The End of the Empire. While both Prussia and Austria became forgetful of the obligations imposed upon them by their common German destiny and nationality, most of the other European countries went through revolutionary developments which in the end proved fateful to Germany as a whole. England, which had become the foremost maritime and colonial power of the world, lost her North American colonies in the American War of Independence (1773–1783). The North American Republic was founded and based on a constitution which embodied those principles of the sovereignty of the people and the supremacy of the natural law that in part had been handed down from the political theorists of the Middle Ages and their interpreters in the sixteenth and seventeenth centuries (cf. p. 304 sq.) and in part were derived from the political doctrines of the contemporary philosophers.

Sentiment against all absolutistic state governments was running high, and wherever tyranny exercised its oppressive rule popular reaction appealed to the "inalienable rights" of the individual. The extent to which even enlightened despotism in Germany had become susceptible to the social trend of the times is shown by the fact that Frederick the Great had been the first monarch to acknowledge the young American republic, and that Prussia was the first sovereign state to conclude a treaty with the new nation overseas.

a) *The French Revolution*. France, burdened with debts and faced by national insolvency, was drifting along under the benevolent but weak and shiftless regime of Louis XVI (1774-1792). The *"ancien régime"* was overthrown in 1789, and the king died under the guillotine in 1793.

But the French revolutionary movement did not stop at the boundaries of France: in its aggressive dynamism it spread to the Spanish Peninsula and the Netherlands and could only be halted by the force of arms. The German reaction to the revolution was chiefly emotional for the time being. Before the reign of terror dispelled the beautiful dreams of an earthly paradise under the banners of "liberty, equality, and fraternity," the German intelligentsia had welcomed the French uprising in speeches and poems. The alienation between the two countries that resulted from disappointed hopes was all the more radical, and it was only two generations later that the political reverberations of the ideology of 1789 were definitely felt in Germany.

King Frederick William III of Prussia (1797–1840) was in no way a match for the statesmen and generals of the French Revolution. His attempt to preserve Prussia's neutrality in the Coalition Wars against France proved suicidal, and when Prussia finally, singlehanded, took up arms against Napoleon Bonaparte, it was too late.

The adversaries that France had to respect and fear were England and Austria. The British Isles, owing to their geographical position and the constitutional and moderately parliamentary form of the British government, were comparatively safe from being infected by the germ of the Revolution. England was only too willing to lend a hand in halting the revolutionary wave and in this way to preserve the proverbial European "balance of power" and keep France from challenging Britain's naval superiority. The German Empire, on the other hand, lay directly in the pathway of the advancing French armies, and only the fullest amount of co-operation between the leading German states could have stemmed the tide. Both England and Austria felt themselves as the defenders of human freedom against revolutionary terror and nihilism, but without the active participation of Prussia the victory of France over the Empire was a foregone conclusion.

b) *The Aims of French Aggression*. It is interesting to note that the leaders of the French Revolution resumed Louis XIV's policy of national expansion, that they tried to carry to a successful conclusion what the greatest of the French monarchs had been unable to accomplish, and that they reproached Louis' decadent successors for having forgotten and betrayed France's traditional national interests. Napoleon Bonaparte knew what he was talking about when he told one of the Prussian envoys: "I shall play the role that Richelieu has assigned to France."

We recall that it had been Louis XIV's great ambition to overthrow the dominion of the Hapsburg emperors, to gain possession of the left bank of the Rhine, and to subject the German states to French supremacy. It would have been the crowning achievement of his life if all these designs had finally converged in the resurrection of the Empire of Charlemagne, with Louis in the possession of the imperial crown. Louis had succeeded in realizing only a fractional part of these far-reaching aims, but the leaders of the Revolution were as good imperialists as their one-time monarch. In 1793 Danton, who at that time had assumed dictatorial powers, declared: "In vain, I say, they try to scare us with the idea that this Republic might grow too large. Its boundaries are marked out by nature. We shall definitely reach them — on the Rhine! It is there that the marches of our Republic must end, and no power on earth shall prevent us from attaining them."

c) *The Coalition Wars.* This, then, was the prize at stake in the several wars between France and Germany that were fought between 1792 and 1805 and that ended with the destruction of the Holy Roman Empire and the temporary extinction of Prussia and Austria as sovereign states.

The Convention of Reichenbach (1790) had made it possible for Austria and Prussia to enter upon the first Coalition War side by side. The legend that this war was forced upon France by the enemies of the Revolution deserves little credence. It is true that Emperor Francis II was impressed by the plea of the French refugees and the plight of Louis XVI. But it is also a well-established fact that the war was declared by the revolutionists when Francis II turned down a French demand for disarmament. There is no doubt that the French leaders needed success in the foreign field in order to be able to master an increasingly complex situation at home.

In 1792 small detachments of the Austrian and Prussian armies marched into the French Champagne but withdrew after the battle of Valmy (cf. Goethe's description in his *Campaign in France*). The French Republican Army of the Rhine followed the retreating allies beyond the Rhine and carried its march of conquest into Flanders. In the following year the First Coalition was formed, comprising England, Holland, Spain, Sardinia, Naples, and Portugal. Two years of warfare proved indecisive, and the Coalition broke up when Prussia concluded with France the separate Peace of Basel (1795). In the following year Archduke Charles of Austria, brother of Emperor Francis II and generalissimo of the Austrian armies, forced the French out of Franconia and Bavaria and back across the Rhine. Prussia, preoccupied with the consolidation of her Polish spoils (cf. p. 322), declared herself completely disinterested in the affairs of the Empire and even gave up her resistance against the annexation of the left bank of the Rhine by the French. Austria and England continued the fight, but in the Treaty of Campo Formio (1797) Austria had to agree to the cession of the left bank of the Rhine.

In the meantime the star of Napoleon Bonaparte (1769–1821) had started on its dazzling course. At the age of twenty-seven the heir, executor, and conqueror of the French Revolution had become commander in chief of the French armies. When the second Coalition War (1799–1802) began, he had made himself "First Consul" of the French Republic. This time Russia, England, Austria, Turkey, Naples, Portugal, the Italian and the Papal

States were united against France, while Prussia stood passively aside. The Austrians, successful in southern Germany and in Switzerland under the command of Archduke Charles, were defeated in the battles of Marengo and Hohenlinden (1800). Several Russian defeats in Switzerland and Holland were followed by Tsar Paul I's withdrawal from the Coalition. In the Peace of Lunéville (1801) the cession of Flanders (Belgium) and the left bank of the Rhine to France was confirmed and Lombardy was added to the French conquests. An imperial deputation was to compensate those German princes who had sustained losses by the French annexation of their territories on the left bank of the Rhine. The result of the *Principal Decree of the Imperial Deputation* of Regensburg (1803) was a complete remaking of the map of Germany. The secularization of all ecclesiastical territories provided the indemnification demanded by the princes of Prussia, Wurtemberg, Bavaria, Baden, Hesse, and Nassau. This arbitrary redistribution of lands and possessions signified the destruction of the ancient imperial constitution and absolutely ignored and denied the rights and prerogatives of the emperor. The German empire was transformed into a loose federation of medium-sized states.

The new order, inspired and supervised by Napoleon, marked the final triumph of all the aims of French imperialism. It was only logical when, in 1804, Napoleon crowned himself emperor of the French. Europe's answer was the formation of the third Coalition, including England, Russia, Austria, Sweden, and Naples, Prussia again maintaining her neutrality. In the Peace of Pressburg (1805) that followed the Austro-Russian defeat in the "Three-Emperors' Battle" (Francis II, Tsar Alexander I, Napoleon) at Austerlitz, Nemesis descended upon Prussia. While Napoleon rewarded his servile vassals and allies, Bavaria, Wurtemberg, and Baden with German land and promoted the dukes of Bavaria and Wurtemberg to the kingship, Prussia was compelled to enter into a humiliating alliance with France (1806). The principalities of southern Germany formally announced their resignation as member states of the Empire and formed the "Confederation of the Rhine" (*Rheinbund*) under the protectorship of France. On August 6, 1806, Emperor Francis II abdicated, and the Holy Roman Empire had come to an inglorious end.

Prussia had actually gained territorially by the secularizations, and her policy of neutrality had saved her from the afflictions of the war. But she had lost in power and prestige, and under the rule of a weak and irresolute king, isolated politically, she had to suffer further humiliations from the Corsican conqueror. And Napoleon was firmly determined to complete his work by the destruction of the last independent state on the European continent.

By breaking solemnly sworn treaties and by a series of other provocations Napoleon finally forced the wavering Frederick William III into the dreaded armed conflict. The Prussian armies and with them the Prussian State were defeated and crushed in the battles of Jena and Auerstedt

(1806), and in the following year the emperor of the French staged his
triumphant entry into Berlin. Frederick William III fled to East Prussia,
and in the Peace of Tilsit Prussia was forced to cede half of her territory,
including all the formerly Polish provinces. All that remained in her
possession was the lands east of the Elbe.

French occupation, heavy war indemnities, compulsory disarmament:
Prussia was spared none of the humiliations of a nation that had been
deprived of her independence and her honor by a merciless victor. Napoleon's
brother, Jerome, was made king of Westphalia, and the elector of Saxony
was presented with the newly created duchy of Warsaw. France ruled over
Holland and the greater part of Germany. The Empire and Crown of
Charlemagne had been restored and usurped by Napoleon. Austria survived
in a greatly weakened state, and her population was composed of many
non-Germanic (Slavic, Magyar, Italian) and heterogeneous elements. In
1809 she made one more attempt to challenge Napoleon's domination of
Europe. This time Napoleon marched upon Vienna, and the Peace of
Schönbrunn deprived Austria not only of her position as a great power
but of some of her most valuable provinces as well. It left the state on the
verge of complete financial collapse. Once more the future of Germany
looked very dark indeed.

Chapter 11

CIVILIZATION IN THE AGE OF ABSOLUTISM AND ENLIGHTENED DESPOTISM

The Growth of the Absolutistic State. The world which emerged from the turmoil of the Thirty Years' War, and which bears all the earmarks of the civilization that extends into our own time, was characterized by the central position occupied by the secular State and its representative, the prince. In the following centuries the concept of the State becomes more and more abstract, divorced from the personality of the ruler: the absolutism of the prince is followed by the absolute sovereignty of "the State." But during the period which begins with the Renaissance and ends with the French Revolution of 1789 all political power is concentrated in the person of the sovereign who is responsible to no one but himself, in accordance with the political principles of Machiavelli (cf. p. 247 sq.) and the juridical maxims of Jean Bodin (cf. p. 304). "The royal throne is not the throne of a man but the throne of God Himself. . . . The King's majesty is an adequate expression of God's majesty," wrote Jacques Benigne Bossuet (1627-1704), bishop of Meaux, the most celebrated theologian in the age of Louis XIV.

This absolutistic concept of the State and its leader was the exact reverse of the social and political ideas of the Middle Ages, when the State was linked up with universal and other-worldly ends, and when a vocational division of powers and functions had given the individual his share in social and political administration. In the medieval cities this graduated order of rights and duties had received its fullest realization. But it was there, too, that some of the essential features of the modern State could be recognized: the unified economic territory of the city was strictly regulated and disciplined by local administration, and this administration itself resembled closely the political rule of the later absolutistic monarchies. Whereas the chancellors of the medieval emperors had been bishops and feudatories, the city clerk was a professional jurist, a layman, and thus the precursor of the chancellors of the absolutistic monarchs.

A further important characteristic of the absolutistic State is its predominantly or even exclusively secular nature, which in itself is indicative of the complete secularization of politics and morals that was the fruit of Renaissance and Reformation. The absolutistic State, in proclaiming its autonomy, refused to share its power with any other agency or to recognize any law and sanction beyond or above itself, and therefore was as much opposed to a universal empire as to a universal Church. The territorial State was the ideal absolutistic State and the "reason of State" (*ratio status, Staatsraison*) was its supreme law, whose exigencies fully justified alliances with "heretics" and pagans.

The absolutistic idea of State omnipotence, waging relentless warfare against every rival power and corporative organization, led logically to the destruction of the last remnants of feudalism and to the paralyzation of parliamentary government, wherever it existed. While it is true that social divisions and class distinctions in the age of absolutism were as conspicuous as ever, they were practically nullified by the fundamental and all-important distinction between the "sovereign ruler" and the "subject." The members of all social ranks were equally without rights and powers as against royal omnipotence. In thus eliminating the intermediate steps of a graduated social order the absolutistic State unknowingly prepared the way for the revolutionary ideas of social equality.

State and society were no longer conceived as organisms, as had been the case in the sociological speculation of Aristotle and Thomas Aquinas. The absolutistic State became a gigantic mechanism, a wonderfully constructed machine, thus reflecting the all-pervading influence of the new mechanical and mathematical sciences. Frederick the Great compared a well-conducted government with the faultless consistency of a well-constructed philosophical system. He was convinced that social and political structures can be scientifically calculated and mechanically preconditioned, in accordance with the laws of induction, observation, comparison, and generalization. Reason and nature join in the construction of the well-ordered police State, in which nothing is left to chance but everything controlled and directed by the will of that abstraction called "the absolute State."

Economy in the Absolutistic State. The economic system which served to provide the abundance of material means for the satisfaction of the selfishness of absolutistic government is associated with the name of Jean Baptiste Colbert (1619–1683), Louis XIV's minister of finance, the creator of "Colbertism" or "mercantilism" in national economy. Mercantilism is merely another name for economic absolutism. The absolutistic State was truly totalitarian in the modern sense, in that it deprived all its subjects of their personal rights and liberties in order to enlist all their physical and mental faculties in the supreme effort of assuring internal prosperity and external security.

Colbert and his imitators in other countries considered a State-controlled economy an essential prerequisite for national aggrandizement. He tried to achieve his aim by devising a new system of taxation and internal revenue, in which the major burden fell on the economically and socially privileged classes; by encouraging domestic trade and commerce and the home industries, in order to make the State self-sufficient and independent of foreign imports; and by creating a favorable balance of trade by means of steadily increasing exports of finished goods and prohibitions on the export of raw materials. Such a favorable balance of trade was to fill the coffers of the mercantilist State with precious metals, while colonies were to provide both raw materials and markets. The absolutistic State used its military and political power to gain economic advantages, and it utilized in turn its increasing economic prestige to feed its political and national ambitions. In this process the absolutistic state and the rising middle classes were natural allies. They were both opposed to the medieval system of land tenure and agricultural economy, and the "Third Estate" (the middle class) was willing to sacrifice liberty and self-respect for the sake of material gain and the economic security and protection that was guaranteed by the new State paternalism. When finally, in 1789, the *Tiers état* (Third Estate) had acquired economic strength and self-sufficiency, its members felt that the moment had come to reclaim their civic and human rights and to revolt against the centralized State.

The secularization that characterizes the tenets of absolutistic political theory is no less in evidence in the economic sphere. Political economy shows itself no longer inspired by religious or moral motivations but by the scientific calculations of mathematics and physics. Economy in the absolutistic State anticipates the essential principles of the "economic liberalism" of Adam Smith (1723–1790) and the French "Physiocrats" in that it makes economic self-interest the source of all values in State and society. Self-interest, being inherent in the operation of a providential plan, must not be stifled but rather developed, enlightened, and rationalized. The striving for material abundance must be made the basis of social ethics. A pre-established harmony is said to permeate the cosmic as well as the social universe, so that the individual who seeks his own advantage works at the same time for the well-being of all: the progress of society as a whole is nothing but the sum total of the progress of all the individuals of whom it is composed.

With François Quesnay (1694–1774), the court physician of King Louis XV of France, the French Physiocrats and their German disciples demanded that all governments conform to the "natural order of things." They were convinced that economic laws were as fixed and inexorable as the laws of nature. The main function of the State is the removal of impediments that prevent nature from following its lawful course. The best government, therefore, is that which governs least. Stressing the importance of agriculture for the well-being of society, they denounced the mercantilistic theory as unsound and maintained that the real wealth of a State did not consist in the accumulation of gold but in the natural resources of the soil, the *"produit net"* — the surplus of natural products. They advocated a single tax, the ground tax, and defined the peasant as "the prime motor of the social machine."

Art and Culture of the Age of Baroque and Rococo. The period that follows the great upheavals of the age of the Reformation and that ends with the triumph of "Enlightenment" (cf. p. 368 sqq.) in the eighteenth century is known as the Age of Baroque and Rococo. The latter term designates the end phase of Baroque, coming to a rather abrupt termination in the years of the French Revolution at the end of the century. The Baroque* runs parallel in part with such intellectual movements as the Catholic Restoration, the theory of the absolutistic State, Rationalism, and Pietism. As a matter of fact it embraces unreconciled such opposites as rationalism and irrationalism, sensuality and spirituality, cynical sophistication and mystical ecstasy, stilted artificiality and the craving for the simplicity and harmony of nature. It is a period and a style filled with paradoxical antitheses and deriving its dynamic vitality from the unceasing and ever failing endeavor to overcome these dualisms in the synthesis of a newly conquered unity of thought and culture.

a) *Origins of Baroque Culture.* As an artistic style and a specific medium of cultural forms and forces Baroque represents the last great universal manifestation of the unity of Western civilization. It is Catholic in its essence, both in the denominational and the more general sense of the term, and its beginnings are inseparably linked with the militant and aggressive spirit of the Catholic Restoration (cf. p. 253 sqq.). It recognizes nevertheless its indebtedness to the cultural and artistic achievements of the Renaissance, whose individualism and cult of sensuous and natural beauty it adopted, rejecting however its paganism and subjecting man and nature to the dictates of a spiritually informed and divinely ruled universe. It may not be amiss, therefore, to characterize the Baroque age as a combination of certain characteristics of the Gothic and Renaissance cultures.

Baroque culture originated in Rome, the seat of the papacy. The popes were the chief patrons and propagators of the new style of thinking, building, and living, employing those artists (e.g., Michelangelo, Bernini) who created the resplendent symbols of the spirit of incipient and mature Baroque: the new circular structure of St. Peter's Cathedral and its adjacent colonnades and buildings.

b) *Political Aspects of Baroque Culture.* The political exponents of Baroque culture were the absolutistic princes and those ecclesiastical rulers who, like Richelieu, made the Church subservient to princely ambitions and the imperialistic designs of nationalistic policies. The result of this fusion of nationalism and religion was a steady weakening of ecclesiastical authority, until in the eighteenth century the popes became mere puppets in the game of Franco-Spanish power politics, finding their influence almost completely restricted to the small territories of the Papal States. The idealism that had inspired the reforms of the Council of Trent (cf. p. 257 sq.) had in many instances degenerated to a mere formalism whose emptiness had to be

---

* The name is derived from the Portuguese word *barocco:* "an odd-shaped pearl." The name "Rococo" is derived from the French word *rocaille,* denoting "shell ornament."

artificially filled with the pathos of heroic gestures and exaggerated emotions. The political reality was endowed with an accent of pessimism and melancholy resignation.

As early as 1637 the Spanish Jesuit, Baltazar Gracian, one of the greatest stylists of Spanish literature, wrote in his *Manual of the Art of Worldly Wisdom* (*Oráculo manual y arte de prudencia*): "Unhappy is he who like myself has been living among men, for every one is like a wolf unto the other, if not worse." And: "Believe me: neither wolf nor lion, nor tiger, nor basilisk are as cruel as man." And again: "Whoever does not know thee, oh life, he may well esteem thee; but he whose eyes have been opened, would prefer to proceed from the cradle straightway to the coffin." It is not surprising that Arthur Schopenhauer (1788–1860), the philosopher of an all-pervasive pessimism, became the best German translator of Gracian's *Manual*.

It is evident that this Spaniard's political pessimism represents the reaction of a sensitive intellectual to the general adoption of Machiavellian principles in national and international life. The traditional idea of the State as an organism based on the natural and moral law and informed by reason, custom, and freely determined human action, had been abandoned in favor of the new doctrine of the "Reason of State," serving as the sole criterion for every deed and misdeed.

c) Social Significance of Baroque Culture. With its special liking of the spectacular, theatrical, and representational, Baroque culture expressed most adequately the world of courtly form and etiquette as it was embodied in the two foci of the age — State and Church: the former more and more encroaching upon the ancient prerogatives of the latter.

If Rome was the birthplace of Baroque culture, the typical Baroque State was first realized in Spain and subsequently in France, where its political implications were most fully and effectively developed. Its artistic form language was most distinctly in evidence, however, in southern Germany and Austria and, with some racial and national modifications, in the southern part of the Netherlands, in Spain, Portugal, and their colonial possessions overseas. In France the king and his court were the center of the social culture of the Baroque age, representative of a style of life in which the solemn measures of classical antiquity and the worldly splendor of the Renaissance blended with Spanish *"gravidad"* and French grace and frivolity. German and Austrian Baroque, on the other hand, was not confined to a courtly social elite but penetrated all social groups and met with an enthusiastic response among the common people and peasants. This is especially true of the religious and artistic components of Baroque culture as manifested in a newly flourishing monastic life, a revival of the liturgical arts, colorful processions and pilgrimages, and a wave of mystical devotion.

In France the death of Louis XIV in 1715, the brief regency of Duke Philip of Orléans, and the following rule of Louis XV (1715–1774) brought about a relaxation of the shackles of courtly conventions and marked the triumph of the more lighthearted and careless social climate of the Rococo. This final phase of Baroque culture is characterized by many symptoms of social decay; by a lack of vitality, an atmosphere and attitude which is artistically expressed in the preference for subdued and broken colors and shaded autumnal nuances, by the virtual obliteration of all formal barriers between architecture, sculpture, and painting, with a marked emphasis on rhythmical musicality and pictorial decorative design.

d) Fashion in the Age of Baroque. As in every other department of civilization so in the realm of fashion France and her all-powerful king set the absolute standards. By the manner of his dress the *galant homme,* style Louis XIV, tried to convey the impression of majestic and imposing splendor. His head was crowned with a leonine periwig with long, flowing curls that covered neck and shoulders. He wore short and tight knee breeches, silken stockings, buckled shoes, a richly embroidered vest, and a long laced coat with narrow waist. A lace necktie, lace cuffs, and a rapier added to the picturesque appearance of the typical *gentilhomme.* The beard was sacrificed for the greater glory of the periwig.

The age of Louis XV favored a fashion of softer and more graceful design, and King Frederick William I of Prussia, in protest against the artificiality of the periwig, introduced the famous pigtail or queue (*Zopf*) and made its adoption compulsory in the Prussian army. It was soon adopted by the military and other classes in every country. Later on, the *Zopf* came to be considered as a somewhat grotesque symbol of every philistinism, bureaucracy, and pedantry in past and present. In art the *Zopfstil* designates a mode of the decorative design of the dying Rococo, comparable to the French *"Louis Seize"* (style under Louis XVI), that reigned about 1770 and was characterized by sober plainness, a peculiar lack of imagination, and regularity in ornament.

The noble lady in the age of Louis XIV wore a narrow-waisted upper garment with laced sleeves of moderate length. As in the preceding period the richly pleated skirt ended in a long train, and the entire dress was lavishly decorated with lace embroidery and multicolored ribbons. After the second decade of the eighteenth century (*c.* 1720–1760) the hoop petticoat (farthingale, crinoline) returned and became known in Germany as the *Hühnerkorb* (chicken coop). Its framework was made of hoops of iron, wood, or whalebone, and it was covered by a petticoat, skirt, and robe of the finest silk, in choicest colors, and adorned with ribbons, laces, embroideries, and artificial flowers. The upper part of the body and the almost disappearing waist were enclosed and compressed by a tight corset. The towering laced hood (*Fontange*) that served as headdress in the age of Louis XIV disappeared after the king's death and gave way to a simple laced bonnet, worn on top of the combed-out hair. In the seventies of the eighteenth century the towering coiffures of the "fashion *à la mode*" staged once more a victorious comeback.

From Spain the artistically decorated fan, wrought of costly lace and covered with dainty paintings, had been imported. It was as indispensable to the fashionable lady as was the rapier to the well-dressed beau. Ladies of social standing were rarely seen without their snuffboxes, which were made of silver, ivory, steel, horn, or wood and adorned with delicate relief work or miniature paintings upon enamel. When out-of-doors, the lady carried a cane to which colored ribbons and flowers were attached, or a parasol to protect her face from the glaring sunlight.

The age of Baroque and Rococo paid less attention to even the minimum requirements of personal and public hygiene than any other period in European history. Beyond a water can and bowl the costly equipment of castle, palace, and private residence did not normally include any facilities for bathing and washing. One may even say without exaggeration that bathing and washing were most unpopular. Public bathhouses were ill reputed, and bathing in rivers and brooks was considered as indecent or in bad taste. This neglect of the most primitive demands of physical hygiene explains the universal use of enormous quantities of cosmetics, smelling salts, perfumes, and so forth, of "fragrant essences and ingredients."

e) Eating and Drinking. Table manners and the arts of the cuisine took their directives from France. Courtly etiquette exerted a restraining influence on the habitual German overindulgence in food and drink. The nonalcoholic beverages, such as coffee, tea, and chocolate, became very popular after they had conquered the society of the French court at the end of the seventeenth century. The first German coffeehouse was opened in Hamburg in 1680, and these establishments together with the "coffee gardens" gained the favor of the middle class and became centers of social intercourse, divertisement, and relaxation.* The politically interested *galant homme* would spend many hours in the coffeehouse, reading the latest newssheets, playing billiard or card games. The great popularity of coffee and tea resulted in the sharply decreasing consumption of wine and beer. In the year 1721 no less than 4,100,000 pounds of tea were imported into Europe by English, French, and Dutch trading companies.** These nonalcoholic drinks, as well as the newly acquired habits of smoking and snuffing, captured the imagination of all classes by their novelty and exotic charm and soon became the objects of poetic panegyrics. Foreign tobaccos were imported and taxed by the governments, and in the period of mercantilism (cf. p. 328 sq.) the princes encouraged the planting of tobacco in their own territories. At the end of the seventeenth century tobacco was grown in Alsace, the Palatinate, Hesse, Saxony, Thuringia, Brandenburg, and Mecklenburg.

---

* Coffee was brought from Africa to Arabia (Mecca = Mocha) in the seventh century A.D.; it reached Constantinople (via Asia) in 1554 and was imported into Europe in the seventeenth century.

** Tea has been known and used as a beverage by the Chinese since the fourth century A.D. and by the Japanese since the eighth century A.D. Dutch traders made it known in Europe about the middle of the sixteenth century. About a hundred years later it became popular with the European aristocracy.

f) Eros. Sexual relations, moral concepts, and the resulting love codes and conventions of the Age of Baroque and Rococo were partly conditioned by the position and evaluation of women during this period. The total abandonment of moral standards that became the conspicuous characteristic of the French court under the rule of Louis XV and among his German imitators is scarcely found in the age of Louis XIV. But even during the lifetime of the *"roi soleil"* that new and refined eroticism was developed that permeated and saturated the culture of the Rococo. Although in some respects the cult of the noble lady looked like a revival of the chivalresque *"Minne"* (cf. p. 155), this latest fad of European society was too much imbued with sophistication, frivolity, and morbidity to be mistaken for anything but the hectic proliferation of a waning civilization.

From the beginnings of European history to the end of the seventeenth century European society had shown distinctly masculine features, despite the fact that occasionally women would rise to positions of leadership in the spheres of religious and secular culture. But in the main women had been confined to the home and had recognized man as the natural political and social leader, finding their own happiness and contentment in the care of household and children and in rather narrowly limited social activities. During the seventeenth century, however, the European lady gradually advanced to a central position in society. Women began to play their part in the scholarly culture of the age.

Princesses and noblewomen of great erudition and culture became renowned for their genuine interest in intellectual pursuits and broke down the social prejudices that had hitherto barred them from the precincts of the arts and sciences. The "scholarly woman" (*das gelehrte Frauenzimmer*) becomes a familiar type in seventeenth-century culture.

Sophie Charlotte, the wife of the first king of Prussia, studied the philosophical systems of Descartes, Spinoza, and Leibniz and is known as one of Leibniz's closest friends. Anna Maria Schurmann, a deeply religious personality of pietistic leanings, a native of Cologne, wrote verses and letters in Latin, Greek, Hebrew, and French, and is said to have mastered fourteen languages. She was proficient in music, painting, etching, and wood carving and deeply interested in mathematics, history, philosophy, and theology. Elizabeth Charlotte of Orléans (*"Liselotte von der Pfalz,"* 1652–1722), the wife of Louis XIV's brother Philip, a German princess of the Palatinate, was a woman of remarkable originality and independence of judgment, retaining the integrity and naturalness of her character in the midst of the frivolous environment of the French court and showing wit and a keen sense of observation in her letters, in which she offers a running commentary on her startling experiences.

In the period of the Rococo, fashion, manners, and customs point to the growing effeminacy of the general taste and to the predominating influence of the feminine element in society. The decadent and effeminate *cavalier* became the obedient and abjectly admiring slave of a lady and mistress of superior taste, culture, and education. The marriage ties were loosened to such a degree that adultery on the part of both sexes was considered a conventional rule rather than a deplorable exception. Social honors were showered on famous and infamous courtesans and mistresses, the debauchee was celebrated as a hero, and a general reversal of moral values raised the unnatural to the status of the normal and natural.

g) Festivities and Social Amusements. Following the example of the ancient Roman emperors, the absolutistic princes tried to keep themselves and their subjects in good humor by never ending cycles of brilliant festivities and spectacular social entertainments. Marriages, baptisms, coronations, receptions, military victories offered a variety of occasions for colorful parades, processions, fireworks, ballets, masquerades, and multiform other theatrical and musical divertisements. The favorite dance was the gracefully stilted Minuet, an adaptation of a peasant dance of Poitou in France, introduced at the court of Louis XIV in 1663. It became an integral part of the preclassical and classical sonata and symphony of the seventeenth and eighteenth centuries and was transformed into the "Scherzo" movement by Ludwig van Beethoven. At the court balls and masquerades (*Redoute:* from the Italian *Ridotto*) nobles and burghers were carefully separated by a rope or railing.

Everyone paid his tribute to the gambling and card-playing craze, and gambling tables were never missing at social entertainments. In the accounts and balance sheets of wealthy burghers the gambling allowance for their wives figured as an important item, and in princely families definite figures for gambling money were included in the marriage contract. The most popular card game was the "royal" *L'hombre,* of Spanish origin, introduced into France and other European countries in the period of Louis XIV.

A favorite pastime during the winter season was the elaborate sleighing parties, combined with carnival festivities, with phantastically decorated sleighs, jinglets, masked noblemen and their ladies, and a long train of horsemen, lackeys, pages, and trumpeters. In summertime the princes arranged encampments (*Lustlager*) in the open air, with military display, concerts, ballets, *tableaux vivants,* and the varied pleasures of the chase.

The complexity and artificiality of the culture of Baroque and Rococo stood as barriers between nature and society. Even if at times in sentimental yearning men and women dreamed of nature as a haven of repose and an escape from the tyranny of rules and conventions, they were too much the children of their age not to value these laws and rules above everything else. The frail beauty of their culture shines forth from the pleasure castles (*Lustschlösser*) which they erected in the countryside and whose very names suggest a secret longing for solitude, peace, and rest (*Solitude, Sans-Souci, Eremitage,* etc.); yet even in the pastoral costume and environment they remained the slaves of their unnatural conventions. They even felt impelled to impose the artificiality of their culture on the free growth of nature, subjecting trees and hedges, shrubbery and flower beds to the regularity of geometrical design and the added artistic and mechanical devices of fountains, cascades, grottoes, statues, and every sort of plastic decoration. An age that had made the cult of pleasure its final goal was in the end haunted by its own restlessness and had become unable to enjoy the fruits of its cravings. An undertone of sadness vibrates in all the manifestations of this overripe culture of European aristocracy.

h) Religious Currents. The spiritual unrest of the Baroque age expressed itself in manifold ways, but it was most intensely alive in the circles that carried forward the impulses of the Catholic Restoration and among the leaders of a spiritual revival in the Protestant sects. These religious movements were reflected in a new ascendancy of mystical theory and practice, in the foundation of new religious orders, in the philosophical renascence, in the religious life and customs of the people, and in the symbolic language of plastic art, literature, and music.

The major source of the mystical and religious components of Baroque culture was Spain, where St. Teresa of Ávila (1515-1582) had carried out the reform of the Carmelite Order, founding seventeen convents and fifteen monasteries. In her autobiographical *Libro de su Vida* as well as in her other works she gives evidence of an extraordinary understanding of human psychology and a remarkable combination of mystical contemplation, eminent will power, and good practical sense. Her collaborator in the work of monastic reform was St. John of the Cross (1542-1591), a mystical writer and poet of great fervor, spiritual depth, and unusual literary talents, who brought the mystical revival in Spain to its full bloom and who influenced most of the German and French mystical authors of the following centuries.

The rebirth of scholastic philosophy (cf. p. 141 sqq.), that had been effected in the Universities of Salamanca and Coimbra in the course of the sixteenth century, soon spread to the Catholic institutions of higher learning in southern Germany and Austria. The works of the Portuguese Jesuits as well as the *Disputations on Metaphysics* of the Spanish Jesuit Suarez (1548-1617) were adopted as standard texts in German Catholic and Protestant universities and colleges. Christopher Scheibler, professor in the University of Giessen, wrote a work on Metaphysics (*Opus Metaphysicum, 1617*) which became known as the "Protestant Suarez." This happened at a time when the Jesuit Mariana's work *On the King* (1605, 1611), obviously advocating tyrannicide, was causing a stormy controversy between Jesuits and Protestants.

Swinging back and forth between extremes, Baroque mentality produced strange and one-sided religious attitudes in both Catholic and Protestant countries and individuals: Jansenism* and Quietism** in France, and

---

* Jansenism is a rigoristic ethico-religious system, developed by Cornelius Jansen (1585-1638), bishop of Ypres. He approached Luther's and Calvin's views in his pessimistic evaluation of human nature, his denial of free will, and his doctrine of absolute predestination.
** Quietism, as taught in the later Middle Ages by the "Brethren and Sisters of the Free

Pietism (cf. p. 364 sqq.) in Holland and Germany. In these movements an antirational sentiment is conspicuous, an emotional reaction against the rationalistic trends of the age.

The most popular preachers of the seventeenth century were those who appealed to religious feeling and imagination. But it must be said that the people at large were relatively little affected by the hysterical exaggerations of certain types of Baroque mentality. On the contrary, the lower classes had preserved their gay naïveté, their sense of humor, and their unvarnished vitality. They were unbroken in their moral and emotional life and, as in Luther's time, responsive to the one who had learned to think their thoughts and to speak their language.

Among the famous Catholic preachers in German lands was Procopius of Templin (c. 1607–1680), a Capuchin monk,* the author of three volumes of spiritual songs, comparable in their mild serenity to the better known hymns of Paul Gerhardt (cf. p. 298 sq.). Most effective as a pulpit orator and popular writer was Abraham a Santa Clara (Johann Ulrich Megerle, before he entered the Augustinian Order), 1644–1709,** the son of an inn-keeper in the province of Baden. His fiery and soul-stirring sermons, perfect specimens of the art of rhetoric, represent in their pointed, antithetical style and rich imagery Baroque prose at its very best. His powerful word fanned the heroic spirit of the Austrian people in their determined resistance against the Turks and consoled them in the tribulations of the year of the plague (1679). In 1677 Emperor Leopold I made the Augustinian monk chaplain of the imperial court.

Widely read and thoroughly enjoyed by the common people were the didactic and devotional works of Martin of Cochem (1634–1712), a Capuchin monk of the Moselle region, who was equally famous as author and preacher and whose *Life of Christ* (1677) served as a textual pattern for several Passion plays.

  i) *Arts and Crafts.* The style of the Renaissance had been given a cool reception in the northern countries of Europe and especially in Germany. Here the great masters on the whole continued the late Gothic tradition, although, with the exception of Grünewald (cf. p. 198 sq.), they welcomed the technical innovations and some of the formal values of the classical revival and embodied them in their creations.

It was this preponderance of the medieval tradition in German art that made it a particularly favorable medium for the stylistic tendencies of the

---

Spirit" and in the seventeenth century by Mme. de Guyon and, in a more moderate form, Archbishop Fénelon of Cambrai (1651–1715), demanded the complete annihilation of all active faculties of the mind ("mystical death") for the sake of absolute surrender to the will of God.

  * The Capuchins, a branch of the Franciscan Order (cf. p. 134 sq.), were organized in 1525 to restore the original purity of the Franciscan ideal. In their external appearance they are distinguished from the Franciscans by their beard and a large cowl (capuche: *Kapuze*).

  ** Schiller (cf. p. 422) used Abraham a Santa Clara and his figurative language in the famous *Kapuzinerpredigt* of the first part of the Wallenstein trilogy (*Wallenstein's Camp*).

Baroque age, which in its very essence was a composite of Gothic and Renaissance, of spiritual fervor and beautiful natural form. It is nevertheless undeniable that artistically as much as intellectually the new Baroque style originated in Italy and Spain, the countries that had taken the lead in the Catholic reform movement. The extension of the Counter Reformation into southern Germany and Austria was soon followed by the adoption of the new art forms. As far as France is concerned, the heritage of antiquity and Renaissance was strong enough to preserve the classical artistic tradition essentially unimpaired even under the veneer of Baroque and Rococo. The style of the eras of Louis XIV, Louis XV, and Louis XVI are variations of an identical theme: they are a direct outgrowth and expression of courtly absolutism and political as well as cultural imperialism.

Hardouin-Mansard and Le Vau, the two architects of Louis XIV, the builders of the castle and palace chapel of Versailles, and Lenôtre, the creator of the royal gardens, set the standard of artistic taste for all France. Bernini's Baroque plan for the façade of the Louvre was rejected by the king in favor of the classical designs of Claude Perrault, in which grace and dignity combined to produce an effect of monumental simplicity.

The first powerful manifestation of Baroque sentiment in art may be found in the mature works of Michelangelo, in which the law of classical proportion and harmony gives way to a forceful and dynamic expressionism. From Michelangelo's design for the renovation of St. Peter's Cathedral in Rome to Bernini's (1598–1680) semicircular colonnades on St. Peter's Square a steadily growing mastery of the problems of space and architectonic masses may be observed. The architects of this period and their employers, the absolutistic princes, were beginning to plan and build entire cities as grandiose works of art, feeling themselves as sovereign masters of the realm of nature with its unlimited possibilities. In dictatorial fashion they applied to any given situation or problem a rule and order of their own making. Thus the typical Baroque city shows the same systematic uniformity as the absolutistic State, the princely army, and civic administration. Rome, the Eternal City, with its vast perspectives, its system of radiating streets whose lines converge in the focal *Piazza del Popolo,* provided the incomparable exemplar that was imitated and approximated in such German cities as Würzburg, Mannheim, and Karlsruhe. In the latter city the fanlike arrangement of streets serves only to emphasize the central and dominating structure of the princely castle. From his palace the prince overlooks the entire city, while in a graduated order the houses of nobles, court officials, merchants, and craftsmen are grouped in well-measured and increasing distances from the focal point. Since the times of Graeco-Roman antiquity city planning had not been practiced on such a large scale and with similar ingenuity and consistency.

In individual buildings the new consciousness of space expressed itself in multiple spatial combinations, the refracted light emanating from various hidden sources, resulting in a phantastic transfiguration of reality. As

Tabernacle in the Monastery at Andechs on the Ammer Lake.

distinguished from the planned city the individual building shuns symmetrical design, providing instead for constant change and a confusing variety of directions. All clear limitations and solid boundaries are obliterated by the play of unexpected and irrational impulses. Architecture, sculpture, and painting fuse in a festive phantasmagoria of light and color. Whereas the Gothic master builders endeavored to dematerialize even those things that were most deeply steeped in matter, the Baroque architect and sculptor materializes even the most immaterial objects, fashioning plastic rays of light and tangible clouds. The result was a kind of exaggerated realism, feverish, convulsive, and overdescriptive. Angels are represented as healthy, naked, and precocious children and coquettish girls, and heaven becomes a glorified extension of the earth. Asceticism deteriorates into an enjoyment of pain or into sensual ecstasy or vice versa, revealing an almost pathological confusion of emotions.

The peculiar characteristics of the Baroque style may in part be explained by the universally felt urge for religious propaganda, for which art provided a symbolic language. In a world in which the Church had been forced to share its rule over men's minds with secular powers, the ancient spiritual message had to be convincingly and strikingly reaffirmed by every available means. By addressing men's senses and imagination the Church tried to reach man's intellect. In Protestant northern Germany the subtle and sublime language of music served as the exclusive artistic medium, while in the Catholic South all the arts in unison engaged the entire sensuous and intellectual organism of the human being. As in the age of the Reformation, the masses were once more stirred and moved by Christian impulses. In movement and countermovement, in attack and defense, in continuous agitation and struggle, the Baroque style acquired its distinctive features.

This new style was gratefully adopted, developed, and propagated by the Jesuits (cf. p. 254 sqq.), who formed the vanguard of the Catholic Restoration. This fact gave rise to the misnomer "Jesuit-Style," which term in its generalization by no means exhausts the rich possibilities of Baroque art. Nevertheless, the religious experiences of the age and certain changes in the liturgical and devotional practices of the Church found their expression in architectural form and were especially noticeable in the numerous Jesuit churches that covered city and countryside. Additional choir and nave space was to enable large congregations to follow the popular sermons and to have an unobstructed view of the pulpit, the great altar, and the liturgical ceremonies. The mysterious semidarkness of the medieval cathedral gave way to a brightly lit and loudly decorated interior. In the larger churches a second story in the form of an aisle gallery and enclosed box seats for the nobility and the court were added. While every Gothic church dominated all the surrounding buildings of the city, town, or village, the Baroque church is frequently co-ordinated with private or public buildings. In the Benedictine monastic settlement of Melk on the Danube the structural unit of the church is hardly distinguishable from the rest of the buildings.

Façade and interior show great vitality of architectural and sculptural design, plantlike tropical richness and plastic massiveness, and a tendency to create an effect of disconcerting unrest by a maze of opposing lines and broken or unfinished forms.

The first Baroque and Rococo churches and secular buildings on German soil were the work of Italian and French architects: the Church of St. Cajetan (*Theatinerkirche, 1663–1675*) in Munich was built by Agostino Barello, a native of Bologna, while the *"Residenztheater,"* the Amalienburg, and the interior of the royal palace (*"Residenz"*) in the same city are samples of the gay and delicate taste of François de Cuvilliés, a Walloon who came to Munich in 1724 and was most successful in introducing the elegance of French Rococo into Germany. But the Italian and French masters were soon superseded and surpassed by their German pupils, who became the creators of German Baroque as a national style.

In analogy to the Gothic style three major phases in the development of German Baroque may be distinguished: Early Baroque (*c.* 1580–1630), High Baroque (*c.* 1670–1720), and Late Baroque or Rococo (*c.* 1720–1770). The Thirty Years' War and its cultural consequences caused a temporary period of stagnation (*c.* 1630–1670). Architecture as the leading and socially most significant art proved equally creative in the ecclesiastical and secular spheres. Among the works of secular architecture the princely residences, palaces, pleasure castles, and parks rank foremost. The most fruitful regions are Austria, Bohemia (Prague), Bavaria, Franconia, Silesia, and Saxony (Dresden). The outstanding master builders are Fischer von Erlach (St. Charles Church, Vienna); Lucas von Hildebrandt (Belvedere Castle, Vienna); Daniel Pöppelmann (Zwinger, Dresden); Georg Bähr (*Frauen-kirche,* Dresden); Jakob Prandauer (Monasteries Melk and St. Florian, Austria); Johann, Christoph, and Ignaz Dientzenhofer (Cathedral of Fulda and numerous buildings in Prague); Joseph Effner (Nymphenburg and Schleissheim Castles near Munich); Dominicus Zimmermann (churches Steinhausen, Wies in Bavaria); Michael Fischer (churches Zwiefalten, Ottobeuren in Swabia); Balthasar Neumann (Würzburg Castle; churches Vierzehnheiligen, Neresheim in Franconia and Swabia); and Andreas Schlüter. The last named master, a native of Danzig, is the creator of the Berlin Castle and the equestrian statue of the Great Elector, the only representative master of the much more austere and almost classical Baroque style of the Protestant North. The leading Baroque sculptors this side of the Alps are Raphael Donner in Austria and Andreas Schlüter in Germany. The brothers Kosmas Damian and Egid Quirin Asam of Munich (Church of St. John Nepomuk) are masters of the fully grown Rococo, unsurpassed in the fragile lightness and picturesque melodiousness of their figural compositions, their altarpieces, and their stucco decoration.*

---

* According to their birth dates the great Baroque architects belong in the following two generations of the seventeenth century: (1) Fischer von Erlach, Christoph and Johann Dientzen-

Zwinger, Dresden, by Daniel Pöppelmann.

Benedictine Monastery in Weingarten, Wurtemberg.

Baroque painting achieved its greatest fame in Italy (Caravaggio, Tintoretto, Tiepolo), Spain (El Greco, Velasquez, Murillo, Zurbarán), Flanders (Rubens, van Dyck), Holland (Rembrandt), and England (Hogarth, Gainsborough). Most of the German masters were of second and third rank, but with their al fresco murals they provided a suitable background for the great works of the architects and sculptors. In their painted ceilings they create an imaginary heaven and the illusion of infinite space, a feast of dazzling light, silvery clouds, and radiant atmosphere, wherein angels and saints move with perfect ease. The prince-bishop of Würzburg had the central staircase and Emperor's Hall of Balthasar Neumann's magnificent castle decorated with paintings from the brush of Tiepolo, the great master of Venice.

The art of portrait painting, satisfying the thirst for fame and glory of princes and nobles, bishops and abbots, flourished no less than in the period of the Renaissance with its cult of individualism. The Baroque painters portray the cavaliers in heroic poses and the ladies as glamorous goddesses of love. Eighteenth-century Rococo developed the art of pastel painting (crayon painting) as a new and delicate pictorial technique, of which the earlier works of Anton Raphael Mengs (1728–1779), the court painter of King Augustus III of Saxony-Poland, are excellent examples. The arts of etching and engraving are best represented by the genrelike and at the same time more realistic works of Daniel Chodowiecki (1726–1801), who acquired fame with his illustrations of some of the masterpieces of German eighteenth-century literature (Klopstock, Gellert, Lessing, Goethe, Schiller, etc.).

The high quality of German craftsmanship held its own throughout the Age of Baroque and Rococo. The goldsmiths provided the sacristies and altars of the churches with precious chalices, monstrances, and variegated ornamental decorations. The arts of weaving and embroidery reached new heights in the making of tapestries, carpets, and liturgical vestments. The artistic locksmiths and blacksmiths created beautifully shaped table utensils and elaborately wrought and fancifully decorated iron gates. The refined taste as well as the frail iridescence of the Rococo shines forth from the graceful products of the porcelain factories of Dresden and Meissen, later on also of Berlin, Frankenthal, Ludwigsburg, Nymphenburg, and Vienna.*

---

hofer, Pöppelmann, Schlüter, Bähr, Hildebrandt, Prandauer were born in the fifties and sixties; (2) Zimmermann, the Asams, Joseph Effner, Balthasar Neumann, Michael Fischer, and Ignaz Dientzenhofer were born in the eighties and nineties. Many of the great monuments of German and Austrian Baroque architecture were destroyed during World War II.

*Porcelain clay for the manufacture of pottery was first used by the Chinese (seventh century A.D.). In Europe this ancient technique was rediscovered by Johann Friedrich Böttger (Meissen) at the beginning of the eighteenth century. The porcelain factory of Meissen was founded in 1710. The related process of the manufacture of faïence (from the Italian city Faënza) is of even earlier origin (Egypt, Babylon, Persia). It was cultivated by the Mohammedans in the Orient and by the Moors in Spain (c. 1100–1500). In Italy faïence is known as Majolica. The first German faïence factories were those of Hanau (1661) and Frankfurt (1666).

j) Literature. The major theme of drama and novel in the age of Baroque is the freedom of the human will to choose good or evil, heaven or hell. The struggle of the hero with the apparent arbitrariness of life and the inscrutable decrees of "Fortuna" (Roman goddess of Fate) has as its object and final goal the purification and mastery of the passions by the exercise of reason and free will.

Although some of the literary trends and creations of the early Baroque had to be discussed in connection with the social and cultural conditions of the period of the Thirty Years' War (cf. p. 284 sqq.), their significance can be more adequately appreciated if the spirit of the age of Baroque is used as a frame of reference. This is especially true of such authors as Jacob Böhme, Andreas Gryphius, Martin Opitz, Grimmelshausen, and others.

Two definite tendencies or branches are easily distinguished in the creations of Baroque literature: (1) a group of authors whose works bear the marks of courtly representation and didactic rationalization, and (2) the works of those writers who wish to express not the experiences of an entire class but personal and intimate feelings of merely private concern. The members of the first group are the creators of the truly representative works of Baroque literature, while the authors who belong to the second group fulfill the no less important historical function of preparing the way for the literature of the age of sentimentality (cf. p. 392 sq.) and enlightenment (cf. p. 368 sq.). What both groups have in common is a certain lack of moderation and proportion and the overstraining of either reason, emotion, or will.

The spiritual dynamism of the age is most poignantly alive in those dramatic works that were written by members of the Jesuit and Benedictine Orders. The authors were professors of Catholic colleges and universities, and their works were among the most effective instruments of religious propaganda in the period of the Catholic Restoration. The stage assumed the function of a great moral and educative agency by means of which the spectators were to experience the wished-for synthesis between earth and heaven, nature and supernature. The intended moral effect was contrition, repentance, and ultimate conversion. While the Protestant school drama used both the German and Latin tongues, the religious drama of the Catholics and particularly the Jesuits cultivated a neo-classical Latin style of great elegance and lucidity.

The sources and patterns from which the leading Jesuit dramatists derived inspiration were morality plays of the type of *Everyman,* which flourished especially in the Low Countries; the Humanistic school theater with its revival of the classical Roman comedy of Plautus (*c.* 250–184 B.C.) and Terence (*c.* 190–159 B.C.); and the biblical folk plays which were frequently produced in public squares.

The most talented Jesuit playwright of the early Baroque is the Swabian, Jacob Bidermann, whose *Cenodoxus* or *Doctor of Paris,* written when the author was twenty-four years of age, deals with the Faustian theme of the life, death, and judgment of a self-styled "superman." It is recorded that after the first performances several high-ranking courtiers were so deeply moved that they changed their entire mode of living, and that the actor who played the title role became a member of the Jesuit Order. The Catholic religious drama reached its perfection in the works of the Tyrolese Jesuit, Nicholas Avancini (1611–1686) and the Benedictine writer Simon Rettenbacher (1634–1706) of the monastery of Kremsmünster in Upper Austria.

The unreal, superrational, and allegorical character of these plays necessitated revolutionary changes and innovations in the art of stagecraft, for which again the Jesuits provided guidance and inspiration. The Baroque stage of the religious orders presents an utter contrast to the homely and often uncouth performances of the wandering troupes, whose members had to be satisfied with the most primitive equipment and who had no social standing. Nothing, on the other hand, was too costly and extravagant for the princely or monastic stage. Special consideration was given to elaborate costuming and stage setting. Artists and technicians of great reputation put their talents at the disposal of their ecclesiastical and secular employers. Ever new problems presented themselves, whose solution required the intuition and dexterity of artistic genius. Complicated mechanical devices and machinery had to create the illusion of pouring rains, flying clouds, howling storms. The scene had to be set for the convenience of the incalculable whims of the gods and goddesses of the classical pantheon as well as for the visions of saints and the apparitions of angels, demons, monsters, and phantoms. Up to the middle of the seventeenth century change of scenery had been effected by movable painted prisms ("Telari-Stage"), which enclosed a well-defined and limited static space. The Baroque period introduced the wings with painted perspective, thereby giving the scene additional depth and allowing for ever changing prospects and extended horizons. The most ingenious theater architects, stage designers, and stage decorators were three members of the Italian family Galli da Bibbiena (Fernando, 1657–1743; Giuseppe, 1696–1757; Antonio, 1700–1774). They exercised a noteworthy influence on the space concepts of Baroque architecture.

The ideal goal of Baroque drama and stagecraft was in a way an anticipation of Richard Wagner's (cf. p. 494 sqq.) theatrical *Gesamtkunstwerk* (the total or universal work of art), in which all the different arts unite and fuse. The physical magnitude and the processional and representational character of the performances proved favorable for the development of the open-air theater, in which a fitting background and setting was provided by the highly formal and decorative garden architecture or by triumphal arches, halls and temples of honor which were constructed for some particular occasion. The art of the drama tended to merge with parade, procession, ballet, festival play, Oratorio, and Opera.

Baroque drama as cultivated outside the religious orders, and the works of such authors as Andreas Gryphius (cf. p. 299) which had grown out of the religious premises of the Protestant Reformation, were either farcical slapstick comedy or dramatizations of grand historical and political events (*Haupt- und Staatsaktionen*). The comedies were frequently built around the dominant figure of the clown (*Hanswurst, Pickelhäring*) and were without literary significance. The *Haupt- und Staatsaktion* was a bombastic and bloodcurdling affair, with a heroic or phantastic plot, and from the linguistic point of view a medley of German, French, Italian, and Latin.

Comedy and *Staatsaktion* were combined in the offerings of the touring companies or troupes, especially the "English Comedians" who, between 1585 and 1660, produced more or less crude versions of Elizabethan and Shakespearean drama at German courts and in German cities. Their stage was of the simplest kind: a wooden framework, draped with curtains or rugs. The English language gradually gave way to German, and German touring companies eventually replaced the foreign troupes. Despite their often primitive taste the members of these companies were professional actors and therefore capable of improving the artistic quality of theatrical performances and of enlarging the scope of the dramatic repertoire. Johannes Velten (1640–1692), a German actor of excellent literary taste, worked unceasingly for the advancement of the German stage and was the first to enrich the offerings of his troupe by the inclusion of the works of the classical French authors.

Typical of the Baroque *novel* are the works of Lohenstein (1635–1683), Zesen (1619–1689), and Anton Ulrich, duke of Brunswick (1663–1714). They have in common the antithetical structure and the rhetorical artificiality of style and composition. For Lohenstein (*Arminius,* etc.) the ideal hero is somewhat like a map or mirror of the universe; he is an instrument in the hands of an incomprehensible universal intellect, not an unknowing or passive tool, to be sure, but an intelligent agent himself, who perseveres in temporal tribulations and achieves moral triumph in the ultimate mastery of the complexities of life. Zesen's *Adriatic Rosemund* has an educational, didactic, and nationalistic tendency, and his *Assenat* is a Baroque version of the biblical story of Joseph in Egypt. The latter takes the form of the political "Utopia" when it attempts a moral justification of royal despotism: Joseph succeeds in his scheme of a planned economy by reducing the Egyptian population to the status of serfdom. Ulrich von Braunschweig's (Brunswick) *Roman Octavia* depicts life as a "school of patience," in which the good are eventually rewarded, the wicked punished. The heroines are models of moral perseverance and representatives of perfect courtly decorum. The varying aspects of historic evolution reveal the essentially identical nature of man and the natural and divine law. The Baroque striving for universality is realized by making the novel a mosaic of epistles, orations, narratives, and lyrics. The ideology of the age of "Enlightenment" (cf. p. 368 sq.) is foreshadowed by a belief in a universal moral law, residing in human nature beyond and above all dogmatic distinctions.

France was the first country to revolt against the high-sounding verbosity and grandiloquence of Baroque literature. Molière's (1622–1673) comedies had ridiculed the stiltedness of the culture of his age, and Boileau (1636–1711) had demanded clarity, naturalness, and simplicity as requisites of a beautiful literary style. French literature had already adopted these very principles and had achieved a somewhat too faultless and academic classical perfection in the works of Corneille (1606–1684) and Racine (1639–1699). In Germany the first opposition to the exaggerations of Baroque literature likewise dates back to the seventeenth century. The taste of the middle class began to rebel against courtly bombast and demanded honesty and intelligibility of literary expression. And the opposition that came from mystico-religious quarters wanted to see the "language of the heart" reflected in the clarity, simplicity, and truthfulness of literary style. Enlightenment, Pietism, and Rococo were united in their antagonism to Baroque ostentation and pompous extravagance, although their opposition sprang from different sources. But all the anti-Baroque forces seemed crystallized in the works of Christian Gellert (1715–1769), who was the favorite author and the exponent of all three tendencies that characterized the period between Baroque and "Storm and Stress" (*Sturm und Drang,* cf. p. 394 sq.): rationalism, sentimentalism, and the smooth elegance of the Rococo. For Frederick the Great Gellert was "the most sensible" of the German men of letters, and Goethe, despite a more critical appraisal, saw in this poet's mediocre talents the bases of moral culture in Germany. In Gellert's fables and hymns we find moralism and introspection, common sense and the rational veneration of a deistically conceived Godhead, while in his novels virtue and vice are arrayed against each other in a forced and primitive chiaroscuro technique.

The authors of both Rococo and Enlightenment were animated by the comforting conviction of living in the best and most reasonable of all possible worlds. This is especially true of the "Anacreontics," * a group of poets who created for themselves an idyllic and hollow fools' paradise, wherein they could enthusiastically give vent to their epicurean dreams of wine, women, and song. Although their pale epicureanism remained confined to the printed page, they enriched German lyric poetry by new emotional accents. Ewald von Kleist (1715–1759), the most talented of their number, became the lyrical panegyrist of the Frederician army, marking the transition from the lighthearted Rococo to the heroic pathos of the "Storm and Stress" poets.

German literary Rococo reaches its peak in the later works of Christoph Martin Wieland (1733–1813), in which the pietistic sentimentalism of his youth gave way to the mildly skeptical and partly ironical mentality of the Rococo, in which a graceful and tolerant art of living is embodied in the form of a new and refined humanism. The high cultural acumen that is achieved by Wieland is evidenced by the broadness and flexibility of his

* The name refers to the Greek lyric poet Anacreon (sixth century B.C.).

literary taste and by the gift of empathy that enabled him to appreciate such widely divergent modes of artistic expression as those represented by Shakespeare (many of whose works he translated), the young Goethe, and Heinrich von Kleist (cf. p. 483 sqq.).*

k) Music and Opera. The churches, abbeys, and castles of the age of Baroque and Rococo, with their flowing façades, majestic porches, halls, and staircases, the soft lyricism of their interior decoration, signify the submersion of plastic architectural form in the spirit of music. The musical art forms therefore are not merely an important part of Baroque style but they seem to express its very essence. Some of the finest specimens of Rococo architecture before World War II, such as the famous "Gloriette," a hall of columns of fragile beauty in the park of Schönbrunn near Vienna, or the arcades and pavilions of Pöppelmann's "Zwinger" in Dresden, part of which housed one of the most famous art collections of Europe, looked like Mozartian Minuets in stone, like frozen music.

German church music in the seventeenth century received its chief inspiration from Italy, where two major schools may be distinguished: the Romans and the Venetians. The Romans, following the style of Palestrina (cf. p. 282), are more austere; the Venetians, most gloriously represented by Giovanni Gabrieli (1557–1612), are more worldly and richer in their vocal and instrumental color schemes. It was the Venetian school that exerted a direct influence on the German composers of the age of Baroque and Rococo.

Heinrich Schütz (1585–1672), Georg Friedrich Händel (1685–1759), and Johann Sebastian Bach (1685–1750) are the great German masters of the Baroque period. Schütz, a native of Thuringia, studied in Venice under Giovanni Gabrieli and subsequently received an appointment at the court of the elector of Saxony in Dresden. Most of his works are of distinctly religious character. He combined the polyphonic tradition of the sixteenth century with the new style (*nuove musiche, stile nuovo*) of the harmonically accompanied monody, and developed the standard forms for the biblical oratorio and "Passion." In his "Passions" and "Spiritual Concerts" he is the direct precursor of J. S. Bach. In his opera *Daphne,* for which Martin Opitz (cf. p. 299) wrote a German version of Rinuccini's Italian libretto, he introduced the recitative** vocal style.

Likewise a native of Thuringia was the great Johann Sebastian Bach, to whom, according to Schumann (cf. p. 493), "music owes almost as great a debt as a religion owes to its founder." He is the towering genius of the

---

* Of Wieland's works the drama *Lady Johanna Gray* and his prose translation of Shakespeare breathe the spirit of Enlightenment. His educational novel *Der goldene Spiegel (The Golden Mirror)* praises the representative of enlightened despotism. The novels *Agathon* and *Abderiten* construe a world of ideal classical culture, opposing exaggerated spiritualism and sensism. The narrative in verse, *Oberon,* is a masterpiece of the literary Rococo.

** The recitative style in music is based exclusively on the spoken word of the text, relinquishing all independent melodic and rhythmical paraphrases. It forms an integral part of the "representative style" (*stile rappresentativo*) of the early opera.

great musical heritage of German Protestantism. In him the style of musical Baroque reaches its greatest spiritual depth, while at the same time he marks the height and consummation of a development of musical form that extends over a period of three centuries, leading from the late Gothic, Renaissance, and early Baroque polyphony to modern homophony (harmony). Bach is the only composer who embraces and unites in his works these two distinct musical styles.

Bach, the father of twenty children, several of whom achieved fame as composers and musicians, passed the greater part of his uneventful life as an organist and cantor in the petty towns of Thuringia and in the neighboring city of Leipzig. After having completed his studies he was appointed as court organist and concertmaster in Weimar in 1714 and three years later as conductor (*Kapellmeister*) to the court of Prince Leopold of Anhalt-Cöthen at Cöthen. In 1723 he became cantor at the Thomas School in Leipzig and director of music in the two main churches of that city. In the beginning he entertained friendly relations with the literary and academic circles in Leipzig, among others with Johann Christoph Gottsched (cf. p. 378 sq.), who exercised a kind of literary dictatorship in Germany, but later on he withdrew more and more from social intercourse. In 1736 Bach was appointed as honorary court composer to the elector of Saxony, and in 1747 he accepted an invitation to visit the court of Frederick the Great, where his son Emanuel was employed as a cymbalist. The constant strain on his sight from early youth brought about his total blindness one year before his death (1750).

Bach's musical compositions reveal a complete mastery of technical means, logical structure, monumental form, and the sublimity of religious experience. The vocal arrangements of church chorals, in which the solo arias function as lyrical interpretations of the musical core, grew out of the sphere of organ music.* In the "Passions" of John and Matthew, the two hundred church cantatas, the Magnificats, oratories, and masses we have examples of Bach's perfected personal style. In the *High Mass in B minor,* written for the Catholic court of Saxony, the subjective elements of Bach's spirituality blend admirably with the severe objectivity of the Gregorian Chorale.

The composer's instrumental works include the numerous preludes and fugues for organ and clavier, the sonatas, suites, concertos, and overtures for various instruments and full orchestra. In the Cöthen period he composed instrumental chamber music, while in the Leipzig period he produced his greatest church music. In his fugues Bach developed the art of harmonic

---

* Piano and organ music were closely allied musical arts in the sixteenth and early seventeenth century. The credit for having created a genuine style of piano music belongs to the English composers of the Baroque age (William Byrd, Orlando Gibbons, etc.). The early forms of the pianoforte ("clavier," *Hammerklavier,* invented in the eighteenth century) were the clavichord and the harpsichord, the former of soft, the latter of hard and metallic tonal quality.

counterpoint* to its final perfection, achieving a complete synthesis of melodious and harmonious elements.

Georg Friedrich Händel, born in Halle in the province of Saxony in the same year as Bach, was a composer of much more cosmopolitan taste. Three years he spent in Italy and, after a short engagement in Hanover, he journeyed to London, where he stayed as director of the opera until his death (1759). He lies buried in Westminster Abbey.

Having familiarized himself at an early age with the musical styles of Italy, France, and England, Händel was ideally prepared to become a creative innovator in the universally cherished musical forms of oratorio and opera, English influence prevailing in the former and Italian influence in the latter. The dramatic intensity and dynamic rhythm of his works make Händel the foremost representative of a festive, majestic, and fully seasoned Baroque style. After the venture of the London opera had ended in failure, Händel gave his attention almost exclusively to the oratorio. In his instrumental compositions he continued and perfected the tradition that had been established by such Italian masters as Corelli (1653–1773) and Vivaldi (c. 1680–1743). His works include forty operas, thirty oratorios and Passions; Te Deums, cantatas, arias, Concerti Grossi, and numerous pieces of chamber music.

The most original contribution that the seventeenth century made to the development of musical styles was the creation of the new forms of *opera* and *music drama*. The immediate ancestor of the opera was the Italian and German *madrigal*, the most favored form of musical entertainment in the age of the Renaissance. In the madrigal several harmonically interrelated voices followed the lead of the upper voice in the interpretation of a poetic text, thus preparing the way for the recitative solo arias of the new operatic style.

The first great master of the European opera was Claudio Monteverdi (1567–1643), whose Opera *Ariadne*, first produced at the court of Mantua in 1608, moved the audience to tears. In the new *stile rappresentativo e recitativo* declamation and acting were harmoniously combined. As early as 1594 Jacobo Peri's (1561–1633) *Daphne*, with text by Rinuccini, had been performed in private before a group of Florentine connoisseurs. The first public opera house was opened in Venice in 1637. Ten years earlier Rinuccini's *Daphne* in Opitz's German version and with Schütz's music had been produced for the first time in Germany, and about the middle of the seventeenth century the art of the opera had conquered all the German court theaters.

For some time, however, the opera on German soil retained all the

---

* Counterpoint (Latin, *contrapunctus: punctus contra punctum:* "note against note") denotes the art of combining independent melodies in accordance with definite laws of musical composition. We distinguish a preharmonic and a postharmonic phase in the historical development of counterpoint. The preharmonic period reaches from the early medieval chant to the musical style of Palestrina. The postharmonic period begins at the end of the sixteenth century; its unsurpassed master is Bach and its ideal musical form is the fugue.

earmarks of the land of its birth: text, music, and singers were mostly Italian. In Vienna, Dresden, Munich, and elsewhere the courts cultivated the Italian type of opera and employed Italian composers, conductors, stage directors, and performers. Even in Hamburg, where the most serious attempt was made to create an indigenous operatic taste, many of the operas that appeared on the stage were German only in name but Italian in spirit and atmosphere.

Although Frederick the Great stated that he would "rather listen to a neighing horse than allow a German prima donna to sing at the Royal Opera," the Italian taste in music was gradually waning in the course of the eighteenth century. One of the reasons for this change was the growing melodramatic superficiality of the Venetian and Neapolitan styles. The serious-minded music lovers in Germany demanded depth, simplicity, and true feeling in place of ornamental flourishes, decorative trimmings, and sentimental lamentations.

Under the influence of the renewed interest in classical antiquity the Frankish composer, Christoph Willibald Gluck (1714-1787), convinced of the shallowness of Italian opera, became the creator of a new music drama that took its inspiration from Greek tragedy, subordinating the musical idiom to the propensities of a classically ennobled literary style and dramatic plot, and enriching the art of musical characterization by the reintroduction of chorus, dance, and orchestral accompaniment. The texts of Gluck's collaborator, Raniero di Calzabigi, show a keen realization of the German composer's revolutionary ideas, with which Gluck was able to turn the tide and break the stranglehold that Italy had gained on German music. The composer himself commented on his musical principles in the words with which he dedicated his opera *Alceste* (1767) to the duke of Toscana, the future Emperor Leopold II: "It has been my intention to confine music to its real task, i.e., to serve poetry for the sake of verbal expression and literary interpretation, without interrupting or weakening the plot by the addition of futile and unnecessary embellishment. It has been my further intention to do away with all those excesses, against which for some time common sense and good taste have revolted. I have considered it my special task to try to achieve a beautiful simplicity and to avoid the mistake of parading clever technical tricks at the expense of clarity."

The spirit of the Rococo and the neo-classical tendencies blend perfectly in the works of Joseph Haydn (1732-1809) and Wolfgang Amadeus Mozart (1756-1791). Together with Beethoven (cf. p. 426 sqq.) they are considered as the leaders of the new musical classicism of the Viennese school. Although Haydn's operas, masses, and other works of vocal music rank high, he is above all the great master of instrumental composition, especially of symphony and chamber music (string quartets), unequaled in the joyful and childlike optimism that permeates all of his works, revealing symbolically the placid beauty of the Austrian landscape and expressing the simple piety of the Austrian folk spirit. Haydn's oratorios are influenced by the choral style of Händel, adding to it the new elements of the rediscovery and musical illustration of nature.

Haydn and Mozart were the first and foremost creators of a popular musical style, breaking down the artificial barriers that separated the different classes of the German population and finding a way not only to the heart and soul of the people at large but demonstrating at the same time the possibility of a homogeneous and indigenous German culture.

In Mozart the delicate style of the Rococo experienced its final transfiguration. A child prodigy of extraordinary gifts but of unassuming modesty, Mozart achieved an early maturity of musical form, a sparkling gaiety, crystalline clarity, and sublime intelligibility, issuing from a great sensitivity and soft melancholy of mind and a profound realization of the tragic texture of life.

On his journeys to France, England, Italy, and the Netherlands Mozart was greeted with unending applause. His indebtedness to the Italian musical tradition, documented particularly in the Italian texts of his operas, did not prevent him from feeling deeply his obligations to the country and civilization of his birth. "I ask God every day," he told his father in a letter from Paris, "that He grant me to work for the greater honor of . . . the entire German nation."

In his works Mozart makes use of all the technical devices that his predecessors, above all Bach, Händel, Gluck, and Haydn, had developed and that were at his disposal. The thematic structure of Haydn's compositions became more expressive in Mozart's richer instrumentation. In the field of the opera he started out from the neo-Neapolitan *Opera Seria* but soon developed his own distinctive style in such operatic gems as *The Marriage of Figaro, Don Giovanni,* and *Cosi fan Tutte (All Act Alike)*. His *Magic Flute (Zauberflöte)* became the paragon and adored model of the Romantic fairy opera (cf. p. 494 sq.).

The larger number of Mozart's more than six hundred works belong to the categories of the symphony (41), the sonata (53), and various types of chamber music. Several of his church compositions (masses, cantatas, vespers, litanies, etc.) and many of his arias and "Lieder" have achieved immortal fame. Mozart's swan song and a kind of funeral chant of the Rococo is the beautiful *Requiem* that he composed in 1791, in memory of the countess of Walsegg.

The Age of Rationalism. The modern world had taken its start from the individualism of Renaissance and Reformation. In Italy the ideal of the *uomo universale* (the universal or total man) had been conceived. In Germany Martin Luther had tried to establish a new church and society whose norms were not to be imposed from without but were to grow from the inwardness of the individual soul. In the following centuries the sovereign individual extended his dominion over the several provinces of life and civilization, conquering them one by one and step by step:

State, society, politics, economics, the arts, philosophy, morality, and religion.

a) Philosophy and the New Scientific Methods. In a seemingly disenchanted world, however, man began to discover new miracles. The great scientific geniuses of the seventeenth century found a new world in the study of nature: a world that appeared as self-sufficient, self-conserving, deprived of purposes and ends; a world that could be experimentally measured and rationally comprehended and explained. It appeared entirely possible to interpret all the phenomena of life in rational terms: religion and morals, State and society, art and science.

The new science itself was almost exclusively interested in observation, description, and experimentation, paying little attention to causal or genetic relations. It was engaged in reducing all qualitative distinctions to quantitative, extended, and therefore measurable entities. The many and perplexing phenomena of an atomistically split universe were rallied by the piercing intellect of Descartes (1596–1650), who forged a new theory of cognition and established a new unity of knowledge on the "infallible" authority of the science of mathematics. It was in 1619, the second year of the great war, that Descartes, then a soldier in the army of General Tilly, in his quarters in Neuburg on the Danube believed he had discovered the criterion of indubitable certitude in that self-consciousness of the thinking and doubting ego, which became for him the cornerstone of his philosophical system (*cogito, dubito — ergo sum:* "I think, I doubt — therefore I am"). Mathematically clear and distinct ideas and principles became for him the criteria of all truth.

However, the integral rationalism of Descartes was unable to bridge the gulf that separated mind and body, spirit and matter, "thought" and "extension." This unreconciled dualism remained a stumbling block and an open challenge for all the followers of Descartes to this day. Nevertheless, the Cartesian system presented itself as a tool for the rationalization of life in its entirety. Cartesian reasoning aided in the great discoveries in mathematics, physics, chemistry, biology, geology, and many related fields. Descartes himself was the creator of analytical geometry, whereby geometrical data may be translated into algebraic symbols and vice versa, and both Isaac Newton (1642–1727) and Gottfried Wilhelm Leibniz (1646–1716) discovered independently the differential calculus.

Baruch (Benedict) de Spinoza (1632–1677) developed his system of philosophical pantheism* *"more geometrico,"* making use of the method and terminology of Euclidean geometry. The world emanates with mathematical necessity from the one divine substance which man recognizes in only two of its infinitely many attributes: extension and consciousness, body and mind. The more the human mind becomes conscious of the divine origin and necessary constitution of the universe, the stronger is its control

---

* Pantheism denotes the identity of God and the universe, both being considered as parts or expressions of one and the same substance.

over emotions and passions and the greater its happiness. Although Spinoza did not share Descartes's and Newton's belief in a personal Creator and was excommunicated as a heretic by the synagogue of his native city of Amsterdam and denounced as an atheist by many of his contemporaries, his heart and mind were filled with religious reverence, with what he called the "intellectual love of God" (*amor intellectualis Dei*).

Rationalism and its Cartesian premises were carried to their extreme yet logical conclusions by the French philosophers of the age of "Enlightenment" (cf. p. 368 sq.), who prepared the way for the coming revolution. By their denial of God, the immortality of the soul, and free will, they resolved Descartes's metaphysical dualism into an all-embracing materialism and atheism. Julien de Lamettrie (1709-1751) defined man as a machine whose proper functioning is regulated by a reason which is itself the product of material and mechanical forces. The theorists of the French Revolution of 1789 transferred the method of scientific experimentation to a thoroughly planned and rationalized political and social economy. By a strange and paradoxical reversal of emphasis the freedom of the sovereign individual issued in the rule of the masses and the rise of collectivism.

While philosophical rationalism advanced triumphantly on the European continent, the British philosophers perfected the experimental method, based on sense experience and observation. Francis Bacon (1561-1626), the English lord chancellor, extolled critical judgment, gained by practical experience above mere book learning, and denied the existence of innate ideas. He expressed the conviction of most of his contemporaries when he coined the phrase: "Knowledge is power. We have as much power as we have knowledge." Thomas Hobbes (1588-1679), who for several years had been Bacon's secretary, became the philosophical spokesman of the absolutistic age when he described the State as the ferocious "Leviathan," devouring those who will not submit to its rule without questioning. The State, as the embodiment and supreme arbiter of all law, establishes, determines, and interprets all religious and moral values. John Locke (1632-1704), George Berkeley (1684-1753), and David Hume (1711-1776) carried the empirical* premises of their predecessors to their extreme conclusions: Locke denying the existence of substances, Berkeley denying the existence of an objective reality, and Hume espousing a complete skepticism.**

b) *Philosophy and Natural Religion* (*Deism*). The scientific spirit of the age of rationalism gradually developed a new religion of its own making, a scientific or natural religion, which took hold of pulpits, lecture halls, and the printed page. Its faithful adherents were convinced that the age of natural science had ushered in a golden age of supreme perfection, that it was to raise man to a higher level of existence, that it would bring forth a

---

* Empiricism derives all knowledge from experience. Only that is real which can be experienced. If intellectual experience is denied and only sense experience admitted, empiricism becomes sensism. Positivism, naturalism, and agnosticism are derivations of empiricism.

** Skepticism implies the denial of the existence or knowability of truth. Religious skepticism is often called agnosticism.

race that was more prudent, more contented, and infinitely happier. Descartes himself had visualized in his *Discourse on Method* that henceforth humankind would painlessly reap the fruits of the earth, that the evils and frailties of sickness and old age would disappear with the discovery of their causes, and that nature itself, once it was properly known, exploited, and dominated by man, would provide every aid that was needed for the salvation of mankind.

In the realm of religion, revelation and every supernatural, mystical, and miraculous element was eliminated, and religious dogma was subjected to the "natural light of reason" that was the common property of all men. What remained after this cleansing process was a so-called "innate" conviction of the existence of God, and a likewise "innate" consciousness of the moral law, the freedom of will, the immortality of the soul, and the dignity of human nature.

Luther's friend Melanchthon (cf. p. 331 sq.) had been the first one to outline the principles of a rationalistic theology, while Erasmus of Rotterdam (cf. p. 249 sq.) had set the first example of a rationalistic interpretation and criticism of the Scriptures. Spinoza in the seventeenth, and Kant (cf. p. 371 sqq.) in the eighteenth century continued and concluded the rationalization of religious beliefs, the latter making religion the servant of a self-sufficient (autonomous) morality.

The new religion of the rationalistic age was called "Deism." It retained the belief in a transcendent God as the "author" of nature. But while the Deists emphasized God's transcendence (His existence above the world, as its "Author"), they denied God's immanence (His existence within the world as its Sustainer). Once created, they claimed, the world is then left to follow its own intrinsic laws, without further interference by the extra-mundane God.

One of the earliest proponents of the system of natural religion was Lord Herbert of Cherbury (1581-1648), who mentioned the following five principles as bases of a rational theology: (1) there is a supreme being; (2) we owe reverence to this supreme being; (3) this reverence finds its expression in virtue and piety; (4) our trespasses must be atoned for by repentance; (5) God rewards and punishes us in accordance with His goodness and justice. Whatever else beyond these five principles is contained in any religious creed, is the result of clerical fraud or poetic fancy.

John Locke (1632-1704) advocates religious toleration and freedom of worship but wants to see atheists and Catholics deprived of these benefits, the former because they cannot swear any oath of allegiance, the latter because they themselves are intolerant. Locke admits the demonstrability of the existence of God and the possibility of God's extraordinary interference with the course of natural events. According to this philosopher the human mind is entirely passive, an "empty slate" (*tabula rasa*), upon which observations and experiences are inscribed. The term "empty slate," used in reference to the human mind, was first employed by Thomas Aquinas (cf. p. 145 sq.), who had linked it with the important concept of the "active intellect," denoting that mental spontaneity that reacts to external stimuli and draws universal ideas from particular observations (faculty of abstraction).

c) *Rationalism in Germany.* Among the first German scholars who adopted the rationalistic tenets of the French and English writers was the jurist and historiographer Samuel von Pufendorf (1632–1694). He was influenced by Thomas Hobbes and the Dutch jurist Hugo Grotius (1583–1645), who in his work "On the Law of War and Peace" (*De iure belli et pacis*) had laid the foundations of modern international law. Grotius based his concept of the "natural law" on the nature of man and that law and order which we observe in the universe. Pufendorf, who taught in the Universities of Heidelberg and Lund (Sweden), published his famous work on natural and international law (*De iure gentium et naturae*) in 1672. He considered human nature as the basis of all law, and human reason as its supreme authority. In his treatise on *The Christian Religion and its Relationship to Civic Life* (1687) he defended the absolute sovereignty of the State and called it a duty of all monarchs to provide for the happiness of their subjects, if necessary even against their will and by the use of force. The book won the admiration of the Great Elector (cf. p. 310 sq.) and gained for its author the titles of Privy Councilor and Royal Prussian Historiographer.

In the first half of the seventeenth century the great advances in mathematical studies were documented in such epochal works as John Kepler's *New Stereometry* (*Nova Stereometria,* 1615) and Cavalieri's *Geometry of Indivisibles* (*Geometria Indivisibilium,* 1635), both men introducing the notion of infinity into geometry. Transcending the limitations and the one-sided dogmatism of most of the rationalist doctrinaires, the universal genius of Gottfried Wilhelm Leibniz (1646–1716) rethought and reinterpreted the knowledge of his age in the terms of the past, the present, and the anticipated future. His synthetic mind was ever alert in discovering possibilities of unifying that which seemed to be irreparably divided and of reconciling apparently insolvable antinomies. Thus he endeavored to combine the scholastic-Aristotelian philosophy of the past with the mechanism and empiricism of his own scientific age. Against the rationalists he defended the integrity of the Christian concept of the Deity that both transcended the world and yet was essentially represented in its every part (Theism). He dreamed of a reunion of the separated religious denominations, and in his *Theodicy* (1710)* expounded in a novel way the principles of natural and supernatural theology. He tried to justify the dogma of the Trinity, the real presence of Christ in the consecrated Host (Sacrament of the Altar), and the doctrine of eternal damnation. The idea of a "perennial

---

* The term *Theodicy,* coined by Leibniz, denotes the philosophical and scientific attempt to justify the existence of God and to reconcile the divine attributes of infinite goodness, wisdom, and omnipotence with the actuality of physical and moral evil.

philosophy" (*philosophia perennis*), an expression first used by Augustinus Steuchus, librarian of the Vatican in Rome, in a book of the same title (1540), was resumed by Leibniz: he outlined the principles of a perennial philosophy that was to embrace the elements of truth contained in all the major philosophical systems of the past and present.

In his *Monadology* (1714) Leibniz developed some of the metaphysical concepts as contained in the nature philosophy of Giordano Bruno (cf. p. 275) and the Neo-Platonists of the early centuries of the Christian era. He described the world as a harmonically ordered system of "monads" — infinitely small, indivisible, and spiritual units, representing and reflecting the universe in varying and rising degrees of consciousness. God, the ab-original monad (*Urmonade*), is also the one which possesses supreme and universal consciousness, the one which has preordained the substances and activities of all the other monads in a system or cosmos of "pre-established harmony." God Himself therefore is mirrored in the various gradations of being: in mineral, plant, animal, man, and the pure spirits. In such a magnificently ordered world physical and moral evil can only serve to contribute to the greater harmony of the whole by providing contrast motifs and complementary colors. As Leibniz considers the perfection of the universe more from an aesthetic than a moral or metaphysical point of view, he is bound to arrive at the optimistic conclusion that a world in which such harmony, unity, and integrity is achieved must be the best of all possible worlds.

With his insistence on the spiritual character of the individual monads Leibniz broke the chain of purely mechanical causation and reintroduced the Aristotelian and scholastic notion of purposes and ends (final causes). His deep insight into the nature of an organically developed individuality and personality made him the intellectual ancestor of German Idealism (cf. Chap. 9) and Romanticism (cf. Chap. 14), as represented philosophically by Herder, Goethe, Schiller, Kant, Fichte, and Hegel.

In the encyclopedic catholicity of his interests Leibniz was a typical Baroque philosopher. He is, however, remembered not only as a philosopher but as a great scientist and jurist as well. He made important discoveries in the fields of mathematics and physics and lasting contributions to the disciplines of history, political economy, international law, and linguistics. One of his most cherished projects aimed at the foundation of an inter-national academy of sciences, and he finally succeeded in persuading Frederick III, the elector of Brandenburg-Prussia, to establish the Berlin Academy. Leibniz became its first president in 1700. He felt confident that science would eventually bring about an era of universal peace among the nations of the earth, and he greeted with enthusiasm the project of a league of nations that was presented to the Peace Congress of Utrecht by Abbé Saint-Pierre at the end of the Spanish War of Succession (1714).

Leibniz' correspondence extended to the most distant parts of the globe. He exchanged letters with the leading scholars in many countries, even with the Jesuit missionaries in faraway China. His acquaintance with leading statesmen and members of the nobility led to his appointment as German ambassador to the French court in 1672. As historiographer of the dukes of Brunswick Leibniz visited Vienna, Venice, Rome, Naples, Florence, Bologna, and Modena.

Among the several languages he mastered the philosopher gave preference to French, in the admiration of which he concurred with most of his contemporaries. Nevertheless he occasionally advocates the cultivation and improvement of the German language and regrets that the neglect of the national linguistic tradition has outweighed the benefits which otherwise could have accrued from the influence of French style and speech. Leibniz' own works, most of them written in French or Latin, give evidence of the almost universal scope of his interests and his knowledge, but they lack formal coherence and seem more like a monumental collection of ingenious essays than a carefully arranged system of ideas. The authentic edition of all his works that was prepared by the Berlin Academy of Sciences was nearing its completion at the outbreak of World War II.

The so-called "popular" philosophers of German Rationalism were not greatly interested in the depth of Leibniz' metaphysical speculation. What appealed to them were his optimistic views concerning this "best of all possible worlds," because this optimism seemed to substantiate their own belief in the self-sufficiency of the universe and the unlimited perfectibility of man. To Christian von Wolff (1679-1754) belongs the merit, if merit it be, to have diluted and popularized the ideas of the great philosopher so as to make them intelligible to the average reader. From 1707 on Wolff lectured on mathematics, natural science, and philosophy in the University of Halle. He was expelled by order of King Frederick William I of Prussia when the Pietists (cf. p. 364 sqq.) objected to his rationalistic views. Frederick the Great, after his accession to the throne, called him back and made him chancellor of the university. For more than a quarter of a century Wolff's philosophy dominated the philosophical faculties of the German universities, and a whole generation of thinkers acknowledged in him their teacher. For Wolff there were no mysteries in heaven and on earth: everything became perfectly clear, simple, and natural once it was exposed to the tranquil searchlight of reason.

Nature, virtue, and reason were the three main themes of Wolff's speculation. He emphasized the equality of human nature and demanded that the precepts of the moral law be equally applied to all classes. He claimed that even peasants were able to read his treatises on logic. As the "genius of mediocrity" he appealed to members of all strata of society and counted among his pupils representatives of all professions.

The fame of having become the father of the German movement of "Enlightenment" (*Aufklärung,* cf. p. 368 sq.) Wolff shares with his colleague in the University of Halle, the jurist Christian Thomasius (1655-1728). From Leipzig, where he had started his academic career and where he had met with the opposition of Lutheran theologians, he moved to Halle and became one of the most popular teachers of the recently founded local university (1694). His high esteem for the German language as a medium of scientific and literary expression he demonstrated by delivering the first university lectures in German since the days of Paracelsus (cf. p. 273). He showed himself interested in the practical application of knowledge and demanded a thoroughgoing reorganization and vitalization of pedagogy. The cause of toleration and freedom of conscience was dear to his heart, and he fought with great vigor against antiquated and inhuman concepts and procedures in criminal law, especially against the still flourishing trials for witchcraft. Individual and social ethics Thomasius referred to the supreme tribunal of "common sense," and the quintessence of morality to him is the art "to lead a happy, contented, and gallant life by means of reason and virtue."

d) Rationalism in Education. The practical trend of Rationalism was reflected in the curriculums of the schools and universities. The time-honored "humanistic" education, based on formal discipline and proficiency in the liberal arts, was considered as obsolete and foreign to life. The rationalistic teacher was to prepare the student for the practical requirements of life, providing the tools for the acquisition of technical skill by means of vocational training. The "progressive" educators of the seventeenth century demanded that the student be confronted with actual problems and situations in State and society, in art and nature, and that rules and disciplines be enlivened by practical applications, by experiment and demonstration. "Realism" became the catchword of the new philosophies of education. One of the leading "reformers" in this field was Christian Weise (1642–1708), poet, teacher, and later on principal of the *"Gymnasium"** in Zittau (Saxony). He tried to educate his charges, most of them sons of noble families, in the spirit of the new pedagogy and to indoctrinate them with the new ideas.

In August Hermann Francke's (cf. p. 365) *Paedagogium* in Halle the chief emphasis in the curriculum was placed on natural science, mathematics, geography, and history, although, in accordance with Francke's pietistic convictions, all these subjects had their core and living source in religious instruction. The students were taught specific trades and on frequent visits to workshops they learned by observation as well as by practical application. A "Teachers' Seminary" (*Seminarium Praeceptorum*) in Halle was dedicated to the task of teacher training. By introducing his new methods of instruction into his orphanage and his school for poor children, Francke influenced the future development of the public school system in Germany. Public instruction on the grammar and high school level had for some time been in the hands of the Piarist Order, founded in 1597 by St. Joseph

---

* The *Gymnasium* is the earliest type of the German high school and may best be described as an equivalent of a liberal arts college that includes the lower high school grades (nine grades in all). It is distinguished from the later types of the *Realschule* and *Realgymnasium* by its strictly "humanistic" curriculum, embracing the liberal arts and the classical languages.

of Calasanza, a Spanish priest, and of the Congregation of the "Institute of Mary" (*Englische Fräulein*), founded by Mary Ward (1585-1645), an English nun. The members of these two religious orders conducted separate schools for boys and girls.

The opposition to this new progressive "realism" in education was strongest in the universities, which in many instances had become purely antiquarian in their interests and pursuits. In the course of the seventeenth century their vitality had suffered to such a degree that Leibniz proposed to let them die a natural death. Their scholarship was not merely out of tune with contemporary life and its pressing problems, but their blind allegiance to defunct authorities made them oblivious to the progress of science and rendered them incapable of independent research. About the turn of the century a gradual infiltration of the new ideas becomes noticeable. The University of Halle must be considered as the first German institution of higher learning in which the spirit of the modern age triumphantly celebrated its conquest of the past. It was at Halle that the principle of the freedom of teaching was solemnly proclaimed in 1711, when its *Rector* (president), Nicholas Gundling, in a speech delivered in honor of the first king of Prussia, praised the independence of scientific research. He called the university "the vestibule of liberty" and demanded that it lead its students fearlessly to truth and wisdom. He insisted that only free minds and free men would be capable of assuming such leadership as was needed in a university, and that by virtue of the demands of the natural law no man had the right to infringe upon another's freedom of conscience and conviction: "All compulsion in these matters is evil. . . . Teach, exhort, pray! If they listen, it is well; if they don't listen, learn to bear it. Truth rises before us: let him who can, ascend; let him who dares, take hold of her; and we will applaud" (*Veritas adhuc: qui potest ascendat; qui audet, rapiat et aplaudemus*).

e) Methods of Adult Education. In their endeavor to spread the new ideas and to raise the general standard of culture by means of increased knowledge and literacy, the leaders of the rationalistic movement addressed themselves to the general reading public in the new "moral weeklies," which made their first appearance early in the eighteenth century in England and were soon adopted and imitated in Germany. The weekly periodical was an offshoot of the pamphlets and newssheets which originated at the end of the fifteenth century. The first natural agents for the distribution of written and printed news were the postmasters, and in the beginning (*c.* 1500) it was the prevailing custom to add a special newssheet to one's letters. Basel, Strasbourg, Cologne, and Augsburg were among the earliest circulation centers of printed news pamphlets. In many instances the postmasters themselves were the compilers and editors of the news, but frequently princes and wealthy merchants had their own news correspondents who were stationed at the important centers of political and commercial activity.

The first regular weekly journal dates from the year 1609 and was edited in Strasbourg, while the first daily newspaper was published in Leipzig in 1660. The first home of the didactic and moralizing weeklies, however, is England. There the new type of family periodical appeared, designed to raise the intellectual and moral standards of the middle class and to influence individual and social life by means of criticism, satire, and moral instruction and edification. The most popular of the English moral weeklies were Sir Richard Steele's and Joseph Addison's *Tatler* (1707–1711), *Spectator* (1711–1712), and *Guardian* (1713). The most skillful of their German imitators were Johann Jacob Bodmer (*Discourses of Painters,* 1721–1723) and Johann C. Gottsched (*Vernünftige Tadlerinnen,* 1725–1727). More than five hundred different moral weeklies were published in Germany between 1713 and 1800. They represented an effective and novel form of adult education and were more influential than either book or sermon in the formation of public opinion and a general philosophy of life.

f) Social Divisions and Social Conventions. Although the Age of Absolutism and Rationalism had exalted the ruling prince beyond the pale of ordinary mortals, the social divisions among the different classes of subjects endured practically unabated. Peasants, burghers, and nobles, merchants and craftsmen, the learned and the unlettered were living their lives in accordance with definite social patterns, and the members of the upper classes attempted to meet the growing pressure of the less privileged by the erection of artificial barriers of etiquette and convention. The strict observation of all proprieties as to rank and title was the essential prerequisite of well-mannered social intercourse, and any infraction or neglect of one of the rules that referred to questions of precedence in rank was considered an unpardonable social crime.

The self-respecting carpenter, cobbler, tailor, baker, and confectioner, for all his strongly marked class consciousness, would proudly display on the signboard of his store or shop the coat of arms of the ruling princely house, if he was fortunate enough to count the court among his clients. He usually paid dearly for the privilege of calling himself *Königlicher Hofbäcker, Hofkonditor, Hofschneider* (royal court baker, court confectioner, court tailor). These titles often remained with the families and the business establishments of their bearers right down to the fall of the German monarchies in 1918.

Social rank and the powers and luxuries that it implied were considered as the most worthy goals of human endeavor, worthy enough indeed to justify the most abject kind of adulation and the sacrifice of honesty and character. It was the supreme ambition of the wealthy merchant to obtain a patent of nobility and thus climb one step higher on the social ladder. But even if this dream of a lifetime did not come true, he at least imitated the life of the nobility by the erection of palacelike and luxuriously furnished dwellings, by surrounding himself with numerous servants, and by an almost uninterrupted chain of social events, musical and theatrical entertainments, ballets, balls, and other festivities.

Although the absolutistic State had deprived the members of the nobility themselves of their ancient political prerogatives and privileges, they had been compensated by an even greater social prestige and by a definite consolidation of their economic and financial status. The pitiful position of the peasants made the tillers of the soil the prey of greedy nobles, and many of the huge lordly estates, especially in the German East, owe their origin to the exploitation and expropriation of a helpless peasantry.

g) *The Education of the "Cavalier."* The typical nobleman, however, felt truly at home only in the service of the court. As official members of the princely household the nobles occupied the positions of masters of ceremony, equerries (*Stallmeister*), chamberlains (*Kammerdiener*), chancellors, councilors (*Räte*), ambassadors, and army officers. The training of the future courtier or "cavalier" was entrusted to special "Knightly Academies" (*Ritterakademien*): boarding schools for young noblemen, the earliest of which were founded about the middle of the seventeenth century. The sons of Catholic nobles were frequently educated in the schools of the Jesuits.

Among the subjects to be mastered by the young nobleman a thorough knowledge of French and Latin seemed to be indispensable; the former on account of its cultural and literary values, the latter because it was the language of scholars and diplomats. The study of German and other modern languages was considered as desirable but received less emphasis. Poetry was esteemed as a potent means of adulation: to express one's homage and admiration in verse could hardly fail to impress the prince and gain his favorable response.

A person of noble rank was expected to be familiar with the latest developments in natural science and mathematics, with military science, and especially with the arts of fortification and shipbuilding. The study of history was recommended as "one of the most precious adornments of a titled person and, next to political science and common law, the most gallant part of his erudition."* Geography and the related disciplines of chronology, genealogy, and heraldry were highly praised because "without them it is impossible to understand history, to interpret intelligently the news, and to discuss rationally the problems of the modern state."** Most important, however, was a thorough familiarity with the science of politics and a complete mastery of the rules of political prudence.

Physical education and some training in the fine arts were to make the courtier alert and wide awake, socially fit in body and mind, adding to his appearance and behavior an external gloss and polish of physical and intellectual culture. The education of the young German nobleman was given its final touch by extended travel experience in foreign countries, preferably in Holland, England, France, and Italy.

Pietism. Medieval philosophy and theology had united rational and

---

* Dietrich Hermann Kemmerich: *Newly Opened Academy of Sciences,* etc. (1711).
** *Ibid.*

preterrational elements in a system of thought that harmoniously joined together scholasticism and mysticism (cf. p. 141 sqq.). But Luther and Melanchthon, in order to safeguard the edifice of their church, had eventually to eliminate all mystical religious impulses, and thus rationalism finally prevailed in theology as in other fields. In the centuries that followed the Reformation a growing number of individuals, unable to find an outlet for their thwarted emotional life in the rigid forms of orthodox dogmatism, began to segregate and separate themselves from the official churches and to form small groups, sects, and conventicles, in which they tried to satisfy their spiritual yearnings. In the seventeenth century, these timid beginnings converged in the movement which has been named Pietism.

In 1650 the former Jesuit priest Jean Labadie (1610–1674) had joined the Reformed Church in the Netherlands and had gathered a large following with his demand for a religious rebirth under the direct guidance and inspiration of the Holy Spirit. Influenced by Labadie's ideas, Philip Jacob Spener (1635–1705), a native Alsatian, drew up an ecclesiastical reform program (*Pia desideria*, 1675) which formed the basis of the pietistic revival movement. In the prayer meetings which he conducted in private homes and in churches (*Collegia Pietatis*) he preached a practical Christianity, a religion that was to penetrate into the innermost essence of human nature, a faith which was to document itself in works of mercy and charity. Following Spener's example, August Hermann Francke (1663–1727) opened his *"Collegia Biblica"* in Leipzig in 1686; they met with such enthusiastic response on the part of the students of the local university and the population of the city that the orthodox theologians, thoroughly alarmed, began to realize the threatening danger and succeeded in having the meetings prohibited by the civil authorities.

These disturbances in Leipzig, followed by similar ones in Hamburg, were the signal for the release of all the antiorthodox resentment that had been brewing among the laity of the Protestant churches. In this second and decisive stage of its development Pietism grew into a popular movement of large dimensions. The revolt of the laity, centering in the middle class (the *Third Estate*), issued in the first major onslaught against the absolute supremacy of the State and its ally, the Church. Religious "storm and stress" mingled with the manifestations of social and political dissatisfaction, and the revolt against the complacency of hidebound clericalism and secular despotism spread with amazing speed to various parts of Germany. Thus Pietism had reached its third stage. Enthusiastic sects and secret societies made their appearance, ancient and seemingly forgotten doctrines were revived, and all the many voices were passionately united in their outcry for the arrival of the Millennium.

On the surface Pietism showed itself violently opposed to Rationalism. It stressed personal experience, subjective feeling, the values of the inner life. But both Pietism and Rationalism were convinced that the nature of the Divinity could be comprehended empirically: the Pietist claimed that

God could be physically experienced in feeling and imagination; the Rationalist maintained that God could be known conceptually and intellectually. The one drew the Godhead into the individual heart; to the other the Deity became almost evanescent in the realm of impersonal abstraction. Pietists and Rationalists replaced a harmonious balance between emotion, will, and intellect by an exaggerated emphasis upon one of these faculties to the exclusion of the others. Pietism and Rationalism have in common the opposition to the orthodox churches and all forms of State religion; they both accentuate the ethical implications of religious doctrine, and they both believe in the testimony of the "inner light," to which the Rationalists refer as the "natural light of reason."

The ideal goal of the religious cravings of the Pietists was the rebirth of the human soul in Christ. To achieve this end they elaborated a richly graded scale of sensory and imaginative experiences, starting with the fearful sensation of sinful entanglements in a corrupt world, then gradually proceeding to a state of penitence and utter humiliation, and finally culminating in the hoped-for bliss of "conversion." Such an experience called for outward confessional manifestations, and thus the Pietists discovered in human emotions a creative force that softened the arid intellectualism of the age and made German thought and culture more sensitive to the beat of the human heart.

The deep religious feeling of the Pietists created for itself new forms of stylistic and linguistic expression which came to their fruition in the poetry of Klopstock (cf. p. 393 sq.). The elemental passion of the poets of the period of "Storm and Stress" was anticipated by Gottfried Arnold, whose *Unparteiische Kirchen- und Ketzerhistorie* (unpartisan history of churches and heretics) is mentioned with high praise in Goethe's *Dichtung und Wahrheit* (*Poetry and Truth*). It was the first work that applied the psychological method to Church history.

Arnold experienced his "revival" under Spener's guidance, and under Spener's influence he began to oppose the theology of his time. The complex world of his thought, the oscillating ways of his life, and the amazing intellectual range of his works mirror the most significant tendencies of the age. Religious "storm and stress" animates his vehement attacks against the conventional codes and rules of the compact majority in State and Church. He turns away from the disheartening actualities of the present and visualizes in sentimental yearning the fulfillment of his ideals in the times of the Apostles and the Fathers of the early Church. As a scholar, he had received a comprehensive scholastic and humanistic training, and the humanistic concepts of historical evolution are clearly noticeable in his historical works. He resigned as a member of the faculty of the University of Giessen because of the "insipid gossip, the ludicrous arrogance, hypocrisy, and false gravity of the universities."

Like the other Pietists, Arnold believed himself an instrument of the Godhead and wanted to see his poetry printed and published for the sake of the education and edification of others. According to him, genuine poetry has to serve the ultimate goal of life and it has to derive its inspiration from the eternal source of life. Spiritual revival he considered an absolute prerequisite for the poet. Again the humanistic conception of science as a *"magistra vitae"* (guide of life), the humanistic conception of poetry as an "agreeable instruction" suggests a close relationship between Arnold's and the Humanist's point of view. In its striving for a unified and integrated Christian humanism Arnold's "pietism" is clearly distinguished from Luther's piety, which insisted on the actuality and the full preservation of the abysmal dualism between God and the world.

The social incentives of the pietistic movement were realized in Francke's schools and orphanages in Halle and in Count Ludwig von Zinzendorf's (1700–1760) foundation of the "Union of Moravian Brethren" (*Brüdergemeinde*) at Herrnhut in Saxony. The original members of Zinzendorf's religious community were descendants of those Hussites (cf. p. 176 sq.) who had fought against the imperial armies to preserve their religious and national independence. At the beginning of the sixteenth century their sect numbered well over 100,000 followers. Several persecutions, however, as well as a relaxation of their original asceticism led to their gradual disintegration. Many of them migrated to Prussia and Poland, but those who remained became, later on, the nucleus of Zinzendorf's Herrnhut foundation.

The beginnings of German immigration in the United States of America are closely linked with the pietistic movement and its policy of establishing foreign missions overseas. The first German colony in North America (Pennsylvania) was founded by groups of Mennonites (cf. p. 242) from southern Germany under the leadership of Daniel Pastorius (1651–1719), who landed in Philadelphia in 1683. Pastorius was one of Spener's disciples, and the settlers whom he had brought to the New World were the first to raise their voices in protest against the abuses of slavery. Members of Zinzendorf's community journeyed as missionaries to St. Thomas in the West Indies, while others joined their coreligionists in Pennsylvania. Zinzendorf himself paid several visits to their flourishing settlements.

The cultural fruits of Pietism are manifold but are most evident in religious poetry, in the sentimental and autobiographical novel, in the art of letter writing, and in music. With its urge for soul-searching self-analysis, for a heavily charged emotionalism and personalism, Pietism represented a potent element in the formation of the new concepts of personality that inspired the classical writers and thinkers of Germany in the eighteenth and nineteenth centuries. Even the limitations imposed upon the members of the pietistic sects by a certain narrow provincialism and a puritanical denunciation of all worldly concerns could not prevent their movement in the long run from acting as a humanizing force, working for a more irenic and tolerant religious attitude, and from thus meeting halfway the prevalent currents of the age of enlightenment. Many of the leaders of German thought and culture in the following two centuries grew up in the shadow and shelter of this pietistic heritage, acknowledging their debt to a form of spirituality that illumined with its kindly light the years of their intellectual and moral formation (Lavater, Goethe, Jacobi, Schleiermacher, Novalis, Gerhart Hauptmann, etc.).

Enlightenment ("Aufklärung"). From the later Middle Ages and the Reformation to the period of princely absolutism and enlightened despotism the ancient authority of the Christian Church had steadily declined. The culture of the Rococo revealed the shaky foundations of a society whose members were still clinging to certain external forms of the past but had lost contact with all the vital meaning of the spiritual tradition of Western civilization. From the end of the seventeenth to the end of the eighteenth century the social and cultural life of Europe was presenting a splendid façade that carefully covered the symptoms of decay, but at the same time revealed a glittering unrest and a lack of stability and self-assurance that bespoke an uneasy conscience and a growing anxiety as to the final outcome of a dissipated and wasteful existence. When the life of European aristocracy had dissolved into an endless series of love affairs, scandals, festivities, and games, the time seemed to have arrived for the healthier members of the social organism to call for retribution and to restore poise and balance by a process of revolution and rejuvenation.

The production of Pierre Beaumarchais' (1732–1799) *Marriage of Figaro,* an excoriating satire on the decadent nobility, at the Théâtre Français in Paris in 1784, was an event that symbolized the approaching end of *"la folle journée"* (the mad journey).

a) The Origins of Enlightenment. The first and most effective broadside attack against the established authorities of the past came from the "republic of letters," the representative thinkers of the eighteenth century. The symptoms of cultural decline were not confined to any one country and, accordingly, the voices of social criticism were simultaneously heard in every part of Europe. But France, which for a long time had politically and culturally dominated the European scene, and where the disintegration of the monarchy and nobility was most marked, became the center of the revolutionary criticism of the *"philosophes."* The thirty-five volumes of the *Encyclopédie ou dictionnaire raisonné des sciences, des arts et des métiers* (*Encyclopedia,* or *Rational Dictionary of the Sciences, Arts, and Trades,* 1751–1780) became the great collective manifestation of revolutionary thought, wherein the criteria of modern individualism, rationalism, and mechanism were systematically applied to the fields of religion, philosophy, literature, science, and sociology. The editors were Denis Diderot (1713–1784) and Jean D'Alembert (1717–1783), and among the contributors were such illustrious thinkers as Voltaire, Turgot, and Montesquieu. The corruptness of the supposedly Christian civilization of Europe was here for the first time contrasted with the assumed superiority of the "noble savage" and the humane wisdom of Oriental thought. The leader in the attack against official Christianity, against intolerance and bigotry, was François Marie Arouet, better known by his pen name of Voltaire (1694-1778), who in the ninety volumes of his collected works subjected every department of human endeavor to his scathing criticism and who, with his "Essay on the Customs and the Spirit of the Nations," created a new type of critical historiography and cultural history (*Kulturgeschichte*). As the final goal of the human race he visualized an age of enlightened humanism, based on social responsibility and a natural and rational religion.

b) German Enlightenment. In Germany the new ideas met with warm response, but their radicalism was tempered by a certain reverence for traditional values and a more or less academic adherence to the principles of the French thinkers. For Kant (cf. p. 371 sqq.) enlightenment meant "emancipation from an immaturity that man had brought upon himself through his own fault." That immaturity he defined as "the incapability of using one's reason without external guidance. . . . You must be courageous enough," he said, "to make use of your own faculty of reasoning: that is the true motto of enlightenment."

The city of Berlin, where Frederick the Great had encouraged the propagation of the ideas of the French Encyclopedists, became the center and bulwark of German Enlightenment. The most distinguished representative of enlightened thought was Friedrich Nicolai (1733-1811), a Berlin book dealer, whose ideal of a philosopher was Christian Wolff (cf. p. 360), and who in his novels, satires, travel books, and philosophical essays exhibited a narrow, shallow, and intolerant rationalism. Though he was in contact with practically all the illustrious thinkers of the age, he antagonized most of them by his malicious and destructive criticism. In Schiller's and Goethe's epigrams (*Xenien*) of the year 1797 Nicolai is ridiculed as an empty-headed and coarse fellow, and in Goethe's *Faust* he appears as "Proctophantasmist" amidst the spirits, witches, and devils of the "Walpurgisnacht," among a motley crowd of creatures whom his enlightened zeal had all too sweepingly explained away.

Among Nicolai's collaborators, later on known as the "Nicolaites," the most capable was the Jewish popular philosopher Moses Mendelssohn (1729-1786), Lessing's (cf. p. 380 sqq.) friend, a representative of enlightened Deism (cf. p. 356 sq.), a man of the highest intellectual and moral caliber, an untiring worker for the advancement of the human race, and an eloquent advocate of religious toleration. In his aesthetic views he influenced Schiller and Kant, and his speculation on the sensitive faculty contributed to the increasing psychological knowledge of the age. The leading character in Lessing's drama *Nathan the Wise* bears the features of Moses Mendelssohn.

Many of the views of the enlightened German thinkers were transmitted to the reading public through several newly founded periodicals, taking the place of the "moral weeklies" (cf. p. 363), which had fallen into growing disrepute. Nicolai himself edited the "Library of Belles Lettres and the Liberal Arts" (*Bibliothek der schönen Wissenschaften und der freien*

Künste, 1757), the "Letters Concerning the Most Recent Literature" (*Briefe, die neueste Literatur betreffend*, 1759), and the "General German Library" (*Allgemeine deutsche Bibliothek*, 1766). These periodicals, to which Nicolai, Mendelssohn, Lessing, and other authors contributed, tried to review critically the more recent publications in Germany and to spread general information regarding literary affairs. The most influential and long lived of the three journals was the *Allgemeine deutsche Bibliothek*, whose publication ceased in 1806, and which during these four decades molded to a large extent the standards of literary taste and critical judgment.

c) Secret Societies. The principles of enlightened thought were adopted and promoted by a number of secret societies, the most important of which was the institution of Freemasonry, founded at the beginning of the eighteenth century. The first masonic "Grand Lodge" was constituted in England in 1717. The *Book of Constitution* of the year 1723 stated as the purpose of the society the construction of the Grand Temple of Humanity, the education of an enlightened and united mankind that had freed itself from superstition and from the restrictions imposed by religious, political, and social dogmas, parties, and authorities. The individual members were to strive for personal ennoblement and the harmonious integration of their characters, on the basis of humanitarianism and religious toleration. Strict secrecy surrounded the complex organization of the society, whose elaborate symbolic rituals were in part derived from the medieval masonic guilds. The initiation proceeded by degrees from the stage of apprentice to that of journeyman and master.

The masonic movement rapidly gained a large following in all European countries. It was introduced in France and Ireland in 1725, in Scotland, Spain, Portugal, Italy, and North America during the following decade. The leaders of the American and French revolutions, Washington and Franklin as well as Mirabeau and Robespierre, were freemasons.

The first German Grand Lodge was established in Hamburg in 1737. German Freemasonry retained the belief in God and immortality and appropriated the spirit of German classical literature and philosophy, while in the Romanic countries the lodges adopted the atheistic and materialistic outlook of the Revolution of 1789. The antiecclesiastical character of Freemasonry was especially pronounced in Spain, Portugal, France, and Italy. In the latter country the lodge played a leading part in the nineteenth century in bringing about the destruction of the secular power of the papacy, the annexation of the Papal States by Italy, the secularization of education, and the national unification of the country. The Catholic Church has placed membership in the lodge under the penalty of excommunication (Decree of Clement XII of 1738 and canon 2335 of Canon Law, 1918), and the Fascist and National-Socialist governments of Italy and Germany suppressed the masonic lodges in their countries as incompatible with the interests of the national State.

In the eighteenth century most of the political and intellectual leaders of

Germany were admitted to membership in the lodge (Frederick the Great, Nicolai, Klopstock, Wieland, Herder, Goethe, Fichte, Mozart, Haydn, etc.), and in the nineteenth century members of the Hohenzollern dynasty and most representatives of Prussian officialdom were freemasons. Lessing, in his *Discourses for Freemasons* (*Gespräche für Freimaurer*), praised the ideals of Freemasonry as being in harmony with the spirit of enlightenment and true Humanism.

An interesting offshoot of Freemasonry was the "Order of Illuminati" (the Enlightened Ones), founded by Adam Weishaupt (1748–1830), formerly professor of Canon Law in the University of Ingolstadt in Bavaria. Aims, ideals, and organization resembled closely those of the masonic lodges, but the antiauthoritarian tendency was more conspicuous. The Order was suppressed in Bavaria in 1784 but experienced a short-lived revival at the end of the nineteenth century (1896–1933).

d) Critical Philosophy: Kant. The eighteenth century had produced a number of popular philosophers who, like Christian Wolff (cf. p. 360), had made philosophy accessible to the average man and woman, while at the same time depriving it of much of its former earnestness and depth. The limitations of the philosophical foundations of the age of enlightenment were realized by no one more keenly than by Immanuel Kant (1724–1804) who, himself deeply rooted in rationalistic thought, nevertheless succeeded in overcoming the narrowness of its dogmatism.

A native of Königsberg in East Prussia, Kant had attended the local university and accepted the main tenets of the widely acclaimed rationalistic systems of Leibniz and Wolff. He had made his own the scientific and mechanical explanation of nature as presented by Isaac Newton and had heartily approved of Descartes's saying: "Give me matter, and I shall construct a world." Kant's ideas on the origin of the planetary system from chaotic gaseous nebulae, as he laid them down in his "General Natural History and Theory of the Heavens" (1755), were later on resumed by the French astronomer and mathematician, Pierre Laplace (1748–1827), and formulated in the "Kant-Laplace Theory." But Kant was convinced that it was impossible to apply the mechanical explanation of nature to organic life, and he was unwilling to relinquish certain religious premises that had been implanted in his mind by the pietistic influences of his youth and that had been restated in Rousseau's (cf. p. 376) striking phrase: "Gravitation effects in the corporeal world what love creates in the world of the spirit."

Faced by the alternative of an all-embracing rationalism which left no avenue open to spiritual realities, and an integral empiricism which had ended in Hume's skeptical denial of the possibility of objective knowledge, Kant felt the necessity of transcending the limited viewpoint of either of these extreme positions and of combining their partial truths in a new philosophical synthesis.

It was the influence of Hume's philosophy that awoke Kant from his "dogmatic slumber" by shaking his naïve confidence in the absolute reliability of human reason. From now on, the all-important question in his mind concerned the possibility and validity of human knowledge.

In the same year in which he received an appointment as professor of logic and metaphysics in the University of Königsberg (1770), Kant published his epochal masterpiece, *The Critique of Pure Reason*. The author himself likened the significance of this work to the revolutionary discovery of Copernicus: as Copernicus had demonstrated the illusory nature of the seeming revolution of the firmament around the earth, so Kant attempted to prove that human thought was not formed and determined by extramental objects but that the objects in the extramental world depended in their meaning and rational significance on the organization of the human mind. Things as they are in themselves (*"das Ding an sich"*) are inaccessible to human reason. They are only knowable as they appear to us (as *"phenomena"*), not as they actually exist outside the human mind (as *"noumena"*). Objective experience is molded into sensitive intuitions by the *a priori* (innate) forms of sensibility, space and time. The understanding (*Vernunft*) in turn molds these intuitions into objects of knowledge, by means of the main categories of quality, quantity, relation, and modality. Thus the synthetic action of the understanding imparts meaning and coherence to the otherwise unrelated and unconnected series of our perceptions. Extension and duration, therefore, being mere modifications of time and space, are purely subjective, and a "science of being" (ontology, metaphysics) becomes an absolute impossibility.

It was, however, just such metaphysical speculation that had been used by the rationalist philosophers (Descartes, Spinoza, Leibniz, etc.) as well as by the scholastics (cf. p. 141 sqq.) to prove the existence of God, the immortality of the soul, and the freedom of will. And Kant, too, had expressly stated that the primary concern of his speculation was the vindication of the religious claims of the past. It was his intention "to dethrone knowledge in order to make room for faith." How did Kant achieve his aim, and how was he able to combine the pretended subjectivity of all human knowledge with the validity of absolute and necessary norms and laws?

The answer is given in the *Metaphysics of Morals* (1785) and *The Critique of Practical Reason* (1788). In these two works Kant withdraws faith and religion from the sphere of pure reason and places them under the absolute dominion of the "moral law." Both Luther and Leibniz had been in search of objective norms, which were not to be imposed authoritatively from without but were to issue from the innermost essence of the individual. For Kant the realm of human freedom becomes the ground where individual independence (autonomy) and objective necessity meet. For him nothing is as indubitable as "the starry firmament above me and the moral law within me."

The "moral law" confronts man in the form of the "categorical imperative," which exhorts him to act in such a way that the principles of his actions may at any time be applicable to all mankind; to choose such maxims as may be made the bases of a universal law and rule. According to Kant, the freedom of will, the immortality of the soul, and the existence of God are truths that are inherent in the constitution and inclination of the moral nature of man. They cannot be demonstrated by pure reason, but they can and must be "postulated" by "practical reason" if human life is not to be voided of any and all meaning.

If the innate and imperative character of the moral law is admitted, man must also have the power to live up to its demands, i.e., he must have free will. But life on this earth is much too short to allow for the perfect fulfillment of the demands of the categorical imperative: therefore practical reason postulates the immortality of the soul. Furthermore, every human being longs for lasting happiness, and yet even the most perfect obedience to the moral law does not yield that result: there must be a power therefore that fulfills man's desire for eternal happiness, and this power we call God. Finally, the moral law demands justice and retribution, and we know from experience that this demand is frequently not satisfied in this earthly life. Practical reason, therefore, postulates the dispensation of perfect justice by the omniscient and omnipotent God in a life beyond.

In his emphasis on the power of human will as well as in the aesthetic speculation of his *Critique of Judgment* (1790) Kant had given a fuller and truer description of human nature than was current in the age of enlightenment. He had recognized the relative significance of the faculties of thinking, feeling, and willing as against the prevailing one-sided intellectualism. In his religious speculation, on the other hand, he agrees with the other spokesmen of the age in defining a good and noble life as the supreme form of worship. His "autonomous" ethics demands that the moral law be obeyed for its own sake, regardless of eternal reward or punishment and without the aid of dogmas, prayers, and cultic observances. While the philosopher thus upholds with the enlightened thinkers the emancipation of man from the authorities of the past, he does not share their optimistic view of human nature. In the treatise *Religion within the Boundaries of Pure Reason* (1793) he develops an ethical rigorism which insists that the inherent evil in human nature be overcome by a stern sense of duty and by the firm exercise of will power. He goes so far as to maintain that natural inclination and the moral law are contradictory, and that therefore a human action can only be termed moral if it is performed in opposition to the urges of our sensitive nature. Schiller (cf. p. 417 sqq.) who in other respects adopted Kant's moral philosophy, satirized his ethical rigorism in a pointed epigram,* while at the same time trying to overcome it by a process of

---

* *Scruple of Conscience*
  Willingly serve I my friends; but, alas, I do it with pleasure;
  Therefore I often am vexed, that no true virtue I have.
Solution
  As there is no other means, thou hadst better begin to despise them;
  And with aversion, then, do that which duty commands.
                              (Tr. by E. A. Bowring; Belford Clarke & Co., New York.)

education which culminated in the harmonization of natural inclination and the moral law.

Kant saw the meaning of history in the growing realization of moral freedom, eventually leading to the establishment of eternal peace among the nations of the earth (*On Eternal Peace,* 1795). In his personal life the philosopher embodied the very principles of his teaching and thinking, and his sincerity, simplicity, modesty, and moral earnestness made him one of the most admired and influential intellectual leaders of modern times.

e) Enlightened Theology. The movement of enlightenment in Germany tended toward antireligious radicalism only in a few instances. The majority of its representatives were neither atheists nor agnostics. One of the most revolutionary manifestoes of theological criticism was the so-called *Wolfenbüttel-Fragmente,* originally composed by the Hamburg orientalist and theologian, Samuel Reimarus (1694–1768), and later on published by Lessing (cf. p. 380 sqq.) without mentioning the name of the author (1774–1778). These "Fragments" represented part of Reimarus' more comprehensive "Apology for Reasonable Worshippers of God," wherein he attempted to prove the fraudulent character of the New Testament, claiming that the real teaching of Christ was in complete harmony with an enlightened and rational theology. Lessing in an explanatory note made several reservations as to his own critical point of view and insisted that it was the main purpose of his edition to stir up a theological controversy and to demonstrate Christianity as a living spiritual force: "The letter is not the spirit, and the Bible is not identical with religion. . . . There was religion before there was a Bible. Christianity existed before the Apostles and Evangelists wrote. Our religion is not true because the Apostles and Evangelists taught it: they rather taught it because it is true. . . . All the written documents cannot impart to it an inner truth if it has none."

Lessing's own views on the nature of Christianity are contained in an essay entitled "The Education of the Human Race" that was published in 1780, one year before his death. Here the great world religions — Paganism, Judaism, and Christianity — represent successive grades in an educational curriculum, arranged by God, the great schoolmaster. In each grade the presentation of the subject matter is adapted to the mental capacity of the learners. In the childhood stage of mankind (Paganism and Judaism) God had to reveal His will and guide His charges by means of visible and tangible signs, by promises of reward and punishment, while in the stage of adolescence He used the symbolism of the Christian dogmas to lead man's thoughts and endeavors to a higher spiritual plane. But the stage of maturity will be reached in the not-too-distant future, when men will no longer look out for rewards and no longer stand in need of punitive restrictions and coercive dogmas but will practice virtue for its own sake: "The time of a new and eternal Gospel will certainly arrive. Continue on your inconspicuous path, eternal providence!"

These views of Lessing's as much as those of Kant's may serve to illustrate how far the leading minds of the eighteenth century were removed from the comfortable complacency of the popular spokesmen of enlightenment, for whom their own age represented the apex of all that was true, good, and beautiful.

The friends of enlightened thought gradually gained hold of the highest positions in Protestant church administration and began to dominate the theological faculties in the Protestant universities. Being theological rationalists, most of them were opposed to Luther's doctrine of "salvation by faith alone" (*sola fide*), for which they substituted their own idea of "salvation by reason alone" (*sola ratione*). Others followed Luther in drawing a strict dividing line between faith and reason, eliminating every element of rationality from the religious sphere (*Fideism*).

In the Catholic territories of Germany the princes were the most powerful friends and protectors of enlightened thought. Empress Maria Theresa (cf. p. 313 sq.) as well as her son, Emperor Joseph II (cf. p. 320), promoted the ideas of enlightenment as a means of strengthening the foundations of the absolutistic State and of extending its supremacy over the Church. Pope Pius VI, on a special journey to Vienna, fruitlessly attempted to dissuade the emperor from carrying his ecclesiastical reform measures too far. All episcopal seminaries and monastic schools were closed by imperial decree, all contemplative religious orders were suspended and their property confiscated. The proceeds from the sale of the monastic estates were used for the establishment of new parishes and for the support of orphanages, hospitals, and poorhouses. The number of Church holidays was reduced and pilgrimages and processions were prohibited. The liturgy and the divine services were simplified and stripped of all external display.

The ideas of the enlightened age penetrated into Catholic schools and seminaries, into monasteries, convents, and parish houses. Nicholas of Hontheim, auxiliary bishop of Treves (1701–1790), published under the pen name of Justinus Febronius a widely read book on the papacy (*De statu ecclesiae*, 1763) in which he advocated the Conciliar Theory of the later Middle Ages (cf. p. 173 sq.), demanding that the papacy be divested of its absolute teaching and governing power over the clergy and laity.

The idea of a general secularization of ecclesiastical possessions was first conceived in Prussia in 1795. The plan was heartily seconded in the following year by the provincial administrations of Wurtemberg and Baden and received the approval of Emperor Francis II in 1797. The methods of procedure were discussed by the German princes with Talleyrand (1754–1838), formerly bishop of Autun, and at that time one of the chief councilors of Napoleon. The secularization was legally confirmed in the "Principal Decree of the Imperial Deputation" of 1803 (cf. p. 325). This decree of secularization cost the Catholic Church in Germany 1719 square miles of landed property with a population of three and one-half million and an annual revenue of about twenty-two million taler (approximately 66 million Reichsmarks or 17 million dollars).

The spirit of enlightenment was clearly in evidence in the increasing religious toleration between Catholics and Protestants and in several renewed attempts at effecting a reconciliation and reunion of the separated Christian denominations. In Prussia these irenic and ecumenic tendencies resulted in the unification of the Lutheran and Reformed churches in 1817, the year of the third centenary of the Lutheran Reformation. Other German lands imitated Prussia's example in the following decade.

After the death of Frederick the Great the Prussian government relinquished its benevolent protectorship of religious enlightenment. A decree of Frederick William II of the year 1788 threatened punitive action against the unorthodox Protestant clergy, and a royal order in Council of 1791 contained the following: "I can and shall never tolerate that the common people be drawn away from the old and true Christian religion by false doctrines or that writings which try to further such ends be printed in my country."

f) State and Society: Rousseau. The age of enlightenment designated the sovereignty of the people as the supreme norm of the State and its individual members. According to Rousseau (1712–1778), the body politic constitutes a distinct moral person that comes into existence by "the total alienation" of individual rights to the whole community. This is the political and social philosophy that Rousseau advocated in *The Social Contract* (1762), maintaining that lawful government derives its authority from the consent of the governed.

The idea of the sovereignty of the people had been advanced long before Rousseau: Aristotle had defined a citizen as one who shares in governing and in being governed (Pol. I, 12, and II, 2). He had taught that all citizens have in principle a claim to civil power, but that the exceptional individual ought to be made king by the choice of the freemen who constitute the State. Augustine and Thomas Aquinas had defined society as "a multitude, united by juridical consent (*iuris consensu*) and a community of interest" (*Summa Theologica*, 2–2, q. 42, a. 2), and the latter had placed the legislative power in the people or their vice-regent (*Summa Theologica*, 1–2, q. 90, a. 3). The Dominican and Jesuit scholars from the middle of the sixteenth century to Suarez (cf. p. 304 sq.) in the seventeenth century had taught that civil sovereignty is received from God by the people, who in turn entrust it to their rulers by constitutional consent.

Rousseau acknowledged his indebtedness to John Locke (cf. p. 356 sq.) who a century earlier, in his *Second Treatise on Civil Government,* had taught that civil society is juridically established by a covenant of the people, that the law of nature obligates them to observe this contract, and that sovereignty is limited in its power by this social covenant. The innovation in Rousseau's theory of the sovereignty of the people consists in his abandonment of the immutable bases of the natural law, so that the social contract is apt to become an arbitrary rule of the collective sentiment of shifting majorities. Theoretically and logically speaking, Rousseau's "social contract" would have to be renewed by each successive generation.

g) Enlightenment in Education. Convinced of its absolute intellectual superiority over the "dark" centuries of the past, the age of enlightenment attempted to inculcate its ideas into homes and schools. It is because of these didactic tendencies that the eighteenth century has been called "the pedagogical century." The doctrines of enlightenment were taught in the lecture halls of the universities, preached in the pulpits, and proclaimed on the stage. In 1784 Schiller (cf. p. 417 sqq.) delivered his famous lecture, "On the Stage, Considered as a Moral (didactic) Institution," in which he assigned to the theater the educational task of spreading the light of wisdom throughout the State: "Clearer ideas, truer principles, purer emotions emanate from here and flow through the veins of the people; the fog of barbarism, of dark superstition disappears, and night gives way to the victorious power of light." A manual dealing with every phase of social intercourse was published by Baron Adolf von Knigge (1752–1796), containing "precepts concerning human behavior so as to live happily and socially contented in this world, and to impart a like happiness to one's fellow men."

Education became one of the major concerns of enlightened State government. In Brandenburg-Prussia a general school directorate was created by Frederick the Great's minister of education, and in Austria Maria Theresa placed the entire school system under the supervision of a governmental committee. The reorganization of the public schools, however, was not begun until the end of the eighteenth century, although as early as 1717 King Frederick William I of Prussia had issued an edict that imposed on all parents the obligation of sending their children to school. Frederick the Great, his son and successor, considered the schools chiefly as means for the development of political efficiency and economic abundance, disregarding humanistic and truly pedagogical motives.

New educational impulses were awakened by Rousseau and two of his German-speaking disciples, Johann Basedow (1723–1790) and Johann Heinrich Pestalozzi (1746–1827), the former of German, the latter of Swiss nationality. With their deeper understanding of human nature and their broader conception of human life they softened the rigid educational philosophy of the enlightened doctrinaires and sympathized with the pedagogical ideals of the Pietists (cf. p. 364 sqq.). By introducing emotional incentives into education they tried to break away from the purely rationalistic and intellectualistic pedagogy that had prevailed under the influence of Cartesian philosophy and that had found its clearest formulation in the educational theories of Johann Herbart (1776–1841). But in trying to avoid the psychological mistakes of the rationalist educators, these German followers of Rousseau did not always escape the pitfalls of their master's sentimentalism and his all-too-optimistic faith in the intrinsic goodness of human nature "in the raw."

With the support of Prince Leopold Frederick of Anhalt-Dessau, Basedow founded his *Philanthropinum* in Dessau in 1774, a "humanitarian school for teachers and learners," from which corporal punishment was banished and in which the zeal of the student was to be stimulated by the cultivation of his creative self-activity and his social instincts. The formal discipline of the Latin schools was severely criticized as an "unheard-of waste of time." Knowledge was to be acquired not by memorization and drill but by a direct appeal to the nature of the child and by arousing his interest in playful co-operation with the educational aims of the teacher.

Rousseau's contempt of the abstract and theoretical knowledge of contemporary civilization and his glorification of the primitive state of nature was shared by Pestalozzi, the Swiss educator, who was instrumental in introducing the principles of the new pedagogy into the public schools. He was convinced that personal example, not subject matter, was the decisive factor in education. Instruction was to begin with visible demonstration, to proceed from there to the formation of concepts and ideal patterns, always taking account of the relative capacities of the growing child. The goal of all education is for Pestalozzi the harmonious development of the human faculties, the training of "head, heart, and hand" in constant interplay with the vital forces of life. Such a genuinely humane education was to provide the unshakable basis for any kind of vocational training.

To demonstrate the practicability of his theories Pestalozzi established a model institution on his small estate in the Swiss canton of Aargau, where he gave shelter and instruction to fifty beggar children. "For years," he wrote, "I have been sharing the life of fifty beggar-children, in poverty sharing my bread with them, living like a beggar myself, so that I might learn how to teach beggars to live like human beings." In 1799 he opened a second school for children of the poor in Stans, and in 1800 he found employment as a public school teacher at Burgdorf in the canton of Bern, where a few years later he founded a teacher's college that attracted the attention of the leading pedagogues of many countries.

h) Literature and Literary Criticism. For the enlightened mind the purpose of all art in general and of literature in particular was moral instruction, resulting in moral enjoyment, edification, and improvement. However, literary criticism in Germany advanced beyond these limited objectives as soon as it was forced to deal with literary works whose scope transcended the traditional scheme of literary rules.

Johann Christoph Gottsched (1700–1776), professor of poesy and philosophy in Leipzig, ruled for many years as the unopposed leader of the literary representatives of German enlightenment. It was only in his old age that he had to release his dictatorial grip on the world of letters and that his well-meant critical and literary endeavors became the object of scorn and ridicule.

Following the precepts of Horace's (65–8 B.C.) and Boileau's (1636–1711) poetics Gottsched made imitation of nature the criterion of poetic expression. As a disciple of Christian Wolff (cf. p. 360) he considered poetry and art as moral and educational agencies. In the tragedy of the ancients as well as in the neo-classical drama of the epoch of Louis XIV he admired most of all the smoothness and regularity of literary style and artistic form, disregarding altogether the underlying imaginative and emotional elements. Clarity, regularity, and naturalness he considered as the essential requisites of a good piece of literature. Thus, with his widely read *Attempt at a Critical Poesy for the Germans* (1730), published approximately one hundred years after Opitz' poetics (cf. p. 299), he gave evidence that literary criticism in the age of enlightenment was as far removed from the appreciation of the true nature of poetry as it had been in the preceding period of rationalism.

Perusing Gottsched's directions for the composition of a poem or a dramatic plot, it would seem that such a task is beset with few difficulties: "At the outset you must select an instructive moral lesson. . . . Next you must conceive the general outline of certain events in which an action occurs that most distinctly demonstrates the chosen lesson." This having been accomplished, there remains only the simple question: do you wish to turn your idea into a fable, a comedy, a tragedy, or an epic? If a fable, you must give your characters the names of animals; if a comedy, your persons must be burghers; but if a tragedy, you must employ persons of birth, rank, and appearance; and if an epic, "the persons must be the most impressive in the world, such as kings, heroes, and great statesmen, and everything must have a majestic, strange, and wonderful sound." Gottsched's model tragedy, *The Dying Cato* (1732), eclectically pieced together from French and English literary reminiscences, is a practical demonstration of what he considered great dramatic art, and the author encouraged his friends and admiring disciples to proceed along similar lines. Here as in his French models the "three unities" of time, place, and action, as demanded by Boileau, served to combine a swift-moving plot with a streamlined form.

Gottsched's limitations, which were largely those of his age, should not obscure his laudable and successful efforts to purify and ennoble the German language and to improve the repertoire of the German stage. He was as much opposed to the hollow bombast of the *Haupt- und Staatsaktionen* as to the coarseness of the popular *Hanswurstiaden,* and the public burning of a *Hanswurst* dummy on Caroline Neuber's stage in Leipzig was an act of symbolic significance in the history of German drama and the German stage. Caroline Neuber (1697–1760) was an actress and directress of discriminating literary taste who performed with her own troupe in Leipzig, Brunswick, Hamburg, Frankfurt on the Main, Vienna, and St. Petersburg (Leningrad). Though in the end she turned against Gottsched, she was one of his most devoted pupils during the years of his greatest influence.

The rule of Gottsched was finally broken and the artificially repressed forces of feeling and imagination restored in their own rights by the critical works of Bodmer and Breitinger, by the advanced literary theories of Lessing, and by the new aesthetic speculation of Baumgarten, Sulzer, and Kant. The Swiss scholars, Jacob Bodmer (1698–1783) and Johann

Breitinger (1701–1776), like Gottsched were interested in the unification and purification of the German language. But by their retrieval of the irrational and emotional impulses of literary creation they freed German literature from the bondage of sterile intellectualism and pointed forward to the movements of "Storm and Stress" and Romanticism. They called the attention of their contemporaries to the great writers of England and especially to John Milton (1608–1674), who in his *Paradise Lost* had created the great religious epic of Puritan idealism. They rediscovered the buried treasures of medieval German literature, above all the works of the *Minnesänger* (cf. p. 155 sq.) and the *Nibelungenlied* (cf. p. 154). And they had the good fortune of seeing their dreams of a German literary revival come true during their own lifetime.

What Bodmer and Breitinger had demanded and hoped for was fulfilled by the critical and creative genius of Gotthold Ephraim Lessing (1729–1781), in whom the movement of German enlightenment found its greatest literary exponent and its conqueror. His penetrating speculation proceeded from the rationalism of Leibniz (cf. p. 358 sqq.) and Mendelssohn (cf. p. 369) to the moralism of Kant (cf. p. 371 sqq.) and anticipated the humanism of Goethe and Schiller (cf. pp. 404–426). As a poet and dramatist he combined Gottsched's clarity of observation and composition with a rich knowledge of life and human nature, as transmitted to him by personal experience and literary exploration. In his critical wisdom and artistic form the major elements of the classical age of German literature are already in evidence. Although the themes and problems of his works were imposed upon him by his age, his queries were phrased with a pointed personal accent and the answers betrayed a courageous independence of thought and an inexhaustible treasury of information.

Lessing was fully aware that, being a child of a rationalistic age, his critical intellect often encroached upon his creative poetic faculties, and in the severe self-analysis that is contained in the final chapter of his *Hamburg Dramaturgy,* he said of himself: "I am neither an actor nor a poet. . . . I do not feel within me the lifespring . . . that by its own force flows richly, freshly, and purely. I have to force everything to the surface as with the aid of a pressure-pump. I would be very poor, cold, and purblind indeed, had I not learned in modesty to borrow from foreign treasures, to warn myself on foreign hearths, to strengthen my vision by making use of the lenses of art."

For Lessing God is identical with the rational order of the universe, and religion is the free affirmation and acceptance of this order. The meaning of individual and social life is realized in the progress from a blind obedience to urges and instincts, to actions that are informed and determined by the law of reason. Supreme reason and perfect morality converge. While Lessing shares most of these convictions with other representatives of the age of enlightenment, he parts company with them when he moves the final goal of human striving from the finite to the infinite: "Not the truth which any one possesses or supposes to possess, but the sincere endeavor that he has made to arrive at truth, makes the worth of a man. For not by the possession but by the investigation of truth are his powers expanded, wherein alone his ever-growing perfection consists. Possession makes us complacent, indolent, and proud. If God held all truth shut in His right hand, and in His left hand nothing but the ever-restless quest of truth, though with the condition of my erring for ever and ever, and if He should say to me: 'Choose!'—I should bow humbly to His left hand, and say: 'Father, give! Pure truth is for Thee alone!'"

Lessing, the son of a Lutheran pastor, was born in Upper Lusatia and, following the wish of his parents, devoted himself to theological studies at the University of Leipzig. Becoming more and more interested in other disciplines, he turned first to the study of medicine and subsequently to philology and philosophy. From Leipzig, Germany's "little Paris," where he had freely associated with the actors and actresses of Caroline Neuber's troupe, he went to Berlin, the city upon which Frederick the Great had impressed the stamp of his personality, the cultural center of German enlightenment. Together with Moses Mendelssohn and Friedrich Nicolai he edited the *Letters Concerning the Most Recent Literature* (1759–1765). Leading for several years the life of a free-lance writer, he accepted a position as secretary to General von Tauentzien, the governor of Breslau (Silesia) in 1760. In 1767 he received an appointment as dramaturgist and theater critic at the newly founded National Theatre in Hamburg. Although the failure of this ambitious enterprise in the following year left Lessing again without a position, the fruit of his activity as a theater critic, the *Hamburg Dramaturgy,* remains the noblest document of the struggle for the creation of a national stage as the symbol of a growing national consciousness. Lessing's wife, Eva König, whom he married after having been appointed ducal librarian in Wolfenbüttel (Brunswick) in 1769, died in the following year. Lessing himself ended his life in poverty in 1781. He had to be buried at public expense.

In the seventeenth of the *Letters Concerning the Most Recent Literature* Lessing, whom Macaulay has called "the foremost critic of Europe," launched his decisive attack on Gottsched. He blamed Germany's literary dictator for having fostered a type of literature that was foreign to the German temper and mentality. Gottsched, in his blind admiration of the neo-classical drama of France, had lost sight of the genuine classical qualities as they were embodied in ancient Greek tragedy. The misinterpretation of Aristotle's *Poetics* and the slavish observation of the "three unities" had led Gottsched and his followers to a misconception of the nature of tragedy and dramatic art in general. Lessing insisted that "the grand, the terrible, the melancholy appeals more to us [Germans] than the gallant, the delicate, the amorous. . . . He [Gottsched] ought to have followed out this line of thought, and it would have led him straightway to the English stage." Particularly in Shakespeare Lessing found all the depth and grandeur of the ancients and, in addition, a supreme clarity and rationality that made his tragedies superior to those of Corneille and Racine: "Corneille is nearer the ancients in the outward mechanism, Shakespeare in the vital essence of the drama."

It was in accordance with these convictions that Lessing in the *Hamburg Dramaturgy* (1767) demanded that the action of a play ought to grow out of the structural necessities of the individual characters and that these characters themselves ought to follow their intrinsic laws of self-realization. Corneille's tragic heroes call forth admiration, but the real tragic hero evokes fear and compassion in the heart of the spectator. Only in this way does the truly great tragedy succeed in bringing about the Aristotelian "Catharsis," effecting the purification of human emotions and passions. Of the "three unities" the unity of action is the only one that must be strictly observed, while those of time and place are of minor significance.

When Lessing thus advocated the emancipation of German literature from French influence, he was prompted by the twofold aim of making literature a sensitive instrument of vital contemporary thought, and of giving voice to the hitherto suppressed or subdued forces of the German national temper. There was no element of chauvinism in Lessing's deep love of his native country, its tradition and its culture, and he found it perfectly natural to reconcile his cosmopolitanism with his patriotism.

Lessing's *Laocoön* (1766), having as its object the re-establishment of the intrinsic laws and the specific boundaries of poetry and the plastic arts, is a work of chiefly historical significance. The proposed solutions of a highly complex problem suffer from an oversimplification, caused by the defective knowledge of the art of antiquity that was a characteristic mark of art criticism in Lessing's time. Sculptures of the type of the famous Laocoön group,* now known to be works of the decadent Hellenistic period of Greek art (*c.* 50 B.C.), were considered by Lessing and his contemporaries as prototypes of classical Greek style. Unaware of the fact that Greek statuary at the time of its origin was customarily painted with loud and lively colors, the admirers of antiquity in the eighteenth century praised its plainness as a special virtue and a true symbol of the idealization of human form and feeling.

Lessing bases his critical investigation on a comparison between the agony of Laocoön and his two sons as depicted by the ancient sculptors of Rhodos and by the poet Vergil (70-19 B.C.) in his epic *Aeneid*. He arrives at the conclusion that it is in the nature of the plastic arts to depict its objects *simultaneously in space,* while the art of poetry depicts a *sequence of events in time.* The plastic arts therefore must endeavor to select "the most fruit-

---

* The Laocoön group represents a Trojan priest with his two sons in the deadly embrace of two serpents which have been sent by the goddess Pallas Athene to avenge the disclosure of the presence of the "Trojan horse," in which were hidden the Greek warriors who were to open the city gates of Troy to the besieging armies outside the city walls. The Laocoön group was discovered in the palace of Emperor Titus in Rome in 1506 and is now in the Vatican Museum.

ful moment" to characterize a situation, whereas the poet can afford to evolve an action in successive stages, from its inception to its end. Thus Vergil could describe vividly and minutely the prolonged agony of the Trojan priest without violating the laws of poetry, while the Greek sculptors had to tone down Laocoön's wild outcry to a mere groan of pain. But in exercising this restraint and in choosing "the most fruitful moment" the plastic artists have been able to achieve an identical effect in their own proper medium of expression.

Lessing's dramatic works are ingenious applications and exemplifications of his artistic theories. *Minna von Barnhelm* (1763), Germany's first and foremost classical comedy, reflects the ethical and political climate of the age of Frederick the Great and the Seven Years' War (cf. p. 314). In Goethe's judgment it is a work of typically North German character, "the first dramatic creation of vital significance and specifically modern content." The plot is woven around the concept of soldierly virtue, the conflicts arising from the struggle between love and honor, feminine cunning and masculine stubbornness. It is comedy in that highest sense in which tragedy looms as an ever present possibility, and the solution follows from the inherent nobility and gentle wisdom of the leading characters. The logical structure of the play and the final victory of reason over emotions and passions are in line with the enlightened philosophy of its author.

Five years after the completion of *Minna von Barnhelm* Lessing presented Germany with her first classical tragedy. *Emilia Galotti* (1772), a modern version of the story of the Roman heroine Virginia,* is a fearless indictment of the moral corruption of the princely representatives of absolutism, marking the incipient revolt of the middle class against petty tyranny and social inequality. The integrity of the human soul is rated as of higher value than life itself. Carefully observing the conventional unities of time, place, and action, the play is a technical masterpiece of artistic economy and stylistic precision. It illustrates effectively the practicability of the author's theoretical views as expressed in the *Hamburg Dramaturgy*.

A poetic sequel to Lessing's edition of Reimarus' *Fragments* (cf. p. 374), and the greatest literary manifestation of the religious ideology of German enlightenment, is the drama *Nathan the Wise* (1779). In pleading the cause of religious toleration in the dialectic form of the drama, Lessing wrote the final chapter of his heated controversy with Pastor Goeze of Hamburg who had suspected him of being the author of the *Fragments* and had repeatedly attacked him for his supposed antireligious radicalism. When the threat of censorship made it impossible for Lessing to continue the controversy in the accustomed form of the literary tract and pamphlet, he returned to "his old pulpit," the stage, and wrote the story of Nathan, the Jewish sage.

The thesis of the play is most clearly expressed in the Parable of the

---

* Virginia, according to the legend, was killed by her father, the Roman tribune Virginius (*c.* 450 B.C.), to save her from being dishonored.

Three Rings which Lessing had found in Boccaccio's *Decameron* but which was first recorded in the medieval *Gesta Romanorum* (*Deeds of the Romans*), compiled by the monk Helinand at the end of the twelfth century. The fable tells of a ring, endowed with the magic power of rendering its bearer "pleasing to God and men." The ring is in the possession of a family whose members have passed it on from generation to generation, the father in each case willing it before his death to his favorite son, and thereby making his heir the master of the house. In the course of time it happens that the genuineness of the ring is called in question by three brothers whose father, loving each of his sons with an impartial affection, has committed the pious fraud of bequeathing to two of them perfect duplicates of the original ring. The judge to whom the brothers submit their case arrives at the conclusion that by their envy and discord they have proven that none of them could possibly have inherited the original ring with its inherent magic power. But while the ring itself may have been lost, its power may still be made effective if each of the three sons will endeavor to redeem its promises by a life of noble thoughts and deeds, by love for God and men. In other words, it is Lessing's conviction that Judaism (Nathan), Mohammedanism (Sultan Saladin), and Christianity (the Knight Templar) can best prove the validity of their respective claims to the possession of truth by the justice and charity that informs the lives of those who profess these different creeds. True faith, Lessing implies, manifests itself in good and noble conduct.

The religious philosophy that underlies Lessing's polemic treatment of the claims of the world religions is that of Deism (cf. p. 356 sq.). "Nathan's opposition to every kind of positive religion has always been my own," says the author of this play. Dogmas and revelations appear to him as crutches and atavisms of a less enlightened age, impeding true toleration and the realization of a truly humane morality and culture.

Lessing's critical and poetic efforts were at one and the same time revolutionary and conservative. He was progressive in his admiration and appreciation of Shakespeare, whose metrical form he adopted in the five-feet iambics of his "Nathan," thereby establishing a metrical norm for German classical drama. But he remained faithful to the great literary tradition of the ancients in his adherence to the formal principles of Aristotle whom he reinterpreted for his contemporaries and successors. The rules and laws of poetry and drama, in which he believed and which he defended, were never to infringe upon the creative freedom of the poet and artist: they were merely to act as tools and means to the end of poetic perfection. In his own work he demonstrated convincingly that the artistic genius is not the slave of rules but their master.

i) Historiography. It had been Machiavelli's (see p. 247 sq.) contention that the course of political and social history was determined by the prudent use of power and organization. If that was true, then politics was an art that could be learned and could gradually be developed into a science.

It was from Machiavelli that the great historians of the seventeenth and eighteenth centuries accepted the principle of what is called "pragmatic" historiography. It becomes the task of the historian to describe and explain psychologically the purposive actions of individuals in different ages in order to enlarge the scope of political experience and to provide guiding rules for the calculation and formation of future events. In this way the past history of the human race appears as a summation of rationally integrated occurrences and its future almost as a mathematical problem. The development of a strictly scientific method was to make it possible to proceed from one securely established truth to the next, all of them testifying and contributing to the optimistic belief in the solidarity and infinite perfectibility of mankind.

In contrast to the medieval concept of universal history the *Kulturgeschichte* and *Universalhistorie* of the eighteenth century pictured as the meaning and final goal of the history of mankind not the realization of the Augustinian "City of God," but the *"église philosophique"* (philosophical church) of enlightened minds, of an "educated" mankind. This kind of reasoning underlies the great historical works of Montesquieu (*De l'esprit des lois*, 1748), Voltaire (*Essai sur l'histoire générale*, 1754–1758), Hume (*History of England*, 1754–1763), Gibbon (*History of the Decline and Fall of the Roman Empire*, 1782–1788), Frederick the Great (*On Customs, Habits, Industry, and the Progress of the Human Mind in Arts and Sciences*, 1750), and Friedrich Schiller (*History of the Revolt of the Netherlands*, 1788; *History of the Thirty Years' War*, 1790–1792). All these writers considered their task from a scientific as well as artistic point of view and were eager to discover such "laws" as might enable them to predict and predetermine the future course of European history. They were all rationalists and pragmatists, no longer satisfied, however, with becoming the teachers of politicians but animated by the higher ambition of becoming the teachers of mankind. Like the rationalistic philosophers and poets they disregarded or underestimated the significance of the forces of imagination, emotion, and passion in human life and human history. They conceived of the human race as a homogeneous mass of individuals, considering the social, political, and national divisions as so many artificial and unnecessary barriers to universal understanding and mutual enlightenment. Their high esteem for the art and civilization of antiquity caused them to invent the unhistorical tripartition of history — Antiquity, Middle Ages, Renaissance — which afterward became a widely accepted scheme, and in which the intermediate "middle" age was described as a defection from the lofty heights of ancient culture, as a dark era of barbarism and superstition.

The inadequacy of the rationalistic and pragmatic approach to historical phenomena was first realized by Herder (1744–1803, cf. p. 396 sq.), who like Kant and Lessing was himself a child of the age of enlightenment and like them rose far above its limited perspective. He agreed with the pragmatic historians that the history of mankind was marked by a steady progress from the childhood stage of the Oriental civilizations to the adolescence and maturity of Greece and Rome, and the senility of the "dark ages." He, too, pleaded the cause of the education of mankind to true humanity, harmony, and happiness. But at the same time he recognized the relative significance and uniqueness of each historic epoch in its own rights, thereby debunking the myth of universal and infinite progress. With his emphasis on the "folk spirit" (*Volksgeist*) that causes the organic unfolding of aboriginal character traits in different ethnic groups of peoples, he anticipated the nationalistic ideologies of the nineteenth and twentieth centuries and furnished the spiritual weapons for the struggle for "national self-determination." For him every social, corporative, or national unit is more than a summation of its individual members: it is an organism of its own, following an inborn law of genetic and generic evolution. In this way the mechanical theory of State and society had to give way to the organic idea of cultural folk communities (*Kulturgemeinschaften*).

For Herder the unity and harmony of the human race was continuously realized in the concrete and manifold individual and social entities of human history. In his historical masterpiece that bears the title *Ideas on the Philosophy of the History of Mankind* (1784-1791) he demanded that no preconceived standard of measurement should be applied to any past epoch, event, or individuality, but that every such phenomenon be judged according to its own internal structure and the specific conditions and laws of its growth. Giving due consideration to the natural and spiritual forces of cultural formation, to climate and soil as much as to the several faculties of the human body and soul and to their symbolic manifestation in legend, song, and dance, in mythology, folklore, and religion, he led away from the generalizations of his age and became the intellectual ancestor of the historical spirit of the nineteenth century.

In the narrower circle of the provincial social conditions of his native Westphalia, Justus Möser (1720-1794), historiographer, statesman, and sociologist, followed a similar train of thought and arrived at similar conclusions. In England Edmund Burke (1729-1797), leader of the Whigs in the House of Commons and author of the *Reflections on the Revolution in France* (1790), like Möser combined the political and social philosophy of enlightenment with the ideals of a new humanism. Möser considered a healthy and contented peasantry as the safest foundation of a prosperous State, and Burke, though a severe critic of the spirit and methods of the French Revolution, fought gallantly for the ideals of justice, liberty, and humanity. He was opposed to the exploitation of East India, to the burden of taxation imposed on the American colonies, to England's anti-Catholic legislation, and to the policy of oppression in Ireland. He reaffirmed the right of resistance against unlawful authority, but blamed the French revolutionists for having violated the duty of loyalty to the law of nature and the values embodied in sound tradition.

Both Möser and Burke weighed concrete realities and the complexity of human nature against the simplifications of abstract theories, trying to re-establish true liberty and human dignity on the solid rock of the natural law. Both men exercised a decisive influence on the political philosophy of the German Romanticists (cf. p. 470 sqq.) and presented the most valid arguments to the leaders of the counterrevolution and political restoration that followed the defeat of Napoleon. It was Friedrich Gentz (1764–1832), later on Prince Metternich's (cf. p. 461 sq.) right-hand man and one of the chief exponents of the political restoration movement, who in his earlier years had translated and annotated Burke's *Reflections* (1793), thereby popularizing in Germany one of the great classics of political literature and philosophy. Equally strong at the beginning of the nineteenth century was the influence of the political theories of Joseph de Maistre (1754–1821), the French statesman and philosopher, who vigorously and intelligently defended Church and State, the traditional authorities, against the ideas of 1789. But, at the same time, he recognized in the French Revolution a work of Providence and an inevitable result of historical constellations. What distinguished all these men from the representatives of a strictly rationalistic and pragmatic historiography was their closeness to life and their realization of the organic and genetic continuity of historic evolution.

j) The Natural Sciences. The methods of experimentation, measurement, and factual observation, as inaugurated by Galilei (cf. p. 275) and Bacon (cf. p. 356), led to several phenomenal discoveries in the natural sciences in the latter part of the eighteenth century. Enlightenment and natural sciences were linked by many bonds of common interest and agreed essentially in their philosophical premises. France and England, the leading political powers, and to a lesser degree Italy, assumed leadership also in scientific research, while in Germany the scientific endeavors of individuals and institutions were in the main dilettantic rather than systematic. The French *Académie des Sciences* (1666) and *Ecole Polytechnique* (1794), and the English *Royal Academy* (1682) had become the centers of scientific research. In Germany, too, a number of scientific academies were founded, but none of them could compare with their sister institutions abroad. While the English scientists remained always conscious of the limitations of the experimental method, French science in the age of enlightenment suffered from its implicit trust in the materialistic and mechanistic presuppositions of the prevalent philosophy. In Germany a more or less clear realization of the insufficiency of a mechanistic conception of nature led at the turn of the century to the rise of "nature philosophy" (cf. p. 501). This "nature philosophy," born of the protest of the spirit against the claims of materialism, bore rich though somewhat strange fruit in the speculation of the Romanticists (cf. p. 470 sqq.), but in turn acted as a powerful stimulus for the great scientific discoveries of the nineteenth century.

As far as the individual sciences are concerned, the German-speaking countries produced in the eighteenth century a large number of brilliant scientists in various fields. Leonhard Euler (1707–1783), the great mathematician and native of German Switzerland, who taught at the Academies of Berlin and St. Petersburg, and several members of the scholarly Bernoulli family of Basel (Switzerland) provided the theoretical bases for Laplace's astronomical speculation. Friedrich Wilhelm Herschel (1738–1822), a German musicologist and astronomer, constructed several giant telescopes and became widely known for his discovery of the planet Uranus. At about the same time the Italian Lagrange (1736–1813) and the Frenchman Arago (1786–1853) had made their important contributions to optics and astronomical physics.

The Italians Galvani (1738–1798) and Volta (1745–1827), the Frenchman Ampère (1775–1836), the Englishmen Davy (1778–1829) and Faraday (1791–1867), and the Dane Oerstedt (1777–1851) discovered the electrical currents and became the founders of the sciences of electrodynamics, electrochemistry, and electromagnetism. As early as 1663 the German physician Otto von Guericke (1602–1686) had constructed an electrical machine and observed the phenomena of electrical repulsion, conductivity, and induction. The same scholar invented the water barometer that proved the dependence of the weather on atmospheric pressure, and the air pump which utilized the new knowledge of the materiality and dilatation of the air. In 1654 Guericke had demonstrated the phenomenon of atmospheric pressure before the Diet of Regensburg, using two hollow hemispheres, one yard in diameter, which, after the air had been pumped out, could not be pulled apart by twenty-four horses.

The analyses of water and air, based on the experiments of the Englishmen Priestley (1733–1804) and Cavendish (1731–1810) and the Swedish apothecary Scheele (1742–1786), led to the discovery of oxygen and other gases and acids, opening up new possibilities for chemical research. In the first decade of the nineteenth century the chemistry of gases was systematically developed by the French chemist and physicist Gay-Lussac (1778–1850).

Medical science made rapid progress, especially in the field of surgery, after the widespread opposition to anatomical dissection had finally been overcome. Even in the middle of the seventeenth century the knowledge of the anatomy of the human body was in such a primitive stage that the court physicians of one of the margraves of Baden had to carry on lengthy disputes in their endeavor to determine the location of their distinguished patient's heart. The dissection of a pig was finally decided upon to arrive at a solution of the problem by way of analogy.

The earliest work on human anatomy, and for a long time the only one of its kind that was based on results obtained by the dissection of human corpses, was written by Andreas Vesalius of Padua (1514–1564), who thereby undermined the hitherto unquestioned authority of Galenus. It was not until two centuries later, in the age of enlightenment, that Vesalius' fellow countryman, Morgagni (1682–1771), established pathological anatomy as an independent science, laying the foundations for organographic diagnostics and scientific surgery. Gerard van Swieten (1700–1772), the court physician of Empress Maria Theresa, a pupil of Hermann Boerhaave (1668–1738) of the University of Leyden (Holland) where he conducted the first modern clinic, became the founder of the older Viennese school of medical and clinical science. In 1784 Emperor Joseph II established in the same city the *"Josephinum,"* an academy for military surgery, and the General Hospital with maternity ward and foundling house, a model institution that for a long time remained without parallel in Europe.

In the beginning of the eighteenth century pathological physiology was almost in as rudimentary a stage as pathological anatomy. The so-called "ontological" school of physiology explained disease by assuming the presence of independent organisms in the human body. This misconception was first successfully attacked and disproven by the English physician John Hunter (1728–1793), the founder of experimental pathology.

The mechanistic ideas of the French rationalists affected profoundly the physiological views of the eighteenth century. Human metabolism was compared with a hydraulic machine, the organs of respiration with a pair of bellows, the entrails with sieves. Medical science in its entirety was frequently conceived of as a mechanico-mathematical discipline. The many crudities of this physiological materialism found their counterpart in an increasing interest in mysterious and occult forces that were to afford an outlet for suppressed emotional and spiritual urges.

Kant was convinced of the therapeutic force and function of reason, and he wrote an essay in which he tried to demonstrate the "power of the human mind to gain mastery over one's pathological states by a mere firm resolution." But many of his contemporaries substituted for reason and mind a mysterious "live-force" which they endowed with the faculty of working all kinds of miracles. Galvani's experiments with frog legs and the explanation of the irritability and sensitivity of muscles and nerves as presented by the German scientist and poet Albrecht von Haller (1708–1777), gave rise to fantastic speculations as to the possibility of reviving the dead by irritation of the muscular and nervous systems. The German physician Franz Anton Mesmer (1734–1815), the discoverer of animal magnetism, believed in the presence of magnetic fluids and currents in all physical organisms, which might be used for therapeutic purposes. "Mesmerism" was adopted in certain quarters as a philosophy of life which was designed to elucidate the interrelations that exist between the different parts and beings of the universe, between macrocosm and microcosm. From Vienna, where the authorities looked with disfavor upon Mesmer's growing clientele, he went to Paris, where his miraculous cures attracted the attention of the sensation loving aristocracy on the eve of the French Revolution.

Likewise a strange combination of scientist and theosophist was the Swedish philosopher Emanuel Swedenborg (1688–1772), the founder of the "Church of the New Jerusalem," whose doctrines were ridiculed in Kant's *Dreams of a Visionary* (1766). He speculated on the interrelation of body and soul and the prophetic significance of dreams and, at the same time, worked out a coherent mechanico-rationalistic system of nature philosophy. He claimed to have received direct revelations of supernatural

truths by means of his constant intercourse with the spirit world. Swedenborg was the founder of the science of crystallography, and Mesmer was
the first European physician of rank who taught and applied the methods
of what became later known as hypnotic suggestion, psychotherapy, psycho-
pathology, parapsychology, and psychoanalysis.

From his own autobiography and from Goethe's sympathetic description
in the ninth book of *Poetry and Truth* we gain an intimate knowledge of
the charming personality of Johann Jung-Stilling (1740–1817), a writer of
pietistic leanings, a political economist and physician by profession. He, too,
claimed direct intercourse with the spirits of the departed and was at home
in the mystico-theosophical dreamlands of Paracelsus (cf. p. 273) and
Jacob Böhme (cf. p. 270).

The Saxon physician Friedrich Hahnemann (1755–1843), likewise opposed
to the current materialism of medical science, became the founder of
homoeopathy, characterized by the attempt at effecting cures by the application of medicaments which produce in the human body symptoms similar
to those of the disease: treating constipation with laxatives and acidosis with
alcalizing agents. Vaccination against malignant pustules and smallpox,
first practiced by the English country doctor, Edward Jenner (1749–1773),
was a direct application of the therapeutic principles of homoeopathy.

Hahnemann's *Organon of Practical Medicine* (1810) became the classical
handbook of all homoeopathists. His influence extended to England and
North America, and some of his disciples opened the first homoeopathic
institute in Philadelphia, forming the nucleus of the foundation of the
Hahnemann College (1848) with its several hospitals and policlinics. In
Washington, D. C., a public monument was erected in Hahnemann's honor.

Abraham Werner (1749–1817), the "father of geology," who taught at
the internationally famous mining academy at Freiberg in Saxony, was
the chief defender of the theory of "Neptunism," trying to relate all
geological formations and changes to oceanic influences. His views exercised
a certain fascination on Goethe's scientific theories as well as on the
Romantic nature philosophy of Novalis (cf. p. 476), H. Steffens (1773–1845),
and Franz von Baader (1765–1841). The "Neptunist" theory was refuted
by the English geologist James Hutton (1726–1797), whose "Plutonism"
explained geological transformations as the results of volcanic influences.

In the field of biology William Harvey's (1578–1657) hitherto accepted
theory of organic evolution or preformation, maintaining the generation of
plants and animals from original constitutional dispositions of species, was
opposed in the eighteenth century by Friedrich Wolff's (1733–1794) theory
of postformation or epigenesis which taught the spontaneous generation of
new organisms from unorganized matter. Both theories were combined in
the early twentieth century in Hans Driesch's (1867–1941) concept of
"epigenetic evolution," according to which an organism is the result of the
activation of constitutional dispositions, under the influence of biological
factors and environmental conditions.

Chapter 12

GERMAN CLASSICAL IDEALISM

Germany and the Classical Heritage. The "European tradition" had its intellectual roots as much in the culture of antiquity as in the more recent forces of Christianity which superseded the former but never entirely abrogated this ancient legacy. The German tradition, on the other hand, showed itself opposed at several junctures to the smooth formalism and placid equilibrium of classical antiquity, asserting the irrational and mystical impulses of its own psychological and racial heritage. The first real synthesis of Graeco-Roman, Christian, and Germanic culture was embodied in the Carolingian Renaissance (cf. p. 51 sqq.), while the second European classical revival in the fifteenth and sixteenth centuries met with little response on the part of Germany. The religious dynamism of the Lutheran Reformation clashed with the worldly spirit of the Italian Renaissance, and the academic classicism of seventeenth-century France, though feebly imitated in Germany, evoked there at the same time the anticlassical movements of Pietism (cf. p. 364 sqq.), Sentimentalism, and "Storm and Stress." It was not until the latter part of the eighteenth century that the spiritual unrest of the German mind succeeded in achieving a classical harmony and perfection of its own stamp, a cultural and intellectual pattern that resulted from such an ideal blend of form and content as hitherto had only been realized by the singular artistic genius of Dürer (cf. p. 197) and Holbein (cf. p. 197 sq.). But this German classicism was so much a creation of the Germanic race that to this day it appears to prominent literary critics of France and England as unclassical to such an extent that they prefer to call it "Romanticism," grouping it together with the European romantic movement of the early nineteenth century.

The Revolution of Feeling. The classical writers and thinkers of Germany without exception experienced in their youth the influence of Rousseau (cf. p. 376), the European apostle of a new emotionalism, who became the leader of a whole generation in their revolt against the despotism of reason. To Descartes's *"exister c'est penser"* (to exist means to think) Rousseau opposed the slogan *"exister c'est sentir"* (to exist means to feel), calling attention to the neglected powers of will and heart and thereby challenging the complacency of an artificially organized society. For the individualism of rational human beings he substituted an individualism of sensitive hearts and souls. By making the feeling ego the final authority in life and culture he completed the victory of modern subjectivism, rehabilitating the inwardness of sentiment and fancy in the plastic and literary arts and rediscovering the landscape as a mirror of the human soul.

With Rousseau the German classicists started out by affirming strongly the right of nature to assert itself, but they ultimately supplemented and sublimated his message by the demand that nature be perfected by means of human reason and moral action. With Rousseau they shared the conviction that modern civilization had destroyed the fullness and oneness of human nature, but while Rousseau expected the restoration of its original integrity from a return to a primitive state of life, his German disciples pointed forward to the superior culture and the true humanity of a future day and age, to be ushered in by great personalities in whom the faculties of reason, will, and emotions would be reconciled.

Both Herder and Schiller advanced in their constructive criticism beyond Rousseau's one-sided anticultural pessimism, by their contention that civilization, by virtue of its own inherent vitality, could heal the wounds that it had struck. It was their belief that only a sham civilization could harm the integrity of human nature, but that a genuine and fully grown civilization would necessarily lead human nature to its true perfection. And Goethe more than anyone else exemplified in his life as much as in his works the fact that modern man, on his passage through ever rising planes of cultural education, through self-realization and intellectual discipline, could in the end attain to the reborn naïveté of pristine nature. Thus a "beautiful soul" for Goethe and Schiller was a human personality in which the faculties of intellect, will, and emotions were brought to complete harmony.

a) Sentimentalism ("Empfindsamkeit"). The growing importance of the middle classes in the eighteenth century brought about certain changes in the general intellectual, moral, and literary standards and ideals of the age. German culture and literature were no longer dominated by theological or dynastic social and communal interests but became more and more saturated with the individual experiences and concerns of average human beings. A happy and contented human life on this earth became the ideal goal of individual and social striving. This preoccupation with individual life sharpened the eye for the intimate psychological observation and description of human existence and the development of human characters.

Keen introspection, psychological reflection, and self-analysis are clearly manifested in the poetry and fiction of the first half of the eighteenth century and particularly in the sentimental novel, which was imported to Germany from England. Lawrence Sterne's (1713–1768) *Tristram Shandy* and *A Sentimental Journey through France and Italy by Mr. Yorick* were translated into German and infested the German sentimental and romantic novel with their emotional exuberance and somewhat scurrilous humor. James Thomson's (1700–1748) *Seasons,* with its detailed description of nature, found an echo in Haydn's oratorio (1801) of the same title, and

Samuel Richardson's (1689–1761) sentimental novels moved Christian Gellert (cf. p. 349) so deeply that he "was drowned with weeping," that he "sobbed with infinite joy" and considered Richardson a magician who commanded "all that is touching and overwhelming, enrapturing and intoxicating." Rapture and intoxication his English and German readers found in Edward Young's (1683–1765) gloomy *Night Thoughts on Life, Death, and Immortality* (1742–1745) and in James Macpherson's (1736–1796) romantic *Poems of Ossian* (1760–1764) which the Scottish poet falsely advertised as translations of the songs of a Gaelic bard of the third century A.D. Young's nature poetry and Macpherson's sentimental melancholy assumed a new and more vigorous life in Klopstock's odes and Goethe's *Sorrows of Young Werther* (cf. p. 409 sq.).

The sentimentalism that pervades these literary documents, bordering at times on exhibitionism, represented a violent reaction against the conventional and authoritarian culture of Rococo and princely absolutism and has its center in the self-assertion of the individual and his experiences. Letters, diaries, and memoirs became the favorite literary vehicles of personal confession and self-portrayal. All at once the German language lost its stilted artificiality, assuming color and expressive vigor. The science of physiognomics became for Johann Kaspar Lavater (1741–1801) the key that unlocked the sacred shrine of human personality, its riches, its mysteries, its unlimited potentialities. The feeling of universal friendship and brotherhood wove sentimental ties between all members of the human race, between man and nature, between nature and God, and nature itself became the intimate confidant of all sentimental souls: the gentle element that soothes and liberates, that heals and makes man whole and holy again. Thought, speculation, and practical demonstration were all dissolved in the waves of feeling, mystical affection and devotion, and awe-inspired exaltation.

b) Friedrich Gottlob Klopstock (1724–1803). Though an "apprentice of the Greeks" in the metrical form of his lyric poetry, Klopstock was a typical poet of the Germanic North, as far as the spirit and content of his works is concerned. His "expressionistic" style was the medium of his emotion and passion and showed little of the neo-classical "noble simplicity and quiet grandeur." However, in the midst of the sweet and sentimental trivialities of the anacreontic and pietistic poets his work represents another milestone on the road to classical German literature, and with his solemn conviction of the religious, social, and national significance of poetry, he restored to the realm of German letters dignity of form and sublimity of subject matter.

When the first three cantos of his *Messiah* were published in 1748, Klopstock was joyously acclaimed and adopted as Germany's first and foremost poet in modern times. Although the author of this religious poem was influenced in the choice of his theme by Milton's (1608–1674) religious epics, the twenty cantos of the completed work resemble in composition and style more the musical form of the oratorio than the epical narrative of its

English model. The poem is greatest in its lyric and dramatic passages and lacks the plasticity, concreteness, and individuality of objective and descriptive literary forms. In conformity with the Lutheran dogmatic premises of the work the human nature of Christ is completely submerged in the divine attributes of the Redeemer. What interests the author primarily is not so much Christ's passion and death, viewed as historic occurrences, but rather the psychological effects of the work of redemption on human souls, on angels, and on demons.

The characteristic features of the *Messiah* reappear in Klopstock's Odes and in his dramatic attempts. The positive and negative qualities of his poetry are well defined in Friedrich Schiller's critical appraisal: "His sphere is always the realm of ideas, and he makes everything lead up to the infinite. One might say that he deprives everything that he touches of its body in order to turn it into spirit, whereas other poets clothe everything spiritual with a body." God and immortality are the central themes of most of Klopstock's works, and they are all permeated with the conviction of the infinite value of the immortal human soul. Everything earthly and material is seen and evaluated from the point of view of eternity, and his devotion to nature is an eloquent testimony to the omnipresence and omnipotence of the divine spirit, manifesting itself in the circling stars of the skies, in the rhythmic cycles of the seasons, and in the elemental forces of nature. It is Klopstock's historic accomplishment to have freed the German language from the bondage of a sterile rhetorical intellectualism and to have made it a pliant medium for the direct lyrical expression of the impulses and experiences of the individual human soul.

c) Hamann and the "Storm and Stress" Movement. The modern individualistic trend that had found its first powerful manifestation in the Italian Renaissance and in the German Reformation was carried to extreme conclusions by the generation that succeeded that of Lessing and Klopstock. While the sixteenth and seventeenth centuries had still recognized a universal and divinely sanctioned law and order for mankind, the age of Enlightenment had set up humanity or its individual representatives as ends in themselves, so that ultimately man could be proclaimed as the measure of all things. The history of human civilization appeared as a dialectic struggle between individual and superindividual norms, the great epochs of history resulting from the harmonization of individual and social claims, and the epochs of decline revealing their maladjustment and open antagonism. No longer did the individual recognize himself as an integral part of a universal order, but he conceived of himself as an autonomous being whose innate law and individual nature set him apart, in sharp contrast to his age and social environment. In France the revolt of the individual and his victory was decided in the political arena; in Germany the scene of action was the realm of letters, and the victorious forces that were destined to assume the intellectual leadership of their nation were recruited from the awakening middle classes.

In 1760 a small pamphlet was published, bearing the somewhat obscure title *Socratic Memoirs*. Its author was Johann Georg Hamann (1730–1788), the "Magus of the North," who in sibylline language and in glowing colors painted the image of the sage of Antiquity as the true prototype of a great human personality. What were the essential features of this new and ideal type of man, of this new Socrates in whom the age of enlightenment had already seen the precursor of its own aspirations? For Hamann the new Socrates was a genuine product of creative nature, a genius who was impelled by the irresistible dictates of the "daimon" in his own breast, a being predestined from eternity to tragic conflict, to suffering, and death. In his exemplary greatness this new man resembled the heroes of Greek tragedy whose valor was derived from the mysterious depths of their divine origin and from the unconscious forces of nature. With this new concept of human personality Hamann dealt the deathblow to the arrogant humanitarianism and the complacency of the enlightened *"philosophes."* He gained the attention and enthusiastic following of the younger generation, out of whose ranks were to emerge the classical representatives of German culture and literature in the late eighteenth and early nineteenth centuries.

The literary revolution crystallized in the poems and dramas of the "Storm and Stress" (*Sturm und Drang*) movement, which derived its name from the title of one of Maximilian Klinger's (1752–1831) plays. With all "Storm and Stress" poets Rousseau's antirationalism and anticultural pessimism became a kind of obsession. But if Rousseau with his call "Back to Nature!" had indicted a corrupt social system and, in "Emile" and the "Nouvelle Héloïse," had tried to vindicate human emotions and passions, the writers who gathered around Herder and Goethe in Strasbourg mistook anarchy for freedom and arbitrariness for naturalness. Their aesthetic revolution was therefore essentially destructive, aimed, as it were, at all rule and authority and glorifying sensuality, voluptuousness, and the rule of instincts untrammeled. Their total lack of intellectual and moral bearings makes them crave for movement for the sake of movement. The hero of Klinger's "Sturm und Drang," about to join the American Revolution as a volunteer, gives vent to the restlessness and rootlessness of this "lost generation," when he exclaims: "Nowhere rest, nowhere repose . . . glutted by impulse and power . . . I am going to take part in this campaign. . . . There I can expand my soul, and if they do me the favor to shoot me down — all the better." For Wilhelm Heinse's (1749–1803) *Ardinghello,* passion, lust, and crime are necessary and legitimate forms of human life. The only true virtue is power, and weakness is the only real crime.

It would be difficult indeed to read any meaning into this squandering of youthful enthusiasm and poetic talent, if it were not for the fact that it was the historical function of the "Storm and Stress" poets to break up and fertilize the soil which was to nourish the genius of Herder, Goethe, and Schiller. In all the misspent energy and ill-directed idealism of this generation there was the spark of the undying vitality of youth and at the same time a spontaneity and radicalism that were needed as much for destruction as for regeneration.

"What is genius?" asks Lavater in his *Physiognomic Fragments* (1775–1778), and he answers: "Where there are efficiency, power, action, thought, feeling which can be neither learned nor taught by men—there is genius. Genius is what is essentially unlearned, unborrowed, unlearnable, untransferable, what is unique, inimitable, and divine. . . . Genius flashes; genius creates . . . ; it is inimitability, momentaneity, revelation. . . ." Taking this definition as a standard of measurement, none but Herder, Goethe, and Schiller lived up to its requisites.

The "Storm and Stress" poets' cult of Shakespeare was almost a case of mistaken identity: Shakespeare was of course not the "uncultivated genius," who disregarded artistic rules and aesthetic laws, but he was the great master who used them as tools and servile organs of a thoroughly disciplined artistic mind.

d) *Johann Gottfried Herder (1744–1803).** Out of Rousseau's glorification of the forces of primitive nature and out of Hamann's understanding of human personality and creative genius, Herder was able to evolve his own concept of the organic growth of human civilization, from its dark and unconscious beginnings to its mature intellectual documentation in distinct national cultures. As Hamann's most faithful disciple Herder made his own the definition of poetry as "the mother-tongue of the human race." Language appeared to him as a sublime symbol of the human mind, a genuine expression of the spirit of nations, races, and cultures that achieved its purest manifestation in the works of poetry and literature. Together with language and literature, however, he conceived of art, religion, philosophy, law, and custom as direct objectivations and realizations of the lives, instincts, environments, and living conditions of the peoples and nations of the past and present. The "inner form" that worked as an immanent, active principle in poetry and art was born of the spirit of the age; it tolerated no longer the imitation of obsolete styles of the past but demanded original creation born of the experiences of the living generations. In this way he visualized Homer, Luther, Shakespeare, and other great leaders and innovators in the realms of arts, letters, and human thought not only as autonomous personalities but at the same time as true representatives and mouthpieces of the spirit of their age, their people, and their material and spiritual environments. The fundamental unity of the genius and his maternal native soil, race, and cultural heritage was discovered, emphatically asserted by Herder, and transmitted to his great contemporaries of the

---

* Herder was born in Mohrungen (East Prussia), came under Kant's influence at the University of Königsberg (1762) where he studied medicine, theology, philosophy, and philology. From 1764–1769 he was employed as teacher and preacher at the Protestant cathedral school in Riga. In Strasbourg (1770) he associated with Goethe, who later on was influential in bringing about Herder's appointment as general superintendent (of the Church) in Weimar. His last years were embittered by his controversies with Kant and his estrangement from Goethe.

classical age and to the nineteenth century. His disciples and heirs could no longer consider poetry, literature, and art as a pleasant or inspiring pastime: he taught them to understand their endeavors and the finished products of their creative minds as the fruits of the innermost essence of individual and social forces in a given historical situation. Thus literary history was destined to become part and parcel of the history of the human mind and soul, and Rousseau's anticultural pessimism was sublimated and overcome by a joyous acknowledgment of the ever changing plenitude and diversity of intellectual forms and patterns. The immeasurably enlarged vision was enabled to travel far back into the German and European past, to extend its view into an anticipated future, and to survey the panorama of world literature from the static center of a new national consciousness.

It was thus a rare combination of great gifts — those of the philosopher, critic, and poet — that made it possible for Herder to perceive and correct the shortcomings of both Enlightenment and "Storm and Stress," to become the mentor of the young Goethe and the teacher of the writers and thinkers of the classical and romantic periods.

Among Herder's critical and poetic works the following deserve special mention as documents of the perspicacity and universality of his mind: in the *Travel-Journal* (*Reisejournal*, 1769) we discover the fruit of his early preoccupation with the problems of aesthetics, poetry, and pedagogy. He points to a new and true Humanism of the future, speculates on the basic requisites of a liberal constitution for the state of Livonia, and dreams of a renascence of Russo-Slavic civilization. In his *Fragments Concerning the More Recent German Literature* (1767) he continues and supplements the critical analyses of Lessing's *Literaturbriefe* (cf. p. 381). He dwells especially on the significance of poetic rhythm, meter, and style, and describes the evolution of literary expression from its primitive and timid origins in inarticulate sound to an intellectual maturity that subjects emotionalism and metaphorical imagery to order and rational law: a change and cyclical movement that recurs in each national organism and that regularly is marked by the gradual displacement of poetry by prose, leading eventually to abstract intellectualism and sterile rationalism. In comparing cultural and literary growth with the evolution of biological species, passing through the successive stages of primitivity, maturity, and death, only to make room for new beginnings, Herder anticipated Hegel's (cf. p. 502 sq.) "dialectical philosophy" of history as well as Spengler's (1880–1936)* theory of "cultural cycles."

The "Letters for the Promotion of Humanity" (*Briefe zur Beförderung der Humanität*, 1793–1797) contain Herder's condemnation of the vice of national pride which he considered "the greatest of all follies." "Education for humanity" is to bring about the harmonization of the natural, the moral, and the divine, culminating in the final reconciliation of Antiquity

---

* Cf. Oswald Spengler: *The Decline of the West* (New York: Alfred Knopf, 1939), trans. from the German: *Der Untergang des Abendlandes* (München, 1917; 1932).

and Christianity. In collaboration with Goethe and the historian and states-man Justus Möser (1720–1794) Herder published the essays "On German Arts and Customs" (*Von deutscher Art und Kunst*, 1773), to which he contributed his profound studies on Ossian and Shakespeare. He calls attention to the buried treasures of folk poetry and designates the comprehension and interpretation of actual life as the essential function of literature.

To demonstrate the validity of his theories in a practical way Herder displayed in his collection of folk songs and ballads (*Stimmen der Völker*, 1778–1779) the poetic products of the creative *"Volksgeist"* of many nations and races. His poetic intuition faithfully preserves the spirit of the originals, in word, rhythm, and melody, and he shows himself as one of the great masters in the art of translation. It was perhaps his great versatility and flexibility as much as his strongly developed historical sense that deprived his own poetic creations of originality and lasting significance. He lives on as an inspired and inspiring seer, teacher, and pioneer, a leader into a promised land in which others might reap what he had sown.

Neo-Classicism and the New Humanism. Herder appears in his full and imposing stature when viewed as the standard-bearer in the momentous struggle that was being waged in Germany's classical age against meaningless conventions and the barrenness of an icy intellectualism. What he expected from the rebirth of a richer and truer view of life, and from a more complete realization of man's potentialities and innate aspirations, he summarized in the *Letters for the Promotion of Humanity* in these words: "Humanity: if we would give this idea its full vigor . . . if we would inscribe it into our own hearts and those of our fellow-men as an unavoidable, general, and primary obligation—all our social, political, and religious prejudices might perhaps not entirely disappear, but they would at least be softened, restrained, and rendered innocuous."

a) *Greece and Rome*. For Herder's friends and contemporaries the ideal pattern of this exalted type of humanity seemed to be embodied in the world of Graeco-Roman antiquity. The New Humanism in the North, in France as well as in Germany, paid little attention at first to the heritage of ancient Greece. It was rather the ancient republic of Rome that beckoned with the splendid achievements of its art, literature, and intellectual culture. Englishmen were among the first to carry on systematic archaeological research on ancient Roman soil, and from England the new classicistic style of architecture penetrated into northern Germany. The shift of interest from Rome to Greece was chiefly due to the Platonic and Neo-Platonic program of studies in the monastic colleges of Cambridge and Oxford, where Plotinus, the head of the Neo-Platonic schools (203–269), was again read and appreciated in the seventeenth century. It was above all Lord Shaftesbury (1671–1713), the English moral philosopher, who eagerly absorbed these Platonic teachings, reviving in his ethico-aesthetic treatises the Greek ideal of the harmony of the good, the true, and the beautiful. Shaftesbury's ideas, in turn, were adopted and further developed in the philosophical and aesthetic speculation of Herder, Goethe, Schiller, and some of the leaders of the German Romantic School (cf. p. 470 sqq.).

b) *"Noble Simplicity and Quiet Grandeur."* Johann Joachim Winckelmann (1717-1768), on the other hand, was attracted like Lessing to the art and literature of ancient Greece by a real inner affinity. Vexed and irritated by the vainglorious showmanship of the courtly culture of the Rococo and filled with compassion for the peoples and nations that smarted in the servitude of more or less enlightened despots, Winckelmann like Lessing escaped into the more humane climate of Greek democracy and found a haven of intellectual and moral repose in the purer and simpler forms of Greek art and literature. True enough, it was an idealized and partly unhistorical Greece to which both these writers paid homage but it was nevertheless also the Greece of the Homeric epics, of Attic tragedy and prose, of Xenophon, Plato, and Aristotle.

Greek art as Winckelmann knew and interpreted it, the art of "noble simplicity and quiet grandeur" (*edle Einfalt und stille Grösse*), became for him and his age the measure and standard of all artistic creation. "Back to Hellas!" became the battle cry of artists and poets, scholars and educators, burghers and nobles.

In Rome, Florence, Naples, and in the recently excavated cities of Herculaneum and Pompeii, Winckelmann inhaled the spirit of the ancient world. In the Roman copies of the masterpieces of Greek sculpture he admired the unity of form and content, the smoothness and gentle grace of lines and contours, the freedom and ease of the plastic form. Like Lessing he remained unaware of the fact that Greek art and life were not all smoothness, harmony, and ideal beauty, that under a smooth surface loomed tragedy and intense suffering as ever present realities, that the serenity of Apollo was constantly challenged by the dark irrationality of Dionysos, the god of the blind urge, of orgiastic intoxication and demonic lust.

Winckelmann's epochal *History of the Art of Antiquity* (1764), the result of his archaeological studies, contained his classicistic principles of aesthetic contemplation. The influence of the classical Greek writers was reflected in a measured and lucid prose which made the book accessible to many non-German readers.

c) *Neo-Classicism, the French Revolution, and the Style of the Napoleonic Empire.* Despite Winckelmann's conviction that only by imitating the Greeks could German artists and writers achieve real greatness, it was not the spirit of Hellas but the spirit of ancient Rome that appealed more universally to the sober taste and temper of the middle classes.

The struggle between the dying Rococo and the new classicism, beginning in France and Germany in the sixth decade of the eighteenth century, ended with the victory of the unimaginative and somewhat pedantic reincarnation of Roman civic republicanism in the ideology of Robespierre and the French Revolution. Cicero (106-43 B.C.), the great Roman orator, statesman, and philosopher, became the idol of the revolutionary leaders, who admired his legalistic mind and his ethical rigorism. He appeared to them as an ideal combination of a "popular philosopher" and an orator of overpowering eloquence. They quoted freely from him and other Roman authors and derided Danton for not complying with this fashion.

Napoleon, too, commanded all the devices of classical rhetoric and was fully conscious of the dynamic power of the spoken word. To Nietzsche (cf. p. 695 sq.) he appeared as "a statue of Antiquity in the midst of a Christian society." The artists who depicted Napoleon's features were struck by their resemblance to those of Emperor Augustus. The remaining feudal and dynastic political formations of medieval Europe were swept away by the French emperor, to be replaced by a political order of his own making, by a system that showed the characteristic marks of classical symmetry, simplicity, and rationality. By bringing about the "alliance of philosophy with the sword" he strove to resume the task of the Roman Caesars, to give peace to the world by establishing a unified dictatorial rule over the nations of Europe. He tried to revive Roman imperialism in a Christian garb, visited the tomb of Charlemagne at Aix-la-Chapelle, and crowned himself emperor in the presence of the pope. The structure and administration of his centralized empire was fashioned in accordance with the Roman model, and he made Roman law the basis of jurisdiction and Roman political ethics the basis of education. Artists and men of letters worked in the service of the Empire and were entrusted with the task of embellishing and glorifying its universal mission. The new "Punic War"* against the English "nation of shopkeepers" was to restore the absolute hegemony of the New Rome and to make the Mediterranean a "French Lake."

Thus the New Classicism, the style of the "Empire," carried forward by Napoleon's legions, went on its sweeping march of conquest throughout the territories and nations of the Western hemisphere. It found its outward expression in the increasing number of architectural monuments and newly planned cities that arose in the immense area that was flanked by St. Petersburg (Leningrad) in the East, Washington in the West, and Montevideo in the South. The simple lines and symmetrical designs of this cosmopolitan architecture followed the artistic example of ancient Rome and its modern replica, Paris, the imperial metropolis on the Seine.

d) *Neo-Classical Art in Germany*. The disintegration of the Holy Roman Empire and the political misfortunes of Austria and Prussia retarded and partly thwarted the development of the plastic arts in the German-speaking countries. The neo-classical style on German soil acquired significance as a component part of the great achievements of classical idealism in literature and philosophy but remained chiefly eclectic, imitative, and academic in architecture, sculpture, and painting. As the style of the political and social forces of conservation, tradition, and reaction it extended far into the

---

* Rome waged three "Punic Wars" with Carthage (264–146 B.C.) to secure military and economic supremacy over the dominating sea power of her political rival (Punic-Carthaginian Wars). Carthage was finally conquered and destroyed (149–146).

nineteenth century and disappeared only in the period of the revolutionary movements that paved the way for constitutional reforms and the political unification of Germany.

The public buildings and monuments which mark the period from the death of Frederick the Great to the revolution of 1848 (cf. p. 527 sq.) show a regularity and frugal rigidity of design that make them appear as foreign importations rather than as the manifestation of indigenous forces. Their cool and sober intellectualism found little response among the people at large who were much more attached to the still surviving art forms of a colorful popular Baroque or a soulful Romanticism. The representative style of the French *"Empire"* found its rather timid echo in the German *"Biedermeier,"* a manner of living and a style of interior decoration in which the stately neo-classical mannerisms were reduced to the intimacy of a bourgeois culture, whose neatness and narrowness reflected the mentality and social conditions of the German middle classes between 1815 and 1848 (the *"Vormärz,"* cf. p. 461 sqq.).

The most significant architectural monuments of German Neo-Classicism are found in Berlin, Munich, and Karlsruhe. In Berlin the Silesian architect, Karl Langhans (1733–1808), created the famous *"Brandenburger Tor"* (1789–1793), the symbolic gateway to the metropolis of the soldier-kings of Prussia.

The greatest master of the "Prussian style" in architecture was Karl Friedrich Schinkel (1781–1841), whose prolific building activity drew inspiration from the distant and disparate sources of Greek and Gothic architecture. As the son of a historically minded age he felt free to choose among the various stylistic possibilities of the past, but lacked the singleness of purpose and creative spontaneity that are required for the achievement of artistic unity and true originality. To him "Old Berlin" owes its characteristic architectural physiognomy, and his strongly developed sense of orderliness, balance, and clarity of design made him anticipate some of the principles of modern "functional" architecture. The "Old Museum" of Berlin (1822–1828) was the first building of its kind on the European continent (the British Museum was constructed according to the classicistic designs of Sir Robert Smirke between 1823 and 1855), and the Berlin *"Schauspielhaus"* (1818–1821) served as a model for most of the municipal and national playhouses of the nineteenth century. In his more than eighty buildings Schinkel utilized most of the historic styles of architecture with which he had become acquainted on his extensive travels. As a loyal servant of the royal dynasty of Prussia, Schinkel designed the spiked helmet (*Pickelhaube*) that became one of the best known symbols of Prussian militarism and was adopted by both the police force and the army (1842).

The sculptors of the "Prussian style" were Gottfried Schadow (1764–1850) and his pupil Christian Rauch (1777–1857), both of them neo-classicists, but both inclined to translate the classical repose of ancient statuary into the more characteristic and individualistic language of their own political and social environment. Among many other works each of the two sculptors created statues in commemoration of Frederick the Great. The base of Rauch's equestrian monument of the Prussian king in Berlin is largely occupied by the figures of Prussian generals, while to Kant and Lessing an overly modest space is allotted underneath the tail of Frederick's horse.

King Louis I of Bavaria (1825–1848) was one of the few German princes of the neo-classical period who continued the noble tradition of princely patronage of the arts, despite the adverse conditions of the times. Under his rule the neo-classical style experienced a belated flowering in southern Germany. By his consistent and vigorous cultivation of artistic and literary taste he made his court and the royal capital of Munich the cultural center of Germany. He commissioned Leo von Klenze (1784–1864) with the construction of numerous monumental buildings in neo-classical style ("*Glyptothek*" and "*Propyläen*" in Munich; the "*Walhalla*" near Regensburg; the "*Befreiungshalle*," commemorating the Wars of Liberation, near Kelheim).

Karlsruhe, the capital of the margraves of Baden, was transformed into a mathematically construed model city of dignified classicistic taste by Friedrich Weinbrenner (1766–1826), who superimposed on the Baroque ground plan the characteristic elements of the new style, and adorned the city gates, palaces, and many private residences with Doric and Corinthian ornamentation.*

Neo-classical German painting showed considerably less vitality and ingenuity than its sister arts. A quaint mixture of Antiquity and Rococo, of imitative-naturalistic and phantastic-theatralic elements characterizes most of the paintings produced in the age of Goethe and Schiller. Angelica Kauffmann (1741–1807), of Swiss nationality, created a large number of sentimental and genrelike works, allegorical and mythological subjects, gods and goddesses, Vestal virgins and sybils, heroically posing figural compositions and sober, commonplace portraits. Wilhelm Tischbein (1751–1829) is best known for his somewhat spectacular painting of Goethe in the classical setting of the Roman Campagna. Winckelmann's favorite was the court painter of the king of Saxony in Dresden, Anton Raphael Mengs (1728–1779), whom he placed even above his idol Raphael. Today Mengs appears to us as a faithful and diligent pupil of the great masters of the Italian Renaissance, a talented draftsman, but one whose paintings lack coloristic luster and spiritual depth. In the landscapes of Asmus Carstens (1754–1798), however, nature awakes from a trancelike sleep and begins to stir and move underneath the transparent classical veil. It is the spirit of Romanticism that gradually illuminates and transfigures the cool aloofness of the classical scene.

e) The Science of Antiquity ("Altertumswissenschaft"). The archaeological as well as linguistic interest in Antiquity was born of the neo-classical and neo-humanistic tendencies of the eighteenth century. The

---

* Many of the monuments of neo-classical German architecture were destroyed during World War II.

scientific exploration of the ancient civilizations of Greece and Rome (*Altertumskunde, Altertumswissenschaft*) grew out of the pioneer work of German philologists and included eventually every aspect of the life and culture of Antiquity. The actual founder of the new science was Friedrich August Wolf (1759–1824), professor of classical philology in Halle and Berlin, a pupil of Christian Gottlob Heyne (1729–1812) in Göttingen, who had taught him to evaluate classical literature and culture from the aesthetic and artistic point of view. Henceforth the study of the ancient writers was no longer primarily concerned with the imitation of classical figures of speech but was to serve the refinement of taste and the perfection of human character. Another one of Heyne's famous pupils was Wilhelm von Humboldt (1767–1835), a friend of Schiller and Goethe, who later on, as Prussian minister of education, was to introduce the ideas of the New Humanism into the Prussian schools (cf. p. 439 sqq.).

f) The New Humanism. The original philosophical and spiritual forces of the classical age, that are inseparably linked with the names of Goethe and Schiller as its greatest exponents, were Rationalism and Protestantism. It was the Protestant heritage that saved the classical literature and philosophy of Germany from the atomism, materialism, and skepticism with which the period of Enlightenment was befraught in France and England, and it was this Protestant religious and metaphysical component that gave to German "Idealism" its characteristic flavor.

This German Idealism crystallized in its dual poetico-philosophical aspect in the sister cities of Weimar and Jena, located in the idyllic province of Thuringia, in the very heart of Germany. Two small provincial towns, the one a minute princely residence, the other the seat of a university, harbored at the end of the eighteenth century an amazing number of great and unusual personalities, each of whom aided in his own individual way in shaping the German and European culture of the nineteenth century.

It was the great educational and spiritual goal of the New Humanism to lend to the idea of modern individualism a richer and deeper personal note, to visualize the humanizing process in the history of civilization as a victory of spirit over matter, of culture over nature. The cult of the great personality as the teacher and leader of men became the major concern and the central idea of the German intelligentsia, who thus gave to modern subjectivism its most refined and sublime expression. It was their conviction that only in a universal and total view of human life could individuality and subjectivity find their fullest realization. By expanding and extending his inner life into the cosmic reality of his surrounding world man would learn to see wholeness in every part and particle of the universe, he would impart meaning to his own existence and would understand the symbolic language of nature and art by making it part of his own being.

In this give-and-take between the subjective and objective realities, between the ego and the wealth of forms in the outer world, the New Humanist experienced his supreme happiness. His confidence in the self-reliant autonomy of a fully developed human personality revealed the unshakable trust and certitude of a religious creed. Human guilt, error, and blindness were atoned for by the redeeming force of "pure humanity" (*reine Menschlichkeit*). Human greatness was seen as the result of the moral and aesthetic conquest of the subhuman strata of life, and such a mastery of life was the precious reward of the self-discipline and unrelenting moral effort of the poet, the artist, the philosopher. Once more the Greeks provided the ideal pattern of the wished-for "harmony and totality" of life, the Greeks in whose *"Kalokagathia"* (*Kalos*-"beautiful"; *agathos*-"good") this classical harmony had found its verbal and factual expression.

Art was considered by the New Humanists as the most effective of all educative forces, the only one that was capable of truly reforming and reintegrating human life, and beauty was considered as the most trustworthy guide to goodness and truth. Kant's uncompromising dualism of nature and spirit, of sense faculty and reason, appears reconciled in Schiller's idea of the aesthetic education of man, leading to the harmonious development of all human faculties and potentialities. According to Schiller man shares his sensitive nature with the irrational animals, he shares his moral destiny with the spiritual powers, but he is unique in that he alone can embrace and resolve in his own being the opposing forces of matter and mind, of sense and reason, of nature and spirit. It is art that points the way to that ideal realm where true freedom is found in the tranquillity of the "beautiful soul."

In this fervent desire of the New Humanism to attain to moral and spiritual freedom in an ideal subjective and objective world, fashioned by art and resplendent with beauty, the "Religion of Humanity" (*Humanitätsreligion*) reveals its deepest significance: the New Humanism appears as another attempt of modern man to build a unified system of values, an integrated philosophy of life on the bases of modern individualism. The will to autonomy and self-responsibility, now stirring actively in the consciousness of the wide-awake middle classes, found its confirmation in an intellectual aristocracy, a "republic of letters" which was to replace the aristocracy of birth, rank, and title.

Goethe and Schiller. The two men in whom the literary and cultural trends of the post-Reformation centuries converge and climax seem to represent in their mentality and outlook not only two poles of German life but two specific types and possibilities of human existence as such. Coming from different social environments and passing through a different set of experiences, they seemed at first incapable of understanding each other. But when they at last realized that each stood in need of those complementary forces in the other which could serve to integrate their personalities and their works, the friendship they formed transcended in its implications and consequences the sphere of their individual destiny and became an event of the greatest national and inter-European significance. During the years of their mutual intellectual intercourse they both experienced the fruition of their lives and achieved the fullest realization of their literary endeavors.

If we venture to call Goethe a realist and Schiller an idealist, we do well to remain conscious of the limitations which are of necessity attached to such labels. Although the richness and complexity of a great human personality defies in the last analysis the rigidity of such a classification, it may aid nevertheless in circumscribing the ways in which reality is seen, approached, and mastered by individuals of an essentially different physical and intellectual structure. In the case of Goethe and Schiller it is legitimate to say that the one (Goethe) experienced reality unreflectingly with his entire sensuous organism, proceeding from the observation of the individual and concrete to generalizations and the formation of ideal types and concepts. Schiller, on the other hand, lived and moved in a world of ideal essences which, as intellectual experiences, were more real to him in their generality and universality than their feeble images in the world of sense experience.

a) Goethe's Personality. Goethe appeared on the German scene in the historically fateful hour when German civilization was about to throw off the yoke of an all-embracing rationalism. It was his privilege and his destiny to complete this liberation by virtue of a unique combination of the emotional and rational faculties, of elemental passion and tranquil rationality. He was deeply convinced that all life was mysteriously rooted in immeasurable depths and that it was the sacred duty of the human mind to render visible and reveal this secret meaning of life. He felt justified in calling himself the liberator of the Germans "because by the paradigm of my life they have learned that men must live from within, that the artist must work from within. For, no matter what he contrives or how he may act, he will always tend to realize fully his own individuality." In the realization of his own personal destiny, therefore, Goethe followed like Socrates the voice of his "daimon" and recognized in his work the incarnation of universal laws of being. Thus poetry and truth, life and work grew into an inseparable unity and harmony.

He was dissatisfied with the mechanical explanation of nature and mind as offered by the proponents of Cartesian mathematics, rationalist psychology, and descriptive natural science: he was looking for the "spiritual bond" that imparted structural and organic unity to isolated and seemingly disconnected phenomena. In his penetrating analysis of organic and inorganic nature Goethe inaugurated the systematic speculations of the nature philosophers of the nineteenth century and provided an important link between Aristotelian vitalism and the neo-vitalistic science of organic life in our own time.

Goethe appeared to his contemporaries as nature's favorite child, richly endowed with splendid gifts of body and mind, a perfect exemplar of the human species. Napoleon, not given to euphemistic exaggerations in his judgment of men, exclaimed upon meeting Goethe: *"Voilà un homme!"*

Goethe felt himself lovingly and reverently bound to all creatures and to all the mysterious forces of the universe. In silent admiration and awe he stood before the unknown and the unknowable. Like Kant he acknowledged the great ethical command of duty and was ever willing to obey it in the realization of his own self and in the service of the ideals of humanity. With other representatives of Germany's classical age he shared the belief in the common concerns of a united mankind, in a common human fatherland that was not limited by national boundaries. He confesses that as a true cosmopolitan he takes his stand above the nations, experiencing the good and ill fortunes of neighboring peoples as his own. Science and art, he feels, belong to the world, and before them the boundaries of nationality disappear. Only mildly interested in the political struggles of the day and rather indifferent to German national ambitions, he admires in Napoleon the genius of the great ruler and the greatness of a life of unbending heroism.

Goethe aptly characterized his works as "fragments of one great confession." This is especially true of his lyric poems which as autobiographical documents of his intimate feelings and experiences reflect every phase of an amazingly abundant and variegated life. Though surpassed in the epic and dramatic fields by the genius of Homer, Dante, and Shakespeare, he remains the foremost lyricist of the world and is unequaled in the universality of his creative work. He gave German literature the stamp of classical perfection and has gained for it a distinguished place among the literatures of the world. At the same time, he opened up for the German people the treasury of world literature and, in form and content, in style and diction, in poetry and prose, gathered its most precious gems and transplanted them to German soil.

b) Schiller's Personality. In Goethe's judgment the most remarkable of Schiller's qualities was an innate nobility of mind and soul which influenced everything and everyone that entered into the magnetic field of his personality. "Every one of Christ's appearances and utterances tends to make visible the sublime. He invariably rises and raises beyond vulgarity. In Schiller there was alive this same Christlike tendency. He touched nothing vulgar without ennobling it," Goethe wrote concerning his friend. If Goethe possessed or achieved a high degree of harmony within himself and between his own ego and the transsubjective world, Schiller fought a heroic battle against hostile forces within and without. His uncompromising devotion to a world of ideal values and his relentless struggle for the realization of ethical and aesthetic absolutes made his life tense, high pitched, and very lonely, a life that was cut short not only by the frailty of his physical constitution but by the all-consuming force of the spiritual fire that burned within his soul.

In no lesser degree than Goethe, Schiller attained in the end to classical perfection of form, and to mildness, equanimity, and moral greatness of character, but the different stages of his life's way were strewn with thorns and his victories were paid for with sacrifice and suffering. "His face resembled the countenance of the Crucified," wrote Goethe after their first meeting, and years later he said: "Everything in him was grand and majestic, but his eyes were gentle."

Schiller experienced life and world dualistically and dialectically as a struggle between the opposing forces of sensuality and spirituality, necessity and freedom, natural inclination and moral obligation. He was convinced that the breach could be healed and harmony ultimately restored by the moral and aesthetic education of mankind and by the recognition of universal and communal principles and institutions as they are manifested in the social and cultural organisms of family, folk, and fatherland. As moral freedom was the central concept of his life and work, he visualized the ideal human society of the future as resulting from the intellectual and moral greatness of a true leader whose leadership received its sanction from the eternal law of the universe and the inalienable rights of self-determining individuals. He was more interested in a national liberty that rested on these God-given human rights than in the demands of a listless nationalism which derived its justification from common biological and racial characteristics. Thus he was without question a "national poet," but at the same time a poet and thinker whose love and enthusiasm belonged to the entire human family and whose devotion to the weal of mankind made him a pre-eminent educator of his own people.

Great dramatist and moralist that he was, Schiller considered it as the supreme task of the tragic poet to arouse and purify man's moral conscience. He attempted the impossible, however, when he tried to introduce the Greek idea of an inexorable fate into the world of eighteenth-century Humanism and to save and preserve man's freedom and dignity in the face of the inscrutable and impersonal decrees of the ancient "Powers." His ambition to reconcile the ancient fate tragedy of Sophocles (496–405 B.C.) with the modern character tragedy (*The Bride of Messina*, cf. p. 425 sq.) remained unfulfilled, and the author was forced into the recognition that tragic guilt in post-Renaissance drama does not derive from the inflexible decrees of Fate but from the psychological inescapability of human life and personality as such.

c) Goethe's Life and Works. Three major phases in Goethe's development may easily be distinguished: the "storm and stress" of his youth, the classical maturity of his manhood, and the wisdom of his old age when everything transitory had become for him a symbol of the eternal and all human striving an approximation to a lasting peace and rest in God ("*Und alles Drängen, alles Ringen ist ewige Ruh' in Gott dem Herrn*").

Johann Wolfgang Goethe (1749–1832) was a native of the city of Frankfurt on the Main, the scion of a well-to-do patrician family, whose early education was conducive to creating a well-balanced human character and in whom theoretical and practical knowledge and the faculties of intellect, will, and imagination could grow and unfold harmoniously.

At the age of sixteen Goethe entered the University of Leipzig to take up the study of law, in accordance with his father's wish. But his fertile mind was anxious to branch out into other fields, and while submerging joyfully in the glittering atmosphere of the frivolous Rococo society of "Little Paris," he derived lasting benefit from his acquaintance with Adam Friedrich Oeser, the director of the Leipzig Academy of Arts, who encouraged his interest in drawing and introduced him to the aesthetic writings of Winckelmann and Lessing. Goethe's literary style in this period as revealed in his earliest lyrics (*Annette,* 1767) is that of the Rococo (cf. p. 349 sq.) and the Anacreontics (cf. p. 349).

Goethe's stay in Leipzig was cut short by a physical breakdown, caused by a hemorrhage of the lungs, and the young poet had to return to Frankfurt to convalesce in the sheltered atmosphere of his parental home. It was during these months of sickness and gradual recovery that he submitted temporarily to the religious influence of pietistic sentimentalism, embodied for him in a most appealing form in the life and personality of Susanna von Klettenberg, who was one of his mother's friends. *The Confessions of a Beautiful Soul,* filling the sixth book of the novel *Wilhelm Meister's Apprenticeship* (cf. p. 412), represent Goethe's grateful acknowledgment of this early influence, and commemorate the mild and irenic piety of a pure and noble human heart.

In the spring of 1770 Goethe went to Strasbourg to continue his studies, and it was here that he experienced the influence of Herder and the self-styled geniuses of the "Storm and Stress" movement (cf. p. 349 sq.). Herder proved an inspiring and trustworthy guide in pointing out to Goethe the riches of the literary landscape, in revealing to his eagerly absorbing mind the secrets of Homer, Shakespeare, Rousseau, and Ossian, of Hebrew and folk poetry, opening his eyes to the breadth and depth of the realms of the spirit, and arousing in him the titanic force of his slumbering creative genius. Standing in awe before the rhythmical musicality of the rising contours of the Cathedral of Strasbourg, Goethe experienced a close kinship between his own youthful enthusiasm and the prayerful jubilation of the Gothic master builders (*Von deutscher Baukunst,* 1773).

The *Sesenheim Lieder* are radiant with the shimmer and fragrant beauty of young Goethe's love for Friederike Brion, the daughter of the pastor in a neighboring town, while *Goetz* and *Urfaust* speak of Goethe's tragic guilt in sacrificing Friederike's love and happiness to his own "titanic" need for freedom and self-realization.

After another brief stay in Frankfurt Goethe went to Wetzlar, the seat of the *Reichskammergericht* (Imperial Supreme Law Court), to practice law (1772). In the autumn of the same year he was back in Frankfurt. His love for Charlotte Buff, the fiancée of one of his friends, had prompted him to save himself by flight and thus to escape the remorse of another tragic entanglement. The episode itself provided the main theme for the autobiographical novel *The Sorrows of Young Werther* (1774).

The drama *Goetz von Berlichingen* (1773) was the first work by Goethe in which a new content was embodied in a new form and style. As such it became the great model of the "Storm and Stress" poets. But while his imitators admired the freshness and immediacy of Goethe's language and the unconventionality of his dramatic technique, they forgot that with him these devices were only means to convey more forcefully his own personal message. This message was presented in the form of a folk drama, based on the autobiography of the gallant Frankish knight (1480–1562) who in the age of religious revolt and social revolution had made himself the spokesman and leader of the rebellious peasants. Against Emperor Maximilian's "Land Peace" and the jurisdiction of the imperial court, Goetz maintained the law of individual self-help, nevertheless considering himself a loyal imperial knight to the end. To Goethe and his companions Goetz appeared as a symbol of German greatness, a model of personal courage, integrity, and moral conviction in a period of social decay and a purely conventional morality. The struggle between Goetz and his opponents reflects the passionate attack of Goethe's own generation upon the forces of stagnation and rationalistic petrifaction. The technical scheme of the three Aristotelian unities gave way to the dynamic spontaneity of Shakespearean composition, and the vitality of untamed nature broke down the artificiality of every rule that had its *raison d'être* not in the structural laws of character and language.

In the fate of Goetz, Goethe had first realized the tragic destiny of the great leader, the genius, and superman whose titanic will necessarily predestines him to tragic frustration and defeat in the petty world of spatio-temporal limitations. In fragmentary form and free rhythmical verse Goethe subsequently sketches the daimonic force that impels, informs, and devours the lives of Mohammed, Caesar, Socrates, Prometheus, and Faust.

In the original version of *Faust* (*Urfaust*, 1773–1775) titanic passion breaks into the peaceful atmosphere of an idyllic bourgeois world, with destruction and tragedy resulting from the impact. But Goethe's superman himself, in deed and misdeed, in craving, lust, and despair follows merely the dictate of his "daimon," the unbending law of nature itself, and he remains strong even in death and perdition. In Gretchen's songs and prayers, in the solemn invocation of the Earth Spirit, and in the responding chants Goethe reveals himself for the first time as the great master of lyric poetry.

With *The Sorrows of Young Werther* Goethe completes the literary cycle of the works of his youth. This sentimental novel is no less a document of passion than *Goetz* or *Urfaust*, but Werther's passion is "a sickness unto death" for which no remedy can be found in the world of action: from the outset it is condemned to devour itself in silent suffering and utter solitude. The superman of action has been replaced by the superman of emotion, of a feeling whose intensity is heightened and deepened by the gentle rhythm of nature in which it is embedded, carrying it in a predestined course from the crisp awakening of spring to autumnal melancholy and the icy loneliness of winter, from tender hope to passionate yearning and inescapable self-destruction.

For Goethe the completion of *Werther* was an act of liberation: he had freed himself from the sickness to which Werther had succumbed. Thus Werther had to die so that Goethe might be able to live a fuller and sounder life. The novel itself almost immediately became a best seller, and even Napoleon was not immune from the contagion of the "Werther-fever": he confessed that Goethe's novel accompanied him on all of his campaigns.

The beginning of the second major period in Goethe's life and the classical stage in his creative work is outwardly marked by his arrival in the principality and town of Weimar in 1775. He had accepted the invitation extended to him by Charles Augustus, the reigning duke who, as hereditary prince of his duchy, had visited Goethe in Frankfurt and had been charmed by his genial and fascinating personality. In Weimar Goethe soon became the center of courtly society and the intimate friend and counselor of the duke. In this idyllic environment and in the midst of the intellectual elite that gathered together in the shade of the magnanimous princely patronage of arts and letters, Goethe spent with few and brief interruptions the remainder of his life, holding at one time or other the titles and positions of privy councilor, chamber president, minister of finance, prime minister, and director of the court theater.

It was during the first decade of his life in Weimar that Goethe was bound by ties of love and friendship to Charlotte von Stein, the wife of one of the court officials, whose wonderfully balanced character, in its rare unison of the graces of body and mind, corresponded more fully to Goethe's ideal of a "beautiful soul." His "storm and stress" subsided under the ennobling influence of a companionship which in its accord of hearts and intellects rose beyond the sphere of personal relationship into the realm of social responsibilities.

But Goethe's mind was still in the process of growth. His friendship with Charlotte von Stein gave him a presentiment of that classical harmony that was as yet unrealized in his work. His journey to Italy (1786–1788), undertaken as an attempted escape from his manifold social and official duties, symbolizes his actual entrance into the world of his longing, the realm of classical harmony and immaculate formal beauty. The pure and clear contours of the southern landscape, the "noble simplicity and quiet grandeur" of classical art effected in Goethe a poetic and moral renascence: "Together with the artistic sense," he wrote, "it is the moral sense which here experiences a great rejuvenation." As the "Faustian" wanderer from the North he stood in silent admiration before the tranquil beauty of the South, before the art treasures of Rome, Naples, and Sicily, taking the greatest of delight in this temporary refuge and restful haven.

The sojourn in Italy (*Italian Journey*, published 1815–1829) yielded immediately a rich literary harvest: *Egmont* (1787), *Iphigenia* (1787), *Tasso* (1789), and the *Faust-Fragment* (1790) are the dramatic creations that embody the ideal of classical form. In *Egmont* Goethe wanted to portray a historical character who leads his people in their struggle for freedom. Count Egmont (1522–1568), the stadholder of Flanders and Artois, places himself at the head of the Dutch rebellion against the Spanish army of occupation and is executed at the behest of the duke of Alva. As was the case in *Goetz,* the political tendency of the play is democratic and anti-authoritarian. Classical in its stylistic form, the rhythmically moving language in Egmont is musically expressive. The operatic finale and the general lyrical character of the work may have inspired Beethoven's Egmont compositions.

Iphigenia was begun in 1779 (in prose) and completed in Rome in 1787 (in blank verse). Its theme was suggested by Euripides' (*c.* 480–407 B.C.) two dramas (*Iphigenia in Aulis* and *Iphigenia on Tauris*). In Goethe's *Iphigenia* the external motivations of the action as depicted by the Greek playwright are translated into inner, spiritual forces, appeasing and defeating the powers of retribution that haunt Orestes and Iphigenia, the children of Agamemnon, by the irresistible persuasion of love and "pure humanity."

The classical verses of *Tasso* (begun in 1780 and completed in 1789) breathe the "fragrance of the gentle sadness of the departure from Rome." In the portrait of the great poet of the Italian Renaissance Goethe pictures part of his own self. As Torquato Tasso enjoys fame and princely favor at the court of Alfonso, duke of Ferrara, so Goethe was privileged to live and work at the court of Weimar and was favored by the friendship and liberality of Charles Augustus. And Tasso's relation to the princess reflects and immortalizes Goethe's own debt of gratitude to Charlotte von Stein. Goethe's often conflicting duties as a poet and minister of State are mirrored in the antagonism between Tasso, the impractical man of thought and poetic contemplation, and Antonio, the statesman, the realistic man of action. The problem of Tasso is the problem of Goethe, their common goal being the reconciliation between the ideal and the real, between contemplation and action.

The sojourn in Rome with its pagan enjoyment of nature and the free reign of the life of the senses leaves its imprint also on Goethe's mature lyric poetry, especially the *Roman Elegies* (1789) and *Venetian Epigrams* (1790). The former is dedicated to Christiane Vulpius, the daughter of an official of the court library in Weimar, whose light and happy temper and natural simplicity offered Goethe a much needed sensuous complement of his own weighty life and character, and who lived with him as his common-law wife from 1788 until 1806, when the union was legalized.

The unconventionality of his relations to Christiane Vulpius contributed to Goethe's gradual estrangement from the courtly society of Weimar and to his increasing loneliness after his return from Italy. In 1791 he took over the direction of the newly founded court theater and in the following year took part in the campaign against the French revolutionary armies (cf. p. 324). His antagonism to the spirit of the French Revolution was at the same time a determined struggle for the preservation of the world of his own ideals, a world in which personal values maintained their prerogatives as against the claims of a collectivized society. This courageous and uncompromising self-assertion is expressed in poetic form in the crystalline clarity of the classical meters of *Hermann and Dorothea* (1797), an epic poem that sets a genrelike idyl of German middle class life and culture against the dark and bloody background of the French Revolution.

In the meantime Goethe's life and work had received new content and purpose through the friendship with Schiller. In his remarkable letter of August 23, 1794, the younger poet had interpreted Goethe's character and poetic significance with such unusual insight and striking accuracy that Goethe could in all sincerity confess: "You have given me a second youth, you have restored my poetic talents." The epistolary exchange of thoughts between the two princes of German letters lasted until 1799, when Schiller moved from Jena to Weimar to be in even closer contact with his admired friend.

Together the two friends composed a series of epigrams known as *Xenia** (1797), filling the second volume of Schiller's *Almanac of the Muses* (1796–1800), in which they castigated the mediocre literary taste of their contemporaries and ridiculed a number of popular favorites in the realm of letters.

As early as 1785 Goethe had completed the original version of his novel *Wilhelm Meister* (*Wilhelm Meister's theatralische Sendung*). The final version, *Wilhelm Meister's Apprenticeship* (*Lehrjahre*) appeared in 1795–1796 and was soon universally acclaimed as the unexcelled model of a truly poetic and artistic masterpiece. It is a typically German novel in that scenery, situations, and social environment center in the development of a human character (*Entwicklungsroman, Bildungsroman*). The original version tells of the preparation of a sensitive and talented youth for his artistic lifework, using the world of the theater as a social and poetic background. The *Lehrjahre,* on the other hand, paint a broader picture of the personal and social influences that mold Wilhelm Meister's character and to whose guidance and direction he submits, after having overcome such antisocial and undisciplined forces as arise within himself and in the world around him. These forces are personified in the romantic and mysterious figures of Mignon and the Harper, manifestations of that "daimonic" element by which Goethe as much as Wilhelm were both attracted and repelled, ever conscious of its fascination and its danger.

Schiller's death in 1805 was an irreparable loss to Goethe. He tried to forget his grief by turning with redoubled zeal to his earlier preoccupation with the natural sciences. In 1784 he had discovered the intermaxillary bone in the human skull which confirmed for him his theory of biological evolution by establishing a definite relationship and analogy between the lower

---

* *XENIA* (Greek = hospitable gifts) are epigrams whose classical pattern was established by the Roman poet Martial (*c.* 40–102).

and higher animal organisms. The *Metamorphosis of Plants,* published in 1789, demonstrated the leaf as the original organ of all plants, and in his *Theory of Colors* (*Farbenlehre,* 1810) he turned against Newton's ideas concerning the dispersion of light. His scientific research extended to the fields of botany, morphology, mineralogy, and meteorology. In several hymnic essays he expressed his unshakable belief in an omnipresent divine power that informs and animates nature in all its parts and that has designed for every being the law and reason for its existence.

In the years 1807–1808 the first part of *Faust* was completed and published in its final form. Then followed the cycle of the masterpieces of the third major period of his life, including the novel *Elective Affinities* (*Wahlverwandtschaften,* 1809), the autobiographical memoirs of *Poetry and Truth* (*Dichtung und Wahrheit,* 1811–1814), the series of stories and episodes entitled *Wilhelm Meister's Travels* (*Wanderjahre,* 1821–1829), the poem entitled *Trilogy of Passion* (*Marienbad Elegy,* 1823), and the second part of *Faust,* completed in 1831.

Elective Affinities, the first major work of Goethe's old age, uses four main characters to illustrate the parallelism of the moral and natural laws and their immutability in their respective spheres. Elective affinities exert their force of attraction no less in human nature than in chemical elements. The inviolability of the moral law as exemplified in the marriage bond becomes tragically evident in the destruction of two human beings who sacrifice the demands of duty to the urges of passion. For the first time Goethe designates rational self-control, self-limitation, and resignation as the social obligations of an enlightened morality.

In *Truth and Poetry* Goethe gives a poetically colored account of his life from early childhood days to his twenty-sixth year. The work is filled with cultural and literary reminiscences and reveals the author's affectionate attachment to home and family, to all the natural and human forces that had sheltered his youth and shaped his character.

The fruit of Goethe's study of Oriental poetry was the *Westöstlicher Divan* (1814–1819), a collection of original and paraphrased lyrics in an Oriental setting, inspired by his love for Marianne Willemer, who herself contributed some of the poems. In some of the most accomplished verses of the "Divan" (*"Ist es möglich, Stern der Sterne. . . ."*) Goethe followed Dante's example in glorifying love as the symbolic manifestation of that supreme law that moves the stars and sustains the universe.

The most precious jewel, however, of the lyric poetry of Goethe's old age is the *Marienbad Elegy* (1823), in whose majestic stanzas Goethe's renunciation of the last great passion of his life is reflected, the renunciation of his love for Ulrike von Levetzow, a girl who was seventeen years of age when he first met her in Marienbad and in whose blossoming youth the sensuous beauty and rapture of life had beckoned to him once more. The three parts of this *Trilogy of Passion* (*Trilogie der Leidenschaft*) mirror the threefold struggle of passion versus wisdom, ending with a resignation that vibrates with the undertones of a narrowly avoided tragic despair. Once more, as in the stormy days of *Goetz* and *Werther* Goethe freed himself from the impending danger of destruction by entrusting his woe to the magic medium of poetic sublimation: *"Und wenn der Mensch in seiner Qual verstummt, gab mir ein Gott zu sagen was ich leide"* (And where man grows silent in his despair, a God has granted me the poetic gift of expressing my suffering).

d) Goethe's "Faust." "The main business is finished," Goethe wrote in his diary in 1831, the year before his death. At long last he had completed and sealed the manuscript of *Faust,* and therewith he considered his poetic activity closed and consummated. He had begun this great mosaic of his life as a young man, shortly after his return from Leipzig. The *Urfaust* bore the marks of his "storm and stress"; some of the most sublime passages of the first and second part owed their completion and artistic perfection to the influence of Schiller's constructive criticism; the rest embodied the wisdom and mature art of Goethe's old age.

Thus the *Faust* drama in its entirety recapitulates and summarizes the author's life and reflects the major phases of his poetic development. *Faust,* then, is the great master's most complete and authentic biography. But it is much more than that: aside from being Germany's greatest poetic document and one of the rare accomplishments of human genius, the drama represents and illustrates six decades of the literary and cultural history of Germany. And yet, with all its timely documentary values, it spans and covers a much wider area: it is typically German in that it creates timeless symbols of specific Germanic characteristics, and it is profoundly human in that it succeeds in reaching altitudes that permit a survey and inter- pretation of life and reality in their universal and eternal aspects.

When Goethe wrote the first verses of *Faust* Prussia was still ruled by Frederick the Great and France by Louis XV. When he sealed the manu- script shortly before his death Europe was shaken by the aftereffects of the July Revolution in France (1830): Louis Philippe, the "Bourgeois King," ruled in France, and Metternich (cf. p. 461 sq.) controlled the destinies of Europe from the capital of Austria. When Goethe conceived the Gretchen tragedy of the *Urfaust* the structure of the Holy Roman Empire was still outwardly intact. When he published the *Faust-Fragment* Europe began to feel the reverberations of the French Revolution of 1789. When he wrote the classical scenes of the second part the new political order of nineteenth- century liberalism (cf. p. 523 sqq.) began to dawn, Germany was preparing for constitutional government and eventual political unification, the ideas of a system of world trade and world economy were beginning to gain ground, and there was talk of the building of railroads and the construction of the great canal systems of Suez and Panama. All these enormous changes in the outlook of men and in their modes of living are in one way or another traceable in Goethe's *Faust,* so that we may be able to find in its sequence of ideas an expression of the shifting and contrasting problematics of the eighteenth and nineteenth centuries.

The first part of *Faust* differs from the *Urfaust* in that Goethe here no longer dwells on the violent and tragic encounter between a titanic human will and the orderly world of a well-tempered middle class morality, but the emphasis is shifted to the struggle between Faust and Mephistopheles as representing two essential forces and possibilities of human nature. The addition of the "Prologue in Heaven" raises the drama to a perspective which permits a universal view of Faust's destiny within the huge framework of humanity, its aspirations and its aims. The tragedy assumes more and more the character of a morality play.

Faust, dissatisfied with the wealth of human knowledge which he has made his own, penetrates into the spheres of the veiled unknown, with the aid of Mephistopheles, pledging his immortal soul to the devil if ever his intellectual curiosity, his lust for life, his "longing infinite" can be satisfied. The rejuvenated Faust emerges from the fullest enjoyment of sensuous reality with the bitter sensation of remorse, and the "two souls within his breast," his sensual and spiritual desires, remain more disunited than ever: he is farther removed than ever from satiety and complacency.

In the second part of the play Mephistopheles introduces Faust into the arena of social and political action. Faust has learned to confine his desires to the attainable, but within that sphere of measurable and concrete realities he wishes to perform great human and social deeds. He passes through the stages of Goethe's own path of life: at the emperor's court he renders invaluable service to State and society, busying himself with problems of government, finance, and war. At the emperor's request he undertakes his descent to the "Mothers," pictured as personifications of a realm of Platonic ideas, as the aboriginal and eternally creative prototypes of all things. In his encounter with Helen of Troy Faust comes face to face with the absolute perfection of classical beauty, and Helen's catastrophic evanescence makes him realize that he is not prepared as yet to embrace the ideal and rest in its contemplation. But his unfulfilled longing urges him on to the entrance of Hades, Helen's abode. He is granted the rare favor of listening to the mighty heartbeat of the earth, the great mother of life, whose vital forces pass into his own being. The most intimate contact with nature discloses to him the secret of the perfect appreciation of beauty.

The ultimate union of Helen and Faust symbolizes the synthesis of South and North, of Greeks and "Goths," of classicism and romanticism. The off-spring of this union is the child Euphorion,* in whom romantic passion appears enshrined in classical form.

Faust's social and humanitarian efforts are cut short and his vision is destroyed by the blinding breath of the gray figure of "Care" and by Death,

---

*In creating this allegorical figure Goethe had in mind the personality and poetry of Lord Byron.

the great affirmant of the corruptibility of man's physical nature. The satisfaction in the enjoyment of the beautiful present moment that Faust in the hundredth year of his earthly life has not yet experienced, he anticipates as he sinks into his grave. Angelic hosts, battling for his soul, carry his incorruptible self to the feet of the *"Mater Gloriosa"* before whose throne the blessed spirit of Gretchen intercedes for the salvation of her one-time seducer.

According to Goethe the key to Faust's salvation is found in the angels' chant:

> Whoe'er aspires unweariedly
> Is not beyond redeeming.
> And if he feels the Grace of Love
> That from On High is given,
> The Blessed Hosts, that wait above,
> Shall welcome him to Heaven!
>
> (Bayard Taylor's translation)*

The meaning of these verses is amplified by the following pronouncement of the author of *Faust* as recorded by Goethe's secretary J. P. Eckermann, in his *Conversations with Goethe* (1836, 1848): "In Faust himself we find an ever higher and purer activity to the very end, and, coming from above, the succor of Eternal Love. This is fully in agreement with our religious concepts, according to which we are saved not by our own efforts alone but by the supporting divine grace."

In the fifth act of the second part of *Faust* the hero's destiny is no longer determined by the terms attached to the original blood pact with Mephistopheles but by the metaphysically more important wager between God and Satan, which is the major theme of the "Prologue in Heaven." Faust who like Parzival (cf. p. 153) went through earthly life as a "knight errant" has paid the toll and fulfilled the law of his undeviating quest of truth, goodness, and beauty and is thus granted the bliss of eternal rest *"in Gott dem Herrn."*

In the image of Faust's ripening wisdom and in the challenging circumstances which obstructed his plans and efforts Goethe divined the fate of Western mankind in the nineteenth century. He realized the inevitability of the onrushing machine age which would irreverently call in question those personal and spiritual values that imparted meaning and dignity to his own life and which he recognized as a precious heritage and bequest of the past. "The approaching machine age tortures and frightens me: it draws near like a thunderstorm, slowly, slowly; but it continues in its direction, and it

---

* Wer immer strebend sich bemüht,
  Den können wir erlösen.
  Und hat an ihm die Liebe gar
  Von oben Teil genommen,
  Begegnet ihm die selige Schar
  Mit herzlichem Willkommen.

will come and strike" (*Wilhelm Meister's Travels*). He foresaw the coming of a civilization that would enfranchise the masses and disenfranchise the human person, that would develop new methods of production and generate technological advances and material prosperity. And while he welcomed and blessed the spirit of invention and progress, he was nevertheless keenly aware of the price that was to be exacted. He was aware of the dangers that threatened from a preponderance of a purely practical and utilitarian philosophy of life, and he observed clearly the relative insignificance of material progress as compared with the permanency of man's moral nature and problems: "There will be new inventions, but nothing new can possibly be conceived as far as the moral nature of man is concerned."

It had been Faust's intention to utilize technology for the creation of land and opportunities for a free and industrious people, but in carrying out his plans he had to rely on questionable helpers whose aid stained his lofty idealism with the blemish of insufficiency and guilt. The harmony of moral and material development had been Goethe's ideal goal, but he knew full well that the hour was near when the incongruity of material and moral forces would become strikingly evident in the historic evolution of Western civilization.

e) Schiller's Life and Work. The major phases in the development of Goethe and Schiller are identical: from the "storm and stress" of his youth Schiller turned to the classical form of his mature works and in his philosophical writings gave ample proof of that seasoned wisdom which permeates the literary documents of Goethe's old age.

Friedrich Schiller's short life (1759–1805) was as dynamically moving in tempo and rhythm as might be expected when we weigh the magnitude of his work against the scarcely three decades that were granted to him for its execution. He was born at Marbach on the river Neckar, the son of an army surgeon of Charles Eugene, duke of Wurtemberg. His father later on became a captain and overseer of the princely gardens of Solitude Castle near Stuttgart.

Young Schiller attended the Latin school at Ludwigsburg, where his extraordinary gifts attracted the attention of Charles Eugene, who decreed that Friedrich continue his studies at the newly founded military academy (the *"Karlsschule"*). His major fields of interest at that time were theology and medicine, and he was finally permitted by the authorities to substitute the latter for the course in jurisprudence which had been prescribed for him much against his will.

Schiller's craving for free and independent thought and its literary expression was stifled by the rigid discipline and strict censorship in the *"Karlsschule."* The spirit of revolt that was brewing within him was fanned to a feverish pitch by his acquaintance with those writers who had declared war on outmoded conventions and the soulless regimentation of the human mind. The works of Shakespeare, Rousseau, Lessing, Klopstock,

Wieland, and the "Storm and Stress" poets could be acquired and read by the students of the military academy only as bootleg literature, but the enthusiasm that was aroused by these authors was all the greater.

Schiller was eighteen years of age when he wrote *The Robbers* (1777), his first tragedy, bearing the motto *"in tyrannos"* (against the tyrants) and giving vent to his thirst for freedom and his hatred of despotism. The drama was published in 1781 and was produced for the first time on the stage of the National Theatre in Mannheim in the following year. Schiller had secretly attended the performance and witnessed the enthusiastic reception that was given to his play. In the meantime the author had completed his doctoral dissertation *On the Interrelation between the Animal Nature and the Spiritual Nature of Man,* had taken his degree and received an appointment as staff surgeon. Returning from a second secret journey to Mannheim, Schiller was arrested and forbidden by his princely employer "to write any more comedies." Unable to bear any longer the enslavement of his creative mind, he broke the chains of his "Stuttgart Siberia" and fled to Mannheim.

Though the problem of the *Robbers* was suggested by the unfortunate experiences of Schiller's youth and by his growing dissatisfaction with the existing social order, the general tendency remains essentially unchanged in all his future dramas: he strives to depict the world and its inhabitants, not as they actually are but as they ought to be. In the bitter accusations of the *Robbers* he expresses rhetorically his indignation over the moral failings of his "emasculated century" and his hunger for human greatness and moral regeneration. Of the two hostile brothers, Karl and Franz, the former is a victim and symbol of degraded and enslaved humanity, while the latter is the representative of the corruption and demoralization of the upper strata of society. Although the chiaroscuro technique of this drama, with its almost primitive contrasts of good and evil, results in an oversimplification of the leading characters, Schiller's revolutionary thesis is powerfully brought home.

The expected financial aid from Baron von Dalberg, the director of the Mannheim Theatre, was not forthcoming and Schiller's second drama (*Fiesco*) was unfavorably criticized and rejected by the authorities. The homeless and penniless poet found temporary refuge on the small estate of Frau von Wolzogen in Bauerbach near Meiningen, where he completed his third drama, *Love and Intrigue* (*Louise Millerin*). Dalberg finally was persuaded to accept this drama as well as a revised version of *Fiesco* and to appoint Schiller for one year as official dramatic author for the Mannheim National Theatre.

Fiesco (1782) was Schiller's first historical tragedy, dealing with the unsuccessful revolt of an ambitious nobleman against the republic of Genoa. *Love and Intrigue* (*Kabale und Liebe,* 1783), a vivid portrayal of the tragic plight of the middle classes and their desperate struggle against their aristocratic oppressors, derives its color and persuasive force from Schiller's personal ire and resentment. Ferdinand, the son of the all-powerful minister of state Walter, and Louise, the daughter of the town musician Miller, are made the innocent victims of social prejudice and of the damnable intrigues of a dehumanizing system of political corruption.

Love and Intrigue is artistically the most convincing of Schiller's early works, combining the passionate feeling of the "Storm and Stress" poets with the coolly calculating dramatic composition of Lessing's *Emilia Galotti*. As a stage play it proved even more successful than the *Robbers*.

When Charles Augustus, duke of Weimar, paid a visit to the Hessian court at Darmstadt, Schiller was permitted to read to him the first act of his forthcoming drama *Don Carlos* and the duke expressed his approval by bestowing upon the playwright the title of a Councilor of the State of Weimar. Nevertheless, Schiller's external circumstances were very much unsettled. He was suffering from ill health and was brought to the brink of destitution and despair by lack of funds. More than ever before he was in need of friendship and human understanding as well as of material aid. He therefore accepted gratefully the generous invitation of one of his admirers, the youthful jurist Gottfried Körner of Leipzig. In a thoroughly congenial environment he spent two happy and productive years (1785–1787) in Körner's household, first in Leipzig and, after Körner's marriage, in Dresden. The joyful exuberance of this idyllic interlude in Schiller's life is reflected in his *Hymn to Joy* (*Lied an die Freude*), some of whose moving stanzas were embodied in the choral finale of Beethoven's Ninth Symphony.

On Körner's country estate at Loschwitz, near Dresden, Schiller completed his drama *Don Carlos* (1787), the crowning achievement of the dramatic endeavors of his youth and the first of the mature creations of his manhood. Originally it had been Schiller's intention to make Don Carlos, the son of King Philip II of Spain (1555–1598), the hero of a domestic tragedy in the royal family, but four years of intensive preoccupation with the subject matter had shifted the focus of his interest from the personal and psychological to the universally human aspects of the problem. Thus the completed work became Schiller's first great historico-philosophical tragedy. Carlos' idealistic friend, the marquis of Posa, became the central character, the real hero, whose tragic death is not only a moral lesson to the unstable and self-centered dauphin but a voluntary sacrifice to the ideals of freedom of thought and conscience, a sacrificial offering that is no less inspired by the loyal devotion of true friendship than by an even more steadfast devotion to the cause of humanity. As the loose dramatic composition of the earlier works is stylized and tightened by the adoption of the five-foot iambic verse, so the subjective and chiefly negative polemics of Schiller's "storm and stress" gives way to a positive and constructive idealism of classical temper and balance.

A very similar development is noticeable in Schiller's early lyric poetry which culminates in the philosophical poem entitled *The Artists* (*Die Künstler*, 1789). In this poem the author praises art as the unique prerogative of man, deriving the exalted dignity of the artist from his mission and obligation to lead mankind to the heights of intellectual and moral culture.

In 1787 Schiller had moved from Dresden to Weimar. Goethe was still in Italy, but the poet made other valuable contacts with leading representatives of Weimar society. On a journey to the neighboring province of Thuringia he made the acquaintance of Charlotte von Lengefeld, who became his wife in 1790. In the house of the von Lengefelds in Rudolstadt Schiller and Goethe met for the first time. Although no more intimate relationship resulted from this casual contact, for the time being, Goethe was instrumental in securing for Schiller a (poorly paid) position as professor of history at the University of Jena.

In connection with the writing of *Don Carlos* Schiller had felt the necessity of taking up the systematic study of history. The immediate result of these studies was the *History of the Revolt of the United Netherlands* (1788). In 1789 he began his academic activity in Jena with an inaugural lecture on the nature and purpose of universal history (*Universalgeschichte*). In the winter of 1791 Schiller suffered the first serious attack of the lingering disease which gradually undermined his physical strength and made him realize that only his great will power could lengthen the span of his life sufficiently to permit him to complete his poetic mission. His remaining years were an almost continuous struggle against creeping consumption, brought upon him partly by the privations of his youth.

Schiller knew that in order to become Goethe's equal in the realm of letters, and worthy of the great man's friendship, he had to clarify and purify his art so as to achieve a classical perfection and unity of form and content. The study of history served him as a means for the understanding of the meaning of life, the nature of man, and the destiny of mankind. His *History of the Thirty Years' War* (1790–1792) follows the general direction of his dramatic and lyric production, moving away from the subjective and imaginative interpretation of experiences and events toward an objective and sympathetic evaluation of cultural and historical evolution. But the more deeply he delved into the events of the past the clearer it became to him that the knowledge of history was in itself insufficient for a true understanding of its meaning. Therefore, he concluded, a more adequate discipline was needed to clarify those fundamental concepts and principles that could in turn be used as starting points and motivating forces for moral action. Thus he felt the urge to supplement and integrate the study of history by the study of philosophy. He approached both history and philosophy from a practical or pragmatic point of view, looking in both disciplines for a broader and firmer basis of his art and a metaphysical justification of his own poetic existence.

Most of Schiller's philosophical works are the fruit of his preoccupation with Kant and particularly with the *Critique of Practical Reason* and the *Critique of Judgment* (cf. p. 372 sq.). The "Discipline of Morals" that he postulates culminates in the idea of human self-determination and moral freedom. Its basis is the harmonization of that which is and that which ought to be, of natural inclination and moral law and obligation. This harmonization will be the result of a struggle for moral perfection, a struggle that is brought to a happy conclusion in the placid tranquillity of the "beautiful soul." These thoughts in all their manifold ramifications are luminously expounded in the treatise *On Grace and Dignity* (1793). In the *Letters Concerning the Aesthetic Education of Mankind* (1794) he emphasizes once more the moral and cultural significance of art and beauty. The *Letters* were suggested by the noble experiment and dismal failure of the French Revolution, the first practical attempt in modern times to construct a State in accordance with the demands of reason. Why, asks Schiller, was this gigantic undertaking bound to fail? He answers that modern mankind was not sufficiently educated or prepared to risk the dangerous leap from unreason to reason. And how could some future attempt be undertaken with a better chance of success? The commonwealth of reason cannot be established, says Schiller, until all individual members of this ideal State of the future have become reasonable. However, "there is no other way of transforming a sensual into a rational human being but by making him first into an aesthetic being." Aesthetic education only can bring about the reconciliation of nature and reason, sensuality and morality, blind instinct and the sense of duty. It is the privilege of art to lead man through the realm of beauty gradually into the most sublime regions of human civilization.

The most personal of Schiller's philosophical works is the essay *On Naïve and Sentimental Poetry* (1795–1796), in which he attempted a justification of his own art and modern art in general and which provided the succeeding generation of romantic writers with important principles of literary criticism and aesthetic judgment. For Schiller it was a question of artistic self-vindication: he had to prove to his contemporaries and to his own satisfaction that his own and Goethe's poetry represented two equally valid types of literary expression and could thus exist side by side, each in its own right. All poetry, says Schiller, affects us by reflecting the harmony of life and nature. But there is an essential difference in the ways in which ancient and modern poetry achieve this end: the ancient poet was a child of nature, living in intimate relationship with his surrounding world and transposing this harmonious outlook into this poetic works. The modern poet, on the other hand, has lost this original naïveté, in his own nature as well as in his relationship to the outer world. He has intellectually risen above the state of nature and has thus become conscious of conflicts and contrasts that can only be resolved by a supreme effort of his creative genius. While the "naïve" (ancient) poet experiences the objects of reality in their concreteness and simplicity, the "sentimental" (modern) poet experiences and loves the ideas that are manifested in the world of objects. The ancients and those few who, like Shakespeare and Goethe, are their kin in modern times, are like unto nature in their view and rendition of life; the moderns, on the other hand, must strive to regain the lost harmony of nature and a second naïveté by the roundabout and thorny way of reasoned reflection and the resolve of their will.

The time had finally arrived for that unique and blessed friendship that for one decade united idealism and realism in one common effort: the friendship between Schiller and Goethe. The second meeting, so momentous in its consequences, occurred in Jena in 1794, on the occasion of a scientific convention. Five years later, in 1799, Schiller moved from Jena to Weimar in order to be nearer to Goethe and in closer touch with the court theater of Weimar which henceforth was to provide the forum for the products of his dramatic genius.

The influence of Goethe on Schiller's production bore its first fruit, however, in the field of lyric poetry. Always richly and heavily laden with thought, Schiller's lyrics now began to clothe their profound intellectual content with a classical form that was enhanced by the sheen of a new radiance and lucidity. A series of poems that dealt with various phases and aspects of human and social culture was concluded with the masterful *Song of the Bell* (*Das Lied von der Glocke,* 1800), which in reality is a song of domestic and public life, symbolically interwoven with the successive stages of the casting and the social functions of a church bell.

At last, twelve years after he had completed his *Don Carlos,* years filled with unceasing intellectual activity and recurrent mental anguish and physical suffering, Schiller resumed his dramatic production, that mode of literary expression in which he had no rivals and in which his sovereignty remained unchallenged.

Beginning with the *Wallenstein* trilogy in 1799, his classical dramas followed each other in rapid succession. Schiller himself considered the three parts of *Wallenstein* (*Wallenstein's Camp,* a prelude in one act; *The Piccolomini,* a play in five acts; *Wallenstein's Death,* a tragedy in five acts) as a kind of test case to demonstrate to what extent he was able to conform his own style and outlook to that of Goethe. In Goethe's judgment Schiller's *Wallenstein* was "so great that there is no second work that could be compared with it." In the fate of Wallenstein, the great imperial general of the Thirty Years' War (cf. p. 284 sqq.), Schiller wanted to portray "a great and mighty destiny which exalts man while it crushes him." The work is richer in objective description and realistic observation than any other of Schiller's dramas. It is, however, not only the first great example of a modern realistic drama, it is also the first modern historical tragedy that can hold its own when measured by the genius of Shakespeare. Wallenstein, standing at the height of his fame and power, falls victim to the "daimonic" forces of his nature and drags himself and others into the dark abyss of anarchy and annihilation. It was Schiller's intention to illustrate how the precious gift of freedom may cut both ways, because true freedom must rise above chance and arbitrary will and whim, conforming its decisions to the eternal order of a morally meaningful universe.

Goethe-Schiller Monument, Weimar,
by Ernst Rietschel.

In *Mary Stuart* (1800) Schiller dramatizes the tragic tale of Mary, Queen of the Scots, and her hopeless struggle against her implacable adversary, Queen Elizabeth of England. Madame de Staël (1766-1817), in her book *De l'Allemagne* describes Schiller's *Mary Stuart* as the most touching and the most ingeniously planned and executed among all German tragedies. And, truly, in its architectonic grouping of characters and its symmetrical composition it is quite unique and almost in a category by itself.

The Maid of Orleans (1801) Schiller calls a "romantic tragedy," to indicate that his treatment of the subject matter transcends the realistic frame of historical events. The heroine of this play is Joan of Arc (1412-1431), the French peasant girl of Domremy, who at the age of seventeen joined the royal armies of France, leading them in the liberation of Orléans and in their decisive victory over the English. Captured by the enemy, she was tried by an ecclesiastical court and burned at the stake. Vindicated in 1456, she soon became the symbol of French patriotism and was canonized by the Church in 1920.

In Shakespeare's *Henry VI* Joan of Arc, seen through the eyes of English nationalism, appears as a damnable witch whose black magic caused the defeat of the English. In Voltaire's *Pucelle d'Orléans* (1775) the Maid becomes the object of unsavory satire. For Schiller, on the other hand, she is a divinely inspired prophetess, "a noble image of humanity," whose pure features have been defiled by prejudice and cynicism. Conscious of her divine mission and endowed with supernatural power, Joan succumbs to tragic guilt when she opens her heart to human love. However, she atones for a moment of forgetfulness by her final victory and heroic death.

The patriotic fervor of this play contrasted sharply with Goethe's cosmopolitanism and with Schiller's own former convictions as espoused in *Don Carlos*. It was Schiller's first contribution to an awakening national consciousness, a poetic prelude to the beginning struggle for national liberation and unification. An indication of Schiller's fondness for the poetically transfigured *Maid of Orleans* is his words: "You are a creature of my heart; you will be immortal."

After the completion of his "romantic tragedy" with its loose and colorful texture, Schiller felt the desire to write a heroic drama "in Greek manner," a work that would revive the spirit and style of Greek tragedy and would thus offer the author an opportunity to match his own talents with those of the ancients. Form and fable of the *Bride of Messina* (1803) follow closely the Greek models, and Schiller introduces into modern drama that "analytical technique" which was perfected in some of Ibsen's social plays but which had its ancient paradigm in Sophocles' *King Oedipus*. The analytical dramatist delves into the prehistory of the events to unveil step by step the motivations of the ensuing tragic conflicts.

The Bride of Messina bears the subtitle *The Hostile Brothers* and is a "tragedy with choruses." The scene is laid in Messina on the island of Sicily, and the underlying idea is expressed in the two concluding lines: "Life is not the highest of goods, but guilt is the greatest of evils." The inexorable and impersonal "Fate" that arbitrarily rules over gods as well as men takes here the form of a curse, pronounced by the ancestor of a princely family and revived in the mortal hatred of two brothers, a hatred that is fanned by their ardent love for the same girl, who in the end turns out to be their own sister. While adopting in externals the ancient Idea of Fate, Schiller almost imperceptibly introduces certain psychological motivations that make the action more convincing and compatible with human nature as viewed from Christian and modern premises. The tragic guilt of the leading characters has its ultimate source not in the decrees of Fate but in the propensities and moral failings of the individuals. While in Greek tragedy the chorus functioned as an "ideal person," objectively reflecting the "voice of the people" or the abstract principles of universal reason, Schiller's two choruses are decidedly partisan, participating in the action as "real persons" and at the same time as collective magnifications of the mutually exclusive claims and interests of the two brothers.

Schiller's last completed drama was destined to become also his most popular one. The plot of *Wilhelm Tell* (1804) was based on Aegidius von Tschudi's (1502–1572) partly historical, partly legendary account (*Helvetian Chronicle*) of the liberation of the cantons of Schwyz, Uri, and Unterwalden from Austrian supremacy, constituting the beginning of Swiss independence (1291, cf. p. 169 sq.). Never having been able to acquire a firsthand knowledge of the country and people of Switzerland, Schiller had to rely on his fertile imagination and on the study of travel books and scientific descriptions of the Alpine regions, to reproduce local color and to achieve ethnological as well as psychological accuracy.

In making Tell the soul and moving force of the Swiss rebellion, Schiller succeeded in anchoring the national struggle for liberation in the personal struggle of a free man for his inalienable human rights, and by welding three separate actions into one he gave added strength and *élan* to the underlying idea. Thus from the beginning of his dramatic production to the end Schiller remained true to himself, uncompromising in upholding the ideal of freedom and a sworn enemy of all ethical relativism. In *Wilhelm Tell* he created a national festival play that stimulated and sanctioned the national aspirations of the German people.

When death came Schiller was in his forty-sixth year. His physical strength was exhausted but his mind was in the prime of health and vigor. Twenty-two years after his death his earthly remains were exhumed and transferred to the princely tomb at Weimar, where Goethe too is buried.

Musical Classicism: Ludwig van Beethoven (1770–1827). What Goethe and Schiller had accomplished in the media of language and literature was independently achieved by Beethoven in the world of musical sound. Like the literary giants of Germany's classical age, its lonely musical genius, though linked with his great predecessors by intellectual and historical kinship, created his own artistic form, to enshrine in its symbolism the timeless values of his human experience.

The fiery pathos of Beethoven's instrumental music was his exclusive and unique possession, the new and personal organ with which he expressed the creative power of the human spirit and communicated his response to the fundamental questions of human existence. So great was the vitality and unity of content and form in his works, so disquieting and extraordinary the denouement of tragic conflicts and tensions, that the classical temper of Goethe recoiled from such an immediacy of elemental passion. Beethoven's genius, like that of Goethe, embraced world and mankind, but in contrast to Goethe he was always tragically alone with himself and with his art, disdaining and disregarding social conventions and attachments in both his life and his work. Human suffering and human guilt weighed more heavily upon him than on Goethe, and only in his music was he able to triumph over the vicissitudes and contingencies of life. By virtue of his strong and pure artistic will, he forced the complex mass of his emotions into unity and achieved a brilliance of form of whose purifying force he was himself fully aware when he said: "Those who learn to understand my music will free themselves of all the misery with which all the others are burdened." And in a letter of the year 1802, addressed to his brothers, he gives an indication of the deepest motivations of his work as a composer: "Godhead," he writes, "Thou lookest down upon my innermost being, Thou knowest it, and Thou knowest that love of human kind and the will to do good to others abide therein."

Beethoven was born in the city of Bonn on the Rhine, where his grandfather had migrated from Louvain (Löwen) in Belgium and had held the position of *"Hofkapellmeister"* at the court of the princely elector of Cologne. His father, a drink addict, was employed as a tenor singer in the princely chapel and was Ludwig's first music teacher. At the age of thirteen the boy was appointed as second court organist and shortly afterward joined the princely orchestra as a violist. The elector himself paid the expenses for Beethoven's trip to Vienna, making it possible for the young musician to continue his studies under the venerable master Haydn (cf. p. 354 sq.).

The death of his father in 1792 caused Beethoven to prolong his stay in Vienna indefinitely. Aided by excellent recommendations, he was admitted to the circles of the Austrian nobility, and in 1795 he introduced and soon endeared himself to the public as an accomplished pianist and a composer of rank. A few years later he began to feel the effects of a defect in his organ of hearing, a disease which was gradually aggravated and ended in complete deafness. Beethoven, becoming more and more retiring, solitary, and unsociable, retreated into his own self and began to live exclusively in the hidden world of his inner sense of hearing and feeling. But it was during these years of utter loneliness and seclusion that his vision and creative powers were most active, producing some of the most sublime miracles in the realm of musical sound.

In the development of Beethoven's musical style three major periods may be distinguished. In the first group of compositions he shows his indebtedness to the musical forms and the social ideals of the Rococo. The second stage reveals Beethoven as the great master of a new and highly personal musical classicism. In the works of his third and final period the composer encompasses a spiritual realm of a height, breadth, and depth that spans and bridges the chasm between time and eternity.

To the works of Beethoven's youth (1795-1802, op. 1-50) belong his first three piano sonatas, dedicated to Haydn; the First Symphony (1800, op. 21); the first string quartets; and a number of other instrumental and vocal works. The compositions of the classical stage (1803-1815, op. 53-100) include, among others, the Third Symphony (*Eroica*, 1804, op. 55, originally dedicated to Napoleon Bonaparte); the Sixth Symphony (*Pastoral*, 1808, op. 68) with its fascinating musical interpretation of nature ("psychical" program music); the Seventh Symphony (1812, op. 92) with its full scale of emotional and dramatic values, reaching from gentle and dreamlike lyricism to somber mourning and exultant jubilation; and the light and vivacious Eighth Symphony (1812, op. 93), marking a happy equilibrium in the midst of a titanic struggle. To this classical phase of Beethoven's development belong also *Fidelio* (1805), his only opera, his first great *Mass (in C)*, and numerous pieces for orchestra, among them the musical compositions to Goethe's *Egmont*. Among the major works of the third period stand out the *Missa Solemnis* (*Solemn High Mass in D*, 1824), composed on the occasion of the consecration of Archduke Rudolph as bishop of Olmütz, the foremost of Beethoven's ecclesiastical compositions and the most convincing documentation of a sincere piety that had its roots in the Catholicism of his Rhenish homeland. His grandiose Ninth Symphony (1824, op. 125), combining the symphonic form with that of Cantata and Oratorio and thereby creating a novel mode of musical expression, was composed when Beethoven had already lost his sense of hearing. The last movement, ingeniously interwoven with the words of Schiller's *Hymn to Joy,* contains the sum total of Beethoven's life. Its theme is the striving of a human heart that yearns for the blessed pastures of purest joy and lasting happiness but, still caught in the grip of life's anguish and sorrow, attains its victory in a gallant and defiant acceptance and affirmation of the challenge of destiny: "However Life be, it is always good" (Goethe).

PART V. THE RISE OF THE SECOND EMPIRE

1750–1822	Prince Hardenberg, Prussian chancellor (1810–1822)
1755–1813	Gerhard Scharnhorst, Prussian chief of staff
1757–1831	Baron vom Stein, Prussian cabinet minister (1807–1808); dismissed at the request of Napoleon
1773–1859	Prince Metternich, Austrian chancellor and minister of foreign affairs (1809–1848)
1810	Foundation of the University of Berlin
1812	War between France and Russia; defeat of Napoleon's "Grand Army"
1813–1815	The War of Liberation
1813	War of the "Great Coalition" (Prussia, Austria, Russia, England) against Napoleon — Napoleon's defeat in the "Battle of the Nations" (*Völkerschlacht*) at Leipzig — Denmark and the states of the "Confederation of the Rhine" join the coalition
1814	The campaign in France and the first Peace of Paris — Abdication of Napoleon
1814–1815	Congress of Vienna — Reorganization of Europe — The "Holy Alliance"
1815	Napoleon's return from Elba, the "Rule of 100 Days," and the Second Peace of Paris — Napoleon's deportation to St. Helena — Foundation of the German *Burschenschaft*
1817	The Wartburg Festival of the *Burschenschaft*
1818–1819	Enactment of constitutions in Weimar, Bavaria, Baden, and Wurtemberg
1819	Assassination of Kotzebue by Karl Sand — The "Carlsbad Decrees"
1820	The "Final Act" (*Schlussakte*) of Vienna
1823	Convocation of the Provincial Estates of Prussia
(1825–1855)	Nicholas I, tsar "of all the Russias"
1830	"July-Revolution" in France and German revolutionary movements — Enactment of constitutions in the electorate of Hesse and the kingdom of Saxony
1833	Enactment of constitutions in Brunswick, Hanover, and Oldenburg
1834	Foundation of the German *Zollverein* (Customs Union)
1835	The first German railroad, from Nuremberg to Fürth
1835–1848	Ferdinand I, emperor of Austria, son of Francis I
1840–1861	Frederick William IV, king of Prussia, son of Frederick William III
(1846–1878)	Pope Pius IX
1847	Convocation of the United Diet (*Vereinigter Landtag*) of Prussia in Berlin — Foundation of the Hamburg-America Line
1848	Publication of the "Communistic Manifesto" by Karl Marx (1818–1883) and Friedrich Engels (1820–1895); "February-Revolution" in Paris and "March-Revolution" in Germany: revolt in Vienna and flight of Metternich; street fighting in Berlin; convocation of

a Prussian National Assembly; the Frankfurt Preliminary Parliament votes for the convocation of a German National Assembly; revolt in Baden; opening of the German National Assembly in St. Paul's Church in Frankfurt (May); renewed street fighting in Berlin; election of Archduke John of Austria as imperial administrator (*Reichsverweser, 1848–1849*); uprising in Frankfurt; Vienna surrenders to imperial troops; abdication of Emperor Ferdinand I

1848–1916   Francis Joseph I, emperor of Austria, nephew of Ferdinand I

1848–1850   The duchies of Schleswig-Holstein rise against Denmark

1848–1849   Promulgation of constitutions for Prussia and Austria

1849   The Frankfurt National Assembly offers the hereditary imperial crown to King Frederick William IV, who refuses to accept — Revolutionary uprisings in Dresden, the province of Baden, and the Palatinate

1850   Publication of the revised Prussian constitution — Treaty of Olmütz between Austria and Prussia, in which Prussia relinquishes her plans for a union of German states under Prussian leadership

1851   Restoration of the German Confederation (*Deutscher Bund*)

(1852–1870) Napoleon III, emperor of the French, nephew of Napoleon I

1852   Treaty of London, determining the order of dynastic succession in Denmark and the duchies of Schleswig-Holstein

(1853–1856) The Crimean War

1854   Establishment of the House of Lords (*Herrenhaus*) with "Three-Class-Suffrage" (*Dreiklassenwahlrecht*) in Prussia

(1855–1881) Tsar Alexander II of Russia

1855   Prince William of Prussia, brother of Frederick William IV, becomes regent of Prussia

1857   Foundation of the North German Lloyd

(1859)   War between Austria and Sardinia

1861   Promulgation of a new constitution for Austria — Foundation of the Prussian *Fortschrittspartei* (Progressive Party) under the leadership of Virchow

1861–1888   William I, brother of Frederick William IV, king of Prussia and (1871–1888) German emperor

1862   Otto von Bismarck-Schönhausen becomes prime minister (*Ministerpräsident*) of Prussia

1862–1866   Constitutional quarrels in the lower house of the Prussian Parliament

(1863)   The Polish revolt

1863   Diet of the German princes in Frankfurt, Emperor Francis Joseph I of Austria presiding — Foundation of the General Association of German Workers (*Allgemeiner Deutscher Arbeiterverein*) by Ferdinand Lassalle (1825–1864)

1864   War between Prussia-Austria and Denmark and Peace of Vienna — Foundation of the "First (communist) International" in London by Karl Marx (dissolved in 1876) — (The "Second International," founded in 1889, disintegrated during World War I [1914–1918]. The "Third International," on a strictly communistic basis, was created in 1919 with its center in Moscow) — Pope Pius IX publishes the *Syllabus of Modern Errors* to refute the principles of Liberalism and Socialism

1865   Convention of Gastein between Austria and Prussia concerning Schleswig-Holstein

1866   The "Seven Weeks' War" or "German War" between Prussia and Austria: battle of Königgrätz; truce of Nikolsburg; treaty of Prague — Secret defensive treaties of the southern German states with Prussia

1867   Foundation of the North German Confederation

1869   Foundation of the Social-Democratic Party under the leadership of Wilhelm Liebknecht (1826–1900) — (Opening of the "Vatican Council" in Rome; declaration of papal infallibility in *ex cathedra* promulgations on matters of faith and morals; indefinite prorogation of the Council in 1870)

1870–1871   The "Franco-Prussian" or "Franco-German" War — Capitulation of Sedan and capture of Napoleon III; overthrow of the French monarchy; siege and capitulation of Paris (Sept., 1870, to Jan., 1871)

(1870)   Italian troops capture Rome and deprive the papacy of its temporal possessions (Sept.) — Rome becomes the capital of a united Italy — The pope refers to himself as the "prisoner in the Vatican"

1871   Proclamation of the German empire in the Hall of Mirrors in Versailles (Jan. 18) — Peace of Frankfurt — The first German *Reichstag* (Imperial Diet) — Promulgation of the *Reichsverfassung* (Imperial Constitution) and the *Reichs-Strafgesetzbuch* (Imperial Penal Code) — Foundation of the German Center Party under the leadership of Ludwig Windthorst (1812–1891)

Chapter 13

NATIONAL LIBERATION AND
POLITICAL RESTORATION

Reforms in Prussia. While Austria had come out of the first phase of the Napoleonic Wars weakened but not broken, Prussia had lost more than half her territory, having been reduced to but four provinces: Brandenburg, Pomerania, Prussia, and Silesia. Her economic life was completely paralyzed by the immense war indemnities and by Napoleon's "Continental Blockade" of England (decree of 1806), which made it impossible for Prussia to continue the lucrative export of agricultural products to the British Isles. The catastrophe of Jena and Auerstedt (cf. p. 325 sq.) made the political leaders of Prussia realize the mistakes and omissions of the past decades and made room at last for those unselfish and patriotic men who had long voiced their prophetic warnings in vain.

a) Reform of the State: Stein and Hardenberg. Baron Karl vom Stein was the descendant of an old Westphalian family of Imperial Knights, who had preserved the medieval tradition of knightly independence as well as the idea of a unified and centralized German realm under imperial leadership. "I have but one fatherland," he said, "which is called Germany. . . . With my whole heart I am devoted to it, and not to any of its parts." Opposition to the ambitions of the territorial princes, who in the past had given so many proofs of their national unreliability, was therefore part of his social heritage. He was deeply convinced of the necessity and social significance of a moral regeneration of the German nobility, which he considered as an essential factor in any attempt to rescue Prussia and Germany from their deepest humiliation.

In his autobiography Karl vom Stein appears as a man of action whose political realism was inspired by the religious conviction that the State was a moral organism and that everyone of its members was called by Providence to fulfill a definite social function in the service of the commonweal. The salvation of Germany, he believed, could never be brought about as long as Austria and Prussia, the great historical powers, could not be reinstated in their prerogatives of undisputed leadership. He therefore looked upon the several secondary German states which owed their existence to Napoleon with apprehension and disgust, considering them the greatest obstacles to a German rebirth.

In 1804 Stein received an appointment as Prussian Minister of State in the General Directory and was given charge of the departments of finance and economics. He immediately seized the opportunity to carry out some of the much-needed reforms. An edict of 1805 decreed the suspension of the inland duties in Prussia which had proven one of the major stumbling blocks to the development of a unified national economy. The substitution of private ownership of industrial enterprises for State ownership served to break down the economic system of the mercantile State (cf. p. 328 sq.), and the elimination of the corporate restrictions of the guilds was to prepare the way for the introduction of the principle of freedom of trade.

Stein's *Memoir* of 1806, in which he demanded the reorganization of the Prussian cabinet and the whole governmental system for the sake of greater efficiency and responsible leadership, went unheeded until the collapse of Prussia had verified his prophecy that "the Prussian State will either be dissolved or lose its independence, and . . . the love and respect of the subjects will entirely disappear." Stein, who had been dismissed by a royal cabinet order in January, 1807, as "an obstinate, defiant, stubborn, and disobedient state official," was called back in July of the same year, the day after the conclusion of the Peace of Tilsit (cf. p. 326). In October he published his first great Reform Edict, having as its main objectives the abolition of serfdom, the free exchange and disposal of landed property, and the free choice of occupation. Up to this time, two thirds of the population of Prussia had been bound to the soil, unable to leave their homes of their own free will and obliged to render personal service to the manorial lord. In the rural districts the medieval feudal system had survived essentially untouched. It was still illegal for a member of the nobility to engage in trade or to hold citizen or peasant lands. And it was likewise impossible for a peasant or burgher to acquire mortgages on the estates of the nobility. It was therefore a revolutionary innovation when the Edict of 1807 declared that "every inhabitant of our states is competent . . . to possess . . . landed estates of every kind" and "every noble is henceforth permitted . . . to exercise the occupations of a burgher; and every burgher or peasant is allowed to pass from the burgher into the peasant class or from the peasant into the burgher class."

Stein recognized in the sudden and unparalleled breakdown of Prussia the result of a political and social system of bureaucratic and feudalistic tutelage. A partly paternalistic, partly absolutistic form of administration had gradually loosened the mutual bonds of loyalty and unselfish devotion between the people and their government and had bred an attitude of irresponsibility and indifference among all classes of the population. Stein's program of national regeneration received its directives from his clear-sighted diagnosis of the national disease. It became the supreme goal of his short-lived political career to forge out of a reborn Prussia a powerful instrument for the future unification of a greater Germany that was to include Austria.

Although the ethical convictions of the political philosophy of nineteenth-century liberalism (cf. p. 523 sqq.) were embodied in Stein's edict, it would be a mistake to assume that he identified himself with the doctrines of Adam Smith (cf. p. 514 sq.) or the French Physiocrats (cf. p. 329). When we read that "it is just as much in harmony with the indispensable demands of justice as with the principles of a well-ordered national economy" to eliminate everything that hitherto has prevented the individual to attain to that amount of prosperity that he is able to reach in accordance with his capacities, we must not forget that in Stein's opinion only a nation that consisted of free personalities was capable of enlisting the co-operation of all classes and groups. Liberalism for him, then, was a means to an end, not an end in itself. This explains why, for instance, he refused to make the peasants the absolute masters of the soil, but embodied in his reform program certain restraining clauses which were intended to prevent the reduction of peasant holdings to mere merchandise, and to safeguard the continued existence of a healthy landowning peasantry. Thus the purchase and sale of peasant holdings was made dependent on the consent of the government. As far as the entailed estates of the nobility and the law of primogeniture (right of the eldest son to inherit real estate) were concerned, their integrity was to be preserved because Stein believed that an independent, landowning nobility was likewise essential for a healthy State organism. Economic liberalism, on the other hand, as well as the theories of the French Revolution aimed at the confiscation, dissolution, or partition of all entailed estates. It was precisely because of Stein's attempt to steer a sane middle course between conservatism and liberalism that he antagonized both the conservatives and the liberals. As the progressive features of his reform program became more conspicuous, the nobility indignantly began to look upon him as a traitor to his own caste and an avowed "Jacobin" (revolutionary radical, so named after the "Jacobin Club" of the French Revolution, whose meetings were held on the premises of the "Jacobin" [Dominican] monastery).

In the year that followed the publication of the Reform Edict, Stein bestowed on a large number of cities the *"Magna Charta"* of self-government (1808), thereby restoring to them the autonomy that they had possessed in medieval times. In his constitutional reform of city administration the Prussian minister followed the model of the French Revolution, eliminating the merchant and craft guilds and substituting, for the privileges of birth, capital and private property as the principle of social organization. Jews and members of the armed forces were excluded from citizenship, the former for racial, the latter for professional reasons. Members of both categories were considered as "denizens" (*Schutzverwandte*). They were forbidden to own real estate, were excluded from trade and industry, and had no share in city administration.

Late in 1808 Stein was dismissed a second time, upon the interception of a compromising letter that he had addressed to Count Wittgenstein at the court of the elector of Hesse, and in which the Prussian prime minister openly tried to enlist support in Hesse and Westphalia for the incipient revolt against Napoleon. Stein's property was confiscated by the French emperor and a price was set on his head, but before fleeing to Austria he had drawn up his "political testament," a circular letter in which he set forth the ideas that had inspired his reforms. Some of the demands contained in this political document were not realized until 1848, when the March Revolution (cf. p. 527 sqq.) forced, among other things, the establishment of a Prussian parliament, the suspension of the manorial police, and the abolition of patrimonial jurisdiction. The political result of Stein's dismissal was a closer co-operation of Prussia and Russia and the temporary aloofness of Prussia in the struggle for liberation, which for the time being had to be carried on almost exclusively by Austria.

Stein was succeeded in office by Altenstein (1808–1810), whose feeble and inefficient administration was in turn superseded by the appointment of Karl von Hardenberg as State chancellor of Prussia. Despite the divergency of their political philosophies, Hardenberg's name remains closely associated with Stein's reform program which he continued and in some respects completed. A native of Hanover, he considered, like Stein, Prussia as his adopted country and devoted his great political and diplomatic talents to the cause of its liberation, consolidation, and aggrandizement.

Hardenberg was a docile pupil of the enlightened *"Philosophes"* (cf. p. 368 sq.), a statesman endowed with irresistible personal charm, combining a profound knowledge of human nature with an unshakable belief in the sovereign and autocratic rights of the great political leader. Living in forced retirement after the Peace of Tilsit, he composed his famous *Memoir* of 1807, a counterpart of Stein's document of the preceding year. Its quintessence was the demand for social and economic reorganization, in accordance with the principles of an enlightened individualism and, at the same time, the call for a strongly centralized State bureaucracy, with special provisions for some form of "national representation."

Shortly after having taken over the office of State chancellor he issued a number of financial laws, designed to bring about a "revolution from above." A special edict decreed the secularization of all Church property, both Catholic and Protestant, extending the more limited secularizations of 1803 (cf. p. 325). The amount realized by the sale of ecclesiastical estates was applied to the reduction of the national debt. The new tax bills of 1811 introduced a general ground tax, extended the excise (consumers') tax and the duty on luxury articles over the entire country, and proclaimed complete freedom of trade, subject only to the payment of a license tax. Hardenberg agreed with Adam Smith that unlimited competition was "the best incentive and regulative principle of industry." The bases of the new legislation were equality before the law, freedom of ownership, and freedom of contract. Opposition to the new legislation was vociferous, especially among the nobility and the big landowners. They regarded Hardenberg and his associates as "aliens," who were trying to transform the "honest State of Prussia into a new-fangled Jew-State."

In accordance with the changing agricultural theories and methods Hardenberg worked out a series of new agrarian laws. Albrecht Thaer, who had made a name for himself by the publication of his book on *The Principles of a Rational Agriculture* (1809–1812), in which he applied the economic theories of Adam Smith to a scientifically improved cultivation of the soil, was asked to carry out the new agrarian laws. By making the profit motive the basic principle of agriculture the new system dealt the deathblow to the patriarchal economic ethics of the past. According to Thaer "the most perfect agriculture is the one which draws the greatest profits from its activities." Here, too, the representatives of the landed nobility protested against a new system of rationalization, defending the spirit of patriarchal order and sentimental attachment to the soil. With Adam Müller (1779–1829, cf. p. 498 sq.), their spokesman, they tried to preserve or revive a romantic-feudalistic ideal of agrarian organization and management. For them agricultural activity was a moral "office," performed in the service of State and community, and they thought that there was an essential difference between factory and farm, between trade and agriculture. They therefore objected to Thaer's cool impersonalism which cut the ties that were binding the landowner to the soil. With Martin Luther and a majority of medieval economists they saw in the patriarchal system of agriculture a divinely established order, the basis of family and State alike, an order that was arbitrarily threatened and disturbed by the innovators who replaced personal service and obligations by the servile devotion to the impersonal power of money. They were quite generally opposed to the modern preponderance of trade and manufacture over agriculture and pleaded for the restoration of the corporative system of medieval economy. "Knighthood and peasantry are about to perish, and in the end there will be nothing left but merchants, tradesmen, and Jews" (Adam Müller).

It was due to Hardenberg's personal energy, and the great political power that he wielded as chancellor of the State, that he won his victory over the forces of conservation. In his edict of 1812 he went so far as to open the way for the Jews to acquire citizenship and to enter the academic and civil services.

b) Reform of the Army: Gerhard Scharnhorst. The crushing defeat of the Prussian armies at Jena and Auerstedt (1806) had shown the weakness and inadequacy of the military system that had been created by the kings of Prussia in the period of State absolutism and enlightened despotism. In the year (1807) in which Stein headed the Prussian cabinet and worked out the principles of his social and political reform program, he also laid out the general ground plan for a thoroughgoing military reform. He was fortunate enough to find a congenial collaborator in Gerhard Scharnhorst, who, combining sound theory with practical experience, became the creator of the modern armies, recruited from the people and consolidated by patriotic devotion to a common cause. The victories of the colonial armies of North America over the English mercenaries had conclusively proven the superiority of armed forces that were inspired by popular sentiment and loyalty to a common fatherland. But Scharnhorst was convinced that, if the traditional soldierly training and discipline of the Prussian military machine could be preserved and harmonized with the new patriotism, the military might of the new Prussia would become impregnable.

A native of the state of Hanover, Scharnhorst entered the Prussian military service in 1801 and became director of the military academy in 1804. In his writings he elaborated the new military science whose principles provided the bases of military training and strategy down to Moltke (cf. p. 534) and von Schlieffen (cf. p. 635). In his *Memoir* of 1806 he emphasized the significance of moral incentives for successful warfare, designating personal courage and individual responsibility as absolute requisites of soldierly conduct. Taking the revolutionary armies of France as a model, he demanded the creation of a national army in which every citizen was called to military service. This new citizen army was to be founded on the soldierly virtues of courage, gallantry, and honor and was to provide equal opportunities for all. Dishonorable forms of punishment were to be abolished and rewards for bravery in the ranks were to be encouraged. "Sacrifice and fortitude are the pillars of national independence," he wrote. "If our hearts no longer beat for these, then we are lost, even while we still ride on the waves of great victories." These words were written before the defeat of the Prussian armies, and Scharnhorst, like Stein, had to hear himself denounced as a "Jacobin" radical. But even if Scharnhorst's capacities had been duly appreciated, if his counsel had been heeded and he had been given the supreme command, it would probably have been too late to turn the tide.

Scharnhorst's time came when the Peace of Tilsit had been concluded and Prussia had ceased to be a great power. The king, convinced at last of the need of military reform, made Scharnhorst the head of the military commission, and his ideas bore fruit not only in the ensuing War of Liberation (1813) but in the wars of 1866 (cf. p. 539 sq.) and 1870–1871 (cf. p. 542 sqq.) as well.

The military reform was carried out in several stages, each step forward calculated to make the most constructive use of those accomplishments and institutions of the past that were worth conserving. The idea of universal military service had come into being as a measure of national self-defense in the days of the French Revolution, and its acceptance in Prussia was born of the same motive. The principle of conscription itself was nothing new in Prussia, although hitherto it had been beset with too many discriminations as to classes and persons, exempting large groups of the population and working great hardships on the peasants who provided by far the largest contingents of the conscript armies.

Side by side with conscription the system of recruiting and voluntary enlistment was still in existence and imposed a heavy burden on the state treasury. Military discipline was enforced by a brutal penal code that provided severe punishments, including whipping and running the gauntlet, for minor offenses. The humanitarianism of the enlightened age had stopped short of the military barracks, for the simple reason that the political power of the "enlightened despots" rested on a rigidly disciplined army.

The French Revolution had for the first time made legal equality the basis of conscription, while Napoleon reintroduced the system of limited selective service by legalizing exemptions and service by proxy.

The military reforms of Stein and Scharnhorst attributed primary importance to the necessity of limiting membership in the future armies of Prussia to Prussian citizens. The reform plan of 1807 called for a standing army and a national militia, side by side. When Napoleon prohibited the formation of a militia, the reformers realized that their only alternative was the transformation of the standing army into a citizen soldiery (*Volksheer*), in which all citizens, irrespective of class and position, were obliged to serve. At the same time it was absolutely essential for the new army to combine the traditional spirit of order and discipline with the modern ideals of citizenship, human dignity, legal equality, personal freedom, and voluntary service. The new patriotism was to be wedded to the old Prussian military virtues. The military reform therefore included a complete program of education.

The outgrowth of these considerations was the creation of an army of the line and, side by side with it, the so-called *Landwehr* (militia) and *Landsturm* (general levy of the people). The army of the line was based on the principle of universal military service without exemptions. The *Landwehr,* consisting of some 150,000 men between the ages of twenty and thirty-five, was an army of reservists, and the *Landsturm* signalized the general mobilization of the male population in their entirety for the service of their country. The idea of a "total war" of the people was developed in Ernst Moritz Arndt's (cf. p. 480) stirring pamphlet, *What is the Meaning of Landsturm and Landwehr?* (1813.) The *"Landsturm"* accordingly was to include all men over thirty-five. Their services were to be employed only within the confines of the national boundaries, they were to wear no uniforms and were to use any suitable weapon. The real meaning of the creation of the *Landsturm* was then the virtual obliteration of the distinctions between soldiers and civilians, a *"levée en masse"* in which no one was willing to give or could hope to receive any quarter.

Stein and Scharnhorst knew perfectly well that the military reform could only succeed if the traditional exclusive hold of the members of the nobility on the commanding positions in the army could be broken, if class distinctions were eliminated, and if nobility and citizenry could be welded together. They were absolutely firm in their conviction that the only alternative was a radical reform or none at all. Scharnhorst therefore ruthlessly purged the officers' corps of all those commanders who owed their positions to social prestige rather than personal qualification. Only two of the 143 generals who belonged to the Prussian army in 1806 were allowed to continue in service in the War of Liberation of 1813. One of the first resolutions of the newly appointed military commission reads as follows: "In time of peace only technical knowledge and training, and in time of war only the highest type of bravery, activity, and circumspection can establish a claim to a commanding position. It is therefore necessary that all individuals in the entire nation who possess such qualifications be entitled to aspire to the highest posts of honor in the army."

It was this attempt to break down the privileges of the nobility that met with the strongest opposition of the military clique, whose members were anxious to perpetuate their families in the military leadership of the nation and who suspected Stein and Scharnhorst of "Jacobin" tendencies. The reformers, on the other hand, believed in the principle of competition and considered it the duty of the State to enlist the services of all citizens in accordance with their capacities. It was this part of the military reform program that was only partially and temporarily realized; after the War of Liberation the nobility regained their dominant position in the army.

c) Educational Reform: Wilhelm von Humboldt. Shortly before Stein, giving way to Napoleon's pressure, had to resign his post in the Prussian cabinet, he persuaded the king to appoint Wilhelm von Humboldt (1767–1835), Prussia's ambassador to the Vatican (1802–1808), as head of the Ministry of Education (*Kultus und Unterricht*). In his youth Humboldt had associated with the humanistic circles of Weimar and had acquired fame as the author of treatises on aesthetic subjects and as a translator of Greek tragedies. He was a man of sensitive character, highly cultured, many sided in his interests, and cosmopolitan minded. Owing his own education to private tutors, he had never attended a school and was therefore not specially prepared for his new position. Up to the time of his appointment as minister of education (1809) he had been out of touch with the program of the reformers and had to offer no definite program of his own. It needed a good deal of moral persuasion to make him accept the proffered cabinet post, but he soon grew into his task and became the creator of the modern system of "humanistic" education in Germany.

To fall in line with the social and political reforms the new educational program had to combine the ideas of the German Enlightenment and Classical Idealism of the eighteenth century with the new nationalist and liberal ideologies. The term "national education" (*National-erziehung*) had been coined by the philosopher Johann Gottlieb Fichte (1762–1814, cf. p. 500 sq.) who, in the winter of 1807–1808, had delivered his impassioned *Addresses to the German Nation* in Berlin, under the very eyes of the French army of occupation. In these discourses Fichte blamed the unconcern and selfishness of the individual citizens for the downfall of Prussia, and called for the reconstruction of the fatherland by means of sacrifice and devotion and by the steeling of the national will. He referred to Pestalozzi's (cf. p. 377) educational endeavors, to bridge the gap between an educated intelligentsia and the common people, and recommended a unified school system (*Einheitsschule*) as the most solid foundation of a uniform national education.

Pestalozzi had specified the cultivation of a healthy family life as the indispensable basis of a social and national commonwealth and had described the school as the family's natural complement, whereas Fichte assigned to the school an independent and all-inclusive function that necessitated the radical severance of the ties between home and school. This made the education of the child the exclusive prerogative and responsibility of the State. As Scharnhorst had made the State the master of the bodies of the nation's youth, through universal military service, so Fichte's universal and unified school system was designed to make the State the master of their minds and consciences. Both men were convinced that the moral incentives that the State had to offer would result in a spirit of voluntary submission to the State as a supreme moral absolute. The immediate practical outgrowth of these ideas was the creation of a tripartite system of education, consisting of elementary schools (*Volksschulen*), "humanistic" secondary schools (*Gymnasien*), and universities (for graduate and postgraduate study). The exclusive academies for young noblemen (*Ritterakademien*) and the military schools for the children of soldiers (*Garnisonschulen*) disappeared.

Wilhelm von Humboldt's personal accomplishment within the larger framework of the educational reform was the combination of the educational ideals of the New Humanism (cf. p. 403 sq.) with the doctrines of Pestalozzi. He emphasized the creative aspects in the process of learning and the elements of personal spontaneity that constitute true knowledge and wisdom. Both Pestalozzi and the New Humanists were advocates of "formal discipline," insisting on the basic significance of a harmonious exercise and development of mental faculties and rejecting the idea of specialization, professionalism, and utilitarianism in education. They argued that a well-balanced and liberally educated mind was the most suitable and useful instrument in mastering any scientific, practical, and professional problem and situation. For Humboldt, language in particular was a means for the creative development of intellectual forces and faculties, a material symbolization of spiritual realities. In his philosophical speculations on the nature of speech he made the attempt to demonstrate that the languages of different peoples were the truest manifestations of their national individuality (cf. Herder, p. 396 sq.). It was for this reason that he made the study of languages, ancient and modern, the basis of secondary education. That he attributed major importance to the study of the languages of antiquity was due to his conviction that in the thought and speech of the Greeks and Romans the ideal of *Humanität* was most completely and most impressively conveyed to the student.

Humboldt's ideas on higher education received their official sanction in the "statutes for classical education" (*Gymnasialverfassung*) of 1812. The curriculum of the *Gymnasium* was to consist of a ten years' course, and the compulsory major subjects of instruction were to be Latin, Greek, German, and Mathematics. The minor subjects that were to round out the course of liberal and general education were likewise compulsory. At the end of the ten years' course the student was to undergo a comprehensive oral and written examination, the successful passing of which was to be made a prerequisite for his entering a university. Thus secondary education and university education were strictly and organically correlated, and all professional and vocational training was excluded from the *Gymnasium* and relegated to the universities and polytechnical institutes of university rank. For the time being, this standardized type of classical or humanistic education seemed to carry the day, while the more scientifically and technically oriented "Realschulen" (cf. p. 361), stemming from eighteenth-century Enlightenment, were temporarily pushed into the background.

The rehabilitation of the academic standing of the German universities after a long period of decline took its start from the foundation of the Universities of Halle (1694) and Göttingen (1734). The latter institution in particular was destined to become the cradle of modern scholarship and modern science. The Göttingen faculty were instrumental in building up one of the finest libraries in the world, and in 1751 they founded the "Scientific Society" (*Sozietät der Wissenschaften*), which was closely affiliated with the university.

The ideal contents of the new humanistic scholarship were supplemented by the addition of the new idealistic philosophies (cf. p. 499 sqq.) which had their central meeting ground in Jena, where Fichte (cf. p. 500 sq.), Schelling (cf. p. 501 sq.), Hegel (cf. p. 502 sqq.), and Friedrich Schlegel (cf. p. 475) proclaimed their gospel of the unity of all the sciences and the universal mission of higher education. According to Schelling, it is the function of a university to provide authoritative guidance in the search for truth and to pursue knowledge, not for any practical or utilitarian reasons, but strictly as an end in itself.

The attempted university reform in Prussia was abruptly brought to a halt by the collapse of the State, entailing the loss of some of the most prominent institutions and the suspension of others. However, King Frederick William III expressed the feelings of the intellectual elite of his people when he said: "The State must replace its material losses by spiritual gains." Shortly after Prussia's defeat a royal edict was published that commanded the establishment of a general institute of higher learning, in affiliation with the Academy of Sciences in Berlin. Wilhelm von Humboldt, too, felt that such a leading institution in the capital of Prussia could achieve a great deal in restoring the moral prestige of the State: "The foundation of a great and well-organized university which, if it succeeds, must draw students from all parts of Germany, will be one of the most efficient means to win for Prussia the attention and respect of Germany." Thus the creation of the University of Berlin (autumn, 1810) was chiefly the fruit of Humboldt's ideas and endeavors. When the new university opened its portals, Humboldt was no longer in office. The appointment of Hardenberg as State chancellor in June, 1810, had killed his hopes for a truly independent ministry of education. Further co-operation between the two men proved impossible, and Humboldt returned to the diplomatic service, accepting the appointment as Prussian ambassador in Vienna.

In his educational ideals Humboldt anticipated the pet theory of educational liberalism, the concept of an education without ulterior purpose ("*zweckfreie Bildung*"), of a "knowledge without presuppositions" (*voraussetzungslose Wissenschaft*). But although these and similar slogans proclaimed the absolute objectivity of knowledge and science, the intellectual battles that were fought between the "liberal" representatives of multiple schools of thought were as fierce as ever.

For Humboldt, as for the other leading thinkers of the early nineteenth century, the ideal university was to fulfill the dual function of teaching and research. The high standard of the German universities in the nineteenth century was due to the fact that they were able to realize this ideal demand. These institutions succeeded not only in rearing successive generations of great scholars but also in preparing their students for the complex tasks of national and community life. The pre-eminent teacher was regarded as a kind of apostle, whose teachings became living realities in his disciples. The average professor, on the other hand, developed more and more the characteristics of the specialist and scholarly expert. With the growing specialization of the sciences and professions in the later nineteenth century, and with the ultimate failure of the educational reformers to achieve a new synthesis of science, philosophy, and religion, the idea of scholarship frequently degenerated into an unhealthy preponderance of theory over life, resulting eventually in an abstract and sterile intellectualism. Such a development was bound to bring down upon the German universities sooner or later the Nemesis of thwarted emotions and instincts, the revolt of the telluric forces of "blood and soil." The educational program of the national-socialist revolution reflected this violent reaction against the divorce of scholarship and life, but, because of a similar one-sidedness, it failed to offer the much-needed corrective.

d) *Physical Education: Ludwig Jahn* (*1778-1852*).   The educational reform required the mobilization of both the moral and physical strength of the people. The idea of a self-responsible, self-active, and harmonious personality could only be realized if the training of mind and body received an equal share of attention. Ludwig Jahn (the *"Turnvater"**) made it the major concern of his life to restore the German *Volksgeist* on the basis of the strictest physical and moral discipline. After years of restless wander-

---

* Father of gymnastics.

ing Jahn had accepted a teaching position in one of the Berlin secondary schools and in 1811 he started the gymnastic training (*Turnen*) of several hundred students on the *"Hasenheide"* in the outskirts of Berlin. This group of young people formed the nucleus of a nationwide organization of young athletes, united by a common national ideology and strengthened in their spirit of solidarity by their association and intercourse on frequent journeys across the country, in game and play, in athletic drill and gymnastic festivals. The members of the *Turnerschaft,* recruited from every class and calling, uniformly regimented in dress and equipment, and adopting identical slogans, developed into a homogeneous social force and potential fighting unit for "folk and fatherland." Jahn's idea of a self-sufficient national democracy was pugnaciously intolerant and made him hurl abuse and invective against Frenchmen, courtiers, and Jews alike. But in his blunt and rude sincerity he contributed to the growing assimilation of classes and social groups and aided in the educational reform by injecting moral motives into the lives and thoughts of students in secondary schools and universities.

Military Reforms in Austria and the War of 1809. The "Three-Emperors' Battle" at Austerlitz of the year 1805 (cf. p. 325) had sealed the downfall of Austria but had also cleared the way for the forces of reform and regeneration. Count Philip Stadion (1763–1824), a native of Mainz and like Stein the descendant of an old family of Imperial Knights, took the lead in the Austrian reform movement. He was a statesman who loathed the leaders of the French Revolution as much as he hated Napoleon, their heir and self-appointed executor.

At the time of Austria's decisive defeat the Austrian lands were in a more literal sense than any other European territories exclusive possessions of their native dynasty, the Hapsburgs. Nobles and great magnates were more numerous and more influential there than anywhere else. It was therefore for the time being very difficult, if not impossible, to break down the privileges of birth, to free the peasantry, and to carry out those social and political reforms that marked the rebirth of Prussia. It was for these reasons that the reforms in Austria had to confine themselves chiefly to the reorganization of the army. Thus Austria, with her territories free from enemy occupation, could prepare herself more directly and more thoroughly for the future War of Liberation.

The man who was Stadion's chief collaborator and who at the age of twenty-five had been hailed as the "liberator of Germany" was Archduke Charles, the brother of Emperor Francis (cf. p. 324 sq.). After the Peace of Pressburg (cf. p. 325) Charles assumed the supreme command of the Austrian armies and took over the Ministry of War. He had distinguished himself in the campaigns that preceded the defeat and his genial personality endeared him to civilians and soldiers alike.

Anticipating Scharnhorst's reforms, Archduke Charles firmly established the principle of universal military service, reformed the military penal system, and restored military discipline and morale on the basis of individual responsibility. Like Scharnhorst he recognized the significance of a strong army of trained reserves, supplementary to the army of the line. Thus the "Patent" of 1808 decreed the organization of a *Landwehr,* and both Stadion and Archduke Charles prepared their people for an immediate uprising against Napoleon.

In the same year, 1808, there occurred the heroic and memorable rebellion in Spain, where Napoleon had forced the abdication of King Charles VI and placed his own brother Joseph on the Spanish throne. The Spanish uprising was Napoleon's first serious setback. It was aided by an English expeditionary army under the Duke of Wellington (1769–1852), and it could have led to Napoleon's overthrow if Prussia's irresolute king had followed the example of Spain and Austria and had lent his ear to the advice of Baron vom Stein. Instead, Frederick William III, turning to a policy of appeasement, deserted the cause of national liberation and left Austria, Germany, and Europe at the mercy of the superior might of the French emperor. The shame of the Austrian defeat and the Treaty of Schönbrunn (cf. p. 326) is mitigated by the bravery with which this first phase of the War of Liberation was fought by the Austrian people, and more especially by the glorious uprising of the Tyrolese peasants and shepherds who under the leadership of Andreas Hofer offered all Europe an example of inspired patriotism. Andreas Hofer, the heroic innkeeper of the Passei Valley, was eventually captured, court-martialed, and shot (1810), the Tyrolese rebellion was quelled, and the Austrian war lost; but the cause of freedom had won the crown of martyrdom and the sacrifices were not in vain.

Napoleon and England. In the meantime, however, Napoleon's conquest of Europe had proceeded apace in breath-taking strides. When he was named First Consul of the French Republic in 1799, France had already obtained control of Belgium, Holland, Switzerland, and the left bank of the Rhine. Northern and southern Italy had been reduced to the status of French protectorates within the new system of political alliances. After the plebiscite of 1804 had bestowed upon Napoleon the imperial title, he began to carry out his revolutionary designs for a "new order" in Europe. In 1805 he went to Milan and, like Charlemagne, usurped the "iron crown" of the ancient Lombard kings, investing his stepson, Eugène Beauharnais, with the dignity of a viceroy. In 1806 he created the kingdom of Naples and Sicily and enthroned his brother Joseph as its ruler. The remaining Italian territories, including the Illyrian provinces, Rome, and the Papal States, were annexed by France during the following three years.

In Germany as in Italy Napoleon's policy was dictated by the principle *"divide et impera"* (divide and rule). By sowing the seeds of discord between North and South and by making capital of the venality of some of the German princes he won the material and moral support of a number of South German principalities and gained a strangle hold on the German lands in their entirety. In the Treaty of Pressburg Napoleon's German allies received territorial awards and Bavaria and Wurtemberg were given the status of kingdoms. The emperor of the French proclaimed himself the protector of the newly created puppet states which were united in the Confederation of the Rhine (*Rheinbund*).

And yet, despite this almost unprecedented accumulation of power in his hands, Napoleon realized that his triumph remained incomplete and insecure unless he succeeded in breaking the British domination of the sea lanes and in making England acquiesce in the "new order" of Europe. In order to strike against this last and most formidable opponent Napoleon assembled a fleet of transport ships in the French channel ports and prepared for an invasion of the British Isles. He was convinced that once he dominated the English Channel the road to world domination was clear and unobstructed. But quite unexpectedly he abandoned his invasion plans and in a surprise move marched his armies to the interior of Germany, defeating an Austrian army at Ulm (Wurtemberg). One day after this battle the English under Admiral Nelson achieved a major triumph in the destruction of the French and Spanish naval forces at Trafalgar (1805), thereby ending once and for all Napoleon's hopes of gaining a victory over England by means of military conquest. The only avenue that remained open for the French emperor was the prospect of defeating England by cutting off her trade. But in order to carry such an economic war to the finish, Napoleon's domination of the European continent had to be complete. Thus the defeat and partial occupation of Prussia was followed by the creation of the "Grand Duchy of Warsaw" out of the territories of Prussian Poland, and the establishment of a new "kingdom of Westphalia" that included the Prussian lands west of the Elbe and some of the smaller states of northwestern Germany, and that was to be ruled by Napoleon's brother Jerome. With his influence and control extending to the coasts of the North Sea and the Baltic, and having broken up and defeated the Third Coalition (cf. p. 325), the emperor was at the height of his power and seemed to have become truly invincible.

But while the subjected peoples of Europe were smarting under the yoke of the conqueror they were eagerly waiting for the first opportune moment to throw off their chains and regain their independence. The major flaw in Napoleon's calculations was his underestimation of the strength of some of his opponents, especially of the tough fiber and cool determination of the freedom-loving British nation, which set all its inherited tenacity against the Corsican emperor's gigantic onslaught.

Napoleon's Decrees of Berlin (1806) and Milan (1807), promulgating the so-called "Continental System" and forbidding all British imports to European countries, were intended as a knockout blow against British trade. England was to be brought to her knees by social and commercial disintegration and by political revolution.

However, the "Continental System" turned out to be a boomerang: England's answer was the "Orders in Council" by whose directives ways and means were found to utilize the leaks in the "Continental System" to force English wares upon the European markets while at the same time cutting off the export trade of France and her protectorates. Lacking sufficient naval strength, Napoleon was neither able to enforce his paper blockade against the British Isles nor to cope with the tremendous productive capacity of industrial England which with its power-driven machinery was just beginning to reap the fruits of the "industrial revolution" (cf. p. 548 sq.). Thus the economic war against Great Britain yielded no decisive results for either side and showed all the appearances of a stalemate.

The Break With Russia and the War of 1812. In 1810, after having divorced Josephine, his first wife, who had failed to bear him the much-desired heir to the imperial throne, Napoleon married Marie Louise, the daughter of the Austrian emperor, Francis I. In 1812, he forced Austria into a military alliance with France.

By that time the Franco-Russian alliance, dating back to the Peace of Tilsit (1807) had become a meaningless scrap of paper. Napoleon's own cynical disregard for international treaties and loyalties encouraged a like opportunism on the part of his nominal allies. The young Russian Tsar, Alexander I, resented Napoleon's annexation of the North German coastal regions, extending from the Dutch border to the Baltic, as well as the restoration of a Polish puppet state, bordering on the formerly Polish territories now owned by Russia. Alexander threw down the gauntlet to the master of continental Europe by promising the Poles national independence under Russian protection and by declaring Russia's exemption from the system of the continental blockade against England.

Napoleon realized that Alexander's acts jeopardized the success of his whole political scheme and endangered his hegemony over Europe. Russia's attitude was tantamount to a declaration of war, and in the summer of 1812 Napoleon's "Grand Army," consisting of more than 600,000 men and including large contingents of Bavarian, Swabian, Saxon, Prussian, and Austrian troops, marched through northern Germany and Poland against Russia. Pressing on to Moscow, they found the city deserted and huge conflagrations of mysterious origin. This combined with the shortage of food supplies and equipment caused such consternation and confusion in the ranks that Napoleon was forced to give the order to retreat. The homeward march through the frozen Russian steppes became a ghastly epic of horror and privation, with less than one fifth of the "Grand Army" escaping the icy grip of winter and the harassing attacks of the Russian Cossacks. Napoleon had staked his all on one card and had lost.

The War of Liberation. Europe had watched the progress of the Russian campaign with bated breath, but when the news of the colossal disaster found its way into the various capitals, the first incredulous amazement soon gave way to a feeling of relief and renewed hope. The Napoleonic myth crumbled almost overnight. When the emperor arrived in Warsaw, he was fully aware of the gigantic proportions of the catastrophe, but the force of his will was unshaken and he showed genuine greatness in defeat.

a) Prussia and Russia. The destruction of the "Grand Army" was a world-historic event that immediately set in motion the political leaders of the subjugated peoples of Europe. At the outbreak of the Franco-Russian War Karl vom Stein had accepted an invitation of Tsar Alexander and had traveled from his exile in Austria to the general headquarters of the Russian army in Wilna. He acted as the tsar's chief councilor and submitted to him a detailed plan for the organization of a grand uprising in the rear of the Napoleonic armies. This plan provided for the landing of English and Swedish troops in northern Germany, to aid the German peoples in their struggle for liberation. Count August von Gneisenau (1760–1831), quartermaster general and the leader of the Prussian war party, was sent on a diplomatic mission to Sweden and England, while Ernst Moritz Arndt's (1769–1860) literary talents were enlisted for propagandistic purposes.

Stein was convinced that the liberation and eventual unification of Germany could only be achieved if the uprising of the masses was directed by a central national committee that disregarded the wishes and selfish ambitions of the German princes who, as members of the Confederation of the Rhine, had in his opinion usurped a sovereignty to which they were not entitled. They were to be reduced to the status of members of the Reich and subjects of the emperor: "Whenever the princes therefore do or command anything that is contrary to the interests of the fatherland . . . their subjects are absolved from their oath of allegiance" (Stein). Against much opposition Stein succeeded in making Alexander amenable to his ideas. In the *Petersburg Memorial* of 1812 he outlined his military and political strategy and demanded specifically the destruction of the Confederation of the Rhine and the creation of a unified and independent Germany. He repeatedly called attention to the corrupting influence of the petty princely courts, accusing the princes of having undermined the people's sense of justice and dignity and of having made themselves and their subjects the laughingstock of Europe. "In this moment of great decisions," he wrote, "I am absolutely disinterested in the fate of the dynasties; they are merely instruments; it is my wish that Germany become great and strong in order to regain her national independence."

In December, 1812, General Yorck von Wartenburg (1759–1830), the leader of a Prussian auxiliary corps, signed on his own responsibility the Convention of Tauroggen which in effect amounted to the conclusion of a nonaggression pact with Russia and presented the Prussian king with a *fait accompli*. Although Yorck was subsequently dismissed and the Convention of Tauroggen repudiated by Frederick William III, a revolutionary step had been taken that carried with it its own irrepressible momentum. Meanwhile Stein had arrived in East Prussia and, as the emissary of the tsar, had taken over the provisional administration of this province and proclaimed the formation of *Landwehr* and *Landsturm*. This was another revolutionary act and, like Yorck's nonaggression treaty with Russia, designed to force the Prussian king into a war for Prussia's freedom.

Early in 1813 the assembled deputies of the provincial estates of Prussia listened to the declarations that Stein made as the representative of the tsar. Yorck was present and called for a crusade against the French. From then on events moved fast: on Hardenberg's advice, Frederick William, in an attempt to escape the surveillance of the French army of occupation and also to be nearer to Alexander's headquarters, exchanged Berlin for Breslau, the capital of Silesia. Scharnhorst was put in charge of the rearmament program. To speed up the negotiations that were carried on between Prussia and Russia, the tsar gave Stein orders to proceed to Breslau and, though he was given a cool reception by Hardenberg and the king, the result of his visit was an alliance between Prussia and Russia (Treaty of Kalisch). On March 10, the birthday of the late Queen Louise, Frederick William proclaimed the creation of the decoration of the "Iron Cross." On March 15 Alexander I arrived in Breslau and on the following day war was declared against France. The Prussian king issued the stirring proclamation *"To My People,"* reminding his subjects of the sufferings of the past and naming the precious objectives of the great struggle: freedom of conscience, honor, independence; freedom of commercial enterprise; and a rebirth of the arts and sciences.

The armed citizenry was represented in the contingents of the *Landwehr,* while the academic youth in large numbers enlisted voluntarily in the "Free Corps," especially in those districts that were most familiar with the hardships of foreign occupation and the yoke of the conqueror. Theodor Körner (1791–1813) left his native Saxony, whose king had decided to throw his country's lot in with Napoleon, to join the "Free Corps" of Major von Lützow and to serve the cause of freedom with "lyre and sword." As a poet and human character he symbolized the fervent idealism of German youth, and as a soldier he realized the crowning ambition of his life by dying a hero's death on the battlefield. When in his verse he glorified the War of Liberation as "a crusade, a holy war,"* he merely gave poetic expression to a universal conviction. But Körner belonged to that relatively small group of patriots who with the purity of their enthusiasm fanned the spark in the hearts of their fellow countrymen, so that it grew into a devouring flame.

The joint forces of the Prussians and Russians were commanded by the Russian Marshal Kutusoff, while the Russian General Wittgenstein and the Prussian General Blücher were in charge of the divisional command. Yorck was exonerated and entered Berlin at the head of his corps, jubilantly greeted by an aroused populace. Napoleon, on the other hand, could still count on the support of the Confederation of the Rhine and, with the aid

---

* "Dies ist kein Krieg, von dem die Kronen wissen,
   Es ist ein Kreuzzug, 's ist ein heiliger Krieg."

of their contingents and a newly recruited army of the line, marched quickly
through Germany and met and defeated the allied armies at Lützen and
Bautzen, on Saxon soil. The Russo-Prussian forces retreated from Saxony
and were in grave danger of being outflanked, when Napoleon committed
what he himself later characterized as the greatest stupidity of his life: he
entered into an armistice of two months' duration, declaring himself willing
to renounce his claims to Poland and to relax the continental blockade.

b) Austria's Policy and War Aims. These two precious months permitted
Prussia to complete her armaments, while at the same time Austria under
the leadership of Count Stadion and Prince Metternich withdrew from
her alliance with France and made preparations to enter the war on the
side of the allies.

An offer of Metternich to mediate was coupled with definite demands for
territorial adjustments and restitutions and amounted practically to an
ultimatum. In a personal interview with the Austrian chancellor in Dresden,
Napoleon admitted that it was impossible for him to give up any of his
conquests, because he could not afford to face the French people with
a confession of even partial failure. When nevertheless he finally accepted
the Austrian offer of mediation, he did so in order to gain time for more
extensive preparations.

In the meantime, England's promise of aid and Sweden's entry into the
coalition fundamentally changed the character of the war and turned the
odds against Napoleon.

If the war had begun as a struggle for national liberation and self-
determination, this original aim was partially changed by Austria's entering
the ranks of the allies. What Metternich wanted was not a reorganization
of Europe in accordance with national aspirations, but a restoration of the
European balance of power, on the basis of historical and "legitimate"
dynastic and social claims and relationships. The Austrian empire was
a conglomerate of diverse nationalities which had been brought together
and held united by a century-old dynastic policy and by the prestige of the
Hapsburg crown. Metternich realized that the victory of the principle of
national self-determination would of necessity lead to the dissolution of
the foundations of the Austrian monarchy. But in formulating Austria's war
aims the Austrian chancellor looked beyond the boundaries of his own
country: he foresaw that the peace and order of Europe would be jeopardized
by the countless new complications and antagonisms that would arise out
of the triumph of nationalism. As a member of a cosmopolitan-minded
European aristocracy Metternich clung to the heritage of the cultural and
political traditions of a European commonwealth of nations and considered
Napoleon's claims to hegemony as "outside the pale of nature and
civilization."

Prussia and Austria were united in their opposition to the creation of
a universal super-State that threatened by its uniform structure to suppress
all individualism and political independence on the European continent. As

against the universalism of the Napoleonic monarchy Prussia and Austria defended the ideal of European solidarity. But while Baron vom Stein wanted to build the new Europe on the principle of the new nationalism, Metternich still hoped for the conservation of the historico-political structure of the pre-Napoleonic epoch. This contradiction in the ultimate war aims of the two German nations remained invisible as long as Prussia and Austria fought side by side against the common enemy, but they became strikingly evident as soon as the victory was won.

c) Napoleon and the New Military Strategy. In the age of Absolutism and Enlightened Depotism the armies had been the exclusive creation and property of the rulers. Their moves were scientifically calculated, their services methodically and rationally employed. In their build-up and strategy the "cabinet wars" of the absolutistic princes were artistically conceived chess games that aimed less at the destruction than at the paralyzation of the enemy. Frederick the Great was the first military leader who occasionally broke with the traditional rules of warfare and developed a new offensive strategy. But the new methods were perfected by the generals of the French Revolution and especially by the greatest of them, Napoleon Bonaparte. Under their leadership the masses of the citizen armies acquired a new significance in defense and attack, until Napoleon's military genius learned how to combine to the best advantage the methodical warfare of the absolute monarchs with the psychological assets of the new citizen morale in the army. He knew that the masses could be most effectively used if they were inspired by the ideals of personal devotion to a common cause.

The result was a new military strategy that aimed at the annihilation of the enemy, achieved by the force of superior numbers and by a relentless offensive initiative that dictated the law of action to the opposing armies. Napoleon's forced marches, his surprise movements, and his flexible maneuvering were aided and quickened by a well-trained army of polytechnicians, pioneers, and engineers.

The Prussian generals of the War of Liberation were Napoleon's most docile disciples, and Clausewitz (1780–1831) in particular systematically developed the principles of the new strategy in both theory and practice.

d) The Liberation. When the end of the brief armistice came the allies were agreed upon a definite strategic plan. The main army, under the command of the Austrian Marshals Schwarzenberg and Radetzky, was stationed in Bohemia and consisted of Austrian, Russian, and Prussian troops. In their camp were the three allied monarchs, the tsar, the emperor of Austria, and the king of Prussia. A second army under Marshal Blücher stood in Silesia, and a third, under the unreliable Bernadotte (1764–1844),*

---

* Jean Baptiste Bernadotte, a native of France, began his career as one of the generals of the French Revolution, served under Napoleon in Italy and Germany but later on deserted the cause of the French emperor. In 1810 the Swedish estates elected him as crown prince of Sweden and in the same year King Charles XIII adopted him as his successor. He ruled Sweden as Charles XIV (1818–1844).

covered the city and district of Berlin. The three combined armies surrounded Napoleon in a semicircle which, according to the plan, was to close in on the French emperor from three sides. For the first time in his military career Napoleon found himself deprived of the initiative. The clever maneuvering on the part of the allies was designed to avoid a decisive battle until the strength of their opponent would be sufficiently sapped and worn down.

After ten days of skirmishing the French Marshal Macdonald walked into a trap. After crossing the river Katzbach he was attacked by Blücher and his army annihilated. In several minor encounters Silesia was cleared of French troops and an enemy attack on Berlin repulsed.

The main army, in the meantime, was approaching Dresden, the capital of Saxony. Napoleon hurried north in forced marches and attempted an encircling movement. After two days of undecisive fighting the allies carried out a voluntary tactical retreat. But Napoleon failed to follow up this strategic advantage and instead resumed his former advance on Berlin.

The war at this juncture had only lasted two weeks and already the victory of the allies was practically assured. Napoleon had lost more than one third of his army and the morale of the French troops was badly shaken. The allies were gradually gaining superiority in numbers and materiel. Napoleon knew that his only salvation lay in attack and a battle in the field, but none of the allied generals would do him the favor of exposing their armies to such an onslaught. To effect the eventual unification of their forces in a concerted and crushing offensive, they had first to decide on the most favorable terrain to deliver the final blow. In the meantime, the striking power of Napoleon's armies was further weakened by the desertion of Bavaria, which went over to the allies.

Following Blücher's advice the allied armies now began to converge on Leipzig. As they approached from north and south, Napoleon in a desperate move turned northward to attack the united forces of Blücher and Bernadotte. But Blücher's and Gneisenau's strategy not only frustrated Napoleon's counteroffensive but cut off his retreat, so that at last the emperor decided to march upon Leipzig and to accept the battle at the place where it was forced upon him.

The first day of the battle of Leipzig was undecisive. But on the following day the allied ranks were strengthened by reinforcements and the French were driven back into the suburbs of the city. Napoleon, realizing his desperate position, attempted to negotiate an armistice, but his delegates were not even received by the allied commanders. On the third day, Bernadotte's army advanced and closed the gap between the Silesian and Bohemian contingents. While the battle was raging the Saxon and Swabian troops went over to the allies and thus contributed their share to Napoleon's defeat.

On the following morning the concerted attack of the three allied armies on the retreating troops of the enemy was completely successful and

the three monarchs and their generals met on the market square of Leipzig.
Napoleon withdrew in the direction of the Main river and gained his last
victory on German soil when he brushed aside a Bavarian army that had
tried to cut off his retreat.

The larger part of Germany was freed from the enemy, and the allied
headquarters were moved to Frankfurt. The Confederation of the Rhine
was dissolved, and much against the wishes of Baron vom Stein the
disloyal German princes were allowed to retain their thrones. Those who
had been deposed by Napoleon were reinstated in their domains. The three
Hanseatic cities, Hamburg, Bremen, and Lübeck, as well as the old imperial
city of Frankfurt, were given back their autonomy and their senatorial
administration.

If the allies had followed up their victory, they could have crushed
Napoleon so completely that an extension of the war into the following
year would have been unnecessary. But hardly had the battle of Leipzig
been won when the old discords and rivalries among the allies came to the
fore again and gave the enemy the needed time for partial recovery.
Metternich considered the annihilation of Napoleon as undesirable from
the point of view of the European balance of power. He still hoped for
a peace that would break the hegemony of France without denying to her
the satisfaction of certain legitimate historical aspirations. Blücher and
Gneisenau, on the other hand, maintained that Napoleon's "crimes" called
for the overthrow of his regime and the destruction of his military power.
Blücher's goal, therefore, was the capture of Paris, followed by the dictation
of merciless peace terms. Metternich sensed in these proposals a revolutionary
radicalism that seemed to endanger the very principle of monarchical rule,
and in the environment of the Austrian chancellor Blücher's headquarters
were disdainfully referred to as a "nest of Jacobins."

After much futile bickering and more or less academic disputes the
campaign of 1814 finally got under way, Blücher advancing along the
shores of the river Marne and the main army following the course of
the river Seine. At the same time negotiations with Napoleon's plenipoten-
tiaries were begun at Châtillon. But even now, when final victory was
within certain grasp, Blücher's army, owing to the lack of unity among
the allies, suffered several severe setbacks that filled Napoleon with new
hope. He made one last attempt to intercept the supply lines of the allies
and, that failing, withdrew in the direction of Paris, this time followed by
the reunited allied armies. On March 31, 1814, Paris surrendered, the allies
entered the city, and the war was ended. Napoleon, who had taken up
quarters in near-by Fontainebleau, agreed to abdicate to make way for
the restoration of the Bourbon dynasty. Talleyrand, the former Gallican*

* The term *Gallicanism* refers to certain nationalistic and monarchical tendencies in the
Catholic Church of France (Gaul) which received their clearest formulation in the Declaration
of the French Clergy of 1682, drawn up by Bossuet. Its four articles demand that the authority
of the pope be restricted to ecclesiastical affairs and assert the superiority of a general Church
council to the pope (Conciliar Theory).

bishop, who had left the Church and deserted the Monarchy to serve first the Revolution and then Napoleon, returned now as the Bourbon King Louis XVIII's confidant and minister of foreign affairs, and concluded the peace treaty of Paris between France and the allied powers. The new king of France was the brother of the unfortunate Louis XVI who had been executed in 1793.

The terms of the Peace of Paris were very lenient: no war indemnity was imposed and France was allowed to retain all the territories that she had possessed in 1792, including Alsace, and she even received some territories that had not belonged to her former monarchs, such as Avignon, the duchy of Savoy, and the county of Zweibrücken. This leniency on the part of the allies was due to the fact that the restoration of the Bourbons was supposed to ensure peace and stability in Europe and that therefore everything must be done to make the new rulers appear true to their assumed role as saviors of the honor and the territorial integrity of the French nation. The deposed emperor was granted a pension and sovereign rights over the small island of Elba in the Mediterranean, not far from his native Corsica.

e) Alsace and the Rhine. Metternich's call for the restoration of historically "legitimate" political structures in Europe found an echo even among those romantic writers whose ardent nationalism was in other respects diametrically opposed to the cosmopolitan ideals of the representatives of the old European aristocracies. Arndt and Görres (cf. p. 480) no less than Baron vom Stein and other leading German patriots were fighting for the establishment of a national democracy within the borders of the old German empire. Motivated by the dual impulse of the reawakened historical sense and a vigorous national consciousness, they were the first among their countrymen to advance a program of *Machtpolitik* for the realization of legitimate national aspirations. And yet, when these national leaders directed their appeal to the ancient frontier district of Alsace, it was most surprising and disappointing to them to find that the population failed to respond. The same people who in the eighteenth century had still loyally adhered to their German political and cultural heritage had been almost completely won over by the political and social reforms of the Napoleonic era. The peasants enjoyed the newly gained freedom of person and ownership and the middle classes cherished the freedom of trade and commerce that was guaranteed by the unified and modern legislation of the centralized administration under the French regime. This lukewarm attitude of the Alsatians was one of the reasons that prevented the return of Alsace to Germany under the terms of the Peace of Paris.

But with Alsace lost, the German patriots were all the more solidly united in their historic claims for the possession of the Rhine as "Germany's river, not Germany's boundary" (Arndt). The Rhine became a symbol of German nationalism in the era of Liberation and Romanticism (cf. p. 468 sqq.). Even in ancient Roman times both banks of the river had been settled by German tribes, and all the past greatness and glory of the Empire was mirrored in its placid and majestic waters, in the ancient cities that lined its shores, the magnificent cathedrals that towered above the plains, the rugged castles whose ruins recalled a proud and virile past. Here it was that the patriotic German felt it his sacred duty to keep eternal watch against the encroachments of the "hereditary enemy," the French. For Arndt, the Rhenish districts and the Rhenish people represented the heart and the soul of Germany. The river was the artery from which the whole organism received its lifeblood. It was in the recently liberated city of Coblenz, the city of his birth, that Joseph von Görres (1776–1848) edited the *Rhenish Mercury,* a political review that established the fame of its author and editor as the first and foremost of great German publicists, and to which Napoleon referred as "the fifth of the Great Powers of Europe." In the pages of Görres' *Mercury* the contemporaries could read about the historic and cultural significance of the left bank of the Rhine and they could derive new hope and confidence from the prophecies of Napoleon's downfall and the coming liberation and unification of Germany.

f) The Congress of Vienna (1814–1815). The victory of the allies over Napoleon brought to a temporary halt the revolutionary era that had begun with the French Revolution of 1789. The first phase of the struggle between the European monarchies and the principle of the sovereignty of the people ended with a triumph of the defenders of autocratic and authoritarian government. The German people at large had never submitted to any great extent to the intellectual trends of the period of Enlightenment (cf. p. 368 sqq.), and most of the leaders of the movement of Classical Idealism (cf. Chap. 12) had stressed the values of historical continuity and inherited traditions. Thus the forces of the European counterrevolution, when they assigned to the Congress of Vienna the task of the reorganization of Europe, met with sympathetic response on the part of Germany.

The new order of Europe was to be based on the principles of permanency and stability, and Prince Metternich was the statesman whose political ideas dominated that illustrious assembly of great and small powers. The "dancing" Congress of Vienna, unequaled in modern times in its splendor and extravagance, was a social rendezvous of European aristocracy, convoked to celebrate the resurrection of the *ancien régime.* The gay and frivolous elegance of the ancient imperial metropolis on the Danube provided a most suitable background.

The feeling of social equality that had characterized the period of the national uprisings against Napoleon was forgotten as soon as the victory was won, and the traditionalist sentiment of the people accepted the return of social distinctions and privileges as something necessary and unavoidable. The aristocracy, on the other hand, had "learned nothing and forgotten nothing." They were convinced that their rule would be safe and secure if they only succeeded in preserving the people's trust in a divinely instituted system of authoritarian governance. According to Talleyrand, only he who had experienced the period before 1789 was able to appreciate fully "the sweetness of human existence." Among the advocates of the restoration movement the French philosopher Joseph de Maistre (1754-1821) was the only one whose conservatism was enlightened by a statesmanlike vision that was able to look beyond class distinctions and social prejudice. He recognized the constructive values of a temperate nationalism and traditionalism, whose forces must be implanted in the larger organism of human society. For him the notion of a united "mankind" was no empty abstraction: he visualized it as a "society of nations," devoted to the moral advancement of each of its members and to the perfection of their collective association.

The Congress of Vienna had hardly begun its deliberations when the separate interests of the four great European powers — Russia, Prussia, Austria, and England — again asserted themselves openly. France, defeated and internally weakened, was temporarily eliminated from the game of European power politics. As far as England and Austria were concerned, their interests seemed to run parallel. The first Peace of Paris had given England all she needed and wanted: the continental blockade had failed; and the acquisition of Egypt, Malta, Heligoland, the Cape of Good Hope, and other colonial territories made Great Britain the unassailable mistress of the Seven Seas. To compensate Holland for the loss of Capetown and Ceylon, Belgium was arbitrarily united with Holland, to form the kingdom of the Netherlands under William I of the house of Orange: an artificial aggregation of territories and populations that endured for scarcely two decades.

England's main interest on the European continent was the restoration and preservation of the "balance of power" and in this policy she could count on the full support of the Austrian State chancellor. With the defeat of France the danger of Russian hegemony in Europe loomed as a new and equally formidable threat. It was the tsar's intention to create a national and constitutional Polish State under his own supremacy. Alexander's position was greatly strengthened by Prussia's proposal to annex the entire kingdom of Saxony and the Austro-Prussian tension that resulted from these immoderate demands. Austria, Great Britain, and France were equally opposed to the Prussian plans and were willing to prevent the annexation of Saxony, if necessary, by force of arms. Finally, in view of the Russian danger, a compromise was worked out that gave Prussia approximately two fifths of Saxony. While she agreed to surrender the greater part of Prussian Poland to the tsar, she received substantial compensations on the left bank of the Rhine that practically restored the Prussian boundaries of 1806. Thus Prussia emerged from these political deals once more as one of the leading powers of Europe, and by the surrender of her Polish possessions to the tsar she had freed herself from the liability of having alien populations within her boundaries. Tsar Alexander proclaimed himself king of a united Poland and rounded off Russia's European frontiers by taking Finland from Sweden and Bessarabia from Turkey. He antagonized Metternich by his admonition to the European rulers to grant liberal constitutions to their subjects. All the territorial transactions were carried out with utter disregard for the wishes and aspirations of the populations, whereby the principle of "legitimacy" served as a convenient ruse and excuse.

g) *The German Question and the "Act of Confederation."* The most important result of the deliberations at Vienna was the creation of the "German Confederation," signalizing a provisional settlement of the complex "German question." From the beginning of the War of Liberation it had been generally recognized that some definite form of political organization must eventually supersede the defunct Empire. Many still believed in the possibility of resurrecting the "Holy Roman Empire of the German Nation" in a modernized and liberalized form. There was hardly any difference of opinion among the patriotic leaders as to the legitimate claims of the house of Hapsburg to leadership in such a reorganized and revitalized realm. When, in 1813, Baron vom Stein had called for the restoration of the imperial rule of the Hapsburgs, it was Metternich's keen political insight that had realized the incompatibility of the Austro-Prussian dualism with the idea of a centralized national monarchy. He was convinced that a durable political structure could only be erected in the form of a confederation of states that was sufficiently balanced and at the same time elastic enough to allow the coexistence of several autonomous national units, including the two great sovereign powers, Austria and Prussia. Only in such a decentralized union, welded together by a community of certain vital interests, but avoiding all unnecessary infringements on the sovereign rights of the member states, could the "peaceful dualism" of Prussia and Austria prove itself fruitful and creative.

But Metternich's plan of a "perpetual federation" (*foedus perpetuum*) among equals did not meet with the approval of the representatives of Prussia, Hardenberg and Humboldt. They, too, wanted to adhere to the system of a "peaceful dualism," but they demanded absolute supremacy for Prussia in the north and for Austria in the south, calling for the subjection of the smaller central states to the rule of their powerful neighbors. The negotiations of a committee of five, consisting of the representatives of Austria, Prussia, Hanover, Bavaria, and Wurtemberg, finally resulted in the passing of the "Act of Confederation" (1815), which designated Austria as the presiding power in the new Confederation and stipulated the creation of a Federal Diet (*Bundestag*), that was to meet in Frankfurt-on-the-Main.

The defined purpose of the "German Confederation" (*Deutscher Bund*) was "the preservation of the external and internal security of Germany, and the independence and inviolability of the individual German states." The Confederation consisted of thirty-nine sovereign states and included the king of Denmark (representing Holstein), the king of England (who was also king of Hanover), and the king of the Netherlands (representing the Grand Duchy of Luxembourg). A complicated electoral system was devised to prevent the larger states from outvoting the smaller ones and to make it impossible for any combination of the small states to force their will upon the larger ones. Each of the eleven large states had one vote, while the twenty-eight small states were divided up into six groups, each group commanding one vote. This total of seventeen votes made up the "Inner Council." Despite its many shortcomings this confederation of states acted as a check on the practically unlimited particularism that had prevailed in the Empire before 1806. Though still handicapped in its internal policies by too many conflicting interests, the new Confederation was able to present a united front when foreign affairs were concerned.

h) The "Hundred Days" and the End of Napoleon. In the same month of June, 1815, when the new order of Europe was sealed by the decrees of the Congress of Vienna, the dramatic episode of Napoleon's escape from Elba and his short-lived return to power — the rule of the "Hundred Days" — came to an end. Encouraged by the dissensions among the great powers and by the news of France's intense dislike of the Bourbon Restoration, Napoleon had landed on the French Riviera on March 1, 1815, accompanied by his loyal guard which he had been permitted to retain in exile. The French troops who had been dispatched to arrest him, and whom he encountered on his way to Paris, enthusiastically joined the banners of their old commander. The French people, apprehensive of the probability of renewed suffering and bloodshed, observed an attitude of watchful waiting. Although Napoleon in his proclamations declared himself willing to establish a strictly constitutional rule, the powers whose representatives were assembled in Vienna and on whose decisions the fate of his *coup d'état* depended, immediately forgot their quarrels and closed their ranks. They refused to receive the emperor's envoys and, on March 13, solemnly declared Napoleon an outlaw: an "enemy and destroyer of the peace of the world."

Four armies, commanded by Wellington, Blücher, Schwarzenberg, and Tsar Alexander, were hurriedly put into the field and made ready to invade France. Blücher was named commander in chief of the allied armies and Gneisenau was appointed chief of staff. The Prussians marched into the Netherlands but were thrown back by Napoleon who, using his customary strategy, had attacked before the armies of the enemy should have time to rally and unite their forces. The Prussian retreat might have developed into a rout if the superior strategic genius of Gneisenau had not recognized that the Prussians and the British must join their forces at any cost. Thus Gneisenau commanded his troops to relinquish their bases of operation and to withdraw in the direction of the village of Waterloo, south of Brussels. While Napoleon's Marshal Grouchy, assuming that the Prussians were retreating toward the Rhine, discovered too late that he was on the wrong track and had lost contact with the enemy, Napoleon himself turned against Wellington, unaware of the possibility of a joint English-Prussian opposition.

Wellington had moved into a defensive position near Waterloo, after he had received word from Blücher that the entire Prussian army was about

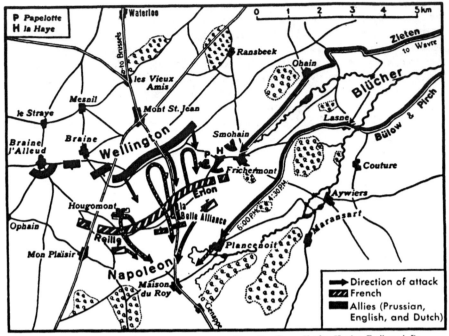

From *Der Grosse Herder*, Herder, Freiburg i. Br.

Battle of Waterloo.

to join the English mercenary troops. Wellington, who combined tenacity
with cool circumspection, was eminently fitted to direct and employ the
minutely calculated methods of defensive operations. While countless French
attacks spent their force on the massive wall of Wellington's army, the duke
calmly gave out the "order of the day": "Our strategy is quite simple: the
Prussians — or night!" When at last the Prussians advanced upon the right
flank of the French army, the British immediately joined in the forward
movement, taking possession of the field of battle. The French retreat became
an irregular flight, and while Wellington stopped and hesitated, the
Prussians followed the enemy, inspired by Gneisenau's "order of the day":
"We have shown how to win a victory; now let us demonstrate how to
chase an enemy!"

After six days the whole campaign was over. In Blücher's headquarters
there was general agreement that the new peace must be dictated in Paris
and that this time the military and national aspirations of Germany must
be given due consideration. Wellington and the English government, too,
wanted the march on Paris, but only to proclaim once more the restoration
of the Bourbons. When the Prussians, attacking the capital of France from
the south, had broken the resistance of the enemy, Fouché, Napoleon's
former minister of police, surrendered the city in the name of the provisional

government. Gneisenau demanded that the emperor of the French be handed over to the Prussians to face a court-martial. Napoleon abdicated a second time and, in order to avoid his being captured by the Prussians, asked his archenemies, the English, for asylum.

In the second Peace of Paris (November 20, 1815) the conservative point of view of the British government prevailed and the Prussian demands for reparations and securities were only partly fulfilled. France, under a restored Bourbon monarchy, retained the boundaries of the year 1792, but she had to pay an indemnity, and the greater part of the stolen art treasures were restored to the various capitals of Europe. An army of occupation under the command of the duke of Wellington was stationed in the northern provinces of France to see that the peace terms would be carried out in good faith.

Napoleon was given the asylum he had asked for: the lonely island of St. Helena in the South Atlantic became his prison for the remaining years of his life (1815–1821). Here he wrote his political testament, the *Memorial of St. Helena* (*Mémorial de Sainte Hélène*), in which he pronounced judgment over past and future and posed as the great pioneer of freedom and universal peace: "I have closed the crater of anarchy and untangled chaos. I have cleansed the revolution, ennobled the nations, strengthened the rulers. I have stimulated competition, rewarded every merit, enlarged the boundaries of fame. That is something. . . . I wanted to give peace to the world, but they have made me into a demon of war." He spoke of his dream of seeing free and creative peoples in a unified Europe, ruled by a constitutional monarch and protected by a citizen army, no longer subjected to the dictates of nobles and priests, but united in the idea of the great occidental commonwealth, the social and democratic Empire of the future. And, truly, with all his failings and unhealthy ambitions, there was dimly alive in this "executor of the revolution" the realization of the significance of the two major social forces of the nineteenth century: liberalism and nationalism. He started Europe's nations on their way to the new liberal economy, the new concepts of constitutional and democratic law, and the new glorification and deification of national destiny.*

Europe and the "Holy Alliance." The leaders of the four great powers which shared in the overthrow of Napoleon and were responsible for the new Europe that took shape at the Congress of Vienna were united in their will to lay the foundations for a lasting peace. Austria, Russia, Prussia, and England were resolved to establish themselves as a permanent council of a League of Nations, to which France was conditionally admitted in 1818, and which was to assume a kind of guardianship over European affairs,

---

* One of the lasting achievements of Napoleon was the creation of the *Code civil des Français*, better known as the *Code Napoléon* (1804). The historical significance of this law code lies in the fact that it incorporated some of the positive accomplishments of the French Revolution in the concepts of *civil law*. It was adopted and retained for shorter or longer periods in the Netherlands, in Luxembourg, in Belgium, in the later Prussian *Rheinprovinz* (in the *Pfalz*, in *Rheinhessen, Baden, Westfalen, Berg,* and *Hanover*), in some Swiss cantons, in Italy, and in Poland. It exerted decisive influence on the contemporary civil law codes of Switzerland, Mexico, and Central and South America.

by means of frequent consultation and mutual co-operation. To further this aim, congresses were held at Aachen (1818), Troppau (1820), Leibach (1821), and Verona (1822). The first rift in this "Concert of Europe" occurred when Great Britain reclaimed her freedom of action and resumed a policy of "splendid isolation." In 1825, Canning, the British prime minister, stated without misgivings that Europe was "once more back to the situation in which every nation is for itself, and God for all."

By reviving the spirit of isolationism England dealt a deathblow to the manifold attempts at international co-operation that were backed by an illustrious tradition, having found speculative expression in the thought of Leibniz, Kant, and others, and having become part of the theory of international law, a creation of the seventeenth and eighteenth centuries.

It was a reborn European solidarity that had vanquished Napoleon, and it was this new Europe that acted collectively in Vienna to defend this solidarity against disturbances from within and without. In the circles of the monarchs, diplomats, and intellectuals assembled at Vienna the idea of a "Christian State" was seriously discussed and finally translated into political actuality by the formation of the "Holy Alliance" (1815). It was Tsar Alexander who first proposed that the monarchs of Europe should act as the "Delegates of Providence" in pledging themselves "to take for their sole guide the precepts of Sacred Religion, namely the precepts of Justice, Christian Charity, and Peace," and to base international relations as well as national and social administration "upon the sublime truths which the Holy Religion of our Saviour teaches. . . . "

The "Holy Alliance," to which all the princes of Europe, with the exception of the pope, the Turkish sultan, and the prince regent of Great Britain, subscribed, was an outgrowth of the pietistic and romantic leanings of the restoration period and of the personal mysticism of the tsar. The monarchs declared that their governments and their peoples were members of one great Christian commonwealth whose only true sovereign was Christ. In three articles they summarized in a programmatic form the leading ideas of the restoration movement: the subjection of political life to the principles of Christian ethics, the adherence to the patriarchal form of government, the belief in the divine origin of all rulership, and the proposal to secure eternal peace by the creation of a League of Nations.

Despite the fact that many of the European princes signed this moral pledge halfheartedly, with mental reservations or even with cynical hypocrisy, the settlement of Vienna and the conclusion of the "Holy Alliance" were followed by forty years of relative calm in the political relations between the great powers. Castlereagh, the British minister of foreign affairs, spoke the mind of the skeptics when he called the pledge of the princes "a sublime piece of mysticism and nonsense," and Metternich's political realism saw in the document an expression of one of Tsar Alexander's pietistic moods, a "high-sounding nothing" that was "useless, to say the least." The pope, on the other hand, objected to the proclamation of the "unity of the great Christian Church in its three branches" (Catholic, Protestant, and Greek-Orthodox), and to the idea of a theocracy of secular monarchs, considering themselves as delegates of Christ.

Metternich and the Principle of Legitimism. Some of the monarchs who pledged adherence to the principles espoused by the originators of the "Holy Alliance" were the same who had based their claims to their hereditary titles and territories on the principle of "legitimacy." They forgot that their ancestors had established their absolute monarchical rule with callous disregard of the traditional rights of the Estates of their realms, and that there was hardly a throne in Europe that had been gained by other means than brute force and illegal encroachments upon the rights of individuals and groups. Nevertheless, the principle of "legitimacy" in itself was an attempt to combat the lawlessness of international relations by relating politics to moral norms, to overcome the Machiavellian separation of political action from moral sanctions by subjecting political rule to the laws of reason and justice. This was, despite its many shortcomings, the inherent tendency and significance of the "Metternich System" that impressed its stamp on the entire period between 1815 and 1848.

Prince Metternich himself was the truest personification of the European counterrevolution. In theory and practice he represented the ideas of conservation, order, and stability and opposed them to the doctrines of social and political revolution. His cool and systematically calculated diplomacy was inspired and strengthened by an almost grotesque vanity and the conviction of his own infallibility. He was averse to any kind of emotionalism, and his dispassionate aloofness made him a stranger to the life and thought of the people and incapable of the self-abandon and personal fervor that characterize the truly great statesman. He felt at home and moved with perfect ease only in the glittering atmosphere of the "*salon*" and the royal cabinet, but was unwilling to expose himself to the political storms that were brewing in the world at large and especially in the growing revolutionary sentiment of the middle classes. The restoration of the European balance of power appeared to him the surest guarantee for the preservation of the graduated feudal structure of Western civilization. It was for this reason that he made the continuation of this historic order the quintessence of his "system" and his "legitimism." His closest confidant and associate was Frederick von Gentz (1764–1832), a publicist of extraordinary genius and dubious morality. He popularized Metternich's reactionary ideas and aided his friend and superior in the development of an ingenious system of political censorship that held Austria and part of Germany in intellectual bondage from the end of the War of Liberation to the days of the "March Revolution" of 1848 (cf. p. 527 sqq.).

In the name of the "reason of state" the organs of Metternich's police organization waged a relentless war against both nationalism and liberalism. Metternich had to carry on this struggle to the bitter end if he wanted to remain true to himself and his deepest convictions. But he was not unaware that the end would spell defeat for him and his entire system of values. Yet his opposition to what he considered the diabolic spirit of the age admitted of no compromise. In his diary of 1820 we read the following words: "I have to live my life in an abominable period. I was either born too early or too late; as it is, I am of little use for anything. Had I lived in an earlier period, I could have enjoyed the spirit of the times, and if I had lived in a later period, I could have served the work of reconstruction. But today I am spending my life in supporting decaying structures. I ought to have been born in the year 1900, with the twentieth century before me. . . . It is my most secret thought that the old Europe is at the beginning of its end. Resolved to perish with it, I shall know how to do my duty. The new Europe, on the other hand, is still in the process of becoming, but there will be chaos between the end and the new beginning."

Restoration in State and Church. The major theme of the political and social struggles of the nineteenth century was the antagonism between monarchical rule and the sovereignty of the people. After France had been readmitted to the "Concert" of the great powers of Europe (1818), the five leading monarchs (of Prussia, Austria, Russia, England, and France) established themselves as a new aristocracy of legislators and administrators. They considered it their principal task to preserve the newly gained stability and to suppress any and all political trends which threatened a resurgence of the revolutionary sentiments of 1789. In their attempt to restore the political and social structure of the *ancien régime* the monarchs welcomed the aid of religion as a handmaid of absolutism, and a reunion of "throne and altar" was to act as a check on the growing popular demand for democratic and constitutional representation.

To justify their antirevolutionary measures the politicians of the restoration movement made use of the arguments that the English statesman Edmund Burke (1729-1797) had advanced in his *Reflections on the French Revolution* (1790). He had distinguished between a legitimate struggle for the inalienable rights of man, as evidenced by the British Revolution of 1688 and the American War of Independence (1774-1783) — a struggle which in the Anglo-Saxon world extended from Magna Charta to the Declaration of Independence and the "Bill of Rights" — and the nihilistic tendencies of the French Revolution of 1789. Frederick von Gentz translated and commentated Burke's *Reflections* and thereby popularized Burke's ideas in the circles of the French emigrants in Germany and Austria. Men like Joseph de Maistre or the poet Chateaubriand (1768-1848) had experienced the Jacobin reign of terror and, in exile and destitution, they had preserved their reverence for the traditional values of home, family, political authority, and religion. They acted as the vanguard of counterrevolution, social restoration, and political reaction. For De Maistre Royalism and Catholicism were natural allies, and in his work on the papacy (1819) he called upon the princes and peoples to overcome anarchy and dissolution by recognizing the universal mission of the Roman pontiff, and by accepting the guidance of the ancient authorities of State and Church. De Maistre's theory of the "organic" and "corporative" nature of State and society was adopted and further developed by the German spokesmen of the restoration period, by statesmen and historians as well as by the representatives of arts and letters. The Congress of Vienna restored Pope Pius VII to his temporal possessions in Italy, and the Jesuit Order (cf. p. 254 sqq.) that had been suppressed in 1773 was re-established and reorganized in 1814.

The "German Movement." In Prussia the War of Liberation had been fought as a crusade of the people, who had been promised by their leaders that victory would carry with it both national independence and a more just social order. The king of Prussia had promised his people a constitution, but as soon as victory was assured he had let himself be dissuaded by Metternich from carrying out the provisions of his pledge. The only German states in which constitutions were granted in the years after the close of the war were Bavaria, Baden, Weimar, Wurtemberg, Hanover, Nassau, and Hesse-Darmstadt. The disillusionment of the war-weary populations was aggravated by a catastrophic failure of crops in 1816–1817 and by a severe economic crisis that was caused by the flooding of German markets with English goods, following the lifting of the continental blockade. The middle classes were utterly discouraged and fell back into their former lethargy and political indifference. Under Hardenberg's chancellorship Stein's political and social reforms were gradually deprived of their meaning and finally completely nullified.

The apathy of the middle classes was not shared by the academic youth, by those young men who had readily offered their lives for the liberation of their country. Those who returned from the battlefields were unable to resign themselves to the idea that their faith and idealism should go unrewarded and that the drab routine of political and social bureaucracy should again settle down on the German lands and stifle the élan of the national awakening. They demanded to have a voice and a share in the molding of their own and their people's future destiny.

Thus the beginnings of the liberal and democratic movement in Germany was in the truest sense a "youth movement." The first important step was the reform of student life, the education of youth for an active and intelligent participation in the political life of a nation in the making. It was only a start but as such it was vigorous though at times ill balanced and prone to overstep its bounds. The way was hard and wearisome, beset with dangers, humiliations, and repressions: the first phase in the slow process of the emancipation of the German middle classes, whose habitual inertia could only be overcome several decades later when the new technological and scientific evolution had provided the requisite social and economic bases for complete success.

In the course of the seventeenth and eighteenth centuries the original groups of "nations" of the medieval universities (cf. p. 137 sqq.) had developed into student corporations (*Verbindungen, Landsmannschaften*) whose members had nominally retained their regional character (Westphalians, Franks, Saxons, etc.), but whose lives and ideas had been influenced by the cosmopolitanism and humanitarianism of the age of Enlightenment. As to social behavior, the students had developed their own code of morals, based on a collective opposition to the well-tempered morality of the bourgeois "philistine." They spoke their own conspicuous lingo, set their own standards in fashion and custom, displayed a supreme disdain of the social conventions of the middle classes, and spent altogether too much time on carousing, dueling, and gambling.

The events at the turn of the century and the changing outlook on life of the generation of the War of Liberation had their profound effects on the thought and habits of the German students. While their associations persisted in their loyalty to the inherited forms of the convivial academic style (the *Komment*), they imparted a new meaning to these external forms. Men like Schiller and Fichte set a living example that acted as a powerful stimulus in the impending reform of academic life. The University of Jena, which for some years had counted both Schiller and Fichte among the members of its faculty, became the model institution of higher learning in the early period of the romantic movement (cf. p. 470 sqq.). In his lectures *On the Idea of Our Universities* the romantic nature philosopher, H. Steffen (1773–1845), described these institutions as "the guardians of the national spirit and the creators of moral freedom." During and following the War of Liberation the corporative students' unions (*Corps*) in all German universities were organized in the "Association of Senior Members" (*Seniorenconvent, S.C.*), acting as the representatives and spokesmen of incorporated and unincorporated students alike. The *Corps* furnished the largest contingents of volunteers, and the common cause made them forget all regional differences and petty factional disputes.

A new plan for the "Order and Institution of the German *Burschenschaft*" had been submitted by Ludwig Jahn (cf. p. 442 sq.) as early as 1811, with the avowed purpose of putting an end to all particularistic tendencies among the academic youth and to enlist all students in Jahn's program of physical education and moral reform. The idea bore fruit in 1818, when the German *Burschenschaften* pledged allegiance to the common ideals of "freedom, honor, and fatherland," and adopted black, red, and gold, the colors of Major von Lützow's heroic "Free Corps," as a symbolic manifestation of their convictions. In proclaiming black, red, and gold as the ancient imperial colors of Germany, the *Burschenschaften* were referring to the imperial standard of the old "Holy Empire" that showed the emblem of a black eagle with red talons, set off against a background of gold.

It was in the circles of the *Burschenschaft* that the idealism of the War of Liberation was kept alive. The only German regions that remained, on the whole, unaffected by the new academic spirit were Catholic Bavaria and Austria, where a patriarchal and paternal relationship between teachers and students still prevailed and where the original affiliation between monastic school and university was still essentially unimpaired.

The year 1817, the year of the third centennial of the Lutheran Reformation and the fourth anniversary of the battle of Leipzig, was chosen by the *Burschenschaften* to manifest publicly their unity and the ideals by which it was inspired. A mammoth demonstration was staged at the Wartburg, the famous castle near Eisenach where Luther had translated the New Testament (cf. p. 226). One of the speakers linked the Protestant Reformation with the struggle for political independence and eulogized "the dual feast of the rebirth of free thought and the liberation of the fatherland." The entire celebration presented an unusual combination of divine service and political demonstration, and it was concluded with prayer, benediction, and the singing of one of the old Protestant hymns.

If this had been all, the meeting at the Wartburg would probably never have acquired its great historic fame. What gave it a spectacular and wholly unexpected prominence was the sequel to the main proceedings, enacted by some radical Berliners, after most of the participants had already left. Imitating Luther's burning of the papal bull in Wittenberg (cf. p. 224), these high-spirited young men built a bonfire and committed to the flames several books by reactionary authors as well as some of the despised symbols of benighted absolutism and political conservatism, among them a pigtail and a corporal's staff. After having defiantly shouted their *"Pereat!"* ("Let it be destroyed forever!"), they went home in peace, proud of having done a day's work.

But Metternich and with him the German princes saw in the Wartburg Festival a serious threat to the monarchical and authoritarian principles of government. They were strengthened in their conviction that revolution was about to raise its ugly head and that something must be done about it when the liberal press praised the student demonstration as an event of great political significance. There followed a diplomatic exchange of opinions between the courts of Berlin and Vienna, the outcome of which was a joint *démarche* with the Grand Duke Charles Augustus of Saxe-Weimar, on whose territory the offense had been committed and who, having granted his people a constitution in the same year, was strongly and rightly suspected as a friend of democratic reforms. But Charles Augustus, who was also the friend of Goethe and the promoter and protector of German Classicism and Humanism, could not be intimidated. He lent further encouragement to the members of the *Burschenschaft* and made it possible for a general student gathering, composed of delegations from fourteen German universities, to meet at Jena (1818) and to draft and adopt a constitution. It was an important document that emphasized the German-Christian character of the *Burschenschaft* and made membership dependent on the profession of an exclusive nationalism, on devotion to "Luther's German God," and on the acceptance of a standardized academic code of honor.

The members of this German youth movement were motivated in their deliberations and actions by a deep-seated resentment against the feudal aristocrats, whose influence still dominated the petty principalities of Germany, whose ideas on culture and education were borrowed from France, and who were separated from their subjects by the barriers of social prejudice and distrust. Their sons began to flock to the fashionable students' *Corps* in increasing numbers and were taught by their elders to look down upon the *Burschenschaften* as the *rendez-vous* of the academic rabble.

The majority of the academic youth, on the other hand, came from the German middle classes. They were proudly conscious of the moral and cultural virtues that they had inherited from the tradition of the Lutheran parsonage. They were joined by those young noblemen who had fought the battle of liberation shoulder to shoulder with them and who shared their contempt of class privilege, sloth, complacency, bureaucracy, the idolization of material possessions and the fecundity of money. And yet, the effects of the academic reform were not very far reaching. After the original élan of the new movement had subsided, the dividing lines between *Corps* and *Burschenschaft* were largely obliterated and pharisaic bigotry and an affected cult of the sophisticated and the unconventional became a characteristic mark of most of the members of the German student fraternities.

The one distinguishing character trait that was retained by the members of the *Burschenschaft* and that made them the standard-bearers of the national movement was their abiding interest in the political destinies of Germany. Practically all the pioneers of German unification grew up under the influence of the *Burschenschaft* and owed to it the pattern of their lives. From the ranks of the more radical of its members the party of the so-called "unconditionals" (*die Unbedingten*) was recruited, aiming at a thorough reform of the governmental system of Germany, with the ultimate establishment of a German republic as their goal. The "unconditionals" were inspired by the glowing fanaticism of Karl Follen (1795–1840) who, together with Karl Schurz (1829–1906) and Franz Lieber (1800–1872), is counted among the early leaders of German Liberalism and who, like Schurz and Lieber, after having been expelled from Germany, found a ready response and a broader field for his activities in the United States.*

In Jena Karl Follen made the acquaintance of Karl Sand, a student of Protestant theology, an idealist whose mental equilibrium had been badly shaken by the emotional strain of the war and the anticlimax that was provided by the broken promises of the German princes. Sand knew no higher ambition than to become a martyr for the exalted cause of social freedom, and he decided that he could best prove himself a true disciple of the teachings of Karl Follen by assassinating the German playwright August von Kotzebue (1761–1819), whose *History of Prussia* had been burned on the occasion of the Wartburg Festival and who, because of his

---

* Karl Follen became one of the leaders of the antislavery movement in the United States. From 1824–1835 he was a member of the German faculty of Harvard University.

close relations with the Russian tsar, was hated by the students as "a paid spy of despotism."

Though Sand paid with his life for his sordid crime, he was hailed by his fellow students as well as by many others of his liberal-minded fellow countrymen as a martyred hero who had sacrificed his life for the honor and future greatness of Germany.

The case of Karl Sand was a real godsend for all those who had long advocated the sternest repressive measures against the liberal and democratic movement. Metternich in particular was firmly determined to make the most of this opportunity "provided by the splendid Sand at the expense of poor Kotzebue," as he caustically expressed his own reaction. The Austrian minister communicated immediately with the government of Prussia to effect, if possible, joint action on the part of both monarchies. Prussia declared her willingness to aid in crushing the spirit of social revolution and, after preliminary negotiations between Metternich and King Frederick William III, the ministers of Austria, Prussia, Bavaria, Wurtemberg, and some of the smaller German states met at the fashionable spa of Karlsbad in Bohemia to work out the famous "Karlsbad Decrees" of 1819, which were shortly afterward ratified by the *"Bundestag."*

Even before the publication of the decrees the persecution and incarceration of suspect persons had begun, and immediately after the document had been ratified a rigid censorship was imposed on all publications and the freedom of speech was radically curtailed. Red, black, and gold, the colors of the *Burschenschaft,* were banned as symbols of the spirit of revolt, and the *Burschenschaft* itself was dissolved. All teachers who were spreading "pernicious doctrines, hostile to public order or undermining existing political institutions" were to be dismissed, and in each university a government official was to supervise all lectures, so as to give them "a wholesome direction, calculated to prepare the studying youth for their future destination."

On May 15, 1820, the "Vienna Final Act" (*Wiener Schlussakte*) was adopted by the *"Bundestag,"* signalizing the triumph of the forces of reaction and putting the final stamp of approval on the repressive measures of the individual governments. The "Karlsbad Decrees" were the most authentic documentation of the "Metternich System." By their ruthless infringements on human rights they arrested a development whose dynamic force, however, could not be permanently halted. It only gathered strength and momentum for the inevitable radical outburst that was to tear apart Metternich's carefully woven web of prohibitions.

Chapter 14

GERMAN ROMANTICISM

Classicism and Romanticism. The world of ideas which inspired the generation that lived through the Wars of Liberation and the ensuing period of political restoration was in many ways a logical outgrowth and culmination of that cult of personality that had been the creed and ideal goal of the leaders of German Classicism (cf. Chap. 12) and the New Humanism (cf. p. 403 sq.). But whereas Goethe and Schiller had sought and achieved a happy balance of human faculties and their expression in literature and society, the Romantic movement of the early nineteenth century dissolved again into its constituent parts the unity and harmony that had been achieved by the classical thinkers and writers. While German Classicism had succeeded in fusing the irrationalism and sentimentalism of "Storm and Stress" with the rationalism of the period of Enlightenment, and had been able to integrate form and content in their works and moral freedom and constraint in their lives, German Romanticism restored to the fullest extent the polarity of these antagonistic forces. The German romanticists believed that the classical synthesis had been achieved at the expense of the depth and breadth of human experience and that an actual unification of the individual and the universal, of personal freedom and objective law, of content and form — nonexistent in the world of appearances — could only be realized in that ideal world to which their yearning aspired.

The proposed classical solution appeared to the romantic authors as merely one solution, but by no means the best and the most desirable. It was their contention that in the attempt to achieve harmonious beauty and formal perfection the classical writers had neglected or suppressed certain vital aspects of reality. For the sake of clarity and intelligibility they had excluded from their abstract speculation and their concrete literary accomplishments the mysterious realms of the preternatural and supernatural, the occult borderland of dreams, visions, and mystical intuitions.

It would be erroneous to designate German Romanticism as a flight from reality. It is more correct to say that Classicism and Romanticism differ in their concept and definition of reality. The classicist experiences with Aristotle the ideal in the contemplation of the individual and concrete, while the romanticist considers with Plato the realm of ideas and universals as supremely real, attributing to the individual object only a borrowed, shadowy, or at best symbolic form of existence. In its endeavor to span all the heights and depths of being, German Romanticism is engaged in a restless search for a wished-for totality, moving from one extreme to the other, always suffering from the fault of excess, always overstating its case, always on the way but never at rest. Life thus reveals itself in its aspects of boundlessness rather than in its limitations, in its dynamism rather than in its static repose and permanence. The "longing infinite" becomes an end in itself, a longing that falls eternally short of its fruition, and all the endeavors and adventures of the human soul are seen as "hieroglyphics of the one eternal love" for the supreme realities of absolute truth, goodness, and beauty. Whereas the classical writer and thinker is concerned with immediate personal values and their realization, the romanticist is always preoccupied with distant goals whose realization transcends and defies the limitations of time and space. Romanticism at its best offers the sublime spectacle of a prodigious quest of the religious and metaphysical meaning of life, nature, and art. At its worst it plunges its protagonists into a chaotic world of shapeless phantasms and hapless imaginings.

Some literary historians have described Classicism and Romanticism as two polar and ever recurrent attitudes of human nature, related and at the same time opposed to each other, as are light and darkness, clarity and formlessness, or male and female. Mme. de Staël (1766–1817) was the first author who dwelt upon the contrast between the "romantic North" and the "classical South," and others have gone further, viewing Romanticism as the truest and fullest manifestation of the northern, Germanic mind.

Historic evidence seems to reveal such rigid classifications as short cuts which fail to do justice to very complex phenomena. One would certainly miss the mark if one were to consider the classical thinkers and writers of Germany as less "Germanic" than those of the romantic age. It is quite obvious, on the other hand, that Germany at certain stages of her cultural evolution has shown decided preference for romantic forms and concepts and that the ideal of classical beauty and perfection has figured historically as a more remote possibility. We feel justified therefore in saying that Classicism and Romanticism reflect a dual aspect of German mentality as perhaps of human nature in general, but that Romanticism as an intellectual pattern and as a medium of literary and artistic expression seems to recommend itself more readily to the Germans.

It is likewise a matter of historical record that just as there are different non-Germanic forms of Classicism so also the romantic movement flourished in the other countries of Europe as well as in the United States of America. The eighteenth-century romanticism of Young's "Night Thoughts" (1742–1745), Macpherson's "Ossian" (cf. p. 393), and Sterne's sentimental novels (cf. p. 392) exerted a strong influence on the German romanticists, as did Walter Scott's novels and Byron's poetry in the early nineteenth century. But even stronger was the impetus that English and American nineteenth-century Romanticism received from Germany, especially during the decades that followed the Napoleonic wars (Carlyle, Poe, Longfellow, Margaret Fuller, and the New England "Transcendentalists"). Italy, France, Spain, the Scandinavian and Slavic nations had romantic movements of their own, more or less remotely related to the contemporary intellectual trends in Germany. French romanticism broke with the classico-rationalistic national tradition, while Italian Romanticism ushered in the literary and political *risorgimento* (national unification, *c.* 1815–1870), and Scandinavian Romanticism marked the "golden age" of the literatures of the northernmost European countries. The general adoption of the term "romanticism" points, to be sure, to a number of common characteristics, but this should not obscure the fact that these several romantic movements carry a widely different meaning within the framework of different national cultures.

"The Romantic School." German Romanticism constituted itself in a literary "school" whose members worked out a new set of aesthetic rules which they opposed to those of the classical authors. But despite this seeming opposition they were still under the spell of Classicism to such an extent that they gave their first periodical a Greek name (*Athenäum*, 1798–1800) and considered Goethe's classical novel *Wilhelm Meister* as the incarnation of everything truly artistic and poetic.

a) Representative Authors. The members of the so-called "older" and "younger" romantic school, though actually belonging to the same generation, represent two distinct phases in the development of the movement. The former laid out the general program and provided the aesthetic theory, the latter translated the romantic ideology into the language of poetry and creative artistic accomplishment.

Jena, Heidelberg, Berlin, and Dresden were the intellectual centers of the movement as a whole, which included among its "older" members: August Wilhelm Schlegel (1767–1845); Friedrich Schlegel (A. W.'s younger brother, 1772–1829); Friedrich von Hardenberg ("Novalis," 1772–1801); Wilhelm Wackenroder (1773–1798); Ludwig Tieck (1773–1853).

Among its "younger" members are: Clemens Brentano (1778–1842); Achim von Arnim (1781–1831); Jakob Grimm (1785–1863); Wilhelm Grimm (J.'s younger brother, 1786–1859); Joseph Görres (1776–1848); Ernst Theodor Amadeus Hoffmann (1776–1822); Joseph von Eichendorff (1788–1857).

More or less loosely related to the "romantic school" were the patriotic romanticists who in prose and poetry glorified the War of Liberation: Ernst Moritz Arndt (1769–1860), Max von Schenkendorf (1783–1817), Theodor Körner (1791–1813); the Swabian romanticists: Ludwig Uhland (1787–1862), Eduard Mörike (1804–1875); the romantic playwrights: Heinrich von Kleist (1777–1811), Franz Grillparzer (1791–1872), and a number of *epigoni* (imitators) who adopted some of the romantic paraphernalia without understanding the romantic spirit as such.

In the process of welding together the different romantic individuals and groups, in establishing bonds of friendship and love, in stimulating enthusiasm and inspiring literary production, the part played by the leading women of the romantic circle and their aesthetic *salons* can hardly be overestimated. Dorothea, the daughter of the philosopher Moses Mendelssohn (cf. p. 369), who married Friedrich Schlegel, and August Wilhelm Schlegel's wife Carolina were the most prominent among a group of highly cultured, intellectually sophisticated, and morally "emancipated" women. It was their influence that kindled the early romanticists' intense interest in the problems of marriage and sexual relations and gave new impetus to their speculations on the interrelation of art, religion, and love.

b) Translators and Historians. It was the feminine element in German Romanticism and the significant role that it played in social life and culture that imparted to romantic thought much of its intuitional character and without doubt contributed its share to making the romanticists masters in the art of translation. In the pages of the *Athenäum* the brothers Schlegel laid down definite rules for the translation of literary masterpieces, stressing the importance of inspirational empathy (*Einfühlung*), whereby the translator was to become "the poet of the poet." He was to transpose himself into a foreign tongue and mentality and, having become one with it, was to re-create the spirit of the work in his vernacular language. By following this advice the romantic translators appropriated for their own nation the poetic treasures of foreign cultures and literatures (Shakespeare, Dante, Tasso, Ariosto, Cervantes, Calderón, Lope de Vega, Camoës, etc.). Thus they brought nearer to realization Herder's and Goethe's idea of a "world-literature" that was to be the common property of all civilized peoples.

Friedrich Schlegel, who described the historian as a "retrospective prophet," exemplified in his own critical works the romanticists' innate and highly cultivated historical sense. It was this sense that enabled them to delve into the cultural deposits of the past and, aided by inner kinship, to rediscover the German and European Middle Ages. They re-evaluated the achievements of the past in art and literature as well as in the fields of political and social endeavor, thereby inspiring their contemporaries with a new love for certain indigenous qualities of German thought, life, and culture. This love for the timeless qualities of the German mind was alive in the fervor of German nationalism in the days of the War of Liberation. And this nationalism was replenished by the poetic glorification of the Holy Empire of the Hohenstaufens and enhanced by the magic charm of a reborn world of quaint medieval cities, of proud castles overlooking the vales and plains and silvery rivers, and of towering cathedrals whose princely majesty stood guard over a sturdy people of valiant nobles, prosperous burghers, and deft and devout artisans. And past and present were linked and enveloped by the same nature in which the spirit of the changing times lived an enchanted life, in which a multitude of voices united in the enduring transfiguration of the mystery of creation.

c) "Longing Infinite" and "Romantic Irony." The endeavor of the romantic writers to embody in their works the entire breadth of life; its lofty heights and dark abysses; the secrets of heaven, earth, and hell, found its expression in Friedrich Schlegel's definition of poetry: "Romantic poetry is progressive universal poetry. It is destined not only to reunite all the separate branches of poetry and to relate poetry with philosophy and rhetoric, but also to fuse and bind together poetry and prose, creative and critical ingenuity, to vitalize and socialize poetry, and to poetize society . . ." (*Athenäum*). For August Wilhelm Schlegel "the poetry of the ancients was that of possession: ours is a poetry of longing; the one rests firmly on the ground of the present, while the other sways to and fro between recollection and presentiment." Thus German Romanticism, at its best, strove for the realization of absolute truth, goodness, and beauty, ever conscious, nevertheless, that infinite and absolute perfection can be approximated only in the form of finite symbols and "hieroglyphics." It was this consciousness of the relative and fragmentary character of artistic and literary forms that became the source of "romantic irony": the supreme effort on the part of the author to overcome the necessary limitations of human accomplishments by the sovereignty of the human spirit which rises above the contingencies of its own creations and ironically contrasts the absolute idea with the frailty of its symbolic representation.

d) The New Medievalism. Despite the fact, however, that the romanticists were most vitally concerned with problems and experiences that had their dynamic center in their own personalities, they aspired to a superindividual realm of ideas and to a communal culture that was to impart added significance to their individual lives and works. They seized upon philosophy and religion in their attempt to unify and integrate personal experiences in a transcendent sphere of values. Living in an age that was witnessing the gradual dissolution of the universal religious and social structures of the past, their yearning for a total view of life attached itself retrospectively to an idealized image of the Catholic Middle Ages, their religion, their thought, and their culture.

Novalis (cf. p. 476), in his essay *Christendom or Europe,* solemnly and passionately sounded the call "back to the Middle Ages!" Himself a Lutheran with pietistic and mystical leanings, he described in glowing colors the unified civilization of medieval Europe as it had emerged from a dark and chaotic world: "Those were beautiful, splendid times, when Europe was one Christian country, when one Christendom inhabited this . . . continent. One great common interest united the most remote provinces of this broad spiritual realm. . . . One sovereign guided and united the great political forces. . . . And how agreeable and well adapted to the inner nature of man this governance and this institution was, is proven by the . . . harmonious development of all human faculties, by the greatness that was achieved by individuals in all the branches of those sciences that constitute art and life, and by the flourishing trade with spiritual and material wares, inside Europe and even extending to the remotest regions of India." The author pictures the Lutheran Reformation as the first phase of the incipient anarchy of Europe, culminating in the rule of Absolutism and the disasters of the French Revolution. He is convinced that Europe's wounds can only be healed and Europe's peace and unity restored by a spiritual power which will be strong and respected enough to lay the foundations for a true League of Nations (*Staatenverein*): "No peace can be concluded among the warring powers . . . , all so-called peace is merely an armistice as long as the point of view of political cabinets prevails. . . . Blood will continue to flow over Europe, until the nations become aware of the horrible insanity which drives them about in a circle, until . . . they again approach their former altars, performing the works of peace and celebrating upon the smoking ruins the great brotherly feast of reconciliation. . . . Religion only can reawaken Europe, provide security for its peoples, and reestablish Christianity in new splendor. . . ."

Like Novalis the early romanticists visualized the "invisible" universal Church of the future and like him they were fascinated by the kindred spiritualistic philosophy and theosophy of Jacob Böhme (cf. p. 270) and the pantheistic speculation of Spinoza and Goethe. They became more and more interested in the mysterious borderlands of the human soul, and by aesthetic considerations as well as by their desire for new metaphysical bearings they were led into the fold of the Catholic Church. While Tieck and Novalis professed a sentimental attachment to Catholicism, Friedrich Schlegel, F. von Stolberg, Zacharias Werner, and others actually embraced the Catholic faith, and Görres and Brentano returned in the end to the abandoned creed of their youth.

e) From Classicism to Romanticism: Jean Paul and Hölderlin. Turning from a general analysis of the romantic movement to a brief consideration of individual authors, the first to demand attention are two precursors of German Romanticism whose works single them out as pioneers, standing on the threshold of a new literary age.

In an obituary speech the poet Ludwig Börne (cf. p. 580 sq.) eulogized *Jean Paul* (Johann Paul Friedrich Richter, 1763–1825) in these words: "A star has gone down, and the eyes of the century will be closed before another of the same magnitude will appear. . . . There will be a time, however, when he will be reborn for all, and they all will then mourn his departure. But he stands patiently at the gate of the twentieth century, waiting with a smile on his lips, until his creeping people will have caught up with him." Jean Paul, a parson's son of a small Franconian town, was both a child of his age and the representative of ideas that heralded the spirit of a liberal and democratic society. One of the greatest stylists of the German tongue, his prose is saturated with a rich and childlike humor, with which he softens and dissolves the tragic dissonances of human life. A born educator, he advocates in both his pedagogical and literary works the ideal of the harmonious development of the faculties of intellect, will, and emotions. As an author he is more interested in standards of truth and righteousness than in formal beauty and artistic perfection. His loving human heart, ever devoted to the woes of his fellow men, makes him an ardent champion of the poor, the weak, and the humble in their defensive struggle against their oppressors and exploiters.

Jean Paul, the writer, is greatest in the literary form of the idyl, in which he encloses a glittering world of quaint characters and occurrences, of princes and fools, eccentric geniuses and pedantic schoolmasters, an abridged universe in which life and death, joy and pain, love and iniquity rest in the embrace of his golden humor. The melodiousness of his style points forward to the rhythmical musicality of romantic prose and sets him apart from the plastic-formal classicism of Goethe and Schiller.

Jean Paul, the moralist and political theorist, expects social and cultural regeneration from a highly developed sense of personal responsibility: "When I read of wars and other calamities . . . I do not curse or whine or remain inactive: rather, since all this misery results from the immorality of some individuals —, I try to extirpate and avoid any and all immorality within myself, well knowing that my own immorality must strike ever new wounds in others." This deep sense of personal accountability, having its roots in the author's virile Protestant faith, made Jean Paul aware of the social significance of his work and made him strive for the reunion of life and literature. Leading art and poetry back from their lofty isolation to the great current of popular tradition, Jean Paul anticipated the ideals of an art that was determined by the ethical motives of social and national consciousness.

Friedrich Hölderlin (1770–1843), a Swabian poet and the second of the great precursors of the Romantic School, shares with Jean Paul the fate of having been rescued from prolonged oblivion by the authors and literary critics of our own century. Although in his youth he associated with Schiller, Schelling, and Hegel, he stands even more apart from his contemporaries than Jean Paul. His life and his poetry were inseparably intertwined. Like the hero of his one and only novel (*Hyperion*, 1797–1799) he lived as a "hermit" in the midst of a society which could offer no satisfactory answer to his longing for a unified world view. In tragic isolation and burdened with a typically Swabian inclination to brooding introspection, he sought in vain to bridge the chasm between subjective experience and objective reality. In vain he tried to find refuge and consolation in nature, in art, and in love, the three symbols and sublimations of his frustrated quest of the divine and its realization in a community of beautiful souls. In the idealized forms and figures of ancient Greece he had visualized the serene harmony of body and mind that seemed denied to him and his generation. And then, quite miraculously, and for the duration of one blessed moment that bore the weight of eternity, the ideal seemed to have assumed human shape in Susette Gontard, the wife of a Frankfurt banker, in whose house he had been engaged as a private tutor. But even this happy idyl was clouded with the hues of impending resignation and profound melancholy. When the hour of parting came, the poet's fate was sealed.

From a brief sojourn in Spain he returned as an aimless wanderer, spending the remaining thirty-seven years of his life in incurable mental derangement.

To Hölderlin's love for Susette Gontard, the "Diotima" of his *Hyperion* and his poems, we owe not only some of the greatest literary documents of the German tongue but also an exchange of letters that rank with the most sublime specimens of epistolary literature. As a poet Hölderlin proved himself a great master of style and artistic form who from inner affinity clothed his experiences in complex Greek meters. In the dynamically moving force of his free rhythms he resuscitated the strong religious individualism of Pindar's (*c.* 520–446 B.C.) Greek odes and anticipated the hymnic language of Friedrich Nietzsche (cf. p. 695 sq.).

f) Leaders of the "Older School." The critical theories of the Romantic School owe their precise formulation to *August Wilhelm Schlegel* and his younger brother Friedrich. August Wilhelm's cultivated sense of literary form and the supple flexibility of his mind made him the master translator of his age. His Shakespeare translation (completed by Tieck's daughter Dorothea and her husband, Count Wolf Baudissin) as well as his translations of Spanish, Italian, and Portuguese masterpieces are contributions of lasting value to German literature. He actually succeeded in making Shakespeare one of the most universally known and revered authors in German lands and one of the most popular ones on the German stage. In his aesthetic and critical works he systematically explored the literary documents of the German past and demanded the reformation of German life and culture in conformity with the ancient indigenous forces of the German mind. For several years the author was the faithful travel companion of Mme. de Staël who with her book *De l'Allemagne* (1810) had been the first to arouse intense interest in her native France in the achievements of classical and romantic German literature. As professor of literature and art history at the newly founded University of Bonn on the Rhine, A. W. Schlegel devoted the years of his mature life to an extensive study of Sanskrit (Hindoo) language and literature.

Friedrich Schlegel, more so than his brother, was given to a passion for rational analysis, evidenced as much in his literary and historical criticism as in the poetic paraphrases of his own self. He interpreted history in terms of personal needs and experiences. In vain he tried to master the discordant urges of his own nature from a focal point in his own personality and, failing in this, he found the desired unity in the "universalism" of the Catholic Church. In the three great works of his later life (*Philosophy of Life; Philosophy of History; Philosophy of Language*) he endeavored to demonstrate the unity of knowledge and faith and "to make manifest to this dissipated age the divine power of the Church in all the sciences and in all human relations." His linguistic and literary studies, especially in the field of Sanskrit and other Oriental languages, have earned him a prominent place in the history of philology and in the newly developing disciplines of systematic literary history and literary criticism.

More creative as a poet and more unified in his world view than the
Schlegels was *Friedrich von Hardenberg,* better known by his pen name
Novalis. His short life was filled to the brim with the romantic "longing
infinite," burning within him as a living spiritual flame and sapping his
physical strength. To his friends he appeared as a stranger from another
planet, but he nevertheless combined with the ethereal and otherworldly
qualities of a romantic poet a remarkably developed practical sense that
enabled him to distinguish himself as a student of law and as a mining
engineer. One of the numerous modern disciples of Plato and the Platonic
mystics and theosophists, he described the human soul as imprisoned in
an earthly body, striving for liberation and longing to return to its divine
source.

The poet more than other human beings has remained conscious of this
exalted dignity of the human soul, and he alone knows of the secret paths
that lead to the spiritual truth that underlies all sense appearances. It is the
task of the poet, therefore, to lead mankind from reason to faith, from
philosophy to religion, through true self-knowledge to the mastery of the
material and spiritual worlds whose motley forms and forces are mere
hieroglyphics of the divine spirit. This "magic idealism" furnishes the key
to the understanding of Novalis' unfinished novel, *Heinrich von Ofterdingen,*
in which the broad realms of nature and history yield their secrets to the
clairvoyant intuition of the poet. The theme of the *Hymns to the Night,*
on the other hand, wherein Death appears as the great liberator and the
longing for Death as the driving force of life, was suggested by the premature death of Sophie von Kühn, the young girl to whom the author had
become engaged. This bittersweet experience confirmed in Novalis the
conviction that an intercourse of the living with the souls of the departed
was possible, and it caused to ripen within him the determination to cut
short his own life and hasten the actual reunion with Sophie by the magic
force of his will.

Wilhelm Heinrich Wackenroder and *Ludwig Tieck,* both natives of
Berlin, were united by bonds of friendship but differed greatly in their
attitude toward life and poetry. As young university students they traveled
together throughout Germany and became the enthusiastic discoverers of
the romantic charms of the old German towns and the soulful beauty of the
native countryside. They were deeply moved by the monuments of the
past that met their admiring eye and mind. Nuremberg, the city of Albrecht
Dürer (cf. p. 197) and Hans Sachs (cf. p. 202), cast its spell over them, and
in breathless admiration they succumbed to the magic enchantment of
ruined medieval castles, overgrown with ivy and bathed in moonlight, the
solemn contours of mountain ranges and lonely forests, bearing witness
that both art and nature were as resplendent and praiseworthy in the inclement North as under the azure skies of sunny Italy. One of the fruits
of these youthful wanderings was Wackenroder's *Confessions of an Art-
Loving Friar* (1797), one of the earliest documents of German Romanticism

and a source of inspiration for the romantic painters of several generations.

Wackenroder died before the romantic movement had really come into its own, but Tieck lived to an advanced age and turned out to be the most flexible and versatile of all German romanticists. Though a prolific writer who tried his skillful hand at every established literary form, many of his works lack the inner necessity and singleness of purpose that we admire in some of the less finished products of his contemporaries. He began with narratives in the mood and style of eighteenth-century Enlightenment but soon paid his tribute to Romanticism in ironic-satirical comedies as well as in dramatizations of legends and folk books with elaborate medieval pageantry, in his paraphrases of the old German folk tales and fairy stories, and in romantic-phantastic novels and short stories of his own invention. Yet he outlived the romantic period and in his later years became a writer of realistic fiction and historical narrative.*

g) *Leaders of the "Younger School."* The names of *Clemens Brentano* and *Achim von Arnim* who married Brentano's sister *Bettina,* the authoress of the widely read but partly fictitious *Goethe's Correspondence with a Child,* are as inseparable as the names of Tieck and Wackenroder. Both poets were members of the younger Romantic School, and together they collected the precious forgotten documents of old German folklore and edited *Des Knaben Wunderhorn* (*The Boy's Magic Horn*), the most renowned anthology of German folk songs.

Brentano was the son of a Frankfurt merchant of Italian ancestry and of Goethe's friend, Maximiliane de Laroche. He was one of Germany's most richly gifted poets but at the same time the most discordant and least balanced character of the entire romantic generation. While the musicality of his lyrics is unsurpassed, the incidental beauty of his prose works (the novel *Godwi*) and his dramatic attempts (*Ponce de Leon*) is marred by an utter lack of logical coherence and aesthetic form. He is at his best in his romantic fairy tales, among which the tragic story of *Casper and Fair Annie* has achieved lasting fame. After having spent four years of his mature life in the company of Katharina Emmerick, a stigmatized nun of Dülmen in Westphalia, he published his recorded observations of her visions, dealing with certain aspects and phases of the life of Christ. He finally found peace of mind and soul in the abandoned Catholic faith of his youth. He will always be remembered as the inventor of the *Lorelay* legend (cf. Violetta's song in *Godwi*) which inspired Heine's (cf. p. 580 sqq.) better known poem of the mysterious maid whose charms lure the skippers to their doom in the watery grave of the Rhine.

Achim von Arnim is known as the author of romantic novels (*Countess*

---

* Representative of the different phases of Tieck's literary development are the following works: *William Lovell* (1794–1796), a psychological novel; *Franz Sternbald's Travels* (1798), a novel depicting the character development of an artist; *Puss in Boots* (1797), a satirical fairy comedy; *Emperor Octavianus* (1804), a romantic drama of partly legendary, partly historical character; *Vittoria Accorombona* (1840), a historical novel; the translation of Cervantes' *Don Quixote* (1799–1804).

Dolores; The Guardians of the Crown) and dramas (*Halle and Jerusalem*) which are carefully planned but poorly executed. A native of the Mark of Brandenburg and the descendant of old Prussian nobility, his heart beat for the cause of the liberation of his homeland from French oppression.

The most talented among the romantic storytellers was *Ernst Theodor Amadeus Hoffmann,* whose versatile genius comprised a strange mixture of seemingly opposite qualities of character and occupation. He was not only a romantic writer, composer, painter, and critic of note but simultaneously an eminent legal expert and an almost pedantic state official. The same mixture of heterogeneous elements is a conspicuous mark of his literary creations and especially of the fragmentary and partly autobiographical novel, *Murr, the Tom-Cat's Reflections on Life* (*Kater Murr*), in which the romantic narrative of Kapellmeister Kreisler's life is grotesquely interwoven with fragments of the tomcat's autobiography. The resulting confusion serves to set off in sharpest contrast Kreisler's idealism and Murr's platitudinous philistinism. Most of Hoffmann's stories present a factual, everyday world, casually and nonchalantly populated with specters and spooks, split personalities, sleepwalkers, and visionaries, a motley array of creatures of a gruesome imagination and a keenly penetrating and realistic observation. The *Tales of Hoffmann* have not only inspired Jacques Offenbach's fantastic opera of the same title, but exerted considerable influence on English and American authors, notably on the fertile genius of Edgar Allen Poe.

Joseph von Eichendorff has been called "the last knight of Romanticism." In his poetry and prose the best that the Romantic School had to offer appears once more collected as in a focus. God, nature, folk, and fatherland are the basic realities that motivate Eichendorff's life and work, and around them his poetic fancy wove a garland of ripe and serene beauty. With Arnim, Brentano, and Görres, who like himself were members of the Heidelberg group of romantic writers, he shares the fondness for folk song and folk tradition. His lyrics, on the other hand, are wider in scope, lending voice to the entire range of human emotions and making nature a symbol and mirror of personal moods and experiences. Eichendorff's love for the Middle Ages and the ideals of chivalry, like that of Novalis, grew out of his longing for a spiritual unification of mankind, and for him, too, the true poet is at once a singer, a seer, a knight, and a priest.

"He who wants to understand a poet thoroughly, must know his homeland," Eichendorff wrote, thus explaining the secret and inimitable charm of his own poetry. It was the radiance of a happy and sheltered childhood and youth, spent in the ancestral castle of Lubowitz in Upper Silesia, that provided the dominant note for Eichendorff's works and that filled them with an unspeakable yearning for a paradise lost and never to be regained on this earth.

After happy student years in Halle and Heidelberg Eichendorff followed the call of his king to the colors and, as a chasseur in the Free Corps of

Major von Lützow, he took part in the war against Napoleon. After the liberation of Prussia he became a conscientious government official, first in Danzig and later on in Berlin.

Among his many works in prose and poetry the tale *Pages from the Life of a Good-for-Nothing* stands out as a real gem of romantic fiction and as one of the most genuine expressions of a thoroughly Germanic poetic temper. All the "leitmotifs" of the Romantic School seem combined and fused in this simple narrative: the glorification and transfiguration of nature with its changing moods and aspects; the scintillating richness of the human heart, its unending cravings, venturing far out and yearning for the home-coming ("*Fernweh*," "*Heimweh*," and "*Wanderlust*"); the sweetness and sadness of human love; and the realization that all our striving is in many disguises nothing but the unquenchable quest for our eternal home, and everything transitory only a symbol of eternity.

While a student at the University of Heidelberg Eichendorff was especially attracted by the vigorous personality of a young *Privatdozent* by the name of *Joseph Görres*. Görres had declared himself emphatically in sympathy with the aims of the Romantic School which by that time had overcome the libertinistic and anarchical rantings of its earliest protagonists and had affirmed its loyalty to the political and social ideas of the reborn Prussian State. Joseph Görres and *Ernst Moritz Arndt* became the two most militant exponents of a political romanticism that was born of their passionately held religious convictions. Although he was no poet Görres ranks among the most prominent members of the Romantic School. He was a native of Coblenz and had been brought up in the crisp atmosphere of eighteenth-century Enlightenment, in the shadow of the speculation of Kant (cf. p. 371 sqq.) and the French *philosophes* (cf. p. 368). His moral rigorism had welcomed the French Revolution of 1789 as the grand fulfillment of the hopes and dreams of the defenders of true progress. In *Results of My Mission to Paris* (1800) he tells of the disillusionment that followed upon observation at close range of the political conditions in the France of the Revolution and of Napoleon. He felt all the heavier the yoke of the French emperor that had crushed the spirit of freedom in his native Rhineland, and both his hatred for the foreign conqueror and his longing for German national unity prescribed for him his true mission as an author. In the service of the German Idea he found himself and became the most important political writer and publicist of his time. He was admired by his friends and fellow countrymen, and both feared and respected by the not easily impressed French emperor. In his essays and editorials Görres fought relentlessly against the spirit of State absolutism and imperialism and for the idea of a national and constitutional democracy, the hoped-for creation of a powerful union of the German people.

In his youth Görres had been chiefly interested in the natural sciences. In his Heidelberg period (1806–1808) he devoted himself to linguistic, aesthetic, and mythological studies and made valuable contributions to the revival of old German art and literature and to the knowledge of Oriental languages. In the period of political reaction that followed the Wars of Liberation Görres barely escaped arrest by his flight to Strasbourg (1819-1827). As professor of history at the University of Munich (1827-1848), where he had been called by King Louis I of Bavaria, Görres became the champion of the new medievalism and of a virile political Catholicism.

The historic significance of *Ernst Moritz Arndt,* the militant Protestant publicist and poet from the Island of Rügen (a Swedish possession at the time of his birth), may well be compared with that of Görres, the Rhenish Catholic. With *Theodor Körner* and *Max von Schenkendorf,* Arndt was one of the "Poets of the Wars of Liberation," but he surpasses them by the wider range of his experience and the more enduring quality of his ideas. Although there was little or nothing of the ethereal and dreamlike in his nature, Arndt concurred with the romantic writers in their glorification of the *Volksgeist* and their vindication of medieval political and social theories and institutions. In his *History of Serfdom in Pomerania and on the Island of Rügen* he deplores the gradual deterioration of the economic, legal, and social status of the peasantry since medieval times and accuses the secularism of the territorial princes and the mechanism of the absolutistic State of having caused this disintegration. He criticizes courageously the totalitarian political maxims of Frederick the Great (cf. p. 316 sqq.) and points out the identical faults in the political system of Napoleon. Like Stein and Görres he advances the idea of the national State against the idea of world imperialism. And again like Stein and Görres he suffers denunciation and persecution, spending many precious years of his life in exile or condemned to involuntary silence.

After having spent the year of 1812 with Stein at the court of Tsar Alexander of Russia, he returned to Prussia in the following year and fanned the enthusiasm of the German youth with his patriotic songs and pamphlets. In 1818 he accepted a position as professor of history at the University of Bonn, but was shortly afterward dismissed because of his active participation in the movement of the *Burschenschaft* (cf. p. 464 sqq.). He was reinstated by King Frederick William IV in 1840 and gained a seat in the First National Assembly of Frankfurt in 1848 (cf. p. 530 sqq.), where he worked for the unification of Germany under Prussia's leadership.

h) German Philology: The Grimm Brothers. As J. J. Winckelmann (cf. p. 399) had established systematic archaeology as an independent discipline, so the brothers *Jakob* and *Wilhelm Grimm* became the founders of the science of Germanistics. From their childhood days they lived together in an intimate communion of thought and work. Both began their academic career as librarians in Kassel, later on accepted professorships in the University of Göttingen, were dismissed in 1837 because of their democratic leanings, and both died as members of the Academy of Sciences in Berlin. Under the influence of the romantic writers they began to study the literary and cultural documents of the German past and systematically endeavored to understand and interpret the German *Volksgeist* in its various manifestations. Following Herder's (cf. p. 396 sq.) profound intuitions they considered the history of language and literature as an inexhaustible treasury of human thought, revealing definite character traits of individual national cultures.

The Grimm brothers started out with the collection of fairy tales that established their fame internationally: *Deutsche Kinder- und Hausmärchen* (1812–1814). They had listened to these tales as they were told by the common people in the intimate atmosphere of their hearths and homes, and they retold them with an unembellished simplicity that preserved their original and natural charm. Once again the tales of "Little Red Riding Hood" (*Rotkäppchen*), "Cinderella" (*Aschenbrödel*), the "Sleeping Beauty" (*Dornröschen*), "Snow White" (*Schneewittchen*), and many others became the property of the entire people, children and grownups alike.

Like Herder and Humboldt the Grimm brothers speculated on the origin of language, and in 1819 the first volume of Jakob's *German Grammar* was published. This is a historic and comparative study of all Germanic dialects that revealed the general structure and morphology of the Germanic languages and was based on painstaking research and personal observation. Here for the first time all those laws of syntax and grammar — *Umlaut, Ablaut,* weak and strong declension and conjugation, sound shift, the rules of phonology, etymology — were developed which today form part of the basic equipment of the German philologist. For Jakob Grimm the history of the German language and grammar was a true mirror of the nature, mentality, and cultural history of the German people. In his *Mythology* (1819) and the *Antiquities of German Law* (1828) he laid bare the common roots of legal and poetic concepts, using as his chief source the judicial case material of the medieval Germanic village communities (*Weistümer*).

After their dismissal from Göttingen the brothers began their last great philological enterprise, the *German Dictionary* (*Deutsches Wörterbuch*), a word encyclopedia of monumental scope which remained unfinished (four volumes) in their lifetime and to which committees of scholars added many volumes after their death.

Reverence for tradition and a sensitive organ for real progress, the two qualities that they most admired in their Germanic forebears, were conspicuous in the life and thought of the Grimm brothers. In past and present they found comfort and encouragement and lovingly understood both as resulting from an unfathomable providential design. They transmitted the fruits of their labors and the high scholarly standard of their work to a number of German linguists of their time, among whom Karl Lachmann (1793–1851) and Karl Müllenhoff (1818–1884) deserve special mention. Their efforts in the field of scientific philology culminated in an uncompleted history of German antiquities, entitled *Deutsche Altertumskunde,* a work that gives clear evidence of the novelty of their methods which were appropriated by several successive generations of German philologists.

The Swabians: Uhland and Mörike. From the same region that had largely contributed to the greatness of German poetry in the golden age of *Minnesang* (cf. p. 155 sq.) came two authors who represented the more sober and conventional aspects of German Romanticism. The chief member of the so-called Swabian School was *Ludwig Uhland,* a poet, a scholar, and a champion of the constitutional rights of the people. His poetry is rooted in the soil and the historic traditions of his homeland and includes romances, ballads, political lyrics, and simple nature songs. All of his poems strive for impersonal objectivity and most of them achieve an admirable clarity and simplicity of form and content. Documents of a healthy mind and a noble and gentle human heart, they approach the artless and sturdy integrity of folk song and folk ballad.

Uhland wrote poetry only in his youth. After having served for three years as professor of German language and literature at the University of Tübingen, his interest in his country's constitutional struggles prompted him to enter the political arena and to take an active part in the fight for liberalism and democracy. His early legal studies in Tübingen and Paris made him well qualified to fulfill the legislative functions connected with his membership in the parliament of the kingdom of Wurtemberg and later on (1848) in the first German parliament at Frankfurt. The bases of his political creed were his profound respect for natural and moral law and his implicit faith in the dignity of man.

In his scholarly contributions to the history of literature and civilization Uhland appears as one of the cofounders of the sciences of Germanistics and Romanistics (Germanic and Romanic philology). In his monographic work on *Walther von der Vogelweide* (1822) he professes his admiration for the greatest lyric poet of the German Middle Ages and makes Walther's voice audible again for modern ears. In the *Myth of Thor* (1830) he lays down the basic principles of mythological research, and in his *Collection of Folk Songs* (1844) he continues and perfects the work of Herder and Arnim-Brentano.

Eduard Mörike, in contrast to his fellow countryman, was one of those quiet and introspective Swabians who are by nature averse to any involvement in political or social controversies, whose intense inner life absorbs all their interest, thus making them strangers to the noisy conflicts and cataclysms of the external world. As a student of Protestant theology in Tübingen, in the quietude of a country parsonage, as a teacher in Stuttgart, the capital of the kingdom, Mörike remained in all these different environments essentially unchanged, faithful to the soft and gentle rhythm of his life, in love with nature's minute and intimate secrets and miracles. In calm detachment he witnessed the death of Romanticism and the rise of new literary fashions, while he himself continued to live in his self-contained poetic realm, the heir of Classicism and of Romanticism, whose sensitive soul combined psychological intuition with formative genius.

In subject matter and metrical form Mörike's lyrics and ballads span a wide range of possibilities, reaching from the simple and direct expression of folk poetry to the classical patterns of antiquity. While in his novel *Maler Nolten* he seems unable to reconcile the classical and romantic, the realistic and phantastic elements, thus falling short of his model *Wilhelm Meister* (cf. p. 412), his story of *Mozart's Journey from Vienna to Prague* is a perfect example of the fusion of romantic fancy, realistic description, and classical mastery of form.

The Dramatists: Kleist and Grillparzer. The romantic mind and temperament expressed themselves most naturally in the subjective literary language of lyric poetry and the lyrically instrumented prose narrative. The members of the Romantic School found it difficult if not impossible to attain to that plastic objectivity and dialectic acuteness that are some of the necessary requisites of dramatic art. While some members of the School exhibited profound and expert knowledge of dramatic theory, their own dramatic attempts, paying no heed to or being unaware of the requirements of the stage, rarely progressed beyond the experimental phase.

Kleist and Grillparzer, the two great dramatists of the romantic age, can only with certain reservations be classified as romantic authors. They shared with the romanticists the fertility and flexibility of mind, their intense idealism, and their opposition to Classicism, but their more realistic appraisal of the possibilities and necessities of the stage and their fuller and firmer grip on life made them succeed where the romanticists failed. The element of tragic frustration that is conspicuous in the life of both authors was due to the fact that both felt the pressing need for the creation of a new dramatic style that was to unite modern individual and psychological characterization with the traditional classical idealization, an undertaking that would have required the combined genius of a Sophocles and a Shakespeare.

Heinrich von Kleist, the descendant of an ancient family of noblemen and army officials of the Mark Brandenburg, was by nature endowed with a morbid and melancholy temper which made him all the more sensitive to his unhappy personal circumstances and to the national disaster that befell his Prussian fatherland under the yoke of the Corsican conqueror. After having taken part in the Coalition War of 1795 (cf. p. 324 sq.) as an ensign, he resigned his army commission and devoted himself to the study of literature and philosophy. His acquaintance with Kant's *Critique of Pure Reason* (cf. p. 372) plunged him into utter confusion and despair, resulting in a complete breakdown, caused by the fearful thought of finding the gateways to the attainment of absolute certitude of knowledge closed once and for all. Partially recovered, his restless mind urged him to find the much-needed relaxation in travels that led him into France, Switzerland, and Italy. In vain he tried, in compliance with the wishes of his family, to earn a living as a petty state official. His failure to conquer the German stage and the German public with his plays, his clashes with the

Prussian censors, the complete fiasco of several ambitious journalistic enterprises, and the ever widening rift with his family finally seemed to leave no avenue open to him but self-destruction. Kleist was thirty-four years of age when he and Henriette Vogel, a casual acquaintance who was suffering from an incurable disease, shot themselves.

The characters of Kleist's plays are magnified symbols of his own urges and ideals. These characters are haunted by the same demonic forces that played havoc with Kleist's own life. They are romantic in that they, too, suffer from the fault of excess. In *Schroffenstein,* his first tragedy, written under the influence of Shakespeare's *Romeo and Juliet* and Schiller's *Bride of Messina* (cf. p. 425 sq.), two families are destroyed as much by the unruly passions of the individuals as by the inscrutable decrees of Fate. *Robert Guiscard,* leader of the Norman conquerors of Sicily, the hero of Kleist's monumental fragment of the same title, falls a victim to his excessive will to power. *Penthesilea,* the queen of the Amazons, the heroine of Kleist's most dynamic play, is destroyed by her boundless love for Achilles. Her love turns into hatred when she believes herself betrayed by the valiant Greek and, joining the maddened pack of her hounds, she mutilates the body of her lover, only to follow him in death in the anguish and agony of unspeakable remorse. It was in *Penthesilea* that Kleist revealed himself as the antipode of Goethe, for whom he nourished a mixed emotion of "love-hatred," similar to Penthesilea's feelings for Achilles. Of *Penthesilea* he said himself: "My innermost being is embodied in it . . . the entire anguish and splendor of my soul," and he felt hurt and humiliated beyond all measure when Goethe coolly described this work and its main character as ill proportioned and bordering on the pathological.

When Goethe, in connection with Penthesilea, spoke of "confused emotions" (*Gefühlsverwirrung*), he named the main deficiency of most of Kleist's characters: they lack balance, proportion, and therewith the prerequisites for unerring and resolute action. *Käthchen of Heilbronn,* the romantic heroine of Kleist's "Great Historical Drama of Chivalry," seems to be the one exception. Kleist describes her as "the reverse of Penthesilea, her opposite pole, a human being that is as great by her passive devotion as Penthesilea is by her action." This drama, Kleist's most genuine contribution to the romantic movement, makes use of the widespread interest in somnambulism and the mysterious forces of nature and mind. Käthchen's unfailing instinct makes her pursue the object of her love and devotion with unfaltering step, so that all the miraculous events and roundabout ways converge quite plausibly in the predestined union of Käthchen and her beloved Count Wetter vom Strahl.

This fairy play and the following realistic comedy *The Broken Jug* are like breathing spells before Kleist's final dramatic effort. The story of Adam, the village judge, who by an overdose of his own cunning and deceit becomes more and more entangled in his self-spun web of lies, is rightly considered as the healthiest and sprightliest of German comedies. It is at the same time the first great example of dramatic realism, embodying in its characters, its plot, and its setting the intimate charm, sparkling vitality, and brisk humor of a Dutch genre picture.

The two remaining dramas of Kleist are affirmations of his fervent patriotism. The *Hermannsschlacht* presents the plight of the Prussian State by means of a portrayal of the analogical struggle of the great Cheruscan leader Arminius (Hermann), "Germany's liberator," against the might of the ancient Roman Empire, ending in the decisive victory of the united Germanic tribes over the Roman legions in the Teutoburg Forest (A.D. 9, cf. p. 20). It is a scarcely disguised call to arms against Napoleon, an outcry of passionate hatred and a document of excessive nationalism. The second patriotic drama, *The Prince of Homburg,* is a more positive presentation of a similar problem. The disguise is even more transparent, the plot dealing with an episode in the military career of the Great Elector of Brandenburg-Prussia (cf. p. 310 sq.) and involving some of the other leading figures in the more recent history of the Prussian State. The theme is the moral education of a Prussian prince who, under the guidance of the Elector's pedagogical wisdom, turns from youthful irresponsibility to a free recognition of the just claims of the State, which confronts the individual as the moral law incarnate, demanding unselfish obedience and supreme sacrifice.

Heinrich von Kleist's prose narratives resemble his dramas in their terse, chroniclelike style, moving inexorably toward a tragic climax. In *Michael Kohlhaas* the author presented Germany with a work of which Friedrich Hebbel, another one of the great playwrights of the nineteenth century (cf. p. 586 sqq.), has well said: "I maintain that in no other German narrative does the horrifying depth of life ... appear as vividly as in this work, in which the theft ... of two horses is the first link in a chain that stretches from the horse-dealer Kohlhaas to the German Emperor. . . ." Kohlhaas, a contemporary of Martin Luther, is characterized by Kleist as "the most upright and at the same time the most frightful individual of his time," a man whose violated sense of justice causes him to become a highway robber and murderer. And, like Michael Kohlhaas, Kleist himself was headstrong, self-willed, and determined not to compromise with conventional tastes and norms. This explains in part his failure to find during his lifetime the response which would have mitigated the tragedy of his personal fate.

Franz Grillparzer, despite his egocentered philosophy of life and his lack of self-harmony, has even less claim than Kleist to be classified as a genuine romanticist. His personality and his works are related to all the great literary styles of the eighteenth and nineteenth centuries, owing as much to the influence of Enlightenment (cf. p. 368 sqq.) and Baroque (cf. p. 330 sqq.) as to that of Classicism and Romanticism, and even foreshadowing some of the essential elements of the realistic modes of the generations of writers that succeeded him.

A true child of his native Vienna, Austria's greatest playwright continues his country's literary traditions and forcefully expresses the positive and negative implications of this cultural heritage. In his searching self-analysis he experienced the weight of his Austrian temperament as a bane rather than a blessing, attributing to it his morbidity, his dissecting criticism, and the lack of concentrated will power which prevented him from mastering the adverse circumstances of his life.

Condemned to spend the greater part of his youth and manhood in the shadow of the Metternich regime, continually vexed and severely handicapped by an arbitrary system of political censorship, he ceased writing for publication at the very height of his literary development. The remainder of his dramatic production, hidden away in his desk, had to wait for the author's death to meet the eye and gain the belated favor of the public.

Personal bitterness, caused by disappointment, frustration, and disillusionment, made Grillparzer preach a doctrine of melancholy resignation and made him seek contentment in a simple and unproblematic life. This aspiration was fulfilled in his old age when, in addition to the gift of peace of heart and mind, the long-coveted universal recognition was granted to him. When he died he was mourned and celebrated as Austria's great "classical" dramatist.

Grillparzer's first important play, *Die Ahnfrau* (the "Ancestress," i.e., the ancestral family ghost), was a distinctive contribution to a peculiar species of romantic drama, the so-called "Fate-Tragedy," of which the East Prussian, Zacharias Werner (1768–1823), was the most talented exponent.* *Die Ahnfrau* is a combination of spook and fate-tragedy, in which motifs of the popular Austrian stage (*Volksdrama*) and the classical rhetoric of Schiller are fused to produce a sweeping melodramatic effect. *Sappho,* conceived in the classical vein under the influence of Goethe's *Iphigenia* (cf. p. 411) and *"Tasso"* (cf. p. 411), is a drama of unrequited love and final renunciation, in which Grillparzer portrays his own disheartening experiences in the guise of the tragic life and death of the great Greek poetess (*c.* 600 B.C.).

The classical setting is retained in two other works of Grillparzer, of which the trilogy *The Golden Fleece* presents a modern version of the Greek legend of Jason and Medea and the expedition of the fifty Greek Argonauts to the Black Sea. The dramatically moving story of the recovery of the "Golden Fleece," of the love and gradual estrangement of Jason and Medea, the effective confrontation of Greeks and Barbarians and their surrounding worlds reveal the author as a master of individual characterization and psychological motivation. In conceiving the Golden Fleece as a symbol of human greed and in portraying its dehumanizing effects

---

* The romantic "Fate-Tragedy" (*Schicksalsdrama*) was born of a misunderstanding of the significance of "Fate" in ancient Greek tragedy. The religious and metaphysical motivation in the dramas of Sophocles, Aeschylos, etc., is here replaced by a "Fate" that attaches itself to external tools or symbols, such as fateful days, weapons, etc.

Grillparzer approaches a synthesis of classical fate-tragedy and modern character drama.

Waves of Love and the Sea is a dramatization and modernization of the legendary account of the unhappy love of Hero, the priestess of Aphrodite, and Leander, the gallant Greek youth, who braves the nightly tempest and the waves of the Hellespontus and whose shattered body becomes a messenger of death for his beloved also.

All of Grillparzer's dramatic works are more or less didactic: they have an ax to grind or a lesson to teach. This is especially true of his historical dramas which deal with certain leading personalities of the ruling dynasty of Austria and are conspicuously pro-Hapsburg. The one comedy he wrote (*Woe to Him Who Lies*) is no exception to this rule: it preaches a humorous and gentle sermon against the fanatics of truth and rectitude, making an eloquent plea for the toleration of the imperfection of all human and earthly things.

Among Grillparzer's posthumous works the most interesting is the psychological character tragedy *The Jewess of Toledo*, whose plot was suggested by Lope de Vega (1562–1635), the great Spanish playwright. King Alfonso, who has become forgetful of his royal duties as a result of his infatuation for Rahel, a seductive but heartless Jewess, regains his true moral stature after Rahel has been put to death at the behest of the queen. While this work marks a further step on the way to dramatic realism, Grillparzer's last and ripest contributions to German Romanticism are his fairy play *The Dream that is Life (Der Traum ein Leben)*, and his mythological play *Libussa*. *The Dream that is Life* is a counterpart of Calderón's Spanish drama, *Life is a Dream*. In it Rustan, the hero, foresees in a dream all the dangers and vicissitudes of his contemplated journey to the Court of Samarkand. He derives from this experience a more sober view of reality and a clearer insight into human relations, resigning himself to the moderate amount of happiness that is found within the narrow confines of man's immediate environment and in the tranquillity of his soul. *Libussa,* the dramatized legend of the foundation of Prague, is the story of a mythological fairy queen of the same name. She sacrifices her royal dignity and descends from her unreal world to be united with her beloved Primislaus, the representative of a new realistic order of practical and creative activity. But, remaining a stranger in this new environment, she withers away and is lost in the ever widening chasm between dream and reality, memory and love, past and present.

Romantic Art. Although the German romanticists were deeply interested in the philosophy of art and the principles of art appreciation, only the arts of painting and interior decoration showed the influence of the romantic modes of thought.

a) Individual Romantic Painters. The preoccupation of the romanticists with the art and civilization of the German past suggested much of the subject matter of the romantic painters. Many of their works were the result of historical retrospection. In the attempt to cultivate an art that was typically and exclusively German they often were too much concerned with the ideal content and neglected the requirements of artistic form. They wanted to tell stories and thus made their works illustrative complements of historical and literary contexts. In this way much of the immediacy and the spontaneous expressiveness of the great German art of the past was lost. Unable to offer a tangible substitute for the discarded formal values of the Italian Renaissance, they either created in accordance with pedantically observed academic rules or abandoned themselves to personal moods, but did not succeed in anchoring their works in the universal consciousness of an artistic style.

Ludwig Richter (1803–1844) and *Moritz von Schwind* (1804–1871) were chiefly illustrators of fairy tales, legends, and the intimate charms of German domestic life. Their works provide a perfect accompaniment of the restrained and self-contained philistinism of the *"Biedermeier,"* the style of family culture and complacent middle class comfort. Both painters, however, deserve the highest praise for their share in the discovery and poetic glorification of the German landscape. Freeing their pictorial compositions from the artificially calculated designs of the Neo-Classicists (cf. p. 400 sqq.), they made nature the sensitive medium of romantic moods.

It was in the field of landscape painting that some of the romantic masters achieved real greatness. Looking at nature they felt, in the words of *Philipp Otto Runge* (1777–1810), "ever more distinctly that in every tree and flower there is hidden a certain human spirit, idea, or feeling." Runge, the friend of Ludwig Tieck, was the most talented of the early romantic painters. His dream of a "synaesthetic" fusion of all the arts points forward to Richard Wagner's *Gesamtkunstwerk* (cf. p. 495), while his theoretical studies on the symbolic values of color and his understanding of the significance of light, atmosphere, and movement place him in the immediate neighborhood of the impressionists (cf. p. 715 sq.) of the later nineteenth century. Characteristic of the symbolic-allegorical tendency of some of his works are his unfinished *Four Seasons* which he had conceived as a romantic "musical poem." The picture of his parents shows Runge's ability as a portraitist and is at the same time a lovable document of German middle-class life and culture at the turn of the century.

The greatest of the romantic landscapists is *Caspar David Friedrich* (1774–1840) who endows the romantic scene with distant horizons and the mysterious sheen of unearthly luminance. His paintings are spiritually alive with the rhythmical breath of almost imperceptible nuances of light and color. His moods are sweet, gentle, and softly melancholy, always truly romantic and never sentimental.

Somewhat apart from the afore-mentioned artists stands *Karl Spitzweg* (1808–1885), whose remarkable genius expresses itself in paintings of miniature size. The warmth and vehement brilliance of his colors and the irresistible charm of his wit and satire make him impart a rare quality

The Poor Poet, by Karl Spitzweg.

of persuasive actuality to his genrelike descriptions of small-town life and characters. No one knew better than Spitzweg the tender emotions, inclinations, and habits that animate a philistine world of the smallest proportions, and he enhanced this petty world by an aura of human greatness and everlasting significance. In his treatment of light and color Spitzweg, like Runge, anticipated some of the innovations of the impressionistic school of painting.

b) The "Nazarenes." The nationalism as well as the medievalism of the romantic movement was expressed in the ideals of a small band of painters who at the beginning of the nineteenth century called for the restoration of an art that was both German and Christian. These "Nazarenes," as they were half ironically called because of their ascetic-pietistic retirement from the world, gathered together in an abandoned monastery in Rome and, like the Pre-Raphaelites in England, tried to imitate the life and work of the religiously inspired schools of painting of the later Middle Ages and the early Renaissance. Their exquisite draftsmanship is best evidenced in their sketches and cartoons, while the completed fresco paintings for the Casa Bartholdy in Rome (now in the National Gallery in Berlin) reveal their insufficient mastery of coloristic patterns. Nevertheless, it remains their great merit to have revived understanding for the tasks of monumental mural design and the almost forgotten technique of alfresco painting.

The leader of the "Friars of St. Luke," as the Nazarenes called themselves, was *Friedrich Overbeck* (1789-1869), a devout Roman Catholic, to whom art was "like a harp on which I would always hear sounding hymns in praise of God." *Peter Cornelius* (1783-1867), another member of the group, more widely known by his illustrations to Goethe's *Faust* than by his series of fresco paintings, became in his advanced age director of the art academy of his native Düsseldorf and worked in Munich in the service of the Bavarian court.

c) Biedermeier. The period between the Congress of Vienna and the March Revolution of 1848 ("*Vormärz*," cf. p. 461 sqq.) was characterized by a mode of living and an artistic taste which derived their peculiar traits from the philistinism of the middle classes. The "philistine" is the "Biedermeier," a name which is sometimes applied to the entire "*Vormärz*" but more specifically refers to the then prevailing fashion of interior decoration. This fashion reflects the homely frugality of life, a culture of small proportions and limited possibilities, which had developed under the influence of the political pressure of the Napoleonic era, the economic depression that followed the Wars of Liberation, and the restrictive measures of the restoration period. As it favored soberness and simple comfort in the style of living, so it encouraged deft and solid craftsmanship and smooth and harmonious design in home furnishings as well as quite generally in the applied arts and crafts.

Romantic Music. All romantic art and literature contained an element of musicality and secretly or openly betrayed a tendency to approximate and imitate the effects of music, the most unplastic of all the arts. Wackenroder, in his essay on *The Miracles of Musical Art,* considers music the most sublime of the arts, because it interprets human feelings in a superhuman way, "because it makes manifest all the movements of the human mind . . . because it speaks a language unknown to us in ordinary life, a tongue which we have learned we know not where and how and which one feels tempted to describe as the language of the angels." Tieck asks: "Should it not be permissible to think in sounds and to compose musically in words and thoughts?" And the philosopher Schopenhauer (cf. p. 505 sq.) sees in the art of music the most immediate realization of the universal "world-will." We are therefore not surprised to find in the works of musical romanticism a genuine and condensed expression of romantic ideas and experiences.

a) *"Lied" and Instrumental Music.* The earliest of the romantic composers was *Franz Schubert* (1797–1828), the youngest of the fourteen children of a Viennese schoolmaster. While he did not break with the musical tradition as established by Haydn, Mozart, and Beethoven, he enriched this heritage by cultivating the style of lyrical music on a grand scale and became the creator of the universally known and loved species of the German *Lied.* When he was sixteen years of age Schubert composed the beautiful musical setting for Gretchen's *Song at the Spinning Wheel* from Goethe's *Faust* and one year later the immortal melody to Goethe's *Erl-King.* Inexhaustible in his melodious resourcefulness, he wrote over six hundred *Lieder* in all, among them such gems as *The Heather Rose, Mignon's Song* (from Goethe's *Wilhelm Meister*), *The Trout, Death and the Maiden,* and the song cycle of *A Winter's Journey.* Schubert's larger instrumental works, including fourteen string quartets and eight symphonies (of which the last, *Unfinished,* is the best known), are highly picturesque and of great lyrical beauty but suffer at times from various defects of composition. Among his many choral works are six Masses and a number of smaller works of a religious nature. Franz Schubert was a largely self-taught artist, whose short life was fraught with much bitterness and disappointment, but who valiantly prevailed over a multitude of adversities.

The second phase of musical romanticism in Germany is represented by *Felix Mendelssohn-Bartholdy* (1809–1847) and *Robert Schumann* (1810–1856). The former was the grandson of Lessing's friend, the popular philosopher Moses Mendelssohn (cf. p. 369). The son of a Jewish banker of the city of Hamburg, Mendelssohn was financially independent and able to satisfy his urge for travel in foreign lands. A citizen of the world, he lacked the distinctive national character traits of other exponents of German Romanticism. His several trips to England and Scotland earned him great popularity in the British Isles and bore fruit in the composition of the *Hebrides* overture and the Scotch Symphony. The romantic fluency of his melodies blends happily with a classical formal equilibrium and his music on the whole is scarcely touched by the complexities of the romantic temperament.

By the time he was fifteen Mendelssohn had already composed twelve symphonies and a large number of other instrumental and vocal works. He paid his tribute to the spirit of the age by the creation of a kind of "elfish romanticism" (*Elfenromantik*) which is best exemplified by his incidental music to Shakespeare's *A Midsummer Night's Dream,* while his *Songs without Words* mark a new departure in the style of romantic pianoforte composition. In his overtures and symphonies Mendelssohn develops his themes and melodies around a definite "program,"* and in his oratorios and choral works he revives and continues the tradition of Bach and Händel (cf. p. 350 sqq.). As director and conductor of the famous "Gewandhaus Concerts" in Leipzig and as cofounder of the Leipzig Conservatory Mendelssohn's judgment carried great weight and he used his influence to bring about a new appreciation of Bach's musical genius.

Robert Schumann was a child prodigy and only six years old when he made his first attempts at musical composition. He grew up to become not only the most astute of the romantic composers of his day but one of the first and greatest of modern music critics as well. As the founder and editor (1834–1844) of the *Neue Zeitschrift für Musik* he laid down the basic principles of the appreciation of music. In 1840 Schumann married *Clara Wieck,* the daughter of his piano teacher in Leipzig, who herself became a noted pianist and a composer of songs and music for the pianoforte. In his later years Schumann showed symptoms of progressive mental derangement; he died in a private asylum which he had entered at his own request.

The fervent subjectivity of Schumann's musical style was held in check by the transparent clarity of musical patterns deriving from an iron discipline of technique and a mature artistic intellect. Equipped with such splendid mastery of musical form and content, Schumann developed a new epigrammatic and miniature style of pianoforte music and became the most distinguished lyrical composer of the second major phase of German romantic music. While the best of his 248 *Lieder* vie in melodiousness and popularity with those of Schubert, his four symphonies and numerous choral works, rich as they are in lyrical and pictorial beauty, suffer not infrequently from the typically romantic faults of antithetical disjointedness and short-winded abruptness.

b) Symphonic Poem and Opera. The third and final major phase of romantic music in Germany has as its chief protagonists *Franz von Liszt* (1811–1886) and *Richard Wagner* (1813–1883). While the earlier romantic

---

* The term "program music," in contrast to "absolute music," is applied to any kind of music which tries to reproduce in musical form certain observed data, events, or images in nature or definite psychological moods and experiences. "Program music" in one form or another was a familiar mode of musical composition in all musical epochs, but it acquires an unprecedented prominence in the second half of the nineteenth century (Liszt, Richard Strauss, etc.).

composers had continued and further developed the traditional classical forms of sonata and symphony and had added as their own major contribution the glories of the German *Lied,* the inventive genius of Liszt and Wagner created the indigenous style of the symphonic poem and the romantic opera. The symphonic poem was an intermediate form between symphony and opera, utilizing the possibilities of both and adapting the symphony to the requirements of descriptive "program music." In this way the symphonic poem becomes capable of expressing poetic values without requiring either actors or a stage setting. The metamorphoses of the musical theme were a further development of the classical "variation" and represent the connecting link between the latter and Richard Wagner's *"Leitmotiv."*

Liszt was above all a brilliant technician and musical improviser, with a decided leaning toward the theatrical and spectacular. As composer he is at his best in his most unpretentious works, such as the Hungarian rhapsodies (19), in which he finds a natural outlet for his forceful musical temperament. In his ecclesiastical compositions he tries to combine the austere melodic structure of Gregorian Chant (cf. p. 83 sq.) with the musical sentiment of modern harmony. His symphonic poems include musical paraphrases of *Tasso, Faust,* and various operatic motifs.

Liszt was born in Hungary of a German mother. He made his first public appearance in Vienna. From the year 1842 dates his association with Weimar, where he stayed for twelve years after having received an appointment as "Court Kapellmeister" in 1849. It was his ambition to make Weimar once again the center of art and culture that it had been in Goethe's and Schiller's time, and even if that dream fell short of its realization, he did succeed in making the city a musical metropolis in which his own warmhearted personality and unselfish endeavors provided guidance and encouragement to a large number of younger composers. In Weimar Wagner's acquaintance with Liszt grew into a solid friendship, and it was in the same city that the foundations were laid for Wagner's future fame.

In *Richard Wagner* the romantic movement in German music reached its culminating point. The "music dráma," his most distinctive achievement, had been anticipated in its general idea in the earlier romantic operas of *Carl Maria von Weber* (1786–1826), whose *Freischütz* (1820) had marked the victory of the German over the Italian style of the opera. Weber's romantic nature feeling, the elegance and nobility of his musical sentiment, and his fervent patriotism made him one of the most popular composers in the period of literary romanticism and in the years of the national uprising against Napoleon. Although the texts underlying his operas were hardly less stereotyped than the cheap and conventional libretti of the Italian operas, his clear understanding of the interrelation of text and music, singers and orchestra, helped him overcome to a large extent the handicap of an unsuitable literary form. His fairy opera *Oberon* became almost a symbol of German musical romanticism.

Weber's highest aspirations, however, were realized by Richard Wagner, who established the desired balance of music and dramatic action. Wagner thus emancipated the German opera once and for all from the tyranny of the Italian *"recitativo"* style which had subjected the musical instrumentation to the requirements of the libretto and of which even Mozart (cf. p. 353 sq.) had not been able to free himself. With Wagner, however, the music was allowed to fulfill its legitimate functions and both music and text were duly balanced and proportioned to each other. The orchestra, assuming the significance of the chorus in ancient Greek tragedy, demonstrated its almost unlimited possibilities in interpreting the secret motivations of the characters and in uncovering the mythological and spiritual background of the action. This was mainly achieved by the introduction and ingenious manipulation of the *"Leitmotiv,"* a device that had been used with great effect by the French composer Hector Berlioz (1803–1869) but that was perfected by Richard Wagner. It consists essentially in the association of short, rhythmically characteristic musical phrases with specific characters and situations; their frequent repetition serves to intensify the effect of identical emotional reactions and also aids in the clarification of the thematic structure of the composition.

It seems that Wagner's task in carrying out these innovations was simplified but at the same time made more exacting by the fact that he was a playwright as well as a composer and therefore his own librettist. But Wagner was not satisfied with achieving fame in the fields of music and drama: it was his ambition to create "the art-work of the future," the *Gesamtkunstwerk* (the total work of art). This was to result from a union and fusion of all the arts, including poetry, song, instrumental music, painting, acting, dance and festival play, and even the arts of the stage machinist and technician. If any man could dare to strive for such a goal without bringing upon himself the lasting odium of wayward presumption, that man was Richard Wagner who, by virtue of his astounding catholicity of tastes and talents, appeared to Nietzsche (cf. p. 695 sq.) as "a great cultural force."

Wagner attained to artistic greatness as well as to public recognition relatively late, after he had been unsuccessful in many early attempts at musical expression. He was born and educated in Leipzig and achieved professional prominence first as a choir director in Würzburg (1833) and an orchestra conductor in Magdeburg (1834) and Königsberg (1836). It was in the latter city that he married the actress Minna Planer, from whom he separated in 1861. From Riga, where he had spent a short time as director of the local opera, he fled to London and Paris to escape his creditors, and before his return to Dresden in 1842 and his appointment as "Court Kapellmeister" of the king of Saxony (1843–1849) he had completed the operas *Rienzi* and *The Flying Dutchman*. These were followed by *Tannhäuser* (1845) and *Lohengrin* (1847), which were both produced by Liszt on the

Weimar stage in Wagner's absence. The composer in the meantime had arrived in the Swiss city of Zurich, on his flight from Dresden, where he had taken part in the revolutionary uprisings of the year 1849.

The period of Wagner's mature creations begins with his "exile" in Zurich (1849–1859). It was during these years that the idea of the Wagnerian "music drama" and the "art-work of the future" assumed its final shape. The plan of the tetralogy *The Ring of the Nibelungs,* textually based on the Scandinavian saga cycle of the *Older Edda,** was first conceived in 1848. The completed *Ring,* comprising the operas *Rheingold, Die Walküre, Siegfried,* and *Götterdämmerung (Twilight of the Gods),* was first produced in its entirety in the Wagner *Festspielhaus* in Bayreuth, August 13–17, 1876. In the same year this new and unique Bayreuth Opera House had opened its doors to the public.

In the *Ring* Wagner had definitely broken with the existing theater, and the new playhouse had been especially designed to fit the requirements of his tetralogy. The seats for the audience were arranged in rising semicircular rows, following the model of the ancient amphitheater. The space that intervened between the proscenium and the first row of seats had been conceived by Wagner as a "mystic abyss" that was to separate the real from the ideal and was to make the dramatic personages appear on the stage at a mythical distance and in superhuman proportions.

Wagner had of course several collaborators who aided him in the practical execution of his ideas, but he was himself intimately familiar with the artistic and technical possibilities and requirements of the stage: he actually lived, worked, wrote, composed, and conducted for the stage and from the point of view of the stage. The *Festspielhaus* was designed by him in close co-operation with Gottfried Semper, a famous Neo-Classical architect. The style of opera developed on this newly created stage marks a definite and significant phase in the history of European music as well as in the evolution of modern stagecraft and stage production.

As a stage director Wagner fostered a kind of romantic historicism that had become popular in the age of Walter Scott and the era of the historical novel and which in the field of the theater had become associated with the efforts of Duke George II of Meiningen (1826–1914). In his court theater the duke had encouraged the trend toward historically accurate and artistically integrated stage productions. This growing interest in historical verisimilitude was in itself a deviation from the indiscriminate medley of styles that was characteristic of the romantic stage proper, with its veritable craze for picturesqueness. In Wagner's operas the stage setting acquires more than historical or archaeological significance: it takes part in the

---

* The *Older Edda* or *Saemundar-Edda* contains next to the *Nibelungenlied* (cf. p. 154) the most important source material of the Nibelungen saga. It is an Icelandic collection of thirty-five songs, compiled in the thirteenth century and consisting of two major divisions: (*a*) the mythological songs of Odin, Thor, etc.; (*b*) the heroic songs of Helgi and the Nibelungs.

dramatic action and becomes a medium for a parallel expression of those voices and forces of nature and spirit that are alive in the musical score.

The realization of Wagner's artistic dream would never have come about without the generous aid and encouragement that he received from Louis II, the "mad" king of Bavaria (1864–1886), who built those phantastic dream castles that adorn some of the most beautiful sites in the Bavarian Alps. He sensed in Wagner's music a world in which his lonely soul could be exalted and soothed in an atmosphere of spiritual kinship. Louis came to Wagner's rescue in the hard and unhappy years that followed the "exile" in Zurich. Wagner was invited to Munich and commissioned to complete the composition of the *Ring*. *Tristan und Isolde* was produced in Munich in 1865, *Die Meistersinger* in 1868. The first performance of *Parsifal* took place in the Bayreuth *Festspielhaus* in 1882. From 1865–1872 Wagner lived in Triebschen near the Swiss city of Lucerne. In 1870 he had married Liszt's daughter, Cosima, the divorced wife of his friend and pupil, the famous conductor Hans von Bülow. The final years of his life Wagner spent in the palatial "Villa Wahnfried" in Bayreuth.

Richard Wagner's philosophy of life was closely linked with the ideological structure of his works. As his own art grew out of the problems of his life, so he demanded of all art that it be humanly and socially significant. He complained of the art of his time that it was nothing but a hothouse plant, that it had no roots in the natural and national soil, and that because of its separation from reality it did not and could not exert a formative influence on social and public life.

With the romanticists Wagner concurred in their high esteem of philosophy, mythology, and religion. Like them he was in love with the Germanic past, intensely interested in the national destiny of Germany, and convinced of the cultural fertility of the German mind. Philosophically he was torn between the opposing influences and urges of Ludwig Feuerbach's (cf. p. 556 sq.) sensualistic materialism and Arthur Schopenhauer's (cf. p. 505 sq.) doctrine of resignation and universal compassion. His friendship with Friedrich Nietzsche (1869–1876) ended with a shrill discord when Wagner in his *Parsifal* paid a glowing tribute to the creative and regenerative forces of Christianity. Nietzsche complained that Wagner, at the end of his life, had "helplessly broken down at the foot of the Christian Cross."

Wagner, in point of fact, expected the renascence of modern mankind from a synthesis of Germanism and Christianity, a line of thought that is followed with a fair amount of consistency from *Tannhäuser* to *Parsifal*. The Christian virtues of self-denial, sacrifice, and compassion are motifs that are interwoven in the dramatic plots of most of Wagner's operas. Those who infringe upon this code of ethics—Tannhäuser, Siegfried, Tristan, Amfortas—atone by suffering retribution and death. Even Siegfried, the nearest personification of Nietzsche's "Superman" (*Übermensch*), the embodiment of the triumphant instincts of strength and power, cannot escape the sanctions of retributive justice and is therefore no exception to the general rule. The complexity of Wagner's heroes and heroines reflects on the whole the composer's own complex personality. As a man Richard Wagner was impelled by the burning ambition to fulfill his mission as an artist. Of this mission he was conscious from the time of his earliest artistic endeavors, and his vanity and naïve egotism were merely outward manifestations of his singular determination to sacrifice everything, including every human loyalty and friendship, to what he considered his supreme task in life.

Political Romanticism. The political and social ideas of most of the leading romantic writers in Germany were as much opposed to eighteenth-century Absolutism as to nineteenth-century Liberalism. They affirmed the value and dignity of the human person but denied the equality of all human beings. As against economic competition, based on the law of supply and demand, they advanced the solidarity of medieval society, with its "divinely willed" inequalities, its pyramidal system of interdependent rights and duties, functions and services, "offices" and "callings," that had been the constitutive principle of the pre-absolutistic social order of Europe.

In accordance with these ideas the three major concerns of political romanticism were: (1) the reawakening of a sense of historic continuity; (2) the re-establishment of social and national unity; (3) the restoration of a society that was inspired by Christian impulses. In formulating their program the political romanticists made use of Herder's doctrine of the enduring characteristics of the "folk spirit" (cf. p. 396 sq.) and of Edmund Burke's (cf. p. 386) conservative and counterrevolutionary ideology which had been partially realized in the political system of Metternich and Gentz.

The State was no longer considered as a mechanical aggregation of individuals but as an organic whole whose functions were not confined to the maintenance of law and order but included the political, social, moral, and religious education of its citizens. Human society in its concrete historic manifestations was to be strictly delimited by a community of linguistic, moral, and racial characteristics.

The most influential spokesman of political romanticism was *Adam Müller* (1779–1829), the friend of Friedrich Schlegel and Heinrich von Kleist and one of the first romanticists to embrace the Catholic Church. For him the State is even more than an organic society: it is a moral personality; it is the "eternal alliance of men among themselves." He disregarded entirely the historic significance of Absolutism and Revolution and set up the corporative society of medieval Feudalism as an absolute ideal, as "the eternal scheme of all true state government, the safeguard of permanence and power." As a partisan of the prerogatives of the nobility who was himself knighted by Metternich, he praised the warlike and knightly spirit of the German race. Giving the lie to his own professed ideal of a restoration of the unity and universality of Western Christian civilization, he visualized a final triumphant rule of Germanic warriors and noblemen over all the "inferior" races of Europe. Although it is certainly

true that the nationalism of Adam Müller and his friends was still checked
by ethical and religious considerations, and that they were entirely sincere
in proclaiming a "holy war" against Napoleon's dream of world conquest,
it cannot be denied that the ruthless *Machtpolitik* of the nineteenth century
was partially carried through with the intellectual armor borrowed from the
arsenal of the political romanticists.

Romanticism and Jurisprudence: Savigny and Eichhorn. The political
romanticists' emphasis on the principles of organic growth and historic
continuity bore fruit in the work of some of the leading jurists of the early
nineteenth century. *Friedrich Karl von Savigny* (1779–1861) and *Karl
Friedrich Eichhorn* (1781–1854) became the founders of the so-called
"historical school" of law as opposed to the rationalistic legal concepts of
the eighteenth century. For both men all human law is the product of
organic growth and as such firmly rooted in the "folk spirit" and one of
the integral and vital elements of national culture. "All law grows and
develops in harmony with the life of the people and it dies as soon as
the people lose their distinctive character traits" (Savigny). If, however,
the people and their culture are the ultimate source of law, there is little
room left for any arbitrary interference with the organic processes of
evolution, and the legal changes and innovations introduced by absolutistic
rulers must be summarily rejected. Thus Savigny's historical method results
in an almost quietistic attitude of *"laissez-aller,"* resenting any progressive
and positive legislation as an interference with the principle of "organic
growth" and as a "break with the laws of history." Such an attitude was
obviously determined by romantic influences, although in other respects,
and especially in his capacity as a scholar and teacher, Savigny was a model
of classical calm and balanced dignity.

To Savigny belongs the merit of having restored the venerable tradition
of "Roman Law" from its original sources to its original purity and in
its historic growth. K. F. Eichhorn, Savigny's colleague in the University
of Berlin, can claim a similar title for the regeneration of "Germanic Law."
The two heads of the "historic school" of law in its "Romanic" and
"Germanic" branches voiced their convictions in the *Zeitschrift für
geschichtliche Rechtswissenschaft* which they founded in 1815. When in
the early years of his academic career Savigny lectured at the University
of Marburg, the brothers Grimm were among his most responsive listeners.
They were greatly impressed by his doctrine of the organic evolution of
the "folk spirit" and successfully applied the "historical method" to the
fields of language and literature.

Romantic Philosophy. The philosophical speculation of the romantic
age, and in fact most of the philosophy of the nineteenth century, is determined by its relationship to Kant (cf. p. 371 sqq.). As far as romantic philosophy as such is concerned, it culminates in the three great "idealistic"*

---

* Philosophical "idealism" means first of all the affirmation of spiritual principles in the
explanation of reality. In its Platonic form it considers the world of visible objects as represen-

systems of Fichte, Schelling, and Hegel. Schopenhauer's philosophico-religious system may be added to this list, if we disregard his personal antipathy for the leading philosophers of his time, and overlook the fact that his own philosophy went unrecognized until the middle of the century.

a) Johann Gottlieb Fichte (1762–1814). It had been Kant's contention that things can never be known by us as they are "in themselves" but only as they appear to us in our subjective consciousness. The mind receives certain sense data as its raw material, so to speak, and out of these data it constructs its conceptual knowledge. But Kant's followers and idealistic critics, more radically and perhaps more consistently, argued that since it was the mind that made the distinction between the mental and the non-mental, between what is objectively given and what is subjectively apprehended, these sense data themselves were no less mental than the concepts the mind forms of them. For this reason Fichte called the distinction between "things in themselves" and appearances an arbitrary assumption, asserting that in human knowledge both object and subject were mental or spiritual realities. For Fichte the form as well as the content of knowledge is derived from the sovereignty of the creative Ego, the spiritual Self which, finding itself confronted with the manifold limitations and restrictions of the "Non-Ego," demonstrates its capacity for spiritual freedom and self-realization by gradually overcoming all that renders it finite. Such a moral and creative evolution of the Ego will eventually result in the submersion of the individual Self in the infinite reality of the universal or "transcendental" Self. Therefore this Universal Ego was for Fichte the supreme reality and the moral force that was capable of transforming and elevating individual and social life. In his *Wissenschaftslehre* (theory of knowledge and learning) he describes the activity of the Transcendental Ego in typically romantic terminology as an "infinite striving," whose goal is an ever increasing clarity of consciousness.

Accused of teaching atheistic doctrines, Fichte had to resign from his professorship in Jena in 1799. He moved to Berlin, where he was enthusiastically received by the members of the Romantic School and where, in 1810, he became the first *Rector* of the newly founded university. His *Address to the German Warriors,* delivered in 1806, at the beginning of the Napoleonic wars, was followed after Prussia's defeat by the *Addresses to*

---

tations or images of eternal ideas. In the epistemological sense "idealism" maintains that the human mind is the basic reality and the main source of the knowledge, comprehension, and structure of the extramental world. For the "subjective idealist" (e.g., Berkeley) this extramental world is merely an idea of the individual ego, while for the "objective idealist" (Fichte, Schelling, Hegel, Schopenhauer) the world is the representation and realization of the Absolute, Universal, or Transcendental Ego or the Absolute Spirit. Almost all philosophical idealists are also pantheists. The idealistic German philosophers of the romantic period have in common an unshakable belief in the constructive power of human thought, coupled with a more or less pronounced disregard for experience and experimental science as sources of knowledge. They all endeavor to reduce the sum total of reality to one fundamental principle (Fichte: the "Transcendental Ego"; Schelling: the "World-Soul"; Hegel: the "World-Spirit"; Schopenhauer: the "World-Will").

the German Nation (1807–1808, cf. p. 439). It was a stirring appeal, citing the faults and neglects that had caused the downfall of Prussia, and it was directed to all social groups. Fichte castigated the complacency of the old and the inertia and indifference of the young, the cowardice and effeminacy of the ruling classes, and the social injustice that had wrought the oppression and exploitation of the poor. Calling for "national education" (*National-erziehung*) as an absolute prerequisite for the rebirth of his country, he maintained that the creation of a perfect State could only be accomplished by "a nation which first of all must have fulfilled the task of educating perfect human beings." And yet he believes that despite the many symptoms of decadence the German people as a racial unity are still best qualified for political and moral leadership.

Fichte constantly stressed the primacy of the moral law as the regulative norm of action for nations and individuals, but he also demanded that individual happiness be at all times subordinated to the welfare of the nation. Thus his *Kulturstaat* was to be a composite of nationalist and socialist incentives, containing in its structure the seeds of State socialism and a new State omnipotence.

b) Friedrich Wilhelm von Schelling (*1775–1854*). German "nature philosophy" (*Naturphilosophie*), as represented by Schelling and some of his romantic friends, was a protest on the part of philosophy against the encroachments of the natural sciences and their mechanistic concepts of nature on the prerogatives of the human spirit. Where the natural sciences seemed to have failed, namely in supplying a satisfactory explanation of the ultimate moving force of the universe, and in offering a solution of the riddle of life, of biological and morphological growth, the German nature philosophers hoped to succeed.

Fichte had approached nature from the point of view of the mind, but Schelling tried to go the opposite way and to explain mental phenomena from the point of view of nature. By starting from the data and observations of the exact sciences and following the forces of nature on their path from the inorganic to the organic forms of existence, he tried to develop a harmonious and all-inclusive philosophico-theological system. For him all the phenomena of nature and mind, of the real and the ideal, are manifestations of an aboriginal force which he calls the "World-Soul" and whose living incarnation is the universe, composed of a graduated series of self-developing and organized forms of being. All being, on both the inorganic and the organic levels, tends toward the fullest realization of the immanent spirituality of the "World-Soul." In the unity of the "World-Soul" nature and spirit are one, but they are separated in the duality of the worlds of nature and mind, and they incessantly strive to become one again by returning to the original source of their unity.

Schelling's speculation, though partly influenced by Fichte's moral idealism, was even more indebted to Spinoza's (cf. p. 355 sq.) pantheistic philosophy and to Jacob Böhme's theosophy (cf. p. 270). The same intuitive transport of mind that caused him to consider art as the highest manifestation of the Absolute, and aesthetic contemplation as the highest form of knowledge, made him anticipate some of Lamarck's and Darwin's discoveries concerning the evolution of organic life, at the same time preserving him from laying too much stress on abstract speculation at the expense of concrete observation.

c) *Georg Wilhelm Friedrich Hegel* (*1770–1831*). How can the freedom of the individual be reconciled with the demands of an all-powerful "World-Spirit" (*Weltgeist*)? This question constituted the major problem and the starting point of the philosophical speculation of Hegel, who undoubtedly was the greatest and most influential of the romantic philosophers. Up to this day his ideas are recognizable in many standard works of political and social philosophy, in the philosophy of history and civilization, in aesthetic theory, and to no lesser degree in political ideologies and their attempted realizations.*

It may be said that Hegel exhausted all the possibilities of idealistic philosophy, carrying it to its extreme conclusions and establishing a metaphysical edifice that rested on the mastery of an immense mass of factual data. While as a metaphysician he created the crowning philosophical synthesis of the nineteenth century, as an observer of reality he prepared the way for the staggering triumphs of the empirical sciences. He absorbed and digested the influences of European Enlightenment and of German Classicism and Romanticism and constructed his own imposing system of thought out of the ingredients of all these intellectual movements.

A rationalist at heart, Hegel proclaimed the identity of thinking and being: "Whatever is rational is real, and whatever is real is rational." Therefore it becomes the task of philosophy to use the data of history and of science to demonstrate the rationality of everything that is real. The world is for Hegel a universe of varying and changing forms in which the gradual evolution of the "World-Spirit" manifests itself. The philosopher is called upon to comprehend these multiform phenomena as aspects and phases of a logical and necessary development. This development follows the scheme of the dialectical triad of "thesis, antithesis, and synthesis": ideas and phenomena cannot be comprehended unless we think and know their opposites. We cannot, for example, define the nature of the good unless we know the nature of evil; we do not know what is rational unless we know what is real. The dialectical thinking and understanding of opposites (theses and antitheses) leads to a synthetic comprehension of the nature of reality.

---

* In 1806, the year of Prussia's defeat, Hegel had finished his first important work, *The Phenomenology of the Spirit*. Between 1812 and 1816 he completed his *Logic*. From 1816–1818 he was professor of philosophy at the University of Heidelberg. In 1818 he took over the chair of philosophy at the University of Berlin, which position he held until his death. Seven of his pupils published a posthumous edition of his works in 17 volumes, arranged in the following order: Vol. 1, Philosophical Treatises; Vol. 2, The Phenomenology of the Spirit; Vols. 3–5, Logic; Vols. 6, 7, Encyclopedia of Sciences; Vol. 8, The Philosophy of Right; Vol. 9, Lectures on the Philosophy of History; Vol. 10, Lectures on Aesthetics; Vols. 11, 12, Lectures on the Philosophy of Religion; Vols. 13–15, The History of Philosophy; Vols. 16, 17, Miscellaneous Writings.

The romantic concept of the organic evolution of an eternally becoming world furnished Hegel the tools with which to explain and justify the necessity and rationality of the individual within the general workings of the "World-Spirit": all things in nature and human life evolve consciously and rationally, but their rationality becomes visible only as they reach the higher stages of consciousness and intelligibility. For Hegel philosophy and religion are identical in that the explications of thought are at the same time the explications of the "Absolute Spirit."

The process of a becoming world is most clearly noticeable in the history of civilization and particularly in the organism of the State, the truest "objectivation" of the "World-Spirit." The "Absolute Spirit" is manifested in ever changing forms in the "folk spirit" itself as much as in its leading exponents; it is incarnate in State and society, in art and religion, in science and economics. But while all these cultural forms are perishable and while one historic epoch gives way to another, the "World-Spirit" as such proceeds unperturbed on its progressive march through history.

All individual life must be understood as being part and parcel of the comprehensive totality of life. Individuality and society are correlated and interdependent, both partakers of the supreme reality of the "Objective Spirit." Individuality becomes real and acquires the attributes of spirituality and morality only as it consciously comprehends itself as determined by and embedded in the universal dynamic movement of the "World-Spirit." For this reason individual freedom and historic necessity are merged by a law of pre-established harmony: the individual may believe he follows his own urges and pursues his own ends, while in reality he serves the higher and still hidden designs of the ruling spirit of the universe. The great political leaders of the past and present may think of themselves as freely moving forces and self-acting agents of world history: in reality they are only the "clerks" of the "World-Spirit" and, after having served its ulterior purpose, they are cast away "like empty shells."

Among the many manifestations of the Universal Reason the State is the highest and the most perfect. It is the realization of the idea of morality, reason, and spirit incarnate, and as such it is partly human and partly divine. The State, in short, is "God walking upon the earth," and therefore the dignity and worth of the human person is ultimately derived from the State.

It was only logical that this political theory should make Hegel an advocate of State omnipotence and a passionate opponent of German Liberalism (cf. p. 523 sqq.). No longer was the State to serve the well-being of the individual, but the individual existed and acted for the aggrandizement of the State. Hegel was consistent, too, in that he placed the State above religion, because religion was concerned with "beliefs," but the State was the possessor of infallible "knowledge." Luther's subservience to all legally constituted authority was transformed by Hegel into the self-sufficiency and moral supremacy of the State, and tolerance henceforth became a "criminal weakness."

This, then, was the ideological framework of the Hegelian *Kulturstaat,* whose essential features the philosopher believed he recognized in the Prussian State of his time and whose structure proved equally suited for the political philosophies of extreme nationalism and of State socialism. There was no room in this scheme of ideas for either moral or international law, the State being no longer the servant of the law but its infallible creator, interpreter, and master. The most powerful State at any given historic epoch was entitled to consider itself as the mouthpiece of the "World-Spirit" and therefore its own advantage was its supreme law. A peaceful society of nations on the basis of equality became an impossibility, the ideal of "eternal peace" was termed an empty abstraction or an idle dream, and the dialectic of history had to justify ever recurring waves of warfare, while international agreements became mere "scraps of paper," whenever practical political considerations made it advisable to disregard them.

Hegel's political philosophy was in its essence an elaborate attempt to justify philosophically the theories of Machiavelli (cf. p. 247 sq.). Might and force were identified with Spirit and Right, and the revolting human conscience was soothed by shifting the responsibility for political crimes to the inexorable laws of the "World-Spirit." Success and failure became the ultimate criteria of the right and wrong involved in political action.

There was a strange contrast between Hegel's comfortable bourgeois existence and the revolutionary implications of his ideas. The same man who in his youth had been a student of Protestant theology in Tübingen and had been associated there in thought and feeling with Hölderlin and Schelling, the romantic enthusiast who in the political confusion of the Napoleonic wars had made no secret of his admiration of the French emperor, whose personality he reverently compared with the dynamic force of the "World-Soul" — he became after the Wars of Liberation the official "State Philosopher of Prussia" and a defender of the worst features of Prussian bureaucracy and autocracy. The same Hegel who in his youth had declared himself in sympathy with the ideas that inspired the French Revolution of 1789 — he became the spokesman of political reaction. He was naïvely satisfied with the belief that his age and his nation had achieved the heights of human and cultural perfectibility and that it was therefore no longer necessary to build actively and creatively for the future but that the time for retrospection and a comprehensive digest of the past had finally arrived.

As Hegel was convinced that in the history of the world today's error might be tomorrow's truth, he was much more interested in the dynamism of historical forces than in their shades of true or false, right or wrong. While on the one hand he encouraged abstract metaphysical speculation to go far beyond the limits of the empirically knowable, his genuine interest in every type of reality made his mentality akin to that of the postromantic "realists" (cf. p. 583 sq.), whose novel ways of thought and life were to supplant the idealistic philosophies of the early nineteenth century.

When Hegel died in 1831, he left behind a band of faithful disciples, well versed in the intricacies of the master's dialectical method and applying it rather indiscriminately to the fields of history, law, natural philosophy, aesthetics, and religion. It was due to Hegel's influence that from now on to the very end of the century the history of philosophy became the leading philosophical discipline and professors of the history of philosophy occupied the most important philosophical chairs.

The Hegelian School was divided into the opposing camps of a Christian-conservative right wing (Old Hegelians) and a radically anti-Christian and materialist left wing (Young Hegelians). This division in itself reflects the ambiguity of Hegel's system and of the dialectical method which lent itself to diametrically contradictory conclusions. The phrase, for instance, "everything that is real is rational," could be used as a strong argument for the preservation of the existing social and political order. But the same phrase, in the negative formulation: "everything that is not rational is not real," contained in it the seeds of utter radicalism and a call for revolutionary action, to make reality comply with the demands of reason. The Young Hegelian radicals made the latter interpretation their own and seemed as much justified in referring to Hegel as their teacher as the Old Hegelian conservatives.

The most astonishing and, historically speaking, the most consequential fate, however, befell the dialectical method at the hands of Karl Marx (cf. p. 556 sqq.), who claimed that Hegelian philosophy, which "had stood on its head," had been put by him "on its legs again." He used the dialectical method, not to explain objective and material reality by referring it back to ideas, but conversely, to explain ideas as resulting from basic material realities. Hegel's dialectical idealism thus provided the methodical foundation for Marx's dialectical materialism. By taking over Hegel's concept of the State and by filling this ready-made mold with a different content, Marx developed "scientifically" the pattern of the classless society and the dictatorship of the proletariat.

d) *Arthur Schopenhauer* (*1788–1860*). Seeing in the universe a wonderfully designed organism, in which each member held its proper place and fulfilled its God-given function by virtue of a "pre-established harmony," Leibniz (cf. p. 358 sq.) had designated the world we know as "the best of all possible worlds." Schopenhauer, on the other hand, weighing the actual amount of good and evil in the world against each other, arrived at the pessimistic conclusion that life was "a business whose profits do not nearly cover its expenses" and that therefore this world of ours was "the worst of all possible worlds." For him the prevalence of evil was the most obvious of facts and he considered the supposed rationality of the universe as an assumption and a product of the wishful thinking of armchair philosophers.

With Schopenhauer the incongruity between thought and life, theory and practice was even more striking than in Hegel's case. The greatest pessimist among philosophers was personally fond of life and good living, fond of good food and drink, and fond of sensual pleasures. His unsociability and his contempt of women were largely the result of the experiences of a lonely childhood, of the premature death of his father and the estrangement from his mother, Johanna Schopenhauer, who was much more interested in writing (worthless) novels and in mixing in literary and social affairs than in the education of her son.

Schopenhauer was a native of Danzig. He traveled in France, England, and Italy for some time to acquire cosmopolitan tastes and to perfect his natural ability in the command of foreign languages. He was a great admirer of Lord Byron, but envied the English poet his luck with women and therefore refused to make his personal acquaintance. As a student of philosophy he attended Fichte's and Schleiermacher's lectures in Berlin and was so unfavorably impressed that he developed a lifelong antagonism against all the representatives of idealistic philosophy. When he temporarily settled down in Berlin as a *Privatdozent,* Hegel and Schleiermacher had become the favorites of the academic world, while Schopenhauer's lectures and writings found no response. He gave vent to his disappointment in bitter attacks against "the professorial philosophy of the philosophy professors" (*die Professorenphilosophie der Philosophieprofessoren*) in general and against Hegel in particular, whom he dubbed a quack, a charlatan, and a servile creature of the Prussian government. The cholera epidemic of the year 1831, which claimed Hegel as one of its victims, caused Schopenhauer to move to Frankfurt, where he spent the rest of his solitary life, with his faithful black poodle as his only companion.

Schopenhauer's philosophy was romantic in that it magnified inner experiences and personal moods into a system of thought which he superimposed on external reality. With Kant (cf. p. 371 sq.) he maintained the subjective origin of time, space, and the categories of pure reason, but against Kant he claimed that the reality (the "thing in itself") that underlies all appearances was knowable. In inner perception and self-knowledge, reality can be recognized as a "World-Will" or a "will to live" that manifests itself in the forms of both unconscious instinct and conscious desire. It is this universal "Will" that causes disease, suffering, and death, that forges the endless chain of souls, migrating from birth to death and rebirth, in different bodies and on different levels of existence.

While in this metaphysical speculation Schopenhauer was chiefly influenced by his profound knowledge of Buddhist philosophy and religion, his ethical convictions represent a blend of Buddhist and Christian ideas. Sympathy with all suffering creatures and mortification he considered as the two pillars of morality. The fatal cycle of births and rebirths can be brought to a halt, the chain of pain and suffering can be broken by an integral asceticism or the absolute negation of the "will to live," whereby all individual wills become one in the universal life stream of the "World-Will," and all restlessness ceases in the eternal quiescence of the great "Nirvana." Suicide, on the other hand, or the self-destruction of the individual "will to live," offers no way out, because it leaves the universal "will to live" untouched.

Schopenhauer describes, however, an intermediate realm between the universal will and its refractions in individuals: in the realm of Ideas the "World-Will" appears "objectified" in the various forms of artistic creation and most poignantly and directly in the world of music. In the contemplation of art human beings may experience a temporary escape from the curse of pain and suffering, but lasting salvation can only be obtained by overcoming desire and in attaining the bliss of "Nirvana."

Schopenhauer, who had a very high opinion of his own works and was fully conscious of his extraordinary qualities as a thinker and a stylist, designated as his *opus maximum* the book entitled *Die Welt als Wille und Vorstellung* (*The World as Will and Mental Representation*). This work was first published in 1818 and republished in 1844, when its author had at last been given the recognition that was his due. It contains his main ideas in a masterly presentation and combines philosophical depth with poetic intuition and a brilliant literary form.

Romantic Theology: Schleiermacher (1768–1834). The greatest Protestant theologian of Germany since the days of the Reformation and one of the most influential religious writers of the nineteenth century was *Friedrich Daniel Schleiermacher*. He was the contemporary and friend of the leaders of the Romantic School, who in his own intellectual and spiritual development had successively experienced the influences of Pietism (cf. p. 364 sqq.), Enlightenment (cf. p. 368 sqq.), Classicism (cf. Chap. 12), and Romanticism. His versatility, his striving for a total view of life, and his religious subjectivism mark him as a romantic character. The central concept of his philosophy of religion was the idea of individuality, and like Hegel he wrestled with the problem of how the claims of the individual could be reconciled with the demands of superindividual realities, be they State, society, a visible ecclesiastical community, or the Deity itself.

A true synthesis of the particular and the universal, according to Schleiermacher, can only be achieved in contemplation and personal "feeling" (*Gefühl*). In his earlier period he defines religion as "the contemplation of the infinite in the finite, of the eternal in the temporal"; later on, as a presence of the infinite in a personal "feeling of absolute dependence." Religion, then, has its roots in human personality, and in taking this position Schleiermacher was as much opposed to the orthodox defenders of "revealed religion" as to the representatives of the "natural religion" of the period of Enlightenment. His concept of religion was most closely related to the ideas of the New Humanists (cf. p. 000) and their religious exaltation of human personality. For them as for Schleiermacher man is a finite incarnation of the infinite spirit, and by consciously developing the divine likeness within him he prepares himself for moral action and emerges as a human character.

The religious community and the organized Church represent for

Schleiermacher the living form and force of the moral law, in whose embrace the individual experiences an awakening of his mind, a strengthening of his will, and an enlargement of his soul. Schleiermacher's *Discourses on Religion, Addressed to the Educated among its Despisers (Reden über die Religion an die Gebildeten unter ihren Verächtern)* picture Christ as the most perfect specimen of humanity, the creative inaugurator of a new and unique destiny of the human race. Christ was the great exemplar, challenging and stimulating the moral courage of men to follow his spiritual leadership. In Church dogmas and cultic observances Schleiermacher saw symbolic expressions of subjective truths and personal religious experiences. As a modern theologian of the "historical school" he was no longer concerned with revelations of supernatural truths that claimed objective validity but rather with the historically conditioned religious contents of the changing individual consciousness. This was a novel approach to the phenomena of religion, favoring the development of the new disciplines of the psychology and comparative history of religion.

Schleiermacher's most unfriendly critic and opponent was Hegel, whose intellectualism and rationalism rose up in revolt against Schleiermacher's vindication of religious feeling. For Hegel religion was an expression of reason, and as such an inferior kind of philosophy. "If religion," he said, "is essentially based on the feeling of dependence . . . then the dog is the finest Christian, for he . . . lives pre-eminently in such a feeling. He even experiences feelings of redemption, at the moment when his hunger is satisfied with a bone."

Chapter 15

LIBERALISM, NATIONALISM, AND THE UNIFICATION OF GERMANY

A. *POLITICAL AND ECONOMIC TRENDS*

The Policy of Intervention. The period of the "Vormärz" (1815–1848) is marked by a latent or open struggle of ideas in practically all European countries. The old Absolutism has to defend itself against the new Liberalism; the principle of "legitimism" (cf. p. 461 sq.) finds itself threatened by the principle of "national self-determination." At the Congress of Troppau (1820) the reactionary governments of Prussia, Austria, and Russia had pledged themselves to intervene, if necessary by force of arms, in the affairs of any country in which the authoritarian regime was endangered by revolution. Thus Austria received the mandate to suppress the liberal movements in Naples and Sardinia (1820), and France, under the restored Bourbon monarchy, was commissioned to execute the "Will of Europe" by crushing the liberal rebellion in Spain (1822). The British government, on the other hand, had shown itself steadily opposed to the policy of armed intervention, and Canning (1770–1827), the British foreign secretary and future prime minister, had proclaimed for the first time the right of the "self-determination of the people."

Both Great Britain and the United States were equally interested in keeping the Metternich System confined to continental Europe and in preventing a reactionary Spain from regaining her Central and South American colonies, which had severed their ties with the mother country during the Napoleonic wars. Canning informed the French government that England would consider the sending of a French expeditionary force to the Americas as a warlike act, and President James Monroe declared in a message to Congress that any attempt made by European powers to extend their political system to any part of the Western hemisphere would be considered as dangerous to the peace and security of the United States (Monroe Doctrine, 1823).

Thus the policies of Metternich's European "Concert" of powers were shattered by the combined forces of Liberalism and Nationalism. The principle of "legitimacy" received its deathblow when Metternich, in the course of the Greek War of Independence (1821–1829), expressed his sympathies for the cause of the Turkish sultan, condemning the Greeks for their rebellion against their "legitimate" ruler. By the joint action of Russia, France, and England, Greek independence was finally secured. In helping Greece to achieve her goal, the mercantile and political interests of the three great powers mingled with idealistic motives, but Metternich's principle of European solidarity no longer played a part in their considerations and actions.

The enthusiasm of Lord Canning for the cause of Greek independence was as sincere as that of Lord Byron, who sacrificed his life for it. In a famous speech of the year 1826 Canning assured all the suppressed peoples of the world of British sympathy and designated the protection of freedom and human rights as the great task of the British empire. It is true that this moral idealism ran parallel with Great Britain's commercial interests. It is equally true that English foreign policy could be just as ruthless as that of any autocratic government whenever British interests were in conflict with the interests of the suppressed peoples (e.g., Ireland, India, the Boer War). By contributing to the liberation of the smaller European peoples England earned their gratitude together with their trade and willingly assumed the role of their protector and guardian. While Gentz (cf. p. 461) spoke of Great Britain as the "source of rebellion" and Metternich had nothing but contempt for Canning's foreign policy, the latter forged an enduring alliance between British Nationalism and the forces of Liberalism. This tradition, once established, was consistently adhered to by Canning's successors, "Lord Firebrand" Palmerston (1784-1865) and Gladstone (1809-1898). The peculiar genius of British statesmanship knew how to enlist the human love of freedom and the popular desire for national independence in the cause of her own aggrandizement. These mixed incentives of British politics provided a temporary bulwark against the increasing amoralism, opportunism, and cynicism that invaded the field of international relations in the course of the nineteenth century.

The Goals of Constitutional Liberty and National Unity. The German people fought as bravely and enthusiastically for their civil liberties and for national unity as any other nation, but a long period of political repression and the historically conditioned particularistic tendencies of the several German states rendered this struggle especially hard and prolonged. The eventual unification of Germany under Bismarck's leadership (cf. p. 546) was an event of such magnitude that it completely overshadowed the issue of constitutional liberty, for which the German Liberals had fought and suffered persecution during the earlier part of the nineteenth century.

Germany Under the Rule of the "German Confederation." The political organization of Germany that had been created by the "Act of Confederation" of 1815 (cf. p. 456 sq.) was the result of a compromise that tried to please everybody but in reality satisfied no one. It was an attempt to deal with a complex situation without disturbing the existing "peaceful dualism" of Prusso-Austrian relations. As a system of government the "German Confederation" was much too unwieldy to function efficiently and to give voice and weight to a national will. It offered conclusive evidence that Germany was not yet a nation in the same sense in which France, England, or Russia were sovereign and relatively homogeneous states.

The "German Confederation" was dominated by the Holy Alliance (cf. p. 459 sq.), which in turn was the instrument of Metternich's political designs. Its endeavors were paralyzed by the selfish interests of the member states and by the latent antagonism between the two largest of them — Austria and Prussia. The fifty years that followed the passage of the "Act of Confederation" witnessed various attempts on the part of the German people to break the political deadlock that was preventing Germany from reaching the goal of her national aspirations.

Political and Social Reaction in Prussia. Frederick William III was fundamentally a cautious conservative who dreaded all revolutionary changes and who was sentimentally attached to the political institutions of the prerevolutionary *"ancien régime."* The events of the years of Prussia's humiliation had forced his hand, and much against his will he had tolerated the work of the reformers who had rescued and liberated the State from foreign oppression. After 1815 the king was glad to join the forces of restoration and reaction and to follow the lead of Metternich and the Russian tsar. Without misgivings he submitted to Austria's growing influence in the "German Confederation," convinced that in the close collaboration with Metternich lay the surest guarantee for the peace and stability of Prussia. In 1815, following the trend of the times, Frederick William III had promised in a proclamation the establishment of representative government in Prussia, but eight years elapsed before the provincial estates were convoked for the first time, and more than forty years before some form of constitutional and representative government was forced upon the State by the will of the people.

In the meantime, Prussia's failure to keep abreast of the changing political and social conditions caused further cleavages in the social structure of the State and contributed to the growing antagonism between Prussia and the more progressive southern German states. The king surrounded himself with bureaucrats of the old school and seized upon every opportunity to restore the former privileges of the nobility as a ruling class. The eight Provincial Diets of Prussia were dominated by the members of the nobility and lacked the most elementary forms of parliamentary rights. They were merely advisory bodies without legislative powers and were subject to the absolute sovereignty of the king. The rural reforms of Stein and Hardenberg were largely undone, and the attempt to liberate the peasants ended with the victory of the manorial lords and the restoration of serfdom or semiserfdom. The result was a huge expansion of the large estates and the creation of a peasant-proletariat. Whereas formerly the peasants had been unfree but socially more or less secure, they now became day laborers without either property or social security, their pay depending on the fluctuations of the markets. This rural proletariat provided the "industrial army of reserves" (Karl Marx), from which the growing industrial civilization recruited its workers: broken existences that doubled and trebled the population figures of the industrial centers by their migration from the rural districts to the big cities. These conditions prevailed above all in the regions east of the Elbe river, while in the Rhineland the influence of the French Revolution and the social reforms of the Napoleonic era aided in creating and preserving a well-to-do and healthy peasantry.

Austria, Prussia, and the "German Confederation." When Francis II had abdicated as German emperor in 1806 (cf. p. 325), it had not been his intention to weaken the ancient prestige of the Hapsburg dynasty or to renounce its claims to political and cultural leadership in the German lands. However, as far as common partnership in the "German Confederation" was concerned, the interests of Prussia and Austria were not identical but contradictory. While Austria's interests lay largely outside the Germanies, in Italy, in Galicia, in the Balkans, and in the Adriatic region, Prussia's interests in all important issues were in harmony with those of all the minor German states. Accordingly, Metternich had devised the "German Confederation" as a large buffer state that was to protect Austria from French attack. This purpose was best served by a loose federation that could rally to a defensive war against foreign encroachments, without being sufficiently consolidated in itself to challenge Austrian leadership.

The Congress of Vienna had returned to Prussia the Polish province of Posnania (*Posen*) in the East and the Rhenish provinces (*Rheinlande*) in the West. Prussia, the immediate neighbor of the Slavs and the French, had thus to assume the responsibilities of a frontier guard on two exposed fronts and had to prepare itself for the risks and dangers involved in a two-front war. As far as Germany as a whole was concerned, this problem was not a new one. Germany's central position on the European continent had compelled German military strategists in the past to take into account the possibility of a dual or triple attack from different directions, and, conversely, French foreign policy from the time of Louis XIV on attempted to threaten and intimidate Germany by means of an encirclement by hostile powers or to force her to fight simultaneously on two or three fronts. But Prussia had not faced this danger since the days of Frederick the Great, and only slowly and hesitatingly did she grow into her new tasks and responsibilities. When she was finally ready to assume the role that destiny seemed to have assigned to her, she had begun to realize that her own existence was inseparably linked with the fate of all the German lands and that she was entitled to consider herself as the champion of a united German nation. In the meantime, however, Prussia tried to ease the burden imposed upon her by the decrees of the Congress of Vienna, advocating a military reorganization and consolidation of the "German Confederation" in order to increase its striking power and make it a more effective instrument for national defense.

Economic Unification: The German "Zollverein." The "German Confederation" proved as inefficient in dealing with the divergent economic interests in the German lands as it had shown itself in solving the political problems. The Empire that had died in 1806 had been burdened with an extreme economic as well as political particularism. All earlier demands for the creation of a uniform currency and the abolition of trade barriers in the form of inland customs duties between the different states and principalities had been foiled by the selfish policies of the territorial princes. Here again the interests of the new Prussia coincided with the economic advantage of the smaller German states in the north and south, while Austria, on the other hand, as an economically self-sufficient unit with favorably located ports and outlets for her markets could not be expected to consider the economic unification of Germany as one of her vital concerns.

While in the rest of Germany the conviction was gaining ground that the creation of a unified German economy was overdue, it remained still doubtful whether the "German Confederation" or the state of Prussia would take the lead in solving this vital problem. The answer to this question of leadership involved much more than a mere matter of priority or even prestige. When Prussia, in 1818, abolished the sixty-seven different tariff schedules in her territories and replaced them by a uniform tariff, thereby making the entire state a single marketing unit, she did it primarily for the economic interests of the big landowners and noblemen (*Junker*) east of the Elbe river. While it is true that this benefited the Rhenish industrialists in the West as much as the *Junkers* in the East, the extremely low export and import duties, as established by the customs law of 1818, were devised to meet the demands of the manorial lords, who were thus enabled to export large quantities of grain, timber, and wool and to import English machines. The Free Trade tendencies of the new customs law worked, however, to the disadvantage of the growing German industry, which found it more and more difficult to compete with England without the benefit of a protective tariff.

It was apprehensions such as these that prompted Friedrich List (cf. p. 514 sqq.) to submit in 1819 to the Federal Diet (*Bundestag*) in Frankfurt as well as to the Diets of the individual German states a memorandum that called upon the "German Confederation" to create by its own initiative a unified German economy and a uniform tariff schedule. Thus the choice between the "German Confederation" and the Prussian State involved, as far as the economic problems were concerned, the choice between a policy of protective tariffs and the principles of Free Trade. But this choice had already been made, not by the German people and their governments, but by Prussia, who imposed her will on the rest of Germany, while the "Confederation" remained a passive spectator. The subservience of the Prussian crown to Austrian political leadership and the endorsement of the policy of "peaceful dualism" did not prevent the allied economic interests of the Prussian monarchy and the landed nobility from gaining a decisive influence on the German markets. Favored by her geographical position, Prussia exerted heavy economic pressure on the other German states by imposing high transit duties on all imports from Holland and England.

Prussia was respected but also feared and distrusted by the non-Prussian governments, and they hesitated to enter into a customs union with such a powerful and ambitious neighbor. But their own disunity and mutual distrust worked slowly yet inevitably into the hands of Prussia. The "South-German Customs Union" between Bavaria and Wurtemberg (1828) was a temporary device that could not halt the logical sequence of events.

The actual economic unification of Germany under Prussian leadership was essentially the work of the Prussian minister of finance, Friedrich von Motz (1775–1830). In 1828 he concluded a customs treaty with Hesse-Darmstadt, thereby extending the Prussian customs policy into the German South. Motz was one of the younger and more progressive members of the Prussian cabinet, a man who had grown up in the era of the Prussian reforms and for whom the political ideas of Frederick the Great were a living legacy. He knew and appreciated the significance of the rising middle class and of the Industrial Revolution (cf. p. 548 sqq.), and as an adherent of Adam Smith's economy of Free Trade and unlimited competitive enterprise he enjoyed the sympathies of the Prussian *Junkers*. In his memorandum of 1829 he explained to the Prussian king the "significance of the tariff and trade treaties concluded with the South German States," adding that "a unification of these States in a tariff and trade association implies an eventual unification in one and the same political system," and that "a truly united . . . and free Germany under the protection of Prussia" would be the final result of a unified economy.

Friedrich von Motz did not live to witness the realization of either of these hopes. The economic unification of Germany was largely achieved by 1834, four years after his death, but the political unification did not come about until 1871. In 1834 the tariff and trade barriers between eighteen of the German states were eliminated, and by the middle of the century all German states with the exception of Austria had joined the Customs Union.

Friedrich List's Doctrine of Economic Nationalism. The Prussian officialdom of the *Vormärz,* indoctrinated with the economic liberalism of Adam Smith, favored the principle of Free Trade, not only because it served best the interests of the *Junkers* but also because free competition seemed to them the most effective stimulus to economic activity. Adam Smith's ideas, as expressed in his masterpiece *The Wealth of Nations* (1776), were embodied in the so-called "classical school" of economy in Germany, early in the nineteenth century. Friedrich List's historic significance lies in the fact that he opposed to the theories of "economic liberalism" his own doctrine of national economy or economic nationalism. Though a liberal by training and inclination, an enemy of princely absolutism and official bureaucracy, he advocates in his *National System of Political Economy*

(1840) the introduction of protective tariffs and shows himself as a forerunner of the "historical school" of national economy.

Persecuted and twice imprisoned by the reactionary government of his native Wurtemberg, because of his participation in the movement for national unity, he was pardoned in 1825 with the stipulation that he emigrate to North America. In the United States he took an active part in the industrial development of the New World, acquired a fortune by his mining operations, and returned to Leipzig in 1832 as consul of the federal government in Washington. "I feel toward my fatherland," he said during this American intermezzo, "as mothers do toward their crippled children: the more crippled they are, the more they love them. In the background of all my plans lies Germany and the return to Germany."

The experiences that he had gathered in the United States turned List against the "cosmopolitanism, materialism, and individualism" of the "classical" school of political economy and made him resume with deeper insight some of the principles of "mercantilism" (cf. p. 328 sq.). The United States, where the policy of protective tariffs was most firmly entrenched from the outset, taught him that a growing national industry in any part of the world depended largely on tariff protection. Free Trade was well adapted to the needs of Great Britain with her technical and industrial superiority and her domination of the world markets. But Free Trade was ruinous for Germany, whose economic conditions were still unstable and whose industry had to fight for its survival in the face of British competition.

These convictions led List to the conclusion that Adam Smith and his followers were wrong when they proclaimed that their teachings were merely an expression of eternally valid economic laws, a doctrine that benefited no one but the British merchants and manufacturers. List maintained, on the contrary, that economic systems and theories were based on considerations of expediency and that it was therefore necessary to renounce the dogmatism of the "classical school" and to free the German mind from its Anglophile preoccupations. He accused the German intellectual and political leaders of lack of realism and practical experience. "It is possible for a nation," he wrote, "to have too many philosophers, philologists, and men of letters, and too few skilled workmen, merchants, and sailors. This is one of the results of a highly advanced and profound culture which is not balanced by a highly developed manufacturing power and a flourishing domestic and foreign trade." In such a nation "there is a surplus of useless books, subtle theoretical systems, and learned arguments, which detract the national mind from useful occupations."

Although List speaks here as the son of a new scientific era and as the teacher of a new nationalistic and capitalistic bourgeois society, it would not be quite correct to call him a materialist. Both he and Adam Smith were intellectually and emotionally influenced by the ideas of Christianity, of Humanism, and of Enlightenment. Adam Smith conceived economic life as a huge rational mechanism, in which egotistic and altruistic interests were harmonized by division of labor, free competition, and the law of supply and demand, and which, if only kept free from the arbitrary interference of states and individuals, proceeded on its predestined course to the goal of general human happiness. List, on the other hand, interposed between the individual human being and the idea of a united mankind the State and the Nation as the major promoters and guarantors of universal progress. According to Adam Smith, the law of supply and demand and the law of the division of labor applies as much to world economy as to an individual factory. If each nation produces those goods for whose manufacture it is best equipped by nature, then it will make its divinely apportioned contribution to the civilization of the entire race. Free trade and free competition, therefore, are the most efficient incentives for all to do their best and fulfill their God-given tasks. In this scheme of things England functioned as the nation which Providence had selected as the standard-bearer of world industry, while other nations were to continue in their agricultural pursuits and to supply the world markets with the produce of the soil.

To List this kind of reasoning appeared fallacious and detrimental when tested by the actual conditions of the world. He demanded that all the peoples of the West should have their share in the industrial evolution, and he declared that England owed her astounding industrial advances not to greater talents or any divine predestination but to more favorable historic circumstances. Furthermore, he was convinced that the natural egotism of all nations was far too great to make possible the free flow of spare products and spare capital from one region or one continent to another, so as to provide sufficient abundance for all. Therefore each nation must shape its own destiny with the resources at its disposal. With reference to Germany, he thought there should be no more talk of Free Trade and cosmopolitanism until Germany had achieved economic equality with England. Nevertheless, List was not concerned with the material development of Germany as an end in itself.

Adam Smith considered economic laws as autonomous mechanisms, pursuing their own ends, independent of the larger contexts and concerns of society and culture. List, however, maintained that all economic activity was interlinked with the different provinces of life and culture and had its vital center and final goal in the perfection of human personality. Thus he considered material power and prosperity as means to "spiritual" and "cultural" ends, to better education, a more just social order, and greater freedom of political institutions.

List wanted to see Adam Smith's principle of the division of labor applied first and foremost to a closed national economy, not to foster unlimited competition and cutthroat practices in national industries and on the labor market, but to unite all individual efforts into a unified national will. From these demands arose his criticism of the prevalence of agriculture over industry. To him the purely agricultural State appeared as a cripple with only one arm, whereas a State that had achieved equilibrium of production by the co-ordinated cultivation of agriculture, trade, and industry seemed "infinitely more perfect."

In all these considerations List never lost sight of the one supreme goal — the creation of a united German nation. He believed that a customs union was a necessary preliminary step toward that end. What he really had in mind was the idea of a "Greater Germany" that was to include Austria and whose territories were to extend from the Adriatic to the North Sea. The next immediate task was an education of the national consciousness for the realization of the great industrial future that lay ahead and for a general program of *Weltpolitik*. Colonies in different continents were to supplement the domestic resources of industry and commerce and to provide the necessary reservoirs of political and economic power. These same colonies were to furnish raw materials and unfinished products and to absorb the manufactured goods of the mother country. List also visualized the possibilities of land settlement and colonization on a large scale in the German East, in Mecklenburg and Prussia, where vast and thinly populated territories were offering invaluable opportunities to German farmers and agricultural workers. The proposed economic unification and reorganization of central Europe was in the last analysis aimed at the economic supremacy of England, whose great industrial genius List envied and admired. In the year of his death he paid a visit to the British Isles, and his last publication dealt with the "Value and Conditions of an Alliance between Great Britain and Germany."

List's ideas were so far in advance of the limited perspective of his contemporaries that the record of his life became an unbroken series of disappointments and failures. The land-owning nobility was opposed to his idea of an industrialized State. The leading economists were specialists in their fields and unable to understand the interrelation of political and economic developments. The practical businessmen were unwilling to follow List into the realm of his farseeing speculations, and the spokesmen of Liberalism were defenders of Free Trade and rejected any interference of the State in the economic sphere. In the very year in which List ended his life by his own hand, England adopted a policy of unlimited Free Trade and thereby decided the victory of economic liberalism in all European countries.

Growth of Population and German Emigration. The peaceful years that followed the Napoleonic wars witnessed a rapid increase of the German population. At the end of the eighteenth century the German-speaking lands counted approximately twenty million people, but by the end of the nineteenth century this figure had more than trebled. This astounding phenomenon is partly explained by the diminishing infant mortality and the prolongation of human life brought about by the advances in medicine, public and personal hygiene, technological science, and, generally speaking, by a much greater stability and security of living conditions.

The absolutistic State of the eighteenth century had looked with favor upon an increase in population and had used various means to encourage immigration from foreign lands. It had appreciated the working capacity of its subjects without being greatly concerned about their social well-being. This frequently resulted in growing destitution among large sections of the rural and urban populations, and this in turn led to occasional waves of mass emigrations to the New World.

Ever since William Penn (1644–1718), the founder of the Quaker State of Pennsylvania, had by his missionary efforts started the wave of German emigration on its westward trail, there followed an unending stream of German emigrants, continuing throughout the eighteenth and to the end of the nineteenth century. Between 1820 and 1870 2,368,483 Germans migrated to the United States. Between 1871 and 1880 the annual emigration amounted to an average of 62,500, and in the following decade even to an annual average of 134,100. Next to the English colonists these German immigrants played a major part in the construction and organization of the civilization of North America.

The gradual realization that this continued mass emigration constituted in the long run an irreparable loss for the mother country and a fatal drainage of its national energies led to legal enactments that placed certain restrictions on further emigration. A nationally planned emigration policy was designed to preserve and strengthen the ties between the German elements abroad and the culture and traditions of their homeland, by means of political, educational, and missionary agencies and activities. The conviction, in turn, that the emigration problem was an issue of great national importance furnished additional arguments for the acquisition of colonies. These colonies, it was argued, would be capable of absorbing the surplus population, without depriving the emigrants of their nationality and without depleting the German nation's creative and productive resources.

Construction of Railroads. Next to the tariff problem the issue of an improved and unified system of transportation played an important part in the considerations of those who worked for the creation of a national industrial State. The free movement of goods within the territories of the Customs Union became an actuality only with the construction of railroads. Friedrich List, by his relentless efforts in behalf of a "national railway system," inaugurated for Germany a revolutionary change in transportation methods. List had actively participated as a shareholder in the development of steam-propelled railway traffic in the United States, and he relates in his memoirs how "in the wilderness of the blue mountain-ridges" of America he dreamed of a German railway system: "It was perfectly clear to me that only in this way could the economic unification [of Germany] be made fully effective." He prophesied that by means of an ever increasing speeding-up process in transportation and economic and cultural exchange the German people would achieve national unity, and the peoples of Europe and the Americas would eventually create a world-embracing system of political and commercial economy.

List was personally responsible for the construction of the railroad that was to connect the Saxon cities of Leipzig and Dresden. However, before the execution of this project was actually undertaken (1839) the first German railroad, covering the short distance between the Frankish cities of Nuremberg and Fürth and propelled alternatingly by horses and steam locomotives, was thrown open to public traffic in 1835, one year after the establishment of the German Customs Union. The Berlin-Potsdam, Berlin-Anhalt, and Berlin-Stettin railroads were built by three different companies between 1838 and 1842. The same years witnessed the opening of several economically lucrative Austrian railway lines, financed by the Viennese branch of the Rothschild banking concern and designed by some of Germany's leading mechanical engineers.

Although these German railways were built with private capital, the State exercised a strict control by means of granting or withholding concessions and by obtaining membership in the administrative boards. The first German state railways were those built between Braunschweig and Wolfenbüttel in the north and between Mannheim-Heidelberg and Basel in the state of Baden in the south (1838). Owing to the spirit of enterprise that animated the German industrialists, the German net of railways soon became one of the most extensive on the European continent, second only to that of Belgium.*

Friedrich List had also been one of the first to point out the military significance of the railway and had frequently used this argument in his negotiations with the German state governments. "The day might come," he wrote, "when France and Russia will join hands, and if that should happen, the advantages of a German railway system are incalculable." The reluctance of the Prussian state to adapt its railway gauge to that of her eastern Russian neighbor was likewise due to military considerations. The real test came in the wars with Denmark (cf. p. 537 sq.), Austria (cf. p. 538 sq.), and France (cf. p. 542 sqq.), when Moltke as chief of the general staff utilized to the full the facilities of the railway system for the speedy mobilization of the armed forces and for the flexible conduct of the military campaigns.

The fact that only a few of the privately financed German railways turned out to be profit-yielding enterprises led to the gradual nationalization of practically the entire German railway system. The only European country in which the railroads were developed and are supported exclusively by private initiative is England. As early as 1814 George Stephenson had built the first steam locomotive in England, and the first railroads, between Stockton and Darlington and between Liverpool and Manchester, had been constructed during the following two decades. While the German railway system assumed a strictly authoritarian character, with an almost militarily organized and uniformed personnel and a rigid code of regulations and

*In 1932, Germany, with a railway net of 58,619 kilometers, ranked first in Europe; Russia second, with 57,500 km.; France third, with 53,561 km.

instructions, the English system preserved the character marks of a liberal institution, relying chiefly on expert training and personal responsibility.

To realize the truly revolutionary significance of the advent of the "railway age" we do well to remember that the means of transportation had not materially changed from the days of ancient Greece to the third decade of the nineteenth century A.D. As road builders the medieval and modern Europeans had never equaled the ancient Romans, and we learn from a vivid description by Moltke of the year 1815 that "the highways of the Middle Ages had come down to us virtually unchanged, the only difference being that the robber-knights have been supplanted by the legalized highway robbery of the customs house officials." The generation that had broken down the customs barriers was the same that created the railway, and it was felt that both innovations were interrelated in that they both were supposed to advance the causes of social progress, national unity, and growing international solidarity. It was still inconceivable to the progressive idealism of the pioneers of this age that the forces of the new technology could be used for evil as well as for good, for destructive as well as for constructive purposes.

Reorganization of the Civil Service. The economic and political unification of Germany owes a great debt of gratitude to the civil service organization in the German states. The territorial changes that had taken place during and after the Napoleonic wars made it necessary to adapt the entire administrative organism of the German states to the requirements of the new political and social constellations. This task was accomplished by the princes and statesmen of the *Vormärz* with such success that up to this day the German civil service is universally admired as a model of thoroughness and efficiency. This is especially true of Prussia, where the "reform period" had created the preliminary conditions for the unified State that grew out of the victoriously fought Wars of Liberation. The Congress of Vienna had added new provinces to the territories of Prussia, and Prussian officialdom, thanks to its excellent training, its moral integrity, and its unselfish devotion to the State, accomplished the difficult task of co-ordinating in its administration the politically and racially heterogeneous populations of Rhinelanders, Westphalians, Saxons,* and Poles.

The peaceful policies of King Frederick William III favored the consolidation of this administrative reform, permitting a gradual amalgamation of the Old Prussian military absolutism and a New Prussian State paternalism that extended its control over the political, economic, and moral activities of its subjects. These subjects as much as the ruling Protestant bureaucracy were determined in their mentality and in their ethical convictions by the religious doctrines of Martin Luther and by the moral philosophy of Kant. Both Luther and Kant had taught them an ethics of duty and discipline

---

* To punish Saxony for having sided with Napoleon in the Wars of Liberation, the Congress of Vienna gave more than half of her territories to Prussia.

("*Pflichtethik*"), making perseverance in one's God-given "calling" (*Beruf*) the test of moral qualification, and demanding unquestioning obedience to the voice of the moral law that issued from the divinely delegated authority of the State.

The New Militarism.   The soldierly and warlike spirit was stronger and more inherent in the national temper and tradition in Prussia than in any other German state. Its rebirth in the nineteenth century was partly inspired by the same forces as the professional ethics of the Prussian civil service. The army bill that was introduced by Hermann von Boyen (1771–1848), the newly appointed Prussian minister of war, was framed in the spirit of Scharnhorst's (cf. p. 436 sq.) military reforms. It provided for universal conscription, retaining the already familiar distinction between the regular army of the line (standing army), the *Landwehr,* and the *Landsturm* (cf. p. 438). Its first paragraph proclaimed that "every individual who has reached the age of twenty is in duty bound to join in the defense of his country." But, "in order to interfere as little as possible with the physical and scientific education" of the young men, they were permitted to apply for military service at the age of seventeen. The forces of the standing army were to spend three years in continuous service and two more years in the army reserves. The two levies of *Landwehr* I and II, extending to the age limit of thirty-nine, included the army of trained reservists "on leave," to be drafted only in case of national emergency or actual war. The *Landsturm,* including the age classes between forty and fifty-five (later on changed to age limit of forty-five), could be called to the colors only in case of invasion and by a special summons of the king. In case of emergency this system of military conscription made available for the Prussian State a trained armed force of half a million men, not including the reserves of the *Landsturm.* The idea of the "people's army" (*Volksheer*) was thus legally incorporated in the structure of the Prussian State, and this Prussian system, which itself had originally borrowed the idea of universal conscription from the armies of the French Revolution, was copied by most of the other continental states in the course of the nineteenth century.*

The liberal idea of a "militia" with periodical short-term levies of the citizenry, that had still prominently figured in Scharnhorst's army reform, was now rejected as contrary to the spirit of professional military training. Nevertheless, a provision was adopted in 1822 that permitted those young men who had attended a secondary school for a certain number of years (four, later on six) and had obtained a qualifying certificate, to serve for one year only and to join an arm of the service of their own choice ("*Einjährig-Freiwilligen-Zeugnis*"). This was a concession to the spirit of an age that was convinced that a liberally or humanistically educated youth was necessarily so much ahead of his fellows in alertness and power of comprehension that his military training could be completed in one third of the

---

* Universal conscription was introduced in Austria-Hungary in 1868, in France in 1872, in Russia in 1874, in Italy in 1875 (in Japan in 1872).

ordinary time. The officers of the Landwehr and subsequently also those of the army reserves were largely recruited from the holders of such "One-Year-Certificates." The provision itself was later on adopted by the armed forces of all the German states that were united in the new German empire (1871) and was in force to the end of World War I.

When early in the second half of the nineteenth century Albrecht von Roon (1803–1879) took over the Ministry of War, the organization of the Prussian army underwent further important changes. A growing cleavage between the conservative professional officers of the standing army, most of them members of the nobility, and the more liberal-minded personnel of the *Landwehr* led to the complete subordination of the latter to the army of the line. This renewed antagonism between an arrogant and socially exclusive army clique and both the middle and working classes destroyed Scharnhorst's, Gneisenau's, and Boyen's idea of the *Volksheer*. The broad Humanism of these great military leaders and educators gave way to the professionalism of the class-conscious military expert and technician. Only the military genius of Moltke (cf. p. 534) was able even within these limitations to attain to a perfection of scientifically calculated military strategy that commands respect and admiration.

The spirit of the "military reform" of the era of the Wars of Liberation lived on, however, in the works of Karl von Clausewitz (1780–1831), the philosopher among the Prussian generals and the author of one of the great classics of military science (*Vom Kriege,* 1832–1834). One of Scharnhorst's most talented disciples, Clausewitz had resigned his commission in the Prussian army after the conclusion of the Prusso-French alliance of 1812. During the Wars of Liberation he had become an officer in the Russian army and had fought against Napoleon; after the war he was first appointed as chief of staff of one of Gneisenau's army corps, and in 1818 was made director of the Prussian Military Academy. This position in itself was rather meaningless, involving chiefly the routine tasks of administration and pedagogic discipline, but it offered Clausewitz sufficient leisure for meditation and writing.

Military strategy is treated by Clausewitz as an inductive science whose methods are dictated by experience and not predetermined by inflexible rules. The new scientific age with its experimental approach to facts and problems for the first time invades here the field of military strategy and supplants the mathematical and mechanical calculations of eighteenth-century rationalism. According to Clausewitz the great strategist has to take into consideration the peculiar circumstances of each individual situation, including the incalculable and unpredictable personal elements that are involved in any such set of conditions, requiring a personal, spontaneous response on the part of the military leader. For him the proper use of the psychological forces of intellect, emotion, and will are the decisive factors in successful warfare.

Clausewitz taught the advantages of a national defense that is ever on the alert and ready to be turned at any moment into a swiftly striking offensive warfare. The general staffs of the Prussian and German armies, however, were unwilling to follow these precepts. They placed the emphasis on attack rather than defense and began at an early date to train their troops for the tactics of the *Blitzkrieg*.

Nationalism and Political Liberalism. After the successful conclusion of the Wars of Liberation King Frederick William III of Prussia had declared: "It is I who shall determine at what time the promised constitutional representation will be granted. . . . It is the duty of the subjects to await patiently the moment that I shall find opportune." As nothing further happened and as the subjects, for the time being at least, were willing "to wait patiently," the political antagonism between those German states in the south, in which various forms of moderate constitutional government had been established, and the despotically ruled Prussian state in the north, became more and more pronounced and retarded the momentum of the movement toward national unity. Austria was ruled even more autocratically than Prussia and, considering her medley of nationalities, the attempt to introduce parliamentary forms of government would have seemed suicidal. For Prussia, on the other hand, constitutional government would have been possible and beneficial, but the fear of impending revolutionary changes made the king and his advisers follow the course of reaction and repression.

a) The Common Root of the National and Constitutional Movements. The constitutional agreements between medieval rulers and the estates of their realm, of which *Magna Charta* furnishes a characteristic example, were no constitutions in the modern sense of the term. They limited and controlled monarchical rule to a certain extent, but they established no national unity that originated with the people as a representative and sovereign power. The American Constitution of 1787 and the French Constitution of 1791, on the other hand, had each been drawn up and proclaimed by a "National Assembly" of the people and could therefore serve as the great models for the constitutional movements of the nineteenth century.

It has been mentioned (cf. p. 304) that medieval political philosophy derived the royal prerogatives from an original popular delegation of powers and that these prerogatives were theoretically limited by contract, custom, and the supremacy of the "moral law." The doctrine of the sovereignty of the people had then been further elaborated by and received additional support from the political theorists of the Jesuit Order in the sixteenth and seventeenth centuries (cf. p. 304 sq.) as well as the Scotch Calvinists, Puritans, and various independent sectarian movements in Europe and in the New World. Nineteenth-century Liberalism, linking these ancient rudiments of constitutional theory with Rousseau's optimistic belief in the unlimited perfectibility of human nature and popular institutions, made the people and their chosen representatives the sole originators and guarantors of legislation, subject only to the exactions of their own creation, the ideal National

State. The common root, therefore, of the national and constitutional movements was given in their common conviction that a nation or a state in the true sense cannot exist without a constitution that guarantees and protects the civic rights of all and thereby transforms a *Machtstaat* (autocratic State) into a *Rechtsstaat* (constitutional State).

b) The "Rechtsstaat" and National Liberalism. The civic and human rights to be guaranteed by the liberal *Rechtsstaat* included freedom and inviolability of person and home; the protection of private property; freedom of speech, press, and assembly; freedom of worship, equality of opportunity, equality before the law, and the universal, equal, and direct form of suffrage. These rights were conceived by the framers of the model constitutions of the American Union and of the French Republic as embodying the "absolute law of reason" and therefore as "eternal rights," existing prior to the State and thus "inalienable," and independent of the State in their validity.

The creation of the *Rechtsstaat* with its clearly defined guarantees of individual rights and the additional safeguard of the three independent branches of government (executive, legislative, and judicial), as originally demanded by Locke and Montesquieu, is the greatest and historically most significant achievement of political Liberalism. Its greatest theoretical proponent in Germany was the philosopher Kant, according to whom the meaning of "political freedom" is not that everyone should be permitted to do what he pleases, but rather that everyone should be free to do anything that is "right," and that no power on earth should ever compel anyone to do what is "wrong." When Kant defined "legal freedom" as the right of the citizen to obey only laws to which he had given his free consent, he thereby expressed the main principle of "government by the consent of the governed."

Kant and the entire political Liberalism of the eighteenth century still believed in absolute values, not necessarily derived from a divine revelation, but inherent in the God-given reason and moral sense of man. They believed in the truth and falsehood of the ideas that underlie social and political structures, and they were convinced that a *Rechtsstaat* was a good form of society precisely because it was based on intellectual and moral truths.

These ideal and rational bases of the older political Liberalism were gradually undermined by the historical and utilitarian spirit of the nineteenth century. While for Kant the purpose of the State was the realization of the idea of "Right," Jeremy Bentham (1748–1832) early in the nineteenth century considered "the greatest good of the greatest number" as the goal of all State legislation, thereby substituting the sociological motives of utility and expediency for the abstract demands of "Right" and "Equity." If the idea of the *Rechtsstaat* was to survive without surrendering its liberal tenets to the ideology of a new *Machtstaat,* it had to look for new norms and sanctions to fill the void created by the abandonment of the old religious and moral standards. Thus Liberalism entered into an alliance with modern

Nationalism, expecting from this union a revitalization of its own creed and the realization of the cultural, social, and political aspirations of modern mankind. If only, in accordance with the principles of Liberalism and Nationalism, Europe could be transformed into a continent of autonomous national and constitutional States, then at last universal peace would be assured!

German Liberalism in particular had not forgotten the teachings and convictions of the Lutheran Reformation and of the New Humanism. It constantly replenished its vigor and vitality with the inspiring thought of a personal freedom and autonomy that were to be used as instruments for individual perfection and the cultural advancement of the race. The idea of the National State was but another means to achieve the goal of a thoroughly personalized culture that could not become a reality as long as the efforts of the individual were not encouraged and aided by liberal political institutions and a national community of ideas and interests.

German Liberalism and Nationalism in Action. While in most of the continental European states the reactionary political system of Metternich seemed firmly entrenched, the liberal movement, carried forward by the awakened middle classes, had gathered sufficient momentum to make itself felt as a force that had to be reckoned with by the monarchical rulers.*

a) The French "July Revolution" and Its Sequel. The signal for the liberal revolt was given in France in 1830, when the reactionary regime of the restored Bourbon monarchy of Charles X (1824–1830) was overthrown and the "Bourgeois King," Louis Philippe of Orléans, was placed upon the throne. The French "July Revolution" marked the first victory of middle class Liberalism over the forces of political reaction on the one hand and over republican radicalism on the other. The parliamentary principle had won the day, with bankers, industrialists, and liberal-minded intellectuals seizing the reins of government. The working class and the Paris radicals had failed in their attempt to restore the Jacobin Republic of 1793, and the privilege of suffrage was still restricted to the "men of property."

The "July Revolution" in France was followed by similar uprisings in other European countries, in which Nationalism and Liberalism worked hand in hand. The Belgians, united with Holland by a decree of the Congress of Vienna, regained their national independence, the German Prince Leopold of Saxe-Coburg becoming the head of a liberal constitutional Belgian monarchy. In 1839, England, France, Prussia, Austria, and Russia agreed to respect and protect the "perpetual" independence and neutrality of the new Belgian State, a pledge that was used by England to justify her entry into the war in 1914, after Belgian neutrality had been violated by Germany.

Poland's attempt to free herself from Russian domination ended in tragic

---

* The term "liberal" was first adopted by the Spanish Cortes (Diet) of 1812 to distinguish the defenders of constitutional government from the representatives of Absolutism. In the following years it became a household word all over Europe.

failure. She lost the semiautonomy that she had possessed as a kingdom under the supremacy of the Russian tsar, and was incorporated into the Russian empire by Nicholas I (1825–1855). Polish Nationalism was crushed, the Constitution abrogated, and the liberal and patriotic leaders exiled. Revolutionary outbreaks in northern Italy and in the Papal States were likewise suppressed with the aid of Austrian troops.

The reverberations of the "July Revolution" were felt in several German states, and as a result some additional local constitutions were granted, but on the whole autocratic rule remained unbroken. Nevertheless, the efforts of Liberals and patriots were not lost. Liberalism and Nationalism had tested their strength and their cause had been consecrated by the blood of heroes and martyrs. In England the news of the successful French Revolution produced a cabinet crisis that brought about the defeat of the Tories and the accession to power of the Whigs. In 1832 the liberal "Reform Bill" was passed by both houses of Parliament, signalizing the victory of the manufacturing interests of the middle class over the landed nobility.

b) The French "February Revolution," the "Second Republic," and the "Second Empire."   The second wave of revolutionary movements in the nineteenth century again took its start in France. The rule of Louis Philippe had rapidly become unpopular, and by his attempts to compromise with both the conservative and progressive elements he had made enemies on all sides. In February, 1848, the Paris mob erected barricades in the streets once more and forced the "Bourgeois King's" abdication. A partly liberal, partly socialist government proclaimed the "Second Republic" of France. A radical socialist revolt of the same year was bloodily crushed, and soon afterward a democratic Constitution, providing for one legislative chamber and a president, elected by universal manhood suffrage, was adopted. But, surprisingly enough, the first general election returned to power a conservative and royalist majority and placed in the president's chair Louis Napoleon, a nephew of Napoleon I and the legitimate pretender to the imperial succession. In a successful *coup d'état* (1851) he substituted a system of councils for the democratic Constitution and, in 1852, he assumed the title of Napoleon III and made himself the head of the "Second French Empire."

c) Revolts in Austria.   Outside France the "February Revolution" of 1848 had repercussions that were more far reaching in their effects than the upheavals of 1830. The revolutionary movement spread rapidly to the Austrian crownlands, to Italy, and to the states of the "German Confederation."

The year 1848 marks the fall of the "Metternich System" and the end of Prince Metternich's political career. The veteran statesman, forced by an angry citizenry to abdicate, went into exile in England, and the liberal Austrian leaders received from Emperor Ferdinand I (1835–1848) the promise of a constitution. In the meantime, Austria had to strain all her forces to check three major rebellions, in Hungary, Bohemia, and in her

Italian provinces of Lombardy and Venetia. The Hapsburg monarchy mastered this difficult task with courage and skill. All the insurrections were quelled, and the armies of Sardinia, which had joined the rebellious Italian states, were routed by the Austrian General, Radetzky. Imperial troops under Prince Windischgrätz recaptured Prague, the capital of Bohemia, and crushed the rebellion in Vienna.

The fiercest rebels were the Hungarian Magyars, whose leader Kossuth had proclaimed an independent Hungarian republic. The Magyars were defeated only with the aid of Russian contingents dispatched by Tsar Nicholas I, who still adhered to the "policy of intervention" (cf. p. 509 sq.) in the interest of the principle of "legitimacy." Hungary was deprived of her constitutional privileges and became one of the several provinces of Austria.

In the midst of these revolutionary upheavals Emperor Ferdinand I decided to abdicate in favor of his nephew, Francis Joseph, who was then only eighteen years of age. Metternich was succeeded in office by Prince Felix von Schwarzenberg, a man of similar political convictions but of much smaller caliber. Metternich himself returned to Vienna, satisfied that once more his system seemed to have weathered a major storm.

In 1849 Emperor Francis Joseph I (1848–1916) promulgated a new Constitution for all the Austrian lands, providing for a centralized administration and leaving the power of autocratic government virtually unimpaired. Her victory over the forces of Liberalism and Nationalism had greatly increased the prestige of Austria as a champion of conservatism and made her a powerful contestant in the bid for political leadership in the "German Confederation."

d) The "March Revolution" in Prussia. When Frederick William IV succeeded his father on the Prussian throne in 1840, the hopes of the Prussian Liberals for constitutional reforms were revived. Those who visualized Prussia as the future leader of the German nation felt that the sympathies of the German South could only be won if Prussia were no longer looked upon as the champion of political and social reaction. The new king seemed at first not disinclined to listen to the arguments of the Liberals, and he began his reign with a proclamation of political amnesty and with the exoneration or reinstatement in office of some of the exiled liberal professors. However, the high expectations of the Liberals were soon turned into bitter disappointment. Frederick William IV was at heart a romanticist whose mind lived in the past rather than in the present, and he looked with growing horror and disgust upon the advancing wave of revolutionary sentiment at home and abroad. Wavering between the desire to redeem his father's and his own promises to give his people a constitutional government and his unwillingness to compromise the exalted dignity and supremacy of the royal crown, he contented himself with half-measures that satisfied no one.

By a royal patent of the year 1847 the king summoned the "United Diet"

(*Vereinigter Landtag*), composed of the eight Provincial Diets of the Prussian State. In his opening address he made it perfectly clear that he felt himself unable to make any substantial concessions to the liberal demands. It seemed inconceivable to him that the natural relationship between the ruler and his people might be transformed into a constitutional contract: "No written sheet of paper," he declared, "shall ever interpose itself like a second Providence between God in Heaven and this land." Sharing in the faith of absolutistic rulers in government by divine right and delegation, Frederick William wanted to rule "in accordance with the law of God and the State," not in accordance with the arbitrary decisions of "so-called representatives of the people" and their shifting majorities.

Thus the deliberations of the "United Diet" led nowhere. The delegates, brusquely rebuffed in their demands for definite constitutional rights, proved obstinate on their part in their refusal to co-operate with the crown and in particular rejected the government's request for a loan. As the opposite points of view of the crown and the delegates appeared irreconcilable, the Diet was finally dismissed without having achieved any tangible objective.

In the meantime, the news of the French "February Revolution" had caused the Diet of the "German Confederation" in Frankfurt to revoke a number of reactionary measures and to announce its eagerness to enter upon a process of reorganization and modernization. As an outward symbol of its change of heart this ultraconservative body adopted the revolutionary colors of black, red, and gold and the emblem of a golden eagle on a black background.

In all the smaller German states the fall of the Bourbon monarchy in France frightened the governments and advanced the cause of Liberalism. New, liberal ministries were recruited from the members of the liberal opposition in the local state chambers, and thus without bloodshed the revolutionary movement had gained a number of important victories.

With the struggle for liberty near its goal, the voices that called for national unity likewise became louder and louder. In the forties, shortly after the accession of Frederick William IV to the Prussian throne, some threatening gestures on the part of France had aroused the national feeling to a high pitch. All eyes instinctively turned toward Prussia, which alone among the German states seemed strong enough to offer organized resistance to a foreign invader. It was at that time that Hoffmann von Fallersleben (1798–1874) wrote the stirring verses of the future national anthem, "*Deutschland, Deutschland über alles, über alles in der Welt.*"*

With Austria engaged in putting down rebellions in her crownlands, it would have been relatively easy for Prussia to seize upon the opportunities that were offered to her by the events of the stormy year of 1848 and to assume leadership in German affairs. But Frederick William IV proved

---

* The opening lines of the German national anthem are often misinterpreted: The phrase "Germany above everything else in the world" does not imply any desire for world domination but simply means that, for every German, Germany ranks foremost.

unequal to the great task. What he abhorred more than anything else occurred under his very eyes: on March 18 the revolution flared up in Berlin and for half a year terrorized and humiliated the king and his cabinet. Prince William of Prussia, the king's brother and the later German emperor (1871, cf. p. 546), wrongly suspected of having given orders to fire on the excited crowds in the castle yard, had to flee to England. The king, in order to save his life and his crown, was compelled to ride on horse-back through the streets of his capital, surrounded by waving banners of black, red, and gold.

But while the prestige of the crown had suffered some damage, the State and its backbone, the army, remained unshaken. The people were averse to revolutionary violence, and in November, 1848, the Prussian troops marched unopposed into Berlin. In December of the same year Frederick William IV proclaimed a Constitution for Prussia that satisfied at least some of the demands of the Liberals. It was adopted in its complete and final form in 1850, providing for a House of Representatives, elected by universal (yet indirect and open) manhood suffrage, but limiting these constitutional gains by dividing the voters into three classes, in accordance with their tax-paying capacity. By means of this *Dreiklassenwahlrecht* (three-class suffrage) the wealthy and propertied classes were always assured a majority over the representatives of rural and industrial labor and other groups of small wage earners.* The democratic features of this constitutional

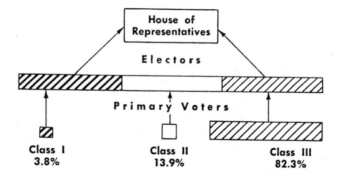

(Each class of the "Primary Voters" chooses one third of the "Electors."
The "Electors," in turn, choose the deputies of the House of Representatives.)

system were further weakened by the creation of a House of Lords (*Herrenhaus*) in 1854, composed of noblemen and manorial lords who were appointed for life and whose offices were made hereditary. Despite an ever growing opposition the Prussian *Dreiklassenwahlrecht* continued in existence until the revolution of 1918.

On the whole, Prussia emerged from the revolutionary tempest of 1848

---

* The inserted graph may serve to illustrate the electoral system of the *Dreiklassenwahlrecht*.

as a civil and military State whose authoritarian character was scarcely touched. The few concessions to liberal sentiment had been made reluctantly and halfheartedly, and the king, in a secret political testament, recommended to his successors that they discredit the Constitution by withholding their oath of allegiance.

The Frankfurt Assembly (1848–1849). Shortly after the violent outbreaks in Berlin had occurred, five hundred men, delegated by a self-appointed committee of fifty-one representatives from the different German states, met in St. Paul's Church in Frankfurt. They deliberated about the most suitable ways and means to give Germany both national unity and constitutional liberty. All were agreed that a German Parliament must be created that was worthy of the name and that was to take the place of the unwieldy and inefficient *Bundestag* (Federal Diet).

The liberal leaders, assembled in Frankfurt, constituted themselves as a "Preliminary Parliament" (*Vorparlament*) and immediately took in hand the preparations for the election of a National Assembly, composed of deputies from all German states.

The National Assembly actually convened on May 18, 1848, but the delegates had hardly begun their deliberations when all the controversial issues that had divided the German lands and peoples for centuries presented themselves with renewed vigor. To the old religious and cultural antagonisms and rivalries between North and South, Prussia and Austria, Catholics and Protestants, there had been added in more recent years the differences of conviction between those who favored a "Greater Germany" (*Grossdeutschland*) that was to include Austria, and those who advocated the creation of a "Smaller Germany" (*Kleindeutschland*) under Prussian leadership and without Austria.

It was a foregone conclusion that the attainment of a workable compromise between these conflicting wishes and opinions would be beyond the ingenuity even of the illustrious men who made up this assembly, among whose almost 600 members were many of Germany's best and noblest minds (Jahn, Uhland, Jakob Grimm, E. M. Arndt, etc.). It was indeed a "Parliament of Professors," a unique forum of scholars who had learned the lessons of German Humanism and Classicism, who as politicians displayed the wisdom of philosophers and the vision of poets, and who unreservedly devoted their knowledge, their strength, and their very lives to the service of their nation. If they failed to translate their ideas into practical political reality, it was certainly not due to lack of enthusiasm and good will but to a combination of adverse circumstances and a series of well-nigh insuperable obstacles.

The National Assembly elected as its president Heinrich von Gagern (1799–1880), a government official of Hesse-Darmstadt, a former member of the *Burschenschaft* (cf. p. 464 sq.), and the leading advocate of a united Germany under Prussian leadership. In his opening address he outlined the aims of the Frankfurt Parliament: "We have to frame a Constitution for

Germany, and we derive our authority for this purpose from the sovereignty of the nation. . . . Germany desires to be one, a single State, ruled by the will of the people. . . . "

Upon the recommendation of von Gagern the assembly elected Archduke John of Austria as *Reichsverweser* or imperial administrator and executive head of the German nation. The archduke had married a commoner and was generally known as a man of liberal sympathies. Thus far the transactions of the legislators made a fairly impressive showing on paper, but it was a hard and cruel fact that the Constitution of the "German Confederation," dating from 1815, could not be changed without the consent of both Austria and Prussia. Neither of these powers showed any inclination to recognize the legislative authority of the Frankfurt Assembly.

While the debates on the nature of the proposed Constitution were dragging on and the difficulties increased, the sudden uprising of the two Elbe duchies of Schleswig-Holstein against Denmark injected a further distracting and controversial issue into the proceedings. The duchies were united with Denmark by a "personal union" with the Danish king. This arrangement dated back to the year 1460, when the estates of Schleswig-Holstein had elected the king of Denmark as their duke and when, together with the provision of this dynastic union with Denmark, the duchies had received a pledge that they should "permanently remain free and undivided." Thus the king of Denmark was also duke of Schleswig-Holstein, although the Congress of Vienna had made Holstein a member of the "German Confederation," which had thereby been given the right to interfere in the political affairs of the southern duchy. While the language spoken in Holstein and southern Schleswig was German and the sympathies of the population were with Germany, the people of northern Schleswig spoke Danish, and many of them considered Denmark's cause as their own. The Danish nationalists wanted to make both duchies part of the kingdom of Denmark, and the growing national sentiment in Germany was equally desirous of seeing them both incorporated in the "German Confederation."

In 1848 the two duchies rose in revolt against Denmark's repeated attempts to deprive them of their independence. The "German Confederation" expressed its sympathies for the cause of the insurgents, and Prussian troops under General Wrangel stormed the "Danewerk," Denmark's ancient frontier wall, and penetrated into Jutland. After the temporary truce of Malmö, brought about by English and Russian pressure, the fight was resumed by Denmark in 1849, with Bavarian, Saxon, and Austrian troops joining the Prussian contingents. Although the war ended with a Danish victory, the Treaty of London (1852) decreed that Schleswig-Holstein should retain its semiautonomous political organization in continued personal union with the king of Denmark. The treaty tried to counteract future complications by stipulating that Prince Christian of Glücksburg, the heir to the Danish crown, should also be made the reigning duke in Schleswig-Holstein.

The struggle for Schleswig-Holstein had demonstrated that the Frankfurt Parliament was unable to make its influence felt in foreign affairs. Its members were without power and authority, and their envoy was not even admitted to the negotiations that led to the Truce of Malmö. Nevertheless, swallowing their pride, they continued their labors and, in March, 1849, completed the draft of a Constitution; two months later they sent a deputation to Berlin to offer the hereditary imperial crown to King Frederick William IV of Prussia.

The Constitution drawn up by the Frankfurt Parliament was a skillful compromise that might have provided a practical basis for conciliating the differing points of view, if all parties concerned had been animated by the same earnest desire for a just and impartial solution as were the members of the assembly. The draft provided for a constitutional monarchy, a "mixed" form of government, in which, as its framers believed, all the good features of monarchical, aristocratic, and democratic rule were combined. The representatives of the people were to be chosen by universal, equal, direct, and secret ballot. In all fundamental principles and in many minor details the German Liberals had drawn freely upon the experiences and political beliefs of France, England, Switzerland, and the American Union, countries which were considered as models of political wisdom, progressive legislation, and free institutions.

It was especially the structure of a federal state, combining the idea of national unity with the interests of particularism and regionalism, that seemed to recommend the American Constitution as worthy of imitation. German Liberalism therefore looked upon the United States as the country that had succeeded in creating the most liberal and most perfect system of government that the world had ever seen. And with all its deficiencies the German Constitution of 1849 was the first attempted realization of the idea of a German Nation, united and organized on the basis of the guiding principles of modern democracy.

Frederick William IV refused to accept the proffered imperial crown from the hands of the people, declaring that such a dignity could be conferred upon him only by the German princes. Austria, on her part, had already recalled her delegates from Frankfurt, offended by the compromise proposal which provided that only the German provinces of the Hapsburg monarchy be included in the German Union.

And so this work, undertaken with such sincerity of conviction and from the noblest of motives, ended in disappointment and failure. Once more revolts broke out, in Saxony, in the Palatinate, and in Baden, giving vent to the resentment of the people, who saw their fondest hopes betrayed by princely whims and dynastic interests. The king of Prussia had to send two army corps under the command of his brother, Prince William, to the German South, to aid in putting down the rebellion.

After thirteen months of deliberations the Frankfurt Parliament was finally dissolved. The restoration of the "German Confederation" and the

"Federal Diet" in 1851 signified another victory of Conservatism over Liberalism. Prussia had made up her mind to follow the reactionary course of Austria, and in the Treaty of Olmütz (1851), usually referred to as the "Humiliation of Olmütz," she formally agreed to relinquish all plans for a German Union under her own leadership.

A New Era in Prussia. The dismal failure of the Frankfurt Parliament was the severest setback that the German liberal and national movement had yet experienced. The decade from 1850 to 1860 found the patriots in silent or open despair. A new wave of censorship and persecution forced many to leave their native land, to continue the struggle for the ideals of freedom and national unity in the New World. Many of these emigrants dedicated their lives to the defense of the American Union during the American Civil War and fought for the liberation of the American Negro slaves. Among them was Karl Schurz (1829–1906), a native of the Rhineland who, having taken part in the revolutionary movement of 1848, had evaded the death sentence imposed upon him by escaping to America in 1852. He devoted his gifts as an orator and publicist to the cause of the Republican party, commanded an army corps in the Civil War, and became a prominent political figure as a United States senator (1869–1875) and Secretary of the Interior (1877–1881).

For those who remained in the home country it seemed to be proven beyond a doubt that their idealism had been misspent. They were slowly getting ready to view the political and national scene with a sober and unsentimental realism. In the light of incontrovertible facts many of the influential leaders in the smaller German states were driven to the conclusion that of the two interdependent issues that had been debated and defeated at Frankfurt, the cause of national unity took precedence over the cause of political liberty. If the former could be achieved, Liberalism might still have a chance, whereas it was doubtful whether political liberty without national unity was even worth fighting for. But it also had been demonstrated that national unity could not be attained unless it was possible to find a solution for the problem of the Austro-Prussian dualism.

As far as their governmental systems were concerned, Austria and Prussia were both committed to a course of political reaction, but Prussia was at least an integral German state, while part of Austria's interests lay outside Germany. Furthermore, there was a slight encouragement in the fact that Frederick William IV, yielding to continuous pressure, had finally promulgated a Constitution, and had done so at the risk of incurring the displeasure of Austria. Finally, as the leading state in the German *Zollverein* (cf. p. 513 sq.), from which Austria was excluded, Prussia seemed to be in a logical position to build up a political leadership that rested on a solidarity of economic interests. Considering all these factors, the smaller German states became more and more reconciled to the thought of accepting the solution of a "Smaller Germany," headed by Prussia, as the most promising compromise under the given circumstances.

Those who nourished such hopes were greatly encouraged by the changes in Prussian administration brought about by the appointment of Prince William, the brother of the childless Frederick William IV, to the regency of Prussia (1857), after the king had become mentally incapacitated by several paralytic strokes. Upon Frederick William IV's death in 1861 the prince regent succeeded to the Prussian throne as King William I (1861–1888; "German emperor" after 1871). These events marked the opening of a new era for Prussia as well as for Germany.

The new king, already sixty-three years of age when he formally took office, was a soldier by training and inclination, and the army ranked foremost among his interests and loyalties. The appointment of *Count Helmuth von Moltke* (1800–1891) as chief of the general staff and of *Count Albrecht von Roon* (1803–1879) as minister of war — two men who combined with the best Prussian military training an intimate acquaintance with modern problems of military science, strategy, and organization — indicated the intention of the monarch to build up the Prussian army to a maximum of strength and efficiency and to make it the most up-to-date military force in the world.

The request for the necessary appropriations to carry out this military program involved the king in a bitter feud with the lower chamber of the Prussian Diet. A majority of the members, having twice reluctantly granted the requested credits, obstinately refused to pass the new army bill of the year 1862.

This defeat of the government was in part due to the newly acquired strength of the "Liberal-Progressive Party," which had been founded in 1861 and had twice gained a majority in Parliament. Its presiding chairman and cofounder was the famous physician and anthropologist Rudolf Virchow (1821–1902). The party program called for the unification of Germany under Prussian leadership, for liberal legislation, and for the reduction of the period of compulsory military training from three to two years. It was a matter of conviction and principle with the "Progressive Party" to oppose every one of the moves of Otto von Bismarck (cf. p. 535 sqq.) from the moment the latter assumed responsibility for the governance of the domestic and foreign affairs of Prussia.

The clash between king and Parliament precipitated a major crisis, in which the rival claims of authoritarian and constitutional government were once more put to a decisive test. The king felt that the prestige of the royal crown itself was at stake, and he was determined to renounce his throne rather than to undergo what seemed to him ignominious surrender to parliamentary pressure.

The document of abdication had already been drawn up when, through the intervention of Albrecht von Roon, the course of events took an entirely different turn and one that was of momentous import for the future destiny not only of Germany but of all Europe. Roon himself had promised to stand by his king, at a moment when even the queen and the crown prince had added their voices to those of the parliamentary opposition. And Roon knew still another man who was willing to come to the support of the king and who had been kept informed by the minister of war of the critical state of affairs. He was an old friend of Roon's and at the time Prussian ambassador in Paris. His name was Otto von Bismarck-Schönhausen.

William I let himself be persuaded by his minister of war to receive Bismarck in private audience before making his decision final. On September 22, 1862, the memorable interview took place that marked the beginning of a new epoch in the history of modern Europe. Without hesitation Bismarck declared his willingness to complete the reorganization of the army against the will of the majority in the Diet. The king decided to continue the struggle with the aid of his newly appointed prime minister who, a few days after the fateful conversation with William I, declared in the Budget Committee of the Chamber of Deputies: "Germany does not look to Prussia's Liberalism but to her power. . . . The great questions of the time will be decided not by speeches and the resolutions of majorities — that was the mistake of 1848 and 1849 — but by blood and iron."

The Policy of "Blood and Iron." Otto von Bismarck (1815–1898), the man who from 1862 to 1890 directed the domestic and foreign policies of Prussia and, after 1871, also those of the Second German Empire, was a descendant of the ancient nobility of the Mark Brandenburg. The future "Iron Chancellor" was born at Schönhausen in the Prussian province of Saxony and had inherited from his forefathers a strong faith in military discipline and in the principles of autocratic government. In 1839 he had retired from the Prussian civil service to devote himself to the management of his father's Pomeranian estate of Kniephof. The historical studies which he pursued in his leisure time deepened his insight into the political problems of his own day, and the intercourse with the families of the neighboring manorial estates served to strengthen his conservative views. At the same time it brought him into renewed contact with the orthodox Lutheran form of piety, from which he had become estranged in his gay and carefree student days at Göttingen, where he had been a member of one of the aristocratic students' corporations (the *Corps* Hannovera).

Bismarck first stepped into the limelight of political life as leader of the conservative right wing in the United Prussian Diet of 1847, pleading for the prerogatives of the crown, for the privileges of the nobility, and for the preservation of the feudal order of society. He had no sympathy with the liberal ideology of the Frankfurt Assembly and had approved Frederick William IV's refusal to accept the imperial crown from the hands of the people's representatives. Prussia's "humiliation" at Olmütz (cf. p. 533) had cured him of his initial admiration of the conservative regime of Austria and confirmed in him the conviction that sooner or later the "German Question" must be settled by force of arms. As Prussian envoy (1851–1858) to the restored "Federal Diet" at Frankfurt he mapped his plans for a

Prussian *Realpolitik* that had as its goal the gradual weakening and final elimination of Austria from an anticipated German Union under Prussian supremacy.

a) Bismarck's Attitude in the Crimean War (1853–1856). When in 1853 Turkey, in alliance with England, France, Austria, and Sardinia, started its campaign against Russian domination in the Black Sea and against the assumed right of Tsar Nicholas I to act as the protector of all Christian denominations in Turkey, it was Bismarck's counsel that prevented Prussia from joining in the war. He knew that Russia's gratitude and friendship were indispensable for the consummation of his political scheme.

The "Crimean War" was concluded by the Treaty of Paris (1856), in which Tsar Alexander II (1855–1881) renounced Russia's protectorate of the Christians in Turkey and the Russian sphere of influence in the Danubian principalities of Walachia and Moldavia, and agreed to the closing of the Black Sea to the warships of all nations. Turkey was formally admitted to the Concert of European Powers on an equal footing. In a special "declaration" the Congress of Paris adopted a number of new rules of naval warfare, outlawing privateering and revising the rights of naval blockade by prohibiting the seizure on the high seas of neutral as well as enemy goods of nonmilitary character (noncontraband goods). In 1861 the principalities of Walachia and Moldavia agreed to unite and together established the independent principality of Rumania.

b) Prussia's Attitude in the Austro-Sardinian War (1859). The struggle for the unification of Germany had its counterpart in Italy, where the kingdom of Sardinia, under the leadership of the great Italian statesman Cavour (1810–1861), played a role similar to that assumed by Prussia in the North. By aiding France in the Crimean War Cavour had managed to gain the support of Napoleon III in his attempt to force Austria out of northern Italy. In 1859 Austria answered the intentional provocations of Sardinia with a declaration of war, and the French emperor sent an army across the Alps to assist in the conquest of the provinces of Lombardy and Venetia. Austria, in launching her Italian campaign, had counted heavily on Prussian support, but Prussia remained aloof and thus further aggravated the strained relations between the two powers. Napoleon III, on the other hand, acutely aware of the power of Prussia and surprised at the unexpected strength of the Italian national movement, that seemed to leave little chance for France's taking over the Austrian sphere of influence in northern Italy, suddenly reversed his policy and concluded the armistice of Villafranca. Nevertheless, in the Treaty of Turin (1860), France received Savoy and Nice as rewards for her intervention on the side of Italy, while the Italian provinces of Lombardy, Tuscany, Parma, Modena, and part of the Papal States were united with the kingdom of Sardinia. Thus Austria lost Lombardy but retained Venetia, and Emperor Francis Joseph declared in a manifesto to the European powers that he had been forced to agree to the peace terms by the desertion of Prussia, his nearest and natural ally.

c) Parliamentary Struggles and Diplomatic Moves. While Europe found itself embroiled in this complex game of political intrigues and rival bids for power, Bismarck followed with ever increasing self-assurance a political course that had become a fixed pattern in his mind. He remained undismayed by lack of understanding and support, by personal vilifications, by threats of impeachment, and by several attempts on his life. The blunt and vehement frankness with which he expressed his opinions had partly been responsible for his appointment as Prussian ambassador to St. Petersburg (1859) and to Paris (1862). It was felt that his presence in the Prussian capital was in itself provocative and a constant source of political friction and diplomatic embarrassments.

When he was finally called back to save the prestige of the crown and to face the hostile majority in the Prussian Chamber, he was prepared for a fight to the finish. For four years (1862–1866) he administered the affairs of the State with a complete defiance of popular and parliamentary opinion. He drew on the treasury without constitutional authorization and without submitting an account of his expenditures; used the powers at his command to enlist the services of censorship, police, and armed force for the suppression of free speech and a free opposition press; and even disregarded the immunity of the members of the Prussian Chamber. Bismarck achieved his objectives systematically one by one, but to many of his contemporaries he appeared either as a ruthless Prussian *Junker* or as a reckless political gambler.

In 1863 Emperor Francis Joseph presided over a Diet of the German princes (*Fürstentag*) at Frankfurt, which had been convoked by Austria to bring about a reorganization of the "German Confederation." Bismarck suspected that the real purpose of the *Fürstentag* was to gain for Austria a predominant position in the German *Bund* and to curb Prussia's increasing influence. On the advice of his prime minister the king of Prussia declined to participate in the deliberations. The only real reform of the *Bund* that Bismarck envisaged was a unified Germany, headed by Prussia. This, however, required first of all the expulsion of Austria, and everything that fell short of this radical solution could only retard the inevitable course of events.

In the same year in which the *Fürstentag* met at Frankfurt (1863) the Poles had staged another revolt against Russia. The liberal sentiment in England, France, and Germany favored the cause of Polish independence and called for strong diplomatic representations in St. Petersburg, even at the risk of becoming involved in war with Russia. But Bismarck, contrary to the general trend of public opinion, decided to give diplomatic support to Russia and thus strengthened the ties of friendship between the tsar and the king of Prussia.

d) The Danish War (1864). While Bismarck was still wrangling with the opposition in the Prussian Chamber, the Schleswig-Holstein question, which was believed to have been settled by the Treaty of London (cf.

p. 531), was revived again. This gave Bismarck the desired opportunity to test the political and military strength of Prussia in the foreign field.

The Treaty of London that had been signed by all the great European powers, including both Prussia and Austria, had declared that, despite the "personal union" of the duchies with the king of Denmark, they were to retain their separate political organization and that the rights of their German population must be respected. However, in 1863, King Christian IX of Denmark published a new Constitution for all Danish territories, including the duchies, and this was considered as a breach of the London agreements. At the same time Duke Frederick of Augustenburg, whose father had renounced his rights of succession in Schleswig-Holstein in favor of the king of Denmark, revived the claims of his line and was supported by the German Confederation.

But Bismarck had his own ideas on the Schleswig-Holstein question. He was neither interested in the claims of the duke of Augustenburg nor in the political independence of the two duchies. From the outset he had made up his mind to incorporate Schleswig-Holstein into the Prussian state, and he used every kind of dissimulation and subterfuge to hide his real aims, until the opportune moment for decisive action had arrived.

The first step in the execution of Bismarck's bold scheme was to persuade Austria to ignore the "German Confederation" and to work hand in hand with Prussia, while he pretended that he himself was as much interested in upholding the terms of the London Treaty as the emperor of Austria. Both powers then agreed that the Schleswig-Holstein question must be decided by force of arms and that the future of the duchies should be determined by the friendly understanding and mutual consent of Prussia and Austria!

In 1864 Prussian and Austrian troops under the command of the octogenarian General Wrangel invaded Schleswig, captured the *Danewerk*, stormed the redoubts of Düppel, and occupied the greater part of Jutland. This first phase of the war was followed by a truce and by subsequent negotiations in London. Bismarck now declared that while Prussia and Austria considered the London Protocol of 1852 invalidated by the actions of the Danish king, the two German powers were still willing to concede political autonomy to Schleswig-Holstein, including a continued personal union with the Danish crown. Upon the refusal of Denmark to accept these proposals, hostilities were resumed and the allied armies advanced deeply into the continental and island territories of the northern kingdom. Then a new Danish ministry asked for a truce, and in the Peace of Vienna Denmark agreed to cede the duchies of Schleswig-Holstein unconditionally to Prussia and Austria. The Danish campaign, whose strategic details had been worked out by Moltke, had lasted from February to October.

e) The "Seven Weeks' War" Between Prussia and Austria (1866). With the handing over of the Elbe duchies to Prussia and Austria the Schleswig-Holstein question was far from settled. The dispute as to what was to become of the spoils of the Danish War occupied the cabinets in Berlin and Vienna and soon brought about a renewed tension in Austro-Prussian relations. There is no doubt that both the emperor of Austria and the king of Prussia honestly wanted peace and mutual understanding, but Bismarck's mind was set on the outright annexation of Schleswig-Holstein and also on a final settling of accounts with Austria. To please his sovereign the Prussian prime minister declared himself willing to agree to the temporary compromise of the Treaty of Gastein (1865), according to which Prussia was to take over the administration of Schleswig and Austria that of Holstein.

But this compromise had hardly been agreed upon when the relations between Prussia and Austria reached a critical stage with the revival of the Augustenburg claims to the two duchies. Austria openly backed the demands of the prince of Augustenburg, chiefly because she found it rather burdensome to administer a distant northern province and would therefore have preferred the establishment of an independent German state of Schleswig-Holstein. The intransigent attitude of Prussia finally caused Austria to carry out her previously announced threat of submitting the Schleswig-Holstein question to the Federal Diet in Frankfurt which, at the request of Austria and by a majority of votes, decreed the mobilization of the federal army. As the Prussian contingents were not included in the mobilization order, it was clear that the measure was directed against Prussia. Bismarck thereupon declared that the Treaty of Gastein had been violated by Austria and that the mobilization also was a breach of the Federal Constitution. As a countermeasure, directed against Austria, Prussia then proposed a new German Confederation without Austria and called for the election of a German Parliament. These proposals were flatly rejected by the majority of the states represented at the Federal Diet.

Thus it seemed that an armed conflict between Prussia, on the one hand, and a majority of the German states, led by Austria, on the other, had become inevitable. But this development contained no element of surprise for Bismarck. Although he had possibly hoped for a certain measure of support from the smaller states, he was prepared for every eventuality.

The international scene seemed favorable for decisive action: Bismarck's previous diplomatic moves had gained him the friendship and secured the neutrality of Russia. England, interested as much as ever in the European balance of power, considered a strong Prussian state as a desirable counterpoise against the continental hegemony of France. Napoleon III, hoping to share in the spoils of the fratricidal German war, intimated that France's friendly neutrality could be bought, and Italy, eager to wrest Venetia from Austria, entered into a secret alliance with Prussia. From a military point of view the stage was likewise carefully set. While in numbers the opposing armies were almost evenly matched, the Prussians were able to rely on their superior discipline, equipment, and leadership.

Crown Prince Frederick and Prince Frederick Charles, commanding the main forces of the Prussian armies, executed their moves in perfect coordination with the carefully planned tactics of von Moltke, the chief of the general staff. In Austria, meanwhile, Ludwig von Benedek (1804–1881), a general of proven courage and ability in the Italian theater of war, only reluctantly accepted the supreme command of the northern armies. His unfamiliarity with the terrain and an ever present presentiment of impending doom contributed materially to the outcome of the struggle.

The essence of Moltke's strategy was lightning speed, aided by perfect teamwork. A union of the armed forces of the minor states aligned with Austria against Prussia had to be prevented. In June, 1866, after having quickly overrun Saxony, Hesse, and Hanover, the Prussian armies marched against Bavaria and the other states of the German South. The Bavarians and their allies were defeated and the cities of Frankfurt, Würzburg, and Nuremberg were taken.

Now the main Austrian forces, stationed in Bohemia, were simultaneously attacked by three Prussian armies that struck from Saxony, Lusatia, and Silesia. The Austrians lost the entire war in the decisive defeat at Königgrätz (July 3), and the victorious Prussians advanced simultaneously toward the Hungarian border and upon Vienna.

In the meantime, however, the Italians, attacking Austria from the south and attempting to seize Venetia, were defeated both on land and on the sea by vastly inferior Austrian forces. But these Austrian victories over Italy had no influence on the outcome of the struggle. The "German War," after having lasted for only seven weeks, was brought to a conclusion by the Truce of Nikolsburg and the subsequent Peace of Prague (August 23). Hostilities were ended just in time to prevent France and Russia from active intervention, as both powers began to show growing uneasiness in view of the amazing efficiency of the Prussian armies.

Bismarck's goal, the elimination of Austria from the affairs of Germany, had been achieved. He wanted no more and vigorously opposed the plan of King William to humiliate Austria by severe peace terms and to annex some of the Saxon provinces. It was the first time that Bismarck demonstrated the wisdom of moderation in victory, carefully refraining from engendering unnecessary bitterness and a desire for revenge in the heart of the enemy. We know from his memoirs that the nervous strain resulting from his heated arguments with the king made him think of retirement from the political scene and, for a brief moment, even of suicide. Only the generously offered moral support of the crown prince gave him the strength to persist in his efforts to make the king amenable to his own point of view.

In the Peace of Prague Austria acknowledged the dissolution of the "German Confederation" and consented to the reorganization of Germany under Prussian leadership. Italy, despite her military blunders, received Venetia as a reward for her participation in the war against Austria, and Prussia rounded out her frontiers and unified her territories by the annexation of Schleswig-Holstein, Hanover, Hesse-Cassel, Nassau, and the city of Frankfurt. The remaining states of northern Germany including Saxony formed with Prussia the North German Confederation (*Norddeutscher*

Bund). The southern German states — Bavaria, Wurtemberg, Baden, and
Hesse-Darmstadt — were persuaded by Bismarck to enter into secret
alliances with Prussia.

Austria, now strictly confined to her own German and non-German territorial possessions, adopted at last a number of liberal reforms which actually
strengthened her internal and international position. In 1867 Emperor
Francis Joseph granted his seventeen provinces a constitution that provided
for a bicameral parliamentary system of government. Hungary became a
semiautonomous kingdom within the dual empire of Austro-Hungary, the
Austrian emperor retaining his title of King of Hungary.

The victorious war of 1866 seemed to have vindicated also Bismarck's
domestic policies. He persuaded the king to conciliate the opposition in the
Prussian Diet. In a solemn speech from the throne William I admitted that
for several years the government had conducted the affairs of state in an
unconstitutional manner and asked for a parliamentary "indemnification"
of the public expenditures of the past four years. This "act of indemnity"
was passed by a substantial majority of votes. The split votes of the members
of the "Progressive Party" subsequently led to the secession of the right wing

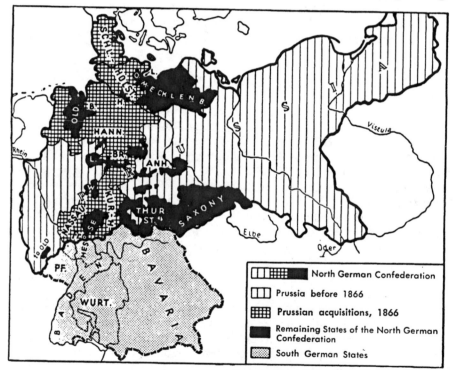

From *Der Grosse Herder*, Herder, Freiburg i. Br.

The North German Confederation.

Liberals, who formed the "National-Liberal" Party, from the intransigent left wing Liberals, who continued their opposition to Bismarck.

f) The North German Confederation. The twenty-one states of northern Germany that had joined the newly created North German Confederation recognized Prussia as their self-chosen leader. In the Federal Constitution, which in its essentials was framed by Bismarck himself and which was published in 1867, the king of Prussia held the hereditary office of president of the Federation. The executive power was vested in the federal chancellor and, to a limited degree, in a *"Reichstag"* (Federal Diet), representing the people and elected by universal manhood suffrage, and in a *Bundesrat* (Federal Council), representing the princes of the different member states. The *Staatenbund* (Federation of States) of the "German Confederation" of 1815 was thus transformed into a *Bundesstaat* (a unified and centralized "Federal State"). The king of Prussia, as president of the Confederation, was commander in chief of the federal army and appointed the federal chancellor, but he had no legislative and no veto power. Bismarck, the prime minister of Prussia, occupied also the post of the federal chancellor.

In this way Prussia had secured for herself the control of the army and of foreign affairs. The Prussian king dominated the *Bundesrat* by virtue of his prestige as a member of the Hohenzollern dynasty and as president of the Confederation. The *Bundesrat* itself was composed of forty-three members, seventeen of whom represented Prussia.

g) The Franco-Prussian War (1870–1871). Prussia's military victories and Bismarck's diplomatic successes at home and abroad had been viewed with growing apprehension by France. Ever since the time of Richelieu (cf. p. 289) it had been one of the aims of French politicians to prevent the rise of a strong and united empire across the Rhine. Napoleon III had remained inactive during the Danish War, chiefly because at that time a French army in Mexico was engaged in the phantastic scheme of establishing a Mexican empire under French protection, to be headed by Archduke Maximilian of Austria, a brother of Emperor Francis Joseph. This farcical adventure, sponsored by Napoleon III, had ended in tragedy when, after the conclusion of the American Civil War, the federal government in Washington seemed ready to deal by force of arms with this flagrant violation of the Monroe Doctrine. France withdrew her troops, and Archduke Maximilian was shot by Mexican insurgents.

In the "Seven Weeks' War" of 1866 Napoleon III again had abstained from active interference, partly because he had hoped for a prolonged conflict that would exhaust Prussia, and partly because he had expected to be paid for his neutrality by territorial compensations. Some broad hints in this connection had drawn evasive responses from Bismarck, until Napoleon, in the summer of 1866, demanded more specifically part of the left bank of the Rhine, including the city of Mainz. It was then that Bismarck categorically refused to cede even one inch of German territory, using simultaneously Napoleon's demands for territorial compensations to arouse the southern German states against France. Napoleon had no better luck when he tried in 1867 to purchase Luxembourg from the Netherlands and to extend French influence into Belgium by a proposal to buy up the Belgian railroad system. Both states were backed in their resistance to these demands not only by Bismarck but also by the governments of England and Russia.

These repeated setbacks in his foreign undertakings added to the growing unpopularity of Napoleon's regime at home. The French Liberals and Republicans had never forgotten the *coup d'état* to which the Second Empire owed its existence, and their opposition in Parliament and in the country at large became more and more vociferous. The monarchists, on the other hand, felt that the waning prestige of the Empire could only be retrieved by a striking success in the field of foreign affairs. And they were convinced that nothing could do more to regain for the emperor the sympathies of the French people than the humiliation and diplomatic defeat of Prussia.

Napoleon, with his armies newly equipped and brought up to full striking power, believed himself equal to the task of checking any further ambitions of the Prussian upstart, by means of intimidation and an impressive show of France's armed strength. Although he had no doubt that the French army was superior to that of Prussia, Napoleon was on the lookout for possible allies in the eventuality of an armed conflict. But secret negotiations with Austria and Italy yielded no positive results. Austria certainly remembered the day of Königgrätz but neither had she forgotten that Napoleon had been instrumental in depriving her of Lombardy. The Italians still resented the way in which Napoleon had acquired Savoy and Nice and the part played more recently (1867) by the French garrison in Rome, where the French had prevented Italian nationalists from wresting the Eternal City from the hands of the papacy. There still remained to Napoleon the hope for the sympathies and possibly the active support of the German South, whose anti-Prussian sentiments had manifested themselves in the past and were still taken for granted, Napoleon naturally being unaware of the secret commitments of these states to come to the aid of Prussia.

Bismarck knew that he held most of the trump cards in his own hands. In a war with France, which he believed unavoidable and for which he therefore worked deliberately, he could count on the armed support of the German South and on the neutrality of the European powers. He foresaw that such a war would irresistibly draw together all the provinces and peoples of Germany and that the anticipated victory would be crowned by the achievement of national unity.

Relations between Prussia and Russia were still friendly, and the dynasties of England and Prussia had aided a rapprochement of their two nations by the marriage of the daughter of Queen Victoria to the crown prince of Prussia. Furthermore, England intensely disliked Napoleon's attempted meddling in the affairs of Belgium.

The Prussian general staff had worked out its strategic plans in every detail and with the utmost precision. The armed forces, including the trained reserves, could be brought to full war strength at the shortest notice, and thus diplomatically and militarily Prussia had reached a state of complete preparedness.

Sooner than he had expected an opportunity seemed to present itself to Napoleon to earn some inexpensive laurels by administering to Prussia a diplomatic rebuff and thus putting her in her place. In 1869 the Spanish throne had been vacated by revolution and the Spaniards had offered the crown to Prince Leopold of the house of Hohenzollern-Sigmaringen, a member of the Catholic branch of the Hohenzollerns and a distant relative of the king of Prussia. Immediately the French government raised a great hue and cry, conjuring up the ghosts of the Austrian-Spanish Hapsburgs and painting all the horrors of a prospective dual Spanish-Prussian monarchy of the Hohenzollerns. For Bismarck the knowledge that the candidature of Prince Leopold was disagreeable to France was a good enough reason to support it, and while King William, anxious to preserve the peace, tried to persuade the prince to decline the Spanish offer, the prime minister behind the scenes used all his influence to secure the acceptance of the candidacy.

When Prince Leopold finally announced that he did not consider himself a candidate for the Spanish throne, the international tension relaxed considerably and Napoleon could have cherished an important diplomatic success. But by listening to the advice of the imperialist extremists in the French cabinet, the French emperor committed the greatest folly of his political career and worked directly into the hands of Bismarck.

In July, 1870, it became known that Napoleon, through the French ambassador to Prussia, had demanded of King William a formal pledge that never in the future would he give his consent to a revival of the Hohenzollern claims to the Spanish throne. The king of Prussia, in an angry mood, asked that Bismarck be informed by wire of the French demands and of William's negative answer. The message was sent to Bismarck from the spa of Ems, where the king was taking the waters, and the Prussian prime minister did not fail to make the most of this incident. He re-edited the dispatch, and made it, by means of several condensations and omissions, to use Moltke's approving words, "sound like a fanfare." In this revised version the "Ems Dispatch" appeared to the Prussians as a gross insult to their king and to the French as an intentional slight of their ambassador. Napoleon's answer was a declaration of war (July 19). Four days earlier, Emile Ollivier, the French prime minister, had declared in the Chamber of Deputies that the French government viewed the imminence of an armed conflict with Prussia "with a light heart."

Bismarck's foresight now reaped its rewards: the German princes immediately rallied to the support of Prussia, placing their armies under the command of the Prussian general staff. Napoleon faced a united Germany whose peoples had forgotten all their political, social, and tribal differences.

Almost overnight Germany had acquired a national will and a national physiognomy.

The nominal commander in chief of the German armies was the king of Prussia, but all military movements and operations were directed by the strategic genius of Helmuth von Moltke. He had divided his forces into three large sectors: a central army under the command of Prince Frederick Charles, a northern right wing under General von Steinmetz, and a southern left wing, consisting of South German contingents, under the crown prince of Prussia.

Six weeks after the start of hostilities a French army of 86,000 men, with the emperor in their midst, were forced to surrender at Sedan (September 2). Two days later the Second Empire of France collapsed and a republican provisional government of National Defense, headed by the French lawyer Gambetta, was proclaimed in Paris. A second French army of almost 200,000 men under the command of Marshal Bazaine was compelled to withdraw to the Moselle fortress of Metz and surrendered after a short siege (October 27). In the meantime, the German armies had marched into the heart of France and had encircled the French capital. Paris offered heroic resistance, but after four months the beleaguered city was finally forced to surrender on January 28, 1871.

A newly elected French National Assembly, convening at Bordeaux, chose Adolphe Thiers, a veteran French statesman and twice prime minister under Louis Philippe, as executive head of the French Republic (1871–1873). He crushed an attempt of the radical "Commune" to establish a socialist regime in France and conducted the negotiations that led to the preliminary peace agreements of February 26. Thirty thousand German troops had staged a symbolic occupation of part of the French capital but were withdrawn after the French National Assembly had accepted the preliminary peace terms.

The final peace treaty was signed at Frankfurt on May 10, 1871. If Bismarck's counsel had prevailed in the peace settlement with France as it had in 1866 in the peace treaty with Austria, the terms would have been severe but would have inflicted no incurable wounds to French pride and self-esteem. He would have been satisfied with a substantial indemnity and the cession of Alsace, the majority of whose population was German in language and cultural tradition. But this time Bismarck was overruled by the men of the army. Without consulting the wishes of their populations the provinces of Alsace and part of Lorraine were annexed by Germany and incorporated into the Prussian system of administration. Administrative autonomy was withheld from both provinces until 1918, and during all these years the Prussian government by a series of psychological mistakes kept alive popular resentment and tried to whip the provinces into line by coercion and intimidation. In addition to these territorial losses France had to agree to German occupation of her key fortresses, until the war indemnity of five billion francs (about one billion dollars) were paid in full. French thrift succeeded in paying off this debt in the surprisingly short time of two years, and in autumn, 1873, the German army of occupation was withdrawn.

The Creation of the Second German Empire. With the defeat of France Bismarck's "policy of blood and iron" had achieved its final triumph. Even before the surrender of Paris the political unification of Germany had become an accomplished fact. In the Peace of Frankfurt France dealt not with Prussia alone but with a resurrected German empire.

The negotiations with the southern states had begun soon after the battle of Sedan. To overcome the hesitations of Bavaria and Wurtemberg, Bismarck declared himself willing to grant these two largest states of the south certain constitutional privileges, chief among which were independent military administration in time of peace and a partially independent railroad, postal, telegraph, and telephone system. The treaties concerning the admission of the southern states into the united empire were signed in November and December, 1870. On behalf of the German princes King Louis II of Bavaria asked King William I of Prussia to accept the hereditary imperial title and therewith the leadership of the German nation. A delegation of the North German *Reichstag* presented the same request on behalf of the people. Before his final acceptance the king had to be persuaded by Bismarck to desist from his original demand of becoming "Emperor of Germany" and to be satisfied with the title of "German Emperor." It was Bismarck's calculation that this latter title was less provocative to the susceptibilities of the minor German princes and might make it easier for them to relinquish part of their sovereignty.

The solemn proclamation of King William I of Prussia as "German Emperor" took place in the Hall of Mirrors of Louis XIV's palace of Versailles, on January 18, 1871. The king's declaration of acceptance was read by Bismarck and contained the following memorable passage: "We accept the imperial dignity, hoping that the German people will be allowed to enjoy the reward of their enthusiastic and unselfish fight in a lasting peace. . . . But to us and our successors may God grant that we be at all times augmenters of the German Empire, not by war and conquest, but by the blessings and gifts of peace, in the welfare and moral greatness of the nation."

The Imperial Constitution ("Reichsverfassung"). The second German Empire was a centralized *Bundesstaat,* dominated by Prussia, which occupied by far the largest territory with almost two thirds of the population of the new Germany. The Empire comprised four kingdoms (Prussia, Bavaria, Wurtemberg, Saxony), six grand duchies, five duchies, seven principalities, three free cities (Hamburg, Bremen, Lübeck), and the territories (*Reichslande*) of Alsace-Lorraine.

The political structure of the Empire rested juridically on the new *Reichsverfassung* which, with few alterations, followed the pattern of the Constitution proposed by the Frankfurt Parliament in 1849 (cf. p. 530 sq.) and the Constitution of the North German Confederation (cf. p. 542). The sovereign rulers of the different states were represented in the *Bundesrat* (Federal Council), a kind of imperial senate, whose members held their offices by princely appointment, not by popular election. In this body Prussia had seventeen votes out of a total of fifty-eight. The representatives of the people, chosen by universal manhood suffrage, formed the *Reichstag*, whose legislative powers, however, were limited by the prerogatives of the *Kaiser*, the *Reichskanzler*, and the *Bundesrat*. The *Reichskanzler*, the appointee of the *Kaiser*, appointed in turn his collaborators in the different governmental offices. The chancellor was responsible only to the emperor and could be removed from office only by imperial decree. Thus it is quite evident that while the governmental system of the Second German Empire was constitutional and representative it was not parliamentary. The *Reichsverfassung* was not as reactionary as the Constitution of Prussia, but it differed even more widely from the democratic parliamentary rule in France, England, or the United States of America, with their far-reaching control of the legislative and executive branches of government.

The political parties in the new *Reichstag* were the same that had functioned before in the individual states and in the North German Confederation. The "Conservatives" were recruited chiefly from state officials and the holders of landed property. The "Liberals," comprising the "national-liberal" monarchists and the "progressive" democrats, were advocates of *"laissez-faire"* and unlimited competition in economics and of "secularism" (freedom from church influence) in politics, culture, and education. The "Center-Party" (seated in the center of the chamber, between Conservatives and Liberals) was originally founded in Prussia (1852) and was reorganized on a national basis by Ludwig Windthorst in 1871. A politico-religious party, it proclaimed the defense of Christian principles in political and social life as well as in education, and it represented especially the interests of the organizations and institutions of German Catholics. The seats on the extreme left of the *Reichstag* were occupied by the "Social-Democrats," the more or less radical disciples of Karl Marx, Friedrich Engels, and Ferdinand Lassalle. Their anticapitalist, pacifist, and internationalist creed as well as their adherence to materialism and atheism placed them in opposition to all the other parties of the Diet, but their gospel of social compassion and of the redemption of the masses from want and social degradation, together with the ability of some of their leaders, gained many converts to their cause and, fortified in their determination by persecution and repression, their party experienced a phenomenal growth during the following decades.

The political unification of Germany was followed by the adoption of a uniform criminal and civil law code (*Strafgesetzbuch, StGB,* 1871) and uniform commercial and industrial legislation, while the administration of justice and the judiciary, with the exception of the Supreme Court (*Reichsgericht,* 1879) in Leipzig, were relegated to the authority of the individual states. The introduction of uniform weights and measures, based on the decimal and metric system, and of a uniform system of currency (the German "Mark," 1871–1924) based on the gold standard, were among the lasting achievements of the reorganized *Zollverein* (cf. p. 513 sq.) of 1868.

B. *INDUSTRIAL REVOLUTION, TECHNOLOGY, AND THE NATURAL SCIENCES*

Men and Machines. In the course of the nineteenth century the European mind experienced an evolution so far reaching in its effects that it left its indelible mark on all modern nations and their cultures. The dynamic activism inherent in the Western belief in cultural and scientific progress had been greatly strengthened by both the rationalist and empiricist trends of the preceding centuries, as also by the neo-humanist cult of the human personality and its self-sufficiency. Lord Bacon's (1561–1626) slogan, "Knowledge is Power," provided the cue for the unprecedented and unparalleled development of industry, technology, and science which characterizes the civilization of the "machine age."

The machine seemed to promise an ardently desired enlargement of the human ego, permitting an extension of human forces into the external world of matter and leading at last to a complete sovereignty of man over inorganic and organic nature. The machine was expected to create more favorable living conditions for all by overcoming the limitations of space and time and by placing within the reach of everyone a multitude of material goods and unheard-of satisfactions.

a) England and the "Industrial Revolution." The country in which the spirit of the new age achieved its first triumphs was England. Here several historic circumstances worked together to lay the foundations for the development of modern industrialism. In the second half of the eighteenth century Great Britain began to reap the fruits of the flourishing colonial empire which she had acquired by the exploits of war and diplomacy. The parliamentary system of government had prevented the establishment of princely absolutism and militarism in the British Isles and had strengthened in the ruling classes the spirit of personal initiative and free commercial enterprise. While the continental states went through a series of destructive wars and economic crises, England's insular position made her practically invulnerable to foreign attack and enabled her to live through the era of the French Revolution and the Napoleonic wars (1789–1815) in relative political and economic stability and thus to prepare herself to become the great arsenal of the industrial capitalism of the nineteenth century. Hence, the decisive changes in the methods of production, in the technical exploitation of the forces of nature, and in the utilization and evaluation of human labor that are commonly associated with the "Industrial Revolution" were first made effective on English soil.

b) Capitalist Industrialism. Up to the latter part of the eighteenth century the technical mastery of nature and its resources had hardly progressed beyond the conditions prevailing from the days of antiquity, and correspondingly the general standards of human life, of comfort, occupation, and recreation were essentially unchanged. The peasantry still comprised by far the largest aggregate number of workers and producers. The majority of the townspeople were still artisans engaged in their home industries and handicrafts, and the chief means of transportation and commercial communication were still the stagecoach and the sailing ship. Life in general was characterized by a relative economic stability resulting from the limitation of both needs and satisfactions.

All this changed almost overnight with the invention of machines and the concomitant advent of capitalist industrialism. Capitalism as such, to be sure, was much older than the industrial system, dating back in its beginnings to the later Middle Ages. But the combination of capital and mechanized industry, favoring the growth of a new money aristocracy on the one hand, and of a propertyless class of wage earners or proletarians on the other, was new. A huge concentration of wealth in the hands of a class of individual owners or of shareholders in various industrial enterprises tended to enthrone the industrial entrepreneurs as leaders of men and states. The labor-displacing machinery made for an increasing insecurity in the life of the workingman, for sharp and ruthless practices in the labor market, and the accompanying evils of unemployment and destitution.

c) The Factory System. Crowded together in the impersonal and unhealthy atmosphere of the factory, the laborers lost the artisans' pride in the quality of their work and became mere "hands" in the big mechanism of industrial mass production. Long working hours, starvation wages, and the employment of women and children added to the wretchedness of living conditions in the factory, frequently reducing human existence to a subhuman level. Various laws were passed in England and in some continental countries to mitigate the hardships and hazards of factory labor, until by the middle of the nineteenth century the worst abuses had been checked. But even these moderate improvements in the factory system were not achieved without violence. The workers, driven to desperation by hunger and destitution, tried to take their revenge on the despised machines that had brought ruin to their homes and families. Early in the nineteenth century the "machine wreckers" in England smashed the weaving frames and power looms in the factories, and in the forties the weavers in Prussian Silesia rose in revolt against their capitalist exploiters.*

The employers found comfort and a moral alibi for their ruthlessness in the *"laissez-faire"* doctrine of economic liberalism, especially in its contention that business and morality don't mix, and that the "survival

---

* For a dramatic account of these tragic events in Silesia, cf. Gerhart Hauptmann's moving play *The Weavers;* Ernst Toller's (cf. p. 729) expressionistic drama *The Machine Wreckers* treats of the revolt in the English factories.

of the fittest" is no less a law of economics than a law of nature. The factory owners were plainly not interested in the lot of their workers as persons but merely in their labor, which they bought, like any other commodity, at the lowest possible rate. When his labor was no longer needed, the workingman joined the ranks of the unemployed, and he and his family faced starvation. Those employers, moreover, who were imbued with the Calvinist teaching of "predestination" and "divine election," felt inclined to look upon poverty as a sign of God's disfavor and upon riches as an infallible proof of a person's being predestined for salvation.

The ideas of economic liberalism found their most formidable expression in such industrial centers as Manchester and Liverpool. Within a short span of time industrial production in these two cities experienced an almost fabulous expansion and the factory owners felt themselves as the executors of a historic and national mission. "Manchesterdom" (*Manchestertum*) became in all European countries a symbol of unlimited industrial competition and of the principle of Free Trade.

d) Flight From the Land. The industrial civilization of the nineteenth and early twentieth century developed into a civilization of city dwellers, marked by the rapid and unnatural growth of big urban centers and a general flight from the land. The big city, with its factories, its educational, cultural, and recreational facilities, and its social and economic opportunities, promised work, advancement, and increasing personal independence. But relatively few of those who were attracted by these allurements were able to enjoy any of the privileges and advantages of city life. The vast majority were forced to spend their lives in overcrowded tenements, in hovels and slums, divorced not only from nature and the soil but shut off from air and sunlight as well. The big city of the nineteenth century was a motley agglomeration of buildings, hastily constructed for reasons of commercial profit, without planning and due regard for the exigencies of nature and the needs of man. It was without beauty and utterly devoid of any distinctive personal or national physiognomy. Many of the new industrial settlements arose in the immediate neighborhood of coalpits, ore deposits, or canals, and the beauty of many historical sites and landmarks was marred or destroyed forever by the tyrannical forces of industry and technology.

In Germany the movement of population into the large industrial centers began about the middle of the nineteenth century. It was indicative of the transformation of the country from an agricultural into an industrial nation. In 1871, 63.9 per cent of the German population were still living in rural districts; in 1895 the percentage had dropped to 50.1; in 1910, to 39.98; and in 1925, to 35.6.

Before long, however, the migration to the city was followed by a flight back to nature. Out of disillusionment and disappointment was born the protest against the artificiality of city life and against the inhumanity of its soulless industrialism. From John Ruskin (1819–1900) and William Morris (1834–1896) to Leo Tolstoi (1828–1910), Eric Gill (1882–1940), and

Mahatma Gandhi (1869–1948) the call for a return to the simple and natural modes of life, for the lost virtues of the artisan, and for a revival of the home industries, as voiced by sensitive artists, writers, and astute reformers, steadily gained in passionate intensity. The German *Wandervogel* and Youth Movement (cf. p. 708 sq.) of the early twentieth century as well as the attempts to revive the folk arts and folk traditions owe their origin to a generally felt impulse to rediscover the beauty of nature and the sanity of natural habits in a seemingly disenchanted and barren world. In the form of *Schrebergärten* (so named after Daniel Schreber [1808–1861], a German orthopedic physician), located at the outskirts of industrial cities and providing small patches of arable land for the laboring and middle classes, or in the form of artistically planned labor colonies, the "back to the land movement" entered the very precincts of the city itself.

e) The Age of Coal and Iron. The "Industrial Revolution" began in England in the latter part of the eighteenth century with the invention of improved methods for the mechanical production of cotton fabrics, for the weaving of silks and woolens, and the knitting of hosiery and lace. A spinning machine, for example, as constructed by Samuel Crompton in 1779, was capable of equaling the work of two hundred manual laborers. As a result England's imports of raw cotton had reached in 1810 the staggering amount of 120 million pounds a year, four times as much as she had imported in 1790. In the relatively peaceful years of the *Vormärz* (1815–1848) the new textile machinery gradually gained a foothold on the European continent, notably in France and Belgium. But the most decisive innovations in machine construction were brought about in those industries that worked with iron and coal, the two most important raw materials of the industrial era. By freeing iron from its ore, and by subjecting it to the processes of smelting and casting, the Industrial Revolution won some of its greatest victories. The traditional building materials of wood, leather, and hemp were replaced by iron, steel, and wire. Similarly the new coal industry revolutionized the older methods of generating heat, light, and power: coke and coal were henceforth used in place of wood, peat, fat, and wax.

Transportation and Communication. Among the nations of the Old and New World only Germany and the United States had accessible coal and iron deposits comparable with those of Great Britain. Germany, however, was prevented by unfavorable political and economic conditions from competing with the industrial development of England, and the United States remained in part dependent on European industry as long as the exploitation of her vast resources was retarded by the sparseness of her population. In England the year 1769, in which James Watt (1736–1819) obtained the patent for his newly invented steam engine, is usually regarded as the beginning date of her Industrial Revolution, though it took nearly half a century until the epochal significance of this invention was fully realized and its productive capacity utilized. The use of this new mechanized source of power supply for railroad and steamship transportation transcended eventually in its effects all national boundary lines and created in the modern world a slowly growing consciousness of the economic interdependence of all nations.

a) Steamships. When the American engineer Robert Fulton (1765–1815) demonstrated on the river Seine his experimental steamboat to Napoleon I, the French emperor showed great enthusiasm and expressed his conviction that this invention would "change the face of the earth." In 1807 Fulton's paddle-wheeled steamboat *Claremont,* equipped with one of Watt's steam engines, successfully completed its first cruise on the Hudson River. In 1819 the steamboat *Savannah* crossed the Atlantic Ocean from New York to Liverpool. The first cruise in 1816 of an English steam-propelled ship without masts, sails, and rudders to the Rhenish city of Cologne caused a great sensation on the European continent. A few years later a regular weekly steamship traffic was established between Rotterdam and Cologne. In 1825 several steamship companies were organized in the Rhineland, and in 1829 the shipbuilding yard of Ruhrort was founded. Regular steamship traffic on the Danube was inaugurated by the "Danubian Steamship Company" (*Donau-Dampfschiffahrts-Gesellschaft*) in 1831. The *Kölner Dampfschleppschiffahrtsgesellschaft* (Steam-Towage Company of Cologne), founded in 1841, specialized in the construction of huge tugboats made of sheet iron and handling most of the goods traffic on the Rhine. Two new trade routes from the Rhine to the Atlantic Ocean were created by the construction of the French Rhine-Rhone Canal and the Rhine-Marne Canal, linking the Rhenish lowlands with the French ports of Marseille and Le Havre.

In the forties of the nineteenth century the paddle steamer was replaced by the screw steamer, an innovation that aided in speeding up the development of overseas steamship traffic. The first steamship line between Bremen and the New World, financed with American capital, was established in 1847, and in the same year the Hamburg-America line (*Hapag*) was founded. The Congress of Vienna had restored Hamburg's privileges as a "Free City" and had thereby greatly stimulated the commercial initiative and the pioneering spirit of the patrician merchants of this proud city-republic, which from then on contributed more than its share to the expanding world trade of the industrial era.

Ever since the rise of England as a colonial power both Hamburg and Bremen had served as the German entrance gates of British commerce and British ideas, and the Hamburg merchants in particular were among the most outspoken advocates of Free Trade policies. In the twenties of the nineteenth century the city of Bremen succeeded in obtaining a strip of land from the neighboring state of Hanover, and in 1827 it established the new port of Bremerhaven at the mouth of the Geeste River. In 1857 the North German Lloyd was founded, the second of the great German transocean lines. Its central administrative offices were located in Bremen, and both Bremen and Bremerhaven offered their port facilities to the incoming and outgoing steamship traffic.

b) Telegraph and Telephone. The revolutionary changes brought about by steam-propelled traffic on land and on the sea were supplemented and completed by the invention of telegraph and telephone, the new means of communication. The so-called "optical telegraph" had been constructed as early as 1793 by the Frenchman Claude Chappe and had proven its usefulness in the service of the revolutionary "National Convent" as well as in the campaigns of Napoleon I. The "optical telegraph" was used for the transmission of messages by means of light signals, and it served almost exclusively the purposes of governmental administration and military strategy.

In 1809 the German physician and mathematician *von Sömmering* (1775–1830) demonstrated before the Bavarian Academy of Sciences "a new little telegraphic machine," which for the first time used electricity for long-distance communication. Sömmering's invention was further developed and improved by the mathematician *Karl Friedrich Gauss* (1777–1855) and the physicist *Wilhelm Eduard Weber* (1804–1891), two German scholars who in 1833 established electrical telegraphic communication between the physical institute and the observatory of the University of Göttingen. The transposition of telegraphic signals into alphabetic symbols was first attempted in 1837 by the German physicist and industrialist *August von Steinheil* and by the English physicist *Charles Wheatstone.* One year later the American inventor *Samuel Morse* obtained a patent for an improved system of electrical telegraphy, the practical value of which was increased by the creation of the "Morse Alphabet." These inventions made it possible for *Werner von Siemens* (1816–1892), a German industrialist and electrical engineer, to build the important state telegraph systems connecting Berlin with the cities of Frankfurt and Cologne, to develop the technics of electrical weak currents, and to become the leading electro-technical industrialist of Europe.

The invention of the telephone (German: *Fernsprecher*) was first conceived of in a rudimentary form by the German schoolteacher *Philipp Reis* in 1861 and was afterward (1872) developed into a practical system of long-distance communication by the English physiologist *Alexander Graham Bell* (1847–1922).

German Industry. In 1765 the Italian popular philosopher Antonio Genovesi, a disciple of Christian Wolff (cf. p. 360), had ventured the prediction that the productive capacity of German trade and commerce would never equal that of England and France. This remained true until the middle of the nineteenth century. But as soon as Germany began to comprehend realistically the new problems presented by the Industrial Revolution, she pushed ahead with typical Germanic thoroughness and tenacity.

Germany was rich in ore and coal deposits and her people had learned discipline of thought and work in the schools and in the army. These acquired habits were complemented by an inborn talent for organization and administration.

The first German industrialist who succeeded in competing successfully with England in the field of machine construction was *August Borsig,* who opened his Berlin railway plant in 1837. Only a few years later Borsig's locomotives not only matched the English machines in speed and power but were actually superior to them. Similar advances were made in the textile industries. The trade of the ancient weaver guilds of Augsburg, for instance, which could take just pride in a long and honored tradition, experienced a revival on the basis of modern capitalist industrialism, a development that carried with it, however, the extinction of the trade and labor concepts of the guilds as such.

The rapidly increasing manufacture of cotton, superseding the time-honored production of linen and woolen goods, was partly responsible for the impoverishment of the linen weavers in Silesia and in other German provinces. It was the linen industry that suffered most severely from the effects of the Industrial Revolution in Germany, and both spinners and weavers felt the full impact of the advancing machine age.

The most impressive accomplishments of the German iron and steel industries are associated with the name of *Friedrich Krupp* (1787–1826) in Essen in the Rhineland and with the work of his son *Alfred* (1812–1887) and his grandson *Friedrich Alfred* (1854–1902). It had been Friedrich's ambition to manufacture a type of cast steel that was to equal if not to surpass in quality the English product. He succeeded at the cost of great personal sacrifices, but lack of funds forced him to close down his newly acquired iron foundry in Altenessen. When he died at the age of 39, his widow and four children were left on the verge of starvation. But on his deathbed he had bequeathed the secret of the production of cast steel to his eldest son Alfred, who was then fourteen years of age. The younger Krupp, confronted with the task of supporting his family and of settling his father's debts, worked his way to success through untold hardships and privations.

Banking and Big Business. With the increasing emphasis on the profit motive in production and business and with the expansion of the capitalist credit system, banking acquired a new significance in financial transactions. The big banking or moneylending institutions date back in their origins to the later Middle Ages and the Renaissance (cf. p. 244 sqq.), but their development in the nineteenth century is characterized by a new factor, namely, the fusion of banking and industrial interests.

The wars of the seventeenth and eighteenth centuries had played into the hands of the Jewish money-changers and moneylenders, who had made themselves indispensable to the absolutistic princes. Even in the first half of the nineteenth century the rulers of states and principalities were depending in their financial enterprises on their "court Jews" (*Hofjuden*) or "court bankers." In the age of Metternich most of the Jewish court bankers of Austria were baronized, although they were still deprived of citizenship.

The most influential of these Jewish banking concerns was the House of Rothschild, whose founder, Meyer Amschel Rothschild (1743–1812), a petty moneylender of the city of Frankfurt, had made his fortune by obtaining government contracts for war supplies during the "Coalition Wars" that followed the French Revolution of 1789. Meyer Amschel's five sons represented the firm in its branch offices in Frankfurt, Vienna, London, Paris, and Naples. During the Napoleonic wars one of the brothers acted as adviser to the French emperor, while the one in charge of the house in London worked hand in hand with the British. When Meyer Amschel died in 1812 he knew that the financial power of his firm had become equally indispensable to both sides in the armed conflict. The founder of the House of Rothschild had regarded it as absolutely essential for financial success to remain politically detached but at the same time to back financially the prevailing sentiments and the political course of the most powerful groups in the different states. Thus when Napoleon's downfall appeared unavoidable, the Rothschild brothers immediately shifted their allegiance to the cause of the Allies and took charge of the shipment of English subsidies to the European continent. After 1815 they lent their financial support to the policies of Metternich and to the forces of the Restoration movement.

Within a bare two decades the family of an obscure moneylender of the Frankfurt Ghetto had risen to a position of international prominence. In 1822 the Austrian Rothschilds were given a patent of nobility. In the early years of the machine age the Viennese and Paris branches financed the Austrian, French, and Belgian railroad systems, but otherwise the Rothschilds refrained from engaging in industrial enterprise.

The first German banks with large capital investments in industrial concerns were the *Schaafhausensche Bankverein* in Cologne (founded in 1848) and the *Bank für Handel und Industrie* (Bank for Trade and Industry) in Darmstadt (founded in 1853). In the second half of the nineteenth century the union of capital and industry led to the formation of large concerns, in which several individual enterprises were collectively organized in the form of huge impersonal corporations, syndicates, and trusts with divided responsibility and limited liability, the individual shareholders hiding under the name of a corporative firm. The capital amassed in some big banking or industrial concerns soon began to wield a power that was all the greater as it was exercised by those who controlled the allotment of credit and therewith the very life source of production. This concentration of money power in the hands of small groups of financial and industrial wizards tended to extend the influence of economic interests over the entire state, its domestic and foreign policies, and into the broad field of international relations, resulting alternately in extreme economic nationalism and international economic imperialism.

In the course of time the multifarious interrelations of industrial and financial interests began to form an intricate web of mutual technico-economic dependencies, superimposing themselves on the traditional manners and customs of life and work and threatening the preservation of the inherited types of national culture. Countless millions in all countries became more and more dependent on the fluctuating price levels of the world market, and the masses began to curse an economic system which produced want in the midst of plenty. The increasing social unrest called for an antidote, and the unbridled ambitions of capitalist industrialism found themselves challenged by the militant forces of socialism and the incipient "revolt of the masses."

Capitalism and Socialism. The fact that the ownership of the means of production and the accumulation of capital provided the employer class with both economic security and political power, while at the same time it forced the masses of wage earners into economic and political servitude, created a growing class consciousness among the dispossessed and led first to the formation of defensive organizations and finally to a violent counter-thrust of the aroused "proletariat"* against capitalist exploitation.

a) Trade Unionism. The earliest manifestation of these combinations of labor groups was the movement of trade unionism, which originated as a direct sequel of the Industrial Revolution and which fought for the right of labor to organize for the purpose of obtaining shorter working hours, improved working conditions, and higher wages. The struggle of the trade unions for recognition was hard and prolonged. They were first fully legalized in England in 1871, while in Germany they were at best reluctantly tolerated but not officially recognized as representative workers' organizations until 1918.**

b) The Socialist and Communist Movement. The majority of trade unionists entered into an ideological and practical alliance with the socialist doctrines of *Karl Marx* (1818–1883), and *Friedrich Engels* (1820–1895). Marx was a German-Jewish economist who, after having joined in the revolutionary movements of 1849, and after having been expelled from continental Europe, had settled in London. There he continued his activities as a publicist, in close collaboration with Friedrich Engels, who had gone through similar experiences and had likewise found refuge in England. Both men were strongly influenced by the dialectical philosophy of Hegel (cf. p. 502 sqq.) and the anthropological materialism of Ludwig Feuerbach (1804–1872), who was himself a member of the "Young Hegelian" school (cf. p. 505). Marx and Engels had subjected the capitalist system of economy to a keen and penetrating analysis and published their conclusions in programmatic form in the *Communist Manifesto* (1848).

---

* The term "proletariat" (from Latin, *proles* = "progeny") was originally used in ancient Rome to designate those citizens who had no money with which to pay taxes and therefore had to place the working capacity of their children at the disposal of the state.

** The socialistic *"Hirsch-Duncker"* and "Free" trade unions of Germany were organized in the sixties of the nineteenth century. The foundation of the interdenominational "Christian Trade Unions" was prompted by the desire to counteract the antireligious tendencies of the Marxist unions. The first German "Christian Trade Union" was founded in 1894.

In 1841 Feuerbach had published his *Essence of Christianity* (*Das Wesen des Christentums*), followed by the *Essence of Religion* (*Das Wesen der Religion*) in 1845. In both works the erstwhile student of theology had maintained that God and the entire realm of the supernatural were a creation of man's hopes and fears: man was not created in the image and likeness of God, but God was created in the image and likeness of man. If man would achieve happiness, Feuerbach claimed, he must not search for it above himself but within himself: theology must be transformed into anthropology.

Marx and Engels greeted this materialistic anthropologism as a sort of revelation, and their trained historical sense traced the beginnings of modern materialism back to the philosophy of Nominalism (cf. p. 142). "Materialism," wrote Engels, "is the natural-born son of Great Britain. . . . Nominalism, the first form of materialism, is chiefly found among the English schoolmen [of the Middle Ages]." And Lenin, the leader of the communist revolution in Russia, described Marxism as a synthesis of German philosophy, English political economy, and French socialism.

The quintessence of the socialist-materialist doctrines as developed by Marx and Engels and presented first in the *Communist Manifesto,* and later on in Marx's *Das Kapital* (1867), is the conviction that "it is not consciousness that determines life, but life that determines consciousness," that "the mode of production . . . conditions the social, political, and spiritual life in general," and that "the history of society is the history of the class struggle." The new materialistic philosophy of history implied in these statements visualized historic evolution as a series of civil wars, culminating in the Industrial Revolution of the nineteenth century. The modern class struggle between capital and labor, employers and wage earners, "bourgeoisie" and "proletariat," was a process of social evolution and interaction that followed the laws of material and biological evolution. Modern mankind was divided by Karl Marx into capitalist "proprietors" and "expropriated" proletarians, and the warfare between these two groups was to end with the "expropriation of the exproprietors."

The class struggle, therefore, was seen by Marx not as an end in itself but as a means to the elimination of classes and class privileges, leading eventually to the abolition of national boundaries and the establishment of the universal co-operative State. There was no doubt in the mind of Karl Marx as to the inevitability of this immanent movement of the "dialectic" of economic forces toward the desired goal. On the day when the means of production would be concentrated in the hands of a few capitalist owners, capitalism would have dug its own grave, and a class-conscious international proletariat would stand ready to take over the system of industrial production and organize the redistribution of wealth with a view to the welfare of all.

While the socialistic theory of Marx and Engels describes the ultimate realization of the ideal proletarian commonwealth as resulting from a necessary evolutionary process, it is admitted that the dictatorial assumption of political power by the workers and the armed repulsion of the forces of counterrevolution might become mandatory during the period of transition and readjustment. The violent overthrow of governments and of the established social order was not compatible with the teachings of historical and dialectical materialism and was consequently not explicitly advocated by Marx and Engels themselves. It was rather advocated by some of their more radical and less philosophically minded disciples and by the protagonists of syndicalism and anarchism of the later nineteenth and early twentieth centuries.

Socialism and communism were united in their antagonism to the institution of private property, in their demand for the socialization of the means of production, and in their protest against the enslavement of human beings by the misuse of the privileges of ownership. In the writings of Marx and Engels the two terms were used almost synonymously. Gradually, however, the term communism came to be generally understood as an extreme form of Marxian socialism. It denoted the increasing emphasis on the more violent aspects of the class struggle and the clamor for the dictatorship of the proletariat, including the demand for the general socialization of economic goods, of articles of production as well as of articles of consumption. In the perfect communistic society the welfare of the individual was to be subordinated to the thoroughly rationalized economic and political mechanism of the proletarian Society, in which economic and social forces claimed such absolute supremacy as to leave little room for the cultivation of moral and cultural values.

Socialization or communization of property had been advocated many times before the advent of the machine age, either in political blueprints for the establishment of an ideal State, such as Plato's *Republic* or Thomas More's *Utopia,* or in communistically organized religious sects (Waldenses, Albigenses, Anabaptists, etc.) and monastic orders. It will also be remembered that common ownership of the soil was the rule in early Germanic times (cf. p. 8). But most of these communistic schemes of an earlier age were limited to one state or region or they were proposed and executed on a religious and voluntary basis, whereas Marxist communism called for a compulsory and world-wide system of socialization. It was to be brought about by a society that had first to be thoroughly secularized and whose social outlook was to be determined by the adoption of the materialistic creed.*

---

* A redistribution of property to combat the evils and social injustices of both communist and capitalist systems is advocated today by the so-called "distributists" (Chesterton, Belloc, etc.), who reject the idea of State ownership and on the contrary demand the widest possible distribution of privately owned property, restoring the means of production to the individual workers. This program seems to be in essential agreement with the social ideas advanced by the French "Jacobins" as well as with those of Thomas Jefferson, who envisaged a solution of the social problem by the creation of a community of landowning small farmers. The British artist and writer Eric Gill cites the following reasons for the restoration of property to individuals:

Small, voluntary social communities, based on the principle of co-operation, somewhat analogous to the religious communist organizations of the past and present, were favored by the French school of social reformers (Cabet, Fourier, Saint-Simon, etc.) in the early nineteenth century. Some of the socialistic ideas of the highly talented and romantically inclined *Ferdinand Lassalle* (1825–1864), German-Jewish social philosopher and political agitator, were well received even by such conservative leaders as Bishop von Ketteler (cf. p. 600 sq.) and Otto von Bismarck (cf. p. 535). Lassalle formulated the program of the "German Workers' Union" (*Allgemeiner deutscher Arbeiterverein*) and thus became the founder of the first German socialist party (1863). His proposed "productive associations" of workers under the protectorship of the State amounted to a moderate form of State socialism. Although Lassalle's theories were rejected by the orthodox Marxists, the merger of his "Workers' Union" with the radical Marxist party organization of *Wilhelm Liebknecht* in 1875 resulted in the formation of the united Social Democratic Party in Germany.

c) The "International." The common international aims of the socialist workers of Europe found their constitutional and organizational representation in the "First International" (London, 1864), whose statutes had been drawn up by Karl Marx himself. After factional disputes had led to its dissolution in 1876, the "Second International" was founded in 1889. In 1907 a radical minority, advocating the instigation of civil wars and headed by Lenin and Rosa Luxemburg (cf. p. 646), seceded from the more moderate majority. World War I brought about further factional and regional divisions, but after the conclusion of the war (1919) the "Third International" was created in Moscow, following a strictly communistic pattern.

A Generation of German Scientists. The philosophy of Hegel and his school (cf. p. 502 sqq.) and the abstract speculations of the "nature philosophers" (cf. p. 501) dominated the intellectual scene in Germany during the early decades of the nineteenth century, and while their intuitions stimulated the spirit of scientific research, their poetico-romantic leanings retarded at the same time the progress of experimental science. The scientifically minded nineteenth century was turning rather sharply from generalization to specialization, from rational speculation to empirical observation. Germany had first to free herself from the spell of Hegelianism before she could make her own vital contributions to the great discoveries and advances in the several fields of the natural sciences.

On the threshold of the age of modern empirical science in Germany stands *Alexander von Humboldt* (1769–1859), Wilhelm von Humboldt's

---

" . . . because property is natural to man; because it is a bulwark against the exploitation of man by man; because unless you own the means of production you cannot control production; because unless you control you cannot be responsible; because responsibility for his deeds . . . is the very mark of man. . . . The injustices of property owners in the past have only been possible because the few owned too much and the many nothing at all. The law therefore should favor ownership, whereas at present it favors exploitation" (Autobiography, Devin-Adair Co., New York, 1941, p. 296 sq.).

(cf. p. 439 sqq.) younger brother, one of the greatest exponents of natural science and a prominent humanist scholar besides. In him the universalistic-philosophical and the empirico-scientific tendencies were equally strong, but he was able to reconcile them by virtue of the synthetic faculty of his mind. Like some of the romantic "nature philosophers" Humboldt had attended in his youth the famous Mining Academy of Freiberg in Saxony, and later on at the University of Göttingen he had undergone a thorough training in scientific method. Nevertheless he did not escape the censure of the contemporary scientific specialists on the one hand and of the philosophers and poets on the other. The former objected to his universalism, the latter to his empiricism.

Humboldt's special field of research was scientific geography, understood as a comprehensive analysis of climate, vegetation, and fauna in their relation to human activities. He collected an inexhaustible wealth of material on his many travels to foreign lands and continents, and of all these expeditions the trip to the Spanish colonies of South America (1799–1804) yielded the richest scientific reward. On his homeward journey he visited Mexico and the United States.

Humboldt's peculiar gift of seeing the interrelations between different branches of science enabled him to make important discoveries in several scientific fields. The sciences of meteorology, geology, and physics are indebted to him for the invention of isotherms, for his research on volcanic formations, and for his investigation of the nature of terrestrial magnetism. In his herbarium he had assembled 5000 newly discovered plant species, and his collection of rare butterflies was unique in its kind. At his own expense, and unafraid of difficulties and dangers, this model research worker accumulated countless specimens of plants, animals, and minerals, of coins, ornaments, weapons, and art objects of various kinds, gathered from many parts of the world. In Paris, in close association with the scientists of the French Academy and the *Ecole Polytechnique,* he organized his treasures and his notes and published the results of his American journey in the French language (*Voyage aux régions équinoxiales du nouveau continent, fait en 1799–1804;* 30 vols., 1834). During the final years of his long life Humboldt completed his *Kosmos,* a monumental compendium of the physical structure of the universe that was soon translated into all the languages of the civilized world. The United States paid tribute to Humboldt's genius by the erection of the Humboldt monuments in St. Louis and Philadelphia.

Another outstanding representative of the first generation of German inductive scientists was *Justus von Liebig* (1803–1873), an eminent chemist, who owed his professorship in the University of Giessen to the recommendation of Alexander von Humboldt. As a young man he had studied in Paris and had received his training in experimental methodology from the leading scientists in the field of physico-chemistry. In his own laboratory he trained several generations of future scientists, teaching them the methods of determining the chemical composition of organic substances and laying the foundations for the development of organic chemistry. By linking chemistry with the physiology of animals and plants Liebig made important contributions to the knowledge of metabolic processes and became the founder of agricultural chemistry. A lifelong friendship bound him to his teacher, the famous French chemist Gay-Lussac, and to Friedrich Wöhler, his most distinguished pupil, together with whom he had experimentally worked out the principles of the new organic chemistry.

After Liebig had been called to the University of Munich by King Louis I of Bavaria (1852), he devoted himself almost exclusively to the problems of agricultural chemistry. By the discovery of new methods of soil conservation and fertilization he became the first great representative of scientific "technical chemistry." In his *Chemical Letters* he popularized his findings, attributing the decay of races and nations to the exhaustion of the soil, brought about by the unmethodical waste of its chemical substance.

A scientist and scholar of the highest rank, equally proficient in the disciplines of mathematics and physics, was *Karl Friedrich Gauss* (1777–1855). His scientific research and his writings are distinguished by their originality and many-sidedness. After having spent his early youth in his native Brunswick, Gauss completed his studies at the University of Göttingen, where from 1807 to his death he was professor of mathematics and director of the local observatory, which he himself had planned and designed.

Regarding arithmetic as the queen of the sciences, Gauss applied his new methods not only to the different branches of higher mathematics but to experimental and mathematical physics, to theoretical and practical astronomy, to geodetics and the science of terrestrial magnetism. Together with the physicist *Wilhelm Weber,* his colleague in the University of Göttingen, he constructed the first electromagnetic telegraph.

Despite his many contributions to applied science, Gauss regarded the practical aspects of his research as of minor significance: "There is for my mind a satisfaction of a higher kind, in regard to which material things are irrelevant. I don't care whether I apply mathematics to some clumps of dirt, called planets, or to purely arithmetic problems; I must confess that the latter have a greater charm for me." His great love and knowledge of nature served only to increase Gauss's humility and his admiration for an all-pervading divine intelligence.

On a vacation trip Gauss made the acquaintance of *Joseph von Fraunhofer* (1787–1826), the greatest optician of the age, who had founded an optical institute of world fame in the Bavarian town of Benediktbeuren. Like Gauss, Fraunhofer had gone through the hard school of poverty and privation, but with inborn genius, industry, and perseverance he had familiarized himself at an early age with the most intricate problems of the science of optics. Together with *Georg Reichenbach* (1772–1826), whom he met in Munich, Fraunhofer had begun to manufacture scientific instruments. It was due to the work of these two men that Munich soon was to step into the place of Paris and London as the leading production center for precision tools. The construction of the leviathan telescope and the so-called "Königsberg Heliometer" were also among the fruits of their combined labors. Fraunhofer's name in particular will always remain associated with the discovery of the "dark lines" ("Fraunhofer Absorption Lines") in the sun's spectrum and with the experiments that first established the exact length of light waves. Fraunhofer's new methods of spectrum analysis were afterward perfected by *Gustav R. Kirchhoff* (1824–1887) and *Robert Bunsen* (1811–1899). The wealth of new information concerning the chemical composition of celestial bodies, derived from the analysis of the spectra of sun, stars, and comets, led in turn to new discoveries in the field of astronomy. Fraunhofer's construction of microscopic instruments was continued with greatly improved methods by the *Carl Zeiss Works* in Jena, founded in 1846. The perfection of scientific methods and instruments was the necessary prerequisite for the phenomenal progress of the sciences dealing with plant and animal organisms, of biology, physiology, botany, zoology, and medicine.

The principle of the "conservation of energy," one of the most fundamental laws of physical and physiological science, was first discovered and formulated in 1842 by *Robert Mayer* (1814–1878), an obscure Swabian country doctor. One year later the English physicist *James Joule* arrived at the same conclusions, and in 1847 the eminent German physicist and physiologist *Hermann von Helmholtz* (1821–1894) demonstrated the validity of the law of the *"Erhaltung der Kraft"* for every branch of the physical sciences. Helmholtz claimed and received all the credit for this discovery, while Robert Mayer was suspected of megalomania and even temporarily confined to an insane asylum. In the sixties of the nineteenth century the English physicist *John Tyndall* rendered a service to the cause of justice and decency when he revealed the tragic fate of Robert Mayer and called attention to his scientific accomplishments. The entire system of modern physics is based on the fact that heat is generated by mechanical forces and that there exists a definite and constant relationship between heat and energy. Robert Mayer's law therefore is as essential to modern physical science as are the discoveries of Galilei and Newton.

In *medicine* as in the other sciences Germany lagged behind France and England in the early nineteenth century but rose to a position of world leadership within a few decades. And, as was the case in the other sciences, the first generation of physicians had to emancipate themselves from the unrealistic theorems of "nature philosophy" in order to be able to transform medicine into an experimental science.

Scientific medicine in the strict sense began in Germany with the anatomical research of *Johann Schönlein* (1793–1864), the inaugurator of modern clinical methodology, whose laboratory at the University of Würzburg became a veritable shrine for the medical students of all European countries. In 1840 Schönlein founded the "German Clinic" in Berlin and thus became the first of a long series of celebrated clinical physicians in Germany.

The great genius, however, in this first generation of German medical scientists was *Johannes Müller* (1801–1858), a shoemaker's son of Coblenz on the Rhine, among whose pupils were some of the most illustrious scientists of modern times, such as Emil Du Bois-Reymond, Helmholtz, and Virchow. Müller taught anatomy, physiology, and pathology, and felt at home in every branch of the biological sciences. In his synthetic approach to scientific problems he followed the lead of Goethe's scientific studies, opposing specialization and endeavoring to comprehend and interpret the vast complex of scientific phenomena in their totality. An adherent of biological "vitalism," he defended the idea of design and purpose in the growth of organic structures against the biological theories of mechanism and materialism. The life force that informs the organism appeared to him as a manifestation of a purposive and creative power.

In the following generation German medical science followed the general trend of the age toward specialization and accepted the mechanistic explanation of inorganic and organic nature. Berlin became the center of inductive medical research in the field of internal medicine as well as in the new science of surgery. As the latter was traditionally associated with the barber's trade, it had to carry on a long fight before being granted recognition as an academic discipline.

Another landmark in the development of modern medical science was reached with the publication of *Rudolf Virchow's* (1821–1902) *Cellular Pathology* (1858). The great pathologist succeeded in linking disease with certain processes of morbid growth or disintegration of cellular structures. For the first time Virchow described the organism as a system of cells subject to various kinds of transformation. Thus the individual cell was recognized as an active agent in the production of disease. *Jakob Henle* (1809–1885), Johannes Müller's oldest and dearest pupil, likewise contributed to cellular research, and in his *Investigations on Pathology* of 1840 he anticipated intuitively the later discoveries of *Pasteur* and *Robert Koch* (cf. p. 565) concerning the microbic nature of certain diseases. He was the first to recognize that some infections of the organism were caused by "parasitical beings, which are among the lowliest and smallest but at the same time most prolific varieties of organisms."

Biological Evolution and Heredity. The new geological evidence of the great antiquity of the earth, produced early in the nineteenth century, vastly changed the ideas on man's function and position in the universe and stimulated scientific inquiry into the origins of life and into the relations that exist between its different manifestations. A new answer was given to these questions by the theory of biological evolution, also known as the theory of "transformism," or, in Germany, as *Abstammungslehre*. The idea as such was not new, and the principle of evolution had been advanced in one form or another by such thinkers as Empedocles (495–435 B.C.), Aristotle (384–321 B.C.), and St. Augustine (A.D. 354–430) in antiquity, by St. Thomas Aquinas in the Middle Ages, and by Leibniz, Lessing, Herder, Kant, and Schelling in modern times. The partly rationalistic and partly intuitive approach of these philosophers gave way in the nineteenth century to the new methods of scientific observation. While this modern research supplemented the older theories by offering a wealth of factual evidence, the materialistic premises of the modern philosophy of science suggested at the same time a set of new and far-reaching conclusions concerning the origin and nature of man. Thus many Darwinists maintained that the theory of evolution exposed the scriptural account of man's creation as a poetic myth and that man was descended both in body and mind from the lower and lowest animal organisms. It might be well to keep in mind, however, that such conclusions have no essential relation to the factuality of biological evolution as such and that, strictly speaking, they rest on a philosophical rather than a scientific basis.

The first two scientists to advance the theory of evolution in the nineteenth century were the Frenchman *Lamarck* (1744–1829) and the German *Treviranus* (1776–1837). They claimed that new needs produced by environmental changes were responsible for organic transformations in the plant and animal kingdom, and that these newly acquired characteristics were transmitted to the descendants of the species.

But these preliminary speculations were almost thrown into oblivion by the appearance of *Charles Darwin's* (1809–1882) *The Origin of Species* (1859) and *The Descent of Man* (1871). The English scientist, adding the theory of "natural selection" to the theory of evolution, demonstrated by a vast accumulation of factual data that organic species are subject to indefinite change. He asserted that in the struggle for existence the fittest individuals of a species have a better chance for survival and adaptation to changing environments than the weaker members, and that this principle of the "survival of the fittest" is the ulterior cause of the biological evolution of infinite varieties of species. If carried to extreme (and logically as well as scientifically unwarranted) conclusions, such a theory might well be used to justify the cruelties and injustices in social and economic life as well as the Machiavellian thesis of "Might is Right" and the idea of a "master race" of "supermen" in international relations. Darwinism was interpreted in this way by the Young Hegelian materialist *Max Stirner* (1806–1856), by the French diplomat and philosopher *Count Gobineau* (1816–1882), by Richard Wagner's son-in-law, the English-born but naturalized German popular philosopher *Houston Stewart Chamberlain* (1855–1927), and most of all by *Friedrich Nietzsche* (cf. p. 695 sq.). It is one of the ironical twists of history that Charles Darwin should thus have unwittingly become the ancestor of the myth of the intrinsic superiority of the "Aryan race." Darwin, however, repeatedly emphasized that the applicability of the theory of "natural selection" was limited in scope, and that the principle of the "survival of the fittest" must take into account the co-operative as well as the competitive, the social as well as the antisocial instincts and reactions of the species.

The most enthusiastic of the German Darwinists was *Ernst Haeckel* (1834–1919), one of Johannes Müller's pupils, who popularized the theory of evolution in his best seller, *Die Welträtsel (The Riddles of the Universe)*. In Jena, where he held the position of professor of zoology at the local university, he founded a museum whose contents were to elucidate the problems of biological evolution. The results of Haeckel's scientific expeditions were made accessible to the public in several illustrated works, revealing the author's brilliance of style and the artistic qualities of his mind.

With the name of the Austrian-Czech botanist and Augustinian abbot *Gregor Mendel* (1822–1884) is associated the discovery of the law of the transmission of hereditary characteristics of the organism. By carrying on over 10,000 individual experiments with specimens of hybrid sweet peas Mendel worked out a method that made it possible to determine with mathematical exactitude the frequency of the reappearance of inherited "unit characters" in the line of descent. However, the significance of Mendel's contribution to the science of biological evolution was not recognized until after his death.

Bacteriology. The greatest progress in the treatment of infectious and epidemic diseases was due to the research of the French scientist *Louis Pasteur* (1822–1895) and the German physician *Robert Koch* (1843–1910). Pasteur proved conclusively that many infections of plants and animals were caused by micro-organisms and that therefore certain diseases might be prevented if these microbes could be either destroyed or antagonized by inoculating the organism with a weakened germ culture of the disease. By the process of "pasteurization" the temperature of the environment of the deadly microbes was raised to a degree that made it impossible for them to survive.

Robert Koch is generally regarded as the founder of the science of bacteriology. His research on anthrax, cholera, and tuberculosis resulted in the isolation of the anthrax bacterium and in the discovery of the micro-organic agents of Asiatic cholera and tubercular diseases.

In 1886 the French Academy of Sciences founded the *Institut Pasteur* which in the early years of its existence devoted all its efforts to the treatment of rabies. In 1899 Pasteur himself was appointed as director of the Institute. The "Robert Koch Institute for the Treatment of Infectious Diseases" was founded in Berlin in 1891 with Robert Koch as its director. *Emil von Behring* (1854–1917), one of Koch's assistants, discovered a serum for the successful treatment of diphtheria in 1894, and both he and Koch were awarded the Nobel Prize.

Experimental Psychology. The methods of psychological research in the nineteenth century were developed in harmony with the spirit of the age of inductive science. Thus psychology, which formerly had been a chiefly rational and speculative science attached to metaphysics and ethics, now became an experimental laboratory science, whose major tools were tests and quantitative measurements of sensations, perceptions, reflex actions, and other mental and emotional processes. With growing insight into the correlation of mental phenomena and brain processes, biological and psychological research became closely linked, and the study of animal behavior was regarded as providing most of the clues for the understanding of human thought and action. Once more the materialistic premises and biases of the contemporary philosophy are clearly recognizable in these attempts to measure thought or to precondition human behavior by the perfection of the new laboratory methods.

In Germany Johannes Müller was the first to establish definite laws relating to a "specific energy of the senses" that makes them respond in certain ways to different kinds of stimuli. *Helmholtz* measured the velocity of nerve messages in 1851, and *Gustav Fechner* (1801–1887) founded the science of psychophysics, which regards material phenomena as physical manifestations of an underlying spiritual reality. The credit for having brought together the many isolated data of experimental psychology to form a consistent scientific system belongs to Fechner's successor in the University of Leipzig, the German philosopher and psychologist *Wilhelm Wundt* (1832–1920), who, in 1879, founded the first psychological laboratory.

Sociology and Social Science. Just as psychology had formerly been treated as a branch of theoretical and practical philosophy, so too had sociology. The works of Plato and Aristotle, of the leading medieval schoolmen, and of many philosophers of the postmedieval centuries abound in sociological speculation. But it was not until the nineteenth century that the attempt was made to convert sociology into an empirical and inductive science.

Sociology in the form of a "social physics" was first developed by the French philosopher *Auguste Comte* (1798–1857). Comte's so-called "positivistic" system of social science was philosophically broadened by *Herbert Spencer* (1820–1903), an English engineer, journalist, and scholar, who in his *System of Synthetic Philosophy* made social science part of a naturalistic and utilitaristic metaphysics.

Comte's endeavor to build up an integral system of social science based on a system of "positive philosophy" was motivated by the breakdown of the *ancien régime* and of the Empire of Napoleon on the one hand, and by his admiration for the great achievements of the natural sciences on the other. In Comte's opinion the past was irrevocably dead, and the future was uncertain. To avoid growing confusion and disintegration of thought and culture he regarded it as necessary to create a new social order anchored in a new system of thought. To bring this about he first of all proclaimed sociology as the standard science, displacing metaphysics, mathematics, and physics, which at various times had held that exalted position.

Comte's "law of the three states" contended that the human mind of necessity passes successively through a theological and a metaphysical phase, to arrive in the end at the mature and "positive" knowledge of the age of science. This third and final state, he claimed, was reached in the nineteenth century, when the inquiry into causes was rendered meaningless and the description and explanation of facts became all important. The modern social scientist is called upon to establish definite laws that are derived from the observation of social facts and that may be used to create a new and better social order. In short, Comte demanded that social science be made the servant of social needs and a tool for the promotion of human happiness and contentment.

It is interesting to note that in order to complete his system Comte felt compelled by the implications of his own thought to streamline the concept of science by arbitrarily excluding all those sciences that would not fit into his theoretical scheme. Then it seemed necessary to formulate a dogmatic "scientism" that had all the earmarks of a substitute religion, including an organized clergy, a supreme object of cultic worship ("Humanity"), and the solemn excommunication of all dissenters — Catholics, Protestants, and Deists alike. "In the name of the Past and of the Future, the servants of Humanity . . . come forward to claim . . . the general leadership of this world. Their object is to constitute a real Providence in all departments — moral, intellectual, and material" (*Catechism of Positivism;* trans. by R. Congreve, London, 1858; Preface, p. 19). Thus, as Etienne Gilson aptly remarks, "the science of sociology gave rise to sociolatry, with love as the principle, order as the basis, and progress as the end" (*The Unity of Philosophical Experience;* Scribner's, New York, 1937, p. 266).

C. CULTURAL TRENDS

The Arts. What appeared evident from the analyses of the artistic styles of the past remains true also in the nineteenth century: artistic expression depends in its form and subject matter to a large extent on the spirit of the age, its religious, philosophical, social, and economic standards and forces. The Baroque Age (cf. pp. 330–354) had witnessed a final demonstration of the formative cultural power of the Church and its princes, a power which it was forced to share with the splendor-loving secular rulers. In the nineteenth century, however, Church and State have to yield their leadership in the arts to the "third estate," the *bourgeois* class. The rise, in turn, of the "fourth estate," the proletariat, after the middle of the century exerts a gradually increasing influence on aesthetic concepts and on artistic creation. In the twentieth century and especially after the upheavals of World War I and the subsequent revolution the collectivist tendencies of society are clearly reflected in both the plastic and literary arts.

a) Art in the Service of the State. Napoleon I in France and King Louis I of Bavaria (1825–1848) were the last secular princes in Europe who pressed the arts into the service of the State and carried on a systematic dynastic art policy on a grand scale. Monumental works of architecture in Munich, among them churches, palaces, and other public and private buildings (Ludwigskirche, Palais Wittelsbach, Feldherrnhalle, Propyläen, the state university and library, etc.) bore witness to Louis' initiative and excellent taste.* The noble neo-classical style of these buildings, which was most conspicuous in the stately structures flanking the Ludwigstrasse and in the palatial beauty of the architectural monuments enclosing the spacious *Königsplatz* (Royal Square), gave Munich its distinguishing mark. By the time the king's grandson, Louis II (1864–1886), succeeded to the throne of Bavaria the vitality of neo-classicism was exhausted, and the king's extravagant taste delighted in a pseudoromantic revival of the palace style of the eighteenth century. In the German North the well-intentioned attempt of Emperor William II (1888–1918, cf. p. 617 sqq.) to promote and direct the arts in his realm by his personal protectorship revealed in its dismal failure the extent to which the truly creative artistic forces had become estranged from the ideals of the ruling dynasty.

b) Museum, "Kunstverein," and Academy. With the waning significance of Church, State, and nobility as standard-bearers of artistic fashions, the individual artists found themselves deprived of their traditional financial protectors and employers. To establish a closer contact between the artists and the representatives of the new *bourgeoisie* and in order to spread aesthetic education among the members of the now leading social groups, the nineteenth century gave new prominence to the internationally established "art museums" and created a new type of art forum in the *Kunstverein* (art association).

The "museum" owes its origin to the princely collectors of Renaissance and Baroque (cf. p. 330 sqq.). In 1793 the French "National Convent" created the first modern type of a national museum by making the treasures of the Louvre accessible to the public. In Germany the demand for the creation of a national center that was to house the art treasures of the past led to the foundation of the Germanic Museum in Nuremberg in 1852 and of the Berlin National Gallery in the seventies of the nineteenth century. Art collection and art appreciation were linked by *Alfred Lichtwark* (1852–1914) who as director of the Hamburg art gallery succeeded in devising a systematic educational program that included serial lectures, conducted gallery tours, and periodically changing exhibits of art works of the past and present. Lichtwark's pedagogic ideas were adopted by the directors of other municipal museums in Germany and met with the liveliest response in the artistic and educational circles of the United States.

While the art museum was primarily engaged in the preservation and presentation of the values and documents of the past, it became the special concern of the *Kunstverein* to encourage the activity of living artists, to

---

* Most of these buildings were destroyed during World War II.

cultivate contemporary art, and to educate the public for its appreciation. The earliest of these German art associations was founded in Karlsruhe (Baden) in 1818. In 1932 they numbered well over one hundred and exercised a power that has unfortunately worked as often to the detriment as to the advantage of art and artists. Especially after the middle of the nineteenth century the *Kunstverein* came to represent more and more the taste and temper of a *bourgeoisie* which intolerantly took its stand against anything that would not submit to its set of aesthetic rules and conventions. Thus many an artist of strong-willed and extraordinary genius found himself ostracized by commercial or artistic cliques and condemned to a solitary struggle against the current of organized public opinion, cut off as it were from those social forces that might have vitalized his artistic style. The lack of such fruitful give-and-take between artist and society was largely responsible for the rise of successive movements and fads that characterized the late nineteenth and early twentieth century, the creations of eccentric minds which, having lost their social and moral bearings, indulged in frantic and often sterile experimentation.

Similar critical reservations apply to the third of the institutions by means of which the nineteenth century had hoped to bring about a revival of the arts and crafts — the Academy. When the first German art academies were founded in the seventeenth and eighteenth centuries, they fulfilled a vital function in supplying the princely employers with a sufficient number of uniformly trained and thoroughly qualified artists and craftsmen.* But with the breakdown of the *ancien régime,* its social ideals and their stylistic manifestation in the arts, the academies lost their *raison d'être,* and the greatest of modern artists actually grew up and achieved their pre-eminence in opposition to and in perpetual struggle with the conventional rules of the academies. This is as much true of the "Nazarenes" (cf. p. 491) and their romantic contemporaries of the early nineteenth century as of the impressionists (cf. p. 715 sq.) in its closing decades. The State-supported academies turned out an overplus of technically well-trained but mediocre artists, the majority of whom were left to shift for themselves, with little chance of steady employment, an artistic proletariat that was forced to commercialize its talents or to submerge in an irresponsible "bohemianism."

National and international "art exhibitions" were held originally in connection with the academies, in order to give a public accounting of the progress of artistic endeavor and to foster more intimate relations between artists and connoisseurs. *Kunstvereine* as well as individual art dealers played a prominent part in organizing such art exhibits all over Germany, and at the end of the nineteenth century permanent "exhibition palaces" were erected in several German cities to provide a dignified setting and a sort of social center for the artists and an art-loving public.

---

* The Academy of Vienna was founded in 1694, that of Berlin in 1764. In 1932 the German academies numbered 24, including several industrial schools for applied arts and crafts.

An important innovation in the methods of art education was achieved in the second half of the nineteenth century. "Master studios" (*Meister-ateliers*) were created for especially talented art students and separate art schools were established for different branches of craftsmanship, such as the arts of goldsmithing (Hanau), lacemaking (Plauen), book printing (Leipzig), and so forth.

The so-called "secessions" of the end of the nineteenth century (*Münchener Sezession*, 1892; *Berliner Sezession*, 1893) were associations of artists who were resolved to fight collectively for their progressive ideas, using commercial organization and periodical exhibitions as major instruments to achieve their goal. But as the members of the original "secessions" grew old, their artistic style became ossified, and they found themselves challenged by new "secessions" of the younger generation, whose right to live and work in accordance with the changing spirit of the age they had intolerantly denied.

c) Architecture. It has been pointed out that German Romanticism (cf. p. 487 sqq.) was artistically creative chiefly in the arts of painting and music, but on the whole unproductive in architecture and sculpture. This statement may be enlarged so as to include much of the development of these arts throughout the nineteenth century. The abdication of Church and State as protectors of the arts made it difficult for architecture in particular to achieve that social and communal expressiveness that is of its very essence. While the more personal arts of sculpture and painting found ways and means to convey a vital message, architecture remained chiefly eclectic and retrospective, dabbling in various styles of the past, without being able to present an integrated artistic interpretation of the cultural forces of the present.

The historical reception of past architectural styles began with the pseudoromantic "Gothic revival." In the latter part of the eighteenth century the English nobility began sentimentally to appreciate the hitherto ignored but still extant monuments of medieval Gothic architecture. The "Gothic revival" in England went hand in hand with the development of the new "English" style of garden architecture. Irregular design and intimate natural charm supplanted the rigid formality of the representative gardens of Renaissance, Baroque, and Rococo and remained in all European countries the prevailing style of landscape gardening to the present day.

With the exception of *Leo von Klenze* (cf. p. 400) even the leading neo-classical architects of Germany submitted to a smaller or larger degree to the influence of the "Gothic revival." To the very end of the nineteenth century neo-Gothic forms of building can be traced in all parts of Germany. The chief impetus for the renewed preoccupation with German Gothic architecture was provided by the German romanticists' intense interest in medieval forms of life and culture. Long after German Romanticism as such had died down the medievalist tendency in architecture held sway over much of the building activity in German lands.

The Cathedral in Cologne.

Interior of Cologne Cathedral.

A culturally significant by-product of the "Gothic revival" in Germany was the restoration of medieval monuments of ecclesiastic and secular architecture. Between 1842 and 1880 the great Cathedral of Cologne, which had come down from the Middle Ages as a monumental fragment, was completed in accordance with the original plans, and the days of its consecration were celebrated as symbolizing the unity of the reborn German empire (1880). The restoration of the Cathedrals of Bamberg and Spires (Speyer) and Ratisbon (Regensburg) was carried out under the protectorate of King Louis I of Bavaria. Besides the churches a large number of medieval castles, among them the Wartburg and the *Heidelberger Schloss,* owed their total or partial restoration to the "Gothic revival."

By far the most important of the historical-minded German architects of the nineteenth century was *Gottfried Semper* (1803–1879), a native of Hamburg. As artist and scholar he exemplifies the dangers that threaten a creative genius in an age of cumulative historical and technical knowledge. Semper was fully aware of the fact that an overdose of theoretical knowledge hampered his best efforts, depriving him of the spontaneity of his artistic vision and making him an imitator of the past rather than a molder of the present. In his critical masterpiece on *Style** he followed the materialistic trend of the age in relating the origins and transformations of art forms to the contingencies of technical and material possibilities and requirements. He had studied the monuments of antiquity and of Renaissance and Baroque in Italy and France, and among the several styles from which his historically trained sense drew inspiration he gave decided preference to the Renaissance. His fruitful building activity in Dresden, which included the construction of the Opera House and the Palais Oppenheim, was cut short by his involvement in the May revolts of 1849. But his years of exile in Paris and London gave him a welcome opportunity to continue his theoretical studies. At the behest of Queen Victoria's husband, the Prince Consort Albert of Saxe-Coburg-Gotha, Semper served as one of the chief advisers in preparing the London International Exposition of 1851 and in designing the plans for the South Kensington Museum. In Switzerland he was commissioned with the construction of the Polytechnical Institute and the observatory in Zurich and of the city hall in Winterthur. In 1871 he was called to Vienna to assume the post of director of building for the *Burgtheater* and the Imperial Museums of Art History and Natural History, together with the Viennese architect *Karl von Hasenauer*. Semper gave evidence of his clear realization of the problematic situation of architecture in his own epoch when he wrote in 1854: "Our architecture is without originality and has lost its pre-eminence among the arts. It will recover it only when modern architects begin to give more attention to the present state of our industrial arts. The impulse for such a happy change will come from the handicrafts."

d) Art and Technology. The possibilities of a "functional" artistic style

---

* *Der Stil in den technischen und tektonischen Künsten,* 2 vols. (Munich, 1860–1863).

that would have suited the new building materials (iron, steel, concrete) and construction methods of the machine age were not recognized by the generation of artists who were contemporaries of the Industrial Revolution. Their love for the decorative design of historically sanctioned art forms prompted them to adorn the architectural façades and the interiors of factory buildings, industrial plants, and railroad depots indiscriminately with meaningless and wholly inappropriate ornamentation. However, the fanciful yet outmoded decorations that were thus pasted on the structural frame satisfied the luxurious but uncultivated taste of the ruling bourgeois plutocracy.

The only positive and direct influence of the new techniques of the machine age on artistic creation is recognizable in the revival of the ancient German craft of bronze casting, a revival that was again due to the initiative of King Louis I of Bavaria. The Munich Foundry produced a large number of sculptural monuments of international fame, among which the symbolic colossal statue of the "Bavaria" ranks foremost. It was the work of *Ludwig Schwanthaler* (1728–1848), the descendant of an old Bavarian family of wood carvers, who completed this unique masterpiece after six years of unremitting labor. *Ferdinand Miller* (1813–1887), the director and ultimate owner of the Munich Foundry, was likewise the heir of several generations of skilled craftsmen. He succeeded in combining the new industrial methods with the co-operative spirit of the medieval craft guilds and thus fulfilled Gottfried Semper's demand of a reunion of art and handicraft.

e) Painting. Whereas architecture and sculpture during the greater part of the nineteenth century remained attached to styles of the past and therefore lacked true originality, the art of painting became the medium of expression for several representative geniuses of the age of liberal individualism and nineteenth-century realism.

In the so-called "Düsseldorf" school the romantic style of historical painting in the "Nazarene" manner (cf. p. 491) lived on as a mere convention, until the Rhinelander *Alfred Rethel* (1816–1851) gave it a new meaning and a strikingly original and realistic note. The new style, combining the indigenous psychological qualities of Albrecht Dürer's graphic art with the figural composition of the Italian Renaissance, became first apparent in Rethel's illustrations of the *Lay of the Nibelungs* and achieved its greatest triumphs in the monumental fresco paintings of the city hall in Aix-la-Chapelle (Aachen). Before Rethel's brilliant mind was destroyed by the ravages of an incurable brain disease he had completed his *Dance of Death*. This realistic sequence of woodcuts is a dramatically moving interpretation of the revolutionary tendencies of his age, and an accomplishment that fully holds its own when compared with Holbein's treatment of an identical theme (cf. p. 198). Rethel's conservatism viewed the revolution of 1848 as a personal and national tragedy brought about by political demagogues. The lamentations and exhortations of his woodcuts move

Dance of Death, by Alfred Rethel.

Three Women in Church, by Wilhelm Leibl.

inexorably to a grand finale: the pathetic figure of Death, crowned with a laurel wreath, his banner unfurled, mounting the top of the barricades.

The most representative realistic painter of Germany in the nineteenth century, however, is *Adolf von Menzel* (1815-1905), a native of Silesia but domiciled in Berlin from boyhood on. He grew up in the forced and unnatural calm of the *Vormärz* (cf. p. 461 sqq.) and experienced the revolution of 1848 as a rough but wholesome awakening from the sleep of philistinism. From his earliest to his latest works he recognized in nature his unfailing guide, and while he never relinquished entirely the romantic inclinations of his youth, he willingly accepted the challenge of the machine age and was one of the first to discover aesthetic values in its sober and matter-of-fact approach to reality.

Menzel was equally proficient in the techniques of lithography and oil painting, and his sympathetic pictorial interpretation of the age of Frederick the Great (cf. p. 316 sqq.), his personality, his court, and his army, striking a timely note of nationalism and patriotism, endeared him to the German people and its rulers alike. Although dividing his attention between the past and the present, he remained ever alert in anticipation of new goals. His long life extended well into the period of impressionistic *plein-air* painting (cf. p. 715 sq.), and early in his artistic career he developed a luminous brilliance of coloristic pattern and composition that was impressionistic in everything but name.

Menzel's greatness towered far above the work of a host of painters of historical subjects and battle scenes, glorifying the military exploits of the German armies and their leaders. The most popular among these politically minded artists was *Anton von Werner* (1843-1915), whose honest but arid naturalism gave a reliable documentary account of Prussia's more recent political and military triumphs. As director of the Berlin Academy, Werner did his best to harness the talents of the younger generation of painters. The limitations of his own aesthetic concepts are evidenced by the fact that he seriously doubted whether the art of painting would be able to compete with the newly developed technique of photography.

In the second half of the nineteenth century Munich began to take the lead in painting as in the other arts. Here *Karl von Piloty* (1826-1886) continued the tradition of Cornelius and Kaulbach in historical paintings whose subject matter was taken chiefly from the Roman and German past. One of his pupils, *Gabriel Max* (1840-1915), a talented colorist and an adherent of spiritism, softened Piloty's naturalism by a touch of reflective sentiment. Another pupil, *Franz Defregger* (1835-1921), the son of a Tyrolese peasant, depicted with deft accuracy and a cultivated sense of form the natural beauty of his homeland and genrelike episodes of his countrymen's struggle for liberation from French oppression (cf. p. 444).

The graphic arts are indebted to *Wilhelm Busch* (1832-1908) and *Adolf Oberländer* (1845-1923), both of whom were gifted humorists and achieved great popularity as illustrators and clever cartoonists. Busch's humor, saturated with a generous dose of Schopenhauer's pessimism, found pointed expression in the textual frames with which he surrounded his graphic narratives and in which he satirized and castigated human weaknesses. His illustrated character sketches, composed in the form of serial sequences and mostly published in the comic weekly *Fliegende Blätter* and in the *Münchener Bilderbogen* (*Max und Moritz, Die fromme Helene, Maler Klecksel,* etc.), became popular classics and served as models for the "comic strips" of American newspapers.

Classicism in painting, which had produced only mediocre talents at the end of the eighteenth century, experienced a revival of more enduring significance in the work of some of the most promising artists of the nineteenth century. *Anselm Feuerbach* (1829–1880) was the grandson of the famous jurist Paul Anselm von Feuerbach, the creator of the criminal law code of Bavaria (1813); his father was an outstanding classical archaeologist, and his uncle the Young Hegelian philosopher Ludwig Feuerbach (cf. p. 556 sq.). By inheritance he was an aristocrat who developed a classical style of painting that bore his personal stamp, although he had been influenced successively by nineteenth-century French realism (Couture, Courbet) and by Venetian, Florentine, and Roman Renaissance and Baroque. In Rome he met Nanna Risi, who became his wife and inspired the ripe classical beauty of some of his masterly portraits (*Medea, Iphigenia,* etc.). When Nanna left him, both his life and his art suffered an irretrievable loss, and the grayish hues of his coloring assumed an ever increasing air of cool detachment and quiet resignation.

The second great master of the classical form in the second half of the nineteenth century was *Hans von Marées* (1837–1887), a native of the Rhineland, whose nobility of character is reflected in the placid beauty and flawless integrity of his works. Aided by the unfaltering devotion of his friend *Conrad Fiedler* (1841–1895), the famous art critic whose understanding and generosity compensated Marées for the indifference or hostility of his contemporaries, he followed the dictates of his artistic conscience with undeviating determination and succeeded in freeing his art from the shackles of a sterile historicism. On his travels in Spain, France, Holland, and Italy Marées experienced the influence of the great masters of the past without ever losing the sturdy independence of his own artistic idiom. The monumental frescoes in the Library of the International Zoological Station in Naples (1873), depicting in the timeless frame of the southern landscape the everlasting vitality of the Neapolitan fishermen and farmers, marked the crowning achievement of Marées' life.

Romantic painting, which had flourished early in the nineteenth century (cf. p. 487 sqq.), likewise came to life again in its second half. In the Swiss master *Arnold Böcklin* (1827–1901) the melodious musicality and brooding symbolism of German thought appeared clothed in the garb of romantic and historically inspired allegory. Endowed with the poet's vision and imagination, Böcklin discovered in nature the many secret voices that bespeak the riddle of life and death and reveal their magic charm in myths and legends. In most of his works the moods of nature appear symbolically condensed in human forms, and the luminosity of local colors is ingeniously used to accentuate the mysterious and phantastic aspects of nature and human life. Böcklin's landscapes and figures are as timeless as those of Marées but more unreal, creations of dream and fancy, even though on the surface the scenery presents reminiscences of the master's beloved Italy. With the greatest German painters of the past Böcklin shares the conspicuously German genius for descriptive illustration and metaphysical interpretation.

A romantic painter of a different type was the Austrian *Hans Makart* (1840–1884), a pupil of Piloty and a protégé of Emperor Francis Joseph. His works reflect his own exuberant temper and extravagant taste as well as the immoderate craving for spectacular display that was characteristic of a Germany thrown off her spiritual balance by the dazzling prospects of a newly acquired political power and economic abundance. The romantic fireworks of Makart's huge historic tableaux, lacking the formal restraint of a disciplined and cultured mind, issued from the frenzy of an aimless enthusiasm. The artist's autointoxication was nourished by the universal acclamation of his public, whose admiration found peculiar forms of expression in the creation of "Makart hats," "Makart bouquets," and so forth.

In an age of science and technology both classicistic and romantic leanings appear out of tune with the basic cultural trends. They were largely born of the isolation, the protest, or the maladjustment of individual artists whose sensitivity, shrinking from the harsh factualness of the present, sought refuge in the shelter of a more or less remote past. Those artists, therefore, who more accurately represented the spirit of the second half of the nineteenth century were masters of realistic observation and factual description. They had nothing but scorn for the dreams and historic revelries of the classical and romantic narrators in the pictorial arts, and they proudly proclaimed themselves as the disciples of nature and life.

One of the first and by far the greatest of these modern German "realists" in the art of painting was *Wilhelm Leibl* (1844–1900), born in Cologne but of Bavarian ancestry, who bade farewell to the fashions of historical retrospection and made man and nature the objects of his aesthetic devotion. In the simple forms of everyday life he discovered a beauty that was entirely of the earth and a spirituality that was inherent in nature itself. "If we paint man as he is," he wrote, "his soul is included as a matter of course." Originally destined to become a mechanical engineer, Leibl soon turned to painting and at the age of twenty entered the Munich Academy. When he found out that his teachers had nothing to offer that he regarded as of vital importance, and that he was on strange soil in the Bohemian atmosphere of the studios, he retired to the Bavarian countryside, pursuing his artistic goals with the singular determination of the old masters. The *Three Women in Church,* his most popular painting, is also his best. It is the work of an artist whose genius derived its enduring greatness from the fact that it was in love with life. Despite his opposition to the Academy and his disinclination to teach, the style of his paintings was eloquent and suggestive enough to attract a number of talented pupils and to give rise to a realistic school of modern German painting.

Literature. The political, social, and economic transformations of the nineteenth century found a more direct response in German literature than in the plastic and pictorial arts. After the "July Revolution" of 1830 (cf. p. 525 sq.) had temporarily strengthened the increasing opposition to literary romanticism, the new wave of political reaction that followed the political uprisings silenced the leaders of liberal thought and gave rise to a mood of pessimism and melancholy resignation. It was the time when Schopenhauer's philosophy (cf. p. 505 sq.) was at last given an enthusiastic reception.

The "March Revolution" of 1848 (cf. p. 527 sq.), marking the end of the reactionary period of the *Vormärz,* brought definitely to the fore the younger generation of writers and poets, whose political and social radicalism was resolutely bent on the destruction of the ideological heritage of German Classicism and Romanticism. All humanistic emphasis on the values of personality was henceforth overshadowed by the ideas of democratic liberation that had been imported from France, England, and the United States, above all the idea of social equality and the demand for political representation and the active participation of the masses in national affairs. In the name of the people and their liberties, literature was drawn from its pedestal. The cult of personality was denounced as a sort of idolatry, and the poet was required to serve the political and social needs of the day and the hour.

a) "Young Germany." The dictatorship of the *Zeitgeist* was openly proclaimed by the members of a literary clique united by the conviction that the technical advances of the machine age ascertained a progressive satisfaction of all human and social needs and that it was the duty of artists and writers to play their part in bringing about the corresponding political and social changes. Whoever excluded himself from this collective effort was regarded as a sterile aesthete or an antisocial reactionary. Thus the movement known as "Young Germany" laid down the rules for German writers and readers, and the predominant influence of its members as publicists and critics condemned to tragic isolation some of the greatest literary talents of the age.

The intellectual leaders of "Young Germany" were Löw Baruch, who adopted the pen name *Ludwig Börne* (1786–1837) and *Heinrich Heine* (1799–1856),* both of German-Jewish ancestry and both embracing Protestantism for reasons of expediency. Both had smarted under the stigma that attached to their race, and Börne in particular worked incessantly for

---

* Other representatives of "Young Germany" were *Laube, Gutzkow,* and *Wienbarg;* the latter, in his *Aesthetische Feldzüge* (1834), coined the name "Young Germany," which was then applied to the entire movement. A decree of the *Bundesrat* of 1835 banned the writings of all the members of the group.

the "emancipation" of the Jews, demanding that they be given full equality of civic rights and complete freedom in choosing their calling.*

Börne, Heine, and their companions, regarding themselves as the authentic spokesmen of the *Zeitgeist,* used the weapons of wit, irony, and scathing satire to arouse their contemporaries and to launch a concerted attack on everything that seemed to retard the march of progress. They were masters in the art of "debunking," but their stylistic finesse and journalistic adroitness exhausted itself in defamation and negation, and their massive materialism and cold intellectualism marred even their best intentions and made them skeptics and cynics against their will. They disdained a world that did not measure up to their ideas and they scoffed at ideals because they despaired of their realization. A good deal of their vaunting melancholy was an empty show and self-parody, and much of their "Byronism" was a mixture of clever play acting and vain pretense. When the novelist *Karl Immermann* (1796–1840) portrayed in his *Baron Münchhausen* (1838) the great master of lying, he created a symbol that exposed the moral instability and rootlessness of an entire generation which had succumbed too readily to the spell of "Young Germany." Immermann's *Münchhausen* novel embodies two distinct styles, the one indicative of the frivolity of the *Zeitgeist,* the other (condensed in the inserted village epic *Der Oberhof*) presenting as an utter contrast a world of lasting values, a saga of the "immortal folk" (*unsterbliches Volk*), firmly rooted in its maternal soil.

As a poet *Heine* towers far above the rest of the Young German writers. And yet Eichendorff's (cf. p. 478 sq.) severe criticism of some typical aspects of the movement applies also to Heine: "Some of them have shielded themselves with the sombre mask of Lord Byron. But Byron's melancholy discordance was real and therefore capable of producing a tragic effect, whereas these poets childishly dissect themselves or rather allow themselves to be dismembered by the imaginary monsters of their own fancy, so that an astonished public may see them bleed to death in picturesque poses. . . ."

Heine was born in the Rhenish city of Düsseldorf. Having spent several years as an apprentice in the business of a wealthy uncle in Hamburg, he subsequently studied law at the University of Göttingen. He traveled for some time in Germany, England, and Italy, and finally settled down in Paris, attracted by the glitter of Bohemian life and the promises of the French revolution of 1830. He lived on the proceeds of his journalistic writings and on a pension granted him by the French government. His marriage to Eugenie (Mathilde) Mirat turned out a failure and became a source of mental torture and self-accusation. In 1847 Heine was afflicted with a progressive spinal disease which made the nine remaining years of his life a prolonged agony. The gloom of these years of suffering was somewhat brightened by his love for Elise Krinitz (Camilla Senden, the *"Mouche"*),

---

* The Jews were granted equality of civic rights in France in 1791, in Prussia in 1812, in the rest of Germany between 1848 and 1869, in England in 1847, in Italy in 1858.

who appeared to the ailing poet as an angel of mercy and who stayed with him through the darkest hours. His deadly disease caused his body to die literally limb by limb.

Heine's most famous collection of lyrics, the *Book of Songs* (*Buch der Lieder*, 1827), was chiefly inspired by his unrequited love for his uncle's daughter Amalie. The natural rhythm and melodic charm of this early poetry was marred only by the author's ever watchful and wistful intellect, which maliciously delighted in turning its mockery and bitter satire against his own self and against the creations of his love and devotion. Many of the poems contained in the *Book of Songs* and in several collections of later date reveal Heine's indebtedness to the Romantic School (cf. p. 470 sqq.). Some of them achieved the simplicity and depth of folk poetry (*Die Lorelei*), while others owe their fame to the fact that they served as texts for some of the greatest of German song composers (Schubert, Schumann, Mendelssohn). The sincerest and artistically most mature poems are contained in the collection *Romanzero* (1853), in which Heine paid his debt of gratitude to Elise Krinitz. These last poems speak at times with the immediacy and passionate fervor of a great confession, revealing in tragic undertones a self-knowledge ripened by suffering and rising to the grand style of biblical lamentation.

Heine's prose* mastered all the nuances of wit and esprit, from subtle irony to bitter sarcasm, combining the plastic imagery of the poet with the sparkling lightness and versatility of the born journalist, but lacking the positive metaphysical qualifications of the genuine satirist.

In December, 1834, while in Paris, Heine wrote a series of essays on the *History of Religion and Philosophy in Germany*. In a penetrating analysis of the philosophy of Kant and his followers the author arrived at the conclusion that "transcendental idealism" constituted a revolution in the realm of thought which was bound to make itself felt in the arena of political action. In almost prophetic words he predicted a sequence of events that would logically follow from the adoption of the philosophical premises of Kant, Fichte, Hegel, and Schelling: "There will be followers of Kant," he wrote at the end of the third book, "who will forsake piety and reverence even in the world of phenomena. Pitilessly they will ransack the foundations of Europe. . . . Followers of Fichte will appear on the scene in full armor. The fanaticism of their will-power can be checked neither by fear nor by selfishness, for like the early Christians they live in a world of the spirit and defy matter. . . . But more horrible than all these will be the 'nature philosophers.' . . . They will re-establish contact with the telluric forces of nature, conjuring up the satanic powers of old-Germanic pantheism. Within their breast there will come to life a war-lust . . . which does not wish to

---

* Heine's major prose works include the *Reisebilder* (*Travel Pictures*, especially *Die Harzreise*, 1826) and *Die romantische Schule* (*The Romantic School*, but with antiromantic tendency); outstanding among his satires are *Atta Troll* (1843) and *Deutschland, ein Wintermärchen* (*Germany: A Winter's Fairy Tale*, 1844).

fight in order to destroy nor in order to vanquish, but which makes fighting an end in itself. . . . If the time should ever come when the Christian Cross will break down, then the savagery of the ancient warriors will reappear . . . ; the ancient gods of stone will rise from their graves. . . . Thor with his hammer will rise and destroy the Gothic cathedrals. We must expect the same revolution in the world of phenomena that we have witnessed in the realm of the spirit. Thought precedes action as lightning precedes thunder. . . . And when you hear it crash as it has never crashed before in the history of the world, then you will know that the German thunder has reached its mark. There will be such a commotion that the eagles will drop dead to the ground, and the lions in the distant deserts of Africa will put their tails between their legs and withdraw to their royal dens. Germany will then offer a spectacle which will make the great French Revolution appear as a harmless idyl. . . ."

b) Literary Neo-Classicism. In literature as in painting the victory of realism was preceded by a brief revival of classicism that was intended as a protest against the sentimentalities of a false romanticism on the one hand and against the uncouth informality of the Young Germans on the other. As painters, sculptors, and architects had been attracted to the court of King Louis I of Bavaria, so poets, scholars, and writers gathered at the court of his successor, Maximilian II (1848–1864). The members of the royal "Symposium," convening at regular intervals in the presence of the king, were united in their conviction that smoothness of form and purity of verse were more important than intensity of feeling or, generally speaking, vitality of content. The prose and verse compositions of the two leading neo-classicists of Munich, *Emanuel Geibel* (1815–1884) and *Paul Heyse* (1830–1914), suffered accordingly from defects which resulted from an aesthetic ideal that was unrelated to life: though sometimes rich in formal beauty, their works were cool and academic, carefully excluding all shrill discords and everything that was disorderly or in any way repugnant to sensitive minds.

c) Poetic Realism. The generation of the Industrial Revolution, of the early machine age, and of the great advances in the sciences was most adequately represented by a literature that was neither romantic and otherworldly nor in the service of social polemics and political propaganda but rather concerned with the realistic observation and description of life in all its aspects. The authors who were thus the spokesmen of the *Zeitgeist* in a more profound sense than the Young Germans may therefore best be characterized as "poetic realists." They were realists in that they were interested in giving an unvarnished account of contemporary life, and they were poets in that they knew how to discriminate between the essential and the trivial, how to select and how to condense, so as to impart to their works both the breath of reality and the shimmer of poetry.

Annette von Droste-Hülshoff (1797–1848), the first of the great nineteenth-century realists in Germany and one of the greatest poetesses of modern times, was a descendant of ancient Westphalian aristocracy. Until 1840 she lived mostly on the secluded estates of her family, but then she moved southward to spend the last eight years of her life in the old castle of Meersburg on the shores of Lake Constance. The unusual qualities of her poetry derive from an equally unusual personality, which was dominated by two steadying influences, the Catholic faith of her ancestors and the austere moorland scenery of her native Westphalia. Calling upon a masculine will to overcome the frail femininity of her physical constitution, she found in religion and nature the sources of her strength of character and of the clarity of her literary form. Her senses were wide awake, registering acutely the wonders of creation and experiencing cosmic order and fruitful abundance in its greatest and smallest manifestations. Her poetic vision penetrated through the physical contours of individuals, objects, and scenes, giving voice, shape, and atmosphere to the hidden creative forces of nature.

Annette von Droste's writings were true to herself, to her spiritual heritage, and to the traditions and local customs of her homeland. She is at her best in her nature poetry and in her verse epics and historical ballads, whose setting suggests the brooding melancholy and somber beauty of the Westphalian heath. Her cycle of religious poems entitled *Das geistliche Jahr* (*The Spiritual Year*), comparable to John Keble's (1792–1866) *Christian Year,* provides poetic paraphrases of the Sunday and feast-day Gospels (*Pericopes*) of the ecclesiastical year. In her village novelette, *Die Judenbuche* (*The Jew's Beech Tree*), she makes Nature herself the avenger of a secretly committed crime and therewith the guardian of moral law and the restorer of the violated cosmic order.

The Silesian *Gustav Freytag* (1816–1895), in his lengthy and ambitious historical novels, was a historian in disguise, like some of the painters of the same period. In *Soll und Haben* (Debet and Credit), however, he made use of his intimate acquaintance with contemporary social and economic trends in presenting a vivid realistic picture of the life of the commercial middle class. In his exuberant comedy *Die Journalisten* he portrays with kindly humor the representatives of the daily press and satirizes the methods of politicians and party bosses. Freytag's most endearing qualities live on in his *Bilder aus der deutschen Vergangenheit* (*Pictures From the German Past*), which in scope and literary form still ranks high among the standard works on German cultural history.

In *Adalbert Stifter* (1805–1868) the genius of Austria made one of its ripest contributions to German literature. Temporarily forgotten or unappreciated, this great novelist was rediscovered by Friedrich Nietzsche (cf. p. 695 sq.), who found in Stifter's works "a world of beauty" and who counted the novel *Nachsommer* (*Mellow Autumn*) among his favorite books.

In Stifter's life and work Austrian Catholicism and German Classical Idealism (cf. Chap. 12) fused. He was instructed in his early youth by monks of the Benedictine Order, and the sense of proportion and harmony embodied in the Benedictine pattern of life and thought became one of the precious assets of Stifter's literary art. His most admired models among modern German authors were Goethe, Herder, and Jean Paul. Contentment, however, he found neither in classical grandeur nor in romantic exuberance, but only in quiet communication with nature, in the great stillness that was born in him when he contemplated the humble forms of minerals, plants, and animals. He looked at nature with the sentiment of a religious devotee and with the eyes of an artist, thus discovering in its varying shapes and nuances "a visible incarnation of the Godhead."

Stifter was a great "poetic" realist, precisely because he was more interested in the moral norm incarnate in reality than in a mere counterfeit or literary double of life. His art was strong enough not to be affected by the innate pedagogical bent of his mind. The characters of his two long novels and of his many short stories* are symbols of a divinely consecrated life and of a human destiny that is shaped by the incentives of will and reason. God's providence extends throughout the universe in all directions, through past, present, and future. God reveals Himself, His designs, and His judgments no less in nature than in history, and the portrayal of the past as much as the description of the present become thus symbolic images of eternal verities.

Realists of an entirely different temper were *Otto Ludwig* (1813–1865) and *Friedrich Hebbel* (1813–1863) who, like Richard Wagner, were born in the year of the "Battle of the Nations" and whose minds reflected an experience of reality that was not unified and harmonized but dialectically broken by the impact of conflicting ideas. It was for this reason that both authors regarded the *drama* as their most suitable means of expression, although Ludwig at first wavered between music and literature and attained to greater artistic perfection in his realistic novels than in his two completed dramas** and his many dramatic fragments.

In accordance with the epico-musical propensities of his talent it was Ludwig's ambition to create an artistic form and technique which in theory at least may be compared with Richard Wagner's idea of the "music drama" (cf. p. 493 sqq.). The epical style of his novels, especially of the tragic village romance *Zwischen Himmel und Erde* (*Between Heaven and Earth*, 1856), comes closest to a combination of the elements of narrative and musical composition. The detailed realistic description of environment and the profound and exhaustive character analyses unite to bring out the dual

---

* The novel *Der Nachsommer* (1857) has as its cultural background the period of the Austrian *Vormärz;* the historical novel *Witiko* tells of the national aspirations of southern Bohemia in the twelfth century. The most accomplished of his novelettes are contained in the two collections *Studien* (6 vols.) and *Bunte Steine* (2 vols.).

** *Der Erbförster* (*The Hereditary Forester*), "a forest tragedy" (1850), whose plot is laid in Ludwig's homeland of Thuringia, and *Die Makkabäer,* the dramatization of an episode recorded in some (partly apocryphal) Old Testament texts, dealing with the persecution of the Jews under King Antioch of Syria, and their successful struggle for liberation (second century B.C.).

characteristics of plasticity and musicality. Ludwig's knowledge of the human soul, its conflicts, its delusions and aberrations, makes him one of the masters of the psychological novel. The stress laid on the conditioning influences of environment and heredity makes him anticipate some of the pet theories of the foremost naturalistic writers of the later nineteenth century (Zola, Ibsen, Hauptmann, etc.). Ludwig's interest in psychology as well as his antagonism to Schiller's idealistic type of drama caused him to delve deeply into the nature of Shakespearean tragedy, and as the fruit of these endeavors he composed two volumes of *Shakespeare-Studien*.

Ludwig's pronounced dislike of Schiller was shared by *Friedrich Hebbel*. This strong-willed playwright and lyricist was born in the North German lowlands of Dithmarschen (Holstein). He had several characteristics in common with his sensitive and introspective contemporary from the Thuringian mountains: both writers were stimulated as well as handicapped by a pungent intellect which in Hebbel's case frequently got the better of his poetic impulses. Both were masters of psychological analysis, both viewed their characters as in part determined by environmental influences, and Hebbel as much as Ludwig was given to philosophical speculation and rationalistic reflection. To this extent their "dialectical" realism appeared to be nourished by identical sources, but aside from such general similarities in their mental constitution they were far apart in their artistic will, in their basic ideological tenets, and in their literary technique.

Friedrich Hebbel, though he wrote lyric and epic poems, never doubted that he was predestined to be a dramatist. He adhered to this conviction with a rare singleness of purpose, undismayed by obstacles, setbacks, and disappointments of many kinds, until at last he achieved not only a high degree of perfection as a playwright but public recognition and also personal happiness in his marital union with the Viennese actress Christine Enghaus.

The son of a poor stonemason, Hebbel went through dark years of privation and humiliating human bondage. Maturing gradually in combat with adversities, he finally attained a philosophy of life which was consistent enough in itself, but whose pessimism reflected the disheartening experiences of his apprenticeship as man and author.

A letter addressed to the seamstress Elise Lensing dates from the years of Hebbel's dismal struggle for his material and spiritual existence. He felt bound to her not by love but by a weighty debt of gratitude, for she was not only the mother of his child, but by her unrelenting toil and sacrifice she had made it possible for the playwright to remain loyal to his literary calling. "You ask me," Hebbel writes, "what deadly disease had me in its grip? My dear child, there is only one death and only one deadly disease, but it is impossible to give it a name. . . . It is the experience of the absolute contradiction in everything. . . . Whether there is a remedy for this disease, I know not, but this I know, that the physician who would cure me (whether he reside above the stars or in the center of my own self), must first of all cure the entire world. . . ."

Hebbel's "pan-tragic" philosophy of life, which seems condensed in this passage as in an outcry of despair and to which the author later on gave forceful speculative and dramatic expression, was clearly suggested by Hegel's dialectics (cf. p. 502 sqq.). The philosophical elaboration of the theory of Hebbel's *"Pantragismus"* we find in his *Diaries,* its dramatic exemplification in his tragedies.

The "pan-tragic" view holds that there is an incurable cleavage in all life, manifesting itself in such antithetical contradictions as life and death, time and eternity, natural inclination and moral obligation, male and female, individual claims and social demands. Thus an irreconcilable dualism cuts straight through the entire realm of creation, inevitably carrying in its wake the seeds of conflict and tragedy. The tragic fate of individuals therefore does not result from personal guilt but rather from some primordial metaphysical guilt inherent in the texture of life itself and necessitated by the very fact of individuation. "In God alone is harmony," says Hebbel, contending that by his individuation man has set up himself against the universe and its Creator. Individuation implies guilt and suffering, because by asserting his individuality the individual clashes of necessity with the laws and conventions of superindividual realities, such as the State, Society, and Religion. The greater the individual personality, the stronger will be his self-assertion or his revolt against the "sleep of the world," the more devastating his encounter with the inexorable decrees of universal laws, and the more tragic his ultimate self-destruction.

By proclaiming that the happiness of the individual must be sacrificed on the altar of the "world spirit," Hebbel reveals his indebtedness to Hegelian metaphysics. The individual, in pursuing his own ends, serves in reality only the higher ends of this Hegelian Deity: while the individual tragically succumbs, the "world spirit" marches victoriously on.

The dialectical method influences also Hebbel's choice of the historical theme and *milieu:* his heroes find themselves placed in the midst of waning and rising cultural forces, and they find themselves involved in and eventually crushed by the impact of the elements of change and progress upon the inert strength of tradition. These heroes and heroines are "supermen" and "superwomen" who by virtue of their keener vision and their greater ambition are foredoomed to personal tragedy. But they were also predestined to be bold leaders in eras of transition (*Schwellenzeiten*), releasing the most vital ideological forces and pointing the way to cultural progress.

Thus Hebbel's most significant dramas are variations of an almost identical theme. In *Judith* the biblical heroine of the same name sets out to free her Jewish homeland from the danger of Assyrian invasion by killing Holofernes, the victorious general of King Nabuchodonosor (sixth century B.C.). Impressed by the commanding vigor of this barbarian chieftain she momentarily forgets her exalted mission. When she beheads the sleeping Holofernes she realizes with horror that her deed was not inspired by heroic patriotism but by the desire to avenge her violated womanhood. What she does not realize is that by an act of personal revenge she has been instrumental in assuring the victory of Judaism over heathen barbarism.

In the preface to the "middle-class tragedy" (*bürgerliches Trauerspiel*) *Maria Magdalene,* Hebbel reproaches his predecessors in this dramatic genre (Lessing, Schiller) for having evolved the tragic conflict from a clash between the middle class and the aristocracy. He proposes to demonstrate in his drama that "crushing tragedy is possible even within the most limited social circle." The result of this attempt fully justified the author's claim: *Maria Magdalene* became the unsurpassed model of modern realistic drama. The tragic conflict derives from the conventional middle-class concepts of honor and morality which seem unable to cope with the elemental emotions of the human heart and with the deepest and truest essence of human personality. "Meister Anton," who by his petrified code of ethics drives his daughter Clara into self-destruction, must confess in the end that he no longer understands a world that has outgrown the limited horizons of his bourgeois mentality.

Returning to the biblical setting of *Judith,* Hebbel develops in *Herodes und Mariamne* the pattern of Hegel's dialectical triad — thesis, antithesis, synthesis — almost in form of a spiral movement: the antithetical opposition between Judaism and Romanism presses irresistibly onward to the dawn of the Christian era. Herod, the representative of an egocentered individualism, is confronted with the progressive forces of Roman collectivism and the new Christian humanism, in which both the individual and social claims find themselves affirmed on a higher plane. Herod's love for Mariamne lacks the element of respect for the rights of human personality, and by violating her spiritual self through distrust and by the use of despotic force he invites the inevitable tragic conflict between the worlds which they both represent: a clash of ideas in which the "world spirit" once more demonstrates symbolically the doom of the one and the victory of the other.

The historic background of the tragedy *Agnes Bernauer* is the German duchy of Bavaria in the period of the early Renaissance (fifteenth century). Again the argument runs along Hegelian lines. Agnes, the "angel of Augsburg," the beautiful daughter of an Augsburg barber, happily married to Albrecht, the son of Duke Ernst of Bavaria, is drowned in the Danube at the behest of the old duke and in the name of the "reason of State." The ultimate approval of this dastardly crime on the part of Duke Albrecht is justified by Hebbel on the ground that, in the case of conflicting interests of the individual and the State, even the noblest individual is to be sacrificed for the greater glory of the State, since the individual is only a fragmentary expression of Morality and Humanity "writ large," as they are embodied in the State.

Gyges und sein Ring (The Ring of Gyges) resumes the thesis of *Herodes und Mariamne,* this time in a partly historical, partly mythological Greek setting. The Lydian King Kandaules, presented by his Greek friend Gyges with a magic ring that makes its bearer invisible, tries to gain through another's testimony the reassurance of his wife Rhodope's matchless beauty by persuading Gyges to enter the queen's chamber, protected by the ring's magic power. The accidental discovery of the truth leads to the destruction of both Kandaules and Rhodope: the king is killed by Gyges in single combat, and Rhodope dies by her own hand. Kandaules and Rhodope are both tragic characters: the former violating the narrowly circumscribed sphere of the moral standards prescribed by Oriental custom, yet seizing upon the wrong means to demonstrate his freedom from meaningless traditions and conventional prejudice; the latter falling a victim to her unthinking abidance by the rigid moral code of her ancestors.

Hebbel's last completed dramatic work, the trilogy of the *Nibelungen* (*Horny Siegfried; Siegfried's Death; Kriemhild's Revenge*), was the first of his plays to be enthusiastically acclaimed by the public. Following closely the sequence of events as recorded in the *Nibelungenlied* (cf. p. 154), the author tries to motivate psychologically the actions of the main characters. The tragic end of the Nibelungen appears as the necessary fate of a world that has to die, so that a new creed may arise from the shattered pagan ethics of revenge and brute force: Dietrich von Bern proclaims the new message of mercy and forgiveness, "in the name of Him who died on the Cross."

The panorama of literary Realism in the nineteenth century is rounded out by the work of five authors, each of whom represents a very definite *milieu* and a clearly circumscribed set of social and literary motifs. Three of these writers are of German-Swiss nationality (Gotthelf, Keller, Meyer) and two are North Germans (Raabe, Storm).

The one who is most significant as an epic poet and as a national educator, but least known outside the narrow circle of his immediate environment, is *Jeremias Gotthelf* (pen name for Albert Bitzius, 1797–1854), by vocation a pastor of the Reformed (Zwinglian) Church of Switzerland. His epic style is marked by a pithy humor, and the characters of his social and pedagogical novels are robust and full of vitality. That Gotthelf's gifts as a writer of the highest rank remained unappreciated by the critics and the reading public of Europe was due not only to his frequent use of the Swiss dialect but even more to his opposition to the liberal *Zeitgeist*.*

The distinctive qualities of Gotthelf's literary art lived on, however, in the works of his younger countryman *Gottfried Keller* (1819–1890). Undecided in his early youth as to whether to turn to landscape painting or literature, Keller became the most popular storyteller and lyricist of his native country. Spending fifteen years of his mature life (1861–1876) as a clerk in the civil service of his home Canton of Zurich, he embodied in his novels, short stories, and poems the indigenous virtues of a solid bourgeois culture and its democratic-liberal ideology. His sturdy humor derives its

---

* Gotthelf's two outstanding novels are *Uli der Knecht* (the farm hand) and its continuation *Uli der Pächter* (the farmer).

amiable naïveté and natural freshness from its closeness to the soil and to popular and national tradition.

Keller's "poetic realism" develops from the subjective immediacy of his early lyrics and narratives to the even flow and contemplative epic temper of his mature style. This important change is illustrated by the two versions of his partly autobiographical masterpiece *Der grüne Heinrich* (*Green Henry*, 1855 and 1879), one of the outstanding examples of the German *Entwicklungsroman* (novel of character development), which as a human document and as an artistic achievement may be said to be on a par with Goethe's *Wilhelm Meister* (cf. p. 412). In several cycles of novelettes, interwoven and united with each other by a common theme or "frame" (*Rahmenerzählung*),* Keller shows himself a master of the short story (*Novelle*). He reaches the heights of Shakespearean or Kleistian tragedy in the simple and austere contours of the village epic *Romeo und Julia auf dem Dorfe* (*A Village Romeo and Juliet*).

The prose and poetry of Keller's contemporary and fellow countryman, *Conrad Ferdinand Meyer* (1825–1898), represent a type of realism which is in some respects directly opposed to the human and cultural values embodied in Keller's art. Meyer, like Keller a native of the city of Zurich, was an aristocrat both by descent and personal taste. The nervously sensitive heir of past ages of daring and doing, he mourned his fate of being born in an era that seemed willing to sacrifice distinctions of character to egalitarian democratic ideals. He turned to the past for inspiration and found models for the main characters of his novels in the age of the Renaissance and Reformation, an age in which the forces of antidemocratic individualism had discovered new forms of passionate self-expression. Pouring the liquid fire of his emotional life into a classically chiseled stylistic mold, Meyer's literary creations linked the cultural and artistic traditions of the Romanic South with those of the Germanic North. Wavering for a considerable length of time between French and German as an adequate medium of his literary expression, Meyer's sympathy for Germany was aroused by the Franco-Prussian War, and in his epic poem *Huttens letzte Tage* he paid an enthusiastic tribute to both German nationalism and German Protestantism. Positively, in the glorification of the tendencies and characters of Renaissance and Reformation, and negatively, in his taunting of medieval institutions, his novels, short stories, and poems are flawless documents of his artistic and spiritual convictions.**

The realism of *Wilhelm Raabe* (1831–1910) is tinged with romantic longing and receives its pessimistic note from the author's abhorrence of the materialistic trends of his age. This north German novelist, a native of

---

* Keller's best known short stories are contained in the series *Die Leute von Seldwyla* (*The People of Seldwyla*), in which the human characters are portrayed in the native setting of a fictitious Swiss town, and in the *"Rahmenerzählung" Das Sinngedicht* (Epigram).

** Characteristic of Meyer's prose works are *Der Heilige* (*The Saint*), an account of the life and martyrdom of Thomas Becket († 1170), archbishop of Canterbury and chancellor of King Henry II of England, and *Jürg Jenatsch*, a novel of the Swiss past.

Brunswick (Braunschweig), whose style, philosophical outlook, and peculiarly melancholy humor are indebted to Dickens, Thackeray, Jean Paul, and Schopenhauer, went in his literary and spiritual development through several distinct phases. His early works were typical expressions of an intellectual crisis marked by the transition from romanticism to realism. The masterpieces of his second period (especially the trilogy, *Der Hungerpastor; Abu Telfan; Der Schüdderump*) portray with merciless realism the mortal combat between the powers of love and steadfast devotion and the demonic forces of sin, error, falsehood, and selfishness. In Raabe's third period a wisdom seasoned by manifold experience replaces his pessimism, and the author attains to a critically balanced and philosophically tempered understanding of human life (*Horacker, Stopfkuchen,* etc.).

Theodor Storm (1817–1888) is a bourgeois poet and novelist of romantic leanings, whose gentle melancholy lacks the dark strains of Raabe's pessimism. His realistic technique succeeds in making his narratives memoirs of the landscape of his beloved native Schleswig, of the vast north German plains, the heath, the marshlands, and the sea, and of the taciturn and sober Frisian people. An ardent German patriot, Storm, who had established himself as a lawyer in his home town of Husum, was forced to leave Schleswig in 1853. He entered the Prussian civil service in Potsdam but returned to his homeland after the Danish-Prussian War of 1864. With great versatility he cultivated every imaginable genre of the short story, at times taxing the reader's patience by the stereotyped repetition of identical motifs, but achieving occasionally a fusion of romantic mood, idyllic charm, and realistic animation which makes such tales as *Immensee* or *Renate* gems of rare beauty. In his lyric poetry Storm shows himself influenced by Eichendorff (cf. p. 478 sq.). Here as in his prose works the varying moods of nature and the emotions of love and longing figure prominently. In his lyrics the subdued gray and silvery hues of the north German landscape with its concomitant intimation of loneliness and ominous dread have found a deeply moving expression.

Historiography. The transition from romanticism to realism found the historians engaged in an endeavor to look at historic evolution from a "realistic" point of view. This implied first of all the narrowing down of the scope of history to include only the political structure of states and the material conditions of their growth, and secondly, the attempt to confine themselves to a strictly factual presentation of historical data. Wilhelm von Humboldt's demand that the historian disregard in his account the ultimate ends of life and history and be satisfied with factual observation and narration, was heeded by *Leopold von Ranke* (1795–1886), who tried in his great historical masterpieces* to understand historic events "as they

---

* *The Roman Popes in the Sixteenth and Seventeenth Centuries* (3 vols., 1834–1836); *German History in the Age of the Reformation* (5 vols., 1839–1847); *World History* (to the eleventh century, 9 vols., 1881–1888), etc. — Ranke's works comprise 54 volumes in all (new ed. of the German Academy, 1925 sqq.).

have actually occurred." In brilliant analyses Ranke describes the gradual emancipation of the modern national states from the universalism of the medieval empire. He found the idea of "Humanity" embodied in the history of individual nations, and in accordance with his theological convictions he maintained that "each epoch stands in an immediate relationship to God." He thus demanded a historiography that recognized the individuality of each epoch but with a view to its significance in the larger context of the universal history of the human race. "Historic epochs succeed each other," he wrote, "so that in their totality be fulfilled what is impossible of fulfillment in each of them individually and that thus the plenitude of the spiritual life infused into the human race by the Deity may become manifest in the sequence of the centuries." In the individual historic States he saw "original creations of the human mind, ideas of God, so to speak."

Ranke was the leading historian of this age of transition precisely because he was able to comprehend the conditioning factors in historical phenomena, without submitting to the materialistic dogmas of cultural determinism and historic relativism. As a historian who had the ambition "to extinguish his own ego," he differed from the eighteenth-century rationalists on the one hand and from the partisan political writers who succeeded him, on the other. As a devout Lutheran Ranke shared Hegel's unquestioning respect for the divinely willed authority of the State and was furthermore convinced of the providential mission of the German nation as the originator and standard-bearer of the Reformation.

Among the other great German "political historians" of the nineteenth century three stand out: *Gustav Droysen* (1808–1884), *Theodor Mommsen* (1817–1903), and *Heinrich von Treitschke* (1834–1896). As a member of the Frankfurt National Assembly (cf. p. 530 sqq.) as well as in his *History of Prussian Politics* (14 vols., 1855–1886) Droysen passionately advocated the idea of Prussian hegemony over all Germany. His studies of medieval history convinced him that the "Holy Roman Empire" was an ideological aberration and that Germany's greatness depended on Prussian leadership. The son of an army chaplain, Droysen had grown up in a military atmosphere in which the tradition of the Prussian soldier-kings blended with the ideals of nineteenth-century liberalism. Success he regarded as the infallible criterion of political action, and the shortest way to the goal of national power seemed to him the surest and therefore the best way.

Mommsen was a historian, jurist, and philologist of liberal-democratic convictions, whose *Roman History* is counted among the standard works of modern historiography. He taught at the Universities of Leipzig, Zurich, Breslau, and Berlin, and his political career included membership in the Prussian Diet and in the German *Reichstag*.

The one-sidedness of pro-Prussian political historiography found its most fanatical protagonist in Treitschke, whose *German History in the Nineteenth Century* (5 vols., 1879) became one of the most widely circulated and most effective documents of Pan-Prussianism and Pan-Germanism. His advocacy of Bismarck's "smaller Germany" under the leadership of Prussia made him a sworn enemy of the principle of federation* and a violent opponent of the supernational aims of Roman Catholicism.

Education. The practical tendencies of the machine age made themselves felt in corresponding changes and shifts of emphasis in the educational curriculum of secondary schools and universities. Training in "dead" languages, such as Greek and Latin, was regarded as unnecessary for the future captain of industry, factory executive, and public official. The new *Realgymnasium* tried to effect a compromise between the liberal arts curriculum of the humanistic *Gymnasium* (cf. p. 441) and the demand for due consideration of scientific and technical training and proficiency in modern languages. Special industrial and technical schools (*Gewerbeschulen*) were to prepare the students for specific practical occupations.

The abstract intellectualism firmly implanted and proudly adhered to in the humanistic *Gymnasium* was met by the educational "realists" with the creation of a new type of *Bürger-Gymnasium* (middle-class gymnasium) or *Realschule,* whose curriculum was made up chiefly of technical subjects, and which had as its object the preparatory training of specialists in commercial and industrial pursuits.

In the same degree in which the "realistic" secondary schools adjusted their curriculum to the practical requirements of the industrial age, the universities on their part submitted to the trend of specialization and assumed the character of professional training centers for scientists, physicians, jurists, educators, and theologians. The increasing demand for advanced technological training led to the creation of polytechnical institutes (*Technische Hochschulen*)** of university rank, open to those who had completed their prescribed course (9 years) of secondary education.

Education on a nationwide scale was thoroughly organized and monopolized, first by the individual state governments and afterward by the centralized national State. While this centralization and State control made possible great achievements in science and industry, it also tended in a steadily increasing measure to thwart true independence of thought. The schools came to function more and more as collective agencies for the propagation of certain governmental policies. Once the hegemony of Prussia over Germany was secured, the entire educational system was pressed into the service of Prussian nationalism and militarism. This important transformation was prepared during the period of the *Vormärz* (1815–1848) and received its systematic consolidation between 1848 and the closing decade

---

* Federalism (*Föderalismus*), as opposed to "unitarism" or centralization, advocates the autonomy or semiautonomy of individual states within the larger frame of a federal national State: it is diversity in unity. The "Holy Roman Empire" may be considered as a model of federalist organization. In modern times the United States and the republic of Switzerland are outstanding examples of federalist nations.

** The first polytechnical institutes in Germany were those of Beuth (1818), Karlsruhe (1825), Nuremberg (1827), Dresden (1828), Stuttgart (1832), and Darmstadt (1836). Later foundations are those of Munich (1867), Aachen (1870), and Breslau (1910).

of the century. While it is obvious that many of the larger and smaller German states contributed their share to educational theory and practice and that at no time the educational institutions of Germany accepted a pattern of mechanical uniformity, it is nevertheless true that the basic tenets adhered to by all German schools were those fostered by the political and intellectual leaders of Prussia. "When I look back upon the forty years during which I have been professor and examiner," wrote the famous anthropologist Rudolf Virchow (cf. p. 563) in 1890, " . . . I cannot say . . . that we have made material advance in training men with strength of character. . . . The number of 'characters' becomes smaller, and this is connected with the shrinkage in private and individual work performed during the pupil's school life."

Philosophy. Hegel's metaphysics (cf. p. 502 sqq.) represented a final attempt during the transitional period between romanticism and realism to unite science, philosophy, and religion in one all-embracing system of thought. We have pointed out (cf. p. 505) that Hegel's own dialectical method was seized upon by the "Young Hegelians" to attack and destroy the idealistic premises of their master's philosophical creed. Positivism (cf. p. 566 sq.) in the form of "historic materialism" no longer saw in history any issues involving truth or falsehood but merely facts and material forces. Even while Hegel was still alive the inductive methods of the empirical sciences began to replace the deductive rationalism of his own system, and metaphysical speculation suffered an almost total eclipse. Auguste Comte's (cf. p. 566) positivism became first a powerful rival of Hegelian thought and then its triumphant conqueror.

German positivism, following in Comte's footsteps, was nevertheless thoroughly German in that it recognized the intrinsic logical conclusions implied in Comte's positivistic premises and accordingly developed a consistent and integral materialism. In the course of the so-called *Materialismusstreit* (quarrel of the materialists), dating from the year 1854, the German Darwinist Karl Vogt published a widely read essay entitled *Köhlerglaube und Wissenschaft** (1855), in which he tried with cynical witticism to dispense with the problem of the human soul. According to Vogt, thought is a secretion of the brain just as the digestive juices are secretions of the stomach, bile a secretion of the liver, and urine a secretion of the kidneys. Three years earlier the physiologist Jakob Moleschott, in his *Kreislauf des Lebens* (Cycle of Life) had expressed similar views. At about the same time the physician Ludwig Büchner launched a violent attack against the "Kant-swindle" and against "Hegel and his accomplices," in a book entitled *Kraft und Stoff (Force and Matter)*, in which he likewise defended the theses

---

* *Superstition and Science*. The term *Köhlerglaube*, referring to the blind faith of the uneducated masses, is said to be derived from a sixteenth-century tale, according to which a *Köhler* (charcoal burner), when questioned by a theologian as to his faith, gives the answer: "I believe what the Church believes," and upon the further question: "What does the Church believe?" responds: "The Church believes what I believe."

of a crude materialism. These theories were in the main a rehash of the teachings espoused by some of the leaders of French Enlightenment in the eighteenth century, of Holbach's (1723–1789) naturalism and Condillac's (1715–1780) sensism. The monistic "energeticism" of Wilhelm Ostwald (1853–1932), on the other hand, reducing matter to the spontaneous movement of atomic structures, was an attempt to salvage cultural and spiritual values without sacrificing the basic convictions of secularism and naturalism.

The severest blow against Hegel, however, was struck not by the materialists but by a representative of the religious individualism of the Christian-Protestant tradition. The Danish religious philosopher Søren Kierkegaard (1813–1855) regarded Hegel's philosophy and the teachings of liberal Protestantism as the two most dangerous anti-Christian forces in modern times. Against Hegel's pantheistic identification of God and world, of human intellect and divine Mind, Kierkegaard emphasized the unbridgeable cleavage between nature and supernature. Against Hegel's and Schleiermacher's (cf. p. 507 sq.) secularization of Christian dogma he preached a God who is the supreme Reality and the absolute Ruler of the universe. Against Hegel's deification of the omnipotent State he proclaimed the "inwardness" of the individual, whose salvation he regarded as of infinitely greater importance than the convolutions of the Hegelian "world spirit."

Kierkegaard's thinking was determined by Luther's contempt of reason on the one hand and by Hegel's deification of reason on the other. Because he was afraid that a positive evaluation of rational knowledge would of necessity lead to the obliteration of the distinctions between nature and spirit and ultimately to a Hegelian "philosophy of identity,"* he discarded reason for the sake of faith. Thus he contributed his share to the self-destruction of philosophy in the nineteenth century. Kierkegaard's epochal significance in the history of ideas was not recognized until more than half a century after his death, when, at the opening of the twentieth century, his numerous works and his *Journals* were not only widely read in his own country but became accessible in German translations.

More deeply and clearly than any other modern author, with the possible exception of Friedrich Nietzsche, Kierkegaard diagnosed the spiritual sickness of the modern age. Again and again he deplored the halfheartedness and intellectual slovenliness of his contemporaries, who lacked the courage and consistency to face the consequences of their own philosophical and religious convictions. He deplored that with the aid of Hegelian philosophy

---

* Kierkegaard's attack on Hegel was seconded from similar motives by Joseph Görres (cf. p. 479 sq.) who in 1842 parodied the "philosophy of identity" in these words: "In the beginning there was Nothingness, and Nothingness was with God, and God was Nothingness, and this Nothingness was with God from the beginning. Everything is made by the same, and without It nothing is made. In It was Life, and this Life was Death, which is the Light of Man, which out of non-existence stepped into existence, and which in Darkness and through Darkness begot individuality and consciousness. And Darkness shone into Light, but Light comprehended It not. There was a man sent forth from God. . . . His name was Hegel."

and liberal Protestant theology it had become an easy and comfortable thing
to call oneself a Christian and actually be a pagan. And he drew a sharp
dividing line between "Christianity" and "Christendom," maintaining that
whereas the former was a spiritual reality, the latter was but an "optical
illusion."

Thus Kierkegaard's thought culminated inevitably in the problem of
"choice," in an all-decisive "either — or," as he formulated this alternative
in the title of one of his profoundest works. "I want honesty," we read in one
of the polemical pamphlets written shortly before his death. "If that is
what this race and generation wants, if it will uprightly, honestly, frankly,
openly, directly rebel against Christianity and say to God: we can but we
will not subject ourselves to this authority . . . , well then, strange as
it may seem, I am for it; for honesty is what I want. . . . An honest
rebellion against Christianity can only be made when we honestly admit
what Christianity is and how we ourselves are related to it."

It is this refusal of compromise, this call for an intellectual honesty that
emanates from the very roots of human existence, which constitutes the
bases of Kierkegaard's influence on some of the most prominent philosophers and theologians of our own day. In the form of "existential"
philosophy (cf. p. 694) and Protestant "Dialectical Theology" (cf. p. 700 sq.)
Kierkegaard's speculation lives on as a challenge to the twentieth century.

Religion. The romantic movement had been instrumental in bringing
about a revival of religious consciousness in Germany among both
Protestants and Catholics. Schleiermacher (cf. p. 507 sq.) had developed his
pietistic theology in opposition to the two prevalent religious trends,
deistic rationalism and Lutheran orthodoxy. He in turn was attacked by
Hegel, whose intellectualism had no use for any exaltation of religious
"feeling." Hegel's philosophy of religion, which was an outgrowth of his
philosophy of history, stimulated the theological speculation of Protestants
and Catholics alike and served to revive the antagonism between the
followers of the two creeds, which had been temporarily alleviated in
the era of Enlightenment.

a) The School of Tübingen. The two opposing camps were entrenched
side by side at the Swabian University of Tübingen, after a Catholic
theological faculty had been attached to this ancient Lutheran stronghold
in 1817. The leaders of the "School of Tübingen" were Friedrich Christian
Baur (1792–1860), the earliest representative of liberal German Protestantism,
and Johann Adam Möhler (1796–1838), one of the most influential Catholic
theologians of the post-Reformation period. Baur was the first German
theologian to apply Hegel's dialectical method to biblical history. His
extended studies of the history of the Christian Church in the early
Christian centuries and his implicit faith in the Hegelian method led
him to the conclusion that the appearance and personal mission of Christ
signified a historically conditioned phase in the dialectical evolution of the
Christian idea, and that the Gospels were polemical pamphlets containing

propagandistic falsifications. The Epistles of St. Paul he regarded as documents reflecting the ideological struggles in the early Christian communities. The Acts of the Apostles he described as the work of one of Paul's disciples who had attempted to effect a compromise by smoothing over the fundamental differences of conviction.* In the Catholic Church Baur saw the final result of this compromise and therefore an imperfect form of Christianity. Despite the revolutionary implications of his ideas Baur was at heart a conservative and personally convinced that Hegel's philosophy could be squared with a strictly theistic point of view. Thus he was far removed from subscribing to the radicalism of his pupil, David Friedrich Strauss.

Möhler contributed to the spiritual revival of German Catholicism in the nineteenth century by drawing on the rich treasury of thought enshrined in the literature and philosophy of German Classicism and Romanticism. He recognized the religious significance of the new ideas for the organic growth of cultural formations and for the principle of historic evolution, and he utilized them for a deeper understanding of the traditional content of faith and dogma. His thorough knowledge of Protestantism enabled him to write his *Symbolik* (1832), in which he presented the dogmatic differences of Catholics and Protestants on the basis of their "symbolic" books, i.e., the officially recognized documents and articles of faith. Möhler's scholarly research in the period of the early Church Fathers laid the foundations for the new theological discipline of "patristics" (from the Latin, *pater,* meaning "father"). In the visible and historic Church he saw the product of organic growth, the "objectivation and living representation of the Christian religion." While he placed strong emphasis throughout on the common heritage of all Christian denominations, he criticized those dogmatic convictions in which the Protestant Churches had laid themselves open to the inroads of naturalism and secularism.

b) The United Protestant Church. Shortly after the War of Liberation and under the emotional stress of the tercentenary celebration of the Reformation (*Reformationsfest,* 1817) a unification of the Lutheran and Reformed Churches was effected in most German states. The first decisive steps in this direction were taken by King Frederick William III of Prussia who, himself a Calvinist, declared in a proclamation that it would please him very much if the year of pious commemoration were to see the birth of a "Christian-Evangelical Church, revitalized in the spirit of its hallowed founder." The most serious obstacle to the contemplated unification was the opposition of the Old Lutheran Orthodoxy, whose spokesman, the Lutheran pastor Claus Harms of Kiel, vigorously stated the case for his coreligionists in ninety-five theses.

---

* According to the best authorities the Acts of the Apostles were written by Luke (*c.* A.D. 63), the collaborator and companion of Paul and the author of the synoptic Gospel that bears his name. In 28 chapters they relate the apostolic activities of Peter and Paul to the end of the latter's first imprisonment in the city of Rome. Cf. Giuseppe Ricciotti, *The Life of Christ* (trans. by Alba I. Zizzamia, Bruce Publishing Co., Milwaukee, 1947, Critical Introduction).

The United Protestant Church of Prussia, which was in the main the creation of the king and his chancellor, Altenstein, was a rigidly organized State Church and constituted a signal victory of the absolute monarchy. While the material contributions of the United Church to ecclesiastical training and discipline and to improved standards in general education will be readily admitted, it cannot be denied that the fusion of secular and ecclesiastical power in the person of the monarch made the Church an instrument of political power. Its splendid external organization was unable to stem the rising tide of religious indifferentism among the educated as well as among the masses.

Disregarding the profound doctrinal differences which had originally caused the cleavage between Lutherans and Calvinists, the Prussian State Church failed to offer a common doctrinal ground and was therefore united only by its opposition to "Roman errors and abuses" (Schleiermacher). As far as theological convictions were concerned, it was a loose federative union, which henceforth existed side by side with the established and unyielding Old Lutheran and Old Calvinist church communities. A full doctrinal unification was achieved in the state of Baden, where the ruling grand duke issued an ecclesiastical constitution and assumed the title of *Landesbischof* (State bishop).

c) The Churches and the Social Question.   The Industrial Revolution and the rise of the proletariat as a class, whose ideology was determined either by atheistic materialism or religious indifferentism, confronted the Christian Churches as a challenge, forcing them to revitalize their spiritual resources. The political revolts of 1830 and 1848 threw the social question into the limelight of public attention and made it incumbent on the Churches to think of ways and means to remedy the abuses of the capitalistic system, if they wanted to retain or regain the allegiance of the masses.

In the Protestant denominations the social impulses of Christianity were stressed and put to the practical test not so much by the orthodoxy as by the smaller Christian sects and groups in Germany, which in their social activities followed the example of the English and American Free Churches. About the middle of the nineteenth century a gradually increasing number of humane societies, poorhouses, nurseries, and other similar organizations for the care of the poor and the welfare of the young came into existence. The pietistic sects (cf. p. 362 sqq.) in particular, which had never ceased to teach and labor in the interests of a practical Christianity, assumed courageous leadership in the new social movement.

Among these Protestant-Pietist reformers of the nineteenth century two personalities stand out by their unselfish devotion to the ideas of social Christianity. Theodor Fliedner (1800–1864), a native of Hesse, had acquainted himself with the methods of organized Christian social endeavor in Holland and England, and he used his experiences in the "Evangelical Asylum," which he founded in the Rhenish town of Kaiserswerth in 1833. This institution was chiefly dedicated to the care and education of female ex-convicts. In 1836 a hospital was established in the same city as a training center for Protestant nurses (*Diakonissen*), the first Protestant institution of its kind and the cradle of an association that extended to every part of Germany. A printing press and a bookstore, attached to the mother house, served to spread the social ideas underlying the foundation. In 1854 Fliedner created in Berlin the first *Hospiz* for unemployed servant girls (*Marthahaus*). Florence Nightingale (1820–1910), the great organizer of the English system of nursing and hospitalization, received her early training in the institutions of Kaiserswerth.

The second great apostle of Protestant organized social work was Johann Heinrich Wichern (1808–1881), who was born in the city of Hamburg. Owing to its many contacts with English life and culture, Hamburg proved a favorable environment for the adoption and imitation of the methods of English charitable institutions. Wichern's *Rauhes Haus* (Tough House) on the outskirts of Hamburg owed its foundation to his own sordid experiences in the slums of his native city, which had strengthened in him the resolve to devote his life to the cause of the outcast and the downtrodden. This house of refuge was the birthplace of the Protestant "Home Missions" (*Innere Mission*), which in their nationwide organization comprised the three major fields of social charity, missionary activity, and constructive social work.

Das Rauhe Haus offered shelter and educational guidance to boys between the ages of five and fourteen, most of them picked from the Hamburg slums. The children were grouped into "families" of twelve or less, and each "family" was placed under the guardianship of a "helper" or "father." Workshops served to prepare the boys for their future trades, and a publishing house provided invaluable aid for the tasks of education and evangelization. Wichern was wholeheartedly attached to the patriarchal order of society with its high regard for the independent work of the craftsman and artisan, and accordingly he tried to kindle in his charges a love for the ancient handicrafts.

Theologically Wichern shared the irenic convictions of the leaders of the pietistic revival movement and their belief in "One True Catholic Church," of which all existing Churches partake. "We believe," he wrote, "in the kernel of Christian Truth that is incarnate in all denominations, because we believe in the presence of the living Christ in all of them." He blamed both the State and the official clergy for their failure to cope with the problems of modern civilization, and he recommended the creation of "free Christian associations" to act as intervening links between home and Church: "If the proletarians no longer seek the Church, then the Church must begin to seek the proletarians," he wrote.

The "Central Committee of the Home Missions" was founded in 1848, the year of the "March Revolution." It was to be a world-wide and supernational organization, but in contradistinction to the "foreign missions" for the conversion of heathens it was to confine its efforts to "baptized Christians, among whom in our days paganism is even more conspicuous than it ever was among devout heathens." The "Home Missions" regarded both the general priesthood of all the faithful and the official ministry as necessary ingredients of a true Christian "Volkskirche."

Within the Catholic Church in Germany, too, the Industrial Revolution caused a re-examination of Christian doctrine in the light of the social question. Even in the early decades of the nineteenth century some of the Catholic romanticists had raised their voices in protest against the degradation of manual labor and the displacement of the laborer by the machine. The romantic philosopher Franz von Baader (1765–1841) was the first to emphasize the original social function of the priestly office, thus reminding the clergy of their duties toward the laboring class.

The actual Catholic-social movement, however, had its beginnings in the thirties and forties of the century and received its main incentives from the teachings of the Church itself. The two pioneers of social Catholicism were Adolf Kolping (1813–1865) and Bishop Emanuel von Ketteler (1811–1877) of Mainz. Kolping, before his ordination to the priesthood, was a poor, migrant journeyman, while Ketteler, a Westphalian nobleman, had been active as a jurist in the Prussian civil service before the influence of Görres (cf. p. 479 sq.) and his friends made him turn to the study of theology. The *Gesellenverein* (Journeymen's Union), founded by Kolping in Elberfeld in 1845 and centralized in Cologne in 1851, was the first symbolic manifestation of a new type of "social ministry" which soon made its appearance in every part of Germany. The individual local *Gesellenvereine*, each of them under the guidance of a priestly *Präses,* were destined to provide shelter for the young journeymen and opportunities for the improvement of their religious and vocational training as well as various recreational facilities.

A patriarchal family life served as the ideal pattern for each "Kolping-House." Kolping regarded it as one of the main objectives of his social endeavors to bring about a social regeneration by rebuilding "the crushed estate of craftsmen and artisans." Thereby he would render innocuous the two abuses of "rugged individualism" and listless collectivism: the society of the future was to rest as much on personal independence as on social responsibility, a combination of qualities that seemed to be prefigured in an exemplary way in the organism of the human family.

Bishop von Ketteler gained prominence as an outstanding leader of Christian-social thought and practical social policies in the stormy year of 1848, when he created a sensation with the social sermons delivered in the Cathedral of Mainz. He sided with the socialist doctrinaire Lassalle (cf. p. 559) in his fight against economic liberalism and took an active part in the trade-union movement among the workers. After an initial hesitation to endorse the enactment of State laws for the protection of the workingmen, fearing a fateful encroachment of the State on personal economic initiative, Ketteler became convinced in the end that private charitable and welfare organizations were unable to cope with the widespread distress of the proletariat, and that only an active and systematic social policy (*Sozialpolitik*) on the part of the State could check the abuses of economic power and protect the interests of the economically weaker members of modern society. Pope Leo XIII in his program of social reform specifically referred to the principles laid down in the writings and sermons of Bishop von Ketteler.*

---

* Cf. *Die Arbeiterfrage und das Christentum*, 1864; *Ausgewählte Schriften*, ed. J. Mumbauer, 3 vols., 1924.

PART VI. THE SECOND GERMAN EM-PIRE, WORLD WAR I, AND THE GERMAN REPUBLIC

1871–1887   *Kulturkampf*
1871–1888   William I, German emperor and king of Prussia, brother of Frederick William IV
1871–1890   Bismarck, *Reichskanzler*
1872   *Dreikaiserbund* (Three Emperors' League): peaceful understanding among William I of Germany, Francis Joseph I of Austria-Hungary, and Alexander II of Russia
1878   *Sozialistengesetz* (antisocialist law) — Congress of Berlin
1879   Protective alliance between Germany and Austria-Hungary — New protective tariffs — German-Austrian alliance
1882   The *Dreibund* (Triple Alliance) between Germany, Austria-Hungary, and Italy
1883   Enactment of health insurance legislation
1884   Neutrality Treaty with Russia — Acquisition of German colonies in South West Africa, Togo, and Kamerun
1884–1887   Enactment of accident insurance legislation
1885   Acquisition of German colonies in East Africa and on South Sea Islands
1887   *Rücksicherungsvertrag* (Reinsurance Treaty) with Russia
1888   Frederick III, German emperor and king of Prussia, son of William I (March 9 to June 15)
1888–1918   William II, son of Frederick III, German emperor and king of Prussia
1889   Enactment of invalidity and old age insurance legislation
1890   Dismissal of Bismarck — England cedes Heligoland to Germany, in exchange for Zanzibar, Wituland, and Uganda (all in East Africa)
1890–1894   General von Caprivi, *Reichskanzler*
1891   *Arbeiterschutzgesetz* (law for the protection of labor) — Commercial treaties with several nations and lowering of protective tariffs
1894–1900   Prince Hohenlohe, *Reichskanzler*
1895   Completion of *Kaiser Wilhelm-Kanal* (North Sea-Baltic Canal)
1898   First naval building program — China leases Kiaochow to Germany (99 year lease)
1899   Germany purchases from Spain the Caroline, Marian, and Palau Islands in Pacific — Construction of Dortmund–Ems Canal
1900   Promulgation of *Bürgerliches Gesetzbuch* (Civil Law Code) — Acquisition of German-Samoa in the Pacific — Navy Bill
1900–1909   Count (later Prince) Bülow, *Reichskanzler*
1902   New Customs Tariff
1905   Wilhelm II's visit to Tangier (first Morocco crisis)
1906   Increased *Reichssteuern* (federal taxes) and program for larger navy — The Algeciras Conference on Morocco

1909   King Edward VII of England visits Berlin — German-French Morocco Treaty

1909–1917   Von Bethmann-Hollweg, *Reichskanzler*

1911   Germany sends the gunboat *Panther* to Agadir (second Morocco crisis) — Agreement with France on Morocco and Equatorial Africa — Promulgation of a unified *Reichsversicherungsordnung* (federal insurance legislation)

1912   The new navy bill — Renewal of *Dreibund*

1912–1913   Balkan Wars

1913   Adoption of new army bill

1914–1918   World War I

1917   The emperor promises reform of Prussian *Dreiklassenwahlrecht* (electoral law) — Annulment of *Jesuitengesetz* (law of 1872, excluding the Society of Jesus from German territory) — *Reichskanzler:* Michaelis (July to October); Count von Hertling (October, 1917, to October, 1918)

1918   Prince Max von Baden, *Reichskanzler* — Mutiny of the German fleet — Revolution — Armistice — Allied occupation of Rhineland — William II abdicates and flees to Holland — Abdication of all German monarchs

1919   *"Spartakisten"* uprisings — Opening of National Assembly in Weimar — *Reichspräsident:* Ebert; *Reichskanzler:* Scheidemann, afterward Bauer — Proclamation of Soviet Republic in Bavaria — Assassination of Eisner — Germany signs *Treaty of Versailles* — Germany adopts *Weimar Constitution*

1920   *"Kapp Putsch"* — Formation of Red army in Ruhr District — *Reichskanzler:* H. Müller, afterward Fehrenbach — Plebiscites in East Prussia, Schleswig, and in Eupen-Malmédy

1921   Plebiscite in Upper Silesia — Communist uprisings in central Germany, Hamburg, and Ruhr District — London Ultimatum on reparation payments — Assassination of Erzberger — Division of Upper Silesia — Wirth, *Reichskanzler*

1922   Conference of Cannes approves reduction of German reparation payments — Conference of Genoa — Treaty of Rapallo — Assassination of Rathenau — Promulgation of *Gesetz zum Schutz der Republik* (law for the protection of the Republic) — Inflation — Cuno, *Reichskanzler*

1923   French-Belgian march into the Ruhr District — Passive resistance movement — Stresemann, *Reichskanzler* — Separatist movements in Rhineland and Palatinate — *"Hitler Putsch"* in Munich — Creation of the *Rentenmark* — Marx, *Reichskanzler*

1924   Second Marx cabinet — Conference of London — Adoption of Dawes Plan

1925   Hans Luther, *Reichskanzler;* Hindenburg, *Reichspräsident* — Withdrawal of French-Belgian occupation forces from Ruhr District — Conference of Locarno and Locarno treaties

1926   Second Luther cabinet — Withdrawal of allied occupation forces from first Rhineland zone — Third Marx cabinet — Germany is admitted to League of Nations — End of allied military control

1927   Fourth Marx cabinet — Continuation of Locarno policy

1928   Second Müller cabinet — Germany signs Kellogg-Briand Pact

1929   Young Plan — Conference of the Hague

1930   Brüning, *Reichskanzler* — End of allied occupation of Rhineland — Germany's September elections (large increase of communist and national-socialist votes) — Reform program and emergency decrees of Brüning cabinet

1931   Second Brüning cabinet — German-Austrian proposal of Customs Union; rejected by Allies — Economic crisis and bank failures — Hoover Plan (reparations Moratorium) — Conferences of German and allied foreign ministers in London, Paris, Berlin, and Rome — Finance Conference of London — Further emergency decrees of Brüning cabinet

1932   Disarmament Conference of League of Nations — Reorganization of German banks — Hindenburg re-elected *Reichspräsident* — Fall of Brüning cabinet — Von Papen, *Reichskanzler* — Conferences on reparations (Basel and Lausanne) — National Socialists win 230 seats in *Reichstag* elections and become strongest political party — Fall of Papen cabinet — General von Schleicher, *Reichskanzler*

1933   Fall of Schleicher cabinet — Hitler-Papen-Hugenberg cabinet — *Reichstag* fire on eve of new elections; National Socialists gain 288 seats in *Reichstag* and, with the aid of 52 deputies of *Deutsch-Nationale Volkspartei,* obtain absolute majority — Parties of the opposition are suppressed or dissolve "voluntarily" — Change of Constitution — Germany withdraws from League of Nations

Chapter 16

POLITICAL AND SOCIAL DEVELOPMENTS

Two Concepts of Empire. As writing is resumed (May, 1946), after an interval of several years, another chapter in the history of Germany and of the human race has been brought to a tragic conclusion. But the destruction of the totalitarian regimes in Germany, Italy, and Japan has so far failed to bring the blessings of a durable peace and the "tranquillity of order" (Augustine) to the tormented peoples of the world. They are still haunted by greed, suspicion, and fear, and by the apocalyptic specters of famine and death. Internal unrest and social strife victimize the nations of victors and vanquished alike, and the burden of armaments is increased rather than diminished with the invention of new and ever more destructive weapons of warfare. National ambitions and international rivalries extend into the council chambers of the United Nations Organization, adding their prodigious weight to the multiple problems which face a confused and rapidly disintegrating civilization. Thus it seems that the words with which Leo XIII described the situation of Europe in 1894 have lost nothing of their prophetic import: "For many years," the pontiff wrote in an apostolic letter (*Praeclara Gratulationis*) addressed to all rulers and peoples, "peace has been rather an appearance than a reality. Possessed with mutual suspicions, almost all the nations are vying with one another in equipping themselves with military armaments. Inexperienced youths are removed from parental direction and control, to be thrown amid the dangers of the soldier's life; robust young men are taken from agriculture or ennobling studies or trade or the arts, to be put under arms. Hence, the treasures of States are exhausted by the enormous expenditures, the national resources are frittered away, and private fortunes impaired; and this armed peace cannot last much longer. . . . To repress ambition, greed, and envy — the chief instigators of war — nothing, however, is more fitted than the Christian virtues and, in particular, the virtue of justice; for, by its exercise, both the law of nations and the faith of treaties may be maintained inviolate, and the bonds of brotherhood continue unbroken. . . . And as in its external relations, so in the internal life of the State itself, the Christian virtues will provide a guarantee of the commonweal much more sure and far stronger than any which . . . armies can afford." Viewing with alarm the general contest for extended empire, the same pope had written in an allocution of 1889: "Since peace is based upon good order, it follows that, for empires as well as for individuals, concord should have its principal foundations in justice and charity."

The new German Empire, a latecomer among the great powers of Europe, was built on the national unity achieved in 1871, and its citizens, on the whole, accepted cheerfully Bismarck's "small-German" solution of the German Question (cf. p. 530). There were, however, dissenting groups, and one of their spokesmen was Konstantin Frantz (1817–1891). He was an astute political thinker and an uncompromising antagonist of Bismarck, who had advocated in his writings the idea of a federated "Greater Germany" (including Austria) which was to become the nucleus of a future world federation. Frantz, and with him all *grossdeutsche* conservative federalists, saw in Bismarck's Empire not a genuine union, but an artifact of Prussian nationalist statecraft and a deviation from the supranational universalist concept of the medieval "Holy Roman Empire of the German Nation." "Can it be the true vocation of the German people," asked Frantz, "to form a great centralized state when their entire history speaks out to the contrary? Can it be their vocation to break with their long historic past, to set up in its place an order dictated solely by utilitarian considerations?" Friedrich Wilhelm Foerster, one of the most severe contemporary critics of the iron chancellor who, according to his own testimony, "grew up in an atmosphere of loathing for Bismarck's work," finds in the writings of Frantz support for his contention that "autocracy superseded federation as the principle of unity. Force replaced the determination and establishment of law and legal rights. Bismarck thus founded that empire which Nietzsche denounced as the extirpation of the German spirit."* Because he excluded from his *Kleindeutschland* the Austrians and Sudeten Germans, Bismarck is for the Austrian historian Richard von Kralik "not the creator but the destroyer of German unity."

It is, then, the unshakable conviction of all these advocates of *Grossdeutschland* that Bismarck's Empire simply absorbed Germany into Prussia and, by dedicating the newly founded *Reich* to the ideas of Prussian *Realpolitik,* forced it into a dangerous and in the long run disastrous competition with the British empire.

Whatever may be the justification of such arguments, their weight was certainly not felt by the majority of those Germans who lived in the newly unified constitutional Empire; an empire which was not even a monarchy in the strict sense, but rather a commonwealth composed of princely (and some municipal) constitutional governments, the sovereignty being vested in the *Bundesrat* (cf. p. 542). The main prerogative of the emperor was

---

* Friedrich Wilhelm Foerster, *Europe and the German Question* (New York: Sheed and Ward, 1940), p. 20.

the appointment of the *Reichskanzler,* while he held no veto power over the legislative enactments of the *Reichstag* and the *Bundesrat.* In case of serious disagreements he could have recourse to the extreme measure of dissolving the *Reichstag* and of ordering new elections, but he could not do so without the consent of the *Bundesrat.* As the emperor became commander in chief of the armed forces only in time of war, his power was more restricted than that of the *Reichspräsident* of the Weimar Republic (cf. p. 649).

As the new empire — consolidated politically and economically by the decisive victory over France, the prompt payment of the French indemnity, and the ensuing expansion of industry, trade, and commerce — rapidly advanced to a leading and pivotal position in Europe, the people found little reason to quarrel with Bismarck or to question the wisdom of his political course. If Bismarck was guilty of nationalism, he shared this guilt with his age: nationalism was in its ascendancy everywhere, and in the struggle for political and economic power the universalistic tendencies of a more or less remote past were forgotten.

As an external symbol of its departure from the *grossdeutsch*-universalist and federalist ideology the new *Reich* adopted black, white, and red as its national colors, combining the Prussian black and white with the red of the Hansa city republics. The black, red, and gold of the Holy Roman Empire, of the followers of Jahn (cf. p. 442 sq.), of the Lützow Free Corps (cf. p. 448), of the revolution of 1848, and of the Austrian federalist movement was incompatible with the nationalistic aspirations of Bismarck's *Kleindeutschland.*

Bismarck's Foreign Policy (after 1871). William I, the new German emperor, and his trusted chancellor who had built the strongest nation on the European continent, found themselves immediately confronted with the task of allaying foreign apprehensions as to the future policies of Germany and therefore of convincing their neighbors that they had nothing to fear from a united and prosperous German nation. "We are satiated," declared Bismarck shortly after the Peace of Frankfurt. "It has always been my aim," he added, "to win the confidence of Europe and to convince it that German policy will be just and peaceful, now that it has repaired the *injuria temporum,* the disintegration of the nation." But aside from the widespread fear of further German expansionist aims, there were many dangerous tensions on the European continent which might precipitate an armed conflict at any time. It required the skill of a great statesman to neutralize these antagonistic forces and to steer the ship of State safely through many a threatening storm. Bismarck succeeded in this with the aid of a political pragmatism which never hesitated to shift friendships and alliances in accordance with the demands of changing political constellations and without much regard for abstract principles.

To isolate France and frustrate her desire for revenge, the German chancellor built a system of defensive alliances with Austria, Russia, and

Italy. In 1872 both Francis Joseph I of Austria and Alexander II of Russia visited Berlin, and Bismarck succeeded in engineering the *Dreikaiserbund* (Three Emperors' League), a friendly accord among the three monarchs which, though it soon lapsed on account of the conflicting interests of Austria and Russia in the Balkans, was temporarily revived after the assassination of Alexander II in 1881. Friendship with the new Italian kingdom was fostered by the Berlin visit of Victor Emanuel II in 1873.

France, in the meantime, had rapidly recuperated from her defeat and had rebuilt her army, bringing it up to an effective strength of 471,000 men (as against Germany's 401,000), and adopting a new conscription law which provided for a five-year term of military service. Germany countered by adding to the fortifications of the frontier fortresses of Metz and Strasbourg. What Bismarck feared more than French rearmament, however, was a royalist restoration in France and a potential Franco-Austrian rapprochement. The Franco-German tension was eventually eased by the defeat of royalist and *revanche*-minded President MacMahon (1879) and the election of Gambetta, who was a Republican and in favor of a conciliatory policy toward Germany. The same end was ably pursued by Bismarck's ambassador to France, Prince Chlodwig zu Hohenlohe (1874–1885), the future German *Reichskanzler* (cf. p. 620). Hohenlohe was a scholar and statesman of international and liberal leanings, a south German federalist who was rooted in the universalist ideals of European culture and who for this reason had the reconciliation of Germany and France at heart.

German-Russian relations which had been friendly ever since the Wars of Liberation (cf. p. 446 sqq.) became strained after the Russian intervention in behalf of the oppressed Christian minorities under Turkish rule. Russia declared war on Turkey in 1877, and to discourage Russian ambitions aiming at Constantinople, England sent a fleet to the Black Sea, while Austria put an army into the field to check Russian moves in the Balkans. In 1878 Russia and Turkey signed the Treaty of San Stefano which guaranteed full independence to Serbia, Rumania, and Montenegro and recognized a "Greater Bulgaria," whose territory was to include the bulk of European Turkey and which was attached to the Russian sphere of influence. England and Austria, alarmed by this increase of Russian power, called for a revision of the Treaty of San Stefano and suggested to submit the issue to an international conference. It was a tribute to the newly won international prestige of the German empire and its chancellor that Berlin was chosen as the meeting place of the contending powers and that Bismarck was permitted to arbitrate the dispute, after he had declared that Germany was not interested in the Near-Eastern question and promised to act as an "honest broker."

The Congress of Berlin (1878) split Bulgaria into three parts, gave Bessarabia to Russia, and permitted Austria to administer the former Turkish provinces of Bosnia and Herzegovina. Although the achievements of the congress were hailed by Disraeli, the British prime minister and chief delegate, as "peace with honor," nothing was really settled, and the Balkans, whose representatives had not even been heard, were left seething with rivalries and unrest. The big powers were too much concerned with their own imperialist aims to judge objectively the issues at hand. While Lord Salisbury, the British foreign minister, shortly afterward regretted that England had "backed the wrong horse" at Berlin, encouraging Austrian expansion at the expense of Russia, Alexander II deeply resented the tripartition of his much coveted "Greater Bulgaria" into a northern independent region, a semiautonomous central section, and a southern Macedonian territory under Turkish control. The tsar blamed Bismarck for the Russian setback, and his veiled threats of war caused the German chancellor to look for a reliable ally to weather a possible Russian attack. Bismarck hurried to Vienna and concluded with the Austro-Hungarian Foreign Minister Andrassy the Austro-German Dual Alliance (1879), providing for mutual assistance in case of Russian aggression and for the benevolent neutrality of either party if one of the two nations should be attacked by France.

Meanwhile the French, in their attempt to extend their dominion in North Africa, occupied Tunis, a Turkish dependency, in 1881 and thereby thwarted the ambitions of Italy, which had hoped that this territory in the neighborhood of Sicily, located at the site of ancient Carthage, could be claimed as an Italian colonial possession on the "dark continent." Despite the fact that Bismarck, to keep France busy abroad and make her forget the loss of Alsace-Lorraine, had encouraged French expansion in Africa, he readily assured Italy of German support in case of a Franco-Italian clash in North Africa. Thus, in 1882, the *Dreibund* (Triple Alliance) of Germany, Austria-Hungary, and Italy was concluded, notwithstanding the Italian grievances against Austria on account of the "unredeemed" territories (*Italia irredenta*) of the southern Tyrol, Istria, and Trieste, whose Italian-speaking population was under Austrian rule. As in the case of the previous Austro-German *Zweibund,* it was agreed that the terms of the *Dreibund,* "in conformity with its peaceful intentions, and to avoid misinterpretation," were to be kept secret.

The second term of the Three Emperors' League expired in 1887, and as both Russia and Austria were adamant in their stand against a renewal, Bismarck, more than ever convinced that friendly relations with Russia were essential for the preservation of peace in Europe, concluded with Tsar Alexander III the secret *Rücksicherungsvertrag* (Reinsurance Treaty) of 1887. This treaty guaranteed mutual neutrality in case of a defensive war, but it was not renewed after its expiration in 1890.

Bismarck's system of alliances, although it had sporadically shown weaknesses and moved gradually toward disintegration, had succeeded in isolating France and in temporarily checking the French desire for *revanche*. This desire, however, was fanned to a new feverish heat by Boulanger, the French minister of war, who came into office after the fall of President Ferry in 1885. Ferry had cultivated the friendship of Germany and had thereby secured the undisturbed growth of the French colonial empire in Africa. In the face of a resurgence of French chauvinism and a threatening Franco-Russian rapprochement, Bismarck, in introducing the new Army Bill of 1887, reaffirmed in the *Reichstag* Germany's peaceful intentions: "We have no warlike needs," the chancellor said, "for we belong to what Metternich called satiated nations. We do not expect an attack from Russia. . . . The difficulty is not to keep Germany and Russia, but to keep Austria and Russia at peace. . . . We risk being called pro-Russian in Austria and pro-Austrian in Russia. That does not matter if we can maintain peace. Our relations with Austria rest on the consciousness of each that the existence of the other as a Great Power is a necessity in the interest of European equilibrium." Then speaking on the situation in the West, Bismarck declared: "We have no intention and no reason to attack France. . . . If the French will keep the peace till we attack, then peace is assured for ever. . . . But we have to fear an attack — whether in ten days or ten years I cannot say. War is certain if France thinks she is stronger and can win. This is my unalterable conviction. . . . If she won, she would not display our moderation of 1871. She would bleed us white, and, if we win, we would do the same to her. The war of 1870 would be child's play compared with a war of 1890 or whatever the date."

By 1887 Boulanger, who shortly afterward was tried *in absentia* for high treason and embezzlement and in 1889 committed suicide in Belgium, had been forced out of the French cabinet. However, in the same degree as Austro-Russian relations grew worse, the prospects for Franco-Russian friendship improved. Thus Bismarck found it necessary in the following year (1888) to review once more the European situation. It was his last major speech on foreign affairs in the *Reichstag*. "Like last year," he said, "I expect no attack. Yet the danger of coalition is permanent, and we must arrange once and for all to meet it. . . . We must make greater exertions than other nations on account of our position. Russia and France can only be attacked on one front; but God has placed us beside the most bellicose and restless of nations, the French, and He has allowed bellicose tendencies to grow up in Russia. We shall, however, wage no preventive war. Nevertheless, I advise other countries to discontinue their threats. We Germans fear God and nothing else in the world." This speech accompanied the introduction and passage of the last army bill endorsed by Bismarck. One month later Emperor William I died at the age of ninety-one, and after the short interval of the ninety-nine days' reign of his son, Frederick III (who succumbed to a cancerous throat ailment), William's twenty-nine-year-old grandson acceded to the throne as Emperor William II.

Bismarck's Domestic Policy (after 1871). The system of changing alliances and coalitions which served the German chancellor so well in conducting his foreign policy provided the pattern also for his dealing with domestic issues. As he could not rule against the will of a parliamentary majority, he sought alternating working agreements with the Progressives, the National Liberals, the Conservatives, and the Center party. Up to the time of William II's accession to the throne the domestic policies of Germany no less than her international policy bore the stamp of Bismarck's personality. In two specific instances, however, he failed to achieve his aims and instead strengthened the forces which he had intended to reduce to impotency. His fight against the "ultramontane" influence of the Catholic clergy resulted in a victory for the Church and a considerably strengthened Center party, and his antisocialist legislation had the effect of vastly increasing the socialist vote and of raising the factional representation of the Social Democrats in the Reichstag from nine seats in 1874 to thirty-five seats in 1890.

*a) The "Kulturkampf."** Bismarck's attitude toward the Catholic Church was determined not by religious but by political considerations. The publication of the *Syllabus* of Pius IX** and even more the declaration of Papal Infallibility as promulgated by the Vatican Council had contributed to the creation of serious frictions between Church and State in Germany. The Center party in the *Reichstag* drew its strongest support from the Catholic population of the German South, among whom also the idea of *Grossdeutschland* (Greater Germany) had its deepest roots and where the critics of Bismarck's solution of the German Question had been most vociferous. In the state of Baden, which was ruled by the National Liberals, anticlerical legislation had been enacted as early as 1867.

Bismarck joined with the National Liberals in questioning the national loyalty and reliability of the Center party, the representative political organization of German Catholicism. Furthermore, he reproached the Center party for championing the cause of political and racial minorities, such as the Poles in Posnania and West Prussia, the Welfs in Hanover, and the French population of Lorraine, all equally opposed to the centralized administration in Prussia and in the *Reich*. Finally, ever apprehensive of potential hostile coalitions, Bismarck feared that in the eventuality of an international conflict involving Catholic powers, a politically organized Catholicism might sympathize with the enemy and thus hamper the German war effort.

German Liberalism, traditionally opposed to religious influences in politics and in education, welcomed the German chancellor's anticlerical campaign. Its hopes for a nationalized *"romfreie Kirche"* (a church free from Rome) received encouragement from the schismatic German *Altkatholiken* (Old Catholics) who had rejected the dogma of Papal Infallibility and had seceded from Rome in 1870. Their representatives were supported by Bismarck in

---

* The term, denoting a "struggle for civilization," was first used by Lassalle, later on by Rudolf Virchow, in an electoral manifesto of the Progressive party, and subsequently became the political slogan of anticlerical Liberalism.
** The *Syllabus,* published by the Papal State Chancery on December 8, 1864, contains a list of "the principal errors of our time." Specifically mentioned are among others, pantheism, naturalism, rationalism, indifferentism, socialism, communism, and liberalism.

their stand against the orthodox members of the German clergy and hierarchy.

The *Kulturkampf* began shortly after the foundation of the Second German Empire, reached its climax about 1875, and was gradually relaxed and finally called off between 1880 and 1887.

On July 8, 1871, the Catholic section of the Prussian ministry of culture and education was abolished, following the charge that its members had supported the Polish minority groups in Posnania and West Prussia. The *Jesuitengesetz* of 1872, which excluded all members of the Jesuit Order and affiliated congregations from the territory of the *Reich*, remained in force until 1917, although it was moderated in 1904. When the Vatican refused recognition to Cardinal Hohenlohe, the German envoy to the Holy See, Bismarck, referring to the historic contest between Henry IV and Gregory VII (cf. p. 71 sq.), declared defiantly: "Have no fear; to Canossa we will not go, neither in body nor in spirit."

In 1873 Adalbert Falk, the Prussian minister of culture and education, introduced the repressive *May Laws* which made all ecclesiastical education, discipline, and appointments subject to State approval and control. In the *Reich* civil marriage was made compulsory in 1875 (later on incorporated in the *Bürgerliches Gesetzbuch, 1900*). The Prussian *Brotkorbgesetz* (breadbasket law) of the same year canceled all State support for recalcitrant members of the clergy. Subsequently, all religious orders and congregations (with the exception of those in charge of the sick) were dissolved, the Catholics' right of organization and assembly curtailed, the Catholic press subjected to rigorous censorship, while many bishops and priests were fined, expelled, or imprisoned.

Bismarck tried to justify these repressive laws and measures in the Prussian *Herrenhaus* in 1873 by characterizing the struggle as "not a fight between faith and unbelievers, but rather the age-old contest between the kingship and the priesthood . . . ; the contest which filled the German Middle Ages down to the disintegration of the Empire; the contest which . . . found its medieval solution when the last heir of the illustrious house of Swabia died under the ax of the French conqueror, who was in league with the Pope."

The *Kulturkampf* was supported not only by Liberals, Protestant Conservatives, and "Old Catholics," but also by a group of Catholic nationalists (*Staatskatholiken*). On the other hand, it was opposed and condemned by many Protestant Conservatives (among them Crown Prince Frederick and his wife, and Empress Augusta), by the socialists, the French of Lorraine, the Poles of Posnania and West Prussia, and the Protestants of Hanover.

In 1878, confronted with the unexpected phenomenon of a greatly strengthened Center party and haunted by the specter of a parliamentary coalition of Centrists and Socialists, Bismarck began to retrace his steps and looked for an opportunity to start peace negotiations with Rome. His diplomatic retreat was made easier by Leo XIII, who succeeded Pius IX in 1879. The new pontiff, in his anxiety for the stabilization and pacification of social and international relations, was willing to meet the German chancellor halfway. Bismarck expressed his gratitude in a speech in the Prussian *Herrenhaus,* in which he paid tribute to Leo's love of peace and justice. "The Pope," he said, "is more pro-German than the Center party and . . . more interested in the consolidation of the *Reich* and the well-being of the Prussian state than the majority of the German *Reichstag* has been at times. . . . The Pope is not Welf or Polish, nor *deutsch-freisinnig* (German-liberal), and he has no leaning toward the Social Democrats. . . . He is simply Catholic. . . . He is free and represents the free Catholic Church. The Center party represents the Church in the service of parliamentarism and vote-getting intrigues. Hence I have chosen to address myself to the absolutely free Pope . . . because from the wisdom of Leo XIII and from his love of peace I expect more success for the internal peace of Germany than I did from the *Reichstag* and the Center party."

In enactments promulgated between 1881 and 1886 the previous legislative measures were so modified as to make them acceptable to the Vatican. The German Liberals who a little prematurely had hailed Bismarck as a second Luther had no further reason to applaud his dealings with Rome.

It was about this time that Bismarck started upon a new fiscal policy which called for protective tariff legislation and thus ran counter to the free-trade inclinations of the left-wing National Liberals. The payment of the French war indemnity had encouraged speculation on the stock market and resulted in overproduction in some industries, and the chancellor felt that the time had come to protect the German landowners, the producers of grain in eastern Germany, and the manufacturers, from the competition of foreign markets. To secure parliamentary approval of the new Tariff Bill he needed not only the votes of the Conservatives, on whom he could safely count in this matter of vital interest to them, but also those of the Center party. He therefore turned from the National Liberals, his onetime strongest supporters, and succeeded in gaining the backing of the Center party and its leader, Windthorst, for a program of moderate protectionism.

b) "*Sozialistengesetz*" *and Social Legislation.* For a second time Bismarck tried persecution as a weapon, in his fight against the rising tide of political socialism, and again he failed. But he had learned from past experience and therefore supplemented his antisocialist measures with a constructive program of social reform and social legislation.

The followers of the dialectic-materialist socialism of Marx and the romantic-idealist socialism of Lassalle (cf. p. 559) joined hands at the Convention of Gotha (1875) and together founded the Social Democratic party, whose tenets represented a compromise between the convictions of the two groups. The party adopted a program of progressive socialization, took a firm stand against the excessive increase of armaments, and opposed colonial imperialism. Since they ignored national boundaries and were eager to collaborate with their fellow socialists in foreign countries, they came to be regarded as *"vaterlandslose Gesellen"* (fellows without a country) and were believed by their political adversaries to constitute a threat to the healthy growth of the new Germany.

While Bismarck in an early meeting with Lassalle had shown an open mind for the just grievances of the working class, he denounced the demands of the Gotha program as "utopian nonsense." In 1878 two attempts were made on the life of William I, in the second of which the emperor was severely wounded. Although the perpetrators were radicals without socialist party affiliations, these incidents served Bismarck as an excuse to introduce his antisocialist bill, the *Sozialistengesetz*. The chancellor, confronted with a parliamentary majority unfavorable to the proposed harsh measures, had the *Reichstag* dissolved. When the newly elected representatives convened the bill was adopted with the votes of the Conservatives and National Liberals and renewed in 1880, 1884, and 1886, the last two times with the additional votes of the Centrists.

The Social Democrats, in the meantime, increased their vote from 500,000 in 1877 to 763,000 in 1887 and to 1,427,000 in Bismarck's last *Reichstag* of 1890. In the election of 1912 they obtained 110 seats (out of 397) and thus had become the strongest party in the *Reichstag*. This success was due not only to the antisocialist legislation (which was allowed to lapse long before 1912) but to the general social problems and conditions of the industrial age and to the able and high-minded leadership of August Bebel and Wilhelm Liebknecht. Bebel, for example, had enough sense of perspective to acknowledge ungrudgingly Leo XIII's efforts in behalf of social justice. "The Pope has stated," he said, "that the Church must work toward the goal of securing a just wage for the workingman. . . . And as the members of the Catholic clergy are in permanent touch with the working classes—far more so than the Protestants—Social Democracy has so far not succeeded in expanding as much among Catholics as among Protestants."

The *Sozialistengesetz* decreed the dissolution of all organizations which, by carrying on socialistic or communistic activities, were believed to constitute a danger to the public peace or aimed at the overthrow of the existing order. All meetings and demonstrations of such a nature were to be supervised and could be dissolved, and all subversive publications were prohibited. Entire districts could be placed under a state of limited emergency, and persons who were suspected of endangering public order could be denied domicile in these restricted areas. The law did not propose, however, to interfere with *Reichstag* debates, election speeches and campaigns, and the rights of suffrage. The *Sozialistengesetz*, like the anticlerical legislation, was gradually mitigated and finally discarded when, in 1890, a majority of Conservatives, Centrists, Progressive Liberals, and Social Democrats voted against its renewal.

Bismarck met the demands of the Social Democrats and the dissatisfaction of the proletarian masses positively by a comprehensive plan of *social legislation* which anticipated by several decades similar enactments in England

Otto von Bismarck, by Franz von Lenbach.

Crown Prince Frederick William.

and France, to say nothing of the much more laggard labor policy of the United States. The chancellor clarified his position in his *Reichstag* speech of April 2, 1881. "For fifty years," he declared, "we have been talking about the social question. . . . Free enterprise is no magic formula; the state can become responsible also for the things it fails to do. I am not of the opinion that the principles of *laissez-faire, laissez-aller,* pure *Manchestertum* in politics — 'let each man himself see to it that he gets along'; 'he who is not strong enough to stand will be run over and trodden down'; 'he that hath, to him shall be given, and he that hath not, from him shall be taken' — can be applied in the paternalistic monarchical state. On the contrary, I hold that those who oppose state intervention for the protection of the weak lay themselves open to the suspicion that they wish to use their strength . . . to gain support and to suppress others in order to establish a party rule. . . . Call this socialism, if you will, I do not care. . . . I desire to see our state, in which the vast majority are Christians, permeated with the doctrines of the religion we profess, especially with those regarding charity toward one's neighbor and compassion for the old and suffering."

The imperial message of November 17 of the same year announced the inauguration of comprehensive labor legislation. The Health Insurance Law, providing for half pay and medical attention for a period of six months in case of sickness, was introduced and adopted in 1883. The Accident Insurance Law, stipulating compensation for partially or totally disabled workers as well as a pension for the dependents of workers killed in the pursuit of their occupation, followed in 1884. The most far-reaching measure, the Old Age Pension Act, securing a retirement annuity for all workers over seventy and for those incapacitated at an earlier age, was passed in 1889. This vast program was supplemented in 1891 by the *Arbeiterschutzgesetz* (law for the protection of labor) which laid down rules for the enforcement of labor rest on Sundays and legal holidays, for State control of safety and health conditions in industry, for the protection of women in the labor market, and for the restriction and eventual abolition of child labor. The *Reichsversicherungsordnung* (federal insurance legislation) of 1911 unified and further implemented all the previous enactments.

Bismarck's Dismissal. Prince William of Prussia, the son of Frederick III and the favorite grandson of Queen Victoria of England, became German emperor and king of Prussia on June 15, 1888. Although before his accession to the throne he had shown great admiration for Bismarck's personality and work, frictions were soon to develop between the young, self-willed, and impetuous monarch and his chancellor. From his uncle, Frederick William IV, the new emperor had inherited the idea of the "divine right" and mission of kings and princes, but a lack of real self-assurance due to inexperience made him feel outweighed and overshadowed by Bismarck's genius. The desire for self-assertion and for popular acclaim caused him to bluster and blunder. Nevertheless, it seemed at first that William II was willing to fall in line with Bismarck's established policies. Heeding the advice of both his grandfather (William I) and his chancellor to cultivate friendship with Russia, he began his round of official state visits in St. Petersburg. As he was an ardent Anglophile, it needed no persuasion to convince him of the need for cordial relations with England. Early in 1889 Bismarck, with the emperor's approval, definitely suggested to Lord Salisbury, then British prime minister, a German-British alliance, arguing that "the peace of Europe can best be secured by a treaty between Germany and England, pledging them to mutual support against a French attack." Salisbury expressed hope for such an alliance in the future, but for the present he wanted "to leave the offer on the table, without saying yes or no." In the summer of the same year the German emperor paid his first visit to England, where he was received with cordiality and feted with great splendor. In 1890 Great Britain ceded to Germany the island of Heligoland, in exchange for the East African territories of Zanzibar, Wituland, and Uganda.

The occasion of the first open conflict between the emperor and his chancellor was a large-scale strike of miners in the Ruhr District (1889). William II, in the hope of increasing his popularity with the working class and their Social Democratic representation in the German *Reichstag* and Prussian *Landtag* by a policy of conciliation, invited a delegation of the miners to Berlin and in a blunt statement unequivocally affirmed the justice of their demands. Bismarck strongly disapproved and saw in the emperor's attitude a capitulation to the forces of radical socialism.

The open break between William and Bismarck occurred in 1890, consequent upon the frequent interferences of the emperor with the policies of Bismarck's cabinet and his direct dealings with individual cabinet ministers, over the head of the chancellor. Bismarck, determined to stop this dangerous procedure, appealed to a Prussian cabinet order of 1852 which stipulated that cabinet ministers could only report to the king after previous consultation with the prime minister. William's demand that this cabinet order be revoked was firmly rejected by Bismarck. The already tense situation was aggravated by a private visit which Windthorst, the Centrist leader, paid to Bismarck to discuss the political situation created by the recent *Reichstag* election, in which the Conservatives and National Liberals had suffered a severe setback, while the Social Democrats had emerged stronger than ever before. When the emperor reprimanded Bismarck for having received Windthorst without previous authorization by the sovereign, the chancellor blandly declared that he would receive any deputy of good manners any time, and that he would never submit to control over his own home. The conflict reached its climax when the emperor accidentally learned of the report of a subaltern consular official in Kiev concerning the movements of Russian troops. William angrily reproached Bismarck for having concealed from him this "terrible danger" and advised him to dispatch a strong warning to Austria. The sharp note containing this accusation was followed by a demand for immediate resignation. In a document which summarized the issues that had brought on the crisis and specified the reasons for submitting his resignation, Bismarck once more stressed the necessity of continued friendly relations with Russia, as any other course "would endanger all the important successes gained by the German Empire in the last decades under the rule of Your Majesty's two predecessors."

Bismarck retired to his estate of Friedrichsruh near Hamburg which during the remaining years of his life became the object of veritable pilgrimages of men and women from many regions and lands and from all walks of life. The first and greatest chancellor of the Second German Empire died on July 30, 1898.

The "New Course." The nominal successors of Bismarck in the Office of *Reichskanzler* during the next two decades were General von Caprivi (1890–1894), Prince Hohenlohe (1894–1900), and Prince Bülow (1900–1909). His actual successor, however, was the sinister Baron Fritz von Holstein who, even after his forced retirement as *Vortragender Rat* (assistant undersecretary) in the foreign office in 1906, retained his pernicious influence on German foreign policy to his death in 1909. The "gray eminence," as Holstein was nicknamed in court and diplomatic circles, was a shrewd and reckless politician, an expert in the manipulation of secret diplomacy, who despite his subaltern rank was the real power behind the throne of William II. Many of the erratic actions commonly attributed to the *Kaiser's* "personal regime" may be traced to the unseen direction of this master of political intrigue. To achieve his ends and impose his will on the emperor and the imperial cabinet, he exploited his knowledge of certain compromising private affairs of high-ranking personages, as well as the conflicting interests of such rival groups as the army, the navy, the heavy industries, the banking concerns, and the Pan-German nationalists. Together with Maximilian Harden (1861–1927), the highly talented but utterly cynical editor of the political journal *Die Zukunft* (the future), he employed his unquestionable skill to discredit the *Kaiser* and his regime at home and abroad.

The nonrenewal of the secret Reinsurance Treaty with Russia, on the ground that it was incompatible with the Austro-German alliance, was largely due to Holstein's hatred of Russia and his friendly feelings toward Austria. The immediate consequence was exactly what William I and Bismarck had dreaded, namely, a "cordial understanding" between Russia and France, leading eventually to the secret military alliance of 1894. Germany thus lost her pivotal position as mediator between the rival ambitions of Russia and Austria, and from a strategic point of view she suddenly found herself exposed on her eastern and western flanks.

As Holstein favored friendly relations with England, Caprivi was permitted to follow his own inclination in this regard and to continue the course charted out by Bismarck. However, for reasons of domestic policy the days of Caprivi's chancellorship were numbered. Yielding to liberal pressure, the German government had entered into trade agreements with a number of neighboring states (Austria-Hungary, Italy, Switzerland, Belgium, Russia, Serbia, Rumania) and subsequently lowered her protective tariffs. The resulting reduction of the prices for agricultural products made the agrarians feel themselves threatened in their vital interests, and in 1893 they formed the powerful *Bund der Landwirte* (Agrarian League) which was destined to play a role of increasing importance in the parliamentary life of Prussia and the *Reich*. The Liberals in turn joined the Social Democrats and Centrists in their opposition to a proposed increase of the armed forces. The new army bill was finally adopted by a newly elected *Reichstag,* but Caprivi resigned shortly afterward and was replaced in 1904 by the aged Prince Hohenlohe, the former German ambassador to France, who very reluctantly took over the burdens of his new office.

It seemed at first as if under Hohenlohe's chancellorship relations with England were to remain correct and even cordial, notwithstanding the fact that Germany's successful competition in the world markets and in the race for colonies (cf. p. 624 sq.) had begun to arouse anxiety and some misgivings in the British Isles. These feelings were intensified by imprudent and provocative utterances of the German emperor on several of his good-will visits to England. One year after Germany had celebrated the completion of the *Kaiser Wilhelm-Kanal* (1895) — linking the North Sea with the Baltic and thereby opening up a new, northern trade route — the first of several serious incidents occurred. William II dispatched the famous *Krüger Telegram* to Paul Krüger, president of the Boer Free State of Transvaal, in which he congratulated the Boer leader on having successfully repulsed the raid engineered by the English-born South African statesman Jameson. As the London Convention of 1884 had given Great Britain control over the foreign affairs of Transvaal, and as the action of the German emperor was coupled with the warning that Germany could not allow any attack on the independence of the Boer Free State, British reaction was naturally most unfavorable and hostile to Germany. Though the incident was soon smoothed over by diplomatic explanations and by an apologetic letter of Emperor William to Queen Victoria, it was never forgotten.

The "new course" in German foreign policy, which is usually dated from the time of Bismarck's dismissal, did not really become very conspicuous until 1897, the year in which Bülow became German minister of foreign affairs and Alfred von Tirpitz was appointed grand admiral of the German navy. Hohenlohe's moderating influence was nullified by the determination of the emperor and his chief advisers to embark on the ventures of a *Weltpolitik* which was to prepare the stage for World War I.

English sympathy was further alienated by William II's challenging declaration that Germany's future lay on the high seas, and that he would never rest until he had raised the German navy to the standard of the German army. When Bülow succeeded Hohenlohe as *Reichskanzler* in 1900, the challenge to British sea power became even more pronounced. The new naval building program of Tirpitz, which aimed at constructing a High Seas Fleet second to none, was met across the Channel with the announcement that England would launch two warships for each German one.

In France, meanwhile, the *revanche*-minded Théophile Delcassé had become minister of foreign affairs in 1898, while in England the Francophile prince of Wales had succeeded Queen Victoria in 1901 as King Edward VII. Although no formal treaty was as yet signed between the two powers, they were drawn together by the mutual sympathies of their political leaders as well as by their common opposition to Germany's "new course."

In 1902 Great Britain and Japan concluded a treaty of alliance which made it possible for England to withdraw part of her navy from the Pacific, while the Franco-British *Entente Cordiale* of 1904 released most of the units of the British Mediterranean fleet for duty in the North Sea. The Russian defeat in the Russo-Japanese War (1904–1905), revealing the weakness of tsarist Russia when forced to rely on her own resources, indirectly paved the way for the *Triple Entente* of Russia, France, and England, which was created in 1907 and officially announced by King Edward VII in 1908. Thus England had at long last been persuaded to relinquish her "splendid isolation," to join a powerful bloc of nations, designed to meet the combination of the *Dreibund*. This decisive step on the part of Great Britain was taken with much hesitation and only after the German emperor had consistently and obstinately refused to consider any limitation of the German fleet.

Europe was now divided into two hostile camps of almost equal numerical strength, but the power potential of the *Dreibund* was more apparent than real, as Italy's partnership in it had grown more and more halfhearted. Extremely vulnerable to an attack by sea, by virtue of her extended shore lines, she could ill afford to antagonize Great Britain. Therefore, while outwardly adhering to her commitments under the terms of the *Dreibund,* she was more than anxious to regain her freedom of action. At the same time the animosity against Austria was kept alive by the partisans of the *Irredenta* movement, who demanded that all Austrian territories inhabited by Italians or an Italian-speaking majority be returned to Italy.

Although the Triple Entente was conceived as a defensive alliance, to become practically effective only in case of overt military aggression, its creation was interpreted by Germany and Austria-Hungary as an actual "encirclement" which, while using intimidation as a temporary means, aimed ultimately at aggression. The growing mutual distrust between the two power blocs, fed by an increasing number of diplomatic incidents, added to the tension and spurred the nations on to redouble their efforts to outbid the armed strength of their opponents. The burden of armaments was reflected in the staggering increases of the national budgets and in the demand for higher taxes to meet the cost of the huge military appropriations.

The German people in their majority confidently followed the course traced out by their political and military leaders. While the Social Democrats and Progressives were often outspoken in their opposition to militarism and imperialism, they were, on the other hand, not insensitive to the danger of foreign aggression, and were determined to meet it at any time shoulder to shoulder with their compatriots. The parties of the Center and the Right (Centrists, National Liberals, and Conservatives) more or less openly supported a vigorous foreign policy. The only group which frankly clamored for national expansion by force of arms was that of the not too numerous but all the more noisy *Alldeutsche* (Pan-Germans). They even dreamed of incorporating into the German orbit the territories of politically separate but racially and linguistically related populations, such as those of Austria, Bohemia, Alsace, Switzerland, Holland, and Belgium. Their ambitions grew even bolder after Germany had taken the first steps toward the creation of a colonial empire (cf. p. 624 sq.). In 1891 they founded the *Alldeutscher Verband* (Pan-German League), an organization which publicly professed and propagated the Pan-German objectives.

The Pan-German call for a union with German Austria and the Sudeten Germans was bound to evoke memories of the *grossdeutsche* movement (cf. p. 530), but there was a vast difference between the advocates of *Grossdeutschland* and those of *Alldeutschland*. Whereas the former had in cosmopolitan spirit aspired to a federation of German states, whose Christian-universalist outlook and culture could bridge the antagonisms between eastern and western Europe and could thus become the nucleus of a world-wide federation, the latter strove for a nationalist Germanic empire of vast dimensions whose claims to power were to rest on the narrow concept of a supposed racial and cultural superiority. The Pan-German movement was thus at best a badly perverted application of the idea of *Grossdeutschland*.

In two instances at least the voices of the domestic critics of the German government's militaristic and imperialistic exploits were heard and sustained by large sections of the German population. In 1908 the indignation which was aroused by an unsigned interview with William II in the *London Daily Telegraph* — in which the emperor reaffirmed his pro-British sympathies, while at the same time accusing the German people of refusing to follow him on his conciliatory course — was so great that even Bülow was seriously perturbed and decided that the time had come to speak plainly to his sovereign. A government crisis, during which William II even mentioned the possibility of abdication, was resolved by the emperor's promise to observe more caution and tact in the future. However, in the following year Bülow, after being charged with having "betrayed" His Imperial Majesty during the critical *Reichstag* debates, was replaced by Theobald von Bethmann-Hollweg.

The second provocation of the home front occurred in the spring of 1914, when the imperial government decided to back an overbearing and misbehaving Prussian lieutenant of the garrison of the Alsatian town of Zabern by decreeing the sternest repressive measures against the aroused populace. This incident more than the many past political and psychological mistakes in the administration of the annexed province, made the *Reich* lose the sympathies of German Alsace. Public opinion was thoroughly shaken out of its habitual quiescence, and the abuses of militarism were severely indicted as never before.

Bethmann-Hollweg, the fifth *Reichskanzler* of the Second Empire, was a conservative with liberal leanings. He was a man of high ideals and a speculative bent of mind (the "chancellor-philosopher"), but was weak willed and therefore unable to hold his ground against the rising tide of militant German imperialism. The Prussian *Junkers* defeated his attempted reform of the Prussian *Dreiklassenwahlrecht* (cf. p. 529), and in the foreign field his efforts to reach a naval agreement with England were doomed to failure by the joint opposition of William II, Admiral Tirpitz, and the Navy League. Characteristically enough, when Lord Haldane, the British secretary of war, visited Berlin at Germany's request in 1912, the negotiations on the proposed naval truce were carried on by Tirpitz, not by Bethmann-Hollweg. It was Haldane's impression that "Tirpitz's school of thought will not be satisfied so long as it cannot dominate British sea-power."

The conversations dragged on and were further complicated by the simultaneous introduction of the new German Navy Bill. Germany's demand that England promise neutrality in a European war in exchange for a limitation of the German naval program was rejected by Great Britain on the ground that such a promise would be incompatible with her obligations to the other signatory powers of the Triple Entente. The drift toward an open break was only halted by the impact of the Balkan Wars of 1912–1913 (cf. p. 626 sq.), which made Germany and England join hands once more in a common attempt to prevent that conflict from developing into a general European war. Before the Balkan crisis Germany had flatly rejected the naval truce suggested by Lord Haldane, but now even Tirpitz hinted at the possibility of a ten to sixteen ratio of German and English capital ships.

However, this slight improvement in Anglo-German relations was more than outweighed by increasing tensions between Germany and France in the West, and between Austria and Russia in the East. Raymond Poincaré, like Delcassé an advocate of an anti-German policy of *revanche,* became prime minister of France in 1912 and succeeded to the presidency in 1913. France decided to raise the term of military service from two to three years, and almost simultaneously Germany adopted another army bill which set aside large appropriations for the further strengthening of the frontier fortresses, for the enlargement and improvement of the artillery, and for an increased gold reserve. The centenary celebration of the battle of Leipzig (cf. p. 451) in 1913 enabled the Pan-Germans to indulge in a frenzy of riotous nationalism, a demonstration which solidified the impression in the camp of the Triple Entente that a major conflict could not be held off much longer.

The Balkan Wars provided Germany with her last opportunity to act as mediator between Russia and Austria. However, the appointment of the Prussian General Liman von Sanders as reorganizer of the Turkish army was interpreted by Russia as a deliberate attempt on the part of

Germany to thwart any Russian advance in the direction of Constantinople and the Straits. The subsequent removal of Liman von Sanders from the command of the First Army Corps of the Turkish forces and his appointment as general inspector of the Turkish army was not enough of a concession to assuage Russian resentment.

Thus the seeds of war were sprouting in every part of Europe, and the international atmosphere was so heavily charged with inflammable matter that only a spark was needed to start off a general conflagration.

The Colonial Empire. As long as Bismarck remained at the helm of the second German empire he adhered to his policy of limited objectives. It was his intention to build Germany as a strong and unified continental power and he was averse to colonial ambitions and adventures. It was only reluctantly therefore that he finally yielded to the increasing demand for colonial markets, to relieve the economic pressure caused by the speedy industrialization of Germany after 1871. Owing to their belated achievement of political unity, the long prevalent agricultural bases of their economy, and their prolonged preoccupation with purely domestic problems, the Germans felt later than other nations the disturbing social and economic effects of the Industrial Revolution. When they finally appeared as industrial competitors and as claimants for overseas markets, the race for colonies was almost over, and the choicest territories had already been parceled out among the colonial empires of Spain, Portugal, Holland, England, and France.

From 1871 on, the dilemma experienced by other highly industrialized nations was brought home to Germany: the domestic food supply could no longer satisfy the needs of a growing population, and the urgency of increased imports of both food and raw materials produced the demand for colonial markets. As Germany, looking for open doors on other continents, became entangled in the intricate web of world economy, clashes with the colonial and imperialist interests of other powers were bound to occur.

In the eighties a merchant from Bremen had acquired control over some territories on the west coast of Africa and asked the German government for protection. Bismarck yielded to this request in 1884 and proclaimed a protectorate over what came to be known as German Southwest Africa. In the same year the West African regions of Togo and Kamerun were obtained by annexation. In 1885 East Africa, part of New Guinea, and some of the South Sea Islands (Marshall Islands) were added to the German colonial possessions. In 1899 the Caroline, Marian, and Palau Islands in the Pacific were purchased from Spain, and in 1900 a German protectorate was declared over the two largest Samoan Islands. The assassination of two missionaries in China had provided the German government with a welcome pretext to obtain from the Chinese government the port of Kiaochow and the coal fields of its rich hinterland on a ninety-nine year lease (1898). By the end of the century the German colonial empire comprised an aggregate area of over one million square miles and a native population numbering approximately twelve million.

German misrule in parts of the protectorate of Southwest Africa led to the violent uprisings of the Hereros and Hottentots in 1904. After their subjugation the economic exploitation of this colony proceeded apace. Immigration from the motherland, which in the beginning had to be stimulated artificially by the propaganda of the colonial office and of private *Kolonialgesellschaften* (colonial associations, e.g., the German Africa Society, 1878), gradually began to flow more steadily, and in the end even the natives began to share to some extent in the higher cultural and economic standards of the colonizers. In 1912 the over-all trade returns from the German colonial empire amounted to about 240 million marks ($60,000,000), a sum total which is not too impressive considering the fact that both politically and economically the colonization had more often proved a liability rather than an asset to the motherland.

The Treaty of Versailles (cf. p. 651 sqq.) stripped Germany of all her colonies. They were nominally placed under the administration of the League of Nations, but actually were added as "mandates" to the colonial empires of the allied powers. The holders of such mandates were legally authorized to expropriate and expel all German nationals then living in these territories. With the exception of the South African Union they availed themselves of this privilege.

Colonial Frictions and International Crises. In the period from 1871 to 1895 the proportion of the rapidly growing German population to the available domestic resources was most unfavorable. Colonial expansion could thus be justified on economic grounds: partly from the need for new markets which were not closed by foreign protective tariffs, and partly from the desire to find outlets for the surplus population of the homeland. The stabilization of German economy during the final years of the nineteenth century, however, invalidated the force of these arguments. England in particular viewed with growing suspicion the renewed German demands for additional colonies. In her own case she regarded the possession of a colonial empire and the command of an adequate sea power for its protection as a matter of life or death, whereas in the case of Germany she recognized no such necessity and therefore interpreted the German demands as a deliberate challenge to the British empire. It is thus hardly surprising that international crises multiplied after 1895, many of them growing out of the rival colonial ambitions of Europe's great powers. And though many of these incidents were disposed of by arbitration or some compromise solution, each of them left a residue of bitterness and distrust which tended to heighten the tenseness of the international situation.

a) The Morocco Crises. The Congress of Berlin of 1884 tried to apportion spheres of influence and adjust rival colonial claims. Despite the fact that the British were considerably irritated by Germany's annexation of African territory bordering on some of their own colonial possessions, they finally agreed to recognize the German protectorates in 1890. Great Britain also acquiesced in France's penetration of Morocco (excepting the Spanish-owned strip of Mediterranean coast line, opposite Gibraltar), but this time Germany objected and thereby provoked three major diplomatic clashes which in each instance brought Europe to the very brink of war.

In 1903 an agreement was reached whereby Morocco was recognized as lying within the French, and Egypt as lying within the British sphere of influence. However, when France proceeded to the occupation of Morocco in 1905, Germany intervened, claiming that her interests had been completely ignored. William II, interrupting his sea voyage to Jerusalem, landed in Tangier on the Moroccan coast and categorically declared that he would be satisfied only with either the complete autonomy of Morocco or its administration under international control. As these demands met with the combined opposition of France and England, the German government proposed to submit the issue to an international conference.

The Algeciras Conference of 1906, while nominally recognizing the sovereignty of the Arab sultan of Morocco, granted France and Spain "police powers" to "maintain order" in the sultanate. At the same time the conference cemented further the Franco-British alliance.

The *second Morocco crisis* came in 1908, when French military police, in search of some deserters from the Foreign Legion, unlawfully entered the German consulate in Casablanca. Germany launched a vigorous protest, and the matter was finally referred for settlement to the Hague court of international arbitration (cf. p. 629 sq.). A compromise was reached by Germany's declaration that her interests in Morocco were exclusively economic, and by France's agreement to safeguard the economic interests of all powers in the Moroccan protectorate.

The *third crisis* occurred in 1911, after French forces had occupied the Moroccan capital city of Fez, following serious disturbances in the interior. Both Germany and Spain charged that this occupation violated the terms of the settlements of Algeciras of 1906 and of the Hague court of 1909. Germany underscored her diplomatic representations by dispatching the gunboat *Panther* to the south Moroccan port of Agadir (the *Panthersprung*). Again Great Britain placed herself firmly at the side of France, thus causing Germany to withdraw the *Panther* and making her agree to another compromise (1912) whereby she was assured freedom of trade in Morocco and was to receive a large slice of the French Congo (New Kamerun), in exchange for German recognition of the French Moroccan protectorate.

b) The Balkan Crises. Bismarck's successors did not share his conviction that the problems of the Balkans and the entire Near East "were not worth the bones of one Pomeranian grenadier." This policy of aloofness toward the Balkans had enabled him to mediate between the conflicting interests of Austria and Russia. The men, however, who were responsible for the "new course" of German foreign policy were soon attracted by the political and commercial possibilities of an extension of German influence into the Near East. This *Drang nach Osten* was bound to involve Germany sooner or later in the cross-purposes of Austrian and Russian imperialism.

In 1888, while Bismarck was still in office, German banking interests, capitalizing on the desire of influential political and military circles in Germany for a sphere of influence in Asiatic Turkey, obtained a Turkish concession to administer the railroad line running from Constantinople to Ismed, and to extend it to Ankara and Konya. This latter point was reached in 1896.

So far the German penetration of Turkey had been purely economic, but from then on the political interests began to predominate. William II, showing himself as indifferent as Bismarck to the complaints of the Eastern Christians against Turkish oppression, defied the concerted opinion of the great powers by making himself the champion of the sultan. In 1898 he journeyed to Constantinople, Syria, and Palestine, and at Damascus reassured the sultan and "the three hundred million Moslems scattered over the earth" that "the German Emperor will always be their friend."

In 1902 Germany was given permission by Turkey to extend the rail line to Bagdad, and from there to Basra and the Persian Gulf. The plans were thus laid for a new and much shortened trade route from central Europe to the Indian Ocean, and the Germans could proudly point to the "Berlin-Bagdad" scheme as being on a par with the much heralded British "Cape to Cairo" railway. Fear of Germany's preponderance in Turkey and her eventual control of the Bosphorus as well as of the route to India caused Great Britain and France to decline a German offer to have the Bagdad project financed and administered by an international consortium. Once more, on his visit to London in 1907, William II tried to ease British apprehensions by offering England control of the Persian section of the railway, but British insistence that the matter must be submitted to France and Russia for their approval nullified this conciliatory gesture. An agreement between Germany and England in this hotly disputed question was finally reached on June 15, 1914. The treaty was signed on July 27, only a few days before the outbreak of World War I. It provided for a German-British board of directors of the Bagdad company, and for cession to a British concern of a section extending from Basra to the Persian Gulf.

The fears of Great Britain and France of German domination in the Near East were not entirely justified, for the road from Berlin to Bagdad had to traverse the territories of the Balkans, the "powder magazine of Europe." It was a foregone conclusion that at least the Balkan Slavs would stubbornly oppose any Germanic penetration or domination. The waves of Slav nationalism were surging higher than usual, and the Serbs, encouraged by Russia, aimed at the creation of a Pan-Slav Balkan state. They strove to include the Slavic populations of Bosnia and Herzegovina, the provinces which, as stipulated by the Congress of Berlin (1878), were policed and partially administered by Austria, although constitutionally they were still under Turkish sovereignty. The Austrian government, alarmed by the Young Turkish revolution of 1908 and eager to forestall the rival claims of Serbs and Turks, annexed both provinces in the same year. Turkey, too weak to resist, was pacified by the payment of an indemnity. The infuriated Serbs, advised by Russia — still suffering from the aftereffects of her defeat in the Russo-Japanese War (1904–1905) — to avoid everything that might lead to an armed conflict, reluctantly abandoned their warlike preparations. Thus the first Balkan storm blew over.

New complications, however, arose in the Near East as an aftermath of the Turko-Italian War of 1911–1912 and led to the *First Balkan War* (1912). Encouraged by England to pursue her colonial exploits in Africa, Italy seized the Turkish possession of Tripoli and defeated Turkey in the ensuing conflict. The evident weakness of the Ottoman state tempted the Balkan states (Greece, Serbia, Montenegro, Bulgaria) to launch a combined attack on Turkey, which was despoiled of almost all its European possessions. But shortly afterward the victors fell out over the distribution of the spoils, and Bulgaria, turning on her erstwhile brothers-in-arms, was decisively beaten by them and forced to yield to Serbia and Greece most of her earlier gains, and part of her own territory besides.

At the Conference of London (1913), which terminated the *Second Balkan War,* Austria and Italy insisted on transforming the former Turkish province of Albania into an autonomous principality, thereby frustrating Serbia's desire for an outlet to the Adriatic.

Serbia and Greece emerged from the Balkan Wars with their territories almost doubled. Serbia received the larger part of Macedonia and some North Albanian regions, while Greece was given southern Macedonia, including Salonika, the western part of Thrace, Epirus, and most of the Aegean Isles. While Bulgaria linked her interests with those of Germany and Austria-Hungary, Serbia was fortified by her territorial gains in her Pan-Slav ideology and in her hostility toward Austria.

As the year 1913 drew to a close, conditions in the Near East were more fraught with dangers and explosive possibilities than before the outbreak of the Balkan conflict. The only ray of hope on the international horizon was the slight improvement in German-British relations which resulted from the mission of Lord Haldane and the progress in his negotiations on a naval truce and on the Bagdad railway.

Peace Movements. The final decades of the nineteenth century and the first decade of the twentieth witnessed not only an international armament race and a general intensification of aggressive nationalism, but also a certain crystallization of the sentiment in favor of a reduction of armaments, of international arbitration, and the creation of suitable instruments for the organization and maintenance of peace. Pacifists of various shades of political and religious conviction added their voices to those of the Vatican, the socialist labor movement, and left-wing liberalism to demand the substitution of international legal institutions for the latent anarchy of a precarious armed peace.

Religious pacifism has its home in England and the United States, and it was in the former country that the first peace societies were founded early in the nineteenth century. The London Peace Society was established in 1816, and the first peace society on the European continent was constituted at Geneva in 1830. The first international peace congress was held at Brussels in 1848, and on this occasion the demands for international arbitration and general disarmament were first advanced. After the Crimean War steps were taken to curb the abuses of unlimited national sovereignty and to humanize sea warfare. The fifteen nations attending the Geneva Convention of 1864 created the organization of the International Red Cross and adopted provisions for the humane treatment of wounded enemy soldiers and prisoners of war. These resolutions were later on incorporated in the codes of martial law of most civilized nations and were further implemented by the peace conferences of the Hague of 1899 and 1907. All these international gatherings were milestones on the way to the reconstruction and further elaboration of the principles of international law, which had never had much sway except in theory, but had completely fallen into abeyance in the age of princely absolutism and excessive nationalism.

Germany was the cradle of "classical pacifism," best documented in Immanuel Kant's tract *Zum ewigen Frieden* (*On Eternal Peace,* cf. p. 374) and conceived by him as "a scientific and practical conquest of the international system of power through the creation of an international system of law." The German *Friedensgesellschaft* (peace society) was founded at Berlin in 1892 by Alfred Fried, Helmut von Gerlach, and Ludwig Quidde. These individual and collective efforts in Germany and elsewhere were supplemented during and after World War I by the creation of several Catholic, Protestant, and interdenominational societies for the promotion of international peace.*

The hopes of the advocates of international peace through collaboration and arbitration were greatly strengthened by a manifesto of Tsar Nicholas II. In 1898 he invited the nations of the world to send representatives to an international conference at the Hague, to devise peaceful and legal ways and means to settle their differences. Although Germany did not refuse to participate in the conference, her attitude with regard to its proceedings and aims was as cool and even cynical as that of England had been on the occasion of a similar Russian initiative in the days of the Holy Alliance (cf. p. 459 sq.). William II was as outspoken as usual when he declared that he was willing to have Germany represented at the Hague in order not to be blamed in Russia and elsewhere for refusing, but that the best guarantee of peace was still the sharpened sword.

When the first Hague conference met in 1899, Prince Münster, the German

---

* The most important were the *Friedensbund deutscher Katholiken* (1917; parallel organizations in England, Holland, Switzerland, Poland, and the United States); Marc Sangnier's *Action internationale démocratique pour la paix* (Paris, 1921); the Protestant World League for Friendship among the Churches (1914); the *Evangelischer Friedensbund* (1931); and the League of Nations (1920–1946). German *periodicals* for the promotion of peace: *Die Friedenswarte* (organ of the *Friedensgesellschaft*); *Der Friedenskämpfer* (Cath.); *Die Zeit* (ed. by F. W. Foerster).

delegate, was specifically instructed by his government to vote against any measure proposing disarmament, and it needed the earnest persuasion of Henry White, the secretary of the United States embassy in London, to make Germany accept at least the Court of Arbitration. At the second Hague conference of 1907 England once more designated the question of disarmament as a matter of prime importance, and again the German government not only made its attendance conditional on the removal of this question from the agenda, but seriously jeopardized the success of the conference by her opposition to the principle of arbitration.

Reviewing the balance sheet of the Hague conferences in the *Reichstag* of the German republic in 1919, Count von Brockdorff-Rantzau, the German foreign minister, declared: "We admit that Germany's attitude at the Hague Conferences toward these two fundamental questions of disarmament and arbitration was an historic sin for which our entire nation must now do penance. It was due not merely to an exaggerated fear of the practical difficulties but to a false estimate of the respective values of might and right."

The Hague conferences owed their greatest and lasting achievement, the creation of the Permanent World Court of Arbitration, to the initiative and the political realism of George W. Holls, the secretary of the United States delegation. The weakness of the Hague Tribunal rested in the absence of any legal supranational power which could compel nations to submit their disagreements to arbitration as well as in the fact that the court itself was without any legal means to enforce its decisions. The chief gain, then, was almost entirely on the moral side: the creation of the Hague Tribunal aided in rallying large sections of world opinion in support of the idea of international justice, solidarity, and co-operation.

Germany As a World Power. Several motivating forces, some of them inherent in the national character, others attributable to historical and geographical circumstances, contributed to the phenomenal growth of the new German empire to a dominant position in Europe and in the world. The boom of 1871 and the crash of 1873 were followed by a speedy stabilization of German economy, a process in which the skillful exploitation of natural resources played a conspicuous part. But the construction of the imposing edifice of German agriculture, industry, and commerce required not only personal initiative and careful planning but even more a talent for large-scale organization and the will to unselfish and disciplined individual and collective action. A country with a soil of less than average fertility and an extremely narrow seaboard could overcome such handicaps only by superb teamwork and a rigid rationalization of its economic forces and resources. It proved a great boon that German private enterprise was traditionally accustomed to accept directives from above. And the fact that these directives were given by industrial and economic experts of more than average intelligence accounts in no small measure for the German success.

The industrial expansion of Germany after 1871 owed much to the willingness on the part of private and public financial agencies to take long-range views and not to shun major risks in providing the necessary credits. The German banking concerns, above all the *Deutsche Bank* (founded in 1870) and the federal *Reichsbank* (founded in 1875) played an important part in the industrial and economic progress of Germany. It was the *Deutsche Bank* which, for example, financed the Anatolian railway project of 1888 and thereby promoted the ambitious scheme of the Bagdad railway.

One of Germany's great early industrial *entrepreneurs,* the electrical engineer Werner von Siemens (1816–1892, cf. p. 553), creator of the German electrical industry, built between 1868 and 1870 the vast network of the Indo-European Telegraph System. In 1866 he invented the dynamo machine; in 1871 he exhibited in Berlin the first electric railway; and in 1881 he completed the first electric streetcar line in Berlin-Lichterfelde. Emil Rathenau (1838–1915), continuing the work of Siemens, acquired the Edison patents for electric bulbs in 1881 and, in 1883, founded the German Edison Company for Applied Electricity which later on developed into the world-renowned AEG (*Allgemeine Elektrizitätsgesellschaft:* General Electric Company).

Germany's vital coal and iron supply came from the mines of the Ruhr District, Upper Silesia, and the Saar region; that of iron ore from the rich deposits of Lorraine (annexed in 1871). The great Krupp works at Essen on the Ruhr, founded in 1811 by Friedrich Krupp (1787–1826), were developed by his son Alfred (1812–1887) into the world's mightiest armament factory (cf. p. 554). The latter's son, Friedrich Alfred (1854–1902), further expanded the vast undertaking, attaching to it the famous *Germania Werft* (shipbuilding yards) in Kiel on the Baltic Sea. In 1903 the huge concern was transformed into a joint-stock company with aggregate holdings of approximately $50,000,000, all the shares remaining in the possession of the Krupp family.

It was with the aid of such "coal and iron barons" as the Krupps and such competitive enterprises as those of Thyssen and Stinnes that Germany before the outbreak of World War I had managed to surpass England in the production of pig iron and to run a close second in the production of coal. In chemical research and applied chemistry she had achieved world supremacy. In several other branches of industry, such as the dye works of Ludwigshafen in Baden, the optical precision instruments of the Zeiss works in Jena, or the toy industries of Nuremberg, she set standards of ingenuity and high-class workmanship which were not matched anywhere in the world.

To utilize to better effect her internal waterways Germany built an ingenious system of canals, and to enlarge the volume of her overseas trade she embarked upon an extensive maritime building program, making the Hamburg harbor into the largest seaport, next to London. The main office of the Hamburg-America Line (founded in 1847; cf. p. 552) bore the

symbolic inscription: *Mein Feld ist die Welt* ("My field is the world").
Its general director from 1899 to 1918 was Albert Ballin, who had worked
his way up from very modest beginnings and whom William II came
to honor with his friendship. Among the 439 ships with a total tonnage
of 1,360,360 which the line owned on the eve of World War I was the
mighty *Imperator* of 50,000 tons, launched in 1913. Bremen, Germany's
second largest North Sea port, was the home of the North German Lloyd
(founded in 1857; cf. p. 552) which in 1914 owned 494 seafaring vessels
with a total tonnage of 983,000.

The closing decades of the nineteenth century showed an increasing
tendency on the part of capitalistic enterprise to eliminate the shocks of
unchecked competition by the concentration of capital in fewer hands.
This tendency led in some countries to the creation of *trusts,* in others to
the formation of *Kartells.* Germany preferred the *Kartell* to the *trust.**
The consequence of the *Kartell* system was the almost complete syndical-
ization of the coal, iron, and steel industries by the end of the century.
The advantages of the system were the prevention of waste and the co-
ordination and unification of the industrial effort. The fact that Germany's
manufacturing output more than trebled and her national income doubled
during the reign of William II is in part at least attributable to this form
of rationalized or "planned" capitalism.

World War I. The year 1914 found the great powers of Europe so en-
meshed in a network of defensive alliances, and so inflexibly determined to
maintain or extend their respective spheres of interest, that any serious
international incident could be expected to touch off a major explosion.
Such an incident occurred on June 28, when Archduke Francis
Ferdinand, nephew of Francis Joseph I of Austria-Hungary, and heir
apparent to the throne of the Dual Monarchy, was assassinated (together
with his wife) while visiting the Bosnian town of Sarajevo. The assassin and
his fellow conspirators were Bosnian nationals, but the crime had been
inspired and planned by the chief of the publicity division of the Serbian
general staff, who was also the presiding officer of the secret Serbian Organization, *The Black Hand,* and closely linked with the Pan-Serbian society,
Narodna Obrana (national defense). It is known from documentary evidence
published by the Bolshevik regime of Russia that both the Serbian government and the Russian military attaché in Belgrade knew in advance of
the preparations for the plot, and that the anti-Austrian movement among
the Slavic subjects of the Austro-Hungarian monarchy had long been
encouraged and materially supported by some of the highest Russian officials.

That the Pan-Slav movement, headed by Serbia, found such ready

---

* The ultimate objectives are identical in both forms of capitalistic concentration, but whereas
in the *trust* the identity of the individual *entrepreneur* is lost, it is retained in the defensive
Kartell. The result in either case is the accumulation of vast economic power in the hands
of a small group of capitalists who are thereby enabled to lay down dictatorial rules concerning production, prices, credit, investments, interest rates, wage levels, etc.

response among the Slavs of the Austrian "succession states," and finally succeeded in creating a united front of anti-Austrian Slavs, was in part due to the failure of the Dual Monarchy to satisfy the justified civil and national aspirations of her Slavic subjects. Although about half of the population of Austria-Hungary were members of the Slavic race, the country was ruled by Germans and Hungarians (Magyars). Archduke Francis Ferdinand became the target of the Serbian nationalists precisely because he was known to favor concessions to the Austrian Slavs, and because the Serbian leaders were convinced that such a policy of conciliation would irreparably damage the Pan-Slav movement. It is the considered opinion of many of the critics of Austrian prewar policies that, if the dual system of the Austro-Hungarian monarchy had been transformed into a Danubian federation granting home rule to Czechs, Slovaks, Croats, and Slovenes, Pan-Slavism would have been deprived of one of its main arguments and incentives.

It was the pro-Austrian King Milan of Serbia who had written in the eighties of the nineteenth century: "If Austria could conciliate the Serbs within her territory by becoming a federal, instead of a dual monarchy, Serbia could join such a federation. In that case my kingdom would be content with the position occupied today by Bavaria, Saxony, and Wurtemberg in the German Empire. But in that case ten million Serbs would be united in one state, and our national unity would be effected. And since the other Balkan states would soon perceive the advantages gained from membership in this Austrian League of Nations, they might also join it."

The fact that none of the statesmen of modern Austria envisioned or attempted such a solution constitutes one of the tragic pages in the chapter of lost opportunities in the history of Austria and eastern Europe. Hence, the situation which prevailed in the summer of 1914, leading up to the climactic events of Sarajevo, presented a dangerous threat to the very existence of Austria-Hungary.

While Bismarck as late as 1887 had declared that "Germany recognizes Russian historic rights in the Balkans," the Germany of William II, as has been noted above (cf. p. 626 sq.), advanced its own ambitious schemes for the penetration of the Balkans, and thus it appeared that both Central Powers were ready to infringe upon the traditional Russian sphere of interest. This despite the fact that the German government had repeatedly tried to exert a restraining influence on the impetuous foreign policy of its Austrian ally. On the other hand, Germany obviously could not afford to hurt the sensibilities and alienate the sympathies of her only reliable partner in the *Dreibund*.

There is no doubt that the government of the Dual Monarchy acted in a very high-handed fashion in the course of events which followed the assassination of the archduke. The contents of the harsh ultimatum which Count Leopold von Berchtold, the Austrian foreign minister, dispatched to Belgrade on July 23 were made known to the German government only twenty-four hours prior to its transmission, and Serbia's conciliatory reply

— taking exception only to some minor points which the Serbian government wished to see submitted to the Hague Tribunal or an international conference — was kept secret for three days. When William II finally was informed of Serbia's submissive attitude he described the Austrian diplomatic success as "a brilliant achievement, considering that only forty-eight hours were allowed." And he continued his gratulatory remarks by saying: "It is more than we could have expected. . . . It removes all reason for war." In a letter addressed to Günther von Jagow, the German foreign secretary, the emperor wrote in a similar vein: "After receiving the Serbian reply which was handed to me this morning, I am convinced that the demands of the Dual Monarchy have in substance been granted. The reservations made on a few points of detail can in my view be cleared up by negotiation. A most humiliating surrender has been effected before the eyes of the whole world, and thus all ground for war has been removed." In a conversation with Jagow in 1929 the British historian G. P. Gooch expressed the following judgment on the causes which led to the general European conflagration of summer, 1914: "We think you could and should have pressed Austria more strongly, just as you think we could and should have pressed Russia. Each of us feared the loss of our friend and ally. The European system was the main cause of the war. Germany was dragged in by Austria, England and France by Russia." Jagow concurred in this view.

While the exchange of notes was taking place between Vienna and Belgrade, the diplomatic and political mills were grinding in the other European capitals. On July 20 Poincaré, the president of the French republic, had paid a visit to St. Petersburg, and the military clauses of the Franco-Russian alliance were then strongly reaffirmed. While telegrams were exchanged between Tsar Nicholas II and the German emperor, Russia had begun preparations for a general mobilization, on July 25. William II implored the tsar to halt the Russian troop movements in the direction of the German and Austrian borders, and the tsar begged the kaiser to help him "to avoid such a disaster as a general European war. In the name of our old friendship, I implore you to do everything in your power to prevent your ally from going too far." On July 25, Sir Edward Grey, the British foreign secretary, proposed a conference of England, France, Germany, and Italy to work out a settlement by negotiation. But neither Germany nor France showed any inclination to act upon this suggestion.

On July 28 the Austrian government, declaring itself unsatisfied by the "evasive" Serbian reply, declared war on Serbia. Immediately the German government urged Austria to disclaim any desire on her part to annex Serbian territory. But the Dual Monarchy paid no heed to this request. On July 29 the tsar ordered the general mobilization of the Russian army. Following another fervent plea of the German emperor, this order was temporarily rescinded, but reissued on July 30. Germany, while declaring a "state of imminent danger of war," delayed mobilization, pending the outcome of the emperor's personal appeal to the tsar. On July 31 a French cabinet meeting affirmed the French government's readiness for war. On the same day William II demanded that Russia halt its mobilization within the next twelve hours. When twenty-four hours had passed without a Russian reply, the emperor announced in the evening of August 1 that a state of war existed between Germany and Russia. In the meantime, in the afternoon of that fateful day, the mobilization of the French and German armies had followed each other within a few hours. A German inquiry in Paris as to the intentions of the French government brought the response that France would be guided solely by her own interests. On August 3 Germany declared war on France. During the night from August 3 to August 4 German troops crossed the frontier of neutral Belgium. On August 4 England declared war on Germany, giving as the official reason for her action the German violation of Belgian neutrality of which both Germany and England were co-guarantors (cf. p. 525).

The German chancellor von Bethmann-Hollweg, who tried both to justify the invasion of Belgium as an act of self-defense (*"Not kennt kein Gebot"*: necessity knows no law) and to apologize for it by promising restitution after the war, did great and irreparable harm to the moral prestige of Germany when he referred to neutrality treaties as "scraps of paper." Actually Germany's invasion of Belgium was an essential and integral part of the strategy which had been devised by General Alfred von Schlieffen (1833–1913), who had intermittently been attached to the German general staff from 1866 on, and its chief from 1891 to 1906. Developing the military doctrines of Clausewitz and Moltke (cf. p. 534) on the tactics of a destructive *Blitzkrieg,* and adapting them to the requirements of the technical age, he had worked out a strategy (the *"Schlieffen Plan"*) which called for a lightning attack on France, enveloping Belgium and Holland in a vast flanking movement, while entrusting the defense of the eastern German frontiers to relatively small task forces. This plan was now put to the test by the order of Helmuth von Moltke (the nephew of the famous military strategist of the Bismarck era), the German chief of staff, without, however, including the Netherlands in the invasion thrust. As England, under the terms of a "gentlemen's agreement" between the French and British governments, had accepted, two days before Germany's invasion of Belgium, responsibility for the protection of the northern coasts of France, her entry into the war could hardly have been prompted solely by the German violation of Belgian neutrality.

To the very last moment Germany had clung to the hope of keeping England neutral, and as a consequence the British declaration of war came as a great shock, producing a violent emotional reaction, especially among the traditionally pro-English German liberals. The sentiments of the disappointed Anglophiles found an outlet in a somewhat artificial campaign of hate which manifested itself in the popular slogan *"Gott strafe England!"* ("May God punish England!") and in such documents as the famed German economist Werner Sombart's *Händler und Helden (Shopkeepers and*

Heroes) or the poet Ernst Lissauer's glowing *Hassgesang* (*Song of Hate*).

The second great disappointment for the German people, if not for their government, was Italy's declaration of neutrality on the ground that the terms of the *Dreibund* called for assistance in the case of a defensive war only, and that in any case Italian policy would be governed exclusively by her own *sacro egoismo*. Italy finally joined the Allies on May 23, 1915, by declaring war on Austria, after having been promised in the secret Treaty of London of April 26 much more than she could have hoped to obtain by bargaining with Austria.* She was promised the southern Tyrol to the Brenner Pass, the Austrian coastal regions, including Trieste, the Dalmatian Islands and the northern part of the Dalmatian coast, occupation rights in Valona, colonial possessions in Asia Minor, plus a guarantee that the papacy was to be excluded from participation in the future peace conference.

While the Central Powers were thus deserted by Italy right at the beginning of the war, their cause derived some additional strength in the first month of the conflict from Turkey's decision to fight on the side of Germany and Austria. The cause of the Allies, on the other hand, was aided by Japan's declaration of war against Germany on August 23, 1914.

The German people — not differing greatly in this respect from the populations in the enemy countries — were familiar only with the surface phenomena and not with the more obscure ultimate causes of the European conflict. They were therefore convinced that Germany had become the victim of a dastardly international plot and that the very existence of the "encircled" fatherland was at stake. Arrayed against the Central Powers was the world's greatest sea power and a potential man power almost three times superior to their own. The Central Powers were favored, on the other hand, by the tactical and strategic advantages of short communication lines and by the German superiority in military training, discipline, leadership, and striking power.

As the German people felt, or were made to feel, that war had been forced upon them, they arose as one man. Forgotten were all internal dissensions, and on August 1, 1914, the Social Democrats of the *Reichstag* faction joined the other parties in a unanimous approval of the war credits. Forgotten also (and not only in Germany) was the international solidarity and the pacifist creed of the proletarian masses. The international labor movement received perhaps its severest blow with the assassination of the great French socialist and pacifist Jean Jaurès, on the very eve of the war. As far as the German socialists were concerned, some of their leaders were among the first to enlist as volunteers. A wave of enthusiasm swept over the entire country, and the air was filled with patriotic slogans. The Kaiser's *"Ich kenne keine Parteien mehr: ich kenne nur noch Deutsche"* ("I no

---

* On May 10, 1915, the Dual Monarchy offered to Italy the cession of southern Tyrol, autonomy for Trieste, occupation rights in Valona, and *désinteressement* of Austria-Hungary in Albania.

longer know of political parties: I know only Germans") and Frederick the Great's *"Viel Feind', viel Ehr"* ("The more enemies, the greater the honor"), spoken in the tragic days of the Seven Years' War, were repeated by young and old, in homes, in workshops, in schools, and in churches.

By December, 1914, the mood of the people had undergone some changes. Spirits were still high, the war bulletins, given out in the characteristic lapidary style of Quartermaster General von Stein, were greatly encouraging, and victory celebrations were frequent. But, nevertheless, there was a general and as yet undefined feeling that something had gone wrong somewhere. It was known, for example, that French-British resistance before Paris and on the Marne river had upset the *Schlieffen-Plan*. It was not so generally known that the chief of staff, with victory almost within his grasp, had suddenly lost command of the situation, issued contradictory orders, and, by his hesitation and evident confusion, had made it possible for the enemy to convert the war of movement into a war of position. The opposing armies threw up entrenchments and formed a stationary double line which extended from the North Sea coast to the Swiss frontier.

In the December session of the German *Reichstag* Karl Liebknecht (the son of Wilhelm Liebknecht, the friend and associate of August Bebel; cf. p. 614) and seventeen fellow socialists voted against the new war credits. In March, 1915, the socialist opposition had increased to thirty-two, almost one third of the Social Democratic party. In the summer of the same year the dissenting party members seceded and formed the faction of Independent Socialists, the nucleus of the future Communist party (*K.P.D.: Kommunistische Partei Deutschlands*). The rifts in the political and social structure of Germany, which had been temporarily closed by the upsurge of patriotic feeling, began to reappear.

Meanwhile the war in the East had yielded important victories for the German armies. After initial successes of small Russian contingents in their advance upon East Prussia, the German forces under the command of Paul von Hindenburg (1847–1934), who had been called back from retirement, were victorious at Tannenberg (late August, 1914), annihilating the Russian Second Army trapped in the swamplands of the Masurian Lakes, and driving the Russian First Army back beyond the Russian frontier. In the summer and autumn of 1915 German troops under the command of General von Mackensen relieved the hard-pressed Austrian armies in Galicia and drove the Russians from Galicia and Poland with staggering losses for the enemy, taking over a million prisoners. The Central Powers were joined by Bulgaria in their drive on Serbia (October, 1915), and by the end of the year Balkan domination had been secured and land communication with Turkey established.

While the opposing armies were stalemated in the West and the Central Powers victorious in the East, the war on the sea, less spectacular and moving more slowly, proved in the end more effective in deciding the final outcome of the conflict. The major sea engagement took place on May 31,

1916, in the North Sea (Battle of Jutland), when the entire German High Seas Fleet under the command of Admiral Scheer managed to fight its way out of a trap laid by the British Admiral Jellicoe. Although victory was claimed by both sides, the British gave unsparing credit to the bravery and strategic ingenuity of the greatly inferior German forces in extricating themselves from an almost fatal predicament.

To meet the mortal danger of the British blockade, Germany early in 1915 declared the waters surrounding the British Isles as "zones of war," using the new weapon of the submarine boat to enforce a "counterblockade" by means of the destruction of increasing volumes of allied shipping space. German submarine attacks, initially confined to allied shipping, and temporarily relaxed after the strong protests of the United States which followed the sinking of the luxury liner *Lusitania* (May 7, 1915), were resumed in full force in January, 1917, when Germany embarked on a campaign of "unrestricted submarine warfare," threatening to destroy any and all belligerent and neutral vessels which entered specified danger zones in the proximity of the coastal waters of the allied powers. Although Germany came dangerously close to its goal — the destruction of a sufficient amount of allied shipping to hamstring the allied operations and force a conclusion of hostilities on German terms — the unrestricted submarine war was a desperate gamble, not only because it drew upon the *Reich* the odium of being insensitive to the injunctions of international law, but also and foremost because it alienated the remaining sympathies of the neutral powers and finally brought the most powerful of them, the United States, into the war on the side of the Allies.

The policy of unrestricted submarine warfare was itself an outgrowth of important changes in the German High Command, caused by the unexpected prolongation of the war and the gradually ebbing morale of the home front. General Erich von Falkenhayn, who had succeeded von Moltke as chief of staff, was dismissed in August, 1916, and replaced by Paul von Hindenburg. Erich Ludendorff, holding the position of quartermaster general, became second in command. Though nominally inferior in rank to von Hindenburg, Ludendorff was the superior strategist and, owing to his military prowess, came to wield a dictatorial power which was by no means confined to the military sphere, but made itself felt in the political sphere as well. A power politician by conviction, he was strongly influenced by the racial, anti-Semitic, and anti-Christian theories of Houston Stewart Chamberlain (1855–1927), Richard Wagner's son-in-law, a native of Great Britain, who had made Germany his adopted country. Ludendorff also maintained close ties with the Pan-Germans, supporting their annexationist war aims, and later on (1917) taking a hand in shaping the program and policies of the rightist and chauvinist *Vaterlandspartei*.

It was Ludendorff's conviction that the stalemate in the West could not be broken unless the morale of the enemy had first been weakened by the methods of ruthless and unrestricted submarine warfare. However, before this fateful course was definitively decided upon, the German government had extended some peace feelers, chiefly to induce the allied powers to make public their war aims. Yet these German overtures of December, 1916, were rejected by the Allies on the ground that they impressed them as "empty and insincere" and only intended to sow seeds of discord in their camp. The German peace initiative almost coincided with President Wilson's first note to the belligerents, in which he asked them to state the objectives they were fighting for. The demand of the American president caused some embarrassment among the allied powers, owing to the fact that (as was revealed in January, 1918, in the New York *Evening Post*) in autumn, 1916, they had concluded some secret treaties whose terms provided for considerable annexations in the East and West, proposed acquisitions of enemy territory which equaled if not exceeded in scope the Pan-German dreams of conquest. In their reply to the presidential note, however, the Allies mentioned as preconditions for peace negotiations only the restoration of the integrity of Belgium, Serbia, and Montenegro; the evacuation of the invaded regions of France, Russia, and Rumania; the liberation of the Italian and Slavic subjects of the Austro-Hungarian monarchy as well as of the non-Moslem populations "under the bloody tyranny of the Turks"; adequate compensation and indemnities, and definite guarantees for the future peace of Europe. These terms, formulated on the presupposition of the sole responsibility of the Central Powers for the war, and involving the dismemberment of Austria-Hungary, were unacceptable to an undefeated Germany and her partners.

The Russian February Revolution of 1917, staged by the socialist *Mensheviki*, and foreshadowing impending military collapse, seemed to work into Ludendorff's hands. To eliminate the eastern front by means of a series of steps which were aimed at effecting the rapid disintegration of Russia from within, the politico-military dictator of Germany decided to grant safe-conduct through the *Reich* to Lenin and other leaders of the radical *Bolsheviki*, who had been living in Swiss exile. The following November Revolution in Russia, plunging the country into utter chaos, had thus the full blessing of the German quartermaster general. In March, 1918, the Russians found themselves compelled to sign the humiliating Treaty of Brest-Litovsk, which ended the war in the East and deprived Russia of her Baltic provinces, Finland, Poland, the Ukraine, and some regions in the Caucasus.

The loss of Russia to the Allies was, however, far outweighed by the gain which was marked by the entry of the United States into the war on their side. Without the foolhardy continuation of unrestricted submarine warfare, in the face of mounting American resentment, United States participation in the struggle might never have gone beyond the financial engagements of private interests which had extended credits to the Allies in the amount of a billion and a half dollars. But the increasing losses of American life and property on the high seas, in addition to German diplomatic blunders and the obnoxious activities of German agents in the United States and in Mexico, finally turned the scales in favor of armed intervention. On April 6, 1917, the United States Congress declared war on the Central Powers.

Early in 1917 another unsuccessful peace offensive had been attempted by Emperor Charles I of Austria-Hungary, who had succeeded Francis Joseph I in 1916. The emperor had gained the conviction — and had so informed the German government — that Austria could not continue the fight beyond the autumn of 1917. He therefore had begun negotiations with the Allies, using as an intermediary his brother-in-law, Prince Sixte of Bourbon, who served as an officer in the Belgian army. But his peace efforts were frustrated by the adamant opposition of Germany on the one hand, and of Italy on the other.

In Germany, too, the sentiment in favor of a negotiated peace was steadily gaining ground and could no longer be stifled even by the most rigid censorship of the press and the attempted thorough regimentation of public opinion. On July 19, 1917, the German *Reichstag,* on the initiative of the Centrist deputy Matthias Erzberger, adopted with 212 votes of the Center party, the Socialists, and the Progressive Liberals against 126 votes of National Liberals and Conservatives the famous "peace resolution." This stated in part that "the Reichstag is striving for a peace of mutual understanding" and that "enforced cessions of territory as well as political, economic, and financial oppression are incompatible with a peace of this kind." It called for the creation of an international organization to guarantee the future peace of the world by means of political and economic collaboration. Erzberger's action had the strong moral support of the papal nuncio in Bavaria, Eugenio Pacelli, the future Pope Pius XII.

The reaction of the High Command was swift and decisive: the conciliatory Bethmann-Hollweg had to resign as chancellor to be replaced by Georg Michaelis, a docile and narrow-minded bureaucrat, who, during the brief period of his chancellorship, acted as Ludendorff's willing tool. Before the year 1917 ended he was forced out of office by an aroused *Reichstag.* But in the months that intervened between his assumption of office and his resignation he had managed to thwart another peace move which had been timed to coincide with and strengthen the peace resolution of the *Reichstag.*

This new peace offensive had issued from the Vatican. In August, Pope Benedict XV had addressed a note to the "Heads of the Belligerent Peoples," in which he had invited the governments at war to agree upon *seven points* from whose common acceptance a just and lasting peace might result. These points included drastic reduction of armaments, creation of an international institution for the arbitration of disputes among nations, provision of sanctions to be applied against any state which should refuse to submit to arbitration, guarantee of the freedom of the seas, complete and reciprocal condonation of all claims resulting from war damages and expenditures, restoration of all occupied territories to their legitimate owners, and co-ordination of all particular interests with the commonweal of human society, in a spirit of equity and justice. The chief negotiations on behalf of the papacy were carried on by Eugenio Pacelli.

The reaction of Chancellor Michaelis to these proposals was largely determined by his intense nationalism and his anti-Catholic bias. On July 24 the pope had dispatched a special preliminary note to the German government to find out in advance what its attitude would be with regard to the papal peace plan. On August 22 Michaelis wrote to Count Wedel, the German ambassador in Vienna: "In my opinion our endeavor must be to throw the odium of a possible failure of the Pope's mediation upon our enemies and show them to be in the wrong. . . . It is therefore my intention to proceed in this matter rather dilatorily."

In response to the papal note of August 1 the British government expressed its willingness to enter into peace negotiations, provided the German government were willing to offer specific guarantees for the restoration and future preservation of the independence and integrity of Belgium. The reaction in Germany to the papal initiative was unfavorable. Some influential newspapers spoke of "papal arrogance," and the Lutheran pastor Dr. Traub, as emissary of the Protestant "Evangelical League," stumped the country in an attempt to counteract the papal peace move, declaring that "as an Evangelical Protestant" he could not "see the end of the war in an untimely peace offered by the Pope in the very year of the jubilee of Luther's reformation" (1517). The German chancellor, making this view his own, subsequently resorted to procrastination, dissimulation, and even falsification to keep the contents of a special dispatch of the papal nuncio from the knowledge of the emperor and the imperial crown council. He furthermore explicitly refused to embody in his answer to the papal note any assurances regarding Belgian independence, assurances which, as he well knew, were an absolute prerequisite to any peace negotiations.

When Nuncio Pacelli received the preliminary draft of the German reply he realized at once that it foredoomed the papal peace move to failure. Reviewing the peace efforts of the Vatican of August, 1917, Archbishop Noerber of Freiburg wrote in 1919: "The war was definitely lost in the moment when the peace of reconciliation which Benedict XV tried to bring about was rejected for no other reason than that it had come from the Pope."

The last hope of the German *Wehrmacht* lay in forcing a decision in the West before the arrival of an expeditionary force from the United States. In October, 1917, while the Austrians routed the Italians at Caporetto, the Germans began preparations for a giant offensive to be launched in the spring of 1918. The privations of the fearful winter of 1917–1918 had brought the German home front near the breaking point. The limit of endurance was almost reached, and the general war weariness found expression in the oft-repeated phrase: *"Lieber ein Ende mit Schrecken als ein Schrecken ohne Ende"* ("Rather an end with terror than a terror without end"). But war weariness also spread among the front soldiers of the belligerents, and the French and Italian High Commands had to use ruthless force to crush several mutinies.

In January, 1918, Woodrow Wilson outlined in an address the "Fourteen Points" which he proposed as a basis for peace. Ludendorff, however, was determined to stake all on one last desperate gamble. In March, 1918, he led his armies in a gigantic assault against the French and British lines in the West, and at the cost of about half a million casualties the Germans reached the Marne river for a second time. But the exhaustion of the German armies provided the Allies with a sorely needed respite, and when Ludendorff, on July 15, launched his final offensive, designed to dislocate and definitively smash the enemy, the allied lines held. Regrouped and reorganized under the command of Marshal Foch, and reinforced by newly arrived powerful contingents from the United States, the Allies counterattacked and turned the second battle of the Marne (July 15 to August 2) into a decisive victory for their armies. On August 8 the British pierced the German lines east of Amiens, and during the following weeks the German forces were pressed back all along their extended front, losing another half million men in valiant rear-guard action.

On September 29, Ludendorff and Hindenburg informed the emperor that the war was lost and that a new German government, to be formed within the next twenty-four hours, must immediately ask for an armistice. During September and October Bulgaria and Turkey collapsed, and the Austrian empire was in a process of rapid disintegration. On November 4 the Dual Monarchy capitulated, Emperor Charles abdicated, and the Polish, Czech, Croat, and Slovene minorities rose in revolt and declared their autonomy.

Yielding to the demand of Ludendorff for an immediate armistice and the formation of a new government, the German emperor agreed to take the necessary steps to have the *Bundesrat* effect the transformation of the German *Reich* into a parliamentary and democratic monarchical State whose chancellor and cabinet were to be directly responsible to the *Reichstag*. On October 3 Prince Max von Baden, the nephew of the then ruling grand duke of Baden, known for his humanitarian work in behalf of the prisoners of war as well as for his democratic convictions, was asked to take over the office of chancellor. He replaced the aged Bavarian scholar and statesman, Count von Hertling, who had succeeded Michaelis.

Prince Max resolutely accepted the arduous task of forming a new government that had the backing of the *Reichstag,* and in his cabinet, in which he himself acted as foreign minister, he included for the first time two leading members of the Social Democrats (Philipp Scheidemann and Gustav Bauer). Pressed and practically coerced by Ludendorff, he finally abandoned his original plan of submitting a detailed blueprint for peace to Woodrow Wilson, and instead, contrary to his conviction, asked the American president for an immediate armistice, accepting as a basis for peace negotiations "the program laid down by the President of the United States in his message to Congress of January 8, 1918, and in his subsequent pronouncements."

Wilson's note of October 14 demanded as a prerequisite for peace "the destruction or reduction to virtual impotency of every arbitrary power anywhere that can . . . disturb the peace of the world." "The power," the note continued, "which has hitherto controlled the German nation is of the sort here described. It is within the choice of the German people to alter it." Wilson's note of October 23 spoke no longer of peace negotiations, but of the "surrender of the military masters and the monarchical autocrats of Germany."

Ludendorff, enraged by the tone and the demands of the American notes, abruptly reversed his decision and advocated continuation of the struggle. But on October 26 he had to yield to the demands for his resignation which were conveyed to him by the emperor. General Wilhelm Gröner, who took over the command of the German armies, was the first to mention to the emperor abdication as the only way to satisfy the stipulations contained in the American notes. The same course was suggested by Scheidemann in a letter addressed to Prince Max, who up to this moment had still clung to the hope of being able to save the monarchy.

In the meantime, dramatic moves were being enacted on the German home front. A revolutionary uprising had slowly but surely gained momentum, and on November 3 mutiny broke out among the naval squadrons stationed at Kiel. The rebellious sailors were soon joined by the workers, and quickly the revolt spread to the other German seaports. On November 7 several of the larger cities in northern and central Germany as well as Munich in the south joined the incipient revolution. In the latter city the establishment of a Bavarian republic was proclaimed by Kurt Eisner, one of the leaders of the radical wing of the Social Democrats. King Louis III of the ancient Wittelsbach dynasty was forced to renounce the throne. On November 9 the revolutionary wave was converging on Berlin. It was then that Prince Max, to avoid bloodshed and ensuing chaos, decided on his own responsibility to announce the abdication of the emperor. "The Chancellor," the proclamation read in part, "remains in office until the questions connected with the abdication of the emperor . . . and the setting up of a Regency have been settled. He intends to propose . . . the appointment of Herr Ebert to the chancellorship, and the framing of a bill to prepare elections for a German Constituent National Assembly."

Reluctantly, after much hesitation, and with grave misgivings William II, yielding to the advice of Generals Gröner and Hindenburg, decided to authorize the announcement of his abdication. On November 10 he crossed the border of Holland, to spend the remaining twenty-three years of his life in the Dutch health resort of Doorn. Thus, after a period of approximately five hundred years of uninterrupted rule, the Hohenzollern dynasty came to an end.

Declining for himself the office of *Reichsverweser,* which was offered him for the interim between the fall of the monarchy and the election of a National Assembly, Prince Max, before retiring from the political scene, persuaded the socialist leader Friedrich Ebert to accept the chancellorship of the German republic.

The Revolution. World War I had involved more than thirty nations, large and small, and approximately sixty-five million men had been under arms. Over eight million soldiers had lost their lives, and almost twenty-five million had been wounded or were among the missing. The total war expenditures have been variously estimated, but they must be figured in the proximity of one hundred and eighty billion dollars. German casualties amounted to one million six hundred thousand dead, over four million wounded, and over two hundred thousand missing. At the end of the war the German national debt stood at one hundred and seventy-six billion gold marks (forty-four billion dollars). The British blockade had caused increasing suffering among the civilian population of the Central Powers, and Germany alone counted about three quarters of a million deaths attributable to malnutrition. The privations of the last winter of the war had sapped the people's remaining strength and finally broken their will to resistance. Thus the defeat of the armies in the field coincided with the physical and moral breakdown of the home front. But the interrelation between the collapse of soldiers and civilians was only temporal, not causal, so that the *Dolchstosslegende* (the story of the home front "stabbing the army in the back," a malicious invention of the resurgent German militarists and rightists of later years) cannot be maintained in the light of historic facts.

The one consolation of the German people in their defeat and misfortune lay in their hope for a new era of political democracy and both social and international justice. Such a new era seemed to be reasonably assured by German acceptance of President Wilson's "Fourteen Points" and by the willingness of the German people to atone for the sins of their political and military leaders. It was this hope and this implicit trust in a saner and juster world order which acted as a moderating influence on the forces of revolution and eventually determined the triumph of constitutional government over leftist radicalism. Despite their many miseries and heartaches the Germans breathed under a freer sky than they had had for many decades, and they took a certain pride in putting their own house in order and in firmly resolving to gain back the confidence of the world.

The way, however, was difficult and dangerous. The first issue which the nascent Republic had to face was the internecine struggle between the Social Democrats (the majority group) and the Independent Socialists of the extreme Left. The workers and soldiers had made the revolution, and it was now a question whether the new Germany was to be ruled by a freely elected National Assembly or whether it was to follow the Russian model and be handed over to a proletarian class dictatorship. In the newly formed Workers' and Soldiers' Councils, meeting in Berlin on November 10, 1918, the Social Democrats received equal representation on a joint committee of the two socialist groups. It was due to the influence of the Social Democrats that the Proclamation of the Council of *Volksbeauftragte* (People's Commissars) of November 12 contained the provision that all future elections, including the one for a Constituent National Assembly, should be based on the universal suffrage of German men and women. Thus the democratic idea of equal popular representation had achieved its first and decisive triumph over those forces which advocated tyrannical class rule.

The twenty-two German monarchs, together with many of those political and military leaders who were linked with the monarchy by tradition and conviction, had disappeared almost overnight. Most of the kings and princes accepted their fate with good grace, and a few of them with a disarming sense of humor. But monarchical feeling had its firmest roots in the army and in the civil service, and it was in these quarters that the slowly growing resistance movement against the Republic found its strongest support. The traditional opposition to democratic ideas and institutions was of the most momentous import in the case of the judiciary, because many judges lacked the mental and psychological disposition to conduct political trials with impartiality. Thus, as a rule, the case of an accused democrat, liberal, or socialist was already prejudged when the hearing began. For the time being, however, these matters were of no immediate relevance. A small minority of the aristocrats and army officers openly sympathized with the revolution, while the majority withdrew for the moment from the scene of action, trying to avoid a premature showdown, and hoping for a comeback at some more opportune time. Ludendorff, for example, thought it the better part of wisdom to seek temporary refuge in Sweden.

The important thing, however, was that Generals Hindenburg and Gröner, who commanded the unreserved loyalty of the returning troops, placed themselves unequivocally at the disposal of the Republic, notwithstanding their sentimental attachment to the monarchical tradition of Germany. By putting the well-being of the nation above all personal considerations they set a noteworthy example and made possible a relative stabilization of the republican form of government.

The provisional government of the new German Republic was headed by the six socialists united in the *Rat der Volksbeauftragten,* with Friedrich Ebert acting as chancellor. The General Congress of Workers' and Soldiers' Councils, meeting in Berlin in mid-December, 1918, endorsed elections for a National Assembly by an overwhelming majority. Thus they delivered a strong rebuff to the dictatorial claims of the "Spartacus League," a group of left-wing extremists, who had been organized by Karl Liebknecht and Rosa Luxemburg in 1916 and had adopted the name of the leader of the rebellious slaves in ancient Rome (73–71 B.C.). A month earlier, a conference of the socialist-controlled State governments of Germany had likewise voted in favor of a National Assembly.

This consolidation of pro-democratic sentiment was materially aided by the united efforts of the Free (socialist) and Christian *Gewerkschaften* (Trade Unions, cf. p. 556) whose well-disciplined members were opposed to political and social radicalism. Their position had been strengthened by an agreement with the representatives of the German employers, negotiated on November 15, which, among other social gains, secured for the German workers the right of collective bargaining and the eight-hour day. It also provided for the establishment of committees of employees in all industrial plants, committees which were later to be centralized in a *Reichswirtschaftsrat* (Federal Economic Council; cf. p. 650 sq.). To facilitate the recovery of German economy the unions pledged themselves not to resort to arbitrary strikes. The Socialization Commission, appointed by the provisional government, met on December 5 and declared itself in favor of the maintenance of private property and opposed to expropriations and untimely experiments in socialization.

As was to be expected, this moderate and conciliatory policy of Majority Socialists and Trade Unions aroused the anger of the uncompromising radical minority. The Independent Socialists refused further co-operation, and before the elections for a National Assembly could be held the provisional government had to enlist the aid of General Gröner and the army to crush an uprising of the "Spartacus League" in Berlin (early January, 1919), in the course of which Karl Liebknecht and Rosa Luxemburg were brutally slain. In Bavaria, too, where the revolutionary movement from the outset had been headed by radical Independent Socialists under the leadership of Kurt Eisner, trouble was brewing. During the final year of the war, Eisner, a Berlin journalist who had moved to Munich in 1910, had organized a Bavarian underground movement and, in November, 1918, following the abdication of the king, had assumed the offices of prime minister and foreign minister of the Bavarian republic. In the hope of obtaining better peace terms from the enemy, Eisner advocated an abject and summary admission of German responsibility for the war and tried to force his opinion on the central provisional government in Berlin, threatening separate peace negotiations of Bavaria in case of refusal. This high-handed procedure as well as Eisner's ruthless suppression of the Bavarian opposition press aroused the indignation of Bavarian patriots and monarchist conservatives. In the elections for a provincial assembly of Bavaria (January 12, 1919) Eisner's Independent Socialists suffered a decisive defeat. The idealist doctrinaire had already resolved to hand in his resignation at the first meeting of the newly elected Diet, when on his way to the assembly he was assassinated by Count von Arco, a monarchist student of the University of Munich. The fact that Eisner was a Jew had contributed considerably to the violent opposition which was stirred up by his political actions.

Elections for the Constituent National Assembly were held on January 19, 1919. On February 6, the elected deputies met in the National Theatre of the city of Weimar, hallowed by the name of Goethe and the tradition of

German Humanism (cf. p. 403 sq.). The Germany which came into being at Weimar was henceforth known as the *Weimar Republic*.

The elections had given 163 seats to the Majority Socialists, 22 to the Independent Socialists, 91 to the Center party, 79 to the Progressives (renamed *Democrats*), 19 to the National Liberals (renamed *Deutsche Volkspartei:* German People's Party), 44 to the monarchist Conservatives (renamed *Deutschnationale Volkspartei:* German National People's Party), and 3 to minor political groups. Out of a total of 421 representatives, 333 supported the republican and democratic form of government (Majority Socialists, Centrists, Democrats), while 88 were either undecided (National Liberals) or outright antidemocratic and antirepublican (Conservatives). But it is interesting to note that even the monarchists of the extreme Right found it necessary to pay lip service to the democratic trend by adding the epithet *"Volk"* to their party label.

On February 11, 1919, Friedrich Ebert was elected *Reichspräsident,* an office which he held until his death in 1925. Gustav Scheidemann was appointed *Reichskanzler* of the Republic. A short-lived Bavarian Soviet dictatorship, proclaimed in April, 1919, which temporarily threatened to upset the fragile stability of the national government, was overthrown with the aid of Prussian and Swabian troops. On July 31 the Weimar Constitution — drafted by the provisional minister of the interior, Professor Hugo Preuss, formerly of the *Handelshochschule* (university for trade and commerce), Berlin — was adopted by a large majority of the National Assembly, against the opposition of the Independent Socialists, the German People's Party, and the German Nationals.

The Weimar Constitution. The committee to which Hugo Preuss's draft for the constitution of the German republic was referred for final action consisted of twenty-eight members representing proportionately the different political factions. It was headed by Konrad Haussmann, a distinguished member of the Democratic party. The compromise worked out by this committee struck a middle course between the tendency to centralize power in the federal government, and the particularist trend of the constituent states. The Constitution provided for a democratic republic of federated states. The individual states were henceforth known as *Länder* (lands). Article 13, which stated that federal law overrides state law, further reduced their still existing semiautonomy. Indicative of this limitation of state rights was the taking over of the German railway system by the *Reich* (a goal which Bismarck had failed to achieve), and Bavaria and Wurtemberg's surrender of their control of post and telegraph services.

The place of the former *Bundesrat* (cf. p. 547) was taken by the *Reichsrat,* in which the *Länder* were represented by members of their respective governments. And, to a larger extent than had been the case in the constitution of imperial Germany, a check was placed on the predominance of Prussia by the provision that no single *Land* was allowed more than two fifths of the total number of votes. Prussia held 26 out of a total of 66 seats, but only 13 of these 26 seats were filled by representatives of the Prussian government, while the remaining 13 were distributed among the administrations of the semiautonomous Prussian provinces.

The major change was not so much in the composition of the *Reichsrat* as in the title of its authority and power. While the old *Bundesrat* had derived its federal power from the Union of Princes, the *Reichsrat* derived its authority from the will of the people. In addition, its power as an administrative and legislative body was greatly restricted by the fact that both its enactments and its vetoes could be overruled by a two-thirds majority of the *Reichstag* or by popular referendum. With all its checks and balances to insure a division of power, the Weimar Constitution leaned toward a unicameral system, centered and anchored in the *Reichstag*.

Konrad Haussmann said of the Weimar Constitution that it was "born in suffering" and that it represented "the law of a people oppressed by the enemy." It reflected the mind of the German people in the hour of defeat, but also their hopes for a better future, and their determination to preserve both their unity and diversity within a legal framework that was to give reasonable assurance for the attainment of justice, progress, and peace. As stated in the Preamble, "this Constitution has been drafted and adopted by the German people, united in its *Stämme* (tribes), and animated by the desire to renew and strengthen its *Reich* on the bases of freedom and justice, to serve the cause of peace both within and without, and to promote the progress of human society."

In Article 1 emphasis is placed on the fact that "the supreme power of the *Reich* emanates from the people," while Article 4 declares that "the generally recognized rules of International Law are integral parts of German Law." Article 17 deals with Electoral Law, stating that "every *Land* is to adopt a Republican Constitution. The representatives of the people are to be elected by the universal, equal, direct, and secret suffrage of all German citizens, men and women (who have attained the age of twenty), in accordance with the principle of proportional representation." The adoption of the French system of proportional representation, while intended to make it possible even for smallest minorities to register their political and social convictions, actually tended to weaken rather than strengthen the parliamentary structure. It encouraged the formation of many small parties reflecting the particular interests of minority groups. Their votes were collected by districts, entered in a *Reichsliste,* and if they added up to the sixty thousand required for the election of a deputy, the minority obtained the status of a party and representation in the *Reichstag.*

Against the opposition of the monarchist-conservative deputies of the Right the Weimar Constitution adopted the colors black, red, and gold — the colors of the Holy Roman Empire and of the Revolution of 1848 — in place of the black, white, and red of the Empire of Bismarck and William II. The ancient black, red, and gold stood for the idea of *Grossdeutschland* (cf. p. 530), whereas the banner black, white, red symbolized the idea of

Bismarck's *Kleindeutschland*. The incorporation of German Austria in the federal organism of the *Reich* was envisaged by Article 2 of the Weimar Constitution, and Article 61 provided for Austrian representation in the *Reichsrat* in a consultative capacity. As early as November 12, 1918, the Austrian National Assembly had endorsed Article 1 of an Austrian Provisional Constitution, stating that "German Austria is a constituent part of the German Republic." Plebiscites held in several regions of German Austria gave evidence of overwhelming sentiment in favor of an *Anschluss,* but both at that time and in later years (cf. p. 669) the realization of this common aspiration of the advocates of *Grossdeutschland* was prevented by the uncompromising opposition of the Allies.

The *Reichspräsident* was to be elected for a period of seven years by the direct ballot of the people, and was re-eligible. His powers were in some respects greater than those wielded by the German emperor. Thus he could dissolve the *Reichstag,* even without the consent of the *Reichsrat,* a measure which in the Imperial Constitution had required the consent of the *Bundesrat.* He could invoke a popular referendum against decisions of the *Reichstag.* He was commander in chief of the armed forces, a power which the emperor had only exercised in time of war. Finally, he could be given extraordinary emergency powers under Article 48 of the Constitution. In case "public safety and order were seriously disturbed," the *Reichspräsident* could rule by decree laws, suspend certain *Grundrechte* (fundamental rights) — the right of *habeas corpus,* secrecy of the mails, freedom of expression, inviolability of the home and of private property, and the right of coalition — and could call on the *Reichswehr* to enforce his emergency decrees. While the exercise of such virtually dictatorial power was theoretically subject to endorsement by the *Reichstag,* this check was almost voided by the provision that the President could dissolve the *Reichstag* and, in the interim of the required sixty days between dissolution and re-election, could rule without a parliament. This article, obviously an offshoot of a period of insecurity and crisis, was later on to prove fatal to the very existence of the Weimar Republic (cf. p. 656 sqq.).

The second major section of the Constitution defined and circumscribed the *Grundrechte* or Bill of Rights and the correlative obligations of citizenship. In this part the spirit of the Weimar Constitution showed the closest kinship with the ideals of the Revolution of 1848 and the Frankfurt Parliament (cf. p. 530 sqq.). The *Grundrechte* were championed in particular by the Catholic Centrists, the Democrats, and the Majority Socialists. All *Grundrechte* were anchored in the dignity of the human person, their common denominator and *raison d'être.* Accordingly, the respective articles deal with those legal decrees and measures which were to safeguard social equality, personal freedom, and social justice. Class privileges were to be done away with. Titles of nobility were to become part of the family name, and no new ones could be conferred. Special guarantees were to protect the right of coalition, the rights of national minorities, the independence of the courts, democratic principles of education, freedom of the press, freedom of worship, and the rights of youth.

The Churches were designated as "corporations of public law," entitled to collect taxes from their members. In the case of the Protestant Churches this change of legal status meant liberation from subservience to the monarchist State whose head had in many instances held the power and exercised the functions of the episcopate. Although the Weimar Constitution tended toward the separation of State and Church, it provided for continued State support of the Churches, and several of the *Länder* subsequently entered into special "concordats" with the Holy See and the Protestant *Landeskirchen*.*

The section dealing with education decreed the abolition of private preparatory schools and established a compulsory common *Grundschule* (basic school) of four grades for all children. Education in general was to aim at "moral training, public spirit, personal and vocational fitness, and, above all, the cultivation of German national character and of the spirit of international reconciliation."

The final and most comprehensive section of the Weimar Constitution was devoted to social and economic problems. Article 153 states that "property imposes obligations; it must be used in the service of the common good." This flexible concept of private property, striking a middle path between the capitalist-liberal idea of an absolute right of ownership and the socialist expropriation theory, harked back to the primitive Germanic and medieval Christian concept of a relative right to private ownership. It thus emphasized the communal component of private property and referred it to its ethical frame and term, the common good of all. The distribution of the soil, for example, was to be controlled by the *Reich,* and land that was needed for the social and economic good of the community might be expropriated or socialized. Entailed estates (*Fideikommisse*) were to be dissolved, and the unearned increment in the value of the soil was to be used for the benefit of the nation. Thus the *Reich* reserved for itself the right to socialize such private enterprises as it considered suitable and "ripe" for such conversion. In these instances the former owners were to be duly compensated.

The most important and socially most progressive innovation in the economic field was the creation of *Wirtschaftsräte* (Economic Councils), to culminate in a central *Reichswirtschaftsrat,* as outlined in Article 165. These economic bodies were to serve as instruments of social peace and social justice and were intended to supplement and complete the system of social legislation inaugurated by Bismarck (cf. p. 535 sqq.). The article stipulated

---

* Article 138 called for the commutation and eventual cessation of financial contributions of the State to the Churches, but State support was never discontinued, not even under National Socialism. Religious instruction in public schools was likewise continued, and the theological faculties at the universities were retained. A *Reich Concordat* with the Holy See was concluded in 1933.

that workers and employees were to "co-operate on an equal footing with employers in the regulation of wages and the conditions of labor, as well as in the general development of the productive forces." To achieve this end it was decreed that workers and employees were to receive "legal representation in the form of District Workers' Councils, Regional Workers' Councils, and a *Reich* Workers' Council." These chosen representatives of labor were then to "combine with the representatives of the employers . . . to form Regional Economic Councils and a *Reichswirtschaftsrat*. Bills dealing with basic social and economic questions shall be submitted to the *Reichswirtschaftsrat* before being presented to the *Reichstag*." These legal directives were further implemented by the laws of February and May, 1920, the former providing for the election of a representative Workers' Council in all enterprises with more than twenty employees (*Betriebsräte*), the latter defining specifically the constitution and the functions of the *Reichswirtschaftsrat*. It was to consist of 326 members, proportionately representing agriculture, horticulture, forestry, fisheries, industry, trade, commerce, finance, communication and transportation, arts and crafts, and consumer interests. Twelve regional economic experts and twelve representatives of the *Reich* government completed the roster of this large and powerful organization.

With the creation of the *Reichswirtschaftsrat* the Weimar Constitution had, in theory at least, pointed a way to resolve the conflict between capital and labor, the two warring contenders in the "labor market," without resorting to the extremes of either excessive capitalist individualism or State socialism. The solution proposed, moreover, embodied much of the best social thinking of the Christian tradition of Europe and many of the suggestions contained in the social encyclicals of Popes Leo XIII and Pius XI.

The Treaty of Versailles. Prince Max von Baden's request for an armistice of October 5, 1918 (cf. p. 642) had been addressed to Woodrow Wilson and had expressed the desire on the part of Germany to accept the "Fourteen Points" as a basis of peace negotiations. The American president referred the German plea to the Allied Powers, and these in turn declared in a joint note to Washington "their willingness to make peace with the government of Germany on the terms of peace laid down in the President's address to Congress of January 8, 1918, and the principles of settlement enunciated in his subsequent addresses." The acceptance of the Allies was qualified, however, by two reservations, one relating to the freedom of the seas, the other to the problem of reparations. To those familiar with the spirit and the letter of the secret agreements and treaties (1915, 1916, 1917) concluded among the Allied Powers — regarding in particular the future disposal of the Rhineland, the German colonies, the Adriatic coast, Constantinople, and the Dardanelles — it must have been obvious even at that time that such far-reaching annexationist plans could hardly be reconciled with Wilson's "Fourteen Points." The French government, for example, had made it clear in September, 1916, that Germany should be deprived of the territory of the Saar and of the entire left bank of the Rhine. These regions were to be transformed into "autonomous republics" under French military supervision. Russia, in return for her approval of the French scheme, was to be given a free hand in the German East.

The note of the American State Department of November 5, 1918, conveyed to the German government the Allies' acceptance of the "Fourteen Points" in their qualified form. The German government in turn expressed its agreement, and a German Armistice Commission left for Paris. At the following "peace conference" the European Allies were represented by their Prime Ministers Lloyd George (England), Clemenceau (France), and Vittorio Orlando (Italy), while the chief spokesman for the United States was President Wilson, who had arrived in the French capital on December 13. Aside from these "Big Four," none of the thirty-odd "Allied and Associated Powers" played any conspicuous part in framing the peace treaties and in determining the future shape of the world's map.

The leader of the German delegation was Count von Brockdorff-Rantzau. He and his associates were excluded from participation in the negotiations, and the terms of the treaty they were asked to sign remained unknown to them up to the moment they were submitted for acceptance *in toto,* on May 7. The German delegates, held *incommunicado* behind barbed wire in a Paris hotel, were, however, permitted to hand in written remarks relating to questions of minor detail and to methods of the fulfillment of German obligations under the treaty.

On May 28, the Germans submitted a set of counterproposals and registered a vigorous protest against the violation of the Pre-Armistice Agreement as embodied in the "Fourteen Points." The answer of the Allies, termed their "last word," made some minor concessions and declared that in case the Germans refused to accept the peace terms as they then stood, the blockade would be continued and Allied troops would occupy the larger part of Germany. As the German High Command insisted that military resistance to invasion was out of the question, the German delegation finally yielded, and on June 22 the National Assembly, confronted with an Allied ultimatum with a time limit of twenty-four hours, accepted the Versailles Treaty against 138 opposing votes. The formal signing took place on June 28 in that same Hall of Mirrors of Versailles Castle where the German empire had been proclaimed on January 18, 1871.

The severest and most ignominious clause of the treaty, and the one to which the vote of the National Assembly had taken specific exception, was contained in Article 231, which stated that Germany acknowledged her and her allies' "responsibility for causing all the loss and damage to which the Allied and Associated governments and their citizens have been subjected as a consequence of the war imposed upon them" by the Central Powers. The German peace envoys had with a heavy heart accepted a dictated peace rather than lay their defenseless country open to invasion and the destruction of its national sovereignty. For thus having squarely shouldered their responsibility as the chosen representatives of the German people they were, before many years had passed, denounced as *November-verbrecher* (November criminals) by the domestic enemies of the Weimar republic.

Opposition to the treaty naturally was strong even among those who had voted for its acceptance. On June 20, Scheidemann resigned as chancellor. He was succeeded by his fellow socialist, Gustav Bauer. The Centrist Erzberger, the new minister of finance, had played an important part in the Armistice Commission and had recommended acceptance of the armistice terms, while to the socialist Hermann Müller, acting as the German plenipotentiary in Versailles, had fallen the onerous and hateful task of putting his signature to the peace document.

According to the terms of the Armistice of November 11, 1918, Germany had to withdraw all her troops from the occupied territories in the West within a time limit of a few weeks. By the end of November this difficult military operation was completed. The withdrawal and the ensuing demobilization had proceeded in good order and without any breach of military discipline. During the same period 5000 locomotives, an equal number of motor trucks, 150,000 freight cars, and immense quantities not only of war material but of farm equipment, including horses (150,000), cattle (880,000), sows (15,000), sheep (897,000), and goats (25,000), had to be delivered to the Allies. These stipulations, too, were fulfilled.

To reimburse the victors for their shipping losses a large part of the German navy and merchant marine had to be handed over, and the German government had to pledge the construction within five years of approximately one million tons of new merchant ships, to be transferred to the Allies after completion (200,000 tons per annum). Added to this were large deliveries of coal, dyestuffs, and other chemical products; the German-owned ocean cables also passed into the hands of the victors. All German rivers were to be internationalized.

The food blockade was not terminated until July 12, 1919. On May 7 of that year Count von Brockdorff-Rantzau had indignantly referred to this fact in addressing the Versailles assembly. "The hundreds of thousands of non-combatants," the German chief delegate had stated, "who have perished since November 11, 1918, as a result of the blockade, were killed with cold deliberation, after our enemies had been assured of their complete victory."

The Treaty of Versailles deprived Germany of about one twelfth of her national territory and population. The German colonies were taken over by Great Britain, the British Dominions, France, Belgium, and Japan, to be administered as "mandates" under the League of Nations. Alsace and Lorraine were returned to France, while the former Prussian districts of Eupen and Malmédy were transferred to Belgium. The Saar region with its rich coal deposits was placed under the sovereignty of the League of Nations for a period of fifteen years, after which a plebiscite was to determine whether this territory should be united with France or with Germany.

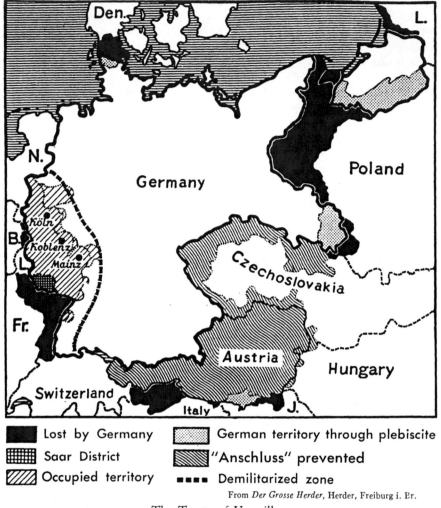

Lost by Germany

Saar District

Occupied territory

German territory through plebiscite

"Anschluss" prevented

Demilitarized zone

From *Der Grosse Herder*, Herder, Freiburg i. Br.

The Treaty of Versailles.

In the East, Germany had to surrender those Polish regions which had been acquired by the partitions of Poland in the eighteenth century (cf. pp. 316, 322). To give Poland an outlet to the Baltic, the Allies created the "Polish Corridor" which separated East Prussia from the rest of Germany and thus became a cause of lasting resentment and multiplying frictions. The predominantly German city of Danzig in East Prussia was declared a "free city," but was incorporated in the Polish tariff system. Its economic life was gradually strangled by the development of the neighboring Polish sea and naval port of Gdynia which succeeded in monopolizing most of the overseas trade.

In October, 1921, the League of Nations divided German Upper Silesia, one of Germany's most important industrial centers, between Germany and Poland, notwithstanding the outcome of the plebiscite of March 20 which had indicated a clear majority in favor of Germany. The dividing line was drawn in accordance with the number of votes cast in the several disputed areas. Memel, the northernmost German city, was awarded to the republic of Lithuania, and Schleswig, in compliance with the expressed wishes of its population, was restored to Denmark.

The left bank of the Rhine was occupied by Allied troops, and Allied bridgeheads were established at Mainz, Coblenz, and Cologne, on the right bank of the river. The German army was to be reduced to a maximum strength of one hundred thousand men, including four thousand officers; the navy to six ships of the line of ten thousand tons each, six small cruisers, twelve destroyers, twelve torpedo boats, and fifteen thousand men, including fifteen hundred officers. The armed forces were to be welded into a strictly professional unit with specified time of service (twelve years for enlisted men, twenty-five years for the officers). The maintenance or construction of heavy guns, tanks, submarines, and military aircraft was prohibited, and all fortifications in the occupied zones of the Rhineland and up to thirty miles east of the Rhine had to be dismantled. The occupied territories were to be evacuated by the Allies in three successive stages within a period of fifteen years, subject to German fulfillment of her obligations under the Versailles Treaty. To "obtain the required guarantees," the Allies reserved for themselves the right to delay evacuation or to reoccupy already evacuated regions (Article 429).

In regard to the fallen imperial regime the German republic was required to hand over to Allied military courts the German "war criminals," including the *Kaiser* and some of the top generals of the army. However, this demand, which immediately aroused a storm of angry protest among Germans from the extreme Right to the moderate Left — a protest which was sustained by the papacy and several neutral countries — was never pressed and finally dropped altogether. Instead, trials of "war criminals" were to be conducted by the German Supreme Court in Leipzig. But by the time these proceedings were instituted, nationalist sentiment had been revived to such a degree that some of the "accused" (notably Hindenburg and Ludendorff) became the objects of popular ovations. More than one of these so-called "trials" was turned into a farce, and practically all of them ended in acquittals.

An Allied Reparations Commission was to assess the damages caused by Germany and to compute the sum total of indemnities and reparations which Germany was expected to pay. At a meeting of this commission in London, in April, 1921, this total was fixed at thirty-three billion dollars (one hundred and thirty-two billion gold marks). It took a decade to convince the political and economic leaders of the Allies of the necessity of scaling down this figure to an amount which could reasonably be exacted from Germany, without upsetting the precarious economic balance of victors and vanquished alike. When reason finally began to prevail, it was too late, because the Weimar Republic was already in its death throes.

It may be asked in conclusion: what actually had become of Woodrow Wilson's "Fourteen Points"? Six of them — relating to the evacuation and restoration of Belgium (VII); liberation of French territory and restoration of Alsace-Lorraine to France (VIII); autonomous development of the non-Germanic peoples of Austria-Hungary (X); self-determination of Rumania, Serbia, and Montenegro (XI); creation of an independent Poland with access to the sea (XIII); creation of a general association of nations, to afford "mutual guarantees of political independence and territorial integrity to great and small states alike" (XIV) — were either wholly or partially realized. The remaining eight points were either entirely discarded — (I) "open covenants, openly arrived at"; (II) freedom of the seas; (III) removal of economic barriers; (V) a "free, open-minded, and absolutely impartial adjustment of all colonial claims" — or so modified that little of the original substance was left.

This is what happened in regard to the guarantees that (IV) "national armaments be reduced to the lowest point consistent with domestic safety"; the demand for evacuation of Russian territory and an opportunity (VI) "for the independent development of the Russian people"; (IX) the promised "readjustment of the Italian frontier" in accordance with "clearly recognizable lines of nationality"; and the pledge of sovereignty for the Turkish portion of the Ottoman empire, plus a guarantee of autonomous development for the other nationalities under Turkish rule: Disarmament (IV) was carried out unilaterally by the vanquished under the terms of the peace treaties. In their attempts to overthrow the Soviets, the Allies repeatedly (1918–1920) interfered with the "independent political development of the Russian people" (VI). The Italian frontier readjustments (IX) placed over half a million Germans and Yugoslavs under Italian sovereignty. And the affairs of Turkey (XII) were finally settled not with the aid of the Allies but despite their adverse interference.

While in accordance with point X and the "principle of self-determination" the Austrian "succession states" were freed from Hapsburg rule and granted autonomy, the rump republics of German Austria and Hungary, under the terms of the treaties of Saint-Germain (September 10, 1919) and Trianon (June 4, 1920) were reduced to a small fraction of the former territories of the Austro-Hungarian monarchy. Both were economically and politically crippled and hedged in to such an extent that their "independent" survival was rendered difficult if not impossible.

The Fate of the Weimar Republic. Born under the most inauspicious circumstances, the German republic made a brave attempt to consolidate its as yet untested forces and to gain a firm footing at home and abroad. The choice of Friedrich Ebert as *Reichspräsident* had been a fortunate one.

The former harness maker was no imposing figure, but he embodied the very best character qualities of the German working and middle classes, and he even gained the respect of his enemies by the calm dignity, the good common sense, and the straightforward simplicity with which he discharged the duties and attended to the functions of his high office. The first *Reichspräsident* was typical in this regard of the officials of the Weimar Republic: while most of them lacked political genius and statesmanlike vision, they were clearheaded men of personal integrity and an abundance of good will, and they were animated by the strong desire to link the well-being of their own country with that of the community of nations and peoples. But being inexperienced in the art of political propaganda and the ritual of international diplomacy, they proved no match for the political demagogues at home and the political strategists abroad.

a) The Kapp Putsch. The young Republic was put to its first test in an uprising staged in March, 1920, by disgruntled monarchist and rightist reactionaries under the leadership of Wolfgang Kapp, an East Prussian landowner who, in 1917, had gained doubtful renown as founder of the annexationist *Vaterlandspartei*. Associated with Kapp were Captain Hermann Ehrhardt, commander of a marine brigade, and General Ludendorff, recently returned from his Swedish exile. Ehrhardt's marines had defied the order of the Inter-Allied Commission to disband; they had marched on Berlin and presented the government with an ultimatum, demanding new elections and active resistance to the dictate of Versailles.

The *Reich* government moved first to Dresden and then to Stuttgart, while the insurgents seized several ministries in Berlin and issued a proclamation abrogating the legality of the Weimar Republic and vesting all authority in Wolfgang Kapp. But this initial success was turned into dismal failure when General Hans von Seeckt, the *Reichswehr* commander, refused co-operation, and the government of the Republic called upon the German trade unions to organize a general strike. Some of the leaders of the *Putsch* were arrested, others went into hiding, and Kapp himself fled to Sweden.

The short-lived revolt had leaned on the armed strength of organized "Free Corps," semimilitary volunteer formations which had been recruited from returning soldiers and sailors and had been employed to aid in putting down communist uprisings in Germany and riots of Polish nationalists in the Silesian frontier districts. They now turned their fighting strength against the German republic, aiming to overthrow the Weimar regime and to free Germany from the shackles of Versailles. Gathering into their ranks large numbers of young men who had lived through the horrors of war and had in their disillusionment become disdainful of all civil law and order, they formed the nuclei of the future antirepublican "private armies" of the *Stahlhelm* (steel helmet), the SA (*Sturmabteilungen:* storm troops), and the SS (*Schutzstaffel:* protective guard; Hitler's bodyguard).

In the Ruhr District the partisans of Kapp ran into the armed resistance of communist labor battalions which quickly gained the upper hand and occupied several Rhenish cities. The *Reichswehr,* entering the Rhineland zone designated as "neutral" in the Versailles Treaty, put down the communist uprising after several bloody encounters. Although the *Reichswehr* had proceeded with the permission of the Allies, France used this incident as a pretext to occupy Frankfurt on the Main, "in the interest of the Allied occupation forces," an action which was strongly reproved by the United States, **Great Britain, and Italy.**

b) Ruhr Invasion and Currency Inflation. Elections for the first *Reichstag* of the Republic were held on June 6, 1920. The results broke up the parliamentary majority of the "Weimar coalition" of Social Democrats, Democrats, and Centrists, the parties which had voted for the acceptance of the Versailles Treaty and had dominated the National Assembly. The moderate parties, with the exception of the Centrists, were greatly weakened, while the Right and the extreme Left increased their representation, the German Nationals from 42 to 56, the German People's party from 22 to 62, and the Independent Socialists (Communists) from 22 to 81.

The cabinet headed by the Socialist Hermann Müller, which shortly after the *Kapp Putsch* had succeeded the Gustav Bauer cabinet, resigned after the *Reichstag* elections. A new government, representing more adequately the parliamentary situation, was formed under the chancellorship of the Centrist Konstantin Fehrenbach.

The major problem confronting the new chancellor and his cabinet ministers was that of reparations. In July, 1920, Fehrenbach went to Spa (Belgium) and three months later to Brussels to attend reparations conferences and obtain accurate information as to the payments, both in money and in kind, which Germany was expected to make. At both conferences Hugo Stinnes, a member of the German People's party and the leading German industrialist, protested sharply against the entire reparations policy of the Allies and even expressed himself to the effect that he would rather see Germany turn communist than submit to the demands of the Allies.

These demands were finally specified and handed to the German delegation at the London Conference of March 1, 1921. Germany was required to pay two hundred billion gold marks (*c.* fifty billion dollars) within a period of thirty years. The German refusal to accept these terms was followed by an Allied ultimatum and the occupation of some additional Rhenish cities. Fehrenbach resigned and was succeeded by Joseph Wirth, a member of the left wing of the Center party, who organized a new government on the basis of the Weimar coalition. Included in the Wirth cabinet was Walter Rathenau, the son of Emil Rathenau (cf. p. 631), the actual president of the AEG (*Allgemeine Elektrizitätsgesellschaft*), a prominent industrialist, an economic expert of more than average capacity, and a sincere believer in international understanding.

On May 11, 1921, the Wirth government accepted the London ultimatum, and Germany, aside from her continued deliveries in kind to France, paid a first reparations installment of one hundred and fifty million gold marks. Both Wirth and Rathenau were henceforth denounced by their domestic foes as the inaugurators of the German *Erfüllungspolitik* (fulfillment policy). Resentment against all those responsible for the signing of the Versailles Treaty reached a high pitch. On August 26, 1921, Matthias Erzberger was murdered in the Black Forest by members of the secret military *Organisation Konsul*, the first of many victims of the gradually emerging forces of counterrevolution and rightist reaction.

The devaluation of the German currency, which had begun during the war, was accelerated in the postwar years by the lowering of German productive capacity caused by territorial and property losses, the dwindling of foreign trade, the lack of international credits, and the payment of reparations. When the fall of the mark reached alarming proportions Germany demanded a moratorium on reparations (December, 1921), and in January, 1922, an international conference convened at Cannes on the French Riviera to straighten out the reparations tangle and stabilize the German financial situation. While the conference was in session, the moderate French cabinet of Aristide Briand was defeated, and the violently anti-German Raymond Poincaré became prime minister of France.

In April the Powers met again, this time at Genoa, and a Russian delegation was invited to take part in the negotiations. The Germans and Russians sprang a surprise on the world by signing the Treaty of Rapallo which waived all reparations and pledged friendship and economic cooperation between the two countries. The text of the treaty had been prepared by Maxim Litvinov, and the secret negotiations had been brought to a successful conclusion by Walter Rathenau, the German minister of reconstruction, and Chicherin, the Russian foreign commissar.

On June 24, Rathenau fell as the second victim of the *Organisation Konsul*. The assassins, when brought to trial, not only maintained that Rathenau had deserved death as a Jew and an *Erfüllungspolitiker*, but they cynically confessed that the execution of the "death sentence" had been necessitated by the very fact that a continuation of Rathenau's foreign policy would have proven advantageous to Germany and would thus have strengthened the prestige of the Weimar Republic.

Poincaré's appointment as French prime minister was followed by another German cabinet crisis. The Wirth government, finding itself compelled to inform the Allies of Germany's inability to meet the payments agreed upon after the London ultimatum of March, 1921, was sustained in its renewed plea for a moratorium on reparations and for an international loan by the British representative on the Reparations Commission. Wirth tendered his resignation on November 14, 1922, one day after he had dispatched his note to the Allies. Wilhelm Cuno, director of the Hamburg-America Line, was entrusted with the formation of a new coalition government which had the strong backing of German industry and consisted of members of the German People's party, the Centrists, the Bavarian People's party,* and the Democrats.

Poincaré viewed the Cuno government with even greater distrust than he had felt toward the Wirth cabinet. He declared himself opposed to any concessions in the question of reparations unless France were given tangible guarantee assets in the form of German State forests and mines in the Ruhr. He even raised again the question of the cession of the Rhineland to France and threatened occupation of the Ruhr in case Germany should fail to meet her reparations commitments.

When Germany, early in January, 1923, was declared in default on deliveries of timber and coal, French and Belgian divisions marched into the Ruhr and occupied the industrial key cities. The Ruhr occupation lasted from January, 1923, to July, 1925, and called forth strong British protests.

The attempt made by France to exploit the rich industrial assets of the Ruhr District was, however, hampered by a German policy of passive resistance and non-co-operation, as decreed by the German government on January 19. Germany's plight aroused increasing sympathy in the United States and Great Britain, and a *démarche* in Paris was undertaken by the Vatican. Thus France found herself not only in a partial economic stalemate but also in a diplomatic situation which became more and more untenable.

In the meantime, the disintegration of the German currency had become catastrophic. The German government had promised to reimburse German industrialists in the Ruhr for forced reparations deliveries and to compensate idle workers for their loss in wages. The printing presses worked overtime to turn out immense quantities of paper money without gold coverage, and soon Germany found herself engulfed in a mad whirlpool of uncontrolled inflation. Before long the equivalent of the dollar was quoted in millions and billions of paper marks. The speed with which the inflation proceeded was such that employers and wage earners had to be paid daily to allow them to catch up with the runaway prices. Even so, the fantastic amounts of paper earnings received became worthless within a few hours.

But what was a nightmare for the average German citizen turned out to be a field day for the holders of foreign currency. The country found itself overrun with foreigners who bought up commodities in such quantities and at such a rate that most stores were completely sold out in the early morning hours, and many were unable to replenish their stocks. The German and non-German holder of foreign currency could purchase industrial plants, ancient castles, land, and real estate for a mere trifle. Savings, insurance policies, and pensions were invalidated, and the entire German middle class was reduced to penury. Resentment against the *nouveaux riches* and

---

* The Bavarian People's party (*Bayerische Volkspartei*) had seceded from the Center party after the Revolution of 1918. This secession was caused by Bavarian opposition to the centralizing tendencies of the Center party as well as by the monarchist sentiment of Bavarian Catholics and their disapproval of the Weimar coalition of Centrists, Democrats, and Social Democrats.

ill feeling against foreigners were on the increase, and a wave of anti-Semitism swept over the country. The economic chaos proved a fertile breeding ground for cynicism, moral license, and political radicalism.

The Cuno cabinet did not survive the economic and financial crisis. It fell in August, 1923, and was replaced by another coalition government which once more included the Social Democrats and was headed by Gustav Stresemann of the German People's party.

c) The Stresemann Government and the Domestic Crisis. The new German chancellor stepped into a heritage that was anything but enviable: German economy and finance were in a state of confusion and exhaustion, and the country as a whole seemed to be on the brink of civil war. Gustav Stresemann (1878–1929), who had developed from an ardent nationalist into an equally determined advocate of international understanding, courageously faced the almost unsolvable problems with which his government was confronted and succeeded within a relatively short time in restoring order at home and securing a *modus vivendi* in the foreign field.

Convinced that the prolongation of the Ruhr struggle could only lead to national ruin, Stresemann called an end to passive resistance on September 26, 1923, and entered into negotiations with France. Thereupon voluntary German reparations deliveries were resumed, and conditions in the Ruhr District gradually returned to normality.

Stresemann's next immediate concern was the stabilization of the German currency. This difficult task was accomplished by the establishment of the *Rentenbank* which in turn issued a new *Rentenmark* (November, 1923), a currency which was not backed by gold but by a mortgage on the entire agricultural and industrial assets of Germany.

On November 23, the combined opposition of the Right and Left led to the fall of the Stresemann coalition government, but in the new cabinet headed by Wilhelm Marx of the Center party* Stresemann was given the post of foreign minister, an office to which he was returned again and again in the several coalition governments of the following years.

While holding the chancellorship of the *Reich,* Stresemann had also efficiently dealt with a triple threat of civil war. Both a monarchist-nationalist revolt of the *Fridericus Rex* movement in Pomerania and communist uprisings in Saxony, in the city of Hamburg, and in several other regions were crushed by the *Reichswehr.* The third threat, however, was the most formidable and the one which bore the earmarks of an organized counter-revolution. The abortive Munich "Beer Cellar *Putsch*" of November 9, 1923, staged jointly by Adolf Hitler and Erich Ludendorff, with the temporary connivance of the monarchistically inclined government of Bavaria, aimed at the abolishment of parliamentary institutions, the suppression of civil liberties, the expropriation of the Jews, and the summary liquidation of political opponents.

---

* This cabinet as well as the following three (1923–1926) renewed the Cuno coalition of German People's party, Centrists, Bavarian People's party, and Democrats.

Adolf Hitler (1889–1945), a native of the Austrian town of Braunau, after having failed in his early attempts as an art student and painter in Vienna, had moved to Munich in 1912. In 1914, he enlisted as a volunteer in a Bavarian infantry regiment. A rabid Pan-German, anti-Semite, and anti-communist, he blamed the Weimar Republic and an international Jewish conspiracy for the lost war, the Treaty of Versailles, and all the subsequent evils which had befallen Germany. In 1919, he and a small band of sympathizers created the NSDAP (*Nationalsozialistische Deutsche Arbeiterpartei:* National Socialist German Workers' party) which gathered a steadily mounting number of recruits from the ranks of uprooted and disillusioned intellectuals, members of the impoverished middle classes, soldiers, and workers. Combining the self-righteousness of the monomaniac fanatic with the persuasive oratory of the revivalist and the cunning of the mass psychologist and political spellbinder, Hitler succeeded in welding his following into a disciplined militia which was bound to the *Führer* by unconditional fealty. Capitalizing on both the nationalist and socialist trends fostered by the political and economic pressures of the postwar years, he held out to the masses the seductive bait of "National Socialism."

The Munich *Putsch* was preceded by the *Führer's* solemn vow that within twenty-four hours he would be master of Germany or dead. However, twenty-four hours later he was neither master of Germany nor dead, but lying flat on the ground in Munich's Odeon Square, trying to dodge the bullets of the Bavarian police. In falling to the ground he had wrenched his shoulder and was carried off by a party physician. Two days later he was taken into custody. The Hitler *Putsch* failed because both the Bavarian government and the *Reichswehr* had refused at the last moment to endorse the extremist program of the *Führer* and his associates.

On April 1, 1924, Hitler was sentenced to serve five years in the fortress of Landsberg in Bavaria, but he was pardoned and released before the year had ended. He had used the months of confinement to write *Mein Kampf,* the future "Bible" of National Socialism, and he emerged from Landsberg with the halo of the political martyr.

Although the Stresemann government had weathered the economic and political crises, it was reproached by the Right for having liquidated passive resistance in the Ruhr, and by the Social Democrats for having been too lenient with the enemies of the Republic. The result of these accusations was the withdrawal of the Social Democrats from the coalition and the above-mentioned emergence of the first Marx cabinet.

d) The Dawes Plan, the Treaty of Locarno, and the Young Plan. Notwithstanding the fact that rightist and leftist radicalism in Germany made some headway during the years following the Ruhr invasion, the period during which Stresemann directed Germany's foreign policy was generally characterized by increasing international co-operation and by a growing willingness on the part of the Allies to aid in Germany's recovery and to restore her to full equality in the family of nations. The spirit of Versailles gradually gave way to what was hopefully called the "spirit of Locarno."

Upon the request of the German government the Reparations Commission appointed two committees of financial and economic experts to deal with the problems of currency stabilization and economic rehabilitation. Charles Gates Dawes, who later became the United States vice-president in the administration of Calvin Coolidge (1925–1929) and was awarded the Nobel Peace Prize in 1925, was the chairman of the first committee. He was a coauthor of the "Dawes Plan" which represented the first attempt to settle the problem of reparations on a purely economic basis, divorced from political considerations. The plan, as adopted on August 16, 1924, by the Conference of London, stipulated that Germany was to pay two and a half billion marks (c. six hundred million dollars) per annum over an as yet unspecified number of years, but provisions were made for reduced payments during the first few years. The sums required for these annual payments were to be raised by mortgages on German railroads and industries, by contributions out of the budget of the German government, and by foreign credits and loans. After a period of five years the annual payments were to be readjusted on the basis of a prosperity index, that is, on the basis of a re-examination of the German capacity to pay. The total German transfer of reparations payments during the five years the Dawes Plan remained in operation amounted to approximately eight billion marks (c. two billion dollars).

The Dawes Plan furthermore called for a reorganization of the German *Reichsbank*, making this institution independent of the State, establishing its control over the circulation of currency and, for a period of fifty years, giving it a monopoly for the issuance of bank notes. The *Direktorium* of the *Reichsbank* was to be composed of fourteen members, seven of them Germans, and the remaining seven representing the United States, Great Britain, France, Italy, Belgium, Holland, and Switzerland.

A second Marx cabinet was formed after the *Reichstag* elections of March 9, 1924. The moderate parties returned weakened, while the extremists of the Right and Left had increased their strength. Nevertheless, the *Reichstag* adopted the Dawes Plan on August 29. Shortly afterward the hope of obtaining a stronger backing for the government's policy of international understanding prompted the *Reichspräsident* to decree the dissolution of parliament and order a new election. The *Reichstag* which convened in December actually indicated in its composition the more conciliatory spirit of the Conference of London and the Dawes Plan: the extremists of the Right and Left lost heavily, while the government parties gained a comfortable majority. The election had also without doubt been influenced by the change of government in England and France. In the former country the labor cabinet headed by Ramsay MacDonald had come into office, while in France the Socialist Edouard Herriot had become president of the Republic.

Nevertheless, political and parliamentary stability in Germany was anything but assured. Progress in the "restoration of Germany to equality among the nations" was much too slow to suit the impatient agitators and politicians of the German Right. To many supporters of the moderate parties it seemed fair and reasonable enough to accede to the Nationalists' bid for representation in the government, thus giving them a chance to make good their claims. It was hoped that the responsibility of office might put an end to their destructive and demagogic criticism and engage them constructively in the rebuilding of Germany and the cementing of international relations.

It was such considerations that led to the resignation of the second Marx cabinet and the formation of a new government, in which the German Nationals obtained representation. Hans Luther, who leaned toward the moderate Right and had held posts as food minister and finance minister in previous cabinets, assumed the office of *Reichskanzler* (January, 1925).

On February 28, 1925, *Reichspräsident* Ebert died. In the following election (April 26) by popular ballot the aged General Field Marshal von Hindenburg, the candidate of the Right, obtained the majority of votes over Wilhelm Marx, the candidate of the parties of the Weimar coalition, and Ernst Thälmann, the candidate of the Communist party. The Centrist Marx was beaten by the decisive vote of the Catholic Bavarian People's party.

Though a conservative Prussian army officer, who had been trained and made his military career under the Hohenzollerns, Hindenburg disappointed all those who had voted for him in the hope of an early swing to the Right and an eventual restoration of the monarchy. He kept his oath of office loyally and gave strong moral support to the policies inaugurated by Gustav Stresemann. It was only after Stresemann's premature death in 1929 that the soldier-president gradually succumbed to the influence of rightist and reactionary politicians.

The crowning achievement of Stresemann's tireless efforts in behalf of the pacification of Europe and international co-operation was the negotiation of the *Locarno Pact*. In this treaty, which was signed by Germany and the Western Allies on October 16, 1925, Great Britain, France, Italy, Belgium, and Germany jointly guaranteed the inviolability of the Franco-German borders as established by the Treaty of Versailles. The only flaw in this international agreement — and, as history was to demonstrate, a major one — was that it left the question of Germany's eastern frontier unsettled. The reason for this omission was Germany's unwillingness to recognize as final the situation created by the "Polish Corridor" and the separation of Danzig from the body of the *Reich* (cf. p. 654). German refusal to follow up French suggestions for the signing of an "eastern Locarno" caused the French government to enter into new military alliances with Poland and Czechoslovakia.*

---

* After World War I the Allies created Czechoslovakia to satisfy the national aspirations of the Czechs and Slovaks. The new nation consisted of parts of the former Dual Monarchy of Austria-Hungary (Bohemia, Moravia, Austrian Silesia, North Hungary, and Lower Austria) and some districts of the former Prussian province of Silesia. The population of Czechoslovakia included approximately 44 per cent Czechs, 16 per cent Slovaks, almost 25 per cent Germans, and several ethnic and linguistic islands of Magyars, Ruthenians, and Poles.

The very substantial positive achievements of the Locarno Pact are to be credited to the close collaboration and combined good will of Gustav Stresemann, Aristide Briand, and Sir Austen Chamberlain: the foreign minister of Germany, and the prime ministers of France and England. In recognition of this fact they were awarded the Nobel Peace Prize for the year 1926. The initiative, however, had come from Stresemann, who had first discussed the possibilities of the plan with Lord d'Abernon, British ambassador in Berlin, who in turn had finally succeeded in convincing the British prime minister of the epochmaking significance of Stresemann's offer.

On November 27, 1925, the Locarno Pact was endorsed by the *Reichstag,* against the votes of the German Nationals, the National Socialists, and the Communists. Even before the signing of the pact the "spirit of Locarno" had borne fruit in the withdrawal of the last Franco-Belgian occupation troops from the Ruhr (1925). The first (Cologne) Allied occupation zone in the Rhineland was evacuated in January, 1926. This was followed by the withdrawal of the Inter-Allied Military Control Commission and the extension of an invitation to Germany to join the Council of the League of Nations.

As far as the German Right was concerned, the Pact of Locarno was, however, nothing to be proud of or grateful for. As Germany at Locarno had voluntarily renounced all claims to Alsace-Lorraine, the signing of the treaty was termed a betrayal of national interests, and the ratification had been preceded by a campaign of personal vilification against Stresemann. The brown-shirted legions of Adolf Hitler, brandishing the *Hakenkreuz* (swastika) banner, and the monarchist-chauvinist *Stahlhelm,* an organization of German war veterans, loyal to the black-white-red of the imperial standard, registered their protests in noisy demonstrations. The supporters of the Weimar Republic countered with mass meetings and parades of the semimilitary contingents of the *Reichsbanner* (founded in 1924), chiefly recruited from liberal and socialist groups and carrying the black, red, and gold banners of the Republic. The Communists on their part were parading their own private army, the *Rotfront,* taking their cues from Moscow and waving the red flag with the hammer and sickle emblem of the Third International.

Obviously, there was small evidence of the "spirit of Locarno" in the violent quest for power of these rival groups. Germany by this time was not only on the way to regaining her former stature as a world power but was also economically on the road to recovery. Therefore, the growth of political dissension and radicalism on the domestic scene must be attributed to the tardiness of the Allies in restoring the occupied zones to German sovereignty, their unwillingness to effect an early relaxation of the burdens of reparations, their refusal to live up to their promise of international disarmament, and their reluctance to remove from the German people the stain of the unfortunate war guilt clause of the Versailles Treaty. The work of peace-loving statesmen, such as Stresemann and Briand, was rendered increasingly difficult by the phalanx of ill will to which the chauvinists of all European nations, including Germany, contributed their weighty share. Thus Stresemann's fervent plea for solidarity in international affairs as well as Briand's call for the creation of a United States of Europe evoked even less response among their own countrymen than across the national boundaries.

On December 10, 1926, the day on which Germany was welcomed as a member of the League of Nations, Stresemann addressed the Geneva Assembly, declaring that "it cannot be the purpose of the Divine world order that men should direct their supreme national energies against one another. . . . He will serve humanity best who, firmly rooted in the traditions of his own people, develops his moral and intellectual gifts to the best of his ability, thus reaching out beyond his own national boundaries, and serving the whole world." These were lofty words, and they were uttered by a man who was anything but a starry-eyed idealist. Stresemann was a man of practical affairs who had learned in the hard school of political experience that even in politics crime does not pay, and that any sound nationalism and true political realism must take account of universal moral principles and incentives if the national State itself is not to fall victim to an international anarchy engendered and sustained by the unchecked will to power.

The acceptance of the Dawes Plan had been followed by a remarkable recovery of German economy, aided by large scale investment (c. sixteen billion dollars) of foreign capital in German industry, public utilities, housing enterprises, and public works. By 1929 both the German national income and industrial production were nearly twice what they had been before the period of inflation. New industrial concerns (*Kartelle*) came into being, savings accounts increased, and in 1927 employment figures were the highest attained since the end of the war. The government could even lower the income-tax rates and raise the salary scale of the civil service.

The bright colors of this picture of Germany's economic and financial status are, however, somewhat delusive. What looked like genuine prosperity was largely an artificially stimulated economic overexpansion, and this artifact rested on unsound foundations. It could only be maintained as long as the flow of foreign credit continued unabated, but was bound to collapse as soon as world prices declined and the international financial situation forced the withdrawal of foreign capital. In 1929, Germany's total indebtedness to foreign creditors amounted to twenty-nine billion marks (c. seven billion dollars).

The new crisis set in with the crash of the stock market in the United States in October, 1929, and the ensuing upheaval in world economy. Even before this critical climax was reached it had become evident that German commitments under the Dawes Plan exceeded the financial and productive capacity of the country and that a readjustment of reparations payments had once more become necessary. Preliminary negotiations in 1927 and

1928 led to the appointment of a special committee in January, 1929, to study the possibilities of a definitive settlement of the problem of reparations. In May, 1929, the *Young Plan,* so named after Owen D. Young, the United States representative and chairman of the Reparations Committee of experts, was completed and presented to an International Conference, meeting at the Hague in August of the same year.

The Young Plan fixed the total of German reparations at 34,9 billion gold marks (*c.* 8,5 billion dollars) and provided for (1) payment of definite annuities covering the period from 1929 to 1988, following a gradually rising scale which was to reach its peak with an annuity payment of approximately two and a half billion marks in 1966; (2) creation of the Bank for International Settlements in Basel (Switzerland), to execute the transfer of payments and to act as a clearinghouse for international war debts; (3) reduction and eventual cancellation (after ten years) of reparations in kind; (4) termination of foreign control over German finances; (5) abolishment of the office of the General Agent of Reparations; (6) complete evacuation of the occupied territories in the Rhineland not later than June 30, 1930.

Meanwhile the German political situation had again undergone some important changes. The success of Stresemann's foreign policy was reflected in the *Reichstag* elections of May, 1928, in which the Social Democrats gained over two million votes and the German Right was considerably weakened. The new party constellation permitted the formation of a coalition government which included the Social Democrats and was headed by the Socialist Hermann Müller. Arrayed against it were the German Nationals, the National Socialists, and the Communists.

On August 27, 1928, Stresemann scored another triumph of his policy of international reconciliation: most of the larger nations of the world, including Germany, put their signatures to the Briand-Kellogg Pact of Paris, outlawing aggressive war and pledging the solution of all international conflicts by peaceful means. The chief shortcomings of the pact were its failure to define aggressive war and to provide for adequate sanctions against aggressors.

In view of the continued successes of the much maligned *Erfüllungspolitik* the German parties of the Right felt that one by one their arguments against the Weimar Republic were losing ground. Already the very structure of the Versailles Treaty, the mainstay of their relentless fight against successive German governments, was crumbling, and soon their opposition would be deprived of its object. These circumstances worked for an ever closer collaboration between the parties of the Right, especially after, late in 1929, the German Nationals had made Alfred Hugenberg — the main shareholder of the powerful *Hugenberg Konzern* which through its ownership of a large chain of newspapers, magazines, news agencies, telegraph companies, and motion-picture enterprises (UFA) controlled a large section of German public opinion — their party chairman.

Gustav Stresemann died on October 3, 1929, without having been able to witness the final adoption of the Young Plan by the *Reichstag* (March 12, 1930). Even before his death the joint forces of Hugenberg's German Nationals and Hitler's National Socialists had initiated a pupolar referendum "against the War Guilt Lie and the Young Plan," asking punishment for the "traitors" who had participated in framing this latest scheme for a reparations settlement. The referendum was held on December 22, 1929, and the initiative was defeated by a large majority of the voters. From then on large amounts donated by Hugenberg and his fellow industrialists, many of whom had made huge fortunes during the period of inflation, went into the coffers of the National Socialist party. These sums were largely used to recruit new storm-troop members from the ranks of the destitute and unemployed, and to defray the expenses of organization and propaganda.

e) The Brüning Government and the End of the Weimar Republic. The economic world crisis which came in the wake of the financial crash in the United States made itself felt in Germany by the flight of capital, the withdrawal of foreign credits, and the rising unemployment figures (almost seven million in 1930). Growing unemployment was in part caused by the far-reaching "rationalization" processes in which German industry had been engaged in the preceding years, and in part also by the abrupt discontinuation of reparations deliveries in kind. The cabinet headed by Hermann Müller, bent upon carrying out certain budgetary reform measures designed to make Germany less dependent on foreign capital, failed to gain the necessary parliamentary backing. As President Hindenburg refused to decree the dissolution of the *Reichstag,* the cabinet resigned, and the task of forming a new coalition government devolved upon Heinrich Brüning who, in 1929, had become the parliamentary leader of the Center party. The new chancellor, though anxious to obtain a broad parliamentary backing, was himself one of the spokesmen of the right wing of his party and came more and more under the influence of those rightist and ultraconservative groups whose spokesmen held key positions in the cabinet.

The Brüning government, which had assumed office on March 30, 1930, obtained a vote of confidence with the aid of the German Nationals, against the opposition of the Social Democrats, the extreme Left, and the extreme Right. The German Nationals felt indebted to Brüning for his extension of a large-scale farm relief program which had been initiated by the preceding cabinet and which benefited the agrarian interests of various agricultural sections of Germany. The temporary rift which the affirmative vote of Hugenberg's party caused in the *bloc* of German Nationals and National Socialists — a *bloc* which dated back to the common opposition to the Young Plan — seemed to justify Brüning's hope of isolating the National Socialists. When, however, during June and early July, the cabinet introduced legislation designed to balance the budget, the German Nationals swung back into opposition, and the government failed by eight votes to obtain a majority. On July 18, the *Reichstag* was dissolved.

In the elections held on September 14, 1930, the National Socialists cashed in on the economic crisis, raising their party's representation to 107 seats, as against 95 in the preceding *Reichstag,* and 12 in 1928. From a small and noisy group of demagogues the followers of Adolf Hitler had grown into the most powerful party with a popular backing of 30 per cent of the electorate. The Communists likewise scored heavily, and from then on the extreme Right and Left were closely, albeit negatively, united in their will to destroy German democracy and the Weimar Republic. In most other respects National Socialists and Communists were mortal enemies and fought each other with ever increasing violence. The "party line" for the German Communists was decreed by Moscow in 1931: they were told to co-operate with all the enemies of the Weimar Republic.

In the same year (1931) German Nationals, National Socialists, and *Stahlhelm* joined forces at a meeting in Braunschweig to form under Hugenberg's leadership the rightist "Harzburg Front" against the Brüning government. However, it became increasingly evident that the political struggle in Germany was turning into a contest between Brüning and Hitler. The *Führer* had been successful in enlisting the support of many conservative Christians by stressing the pledge of the original party platform of 1921, to uphold and defend "positive Christianity." These converts apparently failed to see that many of the other specifically listed aims of the party program flagrantly contradicted such an assertion.

Chancellor Brüning could hold himself in office only with the support of the Social Democrats who, realizing that the choice for Germany was from now on between a moderate authoritarian conservatism and a radical rightist dictatorship, reluctantly gave their backing to a series of *Notverordnungen* (emergency decrees). These decree laws, issued by a *Präsidialkabinett* (presidential cabinet) under Article 48 of the Constitution (cf. p. 649), were to cope with the grave financial and economic situation, on the one hand, and were to curb political radicalism and save what was left of the Weimar Republic, on the other.

The prestige both of the Weimar Republic and the Brüning cabinet was further undermined by determined Allied opposition to an Austro-German customs union negotiated by Ernst Curtius, the German foreign minister, and Johann Schober, the Austrian vice-chancellor, and announced on March 25, 1931. The initiative had come from Austria, but it was generally understood that the governments of both Germanic nations envisaged a future complete economic union and an eventual political *Anschluss,* to redeem Austria from the fatal predicament into which she had been driven by the Treaty of Saint-Germain (cf. p. 656). After England, France, and Italy had registered their protest, the matter was referred to the Hague Tribunal which by an eight-to-seven vote decided against the Austro-German plan.

In the course of the year 1931 the German economic situation also showed further signs of deterioration. The flight of capital, the export of gold, and the withdrawal of foreign credit continued apace, and on July 1 President

Hoover, responding to a personal appeal of *Reichspräsident* Hindenburg, announced a one year's moratorium on all intergovernmental war debts. During the month of July the huge *Nordwolle Konzern* (North German Wool Company) failed, involving in its collapse some of the leading German banks. The German government temporarily closed all banks and immediately issued drastic decrees for the control of foreign exchange, cash payments, and check clearings, with the result that in August the crisis had been mastered and normal banking operations could be resumed. The revolutionizing effect, however, of the government decrees was an almost total nationalization of German finance.

Shortly after the announcement of the Hoover moratorium the Young Plan Advisory Committee and a group of economic experts, working in conjunction with the Bank of International Settlements, arrived at the conclusion that Germany could not be expected to resume reparation payments. They decided that the German economic crisis had to be viewed as an integral part of the world crisis and could therefore be solved only by concerted international action. Finally, the Conference of Lausanne (convened in June, 1932, shortly after the fall of the Brüning government) decided that after a final payment of three billion marks, to be transmitted at the end of three years, all future German reparations should be canceled.

The Brüning government and with it the Weimar Republic could point to some significant achievements both in the domestic and foreign fields. The second major financial and economic crisis of the Republic had been beaten by means of stringent deflationary measures, albeit at the heavy cost of government-decreed reductions of salaries, wages and rates of interest, and the imposition of higher taxes. The government had assumed control over the banks, and all foreign currency in excess of two hundred marks had to be surrendered to the *Reichsbank*. Protective laws prohibited the import of many agricultural products, including butter. Prices for foodstuffs were high, while the general standard of living had been lowered. On the other hand, the overhauling of the entire economic and financial structure of the *Reich* and the radical curtailment of government and private spending had lent additional weight to the government's plea of January, 1932, for the complete cessation of reparations payments and for the cancellation of a large proportion of private indebtedness as well.

It had been demonstrated, furthermore, that the economic problems were directly linked with the political problems and that a stabilization of world economy could only be hoped for if the spirit of Versailles were liquidated at long last. If, then, the enemies of the Weimar Republic did not want to lose out completely they had to make haste, especially in view of the fact that the Genoa Disarmament Conference of February, 1932, gave evidence that there were good prospects of a favorable decision in regard to this last one of Germany's major grievances.

The last chance for the obstructionists of the German Right and extreme Left came with the expiration of President Hindenburg's term of office on May 5, 1932. In view of the tense political situation in Germany an attempt was made to have a two-thirds majority of the *Reichstag* amend the Constitution so as to permit Hindenburg to continue in office for another year, without calling a special election. However, the refusal of Hitler and Hugenberg to concur in such a move made a presidential election mandatory.

In 1928, Hindenburg had been elected to the presidency by the parties of the Right with the aid of the Bavarian People's party. In 1932, the Prussian soldier and monarchist, who had become almost a symbol of the Weimar Republic, campaigned against the enemies of this same republic: against Hitler, the candidate of the National Socialists; Colonel Düsterberg, the candidate of the German Nationals and the *Stahlhelm;* and Thälmann, the candidate of the Communists. Hitler at the time was a man without a country, having lost his Austrian citizenship as a former member of the Bavarian army. He was naturalized, however, by the National Socialist government of Braunschweig.

The first ballot was indecisive. In the second balloting (April 10) Hindenburg obtained nineteen million votes, the absolute majority. Hitler received thirteen million, and Thälmann three million. The candidate of the German Nationals and the *Stahlhelm* had withdrawn in the second race in favor of the National Socialist *Führer.*

Four days after the presidential election General Gröner, minister of the interior and of defense in the Brüning cabinet, decreed the suppression of the private armies of the National Socialists. The result was that in the subsequent elections for the Diets of Prussia and several other German "lands" the National Socialists emerged as the strongest party. General Gröner was forced to resign as *Reichswehrminister,* retaining however the portfolio of minister of the interior.

On May 30, 1932, Chancellor Brüning was dismissed by Hindenburg. In the morning hours of that day he had presented for the President's signature a decree calling for the breaking up of bankrupt *Junker* estates in East Prussia, to provide settlements for German farmers. The *Reichspräsident* had gradually been maneuvered into a position where he had to choose between his bourgeois chancellor and the members of his own caste.

On his eightieth birthday Hindenburg had been presented by rightist German industrialists with the huge ancestral family estate of the Hindenburgs in East Prussia (Neudeck), and the aged President enjoyed spending his days of rest in the circle of his *Junker* friends and neighbors, the owners of the surrounding estates and farm lands. They had finally convinced him that what Germany needed was a strong and ruthless regime. Not only was Chancellor Brüning not the man of the hour, but he was even advocating a policy of "agrarian bolshevism"! Thus, when Brüning submitted his scheme for the parceling of *Junker* estates, the president believed he held the evidence that his friends were right. Brüning had to go.

On May 28, 1932, Franz von Papen, the wily diplomat and rightist politician, the leader of the right wing of the Center party and co-owner of the influential Berlin Centrist newspaper *Germania,* had met with Adolf Hitler to discuss the political situation and the possibilities of joint rightist action. The aristocratic von Papen had little liking for the self-made *Führer* and former lance corporal, but, like Hugenberg and many of the industrialists and *Junkers,* he intended to use Hitler's oratorical and organizational talents to further his own political schemes. Hitler made his "toleration" of a Papen cabinet and any future co-operation contingent on two conditions: the *Reichstag* must be dissolved, and the order suppressing the SA and SS formations must be rescinded.

On June 1, Franz von Papen was appointed chancellor, on the special recommendation of General Kurt von Schleicher, who had long held important posts in the *Reichswehr* ministry and who, as a friend of Hindenburg's son Oskar, had had a hand in the making and unmaking of Brüning. He now was given the portfolio of *Reichswehrminister* (minister of defense) in the Papen cabinet.

On June 4, three days after von Papen's appointment as chancellor, Hitler's first condition for "toleration" and collaboration was fulfilled: the *Reichstag* was dissolved. The second condition was met on June 16: the SA and SS formations were legalized. The decree which outlawed them had really never been enforced.

On July 20, von Papen deposed by an unconstitutional presidential decree the democratic government of Prussia, filling all posts in the administration of the State and the municipalities, including the police force, with rightist officials. The Prussian delegates to the *Reichsrat* were likewise replaced by antirepublicans. Von Papen himself assumed the office of *Reichskommissar* for Prussia.

In the *Reichstag* elections of July 31 the National Socialists received 230 seats, thus more than doubling their strength, and the Communists 89, while the parties of the middle lost correspondingly. The Papen cabinet was largely composed of civilian and military aristocrats and therefore nicknamed "the barons' cabinet." It represented a party coalition of the moderate Right which, without the support of the National Socialists, could rally behind it only 42 of the *Reichstag* deputies. The combined National Socialist and Communist vote, on the other hand, commanded an absolute majority which could obstruct any positive action of the legislative branch of the government. Under these circumstances, and as Hitler had already withdrawn his pledge of "toleration," the cabinet could only rule by decrees countersigned by a docile *Reichspräsident,* and by further bending and twisting the ominous Article 48 of the Constitution.

In September, 1932, the *Stahlhelm,* with von Papen's approval, staged a mammoth parade in Berlin, in which 150,000 war veterans marched, pledging unswerving allegiance to the black-white-red standard of the Hohenzollern monarchy.

The untenable parliamentary situation caused the president to decree the dissolution of the *Reichstag* and to call for new elections. The cancellation of German reparations and the progress in the disarmament talks (cf. p. 670) — to be credited to the foreign policy of Stresemann and Brüning, but taking effect during the early days of von Papen's chancellorship — swung about a million National Socialist votes to the support of the Papen cabinet and another million to the parties not represented in the government. Thus in the elections of November 6, 1932, the National Socialists lost altogether two million three hundred thousand votes and thirty-five *Reichstag* seats.

It was at this juncture that General Kurt von Schleicher reappeared on the scene. He had convinced himself that the reactionary von Papen could not be expected to endorse any extensive program of social reform and public works such as in his opinion could alone save Germany from political and social chaos. On November 17, von Papen resigned, and von Schleicher was appointed chancellor, minister of defense, and *Reichskommissar* for Prussia.

The Schleicher cabinet honestly tried to create a broad front for the tasks of reconstruction. The chancellor called for the transformation of the *Reichswehr* into a democratic people's army and tried to enlist the support of the trade unions and of all other groups which had the true interests of Germany at heart. But both the Social Democrats and the Center party, albeit for different reasons, refused to co-operate. The Social Democrats saw in the new chancellor merely the representative of the hated military caste, and the Centrists had not forgiven Schleicher his share in the overthrow of the Brüning government.

In the meantime, an important meeting between Hitler and von Papen had taken place in Cologne, in the residence of Baron von Schröder, one of the leading German bankers. Papen and some of his political friends and associates had long toyed with the idea of establishing a "corporate state," a type of functional or vocational social order, in which the interests of all social groups were to be welded into an organic and "solidaric" structure. They were even naïve enough to believe that the corporative order as outlined in Pius XI's encyclical *Quadragesimo Anno* (1931) could be harmonized with the "corporatism" of Mussolini's Italy and with the demands of the National Socialist program. They failed to see that the "solidarism" envisaged by the papal encyclical had its frame and term in the free development and perfection of human personality, that it rested on the premise of free service and voluntary association and acknowledged the sanctions of divine, natural, and moral law. Fascist and National Socialist "corporatism," on the other hand, was centered in the absolute power of the State or the Race and proposed the *Gleichschaltung* (co-ordination) of individuals and groups by means of physical and spiritual coercion and regimentation. Hitler, however, was too shrewd to disappoint prematurely this wishful thinking of the Papen group and of those Roman Catholics who had only recently constituted themselves as a subdivision of the National Socialist party.

Acting upon such rather fantastic premises, von Papen used his influence with Hindenburg to persuade the president that the National Socialists should be given a share in a government of a sufficiently conservative stamp to enable it to exert a controlling influence on the National Socialist hotspurs.

The *Reichstag* adjourned on December 9, 1932. Between January 17 and January 28, negotiations between von Papen, Hugenberg, and Seldte (the *Stahlhelm* leader) had brought agreement as to the composition of the new government. On January 28, von Schleicher was dismissed and von Papen commissioned by the president to work out a compromise with Hitler. On January 30, Hitler was appointed chancellor, taking the oath of office to support the Weimar Constitution. The event was celebrated in the evening with a torchlight parade of SA troops marching through the Brandenburg Gate and the Wilhelmstrasse, with Hindenburg and Hitler in the reviewing stand.

The Hitler cabinet included, aside from the *Führer* himself, only two National Socialists. Joseph Göbbels was appointed minister of propaganda and public enlightenment, and Hermann Göring became a minister without portfolio (*ohne Geschäftsbereich*). Von Papen was made vice-chancellor and *Reichskommissar* for Prussia; Hugenberg, minister of agriculture; Seldte, minister of labor; General von Blomberg, minister of defense. Baron von Neurath was retained as foreign minister, and Count Schwerin von Krosigk as minister of finance.

As the government commanded no parliamentary majority, the president decreed the dissolution of the *Reichstag* and set March 5 as the date for new elections. On February 27 a fire of mysterious origin destroyed the *Reichstag* building in Berlin. A feeble-minded Dutch communist, named van der Lubbe, was found on the premises in a dazed condition. He was arrested, "confessed" having set fire to the building, and was later executed.

On February 28, President Hindenburg, again invoking Article 48 of the Constitution, signed a decree "for the Protection of the People and the State," which served as a cover to justify the arrest of thousands of communists, the suppression of the communist press, and the eventual proscription of the Communist party. A supplementary decree established the SA and SS formations as organs of the military police.

The following election campaign turned into a field day for the parties of the Right: communist and socialist meetings were dissolved, their newspapers confiscated; gatherings and publications of Centrists and Liberals were under close surveillance; and all radio stations were operated and controlled by National Socialist functionaries.

The elections were preceded, accompanied, and followed by rioting and bloody excesses. The National Socialists won 288 seats (43 per cent), as against 196 in the previous *Reichstag*. The German Nationals, the Center party, and the Social Democrats suffered only minor losses, while the Communists lost one fifth of their deputies. National Socialists and German Nationals combined polled 51 per cent of the total vote, thus holding a slim majority.

The immediate sequel of the election was a mass persecution unequaled in German history: large numbers of communists, socialists, liberals, Catholics, and Pacifists were arrested, beaten, tortured, and either murdered or sent to concentration camps. State and municipal governments were ousted and replaced by National Socialist administrations. However, the final act of the drama needed for its consummation a screen of legality: The government could obtain dictatorial powers only by a change of the Constitution, for which a two-thirds majority of the *Reichstag* was required. This requirement was fulfilled by outlawing the Communist party, thus preventing the elected Communist deputies from taking their seats in the *Reichstag*.

On March 23 this "rump parliament" convened in the Kroll Opera House in Berlin and passed with the votes of the Right and the Centrists the *Ermächtigungsgesetz* (Enabling Act) which conferred dictatorial powers on Hitler's cabinet for a period of four years. On July 14 all political parties with the exception of the NSDAP were either dissolved or they disbanded "voluntarily."

On August 2, 1934, President Hindenburg died. Shortly afterward Hitler abolished the title of *Reichspräsident* and assumed personally the title and office of *Führer und Reichskanzler*. This step, too, had to be "legalized" by a "plebiscite": the *Führer und Reichskanzler* received a "popular endorsement" of almost 90 per cent. The Weimar Republic had come to an inglorious end.

Here the account of Germany's political destinies must of necessity break off. What follows — the "revolution of nihilism" (Rauschning), the captivity, first of Germany, and later on of Europe, under the Nazi yoke, World War II, the defeat and prostration of Germany — is of too recent date to be seen and evaluated in its true proportions and to permit the detached objectivity required for a historical analysis.

It may suffice therefore to state that from 1933 on the iron rule of the National Socialist *Totalstaat* extended to all departments of public life, culture, and education, and to the most intimate concerns and relations of private and family life. While all civil and human rights were totally abrogated, all duties and responsibilities converged in the *Führer,* the embodiment of *Volk* and *Reich*. Citizenship was limited to "Aryans," and the *Nürnberg Laws* eliminated all Jews from the political, economic, and cultural life of the German *Volksgemeinschaft* (folk community). As has been stated, "positive Christianity" was given a boost in the party program, and freedom was promised to all religious creeds "as far as they do not endanger or are in conflict with the moral ideas of the Germanic race," while at the same time a subtle, insidious, and relentless war of extermination was waged against Christian citizens, churches, and groups of all denominations; while party officials declared Germanism and Christianity as mutually exclusive, and thousands upon thousands of innocent victims lingered and died in concentration camps. The innocent and the guilty: they all became victims of a gospel of hate and the "will to power," embodied in a regime which glorified war and conquest as necessary and normal outlets for a nation's vigor and as "legitimate" means to national glory.

Chapter 17

CULTURAL TRENDS

The Age of Crisis. Baron Karl vom Stein, the leader of the social and political reform of Prussia (cf. p. 432 sqq.), had written in the early twenties of the nineteenth century: "We are overpopulated; we have overreached ourselves in production and manufacture, and we are overfed; our administration has become more and more materialistic, and we have reduced everything to a lifeless mechanism." At about the same time the usually optimistic Goethe had visualized a mankind which would become "more shrewd and more intelligent, but hardly better or happier." He believed he saw "a time approaching when God will no longer be pleased with man, when once again He will have to smash His creation to pieces in order to rejuvenate it."

As the nineteenth century ran its course and turned into the twentieth, such isolated voices of gloom were echoed by many of the prominent thinkers of the West, and the word "crisis" appeared more frequently in learned publications and disputations. In Germany, Paul Lagarde (1827–1891), Friedrich Nietzsche (1844–1900, cf. p. 695 sq.), and Julius Langbehn (1851–1907) were among the first to indict the moral and spiritual bankruptcy of the modern age, and to unmask what Robert M. Hutchins has called the "twin myths of progress and utility." Lagarde, professor of Oriental languages at the University of Göttingen, called for the creation of a new German *Volksgemeinschaft* (people's community) on a religious and moral basis, and was bitterly opposed to political and economic liberalism, moral relativism, and philosophic materialism. Deploring the encroachments of the *Naturwissenschaften* (natural sciences) and of the "scientific method" upon the *Geisteswissenschaften* (French: *sciences morales*), he wrote in 1881: "The predominance of natural science is partly due to the fact that *Geisteswissenschaft* has little to show for itself but the dressed-up subjectivity of individuals and groups, so that honest thinkers develop a loathing for it. . . . The nullity of human kind is at present so pronounced that even the religious urge has taken refuge in the natural sciences. But though the prevalent scientific hypotheses are noisily proclaimed as exact science, they are nothing but scientific dogmas. What do we nonscientists learn in our universities but theories, high-sounding phrases, and empty words? . . . Our judgments on literature, music, and philosophy are such as we find in compendia and review factories; our judgments on political matters are nothing but the spawn of those reptiles who pollute our cities. We have so much education that we no longer have access to ideas."

And Julius Langbehn, in his provocative book *Rembrandt als Erzieher* (*Rembrandt, the Educator,* 1890), joined Lagarde in his fight against the materialism of the age. He praised religious faith, *Volkstum* ("folkishness," national culture), and great art as supreme character builders and asserted in the opening lines that "the spiritual life of the German people finds itself at present in a slow process of decline. Science and knowledge succumb to ever increasing specialization. In thought and literature epoch-making personalities are lacking. The Fine Arts, though distinguished by significant individual accomplishments, have lost the character of monumentality and with it their most compelling force. We have plenty of musicians, but composers and performers of talent are rare. Architecture is the axis of art, as philosophy is the axis of all scientific thought, but at the moment we have neither a German architecture nor a German philosophy. The great masters are dying out; *les rois s'ent vont* (the kings disappear). . . . There is no question but that in all this the democratizing, levelling, and atomizing spirit of this century expresses itself. The entire culture and education of the present age is historical, 'Alexandrian,' retrospective; we are less concerned with the creation of new values than with the registration of old ones. And the greatest weakness of our modern culture is truly this: it is scientific and wants to be scientific, but the more scientific it becomes the less creative it will be."

More radical and more clairvoyant in his criticism than either Lagarde or Langbehn was Friedrich Nietzsche. In the midst of the delusive prosperity, the joyful exuberance, and the noisy nationalism of the *Gründerzeit* (foundation period) which followed the victorious war against France and the proclamation of the German empire (cf. p. 546), he raised his voice in solemn warning: "Of all the evil consequences," Nietzsche wrote in 1873, "which have come in the wake of the latest war with France, the worst is perhaps a widespread, yea even universal mistake: the mistake, namely, of public opinion that German civilization too was victorious in that conflict." Such a delusion, he feared, would eventually "turn the German victory into defeat, yea into the very extirpation of the German spirit in favor of the 'German Empire.'"* He lamented the "unspeakable impoverishment and exhaustion of our existence," and he believed he recognized undercurrents of destructive forces which were prone to endanger the proud edifice of the new Germany: "We are living in an atomic age, an atomistic chaos. Today everything is determined by the coarsest and most evil forces, by the egotism of an acquisitive society and by military potentates. . . . A revolution is unavoidable, and it will be an atomistic revolution." And the preface

---

* Cf. *Unzeitgemässe Betrachtungen* (I).

of *Der Wille zur Macht* (*The Will to Power*) contained the following prophetic passage: "My work," Nietzsche stated programmatically, "shall contain a summary judgment on our century, on the entire modern age, on the kind of civilization which we have attained. . . . What I am going to narrate is the history of the next two centuries. I shall describe what will of necessity come about: the advent of nihilism. . . . Our entire European civilization has long been moving with a tortuous tension, a tension which has been growing from decade to decade, toward the final catastrophe."

About a generation later, Nietzsche's attempt to diagnose the crisis of the modern age and to "narrate the history of the next two centuries" was repeated by Oswald Spengler (1880–1936) in his *Der Untergang des Abendlandes* (*The End of the West,* I and II; 1917 and 1922), a work which sings the swan song of Western civilization and preaches a funeral oration over its allegedly decomposing corpse. For Spengler the modern crisis is a phenomenon inherent in every culture organism: *"Zivilisation"* as such is the end phase of *"Kultur,"* signifying the exhaustion of the culturally creative energies and their replacement by the rationalizing and mechanizing tendencies of science and technology. For him cultural organisms are plantlike growths following in their evolution universal biological laws; they thus pass necessarily through the successive stages or "seasons" of spring, summer, autumn, and winter, and their end or death is both predictable and inevitable.

No attempt is made by Spengler to mitigate or overcome the crisis of the age: he merely describes its symptoms. But this description and the philosophy of history on which it rests are themselves symptoms of the crisis and of that spirit of the age which had been penetratingly analyzed by Spengler's precursors, especially by Nietzsche. Spengler's "scientism" and biologism fail to recognize the essential distinction between human nature and physico-mechanical nature, between that which is materially and biologically predetermined and that which owes its growth to the self-determination of free human agents, between the causality which rules in the natural sciences and the personal and moral imperatives which determine the course of history and the related *Geisteswissenschaften.* Thus Spengler is simply a consistent positivist and materialist when, in his book *Der Mensch und die Technik* (*Man and Technology,* 1931), he arrives at the conclusion that man is a *Raubtier* (beast of prey), that ideals are indicative of cowardice, that man, the "knowing priest of the machine age," is creative not by virtue of his mind, but by virtue of his hand, and that therefore he is not a rational animal but at best a rationalizing brute.

Cultural "crisis" is in the last analysis the manifestation of a lack of confidence in established cultural values and standards. In this respect the crisis of modern Germany is identical with the crisis of modern Europe and America. It is a crisis which, having its roots in significant shifts in the system of values, involves civilization in all its branches: the State, society, economics, education, art, literature, philosophy, and religion. No doubt, both Nietzsche and Spengler had sensed this all-embracing nature of the crisis of their age. But whereas for Nietzsche's basic cultural optimism the mind of Western man could advance to new shores by means of the vitalization of its unused recuperative resources, by means of an *"Umwertung aller Werte"* (transvaluation of all values), for Spengler's cultural pessimism the crisis was indicative not of a transition but of the impending *finale* of Western civilization. To both authors, however, it appeared as the tragedy of modern civilization that the scientific age, which had promised peace, security, and liberation from all illusions and superstitions, was producing on all sides a growing instability and was multiplying revolutionary upheavals; that modern civilization was creating a universe which, to use Aristotle's words, could be inhabited only by beasts or by gods, a universe from which man therefore was excluded. When Nietzsche felt it his "terrible duty" to announce to the world "the death of God," when the romantic longing of his heart projected itself into the chimera of the *"Übermensch,"* the *"blonde Bestie,"* and when he proclaimed the insatiable "will to power" as the new ethical code of his new bestial superman, he provided the precise pattern for Spengler's historic naturalism and *Raubtierphilosophie.*

It was his intense romantic idealism that made Nietzsche say that "the best in us is derived from the sentiments of the past. The sun of our life has set, but the sky still glows with its light, although we no longer see it." His classical-humanist education had taught him to acknowledge and revere the continuity of the Graeco-Roman-Christian heritage of European thought and culture. He recognized in the Western tradition a common stock of ideas by means of which even minds of vastly differing convictions had been able to communicate with each other. And he was all the more disturbed by the revolutionary impact of the age of positivistic science and philosophy which had "atomized" modern mankind by depriving it of those normative and axiological criteria without which a rational system of thought and moral action was impossible.

Nietzsche's description of the predicament of modern civilization became in Spengler's pessimistic view the fatal predicament of modern man: he who had been the master of nature had been reduced to serfdom and slavery by the machine age. The means were revolting against the ends: in a universe constituted exclusively by mechanical and physical laws everything was materially predetermined, and there was no room left for the self-determination of a human person. If both human life and subhuman nature were immersed in such a universe of brutal and morally indifferent facts, the "why?" of the metaphysician and the "ought" of the moralist, the questions as to the nature of being and the ends of doing, became equally meaningless. "The saying 'this ought to be,'" wrote Spengler, "must be replaced by the inexorable 'this *is* so.' . . . A proud skepticism discards the sentimentalities of the nineteenth century. . . . Skepticism is the only philosophical attitude still possible for this age and worthy of it."

According to Spengler, what we are witnessing today is the spectacle of a machine age defeating its own ends. The tired mind of the West seeks escape and refuge either in sports or in exotic religious cults which were scorned and disdained in the age of Darwin. While some of the intellectual leaders are beginning to rebel against their destiny, against the mechanization of life, the masses, having completely succumbed to the spirit of the age, are irretrievably lost. This civilization of "Faustian man" will soon be destroyed and forgotten, as dead and forgotten as are the highways of the Romans, the Chinese Wall, and the palaces of Memphis and Babylon. Spengler therefore admonishes his contemporaries to heed the example of Achilles: let us rather have a short life, full of action and fame, than a long life void of meaning and content. Our fate is inevitable; a return is impossible; optimism is sheer cowardice. Let us then stand firmly at the posts where destiny has placed us, knowing that we are lost, without hope and without redemption. To be able to do this is the mark of our greatness.

The merit of Spengler's diagnosis of the age of crisis and of his counsels of despair lies in his merciless analysis of the "spirit of the age" and in the consistency with which he proceeds from certain given premises to seemingly inescapable conclusions. That his cultural pessimism itself is one of the symptoms of the crisis which he describes is further evidenced by the fact that he fails to see the flaws in the premises. If the premises of materialism and naturalism are correct, then Spengler's conclusions are logical and legitimate. If man's distinguishing mark is his hand, then he achieves his greatest triumph in the creation of "millions and billions of horse-power." But if man's distinguishing marks are his intellect and free will, then the entire picture changes, and the essentially different premises call for essentially different conclusions. If the crisis of the age issues from man's confused mind, from his sick heart, and from his perverted volitional and emotional life, then he and his civilization are not irretrievably lost, because human nature at any historical juncture will be able to rouse itself, to challenge the "spirit of the age" and to recover the wholeness and balance of a truly human life and civilization.

Economic Forces. Viewing with deep concern the turning away of the new German empire from the ideals of the past, the Prussian historian Heinrich von Treitschke (1834–1896, cf. p. 592) said in the German *Reichstag* in November, 1871: "You may believe a teacher of youth who has had an opportunity to watch the younger generation: it must shake the soul of even the most optimistic of us when we see on all sides increasing self-indulgence, materialism, and the abandonment of the ideal values of life." And the realistic novelist Wilhelm Raabe (cf. p. 590 sq.) wrote in one of his books: "Thus the money bag had burst open in the German lands, the thalers were rolling in the streets, and too many hands were eager to grab them. It almost seemed as if this were the greatest gain which the united fatherland had derived from its great world-historic success."

a) Industry. The symptoms of crude materialism to which the above-mentioned complaints allude were most conspicuous during the final decades of the nineteenth and the first decade of the twentieth century. They reflected the transformation of Germany from an agrarian to an industrialized country. This social and economic development was in part determined by the rapid increase of the population, which rose from forty-one million in 1871 to almost sixty-eight million in 1914.* During the same period the city population was growing steadily at the expense of the countryside: while in 1871 two thirds of the German people had lived on the land, in 1914 two thirds lived in big or medium-sized cities.** Industrial mass production gradually penetrated into the rural districts, often superseding the home industries and peasant crafts.

Both Bismarck's policy of protective tariffs (1879) and Caprivi's commercial treaties with neighboring countries (1891) aimed at aiding the development of German industry and effectively served their purpose. The gradual integration of Germany's national economy in the complex structure of world economy likewise stimulated industrial enterprise and strengthened German capitalism.

The industrial expansion of Germany, however, proceeded by no means in a straight upward movement: it was repeatedly retarded by economic slumps and depressions. Thus, the boom of the *Gründerzeit* (1871–1872) was followed by *"der grosse Krach"* (big crash) of 1873. It took Germany some time to recover from this economic disaster, a recovery which was hampered by the competition of other highly industrialized European nations. Between 1873 and 1879 it was generally believed that a policy of free trade would benefit German economic interests, but this view was gradually reversed, and the steady and almost uninterrupted advance of German industry began with the adoption of protective tariffs (1879) and was accelerated by the conclusion of international trade agreements (1891). Prince Bülow, Caprivi's successor in the office of *Reichskanzler* (cf. p. 620 sq.), merely stated the facts when he wrote shortly before the outbreak of World War I: "The industrialization of Germany . . . proceeded from the end of the eighties on with a vehemence which was equalled only by the industrial development of the United States."

The rise of Germany as a leading industrial power was prepared for and aided by an astounding increase in the production of pig iron, the adoption of new mechanical inventions and machines, such as the steam turbine and the Diesel motor, and by pioneering work in the electrical and chemical industries. During the first decade of the twentieth century Germany took the lead in the manufacture of artificial dyes made from coal tar, such as

---

* The territorial losses of World War I reduced the population figures to approximately sixty-three million (1925).

** In 1871, 36.1 per cent of the German population lived in places with 2000 or more inhabitants; in 1880, 41.4 per cent; in 1890, 47 per cent; in 1900, 54.4 per cent; in 1910, 60 per cent; in 1925, 64.4 per cent. In 1871, 4.8 per cent lived in "big cities" (of 100,000 or more inhabitants); in 1890, 12.9 per cent; in 1900, 16.2 per cent; in 1910, 21.3 per cent; in 1919, 24.9 per cent; in 1925, 26.2 per cent; in 1928, 27.9 per cent. Thus, in 1928, almost one third of the population lived in big cities. While in 1871 Germany had 8 big cities, in 1910 it had 44, and 48 in 1928.

alizarin and indigo. During the war years (1914–1918), when the Central Powers were cut off from the outside world, German chemists learned how to gain nitrogen from the air and thus developed a high production volume of artificial fertilizers and explosives. While in 1913 Germany had imported 971,000 tons of saltpeter from Chile and Peru, the new method of nitrogen fixation made her not only capable of satisfying all the demands of the domestic market, but made possible in the postwar years the export of large surplus quantities of nitrogen. The manufacture of artificial silks and dyes opened up new fields in the textile industries, although German textile production never matched that of England and the United States.

Germany's industrial advance was accompanied and followed by a corresponding expansion of domestic and foreign trade and the development of an extended and highly efficient transportation system. The German railroad lines, for example, measured 62,500 kilometers in 1917, as compared with 19,600 kilometers in 1870. Motor transportation on land and in the air made similar strides and, owing to Count Ferdinand Zeppelin's invention of the rigid dirigible airship (1900), Germany for several decades held the lead in this type of air transportation.

b) Agriculture. German agriculture was in a favorable position during the period immediately following the Franco-Prussian War. The productivity of the soil had been heightened by the use of artificial fertilizers and the application of phosphoric acid and potash. The management of farm lands was improved and simplified by the introduction of farm machinery. In 1874, the first *landwirtschaftliche Hochschule* (agricultural university) was opened in Berlin. The German Agricultural Society, founded in 1884, promoted and spread the knowledge of technical agricultural methods and devices, especially by means of publications and periodic exhibitions. Agricultural co-operatives facilitated the purchase of seed grains and fertilizers, the acquisition of machines, the sale of farm produce, and the procurement of money at a low rate of interest.

While these developments greatly benefited German agriculture, the German farmer of the late seventies began to feel more and more the effects of foreign, especially Russian and American, competition. Simultaneously he suffered from the increasing pressure of the industrial age which tended to sacrifice agricultural to industrial interests. Caprivi's commercial treaties favored German industry but resulted in hardships for German agriculture. Prince Bülow's new protective tariffs of 1902, on the other hand, largely repaired the damage, and during the decade preceding World War I German agriculture enjoyed a reasonable amount of prosperity. The war naturally caused a temporary agricultural crisis, but the postwar inflation proved a boon to many German farmers: they were able to liquidate their indebtedness, while at the same time their lands and homesteads retained their value as stable assets.

c) "Handwerk und Gewerbe" (Handicrafts and Trades). The industrial methods of manufacture worked to the disadvantage of the established handicrafts and trades and destroyed many of the home industries and independent *Handwerker*. This process was speeded up by the trade regulations of 1869 and 1871 which abolished the still prevalent trade restrictions of the *Zünfte* (guilds) and decreed complete *Gewerbefreiheit* (freedom of trade). The opposition of the *Handwerker* led to a series of legal enactments (between 1878 and 1897) which partially incorporated certain features of the guild system, reintroduced the *Meisterprüfung* (master's certificate), and made obligatory the procurement of a *Befähigungsnachweis* (aptitude credential, 1908).* These measures actually saved the independent crafts and trades from extinction and guaranteed a high quality of individual performance, especially in the industrial arts and crafts.**

d) *The "Spirit" of Capitalism*. The adverse effects of capitalism and industrialism were analyzed and severely criticized by leading German economists and sociologists. Max Weber (1864–1920) believed he had discovered the ideological roots of capitalism in the *Berufsethos* (vocational ethics) of Calvinism and Puritanism, which placed an ethico-religious premium on "success" in business and on the accumulation of a maximum of economic goods, not to provide leisure and comfort but as an external sign and guarantee of divine favor. Thus, according to Weber, economic activity as such, which had been viewed with suspicion by the theologians and moralists of the precapitalistic era, was endowed with an ethico-religious accent, and immoderate acquisitiveness, formerly condemned as a social vice, came eventually to be regarded as a manifestation of Christian virtue. Weber thus attributed to the capitalistic *Ethos* the creation of the *Homo Oeconomicus* (economic man) whose economic activities were "autonomous" in the sense that they were completely divorced from the exactions of the natural and moral law. Subsequently, in the period of economic liberalism (cf. p. 549 sq.), the capitalist *entrepreneur* looked to the liberal-capitalist State for the protection of the claimed "absolute" right of ownership.

The anticapitalist critique of Werner Sombart (1863–1941) followed a similar line of reasoning. He accused capitalism of having caused the disintegration of family life and of having destroyed the ethical foundations of business life. As negative factors he mentioned in particular the mechanization of labor, the widening cleavage between employers and employees,

---

* The *Gewerbeordnung* (trade regulation) had its legal basis in the enactments of 1869, 1900, and 1929. A qualified *Gewerbefreiheit* was guaranteed in Article 151 of the Weimar Constitution.

** The following are the German technical terms (some of them untranslatable) commonly used to designate the different phases and aspects of *Gewerbe*: (1) *Hauswerk*: the transformation of raw materials in an independent *Hauswirtschaft* (home economy); (2) *Lohnwerk*: paid work, performed with individually owned tools, either in the house of the client (*Stör*) or in the worker's own home; (3) *Verlag*: a group of independent *Handwerker*, working for the same employer; (4) *Manufaktur*: work performed by *unselbständige Arbeiter* (dependent workers) in a manufacturing enterprise; (5) *Fabrik* (factory): work performed by *unselbständige Arbeiter* in an industrial plant, especially machine production in light and heavy industries. These different phases do not necessarily follow each other in a historical sequence, but often co-exist side by side.

the intensification of the class struggle, and the general dehumanization of social relations.

These and similar indictments make capitalism appear as a kind of inverted Marxism because, like Marxism, it adheres to a purely utilitarian and materialistic system of values. It enthrones economics as a supreme ruling power and subordinates to this economic absolutism all cultural, moral, and spiritual activities and interests.

The accuracy of this interpretation seems to be borne out by the fact that in the capitalistic era, culminating in the years preceding World War I, increasing numbers of the younger generation turned from scientific and intellectual vocations and professions to economic and financial pursuits. Science no less than art and literature became largely subservient to capitalistic interests. Those, on the other hand, who refused to follow the general trend condemned themselves to tragic isolation or expended their vitality in fruitless spiritual rebellion. Literature and the arts came more and more to be regarded as luxuries which could be enjoyed only by economically satiated gourmets. While the servile writer and artist might prosper as a hack, responsible and truly creative minds were frequently forced into an eccentric and Bohemian existence, their works reflecting the lack of a popular response.

Technology. Capitalism and industrialism are inseparably linked with the technological development of the modern age. Technology, too, is characterized by its utilitarian and exclusively this-worldly interests. It is free from ethical preoccupations and determined by purely practical and rational-scientific calculations. It excels in the invention of labor-displacing machinery and has thereby contributed to the aggravation and complication of the social problem. On the other hand, it has been praised by such an astute observer as the German physicist Friedrich Dessauer (1881–) as "the greatest earthly power, the root and communal foundation of cultural progress, the liberator of man from the threatening forces of nature . . . unlocking the doors of the universe. . . . It has vastly enlarged the individual sphere of influence and activity and has transformed the ego-centered thinking and doing of man so as to make him a servant of society and humanity. . . . By reducing progressively the immense distances between man and man it has been able to raise the masses to a higher level of spiritual existence."

In Dessauer's optimistic view technology thus appears as a potent factor in the process of human liberation, democratization, and unification. In this positive evaluation of technology Dessauer, the Roman Catholic, is in agreement with most of the leaders of socialism, but in striking disagreement with Spengler. It is interesting to note that the papal social encyclicals no less than Marx and Bebel blame the economic egotism of the ruling classes rather than technological advance for the degradation of the workingman. Bebel in particular saw in the victory of technics over nature a powerful stimulus for the social and cultural advancement of the proletariat. He expected from the steadily rising volume of production numerous benefits for the working class, such as shorter hours of work and more time for recreation and education.

There is no doubt that most of the critics of technology and the machine age were not blind to the many material advantages and the great potentialities of the new methods of production and distribution. Their attacks were usually aimed not at technology as such, but rather at that confusion of means and ends which turned man from a master into a servant of the machine. It was generally recognized that technology had opened up new vistas for creative human endeavor, but deeper minds insisted that technology by itself could not provide the incentives or point the way to higher cultural standards. This important reservation was made by Heinrich von Treitschke, who wrote in his *German History of the Nineteenth Century:* "One has spoken of technology and the facilitation of transportation and communication as if they by themselves constituted civilization, while actually they only offer the *means* for cultural progress. Future generations will not ask to what extent we were able to speed up the transmission of letters but rather whether we had any great human ideas to communicate."* In other words, while technology places new means at the disposal of man, it is indifferent with regard to cultural and moral ends.

Materialism and "Idealism." Although the *neudeutsche Kultur* of the decades between the foundation of the Second Empire and World War I (1871–1914) owed its physiognomy largely to material forces and accomplishments, there was no lack of idealistic and even romantic interests and yearnings. But it appears that the ideal aims and ends themselves were derived from material presuppositions and from the one-sided materialistic preoccupations of the age. Idealism was extolled privately and publicly, in State and Church, in schools and universities. It was a household word in the circles of nationalists and Pan-Germans and among all those historians, educators, preachers, politicians, and military men who wrote and spoke high-soundingly of the eternal mission of *Deutsche Kultur* when what they really meant was *Machtpolitik* and *Realpolitik*. And this materialistically colored "idealism" was especially rampant among the upper classes, the new aristocracy of money and property. "The same generation," wrote Alfred Lichtwark, the Director of the Hamburg Art Gallery, in 1905, "which has acquired the new goods, was only in exceptional instances capable of also attaining to the new culture for whose service these goods were destined. Wealth, too, needs tradition, and there was no tradition of wealth in Germany. . . . In our country one can be very rich, very uneducated, and unwilling to make any sacrifice for cultural ends, without becoming an object of contempt. . . . There has perhaps never been an upper stratum of society with as little cultural significance as in present-day Germany. In

---

* *Deutsche Geschichte des 19. Jahrhunderts,* Vol. V, p. 426.

spiritual and intellectual vitality and interest it lags behind the middle and lower classes."*

Lichtwark himself, of course, and others of a similar mind prove that it would be unjust to indulge in any sweeping generalizations. There have always been many scholars, teachers, preachers, writers, and artists of rank in the new German empire who vigorously opposed both the crude materialism and superficial idealism of their age. But their warnings went largely unheeded as long as the nation as such remained in the grip of a materialistic, utilitarian, and one-sidedly practico-political philosophy of life. On the whole, the contemplative *"Volk der Dichter und Denker"* (people of poets and thinkers) had become a people of political, social, and economic action and was very proud of having accomplished this transformation.

Wissenschaft (Science and Knowledge). As has been previously stated, the new Germany which came into being in 1871 retained and even amplified its leadership in the natural sciences (cf. p. 559 sqq.). Science not only supplied agriculture, industry, and technics with new methods and tools, but entered into a close alliance with nonscientific branches of knowledge, such as philosophy, psychology, historiography, and literary criticism, disciplines which for better or worse availed themselves of the "scientific method."

a) "Naturwissenschaften" (Natural Sciences). Theoretical and physical *chemistry* were given a more solid foundation by the research of Walter Nernst (1864–1941), Albert Einstein (1879–), Arnold Sommerfeld (1868), and Fritz Haber (1868–1934). In the latter's opinion, "the accomplishments of the past fifty years have raised German organic chemistry to such heights that the world has almost come to regard chemistry as a German science."

In *physics,* Heinrich Hertz (1859–1894), a pupil of Helmholtz (cf. p. 562) and one of the last great representatives of the "classical physics" of the nineteenth century, perfected theoretically and experimentally the science of electrodynamics and made important contributions to Maxwell's theory of electricity. He discovered the electromagnetic waves (*"Hertzsche Wellen"*) and thereby laid the foundation for the epoch-making development of wireless telegraphy and radio communication. The revolutionary effects of Albert Einstein's Theory of Relativity and Max Planck's (1858–1947) Quantum Theory transcend in their significance the limited sphere of physical science and are beginning to exert a profound influence on epistemology and even on metaphysics. According to Planck, "the transformation of the physical world picture which has taken place during the past two decades is one of the most thoroughgoing changes that have ever occurred in the evolution of a science. . . . The Quantum Theory has

---

* *Der Deutsche der Zukunft,* p. 8.

finally shattered the much too narrow frame of our former world view."*

Hardly less revolutionary are the recent changes in the fields of biology, anthropology, and psychology. The neovitalism of Hans Driesch (1867–1941), harking back to the Aristotelian "entelechy," has resurrected the idea of plan, design, or "final cause" as prime factors in the evolution of organic life.** Max Scheler's (cf. p. 593 sq.) "metaphysical" anthropology aims at a new understanding of the human person as a *"Leib–Seele–Einheit"* (body-soul unity). The *Ganzheitspsychologie* (Gestalt psychology, structural psychology) of the Berlin and Würzburg schools as well as Sigmund Freud's (1856–1939), Alfred Adler's (1870–1937), Carl G. Jung's (1875–), Ludwig Klages' (1872–), and Rudolf Allers' (1883–) different brands of analytical psychology and "characterology" have, notwithstanding certain psychological and philosophical inconsistencies and shortcomings, materially contributed to a deeper understanding of the human *psyche* as the central core of personality and human behavior.

Whatever will be the ultimate impact of these new scientific theories on modern civilization, this much is certain: they have seriously disturbed and upset the naïve self-assurance of the complacent scientism and agnosticism of the age of Dubois Reymond and Ernst Haeckel (cf. p. 565).

b) Geisteswissenschaften.† In some of the above-named scientific theories, such as Scheler's "metaphysical anthropology," Alfred Adler's "individual psychology," Jung's "analytical psychology," or Klages' and Allers' "characterology," *Naturwissenschaft* has almost become an aspect of *Geisteswissenschaft.* In other words, the former relationship between these two groups of disciplines has practically been reversed: whereas by the latter part of the nineteenth century natural science in its rapid expansion had absorbed into itself every activity and manifestation of the human self, the opening decades of the twentieth century have begun to accentuate once more the basic values and creative impulses of human individuality and personality. This shift of emphasis had its ultimate sources in a changing outlook upon life and a subsequent re-examination of the nature of human knowledge. Such a radical reorientation of thought led of necessity to spirited controversies between the representatives of *Naturwissenschaft* and those of *Geisteswissenschaft,* resulting in a clarification of the mutual relationship of these disciplines and in a redefinition of their respective terms and methods.

1. *Krise der Wissenschaft.* The critical examination of the relative rank and value of the different branches of science and knowledge started from the contention of some German thinkers that different epistemological approaches were required for adequate interpretations in the spheres of

---

* *Das Weltbild der neueren Physik* (1929), p. 16.
** Cf. *Die Philosophie des Organischen* (Engl. trans., *The Science and Philosophy of the Organism* (London: A. and C. Black, 1929).
† The term came into general use after the publication of Wilhelm Dilthey's *Einleitung in die Geisteswissenschaften* (1883).

science and culture. In view of the exaggerated claims of the natural sciences and the encroachments of the "scientific method" on nonscientific modes of human knowledge, the neo-Kantian philosopher Heinrich Rickert (1863–1936) tried at the turn of the century to demarcate the boundary line between *Naturwissenschaft* and *Kulturwissenschaft,* with special reference to the historical disciplines.* A different subject matter, he asserted, requires a different method of approach. The generalizing natural sciences progressively eliminate the distinctive marks of individuality. But it is precisely the individuality and uniqueness of historical and cultural events which characterize the subject matter of the historical and cultural disciplines. The historian is intensely interested in the objects of his research precisely because of their unique and individual nature, and this interest must be satisfied by a method of research which recognizes and responds to the need for a discipline of equal rank with natural science. This discipline, according to Rickert, is *Geschichtswissenschaft* (the "science" of history).

Rickert's argument, however, was not merely aimed at the claimed infallibility and omnipotence of natural science, but equally at those historians who, appropriating the "scientific method," had tried to develop a *Historismus* ("historicism") free of all presuppositions, value judgments, and philosophic interpretations (*voraussetzungslose Wissenschaft*). This attitude had gradually led to a leveling relativism which eventually invaded all the provinces of human life and action, denying the possibility of abiding values and normative judgments in State and society, law and customs, literature and art, philosophy and religion. It was in opposition to this relativization of history and human life that Nietzsche's friend, the classical philologist Erwin Rohde (1845–1898), praised the rugged one-sidedness of men like Nietzsche. "We need such men," he argued, "if we are not to be driven into insanity by the diabolic doctrine that all things have their two sides. In this doctrine lies the whole curse of our 'historicism,' our faithlessness, our faint-heartedness." And Nietzsche himself asserted in his essay *On the Advantages and Disadvantages of History in regard to Life*** that "the oversaturation of an epoch with History makes it hostile and dangerous to life." In his opinion, this kind of "historicism" paralyzed the culturally creative energies and begot first irony and in the end an even more dangerous cynicism.

As, paradoxically enough, the maligned "historicism" itself was born of a desire for "objective" historical truth and could point to great accomplishments in matters of factual research, the dispute obviously was not so much concerned with the ultimate goal as with the problem of the most suitable and promising means and methods to be adopted in the pursuit of that ultimate end.

The real issue of the debate and the cause of the "crisis" was the

---

* Cf. especially *Die Grenzen der naturwissenschaftlichen Begriffsbildung* (1896) and *Kulturwissenschaft und Naturwissenschaft* (1899).
** Cf. *Unzeitgemässe Betrachtungen,* II.

irreconcilable conflict in the scientific and the philosophico-metaphysical concepts and interpretations of "truth." Was truth identical with the phenomenal world of scientific facts, as the scientists claimed, or did it, as the nonpositivist thinkers asserted, transcend these phenomenal data of sense perception? The representatives of the new *Geisteswissenschaft* rejected both scientific phenomenalism and philosophic positivism (cf. p. 594 sq.) and, partly under the influence of German idealistic philosophy (cf. p. 499 sqq.), partly inspired by Bergson's (1849–1941) intuitionism and Bolzano's and Brentano's neo-Aristotelianism (cf. p. 692 sq.), called for a "resurrection of metaphysics." The liberal Protestant theologian and *Kultur-philosoph* Ernst Troeltsch (1865–1923), after having carried in his writings the premises of historicism and relativism to their extreme and ultimately self-contradictory conclusions, found toward the end of his life a meta-physical reorientation of his thinking and a way out of the blind alley of historicism in the religious and philosophical views of his friend Friedrich von Hügel (1852–1925), a British Catholic thinker of German ancestry. He became convinced that "skepticism only *seems* to be a necessary conse-quence of the modern intellectual situation and of modern historicism" and that "it can be overcome by those ethical and ideal forces which emerge from history itself and are mirrored and concentrated in ethical norms.* Others, like Wilhelm Dilthey (cf. p. 691) and, later on, Max Scheler (cf. p. 593 sq.) and Martin Heidegger (cf. p. 694), following the lead of Herder, Goethe, the romantic philosophers (cf. p. 499 sqq.), and Nietzsche, advocated a *Lebensphilosophie* which was to reunite *Wissenschaft* and *Leben* and create a new cultural synthesis by means of an all-embracing and meta-physically anchored philosophy of life and civilization.

2. *"Literaturwissenschaft"* (*Literary Criticism*). The *"Krise der Wissen-schaft"* produced some interesting developments in the field of literary criticism, running largely parallel with the general trend of thought from scientific positivism to a resurgence of metaphysical speculation.

From the eighteenth century on, German literary criticism passed through three principal stages. The first phase was marked by an idealistic awaken-ing under the influence of Platonic and neo-Platonic thought, as mediated in part by Lord Shaftesbury (1671–1713), and embodied in a profoundly personalized manner in the works of Leibniz, Herder, Schiller, Goethe, and the romantic writers and thinkers. The second phase may be described as strictly positivistic or antimetaphysical. It revealed the influence of the doctrines of Auguste Comte (cf. p. 566 sq.) and Karl Marx (cf. p. 556 sqq.) and of the methods of both natural science and dialectic materialism. Comte's principles of the *philosophie positive* were applied to literary and art criticism by Hippolyte Taine,** whose approach to works of literature and art intended to be purely scientific and positivistic. Literature and art, like science, "neither condemn nor pardon; they merely state and explain

---

* Cf. *Die Überwindung des Historismus* (1924), p. 44.
** Cf. *Histoire de la littérature anglaise* (1864) and *Philosophie de l'art* (1865).

facts." The *"milieu"* or *"température morale"* of a literary work or a work of art is constituted by the general state of manners and customs, and the *milieu* produces literary and art forms by way of a Darwinian evolution, eliminating the unfit elements and adopting those which conform to the environmental atmosphere or climate.

Taine's principle of "natural selection" in literature and art was introduced into the methodology of German literary history and criticism by Wilhelm Scherer (1841–1886).* He and his influential school of literary historians abandoned all idealistic and metaphysical criteria of interpretation and thus established the predominance of the positivistic method in German literary research.

The third phase of German literary criticism, dating from the beginning of the twentieth century, reflects the gradual turning away from positivism and the return to some of the principles and methods of the classical and romantic eras, but within a set of intellectual and cultural circumstances which had been rendered much more complex by the problems posed by modern science and by the resultant critical situation of the *Geisteswissenschaften*.

Wilhelm Dilthey (1883–1911),** though still under the spell of positivism, developed on the bases of Hegel's and Rickert's philosophy of history a new method of literary interpretation which emphasized *Verstehen* (understanding) rather than *Beschreibung* (description). His acute insight into the process of literary creation led him to a deeper penetration of the personalities of such German authors as Lessing, Goethe, Hölderlin, and Novalis, and to a novel exegesis of their works. Although in perpetual search of spiritual realities, Dilthey lacked both the philosophical and methodical tools to comprehend fully the spiritual forces of history and civilization. It is fortunate, therefore, that his artistic vision frequently carried him farther than his "scientific" conscience would have given him permission to go.

In the element of artistic vision, superadded to ratiocination and descriptive analysis, contemporary German literary criticism occasionally rejoins and even metaphysically transcends the great tradition of the classical and romantic age. In the work of Joseph Nadler (1884–),† for example, the virtues of the metaphysician, the artist, and the scientist are found in happy union. It is historians and critics of Nadler's type that point the way to an end of sterile specialization, to a future synthesis of the still separated branches of knowledge, and to their hierarchical integration in a harmonious structure of science, knowledge, and wisdom.

3. *Philosophy.*   The epistemological problem concerning the possibility and validity of knowledge, its types and degrees, as corresponding to different

---

* Cf. *Geschichte der deutschen Literatur* (1883).

** Cf. especially *Das Erlebnis und die Dichtung* (1906) and *Einleitung in die Geisteswissenschaften* (1883).

† Cf. especially Nadler's monumental *Literaturgeschichte der deutschen Stämme und Landschaften* (4 vols., 1912–1928).

disciplines, received particular attention within the sphere of strictly philosophic speculation. Hermann Cohen (1842–1918) and Paul Natorp (1854–1924), the founders of the neo-Kantian Marburg School, inquired into the principles and premises of scientific knowledge and clearly delimited and circumscribed in their critical analysis the specific tasks of philosophic research. Both scholars devoted great effort to the elucidation of Kant's (cf. p. 371 sqq.) profound but much disputed concept of the "noumenon" or thing-in-itself, and they like every other neo-Kantian claimed to offer the one and only authentic interpretation of the master's ideas.

Nicolai Hartmann (1882–), too, started out from Kant's idealistic theory of knowledge but, turning against philosophic idealism, he arrived in the end at epistemological realism and laid the foundations for a new realistic metaphysics and ontology.* Hartmann's philosophy thus marks an important turning point in German speculative thought. He consciously reverts to the pre-Kantian and pre-Cartesian tradition of Aristotelian and Thomistic realism. His epistemology like that of Thomas Aquinas starts from the immediate givenness of the object of knowledge. For him as for the medieval philosopher "the relation between subject and object is an ontological one, and it is in the fact that this relation inheres in 'being as such' that the solution of the problem must be sought."

Nicolai Hartmann's return to philosophic realism was in part caused by his temporary association with a group of German thinkers who followed the intellectual leadership of Edmund Husserl (1859–1938), the founder of the school of Phenomenology,** who was himself indebted to the Aristotelianism of Franz Brentano (1838–1917). A priest and at one time a distinguished member of the theological faculty of the University of Würzburg, Brentano had come into conflict with the ecclesiastical authorities and had finally been suspended from his priestly office and relieved of his academic duties. From 1874 to 1895 he was a lecturer at the University of Vienna, and after that lived in retirement in Florence and Zurich.

Brentano's commentaries on the psychology of Aristotle, his theory of value, and in particular his investigations on the nature of justice represent important and lasting contributions to contemporary thought. Among the thinkers whom he attracted to his lectures was Edmund Husserl, a native of Moravia, who, originally a mathematician, had been converted to philosophy by the brilliant oratory and personal persuasive power of Friedrich Paulsen (1846–1908).

Husserl's Phenomenology† is indebted, next to Brentano, to the keen speculation of the Bohemian Catholic theologian, philosopher, and mathe-

---

* Cf. especially *Grundzüge einer Metaphysik der Erkenntnis* (1925).
** Many of the members of this school reside at present in the United States, where they edit *Philosophy and Phenomenological Research* (New York, 1940 sqq.), the successor to the *Jahrbuch für Philosophie und phänomenologische Forschung*.
† Cf. especially *Ideen zu einer reinen Phänomenologie und phänomenologischen Philosophie* (1913); English trans., *Ideas: General Introduction to Pure Phenomenology* (London: Allen and Unwin, 1931).

matician, Bernhard Bolzano (1781–1848). Because of the universality of his preoccupations and interests, Bolzano was known as the "Bohemian Leibniz."* Bolzano's *Wissenschaftslehre* and Brentano's "descriptive psychology" were systematized by Husserl and further elaborated by Max Scheler, Nicolai Hartmann, and Martin Heidegger. All the members of the phenomenological school found in the writings of the two older philosophers (Bolzano and Brentano) welcome support for their attack on the prevalent "psychologism" of Christoph Sigwart (1830–1904) and Benno Erdmann (1851–1909), both followers of Herbert Spencer, and on the exaggerated idealism of the neo-Kantian schools of Heidelberg, Freiburg, and Marburg (Windelband, Rickert, Cohen, Natorp).

Phenomenology soon became the most conspicuous philosophic trend in such prominent centers of German thought as Munich, Berlin, Freiburg, and Marburg, and helped to strengthen the antipositivist movements in France, England, and the Americas.

Phenomenological research stressed the primary importance of "essences" and concentrated its efforts on the analysis of the data of "pure consciousness" as objects of a *Wesensschau* (intuition of essences) which tries to penetrate to the "pure" phenomena underlying the empirical surface phenomena of sense perception. Although Husserl himself never overcame entirely the position of Kantian idealism, he furnished his pupils the methodological tools for a constructive criticism of both epistemological idealism and psychological positivism. It is the conviction of most contemporary philosophers who have adopted the phenomenological method that "it has no necessary connection with philosophic idealism and seems even incompatible with it."**

Among Husserl's disciples, Max Scheler (1875–1928)† and Martin Heidegger (1889–)‡ present the most interesting development. The influence of these thinkers extends far beyond Germany and is especially noticeable in France, Spain, Mexico, and South America. In his *Lebensphilosophie,* his anthropological views, and his concept of human personality Scheler was influenced by Nietzsche (cf. p. 695 sq.), while he owed the basic tenets of his moral philosophy to the teachings of St. Augustine, and those of his metaphysical speculation to Bergson and Husserl. If Husserl's phenomenology had been chiefly concerned with the analysis of "pure consciousness," Scheler's main interest centers in the phenomenological description of the emotions. He claims for man an "axiological sense" or an organ of emotive intuition and evaluation which carries him into the realm of essential and objective values and ultimately determines his position in the

---

* Cf. especially Bolzano's *Wissenschaftslehre* (1837; new ed., 1929).
** Cf. the author's translation of Oswaldo Robles, *Propedéutica Filosófica* (*The Main Problems of Philosophy*) (Milwaukee: The Bruce Publishing Company, 1946), p. 34.
† Cf. *Vom Ewigen im Menschen* (1921) and *Die Stellung des Menschen im Kosmos* (1930).
‡ Cf. especially *Sein und Zeit* (1927); *Vom Wesen des Grundes* (1929); and *Was ist Metaphysik?* (1929).

universe. Values are thus cognized by the spontaneous activity of "emotional consciousness" rather than by the acts of "intellectual consciousness." All values are "intentional objects of pure sentiment," and those values which embody objectively the aims of the pure sentiments of personality rank highest in the hierarchical scale. At one time a convert to Catholicism, Scheler construed later in life under the influence of Schelling (cf. p. 501 sq.) a pantheistic and radically dualistic metaphysics, in which God was conceived as emerging out of the self-redeeming urges of human life and culture.

Martin Heidegger, whose philosophy, like that of Hartmann, aims at a new *Seinslehre* (ontology), and whose "existentialism" in its more negative aspects was recently appropriated by the French philosopher, Jean-Paul Sartre, shows in the several phases of his intellectual formation the influence of such widely diverging thinkers as Aristotle, St. Augustine, Duns Scotus, Pascal, Kant, Rickert, Dilthey, and Kierkegaard (cf. p. 700 sq.). His thought is thus one of the most striking and startling expressions of an age of speculative uncertainty and intellectual crisis.

Heidegger is primarily concerned with the phenomenological analysis and the metaphysical exploration of *human existence*. In the concept of *"Angst"* (anguish), which he adopts from Kierkegaard's writings, he claims he has discovered a new transcendental medium of metaphysical knowledge. In his "existence," which is chained to *Zeitlichkeit* (temporality) and *Geschichtlichkeit* (historicity), man is caught between the two abysses of temporal transitoriness and nothingness. The being of man is thus *Sein zum Tode* (a "being unto death," a "being unto nothingness"). Human *"Angst"* denotes the experience and expresses the tragic situation of man. It aims at an objective world of essences, but it never reaches beyond the limited and fragmentary nature of human existence. In *"Angst"* and *"Sorge"* (care) man attends to things temporal and becomes hopelessly involved in them, although out of the depth of his being he cries out for a world of abiding values. But in this very experience of his forlornness, of a constantly menaced existence, in the very proximity of not-being and death, Heidegger's human being acquires or discovers the deepest significance of his selfhood.

As Heidegger, in the works published up to this date, has confined himself to a phenomenological inquiry into the *being of man,* without having even approached his original objective, the phenomenology of *being as such,* it would be presumptuous and premature to pass a final judgment on his philosophy. It would certainly be unjust to judge him by the misinterpretations and the mental and moral aberrations of some of his self-styled disciples.

A neo-positivist reaction against the "resurrection" of metaphysical speculation in Germany is represented by the "School of Vienna," many of whose members are, at present, residents of the United States and occupy leading positions in American universities. Catering to the empirical and pragmatic bent of the Anglo-Saxon mind, they have managed to command a respect and a following which they at no time enjoyed either in Austria or in

Germany. The "logical empiricism" of this group (Schlick, Carnap, Neurath, Wittgenstein, Reichenbach) claims to be a "scientific philosophy," restricting the field of philosophically "meaningful" questions to experimentally verifiable data, subject to semantic analysis and expressed in logico-mathematical symbols. Whatever cannot be so verified and demonstrated (ideas, moral concepts and judgments, rational inductions and deductions, etc.) is said to be void of meaning and is shoved aside as superstition and tautological trickery. This extreme form of neo-positivism can only be understood when seen as a justifiable corrective of some of the abuses of Hegelian and post-Hegelian idealism (cf. p. 502 sqq.). "Logical empiricism" is justified in recalling philosophy from vague abstractions and generalizations to concrete data, but it succumbs to the fallacies of an opposite extreme when it tries to make of philosophy a purely compilatory discipline and a mere adjunct of science.

The antimetaphysical and in fact antiphilosophical radicalism of the "logical empiricists" illustrates in a very practical manner those dangers of an uninhibited "scientism" which had been first recognized by Friedrich Nietzsche (1844–1900). "What I got hold of at that time," Nietzsche had written in the preface to the second edition of The Birth of Tragedy,* "was something terrible and dangerous, a problem with horns, not necessarily a bull, but certainly a new problem: the problem of science itself, science comprehended for the first time as something problematical and highly questionable." Thus it appears that Nietzsche, though never a systematic philosopher himself, had first discerned the essential difference between the scientist and the philosopher and had categorically emphasized the basic distinction between scientific and philosophic aims and methods.

For Heinrich Rickert (cf. p. 689), who was guided by Nietzsche's poetic and philosophic intuitions in his systematic differentiation between Naturwissenschaft and Kulturwissenschaft, the preacher of the "Superman" and the "Will to Power" was above all a Lebensphilosoph, that is, a philosopher who castigated the separation of both science and philosophy from life and advocated a revitalized and personalized Wissenschaft. Such a demand, however, was highly unpopular in an epoch of scientific specialization, on the one hand, and an abstract, devitalized metaphysics, on the other. It is hardly surprising, therefore, that Nietzsche during his lifetime was not taken very seriously by either scientists or philosophers.

And yet there is no doubt that Friedrich Nietzsche, though often self-contradictory and harshly dissonant in his views, was a thinker in whose sensitive mind and passionate heart all the intellectual vibrations and radiations of the age were gathered and reflected as in a focus. None of the professional philosophers of the Second Empire has, positively and negatively, exerted a comparable influence on all the branches of German

---

* Die Geburt der Tragödie aus dem Geiste der Musik (1886; the first edition had been published in 1871).

thought and culture. His heroic fight against the tremendous odds of an "atomized" society and a disintegrating civilization, his tragic isolation, and his final descent into the listless night of insanity, make him both a witness and a victim of the crisis of the age.

Philosophy was for Nietzsche "love of wisdom" in the Socratic sense, and the philosopher, if he was deserving of his title, was the friend and lover of wisdom. Possessed of the distinctive philosophic character marks of *Redlichkeit, Heiterkeit,* and *Beständigkeit* (integrity, serenity, and consistency), he was first of all called to realize in his own life the virtues of a philosophic existence, and then to shape all human conduct in the image of the true philosopher. This was to be the way of life of *Zarathustra,** the hero of his philosophico-poetic masterpiece, the symbol of Nietzsche's new man and teacher, who first withdraws into solitude to ripen to maturity in communion with nature, and to acquire moral fortitude in his intercourse with the eagle and the serpent, and then returns eventually into the world to spread the glad tidings of the new ethics of the *Übermensch.* This new "Superman," wholehearted in his will and unbroken in his spirit, is now prepared to set about the gigantic task of bringing about the "*Umwertung aller Werte*" (transvaluation of all values). He has banished mercy and compassion from his "heroic" soul, and his ethical code is the "*Wille zur Macht*" (will to power). With Nietzsche, Zarathustra fights against the *décadence* of the bourgeois society of the *fin de siècle,* against a corruption of human values which both the author and his hero blame on the emasculation wrought by the "slave morality" of Christianity, a morality which, according to Nietzsche, is born of the *ressentiment* which the weakling feels in the presence of the lordly power of the master.

To see Nietzsche's anti-Christian polemics in its true perspective it is necessary to point out that the inventor of the *Übermensch* and the advocate of the *Herrenmoral* was the son of a Lutheran pastor and a disciple of Schopenhauer. His idea of Christianity bore the impress of Luther's pessimistic view of human nature (cf. p. 219), on the one hand, and of Schopenhauer's (cf. p. 505 sq.) Buddhistically tainted Christianity, on the other. The Christianity which Nietzsche reproaches for its pure otherworldliness and its lack of moral stamina is certainly not the religion lived, preached, and instituted by Christ.

The unstinted praise which Nietzsche lavished on the "subterranean" instincts of life, and his consecration of all sorrow and suffering in the embrace of a this-worldly eternity, a cyclical perpetual recurrence of all things ("*Wiederkehr des Gleichen*") — ideas with which the poet-philosopher crowns his *Weltanschauung* — represent a desperate attempt to attain to an integrated world view on the basis of Darwinian naturalism. To bring about such a future integration of life and civilization he regarded as the supreme task and duty of the philosopher, the "physician of culture."

---

* Cf. *Also sprach Zarathustra* (1896).

It was Nietzsche's conviction that humanistic culture had utterly failed to live up to its promises and that the originally Christian impulses of Humanism not only shared in this failure but were ultimately responsible for it. To escape, however, the snares of skepticism, cynicism, and nihilism, Western man must let the dead bury their dead and look toward a future in which new values will have to be wrested from the vital forces of the earth, values which will once more determine "the measure, currency, and weight of all things."

The final phase of Nietzsche's controversy with the "spirit of the age" and with the menacing forces of darkness in his own mind was marked by an outcry for a synthesis of "Dionysos and Christ," the personification of the splendor of this life and of the glory of the life beyond, and the profoundest longing of his soul was perhaps revealed in his call for "a Caesar with the soul of Christ."

Nietzsche's message to the age of crisis was above all a great challenge: his deification of telluric forces and his simultaneous merciless dissection of the actually existing culture were signalizing the crossroads to which modern mankind had advanced. The alternative was either a wholehearted new paganism or an integral Christianity.

In 1920, the German Catholic philosopher Peter Wust (1884–1948) published a book entitled *Die Auferstehung der Metaphysik* (*The Resurrection of Metaphysics*), in which manifestly the positive and constructive elements of German idealism and of the speculative thought of Nietzsche and Scheler fused with the ancient tradition of the *Philosophia Perennis*. Wust's attempt at such a synthesis was one of several symptoms of a *rapprochement* between modern secular philosophy and that Graeco-Christian heritage of ideas which had on the whole remained unaffected by the teachings of extreme rationalism, idealism, positivism, and materialism. It seemed to Peter Wust that modern man had "cheated himself out of the ultimate reason for his existence"; that he resembled a lonely wild animal, "roving restlessly hither and thither in the desert which is Western Civilization, hideously crying out his hunger and thirst for eternity."

The neo-scholastic or neo-Thomistic revival, which found an eloquent spokesman in Wust,[*] claimed that the critical realism of the time-tested scholastic philosophy (cf. p. 141 sq.) was fully able to cope with the complexities of modern thought, and to attain to that philosophic synthesis which so far had escaped modern thinkers and modern systems. Theodor Haecker (1879–1945), a disciple and inspired translator of Søren Kierkegaard, had been led to the scholastic tradition by his study of the personality and the works of Cardinal Newman. He went so far as to state that "the highest type of the European and American intelligentsia is on its way home to the natural and supernatural truths of the *Philosophia Perennis*." And, in 1924, the German neo-Kantian philosopher Arthur Liebert, then

---

[*] Other leading German neo-Thomists are Denifle, Ehrle, Fröbes, Hertling, Baeumker, Grabmann, Pesch, Willmann, Mausbach, Geyser, Gredt, Jansen, Przywara, etc.

president of the *Kantgesellschaft,* asserted in an address, delivered at the International Philosophical Congress in Naples, that the neo-scholastic program did not call for the imitation and repetition of outworn doctrines, but was a vital philosophy, capable of facing and solving many of the problems of modern thought and modern science. He further objected to the fashionable designation of Kant and Thomas Aquinas as representatives of criticism and dogmatism, respectively, and called Thomism an indispensable complement of modern critical philosophy.

According to Martin Grabmann (1875–1948), the most prominent Thomistic theologian and philosopher of the University of Munich, scholastic and neo-scholastic philosophy "stress and make secure the natural powers of human thought; they guard the independence of philosophy in its own domain and draw a clear line of demarcation between faith and knowledge." And Grabmann is in essential agreement with all the neo-scholastics in asserting that respect for the fundamental doctrines of tradition does not preclude far-reaching adaptations to modern intellectual and scientific needs and conditions; that neo-scholasticism rejects both absolute traditionalism and absolute relativism; that exclusive traditionalism means petrifaction and death, while exclusive relativism means indifference to values and ultimately the dissolution of the very concept of being. For Erich Przywara, S.J., therefore, the essential requisite of scholastic philosophy is "to go through the world, seeking what was lost rather than hurling condemnations and execrations. The only determining factor in its attitude toward all individual philosophies must be the untiring quest for the kernel of truth they contain. . . . Its anathemas are never directed against *contents* of truth, but against the idolization of particles of truth. Accordingly, its method consists not in drawing the greatest possible number of boundary lines or in digging the deepest possible trenches, but in looking everywhere for the sheen of the all-pervading *Logos.*"

This admonition of the German Jesuit philosopher reflects the spirit of Leo XIII's encyclical *Aeterni Patris* (1879). This encyclical, signalizing an authoritative endorsement of and providing a powerful incentive for the neo-scholastic movement, bore fruit in the foundation of the *Institut Supérieur de Philosophie* of Louvain (Belgium) and similar centers of scholastic studies in various European and American countries, and found an institutional representation in Germany in the Albertus Magnus Academy of Cologne (1922).

Religious Forces and Movements. The surface phenomena of the intellectual, moral, social, and cultural unrest of the modern age had as their deepest source and cause a religious crisis which manifested itself in many and often contradictory movements, all pointing to the undeniable fact that most of the traditional spiritual and moral values of the Western World had become problematical.

In Germany, the period after 1871 witnessed both the radical affirmation of the tenets of antireligious materialism and the re-examination and eventual unconditional reassertion of religious faith and dogma. In between these mutually exclusive positions there was a broad sphere of religious liberalism, ranging from halfhearted lip service to the ideologies of the past to a feverish search for new religious dispensations and cults.

When, in 1872, David Friedrich Strauss had challenged many of his contemporaries with the categorical assertion, "We are no longer Christians,"* Alfred Dove, one of the younger historians of the Second Empire, replied with equal emphasis: "No, we are still Christians, and now more than ever we want to be Christians." It was nevertheless an incontrovertible fact that the secularization of society and culture was proceeding at a rapid pace, especially among the working classes, where the impact of industrialism had been strongest and the inroads of materialism largest.

a) German Protestantism. To halt the progress of secularization proved particularly difficult for the Protestant denominations, because they were doctrinally divided between the orthodox and liberal factions. During the early years of the regime of William II the Lutheran orthodox church, which had commanded great influence by virtue of its association with the highest Berlin court circles, was gradually forced to yield to the advancing forces of theological liberalism. This trend was signally strengthened by the appointment of the liberal Adolf von Harnack (1851–1930), a close friend of William II, to the foremost chair of Lutheran theology at the University of Berlin.

In 1892, the German Lutheran church was severely shaken by the so-called *Apostolikumstreit* (dispute concerning the Apostles' Creed), growing out of the refusal of Pastor Christoph Schrempf of Wurtemberg to use the Apostles' Creed in the administration of the sacrament of baptism. A group of students of theology of the University of Berlin drew up a petition to the *Oberkirchenrat* (supreme church council) to ask for the permanent elimination of the Apostles' Creed from the Lutheran liturgy, but they were advised by Harnack to postpone their action.

The *freireligiöse* (free religious) movement in German Protestantism gained additional strength early in the twentieth century. It was chiefly represented by Karl Jatho and Gottfried Traub, two liberal Lutheran pastors, who commanded a large following but, after severe clashes with the *Oberkirchenrat*, were suspended from office. Jatho and Traub were joined in their fight against Lutheran orthodoxy by the philosopher Arthur Drews who, in his book *Die Christusmythe* (1909), denied the historical existence of Christ, and by the brothers Ernst and August Horneffer, who were disciples of Nietzsche. In the years preceding World War I the attacks of independent Protestant groups upon institutional or "confessional" Protestantism gained such momentum that the orthodoxy seemed to be fighting a hopeless and losing battle. While in the first decade after the Franco-Prussian War the Protestant theological faculties of some of the leading

---

* Cf. *Der alte und der neue Glaube* (1872).

German universities were still dominated by orthodox theologians, the liberal theological "Left" gradually acquired more and more chairs toward the close of the century. Under the leadership of Albrecht Ritschl (1822–1889) of the University of Göttingen, Protestant dogmatic theologians devoted themselves in increasing numbers to *Religionswissenschaft* and *vergleichende Religionsgeschichte* (comparative history of religion), thus introducing the virtues and vices of "historicism" and the "scientific method" into the field of theology.

World War I and its aftermaths produced a strong reaction against theological liberalism and "historicism." While, on the one hand, German Protestantism began to take an active part in the "ecumenical movement" — working for a world-wide reunion of the separated Christian churches, and demonstrating this desire impressively at the international Church conferences of Stockholm (1925) and Lausanne (1927) — it was, on the other hand, called back to the fundamentals of Christian faith by the *Theologie der Krise* (Crisis Theology) or "dialectical theology" of a group of Swiss and German theologians, who followed the leadership of Karl Barth (1886–).[*]

The "dialectical theology" of Karl Barth and his associates was equally opposed to the secularizing tendencies of theological liberalism and to the sterile dogmatism of Lutheran and Calvinist orthodoxy. The new movement, Calvinistic in origin, wanted to endow the Christian message with the fervor and rigor of that unconditional supernaturalism which Barth claimed for the original creeds of Calvin and Luther. The Barthian theology is "Crisis Theology" because it makes man aware of the precariousness of his existence, and it is "dialectical" because it asserts to have its sole ground and *raison d'être* in that Divine Revelation which forces a human response in the form of an all-decisive "yes" or "no." While the Word of God is said to be an eternal affirmation, the word of sinful man is perpetual negation; while God is Eternal Life, man's existence is a "being unto death"; while God is all Holiness, man is all sinfulness.

Being antihumanistic and anti-idealistic, "Crisis Theology" takes issue with the representatives of German humanism and idealism, especially with Schleiermacher's (cf. p. 507 sq.) doctrine of a divine immanence in nature, and with Hegel's (cf. p. 502 sqq.) pantheism. This uncompromising attitude had been anticipated by Søren Kierkegaard (1813–1855), Barth's theological ancestor, and in that Danish thinker's lifelong two-front battle against Hegelianism, on the one hand, and against the liberal secularism of the Danish-Lutheran State Church, on the other (cf. p. 595 sq.).

From his opposition to theological liberalism and Hegelian pantheism, Kierkegaard developed a neo-Lutheran theology which declared war on all philosophy. In particular he rejected the idea of making Christianity a historically conditioned phase in the dialectical self-realization of the

---

[*] Cf. especially *Der Römerbrief* (1918) and *Christliche Dogmatik* (3 vols., 1927 sq.). Other members of the Barth group are Emil Brunner, Wilhelm Thurneysen, and Friedrich Gogarten.

Weltgeist. To him the appearance of Christ and of Christianity signified a unique event of absolute and incomparable value and validity, an event which imposed upon a disciple the fearful responsibility of "becoming a Christian," that is, a follower of Christ. In denouncing "historicism," he was denouncing the finite as against the infinite, the service of time as against the service of eternity.

What then, in Kierkegaard's view, was the position of Christianity in the world and in his own age? "Christianity," he insisted, "is a reality, but Christendom is nothing but an optical illusion." And to his *Journals* he entrusted this reflection: "There must be another reformation, and this time it will be a horrible reformation. Compared with this coming reformation that of Luther will appear as a mere jest. Its battle-cry will clamor for the remnants of faith on earth. And we shall witness millions becoming apostates: truly a fearful reformation. We shall recognize that Christianity is practically non-existent, and it will be a horrible sight to behold this generation, pampered and lulled to sleep by a childishly deformed Christianity — to see this generation wounded once again by the thought of what it means to become a Christian, to be a Christian."

Kierkegaard thus had become the prototype of an "existential" thinker, that is, one who attains to absolute clarity as to where in human life he as an individual experiences the fullest depth of reality, and who expresses this experience in his life and in his work. And it is this same "existential" consistency which is harshly reaffirmed in Karl Barth's "Crisis Theology," which wants to be strictly a *Theologia Crucis,* upholding both Luther's metaphysical dualism between the finite and the infinite and Calvin's Divine Absolutism, which condemns and elects by eternal decree, regardless of human effort or merit. Here, too, is found the radical break with the humanist-idealist doctrine of a divine immanence in the world and in man, on the one hand, and with the Thomistic doctrine of God's ontological indwelling in His creation *"per essentiam,"* on the other.

Karl Barth — before he was deprived by the National Socialist regime of his chair at the University of Bonn, and expelled from Germany in 1934 — had had a large following among German youth. After resuming the teaching of theology at the University of Basel, he continued to watch with deep concern from the vantage point of his native Switzerland the life-and-death struggle of Christian Germany against its "ungodly rulers," trying at the same time to arouse the consciences of Christian men and women in Europe and the Americas to a realization of the acute crisis of contemporary Christendom.

For a long time Barth's doctrines and efforts had not been taken very seriously by both the leading orthodox and liberal German church groups: the Lutheran orthodoxy in the North and Northeast; the "United Church," consisting of the joint Lutheran and Calvinist denominations in central and southern Germany; and the liberal theologians, who had their chief spokesmen in the theological faculty of the University of Marburg. All these theological camps were under attack by the Barthians, because in none of them was theology any longer a living spiritual force molding the thoughts and lives of the people.

It is, however, the never explained paradox of Barthian theology that it advocates a moral and cultural reformation, although its premises of an absolute divine transcendence and a metaphysically evil world, seen exclusively *sub ratione peccati* (under the aspect of sinful corruption) seem to leave no room for cultural activities of moral or spiritual value. From the outset, therefore, it had been clear to Barth's Protestant and Catholic critics that his *Credo* had so overstated the "negative theology" of certain neo-Platonically inclined Christian mystics that the divine First Cause necessarily crushed completely the culturally and morally significant activities of all secondary causes and agents. The order of grace effaced the order of nature, precluding the possibility of a "natural theology" or theodicy, and thus destroying the contiguous relationship of nature and supernature as seen by Catholic theology and Thomistic philosophy. According to the latter, "grace does not efface nature, but rather supports it and leads it to perfection" (*gratia supponit et perficit naturam*). If Barth's theological and metaphysical premises were accepted *in toto,* Christian dogmatics would be turned into a doctrinal body of incomprehensible paradoxes, and Christian faith could save itself only by a *Sprung* (leap) into a *"credo quia absurdum."*

Yet even though the "Theology of Crisis" became involved in some insoluble contradictions (as illustrated, for example, by the controversy between Karl Barth and Emil Brunner, the latter pleading for the elaboration of a "natural theology"), it had without any doubt served to rarefy and clarify the religious atmosphere in German Protestantism. The integral supranaturalism of Barth was soon to collide head on with the equally uncompromising religious naturalism of the *Deutsche Glaubensbewegung* (German Faith Movement) and the Germanized Christianity of the *Deutsche Christen.* While the neo-paganism of the former asserted that Germanism and Christianity were mutually exclusive and went so far as to call Christianity "the religious Versailles of the Germans," the latter, less consistent, wanted to retain a racially "purified" Christianity and eventually proclaimed the identity of the "Third Reich" with the kingdom of God on earth ("one People, one State, one Church, one *Führer*"). In 1934, the Protestant literary critic Karl Kindt, writing in the periodical *Die neue Literatur,* ventured the opinion that God had created Karl Barth and the *Deutsche Christen* to demonstrate "that the one and indivisible truth cannot be taken apart without the most disastrous effects."

It was realistically acknowledged in the opposing camps that an unbridgeable abyss separated the Kierkegaard-Barth position from that of the "German Christians" and the "German Faith Movement." The leaders admitted that it was useless to call for peace where there is no peace and where there cannot be peace. They thus subscribed to Kierkegaard's "either —or." However, in between these extreme positions, the "United Lutherans," including several Calvinistic groups, closed their ranks and re-examined their basic beliefs. In the midst of the religious turmoil that followed the National Socialist revolution they looked for a theological *via media:* on the one hand, they declared their willingness to co-operate, to an extent delimited by the exactions of their Christian conscience, with the totalitarian State and, on the other, they opposed vigorously any *Gleichschaltung* of State and Church. Under the leadership of such men as Martin Niemöller they founded the *Pfarrernotbund* (pastors' emergency league) and organized the *Bekenntniskirche* (Professing Church), and were prepared to suffer persecution, torture, and death for their religious convictions. "The assertion," they declared defiantly, "that the voice of the nation is the Word of God is blasphemy. . . . It is the mission of the Church to educate men for the Kingdom of Christ, not for the German *Reich*. A Church which serves two masters is untrustworthy in every word it preaches. . . . Earthly, material values must not be placed above eternal values. The true meaning of the Gospel must not be interpreted in such a way as to make it pleasing and acceptable to the desires of men. We call heresy the assertion that Christ is the prototype of Nordic Man. We call heresy the Germanization of Christianity. The Christian Church does not and cannot distinguish between baptized Jews and baptized Gentiles. . . . We solemnly deny the State the right to govern the Church, to appoint or depose ministers or to meddle with questions of Church doctrine. Today, the very foundations of Christianity are shaken by error and confusion. This is the time of the great temptation."

Such quotations, to which many more of a similar tenor might be added, illustrate the type of crisis through which German Protestantism is passing, a crisis whose outcome will perhaps decide the future of Protestantism the world over. It is Karl Barth's conviction that the Christian Church must once again cast its lot with the Christian martyrs of the catacombs. He believes that not since medieval times have Christians in every part of the globe faced a situation of more monumental simplicity: a situation which poses questions of such unequivocal clarity that the answers should be easy and self-evident.

b) German Catholicism. In a compendium entitled *Deutschland unter Wilhelm II,* which appeared shortly before the outbreak of World War I and surveyed the several aspects of German civilization under the Second Empire, it was stated by a Roman Catholic contributor: "If anyone has good reason to be grateful to His Majesty, it is the Catholic Church, which has abundantly enjoyed the good graces of the Imperial Sovereign and has been permitted to co-operate in the accomplishment of great national tasks." Notwithstanding the essential correctness of this optimistic estimate, the Catholic Church in Germany underwent several minor crises, some of which, e.g., the *Kulturkampf* (cf. p. 611 sq.), affected German Catholics directly and exclusively, while others reflected more universal religious problems and situations.

Out of the opposition of some groups of German Catholics to the Vatican Council's (1869–1870) definition of Papal Infallibility grew the schismatic movement of *Altkatholizismus* (Old Catholicism) which, though it looked at first rather menacing, remained without serious consequences.

The "Old Catholics" claimed to stand firmly on the principles of the undivided universal Church of the first Christian millennium; they re-affirmed the dogmas of the Trinity, the divinity of Christ, and the absolute authenticity of scriptural Revelation, but rejected the authoritative nature of ecclesiastic "tradition," the dogma of the Immaculate Conception, the primacy of the Roman pontiff, and the infallibility of the pope in *ex cathedra* pronouncements on matters of faith and morals. In addition, they leaned toward the Lutheran interpretation of Mass and Eucharist and demanded the use of the vernacular in the liturgical services. Finally, they denied the obligatory character of priestly celibacy and of the reception of the sacraments; permitted cremation; and refused to accept the Roman Catholic teachings on indulgences, the veneration of saints and images, processions, pilgrimages, sacramentals. The "Old Catholic" constitution provided for independent national churches headed by an episcopate which shared its administrative powers with a synodal council composed of clergy and laity. The movement spread from Germany to some other countries, especially to Austria, Switzerland, Poland, and North America. In 1877, the *Altkatholiken* were represented in Germany by 120 parishes with a membership of 53,640. Old Catholicism was officially recognized and financially supported by the states of Prussia, Baden, and Hessen and was favored by special legislation during the years of the *Kulturkampf*.

About the turn of the century a philosophico-theological movement known as "modernism," which had its origins in France, Italy, and England, began to exert a profound influence on a number of leading German Cath-olic theologians and laymen. Partly for apologetic reasons the "modernists" tried to adapt religious doctrine and practice to modern scientific theories and to the social and cultural conditions of the age. In its German form *Modernismus* combined the *Gefühlstheologie* (the subjective-emotional theology) of Schleiermacher (cf. p. 507 sq.) with biblical criticism and a Darwinian interpretation of the history of dogma and religion. The leaders of the movement (Döllinger, Merkle, Loisy, Tyrrell, etc.) defined religious dogma as a purely symbolic expression of religious truths, to be constantly readjusted to the changing aspects of cultural evolution. Sacraments were explained as fixations of the natural urges of man for a sensuous representa-tion and practice of religious doctrine, and the Church was said to owe its origin to the natural urge of human beings for spiritual intercourse and religious communion. Faith and knowledge were declared as not only completely autonomous in themselves, but as intrinsically contradicting each other.

Pope Pius X, in his encyclical *Pascendi* (1907), designated Modernism as "the sum total of all heresies." The condemnation of the modernist teachings and the censuring and indexing of the writings of several modernist theologians and philosophers was followed by a special papal decree (*Motuproprio Sacrorum antistitum*) of 1910, which demanded of all clerical teachers in Catholic seminaries, schools, and universities, as well as of all pastors and other church officials, the solemn renunciation of all those views that had been singled out as heretical in the encyclical of 1907 (*Antimodernisteneid*). This rigorous measure definitively sealed the fate of the modernist movement.

As a result of the modernist controversy there prevailed for some time an unfortunate tendency among the most conservative groups of German Catholics to denounce as *modernistisch* authors and books which were merely unconventional or marked by originality of thought. This tendency is well illustrated by the so-called *Literaturstreit* (dispute on literature) which followed the publication of Carl Muth's (1867–1944) critical appraisal of Catholic *belles lettres* at the turn of the century.* The future editor of *Hochland,* which was to become one of the leading periodicals of the German Catholic intelligentsia, had asked whether Catholic literature was on a par with the literary production of non-Catholic authors, and had answered in the negative. He had criticized the largely apologetic or purely didactic and moralizing nature of Catholic *belles lettres* and had exhorted Catholic writers to "come out of the ghetto" and face courageously and positively the complex intellectual, moral, and social problems of the modern age.

The attitude of defensive apologetics, which had to a greater or lesser extent prevailed from the time of the Reformation on, had led to a literary isolationism and provincialism which were unwilling and unable to enter into competition and a fruitful exchange of ideas with non-Catholic literary groups and movements. Catholic literature and literary criticism thus were often lacking in vitality and seriousness of effort, and the tendency prevailed to judge literary works by their good intentions and sincere religious devotion rather than by standards of artistic excellence. Many of the works of Catholic authors were "Catholic" only in a narrow and feeble sense and without that breadth and depth which derive from a truly universal view of reality and which are forever exemplified in Dante's immortal poem.

In the face of violent attacks and cries of *"Modernismus,"* Carl Muth carried on the good fight and finally won out. It is in a considerable degree due to this lonely and undaunted *Kulturkämpfer* that Germany possesses today a Catholic literature of high rank, and that German Catholicism, stepping forth from its "ghetto," has become one of the most positive and creative forces in contemporary civilization.

Favored by the political and social constellations of the period following World War I — especially by the increasing influence of the Center party in national and international affairs and by the high quality and exemplary organization of the Catholic daily press — German Catholicism greatly

---

* Cf. Carl Muth, *Steht die katholische Belletristik auf der Höhe der Zeit?* (1898).

increased its material and spiritual assets. Its leading part in the *Catholic Action* movement and in the realization of the tasks of the "lay apostolate," as outlined in several papal encyclicals, was specially commended by Pope Pius XI.*

The freedom of action which the Catholic Church enjoyed under the Weimar Republic made possible the creation of new archbishoprics, bishoprics, and abbeys, and the foundation or reclamation of monastic settlements, many of which had been expropriated and secularized early in the nineteenth century (cf. p. 325).** All of these gains, however, were wiped out by the persecution of the Church which followed the revolution of 1933.

One of the fruits of the "monastic spring" of the early years of the Weimar Republic was the growth of the Catholic *liturgical movement.* Though international in character, it assumed in Germany the dimensions of a popular religious revival under the leadership of the Benedictine abbeys of Maria Laach in the Rhineland and Beuron in the valley of the upper Danube. Without ever leaning on any formal organization, the liturgical movement gradually penetrated into ever widening circles of clergy and laity, gaining a particularly strong foothold among the various Catholic youth groups. Officially sanctioned and encouraged by Pius XI's Constitution *Divini cultus sanctitatem* of 1928, it aimed at a deeper understanding of the liturgy of the Church as the center and cultic expression of Christian faith and life. Translations of liturgical texts and explanations of the liturgical rites, the study of the history of the liturgy, and the fostering of liturgical architecture and the allied arts of painting and music were to instill the liturgical spirit (the *"sentire cum Ecclesia"*) in individual devotion and community service and thus to make the liturgy a living reality in the daily lives of the people.

c) Religious Fermentation. Aside from those religious forces which carried some of the spiritual unrest of the age of crisis into the established churches, there were others, either opposed to institutional religion altogether or attempting to clothe religious ideas in new cults and rituals. While the members of these movements were united in their protest against the "soulless" materialism of modern civilization, they disagreed as to the means to be adopted to combat and overcome the materialistic trend.

The longing for new "absolutes" and for a faith which could unify the *Weltanschauung* of modern man was as articulate in the antirational creeds of religious cranks and enthusiasts as in the circles of serious, God-seeking intellectuals. According to the neo-Kantian philosopher Arthur Liebert, "all our being and all our possessions must of necessity be shattered, unless we have some norms and standards with which to reorient our existence toward a supratemporal and supernatural value." The turning away from

---

* Cf. Leo XIII, *Sancta Dei Civitas* (1880) and *Sapientia Christianae* (1890); Pius X, *Acerbo nimis* (1905); Benedict XV, *Maximum illud* (1919); and Pius XI, *Ubi arcano* (1922).

** Between 1918 and 1933, 1337 new religious settlements (orders and congregations) were established in Germany.

positivism becomes therefore "a moral commandment." Religion alone "can resolve the tensions and antinomies of human life. The problem of religion, therefore, has become the *Schicksalsfrage* (all-decisive question) of our time." This view was shared by all those educators, artists, and writers who called for a moral regeneration on the basis of a religious renascence.

A religious renovation was also advocated by several groups of religious socialists and pacifists, pleading for a human society united by the bond of an "undogmatic" faith. While the sincerity of religious socialism cannot be doubted, its program was too vague and its reasoning too loose to be persuasive beyond the numerically small circles of its immediate adherents.

Similar limitations of an intellectual and moral nature attached to the proselytizing efforts of those who sought the solution of the riddles of life in the revised and revamped teachings of occultism and spiritism. Nevertheless, the feeling of religious homelessness and insecurity, intensified by the experiences of war and revolution, made such doctrines and cults attractive to many who were looking for a religious haven, but were unwilling to accept any of the traditional creeds.

In the seventies and eighties of the nineteenth-century serious-minded scholars, such as Gustav Fechner (cf. p. 566), Friedrich Zöllner, and Baron Karl Du Prel, strongly defended the authenticity of spiritistic and mediumistic phenomena. In the nineties the occultistic movement derived encouragement from the publication of Karl Kiesewetter's *History of Modern Occultism*. After the turn of the century the Munich physician, Baron von Schrenck-Notzing, and the philosopher Konstantin Österreich aroused new scientific interest in the problems of "mediumism," spiritistic "materializations," and the general phenomena of "parapsychology" by their critical-experimental investigations.

The preoccupation of German nineteenth-century scholars with the literature, philosophy, and religion of India brought in its wake a popularization of Buddhistic and theosophical doctrines and practices. A derivative of East Indian and American theosophy was Rudolf Steiner's (1861–1925) "anthroposophy," a mystico-theosophical system, which in the years following World War I attracted tens of thousands of enthusiastic adepts in Germany and Switzerland and which to this day commands the unfaltering allegiance of groups of disciples in Europe and North America.

Rudolf Steiner, a native of Croatia, of Catholic parentage, had become known as an interpreter of the philosophic ideas of Goethe and Nietzsche when, in his endeavor to trace the evolution of the human spirit, he availed himself of the principles elaborated in Goethe's *Metamorphosis of Plants* and established on this basis a gnostico-theosophical anthropology. In 1902, he was appointed general secretary of the German section of the Theosophical Society at Adyar (India) but, after some doctrinal quarrels with Annie Besant, he seceded from that organization and made himself the independent leader of the German Anthroposophical Society (1913). An artist by avocation, Steiner drew the blueprints for the weird structure of the *Goetheanum,* the Anthroposophic Temple at Dornach near the Swiss city of Basel, a work in whose completion anthroposophic architects, sculptors, and painters co-operated. The *Goetheanum,* dedicated to the memory of Goethe, was to be a *freie Hochschule für Geisteswissenschaft,* a "free university" serving the cultivation of "art, letters, medicine, and the natural sciences."

Steiner's "anthroposophy" (the perfect knowledge concerning man) is a synchretistic system of thought, borrowing ideas from Buddhistic, Christian, gnostic, Manichaean, and theosophical sources. Its *"Geisteswissenschaft"* requires a methodical esoteric training which proceeds by way of the successive stages of "preparation, illumination, and initiation," from "imagination to inspiration and intuition," to culminate in the perfectly adequate understanding of human and cosmic nature. In the "temple" of this highest knowledge man is said to learn the truth about the eternal laws of life and about the divine essence of his own being. The evolutionary phases of the human "microcosm" run parallel with the evolution of the "macrocosm" (the world cosmos). This dual evolution is pushed forward periodically by inspired religious leaders, the greatest of whom is the *"Sonnenwesen Christus"* (Christ, the "sun principle"). The individual human being advances through a series of purgative incarnations which in turn are determined by the law of *Karma* (the accumulative sum total of man's moral acts). The entire system is anchored in a blind faith in the spiritual authority of the inspired "leader" and thus tends to withdraw its basic tenets from the scrutiny of critical examination on the part of the disciple.

The amazing temporary success of Steiner's anthroposophy, constituting one of the startling paradoxes of the age of science and technology, justifies an attention which is hardly warranted by its intellectual and religious content. During the hectic years of the postwar period the followers of Rudolf Steiner filled the largest lecture halls in such cities as Munich, Stuttgart, and Basel. Protestant theologians, philosophers, men of letters, artists, scientists, representatives of industry and commerce were gathering in large numbers around this strange and impressive figure, all eager to be handed some infallible recipes for the ardently desired regeneration of modern society. Those who were privileged to witness the manifestations of the anthroposophic movement as critical observers could discover a psychological pattern which was duplicated several years later when another "leader," whose birthplace was located in close proximity to that of Steiner, appeared on the German scene, to turn the aspirations of the masses from the "astral spheres" to the more tangible realities of "blood and soil."

d) "Jugendbewegung" (Youth Movement). Also of a vaguely religious nature was that spontaneous revolutionary movement about the turn of the century with which part of the younger generation in Germany registered their protest against an industrialized and mechanized civilization centered in big cities, and against "conventional lies" of modern bourgeois society.

The German *Jugendbewegung* grew out of a Rousseauan "back to nature" longing, a call for simplicity, truthfulness, consistency in thought and deed, and genuine *Gemeinschaft* (social and communal spirit), as against the sophistication, artificiality, halfheartedness, and selfishness of the liberal-capitalist era. A romantic yearning of youth for a natural and even primitive life in forest and field led at the beginning of the twentieth century to the formation of the first *Wandervogel* (birds of passage) groups. The members pledged abstinence from alcohol and tobacco and dedicated themselves to a self-imposed discipline and to the cultivation of the values of German *Volkstum* ("folkish" values and habits). In the revival of folk songs, folk dances, and folk music, in the nomadic roaming across the country-side, and in the devotion to the ideals of true *Kameradschaft* German youth expressed its desire for a thorough emancipation from the conventions and the external discipline of home and school.

In 1913, the *Freideutsche Jugend* (Free German Youth), composed of thirteen of the youth groups, met on the *Hohe Meissner* in the Hessian mountains to celebrate the centenary of the Wars of Liberation (cf. p. 446 sqq.) and to proclaim the "autonomy" of German youth. Emphasizing the nonpolitical nature of their movement, the famous *Meissner Resolution* formulated the ideals of the groups represented, stating that the *Freideutsche Jugend* proposed to shape the lives of its members in accordance with the demands of "self-determination, personal responsibility, and inner truth-fulness." The values of human personality were thus strongly endorsed and the subjection of man to the dehumanizing influence of a materialistic society severely condemned. All forms and rules of life were acknowledged as binding only if they grew out of the real substance of human nature and expressed man's deepest individual and social aspirations.

World War I not only disrupted the normal evolution of the German Youth Movement, but thoroughly changed it in many of its aspects. While, on the one hand, the movement gained in passionate self-assertion and con-crete elaboration of some of its aims — with the establishment of "free" schools, *Jugendburgen* (youth castles), *Jugendherbergen* (youth hostels), *Volksbildungsheime* (educational centers), *Werkwochen* (weeks devoted to work, intellectual intercourse, and recreation), *Bücherstuben* (reading centers), — it fell a prey, on the other hand, to multiplying factional divisions of a political and sectarian nature, and was finally absorbed by the ideologies of warring political parties. The Catholic youth movement, whose spiritual growth had proceeded in intimate contact with the liturgical movement (cf. p. 706), was unified in 1915 in the *Grossdeutsche Jugend* and a few affiliated groups, composed largely of students of secondary schools and universities. After the National Socialist revolution the entire youth movement was *"gleichgeschaltet"* in the Hitler Youth, and its ideal impulses were shrewdly harnessed to the pseudo religion of the totalitarian State.

The balance sheet of the German Youth Movement shows on the positive side the wholesome effects of a return to simpler tastes and more natural modes of life as well as many of the benefits derived from a keen sense for the many weaknesses and inconsistencies of contemporary civilization. On the negative side it shows the unhealthy consequences of an exaggerated and uncritical esteem for the limited values of adolescence, of an unjustifiable conceit, and of a tendency toward libertinism and extreme subjectivism.

Art, Literature, and Music. The pictorial, plastic, literary, and musical arts of the late nineteenth and early twentieth century mirror the intellectual, moral, social, and religious forces which animate and agitate the age of crisis. Germany shows herself quite as capable as in the past of adding her own creative impulses to those foreign elements which she transforms and nationalizes in the process of adaptation. And, as so often in the past, she occasionally assumes a position of cultural leadership, providing inspiration for the artists, writers, and composers of other lands.

a) Architecture. As Gottfried Semper (cf. p. 573) had predicted in 1854, the principles of a new architectural style were derived from the applied arts and crafts. The eclecticism which prevailed in the seventies of the nineteenth century, and which was marked by the unimaginative repetition of historically dated styles (neo-gothic, neo-renaissance, neo-baroque), gradually gave way to a desire for new and original architectural forms which were to embody the spirit of the modern age. The fulfillment of this desire was first realized in the decorative arts, where an antihistorical and "purist" movement arose in opposition to the borrowed pomp and colossal sham of the buildings and monuments of the *Gründerzeit* and the early decades of the "Wilhelminian" era. This blustering architecture had completely obscured the inner relationship between form and function, and its stucco façades with their extravagant ornamental trimmings had paid no heed to organic structure and artistic decorum.

The new movement in German architecture was indebted to the art theories of the romantic British reform-socialists John Ruskin (1819–1900) and William Morris (1834–1896). Both strove to save the integrity of the artisan and the craftsman from the disastrous effects of the mass-production methods of the machine age. While in their nostalgic "pre-Raphaelite" attachment to medieval art forms they were still history-minded, they conceived of the artistic process not so much in terms of imitation as of original re-creation. And their efforts found an enthusiastic response among German artists and art theorists. At the turn of the century, some of their ideas took shape in the German *Jugendstil,** a decorative style which espoused simplicity of artistic design, but soon violated its own principles by a languid and overly ornate lineament.

While the eccentricities of the *Jugendstil* were soon forgotten, its insistence on simplicity, modernity, and *Materialgerechtheit* (purity and right use of building materials) were to become important ingredients of contemporary German "functional" architecture. The German architects, aware of the tectonic and aesthetic possibilities of the new building materials: iron, steel,

---

* The *Jugendstil* owes its name to the linear technique which was the most characteristic element in Otto Eckmann's (1865–1902) contributions to the German art magazine, *Jugend.*

reinforced concrete, and glass, succeeded in creating an artistic idiom for the revolutionary changes in science, industry, and economy, and at the same time provided an adequate answer to the social needs of the industrial age. The style of the *Neue Sachlichkeit* (new objectivity), reflecting the growing depersonalization and collectivization of modern life, utilized to great advantage the new devices of engineering and the mechanical sciences to achieve a new monumentality in architectural design, while simultaneously contributing to the improvement of living and housing conditions in the crowded areas of the big cities.

The development of the functional style in German architecture proceeded in several phases, each of them associated with the names of some of the leading architects. One of its earliest and most impressive examples was Alfred Messel's (1853–1909) Wertheim department store in Berlin, completed in 1904. It was modern in its huge steel frame of blocklike appearance, but traditional in the neo-gothic design of the surface ornament. Regional elements and the interrelation of architecture and landscape received strong emphasis in the buildings of Hermann Muthesius (1861–1927) and Ludwig Hoffmann (1852–1931). Meanwhile Heinrich Tessenow (1876–) and especially Peter Behrens (1868–1940) achieved an impressive simplicity by means of a strictly abstract-geometrical design, devoid of any kind of ornamentation. Behrens' building for the *AEG* (General Electric Company) in Berlin offered a striking example of a purely rational and functional architectonic structure of cubes and planes. It thus became a kind of paradigm of that international style which owes its characteristic features to the genius of the engineer and in which the form of the building depends entirely on the intrinsic dynamics of the materials of construction: steel, glass, and concrete. The chief German representative of this style came to be Walter Gropius (1883–), whose *Bauhaus* at Dessau was completed in 1926, to serve as an experimental workshop for the development of architecture and interior decoration. The replacement of the massive walls by huge sheets of glass permits illumination of the interior from all sides and thereby gives expression to a new concept of "publicity" which, as it progressively invades even the privacy of the home, symbolically illustrates the dwindling importance of private and personal life.

The development of German secular architecture was paralleled in its main aspects by ecclesiastic buildings. The church architects of the early twentieth century tried to replace the retrospective and imitative historical architectural experiments of the nineteenth century by new modes of construction, taking advantage of the new building methods and materials. They were anxious to embody the timeless Christian content in new forms. Thus the many recent *Catholic* church buildings in Germany are indicative of the attempt to adapt ground plan and interior to the spiritual incentives of the liturgical and Catholic Action movements (cf. p. 706): the place of the liturgical sacrifice is conceived as a broad unit centered in the high altar, and

integrated by a greatly enlarged choir space. As was the case in the early Christian basilica (cf. p. 54), the hall-like character of the interior emphasizes the communal unity of the congregation. Decorative adornments are reduced to a minimum and always subordinated to the simple and massive proportions of the total spatial order. The trend toward simplicity and spatial unity is usually even more pronounced in the new *Protestant* church buildings, where it found strong support in ecclesiastical tradition.*

b) Painting and Sculpture. In architecture both the collective tendencies and the technical genius of the industrial age could express themselves most convincingly. Whenever the other arts tried to become in a similar manner carriers of the scientific-technical spirit, they fell short of their goal because of the inadequacy of their means and methods. In painting and sculpture no less than in the literary arts the late nineteenth and early twentieth century was a period of "movements" and abstract theories rather than of creative ingenuity and great individual artists and writers. And these movements, following each other more and more rapidly, were in themselves symptoms of the intellectual, moral, and emotional instability of their protagonists, of their frantic search for new methods, new techniques, new sensations. Their craving for originality at any price and their endless theorizing often made them oblivious to any rule and norm aside from those imposed by the fixed ideas of their own inflated ego. As a result, the movements which they sponsored remained mostly unintelligible to the majority of their contemporaries, and their sponsors were thus hampered in the communication of an intended message or a professed creed.

There were, however, notable exceptions, especially in the earlier and less radical phase of the development toward modernism. Wherever the *Gehirnkunst* (brain art) engendered by the *Zeitgeist* had not led to the atrophy of heart and soul, romanticism still proved a potent force. Hans Thoma (1839–1924), for example, a son of the Black Forest and its healthy peasant culture, remained in his poetic and romantic realism always close to the thinking and feeling of the common people. His south German and Italian landscapes, his genre paintings and his still lifes continued the romantic tradition of Schwind, Richter, and Böcklin (cf. p. 578 sq.), but were modern in their freedom from any academic canon, in their vivacity and realistic observation. As director of the art gallery of Karlsruhe (Baden) Thoma encouraged the development of a genuine *Heimatkunst* (regional art), while keeping an open mind with regard to modern trends.

Another heir of German romanticism was Max Klinger (1857–1920), who at one time was widely acclaimed as the most popular master of the *fin de siècle,* but whose limitations as a painter and sculptor are today generally

---

* Outstanding contemporary *Catholic* German church architects: Hans Herkomer, Dominikus Böhm, Ludwig Ruff, C. Holzmeister, T. Burlage. *Protestant* architects: G. Bestelmeyer, F. Höger, Otto Bartning. The Catholic painter Willy Oeser, in his monumental religious wall paintings, mosaics, and altarpieces, has succeeded in creating an artistic style which eminently fits the austerity of this architecture.

Church in Bischofsheim Near Mainz. Dominikus Böhm, Architect.

The Shell House in Berlin.

admitted. His works, burdened with too many literary allusions, are peculiarly German in their mixture of romantic-symbolist and naturalistic-descriptive elements. With Richard Wagner he shared the desire to transcend the boundaries of any particular art form and to make all the arts fuse in a *Gesamtkunstwerk* (cf. p. 495). As most of Klinger's works lack that formal perfection to which he obviously aspired, it is hardly surprising that he made his most valuable contributions to modern German art in his brilliant graphic sketches, where he could give free reign to his often riotous imagination and to his predilection for fantastic and symbolic-mystical themes. It is in these sketches that he developed a chiaroscuro technique and a nervously dynamic lineament which pointed forward to the pictorial styles of impressionism and expressionism. This new technique appears at its best in Klinger's dramatic graphic narratives and in his *Brahms Phantasies*.

The antihistorical and antimetaphysical trends of the late nineteenth century found their artistic expression in *naturalism* and *impressionism*. Under the dominant influence of the natural sciences the German artists, following the French example, turned against the traditional academic rules and against the romantic-idealistic thought content of the art of the earlier nineteenth century. Their "back to nature" movement was no longer concerned with ideas, but with "facts" and "things." While for the naturalists these "things" themselves were still of primary importance, the impressionists stripped even the "thing" of its substantiality, retaining only the optical surface appearance, the sensed values of light, shade, and color, their composition and ever changing variations and combinations.

Reviving the eighteenth-century "sensism" of David Hume, the German physicist and philosopher Ernst Mach (1838–1916) provided the speculative basis for an impressionistic epistemology by reducing all reality to a "bundle" of sense perceptions. The world of objects thus became an aggregate of the restless flux and flow of sensations and "impressions," and art became the ability to reproduce these sensed data. Impressionism thus applied to art the principle of positivist philosophy (cf. p. 594 sq.).

Both naturalism and impressionism were antihistorical, antimetaphysical, and antiacademic; both were opposed to any allegorical or symbolic or even philosophical interpretation of reality, simply because both regarded ideas as fictions and phantasms and therefore as meaningless. But whereas naturalism was animated by a revolutionary social fervor — an attitude which accounts for its sympathy with the poor, its criticism of social conditions and institutions, and its characteristic *Armeleutemalerei* (the portrayal of social misery) — impressionism, aside from its vehemently defended aesthetic creed, had no thesis to advance, no cause to sponsor, no ideas to represent. Thus it was as much beyond love, hatred, and passion as "beyond good and evil." Its interest in life was purely *sachlich* (objective), and its art accordingly was "art for art's sake" in the narrowest sense. But it was precisely this exclusive preoccupation with strictly technical-artistic problems that enabled the impressionist to make important discoveries in the limited sphere of sense perception and to depict in his "plain air paintings" of light and color those finest and most delicate nuances which had been beyond the reach of the traditional studio painters.

Naturalistic subject matter and impressionistic technique often fuse in the paintings of Max Liebermann (1847–1935) and Fritz von Uhde (1848–1911). Liebermann, a native of Berlin, shows in the realistic technique and subject matter of his earlier works close kinship with French and Dutch naturalism and realism. Starting out with the portrayal of groups in a setting of semidark interiors, he gradually develops a distinctly personal style of impressionistic landscape painting. The human and social elements in his early canvasses disappear more and more in his cool and factual pictorial renditions of figural and scenic observations, representing chance perceptions without any prearranged structural design. The human person is dissolved in the functional objective relations of luminous planes and in the vibrations of a fluid atmosphere.

While Liebermann was determined in the choice and treatment of his subject matter by the moral indifferentism of a Jewish-liberal *milieu*, Fritz von Uhde, an army officer and the son of a high Protestant church official, made his impressionistic style subservient to a religious and social thesis. His portrayal of Christ as the friend and companion of the socially disinherited scandalized the Protestant orthodoxy, but was acclaimed by socialists and freethinkers. His attempted "socialization" of Christianity was at the same time a rejection of the hieratic idealism of ecclesiastical art. His paintings introduced the Gospel message in a missionary spirit into the simple social relationships of everyday life.

The humanitarian and social thesis was even stronger, although dissociated from the religious component, in the graphic works of Käthe Kollwitz (1867–1946). A member of the socialist party and animated by a deep sympathy with proletarian misery, this woman dedicated her great artistic talent to the single task of a passionate indictment of social injustice. In some of her etchings, as for example in the dramatic scenes depicting the uprising of the Silesian weavers (a theme suggested by Gerhart Hauptmann's drama, cf. p. 732), Käthe Kollwitz rose above any partisan creed to a timeless symbolization of human suffering.

Impressionism in the strict sense, which had celebrated its greatest triumphs in France, the land of its origin, was represented in Germany, aside from Liebermann, by Lovis Corinth (1858–1925) and Max Slevogt (1868–1931). Corinth followed the French impressionists in the dissolution of the tectonic pictorial form and in the depersonalization of the human model. Like Peter Paul Rubens he showed himself enamored of lustrous human flesh, depicting the human nude in endless variations of pose and posture. But while he shared with Rubens the virility of the brush stroke and the ability to vivify his canvasses with the sensuous splendors and the brutal vitality of nature, he lacked the Flemish master's artistic culture and aristocratic restraint. Thus Corinth's religious paintings, unlike those of Rubens, were religious only in name: his interest remained centered in problems of technical dexterity and unrelated to the spiritual significance of his subject matter.

The talent of the Bavarian-born Max Slevogt asserted itself most vigorously in the impromptu creation of brilliant and refreshing coloristic compositions and in the art of book illustration. A master of chiaroscuro, he succeeded in achieving a maximum of expressiveness with a minimum of characteristic line drawing, thus confirming Liebermann's saying that *"zeichnen ist die Kunst, wegzulassen"* (drawing is the art of omission), that is, skill in selecting the essential and omitting the accidental. In 1902, the second year of his stay in Berlin, Slevogt created one of the great masterpieces of German impressionism, the dazzling painting entitled *The White Andrade,* in which he portrayed the famous Portuguese singer in the title role of Mozart's *Don Giovanni.* In its graceful elegance, in the sparkle of golden and silken hues, and in its flashy stage setting, the dramatic-musical quality of Slevogt's art appears at its very best.

The end phase of both French and German impressionism was characterized by an attempt to restore to painting a solid structural form and composition. It was the genius of the great French "post-impressionists" Cézanne and Gauguin and of the Dutch painter van Gogh that finally led the way in the abandonment of the flat impressionistic surface patterns and in the reconquest of a well-defined three-dimensional space. But this newly conquered space no longer obeyed the optical requirements of linear perspective: it was an impressionistically conceived space, constructed by means of functionally interrelated and receding color planes. However, it was the ecstatic-visionary, thoroughly individualistic, and essentially Germanic art of van Gogh rather than the constructivist formalism of Cézanne and Gauguin that was destined to become the greatest inspiration of German *expressionism.*

In its loud and vehement self-assertion, its emphasis on inner experience, and its abstract form-language, the expressionistic movement was typically German or, more precisely, North German. With few exceptions its chief representatives were *Obersachsen.** Although German expressionism claimed to be, and in many respects actually was, the antithesis of impressionism, it remained indebted to the technical innovations of the impressionists. But whereas both naturalists and impressionists had extolled external nature at the expense of mind and ideas, the expressionists idolized mind and contemned nature. To manifest his intellectual sovereignty over the objective external world, the expressionist not only distorted the natural object and arbitrarily destroyed its formal beauty, but he arrived finally at purely abstract patterns. He composed "symphonic" arrangements of lines and kaleidoscopic color schemes and thus approached a style of purely

---

* North Germans, among others: Emil Nolde, Kirchner, Schmidt-Rottluff, Erich Heckel, and Max Pechstein. South Germans: Oskar Kokoschka, Paul Klee, Franz Marc, and Willy Oeser.

ornamental and decorative character. His crude stylizations were not primitive or naïve in the true sense but rather symptoms of nervous fatigue, and his proclaimed kinship with the artistic language of peasants, children, and savages was a manifestation of that same sentimental urge which had started Gauguin on his flight to the South Sea Islands in search for an escape from his own sophistication.

This intellectual sophistication finally prevailed over the creative impulses of the earlier German expressionists. In the end the movement parodied and satirized itself in the aesthetic monstrosities of the German cubists, futurists, constructivists, and dadaists. The latter derided abstract expressionism by reducing their own "compositions" to a jumble of absurd and meaningless associations of line scrawls and color patches. All these extremist movements, originating in the years following World War I and during the inflation period, reflected in their nihilistic and cynical aspects the crisis through which the nations of Europe were passing.

The gradual social and economic reconstruction of Germany under the Weimar Republic produced as its parallel phenomenon in art a healthy reaction against the *Gehirnkunst* of the expressionists in the form of a new realism which took its cue from the *Neue Sachlichkeit* in architecture. This meant a return to nature and matter-of-fact objectivity, on the one hand, and an accentuation of searching and often cruel social criticism, on the other. Thus, the graphic art of George Grosz (1893–) mercilessly dissected the militarist and capitalist pseudo culture of bourgeois society, while in Max Beckmann's (1884–) paintings the human soul appeared dissolved psychoanalytically into bundles of complexes and reflexes, so that the human physiognomy is turned into a grotesquely formless grimace. Or the human being is depicted as a robot in whose head and heart a clockwork performs its automatic functions.

The development of German *sculpture* parallels in the main that of architecture and painting. The partly classical, partly realistic spirit of Hans von Marées (cf. p. 578) was alive in the statues of Adolf von Hildebrand (1847–1921), whose friendship with Marées was to prove of great significance for contemporary German sculpture. He was born in Marburg, educated in Switzerland, and artistically matured in Italy. Hildebrand worked conscientiously in the tradition of the great Renaissance master Donatello and remained forever enamored of classical formal beauty, without relinquishing nature as his most trustworthy guide. His art theory was as much the fruit of many studio talks with friends and fellow artists as of his own creative efforts. Its ingenious application may best be appreciated in such masterpieces as the Wittelsbach Fountain in Munich or the equestrian statue of Bismarck in Bremen.*

The sculptures of August Gaul (1869–1921) and Georg Kolbe (1877–1947) adopted and continued Hildebrand's naturalism, but not his classical ideal-

---

* Cf. Adolf von Hildebrand, *Das Problem der Form* (1893; *The Problem of Form in Painting and Sculpture*, Engl. trans., New York: Stechert, 1907).

ism. Kolbe advanced from naturalist-impressionist beginnings to a sensitive and rhythmically balanced expressionism. The influence of medieval Gothic statuary formed one of the constituent elements in the works of Bernhard Hoetger (1874–) and Wilhelm Lehmbruck (1881–1919). The former added heavy Germanic accents to the loose impressionistic style of his French teacher, Auguste Rodin, while the latter developed a spiritually refined sculptural expressionism on the basis of the firm tectonic pattern of Aristide Maillol's French post-impressionistic sculptures. The kinship with the spiritual content, albeit not with the external form, of medieval Romanesque and Gothic was even stronger in the works of Ernst Barlach (1870–1938), whose cubic wood sculptures defied any of the accepted stylistic categories of modern art. On a journey to Russia, undertaken in 1906, Barlach discovered the metaphysical substance of his artistic creed in the extended horizons of the Russian plains and in the simplicity and unbroken vitality of Russian peasant life. Henceforth Barlach's plastic and graphic as well as his considerable literary production became multiform variations of this experience. The simple creatures whom he modeled with tender love are implanted in the motherly earth, the timeless children of God and nature.

c) Literature. In the seventies of the nineteenth century the poetic realism of the generation of Hebbel and Ludwig (cf. p. 585 sqq.) had outlived itself. Some of its representatives were still alive and productive, but they had lost their audience. Literary tastes were at a very low ebb in the complacent *Gründerzeit,* and the reading public was satisfied with the sugary and sentimental rehash of hackneyed forms and contents of classical and romantic ancestry. A flood of *Unterhaltungsromane* and labored *Professorenromane* testified to the exhaustion of the novel, while the stage cultivated an anemic neo-classicism and moralizing French thesis plays in the manner of Scribe and Sardou; and lyric poetry relished the pseudo simplicity and forced gaiety of mass-produced drinking, soldier, and student songs.

In the meantime, however, the physiognomy and rhythm of German life had begun to change: in the years following the Franco-Prussian War the material wealth of the new German empire had poured largely into the big cities and was contributing to the increase of the social cleavage between capitalists and proletarians. Marxian socialism became a strong force in German life and soon also in German literature.

Among those who heralded the rise of a new literature of social significance was Theodor Fontane (1818–1898). A native of the Mark Brandenburg, he had spent the greater part of his life as a journalist when, at the age of sixty, he published his first novel. As a keen and rather detached observer he described the social transformations which were taking shape in his Prussian homeland. With a mild and melancholy skepticism he viewed the "transvaluation of all values," questioning as much the validity of tradition as the legitimacy of progress. From Darwin he had learned the "law" of the survival of the fittest by means of "natural selection," and from Taine the rules imposed upon human life by the forces of the *milieu*. Man accordingly could not be a free agent, and the moral law, far from being absolute, had to be adapted to the changing situations determined by heredity and environment. Thus Fontane came to regard all values as man-made and subject to the varying requirements of human needs and wants. As everything had two sides, nothing and no one could be said to be absolutely right or absolutely wrong. The world which unfolds itself in Fontane's novels, therefore, and the human beings who populate this world are never determined in their actions by enduring natural or supernatural norms but invariably by chance and circumstance, which add their prodigious weight to the inherent weakness of human nature. There is no longer any room for either heroic action or tragic guilt. The attitude of *tout comprendre c'est tout pardonner* (to understand all is to pardon all) became the source of Fontane's irony and of his soft-spoken bourgeois humanism.*

Two other precursors of the coming literary revolution were the Austrians Ludwig Anzengruber (1839–1889), the playwright, and Marie von Ebner-Eschenbach (1830–1916), the novelist. Anzengruber, a masterly dramatic technician, had inherited Hebbel's realism (cf. p. 586 sq.), and continued and perfected the traditional Viennese *Volksstück* (folk drama). His peasant tragedies and comedies, occasionally pointedly anticlerical and bordering on the melodramatic, excelled in the art of individual characterization and were revolutionary in their trenchant social criticism.**

In her measured and cultivated prose Marie von Ebner-Eschenbach portrayed with warm and rich feeling the aristocratic and popular traditions of the society of the Hapsburg empire.†

The credit for having introduced realism on the German stage and for having thereby prepared it to play its significant part in the literary revolution of the eighties, belongs to Duke George II of Meiningen and his troupe of actors and stage designers. Under the duke's personal direction the *Meininger* made the most painstaking efforts to impart to the dramatic setting a realistic accuracy which resulted from minute historical research. The troupe's Berlin performance of Shakespeare's *Julius Caesar* (1874) was an epoch-making event in the history of the German stage, and the decisive reform of the theaters of the *Reich* capital dates from that year.

The *Deutsches Theater* in Berlin, under the directorate of Adolf L'Arronge (1838–1908), was opened in 1883, marking another important step toward the victory of dramatic realism. To the realistic settings of the *Meininger*

---

* Cf. the social novels *Effi Briest* (1895; Engl. trans. in *German Classics of the 19th and 20th Centuries*, New York: 1913–1915, Vol. 12) and *Der Stechlin* (1898). Of great charm are his *Wanderungen durch die Mark Brandenburg* (1862–1882), a travelogue in four volumes. His ballads show Scotch influence.

** Cf. the dramas *Der Pfarrer von Kirchfeld* (1871, with *Kulturkampf* thesis); *Das Vierte Gebot* (1878; *The Fourth Commandment*, Engl. trans., Pittsburgh: 1912); and *Die Kreuzelschreiber* (1872, comedy). The novel *Der Schandfleck* (1877) tells the moving story of a village King Lear.

† Cf. *Dorf- und Schlossgeschichten* (1883); *Das Gemeindekind* (1887; *The Child of the Parish;* Engl. trans., New York: Bonner [1893]); *Parabeln, Märchen und Gedichte* (1892).

was now added the cultivation of correct enunciation and polished declamation. In the staging of plays requiring elaborate and spectacular sets and the handling of huge masses of actors (*Volksszenen*), the *Meininger* and, to a lesser extent, L'Arronge anticipated some of the devices which later on established the fame of Max Reinhardt (1873–1943), the "magician of the stage," whose overemphasis on the sensuous and optical elements of the scene, however, often tended to distort or obscure the literary values of the drama.

The actual conquest of the German stage by the new realistic or naturalistic movement in German literature was signalized by the foundation of the Berlin *Freie Bühne* in 1889. Both in its name and in its artistic creed and repertory it followed the model of André Antoine's Paris Théâtre Libre (1887–1895). Among the first plays offered to a selected audience of literary connoisseurs were Ibsen's *Ghosts* and Gerhart Hauptmann's *Vor Sonnenaufgang* (*Before Sunrise*). In the theater riots which followed both performances two worlds clashed in irreconcilable antagonism. The naturalistic revolutionaries had challenged the conservatives and traditionalists and, for the time being, *naturalism* had become the passionately defended creed of the younger generation of writers.

German naturalism, in its dramatic creations as well as in its novels and lyrics, had received inspiration from several foreign authors but, above all, from Emile Zola (1840–1902). In his literary theory the French naturalist had followed in the footsteps of his predecessors Balzac, Flaubert, and the brothers Goncourt. Their program called for the application of positivistic and "scientific" principles to literary creations. "Truthful" literature must be scientifically composed literature, that is, a literature in which man appeared as the end product of the forces of heredity and environment. On the speculative bases of materialistic philosophy and scientific theory Zola and his German disciples arrived at a redefinition of art which, in the formulation of Zola, was *"un coin de la nature, vu à travers un tempérament"* (a corner of nature, seen through the medium of a temperament). But in proportion as the individual "temperament" was dissolved or reduced to a bundle of sensory reflexes, the "corner of nature" became all important. In the end the accurate photographic description of the natural object remained as the sole preoccupation of the naturalistic writer.

However, to this purely factual-scientific interest in reality, as suggested by Zola, the German naturalists added an ethico-social component for which the Scandinavians (Ibsen, Björnson, Jacobsen) and the Russians (Turgenev, Tolstoi, Dostoevski) provided the themes. As a consequence, the "corner of nature" was no longer any chance aspect of reality, but one which represented in a condensed form the darkest and most sordid features of life, preferably the *milieu* of a proletarian existence.

This selective method was even retained in the "consistent" naturalism of Arno Holz (1863–1929) and Johannes Schlaf (1862–1941). In the early nineties, at a time when the Austrian poet and critic Hermann Bahr

(1863-1934) was predicting "the end of naturalism," Arno Holz was still busy trying to outline the proper requisites of a consistently naturalistic style. In his opinion, "art has the tendency to be nature." Consequently, naturalistic art, that is, "true" art must strive to be *sachlich* (objective) and close to science. The task of the epic and dramatic writer exacts the most stringent observation of objects, without any attempt at metaphysical interpretation, and without giving any room to the free play of imagination. Nature itself must speak, and the writer's only concern must consist in registering its voice. As to lyric poetry, it must dispense with rhyme, meter, and verse; it must be freed even from those free rhythms which express the emotions and passions of the individual poet, so that it may completely obey the dictation of the external object.

Holz's naturalistic theory of art and literature was thus surely "consistent" enough. But its convincing force was limited to those who accepted with Holz the positivistic concepts of "truth" and of "nature." To those who refused to affirm the "scientific" premises and bases of art and literature the naturalistic theory proved much too narrow.

With one-sided rigor naturalism had presented a picture of man, society, and nature which differed essentially from the view taken by the humanistic idealism of the classical and romantic periods. There human culture had been envisaged as proceeding from a harmonious interplay of human and natural forces. The disenchanted world of the naturalistic writers, on the other hand, had handed man and society over to a telluric determinism. Groping in vain for an axiological center which might impart meaning to a spiritless and depersonalized life, the succeeding generation of writers sought and eventually found escape in a more or less unreal world of shadows and surface appearances. Thus literary *impressionism* came into being as an outgrowth of the desire to transcend the crude domination of matter and as an attempt to sublimate the bitterness of the struggle for existence in detached and unreflecting moods and in exciting sensory and emotive experiences. While *pictorial* impressionism (both in art and literature) enjoyed the thrills provided by colorful series of optical apperceptions, *psychological* impressionism (*symbolism*) indulged in the dissection of inner experiences, and *musical* impressionism (both in literature and music) clung to the tonal-acoustic values of rhythmical sound.

Although these several types of impressionistic literature are rarely found in their purity, but usually mix and overlap, the works of some authors fall readily into one of the three categories. The technique of pictorial impressionism, for example, is easily recognized in the colorful prose sketches of the Viennese Peter Altenberg (1859-1919), whose moody subjectivism (*Wie ich es sehe,* 1896) sounded a keynote of the impressionistic view of life. Psychological and symbolical impressionism is represented in a characteristic variation of personal temper and regional *milieu* in the novels and dramas of Arthur Schnitzler (1862-1931), the Viennese writer and physician.

Schnitzler's works typify in their psychoanalytical technique the *fin de siècle décadence* of cosmopolitan Vienna. His principal characters are frivolous melancholics who play with life and love, which for them are at best mildly exciting pastimes offering ever new opportunities for nervous stimulations and erotic adventures. Schnitzler himself shared to a large extent the subjectivism and relativism of his characters, and he frankly confessed that he too found himself unable to accept any obligatory ethical norms or standards. "I have neither the courage nor the temperament nor the simplicity to adhere to any faith or party," he wrote. And his friend Hugo von Hofmannsthal, in a prologue written for Schnitzler's playlet *Anatol,* expressed in sad though beautiful verse the make-believe texture of psychological impressionism:

> *Also spielen wir Theater,*
> *Spielen unsre eignen Stücke,*
> *Früh gereift und zart und traurig,*
> *Die Komödie unsrer Seele,*
> *Unsres Fühlens heut und gestern,*
> *Böser Dinge hübsche Formel,*
> *Glatte Worte, bunte Bilder. . . .**

Musical impressionism is also ably represented in Hugo von Hofmannsthal's (1874–1929) poems and lyrical dramas. But the melodious rhythmicality of his verse is even surpassed in the early lyrics of Stefan George and in the consummate melodious beauty of the poetry of Rainer Maria Rilke. The latter's art rises above all stylistic categories by virtue of its accomplished union of rich content and immaculate form.

The musical impressionists, sometimes referred to as neo-romanticists, owed a great deal to the symbolism of French and Belgian authors, such as Verlaine, Baudelaire, Huysmans, Maeterlinck, and Verhaeren. Among their German models Friedrich Nietzsche (cf. p. 695 sq.) ranks foremost, and it is from him that they learned once more about the creative possibilities of language and about the rhythmical dynamism of words and verbal patterns.

Even where he chose the dramatic form Hugo von Hofmannsthal was essentially a lyricist who expressed his profound experience of the transitory and enigmatic character of life in a symbolic verse language of great beauty and formal perfection. The moods of melancholy resignation and the twilight hues of the sensed evening glow of Western culture prevail. "We desire not,"

---

* Thus we enact our own plays:
  Prematurely ripened, tender and sad,
  We enact the comedy of our souls,
  The todays and yesterdays of our feelings.
  In smooth words and multi-colored images
  We compose a pretty formula for evil things. . . .

Schnitzler's best known works include the plays *Anatol* (1893; Engl. trans., New York: 1911); *Liebelei* (1896; *The Reckoning,* Engl. trans., New York: 1907); *Der grüne Kakadu* (1899; *The Green Cockatoo,* Engl. trans., London: 1913); the novel *Der Weg ins Freie* (1908; *The Road to the Open,* Engl. trans., New York: 1923), and several volumes of novelettes.

he wrote, "the invention of stories but rather the rendition of moods; not contemplation, but representation; not entertainment, but impression."

Hofmannsthal's modern versions of some of the great dramas of Greek antiquity (Sophocles' *Oedipus* and *Electra*) and of Austrian, Italian, and Spanish medieval and baroque plays (*Jedermann; Das Kleine Welttheater; Das Salzburger Grosse Welttheater*) offered Max Reinhardt unique opportunities for the display of a veritable phantasmagoria of brilliant stage effects, often achieved within the natural setting of a public square or against the background of monumental cathedral architecture. Notwithstanding some distressing neurotic distortions which the Viennese author occasionally allows himself in the portrayal of leading characters, these grand spectacles show Hofmannsthal as one of the legitimate heirs of the medieval and baroque morality play and as a late German representative of a genuine world literature and world culture. With his *libretti* for Richard Strauss's impressionistic operas (*Rosenkavalier; Ariadne; Josephslegende*) he made an important contribution to the development of the post-Wagnerian *Musikdrama.**

Hofmannsthal had originally been loosely associated with a group of poets and writers (the *Kreis der Blätter für die Kunst*) who followed the leadership of the Rhenish author Stefan George (1868–1934). The ways in which George conceived of the poet and of the verbal media of literary expression were new and unheard of only for a generation which had forgotten the accomplishments of German classicism and romanticism. The naturalistic profanity and vulgarity of form and content had left its unmistakable traces on German language and literature. In opposition to the "socialization" of literary values, George and many other symbolist-impressionist writers joined in Horace's dictum *"Odi profanum vulgus et arceo"* (I hate the profane crowd and keep away from it). For George and his school the poet, endowed with the high-priestly qualities of aristocratic leadership, had to stand as a lonely prophet against his time and against the spirit of the age.

In the historic soil of George's native Rhineland the heritage of Roman and Christian antiquity had fused with the introspectiveness of northern spirituality in the form of a broad and highly cultured Catholicism. These historical forces in unison were originally alive in Stefan George. Thus, in a period which lacked spiritual direction and discipline, this Rhenish poet, with his insistence on *Gestalt,* presented a rare phenomenon. In proportion as the romantic moods and remotely Christian reminiscences of his early poetry subsided, there arose in their place an eroticism which pretended to emulate the Greek glorification of divine beauty incarnate in the human form and which finally received its fixation in the *"Maximin-Erlebnis."* The

---

* The *Kleine Dramen* (*Der Tod des Tizian; Der Tor und der Tod*, etc.), though products of his early youth, are among Hofmannsthal's most accomplished works (*Death and the Fool;* Engl. trans. in "Poet Lore" 24 [1913]; *The Death of Titian;* Engl. trans. in *German Classics,* Vol. 17).

physical beauty of a friend who died in the flower of youth thus became the symbol of an idolatrous aesthetic cult. This Maximin cult in turn set the pattern for the oblations offered by George and his *Kreis* at the altars of great historical *Gestalten,* in whom "the divine" appeared *verleibt* (embodied) and the bodily *vergottet* (divinized). As literary manifestations of their cult the disciples of George wrote the biographies of Plato, Caesar, Dante, Shakespeare, Goethe, and Nietzsche.

The members of the *Kreis* set themselves apart from other literary movements, and to accentuate their being different as well as to emphasize the importance of form, rhythm, and sound they created their own typography and orthography, omitting punctuation and abandoning the capitalization of nouns. The hieratic structure and the messianic ambitions of the George school were truncated by the only too obvious intellectual and moral limitations of its individual representatives. "George lacks," wrote the contemporary literary historian, Fritz Strich, "some of the most essential and enduring human qualities. He had to conjure up the past because he and his age had lost the creative power to form timeless symbols of human existence out of their own substance. No truly creative literary accomplishments have emerged from George's *Kreis.*"

Those works which were inspired by George's *Führertum* and which can claim more than passing attention were either translations or of a scholarly rather than poetic nature. Thus both George and his disciple Rudolf Borchardt translated Dante. George translated Baudelaire's *Fleurs du Mal* and Shakespeare's *Sonnets.* Friedrich Gundolf (1880–1931), the author of standard biographies of Caesar, Goethe, and George, presented a new translation of Shakespeare's dramas. Ernst Bertram wrote a highly original biography of Nietzsche, Kurt Hildebrandt one of Plato, and Ernst Kantorowicz that of the Hohenstaufen emperor, Frederick II. All these authors made important contributions to the interpretation of historic personalities and, by virtue of their synthetic understanding of historical events, enriched the methodology of historical and literary criticism. Moreover, both the expressionist and neo-realist movements in German literature were decisively influenced by the vitality of George's verse and by his exaltation of the poet's calling. The shortcomings in George's work and in his *Führertum,* however, may well be summed up in the prophetic words of Friedrich Hebbel (cf. p. 586 sq.), who wrote in his *Diaries:* "It becomes ever more clear to me that only what proceeds from God can be made the subject matter of the highest art. . . . Even in Goethe's *Faust* that which is built on magic is transitory; for a time will come when even the memory of magic and sorcery will be forgotten."*

The poetry and prose of Rainer Maria Rilke (1875–1926) marked both the fulfillment of and the victory over impressionism. Rilke, the descendant of Carinthian Catholic noblemen, was born in Prague, and the picturesque

---

* The best of George's poetry is contained in the volumes *Das Jahr der Seele* (1897), *Der Siebente Ring* (1907), *Der Stern des Bundes* (1907), and *Das Neue Reich* (1929).

romantic charm of that ancient Bohemian city permeates his early impressionistic and folk-song-like lyrics. Like the sculptor Barlach (cf. p. 719) he experienced the spell of the boundless horizons of the Russian and North German plains, and he matured as a literary disciple of Russian and Scandinavian writers and under the steadying personal influence of the French sculptor, Rodin.

In the *Stundenbuch* (*Book of Hours*, 1905) Rilke professes in sublimely beautiful verse a cosmic-pantheistic religion, in which all individual things and beings appear as temporal fixations of eternal cosmic waves and rhythms. While the three major parts of this work (*Vom mönchischen Leben; Das Buch von der Pilgerschaft; Das Buch von der Armut und vom Tode*) are clothed in the symbolism of monastic life, the contents suggest not the mystical surrender of the self-centered ego to the Deity but rather a cosmic expansion of the *ego* and its final dissolution in the divine *All*. Similarly, the *Marienleben* (*Life of Mary*, 1913) celebrates the mother of Christ as a symbol of the spiritual *ego* giving birth and form to the divine.

All the works which Rilke wrote before World War I reflect both his search for and his flight from God. "But the road that leads to Thee," the poet confessed, "is fearfully long, and the track is laid waste because no one has travelled it for so long."*

After ten years of silence Rilke, in 1923, published the *Sonette an Orpheus* and the *Duineser Elegien*,** songs which in their melancholy beauty reflect the experiences of war and revolution and are filled with a heroic despair and the presentiment of death. The mythical singer Orpheus becomes the symbol of a superhuman existence embracing and harboring the antithesis of life and death: "Only in that dual realm sings a gentle voice the songs of eternity." The *Elegies* delve once more into the mystery of life. What is man? He is past and future, life and death; the eternal quest of the "I" for the "Thou," the unstilled longing for God surging against the inexorable actualities of time, world, and death. Human existence is *"Sein zum Tode"* (being unto death) in Rilke's poetry as much as in Heidegger's philosophy (cf. p. 693 sq.).

Rilke's linguistic and metrical form was the medium of his metaphysical urge for the infinite. It expresses an endless movement toward an infinitely distant goal and in its restless rhythmical flux presses on beyond time, space, and *Gestalt*. In form and content this poet appears as the late-born heir of the great culture of Europe who on the highest artistic level and in precious language sang the swan song of German romantic idealism and man-centered humanism.

German literary *expressionism* came into being about the end of the first decade of the twentieth century. Like naturalism, it was endowed with the impetuosity and aggressive radicalism of a literary revolt. It was intimately

---

* *Aber der Weg zu Dir ist furchtbar weit*
   Und, weil ihn lange keiner ging, verweht. — (*Stundenbuch*).
** *Duinese Elegies* (in the original with Engl. trans., London: Hogarth, 1930).

linked with parallel movements in the other arts and had its roots in a changing philosophy of life which left its impress on German civilization in its entirety.

But the expressionistic movement in German literature was even more short lived than either naturalism or impressionism. Flourishing and spending its energies during and following World War I, it came to a surprisingly premature end in the middle twenties of this century. The literary harvest was relatively small, and only a very few works reached the stage of literary perfection. Some critics even assert that the entire movement exhausted itself in pretentious poses, inarticulate outcries, neurotic gestures, and helpless stammerings. An unbiased appraisal, however, will arrive at more positive conclusions.

German literary expressionism voiced the indignation and passionate protest of a generation of writers who felt they had been born into social conditions and were condemned to live in cultural surroundings which they experienced as disgraceful and utterly inhuman. They therefore were united in the idealistic resolve to use their literary talents to change these conditions and surroundings. Furthermore, what was later on termed *Neue Sachlichkeit* (cf. p. 711), the new realistic simplicity in art and literature, the monumental form in functional architecture, the religious fermentation, and the dynamic wave of the Youth Movement (cf. p. 708 sq.) — all this was nourished and fanned by the spirit of expressionistic thinking and writing.

It was an axiomatic assertion of the expressionistic visionaries that their own world was to be in every respect the exact antithesis of the actually existing world of their fathers. Thus the fanatical will to "transvaluate all values" (Nietzsche) captured their hearts and poured from their lips, making them oblivious to the limitations of time and space, tradition and history, logic and grammar, and to any and all of the petty realities of the external world. Instead, the inner world of the soul, the mind, and the spirit was to rule supreme. In short, the expressionistic writers were profoundly convinced that they were burdened with the task or entrusted with the mission of renewing the face of the earth, of reshaping the history of the world.

The expressionistic movement had reached its peak when a defeated Germany seemed politically and socially nothing but a heap of ruins. But far from being dismayed or even surprised by such a spectacle, the expressionist intelligentsia took pride in having actively contributed to the downfall of imperial Germany and in having had its share in the subsequent political and social revolution.

The pronounced *pacifism* espoused by the several expressionistic groups amply justified such claims. Handicapped in their activities and utterances by a rigid censorship, many of the expressionists had taken up residence in Switzerland, and many others had their radical propaganda printed and published abroad and then secretly distributed in Germany.

The literary revolution in *Berlin* used the pages of the two periodicals,

Aktion and *Sturm,* for their manifestoes against power politics and their defense of humanitarianism and cosmopolitanism. In Berlin, too, were gathered the "activists," led by Kurt Hiller and Heinrich Mann (1871), the elder and less famous (though hardly less talented) brother of Thomas Mann. The philosophy of activism, written by Leonhard Nelson (1882–1927), revealed its kinship with the democratic constitutionalism of the French and American Revolutions. The professed radicalism of many activist leaders remained, however, largely confined to the printed page. Assailing the *art for art's sake* slogan of the impressionists, they proposed to make art and literature servile tools of political and social ideas. Unlike Zola, they carefully refrained from mingling with the poor and miserable whose lot they bewailed in impassioned pleas. Thus their voices, coming from the safe and icy distance of aristocratic seclusion, had a feeble and shallow sound, giving the lie to the talkative protestations of their "love for mankind."

The intellectual cleavage and (temporary) personal antagonism between the two Mann brothers illustrated almost dramatically the clash between German literary conservatism and revolutionary radicalism. While Thomas Mann (cf. p. 734 sq.) was esteemed by some of the younger writers as the distinguished heir of Germany's classical and romantic tradition, as the disciple of Goethe, Wagner, Schopenhauer, Nietzsche, and the great Russian novelists, Heinrich Mann was the idol of a rebellious and irreverent literary clique whose members were inspired by the ideology of Western democratic liberalism. And at the very moment when the events on the battlefields of Europe seemed to turn the scales completely in favor of the latter group, Thomas Mann, in his *Betrachtungen eines Unpolitischen* (1918), made a final and almost desperate attempt to exonerate the Prussian conservative world of his Hanseatic forebears, a world in which he still wished to believe and which he therefore defended against the ruthless attacks of the Western *"Zivilisationsliteraten."*

In the German South the *Münchener Kammerspiele* (Munich Little Theater) achieved fame for its sponsorship of the expressionistic *drama.* Homage was paid there to August Strindberg (1849–1912), the great Swedish playwright, who more than any other writer fathered German dramatic expressionism. His influence was strongly felt in the eccentric plays of Frank Wedekind (cf. p. 734), in Karl Sternheim's satirical and cynical comedies, and in the spectacular, technically brilliant *Denkspiele* of Georg Kaiser. The performance of Reinhard Goering's pacifistic drama *Seeschlacht* (*Sea Battle,* 1917) was followed by the first of a series of theater riots, in which pacifist and nationalist sentiments clashed.

The most promising of the pacifist-expressionist playwrights was Fritz von Unruh (1885). Coming from an ancient family of the Prussian nobility and counting among his ancestors many distinguished Prussian generals, he had attended the Imperial Military Academy in close companionship with the Prussian princes. He served as an officer in the war, and had both lost and found himself and his life aim in the horror and anguish of the trenches before Verdun. While his early dramatic production, especially the colorful *Louis Ferdinand* (1913) was in temper and atmosphere (though not in its thesis) akin to some of the plays of Heinrich von Kleist (cf. p. 483 sq.), his postwar dramas gave voice to tortured and defiled humanity. His passionate longing envisaged a new daybreak when the idols of militarism and nationalism would be unmasked and the idea of a mankind united in brotherly love would be universally accepted.*

The stirring socialist dramas of Ernst Toller (1893–1939) were written in a similar vein. His *Masse Mensch* (1920), presenting a poignant indictment of both militarist and communist dictatorship, continued a dramatic pattern in which the collective dynamism of the masses replaces the individual hero, a substitution for which Gerhart Hauptmann's *Die Weber* had provided the paradigm. During the "white" counterrevolution which overthrew the short-lived Soviet dictatorship of Bavaria (1919), Toller was apprehended and sentenced to five years' imprisonment in a Bavarian fortress for his share in Kurt Eisner's (cf. p. 646) socialistic experiment. A political exile after 1933, he took his own life in 1939, in a New York hotel.**

The expressionistic *Weltanschauung* clearly reflected some of the political and social changes as well as the intellectual crisis through which the German nation was passing. The stress which the expressionists placed on human and spiritual-personal values made them disdainful of materialism and positivism. But their spiritualistic subjectivism was as one-sided and unrealistic as had been the materialistic "objectivity" of their naturalist and impressionist antagonists. The inflated *ego* of the expressionist soon became forgetful of *la terre sacrée,* of the reality of matter and nature, and thus his deep longing for an objective realm of values beyond the sphere of a self-centered idealized individualism remained in the main unfulfilled.

Franz Werfel (1890–1945), a native of Prague and a citizen of Vienna prior to Hitler's annexation of Austria, was one of the few initial members of the expressionistic movement who outgrew the metaphysical narrowness of the school and attained to that integrated view of reality which had been anticipated by the French philosopher Bergson and which finally became the common property of the German phenomenological, neo-realist, and neo-Thomist thinkers (cf. p. 697 sq.). In literature as in the arts this neo-realism appeared in the form of the *Neue Sachlichkeit* (cf. p. 711) and in its attempted synthesis of the antithetical positions of naturalism and impressionism, on the one hand, and expressionism, on the other. In a programmatic speech delivered in 1931 and entitled *Realismus und Innerlichkeit* Franz Werfel called for the restoration of a hierarchic order of values in which

---

* Cf. *Opfergang,* a prose epic (1916; Engl. trans., *The Way of Sacrifice,* New York: A. Knopf, 1928), and the dramas *Ein Geschlecht* (1916), *Platz* (1920), *Heinrich aus Andernach* (1925), and this writer's school edition of *Prinz Louis Ferdinand* (New York: Oxford University Press, 1933). Unruh resides in New York.

** Cf. *Seven Plays* (New York: Liveright Publishing Corp.); *No More Peace* (New York: Farrar & Rinehart, 1937); *Pastor Hall* (New York: Random House, 1939); and the autobiography *I Was a German* (New York: W. Morrow & Co., 1934).

matter and spirit, nature and supernature were to receive due consideration. His own later works, especially the drama, *Paulus unter den Juden* (*Paul among the Jews*, 1926; Engl. trans., Mowbray, 1928), and his novels *Barbara oder die Frömmigkeit;* (*The Pure in Heart*, Engl. trans., New York, 1931), *Der veruntreute Himmel* (*Embezzled Heaven*, Engl. trans., New York: Viking Press, 1940), and *Das Lied von Bernadette* (*The Song of Bernadette*, Engl. trans., New York: Sun Dial Press., 1942) were milestones on the road to such an integral literary realism.*

The neo-realist synthesis demanded and partially realized by Werfel naturally found its strongest support among German *Catholic writers* whose works are grounded in the experienced polarity of subject and object, nature and supernature, reason and faith.

In 1912, the convert Reinhard Johannes Sorge (1892–1916), who died in the battle of the Somme, had written the drama *Der Bettler* (*The Beggar*), the first of many ecstatic dramatic confessions of the expressionist movement. In his short life Sorge traveled the long road from the creed of Nietzsche's Zarathustra to a view of life which permitted him to pronounce "Judgment on Zarathustra" (*Gericht über Zarathustra*, 1921). In between he had written several dramatic works in the vein of the medieval morality play. In this revival of the strictly religious play Sorge was followed by the Austrian Max Mell (1882–),** the South German Leo Weismantel 1888–), and others.

Ruth Schaumann (1899–) and Gertrud von Le Fort (1876–1949), both outstanding as lyricists and novelists, and both converts, represent contemporary German Catholic literature at its highest level. Ruth Schaumann, in her work as a sculptor and graphic artist as much as in her writings, reveals a prodigious poetic imagination and a tenderness of feeling which are nourished by her personal experience of the sacred realities of love, motherhood, the human soul, and God. Gertrud von Le Fort's literary style, on the other hand, is more objective and her view of the world more retrospective, enabling her to form timeless culture symbols of Christian truths. In the majestic psalmody of her *Hymnen an die Kirche* individualism and universalism fuse, and the human soul, immersed in the rhythmical sequence of the ecclesiastical year, experiences its own existence as organically linked with the *Corpus Christi Mysticum*. In the novel *Der Papst aus dem Ghetto* (1930; *The Pope from the Ghetto*, Engl. trans., New York: Sheed and Ward, 1934) she tells in the unemotional style of the old chronicles the moving story of Cardinal Petrus of the Jewish family of Pier Leone who, as Anacletus II, the antipope, plunged the Church into the schism of 1130. This narrative views the problem

---

* Other prominent representatives of the *Neue Sachlichkeit* are the lyricists Gerrit Engelke, Jakob Kneip, Adolf von Hatzfeld, and Richard Billinger; and the novelists Joseph Roth, Oscar Maria Graf, Alfred Döblin, Emil Strauss, Hermann Hesse, Erwin Guido Kolbenheyer, Joseph Magnus Wehner, Paul Alverdes, Ernst Wiechert, Franz Kafka, Hans Carossa, Hermann Stehr.
** Cf. *Das Apostelspiel* (1923: Engl. trans., Methuen, 1934); *Das Schutzengelspiel* (1923); *Das Nachfolge-Christi-Spiel* (1927).

of Judaism and of the Jewish people in its profound religious significance and sees its solution in Israel's free acceptance of God's providential design. The novelette *Die Letzte am Schafott* (1931; *The Song at the Scaffold,* Engl. trans., New York, 1933) relates the martyrdom of the Carmelite nuns at the time of the French Revolution, painting against the dark background of a general breakdown of human hopes and values the overpowering reality of divine grace. In *Das Schweisstuch der Veronike* (*The Veil of Veronica,* 1928) and its sequel, *Der Kranz der Engel* (*The Angels' Wreath,* 1948) the action takes place in present-day Rome, the main theme being the meeting of paganism and Christianity in the Eternal City: Rome, the great pagan mother of nations, the city of sublime and enduring beauty, bearing in her womb the secrets of the glories of nature and mind; and that other Rome, the radiant monstrance of the world, the mother of all spiritual blessings, in whose presence the splendors of the pagan city pale, because in the heartbeat of the true *Roma Aeterna* abides the secret of the living God.

After having thus roughly sketched the most important literary movements flourishing in the years which intervened between the foundation of the Second Empire and the end of the Weimar Republic, there remains the task of giving an appraisal of the literary work of some individual authors who resolutely cut across the boundary lines of schools and cliques. While in their philosophy of life and in their artistic-technical means they are no less representatives of the spirit of the age than the members of literary groups, they often succeeded in expressing a common set of social and cultural experiences in a vigorous and distinctly personal style.

Gerhart Hauptmann (1862–1946),* whose beginnings were more or less loosely associated with the naturalistic movement, manifested even in his earliest dramatic production an understanding of human nature and social situations which transcends the narrow doctrinairism of a photographically correct naturalism. His drama *Vor Sonnenaufgang* (1889; *Before Dawn,* Vol. 1), though naturalistic in the accurate description of the sordid *milieu* of a corrupt Silesian family of peasant *parvenus,* derives its moving force from the author's compassion with the fate of his characters. Helen, who in the midst of the debasing influences of her environment has preserved her moral integrity and believes she has found a way of escape in her love for a social-democratic apostle of temperance, takes her own life when her lover, an all-too-faithful adept of the theories of heredity and environment, refuses to marry into a family of drunkards. The main characters of this and the two following plays, *Das Friedensfest,* 1890; *Einsame Menschen* (1891; *The Reconciliation; Lonely Lives,* Vol. 3), are products and victims of external circumstances, unfree in their

---

* Cf. *The Dramatic Works,* New York: Viking Press, 1912–1917; 1924; 1929; 9 vols.

actions, and driven on to their doom by the pitiless forces of heredity and *milieu*. Their actions are no more and no less than *Schmerzreaktionen* (pain reactions). They are weak but not guilty, and therefore not tragic in the accepted sense of the term. However, Hauptmann's *milieu* and character analysis implies not only compassion with these victims of a capitalist-materialist *Weltanschauung,* but at the same time a social criticism and a moral indignation deriving from the religious-pietistic idealism indelibly implanted in the author by the atmosphere and the family traditions of his Silesian homeland.

Gerhart Hauptmann's international fame was firmly established with his drama *Die Weber* (1892; *The Weavers,* Vol. I), in which the historical uprising of the Silesian weavers of 1844 offered the playwright a unique opportunity to depict with great dramatic skill the cumulative dynamism and destructive power of the impoverished proletarian masses. The fact that Hauptmann, himself the grandson of a Silesian weaver, could draw on personal recollections gave the drama an added and convincing force and made it the most authentic social play of contemporary German literature.

"Straight at the heart of German discord" aimed Hauptmann's *Florian Geyer* (1896; Vol. 9), his second drama of social revolution. As the Silesian weavers had risen against their capitalist exploiters, so the hapless peasant masses of the early sixteenth century, under the leadership of the imperial knight Florian Geyer, revolt in the Great Peasants' War (cf. p. 240 sq.) against the German knights and princes. Defying the naturalistic dogma, which had banished history from the stage, Hauptmann wrote a historical drama, but one which carried a stirring message for his German contemporaries. The peasant revolt is crushed and drowned in blood because of the disunity of the several groups and their unwillingness to subordinate themselves to the better judgment of their chosen leader.

In the plays *Fuhrmann Henschel* (1898; *Drayman Henschel,* Vol. 2) and *Rose Bernd* (1903; Vol. 2) the fate of the main characters is no longer determined by heredity and environment but by the unrestrained inner forces of will and instinct. The former drama develops August Strindberg's and Frank Wedekind's favorite theme, the victory of female brutality over masculine weakness and inertia. *Rose Bernd,* on the other hand, seizes upon a popular *Sturm und Drang* (cf. p. 394 sq.) motif, the self-destruction of a woman who has murdered her newborn baby. The symbolistic and romantic elements which enter into the naturalistic setting of the verse drama *Hanneles Himmelfahrt* (1894; *The Assumption of Hannele,* Vol. 4) become dominant in the theme and style of *Die versunkene Glocke* (1896; *The Sunken Bell,* Vol. 4). This is Hauptmann's poetically most accomplished play, in which the fate of Heinrich, the bell founder, becomes a symbol of the destiny of the great artist who, in Hauptmann's opinion, must find in closest communion with nature a compensation for his human and social loneliness.

Hauptmann's succeeding plays deal partly with legendary, partly with historical subjects. *Der arme Heinrich* (1902; *Poor Henry*, Vol. 4) introduces modern psychological motivations into Hartmann von Aue's (cf. p. 152 sq.) medieval tale of the leprous knight who has been promised health by the voluntary sacrifice of a pure maiden, but is finally cured by divine grace. *Der weisse Heiland* (1920; *The White Savior*, Vol. 8) pictures with gross historical bias Montezuma as the "savior" who is put to death by fanatical and gold-hungry Spaniards.

Among Hauptmann's prose works the novels *Der Narr in Christo, Emanuel Quint* (1910)* and *Der Ketzer von Soana* (1918)** stand out; the former for its warmth of human feeling and its original treatment of a religious theme, the latter for its qualities of style. Emanuel Quint is a Moravian God-seeker who attempts to relive the life of Christ in the Silesian mountains, but who, in his pietistic subjectivism and in the growing confusion of his mind, ends by identifying himself with the Saviour, and dies as an outcast in utter loneliness. The story of the *Heretic of Soana* is a panegyric of pagan naturalism, in which the anarchical force of instinct is polemically opposed to the intellectual and moral exactions of Christianity. A young Italian priest forsakes his religious calling to spend the rest of his life as a shepherd in the unbridled freedom of nature. The repulsiveness of the theme is not sufficiently mitigated by the artistic proficiency with which it is developed. Hauptmann's conception of paganism is as distorted and unreal as his idea of Christianity. In none of his many works has he ever succeeded in overcoming the vacillating and vague pantheism and sentimental humanitarianism which from the outset characterized his somewhat ill-balanced philosophy of life.

It was the protest against the relativistic softening of metaphysical and moral values and norms that made Paul Ernst (1866–1933), the one-time socialist, a most determined opponent of naturalism and impressionism and an impassioned advocate of a literary conservatism resting on "the unity of vital experience, social action, faith, and a common ethnic and national destiny." In the treatise *Der Weg zur Form* (1906) Ernst offered a theoretical exposition of his dramatic principles, demanding a return to the spirit and form of Greek and German classical drama which both, in his opinion, had been characterized by a vital union of aesthetic, metaphysical, and moral values. Moral relativism, he asserted, had destroyed the very foundations of the genuine drama by its denial of the absolute nature of good and evil, a negation which had made a tragic conflict impossible. Greek tragedy had succumbed to the moral relativism of Euripides, "the destroyer of the myths" (Nietzsche). Similarly, the classical German drama had been destroyed by the immoralism or amoralism of the naturalists and impressionists: "The sophists ruined the drama of antiquity by their doctrine of the relativity of moral concepts. And the naturalistic drama of

---

* *The Fool in Christ, Emanuel Quint* (Engl. trans., New York, 1911).
** *The Heretic of Soana* (Engl. trans., New York, 1923).

our time is no longer a drama in the true sense because, characteristically enough, it is closely linked with sociological positivism. . . . The essence of being human consists not in our faculty of understanding, but in our capability of discerning ultimate values. . . . Only man can be moral, and therefore all human greatness rests on morality."

Ernst's exclusive interest in the aesthetic and moral components of art and literature set him apart from the expressionists, on the one hand, and from the contemporary religious writers, on the other. While the former placed subjective-spiritual experience above moral content, the latter attempted to ground moral goodness in the superior values of metaphysical and religious truth.*

The antinaturalism of Frank Wedekind (1864–1916) sprang from entirely different roots. With the vehemence of a temperament unchecked by any traditional standards of morality he advocated in his partly serious, partly grotesque dramas the free reign of sexual instincts, convinced "that natural processes are never indecent, but either useful or harmful, reasonable or unreasonable." An inverted bourgeois, Wedekind declared a war to the finish on all "bourgeois morality," borrowing from Nietzsche his call for a new *Herrenmoral* "beyond good and evil," and his plea for the breeding of a new race of "noble human animals." Lacking a moral standard of measurement, Wedekind's social criticism remained purely negative and destructive, unable to create true dramatic symbols of a new order and meaning of reality. The freedom of the individual which he preached had no counterpart in objective moral values and was corroded by the author's cynicism and Bohemian snobbery.**

The contrast between art and life, between the existence and *milieu* of the artist and the bourgeois, became the central problem of the novels of the brothers Heinrich and Thomas Mann. The theme was suggested by the blood heritage of the two authors, the sons of a patrician Hanseatic father and a Creolean mother. While Heinrich Mann† attempted to resolve the art-life antinomy by a twofold escape, first into Bohemianism, and afterward into activist-social expressionism (cf. p. 727 sq.), Thomas Mann (1875–) sought the solution of the problem in a humanistically ennobled *Bürgertum*. Thus Heinrich's way led from a cult of sensuous beauty to social satire, and Thomas proceeded from the experience of the lonely and life-hungry artist (*Tonio Kröger*, 1903; Engl. trans. in *German Classics of the 19th and 20th Centuries*, Vol. 19) to an artistic culture which was sustained by social responsibility (*Königliche Hoheit*, 1909; *Royal Highness*, Engl. trans., New

---

* Cf. Ernst's drama *Brunhild* (1909) and the novel *Saat auf Hoffnung* (1915), both contained in *Gesammelte Schriften* (19 vols., Munich, 1928 sq.).

** Cf. the dramas *Frühlings Erwachen* (*The Awakening of Spring*, 1891; Engl. trans., Brown, 1919); *Erdgeist* (*Earth Spirit*, 1895; Engl. trans., New York, 1914); *Der Marquis von Keith* (1901); in *Gesammelte Werke* (9 vols., Munich, 1912 sqq.).

† Cf. the novel, *Die kleine Stadt* (1909; *The Little Town*, Engl. trans., New York: Houghton, 1931), the best among Heinrich Mann's earlier works; and the socio-political satire, *Der Untertan* (1918; *The Patrioteer*, Engl. trans., New York, 1921).

York, 1926) and a belief in a conservative political democracy. Although both authors surpassed the naturalistic novel by virtue of their deeper and broader understanding of the conflicts inherent in human life and civilization, they tended to satirize or neutralize these conflicts without ever attaining to a metaphysical or cultural synthesis.

Out of the dual endeavor of conscientious factual analysis and sympathetic human understanding was born the melancholic-skeptical irony with which Thomas Mann views the actions of his major characters. Autobiographical features are no less conspicuous in his stories than in his four long novels and his historical play *Fiorenza* (1905). In *Buddenbrooks* (1901; Engl. trans., New York, 1924) Mann, at the age of twenty-five, traced the decay of a patrician family of the Hanse city of Lübeck (the author's birthplace), driving home his thesis that biological and physical health are threatened and eventually doomed by the virus of art and culture. Young Hanno Buddenbrook, biologically unable to carry on the solid patriarchal traditions of his ancestors, is "infected" with music. *Der Zauberberg* (1924; *The Magic Mountain,* Engl. trans., New York, 1927), picturing life in a Swiss Alpine sanatorium for consumptives as a symbolic cross section of decadent European society, almost morbidly underscores Mann's often professed neoromantic "sympathy with death," introducing psychoanalysis as a technical means of characterization. Hans Castorp, the scion of a patrician family of the city of Hamburg, who succumbs to the spell of the "magic mountain," and whose intended brief visit to the mountain resort extends to a period of seven years, is saved from a life of make-believe and utter unreality when he follows the call to arms, meeting death on the battlefields of World War I. The epic tetralogy *Joseph und seine Brüder* (1933 sqq.; *Joseph and His Brothers,* Engl. trans., New York, 1934 sq., 4 vols.) uses a biblical theme for a sophisticated exposition of typically modern psychological and sociological problems and offends by its flippant rationalizations of scriptural texts and personages. *Dr. Faustus* (the "Life of the German Composer Adrian Leverkühn," Engl. trans., New York: A. Knopf, 1949), finally, attempts a psychological and metaphysical interpretation of the ultimate meaning of German history, the German people, and the German mind.

The novelette *Mario und der Zauberer* (*Mario and the Sorcerer,* 1930) more than any of Mann's major works gives evidence of the fact that the author was well aware of the dark and dangerous irrational forces which were closing in on Germany on the eve of the National Socialist revolution. But it appears extremely doubtful whether the revolver shot which in the end kills the sorcerer provides an adequate answer or a really "satisfactory solution." It is quite certain, on the other hand, that Mann's thin-blooded humanism was incapable of offering a more positive answer or a more substantially human solution.

d) Music. The spirit of German classicism and romanticism exerted a more enduring influence on contemporary German music than on the plastic, pictorial, and literary arts. Not only was the classico-romantic musical tradition kept alive, but its continuity was enriched by the creative genius of some great masters who proved fully equal to the task of entering into the great heritage bequeathed to them.

The neo-romanticism of Richard Wagner's music dramas (cf. p. 493 sqq.) had conquered the Western World, so that its influences prevailed not only in the post-Wagnerian opera but also in symphony, chamber music, choral music, and *Lied*. Still, the classical tradition of German music experienced a vigorous revival in *Johannes Brahms* (1833–1897), a native of Hamburg who, after romantic beginnings, developed a distinctly North German classicism of striking originality.

The heavy and severe style of many of Brahms's compositions reveals a typically low-German inclination toward the balladesque and the tragic, elements which prevent his works from being easily accessible to non-Germanic audiences. The richness of his harmonic technique derives from his familiarity with the ancient church modes, while he owes his mastery of vocal polyphony to the influence of Johann Sebastian Bach and the early Dutch masters. From both Palestrina and Bach he drew inspiration for his choral and hymnic music and for his madrigals and concertos, while from Beethoven he learned the logical-synthetic interlinking of themes and motifs. Thus the classical elements prevail, but the romantic components are not lacking. They are manifest in the poetic inspiration of many of his works, in the temperamental rhythm and emotional vivacity of his Hungarian dances and gypsy songs, and in his admiration for medieval and Catholic forms of art and cultic worship. Romantic is also his longing for southern climes and cultures and the mood of a melancholy, unstilled yearning which permeates especially the works of the Viennese period.

In an age which in art and culture paid homage either to listless traditionalism or restless progressivism, Brahms enlivened the sense for lasting forms and values, setting in his own life and work the example of a healthy balance and artistic discipline.*

In his independence of Richard Wagner's style and *Weltanschauung* Johannes Brahms stands almost alone. He had few disciples and founded no school. The heirs, successors, and imitators of Wagner, on the other hand, were numerous. Among them Hans Pfitzner (1869–) stands out as the only one who combined in his operas the three major elements of the Wagnerian music drama: the romantic mysticism of *Lohengrin,* the erotic mysticism of *Tristan,* and the *Parsifal* theme of religious asceticism and salvation by redeeming love (*Erlösungsdrama*).

Pfitzner is Richard Wagner's most legitimate heir, and the purely ideal romantic dreamworld of his operas appears almost as an anachronism in the midst of the materialism of a technical-utilitarian age. In his music-dramatic version of Hartmann von Aue's medieval epic *Der arme Heinrich* (1895) he shows himself as the modern master of the Christian *Erlösungs-*

---

* The works of Brahms include 17 pieces for chamber music, 4 symphonies, 4 concertos, 10 sonatas, and many choral compositions (among them *Deutsches Requiem*).

drama. As a genuine neo-romanticist he combines the charm of the medieval legend with the refinement of modern psychological penetration. His instrumentation broadens and deepens the polyphonic individualism of the post-Wagnerian orchestra by the objective patterns of the medieval *discantus* and the church modes.

The opera *Palestrina* (1916), the musical dramatization of the genesis of the Renaissance master's famous *Missa Papae Marcelli,* contains Pfitzner's artistic *credo:* it is a Faustian drama of the lonely creative artist in the midst of an unfeeling and unresponsive world. In this work as well as in his mature chamber music the composer revives the musical Gothic of Josquin des Près, fusing it with the intricate counterpointal technique of eighteenth-century classicism and with the spiritual animation of German romanticism. The passionate sensualism of Wagner gives way in Pfitzner's music to restrained emotions and occasionally to an ascetic austerity.*

Musical naturalism and impressionism in Germany is most skillfully and colorfully represented by *Richard Strauss* (1864–1949). He achieved world fame with his opera *Der Rosenkavalier* (1911), a work which in its lyrical gaiety leans strongly toward the Viennese operetta, for which *Johann Strauss* (1804–1849),** *Franz von Suppé* (1820–1895), and *Karl Millöcker* (1842–1899) had created the indigenous and lasting pattern.

With *Salome* (1905; text by Oscar Wilde) and *Elektra* (1909; text, as in most of the following Strauss operas, by Hugo von Hofmannsthal, cf. p. 723 sq.) the composer made his most important contributions to the naturalistic operatic style. Both works are actually musical caricatures of the main characters they portray. The clever and exciting tonal effects serve to underscore the psychopathological elements, and the carefully calculated nuances of a lavish orchestration are designed to register and illustrate the most minute nervous reflexes. Wagner's great art of musical characterization is replaced by an episodic and mosaiclike picturesqueness which no longer pays attention to dramatic development and thus dilutes and dissolves the structural form.

The blurring of form and contour and the prevalence of color and *Stimmung* (mood) are most conspicuous in Strauss's impressionistic program music, especially in his tone poems,† which are hardly more than aggregates of brilliant and startling musical *aperçus* or sketchy aphorisms without any tectonic unity. In the *Alpensymphonie* the musical "program" faithfully renders the tonal effects suggested by an alpine scene, including not only the phenomena of nature but even the sound of cowbells. But Strauss's perfect command of all the technical registers of orchestration and

---

* Pfitzner's compositions include, aside from his operas and chamber music, numerous orchestral and choral works, cantatas (*Von deutscher Seele,* 1921), and *Lieder.* He wrote several books in violent protest against modernistic music (*Gesammelte Schriften,* 1926–1929).
** Cf. *Die Fledermaus, Der Zigeunerbaron, Eine Nacht in Venedig,* etc.
† Cf. *Also sprach Zarathustra, Don Juan, Ein Heldenleben, Tod und Verklärung, Alpensymphonie.*

composition can hardly atone for the lack of that profound and comprehensive view of reality which is the indispensable requisite of great art and which Richard Wagner had in mind when he said: *"Ich kann den Geist der Musik nicht anders als in der Liebe fassen"* (In Love alone can I comprehend the true spirit of music).

This deepest love of reality in its plenitude, seen as the handiwork of its divine Maker, was the prime motivating force in the works of *Anton Bruckner* (1824–1896), Austria's greatest musical genius since Schubert's time, and the most accomplished modern master of that monumental symphonic form which Beethoven had created. Bruckner's music is the naïve, unreflected language of the human heart, and both his sacred and secular compositions are permeated by his childlike Catholic faith, by the sturdiness of his ancestral peasant *milieu,* and by the idyllic beauty of his homeland, the landscape of Upper Austria. In the mystic-ecstatic transport of his music Bruckner reveals his kinship with Franz Liszt (cf. p. 493 sq.), although his religious experience has deeper roots and expresses itself in simpler and purer forms. All of Bruckner's works are an affirmation of life: jubilant "feasts of sound" which find the answer to all the dark and perplexing problems of human existence in the supreme clarity of that "dear Lord," to whom the composer dedicated his last (ninth) symphony (*"an den lieben Gott"*).*

The serene religious harmony which in Bruckner's music triumphs over all tragic discord remains a never satisfied longing in the compositions of *Gustav Mahler* (1860–1911), a native of Bohemia, whose international reputation as conductor (Budapest, Hamburg, Vienna, United States) equaled his fame as a composer. Mahler surpasses Bruckner in the firm and often grandiose tectonic structure of his works and in his melodious, though eclectic, versatility. Having received his initial inspiration from Beethoven, he completed the form of the choral symphony which Beethoven had inaugurated with his Ninth Symphony, and he pointed the way to a powerful musical expressionism in his own Ninth Symphony and in the *Lied von der Erde* (Song of the Earth).

Mahler's music is perhaps the purest musical documentation of the cultural crisis of the turn of the century and of the ever repeated attempts to resolve the conflict between *Ich* and *Welt,* between individualism and social collectivism. Filled with a missionary passion for the socialization of the metaphysical and ethical values of music, Mahler wanted to carry his message to the masses by creating the *"Sinfonie des kleinen Mannes"* (the symphony for the little people), by lifting the events of everyday life into the sphere of the sublime, and by striving for the simple grandeur of the folk song.

Mahler's symphonies express and reflect in successive phases his desperate

---

* Bruckner's compositions include nine symphonies (the ninth unfinished), three Masses, one Requiem, one *Te Deum,* one quintet for strings, and several choral and liturgical works.

struggle to free himself from the discords which threatened his own life. A God-seeker in an irreligious age and environment, he invokes the healing and redeeming powers of Faith in the Second Symphony, of Love in the Third Symphony; he flees into the world of dreams in the Fourth; turns his energies to the social tasks of an active life in the Fifth; and, finally, resigns himself to the seemingly inescapable tragedy of life in the Sixth Symphony. This resignation and the romantic "sympathy with death" resound once more with strongest emotional accents in the *Kindertoten-lieder* and in his swan song, the *Lied von der Erde.*

The breadth and depth of both Bruckner's and Mahler's human and artistic penetration of reality was not reached by *Max Reger* (1873–1916), the Bavarian composer, whose exuberant vitality lacked the intellectual acumen which could have acted as a steadying and balancing influence on his unruly talent. Reger's compositions are both conservative and "modernistic," and his historical significance lies in the fact that he combined the classical forms of absolute music with revolutionary innovations in producing chromatic and enharmonic effects. He is undoubtedly the greatest contemporary master of the art of linear counterpoint, and in his magnificent organ music, especially in his fugues and double fugues, he proves himself a loyal and convincing disciple of Johann Sebastian Bach. Yet all too often Reger's scintillating and impetuous temperament arbitrarily disrupts the rigid firmness of this classical frame and expresses itself in the erratic forms of a bulging baroque expressionism.*

Musical *expressionism* as a distinct style growing out of a new and revolutionary theory was introduced into German music by *Arnold Schön-berg* (1874–), a native of Vienna, who succeeded the Italian "futurist" Busoni as director of the Berlin *Hochschule für Musik* and took up residence in the United States in 1933.

Two major phases may be distinguished in Schönberg's development as a composer. In the first he shows himself as a neo-romanticist and enthusiastic follower of Richard Wagner (cf. the choral work *Gurrelieder,* the string sextet *Verklärte Nacht,* and the *Chamber Symphony*). The works of this period, though rich in melodic invention and bold in their polyphonic structure, are lacking in logical coherence and give vent to an unrestrained emotionalism. The second phase is characterized by a fully developed expressionistic style which, indulging in daring cacophonic experiments and disregarding most of the traditional laws of harmony and melody, tends to make Schönberg's compositions purely abstract and therefore unintelligible to the uninitiated (the choral work *Friede auf Erden, Stefan George Lieder, Pierrot Lunaire Lieder, Serenade,* etc.). This type of

---

* Reger's compositions include orchestral works (*Hiller Variations, Mozart Variations, Romantic Suite,* four tone poems, two concerti, choral-orchestral pieces), chamber music (eleven sonatas, seventeen preludes and fugues, five string quartets, etc.), works for piano and organ, about 200 *Lieder,* and *a capella* choruses.

musical expressionism obviously parallels the development toward pure abstraction in literature, painting, and sculpture.

The latest works of Arnold Schönberg thus illustrate on the highest level the fact that contemporary German music, too, was eventually forced to yield to the tendencies inherent in the age of crisis and to mirror even in its most earnest and sincere representatives the progressive disintegration of those values which had constituted the spiritual and moral substance of the German and European past. The artist who is compelled to move as it were in an empty space, unaided by the vital and concrete forces of a *Volkskultur,* which alone could provide the proper frame for his creative work and the proper response to his artistic genius, finds himself isolated in an anonymous no man's land. The historian, on the other hand, who refuses to pose as a major or minor prophet of gloom or cheer, will voice the conviction expressed in Fritz von Unruh's latest novel, namely, that "The End is Not Yet," basing his optimism on that perpetual recuperative power of the human spirit which he finds amply documented in the pages of German history.

BIBLIOGRAPHY*

Achorn, Erik, *European Civilization and Politics Since 1815* (New York: Harcourt, Brace, 1934).

Adam, Karl, *Christ and the Western Mind,* trans. E. Bullough (New York: Sheed & Ward, 1930).

———— *The Spirit of Catholicism,* trans. Justin McCann (New York: Macmillan, 1935).

Allers, Rudolf, *The New Psychologies* (New York: Sheed & Ward, 1933).

Allgemeine deutsche Biographie, ed. Freiherr Rochus von Liliencron, and others; Bayerische Akademie der Wissenschaften (Leipzig: Duncker und Humblot, 1875–1912), 56 vols.

Angelus Silesius (Johann Scheffler), *Der Cherubinische Wandersmann,* a selection from the rhymes of a German mystic, trans. P. Carus (Chicago: Open Court, 1909).

———— *The Cherubinic Wanderer,* trans. J. E. C. Flitch (London: Allen, 1932).

Bahr, Hermann, *Expressionism,* trans. R. T. Gribble (London: Henderson, 1925).

Barth, Karl, *Epistle to the Romans,* trans. Edwyn C. Hoskins (New York: Oxford University Press, 1933).

———— *God in Action,* trans. E. G. Homrighausen and Karl J. Ernst (Edinburgh: T. & T. Clark, 1937).

Bauhaus, 1919–1928, ed. Herbert Bayer, Walter Gropius, and Ise Gropius (New York: The Museum of Modern Art, 1938).

Bebel, F. August, *My Life,* trans. anon. (London: Allen & Unwin, 1912).

Bekker, Paul, *Beethoven,* trans. M. M. Bozman (London: Dent, 1925).

Bethmann-Hollweg, Theobald von, *Reflections on the World War,* trans. G. Young (New York: Harper, 1920).

Bie, Oscar, *Franz Schubert,* trans. J. S. Untermeyer (New York: Dodd, Mead, 1928).

Bielschowsky, Albert, *Life of Goethe,* trans. W. A. Cooper (New York: L. Putnam, 1905–1908), 4 vols.

Bismarck, Otto von, *Bismarck, the Man and the Statesman:* being the *Reflections and Reminiscences* written and dictated by himself, trans. A. J. Butler, Smith (London: Elder, 1889), 2 vols.

———— *The Kaiser vs. Bismarck,* suppressed letters by the Kaiser and new chapters from the autobiography of the Iron Chancellor (New York: Harper, 1921).

Bithell, Jethro, *Modern German Literature, 1880–1938* (London: Methuen & Co., 1939).

———— *Germany. A Companion to German Studies* (New York: Lincoln MacVeagh, The Dial Press, 1938).

---

*For the benefit of the reader the author has in the main listed works that are available in English translation. The bibliography is thus selective and necessarily incomplete.

Boehme, Jakob, *Aurora,* trans. J. Barker and D. S. Hehner, Watkins (London, 1914).

———— *On the Election of Grace,* trans. anon. (New York: Harper, 1932).

———— *Personal Christianity a Science,* trans. anon. (New York: Macoy, 1919).

Brecht, Arnold, *Prelude to Silence. The End of the German Republic* (New York: Oxford University Press, 1944).

Brock, Werner, *An Introduction to Contemporary German Philosophy* (Cambridge: University Press, 1935).

Brentano, Franz, *The Origin of the Knowledge of Right and Wrong,* trans. C. Hague (Westminster: Constable & Co., 1902).

Brunet, René, *The New German Constitution,* trans. Joseph Gollomb (New York: Alfred A. Knopf, 1922).

Bülow, Bernhard von, *Imperial Germany,* trans. Marie A. Lewenz (New York: Dodd, Mead, 1917).

———— *Memoirs,* trans. F. A. Voigt (New York: G. P. Putnam's Sons, 1935), 4 vols.

Burckhardt, Jacob, *The Civilization of the Period of the Renaissance in Italy,* trans. S. G. C. Middlemore (New York: Charles Scribner's Sons, 1878).

Butler, Dom Cuthbert, O.S.B., *Western Mysticism* (London: Constable & Co., 1927).

Cambridge Medieval History (New York: Macmillan, 1926–1936), 8 vols.

Carlyle, R. W., and A. J., *History of Mediaeval Political Theory in the West* (New York: G. P. Putnam's Sons, 1916), 6 vols.

Cathrein, Victor, S.J., *Socialism Exposed and Refuted,* trans. J. Conway (New York: Benziger, 1892).

Chamberlain, Houston Stewart, *The Foundations of the Nineteenth Century,* trans. J. Lees (New York: Lane, 1912).

Clausewitz, Karl von, *On War,* trans. O. J. Matthijs Jolles (New York: Random House, 1943).

Comte, Auguste, *Cours de philosophie positive* (Paris, 1830–1842), 6 vols.

Coudenhove-Calergi, R., *Pan-Europe,* Introd. by N. M. Butler (New York: Alfred A. Knopf, 1926).

Czernin, Graf von, *In the World War,* trans. anon. (New York: Harper, 1920).

Daniels, Dom Augustinus, *Eine lateinische Rechtfertigungsschrift des Meister Eckhart* (Münster: Aschendorff, 1923).

Dante, Alighieri, *The Latin Works of Dante,* trans. A. G. Ferrers Howell and Philip H. Wicksteed (London: J. M. Dent, 1904).

Dawson, Christopher, *The Age of the Gods* (London and New York: Sheed & Ward, 1933).

———— *The Judgment of the Nations* (New York: Sheed & Ward, 1942).

———— *The Making of Europe* (New York: Sheed & Ward, 1934).

Delatte, Dom Paul, O.S.B., *The Rule of St. Benedict,* trans. Dom Justin McCann, O.S.B. (London: Burns, Oates & Washbourne, 1921).

De Maistre, Joseph, *Essai sur le principe générateur des constitutions politiques* (Paris, 1810), Vol. I, Oeuvres complètes.

———— *Les Soirées de St. Petersburg, ou Entretiens sur le gouvernement temporal de la Providence* (Paris, 1821), Vols. IV and V, Oeuvres complètes.

Denifle, H., O.P., *Luther and Lutherdom,* trans. R. Volz (New York: Holy Name Society, 1917).

Denzinger, Heinrich, and Bannwart, Clemens, S.J., *Enchiridion symbolorum, definitionum et declarationum de rebus fidei et morum* (Freiburg: Herder, 1922).

Devas, Dominic, O.F.M., *The Franciscan Order* (London: Burns, Oates & Washbourne, 1924).

Diesel, Eugen, *Germany and the Germans*, trans. W. D. Robson-Scott (New York: Macmillan, 1931).

Driesch, Hans, *Man and the Universe*, trans. W. H. Johnston (London: R. R. Smith, 1930).

———— *The Science and Philosophy of the Organism* (London: A. & C. Black, 1929).

Dürer, Albrecht, *Records of Journeys to Venice and the Low Countries*, trans. R. Tumbo, Jr. (Boston: Merrymount, 1913).

Eckhart, Meister, O.P., *Works*, ed. Franz Pfeiffer, trans. C. De B. Evans (London: Watkins, 1924).

Ehrenberg, R., *Capital and Finance in the Age of the Renaissance*: a Study of the Fuggers and Their Connections, trans. H. M. Lucas (New York: Harcourt, Brace, 1928).

Einhard (Eginhardus, Abbot of Seligenstadt), *Life of Charlemagne*, in *Early Lives of Charlemagne*, trans. A. J. Grant (New York: Oxford University Press, 1922).

Eloesser, Arthur, *Modern German Literature*, trans. C. A. Phillips (New York: Alfred A. Knopf, 1933).

Engels, Friedrich, *Ludwig Feuerbach and the Roots of the Socialist Philosophy*, trans. Austin Lewis (Chicago: Kerr, 1903).

———— *The Peasant War in Germany*, trans. M. J. Olgin (New York: International Publishers, 1935).

———— *Principles of Communism*, original draft of the Communist Manifesto, trans. Max Bedacht (New York: Daily Worker, 1925).

Erzberger, Matthias, *The League of Nations: The Way to the World's Peace*, trans. B. Miall (New York: Hodder, 1919).

Fabre-Luce, A., *Locarno: The Reality*, trans. Constance Vesey (New York: Alfred A. Knopf, 1928).

Ferguson-Bruun, *A Survey of European Civilization* (New York: Houghton Mifflin Co., 1936).

Feuerbach, Ludwig, *The Essence of Christianity*, trans. Marian Evans (London: Chapman, 1854).

Fichte, Johann Gottlieb, *The Way Towards the Blessed Life*, trans. W. Smith (London: Chapman, 1844).

———— *Addresses to the German Nation*, trans. R. F. Jones and G. H. Turnbull (Chicago: Open Court, 1922).

———— *The Science of Knowledge*, trans. A. E. Kröger (Philadelphia: Lippincott, 1868).

———— *The Vocation of Man*, trans. W. Smith (Chicago: Open Court, 1931).

Foerster, Friedrich Wilhelm, *Europe and the German Question* (New York: Sheed & Ward, 1940).

Foerster-Nietzsche, Elisabeth, *The Life of Nietzsche*, trans. A. M. Ludovici (New York: Sturgis, 1912–1915).

———— *The Lonely Nietzsche*, trans. P. V. Cohn (London: Heinemann, 1915).

——— *The Young Nietzsche,* trans. A. M. Ludovici (London: Heinemann, 1912).

Freud, Sigmund, *The Ego and the Id,* trans. Joan Riviere (London: Woolf, 1927).

——— *General Introduction to Psychoanalysis,* trans. anon. (New York: Boni & Liveright, 1920).

Freytag, Gustav, *Pictures of German Life,* trans. Mrs. Malcolm (London: Chapman, 1862, 1863), 4 vols.

Friedell, Egon, *Cultural History of the Modern Age,* trans. C. F. Atkinson (New York: Alfred A. Knopf, 1930–1932), 3 vols.

Froebel, F. W. A., *Chief Writings on Education,* trans. S. S. F. Fletcher and J. Welton (New York: Longmans, Green, 1932).

Fülöp-Miller, René, *Power and Secret of the Jesuits,* trans. F. S. Flint and D. F. Tait (New York: G. P. Putnam's Sons, 1930).

Gasquet, F. A., Cardinal, *The Rule of St. Benedict* (London: Chatto & Windus, 1925).

——— *The Eve of the Reformation* (London: G. Bell & Sons, 1900).

——— *Monastic Life in the Middle Ages* (London: G. Bell & Sons, 1922).

German White Book Concerning the Responsibilities of the Authors of the War, trans. Carnegie Endowment (New York: Oxford University Press, 1924).

Germany, the Federal Constitution of, April 16, trans. Edmund J. James (Philadelphia: University of Pennsylvania, Series in Economy and Public Law, No. VII, 1899).

——— *Preliminary History of the Armistice,* official documents published by the German National Chancellery, trans. Carnegie Endowment (New York: Oxford University Press, 1924).

Gierke, Otto von, *Natural Law and the Theory of Society,* trans. Ernest Barker (New York: Macmillan, 1934).

Gilson, Etienne, *Reason and Revelation in the Middle Ages* (New York: Charles Scribner's Sons, 1938).

——— *The Mystical Theology of St. Bernard* (New York: Sheed & Ward, 1940).

——— *The Spirit of Mediaeval Philosophy,* trans. A. H. C. Downes (New York: Sheed & Ward, 1936).

——— *The Unity of Philosophical Experience* (New York: Charles Scribner's Sons, 1937).

Goethe, Johann Wolfgang von, *Works,* Weimar ed., ed. N. H. Dole (Boston: Nicolls, 1915), 14 vols.

——— *Conversations of J. P. Eckermann With Goethe,* trans. S. M. Fuller (Boston: Hilliard, Gray, 1852).

Gooch, George P., *Studies in Modern History* (New York: Longmans, Green, 1931).

——— *Germany* (New York: Charles Scribner's Sons, 1925).

Grabmann, Martin, *Introduction to the Theological Summa of St. Thomas Aquinas,* trans. J. S. Zybura (St. Louis: Herder, 1930).

———*Die Kulturwerte der deutschen Mystik des Mittelalters* (Augsburg: Benno Filser, 1923).

——— *Thomas Aquinas, His Personality and Thought,* trans. Virgil Michel (New York: Longmans, Green, 1928).

Gregorovius, F., *History of the City of Rome in the Middle Ages*, trans. Annie Hamilton (London: G. Bell & Sons, 1894–1902).

Gregory of Tours, *History of the Franks*, trans. O. Dalton (London: Clarendon Press); selections, trans. Ernest Brehaut (New York: Columbia University Press, 1916).

Grimmelshausen, H. J. C., *The Adventurous Simplicissimus*, trans. A. T. S. Goodrick (New York: Dutton, 1924).

Grisar, Hartmann, S.J., *Luther*, trans. E. M. Lamond (St. Louis: Herder, 1913–1917).

—— *Martin Luther, His Life and Work*, ed. Arthur Preuss (St. Louis: Herder, 1935).

Gropius, Walter, *The New Architecture and the Bauhaus*, trans. P. M. Shand (New York: Museum of Modern Art, 1937).

Gundolf, Friedrich, *The Mantle of Caesar*, trans. J. W. Hartmann (New York: Vanguard Press, 1928).

Haeckel, Ernst, *The Riddle of the Universe*, summarized by Vance Randolph (New York: Vanguard Press, 1926).

Haecker, Theodor, *Virgil, Father of the West*, trans. A. W. Wheen (New York: Sheed & Ward, 1934).

Haller, Johannes, *Epochs of German History*, trans. E. W. Dickes (New York: Harcourt, Brace, 1930).

—— *France and Germany, the History of 1000 Years*, trans. Dora von Beseler (London: Constable & Co., 1932).

—— *Philipp Eulenburg, the Kaiser's Friend*, trans. Ethel C. Mayne (New York: Alfred A. Knopf, 1930).

Händel, G. F., *Letters and Writings*, ed. E. H. Müller (New York: Cassell, 1935).

Harden, Maximilian, *Germany, France, and England*, trans. Cranston Lawton (New York: Brentano, 1924).

Harnack, Adolph von, *What Is Christianity?*, trans. B. Saunders (New York: G. P. Putnam's Sons, 1904).

Hartmann, Eduard von, *The Philosophy of the Unconscious*, trans. C. Coupland (London: Trübner, 1893).

Hartmann, Nicolai, *Ethics*, trans. Stanton Coit (New York: Macmillan, 1932), 3 vols.

Hauptmann, Gerhart, *The Dramatic Works*, ed. Ludwig Lewisohn (New York: Viking Press, 1912–1929), 9 vols.

Hayes, Carlton J. H., *A Political and Cultural History of Modern Europe* (New York: Macmillan, 1932–1938).

Hegel, G. W. F., *Phenomenology of Mind*, trans. J. B. Baillie (New York: Macmillan, 1931).

—— *Lectures on the Philosophy of History*, trans. J. Sibree (New York: Colonial Press, 1899).

—— *Selections*, ed. J. Loewenberg (New York: Charles Scribner's Sons, 1929).

Hegemann, Werner, *Frederick the Great*, trans. Winifred Ray (New York: Alfred A. Knopf, 1929).

Heine, Heinrich, *Works*, trans. G. Leland (London: Heinemann, 1891–1905), 12 vols.

Hielscher, Kurt, *Picturesque Germany* (New York: Brentano, 1924).

Hildebrand, Adolf von, *The Problem of Form in Painting and Sculpture,* trans. Max F. Meyer, and R. M. Ogden (New York: Stechert, 1932).

Hindenburg, Gert von, *Hindenburg, 1847–1934; Soldier and Statesman,* trans. Gerald Griffin (London: Hutchinson, 1933).

Hindenburg, Paul von, *Out of My Life,* trans. A. Holt (New York: Cassell, 1933).

Hodges, H. A., *Wilhelm Dilthey* (New York: Oxford University Press, 1944).

Hohenlohe-Schillingsfürst, Fürst zu, *Memoirs,* ed. F. Curtius (New York: Macmillan, 1906), 2 vols.

Hrotsvitha of Gandersheim, *The Plays of Roswitha,* trans. Cyph. St. John, i.e., Christabel Marshall; with introd. by Cardinal Gasquet (London: Chatto and Windus, 1923).

Huizinga, J., *The Waning of the Middle Ages* (London: E. Arnold & Co., 1924).
———— *Erasmus* (New York: Charles Scribner's Sons, 1924).

Humboldt, Alexander von, *Works* (New York: Appleton, n.d.), 9 vols.

Humboldt, Wilhelm von, *The Sphere and Duties of Government,* trans. J. Coulthard, Jr. (London: Chapman, 1844).

Jaeger, Werner, *Aristotle: Fundamentals of the History of His Development,* trans. R. Robinson (New York: Oxford University Press, 1934).

Janssen, Johannes, *History of the German People at the Close of the Middle Ages,* trans. M. A. Mitchell and A. M. Christie (St. Louis: Herder, 1925), 17 vols.

Jarrett, Bede, O.S.B., *Life of St. Dominic* (London: Burns, Oates & Washbourne, 1924).
———— *Social Theories of the Middle Ages* (London: E. Benn, 1926).

Jaspers, Karl, *Man in the Modern Age,* trans. Eden and Cedar Paul (New York: Holt, 1933).

Jones, W. Tudor, *Contemporary Thought of Germany* (London: William Norgate, 1930, 1931), 2 vols.

Jordan, Max, *Beyond All Fronts:* a Bystander's Notes on This Thirty Years' War (Milwaukee: Bruce Publishing Co., 1944).

Kant, Immanuel, *The Critique of Pure Reason,* trans. Max Müller (New York: Macmillan, 1907).
———— *Critique of Aesthetic Judgment,* trans. J. H. Bernard (New York: Macmillan, 1914).
———— *Perpetual Peace,* trans. Helen O'Brien (London: Sweet & Maxwell, 1927).
———— *Selections,* ed. Th. M. Greene (New York: Charles Scribner's Sons, 1929).

Kantorowicz, Ernst, *Frederick II, 1194–1250,* trans. E. O. Lorimer (London: Constable & Co., 1931).

Karrer, Otto, *Meister Eckehart. Das System seiner religiösen Lehre und Lebensweisheit.* Textbuch aus den gedruckten und ungedruckten Quellen (München: Verlag Josef Müller, 1926).

Kessler, Harry Graf von, *Walter Rathenau, His Life and Work,* trans. W. D. Robson-Scott and Lawrence Hyde (New York: Harcourt, Brace, 1930).

Ketteler, Wilhelm Emmanuel, Freiherr von, Bischof, *Schriften,* ed. Johannes Mumbauer (München: J. Kösel and F. Pustet, 1924), 3 vols.

Keyserling, Hermann Graf von, *The World in the Making,* trans. Maurice Samuel (New York: Harcourt, Brace, 1927).

—— *Europe,* trans. Maurice Samuel (New York: Harcourt, Brace, 1928).

Kierkegaard, Søren, *The Point of View,* trans. Walter Lowrie (New York: Oxford University Press, 1939).

—— *Christian Discourses,* trans. Walter Lowrie (New York: Oxford University Press, 1939).

—— *The Present Age,* trans. Alexander Dru and Walter Lowrie (New York: Oxford University Press, 1940).

—— *Fear and Trembling,* trans. Robert Payne (New York: Oxford University Press, 1939).

—— *The Journals,* trans. Alexander Dru (New York: Oxford University Press, 1938).

—— *Stages on Life's Way,* trans. Walter Lowrie (Princeton: Princeton University Press, 1940).

—— *A Kierkegaard Anthology,* ed. by Robert Bretall (Princeton: University Press, 1946).

Kuehlmann, Richard von, *Thoughts on Germany,* trans. Eric Sutton (New York: Macmillan, 1932).

Kühnemann, Eugen, *Schiller,* trans. Katherine H. Royce (Boston: Ginn, 1912).

Lamprecht, Karl, *What Is History?,* trans. E. A. Andrews (New York: Macmillan, 1905).

Leibniz, G. W., *Monadology and Other Philosophical Writings,* trans. R. Latta (Oxford: Clarendon, 1898).

—— *Philosophic Writings,* sel. and trans. M. Morris (New York: Dutton, 1934).

Leo XIII, Great Encyclical Letters of (New York: Benziger Bros., 1903).

Lessing, Gotthold Ephraim, *Laocoön,* trans. Sir Robert J. Phillimore (New York: Dutton, 1905).

Lichnowsky, K. M., Fürst von, *Heading for the Abyss: Reminiscences,* trans. Sefton Delmer (New York: Harcourt, Brace, 1928).

Loewenstein, Prince Hubertus zu, *The Germans in History* (New York: Columbia University Press, 1945).

—— *The Tragedy of a Nation: Germany 1918–1934* (New York: Macmillan, 1934).

Lowrie, Walter, *Kierkegaard* (New York: Oxford University Press, 1938).

Ludendorff, Erich von, *My War Memoirs,* trans. anon. (New York: Harper, 1920), 2 vols.

Luebke, Wilhelm, *History of Art,* trans. C. Cook and R. Sturgis (New York: Dodd, Mead, 1922), 2 vols.

Luther, Martin, *Works,* ed. Eyster Jacobs (Philadelphia: United Lutheran Publishers, 1915–1932), 6 vols.

—— *Werke; kritische Gesamtausgabe,* ed. J. K. F. Knaake, G. Kawerau, E. Thiele, and others (Weimar: Hermann Böhlau, 1883 sqq.).

Lutz, Ralph H., *The German Revolution of 1918–1919* (Stanford University, Calif.: Stanford University Press, 1922).

—— *The Fall of the German Empire, 1914–1918* (Stanford University, Calif.: Stanford University Press, 1932).

Malleus maleficarum, ed. Jacob Sprenger, trans. Rev. Montague Summers (London: John Rodker, 1928).

Marx, Karl, *Capital, the Communist Manifesto, and Other Writings,* ed. Max Eastman (Modern Library, 1932).

Max, Prince of Baden, *Memoirs,* trans. W. M. Calder and C. W. H. Sutton (London: Scribner; Constable, 1928).

Metternich, Fürst von, *Memoirs,* trans. Gerard W. Smith (New York: Harper, 1881), 5 vols.

Migne, Jacques-Paul, *Patrologiae cursus completus,* a chronological collection of the works of all fathers, doctors, and authors of the Church (Paris, 1844–1880), 382 vols.

Mirbt, Carl, *Quellen zur Geschichte des Papsttums und des römischen Katholizismus* (Tübingen: J. C. B. Mohr, 1924).

Moltke, Helmuth von, *Essays, Speeches, and Memoirs* (New York: Harper, 1893), 2 vols.

Montalembert, Comte de, *The Monks of the West* (London: John C. Nimmo, 1896), 6 vols.

Monumenta Germaniae Historica, founded by Reichsfreiherr Karl vom Stein, ed. Georg Heinrich Pertz and others; *Scriptores* (SS) *rerum Germanicarum in usum scholarum* (German translation, sel., *Geschichtsschreiber der deutschen Vorzeit,* 1884–1928, 96 vols.).

Mozart, Wolfgang Amadeus, *The Man and the Artist,* as revealed in his own words, trans. H. E. Krehbiel (New York: Huebsch, 1905).

Müller-Freienfels, R., *The Evolution of Modern Psychology,* trans. W. Beran Wolfe (New Haven: Yale University Press, 1935).

Muther, Richard, *The History of Modern Painting* (New York: Dutton, 1907), 4 vols.

Nicholas of Cusa, *Opera omnia,* ed. Ernsa Hoffmann and others (Leipzig: Felix Meiner, 1932 sqq.).

Niemann, Walter, *Brahms,* trans. C. A. Phillips (New York: Alfred A. Knopf, 1929).

Nietzsche, Friedrich Wilhelm, *Complete Works,* ed. O. Levy (New York: Macmillan, 1925), 18 vols.

Oesterreich, T. K., *Occultism and Modern Science,* trans. anon. (New York: McBride, 1923).

Olden, Rudolf, *Stresemann,* trans. R. T. Clark (New York: Dutton, 1930).

Otto, Bishop of Freising, *The Two Cities: a Chronicle of Universal History to the Year 1146 A.D.,* trans. C. C. Mierow (New York: Oxford University Press, 1928).

Pastor, L. F. August, Freiherr von, *The History of the Popes From the Close of the Middle Ages,* trans. F. I. Antrobus, R. F. Kerr, and Dom Ernest Graf (London: K. Paul, Trench and Trübner, 1906–1941), 24 vols.

Paulsen, Friedrich, *The German Universities and University Study,* trans. F. Thilly and W. Elwang (New York: Charles Scribner's Sons, 1906).

Pfeilschifter, G., *German Culture, Catholicism, and the World War,* trans. Jos. Matt (St. Paul, Minn.: Wanderer, 1916).

Pinnow, Hermann, *History of Germany,* trans. M. R. Brailsford (New York: Macmillan, 1933).

Pius XI, *Sixteen Encyclicals of His Holiness,* 1926–1937 (Washington: National Catholic Welfare Conference, 1937).

Planck, Max, *The Universe in the Light of Modern Physics,* trans. W. H. Johnston (London: Allen & Unwin, 1931).

Ploetz, Karl, *Epitome of Ancient, Mediaeval, and Modern History,* trans. H. Tillinghast (New York: Houghton Mifflin Co., 1925).

Preger, Wilhelm, *Geschichte der deutschen Mystik im Mittelalter* (Leipzig: Dörffling und Franke, 1874–1893).

Procopius of Caesarea, *Works,* trans. H. B. Dewing and Glanville Downey (London: W. Heinemann, 1914–1940), 7 vols.

Przywara, Erich, S.J., *An Augustine Synthesis* (London: Sheed & Ward, 1936).

Pufendorf, Samuel Freiherr von, *De jure naturae et gentium,* trans. C. H. and W. A. Oldfather (New York: Oxford University Press, 1934).

—— *De officio hominis et civis juxta legem naturalem,* trans. F. G. Moore (New York: Oxford University Press, 1927).

Ranke, Leopold von, *History of the Reformation in Germany,* ed. R. A. Johnson (New York: Dutton, 1905).

—— *History of the Popes,* trans. E. Fowler (New York: Colonial Press, 1901), 3 vols.

Rathenau, Walter, *In Days to Come,* trans. E. and C. Paul (New York: Alfred A. Knopf, 1921).

—— *The New Society,* trans. anon. (New York: Harcourt, Brace, 1921).

Rohde, Erwin, *Psyche,* trans. W. B. Hillis (New York: Harcourt, Brace, 1925).

Rohrbach, Paul, *German World Policies,* trans. E. von Mach (New York: Macmillan, 1915).

Schacht, Hjalmar, *The Stabilization of the Mark,* trans. Ralph Butler (London: Allen & Unwin, 1927).

—— *The End of Reparations: The Economic Consequences of the World War,* ed. G. Glasgow (London: Cape, 1931).

Scheeben, Joseph Matthias, *Natur und Gnade,* ed. Martin Grabmann (München: Theatiner Verlag, 1922).

Scheidemann, Philipp, *The Making of the New Germany: Memoirs,* trans. J. E. Michell (New York: Appleton, 1929).

Scherer, Wilhelm, *History of German Literature,* trans. F. C. Conybeare (New York: Charles Scribner's Sons, 1893), 2 vols.

Schiller, Friedrich von, *Works,* ed. N. H. Dole (Boston: Niccolls, 1915), 10 vols.

Schleiermacher, Friedrich, *Soliloquies,* trans. H. L. Friess (Chicago: Open Court, 1926).

Schnabel, Franz, *Deutsche Geschichte im neunzehnten Jahrhundert* (Freiburg im Br.: Herder, 1929 sqq.), 4 vols.

Schnürer, Gustav, *Kirche und Kultur im Mittelalter* (Paderborn: Ferdinand Schöningh, n.d.).

—— *Katholische Kirche und Kultur in der Barockzeit* (Paderborn: Ferdinand Schöningh, 1937).

—— *Die Anfänge der abendländischen Völkergemeinschaft* (Freiburg: Herder, 1932).

Schopenhauer, Arthur, *The World as Will and Idea,* trans. R. B. Haldane and J. Kemp (London: Trübner, 1896), 3 vols.

Schubert, Franz, *Letters and Other Writings,* trans. Venetia Savile (New York: Alfred A. Knopf, 1928).

Schweitzer, Albert, *Johann Sebastian Bach,* trans. E. Newman (New York: Breitkopf & Haertel, 1911), 2 vols.

Spann, Othmar, *Types of Economic Theory,* trans. Eden and Cedar Paul (London: Allen & Unwin, 1930).

Specht, Richard, *Beethoven as He Lived,* trans. Alfred Kalisch (New York: Macmillan, 1933).

—— *Brahms,* trans. Eric Blom (New York: Dutton, 1930).

Spengler, Oswald, *The Decline of the West,* trans. F. Atkinson (New York: Alfred A. Knopf, 1934).

—— *The Hour of Decision,* trans. F. Atkinson (New York: Alfred A. Knopf, 1934).

—— *Man and Technics,* trans. F. Atkinson (New York: Alfred A. Knopf, 1932).

Spitta, Julius, *Johann Sebastian Bach,* trans. C. Bell and J. A. F. Maitland (New York: Novello, 1899), 3 vols.

Stegemann, Hermann, *The Mirage of Versailles,* trans. R. T. Clark (New York: Alfred A. Knopf, 1928).

—— *The Struggle for the Rhine,* trans. G. Chatterton-Hill (London: Allen, 1928).

Steiner, Rudolf, *The Philosophy of Freedom,* trans. A. Hoernlé (New York: G. P. Putnam's Sons, 1916).

—— *An Outline of Occult Science,* trans. Max Gysi (New York: Rand, McNally, 1914).

Steinhausen, Georg, *Deutsche Geistes-und Kulturgeschichte von 1870 bis zur Gegenwart* (Halle: Max Niemeyer, 1931).

—— *Geschichte der deutschen Kultur.* Neu bearbeitet und erweitert von Dr. Eugen Diesel (Bibliographisches Institut: Leipzig, 1936), 2 vols.

Stöckl, Albrecht, *Handbook of the History of Philosophy,* trans. T. A. Finlay (New York: Longmans, Green, 1911 sqq.).

Stresemann, Gustav, *Essays and Speeches,* Pref. Sir Austen Chamberlain; trans. Chr. R. Turner (London: Butterworth, 1930).

—— *Diaries, Letters, and Papers,* trans. Eric Sutton (New York: Macmillan, 1935).

Suso, Heinrich, O.P., *Little Book of Eternal Wisdom,* ed. C. H. McKenna, O.P. (London: Angelus Company, 1910).

—— *Deutsche Schriften* (Regensburg: G. J. Manz, 1926).

Suttner, Bertha von, *Memoirs,* trans. anon. (Boston: Ginn, 1910), 2 vols.

Sybel, Heinrich von, *The Foundation of the German Empire by William I,* trans. Marshall Livingston Perrin and others (New York: T. Y. Crowell, 1890–1898), 7 vols.

Tacitus, *The Germania,* trans. Arthur Murphy (New York, 1909, in *The Classics,* pp. 354–424).

—— *The Histories, the Annals,* trans. John Jackson and Clifford H. Moore (New York: G. P. Putnam's Sons, 1925–1937), 4 vols.

Tauler, Johannes, O.P., *The Following of Christ,* trans. J. R. Morell (London, New York: Burns & Oates, 1896).

——— *The Sermons and Conferences,* trans. W. Elliott (Washington, D. C.: Apostolic Mission House, 1910).

Tawney, R. H., *Religion and the Rise of Capitalism* (New York: Harcourt, Brace, 1926).

Taylor, H. O., *The Classical Heritage of the Middle Ages* (New York: Macmillan, 1935).

——— *The Medieval Mind* (New York: Macmillan, 1919).

Thomas Aquinas, St., *Opera omnia,* ed. Cardinal Thomaso Maria Zigliara and others (Rome: Typographia Polyglotta, 1882–1930), 15 vols.

——— *Basic Writings,* ed. Anton C. Pegis (New York: Random House, 1944), 2 vols.

——— *On the Governance of Rulers,* trans. Gerald B. Phelan (New York: Sheed & Ward, 1938).

Treitschke, Heinrich von, *History of Germany in the Nineteenth Century,* trans. Eden and Cedar Paul (New York: McBride, 1915–1919), 7 vols.

Troeltsch, Ernst, *Christian Thought, Its History and Application,* ed. Baron F. von Hügel (New York: Doran, 1923).

——— *Protestantism and Progress,* trans. W. Montgomery (New York: G. P. Putnam's Sons, 1912).

——— *Social Teaching of the Christian Churches,* trans. Olive Wyon (London; New York: Macmillan, 1931), 2 vols.

Ueberweg, F., *A History of Philosophy,* trans. G. S. Morris (New York: Charles Scribner's Sons, 1892).

Valentin, Veit, *1848: Chapters of German History,* trans. E. T. Scheffauer (London: Allen & Unwin, 1940).

——— *The German People* (New York: Alfred A. Knopf, 1946).

Wagner, Richard, *Prose Works,* trans. W. A. Ellis (London, 1892–1899), 8 vols.

——— *My Life,* trans. anon. (New York: Dodd, Mead, 1924).

Walzel, Oskar, *German Romanticism,* trans. A. E. Lussky (New York: G. P. Putnam's Sons, 1932).

Watkin, E. T., *Catholic Art and Culture* (New York: Sheed & Ward, 1944).

Weber, Max, *The Protestant Ethic and the Spirit of Capitalism,* trans. Talcott Parsons (New York: Charles Scribner's Sons, 1930).

Wheeler-Bennett, John W., *Wooden Titan; Hindenburg in Twenty Years of German History* (New York: William Morrow, 1935).

Wilhelm II, *The Kaiser's Memoirs,* trans. R. Ybarra (New York: Harper, 1922).

Wilms, Hieronymus, *Albert the Great,* trans. Adrian English and Ph. Hereford (London: Burns, 1933).

Witkowski, Georg, *The German Drama of the Nineteenth Century,* trans. L. E. Horning (New York: Holt, 1909).

Woelfflin, Heinrich, *Principles of Art History,* trans. M. D. Hottinger (New York: Holt, 1932).

Worringer, Wilhelm, *Form in Gothic,* trans. H. Read (New York: G. P. Putnam's Sons, 1927).

Wust, Peter, *The Crisis in the West,* trans. E. I. Watkin (London: Sheed & Ward, 1931).

Zimmern, H., *The Hansa Towns* (New York: G. P. Putnam's Sons, 1891).

Zoepfl, Friedrich, *Deutsche Kulturgeschichte* (Freiburg im Br.: Herder, 1929, 1930), 2 vols.

INDEX